FINES FOR OVERDUE BOOKS

ORDINARY LOANS - 5p per day
SHORT TERM LOANS - 10p per day
OVERNIGHT LOANS - 10p per hour (after 11am)

POSTAGE WILL BE CHARGED FOR OVERDUE LETTERS

PLEASE REPORT ANY LOST BOOKS IMMEDIATELY

COLLINS

BIOGRAPHICAL DICTIONARY OF SCIENTISTS

COLLINS

BIOGRAPHICAL DICTIONARY OF SCIENTISTS

Edited by
Trevor Williams

HarperCollins*Publishers*

HarperCollinsPublishers
P.O. Box, Glasgow G4 0NB

Reprint 10 9 8 7 6 5 4 3 2 1 0

Copyright © 1994 HarperCollinsPublishers

The Author hereby asserts his moral rights to be identified as the Author
of the Work and the Publishers undertake to observe such assertion and
to impose the same condition on its licensees.

ISBN 0 00 470109 7

A Catalogue record for this book is available from the British Library.

Typeset in Linotron Melior
by Rowland Phototypesetting Ltd
Bury St Edmunds, Suffolk

Printed in Great Britain by
HarperCollinsManufacturing Glasgow

PREFACE TO FOURTH EDITION

The third edition of this Dictionary, first published in 1969, has now been out of print for several years. Although this new edition follows the general lines of its predecessors some substantial changes have been made.

First, some 250 new entries have been added, partly to make good some earlier omissions but more particularly to include, for the first time, a number of living subjects. To prepare these I have enlisted the help of 20 new contributors and I am most grateful to all of them for the trouble they have taken in preparing the entries promptly and in conformity with editorial requirements. The Subject Index and the Table of Anniversaries have been appropriately updated and a list of Nobel Prize Winners from the inception of the awards in 1901 is now included.

The notes at the end of each of the existing entries have been rigorously scrutinized and many new references have been added. At the same time, a few of the less apposite ones have been deleted. Additionally, scientists – nearly 900 in all – previously identified in the Appendix only by years of birth and death and an indication of the entries in which their names are mentioned, have now in almost every case been provided with at least one general reference for more detailed biographical information. As a result of all these changes, this new edition contains some 3000 more references than its predecessor and I believe that this will greatly increase its usefulness.

The first three editions of this Dictionary were prepared in collaboration with A & C Black. Now, by friendly agreement between all concerned, responsibility for publication has been assumed by HarperCollins, who, too, have proved most helpful collaborators.

November 1993   T.I.W.

A NOTE ON REFERENCES

Each entry in this Dictionary has been designed to stand on its own, and for many users will suffice to provide all the basic information required. Others, however, may want to be guided to fuller and more critical biographical studies and the references that follow the entries are designed to fulfil this need. Their selection has been pragmatic, but the following considerations have been kept in mind. The emphasis is on books and journals written in English but where important – and sometimes definitive – biographies exist only in foreign languages these have been included. So far as possible at least one reference quoted includes a portrait of the subject. In some cases references quoted may offer substantially the same information but it has been felt important to provide a choice, as for individual users some will be more readily available than others. In this edition, for the first time, at least one reference has been provided for virtually all the scientists listed in the Appendix. It has to be recognized, however, that for quite a number of scientists of distinction rather little biographical information is available.

Biographical details about scientists are to be found in a very wide variety of publications. These include full-length books (including autobiographies); memoirs in the publications of learned societies; studies in journals devoted to the history of science; citations made on the occasion of awards; and obituaries in national and local newspapers. There are, however, a few major reference works devoted solely to scientific biography and in the nature of things these figure prominently in the footnotes to the entries. Among the most important are the following:

Dictionary of Scientific Biography

This is an international work – published under the auspices of the American Council of Learned Societies – concerned mainly with scientists (all deceased) but including workers in allied fields, especially mathematics and medicine, though weak on technologists. In its original form it comprised 14 volumes (1970–80) with entries – by individual authorities – ranging from a few hundred to many thousands of words. Each entry is followed by a very detailed list of references – in many languages – relevant to the subject in question. A number of subjects omitted from the main work will be found in a supplementary volume (XV). A further large volume (XVI) contains an exhaustive name and subject index. A second supplement (volumes XVII and XVIII) appeared in 1990, with entries for scientists who had died since the original lists were prepared. This is by far the most comprehensive work of its kind, but it is a massive, very expensive work rarely to be found outside large or specialized libraries. Unless otherside indicated (as Supp. I or II) the references in this Dictionary are to the original work.

J. C. Poggendorff, *Biographisch-Literarische Handwörterbuch zur Geschichte der exakten Wissenschaften* ('Poggendorff')

This is another massive biographical work, originally published in two volumes in 1863. It then contained some 8000 entries but has since been repeatedly enlarged and now totals some 20 volumes. The earlier volumes have been reprinted in various forms since the last war. Although written in German the style is so succinct that a minimal knowledge of that language suffices to extract the information it offers. Again, a work rarely found outside large libraries.

Nobel Prize Winners

Since the prizes were first awarded in 1901, Nobel Laureates have been recognized as the elite of the scientific world. The Nobel Foundation in Stockholm publishes annual volumes, *Les Prix Nobel*, giving biographical details of the prize winners and the research for which the award was made. However, unless the award was made rather late in life – which it not uncommonly is – much of the prize winner's career is necessarily not recorded. A much more complete record will be found in Tyler Wasson (Ed.), *Nobel Prize Winners* (1987). More recently (1993) a similarly organized work on prize winners in chemistry has been published (Laylin K. James, *Nobel Laureates in Chemistry 1901–1992*).

Biographical Memoirs of Fellows of the Royal Society

This important series of annual volumes began in 1955, as successor to the earlier *Obituary Notices* (1932–54). The entries – now totalling some 1500 – are written by close associates of the subject and run to several thousand words. Each entry is accompanied by a portrait and a comprehensive list of publications. While it largely records the lives of British scientists, the Royal Society has always had a proportion of Foreign Members, who are also commemorated here. Volume 26 (1980) contains a comprehensive index of entries back to 1932 and Volume 36 (1990) one for the previous decade.

The American equivalent is *Biographical Memoirs. National Academy of Sciences*.

Dictionary of National Biography

This is the standard work of reference for the lives of British notabilities, including many scientists. The original work included biographies from the earliest times to 1900. It has been extended by a supplement; by a 20th Century DNB (1901–60); and a succession of decennial (latterly quinquennial) volumes. Lately (1993) a special supplementary volume – *DNB: Missing Persons* – has been published containing entries for more than a thousand subjects who for one reason or another were omitted from all the previous volumes. The *Dictionary of National Biography* again is a massive library work but is much more readily available as the corresponding *Concise Dictionary of National Biography*.

The American counterpart is the *Dictionary of American Biography*. This first appeared as a 20-volume work (1928–36) to which supplements have been added. There is also a *Concise Dictionary of American Biography*.

ISIS Cumulative Bibliography

This is another magisterial work consisting of a critical bibliography of the history of science arranged according to personalities, institutions, subjects, and civilizations and periods. It consists of a complete index and cumulative table of contents to ISIS (founded 1912), journal of the History of Science Society. Volumes 1 to 6 cover the period 1913–65; two later volumes cover the years 1966–75. It is a highly specialized and exhaustive work listing not only general biographies but also scholarly dissertations on minutiae of scientific history.

Because it is a bibliographical rather than a biographical work of reference, this book is not cited in the footnotes. Nevertheless, it should be noted that it can throw much light on the lives and work of a high proportion of the scientists listed in the Dictionary.

CONTRIBUTORS

The styles and descriptions of contributors have not been altered but show them in the appointments they held when they made their contributions. Contributors new to this edition are distinguished by an asterisk.

E P A Edward Penley Abraham, FRS, MA, DPhil.
Professor of Chemical Pathology, Oxford.
P A A Per-Åke Albertsson
Professor of Biochemistry, University of Umea, Sweden.
C A Sir Christopher Andrewes, FRS, MD, FRCP
Formerly Deputy Director, National Institute for Medical Research, London.
A A Angus Armitage, MSc, PhD
Reader in the History and Philosophy of Science, University of London.
W H G A Walter Harry Green Armytage
Professor of Education, University of Sheffield.
A P B Anne Pimlott Baker, BA *
Research Assistant, *Dictionary of National Biography*.
C E H B Cecil Edwin Henry Bawn, FRS, CBE
Emeritus Professor of Physical Chemistry, University of Liverpool.
C B Cyril Bibby, MA, MSc, PhD
Principal, Kingston upon Hull College of Education.
R M B Ronald M. Birse, BSc, C. ENG., MICE, MIHT *
Honorary Fellow, Department of Civil Engineering, University of Edinburgh.
W H B William H. Brock, BSc, MSc, PhD *
Professor of the History of Science, University of Leicester.
J C John Challinor, MA
Formerly Senior Lecturer in Geology, University College of Wales, Aberystwyth.
E C Edwin Clarke, MD, MRCP
Senior Lecturer in the History of Medicine, University College, London.
J D C Sir John Douglas Cockcroft, OM, KCB, CBE, FRS
Late Master of Churchill College, Cambridge; formerly Director of the Atomic Energy Research Establishment, Harwell; Nobel prize winner for physics, 1951.

N C Noel Coley, PhD *
   Reader in the History of Science, Open University.
C C-D C. Cormier-Delanoue *
   Fondation Louis de Broglie, Paris.
E J H C Edred John Henry Corner, CBE, FRS, FLS *
   Emeritus Professor of Tropical Botany, University of
   Cambridge.
J K C John Keith Crellin, B.Pharm., MSc, MPS
   Wellcome Historical Medical Museum and Library.
R H D Richard Henry Dalitz, FRS, PhD *
   Royal Society Research Professor, University of Oxford 1963–90.
K D Keith Dalziel, FRS, MA, PhD *
   Reader in Biochemistry, University of Oxford 1978–83.
G DE B Sir Gavin de Beer, FRS, FSA, DSc
   Formerly Director of the British Museum (Natural History).
T K D Thomas Kingston Derry, MA, DPhil.
   Joint author of *A Short History of Technology.*
R G C D Raymond George Coulter Desmond, FLA
   Librarian, Royal Botanic Gardens, Kew.
J M D John Michael Dubbey, MSc, AKC
   Senior Lecturer in Mathematics, Woolwich Polytechnic; part-time
   Lecturer in the History of Mathematics, University College,
   London.
M P E Melvin Peter Earles, B.Pharm, MSc, PhD
   Senior Lecturer, Chelsea College of Science, University of London.
J C E Sir John Carew Eccles, FRS, FAA, FRSNZ, MB, BS, MA, DPhil.
   Distinguished Professor Emeritus, University of New York at Buffalo.
   Nobel prize winner for medicine, 1963.
W V F Wilfred Vernon Farrar, BSc, PhD
   Nuffield Research Fellow, Department of the History of Science and
   Technology, University of Manchester Institute of Science and
   Technology.
W F Wilhelm Siegmund Feldberg, CBE, FRS, MA, MD
   Head of the Laboratory of Neuropharmacology, National Institute for
   Medical Research, London.
H and A G Helmut and Alison Gernsheim
   Photo-historians and authors.
A P G Alan Philps Graham, MA, FLS, FIBiol.
   Formerly Head of Biology Department, Latymer Upper School,
   Hammersmith, London.
F G S Sir Francis Graham-Smith, FRS, PhD *
   Emeritus Professor of Physics, University of Manchester.

F G Frank Greenaway, MA, PhD, FRIC, FMA
Keeper, Department of Chemistry, Science Museum, London.

L F H L F Haber, BSc (Econ), PhD

W R H Sir William Rede Hawthorne, FRS, CBE
Master of Churchill College, Cambridge, formerly Professor of Applied
Thermodynamics, University of Cambridge.

L S H Leslie Spencer Hearnshaw, MA
Professor of Psychology, University of Liverpool.

J W H John William Herivel, MA
Reader in the History and Philosophy of Science, The Queen's
University, Belfast.

N H Norman Higham, MA, ALA
Librarian, University of Bristol.

R L H Richard Leslie Hills, MA, DIC
Research Assistant, University of Manchester Institute of Science and
Technology.

R A H Robert Aubrey Hinde, CBE, FRS *
Master of St. John's College, Cambridge.

R J H Richard J. Howarth, PhD, FGS *
Visiting Professor of Mathematical Geology, University College,
London.

E H J Ernest H Jellinek, DM, MRCP
Senior Lecturer in Neurology, University of Edinburgh.

R V J Reginald Victor Jones, CB, CBE, FRS, DPhil.
Professor of Natural Philosophy, University of Aberdeen.

B K Sir Bernard Katz, FRS
Emeritus Professor of Biophysics, University College London.

K D K Kenneth David Keele, MD, FRCP
Consultant Physician, Ashford Hospital, Middlesex.

B B K Brian Beverley Kelham, BSc
Nuffield Research Scholar, University of Manchester Institute of
Science and Technology.

N K Nicholas Kemmer, FRS, FRSE, DPhil.
Tait Professor of Mathematical Physics, University of
Edinburgh.

C W K Clive William Kilmister, MSc, PhD
Professor of Mathematics, King's College, London.

D G K-H Desmond George King-Hele, FRS, FIMA, FRAS
Senior Principal Scientific Officer, Space Department, Royal
Aircraft Establishment, Farnborough.

D M K David Marcus Knight, MA, DPhil.
Lecturer in the History of Science, University of Durham.

C L Christopher Langley, BSc, MA, PhD *
Head of Information, Ciba Foundation, London.

R P L Richard Paul Lorch, BA
Department of the History of Science and Technology, University of
Manchester Institute of Science and Technology.

A C B L Sir Alfred Charles Bernard Lovell, FRS, OBE
Director, Nuffield Radio Astronomy Laboratories, Jodrell Bank.

I M McC Irena Maria McCabe, BSc, MSc
Librarian/Archivist, Royal Institution of Great Britain.

L H M L. Harrison Matthews, FRS, SCD
Formerly Scientific Director, Zoological Society of London.

C M Clifford Mawdsley, MB, CHB, MRCP, MRCPE
Senior Lecturer in Neurology, University of Edinburgh.

A R M Anthony R. Michaelis, BSc, PhD, DIC
Science Correspondent of the *Daily Telegraph*; formerly Editor of
Discovery.

P J T M Peter J. T. Morris, MA, D.Phil, GRSC *
Senior Curator, Science Museum, London.

J W N John William Nicholson, BSc, PhD, C. Chem, FRSC *
Senior Lecturer, Department of Biomaterials Science, King's College
School of Medicine and Dentistry, London.

J D N John David North, MA, BSc, DPhil, FRAS
Assistant Curator, Museum of the History of Science, Oxford.

B J N B. J. Norton, BSc, MPhil.
History of Science Department, University of Leicester.

D N Donald Nudds, MA
Lecturer in Computing, University of Bradford.

R C O Robert Cecil Olby, MA, DPhil.
Librarian, The Botany School, Oxford.

A D O Arthur Derek Orange, PhD, MSc
Senior Lecturer, Department of Humanities, Newcastle upon Tyne
Polytechnic.

O P Olaf Pedersen, MSc, DSc
Professor of the History of Science, University of Aarhus, Denmark.

R E P Sir Rudolf Peierls, FRS, MA, DSc
Whykeham Professor of Physics, University of Oxford 1963–74.

H M P Herbert Marcus Powell, FRS, BSc
Professor of Chemical Crystallography, University of Oxford.

A G P Sir Alfred Grenvile Pugsley, OBE, FRS, DSc *
Professor of Civil Engineering, University of Bristol 1944–68.

S J R Sandra Joan Raphael, BA, Dip. Lib.
Editor/Writer.

C A Ro Colin A. Ronan, MSc, FRAS *
Lately The Needham Research Institute, Cambridge.

A E R Archibald Edmiston Roy, BSc, PhD, FRAS
Senior Lecturer in Astronomy, University of Glasgow.

C A R Colin Archibald Russell, MSc, PhD, FRIC
Senior Lecturer in Organic Chemistry, Harris College, Preston.

H S Henrik Sandblad, PhD
Professor, University of Gothenburg, Sweden; Head of Department for
the History of Knowledge and Science.

M S Maurice Schofield, MA BSc, FRIC
Science writer; formerly Senior Lecturer, Wolverhampton College of
Technology.

D S David Shoenberg, FRS, PhD *
Professor of Physics, University of Cambridge.

W N S William Norman Slatcher, BA, MSc
Research Assistant, Department of the History of Science and
Technology, University of Manchester Institute of Science and
Technology.

W T S William Thomas Stearn, DSc, ScD, VMH, FIBiol., FLS
Senior Principal Scientific Officer, Department of Botany, British
Museum (Natural History).

H S H. Suginome *
Professor of Chemistry, Hokkaido University, Japan.

C S Christine Sutton, BSc, PhD *
Research Assistant, Department of Physics, University of Oxford.

G R T Geoffrey R Talbot, BSc, PhD
Assistant Lecturer in the History and Philosophy of Science, The
Queen's University, Belfast.

G P T Sir George Paget Thomson, FRS, DSc
Formerly Master of Corpus Christi College, Cambridge; Emeritus
Professor of Physics, University of London; Nobel prize winner for
physics, 1937.

E A U Edgar Ashworth Underwood, MD, FRCP, FLS
Hon. Lecturer, Department of the History and Philosophy of Science,
University College, London.

J S W Jeannie Sandra Wallace, BSc, DPhil. *

R L W Robert L Weber, BA, PhD
Formerly Associate Professor of Physics, Pennsylvania State
University.

C W Charles Weiner, PhD
Director, Center for History of Physics, American Institute of Physics,
New York.

G J W Geerad James Whitrow, MA, DPhil.
Reader in Applied Mathematics, Imperial College, London.
L P W L Pearce Williams, PhD
Professor of the History of Science, Cornell University, USA.
F P W W F. Peter W. Winteringham, DSc, FIBiol, FRSC, FRSA *
International Atomic Energy Agency/UN Food and Agriculture
Organization 1967–80.

A

ABBE, ERNST Born at Eisenach, Thuringia, Germany, 23 January 1840; died Jena, Saxony, 14 January 1905. Physicist, noted for development of optical instruments.

Abbe was the son of a foreman spinner. He was educated at the universities of Jena and Göttingen. In 1863 he joined the physics faculty at Jena and in 1870 was appointed professor; eight years later he became Director of the Observatory there. In 1875 he met Carl ZEISS), supplier and repairer of instruments for the University of Jena, whose development of high-quality optical instruments was handicapped by his inability to undertake elaborate lens computations. In Abbe, Zeiss found a man whose scientific and mathematical training complemented his own practical experience, and a partnership was established. Progress was still slow, however, as the range of available optical glasses was insufficient to manufacture their hypothetical achromatic compound lenses. In 1879, however, Abbe met Otto Schott (1851–1935), son of a Westphalian glass manufacturer who had been experimenting with lithium glass. This proved valueless to Zeiss and Abbe, but Schott was persuaded to undertake fresh experiments which led to the development of the very useful borate and phosphate glasses, having properties very different from those of crown and flint glass. In 1884 Zeiss, Abbe, and Schott established the glass manufacturing firm of Schott and Sons. Four years later, on Zeiss's death, Abbe became owner of the Zeiss concern, whose reputation for the manufacture of optical instruments of the highest quality became internationally established. He is particularly remembered for the apochromatic objective (1886). His oil-immersion objectives contained at least eight component lenses. To complement the use of his high-power objectives he devised (1872) a substage condenser.

With A. H. L. FIZEAU Abbe devised a very sensitive optical dilatometer for measuring thermal expansion. He is remembered also for the Abbe crystal refractometer.

F. Auerbach, *Ernst Abbe*. 1918.
Dictionary of Scientific Biography.

T I W

ABEGG, RICHARD WILHELM HEINRICH Born in Danzig, Germany, 9 January 1869; died near Tessin, Pomerania, 3 April 1910. Physical chemist.

Abegg studied chemistry at several universities: Tübingen, Kiel, Berlin, Leipzig, and Stockholm. He settled in Göttingen as assistant to W. H. NERNST, and became professor in 1897; in 1899 he moved to a chair in the *Technische Hochschule*, Breslau. He was killed in a balloon accident.

Apart from an early study of chrysene (in the school of A. W. von HOFMANN), Abegg's work was in the field of physical chemistry. He published on such topics as complex ions, depression of freezing-point, transport numbers, and oxidation potentials. He distinguished between the 'normal' and 'contra' valencies of the elements, and his name is remembered in 'Abegg's rule', which states that the sum of these two valencies is always eight.

Berichte der deutschen chemischen Gesellschaft, **46**, 619, 1913. (Portrait.)

W V F

ABEL, SIR FREDERICK AUGUSTUS Born at Woolwich, near London, 17 July 1827; died London, 6 September 1902. Explosives chemist.

Abel was educated at the Royal College of Chemistry and in 1851 was appointed demonstrator in chemistry at St Bartholomew's Hospital, London. The following year saw his appointment as lecturer at the Royal Military Academy, Woolwich, and the beginning of a long career particularly concerned with military explosives. He became the British Government's chief adviser in this field.

In 1845, C. F. SCHONBEIN had shown that an exceedingly powerful explosive (gun-cotton) could be made by treating cotton with nitric acid, but a series of disastrous explosions halted its manufacture in Europe. Abel showed that gun-cotton could be made safe to handle if subjected to prolonged and meticulously careful washing to remove all traces of free acid. This process was worked by the British Government at Waltham Abbey and was later exploited by Alfred NOBEL. In 1889 Abel (with Sir James DEWAR) invented cordite, an important military propellant consisting of gun-cotton and nitro-glycerine gelatinized with acetone and stabilized with petroleum jelly. It was so called because it was finally extruded through dies and emerged in the form of a cord, the thickness depending on the intended purpose of the explosive.

The importance of Abel's work in this field, and in the steel industry, was widely recognized in his lifetime. He was elected F. R.S. in 1860 and was awarded the Society's Royal Medal in 1887. He was knighted in 1883 and made a baronet ten years later. A man of very wide scientific and technological talent, he was also an accomplished musician.

Dictionary of National Biography. 1901–1911.
The Times, 8 September, 1902.
Nature, lxvi, 492, 1902.

T I W

ABEL, NIELS HENRIK Born on the Island of Finnoy, Norway, 5 August 1802; died near Arendal,

Norway, 6 April 1829. Mathematician; proved the impossibility of solving the general quintic equation.

Abel's father, an impecunious Norwegian minister, died when Abel was 18, leaving him to keep the family. He attended the Cathedral School at Oslo, where he was helped, both intellectually and financially, by the enlightened mathematics master. In 1821 he entered the University of Oslo. He spent the winter of 1825–26 with Norwegian friends in Berlin, where he met Leopold Crelle (1780–1855) and encouraged him to found his famous *Journal* – to which Abel contributed many papers. In 1826 he went on a European tour ending at Paris, and in 1827 returned to Norway heavily in debt. He died in poverty before news of the offer of a university post in Berlin reached him.

Modern equation theory is usually considered to date from Abel and E. Galois (1811–32), J. L. LAGRANGE and P. Ruffini (1765–1822) had considered the impossibility of solving the general quintic in radicals: Abel proved it in 1824. He also gave the first rigorous proof of the general binomial theorem. He revolutionized the study of elliptic integrals by introducing elliptic functions, whose theory he developed in rivalry with K. C. J. JACOBI: his most famous paper in this field in his *Mémoire sur une Propriété Remarquable d'une Classe Très Étendues de Fonctions Transcendantes.* (1826).

N. H. Abel, *Œuvres Complètes.* 1839. (New edition 1881, reprinted 1965.)

O. Ore, *Niels Henrik Abel: Mathematician Extraordinary.* 1957. (Portrait.)

E. T. Bell, *Men of Mathematics.* 1937.

R P L

ABRAHAM, SIR EDWARD PENLEY Born in Southampton, England, 10 June 1913. Biochemist notable for work on antibiotics.

Educated at King Edward VI School in Southampton, Abraham graduated in Natural Science from Queen's College Oxford in 1935. He then joined Sir Robert ROBINSON's natural products chemistry school in the Dyson Perrins laboratories to work on the chemistry of lysozyme, an antibiotic discovered in tears by A. FLEMING in 1921. Following a doctorate (1938) and a Rockefeller Travelling Scholarship to study in Stockholm, he returned to Oxford at the end of 1939 to join H. W. FLOREY and E. B. CHAIN in work on the chemistry of penicillin. Abraham worked with Chain on the chromatographic and freeze-drying purification of penicillin which was essential both for its safe clinical trials and for the elucidation of its chemical structure. He supported Chain in the argument with Robinson concerning the beta-lactam hypothesis of penicillin structure that was confirmed by the x-ray studies of Dorothy HODGKIN in 1945. Abraham's work as member of the penicillin team, which included the isolation of penicillinase, a penicillin-destroying enzyme produced by some staphylococci, was crucial to its successful clinical trials.

In 1953 Abraham and Guy Newton (1920–69) isolated cephalosporin C from one of the many types of penicillin previously extracted from the fungus *Cephalosporium acremonium.* This new antibiotic prepared the way for chemical modifications of naturally-occurring substances for pharmaceutical use in the 1960s. Abraham was made a Fellow of Lincoln College Oxford in 1948, reader

in clinical pathology at Oxford in 1960 and professor in 1964. He was elected FRS in 1958 and knighted in 1980. He is the author of several monographs on the biochemistry of antibiotics.

Trevor I. Williams, *Howard Florey: Penicillin and After.* 1984.

E. P. Abraham, *Review of Infectious Diseases,* **1**, 99, 1979.

W H B

ACHESON, EDWARD GOODRICH Born at Washington, Pennsylvania, USA, 9 March 1856; died New York, 6 July 1931. Industrial chemist.

Acheson had little formal education, and worked at humble jobs until 1880, when he obtained a position in the laboratory of T. A. EDISON at Menlo Park. Here he worked on problems connected with electric lamps, but left in 1884 to become an independent industrialist. In 1891 he discovered silicon carbide ('carborundum') and set up a company to manufacture it. This needed cheap power for the electric furnace, and in 1895 he moved to Niagara Falls. The electric furnace was used in 1899 to make 'synthetic' graphite from coke, and in 1906 Acheson discovered how to make lubricants from colloidal graphite ('Aquadag' and 'Oildag'). His later years were largely spent in managing the enterprises he had founded.

Journal of Chemical Education, **33**, 113, 1956. (Portrait.)

W V F

ADAMS, JOHN COUCH Born at Laneast, Cornwall, England, 5 June 1819; died Cambridge, 21 January 1892. Discoverer of Neptune.

John Couch Adams was the son of a tenant farmer. Given a classical education at Devonport, he studied mathematics on his own initiative. His parents managed to send him to Cambridge in 1837. Graduating as Senior Wrangler in 1843, he was immediately elected to a Fellowship at St John's College, and later to one at Pembroke College (1852).

He became Lowndean Professor of Astronomy and Geometry in 1858, and Director of the University Observatory in 1860.

In 1821 Alexis Bouvart (1767–1843) had published tables of Uranus, reluctantly rejecting the earliest observations of the planet's position as being incompatible with later observations. In 1841 Adams learned of these difficulties and soon arrived at a first solution of the problem, convincing himself that the irregularities were due to an undiscovered planet. Within two years he had deduced the elements and position of the new planet, unaware that U. LE VERRIER was working on the same lines in France. In the autumn of 1845 he several times sought to see the Astronomer Royal, Sir George Airy (1801–92), but failed to meet him. He nevertheless left a statement with Airy, which was neglected until, eight months later, it was learned that Le Verrier had arrived at a value for the mean longitude of the unseen planet differing by only one degree from Adams's figure. In September, Le Verrier wrote to J. G. Galle (1812–1910) at the Berlin Observatory, and within five days Galle discovered the object. To intense national enthusiasm in France, J. F. W. HERSCHEL made known the work of Adams, while James Challis (1803–82) announced that he had been searching for the planet, using Adams's predictions, since the end of July. He had even observed it on three occasions without realizing its planetary status. A bitter controversy ensued. With characteristic impartiality, the Royal Society awarded its highest honour, the Copley Medal, to Le Verrier alone. D. F. J. ARAGO wished to call the planet 'Le Verrier', but by general consent the name 'Neptune' was agreed upon.

Adams never forsook his studies of the dynamics of the solar system, and for the rest of his life he was generally recognized as the leading authority on the subject. He was involved in yet more controversy with the French, including Le Verrier, when he found fault with the explanation of P. S. LAPLACE, of the secular acceleration of the Moon's mean motion, but his critics eventually acknowledged that he was right.

> W. G. Adams and R. A. Sampson (Ed.), *The Scientific Papers of John Couch Adams*, 2 vols. 1896–1900.
> W. M. Smart, *John Couch Adams and the Discovery of Neptune*. 1947. (Portrait)
> *Dictionary of Scientific Biography.*

J D N

ADAMS, WALTER SYDNEY Born in Kessab, near Antioch, Syria, 20 December, 1876; died Pasadena, California, USA, 11 May, 1956. Astrophysicist, developed spectral parallax for estimation of star distances.

Adams returned to the United States with his missionary parents in 1885. Graduating from Dartmouth College (1898), he joined Yerkes Observatory on a programme of stellar spectrography. In 1904 Adams joined the team under G. E. HALE to establish the Mount Wilson (Solar) Observatory and he and Hale subsequently examined solar spectrograms. In 1908, they demonstrated from comparison of enhanced spectral lines (first described by J. N. LOCKYER in 1897) with laboratory spark spectra that the spots have lower temperatures than the disk. Adams then examined many star spectra, particularly using pairs of stars of similar spectral type, and therefore similar temperature, but with different luminosities. In 1914 he realised that the luminosity of a star could be deduced from the intensity of key lines and hence its distance away from its apparent brightness relative to its true luminosity. This spectral parallax method became invaluable in determining galactic structure.

Despite administrative work as Assistant Director and Director of the Observatory from 1913–46, Adams continued measurement of stellar spectrograms to the end of his life and used it to deduce radial velocities of thousands of stars. Other contributions included: confirmation of relativistic space-time curvature using the spectrum of Sirius B (1925); detection of CO_2 in the Venusian atmosphere (1932); and of H_2O and O_2 in the Martian atmosphere (1937).

> *Biographical Memoirs of the National Academy of Sciences*, **31**, 1, 1958. (Portrait.)
> *Biographical Memoirs of Fellows of the Royal Society*, 1956. (Portrait.)
> *Dictionary of Scientific Biography*, vol. 1. 1970.
> W. S. Adams, in A. Beer (Ed.), *Vistas in Astronomy*, **1**, 619, 1955.

R J H

ADDISON, THOMAS Born at Long Benton, near Newcastle upon Tyne, England, April 1793; died Brighton, Sussex, 29 June 1860. A founder of endocrinology.

Addison studied medicine at the University of Edinburgh and graduated as a doctor of medicine in 1815. He then migrated to London; was appointed house surgeon to the Lock Hospital; and studied dermatology under Thomas Bateman (1778–1821). He became a Licentiate of the Royal College of Physicians in 1819. Despite the fact that he was now a fully qualified physician, Addison entered as a student at Guy's Hospital about 1820. He was appointed assistant physician to that hospital in 1824, lecturer on materia medica in 1827, and physician in 1837. In 1838 he was elected a Fellow of the Royal College of Physicians. He had a brilliant reputation as a lecturer and as a clinical teacher.

In 1829, in collaboration with John Morgan (1797–1847), Addison wrote the first book in English on the action of poisons on the living body. An early and important paper by him gave an excellent description of the clinical features which he found to be diagnostic of a fatty liver. He laid down the basis of our knowledge of the pathology of lobar pneumonia (1837, 1843). In 1839 there appeared the first volume of the *Elements of the Practice of Medicine*, by Addison and Richard BRIGHT. This volume was mainly by Addison, and Bright's work was to appear in the second volume, which was never published. In this work Addison gave the first adequate description of appendicitis and its results. He discovered the disease xanthoma.

On 15 March 1849 Addison read to the South London Medical Society a paper 'On anaemia: Disease of the suprarenal capsules'. He was primarily interested in the anaemia, and in the three cases upon which autopsy had been performed he had found disease of the suprarenal capsules. He suggested that the existence of anaemia together with disease of the suprarenals was not a coincidence. The paper attracted no attention, although it contained the germ of the discovery of two new diseases. In 1855 Addison extended his theme in a small book entitled *On the Constitutional and Local Effects of Disease of the Supra-Renal Capsules*. In this he gives an excellent description of the features of the 'idiopathic' anaemia, which was soon to be called 'pernicious' or 'Addisonian anaemia'. He explained that originally he had been searching for further cases of this condition when he discovered by chance another disease characterized pathologically by disease of the suprarenal capsules. This was 'Addison's disease', the clinical features of which were great weakness, a peculiar bronze pigmentation of the skin, and, at that time, a fatal result. In the same year Claude BERNARD introduced the term 'internal secretion', and Addison's work led almost at once to physiological studies which showed that the suprarenal capsules were really suprarenal (or adrenal) glands.

> W. Munk, *Roll of the Royal College of Physicians*. 1878.
> H. Dale, *British Medical Journal*, ii, 347, 1949. (Portrait.)
> *Medical Times and Gazette*, **2**, 20, 1860.
> *Dictionary of Scientific Biography.*

E A U

ADLER, ALFRED Born in Vienna, 7 February 1870; died (while on a lecture tour) Aberdeen, Scotland, 28 May 1937. Founder of Individual Psychology.

Adler worked in Vienna as a general physician before becoming associated with Sigmund FREUD. He was one of Freud's earliest collaborators, contact having been made between them as early as 1902. For a time Adler played an important part in the development of the psychoanalytic movement, and served as President of the Vienna Psychoanalytic Society. Differences of opinion arose, ostensibly on the role of the sexual drive in the origin of the neuroses; in 1911, after a series of discussions, Adler and a number of others left the Freudian circle, and set up their own movement, later termed Individual Psychology.

The central concept in Adler's theory of the neuroses was that known as 'the inferiority complex'. His first important book, *A Study of Organ Inferiority* (1907), stressed the role of bodily inferiority in the adjustment of the individual, and the compensatory strivings which result. These strivings may lead to overcompensation, and a craving for superiority, which may in effect cut the individual off from the social group to which he belongs. Adler later developed the concept of inferiority more widely to embrace many sorts of inferiority other than organ inferiority. For example, younger children tended to feel inferior to their older siblings, and women tended to feel inferior to men, and consequently to engage in various forms of 'masculine protest'.

Adler believed that for every individual there was a unique goal, only dimly envisaged and partially understood, which could satisfy his personal needs. It was up to the individual, assisted if necessary by the psychotherapist, to discover the unique 'life style' which would enable him to realize his goal. No individual, however, is separable from the society in which he lives, and what Adler calls 'social interest' is an essential factor in personal adjustment. Maladjustment is the substitution of self-centred superiority strivings, rooted ultimately in inferiority feelings, for social co-operation and social interest.

There is a good deal of common sense in Adler's psychology, but a lack either of trenchant theoretical analysis or of methodological rigour. His key concepts are often vague and poorly defined. In his day he did much to promote child guidance and socially orientated concepts of mental health, but his long-term impact is likely to be less than that of either Freud or C. G. JUNG.

H. L. and R. R. Ansbacher, *The Individual Psychology of Alfred Adler. A Systematic Presentation in Selections from his Writings.* 1958. (Portrait and full bibliography.)

Phyllis Bottome, *Alfred Adler, Apostle of freedom: a Biography.* 1939.

H. Orgler, *Alfred Adler: The Man and his Work* (4th ed.) 1973.

L S H

ADRIAN, EDGAR DOUGLAS (BARON ADRIAN OF CAMBRIDGE) Born London, 30 November 1889; died Cambridge, 4 August 1977. Renowned for his pioneer work on the coding of sensory information in the form of impulse discharges in sensory nerve fibres.

Adrian's life was uniquely bound up with a great academic foundation, Trinity College, Cambridge, with which he was intimately associated for almost 70 years. He entered as a Major Scholar in Natural Science in 1908. After a distinguished double first he was elected a Fellow of the College in 1913, a position he held to the end of his life except for 14 years (1951–65) during which he was Master.

We first encounter Adrian scientifically in 1912 in his experiments with his famous teacher, Keith Lucas (1879–1916), in elegant investigations on summation in the nerve-muscle preparation. Two kinds were described. In one there was summation of the local responses of nerve to subthreshold stimuli. The other was the much more interesting phenomenon of summation of conducted impulses either at a narcotic block or at the junctional region between nerve and muscle. This was investigated by experiments that have become classics. There was a remarkable simplicity and directness in the experimental attack on the properties of nerve and muscle and of the neuromuscular junction. It was a great tragedy when this most fruitful collaboration was broken by the death of Lucas in 1916. Adrian edited a monograph that Lucas left in manuscript form, 'The Conduction of the Nervous Impulse', published in 1917.

In 1914 Adrian relinquished research in order to become medically qualified. The exigences of the First World War caused him to move his interests to the clinical problems of nerve injury and muscle denervation and to war neuroses. He was elected Fellow of the Royal Society in 1923.

A notable postwar contribution was his pioneer review of theories of inhibition in 1924, in which he advanced for the first time the suggestion that central inhibition may be hormonally mediated, on analogy with the recent demonstration by Otto LOEWI of vagal inhibition of the heart.

Then followed a set-back. In 1912 Lucas and Adrian had invented a technique of graded narcosis of nerve as a testing procedure for the strength of the nerve impulse. They presented evidence that there was a progressive decrement of a nerve impulse when it travelled along a uniformly narcotized nerve. On this basis they had carried out many analytical experiments on the nerve impulse. Then came in 1924 and 1926 two monographs by Genichi Kato of Japan that gave a convincing experimental refutation of decremental conduction and consequently of the scientific stories built up by Lucas and Adrian. Adrian accepted the refutation as a good scientist should, but he never returned to this controversial field. For this we can be grateful, because in 1925 and 1926 he was at the outset of the work for which he is most famous, namely a study of the coding of sensory information in transmission to the brain by the discharge frequencies of impulses in nerve fibres. For the first time there was a clear demonstration by Adrian and Yngve Zotterman of the manner in which intensity of stimulation is coded as frequency of firing in single afferent fibres. Later, with Detlev Bronk (1897–1975) the same principle of coding by frequency was demonstrated for the discharge of motoneurones, and so in the control of motor responses.

Contemporary neurobiologists cannot realize the technical difficulties in those pioneer investigations, where the capillary electrometer was the device for recording from single nerve fibres – perhaps the most temperamental instrument ever devised! Encouraged by these successes Adrian and collaborators essayed a study of the discharges of many sense organs. Initially there was concentration on the diverse receptors of skin and muscle. Then in 1927 and 1928 with Rachel Matthews there was a study of the eye, and in 1931 of the ear. It was this fundamental work on nerve impulse discharges that earned Adrian a Nobel prize that he shared with C. S. SHERRINGTON in 1932.

By the early 1930s recording techniques had been greatly improved by the oscilloscope designed by Bryan Matthews. Armed with this instrument Adrian and Matthews made important studies on the Berger rhythm that had been discovered by Hans BERGER some years earlier. Some of their records of evoked potentials and of the influence of various procedures on the alpha rhythm have become classical illustrations. Their work triggered the remarkable development of electroencephalography. Adrian's own brain was an excellent generator of the alpha rhythm. I have heard him remark that in this respect it was as good as a rabbit's brain!

At that period there were several notable studies on the cerebral cortex. The slow potential waves evoked by direct surface stimulation – the superficial and deep responses – have been much investigated since, but I think the full import of these responses is not yet assimilated to our ideas on the functioning of the neocortex. In 1938–9 there were the studies with G. Moruzzi on the electrical responses of motor pyramidal cells and the correlation of these discharges with impulses in the pyramidal tract. This work was related to the clinical condition of epileptic seizure.

Adrian was elected to the Foulerton Professorship of the Royal Society in 1929, relinquishing this attractive research position to take on the arduous duties of professor of physiology at Cambridge from 1937 to 1951.

In the 1940s Adrian made a comparative study of the sensory areas of the neocortex in a wide variety of mammals – rabbit, cat, dog, pig, horse, monkey. There was good correlation with the functional meaning for the animal. Thus in these somatotopic studies the pig's snout dominates the whole of the tactile receiving area of the cerebral cortex, and even in the horse the nostrils occupy half of the tactile receiving area. In contrast, in the monkey the limbs are well represented as well as the head. Adrian's final experimental investigations (1941–3) were on the vestibular receptors of the inner ear and (1937–59) on the extremely difficult problem of olfaction, which he studied by electrical recording from the olfactory epithelium and the olfactory bulb in a wide variety of animals. Progress was slow because those were the years in which he had immense administrative responsibilities.

Adrian was a master of exposition. His communications to the Physiological Society were models of clarity. His three monographs are delightful in their simple elegance: *The basis of sensation* (1928); *The mechanism of nervous action* (1935); and *The physical background of perception* (1946). With growing complexity of neurobiology it seems no longer possible to write such monographs.

In later life he was much in demand as a lecturer,

an art in which he was most accomplished in a wide variety of subjects.

Adrian was a man of great charm and simplicity and was loved and admired by all, but he also had his reticences, resembling in all these respects his devoted friend, Sherrington. He had a most distinguished administrative career. Foreign Secretary of the Royal Society (1946–50); President of the Royal Society (1950–5); and Master of Trinity College (1951–65). But these are only the most notable of a galaxy of University and scientific appointments. Amongst his numerous honours were the Nobel prize; the Order of Merit; the Royal and Copley Medals of the Royal Society; and a Peerage (1955).

In 1923 he married Hester Pinsent and they had two daughters and one son. Hester died in 1967.

Biographical Memoirs of Fellows of the Royal Society. 1979. (Portrait.)

Dictionary of National Biography.

H. Oxbury (Ed.), *Great Britons: 20th Century Lives.* 1985.

Tyler Wasson (Ed.), *Nobel Prize Winners.* 1987. (Portrait.)

J C E

AGASSIZ, JEAN LOUIS RODOLPHE Born at Motier, Switzerland, 28 May 1807; died Boston, Massachusetts, USA, 18 December 1873. Leading American geologist, palaeontologist, and zoologist.

Louis Agassiz, son of the Protestant pastor of Motier, took a medical degree at Munich in 1830. He had already worked out and published a report on the freshwater fishes of Brazil collected by J. B. von Spix (1781–1826) and C. F. P. von Martius (1794–1868) in 1829, and this study gave him a lifelong devotion to ichthyology. He followed it with a *History of the Freshwater Fishes of Central Europe*, and then turned his attention to fossil fish, publishing five lavishly illustrated volumes from 1833 to 1843, having visited all the principal museums of Europe for study. This work led him to formulate a new ichthyological classification which, though now superseded, was a major advance. He followed this with researches on recent and fossil echinoderms, fossil mollusca, and the Old Red Sandstone fishes of Scotland and Russia.

Concurrently Agassiz was studying the glaciers of the Alps and published *Études sur les Glaciers* in 1840, discussing the effects of glacial action on topography, and showing that in geologically recent times widespread glaciation had formed an ice age; he reinforced his theory by the discovery with W. Buckland (1800–74) of evidence of glacial action in Scotland.

In 1846 Agassiz went to the United States to study geology and natural history, and to deliver a course of lectures on zoology at the Lowell Institute of Boston, Massachusetts. The great opportunities for pursuing his favourite subjects, and the financial support available in America, induced him to settle there. In 1847 he was appointed professor of Zoology and geology at Harvard University, and launched into ambitious programmes of research and teaching. He very soon became a public figure through his popular lectures to laymen and his involvement in university politics. His research output was enormous and included four illustrated volumes of *Contributions to the*

Natural History of the United States, 1857–62. He accumulated vast collections from correspondents all over the country, and with them founded the Museum of Comparative Zoology at Harvard.

His collections, the museum and its staff, and lavishly illustrated publications, all needed large sums of money, and he developed great skill in raising funds from public and private sources; but however much he gained his fertile imagination was ever devising new schemes requiring more. Towards the end of his life Agassiz travelled in Brazil, and in the southern States, his journeys resulting in further books. He also established a zoological field station on Penikese Island in Buzzard's Bay, Massachusetts.

Agassiz was a man of such enormous energy and enthusiasm that many of his projects were left unfinished at his death, though the amount of work he accomplished was astonishing as the product of one man. His labours laid the foundation of scientific zoology in America and provided a stimulus to its pursuit all over the world. It is peculiar that notwithstanding his deep studies in palaeontology, he refused to accept the views on evolution developed by Charles DARWIN and professed a belief in successive independent creations.

   E. Lurie, *Louis Agassiz, a Life in Science.* 1960.
     (Portraits.)
   E. C. Agassiz, *L. Agassiz, His Life and*
     Correspondence. 1885.
   C. F. Holder, *Louis Agassiz, His Life and Work.*
     1893.
   A. B. Gould, *Louis Agassiz.* 1901.
   Dictionary of Scientific Biography.
   Gesnerus, **31**, 1, 1974.

                                    L H M

AGRICOLA (GEORG BAUER) Born at Glauchau, Saxony, Germany, 24 March 1494; died Chemnitz, Saxony, 21 November 1555. Pioneer of mining and chemical technology.

As a young man, Agricola studied at Leipzig. He then taught classics at the Municipal School in Zwickau and became Principal in 1520. Later, he studied medicine in Italy (Venice, Bologna, Padua), but then returned to his own country to make an intensive study of the techniques of mining and extraction of metals. For a time he lived in a mining area in Bohemia. He shortly moved to Joachimstal, where he became town physician (1533), and was later made burgomaster of Chemnitz (1546). Geographically, he was almost ideally placed to observe the principal mining and metallurgical processes of the day. He had the further advantage of the patronage of the Elector of Saxony, who gave him a pension and exempted him from taxation. Agricola was a Catholic and could not be buried in the intensely Protestant province of Saxony; his remains rest in the cathedral at Zeitz, Halle.

Agricola was not a great innovator, but he was a keen and critical observer of contemporary practice who interpreted what he saw in terms of the scientific knowledge of his time, with which he was well acquainted. He left a number of books on mining and chemical technology which were of lasting importance; his one medical work (*De Peste*, 1554) is trivial. His first book on mining was the Bermannus (1530), an account of Saxon minerals; it deals at some length with bismuth, but

does not, in fact, represent the first mention of this metal, which is described in the (anonymous) *Nützliches Bergbüchlein (c.*1500). His *De Natura Fossilium* appeared in 1546, and is an attempt at the systematic classification of minerals. However, his great work, on which his reputation mainly rests, is the *De Re Metallica*, first printed at Basle in 1555, and at once acknowledged as outstanding. It appeared in German in 1557 and in Italian in 1563; there was a second Latin edition in 1561. A handsome English edition appeared in 1912, annotated by Herbert C. Hoover (1874–1964), a mining engineer who became President of America (1929–33). The work is in twelve parts, profusely illustrated with woodcuts, some probably copied from the *Pirotechnia* (1540) of Vannucio BIRINGUCCIO. The first eleven parts deal mainly with mining and the smelting of extracted ores; the twelfth is essentially an account of the chemical technology of Agricola's day, much of which was, of course, closely connected with metallurgical processes.

   J. R. Partington, *A History of Chemistry*, vol. 2.
     1961.
   Bern Ditner, *Agricola on Metals.* 1958.
   Dictionary of Scientific Biography.

                                      T I W

AKERS, SIR ALAN WALLACE Born in London, 9 September 1888; died Alton, Hampshire, 1 November 1954. Chemist, wartime Director of UK Atomic Energy Research.

Akers went to Aldenham School and then trained at Oxford as a chemist. He then embarked on an industrial chemical career, first (1911–24) with Brunner Mond and Company (see J. BRUNNER and L. MOND) and then with its successor, Imperial Chemical Industries (1928–53), with whom he was appointed Research Director in 1941.

He was a man of many-sided talent. To purely formal qualification in chemistry (especially thermodynamics) he added a remarkable memory, quick insight, an equable disposition, and complete integrity. To these was added musical talent and an appreciation of the arts; he was a Trustee of the National Gallery, London. This combination of qualities led to his appointment during the war (1941–46) as director of a special organization set up by the British Government in 1941 to deal with all aspects of atomic energy. This involved him in co-ordinating the activities of a rapidly growing team of scientists and in delicate negotiations in both the UK and North America. These services were recognized by the award of a knighthood in 1946. He was elected FRS in 1953, and was an honorary graduand of Oxford and Durham.

   Biographical Memoirs of Fellows of the Royal
     Society. 1955. (Portrait)
   The Times, 2 November, 1954.
   Dictionary of National Biography.

                                      T I W

ALBERTI, LEONE BATTISTA Born in Venice, Italy, 18 February 1404; died Rome, 25 April 1472. Formulated laws of perspective.

Alberti was one of the most gifted men of the Renaissance. Primarily an architect, he was also an accomplished painter, musician, and mathematician. His churches of San Francesco at Rimini and Sta Maria Novella at Florence are outstanding examples of pure classical style. In his designs he was particularly influenced by VITRUVIUS and his *De Re Aedificatoria* (1485) not only did much to interest his contemporaries in the classical style but introduced them to constructional methods practised by Roman engineers.

Alberti has been credited with the invention of the camera obscura, but it is now accepted that this is properly attributed to the Arabian scholar ALHAZEN. He was however, certainly interested in optical devices of this kind, and it was probably these that led him to elucidate the laws of perspective, which had a profound effect on painting style. In a sense, he was the originator of projective geometry, developed in the nineteenth century by J. V. PONCELET.

A. Stokes, *Art and Science.* 1949.
J. Gadol, *Leon Battista Alberti: Universal Man of the Renaissance.* 1969.
P. H. Michel, *La Pensée de L. B. Alberti.* 1930.
Dictionary of Scientific Biography.

T I W

ALBERTUS MAGNUS Born at Lassingen, Swabia, Germany, 1193 or 1206; died Cologne, 15 November 1280. A great naturalist and compiler of Aristotelian writings.

After studying at Padua, Albertus took the Dominican habit in 1223. His life was devoted to teaching and writing on almost every aspect of theology, philosophy, and natural science, with the exception of mathematics. His philosophic and scientific works form a compendium of the writings of ARISTOTLE together with information derived from an encyclopedic knowledge of Islamic and Jewish authors, and neoplatonic works.

Between his arrival at the University of Paris in 1245 and his elevation to the see of Ratisbon in 1260, he composed his most important scientific works in the form of commentaries on, and paraphrases of, Aristotle. The *De Mineralibus* contains descriptions of various chemical substances and ninety-five minerals, many from direct observation. In the *De Vegetabilibus et Plantis* and the *De Animalibus* he proved himself the foremost naturalist of the Middle Ages. As Provincial of the Dominican Order, he had ample opportunities for observation during his long journeys on foot, preaching and teaching. The detailed descriptions of plants and animals, many noted for the first time, bear witness to his powers of observation, but he was incapable of original theorizing and always fitted new facts into the old framework of Aristotle's theories. Thus, though he rejected some old superstitions, such as the legend of the phoenix, he perpetuated many of Aristotle's errors, confusing bats with birds and whales with fishes. After surveying human anatomy, he gave detailed comparisons of the organs of man and various animals, though he had no personal knowledge of anatomy other than of the skeleton. Albertus was not a mathematician and contributed nothing to astronomy. He shared the contemporary interest in astrology, but works ascribed to him are of doubtful authenticity.

Albertus gained considerable reputation, even in his own lifetime, for his enormous energy; the vast amount of his writings was to form a reference library for scholars in centuries to come. Nevertheless, his work is unsystematic and generally uncritical, a compilation of authorities rather than

an organic synthesis. Although he gained undeserved fame as a magician from apocryphal dissertations on magical properties of plants and astrological superstitions, his contemporary title of 'Doctor Universalis' was not unmerited.

L. Thorndike, *A History of Magic and Experimental Science,* vol. 2. 1923.
H. C. Scheeben, *Albertus Magnus.* 1955. (Portrait.)
T. M. Schwertner, *St Albert the Great.* 1932.

J D N

ALBINUS, BERNHARD SIEGFRIED Born at Frankfurt-an-der-Oder, Brandenburg, Germany, 24 February 1697; died Leiden, Netherlands, 9 September 1770. The foremost anatomist of the eighteenth century, and the initiator of a new method of anatomic illustration.

Albinus was the most famous of the sons of Bernard Weiss (1653–1721), professor of medicine at Frankfurt-an-der-Oder, who had latinized his name as 'Albinus'. In 1702 Albinus senior was called to a chair at Leiden, and Bernhard Siegfried received his education there. In 1712 he matriculated in the University of Leiden, where he was a pupil of H. BOERHAAVE and other famous teachers. In 1718 he went to Paris to study anatomy and surgery. But in 1719 he was recalled by the University of Leiden to deputize for J. J. Rau (1668–1719), the professor of anatomy and surgery. Albinus acquitted himself so well that he was created a Doctor of Medicine, and in 1721 he was called to the chair of anatomy and surgery. In 1725 he compiled an excellent catalogue of the anatomical preparations that Rau had bequeathed to the University. Because of his health, Albinus requested in 1745 that he should be relieved of some of his duties, and he relinquished his chair and in its place was appointed professor of medicine. He now devoted himself to anatomy and physiology, and his younger brother became Lecturer in Surgery. Albinus was elected Fellow of the Royal Society in 1764.

Early in his professorship Albinus published several well-illustrated anatomical works for the use of his students. In 1725, in collaboration with Boerhaave, he published a sumptuous edition of the complete works of VESALIUS. In 1737 he edited a new edition of the works of FABRICIUS ab Aquapendente. In this direction he rendered his greatest service by the republication of the anatomical plates of EUSTACHIUS, with his own comments on the dissections illustrated (1744). Albinus had meanwhile moved to his conception that, in the anatomical illustration of an organ or region, what was required was not an illustration of the result of a single dissection but a composite picture illustrating the 'anatomic norm'. For example, in illustrating a particular bone, a large number of specimens were carefully measured and drawn, and a composite illustration, showing the correct proportions of a 'normal' bone, was finally produced. Albinus devised a complex method of viewing the objects to be drawn, so that in making the drawing the artist would always see the relevant parts of the object in the same correct proportions, whether he viewed the object from a distance or from close at hand. The first result of these methods was his *Plates of the skeleton and muscles of the human body* (1747), a magnificent work which occupied him for many years and cost him a great deal of money to produce. In the preparation of this work he had the expert and devoted assistance, as artist and engraver, of Jan Wandelaar (1690–1759).

Allgemeine Deutsche Biographie.
L. Choulant and M. Frank, *History and Bibliography of Anatomic Illustration.* 1920.
F. H. Garrison, *History of Medicine.* 1929. (Portrait.)
Dictionary of Scientific Biography, Supp. I.

E A U

ALBRIGHT, ARTHUR Born at Charlbury, Oxfordshire, England, 3 March 1811; died Chelsea, London, 3 July 1900. Industrial chemist; pioneer in the manufacture of phosphorus.

Albright came of a Quaker family. He attended school at Rochester from 1822 to 1827, and then became apprenticed to his uncle, who was a chemist and druggist in Bristol. He declined the offer of a partnership, and after a somewhat unsettled period he joined (1842) the firm of John and Edward Sturge, who were manufacturing chemists at Birmingham. In 1844 they expanded and purchased a new works at Selly Oak to make white phosphorus. Shortly afterwards Albright met Anton SCHRÖTTER, who described how he had discovered a new variety of phosphorus called amorphous or red phosphorus. It had the advantage of not being spontaneously inflammable, nor toxic, and was therefore easily transportable, but its preparation involved dangers. Albright purchased Schrötter's patent, and improved the method of preparation; in 1852 he was granted a patent for his improvements. A plant was opened at Oldbury in 1851 for making amorphous phosphorus for use in the manufacture of matches, and when the partnership with the Sturges was dissolved, in 1855, Albright retained this plant. In the following year he took J. W. Wilson (1834–1907) into partnership and the firm became known as Albright and Wilson. Albright retained his interest in this firm until his death. He was an ardent campaigner for social reform, and in 1874 was an unsuccessful Parliamentary candidate for East Worcestershire.

R. E. Threlfall, *The Story of 100 years of Phosphorus Making, 1851–1951.* 1951. (Portrait.)
The Times, 4 July 1900.
Dictionary of National Biography (Missing Persons). 1993.

B B K

ALDER, KURT Born at Königshütte, Silesia, 10 July 1902; died Cologne, 20 June 1958. Organic chemist, one of the discoverers of the Diels-Alder reaction.

Alder, the son of a teacher, studied chemistry in the Universities of Berlin and Kiel, where he held (1934) an extraordinary professorship. From 1936 to 1940 he worked in the research department of I. G. Farben at Leverkusen; in the latter year he was appointed to a chair in the University of Cologne, which he held until his death.

The Diels-Alder reaction was discovered (1928) while Alder was research assistant to Otto DIELS at Kiel. It involves the addition of a conjugated diene to a variety of unsaturated compounds (dienophiles), the product usually being a six-membered ring. This reaction, extremely versatile, and often remarkably facile, has become of the greatest importance in synthetic organic chemistry and in the petrochemicals industry. Alder's later career, interrupted as it was by the difficult conditions of 1940–50, was largely devoted to the study and extension of this reaction, and its application to industrial problems. He and his students also made important contributions to the study of stereochemistry.

He was awarded the Nobel prize for chemistry, jointly with Diels, in 1950.

Chemiker-Zeitung, **82**, 489, 1958. (Portrait.)
E. Farber, *Nobel Prizewinners in Chemistry.* 1953. (Portrait.)
Tyler Wasson (Ed.), *Nobel Prize Winners.* 1987. (Portrait).

W V F

ALDROVANDI, ULISSE Born at Bologna, Italy, 11 September 1522; died there, 10 May 1605. Naturalist.

After studying philosophy and medicine at Padua and Rome, Aldrovandi became in 1560 a professor at the University of Bologna, and the first Director of the Botanic Garden there. During the forty years he spent in the University he made great collections of natural objects and employed artists to make drawings of them. His services to science were recognized by the Government of Bologna, which doubled his salary, in return for which Aldrovandi bequeathed his collections and manuscripts to the city. These collections gave him material for his writings on natural history, which were intended ultimately to form an encyclopaedia of living things. Only four volumes of the fourteen – three on birds and one on insects – appeared during his life, but the others, on other animals, plants and minerals, were edited and published in the half-century following his death.

Aldrovandi's books are usually compared with the *Historia Animalium* of Konrad GESNER, the contemporary Swiss naturalist whose work must have influenced him. They differ from Gesner's work in being less critical, although paying more attention to anatomy, citing many more exotic and little-known forms, and having illustrations of a better quality. Aldrovandi has been criticized for the volume of irrelevant material quoted in his books, but nevertheless their influence lasted well into the eighteenth century, until the *Histoire Naturelle* of G. L. L. BUFFON replaced them.

Onoranze a Ulisse Aldrovandi nel terzo centenario dalla sua morte. 1908.
Dictionary of Scientific Biography.

S J R

ALFVÉN, HANNES OLOF GÖSTA Born at Norrköping, Sweden, 30 May 1908. Physicist, noted for pioneering work in magnetohydrodynamics and plasma physics.

Alfvén was educated at the University of Uppsala, where he gained his PhD in 1934, and subsequently worked as a research physicist at the Nobel Institute of Physics. He moved to the Royal Institute of Technology, Stockholm in 1940, becoming professor of electronics in 1945 and professor of plasma physics (a chair specially created for him) in 1963. As the result of a disagreement with the Swedish government he moved to the University of California, San Diego in 1967, but later restored his connection with the Royal Institute in Stockholm.

His early theoretical research into the behaviour of plasmas in electrical and magnetic fields led him to predict that under certain conditions a plasma could be restrained by a strong magnetic field, a phenomenon later confirmed and exploited in experimental research on controlled thermonuclear fusion. By 1942 he had developed his theory to show that hydromagnetic waves ('Alfvén waves') could exist in plasmas such as the ionized gas emitted by the Sun, and although it took some time for his work to be generally accepted it later became the basis for important advances in cosmology. He published *Cosmical Electrodynamics* in 1950, a monograph *On the Origin of the Solar System* in 1956, and (with G. Arrhenius) *Structure and Evolutionary History of the Solar System* in 1975. He was awarded the Gold Medal of the Royal Astronomical Society in 1967, and shared the Nobel prize for physics with Louis NÉEL in 1970, for 'fundamental work and discoveries in magnetohydrodynamics with fruitful applications in different parts of plasma physics'. For a time he was an advocate of nuclear weapons as a deterrent, and of nuclear power for peaceful uses, but after 1970 he changed his stance and joined the anti-nuclear lobby.

Robert L. Weber, *Pioneers of Science: Nobel Prize Winners in Physics* (2nd ed.) 1988. (Portrait.)
Modern Scientists and Engineers, McGraw-Hill. (Portrait.)
Tyler Wasson (Ed.), *Nobel Prize Winners*. 1987. (Portrait.)

R M B

ALHAZEN (ABU 'ALI AL-HASAN IBN AL-HAYTHAM) Born at Basra (in modern Iraq), *c*.965; died Cairo, *c*.1038. Work in optics influential in West until 17th century.

After moving to Cairo, Alhazen entered the service of Caliph al-Hakim who sent him to southern Egypt to find a means of controlling the annual flooding of the Nile. Fearing execution after the failure of this expedition Alhazen feigned madness until the death of the caliph years later in 1021.

His major work was in optics. Building on the work of PTOLEMY and GALEN he discussed the nature of light. Alhazen rejected the ancient Greek theory of vision that held that light was emitted by the eye and was then reflected in the object viewed. He argued that light rays coming from the Sun hit objects and were then reflected into the eye and perceived by the brain. He also studied lenses and mirrors, discovering that it was the curvature of the lens that accounted for its ability to focus light, and developed parabolic mirrors similar to those used in modern reflecting telescopes. Alhazen constructed the first known instance of the camera obscura, observing the form of the image of the Sun cast on a wall during an eclipse using a pin hole in a screen. He also studied rainbows, and realising that they formed in the atmosphere he investigated atmospheric refraction and calculated the height of the atmosphere.

Alhazen's work on optics was translated into Latin from the original Arabic in the 13th century, influencing medieval thinkers including Roger BACON and Robert GROSSETESTE. It was published in Basle in 1572 under the title *Opticae thesaurus*, and remained influential until superseded by the work of KEPLER.

Dictionary of Scientific Biography.

Hamdard, **13**, 1–346, 1970 (Proceedings of 1000th Anniversary Celebrations, Hamdard National Foundation, Pakistan).

A P B

ALPHER, RALPH ASHER Born in Washington, DC, USA, 3 February 1921. Physicist best known for his work on the Big Bang theory of the early Universe.

While working as a physicist at the US Naval Ordnance Laboratory (1940–1944) Alpher graduated in physics in 1943 at George Washington University. He joined Johns Hopkins University in Maryland in 1944, continuing as a part-time graduate student at George Washington University, with George GAMOW as his supervisor. Gamow's interest at the time was in the formation of the chemical elements in an expanding Universe, and this led to his theory of the Hot Big Bang, in which the Universe began in a state of extremely high temperature and density. In 1948, Alpher and Robert Herman (1914–), who also worked at Johns Hopkins University, published a paper on this theory in which they showed that the Universe should be bathed in radiation left over from the Big Bang and now cooled to a temperature of 5 K. This radiation, at 3 K, was discovered in 1965 as 'microwave background' by Arno PENZIAS and Robert Wilson.

Alpher left Johns Hopkins University in 1955, and joined the General Electric Company, where he worked until 1986. Since 1987 he has been Distinguished Research Professor of Physics at Union College in Schenectady, New York, and Senior Scientist at the Dudley Observatory there. He lists his interests as cosmology, astrophysics and the physics of fluids.

Physics Today, p. 24, August 1988. (Portrait.)

C S

ALPINI, PROSPERO Born at Marostica, Italy, 1553; died Padua, 1617. Physician and botanist.

Little is known of the early life of Alpini. He graduated in medicine at Padua. From 1580 to 1583 he travelled in the Greek Islands and in Egypt, being appointed physician to the Venetian Consul in Cairo, Giorgio Emo. In 1593 he was appointed professor in the University of Padua and Director of the Botanic Garden there, to which he introduced a number of Egyptian plants.

His published works reflect his Egyptian experiences. His *De Plantis Aegypti liber* (1592) described, and illustrated with woodcuts, some fifty Egyptian plants, including *Lycium* and the Senegal *Acacia*. He is reputed to have been the first to fertilize dates artificially. He was also the first European writer to describe the coffee plant, which he saw in Cairo. His *De Medicina Aegyptorum* (1591) is an account of Egyptian medical practice, with useful observations on the diseases of the Middle East. His *De praesagienda vita et morte aegrotontium* is an account of medical prognosis. It was widely acclaimed and was published in English translation in 1746 as *The Presages of Life and Death in Diseases*, following a suggestion of H. BOERHAAVE

Agnes Arber, *Herbals*. 1912 (paperback 1986). (Portrait.)
R. H. Major, *A History of Medicine*. 1954.
Dictionary of Scientific Biography.

T I W

ALVAREZ, WALTER LUIS Born in San Francisco, California, USA, 13 June 1911; died there, 1 September 1988. Chiefly remembered for his work in elementary particle physics.

Alvarez studied at the University of Chicago, gaining his BSc in 1932, his MSc in 1934, and his PhD in 1936. He then went to work with Ernest LAWRENCE, at the University of California's Radiation Laboratory at Berkeley. Apart from spells at other laboratories during the Second World War, Alvarez remained at Berkeley for the rest of his life. His major work there was to develop the hydrogen bubble chamber, after meeting Donald GLASER, inventor of the bubble chamber, in 1953. This device makes visible the tracks of subatomic particles as trails of bubbles in a liquid. Alvarez pioneered the use of liquid hydrogen, beginning with a chamber 1 inch in diameter and culminating in 1959 with the 72-inch chamber with which several short-lived subatomic particles were discovered. For this work, Alvarez received the Nobel prize for physics in 1968.

Alvarez has many other discoveries and inventions to his credit, including the Ground-Controlled Approach blind landing system for aircraft; using cosmic rays to show that there is only one chamber in the Second Pyramid at Giza; and proposing (with his son Walter) that 65 million years ago the Earth was struck by an object which caused sufficient dust to screen out the Sun and lead to the demise of the dinosaurs through starvation.

Nobel Lectures: Physics, 1963–1970. 1972.
L. W. Alvarez, Alvarez: Adventures of a Physicist. 1987.
Physics Today, June 1989. (Portrait.)
Robert L. Weber, Pioneers of Science: Nobel Prize Winners in Physics. 1980 (Portrait.)
Tyler Wasson (Ed.), Nobel Prize Winners. 1987. (Portrait.)

C S

AL-RAZI See RHAZES.

ALTER, DAVID Born at Westmoreland, Pennsylvania, USA, 3 December 1807; died Freeport, Pennsylvania, 18 September 1881. Physicist; made contributions to spectrum analysis.

Alter had little formal schooling, but at the age of 21 he entered the Reformed Medical College, New York, graduating in 1831. He spent most of the rest of his life making experiments and inventions in a wide range of subjects. He worked alone, using home-made apparatus; even the lenses and prisms used in his spectroscopic work are reputed to have been made by him. His inventions included a successful electric clock; a model for an electric locomotive, which was never made; and a method for purifying bromine. He also devised a method for obtaining oil from coal, but the discovery of oil in Pennsylvania (see E. L. DRAKE) prevented this from having any commercial success. In 1836 he devised an electrical telegraph, which consisted of seven wires, an impulse through each of which could deflect a needle by varying amounts and so spell out a message. His most important work was concerned with spectrum analysis. He put forward the idea, which was later proved by R. W. BUNSEN and G. R. KIRCHOFF, that each element had a characteristic spectrum, and

this made possible the use of the spectroscope to determine the chemical nature of a gas or vaporized solid. The importance of Alter's work was not at the time recognized in America.
Dictionary of American Biography.

B B K

AMICI, GIOVANNI BATTISTA Born at Modena, Italy, 25 March 1786; died Florence, 10 April 1863. Astronomer and microscopist.

Amici studied at Bologna, and was professor of mathematics at Modena from 1815 to 1825. Subsequently he became astronomer to the Grand Duke of Tuscany and Director of the Observatory at the Royal Museum in Florence. He retired in 1859. He contributed to the improvement of reflecting telescopes by his design of parabolic mirrors. About 1827 he invented a reflecting microscope, which contained a 3-inch concave mirror between objective and eyepiece, all of which were mounted in a horizontal tube. The mirror magnified the image without causing chromatic aberrations.

In 1823, while examining cyclosis in the stigmatic hair cells of the Oleander, Amici saw a pollen grain – which was adhering to the hair cell – put out a tube which grew along the hair. Seven years later he followed the growth of the pollen tube in Orchis morio into the stigma and down the style to the ovary, where it terminated in the mycropyle of an ovule. In 1846 he discovered a granular material in the unfertilized embryo sac which he regarded as the female agent of fertilization. These observations were broadly speaking correct, but with better preparations and microscopes they were refined by the cytologists of the 1880s and 1890s.
Atti dell'Istituto botanico della Università di Pavia, ser. 2, 2, iii, 1908. (Portrait.)
Dictionary of Scientific Biography.

R C O

AMPÈRE, ANDRÉ MARIE Born at Lyons, France, 22 January 1775; died Marseilles, 10 June 1836. Celebrated for his contributions to electrodynamics.

Ampère was largely autodidactic, possessed of a phenomenal memory, and his mathematical powers developed early; like Blaise PASCAL, he had composed a treatise on conic sections by the age of 13. Following his marriage in 1799 he earned a living by coaching in mathematics until his appointment as professor of physics at Bourg. There he composed his Considérations sur la théorie mathématique du jeu, on the strength of which he was appointed to a chair at Lyons and later to a lectureship in mathematical analysis at the École Polytechnique. Thereafter he lived in Paris, being appointed Inspector-General of the Imperial University in 1808 and professor of mechanics at the École Polytechnique in 1809. Later he taught physics at the Collége de France. He was elected FRS in 1827.

The middle period of Ampère's life, from his arrival in Paris in 1805 until the announcement of H. C. OERSTED's discovery in 1820 of the magnetic effects of an electric current flowing in a conducting wire, was remarkable more for the variety of his interests than for any outstanding contribution to knowledge. His standing as a mathematician was confirmed by his election to the mathematical section of the *Académie* in 1814, and he interested himself in physics and chemistry, arriving independently at AVOGADRO's hypothesis in 1814. He also devoted much time to the study of psychology and ethics in the company of P. J. G. Cabanis (1757–1808), A. L. C. Destutt de Tracy (1754–1836) and M. F. P. G. de Birain (1766–1824). The latter exerted a strong influence on the development of his philosophical views.

At a memorable séance of the *Académie des Sciences* on 11 September 1820 Ampère saw Oersted's experiments repeated. Immediately he threw himself into this work, presenting a paper on the mutual interaction between current-carrying wires at the succeeding séance of the *Académie*. Many other scientists besides Ampère were attracted to the same field, including J. B. BIOT and F. Savart (1791–1841), D. F. J. ARAGO, H. DAVY, M. FARADAY, A. J. FRESNEL, and A. A. de la Rive (1801–73). While the respective contributions of other workers to the development of Ampère's thought remain to be assessed, there can be no doubt of the decisive importance of Ampère's own individual contribution as summed up in his classic *Mémoire sur la théorie mathématique des phénoménes électrodynamiques uniquement déduite de l'expérience*. By a masterly combination of theory and experiment Ampère derived a formula for the mutual interaction between two small elements of conductor in terms of the magnitudes of the currents, their separation, and relative orientation. Assuming only the interaction to be in the line joining the two elements, this formula was a mathematical deduction from the experimental facts just as the inverse square law of gravitation formulated by NEWTON had been a deduction from the astronomical facts subsumed in the laws of planetary motion discovered by KEPLER – an example specifically referred to by Ampère in the preface to his memoir.

Besides his formula for the force between elements of current, Ampère introduced the notion of magnetic shells, showing that a closed electric circuit is equivalent in its magnetic effect to a certain distribution of magnetism over any surface bounded by the given current. But his discovery of the motion of a current-carrying conductor in the Earth's magnetic field led him into the error of supposing that this field was necessarily due to electric currents flowing in the interior of the Earth, an opinion reinforced by his ability to explain the action of one magnet on another, or of a magnet on a current-carrying wire, by the assumption that the properties of magnets result from the circulation of currents in their ultimate particles.

The execution of his father, who fell victim to Collot d'Herbois and Fouché at Lyons in 1793, resulted in a prolonged nervous break-down, and the death of his wife in 1804 was a further blow from which he never entirely recovered. In spite of these and other domestic sorrows, and of serious disciplinary difficulties with students, Ampère continued always a warm-hearted, real, and lovable human being. He died of pneumonia following a short illness while on a tour of duty as inspector-general of the university. His name is remembered in the unit of electric current.

D. F. J. Arago, *Oeuvres* (17 vols), 1854–62. (Vols. 1–3, *Notices Biographiques*.)

L. de Launay, *Le Grand Ampère*. 1925. (Portraits.)
Revue des deux mondes, **9**, 389, 1837.
C. A. Valson, *André-Marie Ampère*. 1885.
Dictionary of Scientific Biography.

J W H

AMUNDSEN, ROALD ENGELBREGT GRAVN-ING Born at Sarpsborg, Norway, 16 July 1872; died in the Arctic Ocean, 16 June 1928. Scientific explorer; the first to sail through the North-West Passage; to reach the South Pole; and to fly over the North Pole.

Fascinated from childhood by Arctic exploration, in 1897–99 Amundsen acquired experience as mate in a Belgian expedition which was the first to winter in the Antarctic. In 1903–06 he took the 47-ton, motor-equipped *Gjöa* with a crew of five through the North-West Passage, spending almost two years on the south coast of King William Island, where extensive scientific observations were made in the immediate vicinity of the magnetic pole.

In 1910 Amundsen diverted to the Antarctic an expedition with which he had planned to conquer the North Pole, reached in 1909 by J. E. W. Peary (1856–1920). After preparing a base at the Bay of Whales and supply depots inland, he set out on 19 October 1911 with four companions and dog-drawn sledges for the South Pole, where he spent four days, 14–17 December, and returned to his base on 25 January, one week after Scott in turn had reached the Pole.

In 1918 Amundsen attempted to drift closer than Nansen's *Fram* to the North Pole, but the highly equipped *Maud* was frozen in the North-East Passage for two winters and achieved little success. Meanwhile, Amundsen had begun to experiment with exploration by air, and on 12 May 1926 he flew over the North Pole in an airship constructed and navigated by the Italian, Umberto Nobile, a voyage which finally proved that there is no Arctic continent. His death followed two years later in a seaplane accident *en route* to Spitsbergen.

R. E. G. Amundsen, *My Life As An Explorer*. 1927.
J. A. Hammerton, *Concise Universal Biography*. (Portrait).
B. Partridge, *Amundsen*. 1953.

T K D

ANAXAGORAS OF CLAZOMENAE Born at Clazomenae, Asia Minor, *c*.500 BC; died Lampsacus, in the Troad, *c*.428 BC. The last of the Ionian natural philosophers.

Anaxagoras introduced the scientific spirit into the Athens of Pericles and suffered persecution for his rationalistic views on the nature of the heavenly bodies. He was the author of a scientific treatise *On Nature* of which only fragments survive.

Anaxagoras taught that the Moon received its light solely from the Sun and that its surface generally resembled that of the Earth and was inhabited; that eclipses of Sun or Moon were caused by the interposition of the Moon, Earth, or earthly bodies; that the Sun was a red-hot stone larger than the Peloponnese; that the great meteorite of 467 BC had fallen from the Sun. He attempted to 'square the circle'; and he wrote on the applications of perspective to the problems of constructing scenery for the theatre. In the field of anatomy, he dissected and vivisected animals and discovered the lateral ventricles of the brain. He attributed the annual swelling of the Nile to the melting of mountain snows near the upper waters of the river.

Anaxagoras conceived the Universe to have originated as a chaos of innumerable 'seeds' reduced by 'mind' to order and form through a movement of rotation. He thus adumbrated the philosophic dichotomy of 'mind' and 'matter' and anticipated the role of rotational forces in later theories of planetary or stellar evolution.

> W. K. C. Guthrie, *A History of Greek Philosophy*, vol. 2. 1965.
> G. Sarton, *A History of Science: Ancient Science through the Golden Age of Greece.* 1952.
> *Dictionary of Scientific Biography.*

A A

ANAXIMANDER OF MILETUS Born in *c.*610 BC; died *c.*545 BC. Ionian natural philosopher.

Anaximander is reputed to have invented or introduced the gnomon (a sun-dial with a vertical needle); to have drawn the earliest map of the inhabited Earth; to have written the earliest scientific treatise (now lost); and to have been the first to teach a crude doctrine of organic evolution.

Anaximander's gnomon served to determine the lengths and directions of shadows and thence to measure the lengths of the year and, eventually, of the seasons, by fixing the times of the equinoxes and the solstices.

Anaximander conceived the Universe as boundless and constituted of a primary substance of indeterminate properties. The Earth was a cylinder of height one-third of its breadth, floating in the midst of space, there being no reason why it should fall in one direction rather than another. He explained the heavenly luminaries by supposing the Earth to be encircled by hoops of compressed air having vents at which fire imprisoned within them became visible; and he speculated as to the relative distances of these luminaries from the Earth. He taught that eternal rotation conferred order upon the Universe by sifting out heavier from lighter materials and arranging them in concentric layers.

Anaximander held that life originated with aquatic forms which later adapted themselves to living on dry land, and that man had descended from lower animals.

> W. K. C. Guthrie, *A History of Greek Philosophy*, vol. 1. 1962.
> T. L. Heath, *Aristarchus of Samos, the Ancient Copernicus.* 1913. (Reprinted, 1959.)
> *Dictionary of Scientific Biography.*

A A

ANDERSON, CARL DAVID Born in New York, 3 September 1905; died 11 January 1991. Discovered two elementary particles, the positron and the muon.

Anderson was brought up in Los Angeles and in 1927 graduated in physics and engineering from the California Institute of Technology. He continued as a graduate student with Robert MILLIKAN and gained his PhD in 1930. Millikan persuaded Anderson to stay at Caltech and build a detector to measure the energies of electrons in cosmic rays. Millikan's request was to build a cloud chamber (in which particle tracks appear as trails of droplets in a vapour) to operate in a high magnetic field. Anderson built the device and soon discovered a particle of the same mass as the electron but with positive charge – the positron. In 1936 he was awarded the Nobel prize for physics, which he shared with Victor HESS, the discoverer of cosmic rays.

In continuing his studies of cosmic rays with his student, Seth Neddermeyer, Anderson made his second important discovery, announced in 1936. They found tracks in their cloud chamber that were clearly due to particles of mass larger than the electron, but smaller than the proton. These particles have since become known as muons.

During the Second World War Anderson worked on rocket research at Caltech, and afterwards resumed his studies of cosmic rays. He retired in 1976.

> L. M. Brown and L. Hoddesdon (Ed.), *The Birth of Particle Physics.* 1983.
> H. A. Boorse, L. Motz, J. H. Weaver, *The Atomic Scientists, a Biographical History*, 1989. (Portrait.)
> *Les Prix Nobel en 1936.* 1937 (Portrait.)
> Tyler Wasson (Ed.), *Nobel Prize Winners.* 1987. (Portrait.)

C S

ANDERSON, PHILIP WARREN Born in Indianapolis, USA, 13 December 1923. Solid-state physicist.

After wartime service as a radio-engineer, Anderson resumed his studies in physics at Harvard University. After an appointment in Tokyo he developed a close association with Cambridge University as visiting professor 1967–75. In 1975 he was appointed professor of physics in Princeton University and in the following year also Consulting Director, Physical Research Laboratory, Bell Telephone. At Harvard he worked initially with J. H. van Vleck (1899–1980) whose main interest was in electric and magnetic susceptibilities. After the war Anderson too made major contributions in the field of disordered and magnetic systems. He also developed theoretical explanations of the phenomena of superfluidity and superconductivity, and the nature of the JOSEPHSON effect. In 1977 Anderson shared a Nobel prize with his old mentor van Vleck and Sir Nevill MOTT, another pioneer of solid-state physics. In 1984 he summarized a lifetime's work in *Basic Notions of Condensed Matter Physics.*

> *Les Prix Nobel en 1977*, 1978. (Portrait.)
> Robert L. Weber, *Pioneers of Science: Nobel Prize Winners in Physics.* 1980. (Portrait.)
> *New Scientist*, 20 October, 1977.
> Tyler Wasson (Ed.), *Nobel Prize Winners.* 1987. (Portrait.)

T I W

ANDERSON, THOMAS Born at Leith, Scotland, 2 July 1819; died Chiswick, near London, 2 November 1874. Discoverer of pyridine and other organic bases.

Anderson was educated at the University of Edinburgh, graduating MD in 1841; in 1839–40 he was Hope Prizeman. For a short time he studied under Justus von LIEBIG at Giessen. Returning to Edinburgh, he taught in the extra-mural medical school, and then, in 1852, succeeded Thomas

Thomson (1773–1852), as Regius Professor of Chemistry at Glasgow. In 1845 he was elected Fellow of the Royal Society of Edinburgh and for a time he edited the *Edinburgh New Philosophical Journal*.

Carrying out an investigation of bone oil, he discovered the nitrogenous bases collidine, lutidine, picoline, and pyridine. Picoline (Latin *picatus*, tarry) was probably identical with the odorin obtained by Otto UNVERDORBEN in 1827. He also obtained pyrrole, first noted by F. F. RUNGE, and correctly assigned it the formula C_8H_5N. Another basic substance he obtained (petinine) was shown by C. GERHARDT to be normal butylamine.

J. R. Partington, *A History of Chemistry*, vol. 4. 1964.
Dictionary of National Biography.

T I W

ANDREWS, THOMAS Born in Belfast, Ireland, 19 December 1813; died there, 26 November 1885. Established the continuity of the gaseous and liquid states, and conceived the notion of critical temperature.

Andrews was educated at Belfast, Glasgow, Paris, Dublin, and at Edinburgh, where he graduated MD in 1835. During his first period of study in Paris in 1830 he worked in the laboratory of J. B. DUMAS, the foremost French chemist of the day, of whom PASTEUR and Andrews were the most distinguished pupils, and who encouraged Andrews to concentrate his research on physiochemical problems. Returning to Belfast in 1835, Andrews found time from his medical duties to continue his scientific researches, and his work on voltaic action and heats of combination soon established his reputation. He was elected member of the Royal Irish Academy in 1839, and Fellow of the Royal Society of London in 1849, following the award of a Royal Medal in 1844 for his paper *On the thermal changes accompanying basic substitutions*. In 1845 he was appointed Vice-President designate of the projected Queen's College, Belfast, and in 1849 professor of chemistry, offices which he held with conspicuous success until failing health impelled his retirement in 1879.

Andrews's eminence as a scientist in spite of the wholly un-Victorian slimness of his collected papers was due to his almost total concentration on three main topics: heat of chemical combination, ozone, and the continuity of the liquid and gaseous states. In the first subject Andrews was but one among other workers, though his contribution was of decisive importance. In the second, he was uniquely responsible for proving that ozone from whatever source derived is one and the same body, having identical properties and the same constitution, and is not a compound body but oxygen in an altered or allotropic form. For this work Andrews deserves to be remembered in company with the discoverer of ozone, C. F. SCHÖNBEIN. But it was his work on the continuity of the gaseous and liquid states which constituted Andrews's most enduring claim to fame and which best demonstrated his great skill as an experimentalist. Although Michael FARADAY, Cagniard de LATOUR, H. V. REGNAULT, and K. Natterer (1860–1901) had already investigated various aspects of the subject, it continued in an essentially obscure and chaotic state until Andrews supplied the necessary elucidation in the form of the familiar set of pressure-volume isotherms above and below the critical temperature. The notion of critical temperature thus introduced by Andrews then led directly and inevitably to the liquefaction of the so-called permanent gases by R. P. PICTET, Z. F. von WROBLEWSKI, and L. P. CAILLETET.

T. Andrews: *Scientific Papers*. 1889. (Includes memoir and portrait.)
Nature, **224**, 543, 1969.
Dictionary of Scientific Biography.

J W H

ÅNGSTRÖM, ANDERS JONAS Born at Medelpad, Sweden, 13 August 1814; died Uppsala, 21 June 1874. A founder of spectroscopy.

The son of a country minister, Ångström studied physical science at Uppsala, obtaining his doctorate in 1839. After teaching physics and astronomy for some years there, he was appointed to the chair in physics in 1858, which he occupied until his death. He served for some years as Secretary of the Royal Society in Uppsala, and as University Rector (1870–71).

Ångström's early interest in spectroscopy was expressed in a memoir of 1853 (translated into English in 1855). This includes numerous measurements of atomic spectra, particularly those produced by an electric spark, where lines due to both electrode and gas were noted. Applying L. EULER's theory of resonance, Ångström concluded that hot gases emit and absorb radiation of the same wavelength, anticipating experimental proof of this in 1859 by G. R. KIRCHOFF, with whom he is entitled to be regarded as a founder of modern spectroscopy.

The importance for astronomy of this connection between absorption and emission spectra was quickly realized, since spectra from heavenly bodies could now indicate the elements present. In 1861 Ångström began a study of the solar spectrum which led him to infer the presence of hydrogen in the Sun. In 1868 his map of the *Normal Solar Spectrum* was published, listing about 1000 Fraunhofer lines. (See J. von FRAUNHOFER.) Despite a slight error in his values (about 0.13 per cent), his atlas became the standard reference work for nearly twenty years. His *Researches in the Solar Spectrum* appeared in 1869.

In 1867 Ångström examined the spectra of the aurora borealis. Other optical work included studies of polarization and double refraction by crystals and of spectra of simple gases. He published on heat conduction by the human body and on the temperature of the Earth, on terrestrial magnetism, and the path of Halley's comet.

Ångström's fellow countrymen recognized his merits rather slowly, partly due to his reserved nature and reluctance to court popularity. Abroad, his work tended to be inaccessible at first, as much of it was in Swedish. But recognition came eventually, and he became a member of the Stockholm and Uppsala Academies, and in 1870 a Fellow of the Royal Society of London, from whom he received the Rumford Medal in 1872. His name is immortalized in the spectroscopists' unit of wavelength, 10^{-8} cm, the Ångström unit.

Nature, **10**, 171, 376, 1874.
American Journal of Physics, 32, 298, 1964. (Portrait).

Proceedings of the Royal Society of London, **25,** xviii, 1877.

S. Lindroth (Ed.), *Swedish Men of Science.* 1952.

Dictionary of Scientific Biography.

C A R

APOLLONIUS OF PERGA

Born at Perga, Pamphilia, Asia Minor, and flourished in the second half of the third century BC. Author of a classic treatise on conic sections, superseding all earlier works on the subject.

Of the eight books into which the 'Conics' of Apollonius was divided, four survive in the original Greek, three others in Arabic translation only, and one is lost. Apollonius defines his curves as intersections of a plane with a double cone; and he distinguishes between the three possibilities respectively producing the parabola, the ellipse, and the hyperbola, so named from characteristic properties of the curves expressed in terms of Pythagorean 'geometrical algebra'. The later books deal with the properties of tangents, normals, asymptotes, conjugate diameters, and evolutes of conics. Harmonic properties and rectangle theorems, now familiar, are covered; but there is no reference to the focus-directrix property of conics, probably known to EUCLID and clearly formulated by PAPPUS in the third century AD. Other, minor, works of Apollonius have not survived.

Apollonius, who studied in Alexandria, was involved in the contemporary development of planetary theories, though here his exact contribution cannot be defined with certainty. It was probably he who generalized the hypothesis of epicycles (devised to represent the apparent motions of Mercury and Venus) to account also, by means of movable eccentric orbits, for the observed movements of the outer planets, Mars, Jupiter, and Saturn.

T. L. Heath, *A History of Greek Mathematics,* vol. 2. 1921.

T. L. Heath, *Apollonius of Perga.* 1896.

Dictionary of Scientific Biography.

A A

APPERT, NICHOLAS

Born at Chålons-sur-Marne, France, 17 November 1749; died Massey, 1 June 1841. Pioneer of food preserving and canning.

As the son of an innkeeper, Appert gained experience in brewing and pickling and then became a chef and confectioner. He experimented on 'sealing the seasons' by preserving meat and vegetables for winter use, winning a French Government prize. He published a classic work: *Le Livre de tous les Ménages, ou l'Art de Conserver pendant plusieurs années toutes les Substances Animales et Végétales.* Appert's success (not a financial one) was due to effective heat-sterilization of vessels and contents and to urgent demands for military stores in the Napoleonic period. He used glass jars before turning to cans, the jars being fitted with bungs of waxed cork with pores running horizontally to minimize air leakage. Sponsored by the epicure De La Reynière, he opened a factory at Massey in 1804. Appert used an autoclave, permitting temperatures higher than the boiling-point of water and anticipated pasteurizing of milk. His work was highly praised by the *Société d'Encouragement pour l'Industrie Nationale,* yet he died in poverty and was buried in a common grave.

J. Potin, *Biographie de Nicolas Appert.* 1891.

A. W. Bitting, *Appertizing.* 1937. (Date of birth incorrectly given.) (Portrait.

Canning and Packing, 2–5, 1960.

M S

APPLETON, SIR EDWARD VICTOR

Born at Bradford, Yorkshire, England, 6 September 1892; died Edinburgh, 21 April 1965. Physicist, noted particularly for research on the upper atmosphere.

Appleton was educated at Hanson High School, Bradford, and at St John's College, Cambridge, of which he subsequently became a Fellow (1919). Later, he was appointed Research Demonstrator under Lord RUTHERFORD in the Cavendish Laboratory, Cambridge. In 1924 he became Wheatstone Professor of Experimental Physics in King's College, London (1924–36) and then Jacksonian Professor of Natural Philosophy at Cambridge (1936–39). During the Second World War, and until April 1949, he was Permanent Secretary to the Department of Scientific and Industrial Research. He then went to Edinburgh as Principal and Vice-Chancellor of the University, which post he held at the time of his sudden death.

Appleton's research was concerned mainly with the physics of the upper atmosphere, which he systematically explored using radio techniques. He made important contributions to the development of radar. His interest in radio communication was aroused when, as a young man, he served as a captain in the Royal Engineers during the First World War.

In 1924 Appleton demonstrated experimentally the existence of the electrified reflecting layer in the upper atmosphere postulated by A. E. KENNELLY and O. HEAVISIDE. Subsequently the existence of a second reflecting region above the Heaviside-Kennelly layer was demonstrated: this is often referred to as the Appleton layer. He recognized the importance of international co-operation in research of this kind – especially in relating upper atmospheric conditions to the sunspot cycle – and promoted the work of the International Scientific Radio Union, of which he was President 1938–54. He also played an active part in organizing the second International Polar Year 1932–33.

Appleton was widely honoured. The Royal Society elected him Fellow in 1927. He was President of the British Association in 1953. He was awarded the Nobel prize for physics in 1947. He was an honorary graduand of sixteen universities and an honorary member of many learned societies. He was knighted in 1941.

Nature, **206,** 1094, 1965.

Biographical Memoirs of Fellows of the Royal Society. 1966. (Portrait.)

R. Clark, *Sir Edward Appleton.* 1971.

Tyler Wasson (Ed.), *Nobel Prize Winners.* 1987. (Portrait.)

Dictionary of Scientific Biography.

H. Oxbury (Ed.), *Great Britons: 20th Century Lives.* 1985.

Science and Culture, **31,** 348, 1965.

T I W

ARAGO, DOMINIQUE FRANÇOIS JEAN

Born at Estagel, France, 26 February 1786; died Paris, 2 October 1853. Celebrated for his contributions to physics and astronomy.

After attending the *École Polytechnique,* Arago

was appointed to the Bureau of Longitudes through the influence of LAPLACE. In company with J. B. BIOT he was then charged with completing the measure of an arc of terrestial meridian, continuing this work alone after Biot's return to Paris in August 1807. Returning to Paris two years later after many adventures, he was elected to full membership of the *Académie des Sciences* in place of J. J. F. de Lalande (1732–1807). In the same year (1809) he succeeded Gaspard MONGE in the chair of analytical geometry at the *École Polytechnique*, continuing in this position until 1830, when he insisted on resigning following his election as permanent secretary of the *Académie* in succession to J. B. J. FOURIER.

As an astronomer, Arago is remembered as the discoverer of the solar chromosphere and for his accurate measurements of the diameters of the planets. His public lectures at the Paris observatory between 1812 and 1845 enjoyed great popularity.

In physics, his principal work was in electromagnetism and in light. In the same year (1820) as H. C. OERSTED discovered the magnetic effects of an electric current, Arago found that iron placed in a wire coil could be magnetized by the passage of current from either a Leyden jar or a voltaic cell. In 1824 he discovered the phenomenon of magnetic rotation, in which a rotating copper disk deflects a magnetic needle suspended above it, an effect later explained by Michael FARADAY in terms of magnetic induction. Arago's researches in light commenced with his discovery of chromatic polarization in 1811. Together with F. H. A. von HUMBOLDT he successfully defended A. J. FRESNEL against the criticisms of LAPLACE, S. D. POISSON, and J. B. BIOT. Subsequently Fresnel and he succeeded in elucidating the fundamental laws of the polarization of light in terms of the wave theory. He then determined on a crucial test between the emission and wave theories by comparing the velocities of light in air and in a dense medium. His plans for this test (based on the method of rotating mirrors previously employed by C. WHEATSTONE for measuring the velocities of an electric discharge) were laid down before the *Académie des Sciences* in 1838. Owing to experimental difficulties and to his involvement in the revolution of 1848, the apparatus was still incomplete when his sight suddenly failed in the spring of 1850. J. B. L. FOUCAULT then took over Arago's method, and the retardation of light in a dense medium compared with air was finally demonstrated before Arago's death.

Arago entered politics in 1830 as deputy for the *Pyrénées Orientales*. He sat on the extreme left and in 1848 was elected to the provisional governments as Minister of War and Marine. It was by his direction that slavery was abolished in the French Colonies. A deputy of the Constituent Assembly, he was a member of the Executive Commission which retired in June and he sat in the Legislature. When Louis Napoleon became Emperor, Arago refused to swear allegiance, but escaped prosecution owing to his eminence as a scientist.

H. Chauvet, *François Arago et son temps*. 1954.
M. Crosland, *The Society of Arcueil*. 1967.
Maurice Daumas, *Arago*. 1943.
Dictionary of Scientific Biography.

J W H

ARCHER, FREDERICK SCOTT Born at Bishop's Stortford, Hertfordshire, England, 1813; died London, 2 May 1857. Inventor of the wet collodion process of photography.

Son of a butcher, Archer started as assistant to a silversmith in the City of London, then became a portrait sculptor there. To ensure good likenesses, he took up, in 1847, the Calotype process of W. H. F. TALBOT, but devoted himself less to sculpture than to the improvement of photography and the invention of a camera for travellers. In March 1850 Archer published in *The Chemist* the use of pyrogallic acid as a developer; this substance proved essential in his collodion process, published in the same journal (March 1851) after three years' experimentation. His detailed instruction manual appeared in 1852. Archer's process was a great advance on the daguerreotype (see L. J. M. DAGUERRE) and paper processes, being more light-sensitive and producing finely detailed glass negatives from which positives on paper were printed. The plates had to be exposed and developed before the sensitized collodion dried, necessitating a dark-tent and portable laboratory for outdoor work. Despite this disadvantage, collodion soon superseded all other processes and remained in general use for thirty years. Archer's camera, in which the manipulation was carried out within the apparatus itself, did not prove practicable, but like his fluid lens and triplet lens, was an important forerunner of later constructions.

In collaboration with Peter W. Fry (d. 1860), Archer devised the Ambrotype (1851) – the first cheap form of portraiture, which revolutionized portrait photography.

Talbot's claim that Archer's process was a variant of his Calotype was dismissed in a lawsuit (December 1854). The modest inventor, having devoted all his time to experimentation, died in great poverty.

Helmut and Alison Gernsheim, *The History of Photography*. 1955. (Portrait.)
Dictionary of National Biography.

H and A G

ARCHIMEDES Born in Syracuse, Sicily, *c*.287 BC; killed in the sack of that city 212 BC. The greatest mathematician of antiquity; creator of statics and hydrostatics.

Anticipating the invention of the integral calculus, Archimedes applied a rigorous geometrical technique to the mensuration of curved lines, areas, and solids. In particular, he evaluated the circumference and the area of a circle (involving a close approximation to π), the surface areas of a sphere, a parabolic segment, and a spiral, and the volumes of a sphere, a cylinder, and various conoids. He discovered many of these results by means of his 'Method'. This consisted in finding in his diagram a point about which the elements of, say, an unknown area could be balanced in imagination against the corresponding elements of a known area, the two areas being thus shown to be inversely proportional to the arms of the imaginary balance. This procedure was only preliminary to the rigorous proof of the result thus indicated.

Archimedes reduced statics to a rigorous propositional discipline comparable to what EUCLID had made of geometry. He determined the centres of gravity of the simpler plane and solid figures, and he rigorously derived from first principles the law of the lever, covering the case where the arms are incommensurable. He founded hydrostatics by establishing that a body floating in a fluid displaces a weight of the fluid just equal to its own weight, and that a body sufficiently heavy to sink in the fluid will, when weighed therein, be found lighter than its real weight by the weight of the fluid that it displaces. He proceeded to investigate the stability of a floating paraboloidal segment. The conceptions of the specific gravity of a substance and of the upthrust exerted by a fluid upon an immersed body marked important advances. These hydromechanical achievements of Archimedes are immortalized by the story of his investigation of the adulteration of Hiero's golden crown and by the ascription to him of the so-called Archimedean screw.

The popular legend of Archimedes has always stressed his fertility in mechanical inventions (particularly of engines of war serving for the defence of Syracuse) whose scientific interest, however, is only marginal.

T. L. Heath, *A History of Greek Mathematics*, vol. 2. 1921.

T. L. Heath (Ed.), *The Works of Archimedes*. 1897. (*Supplement*, 1912.)

E. J. Dijksterhuis, *Archimedes*. 1956.

Dictionary of Scientific Biography.

A A

ARISTARCHUS OF SAMOS Flourished in the early third century BC. Greek philosopher.

Aristarchus studied under Strato of Lampsacus, the head of the Athenian Lyceum. He was the first to attempt to determine the relative distances of the Sun and Moon by rigorous geometrical reasoning from observational data. He anticipated the Copernican planetary hypothesis, and invented a hemispherical sundial.

The treatise of Aristarchus *On the Sizes and Distances of the Sun and Moon*, which has survived, consists of eighteen propositions based upon six 'hypotheses' (astronomical assumptions or measurements) and employing a crude form of trigonometry. The underlying observations were so inaccurate that the numerical results reached were worthless; but Aristarchus had taken the first step in the rational determination of the size of the Universe and his work marked a great advance upon the ideas of his age.

He is also credited with the hypothesis that the sphere of the stars was motionless, its apparent daily revolution being, in fact, due to a daily rotation of the Earth upon its axis; and, further, that the Sun was at rest at the centre of the sphere of stars, the Earth and the planets describing circles about the Sun as centre. He asserted that the radius of the sphere of stars was incomparably greater than that of the Earth's orbit, so that the Earth's motion produced no corresponding apparent shift (parallax) in the stars. This planetary scheme was reduced to numerical precision in the sixteenth century by COPERNICUS who was acquainted with the ideas of Aristarchus.

T. L. Heath, *Aristarchus of Samos, the Ancient Copernicus*. 1913. (Reprinted, 1959.)

Dictionary of Scientific Biography.

A A

ARISTOTLE Born in Chalcidice, Greece, 384 BC; died Chalcis, 322 BC. Athenian philosopher.

Aristotle's works constituted an encyclopaedic survey and classification of existing knowledge. He organized and directed research; he established the inductive method; he gave to the sciences a philosophical basis and a terminology that were judged adequate during some eighteen centuries.

Aristotle studied under Plato (427–347 BC) in Athens, cultivated zoological interests in Asia Minor, and was tutor to the future Alexander the Great. Returning to Athens in 335 BC, he founded the Lyceum, a centre of teaching and research. Only his later works survive and these mainly in the form of memoranda or students' lecture notes.

In mathematics, Aristotle drew the earliest clear distinction between axioms and postulates, preparing the way for EUCLID and ARCHIMEDES; and he grappled with the problems of infinity and continuity. In mechanics he formulated the law of the lever and understood the parallelogram of velocities; he maintained that the speed of a moving body was proportional directly to the force applied and inversely to the resistance encountered. He established the doctrine of the four mutually convertible elements conceived to constitute the bodies that form the spherical Earth and its surroundings. These elementary bodies (so he taught) tended towards their appropriate places, travelling in straight lines towards or away from the centre of the finite, spherical Universe, which is also the centre of the Earth. In contrast, the stars and planets were composed of a fifth, incorruptible element, the aether, and were carried round the heavens by a mechanical combination of rotating spheres, according to the contemporary hypothesis of EUDOXUS OF CNIDUS. Aristotle made a reasonable estimate of the size of the Earth.

Aristotle's most valuable contributions were to anatomy and zoology. He classified animals on a scale of nature ascending to man (but not implying evolution); he correctly described the stomach of the ruminants, the development of the chick in the egg, the reproduction of cephalopods and much else besides, On the other hand, he regarded the heart and not the brain as the seat of the intelligence; and his failure to understand the difference between arteries and veins delayed the discovery of the circulation of the blood.

The gathering revolt against Aristotle's physical doctrines came to a head about the middle of the sixteenth century; the excellence of his work in zoology was not fully appreciated until the nineteenth century.

W. D. Ross, *Aristotle*. 1923.

G. Sarton, *A History of Science: Ancient Science through the Golden Age of Greece*. 1953.

H. B. Veatch, *Aristotle: A Contemporary Appreciation*. 1974.

G. E. R. Lloyd, *Aristotle: The Growth and Structure of his Thought*. 1968.

Dictionary of Scientific Biography.

A A

ARKWRIGHT, SIR RICHARD Born at Preston, Lancashire, England, 23 December 1732; died Cromford, Derbyshire, 3 August 1792. Devised the first practical way of mechanical spinning by using rollers.

Arkwright was apprenticed to a barber and when about 18 followed this trade in Bolton. His first wife bore him a son before she died, and he remarried in 1761. He prospered until he took a public house besides his barber shop and he began to lose money; after this failure he travelled around buying women's hair for wigs. In the late 1760s he began spinning experiments at Preston. It is not clear how much Arkwright copied earlier inventions or was helped by Thomas Highs and John Kay (*fl.* 1733–64). In 1768 he left Preston for Nottingham, where, with John Smalley as partner, he took out his first patent. They set up a mill worked by a horse where machine-spun yarn was at last made successfully. The essential part of this process lay in drawing out the cotton by rollers before it was twisted by a Saxony flyer. The partners' resources were not sufficient for developing their patent, so Arkwright found new partners in Samuel Need and Jedediah Strutt (1726–97), hosiers of Derby. Much experiment was needed before they produced satisfactory yarn and a water-driven mill was built in 1771 at Cromford, where the process was perfected. Some of this first yarn was used in the hosiery trade, but sales of all-cotton cloth were limited through the high tax on calicoes. This was lowered in 1774 and marks the beginning of the phenomenal growth of the cotton industry.

While Arkwright had solved the problem of mechanical spinning, a bottleneck in the preliminary stages would have appeared but for another patent taken out in 1775. This covered all preparatory processing, including some ideas not invented by Arkwright with the result that it was disputed in 1783 and finally annulled in 1785. It contained the 'crank and comb' for removing the fleece off carding engines, which was developed at Cromford and solved the difficulty in carding. By now Arkwright had mechanized all the preparatory and spinning processes and began to establish water-driven cotton mills even as far away as Scotland. His success encouraged many others to copy him, so he had great difficulty in enforcing his patent.

Need died in 1781 and the partnership with Strutt ended soon after. Arkwright became very rich, and financed other spinning ventures beyond his immediate control, for example by Samuel Oldknow. In 1786 he received a knighthood, and the following year he became High Sheriff of Derbyshire.

R. S. Fitton and A. P. Wadsworth, *The Strutts and the Arkwrights.* 1958. (Portrait.)

A. P. Wadsworth and J. de L. Mann, *The Cotton Trade and Industrial Lancashire.* 1931.

F. Nasmith, *Transactions of the Newcomen Society*, **13**, 1932.

R. L Hills, *Richard Arkwright and Cotton Spinning.* 1973.

                                                              R L H

ARMOUR, PHILIP DANFORTH Born at Stockbridge, New York, 16 May 1832; died Chicago, 6 January 1901. Pioneer of large scale meat-packing.

A farmer's son, Armour made his fortune initially by speculating in pork prices during the last phase of the Civil War. He dealt in grain as well as pork, but moved to Chicago in 1875 to head a pork-packing firm which had been founded by his brother, H. O. Armour. He brought the animals to the city alive, and adopted elaborate assembly-line methods for slaughtering and for processing of carcasses. He also made a careful study of the utilization of waste products. By organizing refrigerated transport and large-scale canning, he succeeded in selling his pork and other meat in a national, and later a world, market.

Although Armour's reputation was adversely affected by complaints regarding the quality of meat supplied to the US Army at the time of the Spanish War, his wealth is said to have amounted to 50 million dollars, of which he donated about one-half to the Armour Institute of Technology in Chicago and other public objects.

Dictionary of American Biography.

                                                              T K D

ARMSTRONG, EDWIN HOWARD Born in New York City, 18 December 1890; died there, 1 February 1954. Inventor of the superheterodyne radio circuit and developer of frequency modulation for high-fidelity sound transmissions.

Inspired by the story of MARCONI, Armstrong built his own radio transmitter before he was twenty, and graduated from Columbia University with a degree in electrical engineering in 1913. During the First World War, while working on methods of detecting aircraft at a distance, he evolved and patented a radio receiver circuit sufficiently sensitive to pick up the electromagnetic waves from aircraft engines' ignition systems. He called the device a superheterodyne receiver, and the principle was soon found to result in significant improvements in the performance of amplitude modulation radio receivers.

In 1934 he was appointed professor of electrical engineering at Columbia University, at a time when he was trying to eliminate the distortion of radio signals caused by atmospheric electricity or nearby electrical machinery, resulting in what was generally known as 'static'. In place of the amplitude modulation (AM) system of transmission then in use he developed and patented frequency modulation (FM), in which the transmitted signal modulates the frequency, rather than the amplitude, of the carrier wave. The use of FM enables high-fidelity (hi-fi) sound signals in both radio and television to be transmitted without interference, though only over relatively short distances at very high frequencies (VHF).

From the start of his inventive career Armstrong was embroiled in litigation over infringements of his patents, and although he became both rich and successful by the early 1930s he never lost the conviction that there was a conspiracy against him. Eventually, his obsession with real and imaginary business, legal, and financial problems led him to commit suicide by jumping out of the window of his New York apartment.

Current Biography, 23–26 1940. (Portrait.)
Dictionary of Scientific Biography.
Dictionary of American Biography.
Scientific American, **190(4)**, 64, 1959.

                                                              R M B

ARMSTRONG, HENRY EDWARD Born in London, 6 May 1848; died there, 13 July 1937. Chemist and teacher.

Armstrong studied at the Royal College of Chemistry under A. W. von HOFMANN and E. FRANKLAND then at Leipzig under A. W. H. KOLBE. After various posts in technical education in London, he became professor of chemistry (1884) in the Central

Technical College. In 1911 he was compulsorily retired when the College became part of the new Imperial College, London. He married in 1877, and had seven children, including the industrial chemist E. F. Armstrong (1878–1945).

Armstrong's papers are bewildering in number and variety. The sixty papers (1881–1900, partly with W. P. Wynne) on naphthalene derivatives were, though prosaic, of basic importance both to organic chemistry and to the growing dyestuffs industry. This work was prematurely abandoned owing to a petty disagreement with the College authorities. He also published work in the terpene–camphor field, and proposed a 'centric' structure for benzene. He became known, especially after his retirement, for his prolonged and intemperate opposition to the Ionic Theory, and for his provocative, but scholarly, contributions to other topics of public debate (a characteristic recalling his teacher, Kolbe). His deepest interest was in education, in which he was a tireless advocate of the heuristic method.

He was elected FRS in 1876, and was active in the Chemical Society, being Secretary from 1875 to 1893, President for the next two years, and Vice-President for almost the rest of his life.

J. Vargas Eyre, *Henry Edward Armstrong*. 1958. (Portraits.)
Journal of the Chemical Society, 1418, 1940. (Portrait.)
W. H. Brock (Ed.) *H. E. Armstrong and the Teaching of Science*. 1973.
A. Findlay and W. H. Mills (Eds), *British Chemists*. 1947. (Portrait.)
E. Farber (Ed.), *Great Chemists*. 1961. (Portrait.)
Dictionary of Scientific Biography.

                                              W V F

ARRHENIUS, SVANTE AUGUST Born at Uppsala, Sweden, 19 February 1859; died Stockholm, 2 October 1927. Physical chemist, responsible for the theory that electrolytes are dissociated in solution.

Arrhenius came of Swedish farmer stock: his father was an estate manager. He went to Uppsala University, intending to read chemistry, but it was badly taught, and he turned towards physics instead. At Uppsala, however, it was then only possible to do research on light, which he did not wish to do; in 1881 he migrated to Stockholm, to work under Professor E. Edlund (1819–88) on the study of solutions and electrolytes. In June 1883 he presented the results of his work on conductivities of solutions to the Swedish Academy of Sciences. The theoretical section of this paper contains the germ of his theory of electrolytic dissociation. He distinguished between 'active' and 'inactive' molecules of the solute and also introduced the concept of 'activity' as the ratio between the number of ions actually contained in the solution and the number which it would contain if the electrolyte were completely transformed into simple electrolytic molecules. At this stage he did not use the term 'dissociation', but he applied the concept to explain double decompositions.

To his bitter disappointment, his thesis was awarded only a fourth class, which meant that it was very difficult for him to get an academic post. But he sent copies to R. J. E. CLAUSIUS, Lothar MEYER, W. F. OSTWALD, and J. H. VAN'T HOFF, who were impressed. In addition, Ostwald went so far as to visit him in Stockholm. Oliver LODGE wrote an account of Arrhenius's work for the *Report of the British Association* for 1886. Nevertheless, it was not until the turn of the century that Arrhenius received in his own country the honour and recognition which foreign scientists accorded him from the 1880s.

After presenting his thesis, he spent five years going around Europe, supported by a travelling scholarship from the Swedish Academy of Science, and worked with Ostwald, F. W. G. KOHLRAUSCH, L. BOLTZMANN, and van't Hoff; it was during this period of association with the leading workers in the field of physical chemistry that Arrhenius developed his theory. The crucial development which crystallized his thought was the paper on osmotic pressure that van't Hoff produced in 1886, in which he showed that electrolytes behaved in osmotic pressure experiments as though there were more molecules in solution than was, in fact, the case. In March 1881 Arrhenius wrote to van't Hoff asserting that what he had called active molecules must be dissociated molecules, and that at the most extreme dilution all electrolytes were probably completely dissociated.

It had, of course, long been recognized that when an electric current is passed through a solution of an electrolyte, the molecules of solute are decomposed; but the idea that the molecules were dissociated even in the absence of a potential difference across the solution was new, and seemed to many chemists wild. But the evidence from electrolytic experiments and from osmotic pressure determinations produced approximately concordant results for the proportion of molecules dissociated into ions at a given dilution, and the theory gradually prevailed.

By 1887 Arrhenius was regarded abroad as one of the greatest chemists. In 1891 he was offered a chair at Giessen, but declined on patriotic grounds in favour of a post at Stockholm *Högskola*, which rather reluctantly made him a professor in 1895; in 1896 he became Rector of the *Högskola*. In 1902 he was awarded the Davy Medal of the Royal Society; in 1903 a Nobel prize; and in 1905 he was appointed Director of the Nobel Institute for Physical Chemistry, where he had ideal conditions for research and writing.

His theory ran into difficulties because strong electrolytes showed anomalous results; but he was able in 1911 to offer suggestions as to how this anomaly might be explained, and these are reasonably close to modern views.

J. R. Partington, *A History of Chemistry*, Vol IV, 1964. (Portrait.)
J. Walker, ('Arrhenius Memorial Lecture'), *Journal of the Chemical Society*, 1380, 1928. (Portrait.)
Endeavour, **18**, 59, 1959.
E. Farber (Ed.), *Great Chemists*. 1961. (Portrait.)
Tyler Wasson (Ed.), *Novel Prize Winners*. 1987. (Portrait.)
Dictionary of Scientific Biography.

                                              D M K

ASCHOFF, KARL ALBERT LUDWIG Born in Berlin, 10 January 1866; died Freiburg-im-Breisgau, 24 June 1942. A founder of the concept of the role of the reticulo-endothelial system.

Ludwig Aschoff studied at Bonn, Berlin, and

Strasbourg, and qualified in medicine at Bonn in 1889. He was assistant to F. D. von Recklinghausen (1833–1910) in the University of Strasbourg (1891–3), and to J. Orth (1847–1923) at Göttingen (1893–1903). In 1903 he became professor of pathology in the University of Marburg, and in 1906 he was called to the corresponding chair at Freiburg-im-Breisgau, where he spent the rest of his life. There he built up a pathological institute which attracted post-graduate workers from all over the world.

Aschoff published the results of very numerous investigations. In 1904 he described in rheumatic endocarditis the 'Aschoff bodies' found in various parts of the heart, and he wrote much on arteriosclerosis and thrombosis. In 1906 he wrote on the pathological basis of heart failure, and he later advanced our knowledge of gall-stones and of appendicitis. Aschoff did very important work on the conception of the reticulo-endothelial system, constituted by large phagocytic cells found in the spleen, lymph nodes, bone marrow, and the liver. It is to this system that the body owes its day-to-day defence against the inroads of common pathogenic organisms.

Journal of Pathology and Bacteriology, **55**, 229, 1943. (Portrait.)

Lancet, ii, 559, 1942.

L. Aschoff, *Lectures on Pathology*. 1924.

E A U

ASELLI(O), GASPARE Born at Cremona, Italy, *c*.1581; died Milan, 24 April 1626. Anatomist, surgeon, and discoverer of the lacteals.

Aselli became professor of anatomy and surgery at Pavia, but he also had a large practice in Milan, of which he was a freeman. He served as a surgeon-general during active military operations.

On 23 July 1622 Aselli was demonstrating the action of the recurrent laryngeal nerves in a dog. He then opened the abdomen to demonstrate the action of the diaphragm, and noticed many white cords coursing over the intestines and mesentery. At first he thought they were nerves, but suspected his error. He then pricked one, and a milky liquid gushed out. He now appreciated the function of these vessels – viz. to carry the products of digestion (chyle) from the intestine to the body – and he described the valves that they contain. He called them *venae albae et lacteae* (white and lacteal veins). Others had previously seen them, but their function had never been appreciated. It was Aselli's good fortune that the dog used had been recently fed and digestion was in progress. He thought that these vessels carried the chyle to the liver, and it was not until 1647 that Jean PECQUET showed that they discharged to the receptaculum chyli, and others showed the ultimate discharge of the chyle to the venous system.

Aselli's description was published posthumously at Milan in 1627. It is the first medical work to contain coloured illustrations.

C. Daremberg, *Histoire des sciences médicales*, vol. 2. 1870.

M. Foster, *Lectures on the History of Physiology*. 1901.

W. Stirling, *Some Apostles of Physiology*. 1902. (Portrait.)

Dictionary of Scientific Biography.

E A U

ASTBURY, WILLIAM THOMAS Born at Longton, near Stoke-on-Trent, England, 25 February 1898; died Leeds, Yorkshire, 4 June 1961. A founder of molecular biology and pioneer in the application of x-ray analysis to high polymers.

Astbury was the son of a pottery worker and elder brother of the physicist N. F. Astbury. Helped by scholarships to gain an adequate early education, in 1916 he entered Jesus College, Cambridge, to read mathematics and physics. His studies were interrupted by service with the Royal Army Medical Corps x-ray unit but after the war he returned to Cambridge, supplementing physics with chemistry and mineralogy. Studying the latter under A. Hutchinson (1866–1937), he acquired a taste for crystallography that determined both his first appointment and the pattern of his subsequent work.

On leaving Cambridge he joined W. H. BRAGG at University College, London (1921), and in 1923 moved with him to the Royal Institution. His first research was an ambitious, if not wholly successful, attempt to relate the optical activity of tartaric acid to its crystal structure. With Kathleen Yardley (later LONSDALE) he produced the 'space-group tables' which rendered much easier the tasks of x-ray crystallographers. One of his early responsibilities was the development of photographic methods for x-ray analysis. In 1926 he was asked by Bragg, who was giving a series of Royal Institution lectures, to assist in illustrating one with x-ray photographs of fibres. These were so successful that his work received a new direction, and two years later Bragg recommended him as Lecturer in Textile Physics at Leeds University, and Director of the Textile Physics Research Laboratory there. In 1937 he became Reader, and in 1945 Honorary Reader, in Textile Physics. He occupied the first chair of biomolecular structures from 1945 to 1961.

At Leeds he carried out x-ray examinations on wool, hair, and other fibres under a variety of conditions. This work led to a widespread development of the technique for structural investigations on large molecules of all kinds. He conceived the idea that polypeptide chains could be folded and unfolded and that 'denaturation' of a globular protein involves the unfolding of a three-dimensional system. He divided the fibrous proteins into two groups, collagen and the others, and established that mammalian keratin is different from that obtained from birds and reptiles. Flagella were shown to be single macromolecules – rather like hairs, he thought. Much of Astbury's x-ray work opened up the way to later studies on nucleic acids, myoglobin, and haemoglobin.

Astbury was widely honoured, and was elected FRS in 1940.

Nature, 156, 531, 1945; 191, 331, 332, 1961.

Chemistry and Industry, 1174, 1961. (Portrait).

Biographical Memoirs of Fellows of the Royal Society. 1963. (Portrait.)

Dictionary of Scientific Biography.

C A R

ASTON, FRANCIS WILLIAM Born at Harborne, Birmingham, England, 1 September 1877; died Cambridge, 20 November 1945. Inventor of the mass spectrograph.

The son of a merchant, Aston was educated at Birmingham, studying chemistry at the Mason College (later Birmingham University), where from 1898 to 1900 he worked with P. F. Frankland (1858–1946) on optical rotations. After three years with a brewing firm he returned to the College to continue work on discharge tube phenomena which he had studied in his spare time for several years previously. In 1910 he entered the Cavendish Laboratory, Cambridge, under J. J. THOMSON, who was examining the positive rays produced in discharge tubes. Helped by Aston, Thomson passed the rays from a low-pressure tube into electric and magnetic fields applied simultaneously so as to deflect them on to a photographic plate. The parabolic tracks were each characterized by a particular mass/charge ratio. From this work it appeared that neon (atomic weight about 20) had a minor component of mass 22. Accordingly, Aston attempted to fractionate neon, and in 1913 achieved a partial separation by diffusion through pipe-clay.

Aston's research was interrupted by the war, when he worked at the Royal Aircraft Establishment, Farnborough. Meanwhile, however, the concept of isotopes had become clearer and he saw positive-ray analysis as a powerful tool for their study. On returning to Cambridge in 1919 he devised his mass spectrograph. It differed from Thomson's apparatus in that electric and magnetic fields produced deflections in the same plane (though in opposite directions). The image obtained on a photographic plate was called a 'mass spectrum'. With this apparatus (now in the Science Museum, London) Aston examined the isotopic compositions of over fifty elements, concluding that all except hydrogen had integral isotopic weights. An improved apparatus (1925), with an accuracy of 1 in 10 000, showed that this was not quite true. Aston measured the deviations from whole numbers, which he expressed as a 'packing fraction'. This equipment, together with a still more refined version, led to the discovery of many more isotopes.

The mass spectrograph has been indispensable for the study of nuclear physics and chemistry. Recently it has acquired new importance as a tool for structure determination and analysis in organic chemistry.

Aston was a keen photographer and traveller, and took part in several expeditions to observe eclipses. An excellent musician, he became music critic for the *Cambridge Review*.

Amongst numerous other honours, he was made Fellow of Trinity College, Cambridge, in 1920; FRS in 1921; and Nobel Laureate in chemistry in 1922.

Journal of the Chemical Society, 1468, 1948.
Obituary Notices of Fellows of the Royal Society. 1948. (Portrait.)
Dictionary of Scientific Biography.
Dictionary of National Biography.
Tyler Wasson (Ed.), *Nobel Prize Winners.* 1987. (Portrait.)

                                                          C A R

AUDUBON, JOHN JAMES Born at Les Cayes, Santo Domingo (now Haiti), 26 April 1785; died New York, 27 January 1851. American naturalist and artist.

Audubon, the natural son of a French sea-captain-planter and a creole mother, was brought up in France at his father's villa near Nantes, where he early developed a passion for natural history, drawing, and music. He was educated locally and in Paris, where for six months he was a pupil of J. L. David (1748–1825), the painter.

In early life he emigrated, and became naturalized in the United States, where his father owned property, but he was unsuccessful in various commercial ventures. In spite of marriage and a family, and much poverty, he travelled widely, collecting and painting birds and other animals. As no American publisher would take his works, in 1826 he came to England, where the Havells, engravers and art publishers, engraved most of his plates, which he published, with descriptive text, by subscription; the elephant folio *Birds of America* appeared in parts from 1827 to 1838. He remained three years in Great Britain, was elected FRS (1830), and was lionized owing to his flair for publicity, appearing in public clad in the costume of the backwoods. On returning to America he published an octavo edition of the *Birds* with lithographed plates including many supplementary ones. He painted illustrations for the *Quadrupeds of North America*, and prepared the text in collaboration with his sons and John Bachman (1790–1874), who edited and published the final volume after his death. Audubon broke new ground by painting birds life-size in dramatic attitudes, and by his meticulous care in drawing from fresh specimens, never from stuffed ones.

M. R. Audubon, *Audubon and his Journals.* 1887. (reprinted 1960). (Portraits and autobiography.)
F. H. Hewick, *Audubon the Naturalist*, (2nd ed.). 1938.
A. B. Adams, *John James Audubon: A Biography.* 1966.
A. Ford, *John James Audubon.* 1964.
Dictionary of Scientific Biography.

                                                          L H M

AUGER, PIERRE VICTOR Born in France, 14 May 1899. Physicist.

Auger was educated at the Ecole Normale Supérieure and the University of Paris, where he was appointed Assistant in 1927 and professor of physics in 1937. In 1925 he discovered the eponymous Auger Effect, though this had in fact been discovered two years earlier, in a different context, by Lise MEITNER. If an atom becomes ionized by loss of a K electron it can lose energy either by emitting an x-ray photon or by ejecting an outer electron: the latter is the Auger Effect. Observation of this threw much light on the structure of atoms. Auger also published many papers on neutrons and on cosmic and x-rays. After the Second World War, during which he was Research Associate at the University of Chicago (1941–3) and worked with the Anglo-Canadian atomic energy project, he held a number of very senior administrative appointments. These included being director of the natural sciences division of UNESCO (1948–59) and Director-General of the European Space Research Organisation (ESRO). He was an enthusiastic and influential popularizer of science. He was elected a member of the French Academy of Sciences in 1977.

Who's Who, 1993.
International Who's Who, 1993.
Edgardo Macorini (Ed.) *Scienziati e Tecnologi Contemporanei.* 1974. (Portrait.)

                                                          T I W

AVERY, OSWALD THEODORE Born at Halifax, Nova Scotia, Canada, 21 October 1877; died Nashville, Tennessee, USA, 20 February 1955. Bacteriologist.

Although born in Canada, Avery, the son of a Baptist clergyman, spent most of his life in New York City. He graduated from Colgate University in 1900 and qualified in medicine at the College of Physicians and Surgeons, Columbia University, in 1904. From 1905 until 1913 he did bacteriological research at the Hoagland Laboratory, Brooklyn. He was appointed bacteriologist to the Rockefeller Institute Hospital, New York, in 1913, and remained there until his retirement in 1948.

Avery, always known as 'The Professor', devoted his research to the study of the pneumococci, the bacteria which cause pneumonia, stimulated by the publication by F. Griffith (1877–1941) of the results of his study of *Diplococcus pneumoniae*. This led to work on bacterial transformation and the discovery, announced in 1944, that the transforming principle, when one bacterial type was converted to that of a different strain inoculated with it, but heat-killed, was DNA. Avery went on to suggest that DNA might provide the chemical and physical basis of heredity, and dispelled the earlier idea that proteins carried the genetic information. Avery's work paved the way for the discovery by Francis CRICK and J. D. WATSON (1928–) of the double helical structure of the DNA molecule, announced in 1953.

Avery was elected a Foreign Member of the Royal Society in 1944. It was widely felt that he should have been awarded a Nobel prize.

Biographical Memoirs of Fellows of the Royal Society. 1956. (Portrait.)
R. J. Dubos, *The Professor, the Institute, and DNA.* 1976.
F. H. Portugal and J. S. Cohen, *A Century of DNA.* 1977.

                                                                                A P B

AVICENNA (ABU 'ALI AL-HUSAIN IBN ABDAL-LAH IBN SINA) Born at Afshana, near Bokhara (in modern Uzbekistan), AD 980; died Hamadan (in modern Iran), AD 1037. Arab philosopher and scientist.

Avicenna, like many of the great medieval scholars, took the whole of human knowledge as his province and so greatly excelled in this that his is generally regarded as the greatest mind since ARISTOTLE, by whose writings he was greatly influenced. As a boy, he was conventionally educated in the Koran and classical Arabic texts, but he then turned to astronomy and mathematics, mastering the Greek works in these subjects. He mastered also the medical knowledge of his time and was physician to several local rulers, though his career was an unsettled one as a result of constant strife between the warring emirates. He was a prodigious writer and the *Qanun (Canon)* alone, the encyclopaedia of medical knowledge by which he is best known, ran to about a million words. Through this work much classical Greek medical knowledge was reintroduced to Europe. This, however, was only a small fraction of his writings, in which he sought a total synthesis of abstract and practical knowledge, a synthesis of abstract and practical knowledge, a synthesis in which theology held pride of place.

Avicenna was well acquainted with the alchemical knowledge of his time, particularly that of GEBER. He subscribed to the belief that all metals were derived from two ideal elements, sulphur and mercury: these were related to, but not identical with, ordinary sulphur and mercury. He did not, however, believe in the possibility of transmuting base metals into gold. He made a particular study of minerals, on which he wrote a substantial treatise.

In physics, he had a special interest in optics and vision, partly derived, no doubt, from his medical interest in the diseases of the eye that are so prevalent in the Middle East. He appears clearly to have realized that light – which he believed to be corpuscular – proceeds from the object viewed to the eye and forms an image within it. He studied also the nature of time and motion, both practically and philosophically, and concluded that the two must be interrelated: time could have no significance in a totally motionless world. He anticipated the first law of motion formulated by NEWTON, namely that a body remains at rest or moves with constant speed in a straight line unless subjected to an external force. He seems, however, to have thought only in terms of constant velocities and not to have understood the concept of acceleration.

Carra de Vaux, *Avicenne.* 1900.
G. M. Wickens, *Avicenna: Scientist and Philosopher.* 1952.
S. M. Afnan, *Avicenna: His Life and Works.* 1958.
Medical History, **1**, 249, 1957.
Dictionary of Scientific Biography, Supp. I.

                                                                                T I W

AVOGADRO, AMEDEO Born Turin, Italy, 9 August 1776; died there, 9 July 1856. Originator of key hypothesis of molecular constitution of gases.

Lorenzo Romano Amedeo Carlo Avogadro di Quaregua e di Cerreto came of a legal family and himself qualified (1796) in law and was in practice for many years. From 1800 he studied physics and occupied chairs in physics off and on for most of his life. In 1811 he published, in French in the *Journal de Physique*, a paper which should have resolved all the difficulties confronting John DALTON, J. L. GAY-LUSSAC, and their contemporaries about the relation between atomic weights and the properties of gases. He asserted that equal volumes of all gases (under the same conditions of temperature and pressure) contain equal numbers of molecules. By the application of this hypothesis it should be possible to determine the molecular formulae of gases and consequently a self-consistent system of atomic weights. This brilliant conception was ignored for fifty years. There are several explanations. Avogadro used a clumsy nomenclature (e.g. using molecule for both atom and molecule). He offered little experimental evidence. His contemporaries, having been persuaded to swallow the idea of an indivisible atom of an element, would not take to a hypothesis which seemed to (but did not really) imply that the atom was divisible. A. M. AMPÈRE suggested a similar hypothesis in 1814 and he was credited by some later writers (e.g. M. A. A. Gaudin (1804–80)) with being its originator, although Ampère himself accorded Avogadro priority.

Avogadro continued to publish occasional papers on his theory and included it in a large physics text book (1837–41), but with no more success. He published other discoveries in chemistry of no great consequence and died respected for his learning and modesty, but without having achieved anything revolutionary. It was not long after his death that Stanislao CANNIZZARO circulated at the conclusion of the Carlsruhe Chemical Congress of 1860 the *Sunto di un corso di filosofia Chimica*, which expounded a system of atomic weight determinations using Avogadro's work, and thereby put Avogadro's hypothesis in the forefront of chemical theory.

I. Guareschi (Ed.), *Opere Scelte*. 1911. (Portrait.)
W. Tilden, *Famous Chemists*. 1921.
A. N. Meldrum, *Avogadro and Dalton*. 1904.
Dictionary of Scientific Biography.

F G

AYRTON, WILLIAM EDWARD Born in London, 14 September 1847; died there, 8 November 1908. Pioneer in electrical education and engineering.

The son of a barrister, Ayrton studied mathematics at University College, London, and electricity at Glasgow under W. THOMSON (Lord Kelvin). After successful service with the Indian Telegraph Company, and a year with the Great Western Railway, he was appointed in 1873 to the first chair in natural philosophy and telegraphy at the Imperial Engineering College, Tokyo. Here he worked with John Perry (1850–1920), professor of engineering, on dielectric constants of gases; viscosities of dielectrics; terrestrial magnetism; and other topics. Returning to London, he was professor at the City and Guilds of London Institute (1879); Finsbury Technical College (1881); and Central Technical College (1884). He became an outstanding teacher of electrical subjects, often using apparatus he had made himself.

In 1879 Ayrton became the first to advocate power transmission at high voltage. With Perry (who had rejoined him at Finsbury) he invented many electrical measuring instruments, including a spiral-spring ammeter and wattmeter. They also worked on railway electrification, and produced a dynamometer and (1882) the first electric tricycle.

Ayrton's second wife, whom he married in 1885, was Phoebe Marks (1854–1923), later famous for her work on the electric arc. Sponsored by the Admiralty, they worked together on the electric searchlight (1904–8).

Ayrton was elected FRS in 1881, receiving its Royal Medal in 1901. He was President of the Physical Society (1890–2) and of the Institution of Electrical Engineers (1892), whose *Journal* he had edited for eight years.

Nature, **79**, 74, 1908.
Dictionary of National Biography.
R. Appleyard, *The History of the Institution of Electrical Engineers* (1871–1931). 1939. (Portrait.)
Journal of the Institution of Electrical Engineers, **42**, 1, 1909.

C A R

B

BAADE, WILLIAM HEINRICH WALTER Born at Schröttinghausen, Westphalia, Germany, 24 March 1893; died Göttingen, 25 June 1960. Astronomer.

After studying at Münster, Baade was awarded a PhD by the University of Göttingen in 1919. A pupil of the mathematician Felix Klein (1849–1925), his interest in astronomy was aroused by K. Schwarzschild (1873–1916). From 1920 until he emigrated to the USA in 1931 he worked in the observatory at Hamburg-Bergedorf and taught at the University of Hamburg.

In 1931 he joined the staff of Mount Wilson Observatory, Pasadena, California, and worked with F. Zwicky (1898–1974) and E. P. HUBBLE on supernovae and galactic distances. The wartime blackout of Los Angeles cleared the night sky and enabled him to study the Andromeda galaxy, using a 100-inch telescope. He was the first to observe individual stars in the nucleus of the Andromeda nebula. By showing that Andromeda was more than two million light years away he was able to calculate that the Universe must be at least five billion years old. In 1948 Baade discovered the asteroid Icarus, the first asteroid found which approached the Sun within the orbit of Mercury.

In 1948 Baade moved to Mount Palomar observatory and continued his study of star clusters in our galaxy and nearby galaxies. He showed that star formation was continuing within our galaxy and in the early 1950s was the first to notice stellar populations, identifying two classes of stars in the galaxy: hot, young, blue stars in the spiral arms of the galaxy, which he called Population I stars, and older, redder stars in the central region, called Population II stars. In 1952 he was able to show that the galaxies are twice as remote as previously believed.

Baade returned to Germany in 1959 as Gauss Professor at the University of Göttingen. In 1954 he had been awarded the gold medal of the Royal Astronomical Society for his observational work on galactic and extra-galactic objects.

Dictionary of Scientific Biography.

David Abbott (Ed.), *The Biographical Dictionary of Scientists: Astronomers.* 1984.

The Times, 29 June 1960.

APB

BABBAGE, CHARLES Born at Teignmouth, Devon, England, 26 December 1792; died London, 18 October 1871. Pioneer of machine computing.

Babbage was educated privately and at St Peter's College, Cambridge, where he graduated in 1814, although without taking the tripos examinations.

He was a friend of John HERSCHEL and George Peacock (1791–1858), and with them founded the Analytical Society of Cambridge. Although he wrote one or two papers on the calculus of functions, his principal work is first evident in some notices to the Royal Society on the connections between notation and mechanism. His ambition was to eliminate errors in astronomical and mathematical tables, by having machines not only calculate them but print them directly without human intervention. He worked on this problem for almost all his life. The Government reluctantly gave him financial assistance, and he spent a great deal of his private fortune in pursuing his ambition. He travelled extensively in Europe, analysing every sort of machinery, and publishing his findings in *Economy of Machines and Manufactures* (1834).

Babbage's first computer, or 'difference engine', equipped for automatic printing, was largely finished in 1834, although Babbage, having previous to this conceived the idea of a more sophisticated 'analytical engine', wished to change his plan. The Government refused to take on any further financial commitment. The difference engine was used in its early stages to compile tables of logarithms from 1 to 108 000 (1827). Great pains were taken to achieve clarity in the printing of this, changes of typeface being used periodically to assist the eye, and coloured papers being used on the grounds that black on white is a fatiguing combination. The analytical engine was to be capable of performing any sequence of arithmetical operations, and to be programmed by means of punched cards. That this, and Babbage's many other projects, were never brought to a state of completion, was in part due to his own character, in part to lack of adequate financial backing, and in part to the inadequacies of existing precision technology.

Babbage was Lucasian Professor of Mathematics at Cambridge from 1828 to 1839. He wrote profusely on a variety of subjects, amongst other things contributing one of the Bridgewater Treatises (the ninth; 1837), and one or two mathematical tracts on life assurance. With Byron's daughter, he spent much futile effort in trying to evolve an infallible system for forecasting the winners of horse races, losing a great deal of money in the process. Appropriately, he was founder of the Statistical Society (1834).

P. and E. Morrison (Ed.), *Charles Babbage and his Calculating Engines.* 1961.

M. Moseley, *Irascible Genius.* 1964. (Portrait.)

A. Hyman, *Science and Reform: Selected Works of Charles Babbage.* 1989.

J. Fauvel, *Interdisciplinary Science Rviews*, **17**, 304, 1992.

Dictionary of Scientific Biography.

J D N

BABCOCK, HORACE WELCOME Born in Pasadena, California, USA, 13 September 1912. Astrophysicist: pioneered measurement of stellar magnetic fields.

Babcock studied at the California Institute of Technology and the University of California before joining the Yerkes and McDonald Observatories (1939–41). In 1946 he joined the staff of the prestigious Mount Wilson Observatory, where he was Director 1951–80. In 1896 P. ZEEMAN had shown that some spectral lines are split in a strong magnetic field and later (1908) G. E. HALE showed that light from sunspots is split in this way. With his father, Harold Delos Babcock (b. 1882), he developed a very sensitive stellar magnetograph to measure the magnetic fields of sunspots (c 10^{-4}T). They also showed that the Sun's magnetic poles periodically reverse. Turning to stars, they measured many stellar magnetic fields and found that these were often variable. Babcock's research earned him many honours, including the Henry Draper Medal of the National Academy of Sciences (1957) and the Gold Medal of the Royal Astronomical Society (1970).

Who's Who, 1993.

Dunne H. Roller (Ed.), *Perspectives in the History of Science and Technology*. 1971.

T I W

BABCOCK, STEPHEN MOULTON Born at Bridgewater, New York State, USA, 22 October 1843; died Madison, Wisconsin, 2 July 1931. Agricultural chemist; pioneer of research on nutrition.

Babcock was educated at Tufts College, Massachusetts, obtaining the degree of AB in 1866, and at Rensselaer Polytechnic Institute, where he briefly studied engineering. He worked for several years at Cornell University before going to Göttingen, where he obtained the degree of PhD in 1879. Afterwards he returned to Cornell, but did not stay long, and in 1882 became chemist to the New York Agricultural Experiment Station, and there developed a gravimetric method for milk analysis, and a viscometer to detect adulterants in liquids. In 1888 he was appointed professor of agricultural chemistry at the University of Wisconsin, and devised a method for accurately assessing the fat content of milk. This method came into widespread use because of its simplicity and accuracy. Babcock also carried out work on pasteurization and the curing of cheese, but one of his most important investigations was connected with the nutritional value of various animal foodstuffs. This field of study later became important at Wisconsin. Babcock retired in 1913, but continued to take an interest in the University until his death.

E. J. Dies, *Titans of the Soil*. 1949.

E. Farber (Ed.), *Great Chemists*. 1961.

Dictionary of American Biography, Supp. I.

Duane H. Roller (Ed.), *Perspectives in the History of Science and Technology*. 1971.

B B K

BABO, CLEMENS HEINRICH LAMBERT VON Born at Ladenburg, Germany, 25 November 1818; died Karlsruhe, 15 April 1899. An unusually versatile chemist.

von Babo was a pupil of J. von LIEBIG in Giessen; most of his life was spent in the University of Freiburg, finally as professor. His activities as a chemist were remarkably wide. He found (1847) that the vapour pressure of a liquid is lowered by dissolved material, and that the relative fall is proportional to the concentration, but independent of temperature. He studied (with E. Warburg) the relation between the density and viscosity of gases; he worked on analytical chemistry, the physical properties of soil, and the isolation of various natural products. He was also fertile in devising new apparatus ('Babo's tube' for making ozone) and was the first to use a centrifuge as a laboratory tool.

Berichte der deutschen Chemischen Gesellschaft, **32**, 1163, 1899.

W V F

BACKUS, JOHN Born at Philadelphia, Pennsylvania, USA, 3 December 1924. Computer scientist. Invented FORTRAN scientific programming language.

After serving in the US Army from 1943 to 1946 Backus graduated from Columbia University, New York, in 1949, and joined IBM in 1950 as a programmer in the Pure and Applied Science Departments. In 1954 IBM published the first version of FORTRAN (FORmula TRANslator), invented by Backus. This was the first 'high-level language' to be developed, using language close to natural language. Using a notation similar to algebraic notation, it was designed for scientific and mathematical problems. By 1957 FORTRAN had become commercially available for use on an IBM computer, and it became the most widely used scientific programming language. New versions of FORTRAN were developed later, including Fortran 77 and Fortran 90.

In 1959 the Backus Normal Form (BNF), invented by Backus, was taken as the standard notation for describing the syntax of a programming language. This was later modified by Peter Naur (hence 'Backus Naur Form'). This placed the design of computer languages on theoretical foundations, and because it was independent of any particular machine it meant that languages could be used on different machines rather than being written specifically for one machine.

Backus remained with IBM at the Research Center in Yorktown Heights, New York, 1959–65, and then went to the IBM Almaden Research Center in San Jose, California as an IBM fellow. From 1973 he was Manager of Functional Programming.

A P B

BACON, FRANCIS (BARON VERULAM, VISCOUNT ST ALBANS) Born in London, 22 January 1561; died Highgate, London, 9 April 1626. Statesman, essayist, and natural philosopher: author of the so-called Baconian method.

Francis Bacon was the son of Sir Nicholas Bacon (1509–1579), Keeper of the Great Seal. After studying at Trinity College, Cambridge, and Gray's Inn, London, he joined the suite of the English Ambassador in France. After taking his seat in Parliament in 1584 he endured long disappointment in his attempts to gain public office. His fortunes changed with the accession of James I, and he became successively Knight (1603), Member of the King's Council (1604), Solicitor-General (1607), Attorney-General (1613), Keeper of the Great Seal (1617), and Lord High Chancellor (1618). At the height of his success, in 1621, he was convicted of corrupt practices and imprisoned. Though soon released, his public career was finished.

Bacon was obsessed with the idea that he was born to be of service not only to his country but to humanity as a whole, by the production of good through the discovery of truth. He reviewed all the accepted branches of human knowledge, classifying them according to the faculty of mind (memory, reason, or imagination) to which they belonged. His comprehensive scheme he called 'the grand instauration of the sciences', and many of his scattered writings, beginning, for example, with the *Advancement of Learning* (1605), were intended as parts of a final *Instauratio Magna*. In connection with this should be mentioned the *De Augmentis*, which superseded the *Advancement of Learning*, the *Novum Organum* (1620), and many shorter pieces. Bacon often outlined his grandiose scheme, but never completed it.

Bacon was greatly revered by scientists, well into this century, for the so-called Baconian method, which many believed they were following in their work. Bacon argued that hidden among the facts presented to the senses (and stored in the memory) are causes, or forms, and that the great scientific problem is to analyse experience by mechanical means so as to arrive at true conclusions. The means in question was his method of induction, which involved firstly the exhaustive collection of particular instances; and secondly the exclusion of elements not always accompanying the phenomenon investigated. This, a gradual procedure, takes us, according to him, from less to more general propositions.

Bacon influenced philosophy more than science. The Baconian method of induction was further discussed and developed by William Whewell (1794–1866) and John Stuart Mill (1806–73), in the last century. It was not completely new with Bacon, bearing as it does a strong resemblance to certain mediaeval ideas (e.g. the 'method of falsification' developed by Robert GROSSETESTE).

J. Spedding, *Life and Times of Francis Bacon.* 1878.
J. G. Crowther, *Francis Bacon.* 1960. (Portrait.)
A. Wigfall Green, *Sir Francis Bacon.* 1966.
B. Farrington, *Francis Bacon: Philosopher of Industrial Science.* 1961.
Dictionary of Scientific Biography.

                                                                                    J D N

BACON, ROGER

BACON, ROGER Born at Ilchester, Somerset, England, *c.*1214; died Oxford, 11 June 1292. Scholar ('*doctor mirabilis*') and often regarded as the first modern scientist.

Little is known of Bacon's early life; he appears to have come from a wealthy family. He studied first at Oxford, under Robert GROSSETESTE and later (1234–50) at Paris under Peter PEREGRINUS. About 1247 he joined the Franciscan Order, and three years later he returned to Oxford, but it appears that his quarrelsome nature and independence of thought led him into conflict with his colleagues. From 1257 onwards he pursued his studies in iso-

lation – traditionally at a house on Folly Bridge that stood until 1799 – taking no part in University affairs. Then he was for many years (1277–91) kept virtually imprisoned by his Order in Paris. Only for a short time (1265–8), while Clement IV was Pope, was he in favour. In 1292 he returned to Oxford, but died in the same year.

Like most of the great scholars of his day, Bacon took virtually the whole of contemporary knowledge as his province. In science he ranged over alchemy, astronomy, and optics, together, of course, with mathematics. Nevertheless, he believed that all other branches were subordinate to theology. He distinguished two different kinds of knowledge. Firstly, an inner knowledge of divine origin – the 'active intellect'. Secondly, practical knowledge gained by observation and experiment. The two together made up experience. Bacon recorded his ideas in three major works: these were, respectively, the *Opus majus*, *Opus secundum*, and *Opus tertium*. He planned to incorporate these in a general encyclopaedia, but this was never realized.

Over the years, Bacon acquired an undeserved reputation as a magician rather than a scholar. Robert Greene (1560–92) in his posthumously published play *The Honorable Historie of Frier Bacon and Frier Bongay* (1594) recalls the brazen head which Bacon is alleged to have made; while Bacon slept it uttered, and then shattered in pieces. He is credited with the discovery of gunpowder, but this is unfounded.

It is evident from his writings that Bacon had a strong practical streak in his make-up. Alchemy – of which he was a practitioner – he regarded as the most valuable of the sciences, 'because it produced greater utilities'. He had remarkable powers of imagination and many of his prophecies have been fulfilled. They include mechanical transport on land and sea, aerial flight, and submarine exploration. He demonstrated that air is required to support combustion, and experimented with lenses to improve vision. Probably his most valuable contribution, however, was the stress he laid on experiment; he taught that in practical affairs – in developing useful knowledge – speculation was useless without the investigator having first elucidated the facts.

Gordon Leff, *Medieval Thought.* 1958.
A. C. Crombie, *Augustine to Galileo.* 1952.
T. Crowley, *Roger Bacon.* 1950.
A. G. Little (Ed.), *Roger Bacon: Essays Contributed by Various Writers.* 1914.
J. J. N. McGurk, *History Today,* **30**, 445, 1974.
Dictionary of Scientific Biography.

                                                                                    T I W

BAEKELAND, LEO HENDRIK

BAEKELAND, LEO HENDRIK Born at Ghent, Belgium, 14 November 1863; died Beacon, New York, 23 February 1944. Inventor of Bakelite, the first major industrial synthetic plastic.

Baekeland studied chemistry in Ghent under F. Swarts (1866–1940), whose daughter he subsequently married. After three years at the *École Normale* at Bruges, two more at Ghent, and a further period of travel in France and Britain, he settled in the United States in 1889. His first post there was as chemist to a photographic manufacturer. Two years later he set up as a consultant, and devised the first commercially successful photographic contact developing paper – an unwashed silver chloride emulsion. His claim to have invented this 'gaslight' or 'velox' paper is doubtful, but so successful was the Nepera Chemical Company which he founded to make and sell it that the firm was bought by George Eastman (1854–1932) in 1898 for $1 million. In 1900 he turned to the study of electrochemistry and for a few years worked successfully in this field.

In 1905, looking for a substitute for shellac, he examined the reaction between phenol and formaldehyde, as others had done previously. However, Baekeland abandoned the traditional suspicion of non-crystalline organic solids, and discovered a convenient method for the controlled production of the resin which he termed 'Bakelite'. He patented it in 1906 and began manufacture for electrical equipment. By 1911 it was being made by Bakelite companies in Germany and the United States, and in 1922 a merger of the American company with two of its rivals led to the formation of the Bakelite Corporation, with Baekeland as its first President. In 1939 this was absorbed into the Union Carbide and Carbon Company.

The discovery of this dark-coloured thermohardening resin – the first major industrial synthetic plastic – stimulated much further research in the 1920s, and Baekeland must rank as the founder of the modern plastics industry. He received civil honours from France and Belgium, became President of the American Chemical Society, the American Society of Chemical Engineering (from whom he received the Perkin Medal in 1916), and the American Electrochemical Society.

Baekeland became rich early in life and was able to travel extensively, touring Europe by car in 1907. His success owed much to his restless independence and forceful personality. He is recorded as having been a man of great charm and freedom from prejudice.

Nature, **153**, 369, 1944.
Journal of Chemical Education, **41**, 224, 1964. (Portrait.)
M. Mitchell, *American Science and Invention.* 1960. (Portraits.)
J. Gillis, *Leo Hendrik Baekeland.* 1965. (English summary; portraits.)
Dictionary of Scientific Biography.

C A R

BAER, KARL ERNST VON Born at Piep, Estonia, 17 February 1792; died Dorpat, Russia, 28 November 1876. Discoverer of the mammalian ovum and a pioneer of embryology.

Baer, descended from the German nobility of Estonia, was educated at Reval for a military career, but from 1810 he studied medicine at Dorpat. After graduating in 1814 he continued his studies at Vienna. There he realized that he was not a born practitioner, and he then studied anatomy and embryology at Würzburg. After a few months in Berlin he settled as Prosector in Anatomy at Königsberg (1817). In 1819 he became associate professor of zoology there, and in 1822 ordinary professor. In 1829–30 he spent a few months at St Petersburg and, not being called to another German university, he accepted in 1834 the call as an academician of the Academy at St Petersburg. There he remained until he returned to Dorpat in 1867. Baer's very important work in

embryology was done at Königsberg, but at St Petersburg he was active in other fields, such as anthropology and ethnography.

Baer's most important work, *De ovi mammalium et hominis genesi* ('On the origin of the mammalian and human ovum', 1827), resulted from research carried out at Königsberg. At that time the eggs of many animals lower than mammals were known. R. de GRAAF thought at first that the follicles in mammals that bear his name were eggs; but he later discovered in the uterus an egg, in a later stage of development, which was smaller than a Graafian follicle. Albrecht von HALLER thought that the mammalian ovum was formed by coagulation from the fluid of the Graafian follicle. Baer investigated this problem in dogs, and he discovered the ovum as a yellowish spot floating in the follicular fluid.

In his other great work, *Entwicklungsgeschichte der Thiere* ('The developmental history of animals', 1828–37), Baer put forward the 'germ-layer theory', according to which the eggs of vertebrates develop to form four layers of tissue. In these vertebrates each layer gives rise to certain definite organs or tissues of the adult. (Baer's two middle layers were later better regarded as one.) Baer also discovered the notochord in the embryo chick, and he showed that this endodermal – and often transient – structure is present in the embryos of all vertebrates. His conception, later known as the biogenetic law, that during development a higher animal passes through stages which resemble stages in the development of lower animals, was later fruitful in the interpretation of embryology and of evolution.

W. Haacke, *Karl Ernst von Baer.* 1905.
E. Nordenskiöld, *History of Biology.* 1929. (Portrait.)
Dictionary of Scientific Biography.

E A U

BAEYER, ADOLF JOHANN FRIEDRICH VON Born in Berlin, 31 October 1835; died near Munich, 20 August 1917. A great experimental organic chemist, notable for his synthesis of indigo.

Von Baeyer came of a scientific family. He studied chemistry under R. W. BUNSEN at Heidelberg, but his preference for organic chemistry (not encouraged by Bunsen) led him to work in the laboratory of F. A. KEKULÉ, whom he followed from Heidelberg to Ghent. He taught chemistry in the *GewerbeSchule* in Berlin (1860–72), then for three years in Strasbourg University, newly annexed to Germany; in 1875 he became successor to Justus von LIEBIG in Munich, where he remained until his death. He gave only elementary lectures, and the emphasis of his great school was on learning by research rather than formal teaching. His pupils included Emil FISCHER, K. GRAEBE, V. MEYER, and W. H. PERKIN, JUNIOR.

His real importance in organic chemistry is that he seized upon the Structure Theory of his friend Kekulé, and, without any of the philosophical scruples which troubled Kekulé and others, used it as the theoretical base on which to build his life's work. He was a superb experimenter (as Kekulé was not), and in his hands the Structure Theory had its first triumphs.

Some early work on condensation reactions of aldehydes and ketones led him to propose (1870) that the primary photochemical reaction in plants was the combination of water and carbon dioxide to give oxygen and formaldehyde; further condensation of the latter was supposed to give carbohydrates and other plant materials. This theory stimulated research for many decades, but is now abandoned. He discovered the 'phthalein' dyestuffs, and his classical work on indigo, begun in 1865, led to a synthesis (1880), and to the formulation of the correct structure (1883). Von Baeyer refused, however, to collaborate with industry in this matter, and the eventual commercial synthesis of indigo owed little to him directly.

Other topics investigated by von Baeyer and his pupils included uric acid derivatives, polyacetylenes (a class of compounds demanding brilliant experimental technique), and oxonium salts; he proposed a 'centric' formula for benzene, and a 'strain theory' correlating the stability of cyclic compounds with the ring angles.

He was married, and had four children. Among other honours he was awarded the Nobel prize for chemistry in 1905.

K. Schmorl, Adolf von Baeyer. 1952.

Journal of the Chemical Society, 1520, 1923. (Portrait.)

E. Farber (Ed.), Great Chemists. 1961. (Portrait.)

C. de Milt, Journal of Chemical Education, **31**, 91, 1954.

Dictionary of Scientific Biography.

Tyler Wasson (Ed.), Nobel Prize Winners. 1987. (Portrait.)

W V F

BAILLIE, MATTHEW Born at Shotts, Lanarkshire, Scotland, 27 October 1761; died Duntisbourne, near Cirencester, Gloucestershire, England, 23 September 1823. Physician and a pioneer morbid anatomist.

Baillie, the nephew of John HUNTER and his brother William, was educated at Hamilton Academy, and at the age of 14 years he entered the University of Glasgow. There he studied classics, mathematics, and philosophy. He was awarded an exhibition to Balliol College, Oxford, and entered there in 1779. Much of his education was received during his Oxford vacations from his uncle, William Hunter (1718–83), at the latter's famous Windmill Street School in London. Meanwhile, Baillie studied arts and medicine at Oxford; he graduated BA in 1783, MB in 1786, and MD in 1789. William Hunter had died in 1783, and his house and the school were left to Baillie for thirty years. Baillie began to give lectures at the school in 1784–5, before he had graduated in medicine, and he continued to lecture with great success until 1799. In 1787 he was elected physician to St George's Hospital, but his practice as a physician became so great that he resigned that post also in 1799.

Baillie was elected a Fellow of the Royal College of Physicians in 1790. He was a Censor twice, and became an Elect in 1809. He was the last owner of the famous 'gold-headed cane' (now in the possession of the College), which had descended to him from its first owner, John Radcliffe (1650–1714). Baillie was elected a Fellow of the Royal Society in 1790, and he delivered its Croonian lecture in 1791.

Baillie's significant contribution to medical science was his Morbid Anatomy of some of the most Important Parts of the Human Body, published in 1793. In 1799–1803 a Series of Engravings was published as an atlas to illustrate the book. This is the first work which attempted to treat pathology as a subject in itself. In it Baillie arranged his observations by organs instead of by symptoms, as G. B. MORGAGNI had done, and he dealt only with the brain and the organs of the chest and abdomen, fields in which he had great personal experience. He gave the first accurate definitions of cirrhosis of the liver and of hepatization in lobar pneumonia, and he provided excellent descriptions of renal cysts, typhoid ulcers, gastric ulcer, and other conditions. The engravings in the atlas, drawn by the naturalist William Clift (1775–1849), are very fine.

B. W. Richardson, Disciples of Aesculapius. 1900.

G. Wolstenholme and D. Piper (Eds), The Royal College of Physicians of London: Portraits.1964.

Dictionary of Scientific Biography.

E A U

BAIRD, JOHN LOGIE Born at Helensburgh, Dunbartonshire, Scotland, 13 August 1888; died Bexhill, Sussex, England, 14 June 1946. Pioneer of television.

The youngest son of a Presbyterian minister, Baird was educated in Glasgow at the Royal Technical College (now University of Strathclyde) and the University. Persistent ill-health caused him to be rejected for military service in 1914, to resign from the post as electrical engineer which he held during the war years, and to abandon three successive business ventures, in Glasgow, the West Indies, and London. In 1922 he retired after a complete breakdown to live at Hastings.

In these unpromising circumstances he turned to amateur investigations, and after two years' research contrived a primitive television apparatus, capable of transmitting a flickering image over a distance of a few feet. Having conveyed his equipment to two attic rooms in Soho, he gave the first demonstration of true television there on 26 January 1926. In December of the same year Baird showed his 'noctovisor', enabling images to be transmitted from a dark room by means of infra-red rays. Thereafter his time was devoted entirely to pioneering new developments in television.

In 1927 Baird demonstrated television by telephone line between London and Glasgow, and in 1928 between London and New York and to a ship in mid-Atlantic. He also pioneered television in natural colour; stereoscopic and big-screen television; and (1932) ultra-short-wave transmission. He formed the Baird Television Development Company, which on 30 September 1929 was allowed to provide the first BBC television programme. Synchronization of sound and vision was achieved a few months later, and half-hour programmes were shown regularly on five mornings a week, which acquired considerable publicity when they screened the 1931 Derby.

In January 1935, however, a Departmental Committee under an ex-Postmaster-General reported in favour of high-definition transmission, and in September the thirty-line pictures of primitive television were discontinued. For two years Baird's Company operated side by side with its rival, EMI, which had the resources of the Marconi organisation behind it. Baird's system, working on 240 lines, mechanically scanned, then gave place finally to the 405-line electrically scanned system promoted by Marconi-EMI.

R. F. Tiltman, *Baird of Television*. 1933.
Dictionary of National Biography.
A. Briggs, *History of Broadcasting in the United Kingdom*, vol. 2. 1965.
B. Morgan, *Men and Discoveries in Electricity.* 1952.

T K D

BAIRD, SPENCER FULLERTON Born at Reading, Pennsylvania, USA, 3 February 1823; died Woods Hole, Massachusetts, 19 August 1887. Naturalist and zoologist.

Before graduating at Dickinson College in 1840 Baird met J. J. AUDUBON, who started his lifelong interest in ornithology. In 1845 he was appointed professor of natural history at Dickinson, where he taught zoology, physiology, chemistry, and mathematics. In 1850 he became Assistant Secretary to the Smithsonian Institution – founded from the estate of J. M. SMITHSON – and in 1878 Secretary. He had wide interests and was a prolific writer, publishing work not only on many branches of zoology but also on geology, botany, anthropology, and other subjects. His official position brought him into the planning of Government exploring expeditions to the western States, the resulting collections coming under his care at Washington, where he studied and reported upon them.

For many years he worked in close touch with Louis AGASSIZ, supplying him with specimens from the national collections for study and description, but an unfortunate quarrel estranged them and ended in an unsuccessful attempt by Agassiz to exclude him from the National Academy of Sciences. The most important of Baird's numerous publications were his *Mammals of North America* (1859) and, in collaboration with Brewer and Ridgway, his *History of North American Birds* (1875– 84). In 1871 he was appointed US Commissioner of Fish and Fisheries, and took a large part in founding the Marine Biological Laboratory at Woods Hole.

W. H. Dall, *Spencer Fullerton Baird*. 1915. (Portrait.)
Biographical Memoirs of the National Academy of Sciences, III. 1895.
Dictionary of Scientific Biography.

L H M

BAKEWELL, ROBERT Born at Dishley Grange, near Loughborough, Leicestershire, England, 1725; died there, 1 October 1795. Pioneer of scientific agriculture.

Bakewell travelled widely to study contemporary agricultural practice. Inheriting his father's farm, he systematically set about improving its productivity. He was particularly successful in animal breeding, and within thirty years notably improved the old English heavy horse, Leicestershire breed sheep, and Longhorn cattle. He also paid great attention to the organization of his farm in order to simplify its operation.

Understandably, for he could have gained no protection under the law, Bakewell did not disclose his breeding methods. Nevertheless, they had far-reaching effects not only in Britain but abroad. He rarely sold his beasts, but commonly let both bulls and rams by the season. 'Twopounder', his most famous improved Leicester ram, once earned him the then remarkable fee of 800 guineas for one season. Practically every large breeder of the day used his Longhorn bulls. It appears that the key to Bakewell's rapid success was that he pursued a policy of outbreeding to achieve the traits he sought, and fixed these by inbreeding.

At Dishley Grange he dispersed lavish hospitality not only to working farmers but to many great landowners, including royalty, who were anxious to study his methods at first hand. Even his great wealth became exhausted and he became bankrupt in 1776, and died in straitened circumstances.

C. S. Orwin, *A History of English Farming*. 1949.
Dictionary of National Biography.
H. C. Pawson, *Robert Bakewell*. 1957.

T I W

BALARD, ANTOINE JEROME Born at Montpellier, France, 30 September 1802; died Paris, 30 March 1876. Discoverer of bromine.

Balard had one of those small talents which would have shone brighter in duller company. He lived at the same time as many outstanding French chemists, so his useful discoveries seem less meritorious than they were. He studied pharmacy at the School of Pharmacy in Montpellier, becoming assistant to the professor, Joseph Anglada (1775– 1833). He moved to a minor post in the *École Normale* in Paris, and succeeded L. J. THENARD as professor in the Faculty of Science there.

He did some work on cyanogen, but also followed the example of many French chemists and turned to the study of chemical work of economic importance, in his case the properties of the impure salt made by the solar evaporation of sea-water. When investigating the amount of the newly discovered element iodine in sea-water and in marine creatures, he had observed that on treating solar-salt liquor with chlorine he not only got indications of iodine but also a yellow solution with an intense smell. He obtained a dark red liquid by distillation, which turned out to have properties relating it to chlorine and iodine. He announced this in 1825 (more fully in 1826). He wanted to call the substance 'muride', but he was prevailed upon by L. J. Thenard, L. N. VAUQUELIN and J. L. GAY-LUSSAC to call it 'brome' [bromine] after its strong, offensive smell (Gk. *bromos*, stink).

His other work included the discovery of hypochlorous acid, chlorine monoxide (1834), and some organic compounds. One act, as a teacher, is probably more important than any research. He encouraged PASTEUR and used his influence to get him permission to stay on at the *École Normale* instead of being transferred to a teaching post at Tournon. Pasteur was then free to study crystallography and so begin his spectacular career.

Nouvelle Biographie Universelle, vol. 4. 1953.
J. R. Partington, *A History of Chemistry*, vol. 4. 1964.
E. Smith, *Journal of Chemical Education*, **3**, 382, 1926.
Dictionary of Scientific Biography.

F G

BALFOUR, FRANCIS MAITLAND Born in Edinburgh, 10 November 1851; died in the Alps, July 1882. Notable for his brilliant pioneer work on comparative embryology and vertebrate morphology.

Leaving Harrow School in 1870, Balfour entered Trinity College, Cambridge, where he studied under Professor Sir Michael Foster (1836–1907), who inspired his interest in embryology. After taking a first-class degree he went to the Marine Biological Station at Naples, and there commenced his researches on the development of Elasmobranch fishes which subsequently produced valuable knowledge of the origin of the nervous system and the homologies of the urino-genital systems in vertebrates. On being elected a Fellow of his college in 1874 he returned to Cambridge, continuing his researches and engaging in teaching and administration, for which he also displayed great talent.

Balfour published his great treatise, *Comparative Embryology*, in two parts – Invertebrates in 1880, followed by Vertebrates in 1881. The work is monumental on account of its lucidity, perception, and fertility of ideas, and its value was so highly esteemed that the Universities of Oxford and of Edinburgh in turn offered chairs, but Balfour preferred to remain at Cambridge, where the University created a chair for him and in March 1882 elected him as first professor of animal morphology. In this capacity Balfour, tragically, never actively served, for whilst mountaineering during the summer of the same year he and his guide were killed whilst climbing the Aiguille Blanche on the Italian side of Mont Blanc; the exact manner of death and the date (though probably 19 July) are unknown.

For his unselfishness, generosity, and courtesy throughout his short life, Balfour endeared himself to all with whom he came in contact.

Elected Fellow (1878) and awarded a Royal Medal (1881) by the Royal Society. Received honorary LLD from University of Glasgow (1881).

Proceedings of the Royal Society, **35**, xx, 1883.
Science, **2**, 299, 1883.
Dictionary of Scientific Biography.

A P G

BALMER, JOHANN JAKOB Born at Basle, Switzerland, 1 May 1825; died there, 12 March 1898. The first to discover a mathematical relationship between the frequencies of atomic spectral lines.

Balmer was the eldest son of a farmer, prominent in the local administration at Basle. Leaving school in 1844, he spent the next winter at the Karlsruhe Polytechnic Institute, where he studied geometry, mineralogy, French, architecture, and other subjects. After a further period at Berlin he returned to his old school at Basle as teacher of technical drawing (1846). Granted a doctorate by the local University, he became, in 1850, a part-time teacher at a girls' school in Basle, and remained at this post for forty more years, teaching mathematical subjects and Latin. In 1865 he also acquired the right to teach projective geometry in the University, remaining a *Privatdozent* until 1890. He published a textbook on this subject in 1887.

Balmer made his great discovery without having received any specialized training in physics, and when he was almost 60. In 1884 he announced to the Basle Natural Science Society his finding that the frequencies of the lines in the hydrogen spectrum form a convergent series, now called the Balmer series. Several years later he published similar results for helium and lithium spectra.

His interest in atomic spectra was aroused by a physics lecture by E. Hagenbach (1871–1955) and sustained by his encouragement. It appears that his success was due to a combination of mathematical insight and ability to visualize graphical relationships. It started the long search for the meaning of spectroscopic data, culminating in the quantum theory.

Elemente der Mathematik, **16**, 49, 1961. (Portrait.)
American Journal of Physics, **34**, 496, 1966.
G. K. T. Conn and H. D. Turner, *The Evolution of the Nuclear Atom*. 1965. (Portrait.)
Die Naturwissenschaften, **9**, 451, 1921.

C A R

BANKS, SIR JOSEPH Born in London, 2 February 1743; died there, 19 June 1820. Botanist; President of the Royal Society for forty-two years; statesman of science.

Although Banks made surprisingly few direct personal contributions to the advancement of knowledge, he dominated the scientific scene in Britain for roughly half a century and carried great authority abroad.

He was the son of William Banks of Revesby Abbey in Lincolnshire, who died in 1761. In 1764, when he came of age, Banks inherited a large fortune, which he spent lavishly in promoting his scientific interests. Primarily he was a botanist, and resolved to make this his life's interest while still a boy at Eton. His early knowledge he gained from countrywomen who gathered simples near the school, aided by diligent study of the *Herball* of John GERARD. At Oxford, botanical teaching was virtually nonexistent (Humphry Sibthorp (1713–97) is alleged to have given only one lecture in his life), so Banks fetched Israel Lyons (1739–75) from Cambridge to be his mentor. Leaving Oxford in 1764, he persuaded his mother to rent a house in Chelsea, to be near the Physic Garden of the Society of Apothecaries. Two years later, anxious to extend his knowledge of plants beyond those native to his own country, he sailed as naturalist in HMS *Niger*, a Fishery Protection vessel voyaging to Labrador and Newfoundland.

On his return he learnt that the Royal Society, to whose Fellowship he had just been elected, was planning an expedition to the South Pacific to observe the transit of Venus in 1769. Immediately, he realized the opportunities this would offer for botanical work in lands whose rich flora and fauna were then virtually unknown. In due course the expedition, under the command of Captain James COOK, sailed in the *Endeavour* on what is now recognized as one of the great voyages of exploration and observation. Banks, accompanied by a party of seven – the chief of whom was the botanist Daniel Solander (1736–82) – sailed with him; the voyage is said to have cost him £10,000 from his own pocket. He returned, after an adventurous voyage lasting three years, with a vast quantity of material, to find himself a celebrity. He was summoned to Windsor to give a personal account of his experiences to George III; this marked the beginning of a lifelong friendship which helped to give Banks great influence in high places. This was certainly a factor in the election of Banks to the Presidency of the Royal Society in 1778, which he regarded as the greatest of the many honours that befell him in his life: the Society was at odds with the sovereign (through a now absurd controversy on whether lightning conductors should be blunt or pointed) and was anxious to re-establish good relations. In 1781 he was created a baronet.

At that time the Society was in cramped accommodation at Somerset House, and Banks's residence in Soho Square – which he purchased in 1776 and where he entertained lavishly – quickly became the focus of the scientific world of London. There scientists could not only meet their colleagues in agreeable circumstances but, no less important, could also meet leading figures from other walks of life. A man of great strength of character, Banks soon dominated the scientific scene.

In 1772 he had plans to make a further voyage with Cook, in the *Resolution*, but at the last moment the plan fell through owing to his dissatisfaction with the accommodation offered. Instead, he made a voyage to Iceland. He maintained throughout his life a most active interest in the many new species identified on contemporary voyages of exploration. An important manifestation of this was the part he played in establishing the now world-famous Botanic Gardens at Kew. His efforts to bring to Kew seeds and plants from every part of the globe were prodigious, and made possible only by his unique international standing. He conceived Kew as not only a centre for maintaining living specimens of as many species as possible, but as offering an advisory service for making practical use of plants. Examples of Banks's practical interest are his attempt to establish the breadfruit in the West Indies – initially frustrated by the famous mutiny on the *Bounty*, which was carrying the plants – and his concern with the successful project to establish the tea plant in India from its native China. He took an active part in importing, at George III's behest, merino sheep – then closely guarded by the Spanish Government – into Britain.

His voyage in the *Endeavour* was the start of a lifelong interest in Australian affairs, and he took an active part in the establishment of the first colony at Botany Bay in 1788, a project which he had first urged in 1779.

H. C. Cameron, *Sir Joseph Banks*. 1952. (Portraits)
E. Smith, *Life of Sir Joseph Banks*. 1911.
Dictionary of National Biography.
Dictionary of Scientific Biography.

                                                                          T I W

BANTING, SIR FREDERICK GRANT Born at Alliston, Ontario, Canada, 14 November 1891; died (in an aeroplane crash) Newfoundland, 21 February 1941. With others he isolated insulin and demonstrated its action in diabetes.

Son of a farmer, Banting was educated at the University of Toronto. He qualified as a doctor in 1916, and went on active service as a Medical Officer, being awarded the Military Cross for gallantry in the field. Returning to Canada after the war, he went into practice as a surgeon in London, Ontario. In 1920 – after reading an article on the relation of the Islets of Langerhans to diabetes – he conceived the idea that ligation of the ducts of the pancreas would destroy the whole gland except for the Islets of Langerhans; if these islets secreted a hormone it could then be extracted. He

expressed this idea in his notebook thus: 'Tie off pancreatic ducts of dogs. Wait six to eight Weeks. Remove and extract.'

The story of how Banting achieved this programme with the aid of a student, Charles H. Best, and Professor J. J. R. MACLEOD (who provided him with a laboratory and experimental dogs at Toronto University) is one of the most brilliant in medical history. The extract they obtained they called insulin. The difficulties of obtaining this in sufficient quantity and purity to be of use to patients with diabetes were overcome with the aid of a young chemist, J. B. Collip. In February 1922, eight months after they had begun their experiments, Banting and Best announced their success. In the following year Banting and Macleod were awarded the Nobel prize, which they shared with Best and Collip. Insulin revolutionized the treatment of diabetes.

In 1923 Banting was made the first professor of medical research in the University of Toronto. He became Fellow of the Royal Society of Canada in 1926; FRS (London) in 1935; and in 1934 was knighted. In 1930 he moved into the new Banting Institute, where he continued research until the outbreak of the Second World War. Enlisting in the Royal Canadian Army Medical Corps he was employed on important scientific work. Whilst flying on a mission connected with this work his plane crashed in Newfoundland and he was killed.

Lloyd Stevenson, *Sir Frederick Banting*. 1947.
   (Portrait.)
M. Banting Bliss, *A Biography*. 1984.
Obituary Notices of Fellows of the Royal Society.
   1942. (Portrait.)
Dictionary of Scientific Biography.
Tyler Wasson (Ed.), *Nobel Prize Winners*. 1987.
   (Portrait.)

                                                                        K D K

BÁRÁNY, ROBERT Born in Vienna, 22 April 1876; died Uppsala, Sweden, 8 April 1936. Aurist.

Bárány was educated at Vienna University, where he took the doctorate of medicine in 1900 and became in 1905 a lecturer in the Otological Clinic in Vienna. In 1914 his investigations of the physiology of the inner ear were rewarded with a Nobel prize.

In the First World War he served in the Austro-Hungarian Army as a medical officer and was captured by the Russians at Przemysl in 1915. In the following year he was released on account of a knee injury and moved to Sweden, where he took charge of a department for ear, throat, and nose diseases at Uppsala in 1926.

Bárány's work was chiefly concerned with exploring the functions of the labyrinth, or balance apparatus, of the inner ear. This arose from a chance discovery of the effect of the successive application of hot and cold water to the outer ear in causing dizziness and disturbance to the eyes. In 1911 he invented a method of opening the posterior semicircular canal in order to decompress the labyrinth; he also introduced a much-used device for effectively isolating the auditory performance of one ear by creating noise in the other. His systematic investigations laid the foundations of present-day knowledge of the function of the labyrinth.

Bárány published in 1907 his *Physiologie und*

Pathologie des Bogengang-Apparates beim Menschen, and contributed widely to textbooks and periodical literature concerned with his special field and related topics, including sea-sickness. He also wrote papers on some aspects of the surgery of the skull and on psychiatric questions. He became a member of many learned societies and travelled extensively in Europe and North America. One of Bárány's intimates remarks that 'research was the elixir of life for him' and that his migration to Sweden in middle life caused him to withdraw noticeably from general society.

L. G. Stevenson, *Nobel Prize Winners in Medicine and Physics, 1901-50.*
Archives of Otolaryngology, **82**, 316, 1965.
Tyler Wasson (Ed.), *Nobel Prize Winners*. 1987. (Portrait.)
Dictionary of Scientific Biography.

                                                                      T K D

BARCROFT, SIR JOSEPH Born at Newry, Co. Down (now in Northern Ireland), 26 July 1872; died Cambridge, England, 21 March 1947. Physiologist.

Having a Quaker family background, Barcroft attended the Friend's School at Bootham, York. He then went to the Leys School at Cambridge; here, in his last year, he obtained the BSc degree of London University by external examination. He entered King's College, Cambridge, in October 1893 and four years later began as a young graduate his researches on the blood. His first investigation, suggested by J. N. LANGLEY, later professor of physiology, concerned the varying rates of metabolism of an organ under different conditions, and involved the estimation of the amounts of oxygen and carbon dioxide in the artery and vein serving the submaxillary salivary gland in the dog. He submitted his findings in a dissertation (March 1899) which won his election to a Fellowship at King's College. This study was crucial for Barcroft, as from it derived his famous work on the dissociation of haemoglobin and oxygen. To obtain the necessary data for the now well-known graphical sigmoid curve on which lie the points of equilibrium between partial pressure of oxygen and percentage saturation of haemoglobin, Barcroft devised apparatus (tonometer and differential blood-gas manometer) enabling rapid readings to be made using very small samples of blood. The new knowledge gained was contained in his great book, the *Respiratory Function of the Blood*, published in 1914. With growing reputation as a physiologist responsibilities also increased: at King's he became College Lecturer in Natural Science, in the Physiology Department, first junior and then senior demonstrator, and in 1910 he was elected FRS. These appointments involved administration and teaching, for both of which he had great gifts. To gain more information of the combination of haemoglobin and oxygen under various conditions he led two high-altitude expeditions – one to Teneriffe in 1910, the other to Monte Rosa, Italy, in 1911.

His studies on blood were interrupted by the First World War, when in 1917 he became Chief Physiologist at the Government's Experimental Station at Porton, near Salisbury. While there his chief concern was the study of the medical aspects of poisoning by chlorine, phosgene, and other gases, and he conducted a courageous experiment in which he shut himself up with a dog in a respiratory chamber containing some hydrocyanic acid. For his war work he was awarded the CBE in 1918.

In the Second World War he worked again at Porton for the first two years, but in 1941 was back in Cambridge as head of the Animal Physiology Unit of the Agricultural Research Council directing researches on the digestion and metabolism of ruminants.

A Readership in Physiology at Cambridge was created for him in 1919, making it possible for him to devote more time to research and less to teaching; he thus set out to solve the 'diffusion–secretion' problem – whether or not at high altitudes the human lung is able to secrete oxygen into the blood at a higher pressure than that in the inspired air. His most spectacular experiment, in which he remained in a glass respiratory chamber for several days, showed no evidence for oxygen secretion and this was confirmed on another high-altitude expedition (to the Peruvian Andes) in 1922. The second edition of the *Respiratory Function of the Blood* (1928) contained a new section, *Lessons from High Altitudes*. At the end of 1925 Barcroft followed Langley in the chair of physiology: once more he spared much time for teaching, but he continued his own researches while encouraging and directing others. In 1923 he had begun to study problems concerned with changes of blood volume in storage organs (spleen, skin, liver, and uterus) and this led to his last investigations, commenced in 1933, on the physiology of the vascular system of the developing foetus in goats and sheep. The Croonian Lecture he gave to the Royal Society in 1935 was entitled *Foetal respiration*, and his last book, *Researches in Prenatal Life, Part I*, appeared three weeks before his death in 1947. In a second part he intended to consider development of the nervous system and general metabolism of the foetus.

He was knighted in 1935. From the Royal Society he received the Royal Medal (1922) and the Copley Medal (1944): from the Royal College of Physicians, the Baly Medal (1923). He was Fullerian Professor of Physiology at the Royal Institution (1923–6).

Kenneth J. Franklin, *Joseph Barcroft*. 1953. (Portraits.)
Obituary Notices of Fellows of the Royal Society, 1951. (Portrait.)
Dictionary of Scientific Biography, Supp. I.

                                                                      A P G

BARDEEN, JOHN Born in Madison, Wisconsin, USA, 23 May 1908; died Champaign, Illinois, 30 January 1991. Solid-state physicist notable for winning two Nobel prizes.

The son of a professor of anatomy, Bardeen graduated in electrical engineering at the University of Wisconsin in 1928. He first worked in geophysics, moving to the Gulf Research Laboratories in 1930–33. Then, to develop his abilities in mathematical physics, he joined Princeton University, where he became interested in solid state physics under the influence of Eugene WIGNER. He gained his PhD in 1936, after he had already moved to Harvard. After a period at the University of Minnesota, Bardeen worked at the National Ordnance Laboratory 1941–5.

At the end of the war Bardeen joined the solid

state physics group at Bell Telephone Laboratories, New Jersey. It was here that he made his first major contribution to physics, in 1947, with the discovery, with Walter Brattain (1902–87) and William SHOCKLEY, of the transistor effect.

The three won the Nobel prize for physics for this work in 1956, by which time Bardeen was professor at the University of Illinois, where he had moved in 1951. He was already interested in superconductivity, the phenomenon in which at very low temperatures a metal loses its electrical resistance. As early as 1950, Bardeen had realised that 'phonons' – vibrations of the lattice of atoms in the metal – must play a role. The precise way in which this happens was later suggested by Leon COOPER, in Bardeen's group at Illinois. He proposed that at low temperatures pairs of electrons couple via their interactions with the lattice, and provide the superconducting current. Bardeen and Cooper, together with a graduate student Robert Schrieffer (1931–) developed these ideas into a full theory of superconductivity in 1957. They were rewarded with the Nobel prize for physics in 1972, making Bardeen the first person to win two Nobel prizes in the same subject. Bardeen, and many other physicists, regarded the work on superconductivity as the more important to physics, despite the enormous impact the transistor has had in electronics.

Bardeen formed important research groups in both semiconductors (in the Electrical Engineering Department) and quantum liquids (in the Physics Department) at the University of Illinois, and made many other contributions to solid-state physics. He became emeritus professor in 1975, and remained active in physics until his death.

Physics Today, Special Issue, April 1922. (Portrait.)
Nobel Lectures, Physics, 1942–1962, 1964.
Les Prix Nobel en 1972. 1973. (Portrait.)
Tyler Wasson (Ed.), *Nobel Prize Winners*. 1987. (Portrait.)

C S

BARGER, GEORGE Born at Manchester, England, 4 April 1878; died Aeschi, Switzerland, 5 January 1939. Organic chemist.

Barger, who was of Dutch-English descent, was educated first in Holland, then at University College, London, and King's College, Cambridge. For a short time (1901–3) he was Demonstrator in Botany at the University of Brussels, but he then returned to London to join the staff of the Wellcome Physiological Research Laboratories (1903–9). He was then successively Head of the Chemistry Department, Goldsmiths' College (1909–13); professor of chemistry, Royal Holloway College (1913–14); and member of staff of the Medical Research Committee (1914–19). He was then appointed professor of chemistry in relation to medicine at Edinburgh (1919–37), and finally Regius Professor of Chemistry at Glasgow (1938).

As his career indicates, Barger's work was particularly concerned with the medical application of chemistry. His major contribution was the synthesis, with C. R. Harington (1897–1972), of thyroxine, which was first isolated by E. C. KENDALL in 1915. In addition, he made many other contributions to the chemistry of natural products, especially organic bases; his scholarly *Ergot and Ergotism* (1931) is a well-known classic. His book

on *Some Applications of Organic Chemistry to Biology and Medicine* (1930) also enhanced his reputation.

Barger was a notable pioneer in what was then a comparatively new field, and he was widely honoured. The Royal Society elected him to Fellowship in 1919, and the Chemical Society of London awarded him its Longstaff Medal in 1936. He was an honorary graduate of the Universities of Padua, Liverpool, Heidelberg, Michigan, and Lausanne. He is remembered as a gifted linguist.

H. H. Dale, *Nature*, **143**, 108, 1939.
Obituary Notices of Fellows of the Royal Society. 1940. (Portrait.)
Dictionary of National Biography.

T I W

BARKLA, CHARLES GLOVER Born at Widnes, Lancashire, England, 27 June 1877; died Edinburgh, 23 October 1944. Physicist, known for his work in connection with x-rays.

Barkla was educated at the Liverpool Institute, and at University College, Liverpool (later Liverpool University (1903)), where he graduated in 1898. In the following year he obtained his Master's degree, and was awarded an Exhibition Scholarship, which took him to Cambridge. There he was first a member of Trinity College, but the desire to use his musical talents to the full led him to migrate after one year to King's College, where he soon became noted for his choral singing. He worked in the Cavendish Laboratory on the velocities of electric waves along wires of varying material and thickness. During his third year he began work connected with x-rays. In 1902 he obtained the Oliver Lodge Fellowship at the University of Liverpool and continued his research there for three years (DSc 1904). Following this, he held various posts at the University of Liverpool until in 1909 he was appointed to the Wheatstone Chair of Physics at King's College, London. In 1912 he was elected FRS. In 1913 he moved to the University of Edinburgh as the professor of natural philosophy, and retained this post until his death.

W. K. RÖNTGEN, who discovered x-rays, showed that after a gas was exposed to them it became a source of secondary radiation. It was this radiation that Barkla studied for virtually the whole of his life, and on which he published over seventy papers. He showed that when x-rays traversed gases or solids of low atomic weight the secondary emission consisted of x-rays that were essentially unchanged. They were, however, polarized, and this supported the suggestion made by G. J. STONEY, that x-rays were ordinary light of short wavelength. When x-rays traversed an element of high atomic weight, they were selectively absorbed, and secondary emission was obtained that was called by Barkla 'fluorescent emission'. The hardness, or penetrating power, of this was characteristic of the scattering element, and was shown to increase with its atomic weight. In 1917 Barkla received a Nobel prize for his work in this field.

Obituary Notices of Fellows of the Royal Society. 1945–8. (Portrait.)
F. Horton, *Proceedings of the Physical Society*, **57**, 249. 1945.
Tyler Wasson (Ed.), *Nobel Prize Winners*. 1987. (Portrait.)

R. J. Stephenson, *American Journal of Physics*, **35**, 140, 1967.
Dictionary of Scientific Biography.

B B K

BARNARD, JOSEPH EDWIN Born in London, 7 December 1870; died Addiscombe, Surrey, 25 October 1949. Remembered for his development of the ultra-violet microscope.

Barnard's interest in optics began with the gift of a microscope when he was 16. Although committed to the family business (a West End hatter's firm), he studied part time, and soon became known for his work at the Lister Institute, King's College London, and elsewhere. In 1895 he became a Fellow of the Royal Microscopical Society, and later he was three times its President. In 1920 he was made Honorary Director of the Department of Applied Optics at the National Institute for Medical Research, Hampstead, London. Throughout his life he remained an amateur scientist, devoting half of each day to business and half to research.

The photographic aspect of microscopy soon attracted Barnard's attention, and in 1911 he wrote the standard work *Practical Photo-micrography*. Recognizing the improved magnification obtainable with rays of shorter wavelength than those of visible light, he began to apply this photographic technique to ultra-violet microscopy. Starting with a simple German apparatus, he introduced successive improvements, eventually producing an instrument with quartz lenses, capable of using short-wave monochromatic radiation.

With this apparatus Barnard obtained clear photomicrographs of some of the larger viruses, including those of bovine pleuro-pneumonia, foot-and-mouth disease, and vesicular stomatitis. The objects seen were identified with the infective units obtained by ultrafiltration, and recognized as micro-organisms too small for visible microscopy. In 1924 Barnard was elected a Fellow of the Royal Society.

Obituary Notices of Fellows of the Royal Society, 1950. (Portrait.)
British Medical Journal, 1053, 1949.
Lancet, **257**, 865, 1949.
Journal of the Royal Microscopical Society, **71**, 104, 1951. (Portrait.)

C A R

BARROW, ISAAC Born in London, October 1630; died there, 4 May 1677. Mathematician, classical scholar, and theologian.

Barrow was educated at Charterhouse, Felstead School, and Trinity College, Cambridge, where he was successively pensioner (1645), scholar (1647), Fellow (1649), Master (1673), and Vice-Chancellor (1675). In 1655 he set out for France and Italy. Returning in 1659, he took orders, and at the Restoration was made professor of Greek. Subsequently he became professor of geometry at Gresham College, London, and then Lucasian Professor of Mathematics at Cambridge. Among his pupils there was Issac NEWTON, whose great gifts he recognized to be superior to his own. He resigned his chair in 1669 in favour of Newton.

Barrow was known to his contemporaries for his slovenly ways, his excessively long sermons, and his great learning. Today, he is remembered chiefly for his mathematical and optical writings. He pro-

duced important editions of the *Elements* (1655) and *Data* (1657), of EUCLID, as well as versions of works by ARCHIMEDES, APOLLONIUS and Theodosius (*fl.* 75 BC). These editions are noted for their tendency to prefer non-verbal mathematical notations, although he believed that arithmetic should be subsumed under geometry, with algebra relegated from mathematics to logic. That he was a great mathematical genius is a myth created in particular by two of his editors, W. Whewell (1794–1866) and J. M. Child. Barrow's work is, above all, that of a first-rate university teacher. The fact that some of the new propositions he announced were the geometrical equivalents of theorems of the calculus, has led some to argue that he must have used analytical methods, only to translate his working into 'synthetic' terminology for publication.

P. H. Osmond, *Isaac Barrow: his Life and Times*. 1944. (Portrait.)
Mordecai Feingold (Ed.), *Before Newton: The Life and Times of Isaac Barrow*. 1990.
Dictionary of Scientific Biography.
Dictionary of National Biography.

J D N

BARTHOLIN, RASMUS (ERASMUS) Born at Roskilde, Denmark, 13 August 1625; died Copenhagen, 4 November 1698. Discoverer of the double refraction of light.

Erasmus Bartholin was the son of Caspar Bartholin, a medical professor in Copenhagen, and brother to the anatomist Thomas Bartholin (1616–80), who discovered the lymphatic system. During his studies in Holland, England, France and Italy (1646–56), he acquired a profound mathematical education and edited the *Introduction to the Geometry of Descartes* (Leiden, 1651) of P. van Schooten (1634–79), after which he translated the *Optics* of Heliodorus of Larissa (1st century AD) into Latin (Paris, 1654). In 1654 he obtained a medical degree at Padua, and from 1656 to his death he was professor of geometry and medicine in Copenhagen and one of the most influential members of the University. Among his pupils were Ole RØMER and Prince George (later Consort of Queen Anne). He was a prolific mathematical author and also published an edition of observations by Tycho BRAHE (Havniae, 1668), but his main claim to scientific fame is the discovery of the double refraction of light through a crystal of Iceland spar, described in his *Experimenta crystalli islandici disdiaclastici* (Havniae, 1669, German translation in W. Ostwald's *Klassiker*, No. 205). Here he demonstrated the physical and optical properties of such crystals and proved that they split a beam of light into two rays by what he called ordinary and extraordinary refraction. In passing, he described a new method of measuring the ordinary refractive index of crystals without shaping them into prismatic form. He gave no theoretical explanation of the new phenomenon which C. HUYGENS later used as a decisive argument for the wave theory of light. No modern editions of his works exist.

A. Garboe, *Geologiens Historie i Danmark*, vol. 1. 1959.
V. Meisen (Ed.), *Prominent Danish Scientists through the Ages*. 1932.

O P

BARTLETT, NEIL Born Newcastle upon Tyne, England, 15 September 1932. Pioneer of noble gas chemistry.

After graduating in chemistry in the University of Durham, Bartlett spent a year (1957–8) as a school master before joining the chemistry department of the University of British Columbia (1958–66). Later he was professor at Princeton University and since 1969 at the University of California, Berkeley. The new family of gases found in the atmosphere in the 1890s by Sir William RAMSAY were commonly known as the inert or noble gases because of their apparent total resistance to involvement in any kind of chemical reaction. Arising from his interest in the highly reactive gas fluorine, Bartlett in 1962 prepared – by a surprisingly simple technique – xenon hexafluoroplatinate. Subsequently workers at the Argonne National Laboratory investigated the reaction of xenon with a variety of hexafluorides, including that of ruthenium. Since then a variety of noble gas compounds has been prepared, mainly – but not exclusively – of xenon and krypton.

Who's Who, 1993.

T I W

BARTON, SIR DEREK HAROLD RICHARD Born in Gravesend, Kent, England, 8 September 1918. Organic chemist.

Barton was educated at Imperial College, University of London. After research on a Government project and in industry (1942–45) he returned to Imperial College to begin research into the chemistry of natural products. He became professor of organic chemistry at Birkbeck College, University of London (1953), where he worked on conformational analysis, the study of the three-dimensional geometric structure of complex organic molecules, begun while at Harvard (1949). In 1955 he was appointed Regius Professor of Chemistry at the University of Glasgow, but after two years he returned to Imperial College as Hofmann Professor of Organic Chemistry. In 1977 he became Director of the *Institut de Chimie des Substances Naturelles*, CNRS, France. On his retirement in 1985 he accepted a position as Distinguished Professor of Chemistry at Texas A and M University, USA.

Elected FRS (1954) and FRSE (1956), Barton discovered a method for synthesizing the hormone aldosterone in 1960, and since 1970 he has concentrated on the invention and discovery of new chemical reactions which might provide more economical and efficient methods for the manufacture of complex organic compounds.

Barton was awarded the Nobel prize for chemistry in 1969 jointly with Odd Hassel (1897–1981) of Norway; in the same year he was President of the British Association for the Advancement of Science. He has received many scientific honours including the Davy (1961), Royal (1972) and Copley (1980) Medals of the Royal Society. He was knighted in 1972.

Sir Derek H. R. Barton, *Some Recollections of Gap Jumping*, 1991. (Portraits.)

Les Prix Nobel en 1969. 1970. (Portrait.)

W. A. Campbell and N. N. Greenwood, *Contemporary British Chemists*. 1971. (Portrait.)

Tyler Wasson (Ed.), *Nobel Prize Winners*. 1987. (Portrait.)

N G C

BASOV, NIKOLAI GENNADIEVICH Born in Usman, near Voronezh, Russia, 14 December 1922. Physicist: independent inventor of the maser and the laser.

After service as medical orderly on the First Ukrainian Front (1942–5) Basov entered the Moscow Institute of Physical Engineers, graduating in theoretical and experimental physics (1950). He then joined the P. N. Lebedev Physical Institute, becoming Director in 1973. He was elected a member of the Praesidium of the Academy of Sciences of the USSR in 1967 and of the USSR Supreme Soviet in 1982.

In 1952 he began research with A. M. PROKHOROV (1916–) on quantum radiophysics and in 1956 submitted a doctoral thesis on 'A Molecular Oscillator'. This was the beginning of a research project which culminated in the invention of the maser (Microwave Amplification by Stimulated Emission of Radiation). As early as 1917 EINSTEIN had postulated from the Planck radiation formula that when a molecule absorbs energy there must be a complementary emission. If more atoms can be created in a high energy state than in a lower one an 'inverted population' is created, resulting in energy amplification. Basov succeeded in creating such an inverted population and later (1963) succeeded also in making superconductor lasers (Light Amplification by Stimulated Emission of Radiation). For these achievements he and Prokhorov were awarded a Nobel prize in 1964, jointly with C. H. TOWNES who had independently done similar research in the USA.

G. W. A. Dummer, *Electronic Inventions and Discoveries* (2nd ed.) 1978.

Tyler Wasson (Ed.), *Nobel Prize Winners*. 1987. (Portrait.)

Les Prix Nobel en 1964. 1965. (Portrait.)

R. L. Weber, *Pioneers of Science: Nobel Prize Winners in Physics*. 1980. (Portrait.)

T I W

BASSI, AGOSTINO MARIA Born at (?)Mairago, near Lodi, Lombardy, Italy, 25 September 1773; died there, 6 February 1856. The founder of the parasitic theory of infection.

Bassi held a law degree of Pavia where he also studied scientific subjects under A. VOLTA, A. Scarpa (1747?–1832), and L. SPALLANZANI. After graduation he became a Civil Servant, but eye trouble caused him to abandon this profession (c.1816), and to retire to his farm at Mairago. He had bad luck as a farmer, but he wrote on agricultural subjects.

About the time of his retirement from the Civil Service, Bassi became interested in 'muscardine', a disease of silkworms which had caused serious injury to the silkworm industry of Lombardy. In this condition the worm dies and after death its body becomes covered with a chalky substance. After prolonged investigation Bassi showed that the disease is contagious, and that if a fragment of the white covering is injected into a healthy worm, the latter becomes infected. He also showed that the white substance consists of a parasitic fungus, since renamed *Botrytis bassiana*. Bassi published these observations in 1835, and in 1836 he published his important methods for preventing the disease. In later works Bassi suggested that some infectious diseases of man are caused by living parasites.

W. Bulloch, *History of Bacteriology*. 1938.
R. H. Major, *History of Medicine*. 1954. (Portrait.)
Nature, **177**, 255, 1956.
Dictionary of Scientific Biography.

E A U

BATES, HENRY WALTER Born in Leicester, England, 8 February 1825; died London, 16 February 1892. Naturalist and Amazonian traveller; discovered the phenomenon of 'mimicry' in animal coloration.

Bates as a young man worked several years in his father's stocking factory; he was an amateur botanist and entomologist, and made a large collection of beetles. In 1844 he met A. R. WALLACE, whom he introduced to entomology; the two friends decided to study natural history in the tropics, paying their way by the sale of collections. In 1848 they sailed for Para, Brazil, and collected together for two years, after which they parted; Wallace returned home in 1852, but Bates remained in Brazil for eleven years. In 1863 he published *The Naturalist on the River Amazons*, one of the best travel books ever written. In 1861 he read a paper to the Linnean Society of London in which he put forward his observations on the resemblance of animals, and particularly insects, to the colours and patterns of their natural backgrounds, by which many are rendered almost invisible. He called especial attention to the remarkable resemblance in colour and pattern between butterflies of the family Heliconiidae, which are distasteful to predators, and some species of other orders which are palatable. He suggested that the latter, under the influence of natural selection 'mimic' the former, and thus secure a better chance of survival – this phenomenon is now known as Batesian mimicry.

On his return to England his finances were low, but his appointment in 1864 as Assistant Secretary to the Royal Geographical Society secured his position, and he continued in office, with much distinction, until his death. He was elected FRS in 1881.

H. W. Bates, *The Naturalist on the River Amazons*. 1863.
A. R. Wallace, *My Life*. 1905.
Transactions of the Royal Geographical Society, **14**, 245, 1892. (Portrait.)
Nature, **45**, 398, 1892.
Dictionary of Scientific Biography.

L H M

BATESON, WILLIAM Born at Whitby, Yorkshire, England, 8 August 1861; died Merton, Surrey, 8 February 1926. Geneticist.

After studying zoology at Cambridge, where his father was Master of St John's College, Bateson went to Hampton, Virginia, to investigate the marine organism *Balano-glossus*. There he became the first to observe its entire development, as a result of which he identified it as a primitive chordate. Back in Cambridge as a Fellow of St John's College, he turned to the study of variation, an enquiry which took him to Russia and Egypt in search of parallels between local variations of aquatic species and local conditions. This quest having failed, he collected evidence for the view

that variation is discontinuous and not related to the conditions of life. His book on the subject *Materials for the Study of Variation* (1894) brought him into conflict with orthodox biologists, though in the same year he was elected FRS.

A programme of hybridization which Bateson undertook in 1897 did not lead him to Mendel's laws, but it prepared him for their announcement by H. de VRIES, K. E. Correns (1864–1935) and E. von Tschermak (1871–1962) in 1900. Bateson introduced Mendel's work to England and despite only meagre support he formed a research group at Grantchester, near Cambridge, where the genetics of animals and plants were studied. Their work on the inheritance of comb shape in the fowl gave the Mendelian dihybrid ratio 9: 3: 3: 1 and also the following modifications of it: 9: 7, 9: 3: 4, and 13: 3. These they rightly attributed to interaction between two pairs of factors (genic interaction). Work on the Sweet Pea (variety Emily Henderson) revealed only partial independent transmission of the characters pollen shape and flower colour. This deviation from Mendel's law of the independent assortment of characters they suggested was due to the production of the various gametes in unequal numbers, a situation which they termed 'partial gametic coupling'. The most numerous types of gametes were said to have been 'reduplicated'. This explanation did not fit the facts well, but even when F. A. Janssens (1863–1924) discovered the chromosome mechanism to which it is due (1909), Bateson held on to the reduplication hypothesis.

In 1908 Bateson became professor of biology at Cambridge, but within a year he left to become Director of the new John Innes Horticultural Institute at Merton; there work of great practical value was done, but the leadership in genetics went to T. H. MORGAN in America.

Beatrice Bateson, *William Bateson, FRS, Naturalist, his Essays and Addresses*. 1928.
Proceedings of the Royal Society, B, **26**, 101. 1927. (Portrait.)
Edinburgh Review, **244**, 71, 1926.
Dictionary of National Biography.
Dictionary of Scientific Biography.

R C O

BAUER, GEORG See AGRICOLA.

BAYLISS, SIR WILLIAM MADDOCK Born at Wolverhampton, Staffordshire, England, 2 May 1860; died Hampstead, London, 27 August 1924. Physiologist.

In 1881 he entered University College, London, and proceeded, in 1885, to Wadham College, Oxford. After taking a first class in the School of Natural Science (Physiology) he returned to University College, where all his researches were made. His investigations were mainly concerned with the digestive, vascular, and nervous systems, and in 1912 a chair of general physiology at University College was created specially for him. His name and that of E. H. STARLING, with whom he collaborated, will always be associated with the discovery of the hormone secretin in 1902. It was found that an extract of acidified duodenal mucosa, when injected intravenously, produced a secretion of pancreatic juice. The acid (hydrochloric) alone produced no secretion when injected intravenously, but a secretion of pancreatic juice followed when the acid was introduced into a loop of the duodenum whose nerve connections had been severed and which was thus isolated from the pancreas except through the blood circulation. It was therefore concluded that during normal digestion the acid content, after leaving the stomach and reaching the duodenum, stimulated the mucosa to produce a hormone, termed secretin, which was carried in the blood stream and caused secretion by the pancreas. This was the first discovery of a hormone secreted by one internal organ producing a specific effect upon another. Also in collaboration with Starling, Bayliss carried out notable researches on venous and arterial pressures, and on the innervation of the intestine: working alone he studied the nature of vaso-motor reflexes; antidromic vaso-dilator nerve impulses; and the physico-chemical aspects of physiology which were then beginning to attract attention. During the First World War his use of saline injections for the amelioration of surgical shock was widely adopted among the troops.

He was closely associated with the Physiological Society almost from its beginning and served first as its secretary and then for a long period as its treasurer.

Bayliss was much respected for his intellectual integrity and renowned for his ability to penetrate to the core of a problem. He had great learning and his *Principles of General Physiology* (1915) became a standard reference.

Knighted in 1922. FRS 1903. Croonian Lecturer (1904); Royal Medallist (1911), and Copley Medallist (1919) of the Royal Society. Baly Medallist (1917) of the Royal College of Physicians.

Proceedings of the Royal Society, B, **99**, xxvii, 1926.

Perspectives in Biology and Medicine, **4**, 460, 1961.

Dictionary of Scientific Biography.
Dictionary of National Biography.

A P G

BAZALGETTE, SIR JOSEPH WILLIAM Born at Enfield, Middlesex, England, 28 March 1819; died Wimbledon, London, 15 March 1891. Civil engineer.

Bazalgette was a pupil of Sir John MacNeill (?1793–1880) – one of the chief assistants of Thomas TELFORD. In 1842 he was appointed engineer at Westminster, and from 1855 to 1889 was chief engineer to the Metropolitan Board of Works. In this capacity he devised and put into effect a complete new drainage system for the City of London. For these important services – an outstanding advance in public health measures – he was knighted in 1874. In 1884 he was President of the Institution of Civil Engineers.

The Board was set up in 1855, following two major outbreaks of cholera in London (1849 and 1853/4). The main cause was recognized as a drainage system totally inadequate for a city of 7 ½ million inhabitants. The Act establishing it required the Board to 'make such sewers and works as they may think necessary for preventing all or any part of the sewage within the Metropolis from flowing into the Thames in or near the Metropolis'. Bazalgette's radical plan for improvement was put into effect within twenty years. It involved no less than 100 miles of large-diameter sewers, and was the first major civil engineering project to make extensive use of Portland cement, 70 000 tons being used. The system had its outfalls some twelve miles below London Bridge – at Barking in Essex and Crossness in Kent – and incorporated three large pumping stations. The scheme involved a new Thames embankment between Westminster and Blackfriars Bridges, reclaiming forty acres of marsh.

H. Jephson, *The Sanitary Evolution of London*. 1907.

London County Council, *The Centenary of London's Main Drainage 1855–1955*. 1955.

The Times, 16 March 1891.
Dictionary of National Biography.

T I W

BEADLE, GEORGE WELLS Born at Wahoo, Nebraska, USA, 22 October 1903; died Pomona, California, 9 June 1989. Geneticist.

Beadle was born on a small farm, and intended to go back there after studying at the University of Nebraska College of Agriculture. Instead, after graduating in 1926 he went to Cornell University to study maize genetics and was awarded a PhD in 1931. From 1931 to 1935 he worked with Thomas Hunt MORGAN at the California Institute of Technology (Caltech), and began studying the genetics of the fruit fly (*Drosophila melanogaster*) working with A. H. STURTEVANT. He continued this work in Paris (1935–6) at the *Institut de Biologie Physico-Chimique*, studying the genetics of eye colour in *Drosophila* with B. Ephrussi. Beadle now turned his attention to gene function. The relation between gene action and enzyme activity had been suggested by A. E. GARROD in 1908, but this had been ignored at the time. Garrod had realised that certain enzyme deficiencies were inherited, and had suggested that specific genes might control the formation of specific enzymes.

After a year teaching genetics at Harvard, Beadle became professor of biology at Stanford University, California, in 1937. He remained there until 1946. Here he collaborated with E. L. Tatum (1909–75), experimenting with red bread mould, *Neurospora crassa*. After irradiating colonies of *Neurospora* in order to produce mutations, they studied the changes in the mutant strains, and concluded that each gene has one function, which is to control the formation of a single enzyme. They published their results in 1941, proposing the 'one gene, one enzyme' theory.

From 1946 to 1961 Beadle was professor of biology at Caltech. In 1961 he became President of the University of Chicago, and in 1968 was appointed director of the American Medical Association's Institute for Biomedical Research. His many publications included *The Place of Genetics in Modern Biology* (1959) and *The Language of Life* (1966).

Beadle shared the Nobel prize in physiology or medicine in 1958 with E. L. Tatum and J. Lederberg (1925–   ) for his discovery that genes act by regulating definite chemical events.

G. W. Beadle, 'Recollections', *Annual Review of Biochemistry*, vol. 43, 1974. (Portrait.)

Tyler Wasson (Ed.), *Nobel Prize Winners*. 1987. (Portrait.)

A P B

BEAUMONT, WILLIAM Born at Lebanon, Connecticut, USA, 21 November 1785; died St Louis, Missouri, 25 April 1853. Pioneer of the physiology of the human stomach.

Beaumont, son of a farmer, was for three years a village schoolmaster at Champlain, NY. While there he read medical works, and at St Albans, Vermont, he studied medicine regularly with a practitioner (1810). He obtained a licence to practise, and in the war of 1812 he became an assistant surgeon in the US Army and was at the Battle of Plattsburgh. He resigned his commission (1816), and for the next four years practised in Plattsburgh. In 1820 he rejoined, was sent to Fort Mackinac, and also served at other stations. In 1834 he was posted to St Louis, where he remained till he left the Army in 1839. He then practised in St Louis until his death. In 1837 he became professor of surgery in St Louis University.

On 6 June 1822 Alexis St Martin (1804?–80), a Canadian trapper, was accidentally shot at Fort Mackinac. From a distance of under a yard a charge of duck-shot entered his left side from behind. Beaumont was on the spot within minutes. There was a very large wound of exit in the left upper abdomen, with protrusion of some organs and an opening into the stomach. After ten months there was healing with much scarring, but there was also a permanent opening into the stomach, closed at times by a 'valve' of mucous membrane. Beaumont now took St Martin into his home and tended him for two years. In May 1825 Beaumont began his gastric experiments, and St Martin, who was now employed by him, accompanied him to Fort Niagara, Burlington, and Plattsburgh. Then St Martin returned to Canada without permission. Experiments were resumed in 1829, continued to March 1831, and again from November 1832 to November 1833, when they ceased. Beaumont published a preliminary account in 1825, and in 1833 there appeared his great classic, *Experiments and Observations on the Gastric Juice*.

In his experiments Beaumont withdrew gastric juice and foodstuffs from St Martin's stomach at varying times after ingestion, and under varying conditions. He records 238 individual observations. He worked out the properties of gastric juice and confirmed the work of W. PROUT on the importance of hydrochloric acid. He showed the influence of mental states on the secretion of gastric juice, made the first study of the movements of the stomach, and carried out direct investigations on the digestion of many foodstuffs. His fifty-one 'inferences' embody much that is fundamental in the physiology of gastric digestion.

J. S. Myer, *Life and Letters of William Beaumont*. 1912, 1939.
G. Miller, *William Beaumont's Formative Years*. 1946.
W. Osler, *Journal of the American Medical Association*, **39**, 1223, 1902.
F. H. Garrison, *History of Medicine*. 1929. (Portrait.)

                                                                    E A U

BECHE, SIR HENRY THOMAS DE LA *See* DE LA BECHE.

BECHER, JOHANN JOACHIM Born at Spire, Palatinate, Germany, 6 May 1635; died London, October 1681. Chemist; originator of the phlogiston theory.

Becher was the son of a Protestant minister, who was ruined by the Thirty Years War. Although thus deprived of a formal education, he had a successful, though somewhat chequered, career. He was appointed professor of medicine in the University of Mainz (1666) and subsequently went to Munich as physician to the Elector of Bavaria. His interest in economic problems led him to take up an appointment at the Commercial College in Vienna, but in 1678 disputes with his patrons caused him to go to Holland and thence (1680) to England.

In Holland his economic projects included one for converting sea sand into gold by use of silver. The States General set up a committee of inquiry and some preliminary tests were made, but inevitably the scheme was discredited. He suggested also a canal from the Rhine to the Danube, to improve trade between Holland and Austria.

In 1667 Becher published a study of minerals under the title *Physicae subterraneae*. In this he develops the notion that all mineral substances consist of three 'earths', which are not unlike the three idealized elements – salt, sulphur, and mercury – of the alchemists. Of particular interest is his *terra pinguis* (fatty earth), which he conceived to be the active principle of combustion. Georg STAHL subsequently elaborated this conception into the phlogiston theory, which dominated chemical thought until the end of the eighteenth century. Although false, it nevertheless served a useful purpose in systematizing the chemical knowledge of the day.

J. M. Stillman, *The Story of Alchemy and Early Chemistry*. 1960. (First published as *The Story of Early Chemistry*. 1924.)
J. R. Partington, *A History of Chemistry*, vol. 2. 1961.
Dictionary of Scientific Biography.

                                                                    T I W

BECKMANN, ERNST OTTO Born at Solingen, Germany, 4 July 1853; died Berlin, 12 July 1923. Organic and physical chemist.

After serving an apprenticeship to a pharmacist, Beckmann studied chemistry in Wiesbaden and Leipzig; he retained an interest in pharmacy throughout his life. He was an assistant in the *Technische Hochschule*, Brunswick (1879), then a *Privatdozent* in Leipzig (1883), and occupied chairs successively in Giessen (1891), Erlangen (1892), and Leipzig (1897). In 1912 he was appointed the first Director of the *Kaiser Wilhelm Institut für Chemie* in Dahlem, from which he retired in 1921.

Beckmann was primarily an organic chemist, and entered physical chemistry almost by accident. He made his name by the discovery (1886) of the 'Beckmann rearrangement' of ketoximes into amides under the influence of certain acidic catalysts. Aldoximes, however, were converted under similar conditions into what were then thought to be polymers (now known to be geometrical isomers), and determination of the molecular weight of the products was urgently necessary. No general, convenient, and accurate method of doing this then existed, and Beckmann set himself to devise one, based on Raoult's Law. The apparatus for determining elevation of boiling-point is known by his name; so also is the accurate thermometer, with a reservoir for adjusting the range.

Studies stemming from the Beckmann rearrangement, and from the molecular-weight apparatus, occupied most of Beckmann's research effort while he remained in academic life. In Leipzig he had the opportunity to design a new laboratory; to this task he devoted so much detailed thought that many of his innovations are standard practice to the present day. He was also active in the fields of camphor chemistry, and the chemistry of food; he studied the chlorides of sulphur and selenium, and discovered sulphur tetrachloride.

His post in the *Kaiser Wilhelm Institut*, which he took up with such great hopes, was to prove a disappointment. The war of 1914–18 soon diverted the energies of the institute into problems of national emergency, which were often barren of results, and gave him no satisfaction. When he finally retired his health was broken.

Berichte der deutschen Chemischen Gesellschaft, **61**, 87A, 1928. (Portrait.)

Journal of Chemical Education, **21**, 470, 1944. (Portrait.)

G. Lockemann, *Ernst Beckmann, sein Leben und Werk*. 1927.

W V F

BECQUEREL, ANTOINE HENRI Born in Paris, 15 December 1852; died Croisic, Brittany, 24 August 1908. Chiefly remembered for his discovery of radioactivity.

Entering the *École Polytechnique* in 1872, Becquerel proceeded to the *École des Ponts et Chaussées* in 1874, and was appointed *répétiteur* at the *École Polytechnique* in 1876. In 1888 he was awarded his doctorate for a thesis on the absorption of light, and the following year became a member of the *Académie des Sciences*. He was appointed professor at the Museum of Natural History in 1892, and at the *École Polytechnique* in 1895. He was a foreign member of many scientific societies, including the Royal Society of London (1908).

Already familiar with the phenomena of phosphorescence and fluorescence through his own researches (1882–92) and those of his father Edmond Becquerel (1820–91), on the discovery of x-rays by W. K. RÖNTGEN in 1895, Becquerel was naturally led to an investigation of the capacity of these rays for exciting fluorescence. This in turn led him to inquire whether fluorescing bodies can themselves produce x-rays or cathode rays, and in pursuit of an answer to this question he investigated certain salts of uranium remarkable for their capacity to fluoresce. On developing a photographic plate placed beneath a quantity of the double sulphate of uranium and potassium contained in a lightproof wrapping he discovered (1896) a blackening of the plate at a point corresponding to the position of the uranium salt. He then proved that this action occurred long after the salt was exposed to light, and that it was due solely to the presence of uranium. An examination of the properties of the penetrating radiation emitted by uranium proved that it was not reflected like ordinary light, and that it had the property of discharging electrified bodies at a distance. Becquerel's work was repeated and confirmed by other scientists, including William THOMSON (Lord Kelvin),

and formed the point of departure for subsequent researches into radioactivity. For his discovery of radioactivity Becquerel shared the Nobel prize for physics with Pierre and Marie CURIE in 1903.

Apart from his discovery of radioactivity, Becquerel carried out important researches (1876–9) on the ability of various solids and fluids to rotate the plane of polarization of light in a magnetic field, discovering the fundamental relationship between the rotatory power of a substance and its index of refraction. Extending these results to gases, he succeeded in demonstrating the influence of the Earth's magnetic field on its atmosphere (1894). He also investigated the absorption of light by crystals (1886–8).

N. H. de V. Heathcote, *Nobel Prize Winners in Physics 1901–50*. 1953. (Portrait.)

Proceedings of the Royal Society, **83A**, xx, 1909.

O. Lodge, *Journal of the Chemical Society*, **101**, 2005, 1912.

Tyler Wasson (Ed.), *Nobel Prize Winners*. 1987. (Portrait.)

Dictionary of Scientific Biography, Supp. II.

J W H

BEDDOES, THOMAS Born in Shifnal, Shropshire, England, 13 April 1760; died London, 24 December 1808. Chemist and physician.

Beddoes, best known for his work on the medical uses of gases, was a versatile man. At Oxford he not only read classics but taught himself French, German, and Italian, mastered the main branches of science, and began a study of medicine that he completed in Edinburgh in 1787. In 1788 he returned to Oxford as Reader in Chemistry, but his sympathies with the French revolutionaries led to his resignation in 1792. He went to Clifton, Bristol, as a medical practitioner. Convinced of the therapeutic effects of 'Factitious Airs' (oxygen, carbon dioxide, and water-gas) he established the Medical Pneumatic Institute, with the help of Thomas WEDGWOOD and other friends. Here he was joined in 1798 by the 19-year-old Humphry DAVY. At Clifton, Davy observed the anaesthetic properties of nitrous oxide and began his electrochemical experiments. Apart from guiding Davy's chemical studies, Beddoes introduced him to his wide circle of friends. This included not only eminent scientists – among them Davies Giddy, later President of the Royal Society as Davies Gilbert (1767–1839), and James WATT – but distinguished literary men such as Southey, Coleridge, and Wordsworth. In 1794 Beddoes had married Anna Edgeworth, daughter of R. L. EDGEWORTH a member of the Lunar Society of Birmingham; their elder son was Thomas Lovell Beddoes, the poet. This period with Beddoes in Bristol greatly helped Davy to bridge the gap between his humble origins in Penzance and his introduction to London Society when he went to the Royal Institution in 1801. Soon afterwards Beddoes followed him to London and resumed medical practice.

Endeavour, **19**, 123, 1960.

F. F. Cartright, *The English Pioneers of Anaesthesia*. 1952.

Dorothy Stansfield, *Thomas Beddoes MD (1760–1802)*. 1984.

Dictionary of National Biography.

Dictionary of Scientific Biography.

T I W

BEDNORZ, GEORG Born in Germany, 16 May 1950. Co-discoverer of new high-temperature superconducting materials.

Bednorz graduated from the University of Münster in 1976, and went to study at the *Eidgenossiche Technische Hochschule* (Swiss Federal Institute of Technology) in Zürich. He was awarded a PhD in 1982, and then joined the IBM Zürich Laboratory in Rüschlikon to work with Alex Müller, (1927–), who had supervised his postgraduate research at ETH.

In the summer of 1983, Bednorz and Müller began to study oxides of copper and nickel in search of materials that would show superconductivity to relatively high temperatures. At the time, the highest temperatures at which superconductivity – the state in which a metal conducts without any losses – was known to occur was around 20 K. Spurred by studies of superconductivity in barium-lead-bismuth oxides, Bednorz and Müller turned to related oxides of copper and nickel. In January 1986 they made their breakthrough, discovering the onset of superconductivity at 30 K in a barium-lanthanum-copper oxide.

These results, published in September 1986, led to the discovery in February 1987 by Paul Chu at Houston of compounds that are superconducting up to temperatures as high as 90 K. The work was taken up by many teams throughout the world, keen to develop applications for the new superconductors. In 1987, only a year after publishing their first results, Bednorz and Müller were awarded the Nobel prize for physics.

R. L. WEBER, *Pioneers of Science*, 1988.

Physics Today, p. 17, December 1987. (Portrait.)

C S

BEEBE, CHARLES WILLIAM Born at Brooklyn, New York, 29 July 1877; died Arima, Trinidad, 4 June 1962. Pioneer explorer of the ocean depths.

Beebe was a graduate of Columbia University (1898) and then joined the staff of the New York Zoological Gardens, of which he eventually became Director. He was keenly interested in ornithology and played an important part in establishing the Society's collection of birds. His *Pheasants: Their Lives and Homes* (1926) was an important contribution. He is, however, remembered mainly for his explorations of the ocean depths in his Bathysphere. In this he reached, with Otis Barton, a depth of just over 1000 metres off Bermuda in August 1934. He recorded his experiences in *Half Mile Down*. Later the two attained even greater depths, of nearly a mile.

H. C. Tracy, *American Naturalists*. 1930.

The Progress of Science, a review of 1940. 1941. (Portrait.)

T I W

BEHRING, EMIL ADOLF VON Born at Hansdorf, West Prussia, Germany, 15 March 1854; died Marburg, 31 March 1917. Celebrated for his discovery of antitoxins and the successful treatment of diphtheria.

Behring, son of a schoolmaster, studied at the University of Berlin and qualified as a doctor in 1880. After some years in the Army Medical Corps he became (1889) an assistant to Robert KOCH at the Institute of Hygiene, Berlin. Later he held chairs of hygiene at Halle and Marburg.

Behring's studies came at an exciting time in bacteriology, for the germ theory of disease was becoming well established and the science of immunology was developing rapidly. Behring's main contributions were announced during 1890. In two papers, one co-authored with Shibasaburo KITASATO, the immunity of animals to diphtheria and tetanus was fully discussed; for example, the authors had demonstrated that an animal immunized against tetanus and diphtheria produced, in the blood, substances (antitoxins) capable of neutralizing the toxic substances produced by the bacteria. They also showed that an animal previously injected with the serum from an immunized animal was resistant to an otherwise fatal dose of bacteria or toxin. Furthermore, it was shown that an animal treated with the serum after disease symptoms had developed could be cured.

Behring and Kitasato's work opened up new concepts, as ideas on immunity at the time were mainly concerned with phagocytosis (absorption of bacteria by blood cells) or with bactericidal action of the blood. They also opened up an entirely new form of medical treatment, and Behring's special studies on diphtheria aroused particular interest because of the dreadful mortality caused by the disease among children. About a year after publication, on Christmas night 1891, the first human case, a child, was treated with diphtheria antitoxin. Behring was very much concerned with the practical application of his work, although, as a consequence of international interest in the discovery, significant advances were made elsewhere. Specially important was the quantitative method devised by P. EHRLICH for determining the antitoxin value of a sample of serum, defining it by comparison with a reference standard.

In 1913 Behring made another important announcement in connection with diphtheria, the discovery of a preparation which gave more lasting immunity to diphtheria than the serum containing antitoxin. This was a mixture of toxin and antitoxin and a forerunner of modern methods for preventing, rather than treating, the disease. Behring received a Nobel prize in 1901 for his diphtheria studies.

H. Zeiss and R. Bieling, *Behring: Gestalt und Werk*. 1941. (Portrait.)

H. J. Parish, *A History of Immunization*. 1965.

Lancet, **1**, 890, 1917.

British Medical Journal, **1**, 498, 1917.

Dictionary of Scientific Biography.

J K C

BEILBY, SIR GEORGE THOMAS Born in Edinburgh, 17 November 1850; died London, 1 August 1924. Chemist; inventor of many important industrial chemical processes.

Beilby, son of a physician, was educated at Edinburgh University. He developed a particular interest in problems of fuel economy and smoke prevention and for a time (1917–23) was Director of Fuel Research. Earlier (1903), he had reported to the Royal Commission on coal supplies and was a member (1912) of the Royal Commission on Fuel and Engines for the Navy. He also helped to develop the Scottish shale-oil industry. From 1907 to 1923 he was Chairman of the Royal Technical College, Glasgow (now University of Strathclyde). He was elected to Fellowship of the Royal Society in 1906.

Towards the end of the nineteenth century the increasing demand for gold led to the introduction of the liquid cyanide extraction process suitable for relatively poor ores. The original MacArthur-Forrest process of 1887 was at first regarded with scepticism, but within five years was adopted in all the principal gold-mining areas. The demand for cyanide rose rapidly in proportion and in 1893 Beilby sold to the Cassel Gold Extracting Company rights in a process he had invented for synthesizing potassium cyanide by passing ammonia over a heated mixture of charcoal and potassium carbonate.

Beilby occupied a prominent place among Scottish scientists of his time. It was in his house that his son-in-law, Frederick SODDY, coined the word *isotope*, now in universal use.

Chemistry and Industry, 15 August 1924.
Fifty Years of Progress: The Story of the
    Castner-Kellner Alkali Company. 1947. (Portrait.)
Journal of the Society of Chemical Industry
    (Jubilee Issue). 1931. (Portrait.)
Dictionary of National Biography.

T I W

BEILSTEIN, FRIEDRICH KONRAD Born at St Peterburg, 17 February 1838; died there, 18 October 1906. The great encyclopaedist of organic chemistry.

Beilstein was of Russian nationality, but of German descent; his friends and sympathies were mostly in Germany. He studied chemistry in Heidelberg, Munich, Göttingen, and Paris, finally settling at Göttingen as *Privatdozent* (1859). In 1866 he returned to Russia as professor of chemistry in the Imperial Technological Institute, St Petersburg, but he disliked Russian students, and tended to surround himself with those of German origin. He was elected a member of the Russian Academy of Sciences in 1881; this gave him an independent income and laboratory, and he withdrew more and more from the duties of his chair. His election provoked bitter controversies within the Academy between the 'Russian' and 'German' factions. Towards the end of his life he spent much time travelling abroad. He never married.

His own research, done mostly at Göttingen, was competent, but of no great importance; it concerned problems of aromatic isomerism. His fame rests on his *Handbuch der organischen Chemie* (first edition 1881), which was an account of the physical and chemical properties of every well-authenticated organic compound, classified according to chemical type and molecular formula. It was then, and continues to be, one of the organic chemist's most valuable tools. Beilstein himself produced two more editions of ever-increasing size; in 1900 he handed over the task to the German Chemical Society, who still perform it.

Berichte der deutschen Chemischen Gesellschaft,
    40, 5042, 1907. (Portrait.)
Journal of the Chemical Society, 1646, 1911.
Dictionary of Scientific Biography.

W V F

BELIDOR, BERNARD FOREST DE Born in Catalonia, Spain, 1693; died Paris, 1761. French engineer and writer on military engineering.

Son of an army officer, Bernard Forest de Belidor lost his father when five months old and was brought up by an officer friend of his father. Having served with J. Cassini (1677–1756) and P. de Lahire (1640–1718) on the determination of the Paris meridian, he was recommended by them as professor at the artillery school of La Fère, where his lectures attracted, amongst others, delegates at the Congress of Cambrai. Arousing the jealousy of the master of the King's artillery, he had to seek employment in Bavaria and Bohemia with the Comte de Ségur, the Duke of Harcourt, and the Prince of Conti in their campaigns of 1744 and 1746. In 1758 he became inspector of artillery, dying at the arsenal in 1761.

His many publications include *Sommaire d'un cours d'architecture militaire, civile et hydraulique* (1720); *Cours de mathématiques* (1725); *La science des ingénieurs dans la conduite des travaux de fortification et d'architecture civile* (1729–49); *Le bombardier français ou Nouvelle méthode de jeter les bombes avec précision* (1731); *Traité des fortifications* (1735); *Architecture hydraulique* (4 vols 1737–53).

The *Science des ingénieurs*, a very popular manual of rules and tables, was reprinted up to 1830. His *Architecture hydraulique* (1739) was described by H. Staub as 'exerting an influence on design and practice for more than a century to come'. It gives full and accurate drawings of canals, bridges, pumps, naval structures and various other engineering works of his day. It was the first work of its kind to make practical use of the integral calculus.

Belidor's influence was international. John Muller (1699–1784), the German-born professor of fortification at Woolwich, used his work in his *Treatise concerning the Practical Art of Fortifications* (1755). So did Charles Valency (1721–1812). In 1825 the *Société d'Encouragement pour l'industrie Nationale* offered a prize for the first one who could successfully develop the hydraulic turbine proposed by Belidor. Part of the prize was won by Claude Burdin (1790–1873) in 1827 and the rest by his pupil Benoit FOURNEYRON in 1832.

R. S. Kirby and P. G. Laurson, *The Early History
    of Modern Civil Engineering*. 1937.
Transactions of the Newcomen Society, **10**, 10,
    1928–30; **29**, 56, 75, 1941–2.
H. Staub, *A History of Civil Engineering* (trans. by
    E. Rockwell), 1952.

W H G A

BELL, ALEXANDER GRAHAM Born in Edinburgh, 3 March 1847; died Cape Breton Island, Nova Scotia, Canada, 2 August 1922. Inventor of the telephone and of aids for teaching the deaf.

After studying at Edinburgh University, Bell took up teaching, but then undertook medical studies at University College, London. During two years before emigrating to the United States in 1871 (via Canada) he studied the work of Hermann von HELMHOLTZ which led him to make a particular study of sound waves. Hence came the urge to specialize in the mechanics of speech, and later in telegraphic communication. Bell's father, Alexander Melville Bell (1819–1905), had fostered 'visible speech' and speech education; Bell himself set up a Boston training school for the deaf. From 1873, when professor of vocal physiology, at Boston University, Bell began four fruitful years of invention. He experimented on transmitting messages by telegraphy, using an iron strip on a vibrating membrane operated by an electromagnet. Then came work in collaboration with Thomas Watson (1854–1934) on transmitters and receivers based on electromagnetic principles. Three major patents were granted him over the period 1875–7, during which his telegraphic apparatus became the telephone. The invention brought much litigation, but his priority was upheld. Thomas EDISON, however, is credited with the 'variable contact' carbon transmitter, producing strongly audible signals. Throughout his work Bell maintained his two main fields of study: his tuned system of multiple telegraphy and the study of air waves within the ear during reception of voice sounds. In his work on the phonograph also he had Edison as rival, but Bell's grooved wax cylinder with spiral sound track proved superior in his 'gramophone'.

This versatile Scot, who became a naturalized American in 1874, has claims to fame apart from founding a telephone industry in the United States. He founded the journal *Science*. He did valuable work for the Smithsonian Institute, of which he was Regent from 1898, and was Hughes Medallist (1913) of the Royal Society. With S. P. LANGLEY, he investigated the stability of flying machines.

R. V. Bruce, *Alexander Graham Bell and the Conquest of Solitude*. 1973.

C. D. Mackenzie, *Alexander Graham Bell*. 1928.

Dictionary of American Biography.

Dictionary of National Biography

The Times, 3 August 1922.

Biographical Memoirs of the National Academy of Sciences. 1945. (Portrait.)

M S

BELL, SIR CHARLES Born in Edinburgh, November 1774; died Hallow Park, Worcestershire, England, 29 April 1842. Anatomist and surgeon.

Bell learnt anatomy from his elder brother, John (1763–1820), a notable Edinburgh surgeon. Charles qualified in 1799 and was shortly afterwards appointed surgeon in the Royal Infirmary, Edinburgh. In 1806 he moved to London, soon becoming well known as a lecturer on surgery. He was elected a surgeon at the Middlesex Hospital in 1812. In 1824 he became professor of anatomy and surgery at the Royal College of Surgeons and, on the institution of University College, London, in 1828, was appointed the first Principal of the Medical School. In 1836 he was elected to the vacant chair of surgery at the University of Edinburgh and held this appointment until his death.

He received one of the first Royal Medals of the Royal Society (1829) for his important pioneer work on the nature and functions of the nervous system. He discovered the true functions of nerves and pointed out that they were not single units, as previously believed, but consisted of separate filaments, with a common sheath, having different purposes and origins. His views were first expressed (1811) in a short private essay entitled *Idea of a New Anatomy of the Brain*; later (1821) he expanded them in a communication to the Royal Society, and finally incorporated them in his *The Nervous System of the Human Body* (1830). His discovery of sensory and motor nerves, with their separate roots, was as revolutionary as that by William HARVEY of the circulation of the blood.

Bell was described by a contemporary as 'distin-guished by unpretending amenity, and simplicity of manners and deportment'. He was knighted in 1831, and was elected FRS in 1826.

G. Gordon-Taylor and E. W. Walls, *Sir Charles Bell: His Life and Times*. 1958.

Dictionary of National Biography.

Dictionary of Scientific Biography.

A P G

BELL, PATRICK Born at Auchterhouse, near Dundee, Scotland, April 1799; died Carmylie, Arbroath, 22 April, 1869. Inventor of a mechanical reaper.

Son of a farmer, Patrick Bell wondered whether a mechanical shear would not work better and faster than his father's reaper. Making a model, he took it to the Highland and Agricultural Society, whose secretary introduced him to Sir John Graham Dalyell (1775–1851), an antiquary and naturalist with engineering interests. Dalyell recommended that a full-sized model should be made and tried. This was duly done, to such satisfaction that it earned Bell, in 1827, a £50 premium from the Society, then an active supporter of such ideas. Four reapers of Bell's design were sent to the United States, stimulating Cyrus MCCORMICK and others to make harvesters so successful as to threaten the solvency of British farmers. Ironically, the presence of two such American machines at the Great Exhibition of 1851 hastened the recognition of Bell's reaper, hitherto relatively neglected not only because of its expense, but because its operations were hindered by the rough ground characteristic of many Scottish farms. The performance of a Bell reaper at the Perth Show in 1852 in cutting and laying a harvest field won for it a prize and considerable attention. In 1868 Bell was awarded £1,000 and a piece of silver plate as a 'token of his countrymen's appreciation of his preeminent services as the inventor of the first efficient reaping machine'.

By this time, however, Bell had given up his active agricultural interests, for he took orders in 1843 and became minister of Carmylie, Arbroath. St Andrews University awarded him an honorary LLD degree.

Transactions of the Highland and Agricultural Society of Scotland (5th Series), **40**, 1928. (Portrait.)

A. J. Spencer and J. B. Passmore, *Agricultural Implements and Machinery*. 1930.

J. E. Handley, *The Agricultural Revolution in Scotland*. 1963.

Dictionary of National Biography.

W H G A

BELON, PIERRE Born near Le Mans, France, in 1517; died Paris, April 1564. Naturalist chiefly remembered for his descriptions of birds and marine animals.

Belon was the son of poor parents. In his youth his ability attracted the attention of his Bishop, who sent him to Paris to study medicine. In 1540 he went to Germany to study botany under Valerius Cordus (1515–44) and he retained an interest in this subject for the rest of his life. He is reputed to have introduced the Lebanese cedar into western Europe and in 1553 he published a short work on cone-bearing trees. He was familiar with the classical writings and in 1546 he set off on a three-year journey to the eastern Mediterranean for the purpose of identifying the animals and plants referred to by the ancients. His archaeological, botanical, and zoological observations were reported in 1553 in *Les observations des plusiers singularitez et choses mémorables, trouvés en Grèce, Asie, Judée, Egypte, Arabie & autres pays éstranges.*

His first work on aquatic étanimals was published in 1551. The greater part is devoted to a dissertation on the dolphin, in which he identified the animal featured in ancient art as the common Atlantic species. In 1553, in the *De aquatilibus*, he extended the subject to include all animals which inhabit water, including cetaceans, otters, turtles, true fishes, and crustaceans. Although much of the contents derived from observations on his travels and in the fish markets of Europe, it is primarily a compilation. The systematic arrangement is based on Aristotle and many of the woodcuts are believed to have been copied from drawings of the Venetian, Daniel Barbaro (1528–69), whom Belon met in London. Belon's major work was the handsome folio *L'Histoire de la nature des Oyseaux* of 1555 with illustrations by Pierre Goudet. The groupings are again those of Aristotle and the author continues in his endeavours to identify birds mentioned in ancient texts. The birds illustrated are mainly of European origin, although some more exotic species are included. Although the descriptions are meagre, many different kinds of birds are illustrated and described with reference to similarities of structure and mode of life. The work was a major contribution to sixteenth-century science and is of particular interest in the introduction, where the human skeleton is compared with an adjacent figure of a bird skeleton. By indicating the homologies between them Belon may be considered one of the earliest in the important field of comparative anatomy.

The non-payment of a pension from the King presented many difficulties to Belon in the later years of his life, which ended tragically one evening in April 1564 when he was murdered in the Bois de Boulogne. It is not known whether he was the victim of thieves or of the Huguenot troubles.

L. C. Miall, *The Early Naturalists (1530–1789).* 1912.
P. Delauney, *L'Aventureuse existence de Pierre Belon du Mans.* 1926. (Portrait and iconography.)
Dictionary of Scientific Biography.

M P E

BENEDEN, EDOUARD JOSEPH LOUIS-MARIE VAN Born at Louvain, Belgium, 5 March 1846; died Liège, 28 April 1910. Embryologist and cytologist.

Van Beneden was drawn to the cell theory of M. J. SCHLEIDEN and T. SCHWANN when a student. His subsequent researches into the structure of eggs from a wide range of animal species showed that they are all single cells, their differences being due to variations in the nature and quantity of reserve materials, etc. In 1870 van Beneden took charge of the teaching of zoology at the University of Liège, becoming associate professor in 1871 and full professor in 1874. He devoted much time to his teaching, especially to his course on embryology, which was based almost entirely upon his own researches. The manuscripts he wrote on this subject he did not publish, but his student, J. L. A.

Brachet, published them after his death. They concern the segmentation, polarity and gastrulation of the fertilized egg.

Van Beneden's study of fertilization in the intestinal worm of the horse, *Ascaris megalocephala*, revealed clearly for the first time the constancy of the chromosome number per cell; the halving of this number in the formation of the germ cells; and the individuality of the chromosomes within the nucleus. He distinguished two varieties of *A. megalocephala*, namely *univalens* with only one chromosome in its germ cells and *bivalens* with two. He perceived that the chromosome number of the egg nucleus is halved when the first polar body is shed. He failed, however, to observe correctly the way in which this halving is brought about and he misconstrued the significance of the diploid condition, believing that the two sets of chromosomes (or chromatic loops as he called them) in the body cells represent the hermaphrodite condition, the halved number in the germ cells the male and female condition. It fell to A. WEISMANN to provide the correct interpretation and to T. BOVERI to unravel the mechanism of chromosome reduction.

Van Beneden was made an honorary doctor of the universities of Brussels, Edinburgh, Jena, Leipzig, and Oxford. His most important paper, *Recherches sur la maturation de l'oeuf et la fécondation*, is to be found in the *Archives de Biologie* for 1883, the journal which he and C. E. M. van Bambeke founded in 1880.

Académie Royale des Sciences, Biographie Nationale, **26**, 174. 1936–8.
A. Kemna, *P. J. Van Beneden: La Vie et l'Oeuvre d'un Zoologiste.* 1897.
Dictionary of Scientific Biography .

R C O

BENNET, ABRAHAM Born at Taxal, Cheshire, England, 1749 (baptised 20 December); died Wirksworth, Derbyshire, 1799 (buried 9 May). Pioneer of electrical science.

Bennet invented the gold-leaf electrometer (1787), and a simple induction machine (1789). He performed numerous experiments in electricity, and was elected FRS (1789). He showed that many bodies acquired an opposite electrification when separated from other electrified bodies, and conceived the notion that bodies have varying attractions or capacities for electricity. In 1792 he made an unsuccessful attempt to prove that light has momentum by concentrating it by means of a large lens on a piece of paper suspended in vacuo.

A. Bennet, *New Experiments in Electricity.* 1789.
Dictionary of National Biography (Missing Persons). 1993.

J W H

BENTHAM, GEORGE Born at Stoke, near Plymouth, Devon, England, 22 September 1800; died London 10 September 1884. Plant taxonomist.

George Bentham was a nephew of Jeremy Bentham (1748–1832). Although he, too, studied law, he took an active interest in botany from an early age, and was elected Fellow of the Linnean Society in 1828. The affairs of the Royal Horticultural Society prospered while he was its Hon. Secretary (1829–40). He assisted N. Wallich (1786–1854) with the naming of his enormous collection of Indian plants, an exercise which led to his first important work, *Labiatarum Genera et Species* (1832-6).

Being a close friend of Sir William Hooker (1785-1865), Director of Kew Gardens, he generously presented in 1854 his valuable herbarium and library to Kew, where he then worked daily for the rest of his life. He contributed the *Flora Hongkongensis* (1861) and the seven-volume *Flora Australiensis* (1863-78) to the Kew series of Colonial floras. In collaboration with Sir Joseph D. HOOKER he undertook his most important work, the *Genera Plantarum* (1862-83), which occupied him for some twenty-five years. This monumental work in three volumes is still the standard plant classification used by many British botanists, who are also indebted to Bentham for his popular *Handbook of the British Flora* (1858), which went through several editions.

He was elected FRS in 1862, already being a recipient of the Society's Royal Medal (1859). He will long be remembered as a particularly energetic and effective President of the Linnean Society (1863-74).

B. D. Jackson, *George Bentham*. 1906. (Portrait.)
Dictionary of Scientific Biography.
Dictionary of National Biography.

R G C D

BENZ, KARL Born at Karlsruhe, Germany, 25 November 1844; died Ladenburg, near Mannheim, 4 April 1929. A pioneer of internal combustion and automobile engineering.

The son of a railway mechanic, Karl Benz early showed an aptitude for machines, and was trained in mechanical engineering at the Karlsruhe Lyzeum and Polytechnikum (1853-64). After factory experience with Maschinenbau Gesellschaft, Karlsruhe, he spent two years with Schweizer & Cie, Mannheim; there he gained a fortunate promotion, joining the brothers Benkiser at Pforzheim in 1868. Going into business in 1871, Benz set up a small machine-tool works in Mannheim. Faced by financial crisis in 1877, he was forced to turn towards the development of some machine which would have immediate time-saving effects. Benz saw salvation in the internal-combustion engine, but due to the granting of the Otto four-cycle patent of that year (see N. A. OTTO) he had to experiment with the two-cycle engine. Following Dugald Clerk (1854-1932), whose two-cycle engine was always in some danger of exploding, Benz developed an engine in which the fuel would not ignite in the pump, and in which the cylinder was swept with fresh air between each stroke. By 1879 the design was sufficiently refined for the engine to run for long periods with little attention. Benz made preparations for its commercial manufacture, but it was not until 1882 that he obtained financial backing to set up the Gasmotorenfabrik Mannheim. Differences between the partners arose almost at once, and in 1883 Benz left the firm and obtained backing for the creation of a new company, Benz & Cie, Rheinische Gasmotorenfabrik, Mannheim. The revocation of Otto's four-cycle patent in 1886 led Benz to design such an engine specifically for vehicular use, and in that year he patented a 'motor-car with gas engine drive'. The engine had an output of 0.8 hp at 250 rpm; a horizontal flywheel; and a battery-buzzer ignition system. A multitude of detailed improvements followed this

turning-point in automobile history. The exhibition of the car at the Paris Fair of 1889 aroused little interest and, unlike G. DAIMLER, Benz found no Frenchman interested in its manufacture. The 1890s saw the production of a four-wheel car with king-pin steering, followed by a whole series of improved models. Two thousand had been made by 1899, when the company was reorganized as Benz & Cie, Rheinische Gasmotorenfabrik AG, Mannheim. In 1901 there was disagreement among the directors, and in 1903 Benz left the board. Briefly returning in 1904, he finally retired a little later to Ladenburg.

St J. Nixon, *The Invention of the Automobile*. 1936. (Portrait.)
E. Diesel and others, *From Engines to Autos*. 1960. (Portrait.)
I. K. Schnauffer, *Chartered Mechanical Engineer*, **14**, 570, 1961.

W N S

BERG, PAUL Born in Brooklyn, New York, 30 June 1926. Molecular biologist: pioneer of recombinant DNA techniques.

Berg studied biochemistry at Pennsylvania State University – his studies being interrupted by military service – and later worked with A. KORNBERG at Washington University, St Louis, where he became familiar with the chemistry of DNA and RNA. In 1959 he went to Stanford University, latterly (1970) as chairman of the biochemistry department. There he became particularly interested in transfer DNA, which controls the assembly of amino acids into proteins. He isolated many individual tDNAs and the enzymes associated with them.

He then turned his attention to prokaryotic organisms (such as bacteria) which have no defined cell nucleus. By the early 1960s it was known that in the case of *E. coli*, the common experimental organism, viruses invading the cell can replace some of the bacterial DNA with their own. As a result the bacteria begin to manufacture viral protein. Berg wanted to explore the possibility of effecting similar changes in the genes of multicellular organisms. To gain experience he spent a year (1967-8) at the Salk Institute with R. DULBECCO, who was working with a newly discovered virus, polyoma, which causes tumours in rodents. Returning to Stanford he began independent research with the closely related simian virus 40 (SV40). In the early 1970s he succeeded in preparing recombinant DNA using SV40 and bacteriophage lambda. These do not normally interact but by using specific enzymes he was able to cleave their DNA at points which made it possible for the fragments to recombine.

In effect, he had produced synthetic viruses, with unpredictable properties. This potential hazard excited much controversy and research was suspended until 1974, when an international conference laid down guidelines offering acceptable safeguards.

For this research Berg was awarded a Nobel prize for chemistry in 1980, sharing it with W. GILBERT and F. SANGER.

Les Prix Nobel en 1980, 1981. (Portrait.)
Tyler Wasson (Ed.), *Nobel Prize Winners*. 1987. (Portrait.)

T I W

BERGER, HANS Born at Neuses, near Coburg, Bavaria, Germany, 21 May 1873; died Bad Blanckenburg, Thuringia, 1 June 1941. Founder of electro-encephalography.

Berger, the grandson of the poet Rückert, studied mathematics and physics for a year at Jena, then changed to medicine and qualified in 1897. In 1900 he joined the staff of the psychiatric clinic at Jena, and in 1919 succeeded to the chair of psychiatry, retiring in 1938. Berger did not establish a great reputation as a psychiatrist, but he was an accomplished diagnostician of focal brain disorders.

His main interest lay in the physical basis of the mind, and he published monographs on the blood circulation of the brain in 1901; on the temperature of the brain in 1910; and on 'psychophysiology' in 1921. Inspired by the direct recording of electric currents from the exposed brains of animals by A. Caton (1842–1926) of Liverpool in 1875, and by the demonstration of electrocardiography by W. EINTHOVEN, Berger began in 1924 to record, with the very inadequate amplifiers at his disposal, first from the exposed brain of dogs; then from needle electrodes under the scalp of patients who had had brain operations with removal of part of the skull bones; and finally through the intact skull from normal human beings (his own family and volunteers) and from patients with brain disorders. The first paper on human electro-encephalography (1929) was followed by a series of classical observations up till the time of his retirement, describing, inter alia, the alpha rhythm which appears at a rate of about ten cycles per second in the parieto-occipital areas of the brain at rest.

Berger was aware of the possibilities of the new discipline both in the diagnosis of diseases of the brain and in neurophysiology: initially his discoveries were taken up and developed mainly in the Anglo-Saxon countries, and the electro-encephalogram (EEG) has since become a routine investigation in neurological and psychiatric diseases. He was not appreciated in his own country because of his remote and secretive nature; he was an uninspiring teacher, and was not expected to make any discoveries. He had no facilities for EEG work after his retirement, and committed suicide in a fit of depression.

H. Boening, Archiv für Psychiatrie und
    Nervenkrankheiten, 114, 17. 1941. (Portrait.)
R. Ginzberg, Journal of the History of Medicine, 4,
    361. 1949.
W. Haymaker and F. Schiller (Eds), Founders of
    Neurology. 1953. (Portrait.)
Dictionary of Scientific Biography.

E H J

BERGIUS, FRIEDRICH Born at Goldschmieden, near Breslau (now in Poland), 11 October 1884; died Buenos Aires, Argentina, 31 March 1949. An outstanding industrial chemist and man of business.

Bergius, whose father owned a small chemical plant, studied chemistry in Leipzig, Berlin, and Karlsruhe. From his teachers in the two latter places (W. NERNST and F. HABER) he derived an interest in reactions at high pressures and temperatures. In 1911 he became Privatdozent in Hanover, teaching physical and industrial chemistry; in a private laboratory he carried out pioneering experiments in the high-pressure hydrogenation of coal

and crude oil. His business career began in 1914, when he joined Goldschmidt A. G. of Essen as head of the laboratories.

The Bergius process of hydrogenation of coal to petroleum was of great potential importance to Germany during the war of 1914–18, and its development was pushed forward as a matter of national emergency. It came too late, however, to have much influence on that war, but during the interwar years it was extensively worked under licence in several countries, in an attempt to avert a strategic shortage of petroleum which seemed possible. In the Bergius process coal was mixed into a paste with oil and hydrogenated at about 200 atmospheres in the presence of a catalyst. A ton of bituminous coal yielded about 180 gallons of motor spirit. During these years also Bergius developed two other important processes; the high-temperature hydrolysis of chlorobenzene to give phenol, and the direct conversion of ethylene into ethylene glycol.

Bergius's name is also connected with the attempts to make a commercially viable process of the hydrolysis of wood-pulp to sugar and protein. This began in 1917, in collaboration with Erik Hägglund and R. WILLSTÄTTER, and the process was used to a limited extent during the Second World War; it seems, however, to be of little interest under normal economic conditions.

In 1931, Bergius shared the Nobel prize for chemistry with Carl BOSCH. After 1945, he left Germany and worked as a technical adviser in Spain and Argentina, where he died.

Journal of Chemical Education, 26, 508, 1949.
E. Farber, Nobel Prizewinners in Chemistry 1901–
    50. 1953. (Portrait.)
Tyler Wasson (Ed.), Nobel Prize Winners. 1987.
    (Portrait.)

W V F

BERGMAN, TORBERN OLAF Born at Catherineberg, West Gothland, Sweden, 20 March 1735; died Medevi, Sweden, 8 July 1784. Well known for his work on chemical affinity.

Bergman was the son of a tax-collector. At Uppsala he studied first theology and law (to please his father) and then natural science (to please himself). There, in 1758, he began to teach physics and mathematics, and in 1767 he became professor of chemistry and pharmacy. Ill health compelled him to retire in 1780.

His first publications were on physical subjects: the rainbow, aurorae, frictional electricity, and others. In pyroelectricity he showed that the electrification of opposite ends of a tourmaline crystal on warming depends on change of temperature. He published an important treatise on physical geography in 1766.

Bergman's chemistry appears to have been largely self-taught. His first chemical publication, on alum, was in the year he was appointed professor. From then on he and his students produced a large number of dissertations on various aspects of chemistry, including tartar emetic, fulminating gold, nickel, platinum, arsenic, etc. He remained a believer in phlogiston, which he thought was present in all combustibles and probably identifiable with hydrogen.

Bergman inherited the great Swedish tradition in mineralogy, and produced a new chemical classification of minerals, many of which he analysed. He was one of the first to use the blowpipe extensively and systematically as an analytical tool and to stress the need for purity in chemical reagents. Analysis of iron samples led him to the identification of several impurities.

Bergman's most famous – and most ambitious – work was on 'elective affinity'. Following a suggestion of A. Baumé (1728–1804), from 1775 to 1783 he compiled extensive affinity tables, placing acids in a sequence determined by their relative affinities for a given base, those with stronger affinities displacing those with weaker. Similarly, bases were ranged in the order of their affinities for each acid. Altogether, 59 substances were taken, each with two entries – one for 'wet' reactions, one for 'dry'. Ill health prevented completion of the thousands of new experiments necessary, and the unfinished task lacked due recognition of the influence of external conditions. Nevertheless, his results stimulated later workers to develop clearer ideas on both 'affinity' and combining weights.

Bergman succumbed to tuberculosis when only 49, two years before the death of his younger friend K. W. SCHEELE. He was a member of the Swedish Academy and (from 1765) the Royal Society.

B. Moström, *Torbern Bergman*. 1957.

J. R. Partington, *A History of Chemistry*, vol. 3. 1962. (Portrait.)

G. Carlid and J. Nordström, *Torbern Bergman's Foreign Correspondence*, vol. 1. 1965. (Portrait.)

W. A. Smeaton, *Endeavour* (New Series), **8**, 71, 1984. (Portrait.)

J. A. Schufle, *Chymia*, **12**, 59, 1967. (Portrait.)

Dictionary of Scientific Biography.

C A R

BERGSTRÖM, SUNE Born in Stockholm, 10 January 1916. Biochemist and Nobel Laureate.

Bergström trained as a doctor at the Royal Caroline Institute in Stockholm. Following his MD and postgraduate studies, he was appointed professor of biochemistry at the University of Lund in 1947. In 1958 he rejoined the Caroline Institute as professor of biochemistry. He was Rector of the Institute from 1967 to 1977 and Chairman of the Nobel Foundation 1975–1987. In 1935, Bergström's teacher, Ulf von EULER (1905–83) had isolated a hormone from human semen which he named prostaglandin (i.e. from the prostate gland). He had found that it induced contractions in smooth muscle as well as lowering blood pressure. Prostaglandins were subsequently found present in many cells. In 1957, encouraged by von Euler, Bergström, together with his pupil, Bengt I. Sammuelsson (1934–), succeeded in isolating and purifying two of what turned out to be a whole family of prostaglandins. In 1962, using gas chromatography and mass spectrometry, Bergström was able to deduce that they were complicated unsaturated fatty acids. Some of these were synthesized in 1968 by E. J. COREY in America. Prostaglandins have found considerable clinical use in the treatment of high blood pressure and as abortive agents. In 1982 Bergström shared the Nobel prize for physiology or medicine with Sammuelsson and the British pharmacologist, John R. Vane (1927–) for work on the formation and function of this important biochemical group.

New Scientist, **96** (14 October 1982), pp. 82–3 (Portrait.)

Science, 19 November 1982.

Tyler Wasson (Ed.), *Nobel Prize Winners*. 1987. (Portrait.)

W H B

BERNARD, CLAUDE Born at Saint-Julien, Villefranche, France, 12 July 1813; died Paris, 10 February 1878. The founder of experimental medicine.

Bernard was educated at Villefranche and at Thoissey, Ain, and then assisted a pharmacist at Lyons. In 1834 he entered the School of Medicine at Paris. He became *préparateur* to F. MAGENDIE at the *Collège de France* in 1841, and two years later graduated as a doctor of medicine, after which he devoted himself entirely to physiology. In 1847 he was appointed 'substitute' to Magendie, and thereafter they shared the lectures at the *Collège*. In 1847 also he was awarded the prize in experimental physiology of the *Académie des Sciences*, and in 1854 he became a member of that *Académie*, of which he was president in 1869. In 1855 he succeeded Magendie at the *Collège de France*, where most of his experimental work was done. In 1861 he was elected a member of the *Académie de Médecine*; in 1864 a Foreign Member of the Royal Society of London (Copley Medallist 1876); and in 1869 a member of the *Académie Française*.

Bernard's main contributions to physiology were:

(*a*) He discovered the glycogenic function of the liver. He fed an animal on a sugar-free diet and found glucose in the hepatic vein and in the liver tissue. He thought (1855) that the glucose was secreted by the liver, and this was the origin of the term 'internal secretion'. But after washing a liver completely free from sugar, he kept it for twenty-four hours, and then found that it contained abundant sugar. He concluded that some sugar-forming substance in the liver had been changed to sugar. In 1857 he isolated this substance and called it glycogen. He demonstrated (1849) that puncture of the floor of the fourth ventricle of the brain causes sugar to appear in the urine – the inference being that sugar production in the liver is controlled by the nervous system.

(*b*) It was thought that the pancreas was a salivary gland. Bernard noted in a meat-fed rabbit that the lacteals in the mesentery were filled with a white fluid – indicating digestion of the fat of the meat – but only below the entry of the pancreatic duct to the duodenum. He concluded that the fat was acted upon by the pancreatic juice, and *in vitro* he showed that if crushed pancreas is mixed with neutral fat and kept at body temperature, the fat is split into fatty acids and glycerol. He then showed that the passage of the acid stomach contents into the duodenum induces a flow of pancreatic juice; and that, if the pancreatic duct is blocked, fat is not digested. He also demonstrated that the pancreatic juice changes starch into maltose.

(*c*) In 1851 Bernard cut the cervical sympathetic and found increase of temperature on that side. He later showed that the action was on the capillaries, and he – and C. E. BROWN-SÉQUARD independently – demonstrated that stimulation of the cut cervical sympathetic causes their contraction. The existence of vasoconstrictor fibres was therefore demonstrated. In 1857 he discovered that the nerve supply to the submaxillary gland contains vaso-dilator fibres. He had therefore discovered vasomotor nerves and their effect in controlling blood-flow.

(d) In 1844 Bernard started experiments using the South-American arrow poison, curare. By 1857 he had shown that, when injected, it poisons the endings of the nerves in muscles throughout the body. His experiments proved the independent contractility of muscle. In 1846 he began his studies on the poisonous effects of carbon monoxide, and by 1856 he had concluded that the erythrocytes are responsible for the respiratory function of blood, and that the oxygen is not in solution, but is bound to some substance in the erythrocyte. In 1857 E. F. HOPPE-SEYLER discovered this substance and named it haemoglobin.

(e) Bernard first stated his theory of the 'internal environment' in 1857, and he developed it in 1865. He regarded life as dependent upon the constancy of the internal environment, constituted by the blood and lymph which bathe all the cells. This theory is important in modern physiology.

J. M. D. Olmsted, *Claude Bernard, Physiologist.* 1938. (Portrait.)

M. Foster, *Claude Bernard.* 1899.

J. Schiller, *Claude Bernard et les Problémes scientifiques de son temps.* 1967.

Dictionary of Scientific Biography.

E A U

BERNOULLI, DANIEL Born at Gröningen, Netherlands, 8 February 1700; died Basle, Switzerland, 17 March 1782. Mathematician: made important contributions to hydrodynamics and differential equations.

The son of Jean BERNOULLI, Daniel is the most famous member – apart, possibly, from his father, and his uncle, Jacques BERNOULLI – of the Bernoulli family, which produced an outstanding number of talented mathematicians. He was the younger brother of Nicolaus (1695–1726), best known for his work on the 'St Petersburg problem' in probability. Having got his doctorate in medicine for his thesis on the action of the lungs, Daniel became professor of mathematics at St Petersburg in 1725; he found the conditions rather primitive there, and in 1733 returned to Basle to become professor successively of Anatomy and Botany and of Natural Philosophy, vacating the chair in 1777. He was awarded ten prizes by the *Académie des Sciences*: he shared one of these with his father, which occasioned a difference between them. He was the intimate friend of L. EULER and J. Le R. D'ALEMBERT. In 1748 he succeeded his father in the *Académie*, and was elected FRS in 1750.

His magnum opus, *Hydrodynamica*, appeared in 1738, though it was almost finished in 1733. It is in thirteen sections, the first of which is devoted to the history of the subject. Daniel develops hydrostatics and hydrodynamics using NEWTON'S laws of force together with the *vis viva* of G. W. LEIBNITZ, though – to avoid controversy – he uses the latter in a more acceptable form similar to that employed by C. HUYGENS. Part 5 of section XII contains the idea of 'Bernoulli's Theorem', but he does not state it explicitly. Perhaps the most impressive part of the work is section X, which starts by propounding a kinetic theory of gases which is very like the modern one, and continues (not using the theory) with a significant discussion of the *vis viva*

of elastic fluids. An important part of the book is the wealth of practical applications of the theoretical results. In other fields his most important contribution is to differential equations: he solved the differential equation of J. F. Riccati (1676–1754), and did much work on partial differential equations – particularly in connection with problems of vibrating strings, which he studied with D'Alembert and Euler – and he was a pioneer in the use of trigonometrical series. Daniel published papers on probability, into which he introduced the idea of 'moral expectation', and in which he showed how differential calculus could be used. He also wrote on continued fractions, astronomy, and the computation of trigonometrical functions.

C. A. Truesdell, *Rational Fluid Mechanics 1687–1738*, in *Leonhardi Euleri Opera Omnia*, (series II, vol XII). 1954.

C. Hutton, *A Mathematical and Philosophical Dictionary.* 1795.

D. E. Smith, *History of Mathematics.* 1923 (Paperback 1958). (Portrait.)

Dictionary of Scientific Biography.

R P L

BERNOULLI, JACQUES Born at Basle, Switzerland, 27 December 1654; died there, 10 August 1705. Mathematician; made important contributions to calculus and probability theory.

A member of a wealthy merchant family which had moved from Antwerp to Basle in the previous century, Jacques began by studying theology, though on his own initiative he read the *Géometrie* of R. DESCARTES and such works of J. WALLIS, F. van Schooten (1615–60), I. BARROW, and others that came his way. In 1676 he set out on his travels, becoming acquainted with the new philosophy in Holland and England, where he met Robert BOYLE and other English philosophers. In 1681–2 he propounded an incorrect theory of comets, and in 1682 returned to Basle to lecture on mechanics and experimental philosophy. In the same year he wrote *De Gravitate Aetheris*. He refused a church appointment, and in 1687 he was appointed professor of mathematics at Basle (a post he retained till his death), and began his correspondence with G. W. LEIBNITZ, whose papers a few years earlier in *Acta Eruditorum* had decided him to devote himself to mathematics.

He wrote a large number of papers for this journal, among the more important being on the problem of the quadrisection of a triangle by two mutually perpendicular lines (1687), which he solved algebraically; on infinite series and their finite sum (1689) – this contains some results lifted from Barrow; a theorem on conics (1689); analysis (1690) of the problem of the catenary (solved by his brother Jean BERNOULLI, and also by C. HUYGENS and Leibnitz) and of the isochrone – the curve along which a heavy body moves so that the vertical component of its velocity is constant – which was posed by Leibnitz earlier in the year; on the centre of oscillation of the pendulum (1691, 1703) – important for the formulation of d'Alembert's principle (see J. le R. D'ALEMBERT); two papers which showed how to find tangents, length of curve, area, evolute, etc., of a curve by applying his method to examples including the logarithmic spiral (1691), where he used the equivalent of polar co-ordinates; on cycloidal curves and their evolutes, caustics, etc. (1692) – this paper is mostly on the logarithmic spiral; on transcendental curves (1696); and on isoperimetry (1700, 1701) – these papers contain the first principles of the calculus of variations, which Jacques helped his brother found. In Jacques's *Ars Conjectandi* (1713 – posthumous), a treatise on probability, appear the Bernoulli numbers, and also the 'Theorem of Bernoulli'. He was so impressed by the logarithmic spiral's property of reappearing after so many mathematical transformations that he willed it to be carved on his tombstone, with the inscription *Eadem Mutata Resurgo* (I shall arise the same, though changed).

> *Opera*, 2 vols. 1744. (Contains biography by J. J. Batterius.)
> D. E. Smith, *A History of Mathematics*, vol. 1. 1923. (Paperback 1958). (Portrait.)
> *Dictionary of Scientific Biography.*
> *Neue deutsche Biographie II.* 1955.
>
> R P L

BERNOULLI, JEAN Born at Basle, Switzerland, 7 August 1667; died there, 1 January 1748. Mathematician; an important figure in the development of the calculus.

Jean was the younger brother of Jacques BERNOULLI. The contributions of the two brothers are often difficult to separate: certainly they themselves often quarrelled over questions of priority – as indeed they quarrelled severally with G. W. LEIBNITZ. Jean started his career by studying medicine, though he also studied mathematics under Jacques. In 1691 he went to Paris, where he impressed the circle of N. Malebranche (1638–1715), and gave private tuition to G. F. A. de l'Hôpital (1661–1704), for whom he wrote *Leçons de Calcul Différentiel et Intégral* – Jean was upset when l'Hôpital published his *Analyse des Infiniments Petits* without giving him the credit. In 1694 he got his doctor's degree on the strength of a celebrated dissertation on muscular movement which contradicted N. STENO and G. A. BORELLI. At the recommendation of C. HUYGENS, he was appointed professor of mathematics at Gröningen, and in 1705 he succeeded his brother at Basle. He helped to propagate the doctrine of the calculus, and sided with Leibnitz in his controversy with NEWTON. He was made a Foreign Member of the Paris Academy in 1699.

In 1691 Jean solved the catenary problem (which was suggested by Jacques in the same year) in a way different from Leibnitz's. He wrote (1692–3) on caustic curves in collaboration with his brother. In 1694 he published an important, if short, paper on ordinary differential equations, to which was appended another on the quadrature and rectification of curves by a 'most general series'. In modern notation he proved that

$$\int_0^x y \, dx = xy - \frac{x^2}{2!} y' + \frac{x^3}{3!} y'' - \ldots$$

In 1696 he proposed the problem of the brachystochrone (the Bernoullis' term – the curve of quickest descent joining two points), to which GALILEO had given an incorrect solution: he solved it himself (the answer is the cycloid) in 1697. It is due to his work on this problem and that of finding the curve of given perimeter which will enclose the greatest area that he is considered one of the founders of the calculus of variations. He is also remembered for his work on the exponential calculus; on geodesics; on complex numbers; and his treatment of trigonometry as a branch of the calculus. He won a prize from the Academy in 1730 for his attempt, refuted by J. Le R. D'ALEMBERT, to reconcile the vortices of R. DESCARTES with the third law of J. KEPLER.

> D. E. Smith, *A History of Mathematics*, vol. 1. 1923 (Paperback 1958). (Portrait.)
> O. Spiess, *Die Mathematiker Bernoulli.* 1948.
> *Dictionary of Scientific Biography.*
>
> R P L

BERT, PAUL Born at Auxerre, Yonne, France, 17 October 1833; died Hanoi, Tonking, Indo-China (now Vietnam), 11 November 1886. A pioneer in the physiology of respiration and gaseous exchange in the body.

Bert qualified in law at Paris, but as a result of chance observations in Algeria he was led to study tissue grafts. On returning to Paris he studied science and took his doctorate in 1863. In 1868 he became assistant to Claude BERNARD, and he lectured at the Sorbonne on the comparative physiology of respiration. Bert was a close friend of Léon Gambetta (1838–82), the statesman and lawyer, and during the Franco-Prussian War he was appointed Prefect of the North. After the war he was called to the chair of physiology at the Sorbonne, but as he was elected to the *Chambre des Députés* almost at once he did little teaching there. As a politician he was largely responsible for advances in higher education and for the State's assumption of the control of elementary education. During Gambetta's ministry Bert was for a short time Minister for Education, but his policy was not successful. Early in 1886 he was sent by the Government as Resident at Tonking, and his death there was due to dysentery.

From about 1868 Bert had been studying the physiological effects of high and low atmospheric pressures. His work became well known, and he advised Gaston Tissandier (1843–99) before the latter's balloon ascent with two companions on 15 April 1875. Bert's advice was not taken, and the result was that only Tissandier survived. In 1878 Bert collected his observations and experiments in a book, *La pression barométrique*, which is one of the classics of physiology. His results were largely overlooked and completely forgotten, and much erroneous work was done as a result by his successors in the next sixty years. In 1943 his book was translated into English and published because of its value in research then current.

Bert studied the effects of both low and high atmospheric pressure, both on animals and on himself. His fundamental conclusion was that the physiological effects of oxygen and other gases in the blood are due not to their proportions but to their partial pressures. He made rough estimations of the amounts of oxygen lost by the blood when the atmospheric pressure was reduced by varying amounts. He was the first to carry out a thorough investigation of the effects of low atmospheric pressures, and he demonstrated that they were due to a diminished partial pressure of oxygen, and that reduction of mechanical pressure in itself produced no ill effects. His experiments on animals, and on himself in a steel chamber, suggested that in balloon ascents oxygen could be used to avert the dangerous effects of rarefied air.

Bert's work on high atmospheric pressures – such as those encountered by divers and caisson-workers – were even more important. He showed that the effects were due to increased partial pressures of gases in the air breathed, and he demonstrated that the symptoms and signs produced were due to liberation in the tissues of bubbles of gases, mostly nitrogen. As a preventive of 'bends' and 'caisson-sickness' he recommended slow and partial decompression, and he experimented with recompression. Finally, he showed that, for all forms of animal life, oxygen at high partial pressures is a poison. Since his time Bert's conclusions have been extended, but they have never been invalidated.

Lancet, ii, 1004, 1886.
J. S. Haldane and J. G. Priestley, *Respiration*. 1935.
P. Bert, *Barometric Pressure*. 1943. (Portrait.)
L. Dubreuil, *Paul Bert*. 1935.
Dictionary of Scientific Biography.

E A U

BERTHELOT, PIERRE EUGÈNE MARCEL(L)IN

Born in Paris, 25 October 1827; died there, 18 March 1907. Distinguished in organic and physical chemistry, history of early chemistry, and in the public service.

Marcellin (or Marcelin) Berthelot, son of a physician, won a philosophy prize at the *Collège Henri IV* in 1846, studied medicine at the *Collège de France*, but concentrated on chemistry, becoming professor at the *École Supérieure de Pharmacie* (1859–76) and at the *Collège de France* (1864 until his death). He influenced the progress of chemistry in four main ways.

Firstly, he showed how the relations of organic compounds can be studied on the basis of the synthesis of the most simple compounds directly from their elements. Until his day organic chemistry had developed mainly from the study of naturally occurring substances and their breakdown products. The few attempts to build up larger organic compounds from smaller ones or from the elements were without system or connection. From 1855 onwards Berthelot showed how there could be synthesized (in effect) from the simplest carbon compounds, like carbon monoxide, organic compounds of sufficient complexity to justify the belief that an unlimited number of compounds could be derived by stages from the elements. This not only banished the concept of 'vitalism' from chemistry, but also gave chemists a new basis for the planning and purpose of their researches.

Secondly, with L. Péan de Saint-Gilles (1832–63), he showed the significance of reaction velocity (1862–3). Although not the first, he took the subject further than anyone before C. M. GOLDBERG and P. WAAGE formulated the Law of Mass Action.

Thirdly, he made an intensive study of heats of reaction, devising the bomb calorimeter for combustions in oxygen, and formulated the idea of exothermic and endothermic reactions. Although his thermodynamic 'principle of maximum work' was defective, it greatly assisted progress to the idea of free energy and elucidation of the conditions of chemical equilibrium. He extended his ideas into the behaviour of explosives, studying the speed of explosion waves and gaseous products.

Fourthly, he made an outstanding contribution to the study of the history of chemistry by his work on ancient and medieval alchemical texts, for which he got the co-operation of many fellow scholars in the arts. His editions of alchemical works are still unsurpassed.

Like many French scholars, he played an active part in politics and administration. He was active in the defence of Paris 1870, was Inspector of Higher Education in 1876, Senator in 1881, Minister of Public Instruction in 1886, and Foreign Minister in 1895. He was elected to the *Académie des Sciences* in 1873, becoming its Permanent Secretary in 1889. He died within an hour or so of his wife; the two received the unique state honour of being buried together in the *Panthéon*.

Proceedings of the Royal Society, **80**, iii, 1908.
H. Dixon, *Journal of the Chemical Society*, 2353, 1911. (Portrait.)
E. Jungfleisch, *Bulletin de la Société Chimique de France*, **13**, i, 1913. (Portrait.)
E. Farber (Ed.), *Great Chemists*. 1961. (Portrait.)
Dictionary of Scientific Biography.

F G

BERTHOLLET, CLAUDE-LOUIS

Born at Talloire, near Annecy, Savoy, France, 9 December 1748; died Arcueil, near Paris, 6 November 1822. Innovator in physical and applied chemistry.

Son of French parents, in the (then) Italian Savoy, Berthollet studied medicine at the University of Turin, graduating MD in 1768. He became physician to Madame de Montessor. He studied chemistry in Paris under P. J. MACQUER and became a Paris MD in 1778. With other French chemists he was an early member of the staff of the *École Polytechnique* (1795). He was too immersed in his subject to be a good teacher, but was an inspiring research worker. He was a friend of Napoleon, who sent him to Italy in 1796 to collect art treasures and to Egypt in 1798 to help found the Institute of Egypt. He became a Senator in 1804. He lived at Arcueil, where he could enjoy his garden.

With LAPLACE he founded (1807) a *Société d'Arcueil*, a short-lived but influential scientific society. In 1814 he voted for the deposition of Napoleon out of concern for the good of France. Louis XVIII made him a count.

He was one of the first (1785) to adhere to the anti-phlogiston theory of LAVOISIER. He made many original discoveries in inorganic chemistry, establishing the composition of ammonia, prussic acid (1787), and sulphuretted hydrogen. In 1784 he succeeded Macquer as inspector of dyeworks and director of the Gobelins factory. With A. F. FOURCROY, J. A. C. CHAPTAL, and others he promoted many chemical and metallurgical manufactures after the Revolution. His theoretical researches on chlorine and its compounds founded the modern chemistry of this element. He took the important step of introducing chlorine into bleaching, and was one of the originators of volumetric analysis; his idea for testing the strength of a bleaching solution by titration with an indigo solution was perfected by F. A. H. Descroizilles (1751–1825).

His most important work was that on chemical reactions and chemical composition, many of his ideas developing out of his industrial work. In his *Essai de Statique Chimique* (1803) he argued that the forces of chemical affinity, like those of gravitation, must be proportional to the masses of the reacting substances. While this does resemble a modern view, Berthollet developed it to conclusions which came in conflict with the available evidence, and he was involved in a long, energetic but courteous controversy with Joseph Louis PROUST. Berthollet maintained that the composition of a compound varies with the proportions of the reactants from which it is formed and the physical conditions of the reaction; Proust maintained that a compound has a definite composition, however formed. Most chemists agreed with Proust, even before the atomic theory of John DALTON, requiring a law of definite proportions, came on the scene. Berthollet's position was vindicated half a century later by the Law of Mass Action enunciated by C. M. GULDBERG and P. WAAGE, and much other physico-chemical work, although the new interpretations differed from both his and Proust's.

F. Hoefer, *Histoire de la Chimie.* 1866–9.

M. Crosland, *The Society of Arcueil.* 1967. (Portrait.)

M. Sadoun-Goupil, *Le Chimiste Claude-Louis Berthollet.* 1977.

S. C. Kapoor, *Chymia*, **10**, 53, 1965.

Dictionary of Scientific Biography.

F G

BERTHOUD, FERDINAND Born at Placemont, Neuchâtel, Switzerland, 19 March 1727; died Groslay Montmorency, near Paris, 20 June 1807. Clockmaker; remembered for his technical writing.

Berthoud early showed mechanical ability and began his training as a watchmaker in 1743. Moving to Paris in 1748, he specialized in precision clockmaking and was attracted to the problem of longitude measurement at sea, by then reduced to improved timekeeping in the spring-driven watch. To this end he designed an automatic fusee engine, an early machine tool dependent for its accuracy on the skill of its maker rather than its operator. He was appointed *Horloger de la Marine* in 1762. By 1760 Berthoud had used a detached pendulum escapement containing all the essentials of a pivoted detent chronometer escapement. Making about seventy chronometers during his lifetime, he constantly improved their design. By 1780 he had developed a spring detent escapement, and has as good a claim to its invention as John Arnold (1736–99) or Thomas Earnshaw (1749–1829).

Berthoud was a prolific writer, and it is as such that he is remembered today. His first work, *L'art de conduire et de régler les Pendules et les Montres* (1759) became a standard textbook. Aspects of the application of machine tools to precision work were treated in his *Essai sur l'Horlogerie* (1763–86), and his *Traité des Horloges Marines* (1773) is important. In later life he wrote a standard history, *Histoire de la Mesure du Temps* (1802).

F. J. Britten, *Old Clocks and Watches.* (7th ed.) 1956.

R. T. Gould, *The Marine Chronometer.* 1923.

W N S

BERZELIUS, JÖNS JACOB Born at Väversunda, Sweden, 20 August 1779; died Stockholm, 7 August 1848. One of the nineteenth century's greatest chemists.

The son of a clergyman-schoolmaster, Berzelius was brought up by relatives after the early death of both his parents. In 1796 he began the study of medicine at Uppsala, graduating MD six years later with a dissertation on the (negligible) therapeutic effects of galvanism. Preferring to study chemistry, he took an unpaid position in the Stockholm School of Surgery. After two further years as physician to the poor, in 1807 he became professor of medicine (later chemistry) and pharmacy at the School. In 1808 he became a member of the Swedish Academy of Science, and ten years later was appointed its Secretary. He resigned his professorship in 1832 to devote himself to the Academy.

Berzelius's early preoccupation with galvanism led to an interest in electrochemistry that dominated all his later thought. In 1803, with W. Hisinger (1766–1852), he electrolysed solutions of salts, anticipating H. DAVY in several respects. With M. M. Pontin (1781–1858) in 1808 he introduced the mercury cathode and discovered 'ammonium amalgam'. Electrolytic phenomena led him to regard all compounds as divisible into positive and negative parts and to inject into chemistry a dualism that has never completely vanished. His 'electrochemical theory' was expounded in a paper on nomenclature reform based on Latin names (1811); in a treatise on mineralogy (1814); and especially in his *Essay on Chemical Proportions* (1819). In this last book he linked electrochemistry with the atomic theory and emerged as the new prophet of atomism. His enthusiasm sprang from his interest in chemical proportions. Having begun a systematic study of combining weights, he heard of the atomic theory of John DALTON, realized its significance, and returned to his work with redoubled energy. By 1818 he had determined the atomic weights of all but four of the 49 elements then known. Only six of these were examined by his assistants, the rest being handled entirely by himself. But his greatest service to atomism lay in his system of notation, whereby composition was denoted by letters and numbers, as today, and molecules were written in terms of their constituent atoms.

Like T. BERGMAN, Berzelius became adept at mineralogical analysis and used the blowpipe extensively for this. He discovered three new elements: cerium (1803), selenium (1817), and thorium (1829). His assistants added to these lithium (J. A. Arfwedson, (1792–1841), 1818), vanadium (N. G. Sefström (1787–1845), 1830), and several lanthanides (C. G. MOSANDER, 1839–43).

With his medical background Berzelius naturally concerned himself with organic substances, and in 1812 began to analyse them, finding that the combining laws applied there also. Thus he brought organic nature within the atomic concept, though he maintained a vitalistic view regarding the origins of organic substances. He examined many natural products, including bile, blood, faeces, and much else. To Berzelius we are indebted for the discovery of pyruvic acid, the name 'protein', and the concepts of isomerism and catalysis. Application of his dualistic views to organic substances, though successful at first, became increasingly untenable.

In this matter, as in his theory of gaseous volumes and his long refusal to admit that chlorine was an element, Berzelius was badly mistaken. But his achievements were so massive and his knowledge so encyclopaedic that he continued to dominate European chemistry. His views were conveyed by his comprehensive *Textbook* (in six languages, though not English); his monographs and papers, and his magisterial annual reports on chemical progress. Many of his assistants rose to eminence and helped to propagate his ideas.

Berzelius brought a new unity to chemistry and determined the direction it should take for nearly a century. Created a baron on his marriage in 1835, he was also honoured by no less than 94 learned societies.

H. G. Söderbaum, *Jac. Berzelius, Levnadsteckning.* 1929–31.

J. E. Jorpes, *Jac. Berzelius, His Life and Work* (trans. B. Steele). 1966. (Portraits.)

F. Greenaway, *Endeavour*, **3** (New Series), 138, 1979.

E. M. Methado and T. Frängsmyr, *Enlightenment Science in the Romantic Era: The Chemistry of Berzelius and its Cultural Setting.* 1992.

E. Farber (Ed.), *Great Chemists.* 1961. (Portrait.)

Dictionary of Scientific Biography.

C A R

BESSEL, FRIEDRICH WILHELM Born at Minden, North Rhine-Westphalia, Germany, 22 July 1784; died Königsberg, Prussia, 17 March 1864. Prominent German astronomer.

Bessel worked as a young man in the counting-house of a merchant in Bremen. To prepare himself for overseas travel he studied navigation and, therefore, astronomical theory and practice. In 1804, as a test of his own understanding, he reduced a set of 200-year-old observations by T. HARIOTT on Halley's comet, and communicated his results concerning the orbit to the astronomer H. W. M. Olbers (1758–1840). The good impression this caused led to Bessel becoming, in 1806, an astronomical assistant to J. H. Schröter (1745–1816) at Lilienthal. In 1810, at the age of 26, Bessel was appointed Director of the new observatory at Königsberg, and embarked upon a study of the corrections necessary for the production of accurate results, following this work with a series of determinations of approximately four thousand star places. His reduction of the Greenwich observations of James BRADLEY was published in 1818 in *Fundamenta Astronomiae*; this treatment of Bradley's results earned him much acclaim – it was described as inaugurating a new era of practical astronomy. He followed this up with *Tabulae Regiomontanae*, published in 1830, establishing a uniform system for the reduction of observations. Later articles reported his observations on the twin stars 61 Cygni, from which he calculated their distance. This major achievement, published in 1838, was highly praised. J. F. W. HERSCHEL wrote to Bessel of this as 'the greatest and most glorious triumph which practical astronomy has ever witnessed'.

In 1834 Bessel's observations on the wavelike motion of Sirius led him to initiate a series of investigations leading to the conclusion that Sirius has a companion, a dark star. He reported this in 1841; ten years later the orbit was calculated and the companion was actually observed by A. G. Clark (1804–87) in 1862.

In this period Bessel worked on the determination of the mass of Jupiter, his results being published in 1842. By studying the orbital period of each of the major moons of Jupiter, Bessel computed the mass and volume of the planet, showing that its overall density was only 1.35 times that of water.

Apart from his astronomical work, Bessel made a major contribution to applied mathematics by his inauguration of the systematic study and use of Bessel functions.

Particular cases of these functions had been examined previously by D. BERNOULLI, L. EULER, J. L. LAGRANGE, and others, but the general treatment was due to Bessel. In 1817 he first made use of such functions, and then, in 1824, he published in a paper on planetary perturbations his account of some general properties of these functions. He investigated systematically the functions

$$J_n(z) \text{ defined by } J_n(z) = \frac{1}{2\pi} \int_0^{2\pi} \cos(nu - z \sin u) \, du$$

In his work on the perturbation of orbits he expressed the eccentric anomaly θ as an expansion in terms of the mean anomaly ψ:

$$\theta = \psi + \sum_{n=1}^{\infty} A_n \sin n \, \psi$$

where $\frac{1}{2}n A_n = J_n(z)$, the nth order Bessel function of z. Later treatments of these functions have produced the (above) modern notation and defined the functions as solutions of a differential equation, Bessel's equation – fundamental in the investigation of many problems in mathematical physics.

W. Stein, *Von Bremer Astronomen und Sternfreunden.* 1958.

J. A. Repsold, *Astronomische Nachrichten*, **210**, 161, 1919.

Allgemeine deutsche Biographie, Pt 9. 1875.

Dictionary of Scientific Biography.

D N

BESSEMER, SIR HENRY Born at Hitchin, Hertfordshire, England, 19 January 1813; died London 15 March 1898. Inventor of Bessemer process for steel manufacture.

A versatile inventor, Bessemer pioneered the large-scale manufacture of steel by decarburizing iron and died a millionaire; his royalties, he claimed, totalled '1,057,748 of the little gold medals issued by Her Majesty's Mint'. An engineer's son, he left school to enter his father's workshop, but at 17 he set up in London his own small business to produce art metals, fusible alloys, and bronze powder. He invented machines for working graphite for pencils and for composing type, meanwhile improving his knowledge by spare-time education. At 20, he exhibited at the Royal Academy.

In the middle of the nineteenth century steel was still relatively scarce and expensive compared with iron: in 1850 Britain produced 2 ½ million tons of iron, but only 60 000 tons of steel. The basis of Bessemer's invention was his realization that the removal of carbon from iron – essential for its conversion to steel – could be effected simply by blowing a blast of air through the molten metal. His first experiments were carried out in 1855, using a fixed converter. Later, in 1860, he introduced in his Sheffield steel works a tilting converter which was very much faster in action. It was soon widely used in Europe, being introduced into France (1858), Germany (1862), and Austria (1863). Bessemer steel was first made in the United States in 1864, but under the patent of William KELLY. Apart from the manufacture of armaments, there was soon an enormous demand for Bessemer steel for the world's rapidly developing railway systems.

Bessemer received many honours, including a number from foreign countries. He was elected to Fellowship of the Royal Society in 1877, and was knighted two years later. He was President of the Iron and Steel Institute of Great Britain 1870–1.

W. C. Carr and W. Taplin, *History of the British Steel Industry.* 1962. (Portrait.)

F. M. Osborn, *The Story of the Mushets.* 1952. (Portrait.)

Dictionary of National Biography.

M S

BETHE, HANS ALBRECHT Born in Strasburg, Alsace-Lorraine, (then in Germany), 2 July 1906. Well known for his extensive work in theoretical nuclear physics.

The son of a professor of physiology, Bethe studied at the University of Frankfurt and at Munich, where he received his PhD at the age of 22. His many contributions to nuclear physics started soon after with work on the energy loss of charged particles travelling through matter, which later allowed experimenters to measure the energies of particles from their range in matter. In 1933 Bethe left Nazi Germany, and in 1935 joined Cornell University, at Ithaca, New York, where he has remained ever since. Shortly after moving to the US he published three major articles on nuclear physics in *Reviews of Modern Physics*, which became known as 'Bethe's bible'.

Bethe has been described as 'having the rare gift of rapidly grasping the essence of a physical problem', and he has made important contributions to several fields, including solid-state theory. He is probably most widely known for his work in 1938 on the production of energy by the fusion of hydrogen into helium in the Sun and other stars. He showed that only two reaction chains are possible. One, based on reactions between protons, occurs in the Sun and similar stars; the other, which involves carbon as a catalyst, occurs in stars brighter than the Sun. For this work, Bethe was awarded the Nobel prize for physics in 1967.

Nobel Lectures: Physics, 1963–1970. 1972.

H. A. Bethe in *From a Life of Physics.* 1989.

H. A. Boorse, L. Motz, and J. H. Weaver, *The Atomic Physicists, a Biographical History.* 1989. (Portrait.)

J. Bernstein, *Hans Bethe: Prophet of Energy.* 1980

Tyler Wasson (Ed.), *Nobel Prize Winners.* 1987. (Portrait.)

C S

BEVAN, EDWARD JOHN Born at Birkenhead, England, 11 December 1856; died London, 17 October 1921. Co-inventor of the 'viscose rayon' process.

Bevan began his working life as a chemist in a soap works at Runcorn, but later studied chemistry at Owens College, Manchester. Here he formed a friendship with C. F. CROSS; after a period in a paper mill in Scotland, he and Cross set up in partnership together in London (1885) as consulting and analytical chemists. Their work was mainly concerned with the industrial utilization of cellu-

lose, and with the problems of the paper and jute industries. In 1892 Cross, Bevan, and Clayton Beadle (1868–1917) took out the patent which was to be the foundation of the 'viscose rayon' industry. Cellulose (usually in the form of wood pulp) was dissolved in a mixture of carbon disulphide and aqueous alkali (sodium xanthate), and squirted through fine holes into dilute acid to regenerate cellulose as spinnable fibres.

In 1892 Bevan left the partnership to become Public Analyst to Middlesex County Council, a post which he held until his death. He was prominent in the affairs of the Society of Public Analysts.

Transactions of the Chemical Society, 2121, 1921.

Journal of the Society of Chemical Industry, 418R, 1921.

Dictionary of National Biography (Missing Persons). 1993.

W V F

BHABHA, HOMI JEHANGIR Born in Bombay, India, 30 October 1909; died (in an air crash in the Alps) 24 January 1966. Atomic physicist.

A Parsee by birth, Bhabha received his early education in India. Then, in 1932, a scholarship brought him to Cambridge (Gonville and Caius College) at a time when atomic physics at the Cavendish laboratory was going through a particularly exciting phase. His main interests were in cosmic rays and in atomic physics, and he gained his PhD degree in 1935. Returning to India, he was appointed Reader in Theoretical Physics at the Indian Institute of Science at Bangalore, and began a career which established him as not only the acknowledged leader of atomic physics in India but as a man who was listened to with respect throughout the world. His death at the peak of his powers was a great loss. In 1941, at the early age of 32, he was elected to Fellowship of the Royal Society. A year later he became professor of cosmic ray research at the Indian Institute of Science. In 1945 he became Director of the Tata Institute of Fundamental Research in Bombay, which shortly moved into a modern and well-equipped laboratory. Here he was able to pursue his cosmic ray research and to develop work in biology, mathematics, and astronomy.

When atomic-energy research was initiated in India after the war, Bhabha was the natural choice of leader; in 1948 he was appointed Secretary of the Department of Atomic Energy. At Trombay, he established an outstanding institution for both research and production in this field. Reactors established with some help from Britain, and then from Canada, made it possible to produce plutonium on a substantial scale. Potentially, this could be used for the manufacture of plutonium bombs, though at the time of Bhabha's death Indian policy was firmly against this. Bhabha was also actively engaged in the development of atomic power stations in India.

Inevitably, these expensive and advanced programmes in a country where poverty and famine are ever-present realities led to criticism. Bhabha countered this by using his institute not only as an active centre of research and technology but as a training-ground from which highly skilled men could go out to fertilize research.

Bhabha's international prestige led, in 1955, to his being invited to become President of the International Conference on the Peaceful Uses of Atomic Energy, held at Geneva. At the time of his death he was Chairman of the Indian Atomic Energy Commission.

The Times (obituary), 25 January 1966. (Portrait.)
Biographical Memoirs of Fellows of the Royal Society. 1967. (Portrait.)
J. Cockcroft and M.G.K. Menon, *Proceedings of the Royal Institution of Great Britain*, **41**, 411, 1967.
Dictionary of Scientific Biography, Supp. I.

T I W

BICHAT, MARIE FRANÇOIS XAVIER Born at Thoirette, Jura, France, 11 November 1771; died Paris, 21 July 1802. Physician, pathologist, and the founder of animal histology.

Bichat read medicine at Montpellier and Lyons, and then served in the army. He resumed his studies at Paris (1793), and became the protégé of P. J. Desault (1744–95). In 1797 Bichat began to lecture unofficially on anatomy, physiology, and pathological anatomy. In 1800 he became physician to the *Hôtel-Dieu*, and he now lived mainly in the dissection-room. He is credited with having performed 600 autopsies in one year. He died with his last work uncompleted.

In 1800 Bichat published two important small books. The old humoral pathology was still influential, though G. B. MORGAGNI had emphasized that the seat of a disease was in the organs of the body. Bichat now investigated the structure of the body generally. By various processes, such as teasing or maceration, he broke up the organs into elementary types of material which he called 'membranes' or 'tissues'. He recognized twenty-one different tissues, and an organ might embrace several different tissues, forming a 'web'. In his book *Anatomie générale* (1801) Bichat claimed that a disease does not affect an organ as a whole, but only some of its constituent tissues. Bichat's work would have been facilitated had he used a microscope, but he distrusted that instrument. In his time it was little used, and the animal cell had not yet been discovered.

Bichat's work had great influence. It remains as the fundamental intermediate stage between the organ pathology of Morgagni and the cellular pathology of R. VIRCHOW.

H. E. Sigerist, *Great Doctors*. 1933. (Portrait.)
Bulletin de la Société Française d'Histoire de la Médicine, vol. 1, 1902 (reprint 1967).
N. Dobo and A Role, *Bichat: La Vie Fulgurante d'un Génie*. 1991.
Dictionary of Scientific Biography.

E A U

BICKFORD, WILLIAM Born in Devon, England, 1774 (baptised 23 January); died Tuckingmill, near Camborne, Cornwall, 1834 (buried 7 October). Inventor of safety fuse for explosives.

Though unconnected with Cornish mining, William Bickford, leatherseller and a steward of the Wesleyan society at Tuckingmill, was disturbed by the frequent accidents caused by the crude methods of shotfiring then employed. He sought to carry the flame surely and slowly to the charge by adding gunpowder to rope during its manufacture. After several attempts, flax yarn was successfully used to contain the gunpowder. To strengthen this loose rope another twist of rope was laid across the first; and the whole made

watertight with varnish or tar. The fuse was patented in September 1831, and in the manufacture commenced by Bickford and his son-in-law George Smith (1800–68) lay the origin of the highly successful Bickford-Smith fuse-making concern.

T. G. Tullock (Ed.), *The Rise and Progress of the British Explosives Industry*. 1909. (Portrait.)
I.C.I. Magazine, **34**, 258, 265, 1956. (Portrait.)
Dictionary of National Biography (Missing Persons). 1993.

W N S

BIFFEN, SIR ROWLAND HARRY Born at Cheltenham, Gloucestershire, England, 28 May 1874; died Cambridge, 12 July 1949. Geneticist and plant breeder.

After graduating from Cambridge University, Biffen joined a small expedition to Brazil, Mexico and the West Indies to study rubber production. On his return he was appointed University demonstrator in botany under H. Marshall Ward (1854–1905). In 1899 he became botanist to the recently formed School of Agriculture at Cambridge. At once he undertook a series of crop trials with varieties of cereals from many countries. His first major triumph was his discovery that the disease of wheat known as yellow rust was inherited as a simple Mendelian recessive. Biffen applied the study of heredity to the improvement of cultivated plants through hybridization. His *Mendel's Laws of Inheritance and Wheat Breeding (Journal of Agricultural Science*, 1905) exemplifies his pragmatic attitude.

In 1908 he became professor of agricultural botany, and when a Plant Breeding Institute was established at Cambridge in 1912 it was inevitable that he should be its first Director. Mainly through his efforts, agricultural botany evolved as a distinct field of study, and the earlier empirical approach to plant breeding was replaced by scientific method.

His advice was frequently sought; in 1926–27 he made a special study of the wheat-rust problem for the Government of Kenya. He was knighted in 1925, and his academic distinctions included Fellowship of the Royal Society (1914) which awarded him its Darwin Medal in 1920.

Obituary Notices of Fellows of Royal Society. 1950. (Portrait.)
Dictionary of National Biography.

R G C D

BIGELOW, ERASTUS BRIGHAM Born at West Boylestone, Massachusetts, USA, 2 April 1814; died Boston, Massachusetts, 6 December 1879. Inventor of mechanical carpet looms.

Bigelow's father struggled as a farmer, wheelwright, and chairmaker in rural Massachusetts. Before he was 20, Bigelow had many different jobs, among them farm labourer, clerk, violin player, and cotton-mill employee. In 1830 he went to Leicester Academy, Massachusetts, but could not afford to go on to Harvard. He sought work in Boston, New York, and elsewhere, making various inventions. The most important of these was the power loom of 1837 for making coach lace. This contained all the essential features of his carpet looms which he developed and patented two years later. He formed the 'Clinton' company for manufacturing carpets at Leicester, but the factory became so large that it gave its name to the town. The next twenty years saw various mechanical discoveries, while his range of looms was extended to cover Brussels, Wilton, tapestry, and velvet carpets. Bigelow has been justly described as the originator of every fundamental device in these machines, and at the Great Exhibition in England in 1851 it was declared that his looms made better carpets than any from hand looms. He also developed other looms for special materials.

He became a noted American economist, writing two books about tariff problems, advocating that the United States should not abandon its protectionist policies. In 1860 he was narrowly defeated in a Congress election, and the next year he was a member of the committee which established the Massachusetts Institute of Technology.

National Cyclopedia of American Biography, III. (Portrait.)

F. H. Sawyer, *Clinton Item*. 1927.

Dictionary of American Biography.

R L H

BINET, ALFRED Born at Nice, France, 8 July 1857: died Paris, 18 October 1911. Psychologist; pioneer in the development of mental testing.

Binet went to Paris in 1871 intending to become a lawyer. Impressed by the fame and personality of J. M. CHARCOT, he gave up this intention and studied first neurology and later psychology. He worked in the laboratory of physiological psychology at the Sorbonne (1889) and became its Director in 1895.

Binet was a prolific and somewhat prolix writer. With Henri Beaunis (1830–1921) he founded the *Année psychologique* in 1895, and from 1897 until his death was the editor of this annual and in it published much of his work. He was particularly interested in experimental and applied psychology and in the abnormal aspects of the subject. Several studies of hypnotism and hysteria were among his publications. The most notable of his contributions were investigations into the development and measurement of intelligence. In *L'étude expérimentale de l'intelligence* (1903) he described the intellectual processes of his two small daughters. He pursued this topic with T. Simon in *Les enfants anormaux* (1907), and in *Les idées sur les enfants* (1909). He is best remembered for the series of mental tests, devised in collaboration with Simon, which were first published in 1905. This was one of the first attempts to measure intellectual abilities and to define objective criteria of normal attainments in children of different ages.

M. H. Piéron, 'L'Oeuvre d'Alfred Binet', *Revue de Psychiatrie*, **16**, 244, 1912.

American Journal of Psychology, **23**, 140, 1912.

R. Martin, *Alfred Binet*. 1925.

C M

BIOT, JEAN BAPTISTE Born in Paris, 21 April 1774; died there, 3 February 1862. Pioneer of polarimetry.

Biot's career began with service in the artillery. On leaving, he entered the *École Polytechnique*, his first post after this being as teacher in a school at Beauvais. At the early age of 26 he was recalled to Paris, to occupy the chair of physics at the *Collège de France*. He became a member of the *Académie des Sciences* in 1808.

He accompanied J. L. GAY-LUSSAC on his first balloon ascent. He was nominated to the *Bureau des Longitudes,* and, in the company of D. F. J. ARAGO, he went to Spain to measure an arc of the meridian, the first of a number of important geodetic and astronomical expeditions, among them one to the Orkneys. Other subjects in his wide range were the refractive indices of gases (with Arago) and the composition of meteorites. He also studied the astronomy of the ancients, reporting notably on the celebrated Zodiac of Dendera.

His most influential work, gaining him the Rumford Medal of the Royal Society in 1840, was on optical activity. Some consequences of optical activity had previously been observed by Arago, but it was Biot who first recognized the phenomenon of the rotation of the plane of plane-polarized light. He first reported the phenomenon (1815) in oils of turpentine, laurel and lemon, not reporting it in sugar until 1818. He also characterized rotatory dispersion and noted anomalous rotation of tartaric acid in 1832.

From his work sprang polarimetry as an analytical method, and also the line of research on which Pasteur was to build so great a superstructure.

J. R. Partington, *A History of Chemistry*, vol. 4. 1964.

E. Picard, *La vie et l'oeuvre de J. B. Biot*. 1927.

M. Crosland, *The Society of Arcueil*. 1967. (Portrait.)

Endeavour. **21**, 63, 1962.

Dictionary of Scientific Biography.

F G

BIRDSEYE, CLARENCE Born in Brooklyn, New York, 9 December 1886; died Gloucester, Massachusetts, 7 October 1956. Pioneer of the modern deep-frozen food industry.

While Birdseye was working as a field naturalist and fur trader in Labrador he observed the methods adopted by the Eskimos for the long-term preservation of fish by freezing, and realised that it was the speed of freezing, rather than extra low temperatures, that kept the fish fresh. He bought a share in a Massachusetts fishery business with an investment of $7, and from 1916 to 1928 worked to improve techniques for the fast freezing of food. In 1924 he formed the General Seafoods Corporation which he sold for $22 million five years later, along with 168 quick-freeze patents. The company was renamed the General Foods Corporation, continuing to use the split name 'Birds Eye' as a trademark which is still one of the most popular for frozen foods of all kinds.

He later widened his interests, inventing a kickless harpoon and an anhydrous method for dehydrating foods, and becoming president of the Birdseye Electric Company (1935–38). In all, he was granted almost 250 US and foreign patents in the fields of food preservation and incandescent lighting.

Current Biography, 44–46, 1956 (Portrait.)

Who Was Who in America, **3**.

R M B

BIRINGUCCIO, VANUCCIO Born at Siena, Tuscany, Italy, 1480; died Rome, 1538/9. Mining engineer.

Little is known of Biringuccio's life, but his *De la Pirotechnia* (1540) ensures him lasting fame. This is an account, richly illustrated with woodcuts, of the techniques of his day for mining metalliferous ores and extracting the metals from them; it is comparable with the *De Re Metallica* (1555) of Agricola (Georg BAUER). In addition, it describes many of the industrial techniques of the day, including the militarily important manufactures of cannon and gunpowder. The title of the work is somewhat misleading, for it is only the tenth and final section that deals with what we would now regard as pyrotechnics.

As a young man, Biringuccio entered the service of Pendolfo Petrucci (1450–1511), the tyrant of Siena, by whom he was sent to Germany to study technological processes. Later he served the Duke of Parma, Alphonso I of Ferrara, and the Republic of Venice. Finally, he was Director of the Papal arsenal.

J. R. Partington, *A History of Chemistry*, vol. 3. 1962.

J. M. Stillman, *The Story of Early Chemistry*. 1924. (Reprinted 1960 as *The Story of Alchemy and Early Chemistry*.)

Isis, **2**, 90, 1914.

Dictionary of Scientific Biography.

T I W

BIRKELAND, KRISTIAN OLAF BERNHARD Born at Christiania (Oslo), Norway, 13 December 1867; died Tokyo, 15 June 1917. Chiefly remembered for his part in developing, with Samuel EYDE, the first commercially successful process for the fixation of nitrogen.

Birkeland studied physics in Paris, Geneva, and (briefly) under H. R. HERTZ at Bonn, and from 1898 held the chair of physics at the university in Christiania. His first interest was in mathematical physics; his solution of the Maxwellian equations appeared in the *Archives de Genève* in 1895. He headed three expeditions to study the Aurora Borealis, and established a geophysical observatory at 70°N.

At the end of the nineteenth century there was growing concern at the rapid depletion of natural sources of nitrogenous fertilizers for agriculture; Sir William CROOKES drew attention to this in a famous presidential address to the British Association in 1898. The question was also of great strategic importance, for nitric acid was essential for the manufacture of high explosives.

There was therefore growing interest in the possibility of 'fixing' atmospheric nitrogen, i.e. bringing it into chemical combination as a route to synthetic nitric acid. As early as 1784 Henry CAVENDISH showed that the nitrogen and oxygen of the air combined in an electric spark to form nitric oxide, and in 1895 Lord RAYLEIGH made use of this to isolate the rare gases of the atmosphere. Attempts were made to exploit the process industrially, but the first to achieve commercial success were Birkeland and Eyde. Norway was a natural site for this manufacture, as very cheap electricity is essential for its success. The Birkeland-Eyde process was soon overshadowed by an alternative one devised by Fritz HABER and Carl BOSCH.

Birkeland eventually moved to Cairo, partly for reasons of health and partly to resume his astronomical observations; he died while returning to Norway by a roundabout wartime route.

Nature, **99**, 349, 1917.

S. Mortensen and P. Vogt (Eds), *One Hundred Norwegians*. 1955.

Chemistry and Industry, 327, 1967.

T K D

BJERKNES, JACOB AALL BONNEVIE Born in Stockholm, 2 November 1897; died Los Angeles, USA, 7 July 1975. Meteorologist.

Jacob Bjerknes was a third-generation Norwegian scientist. His grandfather Carl Anton Bjerknes (1825–1903) was professor of physics in the University of Christiania (Oslo). His father, Vilhelm Frimann Koren Bjerknes (1862–1951), was also a physicist and Jacob was born while he was professor of applied mechanics and mathematical physics in the University of Stockholm (1895–1907). In 1907 the family returned to Christiania, which meanwhile (1905) had become the capital of a Norway independent of Sweden, where Vilhelm was appointed to a chair of mechanics and mathematical physics. Jacob entered Christiania University, gaining his doctorate in 1924.

They were in all respects a closely knit family. Vilhelm took up his father's interest in hydrodynamics and developed theories of atmospheric movements that he believed would be a sound basis for long-term weather forecasting: his work was supported by the Carnegie Foundation for nearly forty years. With his son Jacob he established a network of meteorological observing stations in Norway during the First World War, and from their results they had by 1919 formulated the concept of air masses – cold polar air masses and warm tropical ones – which substantially preserve their identity for long periods. These masses are separated by fronts. Jacob Bjerknes presented these ideas in 1919 in a pioneer paper 'On the Structure of Moving Cyclones' in *Geofysiske Publikasioner*.

In 1920 Jacob Bjerknes was appointed director of the Weather Forecasting Centre in Bergen and ten years later to the professorship of meteorology in the University there. During these years he established an international reputation and became a consultant to national meteorological offices in Britain, Switzerland, the United States and Canada. In 1940 he settled permanently in America – where he happened to be at the time of the German invasion of Norway – as professor of meteorology in the University of California, Los Angeles. There he was able to extend the range of his observation with the aid of unmanned balloons and, later, satellites. At the same time he extended his theories to include heat exchange between the atmosphere and the oceans. His mature conclusions were summarized in his *Dynamic Meteorology and Weather Forecasting* (1957), written with C. L. Godske. He took a particular interest in 'El Niño', a sudden warming of the sea off the west of Peru that profoundly influences the local fisheries. He studied, too, the relationship between atmospheric circulation in the equatorial Pacific region and weather in middle latitudes.

Under Bjerknes' leadership the department of meteorology at UCLA was one of the world's great centres for research and teaching in this field. During the Second World War it undertook a major training programme for more than a thousand weather officers in the US Army and Navy. In more than half a century of active research Bjerknes himself wrote more than 50 papers.

Bjerknes received honours from learned societies in many countries. In the United States he was awarded the Presidential Medal and an honorary degree of the University of California. Through-out his life he retained his interest in Norway and after the war made frequent visits there. He was awarded the Order of St Olav in 1947.

Jacob Aall Bonnevie Bjerknes: Selected Papers.
   1975.
Bulletin of the American Meteorological Society.
   1975.
University of California Obituaries. 1975.
Dictionary of Scientific Biography, Supp. II.

                                                                                                         T I W

BLACK, SIR JAMES WHYTE Born at Cowden-beath, Scotland, 14 June 1924. British pharmacol-ogist and Nobel Laureate.

After reading medicine at St Andrews Univer-sity, Black taught physiology at the Universities of Malaya (1947–50) and Glasgow (1950–58). Sub-sequently he left academia in order to direct phar-macological research in ICI (1958–64), Smith Kline (1964–73), and, finally, Wellcome, before (in 1984) becoming professor of analytical pharmacology at King's College Medical School in London. In 1948 the American pharmacologist, Raymond Ahlquist (1914–) suggested that different, alpha and beta, receptors in smooth muscle mediated the relaxing or contracting effect of hormones such as adren-aline. In 1964, together with W. Duncan, Black suc-ceeded in blocking the beta receptor sites with propranolol and so, in the case of heart muscle, reducing the heart's work load during hormonal stimulus. Propranolol and other so-called 'beta-blockers' revolutionized the clinical treatment of hypertension. By similar reasoning, in 1972, Black found that cimetidine (Tagamet) was an effective blocker of histamine receptors in the gut wall that were the principal sites of stomach ulcers. In 1988 Black shared the Nobel prize for physiology or medicine with the Americans Gertrude Elion (1918–) and George Hitchings (1905–) for their creation of designer drugs. He was elected FRS in 1976 and was knighted in 1981. He was appointed Chancellor of the University of Dundee in 1992.

New Scientist 22 October 1988, p. 26. (Portrait.)
Les Prix Nobel en 1988. 1989. (Portrait.)

                                                                                                         W H B

BLACK, JOSEPH Born at Bordeaux, France, 16 April 1728; died Edinburgh, 6 December 1799. Pioneer in chemistry of gases; originated theory of specific and latent heat.

Son of a Scots-Irish wine merchant settled in Bordeaux, Black was educated in Belfast, then (1746) at Glasgow University, studying first lan-guages and natural philosophy, then (1748) anat-omy and medicine under W. Cullen (1710–90), in whose laboratory he worked for three years. About 1751 he moved to Edinburgh, where, in 1754, he presented his MD dissertation *De humore acido a cibis orto, et magnesia alba* (On the acid humour arising from food, and on magnesia alba). The work described was extended in a paper of 1756. It con-stitutes a uniquely logical series of experiments on the alkalis and their relations with carbon dioxide ('fixed air'). It is a model of chemical experimenta-tion, being contrived in a cyclic form. For example: a weighed amount of limestone when heated is converted to quicklime; the quicklime when treated with water becomes slaked lime; when this

is boiled with mild alkali (potassium carbonate) the original weight of limestone is recovered. By similar experiments, in which the balance was continually used, he demonstrated a quantitative chemistry of the alkalis, and of the 'air' which entered into combination with them. This was one of the principal foundations of the quantitative chemistry which was built up over the next half century. One of its most important features was the demonstration that gas could be studied in combination by weight measurements. Black pre-ferred to call the particular gas he was dealing with 'fixed air' rather than invent a new one until more was known about the substance, but he had shown the way to the management of gases as distinct chemical entities. In 1756 he returned to Glasgow to succeed Cullen, whom he again succeeded at Edinburgh in 1766.

He published very little, his other great dis-covery being communicated only in his lectures. About 1763 he demonstrated the phenomenon of latent heat, that is, the heat necessary to produce a change of state from solid to liquid or liquid to vapour), and later established clearly the distinc-tion between heat and temperature, at the same time demonstrating the property of specific heat (the relative heat capacity of substances).

His lectures were greatly admired and well attended. He never published them, but many stu-dents' notes survive and a complete set was pub-lished by John Robison (1739–1805) in 1803. His lecture demonstrations were original and striking: for example, decanting 'fixed air' over a candle to extinguish it, and proving that exhaled breath con-tains fixed air by blowing through a tube into lime-water, causing it to become turbid. He never became a FRS, but founded a chemical society for his students, one of the first in the world.

W. Ramsay, *Life and Letters of Joseph Black.* 1918.
   (Portrait.)
H. Guerlac, *Isis*, **48**, 124, 433, 1957.
E. Robinson and D. McKie, *Partners in Science;*
   Letters of James Watt and Joseph Black. 1970.
A. R. C. Simpson (Ed.), *Joseph Black (1728–1799).*
   1982.
Dictionary of National Biography.
Dictionary of Scientific Biography.

                                                                                                         F G

BLACKETT, PATRICK MAYNARD STUART (BARON BLACKETT OF CHELSEA) Born in London, 17 November 1897; died there, 13 July 1974. Distinguished for his researches on cosmic rays; his development of operational research during the Second World War; and as one of the architects of post-war scientific and technological policy in Britain.

Blackett's early career gave little indication that he was to become one of the most distinguished scientists of the 20 Century. He entered Osborne Naval College as a cadet at the age of 13, but his training at Dartmouth was interrupted when war broke out in 1914. He was involved in action in the Falkland Islands and at the Battle of Jutland. In January 1919, with the other officers whose training had been interrupted by the war, he was sent to Cambridge for a course of general studies, but he soon resigned from the Navy in order to become a student of physics. In 1921 he began his scientific career under the direction of Lord RUTHERFORD at the Cavendish Laboratory.

Rutherford set Blackett the task of obtaining visible evidence of the disintegration of the nitrogen nucleus by fast α-particles using the cloud chamber technique. By 1924 he had photographed nearly half a million α-particle tracks, eight of which provided the unambiguous and visible evidence for the disintegration process. In 1932 G. P. S. Occhialini arrived from Italy and introduced the method of coincidence-counting of cosmic rays. Within a few months they had obtained the evidence for the existence of the positive electron.

In the year (1933) in which he was elected Fellow of the Royal Society he moved to Birkbeck College, London, as professor of physics. There he developed his researches on cosmic rays, and began his detailed studies of the energy spectrum. This soon led him into the centre of the controversy as to whether the quantum theory of radiation failed at energies greater than about 2×10^8 eV or whether a new type of penetrating particle with a mass intermediate between that of an electron and proton existed. In the autumn of 1937 Blackett moved from Birkbeck to Manchester succeeding W. L. BRAGG as Langworthy Professor of Physics. There he soon created a major research centre for cosmic rays.

Since 1935, as a member of the Air Defence Committee under H. T. TIZARD, Blackett had been deeply involved with the problem of the defence of the country against air attack. The Committee gave full backing to the development of radar but the internal conflict with F. A. Lindemann (later Lord CHERWELL) had the consequence that when Churchill became Prime Minister it was Lindemann who became the effective scientific adviser and the Tizard-Blackett group lost their great influence. Early in the war Blackett divided his time between Royal Aircraft Establishment (RAE) and various committees. He was involved with the design of the Mark 14 bombsight, but in the late summer of 1940 he became scientific adviser to General F. A. Pile, C-in-C Anti-Aircraft Command. In seven months he introduced fundamental changes in the use of the anti-aircraft guns and the associated radar.

In March 1941 the C-in-C Coastal Command, Air Marshal Sir Philip Joubert de la Ferté, took the initiative which led to Blackett's transfer to his staff and to the formation of the Operational Research Group which was to have far-reaching consequences on the operations of Coastal Command. After nine months, Blackett transferred to the Admiralty where he assembled an operational research group to deal with naval problems. He remained with the Admiralty until the European war was over and during those years he exerted an immense influence. A classic example concerns his analysis of the losses of ships in convoys in relation to the size and speed of the convoy. In 1943 he persuaded the Admiralty to increase the size of convoys, thereby saving some million tons of shipping. During these years he became involved in a bitter dispute with Cherwell about the use of heavy bombers.

His official connection with the development of atomic weapons began in the summer of 1940 when he became a member of the Maud Committee under G. P. THOMSON. Blackett dissented from the view of this Committee that Britain could produce an atomic bomb by 1943 at a cost of £5 million: his minority recommendation that the project should be discussed with the Americans was supported and promulgated by the Ministry. In August 1945 when the Prime Minister (Attlee) set up an Advisory Committee on Atomic Energy, Blackett became one of the scientific members. His view on the policy and international control of atomic weapons diverged rapidly and completely from the majority opinion. The publicity which he gave to his views in his book *Military and Political Consequences of Atomic Energy* (1948) was a source of great concern and annoyance to the UK and USA administrations since at that period his opinions appeared to be predominantly pro-Russian. He was excluded from the inner advisory circles of the Government for the next 16 years and for some time was not allowed entry to America. Ten years after the publication of this book many of Blackett's views were realized to be correct and he was recognized as an acute strategist.

In the summer of 1945 Blackett returned to Manchester and quickly re-established a powerful research group. He encouraged and supported Bernard Lovell (1913–   ) in the development of the researches at Jodrell Bank which subsequently became one of the formative elements in the new science of radio-astronomy. Although Blackett continued to exert a powerful influence on the cosmic ray researches in Manchester and elsewhere his own research interests soon turned to fundamental problems in magnetism. He revived an idea of A. Schuster (1851–1934) that a massive body has, in its own right, a magnetic moment, in addition to any effects produced by ferromagnetic materials or electric currents. He noticed that for the Earth and the Sun the magnetic moments were nearly proportional to the angular momenta, and when he learnt of H. D. BABCOCK's measurement of the magnetic field of the star 78-Virginis, Blackett believed that he had solved the problem of the origin of the magnetic field. His paper *The magnetic field of massive rotating bodies* (1947) had unexpected and far reaching consequences. As a test of his theory he suggested that a laboratory measurement on a rotating sphere could be decisive. In the following years Blackett revealed his superb experimental skill in the construction of a magnetometer which could detect fields of only 10^{ms9} to 10^{ms10} gauss.

By the spring of 1951 he had concluded that the effect did not exist. By that time his interest had shifted to palaeomagnetism, for which his new magnetometer was admirably suited. In 1951 he assembled a research group to study the magnetism of rocks and in a few years he concluded that 150 to 200 million years ago the land mass which now forms Britain was in a position near the Equator. By 1960 he had concluded that continental drift was by far the most likely explanation of the results of the rock magnetic measurements.

In 1953 Blackett succeeded Sir George Thomson as professor of physics at Imperial College. He retired in September 1965, but remained Emeritus Professor and a Senior Research Fellow until his death in 1974. That last decade saw the culmination of his political activities. He had emerged from the nadir of his political fortunes when Harold Wilson succeeded to the leadership of the

Labour Party in 1963. For the previous decade he had been the senior member of a group which evolved a scientific and technological policy for Britain. The Ministry of Technology, created after the Labour victory in 1964, evolved from the ideas of this group. Blackett served as deputy chairman of an Advisory Council on Technology but he soon lost a good deal of faith in the effectiveness of the new technological policies in the face of the industrial troubles with which they became involved. The climax of his career was reached in November 1965 when he was elected President of the Royal Society. Blackett was made a Life Peer in 1969 but spoke only four times in the House of Lords, mainly on the plight of the developing countries – a subject in which he had been passionately involved since a visit to India in 1947. He accepted Nehru's invitation to be his adviser on the research and development needs of the Indian armed forces and for the next 20 years Blackett was a frequent visitor to India. In this association with India Blackett found full expression for his passionate concern with the underdeveloped and the poor, and for his deep conviction that their problems could be solved by the application of science and technology.

Blackett was appointed Companion of Honour in 1965 and invested with the Order of Merit in 1967. He was richly endowed with many other distinctions. In 1948 he was awarded the Nobel prize for physics, and from the Royal Society the Royal Medal in 1940 and the Copley Medal in 1956. He held 20 honorary degrees. Blackett made outstanding contributions to the cause of human emancipation. It is remarkable that this can be said of a man who distinguished himself in three distinct fields of fundamental research; who made vital contributions to the war effort; and who exerted such a powerful influence on the policies of the post-war Labour Party.

Biographical Memoirs of Fellows of the Royal Society. 1975. (Portrait.)

H. Oxbury (Ed.), *Great Britons: 20th Century Lives.* 1985.

Dictionary of National Biography.

Tyler Wasson (Ed.), *Nobel Prize Winners.* 1987. (Portrait.)

ACBL

BLAGDEN, SIR CHARLES Born at Wotton-under-Edge, Gloucestershire, England, *c.*19 April 1748; died Arcueil, near Paris, 26 March 1820. Chemist.

Blagden was a medical man by training, taking the MD of Edinburgh University in 1768, after which he became an army surgeon, holding this position – at least in a titular capacity – until 1814. He was elected to Fellowship of the Royal Society in 1772, and was its Secretary from 1784 to 1797; he became an intimate of its great President, Sir Joseph BANKS. From 1782 to 1789 he was assistant to the eccentric Charles CAVENDISH, and in this capacity became involved in the great 'Water Controversy' concerning the relative claims of Cavendish, WATT, and LAVOISIER to have been first to discover the composition of water. It was through Blagden that Lavoisier learnt of Cavendish's important experiments on 'inflammable air' (hydrogen). Cavendish, a man of great wealth, gave Blagden an annuity of £500 and left him a legacy of £15,000. Blagden was a frequent visitor to Paris

and knew intimately the leading French scientists of the day; later, he unsuccessfully courted Lavoisier's widow, who ultimately married Count RUMFORD.

Blagden's own researches covered a wide field. He carried out considerable, and very accurate, researches on the freezing-points of solutions, discovering (1788) that the depression of the freezing-point is proportional to the concentration of the solution (Blagden's Law). He also investigated the phenomenon of super-cooling of water below its freezing-point without congelation. He also published important papers on the freezing-point of mercury and extended his interest to the restoration of faded writing. He was knighted in 1792.

Dictionary of National Biography.

V. J. R. Partington, *A History of Chemistry*, vols. 3 and 4. 1962, 1964.

F. H. Getman, *Osiris*, **3**, 69, 1937.

Dictionary of Scientific Biography.

TIW

BLAKESLEE, ALBERT FRANCIS Born at Geneseo, New York, 9 November 1874; died Northampton, Massachusetts, 16 November 1954. American botanist and geneticist.

Blakeslee graduated from Wesleyan University, Connecticut, in 1896 and then studied and instructed in botany at Harvard, where he received his PhD in 1904 and the Bowdoin Medal in 1905. Blakeslee held several academic appointments, including the professorship of botany at Connecticut Agricultural College from 1907 to 1914; after retirement in 1942 until his death he served as Visiting Professor of Botany and Director of the Genetics Experimental Station at Smith College, Northampton, Massachusetts. He made numerous and varied discoveries; his observations were shewd and accurate, but apart from his studies on fungi he never ventured far in formulating theories. His earliest discovery, made in 1904, was the phenomenon of heterothallism in common bread moulds (Mucorales), followed by his observation that sexual reproduction in fungi is restricted by genetic incompatibility. He commenced in 1924, and pursued for the rest of his life, his best-known researches on changes in arrangement of chromosomes. He showed that polyploidy can be induced in numerous plants with the aid of an alkaloid, colchicine, derived from the corm of the autumn crocus, *Colchicum autumnale.* This research made possible the commercial production of seeds giving rise to giant-size varieties of well-known flowering plants. He carried out other important genetic researches on chimaeras, and on the culture of excised plant embryos as a means of growing otherwise inviable hybrids. He investigated the inheritance of fragrance in plants and the faculties of taste and smell in man. He was a Fellow and President (1940) of the American Association for the Advancement of Science; an Honorary Fellow of the National Institute of Science of India; and in 1935 was elected a Foreign Member of the Linnean Society of London.

Nature, **174**, 1037, 1954.

New York Times, 17 November 1954. (Portrait.)

APG

BLANE, SIR GILBERT Born at Blanefield, Ayrshire, Scotland, 29 August 1749; died London, 26

June 1834. Physician and naval hygienist; responsible for the disappearance of scurvy from the Royal Navy.

Blane studied arts and medicine at Edinburgh, graduated as a doctor of medicine at Glasgow (1778), and then came to London with an introduction to Admiral Lord Rodney (1719–92). He went with Rodney on the expedition of 1779 to the West Indies, and was appointed physician to the fleet. He returned home in 1783. The officers of the fleet recommended Blane for a special reward, and this was granted in the form of a pension from the Crown. While on leave in London with Rodney, Blane was admitted a Licentiate of the Royal College of Physicians. In 1783 he was elected a physician to St Thomas's Hospital, a post which he resigned in 1795, when he was appointed one of the commissioners for sick and wounded seamen. His term of office ended in 1802. One of his most important official services related to the Walcheren Expedition (1810). Disease ravaged the troops who formed the expedition, and the Army Medical Board had lost the confidence of the Government. The War Office sent out Blane to report. It was decided to recall the expedition Blane was entrusted with the arrangements for bringing home the sick and wounded. A baronetcy was conferred on him (1812). On the accession of George IV he became one of his physicians in ordinary. He was elected Fellow of the Royal Society in 1784, and delivered its Croonian lecture in 1788.

Blane's most important work related to the health of seamen in the Royal Navy. Despite the researches of James LIND, scurvy was still rampant. In 1781 Blane presented a memorial to the Admiralty in which he showed that on the West Indies station one man in seven died of scurvy in one year. He advised the provision of fresh fruit and other antiscorbutics, and the enforcement of stricter discipline in matters of hygiene. Nine months later he reported that the mortality had been reduced to one in twenty. In 1780, Blane published a book on the best means of preserving the health of seamen, and in 1785, his classic work, *Observations on the Diseases of Seamen.* Blane was the one man who procured action against scurvy. In 1793 he recommended to one of the Lords of the Admiralty the use of lemon juice as a preventive. The results were so good that in 1795 regulations were issued for the universal use of lemon juice in the Royal Navy.

G. Wolstenholme and D. Piper (Eds), *The Royal College of Physicians of London: Portraits.* 1964.

Dictionary of National Biography.

E A U

BLOCH, FELIX Born in Zürich, Switzerland, 23 October 1905; died Zürich, 10 September 1983. Physicist who first used nuclear induction for measuring the magnetic properties of atomic nuclei, leading to the discovery of nuclear magnetic resonance.

Bloch intended originally to become an engineer, studying at the Swiss Federal Institute of Technology in Zürich, but after his first year he switched to physics, and later transferred to the University of Leipzig, where he was awarded a PhD in 1928. He left Germany when Hitler came to power in 1933, and in the following year joined the staff of Stanford University as associate professor of physics, becoming full professor two years later. By this time he had become particularly interested in nuclear magnetism, and in 1939 made the first accurate measurement of the magnetic properties of the neutron. During the Second World War he was engaged in research on radar, and as a result of this experience he realised that radio techniques could be applied to atomic nuclei. He used a radio transmitter in resonance with the precession frequency of the nucleus, and a radio receiver to detect the voltage induced in a coil surrounding the specimen. Measurements of the nuclear magnetic resonance yielded a great deal of hitherto unknown information about the structure of atomic nuclei; they also led to the construction of very sensitive magnetometers, and provided new data relating to the chemical composition and structure of gases, liquids and solids.

In 1952 Bloch shared the Nobel prize for physics with Edward PURCELL, who had independently developed a slightly different method of studying the magnetic properties of atomic nuclei. In 1954 Bloch was appointed the first director-general of CERN at Geneva.

Robert L. Weber, *Pioneers of Science: Nobel Prize Winners in Physics,* (2nd ed.) 1988. (Portrait.)

American Journal of Physics, 1970, **38**, 897–904.

M. Chodorow *et al.* (Eds), *Felix Bloch and Twentieth Century Physics.* 1980. (Portrait.)

Tyler Wasson (Ed.), *Nobel Prize Winners.* 1987. (Portrait.)

R M B

BODE, JOHANN ELERT Born at Hamburg, Germany, 19 January 1747; died Berlin, 23 November 1826. Astronomer, whose name is remembered in 'Bode's Law'.

Having been devoted to astronomy from youth, Bode at length exchanged teaching commerce for teaching mathematics and astronomy. An elementary treatise on astronomy (1768) proved immensely popular, going into ten editions, and in 1772 he was called to Berlin to assist in the computing of ephemerides. Two years later he founded the justly famous *Astronomisches Jahrbuch,* which he edited for more than half a century. From 1786 he was Director of the Berlin Observatory. His works included star maps, and catalogues of stars and nebulae.

In 1772 Johann Daniell Titius (1729–96), of Wittenberg, suggested a law which, much publicized by Bode, became known as 'Bode's Law'. The so-called 'law' is a fairly accurate summary of the mean radii of the planetary orbits. It was said that the successive mean solar distances of the planets, beginning with Mercury, are (in astronomical units) one-tenth of the sum of 4 and the appropriate term of the series 0, 3, 6, 12, 24, 48, 96. (The fifth term gives the mean distance of the asteroid belt, not then known.) The law covers the then undiscovered planets tolerably well. It was actually used by both J. C. ADAMS and U. Le VERRIER to give a first approximation to the orbit of Neptune. The first theory of the formation of the planetary system which came at all near to explaining this remarkably simple principle was C. F. von Weizsäcker's in 1943.

Soon after the discovery of Uranus by Sir William HERSCHEL, Bode suggested that the planet might have been previously catalogued as a star, and, in fact, no fewer than nineteen previous observations were identified, going back to that of '34 Tauri' in 1690 by John FLAMSTEED.

J. C. Poggendorff, *Biographisch-literarisches Handwörterbuch.* 1883–1903.

Allgemeine deutsche Biographie. 1876.

J D N

BODMER, SIR WALTER FRED Born at Frankfurt-am-Main, Hessen, Germany, 10 January 1936. Geneticist.

Bodmer was educated at Manchester Grammar School and Clare College, Cambridge, graduating in 1956. He was awarded a PhD three years later, and was a research fellow of Clare until he became a Fellow in 1961. From 1962 to 1970 he held posts in the department of genetics at Stanford University, California, before returning to England as professor of genetics at Oxford University 1970–9. His publications during this period included *The Genetics of Human Populations* (1971, 2nd ed. 1978) and *Genetics, Evolution and Man* (1976). He was director of research for the Imperial Cancer Research Fund 1979–91, and Director-General from 1991 onwards. His research was particularly concentrated on the immune response to cancer.

In 1990 Bodmer became president of HUGO (Human Genome Organization), an international council co-ordinating information from the various national projects to map and sequence the human genome. HUGO was set up in 1988 with offices in several countries and privately financed by the Wellcome Trust and the Howard Hughes Medical Institute. It also took over the task of organising the Human Gene Mapping Workshops which had been taking place since 1973. He was knighted in 1986.

Who's Who. 1993.

A P B

BOERHAAVE, HERMAN Born at Verhout, near Leiden, Netherlands, 31 December 1668; died Leiden, 23 September 1738. Chemist and physician.

Boerhaave was the son of a Dutch minister; as a young man it was his intention to enter the ministry. Not until his mid-twenties did he forsake this in favour of a career in medicine and chemistry. He entered Leiden University in 1684, and proved almost omnivorous so far as the available courses were concerned: he studied not only chemistry and medicine but philosophy, languages, and botany. He graduated in natural philosophy in 1687, and then resolved – rather surprisingly – to go to Harderwijk, a lesser university, to qualify in medicine, which he did in 1693. Returning to Leiden, he established himself in private practice and did some medical teaching. At the same time, he became an active practitioner of chemistry and began to teach this subject, too. In 1703 he was invited to a professorship at Groningen, but declined on the understanding that the first professorship to fall vacant in Leiden should be his; this proved to be the chair of medicine and botany (1709). In 1714 he was made professor of physic and in 1718 succeeded also to the chair of chemistry: thus he was simultaneously professor of chemistry, botany, medicine and clinical medicine.

Boerhaave is a somewhat anomalous figure in the history of science. A man of immense learning, and a gifted teacher, his contemporaries esteemed him as comparable to NEWTON. The Royal Society elected him to Fellowship in 1730, and a year before his death accorded him the honour of dedicating to him a volume of its *Philosophical Transactions*. He was elected to the French Academy in 1728. Yet no major discovery can be attributed to him and basically his reputation is that of an outstanding teacher and writer. Probably it would be fairer to compare him to Sir Joseph BANKS than to Newton. Banks, too, made no great discovery, but yet he profoundly influenced the European scientific scene for half a century.

In medicine, the substance of Boerhaave's lectures were published as the *Institutiones medicae* (1708) and the *Book of Aphorisms* (1709), and remained in use for a century. In botany, similarly, there appeared his *Index Plantarum* (1710) and an *Historia plantarum* – the last an unauthorized version of his lectures published by his students. But his greatest work, and his real claim to lasting fame, was his *Elementia chemiae* (1732), which he published to counteract an unofficial version of his chemical lectures, which he repudiated, published by his students in 1724 (as *Institutiones et experimenta chemiae*). This was immensely successful; it was translated into the principal European languages and remained in use for the best part of a century. Eighty years after it appeared it was described as 'the most learned and most luminous treatise on chemistry that the world has yet seen'. In an age when chemistry was still far removed from an exact science and still contained a considerable element of mysticism, Boerhaave's direct approach, was a most valuable alternative to the speculative and philosophical writings of most of his contemporaries.

H. E. Sigerist, *Great Doctors.* 1933.

E. Farber (Ed.), *Great Chemists.* 1961. (Portrait.)

G. Wolstenholme and D. Piper (Ed.), *The Royal College of Physicians of London: Portraits.* 1964.

G. A. Lindeboom, *Herman Boerhaave.* 1968.

Endeavour, **28**, 2, 1969.

W. A . Smeaton, *Endeavour* (New Series), **12**, 139, 1988. (Portrait.)

Dictionary of Scientific Biography.

T I W

BOHR, AAGE NIELS Born in Copenhagen, 19 June 1922. Physicist best known as co-developer of the collective model of nuclear structure.

Son of the well known physicist Niels BOHR, Aage Bohr was educated in Denmark. In 1943 the family left the country to escape the Nazis, and Aage worked with his father on the atomic bomb project, in particular at Los Alamos from 1944–5. In 1946 he returned to Copenhagen and joined the Institute of Theoretical Physics. He gained his PhD in 1954.

While visiting Columbia University, New York, in 1949–50, Aage shared an office with Leo James RAINWATER. Rainwater had proposed that discrepancies between experiment and the predictions of the shell model of nuclei (due to Maria GOEPPERT MAYER and Hans JENSEN (1907–1973)) could be explained if certain nuclei took on a spheroidal rather than a spherical shape. Bohr became interested in the dynamics of such nuclei, and back in Copenhagen, together with Ben MOTTELSON

(1926–), he developed the collective model of nuclei, in which the nucleons behave not only as individual particles but also act collectively. In 1975 Bohr, Mottelson, and Rainwater were awarded the Nobel prize for physics for this work.

From 1963 to 1970, Bohr was director of what is now the Niels Bohr Institute, succeeding his father who died in 1962. He later became director of the Nordic Institute for Theoretical and Atomic Physics (NORDITA), from 1975–1981.

Physics Today, December 1975. (Portrait.)
Les Prix Nobel en 1975. 1976. (Portrait.)
Tyler Wasson (Ed.), *Nobel Prize Winners.* 1987.
  (Portrait.)

C S

BOHR, NIELS Born in Copenhagen, 7 October 1885; died there, 18 December 1962. Formulated the quantum theory of the electronic structure of the hydrogen atom and of the origin of the spectral lines of hydrogen and helium.

Niels Bohr was the eldest son of Christian Bohr, professor of physiology in the University of Copenhagen. He studied at the University and obtained his Doctorate in 1911. He came to Manchester in March 1912 to work with E. RUTHERFORD, who had published (1911) his nuclear model of the atom to explain scattering of α-particles. The difficulty about this model, in which electrons circulate in orbits round the nucleus, was that on classical electrodynamic theory the electrons should irradiate and lose energy; they should therefore spiral into the nucleus. Bohr made the very daring step of postulating that the orbital momentum of the electron was quantized, and that radiation was emitted by quantum jumps only when a transition was made between one quantum orbit and another. This enabled him to interpret the spectra of hydrogen and to calculate the empirical constant $2\pi^2me^4/h^3$ of J. R. RYDBERG. This combination of classical mechanics with the quantum theory to describe the motion in the electronic orbit revolutionized atomic theory. Nevertheless, the theory was only slowly accepted by physicists; even Max PLANCK remained reluctant for a long time to accept the drastic break with classical physics to which his own quantum hypothesis seemed to lead. At the British Association in Melbourne in August 1914 Rutherford said: 'Niels Bohr has faced the difficulty of bringing in the idea of the quantum in a novel way.'

In the autumn of 1914 Bohr became Reader in Theoretical Physics at Manchester University, remaining there until 1916, when he returned to Copenhagen. In 1918 he became the first Director of the Institute for Theoretical Physics in the University of Copenhagen, an Institute which rapidly became a Mecca for theoretical physicists from all over the world. Bohr said himself that 'in these years a unique co-operation of the whole generation of theoretical physicists from many countries created step by step the logically consistent generalization of quantum mechanics and electromagnetics and has sometimes been designated as the heroic age in quantum physics. To everyone following this development it has been an unforgettable experience to witness how through the combination of different lines of approach and the introduction of appropriate mathematical methods

a new outlook emerged requiring the comprehension of physical experience.'

A major development of Bohr's philosophical views was put forward in a lecture to the International Physical Congress held at Como in September 1927. In this he introduced the idea of 'complementarity'. He pointed out the impossibility of any sharp separation between the behaviour of atomic objects and their interaction with the measuring instruments which served to define the conditions under which the phenomena appear. This principle was used to remove the difficulties and paradoxes in discussing the wave and particle aspects of electrons and protons.

In the 1930s Bohr took a great interest in the development of nuclear physics following the application of accelerators to transmutation of atomic nuclei. He produced one idea of outstanding importance in relation to the problem of collision of neutrons with nuclei. He pointed out that a nucleus must be regarded as a cluster of many particles, protons and neutrons, all strongly coupled together like the molecules in a drop of water. From this it followed that the effectiveness of neutrons in collisions would not depend sensitively on their energy and that the radiative capture of neutrons should be a rather rare event. The theory explained the many extremely sharp resonances in the cross-section for neutron collisions as due to quantum levels of high excitation energy. This picture of the compound nucleus had a profound influence on the theory of nuclear reactions.

Bohr also took a great interest in the mechanics of uranium fission. His paper with G. V. Wheeler in 1939 showed in detail how to understand the competition between the decay of the compound nucleus by fission, radiation, and neutron emission, as well as the different behaviour of fast and slow neutrons and the parts played by the two uranium isotopes. In particular, he showed with Wheeler that it was mainly the uranium isotope U235 which was fissioned by slow neutrons, whilst the U238 isotope would usually absorb the neutrons without fission. This led to the realization that, in general, isotope separation to produce U235 would be necessary to produce a fast chain reaction.

Bohr remained in Copenhagen until the autumn of 1943, when he was in danger of imprisonment as a patriot. However, he became aware of this intention and escaped with his family in overcrowded fishing boats to Sweden. After his arrival in Stockholm, the British authorities arranged to transport Bohr and his younger son Aage BOHR to London. On 6 October 1943 he was flown in an unarmed Mosquito to England.

After the resumption of co-operation in atomic energy between the United States and the United Kingdom in September 1943, it was arranged that Bohr should visit the United States as a consultant to the directorate of Tube Alloys, as the UK organization was known, as part of the UK team. Bohr spent a good deal of time in Washington and at Los Alamos, where he made some technical contributions to the atomic bomb development. He was also useful as an elder statesman in the supercharged atmosphere of Los Alamos, which was full of scientists of great distinction.

Bohr's main interests were, however, in the implications of atomic bombs for the future of the world, and in February 1944 he wrote to Sir John Anderson (Lord Waverley (1882–1958)), the UK Minister in charge of the Tube Alloys project, expressing his concern about the future control of these enormous powers. An interview with (Sir) Winston Churchill was arranged, but was not successful.

When Bohr returned to Copenhagen after the war these international problems remained one of his principal preoccupations, and he continued to discuss them with Sir John Anderson on his visits to England. In 1950 he published in a letter to the United Nations a plea for 'an open world where each nation can assert itself solely by the extent to which it can contribute to the common culture and is able to help others with experience and resources'.

During the 1950s Bohr took a leading part in the foundation of CERN (the European Centre for Nuclear Research at Geneva) and was a Council member for most of the rest of his life. He was also responsible for the foundation of a joint Scandinavian Research Institute in Theoretical Physics ('NORDITA') built alongside his own Institute.

Bohr became chairman of the Danish Atomic Energy Commission on its foundation, and was responsible for the initiation of the RISO Atomic Research Establishment, which has three nuclear reactors; this was a very ambitious project for a country of the size of Denmark. He was President of the Royal Danish Academy of Sciences from 1939 until his death.

Whilst at the Lindau Conference for Nobel Laureates in June 1962 Bohr had a slight stroke, but appeared to have made a good recovery. On Friday, 18 November 1962, only two days before his death, he chaired a meeting of the Danish Royal Academy of Sciences.

Biographical Memoirs of Fellows of the Royal Society. 1962.

S. Rozental (Ed.), *Niels Bohr; his Life and Work seen by his Friends and Colleagues.* 1967.

A. Pais, *Niels Bohr's Times in Physics, Philosophy and Polity.* 1991.

Tyler Wasson (Ed.), *Nobel Prize Winners.* 1987. (Portrait.)

Dictionary of Scientific Biography.

J D C

BOLLSTÄDT, ALBRECHT VON *See* ALBERTUS MAGNUS.

BOLTWOOD, BERTRAM BORDEN Born at Amherst, Massachusetts, USA, 27 July 1870; died Maine, 15 August 1927. Pioneer in radiochemistry.

The son of a lawyer, Boltwood studied chemistry at Yale (1889–92) and Munich (1892–4), returning to Yale to teach analytical and physical chemistry. From 1900 to 1906, mostly in partnership with the geologist J. H. Platt, he worked as a private consultant. Mineralogical analysis doubtless stimulated his interest in radioactive minerals, and he deduced that radium is a disintegration product of uranium from the ratio of their occurrence in ores. He suggested also that their ultimate degradation product is lead, and showed how the age of uranium minerals may be calculated from their lead content. He demonstrated that actinium is formed from uranium, but by a different line from

radium. Other work included a study of radioactivity in natural waters.

Boltwood became professor of physics at Yale in 1906, and in 1909–10 spent a year with Ernest RUTHERFORD at Manchester. Returning to Yale, he became professor of radiochemistry (1910) and of chemistry (1918). His most notable work in this period was the discovery of 'ionium', a precursor of radium and separable from actinium. His efforts to separate it from thorium were unavailing, however, since the two substances are isotopes. This was one of the earliest observations that led to the concept of isotopy.

Boltwood's work was widely respected. His last years were clouded by illness brought on, it appears, by overstrain, and three years after a breakdown he took his own life.

American Journal of Science, **15** (5), 189, 1928. (Portrait.)

Dictionary of American Biography.

Journal of Chemical Education, **6**, 602, 1929; **10**, 82, 1933. (Portraits.)

Nature, **121**, 64, 1928.

Dictionary of Scientific Biography.

C A R

BOLTZMANN, LUDWIG Born in Vienna, 20 February, 1844; died Duino, near Trieste, Italy, 5 September 1906. Celebrated for his contribution to the kinetic theory of gases and to statistical mechanics.

After studying at the University of Vienna, where he took his doctorate in 1866, Boltzmann successively held professorships in Graz (1869–73, in theoretical physics); Vienna (1873–6, in mathematics); Graz (1876–9, in experimental physics); and thereafter in theoretical physics at Munich (1889–93); Vienna (1894–1900); Leipzig (1900–2); and Vienna (1902–6). He was elected FRS in 1899.

The beginning of Boltzmann's scientific career, around 1866, belonged to the most creative and revolutionary period in theoretical physics since the appearance of Newton's *Principia* some two centuries earlier; the pioneer work of Sadi CARNOT had been transformed and completed by the formulation of the second law of thermodynamics by R. J. E. CLAUSIUS and W. THOMSON (Lord Kelvin) on the basis of the mechanical theory of heat; Clausius and J Clerk MAXWELL had made large steps towards the foundation of a sophisticated kinetic theory of gases based on the laws of dynamics and probability theory, and Maxwell had made a beginning to his new theory of electromagnetism. Boltzmann's great talents as a theoretical physicist were largely devoted to these three fields. In electromagnetism he was one of the small number of Continental scientists who early recognized the importance of Maxwell's work, which he then expounded in lectures and in a treatise of his own (*Vorlesungen über Maxwell's Theorie*, 1891). His experimental determination of the dielectric constant of a gas provided one of the first verifications of Maxwell's theory. He made fundamental contributions to the kinetic theory of gases, especially in regard to viscosity and diffusion, and he introduced the so-called Maxwell-Boltzmann integro differential equation governing the change in distribution of atoms due to collisions. Much of his work in this subject was published together in his *Vorlesungen über Gastheorie* (2 vols, 1896, 1898).

In thermodynamics he is remembered by his characteristically ingenious derivation of the law of black-body radiation formulated by J. STEFAN. Perhaps his most original contribution to science was his profound intuition – ridiculed at the time by the energeticist school headed by W. F. OSTWALD – that thermodynamic phenomena were the macroscopic reflection of atomic phenomena regulated by mechanical laws and the play of chance. This belief he illustrated by his work on the equipartition of energy and his attempted derivation, dating from his first published paper in 1866, of the second law of thermodynamics. Boltzmann was thus the founder of the modern subject of statistical mechanics, and although he never achieved a satisfactory statistical-mechanical derivation of the second law of thermodynamics, his attempts to do so, including his discussion of irreversibility and his correlation of entropy with probability, were of decisive importance in the later developments of the subject at the hands of Willard GIBBS, Max PLANCK, and other workers.

Nature, **74**, 569, 1906.
E. Broda, *Ludwig Boltzmann*. 1955.
R. Dugas, *La Théorie physique au sens de Boltzmann*. 1959.
W. Stiller, *Ludwig Boltzmann, Altmeister der Klassischen Physik*. 1991.
Physics Today, **45**, 44, 1992.
Dictionary of Scientific Biography.

J W H

BOLYAI, JOHANN (BOLYAI JÁNOS) Born at Kolozsvár, Hungary (now Romania), 18 December 1802; died Maros-Vásárhely, 27 January 1860. A discoverer of non-Euclidean geometry.

Johann Bolyai was the son of the mathematician Wolfgang Bolyai (Bolyai Farkas), by whom he was instructed in mathematics from an early age. Taking a course (1817–22) at the Royal College for Engineers at Vienna (from which he took his commission in the Austrian Army), he met another mathematician, Karl Szász, who shared his interest in the theory of parallels. Before 1820 it seems that Bolyai hoped to discover a proof of the parallel postulate of EUCLID, as many had tried before him. He now, however, set about formulating an 'absolute theory of space', using Euclidean methods, but keeping an open mind about the truth or falsity of the parallel postulate itself. By 1823 he was convinced of the legitimacy of discarding the postulate, and had found a formula relating the 'angle of parallelism' of two lines with a term characterizing the lines. Like N. I. LOBACHEVSKI, he considered only hyperbolic geometry – not, of course, using the name nor realizing the alternative. In 1823 he sent a copy of his work to his father, who added it as an appendix to his own book *Tentamen Juventum* (1831). The appendix points out that Euclidean space is a limiting case of his own, and introduces formulae involving what was later called the space-constant. His treatment is less analytical than Lobachevski's, and more concerned with the logical status of his work. A copy of the work was sent to K. F. GAUSS, who claimed to have been thinking on the same lines for some thirty years.

Bolyai continued to work at his absolute geometry, trying in particular to prove rigorously that Euclid's postulate was independent of the remaining postulates and axioms. He never proved this, and indeed for a time he thought that he had proved the absolute validity of the parallel postulate. He learned of Lobachevski's work on the same subject only in 1848. He was never reconciled to the thought of his rivals, and had some hard things to say about them. His haughty spirit was, in fact, renowned, costing him his retirement from the Army in 1833. He is reputed to have engaged thirteen cavalry officers in duels on a single day, leaving thirteen adversaries on the square, interspersing the duels with violin solos.

P. Stäckel (Ed.), *Wolfgang and Johann Bolyai, Geometrische Untersuchungen*, part 1. 1913.
R. Bonola, *Non-Euclidean Geometry*. 1906.
Dictionary of SCientific Biography.

J D N

BONDI, SIR HERMANN Born in Vienna, 1 November 1919. Theoretical astrophysicist, best known for having helped to develop the 'steady state' theory of the origin of the Universe.

Having acquired an early interest in mathematics, Bondi entered Cambridge University where his talent was soon recognised and he was awarded an exhibition in his first year. While interned as an 'enemy alien' in 1940 he gained his BA, and also met Thomas GOLD who became his close friend and collaborator. He was allowed to return to Cambridge in 1941, and soon afterwards met Fred HOYLE, with whom both he and Gold theorised about cosmology, and in particular the origin of the Universe. They were not satisfied with the currently popular 'big bang' explanation for the origin of the expanding Universe, and in 1948 they proposed the alternative 'steady state' theory.

At the time it was consistent with practically all that was known about the Universe, and during more than a decade of heated controversy astronomers were unable to decide which of the two theories was the more credible. In 1965, however, PENZIAS and R. W. WILSON discovered the universal background radiation predicted by George GAMOW which could readily be accounted for as a consequence of the 'big bang'. Since then, almost all the advances in our understanding of the Universe have pointed firmly towards a 'big bang', of one kind or another, as its origin.

Bondi became a British citizen in 1947, and after a short stay in the United States returned to England to take up the chair of Applied Mathematics at King's College, London, in 1954. He was elected Fellow of the Royal Society in 1959, and has served as scientific adviser to several government departments; he was knighted in 1973. Since 1983 he has been Master of Churchill College, Cambridge.

Biographical Encyclopedia of Scientists. 1981.
D. Abbott (Ed.) *Biographical Dictionary of Scientists: Astronomers*, 1984.
Who's Who. 1993.

R M B

BONNET, CHARLES Born at Geneva, Switzerland, 13 March 1720; died there 20 June 1793. Swiss naturalist.

Bonnet, a member of a wealthy family, originally studied law, but eventually devoted himself entirely to natural history. In this he was largely influenced by R. A. F. De RÉAMUR. His most lasting work lay in the field of insect biology, as can be seen in such publications as his *Traité d'insectologie* (1745). In this field he made a number of important observations – including many studies on the metamorphosis of insects – but especially important were his observations on parthenogenetic reproduction. By studying the reproduction of aphids he established that a number of females, without being fertilized, produced live offspring.

Bonnet, in fact, made many contributions to the subject of the development of animals and became involved in the question as to whether animals were 'preformed' or whether they developed epigenetically. He himself held a theory of preformation which argued that every female contained the 'germs' of all subsequent generations.

Owing to an eye disease, Bonnet turned to the study of botany, where he made many contributions especially in studies on nutrition. These formed the basis of his *Recherches sur l'usage des feuilles des plantes* (1754). In his later years he became a speculative thinker. In fact, much of his scientific writing shows the same tendency, and though many of his views have not stood the test of time he had a considerable impact on eighteenth-century science.

E. Nordenskiöld, *The History of Biology.* 1929.

L. C. Miall, *The Early Naturalists: Their Lives and Work (1530–1789).* 1912.

R. Saviez, *Mémoires autobiographique de Ch. Bonnet de Genève.* 1948.

Dictionary of Scientific Biography.

J K C

BOOLE, GEORGE Born at Lincoln, England, 2 November 1815; died Blackrock, near Cork, Ireland, 8 December 1864. Chiefly remembered for his work in mathematical logic.

Boole was the son of a small shopkeeper and was largely self-educated. He first studied the classics, turning later to mathematics, in which he received his first lessons from his father. After some years as a school teacher his mathematical reputation resulted in his appointment to the chair of mathematics at Queen's College, Cork (1849), where he remained for the rest of his life.

Boole's first paper, entitled 'Theory of analytical transformations', was published in the *Cambridge Mathematical Journal* for 1839, edited by D. F. Gregory (1813–44). This both earned him the friendship of Gregory and introduced him to a large public. At the same time it set a pattern for his first important discovery (1841), namely that a linear homogeneous transformation of the variables in a quadratic form converts the form into a second, with discriminant equal to the original discriminant multiplied by a factor depending only on the coefficients of the transformation. This extension of a simpler result obtained by J. L. LAGRANGE in 1773 was accompanied by a result in which the notion of 'joint invariance' first occurs. In the following year he discovered the first covariants, and for the rest of the century gave algebraists their taste for the theory of algebraic forms – the first outstanding names here being those of A. CAYLEY and J. J. SYLVESTER.

Boole wrote many articles, but only two books of any length on mathematics, and two on logic. The first two, a well-known *Treatise on Differential Equations* (1859) and *Treatise on the Calculus of Finite Differences* (1860), were unusual in exploiting to the full the calculus of operators, rigorously distinguished from their operands. Gregory's influence was evident here. Boole's name will be longest remembered, however, in connection with mathematical logic and Boolean algebra. He realized the possibility of an algebra of entities that were not in any sense numbers, and that the laws which hold for different types of numbers need not all be valid in a system not applicable to numbers. His system of mathematical logic first appeared in a pamphlet (1847), and was given a more satisfactory form in *An Investigation of the Laws of Thought on which are Founded the Mathematical Theories of Logic and Probabilities* (1854). Boole's mathematical logic is so different from anything that had gone before that it is impossible to describe his contribution briefly. It is interpretable as a calculus of classes (with operations of complementation, logical sum and product, and so on), and is isomorphic with a selected part of the functional calculus of first order. The term 'Boolean algebra' is usually reserved when the system is uninterpreted.

W. Kneale, 'Boole and the Revival of Logic', *Mind*, **57**, 149, 1948.

A. Macfarlane, *Lectures on Ten British Mathematicians of the Nineteenth Century.* 1919. (Portrait.)

Notes and Records of the Royal Society of London, **12**, 44, 1956.

Dictionary of National Biography.

Dictionary of Scientific Biography.

J D N

BORDA, JEAN CHARLES DE Born at Dax, Landes, France, 4 May 1733; died Paris, 20 February 1799. Nautical astronomer and mathematician.

Borda was educated at La Flèche (as were M. Mersenne (1588–1648) and R. DESCARTES), after which he began a career at the Bar, turned to mathematics teaching, and then obtained a commission in the cavalry. As a military engineer he devoted himself to harbour construction; problems of ballistics (a memoir of 1756 on this subject earned him membership of the Academy of Sciences); and finally to experiments in hydraulics. After the Battle of Hastembeck, at which he was present, he entered the Navy (1767). In 1782, commanding a vessel in the American War, he was captured, with his frigate, and taken to England. He returned almost immediately on parole to France. After the Revolution he played a leading part in establishing the decimal system of weights and measures, the word 'metre' being his. He was indeed associated closely with J. B. J. DELAMBRE and P. F. A. Méchain (1744–1804) in determining the arc of the meridian on which the standard metre was based.

Borda made a number of small improvements to existing nautical astronomical instruments (quadrant, reflecting and repeating circles, etc., the latter finding a use in crystallography), but his most important work was in hydraulics. This was done, for the most part, in his early twenties, while at Dunkirk. He investigated the resistance offered by fluids to objects of different geometrical shapes, using a rotating-arm apparatus (publications of 1763 and 1767). By these means he confirmed the prevalent theory that the resistance is proportional to the square of the relative velocity. He showed that higher powers may be involved if surface waves are produced. But he perpetuated the fallacy that, since a sphere and a hemisphere with the convex side upstream experience much the same drag, therefore it is the shape of the front, rather than that of the rear, that is significant in all cases.

Better remembered is his theoretical and experimental analysis (published 1766) of the efflux problem, on which the findings of J. BERNOULLI and J. Le R. D'ALEMBERT did not agree. Borda introduced the concept of elementary stream-tubes, rather than normal slices, and showed that, in addition to the contraction of the jet, energy loss on efflux must be taken into account when formulating the discharge velocity.

J. B. Biot, 'Notice sur Borda', *Mémoires de l'Académie des Sciences*, **4**, 1814.

H. Rouse and S. Ince, *History of Hydraulics*. 1957 and 1963. (Portrait.)

Dictionary of Scientific Biography.

J D N

BORDET, JULES JEAN BAPTISTE VINCENT

Born at Soignies, Belgium, 13 June 1870; died Ixelles, 6 April 1961. Famed for his studies on immunology.

Bordet, son of a schoolmaster, graduated in medicine from the Free University of Brussels in 1892. Before 1901, when he became Director of a new bacteriological institute in Brussels (named the Pasteur Institute in 1903), he had worked for some years at the Pasteur Institute in Paris. In 1907 he was appointed professor of bacteriology in the Free University of Brussels.

Because of his wide range, Bordet's scientific career is not easy to summarize in a short notice, even though most of his research falls neatly into the following four areas of study: bacteriophages, blood coagulation, whooping-cough, and immunology. Many of his studies were carried out with co-workers and not the least of his influence was his impact as teacher and research director.

Bordet, in 1906, was the first to culture the causative organism of whooping-cough, and, subsequently, he developed a vaccine which had some beneficial effects on the disease. The whooping-cough organism used to be known as the Bordet-Gengou bacillus after its discoverers. His work on bacteriophages and blood coagulation provided much basic information about the nature and mechanism of these processes.

But his most far-reaching work was in immunology, for which he was awarded a Nobel prize in 1919. One of his best-known discoveries, on which he first published in 1895, was that for lysis or destruction of an invading bacterium by the host organism two substances are required: a relatively stable, specific antibody and a non-specific thermolabile substance (now known as the complement). The complement is present in both immune and non-immune sera, but antibodies only in immune sera. This fundamental observation had led to the knowledge of many useful immunological reactions. Bordet himself showed that one could differentiate between apparently related bacterial species; for example, complement-free serum from an animal immunized against cholera would agglutinate cholera bacteria but not closely related organisms.

One of the most important tests, depending on knowledge of the complement, is the Wassermann test for syphilis (see A. von WASSERMANN), which depends on the detection of the antibodies in the serum of a syphilitic. Bordet studied many other reactions still used by immunologists – agglutination, agglutinin-absorption, precipitation, etc. – making important contributions to each. His exacting techniques, with a clear understanding of the need for proper controls, did much to establish the science of immunology.

Biographical Memoirs of Fellows of the Royal Society. 1962. (Portrait.)

Journal of General Microbiology, **29**, 1, 1962.

Dictionary of Scientific Biography.

Tyler Wasson (Ed.), *Nobel Prize Winners*. 1987. (Portrait.)

J K C

BORELLI, GIOVANNI ALFONSO

Born at Castelnuovo, Naples, Italy, 28 January 1608; died Rome, 31 December 1679. The founder of iatrophysics.

Borelli's father was probably an officer who had served in the armies of Philip III of Spain. Little is known of Borelli's early life, and it is doubtful whether he studied medicine professionally. He certainly studied mathematics at Rome under Benedetto Castelli (1577–1644). Before 1640 he was called to the chair of mathematics at Messina. In 1642 he made a prolonged visit to Florence to meet GALILEO and Evangelista TORRICELLI, but Galileo died in the same year. In 1656 Borelli was called to the chair of mathematics at Pisa, and later in the year M. MALPIGHI was also appointed to a chair there. The two men became friendly and it is probable that Borelli now studied anatomy. Both men were leading members of the *Accademia del Cimento*, founded at Florence in 1657. At Pisa, Borelli published mathematical, physical, and astronomical works, but his lectures dealt also with the subject of his *De motu animalium* ('On the Movement of Animals'), which he was then writing. In 1668 he accepted a recall to his chair at Messina, but six years later he was suspected of political conspiracy and he fled as an exile to Rome. There he was befriended by the ex-Queen Christina of Sweden.

Borelli's most influential work was his *De motu animalium*. Although much of this was written when he was at Pisa, it was not quite complete at his death, and was published posthumously in 1680–1. This book is more than its title indicates, as it is really a treatise on those parts of physiology that could be dealt with by Borelli's method.

The first part of the work treats of the movements of individual muscles and groups of muscles. These are treated geometrically on mechanical principles, and articulations are similarly studied. The first part also deals with posture in man and animals, and also flight and swimming. Probably no single individual has ever studied these matters as successfully as Borelli.

In the second part Borelli dealt with the essential cause of contraction in all muscles. With N. STENO he recognized that the muscular fasciculi are the contracting elements, and that the fibres of the tendons play no part. He thought that, as the contraction of the heart muscle obliterates the ventricular cavities, the volume of a muscle must increase on contraction. He concluded that contraction was due to a sudden fermentation in the muscle, which was triggered off by a physical reaction travelling from the brain in the nerve to the muscle. He calculated the forces exerted by various muscles on contraction. He held that the continuous flow of blood from arteries to veins was due to the elastic reaction of the arterial walls. He rightly concluded that in inspiration the contraction of the respiratory muscles enlarges the capacity of the chest and that air enters to fill the enlarged space in the lungs; when the contraction ceases the chest wall falls in and expiration results. He held that, in animals other than fishes and birds of prey, digestion is a physical process of trituration, due to the movements of the stomach, and that chemical ferments play no part.

M. Foster, *History of Physiology*. 1911.

M. Neuburger and J. Pagel, *Handbuch der Geschichte der Medizin*, vol. 2. 1903.

A. Castiglioni, *History of Medicine*. 1947. (Portrait.)

Dictionary of Scientific Biography.

E A U

BORN, MAX Born at Breslau, Silesia, (then in Germany), 11 December 1882; died Göttingen, 5 January 1970. Theoretical physicist: a founder of quantum mechanics and the originator of its probabilistic interpretation.

Born was the son of a distinguished embryologist, Gustav Born, who was professor of anatomy in the University of Breslau, and of Margarete (née Kaufmann) from whom he probably inherited his love of music. On his father's advice he attended courses at Breslau University on a wide range of subjects in both the sciences and the arts, including philosophy. He also studied at Heidelberg and Zürich, concentrating on mathematics. At Heidelberg he met James FRANCK who was to become his life-long friend and his colleague at Göttingen, the university to which Born first went in 1904 on learning that it was the Mecca of German mathematics. His principal teachers were David Hilbert (1862–1943) and Hermann MINKOWSKI, but he also attended lectures by the philosopher Edmund Husserl (1859–1938), although he adhered neither to his nor to any other philosophical school. He also met the Greek mathematician Constantin Caratheodory (1873–1950), and their discussions on the foundations of thermodynamics led some years later to the latter's famous mathematical reformulation of the subject.

In order to learn more about fundamental problems in physics, Born spent six months in 1907–8 as an advanced student at Caius College, Cambridge, where he received much stimulation from the lectures and demonstrations given by J. J. THOMSON. Soon after returning to Breslau he discovered the 1905 paper on special relativity by EINSTEIN. By combining Einstein's ideas with Oskar Minkowski's mathematical methods, he found a new and better way to calculate the electromagnetic mass of the electron. As a result, Minkowski invited him to Göttingen in December 1908 to assist him in his work on relativity. Unfortunately, Minkowski died the following month, after an appendicitis operation. Born remained in Göttingen and in due course was offered a lectureship (*Privatdozent*) by Woldemar Voigt (1850–1919), whose course in optics he had attended as a student. Until 1913 – when he married Hedwig Ehrenberg, daughter of the professor of law at Göttingen – he shared a house with Theodor von Karman (1881–1963) with whom he worked on the theory of crystal structure and founded the subject of lattice dynamics in a joint paper published in 1912. This theoretical work was based on the assumption that the lattice structure of crystals is a physical reality, even though the experimental proof of this by M. T. F. von LAUE and by W. H. BRAGG and W. L. BRAGG had not then been given.

The main application of crystal dynamics initially was to the theory of specific heats. Although the dynamical part of this work was based on the classical physics of vibrating systems, its application to thermal properties depended on the quantum idea first put forward in 1900 by Max PLANCK. Born's work on the specific heat of solids opened up for him the two main lines of his subsequent research – lattice dynamics and quantum theory. His first objective was to derive all crystal properties on the basis of a lattice whose particles could be displaced by internal forces. Born proved that the vibrational spectrum predicted by lattice dynamics consisted of two types, optical and acoustical, the latter being associated with low-frequency vibrations. In 1914 he applied his ideas to diamond, the crystal structure of which had recently been established by the Braggs. He also incorporated the theory of electromagnetic waves in crystals developed by P. Ewald (1888–1985).

The outbreak of war in 1914 coincided with Born's acceptance of a chair in the University of Berlin. In 1915 he was commissioned in the artillery and assigned to research on sound ranging. At this time he became friendly with Einstein who had recently arrived in Berlin and was perfecting his general theory of relativity. In 1919 Born exchanged chairs with von Laue in Frankfurt-am-Main, and two years later accepted the post of Director of the Physical Institute at the University of Göttingen, but persuaded the authorities to appoint James Franck to take charge of the experimental side.

At Göttingen, Born's main interest soon turned to quantum theory, and he was particularly fortunate in having as his assistants Werner HEISENBERG, Wolfgang PAULI and Pascual JORDAN. In 1925, starting from the principle of rejecting certain unobservable properties of electronic orbits, Heisenberg developed a new formalism for quantum mechanics which Born recognized as equivalent to matrix algebra. The new theory was developed systematically in a famous paper by Born, Heisenberg, and Jordan (1902–1980). Shortly afterwards Erwin SCHRÖDINGER formulated his wave mechanics, which he later showed was mathematically equivalent to quantum mechanics. Although Schrödinger believed that he had reinstated classical continuity in physics, Born was convinced by Franck's experiments on atomic and molecular collisions of the essential role of the particle idea and he sought to reconcile it with the wave concept. He found the connecting link in probability. He suggested that the square of the psi-function in Schrödinger's wave-equation represents probability density in configuration space. By describing collision processes as scattering of waves, Born's idea was confirmed and won general acceptance, although nearly thirty years were to elapse before this fundamental contribution to physics received, in 1954, its due recognition by the award to Born of a Nobel prize for physics.

In the later 1920s Born's department became a world centre of attraction for theoretical physicists and the resulting strain on his health forced him to interrupt his teaching and research for a year. During this time of reduced activity he wrote a masterly major treatise on optics (*Optik*, 1933).

On Hitler's rise to power in 1933, Born was one of the first Jewish professors in Germany to lose his chair. After a short stay in the Dolomites, he went to Cambridge, where he was appointed Stokes Lecturer. In 1936 he succeeded Charles Darwin (1887–1962) as Tait Professor of Natural Philosophy in the University of Edinburgh. The following year he was elected Fellow of the Royal Society. At Edinburgh, where he was later joined by R. H. Fürth of Prague, he built up a considerable research school in the theory of the solid state, the molecular theory of liquids, and other topics, most of his students coming from abroad. One was the later notorious nuclear spy Klaus FUCHS.

On reaching the age of 70 Born retired to Bad Pyrmont, a spa near Göttingen, the post-war German government having made amends for his treatment by the Nazi regime. Although he continued his scientific work, he wrote mainly on the philosophy of physics and on the social responsibility of scientists. He also brought out new editions of several of his books; his *Atomic Physics* attaining unrivalled popularity throughout the English-speaking world as an undergraduate text.

Biographical Memoirs of Fellows of the Royal Society. 1971. (Portrait.)

Max Born, *My Life and Views*. 1968.

Max Born, *My Life: Recollections of a Nobel Laureate*. 1978. (Portrait.)

Dictionary of Scientific Biography, Supp. I.

Tyler Wasson (Ed.), *Nobel Prize Winners*. 1987. (Portrait.P

G J W

BOSCH, CARL Born at Cologne, Germany, 27 August 1874; died Heidelberg, 26 April 1940. Developed industrial ammonia synthesis.

Bosch was the eldest son of a south German engineer. The boy did well in school science, and before going to university spent a year as metal-worker. He read chemistry under J. A. WISLICENUS at Leipzig, where he took his doctorate in 1898. The following year he got a job with the Badische Anilin-& Soda-Fabrik (BASF), a very large German chemical company making dyestuffs. Between 1902 and 1907 he spent much of his time investigating various nitrogen-fixation processes.

In 1908 Fritz HABER told BASF of his ammonia synthesis, and the next year Bosch was given the responsibility for developing Haber's process to the industrial scale. Bosch directed and inspired a large team of chemists and engineers, and his technical knowledge now proved invaluable. He designed the massive high-pressure converters, and was the first to use the water-gas shift reaction ($CO + H_2O \leftrightarrow CO_2 + H_2$) to obtain the large volume of hydrogen necessary for the ammonia synthesis.

By the end of 1913 Bosch had successfully completed the then largest undertaking in chemical engineering, and at the Oppau works of BASF a plant using the Haber-Bosch process was making

36 000 tons a year of sulphate of ammonia. In the next few years Bosch, who had been made director in 1914, enlarged Oppau and built a much larger factory at Leuna. In 1918–19 he was technical adviser to the German delegation at the armistice and peace conferences.

BASF, thanks to Bosch, retained the leadership in high-pressure technology during the 1920s. He supported the synthesis of methanol, and the long and costly development to make petrol by the hydrogenation of coal tar and lignite, but he was mainly absorbed in problems of organization. When BASF and the other German chemical companies merged in 1925 to form the vast *I. G. Farbenindustrie AG*, he became chairman of its management board, and ten years later of its supervisory board. Frequent illness prevented him from playing an active role for several years before he died in 1940.

Bosch was of a retiring nature, wrote little, and made infrequent public appearances. His outstanding contribution to chemical engineering was recognized by numerous honorary degrees, and the award of the chemistry Nobel prize for 1931 jointly with F. BERGIUS for his work on high-pressure synthesis.

K. Holdermann, *Carl Bosch, Leben und Werk*. 1953.

E. Farber (Ed.), *Great Chemists*. 1961. (Portrait.)

Tyler Wasson (Ed.), *Nobel Prize Winners*. 1987. (Portrait.)

Dictionary of Scientific Biography.

L F H

BOSE, SATYENDRA NATH Born in Calcutta, India, 1894; died there, 4 February 1974. Theoretical physicist, chiefly remembered for the development of 'Bose-Einstein statistics'.

Bose started academic life at Calcutta University, where he obtained a degree in applied mathematics and became a lecturer in the physics department. He later moved to Dacca University, and it was there in 1924 that he wrote his most famous paper, 'Planck's law and the hypothesis of light quanta', which he sent to EINSTEIN for comment. Einstein was so impressed with the paper that he translated it into German and had it published in the prestigious journal *Zeitschrift für physik*. Bose's achievement had been to derive PLANCK's formula for black body radiation in purely quantum terms, without referring to classical oscillators as Planck had done. This required thinking of the radiation as a collection of photons, in itself a novel concept at the time. Einstein later applied Bose's technique to a collection of particles, and the treatment has become known as 'Bose-Einstein' statistics.

Bose followed a distinguished career, determined to promote the intellectual side of Indian life. His interests later mainly concerned unified field theory and the theory of numbers, but he also remained dedicated to his role as a teacher. In 1945 he moved back to a chair at Calcutta University, and in 1958 became vice-chancellor of Vishwabharati University.

Physics Today, p. 129, April 1974. (Portrait.)

H. A. Boorse, L. Motz and J. H. Weaver, *The Atomic Physicists, a Biographical History*. 1989.

Dictionary of Scientific Biography, Supp. I

C S

BOULTON, MATTHEW Born at Birmingham, England, 3 September 1728; died there, 18 August 1809. A great manufacturer and a pioneer in technology.

Matthew Boulton was the son of a manufacturer of buckles in Birmingham. He left school at the age of 14, had become partner with his father by 1750, and inherited the business in 1759. Boulton had a restless energy which drove him to expand his business and continually improve his products. In 1758 his interest in science was stimulated by the visit of Benjamin FRANKLIN to Birmingham, and by meeting Erasmus DARWIN. Boulton and Darwin, together with William Small (1734–75), Boulton's doctor and scientific adviser, were the founders of the Lunar Society of Birmingham.

In 1761 he began building a fine new factory at Soho, north of Birmingham, where he manufactured a wide variety of metal products, mostly small items, such as silver plate, buttons, snuffboxes, and *objets-d'art*. He was often in financial difficulties, but this never deterred him from starting new projects.

He first took an interest in steam engines about 1764, when Darwin proposed constructing a steam carriage. In 1767 Darwin and Small met James WATT and became enthusiastic about his improved steam engine. Boulton at once saw its immense potentialities and determined, if possible, to share in its development. The chance came in 1773 after the bankruptcy of John ROEBUCK, who had been working on the engine with little success. In 1775 Boulton secured an extension of the patent for twenty-five years and went into partnership with Watt, to develop the invention commercially. In the 1780s they succeeded, and the Boulton and Watt engines became prime movers of the Industrial Revolution. For this achievement much credit must go to Boulton: his over-optimism, commercial skill, and drive were just as vital as Watt's engineering genius. In the 1780s Boulton was recognized as the leading manufacturer of England, and his factory at Soho was one of the wonders of the age.

Boulton had many other interests besides steam engines. In the world of art he is famous as a silversmith and for his work in ormolu. In the 1790s he set up steam-driven coining machines, which put counterfeiters out of business and gave people real confidence in the coinage. He established the Birmingham Assay Office and the General Hospital. He was elected FRS in 1785, but wrote no scientific papers. He was the leading spirit in the Lunar Society of Birmingham, which did much to stimulate the Industrial Revolution by bringing together scientists and Industrialists. James KEIR, Joseph PRIESTLEY, Josiah WEDGWOOD and Erasmus Darwin were all close friends of Boulton.

H. W. Dickinson, *Matthew Boulton*. 1936.
(Portrait.)
R. E. Schofield, *The Lunar Society of Birmingham*. 1963.
Dictionary of National Biography.

D G K-H

BOUSSINGAULT, JEAN-BAPTISTE JOSEPH DIEUDONNÉ Born in Paris, 1 February 1801; died there, 11 May 1887. French agricultural chemist.

On leaving school, where he displayed no great ability, Boussingault became, in 1819, a student at the School of Mines in Saint-Étienne, and later served there for a short time as an Assistant Lecturer in Chemistry. After obtaining his diploma, he was employed by an English firm to direct operations for mining precious metals in the State of Bolivar, Venezuela. He spent ten years in South America and travelled extensively in the terrain between Cartagena and the delta of the Orinoco in Venezuela. As a result of these travels he was enabled to send valuable reports of his geological, topographical, and ecological observations to the *Institut de France* in Paris, thus gaining a considerable reputation. He returned to France in 1832, and received the degree of *Docteur ès Sciences*; and he was appointed professor of chemistry, and Dean of the Faculty of Sciences, at the University of Lyons. His main scientific interest became the application of chemical principles to agriculture. He was one of the first to show the utility of inorganic nitrogen and phosphorus as soil-fertilizers: he also studied digestive processes in herbivores. In 1839 he followed J-B. DUMAS as professor of chemistry at the Sorbonne and was elected a member of the *Académie des Sciences*; he was also appointed to the chair of agriculture at the *Conservatoire des Arts et Métiers*. After the revolution of 1848 he decided to enter politics: he was elected a deputy for the department of Bas-Rhin in the Constitutional Assembly and later became a member of the Council of State. He resigned office after the *coup d'état* of 2 December 1851, retired from public life, and took up his former appointments. As a chemist, Boussingault is well known for his discovery of the use of barium oxide in the preparation of oxygen, and, in collaboration with Dumas, for the gravimetric estimation of the relative proportions of the gases of the air.

His best-known publications on agronomy are *Mémoires de chimie agricole et de physiologie* (1854) and a treatise entitled *Agronomie, Chimie agricole, et Physiologie* (reprinted 1884).

M. Prévost and Raman d'Amat, *Dictionnaire de Biographie Française*. 1956.
Journal of Nutrition, **84**, 1, 1964.
Dictionary of Scientific Biography.

A P G

BOVERI, THEODOR Born at Bamberg, Germany, 12 October 1862; died Würzburg, 15 October 1915. A pioneer of cytology.

Boveri studied science at Munich and graduated in 1885, with special reference to anatomy. He then studied zoology under Richard Hertwig (1850–1937), and in 1887 became a lecturer at Munich in zoology and comparative anatomy. In 1893 he was called to the chair of these subjects at Würzburg, and this chair he occupied until his death.

Much of Boveri's early work was related to the centrosome. This cellular structure was discovered by E. van BENEDEN in 1876, and in 1887 both he and Boveri independently discovered that it does not disappear at the end of the process of mitosis. The term 'centrosome' is due to Boveri, who introduced it in 1888. In 1887 he published his important work on the round-worm, *Ascaris*. He was able to trace the embryonic cells back to the first cleavage of the fertilized ovum. He showed how in the first few divisions the germ cells are differentiated from those cells which will subsequently form the animal's body. In 1887 also Boveri gave the first accurate description of the formation of the polar bodies in cell division. Between 1887 and 1902 he evolved the theory of genetic continuity of the chromosomes, and in 1892 he worked out the development of spermatozoa and ova.

Allgemeine Deutsche Biographie.

H. Freund and A. Berg, *Geschichte der Mikroscopie*, vol. 1. 1964. (Portrait.)

F. Baltzer (tr. D. Rudnick), *Theodor Boveri: Life and Work of a Great Biologist 1868–1945*. 1967.

Dictionary of Scientific Biography.

E A U

BOVET, DANIELE Born in Neuchâtel, Switzerland, 23 March 1907; died Rome, 8 April 1992. Physiological chemist.

The son of an educationalist, Bovet studied at the University of Geneva, graduating in 1927, and then did two years research in physiology before moving to the Pasteur Institute in Paris. In 1927 G. DOMAGK of I. G. Farbenindustrie began a systematic screening of all his company's products in search of an effective antibacterial agent. In 1932 it was discovered that a new red dyestuff, Prontosil Rubrum, was highly effective in controlling streptoccal infections in mice. Bovet and his colleagues showed that it was only the sulphanilamide moiety of the molecule that was active. As this had been prepared and described in 1908 it was not patentable, to the disappointment of I.G. This opened the way to the very important sulphonamide drugs, not rivalled until the advent of penicillin in the early 1940s. In 1936 Bovet became head of the Therapeutic Chemistry Department and turned his attention to the relationship between histamine and allergies such as hay fever and asthma. A visit to Brazil aroused his interest in the muscle-relaxing properties of the arrow poison curare and this had important surgical repercussions. In 1947 he went to the *Istituto Superiore di Sanita*, Rome, becoming an Italian citizen. Increasingly he turned his attention to the chemistry of the brain and the relationship between chemical structure and pharmacological activity. He was awarded a Nobel prize in 1957.

Tyler Wasson (Ed.), *Nobel Prize Winners*. 1987. (Portrait.)

Daily Telegraph, 16 April 1992. (Portrait.)

Les Prix Nobel en 1957, 1958. (Portrait.)

Who's Who, 1992.

T I W

BOWER, FREDERICK ORPEN Born at Ripon, Yorkshire, England, 4 November 1855; died there, 11 April 1948. Plant morphologist.

On completing his botanical studies at Cambridge, Bower worked in Germany under J. von SACHS. When he returned to England he undertook research on the germination of seeds of *Welwitschia* at the Jodrell Laboratory, Kew Gardens. In 1885 he was appointed to the chair of botany at Glasgow where he was to acquire during the next forty years an impressive reputation in both teaching and research.

In the early years of his career he covered a wide range of plants and problems, but gradually concentrated on the evolutionary morphology of the Pteridophyta. A masterly exposition of his views was presented in what was the most significant work in morphological botany at that time – *The*

Origin of a Land Flora (1908). An abiding devotion to the Filicales resulted in *The Ferns* in three volumes (1923–8). His major work after retirement from Glasgow in 1925 was *Primitive Land Plants* (1935), in which he stated his opinions on all classes of Bryophyta and Pteridophyta. His original observations and skilful marshalling of new facts characterized all his contributions to morphology.

He wrote, or collaborated in, a number of good textbooks, among them being *Practical Botany for Beginners* (1894) and *Botany of the Living Plant* (1919). A Fellow of the Royal Society, and a recipient of its Royal Medal in 1910, he served as President of the Royal Society of Edinburgh (1919–24) and of the British Association (1930).

Obituary Notices of Fellows of Royal Society. 1949. (Portrait.)

Dictionary of National Biography.

R G C D

BOWMAN, SIR WILLIAM Born at Nantwich, Cheshire, England, 20 July 1816; died near Dorking, Surrey, 29 March 1892. A pioneer histologist and a great ophthalmic surgeon.

Bowman was apprenticed to a Birmingham surgeon, and in 1837 came to King's College, London, as the Physiological Prosector. In 1838 he studied at eight European universities, and in 1839 he qualified as a Member of the Royal College of Surgeons of England. He was then appointed Demonstrator of Anatomy and Curator of the Museum at King's College, London, and in 1840 he became assistant surgeon to the newly founded King's College Hospital. Four years later he was elected a Fellow of the Royal College of Surgeons. He was appointed assistant surgeon to Moorfields Ophthalmic Hospital in 1846 and full surgeon in 1851. In 1856 he was promoted to full surgeon to King's College Hospital. He was created a baronet in 1884.

As an ophthalmic surgeon Bowman was in the first rank. He was one of the first in Britain to become expert in the use of the ophthalmoscope, invented in 1851 by Hermann von HELMHOLTZ, and he was also one of the first to adopt the operation of iridectomy in the treatment of glaucoma, devised by Albrecht von Graefe (1828–70).

When Bowman was appointed to the Physiology Department at King's College, Robert Bentley Todd (1809–60) had recently been appointed professor, and the association of the two men was very fruitful. Bowman concentrated on histology, and in 1840 Todd read to the Royal Society a communication by Bowman on the minute structure and movements of voluntary muscle. In this Bowman gave the results of his examination of the muscle fasciculi in different divisions of the animal kingdom. He considered that muscle substance is composed of a series of particles joined together closely side by side into disks, and less closely end to end into fibrils. This theory held the field for many years, but was later shown to be not completely satisfactory. He was the first to describe the sarcolemma, and he introduced that name. His also was the conception of the sarcous element. For this paper Bowman was elected a Fellow of the Royal Society in 1841.

In 1842 Bowman read to the Royal Society a paper on the structure and use of the Malpighian bodies of the kidney (see M. MALPIGHI). This research also was based on the study of many kinds of animals. He described how the Malpighian tuft was enclosed in a capsule, which was the dilated extremity of a uriniferous tubule. Since then this structure has been known as Bowman's capsule. For this research Bowman was awarded a Royal Medal by the Society in 1842. He also worked on the Pacinian corpuscle, and his name is also attached to the serous glands under the olfactory epithelium. In 1847 he read an important paper on the anatomy of the eye, in which he showed the structure and function of the ciliary muscle.

In 1843 Bowman published (with Todd) *The Physiological Anatomy and Physiology of Man* (2 ed., 1856). In this work the term 'physiological anatomy' was used instead of the more common 'general anatomy'. The work contains much more pure histology than had been usual in similar works. Bowman was also indirectly associated with Todd in the publication of the latter's *Cyclopaedia of Anatomy and Physiology* (1836–59).

D'A. Power *et al.* (Eds), *Plarr's Lives of the Fellows of the Royal College of Surgeons of England.* 1930.

H. Power, Prefatory memoir to Bowman's *Collected Papers.* 1892.

B. Chance, *Annals of Medical History,* **6**, 143, 1924.

A. Castiglioni, *History of Medicine.* 1947. (Portrait.)

British Medical Journal, **1**, 742, 1892. (Portrait.)

Dictionary of National Biography.

Dictionary of Scientific Biography.

E A U

BOYER, HERBERT WAYNE Born at Latrobe, Pennsylvania, USA, 10 July 1936. American molecular geneticist.

Boyer studied bacteriology at the University of Pittsburgh and then joined the Department of Genetics at the University of California at San Francisco as a biochemist in 1966. He became professor of biochemistry in 1976. At Stanford University in the early 1970s, Paul BERG showed that viruses could be used to transfer genes (DNA) from one cell to another, a discovery which raised the possibility of genetic engineering. In 1973, in collaboration with Stanley COHEN of Stanford, and using *E. coli* bacillus, Boyer showed that segments of two deoxyribosenucleic acid molecules from different bacterial plasmid sources could be spliced and recombined together. The resultant 'chimera' DNA (or rDNA) was found to replicate normally, the new bacterium showing characteristics derived from both original sources. Boyer then demonstrated that the technique of recombinant DNA could be used to synthesize and manufacture important proteins such as insulin and the growth hormone somatostatin. In 1976 he formed the company Genentech to exploit the technique. Boyer's and Cohen's decision to patent their splicing technique (filed 1974, granted 1980) has proved controversial, though royalties were assigned to their respective universities. Boyer was one of the signatories to a letter in *Science* in 1974 which warned of the possible biohazards of recombinant DNA. Together with S. NICOSIA, Boyer edited the book *Genetic Engineering* in 1978.

Shelson Krimsky, *Genetic Alchemy: The Social History of the Recombinant DNA Controversy.* (1982).

Science, **185** (26 July 1974), p. 303.

W H B

BOYLE, ROBERT Born at Lismore Castle, County Cork, Ireland, 25 January 1627; died London, 30 December 1691. Natural philosopher.

Robert Boyle was the seventh son of Richard Boyle, 1st Earl of Cork (1566–1643). Educated privately and at Eton, he early displayed a prodigious memory and great talent for languages. In the troubled years 1639–44 he completed his education by extensive travels in France, Switzerland, and Italy. On returning to England, he lived from 1645 to 1652 at Stallbridge, Dorset, where he read widely in philosophy, science, and theology, and began to perform scientific experiments. At this period he met Sir William Petty (1623–87), who acted as his physician during a stay in Ireland from 1652 to 1654. On returning to England in 1654 he settled in Oxford where he became friendly with various members of the Oxford group, including John WALLIS and John WILKINS, later to become (as did Petty) foundation members of the Royal Society. Robert HOOKE became his research assistant, especially in the improvement of the air pump devised by Otto von GUERICKE. In 1668 he moved to London where he lived with his sister for the rest of his life. Boyle steadily refused all titles and positions, and declined to become President of the Royal Society in 1680 through his unwillingness to subscribe to the necessary oaths.

Boyle's most important early experiments were based on the use of the air pump. Having repeated all the experiments of Guericke as described by Kaspar Schott (1608–66) in his *Mechanica Hydraulica-Pneumatica* (1657), he added certain new ones of his own such as the fact that warm water boiled under reduced pressure. These experiments were gathered together in the *New Experiments Physico-Mechanicall* (1660). In an appendix to a new edition of this latter work, he published the famous law which goes by his name, though this was, in fact, discovered by one of his assistants, R. Towneley (1629–1707). In his last work, the *General History of the Air* (published posthumously, 1692), he returned to the same subject again, giving a very clear qualitative expression of the notion of heat as due to an increase in the motion of the ultimate particles of a gas.

On the basis of some earlier work, especially that of J. B. van HELMONT, Boyle attacked the chemical views of the alchemists and Aristotelians in works such as the *Physiological Essays* (1661) and more especially the very famous *Sceptical Chymist* (1662). In these and other works he advanced an atomistic theory according to which the ultimate constituents of matter were made up of certain primitive, simple, and perfectly unmingled bodies which by combining together gave all the natural variety of matter. A definitive expression of his atomistic views was given in his *Origin of Forms and Qualities* (1666), in which atoms in motion were regarded as responsible for most of the phenomena of nature. Like DESCARTES and unlike EPICURUS, Boyle assumed that the motions of atoms were derived ultimately from God. In this and other works he gave numerous experiments in favour of the atomic hypothesis. Boyle supposed that in fluids the atoms were able to move with considerable freedom, whereas in solids they were at rest. But unlike Descartes, who supposed that inertia was the sole ground of the solidity of bodies, Boyle supposed that this was also due to the shape of the atoms and their connections with each other.

In his famous *Experiments and Considerations Touching Colours* (1663) Boyle argued that colours had no intrinsic separate existence, being due to the modification of light at the outer surface of bodies. He made many interesting and important observations including some on the colours of thin films.

Suffering much ill health himself, Boyle was deeply interested in diseases of all kinds and in the period 1684–91 he wrote a series of books on medical subjects. None of these are comparable in importance to the writings of scientists such as William HARVEY or T. WILLIS, but they are full of interesting observations and throughout there is the notion that medicine is a subject which must be treated as a branch of science based on experiments and observation rather than on hypotheses and speculations.

During his own lifetime and beyond, the originality of Boyle's scientific work tended to be somewhat overestimated. In fact, with few exceptions, all his experiments touching the vacuum and the spring of air were derived from those which had been performed by Guericke and his disciples in Germany. Likewise there was no great element of originality in his views on atomism, which were taken largely from the writings of thinkers such as P. GASSENDI, DESCARTES, and the ancient atomists. What was original in Boyle was his enormous ingenuity in constructing experiments in support of the atomistic hypothesis. Through his writings a belief in atomism in Europe was greatly strengthened. He was also very influential for the example he provided of the prosecution of the experimental method in science in the manner of GALILEO and his Florentine successors.

M. B. Hall, *Robert Boyle and Seventeenth Century Chemistry*. 1958.

Dictionary of National Biography.

T. Birch, *Life of the Honourable Robert Boyle*. 1744.

F. Masson, *Robert Boyle*. 1914.

L. T. More, *Life and Works of the Honourable Robert Boyle*. 1944.

R. E. W. Maddison, *Life of the Honourable Robert Boyle FRS*. 1969.

Dictionary of Scientific Biography, Supp. I.

J W H

BOYS, SIR CHARLES VERNON Born at Wing, Rutland, England, 15 March 1855; died Andover, Hampshire, 30 March 1944. Physicist.

Boys was the son of a clergyman. In 1869 he went to Marlborough College, and in 1873 to the Royal School of Mines, London. He graduated in 1876. From then until 1881 he was a private assistant to his old teacher, F. Guthrie (1833–86). Guthrie was a founder of the Physical Society, and in 1880 he made Boys a life member. From 1881 to 1897 Boys worked at the Royal College of Science in South Kensington (prior to 1890 it was known as the Normal School of Science), first as a demonstrator in physics and then as an assistant professor. He resigned in 1897 to become one of the Metropolitan Gas Referees, and he held that position until 1920, when he became one of the three Gas Referees appointed for the whole of Great Britain. From 1893 onwards he developed a lucrative practice as an expert witness, mainly in patent cases.

Early in his career Boys prepared quartz fibres – ingeniously made by attaching molten quartz to an arrow fired from a bow – for use instead of silk in delicate suspensions. The great strength and resistance to set of these fibres made them particularly valuable, and he used one in the torsion balance which he designed to determine the constant of gravitation by measuring the attraction between two masses. His results gave the density of the Earth as 5.5270 g/cm;. He constructed a radiomicrometer, which was a combination of a thermocouple and a delicate coil galvanometer, so sensitive that it could detect the heat from a candle a mile away. He used it to detect the heat of radiation from the Moon and planets. In the late 1880s he carried out a series of experiments on soap bubbles, which added to our knowledge of surface tension and the properties of thin films and provided the material for lectures to the Physical Society and at the Royal Institution, and eventually resulted in his popular book, *Soap Bubbles and the Forces which Mould Them*. In 1900 he developed a camera with a moving lens, and with it was able to take some remarkable photographs of lightning flashes.

After his appointment as a Metropolitan Gas Referee, Boys designed a calorimeter for determining the calorific value of coal gas; this became the standard method of testing gas in London and was later used throughout the country.

Boys was elected FRS in 1888 and was knighted in 1935. He was an Honorary member of the New York Academy of Sciences and of the Physical Society of Moscow.

Obituary Notices of Fellows of the Royal Society. 1942–4. (Portrait.)

R. A. S. Paget, *Proceedings of the Physical Society*, **56**, 397. 1944.

C. T. R. Wilson, *Nature*, **155**, 40. 1945.

Dictionary of National Biography.

B B K

BRADLEY, HUMPHREY Born *c*.1584, probably at Bergen-op-Zoom, Netherlands; died *c*.1625. Drainage engineer.

Of Dutch birth, but with an English father, Humphrey Bradley first appeared in England in 1584, advising Sir Francis Walsingham on Dover Harbour. He was recommended by him to the Commissioners of Sewers in the Fen counties and put forward the first comprehensive proposal for recovering land there in *A Treatise Concerning the State of the Marshes or Inundated Lands (Commonly Called Fens) in the Counties of Norfolk, Huntingdon, Cambridge, Northampton and Lincoln* (1589). This showed that the chief obstacles to the drainage of the fens were not engineering ones. In 1593 he wrote to Lord Burghley suggesting that an Act of Parliament should be passed to overcome these obstacles, but before such an Act was passed – in 1600 – he returned to Bergen-op-Zoom. In 1596 he was sent to France in response to a request from King Henry IV, who appointed him Master of the Dykes in 1599 and exempted his workmen from the *taille*. Bradley organized on the model of the three-hundred-year-old *Hoogheemradschappen* an *Association pour le desséchement des marais et lacs de France*, which lasted until the revocation of the Edict of Nantes in 1685. He drained areas in Chaumont-en-Vexin (Oise),

Saintonge, Poitou, Normandy, Picardy, Langue-doc, Provence, and the lake of Sarlièves (Puy-de-Dôme), as well as participating in canal projects to link the Seine-Saône (the origin of the Canal de Bourgogne) and the Loire-Loing.

H. C. Darby, *The Draining of the Fens.* 1940.

L. E. Harris, *The Two Netherlanders: Humphrey Bradley and Cornelis Drebbel.* 1961.

W H G A

BRADLEY, JAMES Born at Sherborne, Gloucestershire, England, March 1693; died Chalford, Gloucestershire, 13 July 1762. Discovered the aberration of light.

James Bradley was the nephew of the astronomer James Pound (1669–1724), who introduced him into the leading scientific circles of the time. In 1711 he entered Balliol College, Oxford, and took orders in 1719. He resigned his living at Bridstow on being appointed Savilian Professor of Astronomy at Oxford in 1721. In 1742 he succeeded Edmond HALLEY as Astronomer Royal.

Together with Samuel Molyneux (1689–1728), who owned a small observatory at Kew, Bradley, in 1725, methodically observed the star γ Draconis, hoping to discover a parallactic motion of the stars, mirroring the Earth's motion round the Sun. Observing small seasonal shifts forming an ellipse of axis 40 seconds of arc, he concluded that the effect arose, not from parallactic motion, but from the aberration of light due to the Earth's annual motion in its orbit. (Bradley drew attention to the discovery by O. ROEMER that light had a finite velocity. He showed that the velocity of light obtained from aberration measurements was more or less equal to the mean of values obtained by using Roemer's method in conjunction with his own observations of Jupiter's satellites.) Bradley stated the constant of aberration as between 20 and 20.5 seconds, the modern value being 20.47 seconds. His results were published in the *Philosophical Transactions of the Royal Society* in 1729. His work is remarkable to the extent that he considers the possibility of a change in the velocity of light before and after its reflection, with distance travelled, with direction in space, and as between sunlight and starlight.

Bradley discovered the effect known as nutation, that is, the oscillation of the Earth's axis caused by the changing direction of the gravitational attraction of the Moon for the Earth's equatorial bulge. The discovery arose out of his work on aberration. Even after this was allowed for, he realized that the polar distances of stars were subject to small variations, the distribution of which, over the celestial sphere, suggested their origin. Reasoning from the discovery by NEWTON that the precession of the equinoxes was caused by the joint gravitational action of the Sun and Moon upon the Earth, he concluded that nutation must arise from the fact that the Moon is sometimes above and sometimes below the ecliptic, and it should therefore have the periodicity of the lunar nodes, i.e. approximately 18.6 years. His observations, covering the period from 1727 to 1747 (i.e. more than a complete nodical cycle), were published as soon as they were completed.

At Greenwich, Bradley made a series of observations of the eclipses of Jupiter's satellites, permitting him to improve Cassini's tables. After 1749

he obtained improved instruments, including an 8-foot mural quadrant, and subsequently devoted himself to compiling a new catalogue of star positions, listing over 60 000 observations in the last twelve years of his life. The catalogue was published posthumously (1798 and 1805, two volumes). In 1818 F. W. BESSEL published his well-known catalogue of 3000 stars based on Bradley's observations.

Little is known of Bradley's personal life, and it is a surprise to find that all his published prose amounts to well under a hundred pages. Newton, much his senior, referred to him as the best astronomer in Europe.

S. P. Rigaud (Ed.), *Miscellaneous works and correspondence of James Bradley.* 1832.

Quarterly Journal of the Royal Astronomical Society, **4**, 38, 1963. (Portrait.)

Dictionary of National Biography.

Dictionary of Scientific Biography.

J D N

BRAGG, SIR WILLIAM HENRY Born at Westward, Cumberland, England, 2 July 1862; died London, 12 March 1942. Founder of the science and art of crystal structure determination by x-ray diffraction methods.

Bragg went to Trinity College, Cambridge, and was placed Third Wrangler in the Mathematical Tripos, Part I (1884). After a further short period in Cambridge he was appointed professor of mathematics and Physics at the University of Adelaide, Australia. A few years later W. K. RÖNTGEN made the momentous discovery of x-rays and Bragg began to make experiments on them and some years later on α-particles, their range, and their power to produce ionization in gases. He did basic work on the behaviour of secondary electrons and as a result of his studies, particularly on secondary electrons produced by γ-rays, began to form views on the nature of x-rays. In 1908 he became Cavendish Professor of Physics at Leeds. The discovery of diffraction of x-rays by crystals belongs to M. von LAUE, W. Friedrich (1883–1968) and P. Knipping (1883–1935). This was in 1912 and immediately Bragg saw its importance in relation to corpuscular and wave-theories of x-rays and showed particular insight in his judgement that what was needed was a single theory which should embrace the two. At the same time he reinterpreted von Laue's theory of diffraction of x-rays by a crystal acting as a three-dimensional grating. He considered each diffracted x-ray beam as the reflection of the waves of the narrow incident beam from a large number of parallel equally spaced planes, and in 1912 gave the Bragg law, originally in the form $n \lambda = 2d \sin \theta$, where d is the spacing of the planes and θ is the glancing angle. It enabled him and his son (William Lawrence BRAGG) in two or three years to work out structures showing the exact positions of atoms or ions, which compose crystals of a number of simple substances – diamond, copper, potassium chloride, and others. After the war Bragg moved to University College, London, and later became Director of the Royal Institution. He was responsible directly or indirectly for a good deal of the spread of crystal structure methods to those areas where it had profound effects; fundamental work on the structures of organic molecules, aliphatic and aromatic types, came from the Royal Institution, and the sciences of metals and of minerals began over again. Interpretation of the properties and behaviour of a vast variety of substances could be related to the position of their constituent atoms; this applies to the highly ordered structures of some crystals, endless gradations of less-ordered structures in other crystals, fibres and polymers both natural and synthetic, liquid crystals, and other molecular aggregates. The extension to biology followed.

He was President of the Royal Society (1935–40). With his son W. L. Bragg, he was awarded the Nobel prize for physics in 1915. His powers as writer and lecturer, illustrated in his Christmas Lectures at the Royal Institution, had an extensive influence on the general public. He was a gentle man.

Obituary Notices of Fellows of the Royal Society. 1942–44. (Portrait.)

G. M. Caroe, William Henry Bragg 1862–1942. 1978.

H. Oxbury (Ed.), Great Britons: 20th Century Lives. 1985.

Tyler Wasson (Ed.), Nobel Prize Winners. 1987. (Portrait.)

Dictionary of National Biography.

Dictionary of Scientific Biography.

H M P

BRAGG, SIR WILLIAM LAWRENCE Born at Adelaide, South Australia, 31 March 1890; died London, 1 July 1971. Founder and prime developer of the science and art of crystal structure determination by x-rays.

Bragg was educated at St Peter's College, Adelaide, Adelaide University, and Trinity College, Cambridge, where he was a Scholar and, later, Fellow and Lecturer. He was appointed professor of physics at Manchester (1919); Director of the National Physical Laboratory (1937); Cavendish Professor, (after RUTHERFORD), at Cambridge (1938); and Resident Professor and Director of the Royal Institution of Great Britain (1953–66).

In 1912, about a year after the discovery of x-ray diffraction by M. T. F. von LAUE, W. Friedrich (1883–1968) and P. Knipping (1883–1935), he was a research student. His father W. H. BRAGG, then professor at Leeds and an expert with x-ray tubes and ionization chambers, was intensely interested in the theory of x-rays and consequently in von Laue's work. Father and son talked much about it. Back at Cambridge, Lawrence explained von Laue's results as being due to the reflexion of a band of 'white' radiation by the planes of the crystal. This interpretation of the diffraction leads to the Bragg law of x-ray reflexion. He also showed that von Laue's diffraction picture from zinc blende was characteristic of a face-centred lattice. He made Laue photographs and deduced the structures of sodium chloride and related crystals. His father developed the x-ray spectrometer which superseded Laue photography as a means of obtaining x-ray diffraction information. Together they published the structure of diamond. The father was especially interested in x-rays, establishing wave lengths based ultimately on the son's sodium chloride structure, and the son used the spectrometer mainly to investigate more crystal structures. The father published a fundamental work for crystal structure analysis, The intensity of reflexion of x-rays by crystals; the son, after the

war, used this and other x-ray studies to develop quantitative methods for determining complicated structures and wrote (with J. West) A technique for the Examination of Crystal Structures with many Parameters (basically, for finding the position of many atoms).

Lawrence Bragg left inorganic chemists with the stimulus, the problems, and the means of solution that his earliest work had created for them; he then turned to minerals, especially silicates which traditional chemistry largely had not explained in satisfactory atomic terms. The structures showed oxygen atoms dominant, effectively filling the space, with other smaller atoms in the interstices, and a constant coordination of four oxygen atoms, whatever the silicon:oxygen ratio. These factors and the resulting variety of complex anions, many extending throughout the crystal, accounted for the chemical and physical properties of silicates, and Bragg moved on.

In the laboratories that he directed he gathered teams and individuals from all over the world who tackled other and more complex structures, metallic alloys at Manchester, large 'biological' molecules at Cambridge and at the Royal Institution. Among the products of these workers were the structures of γ-brass, magnetic alloys, and many others basic to the development of the modern theory of metals. Bragg himself wrote on order–disorder in alloys. The biological molecules include the very complicated and vital DNA and the proteins myoglobin and haemoglobin.

Bragg delighted in the simple and, where possible, visual presentation of ideas – his drawing and painting were skilful. He developed optical analogues of x-ray diffraction, replacing roundabout calculations that ended in numbers by direct and instant pictures of a diffraction pattern or of the atomic distribution in a crystal. Some of the complexities of metal structures were shown by an array of bubbles on a bath. His quality of verbal and visual clarity had full scope at the Royal Institution which, under his leadership, was alive with young men and others engaged in 'the diffusion and extension of useful knowledge.'

With his father, Lawrence Bragg was awarded the Nobel prize for physics in 1915.

W. L. Bragg and others: Dedicated to Sir Lawrence Bragg on his Eightieth Birthday, Acta Crystallographica A, Vol 26. 1970. (Portrait.)

Biographical Memoirs of Fellows of the Royal Society. 1979. (Portrait.)

Dictionary of Scientific Biography.

Dictionary of National Biography.

Tyler Wasson (Ed.), Nobel Prize Winners. 1987. (Portrait.)

J. M. Thomas and D. Phillips (Eds), Selections and Reflections: The Legacy of Sir Lawrence Bragg. 1991.

H M P

BRAHE, TYCHO (or TYGE) Born at Knudstrup, Skaane (then Danish), 14 December 1546; died Benatky, near Prague, 24 October 1601. Greatest astronomical observer before the era of the telescope.

Tycho Brahe was the eldest son of Otto Brahe, a Danish nobleman. When only a year old, he was carried off by stealth by his uncle Jörgen Brahe, who was childless, and Otto allowed him to remain. Jörgen sent the boy to Copenhagen (1559) to study philosophy and rhetoric. Whilst there, and whilst reading law at Leipzig (1562–5), he studied astronomy assiduously on his own. Later he studied chemistry at Augsburg (1570–2), during which time he persuaded a maternal uncle to install a laboratory in his castle at Herritzwad. It was from there that Tycho saw the nova in Cassiopeia, on 11 November 1572, which was the occasion of his first work, *De nova stella* (1573; not to be confused with the *De stella nova* of Johannes KEPLER). Consideration of the absence of both parallax and retrograde motion, which he established by careful observation, led him to conclude that the new star was neither sublunar nor attached to the planetary spheres. It lacked the proper motion of a comet (which, according to ARISTOTLE, would have been sublunar), quite apart from its totally different appearance. Despite the attempts he made in his book to ascertain the astrological significance of the nova, his account is, on the whole, greatly superior to contemporary accounts. An improved treatment of the subject was later included in his principal work, the *Progymnasmata* (1602–3).

After marriage with a peasant-girl had strained family relations (1573), he received a royal command to deliver lectures in Copenhagen. In 1575 he made himself known to astronomers throughout Germany, when he travelled there. He would have settled in Switzerland, had not the King of Denmark presented him with a generous pension, together with the gift for life of the island of Hveen, on which Tycho built the famous observatory of Uraniborg. Begun in 1576, this was never completed to Tycho's satisfaction, since the next king withdrew both his pension and his rights to the island. The twenty-one years he spent there nevertheless allowed him to carry out a gigantic programme of observation. He left Denmark in 1597, and after a period of observing from a castle near Hamburg, arrived in Prague in 1599. Presented with the castle of Benatky and a pension by Rudolph II, he had his instruments shipped from Hveen. In 1600 he was joined by Johannes Kepler, who was not yet 30, but their collaboration was short-lived, for within two years Tycho Brahe was dead.

Tycho's *Astronomiae Instauratae Progymnasmata*, already referred to, was published posthumously, with Kepler as editor. The places of 777 fixed stars which are listed in the first volume were the basis of Kepler's so-called 'Rudolphine Tables' (1627). Tycho's ideas were not new to the learned world, however, for the second volume of the *Progymnasmata* had appeared under another title in 1588. Although mainly concerned with the comet of 1577, this work contains the system of the world which is now generally known as the 'Tychonic' system. With the Earth still at the centre of the cosmos, the Moon and Sun revolved about it, the remaining planets being centred on the Sun. It is now known that Christopher Rothmann (*d.* 1599) had previously arrived at this compromise between the systems of PTOLEMY and COPERNICUS but others also laid claim to it. One of these was Nicolas Reimers (Ursus or Baer), who in 1597 issued his *De Astronomicis Hypothesibus*, containing a scurrilous attack on Tycho, accusing him of plagiarism. In this he quoted out of context a letter

written by Kepler, extravagantly praising Reimers, and apparently supporting him in his criticism of Tycho. Although he finally accepted Kepler's explanation, Tycho was never absolutely sure of his trust. He persuaded Kepler to write an *Apologia* on his behalf, but this was not published until 1858.

Tycho had astronomical instruments of almost every known variety, and in most cases they were built on a colossal scale, in wood, brass, and iron. One of the most useful was a large mural quadrant, an instrument which he wrongly claimed to be of his own invention. The accuracy of his measurements was enhanced by the use of averaging procedures, as well as other means of allowing for instrumental errors and for atmospheric refraction. He introduced the use of transversal scale divisions on his instruments, for increased accuracy, and he much improved the design of their sights. His measurements were often accurate to better than half a minute of arc, and as a result he was enabled to improve, often by drastic amendment, almost every single parameter of astronomical theory. A notable exception was the horizontal parallax of the Sun, which like all astronomers from the time of Ptolemy he took to be 3'. His failure to work out his own value had unfortunate consequences for his theory of refraction, which was none the less remarkable.

Tycho, unlike the ancient astronomers on whose observations Ptolemaic astronomy rested, observed the Moon throughout her cycle, and not merely at syzygy (conjunction or opposition) and quadrature. As a result he discovered a third inequality in her motion in longitude, known as variation. Later he found yet a fourth inequality, with the solar year as period (this is the so-called annual equation). The modification to the system of lunar epicycles necessary to account for these inequalities frightened him, and he left the theory half finished – but not before he had revised the accepted theory of motion in latitude. This, his lunar theory, must rank with his proof that comets are celestial objects, and his discovery of the variation of the obliquity of the ecliptic, as his greatest achievement.

J. L. E. Dreyer, *Tycho Brahe*. 1890 (reprint 1963). (Portrait.)

J. A. Gade, *The Life and Times of Tycho Brahe*. 1947.

V. E. Thoren and J. R. Christianssen, *The Lord of Uraniborg: A Biography of Tycho Brahe*. 1991.

Dictionary of Scientific Biography.

J D N

BRAMAH, JOSEPH Born at Stainborough, Yorkshire, England, 13 April 1749; died Pimlico, London, 9 December 1814. Engineer.

Prevented by an accident from following his father as a farmer, Bramah was apprenticed as a carpenter and then went to work in London. Of an ingenious turn of mind, he made many inventions, including a lock which remained unpicked until 1851; a beer engine; a machine for numbering bank-notes; and a planing machine. He was interested also in the screw propulsion of ships.

His chief invention, however, was his hydraulic press, capable of exerting forces of several thousand tons necessary for shaping heavy pieces of iron and steel. In developing this machine Bramah was assisted by Henry MAUDSLAY, who left him shortly afterwards to set up his own engineering works. Bramah's press, like NASMYTH's steam hammer, was itself one of the great instruments of the industrial revolution. Without it, Stephenson could not have built his bridges nor Brunel have launched the *Great Eastern*.

H. W. Dickinson, *Transactions of the Newcomen Society*, **22**, 169, 1941–2. (Portrait.)

Dictionary of National Biography.

W H G A

BRAND, HENNIG Born at Hamburg, Germany; *fl.* 1670. Discoverer of phosphorus.

Brand is often regarded as the last of the alchemists, and certainly one of the objects of his experiments was the elusive philosopher's stone. Nevertheless, his experimental methods give him some claim to be regarded as one of the first of the chemists.

Very little is known of Brand's life, and his main claim to fame lies in his discovery of phosphorus, about 1669, which he obtained by pyrolysis of sand and concentrated urine. Although the clear conception of a chemical element did not emerge until 1661 (when *The Sceptical Chymist* of Robert BOYLE appeared), and did not gain general currency for a considerable time afterwards, this discovery is of particular interest, for very few new elements had previously been added to those familiar to the ancient world. These were carbon, sulphur, iron, tin, lead, copper, mercury, silver and gold. To these had been added, up to 1600, only arsenic, bismuth, and zinc.

Phosphorus was long known as 'English phosphorus', as it was independently discovered in 1680 by Boyle, who published (1692) a detailed account of its preparation, unlike Brand, who kept his method secret.

M. A. Weeks, *Discovery of the Elements* (5th ed.). 1945.

Maxson Stillman, *The Story of Alchemy and Early Chemistry*. 1960. (Published as *The Story of Early Chemistry*, 1924.)

T I W

BRAUN, KARL FERDINAND Born at Fulda, Germany, 6 June 1850; died New York, 20 April 1918. A pioneer of wireless telegraphy, and inventor of the cathode-ray oscilloscope.

Braun was educated at the universities of Marburg and Berlin, where he received a doctorate in 1872. He subsequently held positions at the universities of Leipzig, Marburg, Karlsruhe, Tübingen and Strasbourg, where he founded an Institute of Physics. In 1885 he returned to Tübingen as professor of physics, and ten years later moved back to Strasbourg as professor and Director of the Institute.

In 1874 he discovered that some semiconducting crystals act as rectifiers, and this property was later used as the basis of crystal ('cat's whisker') radio receivers in the early years of the 20th century. Just before the turn of the century he began to seek ways of improving the range of radio transmissions, then no more than about 15 km, and in 1899 he patented the principle of magnetic coupling of the antenna circuit which achieved the desired effect, and has since been adopted also in radar and television. For this work he shared the 1909 Nobel prize in physics with Guglielmo MARCONI.

His other major contribution to science, in 1897, was his use of the cathode-ray tube as an oscilloscope (or Braun tube), for the study of the high-frequency alternating currents in which he was interested. His discovery that a fluctuating voltage or magnetic field could be used to deflect the electron beam in a cathode-ray tube led directly to the application of the same principle in television receivers and a great variety of measuring instruments.

Robert L. Weber, *Pioneers of Science: Nobel Prize Winners in Physics*. (2nd ed.) 1988. (Portrait.)

Scientific American, **230(4)**, 92–101, 1974.

F. Kurylo and C. Susskind, *Ferdinand Braun: a Life of the Nobel Prizewinner and Inventor of the Cathode-ray Oscilloscope*. 1981.

Dictionary of Scientific Biography.

Tyler Wasson (Ed.), *Nobel Prize Winners*. 1987. (Portrait.)

R M B

BRAUN, WERHNER MAGNUS MAXIMILIAN VON See VON BRAUN.

BREARLEY, HARRY Born in Sheffield, Yorkshire, England, 18 February 1871; died Torquay, Devon, 14 July 1948. Steel metallurgist.

The son of a Sheffield steelmelter, Brearley joined Thomas Firth and Son at the age of 11. In 1883 he became bottle-washer in the laboratory and was encouraged to master the principles of chemical analysis. In 1901 he went to Riga, Latvia, as Chief Chemist to Firth's Salamander Works. In 1907 he established in Sheffield a new joint Laboratory for Firths and John Brown. In 1912 a reported failure of rifle barrels through corrosion led him to investigate alloys containing over 10 per cent chromium. This eventually resulted in the development of 'stainless' steels, especially for cutlery. Brearley did not invent such steels, for they had earlier been investigated in Germany and France, but he undoubtedly pioneered their commercial development. In this connection Brearley quarrelled with Firths, whom he believed had deprived him of his just rewards, and he joined Brown Bayley Steelworks in 1914, eventually as Technical Director.

Dictionary of National Biography: Missing Persons. 1993.

J. H. G. Moneypenny, *Journal of the Iron and Steel Institute*, August 1948.

British Steel Stainless, *75 Years of Stainless Steel 1913–1988*, 1988. (Portrait.)

T I W

BREIT, GREGORY Born in Nikolaev, Russia, 14 July 1899; died in Salem, Oregon, USA, 13 September 1981. Known for many contributions to physics.

Brought up in the USA, Breit studied electrical engineering at Johns Hopkins University, where he graduated in 1918 and received his PhD in 1921. After time at the Universities of Leiden (where he was influenced by Paul Ehrenfest (1880–1933) and Kammerlingh ONNES), Harvard and Minnesota, Breit joined the Carnegie Institution's Department of Terrestrial Magnetism in Washington. Here he worked with Merle TUVE (1901–1982), at first using radio waves to study the conducting layers of the atmosphere. Around 1926 they began work on developing high voltages with the aim of accelerating protons, and eventually succeeded in building a 1.25 million volt electrostatic machine in 1932.

Breit moved to New York University in 1929 and on to the University of Wisconsin in 1934. During the Second World War he worked for a while on the fast neutron project at the University of Chicago and from 1943–5 on ballistics at the Aberdeen Proving Ground in Maryland. In 1947 he became professor at Yale University where he remained until retiring in 1968. Over the years he had published some 250 papers, many of great importance, mainly in the area of nuclear physics. He is particular remembered for the Breit-WIGNER formula for resonances in particle interactions, derived in 1936 during studies of nuclear reactions.

> D. A. Bromley and V. W. Hughes (Eds), *Facets of Physics*. 1970. (Portrait.)
> *Physics Today*, p. 102, October 1983.

C S

BRENNER, SYDNEY Born in Germiston, South Africa, 13 January 1927. Molecular biologist.

After graduating in the Universities of the Witwatersrand and Oxford, Brenner joined the MRC Laboratory of Molecular Biology in 1957 and was Director 1979–86. He was elected Fellow of the Royal Society in 1965, and was awarded the Society's Royal Medal in 1974 in recognition of his outstanding contributions to molecular biology.

Brenner is regarded as a founder of molecular biology as a distinct discipline. He developed a negative staining technique for electron microscopic studies of viruses, demonstrating their structural subunit form. He was the first to describe the detailed structure of bacteriophages. This work led to the elaboration of chemically-induced mutations. He also established the identity of the suppressor mutation and discovered that the gene and its product are colinear. He also showed that messenger RNA was essential in programming ribosomes to make new and distinct proteins following infection with bacteriophage particles.

He initiated the study of the nematode worm *Caenorhabditis elegans* in the 1960s at the Laboratory of Molecular Biology, Cambridge. His aim was to map the relatively small number of cells which make up the animal's simple nervous system and the various cell lineages involved, and thence to understand the molecular genetics of behaviour. These initial studies and the elucidation of the cell lineages using genetic mutants established by Brenner and his co-workers have led to groups across the world using the nematode as a model for the understanding of cell patterning. Currently over 10 000 mutations have been generated and stored by the international groups working on this animal.

Brenner established genetic manipulation as a research tool in the UK and was a member of the Williams Committee which set up the Genetic Manipulation Advisory Group (GMAG), making significant contributions to containment practice necessary for the safe handling of genetically altered organisms.

After becoming Director of the Laboratory of Molecular Biology Brenner continued his interest in the nematode work, becoming involved in genome mapping in other species. He relinquished his post as Director to become head of the Medical Research Council's Molecular Genetics Unit in Cambridge (1986) where he became involved in the UK Human Gene Mapping Programme.

> *Medical Research Council News* No. 32, Sept, 1986.
> *Who's Who.* 1993.

C L

BREWSTER, SIR DAVID Born at Jedburgh, Roxburghshire, Scotland, 11 December 1781; died Allerby, Melrose, 10 February 1868. Chiefly remembered for his work in optics.

Entering Edinburgh University at the age of 12 to study for the ministry, Brewster completed his theological studies but was diverted from the Church by his interest in science, especially in optics. He was elected Fellow of the Royal Society of Edinburgh in 1808, and of the Royal Society of London in 1815, being awarded the Copley and Rumford medals of the latter Society in 1815 and 1818 respectively. He played a leading part in the formation of the British Association for the Advancement of Science. He was knighted in 1832. From 1838 to 1859 he was Principal of the United Colleges of San Salvador and St Leonard of the University of St Andrews. From 1859 until a short time before his death he was Principal of Edinburgh University.

Of a strongly positivist turn of mind, totally averse to any kind of speculation, Brewster's scientific work consisted largely in his collection and publication of great numbers of careful measurements of optical and other phenomena. The Royal Society catalogue of scientific papers contains the titles of no less than 299 of his papers. His most important and original work dealt with the reflection, absorption, and polarization of light, and he discovered the law bearing his name which states that the polarization of light reflected from a glass surface becomes complete when reflected and refracted rays are at right-angles. In 1816 he invented the kaleidoscope.

Besides his scientific work, Brewster was much involved in the editing of various journals including the *Edinburgh Philosophical Journal*, the *Edinburgh Journal of Science*, and the *Philosophical Magazine*. He was a frequent contributor of reviews and articles to other magazines, especially the *North British Review* and the *Edinburgh Review*, and he also wrote a number of works of scientific biography of which the most important was his memoir of NEWTON. Brewster played a leading part in the popularization of science in Britain in the nineteenth century. He was also interested in the application of science to industry and other fields, being responsible for persuading the British authorities to adopt the dioptric apparatus perfected by A. J. FRESNEL for use in lighthouses.

> *Proceedings of the Royal Society*, **17**, lxix, 1868–9.
> M. M. Gordon (Brewster), *The Home Life of David Brewster*. (2nd ed.) 1870.
> *Dictionary of National Biography.*
> *Dictionary of Scientific Biography.*

J W H

BRIDGMAN, PERCY WILLIAMS Born at Cambridge, Massachusetts, USA, 21 April 1882; died Randolph, New Hampshire, 20 August 1961.

Studied the behaviour of substances under very high pressures; wrote on philosophy of science.

Bridgman's entire career was spent at Harvard University; he went up as an undergraduate in 1900, and stayed to do research. He had been excited by the researches of L. P. CAILLETET and E. H. AMAGAT (1841–1915) on the behaviour of fluids under pressure; it was to be his achievement to extend the range of pressures under which substances could be examined from Amagat's maximum of about 3000 atmospheres to 100 000 atmospheres. This enormous increase marks him as one of the greatest of experimental physicists. At first, he met great difficulties in obtaining steel of sufficient tensile strength. About 1909 he invented a self-tightening joint; as the pressure was raised the packing was tightened. Between 1911 and 1915 he published a series of papers on the thermodynamic properties of liquids at high pressures and under a range of temperatures. He discovered two new forms of ice, found their triple-points, and mapped their regions of stability. He then became interested in the theory of fluids, and between 1925 and 1927 published a series of papers on the changes of viscosity with pressure for more than fifty different liquids. They all behaved alike, except for water, in that their viscosity increased rapidly with increased pressure.

From about 1927 he began to feel a need to understand the foundations of physics, and wrote on the philosophy of science. He believed that 'we do not know the meaning of a concept unless we can specify the operations used in applying the concept in any concrete situations'. Critics have felt that this 'operational' approach would exclude many of the hypothetical entities which play a useful – indeed invaluable – role in the theoretical parts of the sciences.

Bridgman took very little interest in administration, or in lecturing; and his lectures were apparently disjointed and difficult, but rewarding if students persisted. He spent the summers on a farm in New Hampshire, where he built a cabin in the grounds in which he would write for some four or five hours a day, in complete isolation. He was awarded a Nobel prize in 1946 for his work on liquids under high pressure; was elected a Foreign Member of the Royal Society in 1949; and received numerous other honours from all over the world. In the end, struck down by a painful and incurable disease, he shot himself.

Biographical Memoirs of Fellows of the Royal Society. 1962. (Portrait.)

Proceedings of the Physical Society, **79**, 1301, 1962. (Portrait.)

Maila L. Walter, Science and Cultural Crisis: An Intellectual Biography of Percy William Bridgman. 1991.

Tyler Wasson (Ed.), Nobel Prize Winners. 1987. (Portrait.)

Dictionary of Scientific Biography.

D M K

BRIGGS, HENRY Born at Warley Wood, near Halifax, Yorkshire, England, 1561; died Oxford 26 January 1631. Mathematician, chiefly remembered for his dissemination of John NAPIER's invention of logarithms.

Henry Briggs entered St John's College, Cambridge in 1577 (BA 1581; MA 1585), of which he was made a Fellow in 1588. In 1592 he was made reader of the Linacre Lecture, and four years later first professor of geometry at Gresham House (later College), London. There he proposed to alter Napier's scale of logarithms to something close to what has since become the common scale. (In modern terms we may write: $\log_{Briggs} x = 10^{10} (10 - \log_{10} x)$.). In 1616 and 1617 he discussed the change with Napier, who acquiesced. (Existing Napierian logarithms were such that $\log_{Nap} x = 10^7 (\log_e 10^7 - \log_e x)$.). The first table of common or decimal logarithms was calculated by Briggs, and published in 1617 (up to 1000). His Arithmetica Logarithmica (1624) contained logarithms of numbers up to 20 000, and from 90 000 to 100 000, to fourteen places. Briggs improved on Napier's method of constructing logarithms, and he discovered some unusually advanced interpolation techniques.

In 1619 Briggs was appointed to the Savilian Chair of Geometry at Oxford. There he pursued a mathematically undistinguished but immensely useful career, calculating tables of logarithmic sines and tangents, natural sines, tangents, and secants, all to between ten and fifteen places. Published as Trigonometria Britannica in 1633, it remained in general use until the early nineteenth century.

Briggs wrote several lesser tracts, including one on the North-West Passage, two on navigation, and on the magnetic compass.

Dictionary of National Biography.
Dictionary of Scientific Biography.

J D N

BRIGHT, RICHARD Born at Bristol, England, 28 September 1789; died London 16 December 1858. Physician; described Bright's disease (chronic nephritis).

Bright was educated privately in Exeter and Edinburgh. In 1809 he became a medical student in Edinburgh, later travelling to Iceland. On his return he studied at Guy's and St Thomas's Hospitals, London, and graduated in Edinburgh in 1813. After a long continental tour, he was appointed Assistant Physician to Guy's Hospital 1820; full Physician 1824; Fellow of the Royal College of Physicians 1832; and Physician Extraordinary to Queen Victoria 1837.

Bright brought the study of morbid anatomy in the living patient to a new level, and he inaugurated the biochemical study of disease by working with chemists to show that urea is retained in the body fluids in renal failure. Bright's clinical genius was not confined to diseases of the kidney; his contributions included new insights into many cerebral and abdominal disorders. His observations are to be found in the Guy's Hospital Reports (1836); in vol. 1 of his Elements of the Practice of Medicine (written with Thomas ADDISON), and in Clinical Memoirs on Abdominal Tumours (1860).

A. A. Osman, Original Papers of Richard Bright on Renal Disease. 1937.

Sir W. Hale-White, Great Doctors of the Nineteenth Century. 1935.

Guy's Hospital Reports, 107 (4). 1958. (Centenary issue, with portrait.)

Bulletin of the History of Medicine, **8**, 909, 1940.

Dictionary of National Biography.

Dictionary of Scientific Biography.

K D K

BRINDLEY, JAMES Born near Buxton, Derbyshire, England, 1716; died Turnhurst, Staffordshire, 27 September 1772. Canal builder.

Brindley was the son of a poor cottager; he worked as a labourer from a very early age, and in 1733 was apprenticed to a wheelwright and millwright near Macclesfield. In 1742 he established a business in Leek, repairing and setting up machinery of many kinds, including the flint mills required by Josiah WEDGWOOD for his pottery. In 1758 he patented an unsuccessful attempt to improve the Newcomen engine, and was employed in a survey for an abortive project for a Mersey–Trent canal route.

Brindley's famous association with the Duke of Bridgewater began in the following year, when the Duke was reconsidering his Worsley Canal scheme with a view to avoiding a costly descent by locks to the River Irwell. Brindley proposed an aqueduct, and was subsequently employed to make both the Worsley Canal, completed in 1761, and its extension to Runcorn in 1767–7. The Duke was also one of the main promoters, with Wedgwood, of Brindley's biggest achievement, the Grand Trunk Canal linking Mersey and Trent across Cheshire and Staffordshire. Although this canal was not completed until six years after Brindley's death, he had found time to lay out six others, making a total canal mileage of 365.

Experience taught him many things, but the ability of this semi-literate workman to solve the problems of such major works as the Barton aqueduct and the Harecastle tunnel is hard to explain.

S. Smiles, *Lives of the Engineers*, vol. 1 (revised ed.). 1874.

L. W. Meynell, *James Brindley, The Pioneer of Canals*. 1956.

H. Bode, *James Brindley, an Illustrated Life*. 1973. (Portrait.)

C. T. G. Boucher, *James Brindley, Engineer 1716–1772*. 1973.

Dictionary of National Biography.

T K D

BRINELL, JOHANN AUGUST Born at Bringetofta, Småland, Sweden, 21 November 1849; died Stockholm, 17 November 1925. Engineer, remembered for his method of determining the hardness of steel.

Brinell attended Borås Technical School, and on leaving worked as a designer. In 1875, he was appointed engineer at the ironworks at Lesjöfors, and became interested in metallurgy. In 1882 he moved to the Fagersta ironworks as chief engineer; and in 1903 to the Jernkoteret. In 1885 he published a paper on the textural changes of steel during heating and cooling; and his work on the chemical composition and hardening of steel was acclaimed at the Paris Exhibition of 1900. At the same exhibition his instrument for determining the hardness of steel, which is now named after him, was exhibited. He also carried out investigations into the abrasion resistance of materials.

C. Benedicks, *Journal of the Institute of Metals*, **35**, 441, 1926.

Dictionary of Scientific Biography.

B B K

BROCA, PIERRE PAUL Born at Sainte-Foy-la-Grande, Gironde, France, 28 June 1824; died Paris, 9 July 1880. Neurologist and a founder of physical anthropology.

Broca read medicine in Paris (1841–3). In 1853 he became surgeon to the hospitals of Paris, and in 1868 he was appointed to the Paris chair of surgical pathology. In 1859 he and some other scientists held the first meeting of a group which soon became the *Société d'Anthropologie*. He was mainly responsible for the foundation of the *Institut d'Anthropologie* (1876). In 1880 he was appointed to represent science as a perpetual member of the Senate of the Republic.

Broca did important work on the pathology of the bones and joints, on cancer, and on tumours generally. In 1856 he published a fundamental work on aneurysms, including arterio-venous aneurysms. In 1861 Broca had a surgical patient who, incidentally, had for ten years been unable to articulate. The patient died and at autopsy Broca found an area in the left inferior frontal gyrus of the brain more prominent than that area on the right side. He described this area as the motor centre for speech (Broca's convolution). For the condition he coined the term 'aphemia', very soon changed by A. Trousseau (1801–67) to 'aphasia'. Recent work has shown that the area for articulation is not so circumscribed as Broca thought, and 'motor aphasia' has been distinguished from 'sensory aphasia'. Broca wrote many articles on craniometry and physical anthropology, and he invented measuring instruments such as the goniometer and stereograph which are used today.

W. Haymaker and F. Schiller (Eds), *Founders of Neurology*. 1953. (Portrait.)

R. Dumesnil and F. Bonnet-Roy (Eds), *Les Médecins Célèbres*. 1947.

The Lancet, **2**, 153, 1880.

Dictionary of Scientific Biography.

E A U

BRODIE, SIR BENJAMIN COLLINS Born at Winterslow, Wiltshire, England, in 1783; died Broome Park, Surrey, 21 October 1862. Physiologist and surgeon.

Brodie was educated largely at home, and then studied surgery under John Abernethy (1764–1831), and anatomy at the Great Windmill Street School, London. He also studied at St George's Hospital. He qualified as a Member of the Royal College of Surgeons in 1803 and became assistant surgeon at St George's (1808); he also lectured at the Windmill Street School. Brodie became surgeon to St George's in 1822. He was surgeon to George IV and serjeant-surgeon to William IV and to Queen Victoria. A baronetcy was conferred on him in 1834. Brodie was one of the Original Fellows of the Royal College of Surgeons when that order was created in 1843, and he was President of the College in 1844. In 1858 he was the first President of the newly constituted General Medical Council. In 1810 he was elected a Fellow of the Royal Society, which awarded him its Copley Medal in 1811, and Royal Medal in 1850. To it he delivered Croonian Lectures in 1810 and 1811. He was President of the Royal Society from 1858 to 1861.

As a surgeon Brodie was particularly interested in diseases of the joints and of the urinary organs, on both of which he wrote standard works. His name is now associated with a chronic abscess of the tibia and with a rare disease of the breast, both of which he first described. He was the first to perform a subcutaneous operation, and he is known for his advocacy and practice of conservative surgery. He received many foreign honours.

Brodie's best-known physiological researches related to the influence of the nervous system on body temperature. He showed that if an animal was decapitated, or if its spinal cord was divided high in the cervical region, the temperature fell more quickly than in the dead animal. But if the circulation was arrested by ligature of the heart, the fall in temperature was greatly retarded. He investigated the effect of curare and other drugs on these phenomena. His researches led to much similar work by other physiologists.

T. Holmes, *Sir Benjamin Collins Brodie.* 1898.
Autobiography, in Brodie's *Collected Works.*
Dictionary of National Biography.
Dictionary of Scientific Biography.

E A U

BRONGNIART, ALEXANDRE Born in Paris, 5 February 1770; died there, 7 October 1847. Geologist; the first to classify the Tertiary formations.

Alexandre Brongniart, son of an eminent architect and father of the famous botanist A. T. Brongniart (1801–76), was himself one of that band of pioneers who made fundamental detailed researches in the field during the first two decades of the nineteenth century and who thereby gathered together a corpus of knowledge essential to establish geology as a science. He served in the medical department of the army until, in 1794, he became a mining engineer. In 1800 he was made director of the Sèvres porcelain works; as a young man he had published a work on enamelling. He wrote a work on reptiles in 1805 and one on mineralogy in 1807. But henceforth his scientific energies were concentrated on stratigraphical geology. He became the collaborator of G. L. C. CUVIER and the two produced their great work on the geology of the environs of Paris, which first appeared in the *Journal des Mines* in 1808; was then published with additions as a separate work in 1811; and was further enlarged in 1822. This was mostly the work of Brongniart. In it the Tertiary rocks were set in order, and it became clear that strata of different ages were characterized by particular fossils, a principle being independently established in Britain (in Mesozoic rocks) by William SMITH. The existence of formations formed under freshwater conditions was recognized; again a discovery being independently made in Britain at about the same time (by Thomas Webster (1773–1844)). In 1822 Brongniart succeeded R. J. Haüy (1743–1822) as professor of mineralogy in the Museum of Natural History in Paris.

L. de Launay, *Les Brongniart, Une Grande Famille de Savants.* 1940. (Portrait.)
Dictionary of Scientific Biography.

J C

BRØNSTED, JOHANNES NICOLAUS Born at Varde, Denmark, 22 February 1879; died Copenhagen, 17 December 1947. Distinguished physical chemist.

Brønsted, the son of a civil engineer, began to study engineering at the Polytechnic Institute of Copenhagen, but turned to chemistry after one year. After graduating, he spent a period in industry, but returned to academic life as assistant in the University of Copenhagen (1905). Only three years later, he was made professor of physical and inorganic chemistry, a position which he held until his death.

The recurring theme of Brønsted's research work was the application of thermodynamics to physical-chemical problems. He carried out an elaborate series of solubility measurements (partly with V. K. La Mer) which proved to be in agreement with the Debye-Hückel theory (1923), and indeed constitute its strongest experimental support. His studies of the kinetics of reactions in electrolyte solutions (1920–4) led to the definition of the 'secondary salt effect'. Much of his experimental work was done using the cobaltammines left by his predecessor S. M. Jørgensen (1837–1914). His new definition of acids and bases (1923, simultaneously with T. M. LOWRY) has proved very fruitful in many branches of chemistry.

In his later years Brønsted became interested in the theoretical foundations of thermodynamics, and became involved in inconclusive controversies. He also turned to politics, and was elected to the Danish Parliament, but his final illness prevented him from taking his seat.

Journal of the Chemical Society, 409, 1950. (Portrait.)
Nature, **161**, 269, 1948.
E. Farber (Ed.), *Great Chemists.* 1961. (Portrait).
Dictionary of Scientific Biography.

W V F

BROOM, ROBERT Born at Paisley, Scotland, 30 November 1866; died Pretoria, South Africa, 6 April 1951. Palaeontologist.

After early education in Glasgow, Broom qualified as a doctor at the university there in 1889, then spent the years 1892–6 in Australia, where he studied marsupial fossils. In 1897 he moved to South Africa and practised medicine, first in Namaqualand, then in Port Elizabeth, and later at Pearston in the Karroo, where he began to explore and publish descriptions of rich deposits of fossil reptiles. From 1903 to 1909 he was a professor of zoology and geology at the college that later became Stellenbosch University, spending his vacations collecting in the Karroo. During the First World War he served in the RAMC before returning to medical practice in South Africa until his final appointment in 1934 as Curator of Palaeontology in the Transvaal Museum, Pretoria.

Though his work on fossils had begun as a hobby, his studies of the evolution and classification of Permian and Triassic reptiles led to further work on the relationship between reptiles and mammals, published in a series of papers between 1895 and 1935, as well as a book, *The Mammal-like Reptiles of South Africa and the Origin of Mammals* (1932). He also investigated the structure of mammalian skulls and the development of mammals before turning his attention to fossil hominids after the discovery by R. A. DART of the Taungs skull (*Australopithecus*) in 1925. His further investigation of Pleistocene remains produced more hominid material, including remains of *Plesianthropus*, from sites at Sterkfontein and

Swartkrans in the 1940s. *The Coming of Man* (1933), *The South African Fossil Ape-Men* (1946, in collaboration with G. W. H. SCHEPERS), and *Finding the Missing Link* (1950) described these discoveries and their importance in the development of man.

Broom was elected a Fellow of the Royal Society in 1920 and received its Royal Medal in 1928.

A. L. Du Toit (Ed.) *Robert Broom Commemorative Volume.* 1948.

R. A. Dart, 'Robert Broom: His Life and Work', *South African Journal of Science*, **48**, 3, 1951.

Obituary Notices of Fellows of the Royal Society. 1953.

Dictionary of Scientific Biography.

S J R

BROUNCKER, WILLIAM (SECOND VISCOUNT BROUNCKER) Born at Castle Lyons, Ireland, c.1620; died London, 5 April 1684. Mathematician; first President of the Royal Society.

Brouncker went up to Oxford at 16, and graduated in medicine in 1647. In 1662 he was appointed Chancellor to Queen Catherine. He became Master of St Catherine's Hospital, London, in 1681. Mathematics, however, was his main interest and in this field he quickly made his name. He was a founder member of the Royal Society and its first President (1662–77). He was a President of Gresham College (1664–7). Although a Royalist, Brouncker was allowed to pursue his studies undisturbed during the Protectorate. He was a gifted linguist and also an accomplished musician. In 1653 he published an English translation of the *Musicae Compendium* (1619) of DESCARTES. This was an unimportant work – Descartes wrote it as a young man while taking part in the siege of Breda – and it is conjectured that Brouncker's motive was to publicise his own version of the musical scale propounded by Marin Mersenne (1588–1648).

In mathematics, Brouncker is remembered for his early use of continued fractions, notably for the evaluation of π. Following John WALLIS, he evolved the formula

$$\frac{\pi}{4} = \frac{1}{1+} \ \frac{1^2}{2+} \ \frac{3^2}{2+} \ \frac{5^2}{2+} \ \dots \ \text{etc.}$$

He was interested also in the quadrature of the hyperbola (*Philosophical Transactions*, 1688) and the rectification of the parabola.

Harold Hartley (Ed.), *The Royal Society: its Origins and Founders.* 1960. (Portrait.)

Dictionary of National Biography.

Notes and Records of the Royal Society, **15**, 147, 1960.

T I W

BROUWER, LUITZEN EGBERTUS JAN Born at Hoorn, Netherlands, 27 February 1881; died Blaricum, 2 December 1966. Mathematical philosopher.

Brouwer went to school at Hoorn and Haarlem, and then to the University of Amsterdam, graduating Doctor of Science in 1907, with a dissertation *On the Foundations of Mathematics*. He remained as External Lecturer (1902–12) and professor of mathematics (1912–51). He was a member of many learned societies, including the Royal Society, and was an honorary graduate of the universities of Cambridge and Oslo; he was appointed Knight in the Order of the Dutch Lion in 1932.

He made important contributions to many major fields of mathematics, notably topology (in which he was a pioneer, enunciating the fixed point theorem), the theory of aggregates, and the theory of functions. It is, however, as a philosopher that he was best known. Rejecting the classical system of deductive reasoning, he established an intuitive school of mathematical thought which, he claimed, was better able to deal with the infinite totalities of modern mathematics. He elaborated his views in his *Wiskunde, Waarheid, Werkelijkheid* (Mathematics, Truth, Reality, 1919). He greatly influenced mathematical thought in the twentieth century.

The Times, 17 December 1966.

Dictionary of Scientific Biography.

T I W

BROWN, ALEXANDER CRUM Born in Edinburgh, 26 March 1838; died there, 28 October 1922. Famous for his work in organic chemistry.

The son of a Presbyterian minister, Crum Brown read medicine at Edinburgh (though probably not intending to practise) and chemistry at Heidelberg and Marburg. He became lecturer in chemistry at Edinburgh in 1863 and later professor (1869–1908).

Crum Brown's MD thesis (1861) *On the theory of chemical combination* contains one of the earliest uses of graphic formulae (atoms linked by lines). Subsequent publications and lectures did much to bring these into general employment. The new symbolism gave powerful support to the theory of structure (A. M. BUTLEROV and others), which was further advanced when Brown disproved Butlerov's distinction between primary and secondary affinity units. He published on organosulphur compounds and on optical activity. With James WALKER he applied the electrolytic synthesis of H. KOLBE to half-esters, and suggested a free-radical interpretation of the reaction. In 1892, with J. Gibson (1855–1914), he proposed the 'Crum Brown-Gibson Rule' for aromatic substitution.

He had remarkably comprehensive scientific interests. In physiology he wrote on the inner ear, and pursued an investigation on the relation between chemical constitution and physiological activity. He envisaged a mathematical theory of chemistry as an ultimate goal for chemists. He was proficient at Japanese and maintained a lifelong interest in systems of knitting.

He gained the first London DSc (1862), and held honorary degrees of all four Scottish universities. He was elected FRS in 1879, and was President of the Chemical Society in 1891–3.

Journal of the Chemical Society, 3422, 1923. (Portrait.)

Ambix, **14**, 112, 1967.

Dictionary of National Biography (Missing Persons). 1993.

Dictionary of Scientific Biography.

C A R

BROWN, ROBERT Born at Montrose, Scotland, 21 December 1773; died London, 10 June 1858. Plant taxonomist: first observer of 'Brownian movement'.

After studying medicine at Edinburgh, Brown joined the army as a surgeon and served in Ireland 1795–1800, developing also his keen botanical interest. A chance meeting with Sir Joseph BANKS in 1798 led to his appointment as naturalist on Matthew Flinders' voyage to Australia (1801–5). Over the next five years he classified the 4000 species of plants brought back, concurrently working as Clerk to the Linnean Society. In 1810 he published the first (only) volume of his *Prodromas florae Novae Hollandiae*, covering 464 genera and 2000 species. Subsequently he worked for Banks (who bequeathed him his house) and after his death in 1820 supervised the transfer of his huge collection to the British Museum. Experimentally, he observed and described the cell nucleas in plants, originally in orchids, but later in Monocotyledons. In 1827 he observed the random movement of pollen and other small particles in fluid suspension. Erudite, diligent, and widely travelled he was internationally esteemed. A. VON HUMBOLDT called him *botanicorum facile princeps*.

W. T. Stearn, *Three Prefaces on Linnaeus and Robert Brown*. 1962.
Dictionary of Scientific Biography.
Dictionary of National Biography VII.

T I W

BROWN-SÉQUARD, CHARLES EDOUARD Born

in Mauritius, 8 April 1817; died Paris, 1 April 1894. Best known for his physiological experiments on the spinal cord, and for his demonstration of the function of the suprarenal glands.

Son of an Irish-American sea-captain, Charles Edward Brown, and a French mother, Charlotte Séquard, Brown-Séquard at the age of 21 persuaded his mother to leave Mauritius for Paris, where he studied medicine, qualifying in 1840. From the first an enthusiastic experimental physiologist, he repeated the studies by GALEN of the effects of hemisection of the spinal cord, thus revealing that loss of the sensations of pain and temperature occurred on the opposite side of the body. Clinically, such 'crossed' sensory changes with hemiplegia are called Brown-Séquard's Syndrome.

Restless in Paris, Brown-Séquard left for Philadelphia, his father's birthplace. Here he married, struggled with poverty, and eventually returned to Mauritius. Back once more in Virginia he published his *Researches on Physiology and Pathology*. By 1856 he was again in Paris, studying the effects of excision of the suprarenal glands, showing the relation between their loss and the symptoms of Addison's disease. In this work Brown-Séquard followed Claude BERNARD as founder of the concept of endocrine disease. Later, in 1878, he was to succeed Bernard as professor of experimental medicine in the *Collège de France*. However, before this event this brilliant, restless man had become a consultant in London, obtaining appointment as one of the first physicians to the National Hospital, Queen's Square; he had accepted the chair of physiology and nervous pathology at Harvard; he had been professor of comparative medicine at Paris; and returned to consultant practice in New York. His last years were occupied in attempting to develop 'testicular juices' as rejuvenating agents in men. He was founder-editor of the *Journal de la physiologie de l'homme et des animaux* (1858–63), and with J. M. CHARCOT and E. F. A. Vulpian (1826–87), of the

Archives de physiologie normale et pathologique (1868–94).

J. M. D. Olmsted, *Charles Edouard Brown-Séquard: a Nineteenth Century Neurologist and Endocrinologist*. 1946. (Portrait.)
W. Haymaker and F. Schiller (Eds), *The Founders of Neurology*. 1970. (Portrait.)
Dictionary of Scientific Biography.

K D K

BRUCE, SIR DAVID Born in Melbourne, Australia,

29 May 1855; died London, 20 November 1931. Noted for his work on parasitology, especially sleeping-sickness.

Bruce qualified in medicine from Edinburgh University and entered the Army Medical Service in 1883. In 1884 he was posted to Malta and began studying the obscure, often fatal disease known as Malta or Mediterranean fever. Within two years he found the cause – a bacterium now named in his honour, *Brucella melitensis*. This and later work eventually led to the eradication of the disease.

From 1889 to 1894, he was assistant professor of pathology in the Army Medical School and worked to improve studies in pathology. In 1894 he went to South Africa and studied nagana, a common, economically important disease of domestic animals. He soon showed that the bite of an infected tsetse fly transmitted the disease. This important result aided his later work on sleeping-sickness. Bruce, as a member of the 1903 Royal Society Commission on the disease, was informed by Aldo Castellani that a trypanosome could sometimes be found in the cerebrospinal fluid of patients with sleeping-sickness. Energetically following this lead, Bruce quickly proved that sleeping-sickness was a trypanosome disease transmitted by a tsetse fly.

In 1912 Bruce was promoted to the rank of Surgeon-General in recognition of his services to medicine. He was elected FRS in 1899 and was knighted in 1908. From 1914 to 1919 he was Commandant of the Royal Army Medical College and made important contributions to the use of tetanus antitoxin. Throughout his life he was ably helped by his wife, Mary Elizabeth Steele, whom he married in 1883, and expressed the wish that her work should always be acknowledged along with his.

Obituary Notices of Fellows of the Royal Society, 1952.
The Lancet, **2**, 1270, 1931.
H. Oxbury (Ed.), *Great Britons: 20th Century Lives*. 1985.
Dictionary of National Biography.
Dictionary of Scientific Biography.

J K C

BRUNEL, ISAMBARD KINGDOM Born at Ports-

mouth, Hampshire, England, 9 April 1806; died London, 15 September 1859. Civil engineer.

The only son of Sir Marc Isambard BRUNEL, Isambard Kingdom was educated at English private schools and the *Collège Henri Quatre* in Paris. He entered his father's office in 1823, and his first important independent work was the Clifton Suspension Bridge, though this was not completed in his lifetime. He also built the Hungerford suspension bridge (1845), of which the wrought-iron chains were re-erected at Clifton in 1862. His miscellaneous employments included the construction of numerous docks and piers and of a floating gun-carriage for the intended attack on Kronstadt during the Crimean War.

In March 1833 I. K. Brunel was appointed engineer of the Great Western Railway, for which he laid out the route and introduced the controversial 7-foot gauge, which was not finally abolished until 1892. He also designed the fine railway termini at Paddington and Temple Meads, Bristol; tunnels, including the Box Tunnel outside Bath; and a series of bridges, culminating in the Royal Albert Bridge, which in 1859 carried the line across the Tamar into Cornwall. The methods he employed here, such as the use of compressed-air caissons, had been tried out previously for his Chepstow railway bridge over the Wye.

Having half-jokingly suggested the proposal, Brunel found support for the building of a steamship designed for the Atlantic crossing, which the *Great Western* duly performed in fifteen days (1838). He followed this by the *Great Britain*, iron-hulled, screw-driven, the largest vessel afloat. Then, in 1853, with the round trip to Australia in view, Brunel proceeded to plan a ship four times as big. This double-skinned, five-deck colossus was economically built with plates and rivets of standard size, and proved immensely strong; it had ten boilers, with engines to drive both paddles and screw. But the *Great Eastern* never reached the East. Its troubles began with the launching, which cost £120,000 more than expected because the vessel had been built broad-side-on to the Thames. Financial and other innumerable worries perhaps made it a blessing in disguise for its designer that he was carried off by paralysis when preparations were being completed for the trials, which showed that the coal consumption was twice the calculated amount: the 'great ship' could never carry its planned 4000 passengers on any voyage of adequate duration, and was eventually used to lay the Atlantic cable of 1865.

Isambard Kingdom Brunel was elected FRS in 1830, and received an honorary DCL from Oxford in 1857.

L. T. C. Rolt, *Life of Isambard Kingdom Brunel.*
    1959.
D. Goddard, *Eminent Engineers.* 1906. (Portrait.)
Alfred Pugsley (Ed.), *The Works of Isambard
    Kingdom Brunel.* 1980. (Portrait.)
A. Vaughan, *Isambard Kingdom Brunel:
    Engineering Knight Errant.* 1991.
R. James, *Isambard Kingdom Brunel 1806–1859:
    An Illustrated Life.* 1972. (Portrait.)
Dictionary of National Biography.
                                                            T K D

BRUNEL, SIR MARC ISAMBARD Born at Hacqueville, Normandy, France, 25 April 1769; died London, 12 December 1849. Engineer and pioneer of mass-production.

Marc Brunel, originally educated for the Church, served as an officer in the French Navy, 1786–92; fled from the Revolution to the United States, where he found employment as a civil engineer and architect; and came to England in 1799, with a view to exploiting his ideas for mass-production of pulley blocks, of which the Admiralty required about 100 000 a year. Sir Samuel Bentham (1757–1831), the Inspector-General of Naval Works, hav-

ing recommended his project as superior to one of his own, Brunel was authorized to set up his machinery at Portsmouth, where his designs were executed mainly by Henry MAUDSLAY. A total of forty-three machines were erected, several of which remained in service for a century and a half. Driven by a 30 hp engine, they converted elm logs into blocks ready for fitting and polishing, and reduced the labour required from 110 skilled to ten unskilled workmen. This was in full swing by 1808, and when the Napoleonic Wars ended Brunel had just prepared a second project of mass-production, boot-making machinery for the army.

Although a very fertile inventor, Marc Brunel lacked commercial talent, and he was for a time imprisoned for debt. From 1825, however, with the help of his son, Isambard BRUNEL, he was engaged to construct the first Thames tunnel, designed for foot passengers but taken over later for the London Underground. He made use of a three-tier cast-iron shield as a stand for the excavators, with screw-jacks to press it against the working face and the completed masonry. The scheme, held up five times by inundations, was completed in 1843, two years after he had received the honour of knighthood.

J. A. Hammerton, *Concise Universal Biography.*
    (Portrait.)
Dictionary of National Biography.
R. Beamish, *Memoir of the Life of Sir Marc
    Isambard Brunel.* 1862.
P. Clements, *Marc Isambard Brunel.* 1970.
                                                            T K D

BRUNNER, SIR JOHN TOMLINSON Born at Everton, near Liverpool, England, 8 February 1842; died Chertsey, Surrey, 2 July 1919. Chemical industrialist.

John Brunner was the second son of a Swiss clergyman who kept a school in Liverpool. He was educated by his father, with the intention that he should follow a commercial career, and worked as an accountant for John Hutchinson (1825–65), a leading alkali manufacturer in Widnes. Here he became friendly with Ludwig MOND, and in 1872 set up in partnership with him at Winnington Hall, Cheshire, to manufacture soda-ash by the newly perfected ammonia-soda process of E. SOLVAY. Brunner was no chemist, but he was the business brains of the partnership, and much of the eventual success of the firm (later Brunner, Mond & Co. Ltd) must be credited to him. His attitude towards labour was remarkably enlightened for his times; in later life (1885) he went into politics, and became a Liberal M. P. (for Northwich) of pronounced Radical opinions. He was made a baronet in 1895.

Journal of the Society of Chemical Industry, **38**,
    277R, 1919.
J. M. Cohen, *The Life of Ludwig Mond.* 1956.
    (Portrait.)
J. I. Watts, *The First Fifty Years of Brunner, Mond.
    & Co.* 1923. (Portrait.)
*Dictionary of National Biography (Missing
    Persons).* 1993.
                                                            W V F

BUCHNER, EDUARD Born in Munich, Bavaria, Germany, 20 May 1860; died Focsani, Romania, 13 August 1917. Chemist; discovered cell-free alcoholic fermentation of sucrose.

After working for a few years as chemist in a

sweet factory, Buchner studied in the University of Munich under J-F. W. A. von BAEYER and T. C. Curtius (1857–1928). He became *Privatdozent* in Kiel (1893), assistant professor in Tübingen (1896), and then professor in the *Landwirtschaftliche Hochschule* in Berlin (1898), briefly at Breslau, and finally at Würzburg (1911). As a reserve officer he was called to the Army in August 1914, but returned to Würzburg in 1916. A year later he rejoined the Army, and died of a grenade wound in a military hospital in Rumania.

Buchner's research interests were twofold. He pursued classical organic chemistry, often in collaboration with Curtius, in his studies of the aliphatic diazo-compounds, especially their reaction with benzene to give norcaradiene derivatives. Of more ultimate importance, however, was his work on fermentation, partly in collaboration with his elder brother Hans. It was during his brief period in Tübingen that he discovered the answer to a problem that had remained unanswered for decades, and for which he was awarded a Nobel prize for chemistry in 1907. By grinding yeast cells with sand at a controlled temperature he was able to prepare a cell-free extract that would ferment sucrose to ethanol, a property which he ascribed to an hypothetical enzyme 'zymase' (later shown by A. HARDEN to be very complex). This work showed that living yeast cells were not essential for fermentation (as PASTEUR and others had supposed), and marks the beginning of modern enzyme chemistry.

Berichte der deutschen Chemischen Gesellschaft, **50**, 1843, 1917. (Portrait.)

Tyler Wasson (Ed.), *Nobel Prize Winners*. 1987. (Portrait.)

W V F

BUFFON, GEORGE LOUIS LECLERC, COMTE DE Born at Montbard, Côte d'Or, France, 7 September 1707; died Paris, 15 April 1788. Encyclopaedist of natural science.

Buffon, the son of Benjamin François Leclerc de Buffon, a magistrate and councillor of the Burgundy Parliament, was educated at the Jesuit's College in Dijon, neglecting study of the law for mathematics and astronomy. At the College he met Lord Kingston (1711–73) and his tutor, with whom he travelled to Italy and returned to England. He inherited a large fortune from his mother and became free to follow those pursuits that interested him. About the age of 25 he returned to Montbard, where he settled down to a lifetime of scientific labour that was uninterrupted for fifty years. He worked regularly for some hours each day in a pavilion in his garden, but when work was done he indulged in frequent 'irregularities of conduct'.

In 1735 he published a translation into French of the *Vegetable Staticks* of Stephen HALES, in 1740 one of the *Fluxions* of NEWTON, and in his earlier years many papers on physics and agriculture. He carried out a series of elaborate experiments to discover the credibility of the story of ARCHIMEDES setting fire to the Roman fleet under Marcellus by focusing the sun's rays upon the ships when distant a bowshot. By using 168 mirrors six inches by eight in size in an adjustable framework he was able to inflame wooden planks at a distance of 150 feet, and a mixture of wood chips, sulphur, and charcoal at 250 feet, and satisfied himself that Archimedes' exploit was perfectly feasible.

In 1739 Buffon was elected Associate of the Academy of Sciences, and was appointed Keeper of the *Jardin du Roi* and of the Royal Cabinet; the contents of the museum attracted his attention to natural history, and led him to plan a comprehensive work describing every part of the animal kingdom, preceded by a history of the Earth. He enlisted the help of several naturalists, especially of L. J. M. Daubenton (1716–1800), in this compilation. The first volumes of the *Histoire naturelle, générale et particulière* appeared in 1749, and publication continued until 1804 in forty-four quarto volumes beautifully illustrated with engraved plates; the last eight volumes, which were published after Buffon's death, were completed by B. G. E. de la ville Lacepède (1756–1825).

In 1753 Buffon became a member of the French Academy, and in 1771 Louis XIV created him Comte; he was elected FRS (1739), and member of the principal academies and learned societies of Europe. His one son entered the Army and perished in the Revolution.

Buffon's chief work is not the result of original research, but a compilation based on wide reading, written in a clear and attractive manner. It was the first attempt at a comprehensive treatment of the entire natural world, and although it has many defects, particularly in its generalizations, it had a wide and stimulating influence on the growing science of natural history.

Buffon expressed his personal vanity in his dress and mode of life, but was an indulgent and popular proprietor to the tenants and employees of his estates. He suffered much in his last years from vesicular calculus and, refusing operation, died from it at the age of 81; at post-mortem, fifty stones were found in his bladder.

Compte de Lacepède, 'Notice sur la vie de Buffon' in *Oeuvres complètes de Buffon*. 1825. (Portrait.)

L. Bertin, *et. al.*, *Buffon*. 1952. (Portrait.)

O. E. Fellows and S. F. Milliken, *Buffon*. 1972.

Janet Brown, *Endeavour* (New Series), **12**, 86, 1988. (Portrait.)

Dictionary of Scientific Biography.

L H M

BULLARD, EDWARD CRISP Born in Norwich, England, 21 September 1907; died La Jolla, California, USA, 3 April 1980. Pioneer of marine geophysics.

Graduating from Clare College, Cambridge (1929) Bullard began research on electron scattering but joined the newly-formed Department of Geology and Geophysics in 1931, completing his PhD in 1932. In 1937 he visited W. M. EWING, undertaking early marine seismic investigations of the US continental shelf. Bullard began a similar programme on the eastern Atlantic margin in 1938, together with land-based heat flow measurements. Following war service with the Admiralty (1939–45), he moved from Cambridge to the University of Toronto and in 1948 began joint investigation with Scripps Institute of Oceanography of ocean-floor heat flow. This continued following his return to England as Director of the National Physical Laboratory. By 1956, when he returned to Cambridge, it had established the surprising equality of sub-continental and sub-oceanic heat flows and later showed that mid-oceanic ridges have associated high-temperature anomalies. In 1965 Bullard demonstrated the remarkable match of continental shelf edges across the Atlantic, using EULER's theorem (remembered from his undergraduate mechanics lectures) to obtain the pole and rotation angle minimizing their misfit. Coupled with evidence of symmetrical magnetic anomalies centered on the Mid-Atlantic Ridge, the following year Bullard became a convinced advocate of sea-floor spreading. Knighted in 1953 for his services to the government, he received the Vletsen Prize in 1968 and in 1974 retired to Scripps.

Dictionary of Scientific Biography, Supp. II.
Biographical Memoirs of Fellows of the Royal Society 1987. (Portrait.)
S. P. Parker (Ed.), *McGraw-Hill Modern Scientists and Engineers*, 1980. (Portrait.)
W. Glen, *The Road to Jaramillo*, 1982. (Portrait.)
R. Muir Wood, *The Dark Side of the Earth*, 1985.
                                  R J H

BUNSEN, ROBERT WILHELM Born at Göttingen, Germany, 31 March 1811; died Heidelberg, 16 August 1899. One of the great experimental chemists of the century, and a pioneer of chemical spectroscopy.

Bunsen, whose father was librarian and professor of linguistics in the University of Göttingen, studied chemistry there and graduated PhD in 1830. After appointments in various universities (Göttingen, Kassel, Marburg, Breslau), he succeeded L. GMELIN in the chair of chemistry at Heidelberg (1852), where he remained until his retirement in 1889. There he built up a fine school of chemistry, with emphasis on practical technique; the number and fame of his students is equalled only by those of Justus von LIEBIG and F. WÖHLER. He never married, and devoted his whole life to his laboratory and his students, among whom his genial and approachable personality made him very popular. Bunsen was essentially an experimenter, with little taste for classifying, theorizing, or speculation; his famous lecture course (*Allgemeine Experimentalchemie*) was much the same at the end of his career as at the beginning, and just as successful. He continued to work and publish until he was almost 80.

His first important research, on cacodyl compounds, was mostly done during his Marburg period. From the foul-smelling, spontaneously inflammable distillate of a mixture of arsenious oxide and potassium acetate (discovered by L. C. Cadet (1731–99) in 1760), Bunsen isolated a pure compound $C_4H_{12}As_2O$, which he regarded as the oxide of a radical 'cacodyl' $C_4H_{12}As_2$. Numerous other derivatives of cacodyl were prepared and formulated similarly, culminating in the isolation of what Bunsen regarded as the free cacodyl radical (now known to be tetramethyl diarsine). This work was an important buttress for the theory of 'compound radicals' in organic chemistry; it also helped Sir Edward FRANKLAND in his development of the concept of valency. From the practical viewpoint it was exceedingly difficult, highly unpleasant, and dangerous to an extent not then fully realized; it is remarkable that it was done without loss of life. It seems to have prejudiced Bunsen against organic chemistry, which he would never allow to be studied in his Heidelberg laboratory.

Bunsen's most seminal work was his pioneer study of chemical spectroscopy, in collaboration with G. R. KIRCHHOFF (1860). This quickly led to the detection and isolation of two new alkali metals, rubidium and caesium, and (in other hands) to the discovery of several new elements. It was the foundation of a whole new science, which extended chemical research from the earth to the sun and stars. With Sir Henry ROSCOE (1857), Bunsen was also one of the founders of photochemistry, in a classical study of the light-induced combination of hydrogen and chlorine.

Bunsen's minor researches are very numerous, and, in conformity with his practical nature, mostly concern matters of laboratory technique. He greatly extended the accuracy and scope of gas analysis, and wrote a book on it; he used it with great success in studies of blast-furnace gases (one of his few ventures into industrial chemistry). He was less successful in the difficult field of combustion and flame, where his often erroneous conclusions were later corrected by M. P. E. BERTHELOT, H. B. DIXON and others. He invented the Bunsen cell and the Bunsen ice calorimeter; in the invention of the Bunsen burner he seems to have played only a small part, though it was made in large numbers for sale under that name by his technician C. Desaga.

G. Lockemann, *Robert Wilhelm Bunsen,
   Lebensbild eines deutschen Naturforscher.* 1949.
H. Debus, *Erinnerungen an R. W. Bunsen.* 1901.
Journal of the Chemical Society, 514, 1900.
   (Portrait).
Berichte der deutschen Chemischen Gesellschaft,
   41, 4875, 1908. (Portrait.)
Dictionary of Scientific Biography.
                                  W V F

BURNET, SIR FRANK MACFARLANE Born at Traralgon, Victoria, Australia, 3 September 1899; died Melbourne, Australia, 31 August 1985. Immunologist.

Educated at the Victoria State School and Geelong College, Victoria, Burnet studied medicine at the University of Melbourne, graduating in 1923. Research at the Walter and Eliza Hall Institute of the University of Melbourne led to one year at the Lister Institute in London as Beit Memorial Fellow, and he was awarded a PhD in 1928 for his research on bacteriophages. He returned to the Walter and Eliza Hall Institute, where he became assistant director in 1934 and Director in 1944. He was also professor of Experimental Medicine at the University of Melbourne from 1944 to 1965.

During the earlier part of his career Burnet did extensive research on viruses, studying viruses in living chick embryos. This led to the study of the influenza virus and methods of immunization against it. He isolated a strain of 'influenza A' virus in 1935. He also showed that there were several types of poliomyelitis virus, and studied the organism causing Q-fever, later named *Rickettsia burneti*.

In the late 1940s Burnet turned his attention to immunology, publishing *The Production of Antibodies* with F. J. Fenner (1914–) in 1949, in which he suggested that the ability to produce a particular antibody was not innate. This was confirmed by Peter MEDAWAR in 1951. In 1957 he formulated his 'clonal selection' theory of antibody formation, showing how the body distinguishes between its own and other living cells, 'self and non-self' substances. Burnet's theory that antibodies could be produced artificially in the body to develop a specific type of immunity led to the discovery of acquired immunological tolerance. It was for this that Burnet was awarded the Nobel prize for physiology or medicine in 1960, jointly with Medawar. This discovery was to be of great importance in the development of tissue transplant surgery.

Elected a Fellow of the Royal Society in 1942, Burnet was knighted in 1951, and awarded the Order of Merit in 1958, and the KBE in 1969. His publications included *Viruses and Man* (1953) and *The Clonal Selection Theory of Acquired Immunity* (1959).

Christopher Sexton, *The Seeds of Time. The Life of Sir Macfarlane Burnet.* 1992.
Biographical Memoirs of Fellows of the Royal Society 1987. (Portrait.)
Sir Macfarlane Burnet, *Changing Patterns: An Atypical Biography.* 1968.
Tyler Wasson (Ed.), *Nobel Prize Winners.* 1987. (Portrait.)

A P B

BURTON, ROBERT Born at Lindley, Leicestershire, England, 8 February 1577; died Oxford, 25 January 1640. Author of the *Anatomy of Melancholy*.

Burton was educated at Sutton Coldfield and Nuneaton Grammar School. In 1593 he entered Brasenose College, Oxford. In 1599 he was elected a Student of Christ Church, Oxford, where he lived until the day of his death. In 1616 he was made Vicar of St Thomas, Oxford, and in 1630 was presented to the living of Seagrave, in his native Leicestershire.

Burton is among those whose claim to fame rests on a single achievement, in his case the writing of the *Anatomy of Melancholy*, which occupied him for thirty years. Apart from this he wrote only one other substantial work, a comedy, *Philosophaster*, which was never published. The *Anatomy*, a work combining immense erudition with exceptional literary talent, is in effect the first serious treatise on morbid psychology, and in the breadth of his interest, and in his conclusions about human motivation, many see Burton as the precursor of Sigmund FREUD. Certainly its 'Third Partition, on Love Melancholy', is a frank and extremely well-documented exposition of erotic psychology. The *Anatomy* first appeared in 1621, and in an enlarged form in 1624. Four other editions were published before the end of the seventeenth century, and many others since. Samuel Johnson records that it was the only book that ever took him out of bed two hours sooner than he wished to rise!

Burton was keenly interested in astrology and he is said to have died on, or very near, the date he had himself predicted in making the calculation of his nativity, which is reproduced on his tomb in Christ Church.

Proceedings and Papers of the Oxford Bibliographical Society, vol. 1, pt. 3. 1926.
E. Bensly, *Notes and Queries.* 1897–1908.
C. Whibley, *Literary Portraits.* 1904.
Dictionary of National Biography.
A. Brownlee, *Nature,* **219**, 125, 1968.

T I W

BUSH, VANNEVAR Born at Everett, Massachusetts, USA, 11 March 1890; died Belmont, Massachusetts, 28 June 1974. Electrical engineer, a pioneer in the design and construction of early analog computers.

After graduating BS and MS from Tufts College in 1913, Bush joined the General Electric Company for some practical experience before taking his DEng, after only one year of study, at the Massachusetts Institute of Technology (MIT) in 1916. During the latter part of the First World War he was engaged on research into magnetic methods of submarine detection, then in 1919 returned to MIT as associate professor of electric power transmission. His research into various problems of electricity distribution involved him in increasingly tedious mathematical computations, and in 1925 he embarked on the development of a series of electro-mechanical calculating machines capable of solving differential equations of increasing complexity. He was thus the first man to achieve what Charles BABBAGE had attempted unsuccessfully to do almost exactly a century before.

In 1931 he began building his almost entirely mechanical differential analyser, which could handle as many as 18 independent variables simultaneously. Within the next ten years many similar machines were constructed, but further advances had to await the theoretical pathfinding of Norbert WIENER's *Cybernetics* in 1948, and the development of solid-state micro-electronics launched by the invention of the transistor by SHOCKLEY, Brattain and BARDEEN in the same year.

Bush was appointed dean of the school of engineering at MIT in 1932, and held the office of president of the Carnegie Institute of Washington from 1938 until his retirement in 1955. During the Second World War he acted as scientific advisor to the US government, and played a leading role in the initiation of 'Project Manhattan' which resulted in the detonation of atomic bombs over Japan in 1945. In addition to his many technical publications, he wrote *Modern Arms and Free Men* (1949), *Science is Not Enough* (1967), and *Pieces of the Action* (1970).

Biographical Memoirs of the National Academy of Sciences, **50**, 89, 1979.
Modern Scientists and Engineers. McGraw-Hill. (Portrait.)
Who Was Who in America, **6**.
Dictionary of Scientific Biography, Supp. II.

R M B

BUTEMENT, WILLIAM ALAN STEWART Born at Masterton, New Zealand, 18 August 1904; died Australia, 25 January 1990. Inventor of the proximity fuse.

Born in New Zealand, Butement was educated in Australia at Scots College, Sydney, before coming to England to University College, London, where he gained his BSc. In 1928 he joined the Signals Experimental Establishment at Woolwich as a scientific officer.

In 1931 Butement was one of the first to see the possibility of long-range detection by radio waves when with P. E. POLLARD he submitted a memo to the director of the SEE on 'Coastal Defence Apparatus (apparatus to locate ships from the coast or other ships, under any conditions of visibility or weather)'. Working in their spare time they developed a pulsed radio transmitter which was able to detect a sheet of corrugated iron at over one hundred yards, but lack of War Office support led them to abandon the experiments.

In 1938 Butement joined the group of War Office scientists at the Bawdsey Research Station who were working on the application of radar to the Army's requirements, and devised a system of coastal defence radar which could detect the approach of low-flying aircraft.

At the end of 1939 Butement was transferred from the War Office to the Ministry of Supply and posted to the Air Defence Experimental Establishment at Christchurch, Hampshire. Encouraged by (Sir) John COCKCROFT he invented a radio-operated proximity fuse which could be used to detonate shells automatically when the target was within a specific range of the weapon. In July 1940 the Tizard Mission passed on details of the proximity fuse to the Americans, who began to manufacture it in large quantities from 1941 onwards for use by the US Navy. It was first used in Britain in combination with the SCR 584 centimetre wave radar set in July 1944 against the V-1 flying bombs, and was first used in a land battle in December 1944 in the Ardennes.

After the Second World War Butement became involved in guided missile projects. He was the first chief superintendant of the Long Range Weapons Establishment from 1947–9, and from 1949 to 1967 he was Chief Scientist in charge of Australian Defence Scientific Research and Development, which included the Rocket Range at Woomera. Butement was awarded the CBE in 1959.

> Guy Hartcup, *The Challenge of War: Scientific and Engineering Contributions to World War Two.* 1970.
>
> Russell Burns (Ed.), *Radar Development to 1945.* 1988.

A P B

BUTLEROV, ALEKSANDR MIKHAILOVICH Born at Chistopol, near Kazan, Russia, 6 September 1828; died Butlerovka, near Kazan, 17 August 1886. Organic chemist, notable for his championship of the theory of structure, and for the concept of tautomerism.

Butlerov came of a family of landed gentry, with military traditions. He studied at the University of Kazan, graduating first in zoology, then chemistry. His teachers (N. N. Zinin (1812–80) and K. K.

Klaus (1796–1864)) were distinguished chemists, but out of touch with current thought; he taught himself from books. In 1857 he was made a full professor in Kazan, and immediately took the opportunity to visit chemistry schools in western Europe. He spent most of his time in the laboratory of A. WURTZ in Paris, where he met A. S. COUPER; he also met F. A. KEKULÉ in Heidelberg. In 1859, after his return to Kazan, he wrote a paper criticizing Couper's revolutionary ideas about structure, but by 1861 we find him at a conference in Speyer, ably advocating the Structure Theory in its most complete form. This position he maintained, both in teaching and research, for the rest of his life, though his contributions tended to be little noticed, except in Russia.

In 1860, Butlerov was made Rector of the University of Kazan, a difficult position which he filled with ability and dignity through three years of incessant student unrest. He also built up a great school of organic chemistry; V. V. Markovnikov (1838–1904) was his best-known pupil. In 1868 he left remote Kazan for the University of St Petersburg. Here he became involved in the bitter disputes in the Academy of Sciences between the Russian and the German factions, and took his stand firmly with the former. He resigned his chair in 1880, and went to live at Butlerovka, his family estate, where he carried on research in his private laboratory. This work concerned variability of atomic weights, and was left unfinished and unpublished at his death.

Butlerov studied formaldehyde for the first time, and observed its polymerization to a mixture of sugars under alkaline conditions. His grasp of structural possibilities enabled him to predict the existence of tertiary alcohols, and to synthesize tertiary butanol. In 1876, in his important paper on isodibutylene, he had all the essentials of the concept of tautomerism, though the implications were not clearly spelled out. Under conditions which were nearly always difficult, he achieved a great deal in chemistry, yet was still able to pursue his other interests, which included bee-keeping and spiritualism.

> L. Gumilevski, *Aleksandr Mikhailovich Butlerov*. 1952. (Portrait.)
>
> E. Farber (Ed.), *Great Chemists*. 1961. (Portrait.)
>
> *Journal of Chemical Education*, **17**, 203, 1940. (Portrait.)
>
> *Dictionary of Scientific Biography*.

W V F

C

CAILLETET, LOUIS PAUL Born at Chatillon-sur-Seine, France, 21 September 1832; died Paris, 5 January 1913. Chiefly remembered for his work on the liquefaction of the permanent gases.

After passing through the *École des Mines* at Paris, Cailletet entered his father's ironworks, later becoming manager. His early scientific research was in metallurgy, especially on the properties of iron. Following the introduction of the notion of critical temperature by T. ANDREWS, it became evident that the failure of all previous efforts to liquefy the so-called permanent gases had been due to pressure being applied at insufficiently low temperatures. Cailletet was thus led to reinvestigate the liquefaction of oxygen, and on 2 December 1877 he finally obtained the liquid in the form of a cloud at 300 atmospheres pressure and −27 °C. In later experiments he liquefied hydrogen, nitrogen and air. Working independently, R. P. PICTET also succeeded in liquefying oxygen in the same year. There ensued a considerable discussion over the question of priority.

Apart from his work on liquefaction, Cailletet also engaged on researches into the general properties of matter at low temperatures and on the passage of gases through metals. He constructed high-pressure manometers and an altimeter for measuring the height of an aeroplane. He was elected to the *Académie des Sciences* in 1884.

Le jubilé académique de L. P. Cailletet. 1910.
(Portrait.)
Nature (Paris), **41**, 143, 1913.
Dictionary of Scientific Biography.

J W H

CAJAL, SANTIAGO RAMÓN Y *See* RAMÓN Y CAJAL.

CALMETTE, LEON CHARLES ALBERT Born in Nice, France, 12 July 1863; died Paris, 29 October 1933. Physician.

Leon Calmette, who was educated at Clermond, Rennes, Paris and The Naval Medical School, Brest, qualified in medicine in Paris in 1886. While on active service in Hong Kong, he became interested in micro-organisms as causes of diseases. Subsequently he worked in French colonies.

In 1890 he returned to Paris to study bacteriology under PASTEUR who, a year later, sent him to Saigon to establish the first Pasteur Institute outside Paris. His research and administrative talents came to the fore. He initiated the local manufacture of smallpox vaccine; the preservation of spinal cords of rabies-infected rabbits, used for the treatment of hydrophobia; and investigated the local manufacture of alcohol from rice. He found that a locally used fungus hydrolysed the starch into sugar which was then fermented by the yeast. This method was adopted in France and elsewhere to obtain alcohol from grain. His work on treating snake bites with horse serum containing the antibodies to the toxin gained recognition.

In 1895 Calmette established another Pasteur Institute, at Lille, which soon gained a reputation as a centre of excellence. As in Saigon, Calmette aimed to improve public health in the region. As professor of hygiene from 1898, he concentrated on the treatment and prevention of tuberculosis and, with his assistant, Camille Guérin (1872–1961), had by 1914 isolated a strain of Bacillus BCG (Bacillus Calmette Guérin) which became the source of vaccine used throughout the world since the late 1920s. In 1919, he took up the post of Deputy Director at the Pasteur Institute in Paris.

Honoured by many learned societies, he became a Foreign Member of the Royal Society, London, for his contributions to Immunology.

Annals of Medical History, **6**, 290, 1934. (Portrait.)
Obituary Notices of Fellows of the Royal Society, **1**, 314, 1935 (Portrait).
N. Bernard, *La vie et l'oeuvre D'Albert Calmette.* 1961.
Dictionary of Scientific Biography.

I M McC

CALVIN, MELVIN Born in St. Paul, Minnesota, USA, 8 April, 1911. Nobel prize-winning pioneer in the use of radioactive carbon-14 labelled carbon dioxide for elucidating the basic metabolic pathways of fixed carbon in plant photosynthesis.

Melvin Calvin graduated in chemistry at the Michigan College of Technology in 1931 and gained a PhD (chemistry) in the University of Minnesota in 1935. His post-doctoral studies included two years (1935–1937) with Professor Michael Polanyi in the University of Manchester, UK. On returning to the USA in 1937 he undertook teaching, research, consultancy and advisory work in the University of California. His studies of plant photosynthesis soon became internationally recognized and provided the biochemical basis for the C_3, C_4, related systems, their kinetics, and critical significance for plant growth under the different conditions of insolation, ambient carbon dioxide levels, water stress, etc. He was awarded the Nobel prize for chemistry in 1961, the Davy Medal of the Royal Society in 1964, and many other honours and prizes. These included 13 honorary Doctorates of Science from American and European universities and fellowships of many distinguished academic Institutions (in Finland, Germany, Ireland, Japan, Netherlands, the UK and the former USSR).

Calvin is distinguished not only by his studies

of what is probably the most important basic metabolic pathway of the entire biosphere, but also for his later contributions to the increasingly important questions of renewable energy resources based upon harvested or cultivated plant biomass. He has studied several potentially important hydrocarbon oils from various plant species, such as the euphorbs and the legume tree *Copaifera multijuga* of the Amazon forests. The C_{15} hydrocarbon of the latter can be tapped and used as a diesel oil fuel substitute. Of exemplary significance in today's world of expanding science, with its inevitable scholastic specialization, is Calvin's clear resolve not to lose sight of the forest for technical trees. His more than 600 published papers and seven books include those ranging from the molecular biology of hydrocarbon biosynthesis to the global interactions between chemistry and trends in population and human resources.

This remarkable scholar has not only contributed many internationally distinguished lectures but also served on a range of national and international committees addressing problems ranging from mental health, national security and global warming to space exploration.

Les Prix Nobel en 1961. 1962. (Portrait.)

Who's Who. 1993.

D. Ridgway, *Journal of Chemical Education,* **50,** 811, 1973.

Tyler Wasson (Ed.), *Nobel Prize Winners.* 1987. (Portrait.)

F P W W

CAMERARIUS, RUDOLPH JACOB Born at Tübingen, Germany, 17 February 1665; died there, 11 September 1721. Botanist.

Camerarius's life and work were centred on Tübingen. He graduated there in philosophy and medicine and, after two years of European travel during which he visited England, he returned in 1688 to become Professor Extraordinary and Director of the Botanic Garden; the following year he obtained the post of professor of natural philosophy, and in 1695 succeeded his father as First Professor of the University.

He was a botanist of some repute who communicated his work in letters to his colleagues in other universities. On 25 August 1694, in his celebrated letter, *De sexu plantarum,* to Professor B. Valentin at Giessen, he reported the failure of pistillate flowers to produce seed in the absence of staminate flowers. He concluded that the 'apices' or anthers with their pollen were the male organs, and that the style and ovary constituted the female parts of the flower.

Some historians have credited the discovery of sexuality in plants to him but this claim is not strictly accurate since both Nehemiah GREW and John RAY had discussed this question a few years before his letter was written. Camerarius's claim to fame lies in his confirmation by scientific experiment of their speculation.

J. von Sachs, *History of Botany (1530–1860).* 1890.
Dictionary of Scientific Biography.

R G C D

CANDOLLE, AUGUSTIN PYRAMUS DE Born at Geneva, Switzerland, 4 February 1778; died there, 9 September 1841. Plant taxonomist.

A member of a Provençal family which had fled from religious persecution to Geneva, Candolle returned to France in 1798 to continue his botanical studies. In Paris he met prominent French naturalists, and wrote numerous smaller monographs including *Plantarum Historia Succulentarum* (1799–1829) with illustrations by P. J. Redouté (1759–1840). His revision of LAMARCK's *Flore française* (1805–15) introduced some new and significant principles of plant classification.

Candolle's classification was based upon that of A. L. De JUSSIEU, with modifications that he elaborated in his famous *Théorie élémentaire de la botanique* (1813). He developed the thesis that morphology, to the exclusion of physiology, is the sole basis of taxonomy. He proposed a theory of symmetry in the structure of plants, especially of the floral organs. 'The whole art of natural classification', he maintained, 'consists in discovering the plan of symmetry.' He adopted the three main groups used by Jussieu: Dicotyledons, Monocotyledons and Acotyledons. His arrangement for the Phanerogams was widely used until the improved classification of G. BENTHAM and J. D. HOOKER more than fifty years later.

In 1808 he became professor of botany at Montpellier until 1816, when he returned to Geneva and created the present Conservatoire Botanique and Botanical Garden. Before his death in 1841 he wrote most of the first seven volumes of the *Prodromus Systematis Naturalis Regni Vegetabilis* (1824–73), the remaining ten volumes being completed by his son Alphonse (1806–93). This monumental work is a descriptive account to specific level of the Dicotyledons and Gymnosperms.

J. von Sachs, *History of Botany (1530–1860).* 1890.
A. P. de Candolle, *Mémoires et Souvenirs.* 1862.
W. Trelease, *Scientific Monthly,* **19,** 53, 1924.
Archives des Sciences Physiques et Naturelles, **1,** 5, 1919. (Portrait.)
Dictionary of Scientific Biography.

R G C D

CANNIZZARO, STANISLAO Born at Palermo, Sicily, 13 July 1826; died Rome, 10 May 1910. Distinguished Italian chemist remembered for his revival of Avogadro's Hypothesis.

Cannizzaro studied chemistry and physics in the Universities of Palermo, Naples and Pisa, and attracted the favourable notice of M. Melloni (1798–1854) and R. Piria (1815–65). In 1847 he threw up his career to join, as an artilleryman, a rebellion in his native Sicily. When the rebellion failed (1849) he went to Paris, where he resumed his studies in the laboratory of M. E. CHEVREUL. Two years later he returned to Italy, becoming a schoolteacher in Alessandria. He was then professor successively in Genoa (1855), Palermo (1861) and Rome (1870), a career interrupted only by a brief military excursion with Garibaldi's forces in 1860. In 1871 he was made a Senator, and concerned himself with questions of public health, and with the establishment of a customs laboratory. He married an Englishwoman, Henrietta Withers, daughter of a pastor, and had two children.

Almost throughout his life Cannizzaro was hampered by lack of laboratory space, and of all but elementary equipment. Despite this, while at Alessandria, he discovered 'Cannizzaro's reaction', the disproportionation of benzaldehyde into benzoic acid and benzyl alcohol in presence of strong alkali. Later, in Rome, he did some important work on the natural vermifuge, santonin, which he established to be a naphthalene derivative. He is mainly remembered, however, as the first major chemist to appreciate the significance of the hypothesis formulated by A. AVOGADRO and to realize that, by its application, the half-century of confusion about atomic weights could be ended. His ideas were published in the form of a pamphlet (1858) *Sunto di un corso di filosofia chimica* (Epitome of a Course of Chemical Philosophy), which he took the opportunity to distribute at the famous Karlsruhe Conference of 1860. Although it had no effect on the deliberations of the Conference, the conclusions of the pamphlet were rapidly accepted in the chemical world, and made their contribution to the great simplification of chemical thought which took place in the 1860s. Cannizzaro pointed out that the molecular weights of volatile compounds could be deduced from measurements of their vapour density. Correct atomic weights made possible, among other things, the discovery of the Periodic System a few years later.

E. Farber (Ed.), *Great Chemists*. 1961. (Portrait.)
Chemical Society Memorial Lectures, 1901–13. (Portrait.)
J. R. Partington, *A History of Chemistry*, vol. 4. 1964.
L. C. Newell, *Journal of Chemical Education*, **3**, 1361, 1926.
W. A. Tilden, *Journal of the Chemical Society*, **101**, 1677, 1912.
Dictionary of Scientific Biography.

W V F

CANTOR, GEORG FERDINAND LUDWIG PHILIP

Born in St Petersburg, 3 November 1845; died Halle, Saxony, Germany, 6 January 1918. Founded modern theory of infinite sets.

Cantor was a cosmopolitan. He was of Jewish descent; his father came from Denmark; he was born in Russia; he was educated at Zürich, Frankfurt, Berlin and Göttingen; and most of his academic life was spent at Halle – where he became professor in 1872. He suffered several nervous breakdowns in later life. He started his mathematical career as a follower of K. F. GAUSS – he got his doctorate for a dissertation on indeterminate equations – and he did some work on Fourier series before turning to the theory of sets. His first paper (1874 – published in Crelle's *Journal*) on this contained a proof that the set of algebraic numbers may be put into one-to-one correspondence with the set of integers. His best-known publication is his *Beiträge zur Begründung der Transfiniten Mengenlehre* (1895–7), in which he propounds his theory of infinite sets, infinite cardinals and infinite ordinals. In opposition to L. Kronecker (1823–91), Cantor treated infinites as actual, not merely potential, and he recognized that his approach owed much to the scholastic discussions on the subject. Cantor's work was bitterly attacked by Kronecker, but C. Hermite (1822–1901), J. W. R. DEDEKIND and others were sympathetic: it was not until the turn of the century that it was recognized that it was of fundamental importance to mathematics, and especially to analysis.

E. T. Bell, *Men of Mathematics*. 1937.
D. J. Struik, *A Concise History of Mathematics*. 1954. (Portrait.)

J. Grattan-Guinness, *Annals of Science*, **27**, 345, 1971.
Dictionary of Scientific Biography.

R P L

CARDAN, JEROME See CARDONA.

CARDANO, GIROLAMO (JEROME CARDAN)

Born at Pavia, Lombardy, Italy, 24 September 1501; died Rome, 21 September 1576. Mathematician, astrologer, physician.

Cardano was the illegitimate son of a Milanese lawyer, who taught his son some mathematics at an early age. Girolamo was educated at the Universities of Pavia, Padua and (after difficulties over his illegitimacy) at Milan – mainly in medicine, a subject then still bound up with astrology. His first notable works were on arithmetic (1539), astrology (1543) and algebra (1545). The first of these occasioned a correspondence with Niccolo TARTAGLIA, who sent him, under pledge of secrecy, his newly discovered solution of cubic equations of the forms lacking either the square or the linear term. Cardano, however, published it in his algebra, and it is now commonly known as Cardan's solution. Cardano, on the other hand, reduced the general cubic equation to a type which was solvable; he discussed the irreducible case and recognized the existence of three solutions – negative solutions were previously discarded. He also expressed the sum of the roots in terms of the coefficients.

Cardano's works having earned him a wide reputation, he was appointed professor of medicine at Pavia (1547). Three years later his most famous work, *De Subtilitate Rerum*, was published, being followed in 1557 by what amounts to a supplement, *De Varietate Rerum*. His fortunes waned in the 1550s. Banished from Milan, he took up a professorship at Bologna (1562), where he was later imprisoned for heresy. Released, he went to live in Rome.

Cardano's best work was in algebra, his *Ars Magna* (1545) being the first important printed treatise on the subject. It also includes the solution of the biquadratic, found by his pupil Luigi Ferrari (1522–65), after he – challenged by Zuanne de Tonini da Coi in 1540 – had failed. But if Cardano was not in the highest rank as a mathematician, he was very influential in scientific circles. His *De Subtilitate* and *De Varietate* are compendious summaries of the scientific lore of the times, often very naïve. Cardano's mechanics, for example, is decidedly inferior to Tartaglia's, from which it is taken. He believed that all animals were originally worms. Since he argued from the infinite variability of species, some writers have found in him a forerunner of Charles DARWIN.

Cardano claimed to have invented the method of proof known as *consequentia mirabilis*, but this had already been used by EUCLID and Theodosius (*fl.* 75 BC). The so-called 'Cardan suspension' is at least as old as the thirteenth century.

O. Ore, *Cardano the Gambling Scholar*. 1953. (Portrait.)
J. Cardano, *The Book of my Life* (trans. J. Stoner). 1931.
Dictionary of Scientific Biography.

J D N

CARLSON, CHESTER FLOYD Born in Seattle, Washington State, USA, 8 February 1906; died New York, 19 September 1968. Inventor of xerography.

After graduating from the California Institute of Technology in 1930 Carlson worked briefly with the Bell Telephone Company, then found a job in the patent department of an electronics firm in New York, where he quickly became aware of the large number of copies of patent specifications and other documents that had to be made, and the deficiencies inherent in the existing carbon paper and photostat copying processes. He decided that the electrostatic principle held most promise, and after four years of experimentation he succeeded in 1938 in producing the first copy of an original document by xerography (Greek: dry writing).

He used the semiconductor selenium as the primary transfer medium, and the copying process described in his patent of 1940 remains substantially the same today. At the same time he had been studying law at night at the New York Law School, where he received his degree in 1939 and gained admission to the Bar in the following year.

He experienced great difficulty, however, in attracting any commercial support for his invention, and it was not until 1947 that a small New York company, which later became the Xerox Corporation, agreed to purchase the manufacturing and marketing rights. They gave the first public demonstration of the xerox process a year later, but it was not until 1959 that the first commercial model was put on the market by Rank Xerox, a company jointly owned by the Rank Organisation and the Xerox Corporation. Today xerox copiers are standard office equipment, and have been developed to copy coloured images, to reproduce enlarged or reduced copies of an original, and to produce colour copies. Carlson took no personal part in the later development and marketing of his invention, but competitors could find no loophole in his patents and he became a multi-millionaire on the strength of his royalties and dividends.

Webster's American Biographies.
Encyclopedia of American Biography.
Scientists and Inventors. (Portrait and illus.)

R M B

CARNEGIE, ANDREW Born at Dunfermline, Scotland, 25 November 1835; died Lenox, Massachusetts, USA, 11 August 1919. Steel magnate and philanthropist.

The father of Andrew Carnegie was an impoverished handloom weaver of strong Radical leanings, his mother an impassioned believer in education and in the opportunities of the New World, to which the family emigrated in 1848. Andrew started as a bobbin boy in a cotton factory; at 14 he was a messenger in a telegraph office, where he became a skilled operator; and in 1853–65 he rose rapidly in the service of the Pennsylvania Railroad, playing an active part in troop transportation during the Civil War. Pullman sleeping cars and iron railway bridges were among his early financial interests, but it was not until 1873, by which date he had made contact with Henry BESSEMER and other British steel-makers, that Carnegie decided to concentrate on steel.

The building of the J. Edgar Thomson Steel Mills began a period of twenty-eight years during which he developed the biggest steel business in America, as part of the movement, facilitated by high tariffs and cheap immigrant labour, in which the American steel industry as a whole rose from modest beginnings to be by far the largest in the world. Carnegie's personal triumph was based on a variety of factors. He pioneered the enlargement of the hearth in the blast-furnace, which made 'rapid driving' possible. He practised vertical integration, moving his own iron ore and coke on his own steamship lines and railways. Above all, his unflinching confidence in the mounting prosperity of his new country caused him always to expand his enterprises during periods of temporary depression, so that he was in a position to sell vast quantities of steel cheaply but very profitably as soon as trade began to recover. In 1901 Carnegie sold out his interests to the newly formed United States Steel Corporation for $250,000,000 in 5 per cent gold bonds redeemable in fifty years.

This vast sum was of public significance, for its owner practised as well as preached 'the gospel of wealth'. Though a believer in ruthless economic competition as the basis of society, Carnegie believed equally in the duty of the rich to use their wealth for 'the improvement of mankind', and founded a series of charitable trusts both in the United States and in Britain. In his lifetime the best known was probably that which had built and equipped 2505 library buildings, beginning in 1881 at his native Dunfermline; but the Carnegie Endowment for International Peace, established in 1910, is the most famous memorial of the Spencerian optimist whose health declined with the shock of the First World War.

A. Carnegie, *The Gospel of Wealth.* 1900.
A. Carnegie, *Autobiography.* 1920.
B. J. Hendrick, *Life of Andrew Carnegie.* 1933.
Dictionary of American Biography.
J. B. Conant, *Science,* **82**, 599, 1935.

T K D

CARNOT, NICOLAS LÉONARD SADI Born in Paris, 1 June 1796; died there, 24 August 1832. Celebrated for his contributions to thermo-dynamics.

Apart from a few months' preparation for entry to the *École Polytechnique,* Carnot was educated at home, his father, Lazare Carnot (1753–1823) – the 'organizer of victory' during the Revolution – devoting himself to his son's education on his temporary retirement from public life in 1800. In 1812 Carnot was admitted to the *École Polytechnique.* Passing out sixth of his year in 1814, he proceeded to Metz. In 1819 he was transferred to the headquarters' staff at Paris, and soon after to the reserve. The remainder of his life was spent quietly in Paris, apart from a short visit to his father in exile in Magdeburg in 1821, and two years of renewed military service from 1826 to 1828. Excessive work led to a serious illness towards the end of June 1832. After a partial recovery he had a relapse and was carried off in a few hours by cholera.

In composing his masterpiece, and unique published work, the *Réflexions sur la puissance motrice de feu* (1824), Carnot was motivated by the realization that the enormous industrial importance of the steam engine, and the great improvements which had been effected in its design by a succession of British engineers, was matched by an almost total ignorance of the theory behind its working. The *Réflexions* was intended as a contribution towards such a theory. A work of genius, it contained the notion of a reversible cycle of operations. Assuming the conservation of caloric, and the impossibility of perpetual motion, it proved (Carnot's Theorem) that all reversible heat engines working between a given pair of temperatures must necessarily have the same efficiency, the maximum possible for the temperatures in question. Manuscript notes found among Carnot's papers conclusively prove that he had given up the caloric theory of heat in favour of the mechanical theory of heat before his death in 1832.

The *Réflexions* was presented to the *Académie des Sciences* soon after its publication, and a favourable report read on it by P. de Girard (1775–1845) some six weeks later. This report was later published in the *Revue Encyclopédique*. But the work attracted no further attention, probably because its abstract nature had little appeal for engineers, and it might then have been entirely forgotten if it had not been for a reference to it in 1834 in a paper by B. P. E. Clapeyron (1799–1864) through which it was rediscovered by W. THOMSON (Lord Kelvin) and R. J. E. CLAUSIUS and made the basis of their independent formulations of the second law of thermodynamics.

Judging by the *Réflexions* and the posthumous manuscript notes, Carnot was the most profoundly original of all French physical scientists of the first half of the nineteenth century with the possible exception of A. J. FRESNEL, and his death at the early age of thirty-six the most serious loss to French science in the same period apart, again, from that of Fresnel.

> Sadi Carnot, *Réflexions sur la puissance motrice du feu.* 1878. (This edition contains biographical notes by his brother Hippolyte, excerpts from manuscript notes, and portrait.)
> *Idem, ibid.* (Fascimile reproduction of original text, with complete manuscript notes.) 1953.
> E. Mendoza, *Archives internationales d'histoire des sciences*, **12**, 377, 1959.
> *Dictionary of Scientific Biography.*
>
> J W H

CAROTHERS, WALLACE HUME Born at Burlington, Iowa, USA, 27 April 1896; died Philadelphia, Pennsylvania, 29 April 1937. Industrial chemist; discovered the fibre-forming polyamides (nylons).

Carothers, the son of a teacher, studied and taught chemistry in Tarkio College, Missouri, and the Universities of Illinois, South Dakota and Harvard. As a promising, though not yet outstanding, young chemist, he was selected by the firm of E. I. du Pont de Nemours to lead the organic section of their research department at Wilmington, Delaware. A tireless worker, he suffered from recurrent periods of depression, in one of which he took his own life. He married not long before his death, and a daughter was born posthumously.

When Carothers began work at Wilmington he set out to prepare organic compounds of high molecular weight and to examine their physical properties. The first fruit of this study was the rubber analogue, neoprene, the first successful synthetic rubber (see J. A. NIEWLAND). A workable process had to be devised to make the intermediate chloroprene from the hitherto little-known and unstable vinylacetylene. Carothers also studied polycondensation, a process in some respects more chemically versatile than polymerisation. From dibasic acids and dihydroxy-compounds he prepared a series of polyesters, but the physical and chemical properties of these appeared unpromising. (By following this road a little further, J. R. WHINFIELD and J. T. Dickson later discovered the polyester fibre 'Terylene'). Polyamides similarly prepared from dibasic acids and diamines, however, could be melt-spun into fibres having attractive properties, or made into transparent film. The product from adipic acid and hexamethylenediamine (Nylon 66) rapidly achieved great commercial success as a synthetic fibre.

> E. Farber (Ed.), *Great Chemists.* 1961. (Portrait.)
> R. F. Wolf, *The Scientific Monthly*, **79**, 69, 1952.
> *Biographical Memoirs, National Academy of Sciences*, **20**, 293, 1939.
> *Dictionary of American Biography.*
> *Dictionary of Scientific Biography.*
>
> W V F

CARREL, ALEXIS Born at Lyons, France, 28 June 1873; died Paris, 5 November 1944. Best known for his work on joining the ends of blood vessels and on the transplantation of organs.

Carrel, after a broadly based university education, received his doctorate in medicine in 1900. In 1906 he became attached to the Rockefeller Institute in New York, where he undertook many of his studies on the suturing of blood vessels and on transplanting organs, for which he received a Nobel prize in medicine in 1912.

Earlier attempts to transplant organs (in order to replace diseased organs or amputated limbs, etc.) had failed through, among other reasons, the lack of a method for re-establishing a normal blood circulation through the transplanted organs. An invariable cause of failure was the development of thrombosis or stenosis. Carrel, who began studying the anastomosing of vessels in 1902, systematically analysed all possible complications and developed techniques to overcome these causes of failure; for example, the enforcement of rigid asepsis and careful attention to details about the use of instruments, needles and suturing.

Using his new techniques, he was able to remove entire organs such as the kidney and to replace them in their original location or, occasionally, in different parts of the body where they still functioned. These studies were far reaching and paved the way for innumerable advances in vascular surgery. His techniques also found application in transfusing blood from donor to recipient, a technique used before methods of preventing blood coagulation had been found.

Carrel is also renowned for his work on tissue culture. Following the pioneering studies by R. G. HARRISON in 1907 Carrel (with associates) made significant contributions to its development, and first demonstrated his tissue fragments in 1910. He was also celebrated for his methods of treating deep wounds by constant irrigation with a mild antiseptic, during the First World War, and for the development of a mechanical heart which was announced in 1935. Many advances in biology and medicine developed out of his work which, though they cannot be mentioned in so short a notice as this, helped to make Carrel a tremendously important figure in twentieth-century science.

Carrel held many positions throughout his life and at his death was Director of the Carrel Foundation for the Study of Human Problems. His influence was also felt through many books, which included the very popular *Man the Unknown* (1935).

T. L. Sourkes, *Nobel Prize Winners in Medicine and Physiology, 1901–1965*. 1967.

H. Freund and A. Berg, *Geschichte der Microscopie*, vol. 2. 1964.

J. J. Antier, *Alexis Carrel*. 1970.

Tyler Wasson (Ed.), *Nobel Prize Winners*. 1987. (Portrait.)

Dictionary of Scientific Biography.

J K C

CARRINGTON, RICHARD CHRISTOPHER Born in Chelsea, London, 26 May 1826; died Churt, Surrey, 27 November 1875. Determined the elements of the Sun's rotation, and photospheric drift.

Carrington was the son of a brewer. Destined for the Church, he preferred astronomy and became an observer at the University of Durham. In 1853 he established his own observatory at Redhill, Surrey, and worked for three years producing a catalogue of stars within nine degrees of the North Pole.

He is chiefly remembered for his work in solar physics. From 1853 to 1861 he undertook a systematic series of observations of sunspots, in order to determine the exact period of rotation of the Sun. He discovered a systematic drift of the photosphere, which caused the rotation period of sunspots to increase with latitude (similar results were discovered independently by G. SPÖRER).

Carrington was the first to observe a chromospheric flare (1859). The flares were accompanied by a violent terrestrial magnetic disturbance, and were followed eighteen hours later by a magnetic storm associated with magnificent displays of the aurora.

Monthly Notices of the Royal Astronomical Society, **36**, 1876.

M. Barnes, *Journal of the British Astronomical Association*, **83**, 122, 1973.

Dictionary of National Biography.

Dictionary of Scientific Biography.

J D N

CARTWRIGHT, EDMUND Born at Marnham, Nottingham, England, 24 April 1743; died Hastings, Sussex, 30 October 1823. Invented a mechanical loom from which modern power looms have been developed.

Edmund Cartwright, the fourth son of William Cartwright, was educated at Wakefield Grammar school, and at 14 went to University College, Oxford. By special act of Convocation in 1764, he was elected Fellow of Magdalen College. He received the living of Marwood, Leicestershire, in 1779, where he wrote poems, reviewed new works, and began agricultural experiments. A visit to Matlock introduced him to the inventions of Richard ARKWRIGHT, and he asked why weaving could not be mechanized in a similar manner to spinning. This began a remarkable career of inventions.

Cartwright returned home and built a loom which required two strong men to operate it. This he proudly patented and then went to look at hand looms. Further improvements to his own, covered by two more patents, produced a machine that showed possibility, but the Manchester merchants whom he visited were not interested. In 1786 he established a factory at Doncaster with power looms which were the ancestors of modern ones. Twenty-four looms driven by steam power were installed in Manchester in 1791, but the mill was burnt down and no one hurried to repeat the experiment. The Doncaster mill was sold in 1793, Cartwright having lost £30,000; in 1809, however, Parliament voted him £10,000, as his looms were then in general use.

In 1789 and 1790 he patented a wool-combing machine which in output equalled twenty hand combers. Infringements were frequent and costly to resist; the patent was prolonged for fourteen years after 1801, but even then Cartwright did not profit. Other inventions included metallic packing for pistons in steam engines, and bread-making and brick-making machines. In 1792 he obtained a patent for a machine to make ropes, and about then he returned to agricultural improvements. He put forward suggestions for a reaping machine in 1793, and in 1801 received a prize from the Board of Agriculture for an essay on husbandry, which was followed in 1805 by a gold medal for his essay on manures. He was elected FRS in 1821.

From 1786 to his death he was a Prebendary of Lincoln; about 1810 he bought a small farm near Sevenoaks, where he continued his inventions, both agricultural and general. Inventing to the last, he died at Hastings and was buried in Battle church.

A. Barlow, *History of Weaving*. 1878.

M. Strickland, *Memoir of the Life, Writings and Mechanical Inventions of Edmund Cartwright, D.D., F.R.S.* 1843.

Dictionary of National Biography.

R L H

CASIMIR, HENDRIK BRUGT GERHARD Born at The Hague, Netherlands, 15 July 1909. Physicist.

Casimir, the son of a schoolmaster who was also a professor of education at Leiden University, entered Leiden University in 1926, obtaining his doctorate in 1931. He spent part of his time between 1929 and 1931 in Copenhagen working with Niels BOHR. From 1931 to 1932 he worked as assistant to P. Ehrenfest (1880–1933), professor of theoretical physics at Leiden University, and from 1932 to 1933 he was in Zürich as assistant to Wolfgang PAULI. He returned to Leiden in 1933, and until 1942 became involved in low temperature research, working with C. J. Gorter (1907–), and as senior assistant to W. J. de Haas (1878–1960) from 1936.

Working on superconductivity, the phenomenon that the electrical resistance of certain metals drops to zero below a critical temperature, in 1934 Casimir and Gorter advanced the two-fluid model of superconductivity to explain the relationship between thermal and magnetic properties in superconductors. They proposed the existence of two sorts of electrons, normal and superconducting. Casimir's most important work was done during his years in Leiden. He published *On the Interaction between Atomic Nuclei and Electrons*

(1936) and *Magnetism and Very Low Temperatures* (1940).

The problems the Dutch universities faced during the German occupation led Casimir to accept a post at the Philips Research Laboratories at Eindhoven in 1942. He stayed on after the war, turning down offers of academic posts in the USA. He became Director of Research in 1946, and a member of the Board of Management in 1956. He is now emeritus professor at Leiden University. He retired from Philips in 1972.

    H. B. G. Casimir, *Haphazard Reality: Half a Century of Science.* 1983.

A P B

CASSEGRAIN, N — (?) *fl.* 1672. Designer of the Cassegrain reflecting telescope.

Cassegrain was a physician who taught at the College of Chartres. He was cited by M. Bercé in the *Journal des Scavans* of 1672 as the inventor of a telescope 'more perfect than Newton's' — although his grounds for saying this were mistaken, and the diagram he gave shows that he little understood the instrument. Whereas the second, small, mirror of Newton's reflector was plane, and merely served to reflect the ray pencil at right-angles to the tube, Cassegrain advocated the use of a convex mirror, with centre of curvature outside the prime focus of the objective, this second mirror both reflecting the rays through a hole in the centre of the objective into the eyepiece beyond and increasing the angular magnification of the instrument.

James Short (1710–68) was one of the first to construct telescopes to Cassegrain's design (*c.*1740). Although he favoured the Gregorian, his instruments were often supplied with an auxiliary convex mirror for use as an alternative to the concave.

Little is known of Cassegrain's life. His family had been doctors and surgeons from the fifteenth century, in Chartres, but there is even uncertainty about his initial.

    Nouvelle Biographie Générale, vol. 9. 1854.

    E. Menault, *Hommes remarquables d'Angerville la Gate.* 1859. (Some family details.)

    Dictionary of Scientific Biography.

J D N

CASSINI, GIOVANNI DOMENICO Born at Perinaldo, near Nice, France, 8 June 1625; died Paris, 14 September 1712. Astronomer with many planetary discoveries to his credit.

Giovanni Cassini was educated by the Jesuits in Genoa. His reputation in astronomy gained for him the professorship in the subject at Bologna, in 1650, where he wrote a treatise on the comet of 1652. After some years in papal service, Cassini was nominated a member of the French Academy by Louis XIV, and invited in 1669 to work in the new Paris Observatory. Although Pope Clement IX insisted that the appointment was to be temporary, Cassini, in fact, never returned permanently to Italy and became a naturalized Frenchman in 1673.

While at Bologna, Cassini determined the rotation periods of Jupiter, Mars, and Venus. He noted the seasonal changes in the characteristic conformation of Mars, and was the first to describe accurately the bands and spots visible on Jupiter. In his *Ephemerides Bononienses Mediceorum Sid-erum* (1668) he succeeded in computing the configurations of the four satellites of Jupiter discovered by GALILEO, and thus made possible the discovery by Olaus ROEMER of the velocity of light.

Although he was unable to persuade Louis XIV and his architect Claude PERRAULT that the Paris Observatory should be devoted solely to astronomy, Cassini began a series of observations using instruments made by Campani and Divini, pupils of Galilei and TORRICELLI. With an object lens having a focal length of approximately 16 feet, he discovered four new satellites of Saturn between 1671 and 1684. In 1675 he observed the division in Saturn's ring, first noted by William Balle (1627–90) in 1665. This division now bears Cassini's name. He described Saturn's ring as being composed of swarms of tiny satellites moving in two concentric rings of differing densities. Cassini planned a series of simultaneous observations, 6000 miles apart, of the distances between Mars and nearby stars. From these he calculated the distance of Mars from the Earth, the dimensions of the planetary orbits, and the Earth's distance from the Sun, all with considerable accuracy. He also made the earliest continuous observations of the Zodiacal light. After 1682, he was aided in his observations by a 'parallactic machine', driven by clockwork, to impart the diurnal motion of his telescope. This is often wrongly ascribed to Roemer.

With the advent of Newton's theory of gravitation in the last years of the century, a great deal of interest was stimulated in the problem of determining the dimensions and form of the Earth. Already in 1669 Jean PICARD had measured an arc of the meridian with some accuracy, treating the Earth as a sphere, like all before him. Jean Richer, noticing the changing rate of a pendulum clock on a voyage to South America, caused NEWTON to offer two possible explanations of it in the third book of the *Principia*, one of which involved a non-spherical Earth. Between 1684 and 1718 Cassini and his son, starting from Picard's base, triangulated the so-called meridian of France from Paris to Dunkirk, and south from Paris to Collioure. They concluded that the Earth was a prolate spheroid, thus contradicting the theoretical work of Newton and HUYGENS. The measurements were completed only after the death of the elder Cassini, however, and he did not live to see either the controversy which centred on them or the vindication of Newton.

Cassini became blind in 1710. He was succeeded as Director of the Paris Observatory by three generations of descendants, the last of whom died in 1845.

    J. D. C. Cassini, *Mémoires pour servir à l'histoire des sciences.* 1810. Contains a partial autobiography.

    C. Wolf, *Histoire de l'Observatoire de Paris.* 1902.

    Dictionary of Scientific Biography.

J D N

CASTNER, HAMILTON YOUNG Born at Brooklyn, New York, 11 September 1858; died Saranac Lake, New York, 11 October 1898. A pioneer in the field of industrial electrochemistry.

After studying at the Brooklyn Polytechnic Institution and the School of Mines of Columbia University, Castner set up as a consultant in New York in 1879, and invented a process for manufacturing sodium by reducing caustic soda with carbon. Failing to interest American industrialists, he went to London in 1886, and came in contact with the Webster Crown Metal Company, Birmingham, which required sodium for the manufacture of aluminium – then a very expensive metal – by reduction of aluminium chloride. In 1888, a factory was built at Oldbury to produce 100 000 lb of aluminium annually. Unfortunately, this promising venture was quickly killed by the exploitation in 1889 of a much cheaper electrolytic method for preparing aluminium, invented independently by C. M. HALL in America and P. L. T. HÉROULT in France in 1886. Castner's only remaining asset was his process for making sodium cheaply, but by exploiting this he won success from failure. First, he developed a process for manufacturing sodium peroxide by burning sodium in a current of air. In 1894, he patented a process for manufacturing sodium cyanide by reaction between sodium, charcoal and ammonia; the product found a growing market in the American, South African and Australian goldfields, and for electroplating.

Castner then sought a better method of manufacturing sodium; he developed a process for doing so by electrolysis of molten sodium hydroxide, but encountered difficulties due to the impurity of the best caustic soda then available. This led him to seek a better process for caustic soda manufacture, resulting in the now world-famous mercury cell for the electrolysis of brine. In this, sodium was discharged at a mercury cathode, forming a weak amalgam. A rocking device circulated the amalgam, which reacted with water in a separate compartment to form very pure caustic soda. The process was soon established in many parts of the world. In Germany, patent difficulties were encountered because Karl KELLNER had filed details of a similar process. To avoid litigation, agreement for an exchange of patents and processes was reached, and the process is generally known as the Castner-Kellner process. It was first worked in Cheshire in 1897 by the Castner-Kellner Alkali Company, of which Kellner was for a short time a director. With modification of detail, though not of principle, it is still worked in many parts of the world.

Castner is recorded as an unassuming man and an excellent experimentalist. Unhappily, he contracted tuberculosis and died at the early age of 41.

Alexander Fleck, Castner Memorial Lecture. *Chemistry and Industry*, 515, 1947.
Fifty Years of Progress: the Story of the Castner-Kellner Alkali Company. 1947. (Portrait.)
Wyndham D. Miles (Ed.), *American Chemists and Chemical Engineers*. 1976.
Dictionary of National Biography (Missing Persons). 1993.

T I W

CAUCHY, AUGUSTIN LOUIS Born in Paris, 21 August 1789; died Sceaux, France, 23 May 1857. Leading French mathematician in the field of analysis.

The Cauchy family stayed in the village of Arcueil during the Terror, and it was there that Augustin received his early education from his father, from whose teaching he gained a fluency in French and Latin verse – on the advice of J. L. LAGRANGE he was given a good literary education before being introduced to mathematics – as well as an uncompromising piety which was to make him sometimes disliked in later life. He attended the *École Polytechnique*, and became a military engineer. He had an enormous capacity for work, and despite numerous other commitments, produced in 1811 a first-rate paper on polyhedra; on seeing this A. M. Legendre (1752–1833) suggested an analogous problem whose solution Cauchy gave in 1812. In 1815 he lectured at the *École Polytechnique*, where he was made professor of mechanics in 1816. In the same year he accepted a place at the Academy from which Gaspard MONGE had been expelled for political reasons. By this time his only serious rival was K. F. GAUSS, who was slow to publish. In 1830 he went into exile with Charles X and accepted a professorship at Turin. In 1832 he was elected Fellow of the Royal Society. In 1838 he returned to Paris, and from 1848 to 1852 was professor of astronomy at the University.

Cauchy was a prolific writer – he produced more than 700 papers, many of them hundreds of pages long. With Gauss he virtually created the modern form of complex analysis, his first contribution to this being in 1814, on complex integration. He introduced complete rigour into the calculus, in which he preferred to regard the integral as the limit of a sum, rather than the inverse of differentiation. He was one of the first to recognize the importance of convergence in dealing with series, and devised several tests, some of which still appear in textbooks under his name. He reorganized the theory of determinants and made advances in group theory, though he dealt in substitution groups and not abstract groups. To the theory of equations he contributed an elaborate proof of the fundamental theorem of algebra, and proved (1815) the conjecture of P. de FERMAT about the sum of figurate numbers. He also wrote many important papers on physics and astronomy; among other things he helped to establish the undulatory theory of light.

E. T. Bell, *Men of Mathematics*. 1937.
J. F. Scott, *A History of Mathematics from Antiquity to the Beginning of the Nineteenth Century*. 1958.
D. E. Smith: *History of Mathematics*, vol. 1. 1923 (Paperback 1958). (Portrait.)
C. Valson, *La Vie et les Travaux de Baron Cauchy*. 1970. (Reprint of 1868 ed.)
Dictionary of Scientific Biography.

R P L

CAVALIERI, BONAVENTURE Born at Milan, Italy, 1598; died Bologna, 1 December 1647. Italian mathematician, famous for his Method of Indivisibles.

Cavalieri was professor of mathematics in Bologna from 1629 till his death: he was a Jesuit, and his appointment was recommended by the Order. He wrote on logarithms (1629) – he did much to popularize them in Italy – and trigonometry (1632, 1638, 1643); conics (1632); optics; astronomy (1648, 1682); astrology (1639); and other subjects. He was at one time a pupil of GALILEO; in a letter (1626) to him Cavalieri said he was going to write on indivisibles, but it was not until 1635 that he produced his famous *Geometria Indivisibilis Continuorum Nova Quadam Ratione Promota*, in which many quadratures, cubatures and centres of gravity are found. He considered a plane surface as made up of parallel lines, a solid of planes, etc.

To compare the areas of two surfaces, or the volumes of two solids – in the tradition of the Greek geometers, he never determined an area or volume absolutely – he compared the sums (found by use of series) of the lengths of the component lines (or of areas of component planes). He was clearly influenced by the medieval 'calculators', as is shown both by his general approach and by his terminology; but he would not take sides in the dispute of potential versus actual infinity, and regarded his method as a useful device which worked. However, in his *Exercitationes Geometriae Sex* (1647), he defended his methods against Paul Guildin (1577–1643).

C. Boyer, *History of the Calculus.* (Paperback 1959.)

American Mathematical Monthly, **22**, 447, 1905.

D. E. Smith, *History of Mathematics*, vol. 1. 1923 (Paperback 1958). (Portrait.)

Dictionary of Scientific Biography.

R P L

CAVENDISH, HENRY Born at Nice, France, 10 October 1731; died London, 24 February 1810. Made discoveries in composition of gases, electricity, geophysics.

Henry Cavendish was the eldest son of Lord Charles Cavendish, brother of the 3rd Duke of Devonshire; he attended school in Hackney, and was at Peterhouse, Cambridge, from 1749 to 1753, but took no degree. After some time in Paris, studying physics and mathematics, he lived in and near London (at Clapham and Bloomsbury). He became very well known in scientific circles, becoming a Fellow of the Royal Society in 1760, but apart from with his scientific friends he aimed at the minimum contact with other people. After years of moderate means, he received a large legacy and was thereafter well described as 'the richest of the learned, and the most learned of the rich'. He never married. At his death he left a fortune of the order of a million pounds. He was buried in All Saints' Church, Derby, which is now the cathedral church and contains a monument to him.

He published the results of three major investigations in his lifetime. In 1766 he gave, in the paper on 'Factitious Airs', what amounted to a demonstration of the existence of hydrogen as a distinct substance ('inflammable air'). He also studied the properties of carbon dioxide ('fixed air') showing that the 'air' produced by putrefaction and fermentation is identical with that produced by the action of acid on marble. In 1767 he published an analysis of some London pump-water (the Rathbone Place water), in which he showed that a water could have calcareous matter held in solution by excess fixed air (that is, he had found the existence of calcium bicarbonate).

In 1783 he showed that the composition of the atmosphere, at different times or at different places, is constant. In 1784–5 he established that water was a compound. (The claim made for James WATT that he was first to show the composition of water, is not now much upheld.) Cavendish was formally a phlogistonist, but recognized that his results could as well be explained on the Lavoisier system.

His other great achievement was the determination of the density of the Earth (1798). Previous attempts had been made by P. Bouguer (1698–1758) (1740; length of seconds pendulum at different places) and Nevil MASKELYNE, (1774; attraction of mountain mass). Cavendish's method had been devised by John Michell (1724–93) whose apparatus Cavendish reconstructed after his death; the attraction of a large lead sphere on a small one is measured by a torsion system. The results are not surpassed in accuracy for a century or more.

His unpublished work was without corresponding influence, but was seen when it was edited from 1879 onwards to be quite as remarkable. In electricity he anticipated much work of C. A. de COULOMB, Michael FARADAY and others, discovering specific inductive capacity, the fact that electrostatic charge is confined to the conducting surface, and he showed that the inverse square law holds to within 2 per cent. A fascinating research was that on the torpedo fish. By making an artificial fish he was able to imitate its electrical behaviour.

His name is commemorated in the great Cavendish Laboratory in Cambridge. The designation 'Honourable', although often used, is not one to which he seems entitled by his status.

G. Wilson, *The Life of the Honourable Henry Cavendish.* 1851.

A. J. Berry, *Henry Cavendish: his Life and Scientific Work.* 1960.

J. G. Crowther, *Scientists of the Industrial Revolution.* 1962. (Portrait.)

E. Farber (Ed.), *Great Chemists.* 1961. (Portrait.)

Dictionary of Scientific Biography.

F G

CAVENTOU, JOSEPH BIENAIMÉ Born at St Omer, France, 30 June 1795; died Paris, 5 May 1877. The founder (with J. PELLETIER) of alkaloid chemistry.

Caventou, the son of an army apothecary, studied pharmacy in Paris. After a short military interlude at the time of Waterloo, he eventually became professor of toxicology in the *École de Pharmacie* (1835–60). Like his friend Pelletier, he had his own pharmacy business as well.

Caventou began work with Pelletier about 1817, quickly learning the older chemist's skill in separating the pure constituents of crude drugs by the gentle methods of solvent extraction, and treatment with dilute acid and alkali. Together they isolated colchicine, veratrine, strychnine, brucine, cinchonine, and, most important of all, quinine (1820). These brilliant discoveries were marred by their insistence that these 'vegetable bases' did not contain nitrogen, though they were well aware of their resemblance to ammonia and its salts. This curious error was corrected in 1823. Caventou continued to publish papers on *materia medica* and related topics, sometimes alone, more usually with Pelletier, until the latter's death in 1842, after which he published nothing.

Journal of Chemical Education, **28**, 454, 1951. (Portrait.)

Chemistry and Industry, **56**, 1084, 1937. (Portrait.)

W V F

CAYLEY, ARTHUR Born at Richmond, Surrey, England, 16 August 1821; died Cambridge 26 January 1895. Mathematician whose output of published work is rivalled only by L. EULER and A. L. CAUCHY.

Cayley graduated from Trinity College, Cambridge, in 1842 as Senior Wrangler and Smith's

Prizeman. After a seven-year Fellowship at Trinity, he worked in law for fourteen years before returning to Cambridge as Sadlerian Professor of Mathematics. He was President of the British Association in 1883. His 967 published papers have been collected in a work of thirteen volumes. His only book, *A Treatise on Elliptic Functions*, was published in 1876.

Cayley may be considered the inventor of the theory of matrices. He derived the rules of the non-commutative algebra associated with them, and showed that each matrix satisfied an algebraical equation of its own order.

He also created the subject of abstract geometry of n dimensions by discovering that metrical properties of a figure could all be replaced by descriptive ones. By relating such properties to the equations $x^2 + y^2 \pm z^2 = 0$ (which he termed the 'absolute conics') he obtained a generalized geometry with the geometries of N. I. LOBACHEVSKI, G. F. B. RIEMANN and EUCLID as special cases. He proceeded to develop the analytic geometry of curves and surfaces, extending Newton's classification of cubic curves, and discovered general theorems concerning the intersection of curves of any degree.

Another of his major discoveries was influenced by the work of G. BOOLE on linear transformations. Cayley attempted to find all the derivatives of any number of functions which have the property of preserving their form unaltered after any linear transformation of the variables, and this led him to develop the resulting theory of invariants and covariants.

Among his other important work, he wrote on the symmetric functions of the roots of an equation; on rational and integral functions together with the equations and loci arising from them; on the non-commutative algebra of groups, considering mainly those of a finite and discontinuous nature; and the theory of periodic functions, especially elliptic and theta functions, recognizing the connection between elliptic functions and doubly infinite products.

He wrote fewer papers on applied mathematics, but his work in this field included theoretical dynamics, potential theory, attractions, and the development of functions arising from planetary and lunar theories.

He received honorary doctorates from eight universities, and was a Fellow of most European scientific societies, including the Royal Society (1852). He had a modest, generous nature, was a gifted teacher, and was in great demand as a referee owing to his encyclopaedic knowledge of mathematics.

A. R. Forsyth, *Proceedings of the Royal Society*, **58**, i, 1895. (Portrait.)

G. Prasad, *Some Great Mathematicians of the Nineteenth Century*, vol. 2. 1933.

R. W. Feldmann, *Mathematics Teacher*, **55**, 482, 1962.

Dictionary of Scientific Biography.

J M D

CAYLEY, SIR GEORGE Born at Scarborough, Yorkshire, England, 27 December 1773; died at Brompton Hall, Yorkshire, 15 December 1857. Pioneer of aerial navigation and founder of aerodynamics.

Although Cayley never achieved his goal of powered flight in a heavier-than-air machine, his experiments were so carefully thought out, and brought him so near success, that he well deserves the title of 'Father of Aerial Navigation' given him by W. S. Henson (1805–88) in 1846. In 1909 Wilbur WRIGHT wrote: 'about 100 years ago an Englishman, Sir George Cayley, carried the science of flying to a point which it had never reached before and which it scarcely reached again during the last century'.

As a boy, he went to school in York, and then became a private pupil of George Walker (c.1734–1807), a Dissenting Divine, in Nottingham. Walker must certainly have influenced Cayley's career considerably: an FRS (1771), he was not only well read in mathematics and navigation but a skilled practical mechanic. After a year there, Cayley spent a short time at Southgate, London, as a pupil of G. C. Morgan (1754–98), well known for his lectures on electricity.

Cayley, of independent means, devoted almost his whole life to study and experiment on the basic principles of flight. In 1853 he constructed a glider which carried his coachman on a flight of some 500 yards across a valley. Practical powered flight was beyond him, as he well understood, because of the lack of an engine with high enough power/weight ratio; he calculated very precisely the power required for a given load and speed. With model gliders he experimented with twisted rubber as a source of power.

Cayley understood the lift given by a cambered wing, and distinguished this from drag. After some experiments with flapping-wing models, he recognized the advantages of the fixed-wing design. He clearly formulated the concept of vertical tail surfaces, of the rudder for steering, of rear elevators, and of the airscrew.

He was interested also in airships and was the first to suggest and design (1816) a semirigid vessel. In the following year he proposed enclosing the gas in a series of separate cells.

Cayley is remembered also as a founder (1839) of the Royal Polytechnic Institute, Regent Street, London, and a sponsor of the first meeting (York, 1832) of the British Association for the Advancement of Science.

C. H. Gibbs-Smith, *Sir George Cayley's Aeronautics*. 1962. (Portrait.); *Sir George Cayley 1773–1857*. 1968.

J. L. Pritchard, *Sir George Cayley*. 1961. (Portrait.)

Dictionary of National Biography (Missing Persons). 1993.

T I W

CELSIUS, ANDERS Born at Uppsala, Sweden, 27 November 1701; died there, 25 April 1744. Astronomer, but chiefly remembered for the centigrade thermometric scale that bears his name.

From 1730 until his death Celsius was professor of astronomy in his native town. For much of this time he travelled in France, Germany and Italy, and whilst in Nuremberg published some of the first systematic observations of the aurora borealis, made between 1716 and 1732. Celsius wrote a number of short astronomical works, but none was very remarkable, although he has to his credit some approximate measurements on the relative brightness of stars. (Astronomical photometry proper does not begin until the work of Pierre Bouguer (1698–1758).)

Whilst a group of astronomers was in South America to ascertain the length of a degree of latitude in the neighbourhood of the equator (1735–43), Celsius spent some time with P. L. M. de MAU-PERTUIS, A. C. Clairaut (1713–65), C. E. L. Camus (1699–1768) and P. C. Lemonnier (1715–99) measuring a meridian arc in Lapland. Although his companions were more illustrious than those on the Southern expedition, the results they obtained were less valuable.

Celsius's most memorable achievement was to persuade scientists of the value of the centigrade thermometric scale. This, still known in Europe as the Celsius scale, was presented in a memoir read before the Swedish Academy of Sciences in 1742.

W. Ostwald, *Klassiker der exacten Wissenschaften*, No. 57. 1904.

N. V. E. Nordenmark, *Anders Celsius*. 1936. (Portrait.)

S. Lindroth, *Swedish Men of Science*. 1952.

Dictionary of Scientific Biography.

J D N

CELSUS, AULUS CORNELIUS *fl.* AD 14–37; may have been born at Narbonne, *c.*25 BC. Roman author of one of the greatest medical works of antiquity.

Nothing certain is known of the life of Celsus. He was probably of a patrician family, and if so he certainly felt responsible for the treatment of his slaves. The only complete work by Celsus that has survived is his *De medicina*, but from various other fragments it would appear that he was responsible for a large work dealing with rhetoric, philosophy, jurisprudence, the military arts, agriculture and medicine. All of this, except the section on medicine, is lost.

There are various opinions regarding the relation of Celsus to the *De medicina*. It is widely held that, though Celsus may have been a 'doctor', he was not a 'practising doctor'. Others consider that he was a mere compiler, but the quality of his work is against this view. Some hold that the *De medicina* of Celsus is a direct translation from a lost Greek original written in Rome, the author of which was possibly Menecrates (*fl.* AD 30), the imperial body-physician. Still others consider that, though the work is not a translation, Celsus used only one original work in its compilation. Finally, there is the school which holds that Celsus, in preparing his book, had access to all the medical works of antiquity, most of which are now lost.

The work consists of a *proemium* (introduction) and eight books. The *proemium* is an excellent history of ancient medicine, and in the whole work Celsus mentions about eighty writers. He is very sympathetic to Hippocratic practice, and his references to the Hippocratic Corpus are very accurate. During the time of Celsus the rival Schools of Methodists and Empiricists were the most important of several Schools of medicine in Rome, and he preserved an admirable balance between them. He emphasized the importance of anatomy for the practitioner, and he knew that arteries contain blood under pressure. The therapeutic methods of Celsus were treatment by diet, drugs and surgery. He gives detailed diets for diseases such as rheumatism and gout. His drugs consist mainly of herbs

and vegetables, but he also mentions animal remedies. The seventh book deals with surgery. The descriptions of instruments are excellent, and he gives accounts of several difficult operations. Some of these descriptions are crystal clear, and in later centuries they became classical.

With the decline of Greek scholarship the influence of Celsus increased. He wrote in very pure Latin, and from the aspect of style he did for medicine what Cicero did for philosophy. The *De medicina* was the first medical work to be printed (1478), and until about the middle of the last century its Latin original was still a standard textbook for medical students.

T. C. Allbutt, *Greek Medicine in Rome*. 1921.

W. H. S. Jones, in *Celsus*, (Ed. and trans. W. G. Spencer). vol. 1, 1935.

O. Temkin, *Bulletin of the Institute of the History of Medicine*. **4**, 159, 1936.

M. Wellmann, *Archiv für Geschichte der Medizin*, **16**, 209, 1925.

Dictionary of Scientific Biography.

E A U

CESALPINO, ANDREA Born at Arezzo, Tuscany, Italy, 6 June 1519; died Rome, 23 February 1603. Physician and botanist.

Cesalpino studied under L. Ghini (1500–56), professor of medicine and director of the Botanic Garden at the University of Pisa, and succeeded him in 1555. In 1592 he was summoned to Rome to be physician to Pope Clement VIII and professor at the Sapienza University.

In Cesalpino's day herbalists arranged plants according to their medicinal properties or merely in alphabetical order. He sought a classification that employed the characters of the fruit and seeds, and in *De Plantis* (1583) gave a full exposition of the whole of theoretical botany. *De Plantis*, probably the most philosophical botanical treatise since the time of THEOPHRASTUS was divided into sixteen books, fifteen of which described some fifteen hundred plants. The most valuable part, however, was the first book, which recognized that plants could be grouped by certain characters of the reproductive organs. Unfortunately, Cesalpino retained the classic divisions of woody and herbaceous plants, and allowed his Aristotelian philosophy to speculate on matters such as the exact location of the plant soul. From his classification sprang all the artificial carpological schemes culminating in that of J. Gaertner (1732–91) in 1788. His work had a profound influence on later botanists, such as J. P. de Tournefort (1656–1708) and LINNAEUS.

He wrote a number of anatomical books, and to a certain extent anticipated the theory of the circulation of the blood enunciated by W. HARVEY.

J. von Sachs, *History of Botany (1530–1860)*. 1890.

L. C. Miall, *The Early Naturalists*. 1912.

Agnes Arber, *Herbals*. 1986. (Paperback).

Dictionary of Scientific Biography, Supp. I.

R G C D

CHADWICK, SIR JAMES Born at Bollington, near Macclesfield, Cheshire, England, 20 October 1891; died Cambridge, 24 July 1974. Discoverer of the neutron.

James Chadwick attended Manchester Grammar School, entered the University of Manchester in

1908, and graduated from the Honours School of Physics in 1911. Under Ernest RUTHERFORD he worked there on radioactivity from 1911 to 1913, when he received his MSc. On an 1851 Exhibition Scholarship, Chadwick worked with H. W. GEIGER at the *Physikalische-Technische Reichsanstalt* in Berlin until he was interned (1914–18), quartered in stables of a racecourse at Ruhleben, near Spandau. With money from England and kind help from Max PLANCK, H. W. NERNST and Lise MEITNER, Chadwick was able to do some work on physics even during the war. In the camp he met C. D. Ellis, an engineer; later, the co-authors of the renowned *Radiations from Radioactive Substances* (1930) were Rutherford, Chadwick and Ellis.

Chadwick was awarded the Wollaston Studentship at Gonville and Caius College, Cambridge, in 1919. In 1921 he was elected a Fellow of the College and in 1923 he was appointed assistant director of the Cavendish Laboratory. His research there was chiefly on the artificial disintegration of elements under bombardment with alpha particles. In 1932 he clarified an experiment which had puzzled W. W. G. Bother (1891–1957) and I. JOLIOT-CURIE and J-F JOLIOT, in terms of the neutron, a neutral particle having approximately the mass of a proton, whose existence had been foreseen intuitively by Rutherford. Chadwick proposed that alpha particles knocked neutrons out of nuclei of beryllium atoms, and that these neutrons in turn knocked protons out of the hydrogen-rich paraffin to produce the effects observed by the Joliot-Curies. Energy measurements confirmed Chadwick's suggestion. From data on different targets he calculated the mass of the neutron, giving experimental confirmation of Rutherford's intuition. For this discovery he was awarded the Nobel prize for physics in 1935.

Chadwick was Lyon Jones Professor of physics at the University of Liverpool, 1935–48. He headed the delegation of British technical experts to the USA in 1943 and was active in experiments which led to the development of the atomic bomb. He returned to Britain in 1946 exhausted by the political and physical strains of this project.

After the war Chadwick participated in three rather distinct efforts: the development of nuclear energy in Britain, pure research in nuclear and particle physics in universities, and specific academic matters at Liverpool and Cambridge. He believed that fundamental research in nuclear physics should be undertaken in universities. He objected to Cockcroft's heading a government laboratory for such research at Harwell. When Chadwick left Liverpool to become Master of Gonville and Caius College (1948) he faced problems in finance as well as in physics. There was improvement when he put some endowment into an equity fund which he managed successfully. However, uncomfortable about divergent views about university policy, Chadwick resigned as Master in 1958 and retired to a cottage in North Wales. In 1969 he and Lady Chadwick returned to live in Cambridge to be near their twin daughters.

Biographical Memoirs of Fellows of the Royal Society. 1976. (Portrait.)

Physics Today **27**, 87, 1974. (Portrait.)

H. Oxbury (Ed.), *Great Britons: 20th Century Lives.* 1985.

Dictionary of Scientific Biography.

Dictionary of National Biography.

Tyler Wasson (Ed.), *Nobel Prize Winners.* 1987. (portrait.)

R L W

CHAIN, SIR ERNST BORIS Born in Berlin, 19 June 1906; died Mulranny, County Mayo, Ireland, 12 August 1979; initiator, with Howard FLOREY, of research that led to the discovery of the systemic chemotherapeutic properties of penicillin.

Ernst Boris Chain was the son of a Jewish chemical industrialist who had emigrated from Russia. His father died when Ernst was thirteen and his mother (*née* Margarete Eisner) and sister died later in a German concentration camp after Hitler had come into power. Ernst Chain was educated at the Fredrich-Wilhelm University of Berlin and emigrated to England in 1933. He spent six months in the laboratory of Charles Harington (1897–1972) at University College London and then, with the help of J. B. S. HALDANE, obtained a place in the School of Biochemistry at Cambridge under Frederick Gowland HOPKINS.

In 1935 Chain went to the Sir William Dunn School of Pathology at the invitation of Howard Florey (later Lord Florey) who had recently been appointed professor of pathology and believed that experimental pathology could benefit greatly from the collaboration of pathologists with chemists. At Florey's suggestion, Chain took up a study of the substrate of lysozyme, a bacteriolytic enzyme, discovered by Alexander FLEMING, that had been found in a number of animal secretions. This led him to read about the many antibacterial substances that had been reported to be produced by micro-organisms. In the course of discussions with Florey, he suggested, and Florey agreed, that a survey should be made jointly of the properties of such substances. Fortunately, one of the first to be chosen for further investigation was Fleming's penicillin. In consequence, Chain, Florey and a small group of colleagues, including N. G. Heatley (1911–) and E. P. ABRAHAM, carried out the work in Oxford which resulted in the demonstration in 1941 of the remarkable therapeutic powers of penicillin in man. Chain shared with Florey and Fleming the Nobel prize for medicine in 1945.

During the war years Chain discovered, with Abraham, the first penicillinase and in 1943 they proposed the then controversial β-lactam structure for penicillin. By this time Chain had become an enthusiastic member of a small group in Oxford, headed by Robert ROBINSON, which took up the study of the chemical and biochemical properties of penicillin and became part of a large but unsuccessful Anglo-American enterprise, whose objective was the production of penicillin by chemical synthesis.

Later Chain expressed dissatisfaction with conditions in Oxford and left in 1948 to organize a department of biochemistry and set up a fermentation plant in Rome. There he became Scientific Director of the International Research Centre for Chemical Microbiology at the *Istituto Superiore di Sanita*. While in Rome he initiated fruitful research on the ergot alkaloids and suggested in 1954 to the then chairman of the Beecham Group that the Company should make further studies of penicillin instead of searching for new and different antibiotics. This led scientists at Beecham to the isolation of 6-aminopenicillanic acid and the production of new and valuable penicillins. In 1961 Chain returned to England and for twelve years was professor of biochemistry at Imperial College, London, where he stimulated work on fusicoccin phytotoxins and glucose metabolism.

Ernst Chain was a highly gifted man. He spoke five languages fluently and was a pianist of distinction who had to choose between music and science at an early stage of his career. He expressed strong views on the organization of academic science and its relationship with industry, but these views were not generally popular and they brought him into conflict with official policy. He married in 1948 Dr Anne Beloff and they had two sons and a daughter. He was elected a Fellow of the Royal Society in 1949 and was knighted twenty years later.

Biographical Memoirs of Fellows of the Royal Society. 1983. (Portrait.)
Dictionary of Scientific Biography, Supp. II.
Dictionary of National Biography.
Tyler Wasson (Ed.), *Nobel Prize Winners.* 1987. (Portrait.)
H. Oxbury (Ed.), *Great Britons: 20th Century Lives.* 1985.
R. W. Clark, *The Life of Ernst Chain.* 1985. (Portrait.)

E P A

CHANCE, ALEXANDER MACOMB Born at Birmingham, England, 28 June 1844; died Torquay, Devon, 1917. Industrial chemist.

Chance – named after his American great-uncle, General Alexander Macomb – was the son of a Birmingham glassmaker, who set up as a soda manufacturer in order to provide one of the basic raw materials required for the family works. He was appointed manager of the Alkali Works in 1868, at a time when the ammonia-soda process had just been perfected by E. SOLVAY, but chose to use the long-established process devised by N. LEBLANC. He introduced an innovation in Leblanc's process that was to give it a new lease of life in the face of strong competition from Solvay's.

The Leblanc process left as a residue large quantities of waste known as galligu. This contained large amounts of calcium sulphide, and apart from being extremely unpleasant and difficult to deal with, locked up valuable sulphur derived originally from sulphuric acid. Many attempts were made to recover this sulphur in an economic industrial process, but Chance was the first to succeed, with a process developed between 1882 and 1887.

Following William GOSSAGE, who had unsuccessfully tackled the same problem, Chance blew carbon dioxide gas through the waste, expelling the sulphur as hydrogen sulphide. At first he proposed to oxidize the hydrogen sulphide to sulphur dioxide, for sulphuric-acid manufacture, but he realized that in the lately patented Claus kiln (1882) the gas could be partially oxidized, to yield sulphur. The Chance process, the last major improvement in the Leblanc process, was quickly adopted and by 1893 some 35 000 tons of sulphur were recovered by its means in UK factories alone. With the removal of the sulphur the galligu was converted to innocuous calcium carbonate. The success of Chance, proceeding along similar lines

to Gossage some forty years earlier, is attributed to the improvement in the interval of the technique of pumping gases.

D. W. F. Hardie, *A History of the Chemical Industry in Widnes.* 1950.
Kenneth M. Chance, *Chemistry and Industry*, 19 August 1944. (Portrait.)
Dictionary of National Biography (Missing Persons). 1993.

T I W

CHANDRASEKHAR, SUBRAHMANYAN Born in Lahore, India, 19 October 1910. Theoretical astrophysicist, best known for his work on white dwarfs and black holes.

Chandrasekhar gained his first degree at the Presidency College, Madras, in 1930, and then travelled to England to study for a doctorate in theoretical physics at Cambridge University. On the journey he investigated the theory of white dwarfs – the dense but hot remains of stars that have collapsed after burning all their fuel. He showed that the mass of such stars had to be less than 1.4 solar masses – now known as the Chandrasekhar limit – otherwise they would continue to contract, ultimately to black holes. He published a complete theory of white dwarfs in 1934, after gaining his PhD in 1933.

Chandrasekhar remained at Cambridge until 1937 and then moved to the University of Chicago, becoming Morton D. Hull Professor of Theoretical Physics in 1952. During this time he studied stellar dynamics, and the interaction of radiation with stellar and planetary atmospheres. After this he turned to investigating stability in stars and discovered two types of instability due to the effects of general relativity. Then in the early 1970s he began a systematic study of black holes, which culminated in his definitive textbook, *The Mathematical Theory of Black Holes.*

In 1983, Chandrasekhar was rewarded for his work on the structure and evolution of stars with the Nobel prize for physics, which he shared with William A. Fowler (1911–) who has made important contributions to the understanding of nuclear processes in astrophysics.

Physics Today, January 1984. (Portrait.)
A. L. Hammond (Ed.), *A Passion to Know.* 1984
Tyler Wasson (Ed.), *Nobel Prize Winners.* 1987. (Portrait.)
Les Prix Nobel en 1983. 1984. (Portrait.)
K. C. Wali, *Chandra.* 1992.

C S

CHANG (ZHANG) HENG Born in Nanyang, China, AD 78; died Luoyang, AD 139. Mathematician and astronomer.

Chang Heng was Imperial Historian and official astronomer during the Han Dynasty. His official duties included recording the occurrence of earthquakes in China, disasters to which the country has always been prone. To assist him he devised (AD 132) the world's first seismograph. This drum-shaped instrument contained a delicately balanced system of pendulums and levers, supporting eight metal balls equally spaced around the circumference. An earthquake shock would dislodge the ball directed towards the epicentre. The original has perished but models constructed on the basis of contemporary records prove its practicality. It was

1700 years before comparable instruments were devised in the west. He devised also a celestial globe whose motion was regulated by a clepsydra, and improved the accuracy of the calendar by making corrections for minor fluctuations in the Moon's motion. In mathematics he improved the accuracy of the value given to π, expressing this as $\sqrt{10}$ (3.162) or 92/29 (3.172). He is also credited with devising differential gearing for a 'South-pointing' chariot.

Chinese Academy of Sciences, *Ancient China's Technology and Science*, 1983.

Colin A. Ronan, *The Shorter Science and Civilisation in China*, Vol 2. 1981.

T I W

CHAPPE, CLAUDE Born at Brulon, Sarthe, France, 25 December 1763; died Paris, 23 January 1805. Inventor of semaphore telegraph.

His intended career in the Church having been terminated through the French Revolution, Chappe experimented with long-distance communication by sound, electricity and visual signals. His electrical device employed synchronized clocks, significance being attached to the position of the second hands at the moment of discharge from a Leyden jar, but the insulation of the conducting wire proved too difficult. Instead, by March 1791 he devised a system of conspicuous semaphores, consisting of a wooden beam pivoted at the centre and provided with additional movable arms at the ends.

In spite of political uncertainties and mob violence, which twice destroyed his apparatus in Paris, in August 1793 Chappe was authorized to build a line from Paris to Lille. With the help of his two brothers he erected fifteen relay stations in twelve months, in time to bring to the capital the news of the recapture of Le Quesnoy. Orders were given for a second line, and the inventor began to plan for commercial uses and weather reports; but financial worries and attempts to contest the priority of his invention drove him to commit suicide at the telegraph workshops in 1805. His methods were adopted in England in 1811–15 and were not finally abandoned in France until 1852.

Nouvelle Biographie Universelle. 1852–66.

T K D

CHAPTAL, JEAN ANTOINE CLAUDE (COMTE DE CHANTELOUP) Born at Nogaret, Lozère, France, 4 June 1756; died Paris, 30 July 1832. Chemical encyclopaedist and administrator.

Chaptal, son of an apothecary, studied chemistry at Montpellier to such good effect that the authorities founded a chair of chemistry specially to enable him to teach chemistry at the medical school. He was one of the first to adhere to the anti-phlogiston doctrine of LAVOISIER. He had a life-long interest in chemical manufacturer and achieved success in its commercial as well as its scientific side. He set up the first French factory for the commercial production of sulphuric acid. He also manufactured soda, white lead, and other heavy chemicals.

During the revolution he managed an important saltpetre works at Grenelle. In 1799, after the *coup d'état* of 18 Brumaire (9 November), he was made a Councillor of State. He succeeded Lucien Bonaparte as Minister of the Interior. His talents found outlets in improving the State chemical industry, and in setting up a school of arts and a society of industries. He also took an interest in hospitals. He was one of the leaders in the introduction of the new metric system of weights and measures. Napoleon conferred on him the title of Compte de Chanteloup. During the Hundred Days, Chaptal held ministerial rank and was Director-General of Commerce and Manufactures. After the second restoration his administrative talent remained in demand and Louis XVIII created him a peer of France in 1819.

He was a prolific writer on technical chemistry and both by his example and his power of exposition made a major contribution to modern scientific chemical industry. His principal works, *Elémens de chimie* (1790, etc.) and *Chimie Appliquée aux Arts* (1807) were very popular. The latter contains some of the best accounts available of the technical and commercial details of the industrial chemistry of his time. His name is remembered in 'chaptalization', a process for enriching wine by addition of sucrose.

Chaptal's administrative talent gave him a certain independence of the somewhat inbred academic scientific circle in Paris. To this extent he was a man in advance of his time.

J. Pigeire, *La Vie et l'Oeuvre de Chaptal.* 1932.

M. Crosland, *The Society of Arcueil.* 1967. (Portrait.)

Dictionary of Scientific Biography.

F G

CHARCOT, JEAN-MARTIN Born in Paris, 29 November 1825; died Auberge des Settons, near Vézelay, 16 August 1893. Physician, neurologist and teacher.

Charcot studied medicine in Paris; after failing the competitive examination in 1847, he was elected Interne at the Salpêtrière in 1848. His MD thesis in 1853 helped to differentiate rheumatoid arthritis from gout and other diseases of the joints. In 1858 he first described intermittent claudication. When he was appointed to the staff of the Salpêtrière in 1862 at the age of 37 he found this ancient institution full of long-stay patients with undiagnosed or unknown chronic afflictions of the nervous system. During the next eight years he set about a systematic clinical study and correlated his findings with meticulous postmortem observations. Classical descriptions resulted of multiple or disseminated sclerosis, previously sketched by Sir Robert Carswell and Jean Cruveilhier (1791–1874); of amyotrophic lateral sclerosis (a variant of which had been described by Charcot's teacher, G. B. A. Duchenne de Boulogne (1806–75), which subsequently became known as Maladie de Charcot); of cerebral haemorrhage; a familial neuropathy now known as Charcot-Marie-Tooth disease; of tabes dorsalis (a form of neurosyphilis) and of its peculiar complication, a destructive and painless arthritis which is still known as Charcot's Joint. He pushed observations and ideas about poliomyelitis as far as was possible at the time. He never lost interest in general medicine and wrote about various aspects of thyroid and liver disease.

Charcot initiated laboratory work, but was opposed to animal experimentation; however, he defended Pasteur when he was attacked for his rabies vaccination. His clinical demonstrations and lectures at the Salpêtrière became increasingly popular and his *Leçons sur les maladies du système nerveux faits à la Salpêtrière* (1872–1873) was translated into many languages. He was made professor of pathologic anatomy at the Sorbonne in 1872, and in 1882 he was created the first professor of disease of the nervous system at Paris.

Latterly he studied the problems of cerebal localization, in which he agreed with the ideas of J. Hughlings Jackson (1834–1911), and of aphasia, where he disagreed with P. P. BROCA. The most dramatic aspects of his work were his demonstrations of hysteria, which attracted fame outside his own profession and were criticized on the ground that he and his assistants suggested the 'crisis' to the patient, as described later in *The Story of San Michele* by Axel Munthe. However, Charcot's ideas on hysteria were sound, and inspired the work of Sigmund FREUD, one of his many pupils to achieve fame. His best-known medical disciples included Pierre Marie, J. F. F. Babinski and V. M. Bechterew.

Charcot had artistic talents and his caricatures and drawings are preserved at the Salpêtrière. He wrote books on *Les Démoniaques dans L'Art* and *Les Difformes et Les Malades dans L'Art*. His own bronze statue outside the Salpêtrière was melted down during the occupation of Paris in 1942. He was the outstanding figure of the Paris Medical School at its apogee and the founder of a great French school of neurology. His only son Jean abandoned medicine after his father's death and became the foremost French polar explorer.

Georges Guillian, *J. M. Charcot* (edited and translated by Pearce Bailey). 1959. (Portraits.)
Dictionary of Scientific Biography/

E H J

CHARGAFF, ERWIN Born at Czernowitz, Bohemia [now Cernovice, Czech Republic], 11 August 1905. Biochemist notable for work on nucleic acids.

Chargaff studied chemistry in Vienna (DPhil. 1928), Yale, Berlin and Paris before deciding to emigrate to America in 1935 because of the European political situation. His entire career until his retirement in 1974 was spent as a professor of biochemistry at Columbia University, New York.

Chargaff's initial research there concerned the coagulation of the blood which involved the investigation of the chemistry of fats (lipids). In 1944, however, inspired by the findings of O. T. Avery (1877–1955) that deoxyribosenucleic acid (DNA), was responsible for the heritable transformation of bacteria, as well as by E. SCHRÖDINGER's suggestion in *What is Life?* (1944) that chromosomes carried a hereditary code, he turned to nucleic acid research. Using the new techniques of chromatography and uv spectrometry, in 1950 he showed that the bases that formed important components of DNA fell into complementary pairs. Not only was the number of purine bases, adenine and guanine, equal to the number of pyrimidine bases, cytosine and thiamine, but the numbers of adenine bases were equal to those of thiamine and those of guanine equal to those of cytosine. These 'Chargaff Rules' played a crucial role in the model-building activities of F. CRICK and J. D. WATSON, when, in 1953, they announced the double helical structure of DNA.

An elegant writer of English prose, his books include (with J. N. Davidson (1911–72)), *The*

Nucleic Acids (1955–60) and autobiographical reflections, *Heraclitean Fire*. The latter, together with *Serious Questions* (1986) reveal an articulate, critical person who is disillusioned by science and the modern university, and pessimistic concerning man's future.

E. Chargaff, *Heraclitean Fire: Sketches from a Life before Nature*, 1978.
McGraw-Hill Modern Scientists and Engineers, Vol 1. 1980 (Portrait.)

W H B

CHARLES, JACQUES ALEXANDRE CÉSAR Born at Beaugency, Loiret, France, 12 November 1746; died Paris, 7 April 1823. Remembered for his work on balloons and the expansion of gases.

Attracted to experimental science through Benjamin FRANKLIN's researches on lightning, Charles built up an important collection of physical apparatus and became celebrated for his public lectures illustrated by ingenious experiments. Familiar with the preparation of gases by J. PRIESTLEY and H. CAVENDISH, Charles began experiments on the filling of balloons with hydrogen, and on 27 August 1783, in collaboration with the brothers Robert, he effected the first unmanned ascent of a balloon filled with hydrogen. On 1 December 1783 he and the younger Robert brother were the first to ascend in such a balloon, later ascending alone to a height of 3000 metres. These successful ascents led to unprecedented public enthusiasm and Charles was subsequently invited by the king to install his physical apparatus in the Louvre. When the Tuileries were invaded on 10 August 1792, Charles owed his life to his presence of mind in recalling his balloon ascents to the infuriated mob.

Charles anticipated the law of constant rate of expansion of gases at constant pressure, later definitively established by J. L. GAY-LUSSAC and John DALTON. He is also remembered for his improvement of the heliostat of W. J. S. vans' Gravesande (1688–1742) and for his invention of a number of ingenious physical instruments including a thermometric hydrometer and a reflection goniometer. He was elected to the *Académie des Sciences* in 1795.

J. B. F. Fourier, *Notice*. 1825.
Dictionary of Scientific Biography.

J W H

CHARPAK, GEORGES Born in Poland, 1 August 1924. Atomic physicist.

Charpak is now a French citizen. He took his PhD at the *Collège de France* in 1955. Since 1959 he has worked at CERN in Geneva, where his main interest has been in very rare particle interactions, often seeking one specific reaction from among as many as a billion. For this, existing photographic systems of detection were inadequate and in 1968 Charpak developed a new type of wire chamber, derived from the conventional Geiger-Müller tube. By connecting the detector directly to a computer he succeeded in improving sensitivity a thousandfold. By using a succession of spaced chambers the particle trajectory can be determined precisely. The introduction of such super-sensitive detectors has had important consequences. In 1974 S. C. C. TING and B. RICHTER used it to discover the charm quark and some years later (1982) physicists at CERN used it to discover intermediate bosons.

Today, such detectors are being increasingly used outside physics; for example, in medicine to detect x-rays.

Charpak was elected to the French Academy of Sciences in 1985 and in 1989 received the High Energy and Particle Physics Prize of the European Physical Society. Since 1984 he has been Joliot Curie Professor at the *Ecole Supérieure de Physique et Chimie*, Paris. He was awarded the Nobel prize for physics in 1992.

Les Prix Nobel en 1992. 1993. (Portrait.)
Physics World, November, 1992.
La Recherche, December, 1993. (Portrait.)
CERN Courier, Vol 32, No 10, 1992. (Portrait.)
Physics Today, January 1993.

T I W

CHERENKOV, PAVEL ALEKSEJEVIC Born in Voronezh Region, Russia, 28 July 1904; died Moscow, 6 January 1990. Physicist, discoverer of the 'Cherenkov effect'.

The son of a peasant family, Cherenkov graduated from the Voronezh State University in 1928, and joined the P. N. Lebedev Institute in Moscow in 1930 to study under S. I. Vavilov. His thesis work was to investigate the penetration in fluids of radiation from radium. The blue light emitted under such circumstances had been thought to be due to fluorescence, but Cherenkov became convinced that a different effect was involved. In 1936 he discovered that the light is emitted at an angle to the direction of the incident radiation. A year later, his colleagues I. M. Frank (1908–   ) and I. E. Tamm (1895–1971) showed that the light was in effect a shock wave due to charged particles travelling faster than the speed of light in the liquid. (The particles were electrons knocked out of atoms by the incident radiation.)

With the development of light-sensitive phototubes in the 1940s, the Cherenkov effect became important for detecting charged subatomic particles. Water-based Cherenkov detectors are used in large-scale cosmic-ray detectors, while smaller devices based on a variety of fluids allow particles to be identified through their differing velocities.

Cherenkov remained at the Lebedev Institute for the rest of his career, working on experimental particle physics. He was awarded the Nobel prize for physics in 1958, sharing it with Frank and Tamm.

Nobel Lectures: Physics, 1942–1962. 1964.
Tyler Wasson (Ed.), *Nobel Prize Winners*. 1987. (Portrait.)

C S

CHERWELL, VISCOUNT See LINDEMANN.

CHEVREUL, MICHEL EUGÈNE Born at Angers, France, 31 August 1786; died Paris, 8 April 1889. A versatile and long-lived chemist, notable for his pioneer work on fats.

Chevreul, son of a surgeon, became assistant to L. N. VAUQUELIN while still a boy, and received his chemical training from him and from A. F. FOURCROY. Apart from various teaching appointments, he was made (1810) assistant in the Museum of Natural History, promoted to professor in 1830, and finally (1861) made Honorary Director for life. He was also (1824) Director of Dyeing at the Gobelin tapestry factory. After the death of his wife in 1862 he lived almost as a recluse in his apartment

at the Museum; but he continued to work and published almost up to his death. He was elected to the *Académie des Sciences* in 1826, and was twice President (1839, 1867).

During his long life Chevreul had time for many investigations, but his reputation rests largely on his early studies of the composition of oils and fats, summarized in his *Recherches sur les corps gras* (1823). He isolated several solid fats as pure substances, analysed them, and showed that they were 'ethers' (esters) of glycerol and the solid fatty acids. The liquid fats were shown to be similar 'ethers' of glycerol and a liquid acid (oleic acid). Soaps were recognized for the first time as alkali-metal salts of the fatty acids. This work had an immediate effect in rationalizing soap boiling, and in replacing the malodorous tallow-candle with 'stearine' (crude stearic acid). It was also important as the exemplar of what could be achieved in the study of apparently intractable natural products.

Chevreul also worked on the chemistry of drying oils (he showed that they absorb oxygen), on spermaceti and cholesterol, and on natural colouring matters (haematoxylin, quercitrin and many others). He wrote a book on his investigations of the divining rod, which is now very rare. In his later years, he was interested in theories of colour, and wrote some distinguished studies of the history of chemistry and alchemy.

G. Bouchard, *Chevreul, le doyen des savants*. 1930.
A. B. Costa, *Michel Eugène Chevreul, pioneer of organic chemistry*. 1962.
E. Farber (Ed.), *Great Chemists*. 1961. (Portrait.)
Journal of Chemical Education, **25**, 62, 1948. (Portraits.)
J. R. Partington, *A History of Chemistry*, vol. 4, 1964. (Portraits.)
W. A. Smeaton, *Endeavour* (New Series), **13**, 89, 1989. (Portrait.)
Dictionary of Scientific Biography.
H. E. Armstrong, *Nature*, **116**, 750, 1925.
Paul Nadar, (Seven) Candid Photographs of Chevreul, *Life*, 11 January 1937.

W V F

CHITTENDEN, RUSSELL HENRY Born at New Haven, Connecticut, USA, 18 February 1856; died there, 26 December 1943. Celebrated as the 'Father of physiological chemistry in the United States'.

Against a background of financial difficulty Chittenden became a special student at Yale College in 1872 through diligence and hard work. He graduated in 1875, but remained to teach physiological chemistry to premedical students. A year earlier, as an undergraduate, he had been teaching practical physiological chemistry to a small number of students at the Sheffield School of Science at Yale – the first physiological chemistry laboratory in the United States. In 1882, after obtaining a PhD and studying in Germany for one year, he was appointed professor of physiological chemistry at Yale, a position he held till his retirement in 1922. While in Germany he had come under the influence of W. KÜHNE at Heidelberg and this led later to joint research on proteolytic enzymes. At Heidelberg, Chittenden also studied chemistry with R. W. BUNSEN.

Chittenden's scientific work falls broadly into three areas: (*a*) enzyme studies, particularly in relation to digestion, such as the action of saliva;

(b) toxicology studies which included examining the effects of heavy metals, organic compounds and alcohol on the human body; and (c) investigations on nutrition, for example on minimum daily protein requirements.

But Chittenden's tremendous influence on American physiological chemistry is perhaps most readily appreciated by his activities in promoting scientific societies and as a teacher. He was a charter member of the American Physiological Society when it was formed in 1887, and the first President of the American Society of Biological Chemists organized in 1906. His success as a teacher is reflected by the subsequent eminence of some of his pupils, for example, Lafayette Mendel (1872–1935), who did so much in establishing the eminence of the Sheffield School of Science.

Chittenden also found time to write a number of books. Notable were *Digestive Proteolysis* (1895) *Physiological Economy in Nutrition* (1904), and *The Nutrition of Man* (1907). In addition to such books dealing with his own scientific subjects, he wrote valuable historical studies on his chosen field, such as *The Development of Physiological Chemistry in the United States* (1930). He was also connected with a number of journals: for example the *Journal of Physiology*, the *American Journal of Physiology*, and the *Journal of Experimental Medicine*.

E. N. Todhunter, *Alabama Journal of Medical Science*, **2**, 337, 1965. (Portrait.)
Dictionary of Scientific Biography.

J K C

CLAISEN, LUDWIG Born at Cologne, Germany, 14 January 1851; died Godesberg, 5 January 1930. A master of synthetic organic chemistry.

Claisen studied chemistry in Bonn and Göttingen, and returned to Bonn as assistant. The years 1882–5 were spent in Manchester, which he disliked intensely. He became *Privatdozent* in Munich (1886), and professor successively in Aachen (1890), Kiel (1897) and Berlin (1904). In 1906 he retired to Godesberg, where he worked in his private laboratory. His last thirty years were dogged by ill health; he never married.

Claisen deliberately restricted his scientific activity to the thing he could do best; the study of organic syntheses and reactions. It would be impossible to summarize his huge output of work in this field. His name is remembered by the 'Claisen condensation', a large group of reactions in which carbon-carbon bonds are formed under the influence of alkaline catalysts such as sodium ethoxide; and by the 'Claisen flask', a simple piece of apparatus for distillation. He was the first (about the same time as J. A. WISLICENUS) to isolate the two forms of a tautomeric compound as chemical individuals (1892); this work did much to clarify current opinion about tautomerism, or, as he preferred to call it, pseudomerism.

Berichte der deutschen Chemischen Gesellschaft, 69, 97A, 1936. (Portrait.)
Dictionary of Scientific Biography.

W V F

CLAUDE, GEORGES Born in Paris, 1870; died Saint-Cloud, 23 May 1960. Engineer, best known for his process for the liquefaction of air.

After finishing the course at the *École de phy-*sique et chimie* in 1886, Claude worked in the laboratory of an electricity company, and later as an engineer in a number of industrial concerns. He was a first-rate technologist, apparently indefatigable in his search for new techniques. He was responsible for a number of major innovations of great industrial importance.

About 1896 he discovered that acetylene is soluble in acetone, and may be transported in safety, without fear of explosions, when thus dissolved. This technique was generally adopted, and one could say that Claude was thus the founder of the acetylene industry. In 1902 he perfected his process for liquefying air, making it do external work during its expansion. His process can be seen as a modification of those of William Hampson (c.1854–1926) and K. VON LINDE, in which cooled gas was further cooled by allowing it to expand from a high pressure through a valve (Joule-Thomson effect). Lord RAYLEIGH had suggested that the efficiency of the process could be made higher if the gas could be made to do external work in its expansion; and Claude carried this into effect by making the gas expand into a cylinder or through a turbine. Using this process he prepared oxygen and nitrogen on the industrial scale. As early as 1910 he pointed out the economies which would result from the use of pure oxygen in iron-smelting, a technique not adopted until after the Second World War.

Also in 1910, Claude worked out a process for making neon lights for signs; in 1917 he invented a synthetic ammonia process similar to that of F. HABER, but involving much higher pressures – 1000 atmospheres instead of 250. In 1924 he was elected to the *Académie des Sciences*. From 1927 on he was concerned with finding sources of energy, and in particular with experiments to generate electricity using the temperature difference between the top and bottom of the sea. The results were not altogether satisfactory, but projects like the wartime PLUTO – the trans-Channel pipeline – were apparently based in part on these pioneer experiments with pipelines under the sea.

In 1944 Claude was expelled from the *Académie* for having collaborated with the Germans; he was sent to prison as a collaborator in 1945, but released in 1949.

Nature, 187, 829, 1960.
Grand Larousse Encyclopédique, vol. 3. (Portrait.)
G. Claude, *Ma Vie et mes Inventions*. 1957.
Dictionary of Scientific Biography.

D M K

CLAUSIUS, RUDOLF JULIUS EMMANUEL Born at Cöslin, Pomerania, Germany, 2 January 1822; died Bonn, 24 August, 1888. Celebrated for his many contributions to theoretical physics.

After attending the University of Berlin from 1840 to 1844, Clausius took his degree at Halle in 1848. In 1850 he was appointed professor of physics in the Royal Artillery and Engineering School, Berlin. In 1855 he became ordinary professor at the Polytechnic School at Zürich and later professor at the University there. He moved to Würzburg in 1867 as professor of physics and two years later was appointed to the same chair at Bonn, a position which he held until his death.

Towards the middle of the nineteenth century it had become evident that CARNOT's proof of his fundamental theorem in thermodynamics was inconsistent with the mechanical theory of heat then rapidly establishing itself. The dilemma was squarely posed by William THOMSON (Lord Kelvin), in his *Account of Carnot's Theorem* (1849). On the one hand, the mechanical theory of heat could not be reconciled with Carnot's use of the caloric theory; on the other, it was becoming evident that the consequences of Carnot's theory had to be accepted as true. It was Clausius who resolved this dilemma in his epoch-making paper *Uber die bewegende Kraft der Wärme* (1850), in which he showed that Carnot's theorem could be maintained in company with the mechanical theory of heat provided only it was assumed that heat could not by itself pass from one body to another at a higher temperature. In the following year, Thomson arrived independently at an equivalent formulation of this, the second law of thermodynamics. The law was given a more precise mathematical expression by Clausius in 1854, but it was only much later, in a series of papers between 1859 and 1865, that he eventually rallied to the notion of the dissipation of energy put forward by Thomson in 1852. In 1865 Clausius first introduced the term entropy, expressing the law of dissipation of energy in terms of the tendency of entropy to increase. In the long-drawn-out controversy which followed the enunciation of the second law of thermodynamics Clausius was the foremost champion of the new theory, successfully warding off all the attacks of the opposition.

Following the earlier papers of J. P. JOULE and A. K. Krönig (1822–79) on the kinetic theory of gases, Clausius contributed a fundamental paper *Uber die Art der Bewegung welche wir Wärme nennen* (1857) in which he calculated a mean speed for gas molecules in terms of the pressure. This calculation ignored molecular collisions, and assumed all the molecules to be moving with the same speed. But the allowance for all possible directions of molecular motion represented an important advance on previous work. In 1858 Clausius introduced the important concepts of mean free path and effective radius of a molecule later taken over by J. Clerk MAXWELL and Lothar MEYER. Clausius was able to show that these concepts accounted in principle for the observed small values of diffusion rates and heat conductivities in gases in spite of the very large mean speeds of the gas molecules.

Apart from Clausius's work in thermodynamics and the kinetic theory of gases, we may note his fundamental contribution to the theory of electrolysis (1857) based on the notion of continuous partial dissociation of ions in solution in the absence of any electro-motive force. He also wrote an important paper on electrodynamics in which he advanced a formula for the kinetic potential between two electrons different from those of W. E. WEBER or G. F. B. RIEMANN. Inevitably incorrect as it stood, being based on the assumption of action at a distance, this formula nevertheless proved important when later amended by H. A. LORENTZ and combined with Maxwell's theory to yield the pondermotive force on an electron.

Clausius was one of the most original theoretical physicists of the nineteenth century, unsurpassed for his profound physical intuition and his ability to make large deductions with a minimum use of complicated mathematical analysis.

E. Riecke, *Rudolf Clausius.* 1889.

S. G. Brush, *Annals of Science*, **14**, 185, 1958.
Proceedings of the Royal Society, **48**, i, 1890.
H. Crew, *Scripta Mathematica*, **8**, 111, 1941.
Dictionary of Scientific Biography.

J W H

COCKCROFT, SIR JOHN DOUGLAS Born at Todmorden, Yorkshire, England, 27 May 1897; died Cambridge, 18 September 1967. Pioneer atomic physicist; the first (with E. T. S. Walton) to split the nucleus.

Cockcroft, who came of a cotton-manufacturing family, was educated at the local secondary school in Todmorden. In 1914 he went to Manchester University to study mathematics, but the following year left to join the Army (Royal Field Artillery); he was one of the few who served unscathed through almost all the great later battles. After the war, he was apprenticed to the engineering firm of Metropolitan Vickers, who, discovering his talents, sent him to read electrical engineering – a training unusual among atomic physicists, which was later to stand him in good stead – at the College of Technology, Manchester. Thence he went to St John's College, Cambridge, to read mathematics, taking the Mathematical Tripos in 1924. On graduation he joined (1922) the great team assembled by Ernest RUTHERFORD at the Cavendish Laboratory; at first his chief collaborator was the Russian scientist P. KAPITZA. It was there that he performed in 1932 (with E. T. S. Walton (1903–)) the classic experiment in which nuclei of lithium and boron were split by bombardment with protons accelerated in an ingenious machine of their own construction. For this work he and Walton were awarded the Nobel prize for physics in 1951. This was not, however, the only major field of science to which he made outstanding contributions; he also played a leading role in the development of radar for defence purposes. He was a member of the Tizard Mission to the United States in 1940 (see H. TIZARD). During the war he was Chief Superintendent of the Government's Air Defence Research and Development Establishment (1941–4). Simultaneously (1939–46) he was Jacksonian Professor of Natural Philosophy at Cambridge.

He then found his way back into the field of atomic physics as Director of the Canadian Atomic Energy Commission, in charge of the Montreal and Chalk river Laboratories. When war ended he was a natural choice as head of Britain's first atomic energy research laboratory at Harwell. When the UK Atomic Energy Authority was set up (1954), to control this and other establishments, Cockcroft was appointed member for scientific research. Finally (1959) he took up the appointment he held until his death, that of Master of Churchill College, Cambridge, a new college – founded as a tribute to Winston Churchill – devoted particularly to the advancement of science and technology.

In the postwar years Cockcroft emerged as a leading statesman of science. His own great contributions gave him the highest standing among research workers. To this he added a gift for the administration of great projects, and personal qualities which earned him the affection and complete trust of all those – young and old – with whom he had to deal.

Many honours were accorded him in his lifetime. The Royal Society elected him to Fellowship in 1936, and awarded him their Hughes (1938) and Royal (1954) medals. More than twenty universities conferred honorary degrees upon him and he was Chancellor (1961–5) of the Australian National University, Canberra. In 1967 he was President of the British Association for the Advancement of Science. He was knighted in 1948 and the KCB was conferred on him in 1953. Four years later he was awarded the outstanding distinction of admission to the Order of Merit. He received the Atoms for Peace award in 1961.

Nature, **216**, 621, 1967. (Portrait.)
Biographical Memoirs of Fellows of the Royal Society. 1968. (Portrait.)
G. Hartcup and T. E. Allibone, Cockcroft and the Atom. 1984.
Tyler Wasson (Ed.), Nobel Prize Winners. 1987. (Portrait.)
H. Oxbury (Ed.), Great Britons: 20th Century Lives. 1985.
Dictionary of National Biography.
Dictionary of Scientific Biography.

T I W

COCKER, EDWARD Born in England, 1631; died 1675. Arithmetician.

Although little is known of the life of Cocker, his name is remembered wherever the English language is spoken; 'according to Cocker' is synonymous with something well done. In 1657 he was running a small school, teaching writing and arithmetic, by St Paul's Churchyard in London. His Arithmetick, being a Plain and Easy Method appeared in 1678, edited by John Hawkins (fl. 1686–1707). This remarkable work ran through over a hundred editions, and influenced the teaching of mathematics in England for more than a century. His Algebraical Arithmetic, or Equations, on algebra, appeared in 1684, but was less successful.

Cocker's fame was enhanced by the play The Apprentice (1756) by Arthur Murphy (1727–1805) in which one of the characters expresses extreme reverence for his arithmetic.

D. E. Smith, History of Mathematics, vol. 1. 1923. (Paperback 1958.)
Dictionary of National Biography.

T I W

COCKERILL, WILLIAM Born in Lancashire, England, 1759; died near Aachen, Germany, 1832. A founder of the continental textile machinery industry.

Cockerill possessed an extraordinary mechanical genius and could make models of almost any machine. He began his career in Lancashire by building 'roving billies' and flying shuttles. In 1794 he migrated to St Petersburg, Russia, but the death of Catherine II only two years later ruined his prospects. Her successor, the madman Paul, sent him to prison because he failed to finish a model on time, but he escaped to Sweden. Here he unsuccessfully tried to introduce textile machines, and so in 1799 he established himself at Verviers, Belgium, as a manufacturer of textile machinery. In 1802 he was joined by James Holden, who before long set up his own machine-building business. In 1807 Cockerill moved to Liège, where, in association with his three sons (William, Charles James, and John), he made carding machines, spinning frames, and looms for the woollen industry. He

secured for Verviers supremacy in the woollen trade and introduced at Liège an industry of which England had so far possessed the monopoly. His products were noted for their fine craftsmanship, and in the heyday of the Napoleonic régime about half of his output was sold in France. In 1814 he retired from the firm and died in 1832 at the residence of his son Charles James at the Chateau de Behrensberg, near Aachen.

W. O. Henderson, The Industrial Revolution on the Continent. 1961.
Dictionary of National Biography.

R L H

COFFEY, AENEAS Born (probably in Dublin) 1779/80; died Bromley, Middlesex, England, 26 November 1852. Remembered for inventing a widely used fractionating still which bears his name.

Coffey was Surveyor and Inspector-General of Excise in Ireland, and in that position he was responsible for the suppression of illicit distilleries. In 1818 he published a pamphlet answering charges of oppression and cruelty by Irish revenue officers. In 1831, when he was a distiller in Dublin, he took out a patent for an improved still, known as the patent or Coffey still. It soon came into general use in the manufacture of whisky, as it accomplished in one operation what had required several operations using the old pot still. It is still widely used in making potable spirits. It consisted of two adjacent columns known as analyser and rectifier; steam was passed through the wash, in the analyser, and carried off the volatile products, which were fractionally condensed in the rectifier.

E. J. Rothery, Annals of Science, **24**, 53, 1968.
Dictionary of National Biography (Missing Persons). 1993.

B B K

COHN, FERDINAND JULIUS Born at Breslau, Silesia, 24 January 1828; died there, 26 June 1898. Distinguished botanist and a founder of bacteriology.

Cohn studied botany at Breslau from 1844, but in 1846 transferred to Berlin, where he was attracted by the work of C. G. EHRENBERG. He graduated in science at Berlin (1847), returned to Breslau and was appointed a Lecturer (1850). He became associate professor of botany there in 1854, and full professor in 1872. The theme of his doctoral thesis had been the principle that the State must establish institutes for plant physiology, and in 1866, with the support of the faculty, he called upon the Minister to take this action at Breslau. The institute was founded and opened in 1868, and Cohn was its Director until his death. In 1870 Cohn founded his new journal of plant biology (Beiträge zur Biologie der Pflanzen). On 22 April 1876 Robert KOCH wrote to Cohn informing him that he had discovered the complete life-history of the anthrax bacillus. At Cohn's invitation Koch arrived at Breslau on 30 April, with his specimens and records. For three days Koch demonstrated to Cohn his methods and results. Cohn was convinced, and he hastened to publish Koch's epoch-making paper in his new journal (1876).

During most of his early scientific career Cohn worked on the microscopic algae and fungi, and also on the development of rotifers and infusoria.

About 1866 he became interested in bacteria, and from 1870 until the early 1880s, when bacteriology was becoming more and more medical, he worked almost entirely on that subject. In about 1885 he returned to plant physiology, and by the time of his death he had published the first three volumes of his Cryptogam-flora of Silesia.

Cohn was the first to demonstrate the fixity of bacterial species; for example, even under varying conditions he was never able to obtain cocci from bacilli, or vice versa. He also showed that bacteria can be classified in genera and species. His classification was widely accepted, and its basic elements remain in modern classifications. He was the first to discover the fact that some bacteria (e.g. *Bacillus subtilis*) form spores, which are resistant to harmful physical agents. He showed that many bacteria are killed by boiling for twenty minutes, and he studied the effects of submitting bacteria to electric currents. He was also one of the first to study the movements of the motile organisms.

Deutsche medizinische Wochenschrift, 24, 482, 1898.

P. Cohn, *Ferdinand Cohn*. 1901.

W. Bulloch, *History of Bacteriology*. 1938. (Portrait.)

Bulletin of the History of Medicine, 7, 49, 1939.

Dictionary of Scientific Biography.

E A U

COHNHEIM, JULIUS Born at Demmin, Pomerania, Germany, 20 July 1839; died Leipzig, 15 August 1884. A pioneer of experimental pathology.

Cohnheim studied at the Universities of Würzburg, Marburg, Greifswald and Berlin. He graduated at Berlin in 1861. After a short period in Prague he was appointed as an assistant in the institute of R. VIRCHOW in Berlin; he was probably Virchow's greatest pupil. In 1867 he was called to the chair of pathological anatomy and general pathology in the University of Kiel, and in 1872 he was appointed to the corresponding chair in Breslau (Wroclaw). Six years later he was called to the chair of pathological anatomy in the University of Leipzig, where he remained until his untimely death. Both at Breslau and Leipzig he attracted large numbers of very able students, both from Germany and abroad. Among the most famous were C. WEIGER and W. H. WELCH. His *Lectures on General Pathology* (1877–80) has remained a classic.

Cohnheim worked at first on normal histology, and shortly after graduating he devised the important freezing method of sectioning fresh tissue. In 1867 he introduced the method of staining by gold impregnation. In 1867 also, with his long study 'On inflammation and suppuration', he reopened a subject supposed to have been closed by Virchow's views on the local origin of pus corpuscles. Cohnheim showed in masterly fashion the early changes in the blood-vessels as a result of injury or irritation; and, even more important, he demonstrated that at the site the leucocytes pass through the walls of the capillaries. This proof that the pus corpuscles were really degenerating blood corpuscles had far-reaching implications. Cohnheim now devoted himself entirely to experimental pathology. Despite the convincing demonstration by J. A. VILLEMIN that tuberculosis can be transmitted to an animal by injecting it with tuberculous material, his view that the disease is infectious had not been widely accepted. In 1868 Cohnheim inoculated tuberculous matter into the anterior chamber of the eye of a rabbit, and thereafter he observed through the transparent cornea the development of the tuberculous process. In 1872 he published important observations on embolism and the production of infarcts. Of importance also at the time was Cohnheim's theory that malignant growths arise as a result of some aberration in the course of embryonic development.

Allgemeine Deutsche Biographie.

Lancet, ii, 391, 1884.

E. R. Long, *History of Pathology*. 1928. (Portrait.)

E A U

COKE, THOMAS WILLIAM (EARL OF LEICESTER) Born at Holkham, Norfolk, England, 4 May 1752; died Longford Hall, Derbyshire, 30 June 1842. Agriculturist.

Coke was educated at Eton and after a period of Continental travel lived for a time in Rome. In 1774 he returned home, and two years later inherited the family estates in Norfolk. Two of his farms falling vacant, he decided to work them himself. His improvements in agricultural practice and estate management were so successful that the annual Holkham sheep-shearing became internationally famous and attracted many visitors. Coke was Member of Parliament for Norfolk 1776–1806 and again 1807–32. He was raised to the peerage, as the first Earl of Leicester, in 1837. At his death a huge memorial – 125 feet in height – was raised in his memory at Holkham.

Coke's great contribution was to show what could be achieved in a basically poor farming area with light sandy soil. Following Lord TOWNSHEND, he introduced the turnip as winter fodder; he replaced rye by wheat; introduced Red Devon cattle and Southdown sheep; improved the local breed of pigs; and improved the land by marling. He encouraged his tenants to introduce his methods by granting leases giving them security of tenure and compensation for improvements. His success is measured by the fact that over forty years his rents rose from £2,000 to £40,000 per annum.

Dictionary of National Biography.

C. S. Orwin, *A History of English Farming*. 1949. (Portrait.)

A. M. W. Stirling, *Coke of Norfolk and his Friends*. 1908.

T I W

COLOMBO, MATTEO REALDO Born at Cremona, Italy, c.1510; died Rome, 1559. Distinguished anatomist; a discoverer of the lesser circulation of the blood.

Realdo Colombo, son of an apothecary, served an apprenticeship of seven years to a surgeon, and studied medicine and anatomy under VESALIUS at Padua. When Vesalius went to Basle in connection with the printing of his *Fabrica*, Colombo was appointed as his deputy. Vesalius resigned his chair in 1544 and Colombo was called as his successor. In 1546 the chair of anatomy at Pisa became vacant, and the University attempted unsuccessfully to obtain the release of Vesalius from his new post at the imperial court in order to fill it, so in 1546 the University appointed Colombo to the chair. In 1549 Colombo accepted the call of Pope Pius IV to a corresponding chair in the *Sapienza* at Rome, where he spent the remainder of his life.

Colombo's only medical book, *De re anatomica*, was published posthumously at Rome in 1559. He was an excellent anatomist, and his book – which is not illustrated – is very clearly written and arranged. He was, however, boastful and prone to attribute to himself the discoveries of others. Though he certainly had great experience of dissection, he did not anatomize as many bodies as he claimed. He was treated kindly by Vesalius, in the first edition of the *Fabrica* (1543), and he repaid Vesalius by criticizing him and his discoveries in public. The ensuing breach between the two anatomists was never healed. In his book Colombo leaned heavily on the work of Vesalius, but he was the first to describe the lens of the eye in its correct position in the anterior part of the globe, and he gave a good account of the eye muscles, the mediastinum, the pleura, and the peritoneum. The most important part of his book is his clear description of the lesser circulation, derived from clinical observations, dissections, and experiments on animals. In a vivisection on a dog he cut the pulmonary vein and showed that it contained blood and not air. Further, the blood was bright red in colour, and he correctly believed that in the lungs it had been rendered 'spirituous' (i.e. oxygenated) by admixture with air. It was long suggested that Colombo may have derived the idea of the lesser circulation from the *Restitutio Christianismi* (1553) of SERVETUS. But it now seems possible that Colombo was teaching his views as early as 1546, and in any case the views of Servetus were not based on dissection and experiment. Both Servetus and Colombo may have been influenced by the work of the thirteenth century Arabian writer, Ibn an-Nafis.

H. P. Bayon, *Annals of Science*, 4, 98, 1939.

A. Castiglioni, *History of Medicine*, 1947. (Portrait.)

E. D. Coppola, *Bulletin of the History of Medicine*, **21**, 44, 1957.

Dictionary of Scientific Biography.

E A U

COLT, SAMUEL Born at Hartford, Connecticut, USA, 19 July 1814; died there, 10 January 1862. Inventor of revolving-barrel pistols.

The son of a textile manufacturer, Colt had early experience in dyeing and bleaching and for some years made his living from popular lectures on chemistry. But he is said to have first conceived his idea of a revolving-breech firearm while he watched the wheel turn during his voyage to India as a deck hand. His invention, which was originally meant to apply to pistols, rifles, and shotguns alike, had as its principal feature the automatic rotation of the cartridge-holding cylinder when the weapon was cocked: a ratchet on the end of the cylinder was to be engaged by a pawl on the hammer. Colt described this to the United States Patent Office in 1832, but did not patent it there until 1836, having secured English and French patents during a visit to those countries in the previous year. He then formed a manufacturing company which failed in 1842, but success came with a big Federal order for pistols at the outbreak of the Mexican War in 1846.

Colt assigned this first contract to the Eli WHITNEY arms factory, but subsequently established his own business at Hartford, which became the largest private armoury in the world, employing 1400 machine tools in a thoroughly worked out system of interchangeable manufacture. Colt also experimented with a submarine battery and electrically exploded mines, and in 1843 he operated a submarine telegraph between New York and Coney Island.

Dictionary of American Biography.

E. Wildman, *Famous Leaders of Industry* (2nd series). 1921. (Portrait.)

T K D

COMPTON, ARTHUR HOLLY Born at Wooster, Ohio, USA, 10 September 1892; died Berkeley, California, 15 March 1962. Discovered the Compton Effect; worked on the atomic bomb.

Compton was the son of a Presbyterian minister who taught philosophy in the College of Wooster, Ohio. He was educated there and at Princeton. After various university posts he became in 1923 professor of physics at Chicago, leaving there only in 1945 to become Chancellor of Washington University. From 1954 to 1961 he was Distinguished Service Professor at Washington, and in his last year a professor at large.

Compton was early interested in x-rays, and in 1923 showed that they were scattered by a block of paraffin wax, with the issuing radiation having a longer wavelength than the primary rays; that is, lower energy. This Compton Effect, inexplicable on the wave theory of light, was readily explained by Compton and P. J. W. DEBYE. It implies an elastic collision between two particles, an electron and the light quantum, with kinetic energy passing to one from the other. Compton found a formula connecting wavelength change with angle of scattering, and showed that recoil electrons left tracks in the Wilson cloud chamber. This result showed that radiation could have the corpuscular characteristics of energy and momentum. It paved the way for L. de BROGLIE's hypothesis that matter also can show a wave/particle dualism (1925). For this work Compton was awarded, with C. T. R. WILSON, the 1927 Nobel prize in physics. He also devised a diffraction method for measuring x-ray wavelengths.

In the 1930s he worked extensively on cosmic rays, and (with his colleagues) developed an improved ionization chamber for measuring their intensity. He organized a world-wide survey in 1933, using sixty-nine stations similarly equipped. This confirmed findings of J. Clay (1882–1955) that cosmic-ray intensity varies with geomagnetic latitude. Later, he showed that it also varies with time of day and year; with the period of the Sun's rotation (twenty-seven days), and with sidereal time. This last variation he ascribed to the entry of the rays into our rotating galaxy from outside.

In 1941 Compton was appointed to a US committee to explore the possibility of an atomic bomb, with special responsibility himself for developing plutonium production. Under the code name 'Metallurgical Project', production began at Chicago under Compton's direction in 1942, and culminated in the atomic bombs of 1945. Compton was a man of deep religious convictions and undertook this work with great reluctance and in the belief that only the atomic bomb could bring the war to a quick conclusion.

A. H. Compton, *Atomic Quest: A Personal Narrative*. 1956. (Portraits.)

Physics Today, **15** (5), 88, 1962.
Biographical Memoirs, National Academy of Sciences. 1965.
Tyler Wasson (Ed.), *Nobel Prize Winners.* 1987. (Portrait.)
Dictionary of Scientific Biography.

C A R

CONDAMINE, CHARLES-MARIE DE LA *See* LA CONDAMINE.

CONDON, EDWARD UHLER Born at Alamogordo, New Mexico, USA, 2 March 1902; died Boulder, Colorado, 26 March 1974. Physicist, US government official.

In his work as civil engineer, William Condon, Edward's father, moved about the West; Edward attended fourteen grammar schools before settling down to four years at Freemount High School in Oakland, California. After three years as a newspaper reporter, he earned his BA with highest honours in 1924 and his PhD degree in 1926, both from the University of California, Berkeley.

On a National Research Council fellowship, Condon studied in Göttingen and Munich in 1926–7 and immediately grasped the significance and power of the new quantum theory. He then embarked on an academic career which took him from Columbia to Princeton, to Minnesota, and back to Princeton where he taught until 1937. He was associate director of Westinghouse Research Laboratories 1937–45; director of National Bureau of Standards 1945–51 (he built the NBS Boulder Laboratories); director of research, Corning Glass Works 1951–4; professor of physics, Washington University (St Louis) 1956–63; and professor at the University of Colorado from 1963.

While especially interested in quantum mechanics, Condon was to a rare degree a generalist in physics. The basis for much work on the separability of electronic and vibrational motions in molecules, the Franck-Condon principle (see J. FRANCK) was in his Berkeley thesis. With P. M. Morse he wrote *Quantum Mechanics* (1929) and with G. H. Shortley *The Theory of Atomic Spectra* (1935). As consultant to the National Defense Research Committee, Condon helped to organize the Radiation Laboratory at Massachusetts Institute of Technology (1940). Early in the war he assisted in organizing the rocket research programme and he served on the President's committee which in January 1942 started the formidable programme which culminated in the production of the atomic bomb.

Condon was scientific adviser to the Senate Special (McMahon) Committee which supported Federal operation of atomic energy plants by a civilian atomic energy commission. He emphasized the need for an effective international control of nuclear weapons through the United Nations Atomic Energy Commission. In 1946 Condon fought 'any attempt to perpetuate into peacetime the restrictive practices' which were used during the war in the military control of nuclear physics.

As editor of *Reviews of Modern Physics* 1957–8, and co-editor (with Hugh Odishaw) of the *Handbook of Physics*, Condon demonstrated his facility for dealing with the full range of topics in physics. In all the positions Condon held in government, industry and universities, he was valued for his keen ability for analysis and teaching and for his success in removing administrative encrustations.

Condon was married when he was only twenty to Emilie Honzik. They had one daughter and two sons. Condon, a square-built man with a closely cropped brush of black hair, was approachable and colloquial. Odishaw has said that Condon was 'outgoing, warm, a wit, a raconteur with an Irish gift for gab.'

Current Biography Yearbook 1946. 1947. (Portrait.)
Physics Today **22**, 68, 1974. (Portrait.)
New York Times, 27 March 1974. (Portrait.)

R L W

COOK, JAMES Born at Marton, Yorkshire, England, 27 October 1728; died Kealakekua Bay, Hawaii, 14 February 1779. Navigator and hydrographer.

Cook was the son of an agricultural labourer. At about 16 he was apprenticed to a Whitby coal-shipper and apart from gaining practical experience of seamanship was taught mathematics and navigation. In 1755 he joined the Royal Navy as an ordinary seaman and in only two years was given his own command, the *Eagle*, in which he sailed to Louisburg for the attack on French Canada. In the course of this expedition he was required to make a hydrographic survey of the St Lawrence, a task he accomplished with such success that it led to further similar commissions. From 1763 to 1768 he was engaged in a survey of the coast of Newfoundland, and this included (1766) an observation of a solar eclipse, of which details were communicated to the Royal Society.

The Society was at this time seeking to organize an expedition to the Pacific to observe the transit of Venus of 1769, which would make possible a precise measurement of the distance of the Earth from the Sun. The Government – interested in such an expedition for political and geographical reasons as well as scientific ones – supported it. Cook was given the command and chose as his vessel the immortal *Endeavour* – an easily careened Whitby collier of a type with which he was very familiar. Apart from facilitating the observations at Tahiti of the scientists – who included the young Joseph BANKS – Cook was charged with seeking the great Southern Continent supposed to balance the great land masses of the northern hemisphere. He was to take possession in the King's name of any new territories discovered. The voyage was highly successful. The scientific observations were duly made; he showed that if a Southern Continent existed it was smaller than was generally supposed; and he showed New Zealand to consist of two islands, whose coasts he charted. He also charted the east coast of Australia and confirmed the reality of Torres Strait.

In 1772–5 he went on a second expedition of exploration, this time with two vessels (*Resolution* and *Adventure*). Apart from casting further doubts on the existence of a very large continent in the South Pacific, the voyage – in which he circumnavigated the globe – was notable for being virtually free of scurvy as a result of Cook's insistence on fresh fruit and vegetables (see G. BLANE, J. LIND). In 1776 he set out on his last, fatal voyage – in the *Resolution* and *Discovery* – the object of which was to seek a northern sea passage between the

Pacific and the Atlantic. His northern exploration had to be abandoned in 1778, through the lateness of the season, and he returned south to the Sandwich Islands, where he was killed in a sudden attack by the natives, apparently the result of a tragic misunderstanding.

Cook's voyages transformed knowledge of the Pacific. On his second and third voyages he was much assisted in his longitude determination by having with him a copy of the famous No. 4 chronometer of John HARRISON. He was elected FRS in 1776.

J. C. Beaglehole (Ed.), *The Journal of Captain James Cook on his Voyages of Exploration* (4 vols). 1961–7. (Portraits.)

Maurice Holmes, *Endeavour*, **8**, **11**, 1949. (Portrait.)

H. Carrington, *Life of Captain Cook*. 1939.

J. A. Williamson, *Cook and the Opening of the Pacific*. 1946.

Trevor I. Williams, *James Cook*. 1974. (Portrait.)

G. M. Badger (Ed.), *Captain Cook, Navigator and Scientist*. 1970.

M. Thiéry, *The Life and Voyages of Captain Cook*. 1929.

C. Lloyd, *Captain Cook*. 1952.

Dictionary of National Biography.

Dictionary of Scientific Biography.

T L W

COOKE, SIR WILLIAM FOTHERGILL Born at Ealing, London, 1806; died Farnham, Surrey, 25 June 1879. Pioneer of the electric telegraph.

Son of a surgeon, William Fothergill Cooke was educated at Durham and Edinburgh University and joined the Indian Army (1826–31) at the age of 20. He resumed his education five years later at Paris and at Heidelberg, where Professor Moncke's demonstration of the electric telegraph stimulated him to return to England in 1837 to pursue its applications for alarm systems and for railway signalling. He was introduced to Charles WHEATSTONE with whom he entered into partnership and took out a joint patent in May 1837 for an alarm system. He persuaded the railway companies to sanction experiments along their lines. From these it emerged that multiple lines and needles were too expensive, so over the next eight years he and Wheatstone reduced them to two wires and one needle. The partnership was an uneasy one, however, and in 1846 Cooke formed the Electro-Telegraph Company, which bought their joint patents for £120,000: three years earlier Cooke had allowed Wheatstone a royalty on mileage of line laid. Though they both received the Albert Medal of the Royal Society of Arts in 1867, Wheatstone was knighted in 1868, a year earlier than Cooke, perhaps representing an official estimate of their relative contribution to the development of the electric telegraph.

J. J. Fahie, *History of the Electric Telegraph*. 1884.

W. T. Jeans, *Lives of the Electricians*. 1887.

Geoffrey Hubbard, *Cooke and Wheatstone and the Invention of the Electric Telegraph*. 1965. (Portrait.)

C. Mackechnie Jarvis, *Journal of the Institute of Electrical Engineers*, **2**, 1956.

Dictionary of National Biography.

W H G A

COOLIDGE, WILLIAM DAVID Born at Coolidgeville, near Boston, Massachusetts, USA, 23 October 1873; died Schenectady, New York, 3 February 1975. Industrial scientist, noted for development of ductile tungsten and the hot-cathode x-ray tube.

Relying mainly on scholarships and loans, Coolidge studied electrical engineering at the Massachusetts Institute of Technology (1896) and went on to gain his doctorate in physics at Leipzig (1899). He then returned to MIT and with A. A. Noyes (1866–1936) embarked on work in a third discipline, chemistry. He thus had an unusual range of qualifications when he first became associated with the General Electric Research Laboratory in 1905. He became its Director in 1932 and his association with GEC continued until 1961. In this capacity he is noted for two outstanding successes.

The first was his discovery of an industrially practicable method of making the highly refractory metal tungsten (m.pt 3380 °C) so ductile that it could be drawn out into the exceedingly fine wires required to make use of the exceptional properties of the metal in incandescent filament electric lamps. The process depended on first creating a small ingot of tungsten by the then unusual technique of sintering the powdered metal; swaging this mechanically at around 1500 °C; and drawing it through a succession of dies of diminishing size. Great difficulties had to be overcome – involving elimination of undesirable impurities and the attainment of a specific crystal structure – in order to obtain a pliable wire. Success was first attained in the laboratory in 1908. Although it was some years before industrial production was achieved, the final result was a revolution in the manufacture of electric lamps. It has been estimated that in the year 1914 the invention diminished the cost of electric light in the United States alone by $2 billion.

Coolidge's second major invention (1913) was the x-ray tube named after him. It was based on the discovery by T. A. EDISON that if a conducting plate is attached to the positive side of the filament in an incandescent lamp, a current of electrons flows from the filament to the plate. From this he conceived the idea of an x-ray tube in which the electron flow is determined only by the temperature of the filament. This made it possible to vary the current and voltage independently.

Herman A. Leibhafsky, *William David Coolidge: a Centenarian and his Work*. 1974. (Portraits.)

Dictionary of American Biography.

T I W

COOPER, LEON N Born in New York City, 28 February 1930. Physicist best known for his work on the 'BCS' theory of superconductivity.

After education at the Bronx High School for Science in New York, Cooper went on to graduate from Columbia University in 1951, and to gain a PhD there in 1954. After a year at the Institute for Advanced Study in Princeton he moved to the University of Illinois as a research assistant. It was here that he did his major work on superconductivity – the phenomenon in which a metal can conduct an electric current with no resistance. In 1956 Cooper showed that electrons can pair together in metals via a relatively weak interaction. Such 'Cooper pairs' became a key feature of the 'BCS' theory of superconductivity, developed together with John BARDEEN and Robert Schrieffer (1931–) at Illinois. In this theory, pairs of electrons with opposite momentum couple together via interactions with the lattice of positive ions. The net result is a state with zero resistivity: in other words, superconductivity.

Cooper was awarded the Nobel prize for this work, together with Bardeen and Schrieffer, in 1972. In 1974, he became Thomas J. Watson Senior Professor of Science at Brown University in Providence, Rhode Island, having moved from Ohio State University, where he worked from 1957 to 1974. His interests now are in neuronetworks and learning systems.

Nobel Lectures, Physics, 1942–1962. 1964.
Physics Today, December 1972. (Portrait.)
New Scientist, 26 October 1972.
Tyler Wasson (Ed.), *Nobel Prize Winners.* 1987.
   (Portrait.)

                                                                     C S

COPERNICUS, NICOLAUS Born at Thorn, Poland, 19 February 1473; died Frauenburg, Ermeland, Poland, 24 May 1543. Founder of heliocentric cosmology.

Copernicus belonged to a wealthy merchant family of German origin. After studying at Krakow University in the early 1490s he became a *canonicus* of the cathedral of Frauenburg, remaining in that office for the rest of his life, though without being ordained. In 1496–1500 he completed his studies in Italy, mainly in Bologna, where he became an *artium magister* in or before 1499 and studied canon law. During that time he was influenced by Italian humanism, and his study of the classics revived by that movement greatly influenced his future life work in astronomy. In 1501 he returned to Italy, studying medicine in Padua and becoming a Doctor of Canon Law in Ferrara (1503). So far, no distinct concentration on astronomy is detectable from the records.

Copernicus's ecclesiastical duties during his remaining 40 years were evidently mainly concerned with administration and economy. He was interested in economic theory, writing a report on monetary value in 1519; he also practised medicine, having a certain reputation as a physician. Moreover, he pursued his humanistic interest, in 1519 publishing a collection of poetic letters by the 7th century Byzantine writer Theophylus Simokatta, translated from Greek to Latin.

Apart from his office, however, his main interest became astronomy, this is evident from the (original) sources; during the 1510s he acquired a European reputation as a distinguished astronomer. His research was based more on literary studies than on observations, however; during his life only about sixty original observations are known to have been made by him. His calculations of planetary motions were primarily based on data derived from earlier literature, during the study of which he developed a theory that offered a simpler explanation of those motions than PTOLEMY's geocentric astronomy. In doing so he received inspiration from certain classical cosmologists, notably the Pythagoreans and, if not from the very start, ARIS-TARCHUS OF SAMOS. Somewhere between 1510 and 1514 he wrote a short, manuscript report, *Commentariolus*, which outlined his new, heliocentric

system. Later, over thirty years, he elaborated this into what became his principal work, *De revolutionibus orbium coelestium libri VI* (1543). He retains the traditional idea that the Universe is finite and spherical in shape, and that, for celestial bodies, the only natural and possible motion is the circular one. Furthermore, he formulates a series of theses that violate the former conception of the universe. He maintains that not all celestial motions have a common centre and also – the radical novelty – that the centre of the Earth is not the centre of universe but only of gravity and of the lunar orbit. The distance between the Earth and the fixed stars had to be immensely greater than previously estimated, and the apparent motion of the firmament was attributed to the Earth diurnally revolving on its axis. Likewise, the apparent motion of the Sun is due to a motion of the Earth, with which we are carried around the Sun in a yearly orbit, as a planet among other planets.

It is the doctrine of terrestrial motion that was essentially new in Copernicus's work, through which he gave rise to the cosmological revolution which signified the ruin of the geocentric and anthropocentric cosmology. To Copernicus, the motion of the Earth was undoubtedly a physical reality, not merely a mathematical hypothesis for calculating planetary orbits, as it was generally regarded and used by the next generations. Because of his confinement to traditional mechanics, however, he never succeeded in formulating his system quite logically, and to himself *De revolutionibus*, printed through the initiation of others, was not a completed work. But his heliocentric theory prompted the new celestial mechanics, which KEPLER, GALILEO and NEWTON developed in the seventeenth century.

L. Prowe, *Nicolaus Coppernicus.* 1883–4.
   (Reprint, 1967).
A. Armitage, *Copernicus.* 1953.
Th. S. Kuhn, *The Copernican Revolution.* 1957.
J. Szperkowicz, *Nicolaus Copernicus.* 1972.
Dictionary of Scientific Biography.

                                                                     H S

COREY, ELIAS J Born in Methuen, Massachusetts, USA, 12 July, 1928. Organic chemist.

After graduating at Massachusetts Institute of Technology (1948) Corey was appointed professor of chemistry at the University of Illinois (1951–9) and Harvard University (1959–). His principal interest has always been in the chemistry of natural products, both identifying molecular structure and effecting synthesis.

In this field he is particularly identified with the concept of retrosynthetic analysis. In essence, this implies starting, as it were, at the end: with the planned structure of the molecule to be produced. This target molecule is very systematically analysed to see what strategically important bonds should be broken. This leads to the identification of successively smaller building blocks, eventually reaching ones which are in one way or another already available. Corey showed that this retrospective analysis is amenable to computer programming, making the process both faster and more reliable.

Retrospective analysis is now being widely adopted and Corey himself has used it to synthesize more than a hundred important natural products. These include the plant hormone gibberellic acid; ginkgolid, the active principle of the ginkgo tree, widely used as a folk medicine in China; prostaglandins; thromboxanes; and many others. To complete these syntheses Corey has developed some fifty new or improved synthesis reagents. In 1992 he was awarded the Nobel prize for chemistry.

Les Prix Nobel en 1992. 1993. (Portrait.)

CORI, GERTY THERESA (née **RADNITZ**) Born in Prague (then in Austria-Hungary), 15 August 1896; died St Louis, Missouri, USA, 26 October 1957. Biochemist, particularly identified with carbohydrate metabolism.

In 1914 Gerty Radnitz entered the German University of Prague to study medicine, graduating in 1920. In that year she married a fellow medical student, Carl Ferdinand Cori (1896–1984). In 1922 Carl emigrated to the USA as biochemist in the New York Institute for the Study of Malignant Diseases, in Buffalo, and soon found Gerty a job there as assistant pathologist. Together they embarked on a lifelong collaboration of research on carbohydrate metabolism, initially in tumour cells. In 1928 they became naturalized Americans and three years later moved to the Washington University School of Medicine, Missouri. There they concentrated their attention on the metabolism of glucose and glycogen, the latter being the form in which glucose is stored in the liver and muscles for future use. The glucose itself derives from the breakdown of dietary starch by the pancreatic enzyme amylase. Together the Coris elucidated the complex mechanism governing the interconversion of glucose and glycogen (the Cori cycle) and demonstrated the key role of the enzyme phosphorylase. This they showed to exist in an active (a) form and an inactive (b) form and they discovered the nature of the activation mechanism. In 1944 they achieved a major success by enzymatically systhesizing glycogen from glucose in a test tube. Concomitantly they investigated the action of insulin, the pancreatic hormone which regulates glucose metabolism in the body. For this research the Coris were jointly awarded the Nobel prize for physiology or medicine in 1947. At the presentation in Stockholm this was described as 'one of the most brilliant achievement in modern biochemistry'.

Gerty Cori went on to investigate diseases arising from defective glycogen metabolism, but she became increasingly handicapped by myelosclerosis and died at the early age of 61.

Dictionary of Scientific Biography.
Tyler Wasson (Ed.), Nobel Prize Winners. 1987. (Portrait.)
C. F. Cori, Annual Review of Biochemistry, **38**, 1, 1969.
S. Ochoa and H. M. Kalckar, Science, **128**, 16, 1958.

T I W

CORIOLIS, GUSTAVE GASPARD (DE) Born in Paris, 21 May 1792; died there, 19 September 1843. Physicist, remembered for his recognition of the Coriolis effect.

Coriolis studied at the École Polytechnique in Paris. After an appointment with the Corps des Ponts et Chaussées he returned to the École Polytechnique as a teacher in 1816, becoming Director

of Studies in 1838. He made important contributions to theoretical mechanics, expressed in his Du calcul de l'effet des machines (1829), powerfully influenced by the work of N. L. S. CARNOT. He also broke new ground by assigning a technical meaning to the word travail (work) in place of the ambiguous vitesse virtuelle, then widely used. A further innovation was the concept of force vive (kinetic energy) as the product $\frac{1}{2}mv^2$.

His originality was recognized by his contemporaries, especially S. D. POISSON, but today few remember him except for his enunciation of the Coriolis effect, which appears in a rotating frame of reference. This has important implications for the movements of the oceans and atmosphere, resulting from the Earth's rotation. A French oceanographic research ship was named after him in 1963. He was elected to the Académie des Sciences in 1836.

Dictionary of Scientific Biography,
J. C. Poggendorff, Biographisch-literarisches Handwörterbuch, vol. 1.

T I W

CORLISS, GEORGE HENRY Born at Easton, New York, 2 June 1817; died 21 February 1888. Improver of the steam engine.

The only son of a physician, Corliss spent four years after leaving school at 14 as storekeeper before going to Castleton Academy, Vermont. In 1842, he obtained his first patent, for a mechanical shoe-stitcher. As a result he joined an engineering firm in Providence, Rhode Island, where he devoted himself to improving the steam engines they manufactured. But his improvements – a system of rocking valves for steam and exhaust ports controlled by a governor in place of the simpler and cheaper slide-valve – needed wider exploitation. Before the first of his many patents in this field was granted in 1849 he took the first steps to set up his own works, which became the Corliss Engine Company in 1856. In this he directed both the business and research sides with such success that, both at the Paris (1867) and the Centennial Exhibition at Philadelphia (1876) his engines attracted wide attention. The 700-ton 1 400 hp Corliss engine selected to drive all the exhibits at the Centennial Exhibition worked continuously for six months.

From their first importation to Scotland in 1859, Corliss engines became very popular in cotton mills, since their smooth running and sensitive controls prevented the fine threads being broken. They were also very economical. By 1864 Corliss valves were being made by Hick Hargreaves in England.

J. Ericsson, Contributions of the Centennial Exhibition. 1876.
Conrad Matschoss, Die Entwicklung der Dampfmaschine. 1908. (Portrait.)
D. Goddard, Eminent Engineers. 1906. (Portrait.)
Dictionary of American Biography.

W H G A

CORMACK, ALLAN MACLEOD Born in Johannesburg, South Africa, 23 February 1924. Invented computer-assisted tomography (CAT).

Cormack was born in South Africa of Scots parents, and educated at the Rondebosch Boys High School, Cape Town, and the University of

Cape Town, where he gained his BSc in physics in 1944. After two years as a research student at the Cavendish Laboratory, Cambridge he returned to South Africa and from 1950 to 1956 was a lecturer in physics at the University of Cape Town. He also worked in the radioisotope department at the Groote Schuur Hospital, and realised the need for more accurate information about the absorption of x-rays by the body tissues in order to work out radiation doses for cancer patients. Seeing that a series of x-ray images was needed in which the beam passed through the body at many different angles, he began to work on the mathematical problem of how to interpret such data.

In 1956 Cormack moved to the USA, first to Harvard University as a research fellow and then to the physics department at Tufts University, Massachusetts, in 1957. He was made a University Professor in 1980. Cormack continued to work on a mathematical theory for image reconstruction, and in 1963 and 1964 published papers describing the mathematical foundations of the technique of computer-assisted tomography whereby x-ray information is reassembled in order to construct images of sections of the body.

The first CAT (or CT) scanner, developed by G. N. HOUNSFIELD at EMI, became available in 1972. The CAT scanner was originally used only as a brain scanner, but in 1975 a whole body scanner was developed. Cormack and Hounsfield shared the 1979 Nobel prize for physiology or medicine.

G. Di Chiro and R. A. Brooks, *Science*, vol. 206, 30 November 1979. (Portrait.)

S. Webb, *From the Watching of Shadows. The Origins of Radiological Tomography*. 1990.

Tyler Wasson (Ed.), *Nobel Prize Winners*. 1987. (Portrait.)

A P B

CORT, HENRY Born at Lancaster, England, 1740; died Hampstead, London, 1800. Pioneer of ironmaking by the puddling process and use of rollers.

In 1765 Cort became a Navy Agent in London. After experimenting with the improvement of wrought iron for naval and ordnance uses, he removed to Fontley, near Fareham, where he set up a forge and slitting mills. In 1783 he patented the use of grooved rollers, which replaced most of the laborious process of hammering. In 1784 he patented the process of puddling: that is, the stirring of the molten pig-iron on the bed of a reverberatory furnace until the decarburizing action of the air causes a 'loop' of pure metal to form. This could be lifted out of the furnace, hammered for the removal of slag, and finished with the rollers described in the earlier patent. Although neither of his inventions was wholly new, the transformation of the British iron industry sprang from their successful combination by Cort.

Unfortunately, he entered into a partnership at Gosport with Samuel Jellicoe, whose father, a naval official, embezzled capital for the business from public funds. Its source may not have been known to Cort, but when the Admiralty discovered what had happened and demanded immediate repayment he lost everything, including the possession of his patents, which rival ironmasters were in any case eager to ignore. In 1794 Cort was conceded a pension of £200 a year by Pitt, one-half

of which was retained by his widow, who survived him with ten children.

'The Inventions of Henry Cort' (ch. iv in T. S. Ashton, *Iron and Steel in the Industrial Revolution*). 1924.

Dictionary of National Biography.

R. A. Mott, (P. Sanger, Ed.), *Henry Cort, the Great Finer*. 1983.

T K D

COTTON, WILLIAM Born at Leyton, near London, 12 September 1786; died at Leytonstone, near London, 1 December 1866. Engineer, especially of textile machinery.

After he left Chigwell Grammar School at 15, Cotton went to the counting house of C. H. Turner. In 1807 he became partner in Huddart & Co., Limehouse, which was concerned with developing on a large scale the inventions of Captain Joseph Huddart (1741–1816) for making cordage by machinery. Here Cotton was soon entrusted with the general management. Many years later, in 1838, when he was the sole surviving original partner, he presented the first machines to the Government, and wrote an account of their construction which earned him the Telford Medal of the Institute of Civil Engineers.

In 1821 he was elected a Director of the Bank of England, which position he held until a few months before his death. He was Governor for three years from 1843 to 1845. Here he invented an automatic machine for weighing sovereigns, which was awarded a prize medal at the 1851 Exhibition. He also made important contributions to the design of hosiery manufacturing machinery.

He was a noted philanthropist with a passion for building churches, being concerned with ten in Bethnal Green alone. He was also interested in the London Hospital; St Anne's School, Limehouse; and was one of the founders of the National Society for Established Schools. He was on the council of King's College, a governor of Christ's Hospital, a supporter of many church charities, and a Fellow of the Royal Society (1821).

Gentleman's Magazine, January 1867.

Manchester Guardian, 27 December 1866.

Dictionary of National Biography.

R L H

COULOMB, CHARLES AUGUSTIN DE Born at Angoulême, France, 14 June 1736; died Paris, 23 August 1806. Celebrated for his researches in electricity and magnetism.

After a long period of service in the *génie* in Martinique, Coulomb returned to France in 1779, being elected to the *Académie des Sciences* in 1781. In 1784 he was appointed intendant of the waters and fountains of France, and in 1786 was given the reversion of the position of superintendent of *plans et reliefs*. During the period 1784–9 he wrote his fundamental memoirs on electricity and magnetism. On the outbreak of the Revolution he gave up all his offices, including his position of Lieutenant-Colonel in the *génie*. Dismissed from the Commission of Weights and Measures, he was finally forced to leave Paris by the law expelling the nobles; he retired to the locality of Blois, followed by his friend J. C. BORDA. On the creation of the Institute in 1795 he returned to Paris, being appointed one of the Inspectors-General of Public Instruction in 1802.

Coulomb's early work on statics and mechanics was gathered together in his great memoir *The Theory of Simple Machines* (1779) concerned in part with the effect of resistance and containing the so-called Coulomb's law of the proportionality between friction and normal pressure. Two years previously he had published a paper on the production of magnets which contained the germs of his later researches. On the basis of earlier experiments of P. van Musschenbroeck (1692–1761) and numerous new ones of his own Coulomb proved that the action of the Earth's field on a magnet is equivalent to a couple proportional to the sine of the angle of deviation. From this he deduced the necessity of employing forces of attraction and repulsion as opposed to vortices in the explanation of magnetic actions. He established the equation of motion of a magnet in a magnetic field and showed how the magnetic moment could be derived from a knowledge of the period of small oscillations.

A series of experiments on the oscillations of a needle suspended from a thread then led him to consider the question of torsion. This was taken up again in 1784 when he corrected an earlier error and gave the correct solution to the problem of the small oscillations of a body subjected to torsion. In his first memoir on electricity (1785) he used his torsion balance to measure electric forces of repulsion, and in a second memoir in the same year he extended his results to the experimentally more difficult case of attractions. He was thus led to enunciate in full generality his famous law of force for electrostatic charges. A further memoir dealt with loss of electricity of bodies, and was followed by three memoirs (1786–8) devoted to the problem of the distribution of electricity on conductors. He proved that all the charge of a conductor lay on the surface, and investigated its distribution.

In later works (1789–1801) he returned to magnetism, for which he established the same law of attraction and repulsion as in the case of electrostatics. He believed in two magnetic fluids bound, however, to the ultimate particles of magnetic material and thus capable only of displacement, as opposed to the full motion possible with the electric fluids.

Coulomb was the complete physicist, rivalled in the eighteenth century only by H. CAVENDISH, combining experimental skill, accuracy of measurement and great originality with mathematical powers adequate to all his demands. His name is remembered in the unit of electricity.

J. B. J. Delambre, *Éloge.* 1807.
J. B. Biot, *Mélanges Scientifiques*, vol. 3. 1858.
C. Stewart Gillmor, *Coulomb and the Evolution of Physics and Engineering in Eighteenth Century France.* 1971.
S. B. Hamilton, *Transactions of the Newcomen Society*, **17**, 27, 1936/7.
Dictionary of Scientific Biography.

                                                                    J W H

COULSON, CHARLES ALFRED Born at Dudley, Yorkshire, England, 13 December 1910; died Oxford, 7 January 1974. Theoretical chemist.

After graduating in both mathematics and physics at Cambridge, and holding appointments in Dundee and Oxford, he was appointed professor of theoretical chemistry in London University (1943). In 1951 he returned to Oxford, initially as professor of mathematics but later (1972) of Theoretical Chemistry. This diversity reflects the remarkable breadth of his scientific talent. His major contribution, however, was in applying quantum theory to the valency bonds, such as those in benzene, which are neither single nor double. It also allowed many bond lengths to be calculated, and his predictions were subsequently shown to be very accurate. His original thinking in this field was summarised in *Valence* (1952), a widely acclaimed work followed by a second edition in 1961.

Coulson was a man of deep religious conviction and spoke and published widely on the relationship between science and religion.

Biographical Memoirs of Fellows of the Royal Society. 1974. (Portrait.)
The Times, 8 January 1974.
W. A. Campbell and N. N. Greenwood (Eds), *Contemporary British Chemists.* 1971 (Portrait.)

                                                                    T I W

COUPER, ARCHIBALD SCOTT Born at Kirkintilloch, Scotland, 31 March 1831; died there 11 March 1892. Organic chemist; the first to recognize the quadrivalency of carbon and its power of combining with itself.

The importance of Couper's work was not recognized until ten years after his death, which occurred in obscurity after long years of mental illness, and little is known of his early life. The son of the proprietor of a cotton-weaving mill, he studied chemistry first at Glasgow and later at Edinburgh. During the period 1852–4 he spent some time studying in Germany, but his poor health made his visits there short ones. In 1856 he moved to Paris and worked with C. A. WURTZ. There he did some minor work on brominated benzene and on salicylic acid. Early in 1858 he asked Wurtz to present to the French Academy a paper he had written *On a New Chemical Theory*. In this he set out clearly the conception that carbon atoms are quadrivalent and capable of combining freely with each other; this is of fundamental importance in assigning structural formulae to organic compounds. Unfortunately, Wurtz procrastinated, and in the meantime F. A. KEKULÉ put forward identical views in his paper *On the Constitution and Metamorphosis of Chemical Compounds and on the Chemical Nature of Carbon*. Shortly afterwards J. B. DUMAS presented Couper's paper, but Kekulé insisted on his priority, and Couper damaged his own case by quarrelling violently with Wurtz. Although he returned to Edinburgh and worked there for a short time, severe mental illness – aggravated by sunstroke – afflicted him, and for the last thirty years of his life he was an invalid.

James Kendall, *Great Discoveries by Young Chemists.* 1953 (Portrait.)
E. Farber (Ed.), *Great Chemists.* 1961. (Portrait.)
R. Anschütz, *Proceedings of the Royal Society of Edinburgh*, **29**, 193, 1909.
Dictionary of National Biography (Missing Persons). 1993.

                                                                    T I W

CRAFTS, JAMES MASON Born at Boston, Massachusetts, USA, 8 March 1839; died Ridgefield, Connecticut, 20 June 1917. Chemist, remembered for the 'Friedel-Crafts reaction'.

The son of a woollen manufacturer, Crafts studied engineering and mining in the United States and at Freiberg. He turned to chemistry with a year (1860) at Heidelberg under R. W. BUNSEN, where he assisted in the discovery of rubidium by means of spectrum analysis. After a period with C. A. WURTZ in Paris, he returned to America, and was eventually appointed to the chair of general chemistry in the Massachusetts Institute of Technology (1870). Owing to poor health, which troubled him all his life, he spent the years 1874–91 in Europe, mainly working with C. FRIEDEL at the École des Mines in Paris. Here they discovered the reaction which bears their names, the alkylation and acylation of aromatic hydrocarbons catalysed by aluminum chloride. The scope and importance of this reaction has broadened with the years, and it continues to find applications both in research and industry.

During this period Crafts also studied organosilicon compounds, and did accurate work in thermometry. He returned to MIT in 1891, and later became President of the Institute, but renewed ill health caused him to retire prematurely in 1900.

Journal of the American Chemical Society, **39**, 171, 1917. (supplement).

Journal of Chemical Education, **5**, 911, 1928. (Portrait.)

Wyndham D Miles (Ed.), *American Chemists and Chemical Engineers*. 1976.

Proceedings of the American Academy of Arts and Sciences, **53**, 801, 1917/8.

W V F

CRAM, DONALD JAMES Born at Chester, Vermont, USA, 22 April 1919. Organic chemist and Nobel Laureate.

Brought up in semi-rural poverty, Cram worked his way through High School and Rollins College, Long Island, where he graduated in chemistry in 1941. Following an MSc at the University of Nebraska, in 1942 he joined the Merck Company's wartime penicillin project. Following postwar doctoral studies at the University of Harvard with Louis Fieser, he joined the staff of the University of California at Los Angeles (UCLA), where he has spent the remainder of his career.

During the 1950s and 1960s Cram worked extensively on unstable bridged-ions, such as the 'phenonium ion', which he showed to be intermediaries in the formation of stereochemical structures. As a result he developed Cram's rule for the steric control of the introduction of a second chiral (asymmetric atom) centre into a stereoisomer. In 1987, together with the Frenchman Jean-Marie Lehn (1939–) and the American industrial chemist Charles J. PEDERSEN (1904–89), Cram was awarded the Nobel prize for chemistry for his work on supramolecules. In 1967 Pedersen, a Du Pont chemist, prepared 'crown ethers' while investigating vanadium catalysts, while Cram and Lehn, working independently, showed how they and other bizarrely-shaped synthetic complexes could be combined with amino acids to mimic the way enzymes attached themselves to substrates. Cram has created a new architectural world of highly-structured complexes such as crytands, spherands, podands, cavitands and cryptaspheraplexes that he christened 'guest-host' or supramolecular chemistry because of the way lock and key shapes of molecules governed reactions. Together with G. S. Hammond, Cram also revolutionized American chemistry textbook writing with the innovative *Organic Chemistry* in 1959.

D. J. Cram, *From Design to Discovery*. 1990. (Portraits.)

McGraw-Hill Modern Scientists and Engineers, 1980, vol. 1, pp. 245–6. (Portrait.)

Les Prix Nobel en 1987. 1988. (Portrait.)

W H B

CRICK, FRANCIS HARRY COMPTON Born Northampton, England, 8 June, 1916. Biophysicist and molecular biologist.

Crick was educated at University College London and Caius College Cambridge. Jointly with James D. WATSON and Maurice Wilkins (1916–) he received the Nobel prize for physiology or medicine in 1962 for the determination of the molecular structure of deoxyribonucleic acid (DNA), the complex nuclear protein which controls heredity and life functions in the living cell. This achievement was one of the most important discoveries in 20th century biology.

During the Second World War Crick worked as a physicist for the Admiralty. In 1947 he began biological research at the Strangeways Research Laboratory, Cambridge, on the three-dimensional structures of large molecules found in living organisms. In 1949 he transferred to the Cavendish Laboratory, Cambridge where in 1951 Watson suggested that the three-dimensional structure of the DNA molecule would reveal its genetic role. Using x-ray diffraction methods Wilkins, Watson and Crick proposed a structural model of DNA involving two intertwined spiral chains of sugar-phosphate units linked horizontally at intervals by organic bases. Crick and Watson suggested that, if separated, each strand of the molecule would serve as a template for the formation of a new sister strand identical to its former partner, accounting for the replication of genes and chromosomes in the cell. They also suggested that the sequence of bases along the DNA molecule represented a code translated by a cellular mechanism into specific proteins responsible for the structure and functions of each particular cell. By 1961 Crick had shown that each group of three bases on a single strand of DNA designates the position of a particular amino acid in a protein molecule. He also helped to determine the base triplets coding for each of the 20 amino acids normally found in proteins and how the cell uses the DNA code to build proteins. The implications of these ideas were discussed in his book *Of Molecules and Men* (1966).

Crick was elected FRS in 1959. In addition to the Nobel prize he has received many honours and awards, notably the Royal (1972) and Copley (1975) Medals of the Royal Society of London. Since 1977 he has been J. W. Kieckhefer Distinguished Professor at the Salk Institute and Adjunct Professor of Psychology and Chemistry at the University of California, San Diego, USA.

F. H. C. Crick, *What Mad Pursuit*. 1988. (a personal view of scientific discovery).

F. H. C. Crick, *Of Molecules and Men*. 1966
Les Prix Nobel en 1962. 1963. (Portrait.)
R. Olby, *The Path to the Double Helix*. 1974
Tyler Wasson (Ed.), *Nobel Prize Winners*. 1987.
   (Portrait.)
James D. Watson, *The Double Helix*, 1968.
   (Portraits.)

N G C

CROMPTON, ROOKES EVELYN BELL Born near
Thirsk, Yorkshire, England, 31 May 1845; died
Ripon, Yorkshire, 15 February 1940. Electrical and
transport engineer.

R. E. B. Crompton, the fourth son of Joshua
Samuel Crompton, had the unusual distinction of
winning the Crimean medal and Sebastopol clasp
at the age of 11 as a naval cadet. He joined the Rifle
Brigade on leaving Harrow and during his service
in India continued experiments, begun whilst a
schoolboy, on steam traction for roads, receiving
official encouragement and help from the Viceroy.

On leaving the army in 1875 he bought a partnership in an engineering works. After recommending
the installation at the Stanton ironworks of dynamos developed by Z. T. Gramme (1826–1901), he
became so convinced of the potential of electric
lighting that he began to make and install generating plant based on the designs of Emil Bürgin of
Basle. Six years later he was awarded the first gold
medal for such work, and in 1886 he formed the
Kensington and Knightsbridge Electric Supply
Company, which aimed at supplying direct current, as opposed to the alternating current of the
London Electric Supply Corporation, of which
S. Z. de FERRANTI was chief engineer. He later
founded and acted as first secretary of the International Electrotechnical Commission in 1906. He
was elected FRS in 1933.

He never lost his first interest in road transport.
From helping to found the Royal Automobile Club
in 1896 to his membership of the Government
Road Board, which began in 1910, he was a keen
promoter of improvements and was one of the
pioneers of bituminous carpeting for roads.

R. E. B. Crompton, *Reminiscences*. 1928.
Obituary Notices of Fellows of the Royal Society.
   1941. (Portrait.)
B. Bowers, *R. E. B. Crompton: An Account of his
   Electrical Work*. 1969.
Dictionary of National Biography.

W H G A

CROMPTON, SAMUEL Born at Firwood, Lancashire, England, 3 December 1753; died Bolton,
Lancashire, 26 June 1827. Inventor of the spinning
mule.

Crompton was the son of a small farmer, who
died in 1759. As a boy he helped his widowed
mother in various tasks at home, including weaving; later he went to work in a spinning mill. In
the course of his work he became familiar with the
spinning jenny designed by James HARGREAVES and
noticed the tendency of the yarn to break. After
five years' work he produced in 1779 his famous
'mule', so called because it was a cross between
Hargreaves's jenny and the water-frame spinning
machine of Richard ARKWRIGHT. The mule was a
very versatile machine, making it possible to spin
almost every type of yarn, and so quickly that there
was soon a demand for faster weaving, encourag-

ing the introduction of the power loom. Crompton
did not patent his invention; perhaps because it
consisted basically of the essential features of
earlier machines, perhaps through lack of funds.
Under promise of a generous subscription he disclosed his invention to the spinning industry, but
was shabbily treated. He eventually saved enough
to set up as a manufacturer himself at Oldham, but
was not successful. Local manufacturers raised a
sum of £500 for him and eventually (1812) he
received a government grant of £5,000, but this
was trifling in relation to the immense financial
benefits his invention had conferred on the industry, to say nothing of his expenses. Later, he set
up as a bleacher, and again as a cotton manufacturer, but only the gift of a small annuity by his
friends saved him from dying in total poverty.

J. Kennedy, *Brief Memoir of Samuel Crompton*.
   1849.
G. J. French, *Life of Samuel Crompton* (2nd ed.).
   1860.
Dictionary of National Biography.

T I W

CRONSTEDT, AXEL FREDRIK Born at Söderman-
land, Sweden, 23 December 1722; died Stockholm,
19 August 1765. Chemist, known for his discovery
of nickel, and for his mineral classification.

Cronstedt was educated under a private tutor
until he was 16 years of age, when he began to
attend lectures at the University of Uppsala as an
unregistered student. He studied chemistry at the
School of Mines, and remained until 1748, travelling extensively to the surrounding mines. Shortly
after leaving he published the *Mineral History of
Westmanland and Dalecarlia* and became a
member of the Swedish Academy of Sciences. In
1758 he published, at first anonymously, his *Essay
on the New Mineralogy*. In this he recognized four
classes of minerals – earths, bitumens, salts and
metals – and classified them according to their
chemical composition, instead of by such physical
properties as colour and hardness. To aid his
investigations of chemical composition, he used
the blowpipe, and became very skilled in its use.
A mineral, described by U. Hjarne (1641–1724),
was known, which had the general appearance of
a copper ore, yet could not be made to yield copper
by the normal process; accordingly it was known
as devil's copper or *kupfernickel*. Cronstedt
obtained from a sample of this a hard, white metal,
quite distinct from copper, which he called nickel.
He reported this in 1751 to the Swedish Academy
of Sciences, but many believed that there was confusion between nickel and cobalt, and it was not
until the early years of the nineteenth century that
Cronstedt's findings were confirmed.

V. Bartow, *Journal of Chemical Education*, **30**, 247.
   1953.
N. Zenzén, *Svenskt Biografiskt Lexikon*. 1932.
J. R. Partington, *A History of Chemistry*, vol. 3.
   1962.
Dictionary of Scientific Biography.

B B K

CROOKES, SIR WILLIAM Born in London, 17
June 1832; died there, 4 April 1919. Remembered
for discovery of thallium and researches on cathode rays.

In 1848 Crookes entered the Royal College of

Chemistry, London, where he became assistant to A. W. von HOFMANN and began his chemical researches, including those in spectroscopy; his first paper was published in 1851. In 1854 he became Superintendent of the Meteorological Department at the Radcliffe Observatory, Oxford, and in the following year was appointed lecturer in chemistry at the Chester College of Science. He returned to London in 1856, and in 1859 became Editor of the newly-founded *Chemical News*, a position he occupied till 1906.

Following hard on the announcement of the spectroscopic discovery of two new elements rubidium and caesium by R. W. E. BUNSEN and G. R. KIRCHHOFF, Crookes's observation of a striking green line in the spectrum of selenium led to his announcement in 1861 of the existence of a new element, thallium. The French chemist C. A. Lamy (1820–78) had isolated the same element independently, and his exhibition of an ingot of the metal at an International Exhibition in London in 1862 led to a controversy over priority. For his work on thallium, Crookes was elected FRS in 1863. Following a protracted series of experiments, which long served as a model for similar investigations, Crookes published (1873) his final, and remarkably accurate, determination of the atomic weight of thallium. The fact that this was not an integral number corroborated for thallium the previous findings of J. G. STAS and J. C. G. de MARIGNAC against the hypothesis of W. PROUT. The necessary use of the vacuum balance in the determination of the atomic weight of thallium then led Crookes to investigate certain irregularities in the weighing of bodies *in vacuo*. There resulted a paper on the *Attraction and Repulsion resulting from Radiation* (1874), followed by a second paper (1875) in which he announced the construction of the famous Crookes radiometer. The origin of the phenomena on which this instrument was based led to a controversy finally resolved in 1876 by the explanation of George STONEY, based on the kinetic theory of gases.

Crookes next proceeded to investigate the electrical discharges in vacuum tubes, a subject which had already been studied by J. PLÜCKER, J. W. HITTORF and others. In his Bakerian lecture of 1878 and his British Association Lecture of 1879, he announced various striking properties of 'molecular rays' including the casting of shadows, the warming of obstacles, and the deflection by a magnet. The title 'Radiant Matter' employed by Crookes in his British Association Lecture of 1879 referred to ordinary matter in a new state in which the mean free path was so large that collisions between molecules could be ignored. Other important work by Crookes included a paper of 1881 containing an experimental confirmation of the prediction by J. Clerk MAXWELL that the viscosity of a gas would be independent of the pressure.

Crookes combined tenacity of purpose, great experimental skill, and a passion for accuracy with a deeply imaginative and intuitive approach to science. He had wide interests apart from science and spiritualism, especially in the commercial application of scientific ideas to various fields as diverse as electric lighting and the extraction of sugar from beetroot. He is particularly remembered for his address to the British Association in 1898 in which he warned the world that it faced starvation if new forms of nitrogenous fertilizers could not be found

to provide food for its rising population. He was the recipient of many honours, including the Royal, Davy and Copley Medals of the Royal Society. Knighted in 1897, he became a member of the Order of Merit in 1910. In 1906 he was elected *Correspondant* of the French *Académie des Sciences*. He was President of the Royal Society 1913–15.

E. E. F. d'Albe, *Life of Sir Wm. Crookes.* 1923. (Portraits.)
A. Findlay and W. H. Mills, *British Chemists.* 1947. (Portrait.)
Proceedings of the Royal Society, **96A, i,** 1919–20. (Portrait.)
W. A. Tilden, *Famous Chemists.* 1921.
F. Greenaway, *Proceedings of the Royal Institution of Great Britain,* **39,** 172, 1962.
Dictionary of National Biography.
Dictionary of Scientific Biography.

J W H

CROSS, CHARLES FREDERICK Born at Brentford, Middlesex, England, 11 December 1855; died Hove, Sussex, 15 April 1935. Chemical technologist, one of the inventors of viscose rayon.

Cross was educated at the Universities of London, Zürich and Manchester. After gaining some industrial experience, he set up in partnership in London with E. J. BEVAN as analytical and consulting chemist, specializing in the chemistry and technology of cellulose and lignin. In 1892 Cross, Bevan and Beadle took out their historic patent on the solution and regeneration of cellulose; wood pulp (or other cheap forms of cellulose) was dissolved in a mixture of carbon disulphide and aqueous alkali (sodium xanthate), and squirted through fine holes into dilute acid to give spinnable fibres of 'viscose'. The modern rayon industry stems from this patent.

Cross was also concerned with the development of viscose films, of cellulose acetate, and with many problems of the paper industry. A cultured man, and a good musician, he was part author of several technical books, notably *Cellulose* (with Bevan, 1895). He was elected FRS in 1917.

Obituary Notices of Fellows of the Royal Society. 1935. (Portrait.)
Journal of the Chemical Society, 1337, 1935.
Dictionary of National Biography.

W V F

CRUM BROWN, ALEXANDER *See* BROWN.

CTESIBIUS OF ALEXANDRIA Dates uncertain; estimates vary between the first and the third centuries BC. Alexandrian mechanician.

Ctesibius was the inventor of the force pump and water organ, and improver of the clepsydra, or water clock.

The force pump combined the cylinder, the plunger and the valves necessary for raising water to an unrestricted height. The water organ, or *hydraulis*, maintained air under hydraulic pressure in a chamber from which it was directed at will into one or other of various pipes upon depressing the corresponding key upon a keyboard. Earlier types of clepsydra had depended upon the outflow of water from a cistern initially full, but in which, as the water ebbed, the head of pressure correspondingly decreased, so that the descent of the liquid surface in the cistern, or its ascent in a second vessel set to catch the escaping water, became slower as the cistern emptied itself. The water clock of Ctesibius marked an advance by providing for the constant replenishment of the water in the cistern, so that the head of pressure, and consequently the rate of outflow, remained constant. The lapse of time was measured by the ascent of a float in the vessel receiving the water. Ctesibius was also credited with the invention of a catapult or of some other such engine of war, but his original writings are lost.

The inventive mechanical tradition of Ctesibius was carried on through antiquity by Philo of Byzantium (*fl.* 150 BC) and Hero of ALEXANDRIA.

> A. G. Drachmann, *Ktesibios, Philon and Heron.* 1948.
>
> G. Sarton, *A History of Science; Hellenistic Science and Culture in the last three Centuries BC.* 1959.
>
> *Dictionary of Scientific Biography.*

A A

CUGNOT, NICHOLAS-JOSEPH Born at Void, Meuse, France, 25 September 1725; died Paris, 2 October 1804. Military engineer and pioneer of steam traction.

Cugnot joined the French army and served for a time in Germany and Belgium, inventing a new kind of rifle used by French troops under the Marshal du Saxe, who encouraged him to work on a steam-propelled gun-carriage. On returning to Paris in 1763 as a military instructor, Cugnot continued his work, obtaining official help from the Duc de Choiseul, then Minister of War. By 1770, a truck, carrying four passengers, ran at a speed of two to three miles an hour before a large crowd of official spectators and Cugnot was commissioned to make a larger truck. The fall of the Duc de Choiseul (1719–1785) led to the project being shelved, and the truck, though built, was not tested. Granted a pension in 1779 from the Ministry of War, Cugnot migrated to Brussels. The pension stopped at the outbreak of the French Revolution. Napoleon asked the *Institut de France* in 1798 to inquire into Cugnot's machine, but nothing came of this, and it was put into the *Conservatoire des Arts et Meétiers* in 1801.

Cugnot's truck was a tricycle with the power-driven front wheel used for steering. Driven by movements of two piston rods working from two cylinders – which, like the boiler, were made of copper – it carried no reserves of water or fuel.

> Augustine Boutaric, *Les grandes inventions françaises.* 1932.
>
> Shelby T. McCloy, *French Inventions of the Eighteenth Century.* 1952.
>
> *Transactions of the Newcomen Society,* **13**, 131, 1932–4; **16**, 21, 1934–6.

W H G A

CULPEPER, NICHOLAS Born in London, 18 October 1616; died there, 10 January 1654. Herbalist.

Culpeper was branded as a charlatan by the physicians of his time, partly because he dabbled in astrology and partly, no doubt, because of his unauthorized translation and publication, in 1649, of the official London *Pharmacopoeia* of 1618. Culpeper took the opportunity of making critical and often offensive comments on the official text, by no means all of them undeserved. The book – *A Physicall Directory* or *A translation of the Dispensatory made by the Colledge of Physitians in London* – was well received and was republished in an extended edition (*English Physitian Enlarged*) in 1653, appended to his famous *Complete Herbal.* Although the latter was unsound in many ways – Culpeper subscribed, for example, to the doctrine of signatures, according to which the outward appearance of a plant was held to indicate its medicinal property – there is no doubt that he and other early herbalists, such as John GERARD, contributed materially to the development of modern botany and pharmacology.

Culpeper was the son of Nicolas Culpeper, a clergyman, and grandson of Sir Thomas Culpeper, a well-known writer on usury. He studied at Cambridge, and after an apprenticeship with an apothecary set up as a physician in Spitalfields. There he had an extensive botanic garden in which he grew many of the herbal remedies he described.

> *Lancet,* **ii**, 1061, 1928.
>
> *Dictionary of National Biography.*
>
> Portrait: frontispiece of *The Complete Herbal* by Nicholas Culpeper. 1653. (Reproduced as Plate XXI in Agnes Arber, *Herbals.* 1912. Paperback 1986)
>
> *Dictionary of National Biography Missing Persons.* 1993.
>
> O. Thulesius, *Nicholas Culpeper: English Physician and Astrologer.* 1992.

T I W

CURIE, MARIE Born in Warsaw, 7 November 1867; died Sancellemox, Savoy, France, 4 July 1934. With her husband the first to discover the nature of radioactivity and to recognize and isolate radium and polonium.

Marya Sklodovska was the fifth and youngest child of a physics teacher in Warsaw. Straitened circumstances compelled her to take posts as governess for six years from 1885. She learned science from books and gained a taste for experimental work in a cousin's laboratory. Going to Paris in 1891, she entered the Sorbonne and studied under conditions of some privation, gaining her Master's degree in physics (1893) and mathematics (1894). In 1895 she married Pierre CURIE and to them were born Irène (later I. JOLIOT-CURIE) in 1897 and Eve in 1904.

Her first scientific work, under G. LIPPMANN, concerned magnetic properties of tempered steel. For her doctorate she followed up the discovery (1896) by A. H. BECQUEREL of what she herself was to call 'radioactivity'. In a disused storeroom at the *École de Physique et Chimie* her work began. Using the electrometer invented by Pierre and his brother, she measured the conducting power of the rays from uranium compounds. Their intensity was shown to depend upon the amount of uranium present, and not on other circumstances (temperature, pressure, etc.). She rapidly extended her investigations to all known chemical elements, finding that thorium also emitted radiation. Turning to mineral samples, she discovered that pitchblende, especially, seemed to be more active than the uranium and thorium it could have contained. Impelled to postulate a new element, she was joined by her husband in an intensive search which culminated in the discovery in 1898 of elements which she named *polonium* (July) and *radium* (December). Their method was the classical group separation, the radium being concentrated in the barium precipitate; successive crystallization of the chlorides gave progressive enrichment in radium, whose chloride was less soluble than that of barium. Polonium was found in the bismuth group. After four more arduous years, they obtained the first pure radium compound from 1 ton of pitchblende waste donated by the Austrian Government. During this period they examined the radiation emitted by their products, and discovered 'induced radioactivity' (contamination of apparatus by radioactive degradation products, though not recognized as such by them at first). They established that β-rays were negatively charged particles. Marie Curie made several increasingly accurate determinations of the atomic weight of radium. Eventually, the two Curies extracted 1 gm of radium from 8 tons of pitchblende. In 1903 they received the Davy Medal, and, jointly with Becquerel, the Nobel prize in physics.

Following the sudden death of her husband in 1906, Marie Curie succeeded to his chair at the Sorbonne and continued her research into radioactivity. She isolated radium metal (with A. Debierne (1874–1949)) and devised a method for its estimation. In 1910 she provided the Paris Bureau of Weights and Measures with 22 mg of pure radium chloride which became the International Radium Standard. She received the Nobel prize for chemistry in 1911.

From then on her scientific work was to consolidate and improve on her earlier achievements, 'protective and maternal, rather than creative' (A. S. Russell). She measured the range of α-particles from polonium; found the half-life of actinium; and did much to establish the independence of rates of radioactive decay on external factors.

In 1914 she became head of the radioactivity laboratory of the newly formed Radium Institute in Paris, but almost at once assisted the French war effort as first director of a radiology service, pioneering a mobile x-ray unit and founding a radiological school for nurses.

After the war she travelled widely, and was honoured extensively by learned societies, universities and civic institutions. She never lost her single-minded devotion to science which was her dominant characteristic. She died of leukaemia, undoubtedly a result of prolonged exposure to high-energy radiation.

Eve Curie, *Madame Curie*. 1938. (Portraits.)

E. Farber (Ed.), *Great Chemists*. 1961. (Portrait.)

Robert Reid, *Marie Curie*. 1974.

A. De Leeuw, *Marie Curie, Woman of Genius*. 1970.

F. Giroud, *Marie Curie: A Life*. 1986.

A. S. Russell, *Memorial Lectures, The Chemical Society*. 1951. (Portrait.)

Tyler Wasson (Ed.), *Nobel Prize Winners*. 1987. (Portrait.)

Dictionary of Scientific Biography.

A R

CURIE, PIERRE Born in Paris, 15 May 1859; died there, 19 April 1906. Husband of Marie CURIE, famous as her co-worker in the new subject of radioactivity, and for his own discovery of piezo-electricity.

The second son of a physician, Pierre Curie was educated privately and at the Sorbonne, where he became assistant in 1878. Together with his brother Jacques, he discovered the piezoelectric effect (electrification of opposite sides of asymmetric crystals of quartz under the influence of pressure), and its converse, the phenomenon of electrostriction. This behaviour was utilized in the Curie electrometer for measurement of small electric charges. In 1882 he was appointed chief of the laboratory of the *École de Physique et Chimie*. His investigations into magnetism led to the enunciation of Curie's Law, that magnetic susceptibility is inversely proportional to absolute temperature. At a certain critical temperature, known as the Curie point, paramagnetism passes over to ferromagnetism (1895).

In 1894 he met Marya Sklodovska and married her in the following year. From early 1898 they worked together in the study of radioactivity, and in their joint communications their individual roles are often indistinguishable. She appears to have concentrated on the chemical, he on the physical, side. With other collaborators at this time, Pierre Curie published on 'induced radioactivity', the heat evolved from radium, and the physiological effects of radioactivity.

After several minor teaching appointments, and following the award of the Nobel prize in physics (jointly with his wife and A. H. BECQUEREL), a chair in physics at the Sorbonne was created for him (1904) and he was elected to the *Académie* in 1905. From now on, the Curies found difficulty in adjusting to the demands of public acclamation, and this, together with ill health, and the demands of his new post, severely restricted his scientific activity. He was tragically killed by a wagon in a Paris street in 1906.

Pierre Curie was one of the finest physicists in Paris at the time, yet he was refused chairs at the Sorbonne in physical chemistry (1898) and mineralogy (1901), and was defeated at the *Académie* elections in 1902. His lofty idealism forbade him to court popularity, and honours eventually offered him were either declined or borne with some resentment for the fame they brought. Despite severe privations, his marriage was very happy, and his wife's success owed much to him.

After his death, Marie Curie published his collected works, and he was honoured in several ways. In 1910 the Brussels Conference on Radioactivity named the unit of radioactivity after him, the *curie*.

M. Curie, *Pierre Curie*. 1927. (Portraits.)

Eve Curie, *Madame Curie*. 1938. (Portraits.)

Les Prix Nobel en 1903. 1904. (Portrait.)

Tyler Wasson (Ed.), *Nobel Prize Winners*. 1987. (Portrait.)

C A R

CURTIS, WILLIAM Born at Alton, Hampshire, England, 11 January 1746; died London 7 July 1799. Founder of *The Botanical Magazine*.

At the age of 14 Curtis, son of a tanner, was apprenticed to his grandfather, a surgeon-apothecary whose premises were next door to the Crown Inn at Alton. One of the ostlers there had a remarkable knowledge of the local wildlife and aroused the boy's interest in natural history. He set himself up as an apothecary in London, but in

1771 sold his practice to establish a botanic garden in Bermondsey. In the following year he was appointed Demonstrator of Botany to the Society of Apothecaries at Chelsea.

In 1775, he initiated the *Flora Londiniensis*, a catalogue of plants in the London area, but the project was not a success and was abandoned in 1798 after two huge illustrated volumes had appeared. In the meantime Curtis had given up his appointment at Chelsea, and had established himself in a new botanic garden in Lambeth, which he opened to the public for a fee.

Then, in 1787, he began his really great work, *The Botanical Magazine*, which has continued to the present day. It was an immediate success; Curtis maintained that the *Flora* brought him praise but the *Magazine* brought him pudding. A feature of the *Magazine*, of which fourteen volumes appeared in Curtis's lifetime, was its rich illustrations of the world's flowers in colour. More than 1770 of the early plates were prepared by Sydenham Edwards (1769?–1819) who had also worked for the *Flora*.

In his later years Curtis moved his garden once again and finally established himself at Brompton. In 1788 his name appeared in the Roll Book of the Linnaean Society as a founder member.

J. W. Hunkin, *Endeavour*, **5**, 13, 1946.
Nature, **157**, 14, 1946.
Dictionary of National Biography.

T I W

CUSHING, HARVEY Born at Cleveland, Ohio, USA, 8 April 1869; died New Haven, Connecticut, 7 October 1939. Founder of modern neurosurgical techniques and investigator of the pituitary gland.

Cushing qualified in medicine in 1895 after training at Yale College and Harvard Medical School. His early practical training was at the Massachusetts General Hospital in Boston and at Johns Hopkins Hospital, Baltimore, with William Halsted (1852–1922), one of the great innovators of techniques in general surgery. At the turn of the century he worked at Berne with Theodor KOCHER, who directed his interests to neurosurgery, and briefly with Sir Charles SHERRINGTON the great English neurophysiologist. Cushing's experimental observations on the effects of artificially raised intracranial pressure in animals had wide clinical applications, especially in the treatment of intracranial tumours. This was to be the main field of his work during the next three decades.

Although intracranial surgery had been practised with occasional success by E. von Bergmann in Germany and by Sir Rickman Godlee, Sir Victor Horsley and Sir William MACEWEN in Britain, the methods were those of general surgery and survival was unusual. At Baltimore and later at Boston, Cushing founded a new discipline of neurosurgery based on meticulous history-taking and examination, and on painstaking operative techniques. His operations lasted many hours, but achieved increasing success over the years. His attractive personality added to the fame of his clinic, and highly gifted pupils started new schools of neurosurgery in their own countries and popularized Cushing's methods of surgical treatment.

He wrote classical descriptions of the natural history of the various types of intracranial tumours which remain valid. In 1917 he published a defini-tive account of tumours of the acoustic nerve, and in the 1930s he classified his immense material relating to intracranial tumours in general and of meningiomas in particular.

He became interested in functions and diseases of the pituitary gland in 1908, and developed a surgical approach to this seeming inaccessible gland at the base of the brain, at first for experimental studies on dogs and then for treatment in man. By 1912 he had investigated fifty patients and established certain aspects of over-and underfunction of this organ, in particular the state of acromegaly in some kinds of overactivity, and dwarfism in underactivity in the growing animal. A peculiar endocrine syndrome resulting from over-activity of one particular type of cell of the pituitary bears his name in clinical medicine. Many cases of blindness arising from pressure on the optic nerves by tumours in the region of the pituitary gland have been cured or improved by Cushing's operations. Cushing was an advocate of reform in medical education and of wider postgraduate training.

A medical historian, he wrote a biography of William Osler (1849–1920). He left his collection of historical books to Yale University.

J. Fulton, *Harvey Cushing: A Biography*. 1946. (Portraits.)

E. H. Thomson, *Harvey Cushing*. 1960.
Obituary Notices of Fellows of the Royal Society. 1941. (Portrait.)
Nature, **144**, 736, 1939.
Dictionary of Scientific Biography.

E H J

CUVIER, GEORGE LÉOPOLD CHRÉTIEN FRÉDÉRIC DAGOBERT, BARON Born at Montbéliard, Doubs, France, 23 August 1769; died Paris, 13 May 1832. Comparative anatomist and founder of palaeontology.

Cuvier, the son of an Army officer, was from boyhood devoted to the study of natural history. He was educated at the Academy of Stuttgart, where he was conspicuous for his application to his studies and for his unusually good memory. In 1795, through the influence of A. H. Tessier (1741–1837) and Geoffroy Saint-Hilaire (1772–1844) he was appointed assistant to the professor of comparative anatomy at the *Muséum d'Histoire Naturelle* in Paris, and in the following year started a course of lectures at the *École du Panthéon*. In 1798 he published his *Tableau élémentaire de l'histoire naturelle des animaux*, based upon his lectures and forming the foundation for his later work on the classification of the animal kingdom. This was followed in 1800 by his *Leçons d'anatomie comparée*, in which he was assisted by A. M. C. Duméril (1774–1860) and G. L. Duvernoy (1777–1855), after he became professor of natural history at the *Collège de France* in 1799. In 1802 he also became professor at the *Jardin des Plantes*, and embarked on extensive researches on various groups of animals.

The results of his work were published in numerous papers in the learned journals, and in a series of impressive volumes. He was particularly interested in the structure and classification of animals, and in the anatomy and systematic position of the many new forms that came to light in the course of explorations in parts of the world where scientific collections were made for the first time.

He produced lengthy works on the mollusca and, in collaboration with A. Valenciennes (1794–1865), on fishes; but his most celebrated researches were on the fossil mammals and reptiles, especially the extinct mammals of the tertiary formations near Paris, the results of which were published as *Recherches sur les ossements fossiles des quadrupèdes* (four volumes, 1812). This was largely collected from his papers in the *Annales du Muséum d'histoire naturelle* and it laid the foundation of modern palaeontology. In parallel with these studies he made extensive investigations for comparative purposes on the osteology of living forms, and published his results in many separate papers. The most famous of all his works, however, is the *Règne animal distribué d'après son organisation*, giving an account of the whole animal kingdom and embodying the results of his researches on animals both living and fossil. This first appeared in 1817 and was followed by numerous editions and translations into several languages.

In later life Cuvier was much concerned with scientific organization and education, was Chancellor of the Imperial University, and Councillor of State under both Napoleon and Louis Philippe. He was a member of all the important scientific societies of Europe – including the Royal Society (1806) – and Perpetual Secretary of the *Institut de France*. In 1831 he was created Baron in the peerage of France by Louis Philippe.

P. M. J. Flourens, *Histoire des Travaux de Georges Cuvier.* 1858.

D. C. Peattie, *Green Laurels.* 1937. (Portrait.)

W. Coleman, *Georges Cuvier, Zoologist.* 1964.

J. Viénot, *Georges Cuvier 1769–1832.* 1932.

Dictionary of Scientific Biography.

L H M

D

DAGUERRE, LOUIS JACQUES MANDÉ Born at Cormeilles-en-Parisis, France, 18 November 1787; died Bry-sur-Marne, 10 July 1851. Inventor of the daguerreotype, the first practicable process of photography, and co-inventor of the Diorama.

Daguerre, the son of a magistrates' court official, was apprenticed (1804) to I. E. M. Degotti, chief designer at the Paris opera. From 1807 on he was for nine years assistant of the panorama painter Pierre Prevost. Daguerre first exhibited at the Salon in 1814, and became an independent stage designer two years later. With Charles-Marie Bouton (1781–1853), he invented the Diorama, an entertainment based on enormous paintings on semi-transparent linen with changing effects caused by transmitted and reflected light, and accompanied by music. Diorama theatres were established in Paris (1822), London (1823), Berlin, Stockholm and elsewhere. Preliminary sketches were made with the *camera obscura* and this led Daguerre to attempt chemical fixation of the images. After experimenting unsuccessfully for several years, he learned (1826) that J. N. NIÉPCE was researching on the same lines, and in December 1829 they formed a partnership to perfect heliography. Continuing with the substances recommended by Niépce, Daguerre discovered the light-sensitivity of silver iodide (1831), and the existence of a latent image that could be developed with mercury vapour (1835), thus reducing the exposure to about twenty minutes. In 1837 he was able to fix his pictures permanently with sodium chloride (from 1839 on, sodium thiosulphate). Having improved heliography out of all recognition, Daguerre felt entitled to call the invention by his name. Through the efforts of François ARAGO the daguerreotype was acquired by the French Government in exchange for pensions to Daguerre and Niépce's son: the manipulatory details were disclosed free to the world on 19 August 1839. Five days earlier, however, Daguerre had patented the process in England.

No other nineteenth-century invention captured the imagination of the public to the same degree, and thirty-two editions of Daguerre's instruction manual, in eight languages, appeared during 1839–40 He was made an Officer of the Legion of Honour and elected to honorary membership of several foreign academies. In 1840 he retired to a small estate at Bry-sur-Marne. Essential improvements to the daguerreotype, and its application to portraiture, were made by others. The daguerreotype was a single direct positive photograph on a silvered copper-plate, with the disadvantage that no copies could be made. For this reason it proved a cul-de-sac in photography, and was superseded by the collodion process of Frederick Scott ARCHER.

Helmut and Alison Gernsheim, *L. J. M. Daguerre: The History of the Diorama and the Daguerreotype*. 1956. (Portraits.)
Helmut and Alison Gernsheim, *The History of Photography*. 1955. (Portrait.)
Nouvelle Biographie Universelle. 1852–66.

H and A G

DAHL, ANDERS Born at Varnhem, Sweden, 17 March 1751; died Åbo, 25 May 1789. Botanist.

Dahl entered the University of Uppsala in 1770 as a medical student, studied under LINNAEUS, and qualified in 1776. On the recommendation of Linnaeus he was employed by Clas Alströmer (1736–96) to take charge of his scientific collections at Gothenburg, and to supervise the establishment of a Botanical Garden at Christinedal. He travelled widely, collecting botanical material, in Sweden and in Germany, where, in 1786, he received from the University of Kiel the honorary degree of MD for his publication, *Observationes botanicae circa systema vegetabilium divi à Linnée*. After financial losses forced Alströmer to abandon his scientific projects, Dahl moved in 1787 to Åbo where he spent the last two years of his life at the University as associate professor of medicine and demonstrator in botany. As a compliment, and in allusion to Dahl's shaggy hair, C. P. THUNBERG, in 1791, gave the name Dahlia to a genus of plants introduced into Sweden from South Africa: in the same year A. J. Cavanilles (1745–1804) of Madrid also so named the different, but more familiar, plant brought from Mexico.

S. Birger, *Svenskt Biografiskt Lexicon*, **9**, 548, 1931.

A P G

DAIMLER, GOTTLIEB Born at Schorndorf, near Stuttgart, Germany, 17 March 1834; died Stuttgart, 6 March 1900. A pioneer of automobile engineering.

Gottlieb Daimler's technical education began in 1848, when he became a gunsmith's apprentice, and continued until 1862. Following a period at technical school in Stuttgart and factory experience (1853–7) in a Strasbourg steam engineering works, he completed his formal training as a mechanical engineer at the Stuttgart Polytechnic. By the time of his return to Strasbourg in 1859 he had recognized the need for a small low-cost engine, but was unable to develop one. With little further interest in steam engines he left the works in 1861 to tour England and France. In Paris his interest was taken by the gas engine devised by E. LENOIR (1860) and the high traffic density in the city.

Daimler spent the next ten years in heavy engineering, with Bruderhaus Maschinenfabrik, Reutlingen (1863–9), as manager, there meeting Wilhelm MAYBACH; and then with Maschinenbau Gesellschaft, Karlsruhe, as director (1869–72). In 1872 he turned to the internal-combustion engine, when he joined Gasmotoren-Fabrik Deutz as chief engineer. With N. A. OTTO and Maybach he was involved in the perfection of the Otto oil engine. In 1875 the Deutz board directed Daimler to develop a petroleum engine, but with the commercial development of the Otto four-cycle engine in the next year this plan seems to have been dropped. Daimler remained at Deutz until 1882, when differences arose and he, with Maybach, set up a factory in Stuttgart for the development of light high-speed internal-combustion engines. From the beginning they had vehicle propulsion very much in mind. At first it seemed that the creation of a reliable self-firing ignition system was impossible, but after many trials a successful design was evolved and patented in 1883. Further refinements followed, and by 1885 the petrol engine had been reduced in size and applied to a motor-cycle. They developed the two-cylinder V-engine giving twice the power from the same space, which, applied to a motor car, was shown at the Paris Exhibition of 1889. The vehicles of both Daimler and K. BENZ were overlooked by the public, but contact was made with R. Panhard (1841–1908) and E. Levassor (1844–97), who established the engines in France. In 1890 the Daimler-Motoren GmbH was created, but following policy disagreements Daimler and Maybach continued their experimental work alone, exhibiting engines at Chicago in 1893, and entering road races to establish the utility of the automobile. Daimler returned to the company in 1895 in full charge, after which time the Daimler engines, under various names, achieved much. The engines were manufactured in Britain by the Daimler Motor Co. Ltd from 1896.

P. Siebetz, *Gottlieb Daimler.* 1942. (Portrait.)

E. Diesel and others, *From Engines to Autos.* 1960. (Portrait.)

                                                                                    W N S

DALE, SIR HENRY HALLETT Born in London, 9 June 1875; died Cambridge, 23 July 1968. Pharmacologist, distinguished for his research on histamine, acetylcholine, and the chemical transmission of nerve effects.

At school, Dale did extremely well in all examinations, but it did not occur to him or to his father, a manager of a pottery firm, that he could go on to university. The opportunity arose through a chance meeting at a Wesleyan Methodist Conference, where Dale's father was introduced to the Headmaster of The Leys School, Cambridge, a leading biblical scholar of his day. Mentioning his son's prowess in examinations, he was advised to enter him for the school's Entrance Scholarship. Dale won this, and at school was directed towards science. Then, with another scholarship, he went on to Trinity College, Cambridge. There, he won a First in Part I and Part II of the Natural Science Tripos, and then spent a further two years in the Department of Physiology before taking up clinical studies. After qualifying in 1902, he returned to research and worked for two years in the Department of Physiology at University College London under E. H. STARLING. But his fundamental discoveries were to come later, during ten fruitful years at the Wellcome Physiological Research Laboratories, and afterwards at the National Institute for Medical Research, London, whose first Director he became in 1928.

Dale loved to dwell on the role played by lucky accidents in his research. In the Wellcome Laboratories he began working on ergot, and the fungus ergot turns up again and again. His work on sympathomimetic amines, histamine and acetylcholine, began with the identification of these substances in extracts of ergot, as the result of lucky accidents. In 1906, he made his first important discovery, also the outcome of a lucky accident. He discovered the sympatholytic action of ergotoxine and thus introduced the first adrenoceptor blocking agent into pharmacology. In 1909, whilst working with ergot, he discovered the oxytocic action of posterior pituitary extract, which led to what is probably the most frequent application of pituitary extract in practical medicine. The year 1910 saw his paper with G. BARGER on the 'Chemical structure and pharmacological action of sympathomimetic amines', which was the beginning of an era of research on structure-action relationship of drugs. In 1913, following up one of his most fortunate accidents, he proved that the anaphylactic contraction of plain muscle resulted from the formation of cell-fixed antibodies. This finding had a lasting influence on immunology and established the relationship between anaphylaxis and immunity. 'Anaphylaxis results from a predominantly cellular fixation of an antibody which, when it circulates in excess is recognized as the cause of immunity.'

Two substances will for ever be linked with Dale's name: histamine and acetylcholine. Nearly all their main pharmacological effects were described by him, and to him we owe the knowledge that they are natural constituents of animal tissues. In this research many of his colleagues took part, the foremost being G. BARGER, H. W. Dudley (1887–1935), P. P. Laidlaw (1881–1940), and A. N. Richards (1876–1966). With the last two, he tried to find out during the First World War what happened in histamine shock, so as to be able to explain by analogy what occurred during secondary wound shock. Histamine was found to produce a deficiency in the volume of circulating blood; the heart received too little blood to propel because the blood was stagnating in the dilated capillaries and, as a result of the increased permeability of their walls, plasma was escaping from the vessels into the tissues, although the larger arterioles were constricted. He concluded that a similar circulatory deficiency occurred in secondary wound shock, and this pointed to plasma or blood transfusion as the most immediately efficient remedy.

In 1914, Dale discovered the dual action of acetylcholine. Firstly, its muscarinic action on plain muscle, heart, and gland cells, which was abolished by atropine. Secondly, its nicotinic action on cells of the adrenal medulla and of autonomic ganglia, which was abolished by excess of nicotine. A third nicotinic action on motor end-plates of skeletal muscle was discovered later. These investigations were to lead twenty years later to a revolutionary change in our concept of neuromuscular and synaptic transmission.

Between 1933 and 1936 one publication after another came out of Dale's department and the nicotinic transmitter function of acetylcholine was established. It came as a real shock that acetylcholine was the neuromuscular and synaptic transmitter. But Dale had already pointed out in 1914 that if there was any evidence for the presence of acetylcholine in animal tissue – this evidence was to be supplied by him and Dudley in 1929 – acetylcholine would be a most suitable transmitter substance for parasympathetic nerve effects. From the evanescence of the acetylcholine effects, he predicted the presence of cholinesterase in the animal body sixteen years before it was discovered. Dale realised the need for a terminology to distinguish nerve fibres not with regard to their anatomical origin but to their chemical transmission and he coined the terms 'cholinergic' and 'adrenergic', now in general use. He also introduced the terms 'cholinoceptive' and 'adrenoceptive' to denote the sensitivity of a structure to the transmitter substance. One other major contribution to science, and particularly to therapeutics, for which humanity owes him a great debt concerns his work on standardisation of extracts containing unidentified pharmacologically active substances. He insisted on the use of a common standard reference preparation and it is greatly due to his efforts that international standards were adopted. As President of The Royal Society during the war years (1940–45), he used his office to defend the freedom of science in often unforgettable words. Of the many honours he received he cherished most the Nobel prize, which he shared with O. LOEWI, in 1936, and the Order of Merit, awarded in 1944.

Biographical Memoirs of Fellows of the Royal Society. 1970. (Portrait.)
Dictionary of Scientific Biography.
Dictionary of National Biography.
H. Oxbury (Ed.), *Great Britons: 20th Century Lives.* 1985.
Tyler Wasson (Ed.), *Nobel Prize Winners.* 1987. (Portrait.)

W F

D'ALEMBERT, JEAN LE ROND Born in Paris, November 1717; died, probably in Paris, October 1783. French mathematician and philosopher who made important contributions to mechanics.

D'Alembert, found near the church of St Jean le Rond, was the illegitimate son of aristocrats: he lived for much of his life in the house of his fosterfather, a glazier. After an education under the Jansenists and abortive studies of law and medicine, he devoted himself to mathematics, contenting himself with the annuity bestowed on him by his natural father. He presented several papers to the *Académie des Sciences*; in the field of calculus he was able to clarify the concept of limits and introduced the notion of different orders of infinities.

In 1741 D'Alembert was admitted to the *Académie* and two years later published his *Traité de Dynamique*. Newtonian in philosophy, he based his ideas on inertia as a property by which the motion of bodies is altered only by gravity (i.e. attraction) or by impact. D'Alembert's Principle then appears as a method of reducing problems of dynamics to ones of statics by superimposing

additional forces corresponding to those which produce actual accelerations.

His principle he applied to many fields of applied mathematics; he obtained, by a lengthy analysis, the general equations for the planar motion of fluids. In 1747 he published his theory of vibrating strings, producing the general solution of the wave equation.

His value as a mathematician was widely recognized and honoured. In his association with D. DIDEROT in the preparation of the great *Encyclopédie* he discoursed on wider fields of scientific and philosophical inquiry.

D. E. Smith, *History of Mathematics*, vol. 1. 1923. (Paperback 1958.) (Portrait.)
Endeavour (New Series), **7**, 78, 1983.
T. Hankins, *Jean d'Alembert: Science and the Enlightment.* 1970.
Ronald Grimsley, *Jean d'Alembert 1717–1783.* 1963.

D N

DALTON, JOHN Born at Eaglesfield, Cumberland, England, (about) 5 September 1766; died Manchester, 27 July 1844. Formulated atomic theory to explain chemical reactions, based on the concept that the atoms of different elements are distinguished by differences in their weights.

John Dalton, propounder of a theory that has profoundly influenced scientific thought for more than a century and a half, rose from very humble origins to be internationally famous. He was the third of six children of a poor hand-loom weaver, Joseph Dalton. Brought up in the Quaker faith, he had the good fortune to have as his schoolmaster another remarkable, but less distinguished, Quaker; this was Elihu Robinson, an experienced meteorologist and instrument maker who instilled in him his own interest in weather observation and scientific experiment. By the age of 12 Dalton himself was teaching in the local school and three years later he and his brother worked as assistant masters at a Quaker school in Kendal; in 1785 he became Principal and taught there until 1793. Again he was fortunate in his associates, for he came under the influence of the blind mathematician John Gough (1757–1825), who was also, rather surprisingly, a competent botanist. At Kendal, Dalton gave some public lectures, and although these were not notably successful they served to make his capabilities more widely known. In 1793 he was invited to become tutor in natural philosophy and science at the Manchester Academy, a Presbyterian College founded in 1786 to take the place of an earlier one that had closed in 1712. However, his teaching duties there left him too little time to pursue his own scientific interests, and in 1799 he resigned the position and thereafter earned his living for many years as a private tutor. Ultimately, in 1833, he was freed of this necessity by the grant of a civil list pension of £150, increased to £300 in 1836.

In Manchester, Dalton found himself in a flourishing scientific community which in 1781 had founded the Manchester Literary and Philosophical Society. This he joined in 1794, and during his fifty years of membership read to it more than a hundred papers. He was appointed Secretary in 1800; Vice-President in 1808; and President in 1819. In 1799 the Society purchased a house at 36 George Street, and here Dalton was given accommodation for teaching and research. Unfortunately, this house, together with most of the Society's records, was almost totally destroyed in a German air raid in 1940. Very recently (1993), however, some fire-damaged papers have been recovered which it may prove possible to restore with modern techniques.

Inspired by Elihu Robinson, Dalton from his early childhood kept a daily record – unbroken until his death – of the local weather. He was conscious of 'the advantages that might accrue to the husbandman, the mariner, and to mankind in general, if we were able to predict the state of the weather with tolerable precision'. This led him to publish, in 1793, his *Meteorological Observations and Essays*. In this he described how to make and use simple meteorological instruments, and added some comments on the aurora borealis and other atmospheric phenomena. It was a not a major work, containing nothing original, and he was probably ill-advised to reprint it unchanged some forty years later. Nevertheless, it can be judged significant in the evolution of his atomic theory. His interest in the weather inevitably gave him a special interest in the atmosphere, and so in gaseous mixtures in general. He formulated the Law of Partial Pressures, according to which the pressure of a mixed gas is the sum of the pressures that each of its components would exert if occupying the same space. Further, he independently formulated the law of the thermal expansion of gases, commonly attributed to J. A. C. CHARLES.

The line of thought that led to the atomic theory may well have derived from this preoccupation with gases. Although there is some evidence that he was activated by a desire to find a physical interpretation of the law of multiple proportions, it was the opinion of Henry ROSCOE – on the basis of some of Dalton's notebooks, now lost – that what was really in his mind was to explain why the constituents of a gaseous mixture remain homogeneously mixed instead of separating into layers according to their density. Certainly there is no doubt that the first allusion to his theory came in October 1803, at the end of a paper on the absorption of gases by liquids. To this, he remarked quite casually, 'I shall just subjoin my results, as far as they appear to be ascertained by my experiments'; the results subjoined were, in fact, nothing less than the first table of atomic weights. The favourable reception accorded this first brief mention led Dalton to develop his theory further. He did so first in lectures at the Royal Institution in 1803–4 and later in his *New System of Chemical Philosophy*, the first part of this appeared in 1808, and in its last chapter he clearly set out his new ideas. Later, William HIGGINS was to claim priority over Dalton, maintaining that he had advanced a similar theory as early as 1789, but today the consensus of informed opinion is that it was Dalton who conceived the fundamental idea that the atoms of different elements were distinguished by differences in their weights. This concept not only provided a logical interpretation of much then recent quantitative research in chemistry but opened up new fields of experiment.

Dalton's atomic theory was his one great achievement; his other chemical work, his meteorological observations, his study of colour-blindness (of which he was himself a victim), were not of sufficient importance to ensure his lasting fame. He was fortunate in being recognized and widely honoured in his own lifetime. The French Academy of Sciences elected him a corresponding member in 1816 and later, on Davy's death, accorded him, in 1830, the great honour of electing him one of its eight foreign associates. In 1822, the Royal Society elected him to Fellowship, and four years later made him their first Royal Medallist. Oxford and Edinburgh gave him honorary degrees. Manchester recognized their greatest citizen by commissioning his statue by Francis Chantrey in 1834. At his death, forty thousand people filed past his coffin, and there were a hundred carriages in the funeral procession – an inappropriate end for one who all his life had remained a simple-minded member of the Quaker faith.

A. Hopwood, *Journal of Chemical Education*, **3**, 485, 1926.

J. R. Partington, *Endeavour*, **7**, 54, 1948. (Portrait.)

F. Greenaway, *John Dalton and the Atom*. 1966.

E. C. Patterson, *John Dalton and the Atomic Theory*. 1970.

A. Thackray, *John Dalton, Critical Assessments of His Life and Science*. 1972.

Dictionary of Scientific Biography.

T I W

DAM, CARL PETER HENRIK Born in Copenhagen, 21 February 1895; died there, 17 April 1976. Biochemist, noted for discovery of Vitamin K.

Dam was the son of an apothecary. He graduated in chemistry from the Polytechnic Institute in Copenhagen in 1920 and after three years at the School of Agriculture and Veterinary Medicine there was appointed (1923) Instructor in Biochemistry in the Physiological Laboratory of the University of Copenhagen. Subsequently he became associate professor in the Institute of Biochemistry (1929–41) before being appointed professor of biochemistry in the Polytechnic in 1941. At that time he happened to be lecturing in the United States, and because of the German occupation of Denmark remained there. He did research first at Woods Hole Marine Biological Laboratories and later (1942–5) in the University of Rochester. From 1945–8 he was at the Rockefeller Institute for Medical Research. He returned to Denmark in 1956 as head of the biological division of the Danish Fat Research Institute, an appointment that reflected his long interest in natural lipids.

In 1929 Dam was investigating the effect of low-fat diets on chicks and observed that they showed haemorrhages in various parts of their bodies and that their blood coagulated abnormally slowly. He first supposed that this was a consequence of Vitamin C deficiency – i.e. a form of scurvy – but the chicks did not respond to this vitamin or any other then known. He concluded in 1934 that the effect was due to an unidentified vitamin, which he called the coagulation vitamin or Vitamin K. He discovered that it was present in hempseed – which is rich in oil – and in the seeds of certain other plants, including cabbage and lucerne. He showed it to be present also in certain animal organs, notably the liver. Later investigation by Dam and by workers elsewhere showed that lack of Vitamin K inhibits formation in the liver of prothrombin, a substance that initiates the blood clotting process.

For this work Dam was awarded a Nobel prize for medicine in 1943, which he shared with Edward DOISY, of St Louis. Although Dam prepared highly active concentrates of Vitamin K, Doisy was the first to isolate it in pure crystalline form (1939). In the event he isolated two very closely related vitamins, K_1 and K_2, from lucerne seed and fish meal respectively. Doisy went on to determine the chemical structure of the vitamin and to synthesize it. It is a naphthaquinone derivative.

Vitamin K has an important role in medicine. Deficiency can cause illness in, for example, patients unable to absorb fat normally, and newborn babies.

Les Prix Nobel en 1940–44. 1946. (Portrait.)
Dictionary of Scientific Biography, Supp. II.
Tyler Wasson (Ed.), *Nobel Prize Winners*. 1987. (Portrait.)
New York Times, 25 April 1976.

T I W

DANIELL, JOHN FREDERIC Born in London, 12 March 1790; died there, 13 March 1845. Remembered for contributions to meteorology and invention of the Daniell Cell.

Daniell's early researches were in chemistry and meteorology and included the development of his dew-point hygrometer, an instrument which transformed the subject of hygrometry. His meteorological papers were published together as *Meteorological Essays* (1823) and included an account of the laws of the Earth's atmosphere; an explanation of the trade winds; and details of the construction of meteorological apparatus. In the second edition (1827) he emphasized the importance of radiation.

In 1835 Daniell began his investigation into voltaic piles, especially into the reasons for their rapid loss of potential. Discovering that this was due principally to the solution of zinc and its deposition on the copper plate, he proceeded to construct a new constant voltage cell which avoided the disadvantages of previous models. This cell provided a powerful impulse to the study of voltaic electricity, including Daniell's own researches into electrolysis, in which he proved that in the decomposition of metallic salts it was the metal that travelled to the positive terminal.

He was elected FRS in 1814, being awarded the Rumford and Copley medals in 1832 and 1837 respectively. In 1831 he was appointed the first professor of chemistry at King's College, London.

Dictionary of National Biography.
J. F. Daniell, *Elements of Meteorology*. 1845. (Includes memoir.)
Dictionary of Scientific Biography.

J W H

DARBY, ABRAHAM Born near Dudley, Worcestershire, England, 1678; died Madley Court, Worcestershire, 8 March 1717. First successful smelter of iron with coke.

In the seventeenth century the development of the iron industry in Britain was limited by two technical difficulties. Firstly, the growing demand for charcoal, then the only satisfactory fuel for blast furnaces, had forced the price up very considerably. Secondly, attempts to improve efficiency by using bigger furnaces were frustrated by the fact that charcoal is too soft to support more than a relatively short column of ore. Not surprisingly, attempts were made to use coal in place of charcoal, but the presence in most coals of sulphur – which spoils the quality of the iron – resulted in only limited success; the claim put forward by Dud Dudley (1599–1684) in 1619 is not now generally accepted. Attention was therefore directed to coke – already used in the smelting of copper and lead – since the coking process eliminates the sulphur. Darby had considerable experience of smelting copper with coke at Bristol – and he had also used coke in malting, where, for different reasons, the presence of sulphur prevents the use of raw coal – and in 1708 turned his attention to iron, founding the Bristol Iron Company. Anxious to make his own iron as cheaply as possible, he acquired premises at Coalbrookdale, on the Severn, close to good local supplies of iron ore and good coking coal. Here, in 1709, he first successfully manufactured good-quality iron in a furnace fired with coke. Initially, much of the iron was used for making pots and other hollow-ware; the quality of his molten iron made it possible for him to make thin castings which competed satisfactorily with heavy brassware then in common use.

The Coalbrookdale manufactory was successful, and Abraham Darby established a dynasty of ironfounders there. The advent of the Newcomen steam engine (see T. NEWCOMEN) gave an important new market; some of the cylinders required for mine-pumping engines weighed as much as six tons, with a length of 10 feet and a bore of 6. By 1758 more than a hundred such cylinders had been cast. In turn, the steam engine improved the manufacture of iron by giving a more powerful and reliable blast for the furnaces than water-power could supply. In 1779, Abraham Darby III (1750–91) designed, cast, and erected the world's first iron bridge, which still spans the Severn just below Coalbrookdale; for this he was awarded a gold medal by the Society of Arts. Later still, in 1802, the Coalbrookdale works built the first railway locomotive, with a high-pressure boiler, for Richard TREVITHICK. His choice was no doubt dictated by the long Darby connection with the Cornish mining industry.

A. Raistrick, *Dynasty of Ironfounders: the Darbys and Coalbrookdale*. 1953; *Endeavour*, **18**, 186, 1959.
Dictionary of National Biography.

T I W

DART, RAYMOND ARTHUR Born at Brisbane, Australia, 4 February 1893; died Johannesburg, South Africa, 22 November 1988. Palaeontologist.

Dart qualified in medicine from the University of Sydney, Australia, in 1917 and served with the Australian Army Medical Corps on the Western Front. He moved to South Africa and became professor of Anatomy at Witwatersrand University, Johannesburg, in 1923, remaining there as Dean of the Faculty of Medicine 1925–1943 and professor until his retirement in 1958.

In 1924 he made what was perhaps the single most important discovery in palaeontology in the 20th century when he identified the fossil skull of a young child in limestone rocks at Taung, near Kimberley. This child, although human in every other way, had a small brain. The orthodox view at the time was that brain enlargement was an essential early step in human evolution. It was also believed that China was the cradle of man. But Dart, who gave the species the name *Australopithecus africanus*, showed that it had been living in the region for two million years. Dart's discovery bridged the gap between ape and man and established Africa as the cradle of mankind, supporting the theory of Charles DARWIN of the evolution of man, although there was much opposition to his views, led by Sir Arthur Keith (1866–1955). The excavation of sites in southern Africa by R. BROOM from 1936 to 1953 vindicated Dart's theories.

During the 1950s Dart developed his 'Bone Tool' theory, first publicized in 1955, based on research into broken bones discovered in the cave of Makapansgat, that before the Stone Age there had been a Bone Age. He believed that the australopithicenes had used the bones of their prey as tools. Although this theory was later discredited, it gave rise to a new scientific discipline, taphonomy, the study of what happens to biological material after death.

From 1966 Dart was professor of Anthropology at the Institute for the Achievement of Human Potential in Philadelphia, USA.

Ruth Moore, *Man, Time and Fossils. The Story of Evolution.* 1962.

R. A. Dart and D. Craig, *Adventures with the Missing Link.* 1959.

Phillip V. Tobias (Ed.), *Hominid Evolution. Past, Present and Future.*

A P B

DARWIN, CHARLES ROBERT Born at Shrewsbury, Shropshire, England, 12 February 1809; died Downe, Kent, 19 April 1882. Illustrious naturalist.

Charles Darwin was the son of Robert Waring Darwin, physician of Shrewsbury, and of Susannah, daughter of Josiah WEDGWOOD. Charles Darwin was thus the grandson of Erasmus DARWIN, the physician-philosopher-poet. Darwin went to Shrewsbury School, from which he derived little benefit, and thence to Edinburgh to study medicine, from October 1825 until April 1827, when it had become clear that medicine was not the career for him. On 15 October 1827 he was admitted to Christ's College, Cambridge, with the intention of taking holy orders, but made the acquaintance of scientists who turned his mind in the direction of natural history. Through them he received an invitation to sail round the world in HMS *Beagle* as naturalist on a voyage which lasted from 27 December 1831 until 2 October 1836, during which time he visited the Cape Verde Islands, South America, the Galapagos, Tahiti, New Zealand, Australia, Mauritius, and South Africa, among other places.

Darwin first made his name as a geologist. His demonstrations of the differences between cleavage and foliation of rocks, the relations of planes of cleavage to geological features over wide areas, of extensive elevations of land and their connection with earthquakes and volcanic eruptions, and his explanation of the formation of coral atolls were contributions to science of the greatest importance. They have been overshadowed, however, by his even more momentous contributions to biology, as a result of his demonstration that evolution of living organisms has occurred, and by his discovery of the principle of natural selection of heritable variation as the cause of evolution.

From his original, orthodox, acceptance of the fixity of species, he was led gradually to a realization of the truth of the origin of species by descent with modification, or evolution, by four lines of observation, the results of his work in South America and the Galapagos Islands. These four lines were the replacement of species in adjacent areas by different but related species; the similarity of type between fossil animals and related living species in the same continent; the South American nature of the birds of the Galapagos Archipelago; and the differences, related to manner of life, between species of birds on the different islands of the Galapagos Archipelago. All these facts fell into place if it could be assumed that species were not originally fixed, but had arisen from previous species and had been modified during descent. The truth of this theory acquired progressive and unvarying support when he found that it explained otherwise inexplicable facts in the sciences of comparative anatomy, embryology, palaeontology, and geographical distribution, to mention only the chief lines of inquiry. With a shrewdness that was quite uncanny in a man who had never had any systematic scientific training, he realized that it was useless to proclaim that evolution was a fact unless he also provided an answer to the question how and by what mechanism it had occurred.

The changes demonstrable in cultivated plants and domestic animals produced by man since the Neolithic Period under the practice of artificial selection convinced him that selection must be the key to evolution of wild species in nature, but the problem was to discover the agent which performed the selection instead of man. By 1838 he had satisfied himself that if heritable variation occurred, the individuals better adapted to their environment would leave more offspring and thus gradually change the type of the species in the direction of more effective adaptation, but he did not yet know how in nature such a change was enforced. On 28 September of that year he read the *Essay on the Principle of Population*, by T. R. MALTHUS, with that author's (fallacious) argument that in man the geometrical rate of increase must outstrip the rate of increase of means of subsistence, with consequent hardship, misery, and death of the poor. Darwin immediately saw that this argument, translated to the case of plants and animals in nature, which cannot increase their food supply, explained the inevitable mortality that must hit the less efficiently adapted and favour the better adapted. His theory of natural selection of favourable heritable variation, expelling inefficient variants from their ecological niches in the environment, and preserving and improving the favourable variants that were rammed into those niches, was then complete.

Darwin published nothing on this subject for over twenty years, during which he completed the publication of his *Journal of the Voyage of the 'Beagle'*; his geological researches; and a long painstaking research on the species of living and fossil barnacles. In 1856 he began to write out his work on species, but was stunned two years later when he received from Alfred RUSSEL WALLACE a perfect summary of the work on which he had himself been working for twenty-one years. Thanks to the intervention of Charles LYELL and Joseph HOOKER, a joint paper was read before the Linnean

Society of London on 1 July 1858, and in 1859 Darwin at last published his *Origin of Species*. this was followed in 1868 by his *Variation in Animals and Plants under Domestication*; in 1871 *The Descent of Man*; and in 1872 *The Expression of the Emotions in Man and Animals*. These epoch-making books contain Darwin's demonstration of evolution, and many other principles besides, such as sexual selection and animal behaviour.

In 1862 he published his *Fertilization in Orchids*, showing that plants have adaptations no less wonderful than those of animals. This was followed in 1875 by two books which took botanists of the world by surprise: *Insectivorous Plants*, which showed the extraordinary adaptations by means of which a plant like sundew captures, digests, and absorbs the substances of the bodies of flies, and *Climbing Plants*, which not only analysed the processes by which plants 'climb', but also showed their importance as an adaptation whereby plants rapidly reach a height where their leaves are well exposed to sun and air, without the expenditure of time and synthesis of woody material required for the growth of the trunk of an independent tree.

In 1876 Darwin published his *Cross-and Self-Fertilization in the Vegetable Kingdom*, which contained the results of over ten years of experimental breeding and demonstrated the all-important fact that, in the majority of cases, the products of cross-pollination are more numerous, larger, heavier, more vigorous, and more fertile than products of self-pollination. This hybrid vigour is favoured by natural selection, and is explained by modern genetics.

In 1887 *Different Forms of Flowers on Plants of the Same Species* was published, revealing the astonishing dimorphisms and trimorphisms of flowers whereby cross-pollination is ensured. His *Power of Movement in Plants*, published in 1880, describing experiments of exposing shoots and root-tips to light, was the starting-point of the whole science of plant hormones and growth-promoting substances.

Darwin's last work, *The Formation of Vegetable Mould through the Action of Worms* (1881), measured the amount of soil sifted, ground to powder, and raised to the surface by worms in given areas in given times. Its importance is only now realized, after abuse of chemical fertilizers and pesticides has reduced the earthworm population, to the detriment of fertility of soil.

In 1839, Darwin married his first cousin Emma Wedgwood and founded a family whose descendants show not only that intellectual ability has an hereditary component but that given good genes inbreeding is not harmful.

For his work, which places him on the same plane as Isaac NEWTON, Darwin received all possible honours from Academies and foreign governments, but nothing from the British Government except burial in Westminster Abbey, on 26 April 1882. The implications of his work, confirmed by every branch of biology, continue to influence all fields of human endeavour.

Gavin de Beer, *Charles Darwin*. 1963. (Portraits.)
Gavin de Beer, *Atlas of Evolution*. 1964.
Gavin de Beer (Ed.) *Charles Darwin and T. H. Huxley*. 1974.
F. Burkhardt and S. Smith (Eds), *The Correspondence of Charles Darwin*. 1985– (continuing). (Portraits.)
Dictionary of Scientific Biography.
A Desmond and J. Moore, *Darwin*. 1991.

G de B

DARWIN, ERASMUS Born at Elston Hall, Nottinghamshire, England, 12 December 1731; died Derby, 18 April 1802. Physician, scientist, and poet.

After studying at Cambridge, Darwin qualified in medicine at Edinburgh. In 1756 he set up in practice as a doctor at Lichfield, where he was to live for a quarter of a century. His professional skill was generally acknowledged.

A man of tremendous energy and intellectual curiosity, his interests ranged widely in the affairs of science and mechanical invention. Among his inventions were improved designs for a carriage, windmill, oil lamp, and a steam engine. Such versatility established him as the presiding genius of the Lunar Society, one of the most brilliant of intellectual circles in eighteenth century Britain. Its members included such eminent men as Joseph PRIESTLEY, James WATT and his partner Matthew BOULTON, Josiah WEDGWOOD, and William WITHERING. A much more modest assembly was the Botanical Society of Lichfield, which consisted of Erasmus Darwin and two others. Darwin edited translations of the *Systema Naturae* and *Genera Plantarum* of LINNAEUS which the Botanical Society published as *A System of Vegetables* in 1783.

Darwin created a small botanic garden at his home in Lichfield, and his interest in botany produced *The Botanic Garden*, a long poem in heroic couplets which became a best-seller. The first part, *The Economy of Vegetation* (1791) was an introduction to the sciences and crafts of the day; the second part, *The Loves of the Plants*, appeared in 1789, and presented an allegorical account of the Linnean system of plant classification. In this extraordinary work the Linnean classes were personified as husbands and wives etc.

His real claim to distinction rests on *Zoonomia, or the Laws of Organic Life* (1794–6). Primarily a pathological work, the most remarkable part is that in which Darwin states his views on evolution. Believing in the mutability of species, he postulated that all creatures possessing what he called 'lust, hunger, and a desire for security' would organically adapt themselves to their changing surroundings. Similar conclusions were reached by the French naturalist J. B. P. A. de LAMARCK. This theory of the inheritance of acquired characters was to be completely discredited by Erasmus's illustrious grandson, Charles DARWIN.

All his works reveal him as a man whose great originality and intellectual vigour presaged a new scientific era.

D. King-Hele (Ed.), *The Essential Writings of Erasmus Darwin*. 1967.
D. King-Hele, *Erasmus Darwin*. 1963. (Portrait.)
R. E. Schofield. *The Lunar Society of Birmingham*. 1963.
D. King-Hele, *Doctor of Revolution: the Life and Genius of Erasmus Darwin*. 1977.
D. King-Hele (Ed.), *The Letters of Erasmus Darwin*. 1981. (Portrait.)
Dictionary of Scientific Biography.

R G C D

DAVAINE, CASIMIR JOSEPH Born at St Armand-les-Eaux, France, 19 March 1812; died near Paris, 14 October 1882. Contributed to medical bacteriology through his studies on anthrax.

Davaine, son of a distiller, studied medicine in Paris. He became a popular medical practitioner, yet spent much of his time researching in many biological fields; for example, plant pathology, teratology, parasitology and, most significantly, bacteriology.

Davaine, with P. F. O. Rayer (1793–1867), began studying the economically important animal disease anthrax in 1850. There were many conflicting ideas about its cause and Rayer soon reported the presence of 'filiform bodies' (bacteria) in the blood of sheep which had died of the disease. In the next decade a number of observations were made on these bodies, but their significance in relation to anthrax remained confused. Against this background, Davaine began, in 1863, a concentrated attack on the problem, publishing, in the same year, a series of important facts. The most significant of these was that anthracic blood was not infectious if the filiform bodies were absent. The next year Davaine studied the 'malignant pustule', a localized human form of anthrax, and showed microscopically, that organisms found in it were identical in shape to those in the blood of animals suffering from anthrax.

Davaine's character was such that he continued vigorously to expound his views despite the widespread opposition to the germ theory of disease. Furthermore he continued to produce more exacting evidence. For instance, in 1869, he diluted anthracic blood in distilled water and after twenty-four hours he injected the supernatant liquid and the bottom layer containing the bacteria into different guinea pigs. The supernatant liquid failed to produce the disease while the bacterial layer did. In 1873 he studied the effects of many substances on anthrax bacteria both *in vitro* and *in vivo*.

Davaine's studies did much to aid the development of bacteriology and to establish the germ theory of disease in the 1860s and 1870s. However, he was unable to stem all the opposition to the idea that a micro-organism caused anthrax, as he had no knowledge of anthrax spores and could not explain the persistence of the disease and its fresh outbreaks in previously contaminated areas. This was finally unravelled by Robert KOCH and Louis PASTEUR. Perhaps one of the most significant features of his work was his undeniable influence on Pasteur. Possibly the greatest tribute Davaine received was Pasteur's statement to him that 'I pride myself for having so often followed up your own learned research'.

J. Théodorides, *Casimir Davaine et les Débuts de la Bactériologie médicale*. 1963. (Portrait.)
J. Théodoridès, *Un Grand Médecin et Biologiste, Casimir Joseph Davaine*. 1968.
Dictionary of Scientific Biography.

J K C

DA VINCI, LEONARDO See LEONARDO DA VINCI.

DAVY, SIR HUMPHRY Born at Penzance, Cornwall, England, 17 December 1778; died Geneva, Switzerland, 29 May 1829. Famous for his discovery of sodium and potassium, and invention of the miners' safety-lamp.

The son of a Penzance wood-carver, and eldest of five children, Davy attended Truro Grammar School, acquiring an interest chiefly in the classics and poetry. Compelled by his father's early death (1794) to support his family, he entered into an apprenticeship with a Penzance surgeon, Bingham Borlase (d. 1813). Nearly three years later his interest in experimental chemistry was aroused by reading the Traité Elémentaire of LAVOISIER, whose ideas he at once began to test. He concluded that light was not a modification of heat, but a constituent of oxygen, and by rubbing ice blocks together until they began to melt deduced that heat was not a substance (caloric) but a form of motion. These variations on Lavoisier were announced with more confidence than the experiments warranted, and Davy was deeply wounded by the scepticism with which they were greeted.

In 1798 he became an assistant to Thomas BEDDOES at the latter's Pneumatic Institution in Bristol, founded to investigate the therapeutic uses of gases. Here Davy discovered how to prepare pure nitrous oxide and examined its physiological effects. His *Researches ... concerning nitrous oxide* (1800) established his reputation as a chemist. News of his prowess reached Benjamin Thompson, Count RUMFORD, who invited him to the Royal Institution, where he became assistant lecturer (February 1801), lecturer (June 1801), and professor of chemistry (May 1802).

The prospect of a medical career was fast receding, for in 1800 Davy had responded to the 'alarm-bell' sounded by the discoveries of A. VOLTA, and was himself becoming a pioneer in electrochemistry. While still at Bristol he began to study voltaic action and concluded that it was caused by chemical reaction. After moving to the Royal Institution, with its heavy demands upon his time, he was unable (or unwilling) to pursue an intensive study of electricity for some years. But his lectures, particularly on chemistry, were a *tour de force*, and helped to revive the flagging fortunes of the Royal Institution. Required by the Managers to lecture upon agricultural chemistry and upon tanning, and to engage in mineralogical analysis, Davy turned his attention to these matters and produced several papers on them. They consolidated his reputation, but he was capable of greater heights, and his opportunity came in 1806. Free from other responsibilities, in five weeks he performed 108 experiments, mainly on electrolytic transfer (through moist asbestos, etc.), and cleared away a mass of misconceptions on electrolysis. Summarizing his results in his Bakerian Lecture to the Royal Society (1806), he proposed theories of electrolysis and voltaic action, and gave the first important electrical explanation of chemical reactivity.

In the following autumn Davy's belief in the power of electricity to reveal the elements of substances was triumphantly vindicated when he discovered potassium by the electrolysis of fused potash, and a few days later isolated sodium (October 1807). For this work, reported in a second Bakerian Lecture, Davy was awarded Napoleon's Fr3,000 prize for the year's best research on galvanic electricity.

In 1808 he received from J. J. BERZELIUS a letter

reporting that amalgams of the alkaline earth metals had been obtained by electrolysis using a mercury cathode. Davy repeated the experiment, and after distilling off the mercury from the amalgams, isolated magnesium, calcium, strontium, and barium. Stimulated by Berzelius's discovery of 'ammonium amalgam', Davy spent months vainly trying to prove that ammonia (like other bases) contained oxygen. He also looked for this in nitrogen, sulphur, phosphorus, and diamond, and, having demonstrated its absence in 'oxymuriatic acid', decided the latter was probably an element, which he named 'chlorine' (1810). Other discoveries included two chlorides of sulphur, phosphorus pentachloride, and chlorine dioxide.

In many ways 1812 was a watershed in Davy's life. The years of experiment and reflection culminated now in his *Elements of Chemical Philosophy*. A few months later (1813) the 'useful' or 'applied' traditions of the Royal Institution were enshrined in his *Elements of Agricultural Chemistry*. On 8 April 1812 Davy received a knighthood, and three days later married Jane Apreece (1780–1855), a rich Scottish widow. There followed the first of several Continental tours that were to constitute a major distraction to sustained scientific effort. The Davys were accompanied by Michael FARADAY, who had recently been appointed to the Royal Institution. During the tour Davy studied the new element iodine in several French laboratories, examined the combustion of diamond in Florence (using a great lens available there), and while at Rome investigated the pigments of classical art and discovered iodine pentoxide.

On his return home Davy was requested to advise on the problem of coal-mine explosions. After six weeks' intensive study on flame phenomena (the first systematic chemical research on combustion), he produced the safety-lamp that now bears his name. It was an immediate success and is still employed. Davy declined to patent his invention or gain any monetary reward.

A second Continental journey (1818–20) was followed by his election as President of the Royal Society (he had been a Fellow since 1803, Joint Secretary (1807–12), Copley (1805), and Rumford (1818) Medallist). For his last major research he returned to electrochemistry (1824); his suggestion that corrosion of copper sheets on warships could be prevented by attachment of zinc plates was only partially successful, but was the first application of cathodic protection.

In 1827 Davy became seriously ill. He went abroad in 1828, but died a year later at Geneva, after a heart attack in Rome.

A man of many parts, Davy was a founder member of the Geological Society, an expert angler, and a poet of some ability who enjoyed the friendship and respect of Coleridge, Southey, and Wordsworth. Lacking a formal scientific training, however, and distracted by the demands of society and scientific administration, he was incapable of an even performance and 'left only brilliant fragments' (Berzelius). For the safety-lamp, the new science of electrochemistry with the spectacular results already achieved, and the 'discovery' of Faraday, posterity owes much to Davy. Yet in the end he failed to find happiness either in his marriage or in fame.

Dictionary of National Biography, XIV.

J. P. Kendall, *Humphry Davy: 'Pilot' of Penzance*. 1954.
Anne Treneer, *The Mercurial Chemist*. 1963. (Portraits.)
Harold Hartley, *Humphry Davy*. 1966. (Portraits.)
C. A. Russell, *Sir Humphry Davy*. 1972; *Endeavour* (New Series), **2**, 161, 1978.
Sophie Forgan (Ed.) *Science and the Sons of Genius: Studies on Humphry Davy*. 1980. (Portrait.)
D. Knight, *Humphry Davy; Science and Power*. 1992.
Dictionary of Scientific Biography.

C A R

DAY, DAVID TALBOT Born East Rockport, Ohio, USA, 10 September 1859; died Washington, DC, 15 April 1925. Petroleum chemist.

Day was educated at Johns Hopkins University (PhD 1884) and then spent two years as demonstrator in chemistry in the University of Maryland. In 1886 he was appointed head of the Mineral Resources Division of the US Geological Survey, being particularly interested in the differing compositions of natural petroleums, especially those present in shales. He came to the conclusions that these differences arose from percolation through mineral deposits. In the laboratory, he showed that if crude petroleum was allowed to percolate through a column of fuller's earth not only was the filtrate different in composition from the original crude material, but certain major constituents of the latter become separated at different points on the column. He realized that this process was of significance not only to the petroleum industry but to the analytical chemist. It is, in fact, identical with the now widely practised analytical technique known as adsorption chromatography, which was later developed by M. S. TSWETT and others. Day gave a detailed account of his experiments to the First International Petroleum Congress (Paris, 1900).

From 1914 to 1920 Day was consulting chemist to the Bureau of Mines, and during this time began to write his *Handbook of the Petroleum Industry* (1922).

Trevor I. Williams and Herbert Weil, *Arkiv för Kemi*, **5**, 283. 1953.
Dictionary of American Biography.
M. R. Campbell, *Mining and Metallurgy*. June 1925.
Wyndham D. Miles (Ed.), *American Chemists and Chemical Engineers*. 1976.
Dictionary of Scientific Biography.

T I W

DEACON, HENRY Born in London, 30 July 1822; died Widnes, Cheshire, 23 July 1876. Industrial chemist.

Deacon was apprenticed at 14 to the engineering firm of Galloway & Sons of London. He was fortunate in that Michael FARADAY was a close friend of his family, who were Quakers, and took an active interest in his career, not only giving him access to the Royal Institution laboratories in London but personally giving him some tuition. Galloway's failed in 1839, but fortune again favoured Deacon and his indentures were transferred to Nasmyth and Gaskell, on the Bridgewater Canal at Patricroft. James NASMYTH was at that time beginning to construct his great steam hammer, required for building the *Great Britain*; it is said that Deacon made the first model of it, required for patent purposes.

About 1848 Deacon joined Pilkington's glassworks at St Helens, and thus came in close contact with the alkali industry, then rapidly growing in that part of England because of the ready availability of coal, lime and salt. Wishing to strike out on his own, Deacon worked for a time as manager in the chemical works of John Hutchinson (1825–65) and then entered into partnership with one of his former employers, William Pilkington (1800–72); the latter withdrew in 1855 and his place was taken by another former employer of Deacon, Holbrook Gaskell (1813–1909).

Deacon's main activity was to manufacture soda by the process invented by N. LEBLANC. For a time he sought to replace this by the ammonia-soda process (ultimately perfected by E. SOLVAY), but failed to overcome the inherent difficulties and, at the insistence of Gaskell, abandoned the project. He did, however, introduce – in collaboration with his chief chemist F. HURTER – an important improvement in the Leblanc process. By the Deacon process the hydrochloric acid, formerly a waste creating a considerable nuisance, was oxidized catalytically to chlorine, which could be converted with lime to bleaching powder, required in very large quantities by the rapidly expanding textile industry.

J. Fenwick Allen, *Some Founders of the Chemical Industry*. 1907. (Portrait.)

D. W. F. Hardie, *A History of the Chemical Industry in Widnes*. 1950. (Portrait.)

Dictionary of National Biography (Missing Persons). 1993.

                                                    T I W

DE BELIDOR, BERNARD FOREST See BELIDOR.

DE BROGLIE, LOUIS, DUC Born at Dieppe, France, 15 August 1892; died Louveciennes, 19 March 1987. Discovered wave properties of material corpuscles, thus pioneering Wave Mechanics, later to become Quantum Mechanics.

Louis de Broglie, heir to an illustrious family known since the 17th century for outstanding services in Army and Politics, started his University studies with history. Later on, under the influence of his elder brother Maurice de Broglie, a leading specialist in x-rays, Louis de Broglie was drawn to study physics. During the First World War he served in the Radio-télégraphie militaire.

His doctoral thesis, presented in 1924 to a jury chaired by Paul Langevin, can rightly be considered as one of the starting points of modern physics. In this work, following earlier studies published in 1923, de Broglie extended the wave-particle duality, already assumed by EINSTEIN for light, to all material corpuscles. The existence of waves associated with moving electrons, revealed in 1927 by C. J. Davisson (1881–1958) and L. H. Germer (1896–   ) was the experimental proof of Louis de Broglie's ideas of 1924, and brought their author the Nobel prize in 1929.

In 1924 he was appointed lecturer at the Sorbonne. Subsequently he was professor of physics in the Henri Poincaré Institute, returning to the Sorbonne in 1932 as Professor of Theoretical Physics.

After the 1927 Solvay Conference, though, de Broglie had to abide by the probabilistic interpretation of the Copenhagen school led by N. BOHR, M. BORN, and W. HEISENBERG, a theory which he taught for over 30 years in the University of Paris and the Institut Henri Poincaré.

During that time, he published some 45 books on various subjects of physics, among which were *La théorie de la quantification dans la nouvelle mécanique* (1932); *Une nouvelle théorie de la lumière* (1942); and *Nonlinear Wave Mechanics* (1960).

After 1952 though, de Broglie's attitude towards the probabilistic trend in microphysics changed completely, and he returned to the precise causal point of view which was already his before 1927. This causal explanation is contained in his *Théorie de la double solution* which he defended during the rest of his active years.

De Broglie's theoretical ideas are currently being further studied by his former students, and other physicists at the Fondation Louis de Broglie in Paris.

Les Prix Nobel en 1929. 1930. (Portrait.)

Louis de Broglie, physicien et penseur. 1953.

M. A. Tonnelat, *Louis de Broglie et la mécanique ondulatoire*, 1966.

G. Lochak, *Louis de Broglie, un Prince de la Science*. 1992.

Robert L. Weber, *Pioneers of Science: Nobel Prize Winners in Physics*, 1980. (Portrait.)

A. Abragam, *La Recherche*, 23, 918, 1992. (Portraits.)

Tyler Wasson (Ed.), *Nobel Prize Winners*. 1987. (Portrait.)

                                                    C C-D

DE BUFFON, GEORGE LOUIS LECLERC, COMTE See BUFFON.

DEBYE, PETRUS (PIETER) JOSEPHUS WILHELMUS Born at Maastricht, Netherlands, 24 March 1884; died Ithaca, New York, 2 November 1966. Physicist and chemist; notable for work on the theory of electrolytes, and on dipole moments.

Debye studied at the Technical High School, Aachen, and went on to postgraduate work in the University of Munich, where he became *Privatdozent*. Between 1910 and 1939 he occupied Chairs of Physics in Zürich (1910 and 1920), Utrecht (1912), Göttingen (1914), Leipzig (1927), and Berlin (1935). In 1935 he was appointed Director of the Kaiser Wilhelm Institute of Physics in Berlin, but he left Germany just before the war, and for the rest of his working life was professor of chemistry at Cornell University. In 1936 he was awarded a Nobel prize for chemistry.

Although he made notable contributions to experimental physics, Debye was more outstanding as a theoretician. He studied the specific heats of solids at low temperatures, and the relationship between chemical structure and dielectric properties. While at Göttingen he developed, with P. Scherrer (1890–1969), a variant of x-ray crystallography, known by their joint names, which employed a powdered sample instead of the well-formed crystal previously necessary; this method has proved of wide utility. This x-ray work, and parallel studies of electron diffraction, was later applied also to gases.

Debye is chiefly remembered for his work on the theory of electrolytes, and electrolytic dissociation in solution. This work, to which important contributions were made by E. Hückel and L. Onsager, was published in 1923, and is usually known as the Debye-Hückel theory. It was essentially a statistical treatment, in which each ion is considered as surrounded by a stationary atmosphere of ions of opposite charge. It made possible accurate predictions of the behaviour of electrolytes in solutions of almost any concentration, in contrast to the previous simple theories, which could deal only with very dilute solutions.

Much of Debye's later work was concerned with the determination and significance of the dipole moments of simple molecules. He and his school built up this study into a powerful tool for investigating problems of molecular structure and of the distribution of electric charge within the molecule. The results of this work contributed to current theories of the chemical bond.

E. Farber, *Nobel Prizewinners in Chemistry*. 1953. (Portrait.)

Nature, **212**, 1302, 1966.

Biographical Memoirs of Fellows of the Royal Society. 1970. (Portrait.)

Dictionary of Scientific Biography.

W V F

DE CANDOLLE, AUGUSTIN PYRAMUS See CANDOLLE.

DE COULOMB, CHARLES AUGUSTIN See COULOMB.

DEDEKIND, JULIUS WILHELM RICHARD Born in Braunschweig (Brunswick), Germany, 6 October 1831; died there, 12 February 1916. Mathematician; developed redefinition of irrational numbers in terms of arithmetical concepts.

Dedekind trained in higher mathematics at the University of Göttingen (1850–52), then undertook his PhD on Eulerian integrals under K. F. GAUSS. In 1855 he began teaching at Göttingen, broadening his mathematical knowledge through lectures by G. F. B. RIEMANN and P. G. L. Dirichlet (1805–59), while himself furthering methods developed by E. Galois (1811–32) for using groups of substitutions to solve polynomial equations in terms of radicals ($^n\sqrt{}$) on the coefficients. In 1858, Dedekind moved to the Zurich Polytechnikum, returning to Braunschweig Polytechnikum as Professor of Higher Mathematics in 1862, becoming Director in 1872–5 and Professor Emeritus in 1894.

As a result of his own early teaching experience, he realised the need for a truly scientific underpinning of arithmetic. He subsequently developed a redefinition of irrational numbers (e.g. $\sqrt{3}$, which cannot be written as an exact ratio of two integers) in 1858, postulating that both rational and irrational numbers form a continuum in which real numbers are located by 'cuts' (*Schnitt*) in the realm of rational numbers. His full development of the theory was published in 1872. In 1879 he introduced the concept of the ideal (i.e. a collection of all algebraic integer multiples of a given integer), a new treatment of integers enabling factorization to be applied to a wider range of algebraic structures than hitherto.

F. G. Ashurst, *Founders of Modern Mathematics*, 1982. (Portrait.)

Dictionary of Scientific Biography.

C. B. Boyer, *A History of Mathematics*, 1985.

Hv. W. Scharlau, *Richard Dedekind*, 1981. (Portrait.)

R J H

DE FERMAT, PIERRE See FERMAT.

DE FERRANTI, SEBASTIAN ZIANI See FERRANTI.

DE FONTENELLE, BERNARD LE BOVIER See FONTENELLE.

DE FOREST, LEE Born at Council Bluffs, Iowa, USA, 26 August 1873; died at Hollywood, California, 30 June 1961. Electronic engineer.

De Forest graduated in mechanical engineering at Yale University in 1896, but thereafter his life-long interest was in wireless communication: his doctorate (1899) was awarded for a thesis on the 'Reflection of Hertzian Waves'. In this field he was a prolific, though often speculative, inventor, being granted over 300 patents. These ranged widely – from regenerative circuitry to film soundtrack – but undoubtedly his greatest invention was the triode valve (1906). This was an improvement of the diode invented by J. A. FLEMING in 1904. Its essential feature was the insertion of a third, control electrode between cathode and anode. It was a highly effective – indeed revolutionary – device for amplifying weak signals and was a key factor in extending the range and scope of radio communication. Fleming successfully challenged de Forest's patent, claiming that it was no more than an extension of his own diode, but years later (1943) the judgement was overturned.

L. de Forest, *Father of Radio* (autobiography). 1950.

New York Times, 2 July 1961.

Proceedings of the Institute of Radio Engineers, **49**, 22A, 1961.

James A. Hijiya, *Lee de Forest and the Fatherhood of Radio*. 1992.

T I W

DE FOURCROY, ANTOINE FRANÇOIS See FOURCROY.

DE GEER, CHARLES Born at Finspaang, Sweden, 30 January 1720; died Stockholm, 7 March 1778. Entomologist.

Charles de Geer belonged to a family of immigrants from the Low Countries, who acquired great wealth and position in seventeenth-century Sweden. He was educated in Holland, and attended the lectures of P. van Musschenbroek (1692–1761) at Utrecht. Returning to Sweden in 1738, he settled down on an inherited estate, which included very valuable ironworks and forests. He was the first of his family to marry a Swedish wife; he took part in political life, and in 1773 was created a baron.

De Geer's interest in insects was roused at the age of 6 by a gift of silkworms; at 17 he had his first paper, on *Aphrophora salica*, printed by the Swedish Academy of Science, which two years later elected him to membership. He was a very close observer, describing 1446 species of insects, and he excelled his famous predecessor, R. A. F. de RÉUMUR, in the accuracy of the drawings he published, which were the work of his own hand.

Though not particularly interested in systematization, de Geer came under the influence of his near neighbour, LINNAEUS, and was responsible for subdividing the *Hemiptera*. He also brought out clearly the part played by insects as pollen carriers.

De Geer's principal publication was his *Memoires pour servir à l'histoire des insects* (7 vols, 1752, 1771–8), of which he read the last proofs on his death-bed. He bequeathed his collections to the Swedish Academy of Sciences.

S. Lindroth (Ed.), *Swedish Men of Science*, 1650–1950. 1952.

T K D

DE GEER, GERARD JACOB *See* GEER.

DE GENNES, PIERRE-GILLES Born in Paris, 24 October 1932. Theoretical physicist distinguished for his contributions to polymer physics and liquid crystals.

De Gennes was educated at the Ecole Normale Supérieure (1951–5), after which he worked for three years as a research engineer at the Atomic Energy Centre at Saclay, obtaining his PhD in 1957. He spent some time at the University of California (Berkeley) in 1959, before serving for two years in the French Navy.

In 1961, de Gennes was appointed assistant professor in the Université Du Paris Sud (Orsay), switching his interests to liquid crystals in 1968. In 1971, he became professor at the Collège de France and was a participant in STRASACOL, a joint action of Strasbourg, Saclay, and Collège de France in polymer physics. Since 1976 he has been Director, Ecole de Physique et Chimie, at the Collège de France.

De Gennes has made two major contributions to physics: (i) the explanation of anomalous light scattering from nematic liquid crystals; and (ii) the development of a mathematical description of polymer motion (so-called 'reptation') that applies both in liquids during self-diffusion and in solids during crack growth. By seeing common features in very different physical systems, de Gennes has been able to describe many complex systems in general terms.

De Gennes' work was recognised by the award of the Nobel prize for physics in 1991. His current research interests involve surface wetting and adhesion.

J. S. Higgins, *Polymer International*, **27**, 295, 1992.
Barbara Goss Levi, *Physics Today*, December 1991.
(Portrait.)

J N

DE GRAAF, REGNIER Born at Schoonhoven, Netherlands, 30 July 1641; died Delft, 17 August 1673. Physiologist; discoverer of the Graafian follicle in the ovary.

De Graaf studied at the University of Utrecht, and then transferred to Leiden, where he worked under Franciscus SYLVIUS. He then studied in Paris and at Angers, and graduated in medicine at Angers in 1665. Thereafter he set up in practice at Delft, where he also carried on his scientific work. In 1672 he declined a call to succeed Sylvius at Leiden; he died prematurely in the following year.

While still a student under Sylvius, de Graaf was the first to obtain specimens of pancreatic juice. He opened the abdomen of a dog and then ligatured the duodenum above and below the entrances of the bile duct and the pancreatic duct. Into the narrow end of the quill of a wild duck he had inserted a plug of soft wood, attached to which was a thread passing down the quill and hanging from its broad end. He now inserted the narrow end of the quill into the pancreatic duct, and attached a small flask to its broad end; the thread was brought out through a hole in the stopper of the flask. After closing the abdomen he pulled the thread, and pancreatic juice began to drip from the quill into the flask. This was a considerable technical advance, but de Graaf's examination of the juice that he had obtained was disappointing. He thought that the juice effervesced with the bile, and thus removed viscid mucus, that might hinder absorption, from the wall of the stomach. He also thought that the juice might in some way separate the useful from the useless parts of the food. De Graaf's dissertation on this subject was published in 1664.

De Graaf wrote treatises on the male and female sex organs, and his description of these was much in advance of his time. In 1672 he described the ovarian follicle that contains an ovum undergoing maturation, and since the time of Albrecht von HALLER, the structure has been called the Graafian follicle. De Graaf did not appreciate the nature of its contents, for the mammalian ovum was not discovered until 1827 (see K. E. von BAER).

Nouvelle Biographie Générale, vol. 21, 1857.
M. Foster, *Lectures on the History of Physiology*. 1901.
F. H. Garrison, *History of Medicine*. 1929. (Portrait.)

E A U

DE HAVILLAND, SIR GEOFFREY Born near High Wycombe, Buckinghamshire, England, 27 July 1882; died Stanmore, Middlesex, 21 May 1965. Aeronautical engineer and industrialist.

The son of a clergyman, de Havilland was educated at St. Edward's School, Oxford, and trained as a mechanical engineer at the Crystal Palace Engineering School. Following apprenticeship with Willans and Robinson in Rugby (1903–6), he worked for the Wolseley Tool and Motor Car Company in Birmingham and the Motor Omnibus Construction Company. He designed his first aeroplane and engine in 1908–9, and taught himself to fly in 1910. From 1911 to 1914 he worked at the Army Balloon Factory at Farnborough, and became chief designer and test pilot for the Aircraft Manufacturing Company at Hendon in 1914. Commissioned in the Royal Flying Corps at the outbreak of World War I, after three months he returned to the design office, and spent the war designing military aircraft. Of the eight planes he designed, five went into war service in large numbers.

In 1920 he founded the de Havilland Aircraft Company in Hendon, and became famous for the Moth, first produced in 1925, a civilian light aeroplane which, as the Tiger Moth, became the standard RAF training plane in the Second World War. During the war de Havilland developed the Mosquito, an unarmed bomber which for most of the war was the fastest aircraft flying. During the war 14 000 de Havilland planes were produced, half of which were Mosquitos. In 1943 he produced the Vampire, the first British jet-powered plane. After the war he developed the Comet, the first passenger jet-propelled airliner, which went into service in 1952 with BOAC and began a regular transatlantic service in 1958. Despite several accidents to the original model, 110 Comets were built. In 1959 the de Havilland Company won the Elmer A. Sperry award, and shortly after that merged with Hawker Siddeley.

De Havilland, knighted in 1944, never made himself chairman of the company, preferring the title of Technical Director. He was awarded the OM in 1962. Two of his three sons were killed in the air.

R. M. Clarkson, 'Geoffrey de Havilland 1882–1965', *Journal of the Royal Aeronautical Society*, **71**, no.674, 1967.

Sky Fever: The autobiography of Sir Geoffrey de Havilland. 1961.

C. Martin Sharp, *D.H. A History of de Havilland.* 1982. (Portrait.)

Dictionary of National Biography.

A P B

DE JUSSIEU, ANTOINE LAURENT *See* JUSSIEU.

DE LA BECHE, SIR HENRY THOMAS Born in London, (?)1796; died there, 13 April 1855. Eminent geologist, founder of the Geological Survey of Great Britain.

Henry De la Beche was the descendant of an ancient Norman family. As a boy he lived for several years in Devon, then in Dorset, at Charmouth, and later at Lyme Regis. Intending to follow his father's profession, he entered the military school at Great Marlow in 1810, but after the peace of 1815 he left the army. He then committed himself to a geological career, initially as an amateur, for he had moderate means derived from an estate in Jamaica. He joined the Geological Society in 1817 and during the next decade carried out various researches at home and abroad. He wrote short but important papers on the geology of the coastal regions of Dorset and Devon, in which the Jurassic and Cretaceous rocks of that important stretch of country were described for the first time, illustrated by admirable panoramic sections. Similar papers were written on the Pembrokeshire coast and portions of the north and south coasts of France. Visiting Jamaica he studied the geology of the island and wrote the first account of it. All these papers appeared in the *Transactions of the Geological Society* (2nd series, vols. 1–4, published 1822–35).

In addition to particular researches, De la Beche wrote books on general geology which were among the first truly scientific and comprehensive works of their kind. These were *Sections and Views Illustrative of Geological Phaenomena* (1830); *Manual of Geology* (1831 and later editions); and *Researches in Theoretical Geology* (1834). Later in life he wrote his best-known book of this kind, *The Geological Observer* (1851 and later editions).

Towards the end of the 1820s De la Beche began in earnest the chief business of his life, his great abilities and energies being reinforced and directed by professional and official employment and by his expanding vision of the founding of a great national institution. The Ordnance Survey were at that time publishing their one-inch maps, and De la Beche took up the task, at first on his own account, of recording the geological features on those of the south-west country. Thus began the systematic geological survey of Britain which grew, almost entirely by his own efforts, into the official Geological Survey, established in 1835, with himself at its head, and, later, the building of the Museum of Practical Geology in Jermyn Street, opened by the Prince Consort in 1851. His single-handed *Report on the Geology of Cornwall, Devon and West Somerset* (1830) is one of the classics of British geology.

De la Beche was knighted in 1842 and was President of the Geological Society, 1847–9, receiving the Wollaston Medal in 1855. Many honours from abroad were conferred on him. To his scientific qualities were added those of the artist and keen lover of nature. He had great physical strength and energy, and his enthusiasm, combined with his cheerful and sympathetic nature, stimulated all who were associated with him.

Obituary notice by W. J. Hamilton, *Proceedings of the Geological Society*, **12**, xxxiv, 1856.

F. J. North, *Transactions of the Cardiff Naturalists' Society*, **65**, 1932; 67, 1934. (Portrait.)

J. S. Flett, *The First Hundred Years of the Geological Survey of Great Britain.* 1937. (Portrait.)

E. B. Bailey, *Geological Survey of Great Britain.* 1952. (Portrait.)

Dictionary of Scientific Biography.

J C

DE LACAILLE, NICOLAS LOUIS *See* LACAILLE.

DELAMBRE, JEAN BAPTISTE JOSEPH Born at Amiens, France, 19 September 1749; died Paris, 19 August 1822. Astronomer and historian of astronomy and mathematics.

Delambre was educated at Amiens and Paris. After a thorough literary training he turned to mathematics and astronomy. In 1771, while private tutor, he attended lectures by the astronomer J. J. Le F. de Lalande (1732–1807), who persuaded his employer to install an observatory. He was given the prize of the Academy of Sciences for his tables of Uranus (1790; see W. HERSCHEL), and was elected a member shortly after. After the foundation of the French Institute (1795) he became, first a member and later perpetual secretary to the mathematical section, to which he presented an historically valuable 'Report on the progress of mathematics' in 1810.

In his lifetime Delambre was best known for the part he played in the measurement of the meridian arc from Dunkirk to Barcelona (1792–9). A detailed account of the operation, published in three volumes, earned him the Decennial Prize of the Institute in 1810. A comparison of the length of the mean degree of latitude in France (stated as 57 025 toises) with that previously found in Peru gave a value for the degree of flattening of the Earth (1/334).

Delambre has some mathematical results to his credit, including some formulae in spherical trigonometry known by his name (1808; derived independently by K. B. Mollweider (1774–1825) in the same year and by K. F. GAUSS in 1809) and some interpolation formulae for logarithms. His most monumental achievement, however, was a series of histories of astronomy which covered all astronomy then known. Like his notes to N. B. Halma's edition of Ptolemy's *Almagest*, they are distinguished by a meticulous attention to detail.

J. B. J. Fourier, Éloge, *Mémoires de l'Academie des Sciences*, **4**, 1814.

J. St Le Tourneur, in *Dictionnaire de Biographie française*, vol. 10. 1962–5.
Dictionary of Scientific Biography.

J D N

DE LA RUE, WARREN Born in Guernsey, Channel Islands, 18 January 1815; died London, 19 April 1889. Pioneer of astronomical photography.

Warren De la Rue was the son of a Guernsey printer, and spent most of his life assisting in his father's business. Having studied science privately, he became a close friend of A. W. HOFMANN after attending his lectures on practical chemistry in 1845. Prompted by James NASMYTH, he turned to astronomy and built a fine reflector. After 1852 he devoted himself to astronomical photography (starting with daguerreotypes), especially lunar and solar studies. It was with his photo-heliographic telescope, used at Kew (now in the Science Museum, South Kensington, London), that Sir John HERSCHEL's proposals to take daily photographs of the Sun were put into effect. De la Rue's observations made during the Spanish eclipse expedition of 1860, which he directed, proved to the satisfaction of most astronomers that prominences ('red flames') are solar, and not lunar in origin. With Benjamin Loewy and Balfour Stewart (1828–87), both of the Kew Observatory, he subsequently investigated many of the simpler properties of sunspots and faculae.

When in his sixties, De la Rue gave his attention again to chemistry and also the subject of electrical discharge through gases. His very first paper, published when he was 21, had concerned a modified version of the Daniell cell, and now he continued to experiment with chemical batteries. One such battery contained no fewer than 15 000 cells.

De la Rue was a microscopist of some originality. He was honoured by many societies in England and France, and was noted for his encouragement of younger scientists.

Dictionary of National Biography.
Nature, **40**, 27, 1889.
Dictionary of Scientific Biography.

J D N

DE LATOUR, CAGN(I)ARD *See* LATOUR.

DE LAVAL, CARL GUSTAF PATRIK Born at Orsa, Sweden, 9 May 1845; died Stockholm, 2 February 1913. Inventor.

Gustaf de Laval came of a family which had emigrated from France to Sweden in the early seventeenth century; he was educated at the Stockholm Technical Institute and Uppsala University. In 1878 he invented the high-speed centrifugal cream separator, incorporating a turbine, which was successfully marketed and brought into use in large dairies all over the world. He followed this up with various devices for the dairy industry, including a vacuum milking-machine perfected in 1913. De Laval's great achievement, however, lay in his further contribution to the development of the steam turbine, which he completed in 1890 after several years of experimentation. In the absence of reliable data on the properties of steam, de Laval solved the problem of the high velocity by special features in the design of the wheel carrying the vanes of the turbine, and that of direction for the stream of particles by the form given to the nozzle through which the steam jet was produced. In 1892 he proposed the marine use of his turbine, though in practice it could not be built large enough, and in 1909–10 he made it reversible.

De Laval resembled Thomas EDISON in the unfailing vigour and variety of his inventive talent. His interests ranged from electric lighting and electrometallurgy to aerodynamics. In the 1890s he employed over a hundred engineers in developing his devices, and the inventions which are exactly described in his diaries (preserved at the Stockholm Technical Museum) are said to number several thousands.

T. Althin, *Life of de Laval.* 1943.
A centenary memorial publication was issued by the Laval Separator Company at Stockholm in 1945.

T K D

DELBRÜCK, MAX LUDWIG HENNING Born in Berlin, 4 September 1906; died Pasadena, California, USA, 10 March 1981. Physicist and biologist.

Max Delbrück, educated in Berlin, Bonn, and Tübingen in mathematics, physics and astrophysics, graduated in 1929, obtained his PhD in 1930. After working for eighteen months at the H. H. Wills Physics Laboratory in Bristol, he moved to Copenhagen on a Rockefeller Fellowship to work with Niels BOHR and then with Wolfgang PAULI in Zürich before returning to Berlin in 1932 to work with Lise MEITNER at the Kaiser Wilhelm Institute of Biology. Bohr's complementarity concept spurred Delbrück to consider the relation of atomic physics to biology. His work in 1933 on the scattering of gamma rays became known as 'Delbruck scattering' after it had been confirmed in the early 1950s. His contact with physicists as well as biologists led him to the quantitative study of genetics, promoting its eventual transformation from an imprecise discipline to an exact science.

In 1937 Delbrück went to work at the California Institute of Technology under the geneticist T. H. MORGAN and with E. ELLIS on the bacteriophage life cycle, applying mathematical methods. In 1940 he moved to Vanderbilt University, Tennessee to teach physics, (associate professor 1947) but contrived to further his interest in biology by elucidating, with S. E. Luria (1912–91) and A. D. HERSHEY, bacterial resistance to viral infection in terms of bacterial mutation, showing that heredity in microorganisms as well as in complex ones involved genes. This work was carried out at Cold Spring Harbor where he was also instrumental in introducing the prestigious annual Phage Meetings, attracting scientists from various disciplines, which generated many stimulating ideas in molecular biology. In 1981 the Max Delbrück Laboratory for research in genetics was opened. He was professor of biology at Caltech 1947–1977 and then Professor Emeritus, which enabled him to continue his interest in transducer physiology, begun in 1953. In 1961 he helped to establish the Institute of Genetics in Cologne where he lectured as Visiting Professor.

Recipient of many honours, he was awarded (with Luria and Hershey) the Nobel prize for physiology or medicine in 1969.

Biographical Memoirs of Fellows of the Royal Society. 1982. (Portrait.)
Les Prix Nobel en 1969. 1970. (Portrait.)

Physics Today, June 1981
Tyler Wasson (Ed.), *Nobel Prize Winners*. 1987.
(Portrait.)

I M McC

DE LE BOË, FRANZ See SYLVIUS.

DE LESSEPS, FERDINAND MARIE, VICOMTE
See LESSEPS.

DE MARIGNAC, JEAN CHARLES GALISSARD
See MARIGNAC.

DE MAUPERTUIS, PIERRE LOUIS MOREAU See
MAUPERTUIS.

DEMOIVRE, ABRAHAM Born at Vitry, Champagne,
France, 26 May 1667; died London, 27 November
1754. Mathematician, best known for his theorem
in trigonometry.

Demoivre was the son of a surgeon, and being a
Protestant decided to leave France on the revocation of the Edict of Nantes in 1685. Still a student
of mathematics, once in London he was compelled
to support himself by private teaching and by lecturing, on both mathematics and natural science.
He became an intimate friend of NEWTON, whose
Principia he is said to have torn into sheets, so as
to carry around a few at a time, mastering them in
his spare moments. Demoivre spent most of his
life in poverty, outliving most of his friends. His
mathematical talents were, however, widely recognized in his lifetime, and after admission to the
Royal Society (1697) he was made a member of the
Berlin and Paris Academies.

Demoivre published a number of papers in the
Philosophical Transactions, and his first book was
on probability (*Doctrine of Chances*, 1718). This
included several innovations, in a branch of
mathematics which only properly began with Jean
BERNOULLI's *Ars conjectandi* of five years before. In
particular, its contains methods for approximating
to functions of large numbers, which later led him
to the notion of the normal distribution curve. In
1725, he published *Annuities on Lives*, which
might be taken as the first important mathematical
work on that subject. It is, however, based on a
law of mortality differing little from one devised
by John Hudd in 1671.

Demoivre was one of the first to make use of
complex numbers in trigonometry. By 1707 he was
in possession of the relation (modern symbolism)

$$2 \cos \theta = (\cos n\theta + i \sin n\theta)^{1/n} + (\cos n\theta - \sin n\theta)^{1/n}$$

which is closely connected with his theorem

$$(\cos \theta + i \sin \theta)^n = \cos n\theta + i \sin n\theta$$

by which he is chiefly remembered. Some related
work by Roger Cotes (1682–1716) was published
posthumously in the same year. These important
results, enlarged upon by L. EULER some twenty
years later, were instrumental in shifting trigonometry from the province of geometry to that of
analysis.

H. M. Walker, 'Abraham de Moivre', *Scripta
Mathematica*, **2**, 316, 1934.
Dictionary of Scientific Biography.

J D N

DE RÉAUMUR, RENÉ ANTOINE FERCHAULT
See RÉAUMUR.

DESARGUES, GÉRARD Born at Lyons, France, 2
March 1593; died there, 1662. French engineer
and mathematician who originated projective
geometry.

Desargues worked as engineer to the Government and was technical adviser to Richelieu,
taking part in the siege of La Rochelle.

The theory of perspective had been formed by
artists, engineers, and so on since the beginning of
the Renaissance: Desargues combined many
theorems on perspective in a form that could be
useful to such people. In 1636 he published his
Traité de la section perspective. He followed this in
1639 with the *Broullion projet d'une atteinte aux
évenements des rencontres d'une cone avec un
plan*, dealing principally with conic sections and
containing most of his important mathematical
results. The fundamental concepts of synthetic
geometry appear – a straight line regarded as a
circle of infinite radius, parallels intersecting at
points of infinity; a type of involution is defined,
with its properties demonstrated; polarity is
described. His ideas, however, were far ahead of
his time, and his influence, except on Blaise PAS-
CAL, little. In the same way, in 1640, the publication of *La coupe des pierres en l'architecture*
brought him into violent controversy with contemporary architects and his views were rejected.

His range was not restricted to engineering and
geometry: he was a lover of music, writing a
manual on composition which was published by
M. Mersenne (1588–1648).

Although Desargues's work was disregarded in
his lifetime, his work was continued by Pascal and
P. de Lahire (1640–1718). It was not until the nineteenth century, however, following the resurgence
of synthetic geometry under G. MONGE that
Desargues's ideas were accepted and developed.

R. Taton, *L'Oeuvre mathématique de Desargues*.
1951.
Dictionary of Scientific Biography..

D N

DE SAUSSURE, HORACE BÉNÉDICT See
SAUSSURE.

DESCARTES, RENÉ (latinized as **RENATUS
CARTESIUS**) Born at La Haye, Touraine, France,
31 March 1596; died Stockholm, 11 February 1650.
Philosopher of great originality, noted particularly
for his analytical geometry.

Descartes was the son of Joachim Descartes, a
Counsellor in the Parliament of Rennes. From 1604
to 1612 the boy studied at the Jesuit school of La
Flèche. He subsequently visited Paris, where he
met the mathematician Claude C. Mydorge (1585–
1647) and renewed the acquaintance of the natural
philosopher Father Marin Mersenne (1588–1648).
When Mersenne left Paris in 1614, Descartes
turned to a serious study of mathematics from what
had hitherto been a gay social life. In May 1617
his studies were interrupted when he set out for
the Netherlands to enlist in the army of the Prince
of Orange. There he met Isaac Beeckman (1588–
1637), Principal of the College at Dort, who became
his close friend, but who later claimed as his own
an essay on music, *Compendium Musicae*, which
Descartes had written at this time.

Campaigning in the Netherlands ceased temporarily, and, bored with inactivity, Descartes left for

Germany, where he entered the Bavarian service in 1619. In the winter of that year he received what has since become his famous philosophical conversion 'in a warm room' – or as some versions have it, 'in an oven' – (dans un poêle). His thoughts are embodied in his *Discours de la méthode* (1627).

After visiting his family home, and making an extended tour of Switzerland and Italy, Descartes settled in Paris for a time (1625). From mathematics his interests had now turned to optics. Apart from an episode when he took part in the seige of La Rochelle (October 1628), he lived in Paris until 1629, when he moved to Holland. There he lived for the next twenty years, visiting France briefly on only three occasions. From Holland he conducted a prolific scientific correspondence with Mersenne, dealing not only with mathematical and physical problems, but also with the theory of music. He studied astronomy, meteorology, and anatomy, as well as optics, paying at least lip-service to Francis BACON's principle of the need to base science on observation and experiment. In astronomy he accepted the system of COPERNICUS, and believed in the infinity of the Universe. He was on the point of completing a work on these lines when he heard of the condemnation of GALILEO (1633). This led him to abandon his book, which he had intended to dedicate to Mersenne, and not until after his death were parts of it published as *Le Monde, ou Traité de la Lumière* (1664). Other works written at this time, and published posthumously in the same year, are the physiological treatises *L'Homme* and *De la formation du foetus*. His philosophical views, first expressed in the *Discours*, were elaborated in *Méditations métaphysiques* (1641), and *Les Principes de la Philosophie* (1644). In the last of these the Copernican theory is adumbrated in a disguised form: the Earth is carried round the Sun in an immense vortex of subtle matter. The Earth moves round the Sun and yet is at rest with respect to the matter surrounding it!

Opposition to Descarte's philosophy, especially the passages in which an attempt was made to prove the existence of God, became more vehement as the years went by. Irritated by the attitude of those around him, and saddened at the deaths of Mersenne and Mydorge, in 1649 Descartes left Holland for Stockholm and the court of Queen Christina, but he died there of pneumonia within five months.

Descartes's science cannot be properly understood without prior reference to his philosophy. He began by systematically doubting everything, before submitting it to his criterion of truth, namely the clearness and distinctness of ideas. Truths which passed the test ('self-evident') were used as premises for other truths. The first reality of which he was assured was that of the thinking self: he could not doubt his own existence – hence the famous aphorism 'I think, therefore I am' (*cogito ergo sum*). He admitted three kinds of substance: God; the Soul-substance of individual men; and created bodies. The last had existence independently of human thought, and their principal property was that of extension. Cartesian physics regards all bodies as resulting from the vortical structure of extension itself. The universe is considered as a mechanical system actuated by God, the First Cause of all motion. Even bodies of animals were held to be automata. He used the work

of VESALIUS and William HARVEY (although occasionally differing from their conclusions) in presenting the workings of the body in mechanical terms. One of the difficulties of his system was that of explaining the interaction of mind and the human body. They interacted, he believed, through the medium of the pineal gland, chosen because it was thought to be the one organ possessed by man but not the lower animals. Descartes's philosophical influence, even as it concerns science, was far too extensive to be outlined in a few words. Well into the lifetime of NEWTON the majority of important scientists regarded themselves as in many ways his disciples.

The essence of the analytic method in geometry is the study of geometric loci by means of their equations. In a sense, the Greeks had known analytic geometry, and claims have also been advanced on behalf of P. FERMAT. Descartes's algebraic symbolism, however, endowed his system with sufficient power for it to be manipulated with ease by mathematicians less competent than Menaechmus (*fl.* 365–350 B.C.), APOLLONIUS and Fermat – hence our name 'Cartesian geometry'. Like Fermat, Descartes found profitable a study of a problem set by PAPPUS. Like all before him, he failed to find a solution by the methods of pure geometry, but in the five or six weeks spent on the problem in 1633 he appears to have formulated the most important parts of his analytical geometry. Abbreviated versions of several related proofs are to be found in *La Géométrie* (1637). Book III of this work is given over to the solution of equations of a higher degree than second by finding the intersections of curves. This is again interesting in that it harks back to the Greek geometers. The third book as a whole is more or less a review of the existing state of algebra, and shows little originality, although worth mentioning on account of the rule now known as 'Descartes' Rule of Signs' in the theory of equations. This was known in an incomplete form to CARDANO, and his own enunciation, with several shortcomings, was criticized by G. P. de Roberval (1602–1675) and J. WALLIS. Thomas HARRIOT had the rule, however, in his *Artis analyticae praxis* (posthumously published, 1631). The intentional obscurity of the first edition of the *Géométrie* prevented its becoming popular at once, but after being translated (1659) into Latin by F. de Beaune (1601–52), and given a commentary by P. van Schooten (1634–79), its fame, like the Descartes legend, grew by geometrical progression.

Descartes's physical theories, found in *La Dioptrique* (1637), *Les Météores* (1637), and *Les Principes de la Philosophie* (1644), ultimately rest, as explained, on the metaphysics to be found in the *Méditations*. In *Le Monde* and *Les Principes* are to be found a crude form of the law of conservation of momentum, and a modern expression of the law of inertia, as well as many less satisfactory laws of impact. In optics, his ambition was to determine the shape of a lens capable of eliminating spherical aberration in order to improve the performance of the newly invented telescope. His solution was mathematically brilliant, but beyond the capabilities of existing grinding technique. His derivation relied on his first finding the correct law of refraction of light, which some have held to have been lifted from a manuscript by Willebrord SNELL. Descartes used this, furthermore, in a generally good account of the rainbow – a phenomenon not fully explained until the discovery by Newton of the dependence of refractive index on colour. In all his science, however, Descartes was a rationalist who allowed his observations and his experimental findings to be subordinated to *a priori* principles. His great strength lay in his incisive treatment of existing problems, and in science, if not philosophy, he was most successful where the problem had been carefully formulated by others.

> J. F. Scott, *The Scientific Work of René Descartes.* 1952 (Paperback 1976).
> L. J. Beck, *The Method of Descartes.* 1952.
> *Endeavour*, **9**, 107, 1950.
> *Dictionary of Scientific Biography.*

J D N

DESCH, CYRIL HENRY Born in London, 7 September 1874; died there, 19 June 1958. Metallurgist.

C. H. Desch attended St John's School, Tottenham, and later Birkbeck School, Kingsland, where he received a good grounding in science, especially in chemistry. He entered the City and Guilds College, London, under the principalship of Silvanus Thompson (1851–1916), and having decided on chemistry as a career joined a firm of industrial chemists. While there he took an external London BSc degree and shortly afterwards worked in Germany, obtaining a PhD of Würzburg University (1902). Returning to England, he studied at University College, London, under Sir William RAMSAY, where he obtained a DSc. His knowledge of metallography, acquired when he was an industrial chemist, was of use to him when Sir Flinders Petrie (1853–1942) asked him to work on metal implements found during excavations at Ur; he acquired a lasting interest in archaeology at this time.

In 1902 he joined the staff of King's College, London, and six years later became lecturer in metallurgical chemistry at Glasgow University under Professor John Ferguson (1837–1916). It was here that he wrote in 1910 his outstanding work, *Textbook of Metallography*, which went through many impressions and editions. In 1911 a research committee was set up under Sir George BEILBY to examine the question of solidification of metals, with Desch as chief investigator. His skilful reports aroused great attention in the metallurgical field, and in 1918 he was appointed to the Chair of Metallurgy at the Royal Technical College, Glasgow. In 1920 he left to become professor of metallurgy at Sheffield. In 1932 he was appointed Superintendent of the Metallurgy Department of the National Physical Laboratory, where he remained until his retirement in 1939.

Though he is best known for his textbook of metallography, his contributions to metallurgy range widely and are to be found in many publications covering solidification, corrosion, metal fatigue, and the chemistry of metal alloys.

> *Biographical Memoirs of Fellows of the Royal Society.* 1959. (Portrait.)
> *Dictionary of National Biography (Missing Persons).* 1993.

N H

DÉSORMES, CHARLES BERNARD Born at Dijon, France, 3 June 1777; died Verberie, Oise, 30 August 1862. Chiefly remembered for his work on the specific heats of gases carried out in collaboration with his son-in-law, Nicolas Clément.

After entering the *École Polytechnique* on its foundation in 1794, Désormes was a student and demonstrator under L. B. Guyton de Morveau (1737–1816) till 1804. Désormes and Guyton are credited with suggesting the fruitless theory that potash and soda were compounds of hydrogen with lime and magnesia respectively; Désormes also wrote on electrochemistry (1801 and 1804) alone, and, in 1802, with J. N. P. Hachette (1769–1834). It is, however, for his joint papers with his son-in-law Nicolas Clément (later Clément-Désormes (1779–1841) with whom he and the MONTGOLFIERS were co-owners of a chemical factory at Verberie, that Désormes is best known. The two recognized the qualitative composition of carbon disulphide (published 1802), and explained the action of nitric oxide as a catalyst in the lead chamber process for sulphuric acid (1806). They also carried out extensive work on carbon monoxide which they discovered in 1801, and on iodine and its compounds (1813). But their most famous work was on the specific heats of gases – published in 1819, but largely foreshadowed in a memoir submitted in 1812 to the *Institut de France* for a prize, which they did not, in fact, win. The paper of 1819 is notable for the first determination of the ratio of the principal specific heats of gases by adiabatic compression, and for its respectful view of the work of John DALTON on heat.

For this paper, Désormes was elected a corresponding member of the Academy of Sciences of Paris, but 1824 marks the last joint scientific paper with his son-in-law. From 1830 Désormes turned to politics, being elected *Conseiller Général* for l'Oise (1830), sitting with the republicans in the *Assemblée Constituante* (1848) and publishing works of local social and political interest (1834, and 1851), including a journal *La Revue de l'Oise* (later *Le Progrès de l'Oise*).

> *Dictionnaire de Biographie Française*, vol. 10. 1965.
> *Dictionary of Scientific Biography.*

G R T

DE VAUBAN, SEBASTIEN LE PRESTRE *See* VAUBAN.

DE VAUCANSON, JACQUES *See* VAUCANSON.

DEVILLE, HENRI ÉTIENNE SAINTE-CLAIRE Born at St Thomas, West Indies, 11 March 1818; died near Paris, 1 July 1881. Chemist and teacher.

While studying medicine in Paris, Deville became attracted to chemistry; he was largely self-taught, and his early work was on turpentine and other natural products. In 1845 he was appointed to a Chair in Besançon, where he made his name by the isolation of crystalline nitrogen pentoxide. He returned to Paris in 1851 as Professor in the *École Normale Supérieure*; he also lectured in the Sorbonne, and was later made titular Professor there. He was evidently a splendid teacher, and much loved by his students. The end of his life was clouded by ill health, partly due to overwork; he finally took his own life.

Deville is best known for his work on the production of aluminium, and for his studies of dissociation. Although small quantities of crude metallic aluminium had been prepared by F.

WÖHLER, Deville was the first to prepare the pure metal in bulk, by reduction of the chloride with potassium (later sodium). He put this process on an industrial basis, but then left its further development to others. But the experience he gained led to important work in many directions: the large-scale production of sodium; the preparation of silicon, boron, and titanium; the design of high-temperature furnaces; the separation of the platinum metals; and the synthesis of artificial minerals. His extensive measurements of vapour density at high temperatures (from 1857, with L. J. Troost (1825–1911) and others) led to the realization that many compounds undergo reversible dissociation; this was of great significance for the infant science of chemical kinetics.

E. Farber (Ed.), *Great Chemists*. 1961. (Portrait.)
Nature, **24**, 219, 1881.
Journal of the Chemical Society, 235, 1882.
J. Gay, *Henri Sainte-Claire Deville, sa vie et ses travaux*. 1889.
Chymia, **3**, 205, 1950.
Dictionary of Scientific Biography.

W V F

DE VRIES, HUGO *See* VRIES.

DEWAR, SIR JAMES Born at Kincardine-on-Forth, Scotland, 20 September 1842; died London, 27 March 1923. A pioneer of low-temperature studies.

In 1859 Dewar went to Edinburgh University, and studied under J. D. Forbes (1809–68), Lyon PLAYFAIR, whose demonstrator he became, and Alexander CRUM BROWN. In 1867 he exhibited to the Royal Society of Edinburgh 'a simple mechanical arrangement adapted to illustrate structure in the non-saturated hydrocarbons'. This apparatus of brass rods, representing valence bonds, indicated seven possible formulae for benzene, including the structures proposed by F. A. KEKULÉ, with alternate double and single bonds, and the excited forms now known as Dewar structures. Kekulé invited Dewar to Ghent, and he spent the summer of 1867 there. In 1869 he became lecturer in chemistry at the Royal (Dick) Veterinary College, Edinburgh, but he continued to assist Crum Brown as well until 1873, when he was appointed Assistant Chemist to the Highland and Agricultural Society of Scotland. This post entailed what he called peripatetic lecturing. Then, in 1875, he was elected to the Jacksonian Professorship of Natural Experimental Philosophy and Chemistry at Cambridge University; and in 1877 to the Fullerian Professorship at the Royal Institution, London. He held both chairs until his death, but because laboratory facilities at that time in Cambridge were poor, his researches were largely carried out in London.

In Cambridge he became a friend of G. D. Liveing (1827–1924), and together they performed a series of important researches on spectroscopy which occupied over twenty-five years. In 1877 Dewar began working on the liquefaction of gases. He had about five years earlier invented that indispensable tool the vacuum flask, in the course of work on the specific heat of 'hydrogenium', that is, hydrogen absorbed in palladium. In 1874 Dewar had published with P. G. Tait (1831–1901) a paper on the use of charcoal as an absorbent in the achievement of high vacua. In 1905 he discovered that the absorbency of charcoal greatly increases at low

temperatures, and highly cooled charcoal was used to achieve high vacua by Dewar in making vacuum flasks, and by workers in atomic physics. In 1878 Dewar demonstrated the apparatus of L. P. CAILLETET for the partial liquefaction of oxygen, before an audience at the Royal Institution; from then on he set about trying to reach lower and lower temperatures, and in particular to liquefy hydrogen and, later, helium. At first he relied on 'cascade' processes, in which the cooling is done in stages with different refrigerants, but from 1895 he employed the Joule-Thomson effect – the cooling produced when an already-chilled gas under pressure is allowed to expand.

In that year he cooled hydrogen to −200 °C using liquid air boiling under reduced pressure; compressed it to 200 atmospheres; and expanded it through a nozzle. Liquid could be seen but not collected. He therefore built a much larger liquid-air machine, and succeeded in 1898 in producing liquid hydrogen in quantity. The next problem was to liquefy helium, discovered on Earth by William RAMSAY in 1895, many years after it had been identified in the Sun by Sir Norman LOCKYER and E. FRANKLAND. Dewar used helium derived from the springs at Bath, in Somerset, cooling it with liquid hydrogen. Unfortunately this helium contained also neon, which froze and blocked the valves, and helium was first liquefied by H. Kamerlingh ONNES, using Dewar's techniques, in 1908.

Dewar was elected FRS in 1877, and was knighted in 1904. He was married in 1871, but there were no children. He had artistic tastes, and was a connoisseur of wine and tobacco. He was brusque in manner on occasion, highly individualistic, and not capable of working in a team. Though as a formal teacher he was indifferent, as a public lecturer he was very good. He was essentially an experimental scientist rather than a theoretician.

Dictionary of National Biography.
Proceedings of the Royal Society, A, **II**, xiii, 1926. (Portrait.)
A. Findlay and W. H. Mills (Ed.), *British Chemists*. 1947. (Portrait.)
Nature, **111**, 472, 1923.
Dictionary of Scientific Biography.

D M K

DICKE, ROBERT HENRY Born in St Louis, Missouri, USA, 6 May 1916. Astrophysicist.

After graduating in physics in the University of Princeton (1939) and Rochester (1941) Dicke joined the Radiation Laboratory of the Massachusetts Institute of Technology, doing development research on microwave radar. In 1946 he returned to Princeton, where he was appointed professor of physics in 1957. In 1964 he predicted, on the basis of the Big Bang theory, that space should be permeated with a remanent radiation in the microwave region of the electromagnetic spectrum. Unaware of this, A. O. PENZIAS and R. W. Wilson almost simultaneously detected experimentally such radiation, corresponding to that emitted by a black body at 3.5 K. Unknown to any of them, G. GAMOW had made a similar prediction in 1948. Dicke studied coherent radiation processes and in telecommunications is remembered for the Dicke radiometer, a sensitive device for detecting weak signals against loud background noise. In 1961 he developed a modified relativistic theory of gravitation: he showed that gravitational and inertial mass were equal to within one part in 10^{11}.

Edgardo Macorini (Ed.), *Scienziati e Tecnologi Contemporanei*. 1974. (Portrait.)

Allen G. Debus (Ed.) *Who's Who in Science*. 1968.

T I W

DIDEROT, DENIS Born at Langres, France, 5 October 1713; died Paris, 30 July 1784. Editor of the great *Encyclopédie*.

Diderot was the son of a master cutler, and received his first education at a Jesuit school, where he showed exceptional brilliance. Destined for the Church, he attended the Jesuit *Collège Louis-le-Grand* in Paris; in 1732 he was awarded a MA of the University of Paris. He did not go into orders, but became an articled clerk in a Paris office, where his studies in law proved less attractive than those of mathematics and languages. He left, and little is known of his activities during the next ten years, except that he did some writing and mixed with the café intelligentsia, among them Jean-Jacques Rousseau. In 1743 he contracted an unhappy marriage. He continued as a publisher's hack and made some translations from English, including one of the *Dictionary of Medicine* of Robert James (1705–76). On the strength of this work he was in 1745 asked to translate Ephraim Chambers's *Cyclopaedia*. This, though a useful work, could not be called controversial, but it sparked off in Diderot a desire to produce an altogether different work, in which all the ideas that he had absorbed in the previous ten years could be formulated in a work of encyclopaedic dimensions. He was able to put this into effect and to enlist the help of revolutionary thinkers of the period. J. Le Rond D'ALEMBERT acted as co-editor at the beginning, but resigned in 1758 after an attack by Rousseau – with whom Diderot also quarrelled – on one of his articles. The lavishly illustrated *Encyclopédie ou Dictionnaire Raisonnée des Sciences, des Arts et des Métiers* (1751–72, 28 vols) – generally described as the literary monument of the Enlightenment – sought to present knowledge as a unified whole and placed emphasis on the progress of the human mind. The work was subject to attack from the Establishment, particularly in clerical circles, and the publisher removed what he considered the more inflammatory passages. But the work that remained is a landmark in the progress of science and technology, and a remarkable achievement in terms of intellectual span and tenacity on the part of its begetter and principal contributor. In his main scientific writings, apart from the *Encyclopédie* – notably *Pensées sur L'Interpretation de la Nature*, *Entretien entre d'Alembert et Diderot* and *Elements de Physiologie* – Diderot appears as a kind of precursor of the evolutionary theory. Though his scientific theories are of interest in themselves, their main value lies in the work of synthesis and brilliant exposition behind them.

Diderot was a prodigious writer, and was the author also of numerous plays, novels, and works of criticism. These are characterized by a wit and insight that redeems their lack of polish.

J. Morley, *Diderot and the Encyclopaedists* (2 vols). 1878.

J. Kemp (Ed.), *Diderot, Interpreter of Nature*. 1937.

C. C. Gillispie (Ed.), *A Diderot Pictorial*

Encyclopaedia of Trades and Industry (2 vols). 1959.

Endeavour (New Series), **8**, 107, 1984.

Dictionary of Scientific Biography.

N H

DIELS, OTTO Born at Hamburg, Germany, 23 January 1876; died Kiel, 7 March 1954. Organic chemist, one of the discoverers of the Diels-Alder reaction.

Diels was the son of the great classical scholar Hermann Diels (1848–1922). He studied chemistry at the University of Berlin under Emil FISCHER, becoming titular professor in 1906. Ten years later he was appointed to a chair at Kiel, which he held until his retirement in 1948. During the Second World War two of his sons were killed on the Eastern Front, and his home and his Department were destroyed in air attacks. Although he wished to retire in 1945, he remained in office, through a period of great difficulty, to begin the rebuilding of the university.

Diels first made his name as an organic chemist by the unexpected discovery of carbon suboxide (1906), by removing the elements of water from malonic acid. He was also active in the then little-understood field of sterol chemistry, and made important advances by his method of selenium dehydrogenation. This drastic process converted sterols into aromatic hydrocarbons, and the later elucidation of the structure of one of these ('Diels' hydrocarbon') was a vital step in the identification of the sterol skeleton. It was another line of work, on the reactions of azo-dicarboxylic ester, which eventually led him in 1928 (with his assistant Kurt ALDER) to the discovery of the 'Diels-Alder reaction'. This versatile reaction involves the addition of a conjugated diene to a large class of unsaturated compounds (dienophiles), to give, typically, a six-membered ring compound. It is of the greatest utility in organic synthesis, and important in the petrochemical industry.

Diels and Alder were jointly awarded the Nobel prize for chemistry in 1950.

Chemische Berichte, **95**, v, 1962. (Portrait.)

E. Farber, *Nobel Prizewinners in Chemistry*. 1953. (Portrait.)

Les Prix Nobel en 1950. 1951. (Portrait.)

Dictionary of Scientific Biography.

Tyler Wasson (Ed.), *Nobel Prize Winners*. 1987. (Portrait.).

W V F

DIESEL, RUDOLF Born in Paris, 18 March 1858; died at sea, 29/30 September 1913. Engineer, remembered for the design and construction of the diesel engine.

After the Battle of Sedan (1870) Germans had to leave Paris, and Diesel and his parents went to England. They lived in poverty, and after a very short time Diesel was sent to stay with an uncle at Augsburg. He attended school there until, in 1875, he went to the *Technische Hochschule* in Munich, where he studied thermodynamics under Carl Von LINDE. He graduated and in 1880 went to Paris to work for Linde's firm, which was building refrigeration plant. In the following year he was promoted to plant manager, and in this position he became interested in the design of an expansion engine based on ammonia. It was unsuccessful, but it paved the way for his later developments. In 1890 he moved to a new post in Berlin, but was still connected with Linde's refrigeration equipment.

About 1890, Diesel conceived the idea for his new engine, and in 1892 he obtained the German patent for it. In a paper entitled *The Theory and Design of a Rational Heat Engine* (1893), he published an account of it, and persuaded two great firms – Maschinenfabrik, of Augsburg, and Krupp, of Essen – to support him in its development. From 1893 to 1897 this was his main concern. In 1897 he was satisfied with his work, and an independent test by Professor M. Schröter (b. 1851) confirmed the engine's efficiency. It was displayed in the Munich exhibition in 1898, and interest in it was world-wide. Diesel early became a millionaire. In 1899 a new factory was founded at Augsburg for building the engines, but owing to Diesel's ill health it was a failure. Nevertheless, development work continued in the works of Maschinenfabrik at Augsburg; of Nobel at St Petersburg; and in France.

In the diesel engine air is compressed to a high pressure, and during this process it becomes hot enough to ignite the fuel, which is sprayed into the cylinder at the end of the compression stroke. There is, therefore, an expansion of the gases which accompanies the downward movement of the piston, and, in consequence, there is no sudden increase of pressure in the cylinder. The diesel engine differs in this respect from that of N. A. OTTO, in which combustion takes place while the volume is constant. The diesel engine uses a heavy oil and is very economical.

Diesel died before his invention was fully exploited; he was drowned after falling overboard from the Antwerp-Harwich mail steamer *Dresden*.

E. Diesel, *From Engines to Autos*. 1960. (Portrait.)

E. Diesel, *Diesel. Der Mensch, das Werk, das Schiksal*. 1937. (Portrait.)

Scientific American, **221**, 108, 1969.

W. R. Nitske and C. M. Wilson, *Rudolf Diesel: Pioneer of the Age of Power*. 1965.

B B K

DIGGES, LEONARD AND THOMAS Leonard,
born 1520 (?) in England, probably in Kent; died in England 1559. Thomas, his son, born in England, 1546 (?); died there 1595. Leonard is credited with the invention of the telescope, Thomas with promoting it and for proposing an infinite Universe.

Leonard Digges, educated at Oxford University, was noted as an applied mathematician, surveyor, and author. His books were all written in English. The first, *A Generall Prognostication*, appeared initially in 1553; a perpetual calendar with much astronomical, meteorological, and other information – together with an explanation of the Earth-centred Universe of PTOLEMY – it was a best seller, went into many editions, and later changed its title to *Prognostication everlasting*. In 1556 his *Tectonicon* on land surveying came out. A third book *Pantometria* appeared posthumously at the hands of his son; it became a seminal work.

By theoretical and experimental research, Leonard devised a reflecting telescope, and almost certainly the refracting telescope as well. In 1554 he was condemned to death for engaging in the unsuccessful rebellion led by Sir Thomas Wyatt, but his sentence was commuted to loss of his estates. He spent the next four years redeeming his property, dying a year later.

His son Thomas, who was about thirteen when Leonard died, had the mathematician John Dee (1527–1608) as his guardian, as his father had wished. Like his father, Thomas made extensive use of Dee's library, noted for over a thousand manuscripts, including important 12th century works on optics. Thomas published his first mathematical work, *Aleu seu Scalae Mathematicae* in 1571. In the same year he produced his father's *Pantometria* in which he openly speaks of Leonard's theoretical and mathematical work on the telescope, and thereafter continued to write only in English. He observed the supernova of 1572, Tycho BRAHE later making use of his excellent observations.

In 1576 Thomas published a new edition of Leonard's *Prognostication everlasting*. This contained Thomas's promotion of the Sun-centred theory of COPERNICUS and, even more significantly, his concurrent announcement that the Universe is infinite. This was probably the result of observations with a telescope.

Thomas was also twice a Member of Parliament, a government advisor and, from 1586 to 1593, Muster-Master General to the English forces in the Netherlands.

Independent confirmation of the work of Leonard and Thomas Digges on the telescope is to be found in a report of the 1570s by William Bourne (d. 1583) to Lord Burghley and in Bourne's *Inventions or Devises* published in 1578.

Journal of the British Astronomical Association, **101** (6), 335, 1991.

L. Digges and T. Digges, *Pantometria*. 1571.

L. Digges and T. Digges, *Prognostication everlastinge*. 1576.

W. Bourne, *Inventions or Devises*. 1578.

Colin A. Ronan, *Endeavour* (New Series), **16**, 91, 1992; **17**, 177, 1993.

Dictionary of Scientific Biography.

C A Ro

DIOPHANTUS Flourished in Alexandria, probably
c.AD 250. Mathematician; author of the *Arithmetica*, the earliest systematic treatise on what would now be called algebra.

Of the thirteen books of the *Arithmetica*, only six survive. These consist almost entirely of problems leading to equations, both determinate and indeterminate, the solutions of which constitute the main interest of the work. It was Diophantus who first employed a conventional algebraic notation; instead of denoting quantities and operations by complete words, he used a special sign for the unknown quantity, though this sign was probably an abbreviation and not a purely conventional symbol. As there was but one sign for the unknown, Diophantus could consider only one such quantity at a time. Powers and reciprocals of the unknown were denoted by the initial letters of corresponding words. He indicated the addition of two quantities by writing them in juxtaposition, but he had a special symbol to indicate subtraction. Coefficients of a quantity were written (in alphabetic numerals) after the sign for the quantity. There was a special sign to denote equality. Diophantus dealt throughout with particular cases and did not attempt to establish general rules for the solution of equations. He recognized only real, rational, and positive roots and avoided equations giving any other kind of value for the unknown.

A fragment survives of a tract by Diophantus on polygonal numbers; and he is believed to have compiled a collection of propositions on porisms. Nothing is known of his life.

T. L. Heath, *A History of Greek Mathematics*, vol. 2. 1921.

T. L. Heath, *Diophantus of Alexandria* (2nd ed.) 1910.

American Mathematical Monthly, **63**, 163, 1956.

Dictionary of Scientific Biography.

A A

DIOSCORIDES, PEDANIUS Born at Anazarbus, Cilicia, *fl.* AD 60–77. A founder of botany.

Dioscorides probably studied at Tarsus and Alexandria, and then became attached to the Roman forces in Asia as a military physician. He travelled widely in search of plants, his interest lying mainly in their usefulness for therapeutic purposes.

Of several works in Greek attributed to Dioscorides the only one that is certainly genuine is that usually known by its Latin name, *De materia medica*. This, one of the earliest and possibly the most famous of herbals, exists in innumerable manuscripts with many variations. It was completed about AD 77, and was still in use in the seventeenth century. The first English translation was made (though not then published) in 1655.

In the earliest versions of this work an attempt was made at an arrangement, which could hardly be called a 'system'. (Of later date are the series of manuscripts arranged alphabetically by names of plants). Dioscorides mentioned about 500 plants, of which about 130 are mentioned in the Hippocratic Collection. Many of the plants are not now identifiable, but some were recognized by J. P. de Tournefort (1656–1708) and others by John Sibthorp (1758–96). Under the name of each plant Dioscorides gave its description, and its place of origin or its habitat. Then followed the method of preparation of the drug and its uses in medicine. A number of these medicinal plants are still found in modern pharmacopœias.

C. Singer, *Journal of Hellenic Studies*, **47**, 19, 1927.

T. C. Allbutt, *Greek Medicine in Rome*. 1921.

R. T. Gunther, *The Greek Herbal of Dioscorides*. 1934.

Agnes Arber, *Herbals*. 1986. (Paperback).

Dictionary of Scientific Biography.

E A U

DIRAC, PAUL ADRIAN MAURICE Born at Bristol, England, 8 August 1902; died Tallahassee, Florida, USA, 20 October 1984. A founder of quantum mechanics and the discoverer of the relativistic wave-equation for the electron.

Dirac, son of a Swiss teacher of French at the Merchant Venturers' Technical College, Bristol, was educated in this College, where his mathematical abilities soon marked him out. In 1921, he graduated in Electric Engineering at Bristol University but remained at Bristol, taking a Mathematics degree in 1923. He then became a research student at Cambridge University, supervised by Ralph Howard Fowler (1889–1944) and supported by a DSIR studentship and a scholarship at St. John's College. In 1925, Fowler gave him a proof copy of an obscure paper by HEISENBERG, the first of his

papers on the development of quantum theory. Dirac quickly realised that Heisenberg's uncertain first steps involved non-commuting physical operators and identified the commutators (A.B–B.A) with the Poisson Brackets A, B of the corresponding classical theory. From this observation, Dirac developed his own form of quantum theory independently, using an operator formalism. After obtaining his PhD, Dirac visited the Institute of Niels BOHR at Copenhagen, where he developed his important 'transformation theory' with which he showed that SCHRÖDINGER's wave mechanics and Heisenberg's matrix mechanics were special cases of his operator theory.

In 1927, Dirac laid the foundations of Quantum Field Theory, by applying quantum theory to the electromagnetic field, using 'second quantization' for the description of its quantum units, the photons. With this, he derived from first principles Einstein's A and B coefficients for the emission and absorption of photons by atoms and the Lorentzian shape for the photon spectrum for a simple atomic transition. Today, these field-theory methods have become highly developed and are used in almost all areas of quantum physics. By this time, Dirac's international recognition was such that, despite his youth, he was invited to speak at the 1927 Solvay Conference at Brussels, where he was accepted as an equal by all those present. At Cambridge in 1927 he was elected a Fellow of St John's College and appointed to a University Lectureship.

In 1928, he achieved his goal of finding a relativistic equation for the description of an electron, using simple but elegant arguments. This 'Dirac Equation' is generally regarded as his outstanding contribution to modern physics. It required automatically that the electron should have intrinsic spin $\frac{1}{2}$, as atomic spectroscopy had already indicated to be necessary, and predicted correctly its magnetic moment; the solution of the Dirac equation for the hydrogen atom gave an energy level pattern in complete accord with observation. It also predicted unphysical negative-energy states for the electron, but he was able to interpret these by his 'hole theory'. He defined 'vacuum' to be the state in which all negative-energy electron states are occupied; when one of these states is unoccupied, the 'hole' appears as a positively-charged anti-electron in a state of positive energy. After C. D. ANDERSON observed such a particle, the anti-electron became named 'positron', the first of many antiparticles subsequently established and used by physicists.

His famous book *The Principles of Quantum Mechanics* was published in 1930. It was the first full and systematic textbook on this subject, now in its fourth edition, still in use and still authoritative on the topics included. Its style is very characteristic of Dirac, abstract but simple, emphasizing the important points and using the clearest logic. In 1932, Dirac was appointed to the Lucasian Chair of Mathematics of the University of Cambridge, and in 1933 he was awarded the Nobel prize for physics, jointly with Schrödinger.

In later years, Dirac was much troubled by the occurrence of infinities in quantum field theory calculations. He rejected the renormalisation procedures with which others obtained results in extraordinarily good agreement with experiment, since they did not follow his dictum 'Physical laws should have mathematical beauty'.

Dirac was elected FRS (1930) and Foreign Member of about twenty National Academies. He received the Order of Merit (1973), the highest civil honour in Great Britain. Upon retirement from Cambridge University (1969) he took up a research professorship in Florida State University, Tallahassee, until his death.

P. A. M. Dirac, *The Principles of Quantum Mechanics.* 1st edition (1930); 2nd edition (1935); 3rd edition (1947); 4th edition (1957 & 1967).

The Physical Interpretation of Quantum Mechanics (Bakerian lecture). *Proceedings of the Royal Society,* 180A, 1, 1942

Biographical Memoirs of Fellows of the Royal Society. 1986. (2 portraits.)

Helge Kragh, *Dirac: A Scientific Biography.* 1990. (3 portraits.)

Dictionary of National Biography.

R H D

DIXON, HAROLD BAILEY Born in London, 11 August 1852; died Manchester, 17 September 1930. Chemist distinguished for his studies of explosions.

Dixon was educated at Westminster School, winning a place at Christ Church, Oxford, in 1870 to read classics. Excessive interest in other pursuits, including sport, coupled with neglect of his studies, almost led to his expulsion from the University. He was rescued from disgrace by A. Vernon Harcourt (1834–1919), the pioneer of chemical kinetics, and set to study chemistry. He obtained a first class degree in the Natural Science School in 1875 and stayed in Oxford to do research under Harcourt.

This research was concerned with the kinetics of explosions, and an early discovery (1877) was that rigorous drying of explosive mixtures of gases such as hydrogen and oxygen stopped them being explosive. He also showed that the law of mass action did apply to gaseous explosions, though BUNSEN in 1857 had claimed that it did not.

In 1887, Dixon moved to Manchester as professor of chemistry at the newly formed University as successor to Sir Henry ROSCOE. He widened the teaching of the Chemistry Department, strengthening the organic side by the appointment at various times of W. H. PERKIN Jnr, Arthur LAPWORTH, and Robert ROBINSON.

Dixon carried out a very accurate determination of the atomic weight of chlorine in 1905, with E. C. Edgar (1881–1938). He was elected FRS in 1885 and was President of the Chemical Society, 1909–11. He retired in 1922.

A. Findlay and W. H. Mills *British Chemists.* 1947. (Portrait.) (Also published in *Journal of the Chemical Society,* 3349, 1931)

Dictionary of Scientific Biography.

J N

DÖBEREINER, JOHANN WOLFGANG Born near Bayreuth, Germany, 15 December 1780; died Jena, Saxony, 24 March 1849. Noted for his 'triads' of chemical elements, and for experiments on the use of platinum as catalyst.

As a coachman's son Döbereiner had no academic training as a young man, yet his practical experience in pharmacies and his attending chemistry lectures proved an effective substitute. Sponsored by an editor, A. F. Gehlen, by L. GMELIN, and by the

Duke Carl August, he rose to become professor at Jena after graduating there. From his early work in pharmacies came the expected contributions on pharmaceutical chemistry, while studies in the inorganic field led to his 'trias' (later 'triads'), when Döbereiner noted that the properties of strontium lay between those of calcium and barium. Similarly, he noted that bromine – discovered by A. J. BALARD in 1826 – was intermediate between chlorine and iodine. Such resemblances paved the way to the Periodic Table of D. I. MENDELÉEFF.

From 1812 Döbereiner worked on crude platina, from which he prepared crucibles, a work extended when Russian platinum became available to him. After DAVY had observed that platinum sponge caused ignition of gas-or alcohol-air mixtures, there came the Döbereiner Lamp, sold throughout Europe in thousands, in which hydrogen ignited on contact with fine platinum. His review of similar processes paved the way for major advances in what is now known as catalysis.

J. R. Partington, *A History of Chemistry,* vol. 4. 1964.

W. Prandtl, *Journal of Chemical Education,* **27**, 176, 1950.

J. P. Montgomery, *Journal of Chemical Education,* **8**, 162, 1931.

Dictionary of Scientific Biography.)

M S

DOBZHANSKY, THEODOSIUS GRIGORIEVICH Born at Nemirov, Ukraine, 25 January 1900; died Davis, California, USA, 18 December 1975. Geneticist and evolutionist.

Dobzhansky was educated in Kiev and graduated from the University of Kiev, in biology, in 1921. After lecturing in genetics at Leningrad University he accepted a fellowship from the Rockefeller Foundation which enabled him to study at Columbia University under the great geneticist T. H. MORGAN. Morgan moved to California in 1928, to set up the Division of Biology at the California Institute of Technology, and Dobzhansky went with him rather than return to the Soviet Union. At CalTech Dobzhansky soon rose to be a full professor of genetics, staying until 1940 when he moved back to Columbia. In 1971 he returned to California, to a part-time post at Davis.

Dobzhansky was a leading contributor to the making of the evolutionary 'New Synthesis' of the 1930s and 1940s – in which biologists reconstructed the view of Charles DARWIN on evolution as due to natural selection upon a basis of Mendelian genetics. This was a considerable achievement, as in the early years of the twentieth century it was widely considered that Mendelism and natural selection were inconsistent. Dobzhansky's contributions were made clear in his aptly named *Genetics and the Origin of Species,* which appeared in three editions (1937, 1941, 1951).

In these various editions, Dobzhansky made frequent reference to the genetical studies which were his hallmark – experimental studies of the distribution, over space and time, of genetical factors in wild populations of *Drosophila pseudoobscura.* This general line of work had been ushered in by one of Dobzhansky's mentors, the great Soviet geneticist S. S. Chetverikov (1880–1959). Particularly noteworthy in this respect were Dobzhansky's studies of chromosomal inversions and his attempts to offer evolutionary explanations of changes in the frequencies of different types of inversions. They may be regarded as genetical studies of evolution in action.

Dobzhansky's interests were not narrowly academic, and he took a lively interest in the putative implications of Darwinism for the human condition. This interest manifested itself in works such as his *Evolution, Genetics and Man* (1955); *The Biological Basis of Human Freedom* (1956); and *The Biology of Ultimate Concern* (1967). This last reveals an interest in, and a respect for, the work of Teilhard de Chardin (1881–1955).

Biographical memoirs of Fellows of the Royal Society. 1977. (Portrait.)

B J N

DOISY, EDWARD ADELBERT Born in Hume, Illinois, USA, 13 November 1893; died St Louis, Missouri, 23 October 1986. Biochemist.

After studying at the Universities of Illinois and Harvard, Doisy served in the US Army and in 1923 was appointed professor of biochemistry at St Louis University, where he spent the rest of his working life. His first interest was in female sex hormones but he later turned to the antihaemorrhagic Vitamin K, then being investigated by C. P. DAM in Copenhagen. Dam had shown that hempseed contains a factor necessary for the coagulation of the blood. It was later found to be present in other seeds and in certain animal tissues. It acts by promoting production of prothrombin and other coagulating factors. By 1938 Dam had prepared highly active concentrates of Vitamin K but it was Doisy and his collaborators who first isolated it in pure crystalline form. It proved to be a derivative of 1,4-naphthoquinone. He later synthesized the vitamin and this greatly facilitated its medical use, especially in treating haemorrhage in newborn babies. Doisy and Dam shared a Nobel prize in 1943.

Les Prix Nobel en 1940–1944. 1946. (Portrait.)
Tyler Wasson (Ed.), *Nobel Prize Winners.* 1987.
  (Portrait.)
R. E. Olson (Ed.), *Perspectives in Biological Chemistry.* 1970

T I W

DOLLOND, JOHN Born in Spitalfields, London, 10 June 1706; died London, 30 November 1761. Optician, remembered for his invention of the achromatic lens.

Dollond was brought up as a silk weaver, and was largely self-educated. In 1752 he joined his eldest son, Peter, who was in business as an optician, and soon became interested in the problem, which Newton had considered insoluble, of making achromatic lenses. Experiments with a combination of water and glass prisms showed that it was possible to get deviation without dispersion; extending this idea at the suggestion of S. KLINGENSTIERNA, he used crown glass and flint glass to make an achromatic lens. Lenses of this type were used in a telescope for which he was awarded the Copley Medal of the Royal Society (1758). In 1761 he was elected FRS, and was appointed optician to the King.

The principle of the achromatic lens was independently discovered by Chester Moor Hall (1703–71), but he failed to publicise it. There is some evidence that Dollond exploited Hall's idea.

J. Kelly, *Philosophical Magazine*, **18, 47**. 1804.

Gentleman's Magazine, **2**, 90, 1820.
H. C. King, *The History of the Telescope.* 1955.
Dictionary of National Biography.
Dictionary of Scientific Biography.

B B K

DOMAGK, GERHARD Born at Lagow, Brandenburg, Germany, 30 October 1895; died Elberfeld, 24 April 1964. Pioneer of chemotherapy; discoverer of the sulphonamide drugs.

Domagk studied medicine at Kiel, graduating (after war service) in 1921. For a short time he was pathologist at the University of Greifswald, and then at Münster in 1928. In 1927 he became associated with I. G. Farbenindustrie as director of research in experimental pathology and bacteriology. In his industrial capacity he embarked upon a systematic search for chemical agents capable of destroying bacteria within the human body. In 1932 he made the outstanding discovery that Prontosil Red, a dye containing a sulphonamide group, could control streptococcal infections in mice. This result was not, however, published until 1935 (*Deutsche Medizinische Wochenschrift*), possibly because of difficulty in repeating the results. Subsequently, Daniele BOVET in Paris found that the antibacterial activity was specifically associated with the sulphonamide grouping and not with the dyestuff itself.

This discovery opened the way to the cheap and effective treatment of a variety of highly pathogenic infections. Dramatically, one of those whose life was saved was Domagk's own daughter, who accidentally infected herself in the laboratory. Domagk was awarded the Nobel prize for medicine in 1939, but the Nazis forbade him to accept it; eventually (1947) he received the medal, but not the prize. He was elected Fellow of the Royal Society in 1959.

Biographical Memoirs of Fellows of the Royal Society. 1964. (Portrait.)
Les Prix Nobel en 1939. 1942. (Portrait.)
Tyler Wasson (Ed.), *Nobel Prize Winners.* 1987.
  (Portrait.)
Dictionary of Scientific Biography.

T I W

DONDI, GIOVANNI DE' Born at Chioggia, near Venice, Italy, 1318; died Genoa, February 1389. Astronomer and clock-maker.

The famous Dondi was the son of a patrician in Padua, who constructed a clock there and later practised medicine at Chioggia. He himself became professor of astronomy at Padua in 1352, and lecturer in medicine at Florence in 1368; two years later, he settled finally at Genoa.

The astronomical clock, which he made for the library at Pavia, took eighteen years to construct. The materials were bronze, brass and copper, and particular ingenuity was shown in providing an auxiliary driving-weight to meet the strain when six of the seven planetary dials had to make their simultaneous nightly advance. In addition to hours, days, and the movements of the sun, moon, and planets, the clock showed the Feasts of the Church elaborated in accordance with a perpetual calendar. Dondi described the whole work with great care in his *Planetarium*, but the technology of his clock was too advanced for succeeding generations to be able to copy it – or even to keep the original in action.

Charles Singer, E. J. Holmyard, A. R. Hall, and Trevor I. Williams (Ed.), *A History of Technology*, vol. 3. 1957.
Nouvelle Biographie Générale, xiv. 1855.
Dictionary of Scientific Biography.

T K D

DONKIN, BRYAN Born at Sandoe, Northumberland, England, 22 March 1768; died London, 27 February 1855. Pioneer of the food-preservation industry, of mechanical papermaking, and rotary printing.

Son of a friend of John SMEATON, Bryan Donkin began as a land agent, but on Smeaton's recommendation was apprenticed to a machinemaker. Here he improved the mechanical making of paper by improving the machine devised by Louis Robert. He erected ever-improved models of such machines, beginning at Frogmore in 1804: by 1851 he had built 191 of them.

As a maker of paper he was also interested in its use in printing, and in 1813 – with Richard Bacon (1775–1844) – patented one of the first rotary printing machines. This was adopted by the Cambridge University Press for Bible printing but was not a success. One feature of it – inking-rollers made from glue and treacle – was, however, soon generally adopted in the printing industry and was an important innovation. Donkin was also interested in the development of colour printing.

Meanwhile, he had turned to the preservation of food, by heat sterilization, devising airtight tins after the model of Nicholas APPERT, building a factory in Bermondsey for this purpose, supplying the Royal Navy among others.

Honoured by the Royal Society of Arts with two gold medals for his revolution-counting machines, he served as chairman of its committee on mechanics. He was a founder of the Institution of Civil Engineers in 1818, and was elected FRS in 1838. He was a keen amateur astronomer, and maintained his own observatory; he served as President of the Royal Astronomical Society.

W. Walker, *Distinguished Men of Science*. (Portrait.)
S. B. Donkin, *Transactions of the Newcomen Society*, **27**, 85, 1959.
Dictionary of National Biography.

W H G A

DONNAN, FREDERICK GEORGE Born in Colombo, Ceylon, 6 September 1870, died Canterbury, England, 16 December 1956. Physical chemist.

Donnan was educated at the Queen's University, Belfast, and at the Universities of Leipzig, Berlin, and London. As a young man he held appointments successively at the Royal University of Ireland (1898–1901), University College London (1902), the Royal College of Science, Dublin (1903–4), and Liverpool University (1904–13). In 1913 he succeeded Sir William RAMSAY as professor of chemistry in University College London, holding this appointment with great distinction until 1937.

Donnan's researches were almost wholly concerned with the physical chemistry of solutions. He is particularly remembered for his thermodynamic interpretation of the principles governing the diffusion of ions through semi-permeable membranes (Donnan equilibrium), described in a series of papers (1911–14).

Earlier researches, in Dublin, concerned the theoretical explanation of the Hall and the Thomson effects for salt solutions. In a study of colloids he introduced the concept of negative surface tension to explain dispersion.

Donnan was internationally honoured in his own lifetime. The Royal Society elected him to Fellowship (1911) and awarded him their Davy Medal (1928). He was Longstaff Medallist of the Chemical Society. He was an honorary member of many foreign chemical societies and an honorary graduand of many universities, including St Andrews, Belfast, Princeton, Coimbra, and Athens. He was a founder-member of the Faraday Society, established in 1903 for the advancement of physical chemistry, for whom he recorded fifty years later his recollection of the development of chemistry during his long and active life.

Nature, **179**, 235, 1957.
W. E. Garner, *Proceedings of the Chemical Society*, 362, 1957.
H. S. Taylor, *Journal of the American Chemical Society*, **83**, 2979, 1961.
Biographical Memoirs of Fellows of the Royal Society. 1957. (Portrait.)
Dictionary of Scientific Biography.

T I W

DOPPLER, CHRISTIAN Born at Salzburg, Austria, 29 November 1805; died Venice, Italy, 17 March 1853. Discoverer of the Doppler Effect.

Doppler, son of a stonemason, gave early evidence of mathematical ability. After studying at the Polytechnic Institute in Vienna, in 1835 he was appointed professor of mathematics at the *Realschule* in Prague. Subsequently he held professorships of mathematics at the Prague Technical College and the Mining Academy in Chemnitz. In 1850 he was appointed to the chair of experimental physics at the University of Vienna, but he died only three years later.

His academic career was thus a distinguished one, which the University of Prague recognized with the award of an honorary degree, but nevertheless his only lasting claim to fame is his enunciation of the so-called Doppler Principle in 1842. This is very widely applicable, and relates the apparent frequency of a wave motion to the velocity, relative to the observer, of the source producing it. A familiar example is the sudden drop in the apparent pitch of a locomotive whistle as a train passes an observer. The principle applies to all forms of wave motion, including radio waves and light. In the case of light – where Doppler's own interpretation was not quite correct – the effect manifests itself as a change in the apparent colour of the source if the velocity relative to the observer is sufficiently high. If the source is approaching, its spectrum will be shifted towards the blue end; if receding, towards the red end. Measurement of the effect makes it possible in appropriate cases to determine the rates of approach or recession of stars and other celestial bodies and provides the main evidence for the theory of an expanding universe.

T. F. van Wagenen, *Beacon Lights of Science*. 1924.

E. N. da C. Andrade, *Endeavour*, **18**, 14, 1959.
(Portrait.)
Dictionary of Scientific Biography.

T I W

DOUGLASS, ANDREW ELLICOTT Born at Windsor, Vermont, USA, 5 July 1857; died Tucson, Arizona, 20 March, 1962. Astronomer; pioneer of dendrochronology.

After graduating at Trinity College, Connecticut (1889) Douglass held several astronomical appointments before becoming professor of physics and astronomy in the University of Arizona, Tucson (1906–18) and Director of the Steward Observatory (1918–38). He made many observations of the solar system – especially sunspots – but his great claim to fame is as inventor of tree-ring dating (dendrochronology). This is based on the fact that the width of annual growth rings in timber depends on local climatic fluctuations, wet and dry seasons producing different results. The passing years thus stamp a distinctive signature on the ring pattern. With some long-lived species this may cover several centuries. Patterns in timbers from archaeological sites can be linked to give a continuous record extending back to as early as 7000 BC. Apart from its intrinsic value, dendrochronology provides a valuable check on the radiocarbon dating technique developed by W. F. LIBBY. Douglass was appointed Professor of Dendrochronology at Tucson in 1936.

A. G. Debus (Ed.) *World Who's Who in Science.* 1968.

Daphne Overstreet, *American West*, 11(5), 1974.

T I W

DRAKE, EDWIN LAURENTINE Born at Greenville, New York, 29 March 1819; died Bethlehem, Pennsylvania, 8 November 1880. Pioneer of oil-well drilling in America.

Though dubbed 'Colonel' Drake by those who sent him to the oilfields, he was a farmer's son who had given up his post as a railway conductor on account of ill health. A stockholder in the Pennsylvania Rock Oil Company, he was sent in December 1857 to inspect its property at Oil Creek, near Titusville, and advocated drilling operations, as used in salt wells and as proposed by G. H. Bissell (1821–84), a promotor of the petroleum industry. Having secured a lease and the assistance of a local blacksmith who had salt-well experience, after nineteen months' work (including three and a half months of actual drilling) Drake struck oil at 69½ feet. This event (27 August 1859) effectively launched the modern petroleum industry.

Drake's well produced only forty barrels a day, which soon fell to fifteen, and he unfortunately failed to patent his chief technical contribution – the use of a pipe down to bedrock to protect the drill-hole. In 1863 he lost his savings in oil speculations and had a further collapse of health; the rest of his life was spent in poverty alleviated by public and private charity.

Dictionary of American Biography.

M. Wilson, *American Science and Invention.* 1954. (Portrait.)

E. C. Miller, *An Investigation of North America's First Oil Well: Who Drilled It?* 1964.

T K D

DRAPER, JOHN WILLIAM Born at St Helen's, Lancashire, England, 5 May 1811; died Hastings-on-Hudson, New York, 4 January 1882. Chemist: pioneer of scientific photography.

Draper studied chemistry at London University before emigrating to the USA *c*.1832, graduating in medicine at the University of Pennsylvania (1836). Subsequently he taught chemistry at Hampden-Sydney College, Virginia (1836–8). He then moved to New York University where he founded the School of Medicine in 1839, later becoming its President (1850). He developed a particular interest in the chemical effects of light and showed that only radiation absorbed by a system effects chemical change (Draper-Grotthuss effect). With the publication of his process by L. J. M. DAGUERRE in 1839, Draper became keenly interested in photography. In that year he took one of the first photographic portraits, by sunlight (exposure 65 seconds), and then proceeded to apply photography to astronomy. In the winter of 1839/40 he took the first photographs of the Moon and later (1843) of the dark lines in the Solar spectrum and lines in the ultraviolet. He was awarded the Rumford Medal of the American Academy of Arts and Sciences in 1875.

Donald Fleming, *John William Draper and the Religion of Science.* 1950.

Dictionary of Scientific Biography.

T I W

DREBBEL, CORNELIS Born at Alkmaar, North Holland, probably 1572; died in the Minories, London, shortly before 7 November 1633. Inventor.

Cornelis Drebbel was the son of Jacob Jansz Drebbel, a burgher of Alkmaar. After leaving school he was apprenticed to Hendrik Goltzius (1558–1617), the painter and engraver, of Haarlem. In 1595 he married Goltzius's sister Sylvia; the marriage was an unhappy one and is said to have been the cause of Drebbel's attaining less success in life than might have been expected from his undoubted talents. Goltzius was also a practising alchemist, and through him Drebbel acquired considerable practical ability in carrying out chemical manipulations; he appears to have had little interest in the search for the elixir of life, the philosopher's stone, and the other mystical elements of contemporary alchemical thought. Apart from this early contact with chemistry, one of Drebbel's friends as a young man was Jacob Metius (d. 1628), a pioneer of the telescope and of the science of optics generally.

Drebbel's interest in engineering lasted long enough for him to prepare, in 1597, a well-known map of the town of Alkmaar, but by then his interest was turning to technology. He designed a water-supply system for the town, and in 1598 the States General granted him a patent for a self-winding and self-regulating clock. The latter has brought criticism on Drebbel on the grounds that he claimed to have invented a form of perpetual motion, which we now know to be an impossibility. In fact, however, he does not appear to have claimed more than a mechanism constantly rewound by atmospheric pressure changes; moreover, greater men than Drebbel – John WILKINS among them – believed in the possibility of perpetual motion at a much later date.

By about 1605 Drebbel was in England, where he spent much of the rest of his life. He demonstrated his *perpetuum mobile* to James I, who installed him at Eltham Park and encouraged his experiments. Rudolf II persuaded Drebbel to visit Prague, and appointed him Chief Alchemist. On Rudolf's deposition in 1611, Drebbel returned to England.

About 1621 he was engaged in experiments with a submarine, and there is evidence that his vessel, propelled by eight rowers, travelled submerged at least from Westminster to Greenwich. Meanwhile he pursued his chemical interests, and introduced the use of tin salts as mordants in dyeing. Of greater interest is the possibility of his having anticipated Joseph PRIESTLEY and K. W. SCHEELE in the discovery of oxygen. In 1604 he published a book *Van de Natuyre der Elementen* in which he refers, somewhat obscurely, to 'saltpeter, broken up by the power of fire, and thus changed into something of the nature of air'. Today, the heating of saltpetre (potassium nitrate) is one of the standard means of preparing oxygen in the laboratory.

L. E. Harris, *The Two Netherlanders: Humphrey Bradley and Cornelis Drebbel*. 1961.

F. M. Jaeger, *Cornelis Drebbel en Zÿne Tÿdgenooten*. 1922.

Gerrit Tierrie, *Cornelis Drebbel*. 1932.

Transactions of the Newcomen Society, **31**, 195, 1957/9.

Dictionary of National Biography.

T I W

DRIESCH, HANS ADOLF EDUARD Born at Bad Kreuznach, Rhenish Prussia, Germany, 28 October 1867; died Leipzig, 16 April 1941. Biologist and philosopher.

Driesch was educated at the Johanneum School in Hamburg, studied zoology under August WEISMANN at the University of Munich, and finally under Ernst HAECKEL at the University of Jena. He graduated from Jena in 1889, presenting a thesis on the morphology of coelenterate hydroid polyps. Driesch was one of the first experimental embryologists. As a result of his researches he became a strong advocate of dynamic vitalism and rejected the mechanistic theories of his former teachers. In 1888, Wilhelm Roux (1850–1924), at the University of Breslau, performed the crucial experiment of pricking with a heated needle one of the first two blastomeres formed after cleavage of a frog's egg. There ensued partial formation of a half embryo, to which the shrivelled lifeless half was still attached. In explanation of this result Roux considered that the living blastomere, derived from half of the parent-egg, was self-differentiating: this was in accordance with Weismann's views that each of the first two embryonic nuclei would contain only half the determinants present in the parent-egg, and so logically lead to the formation of a half embryo. Driesch, at the Marine Biological Station in Naples, where he worked from 1891 to 1900, experimented similarly with the embryos of sea urchins. After two-celled embryos were violently shaken to cause complete separation, each cell was found to give rise to a whole, but half normal-sized, pluteus larva. From these, and like experiments, Driesch concluded that since a living organism can be regenerated from severed parts it cannot be a complex machine, for the parts of any such are unable to reproduce the whole. He therefore conceived the living organism as a harmonious equipotential, rather than toti-

potential, system containing an internal perfecting principle which he called 'entelechy' – a term first used by Aristotle.

In 1900 he settled in Heidelberg, where he forsook experimental biology for abstract metaphysics; he became *Privatdozent* in 1909 and two years later was nominated professor of philosophy at the University. He was subsequently appointed professor of philosophy at Cologne (1919), and at Leipzig (1921). He travelled widely as a lecturer, visiting the Far East (1922–3), and the United States (1925). He expressed his views on vitalism in the Gifford lectures delivered before the University of Aberdeen in 1907, which he entitled *Philosophie des Organischen* (English translation, *Science and Philosophy of the Organism*, 1908). In 1911 he was elected a Foreign Member of the Linnean Society of London.

Festschrift Hans Driesch zum 60. Geburtstag. 1927. (Portrait.)

Dictionary of Scientific Biography.

A P G

DRUMMOND, THOMAS Born in Edinburgh, 10 October 1797; died Dublin, 15 April 1840. Limelight inventor, and administrator.

The son of a lawyer, Thomas Drummond entered Edinburgh University in 1810 and Woolwich Academy in 1813. As a RE officer in 1820 he joined the Ordnance Survey, and in connection with this career he studied under Faraday at the Royal Institution. To assist observation he invented both an improved heliostat and a limelight, the latter being used by him in 1825 while surveying in Ireland. Its action depends on the fact that lime emits an intense white light when heated in an oxyhydrogen flame (see R. HARE). Four years later it was tested with a view to its eventual employment for lighthouses – though its main use was in the theatre – and Drummond began to consider how to reduce the high cost of production. However, in 1831 he made the acquaintance of Brougham and became involved in politics, becoming head of the Boundary Commission for the Great Reform Bill and in 1835 the Under-Secretary (effective head) of the Irish Civil Service. He proved a devoted administrator.

Dictionary of National Biography.

T K D

DU BOIS REYMOND, EMIL HEINRICH Born in Berlin, 7 November 1818; died there, 26 December 1896. Physiologist, and pioneer of the study of the electric phenomena of living tissues.

Du Bois Reymond, son of a Swiss father and a mother of Huguenot descent, was educated in Berlin, Neufchâtel, and at the University of Berlin, where he became assistant to Johannes MÜLLER in 1840. He succeeded Müller in the Chair of Physiology in 1858, and soon began his agitation for a new institute for that subject. In 1877 this institute, then the finest of its kind, was opened, and Reymond was its head for nearly twenty years. In 1851 he was elected a member of the Berlin Academy of Sciences, and from 1867 he was its perpetual Secretary. He was also President of the Physical and of the Physiological Societies. From 1859 to 1877 he was Joint Editor with K. B. Reichert (1811–84) of *Müllers Archiv*, and from 1877 until his death he was sole Editor of the *Archiv für Physiologie*.

Du Bois Reymond's first publication dealt with the electric discharge of certain fishes, a subject to which he later reverted. During his first eight years as assistant to Müller he virtually founded a new science. He was the first to prove that muscular activity is accompanied by chemical changes in the muscle, and also by changes in its electromotive properties. In 1843 he showed that, when a current is led through a nerve by non-polarizable electrodes, electrolytic ions are formed within the nerve. This phenomenon he called electrotonus. He introduced faradic stimulation of nerves, and devised an induction coil for that purpose. His discovery of the resting nerve current, and the difference of electric potential between the cut and the uninjured ends of an excised muscle or nerve, was of fundamental importance. Many of his discoveries were published in his *Untersuchungen über thierische Elektricität* ('Researches on animal electricity'). The first volume of this work appeared in 1848, and the first part of the second volume in 1849. Completion of the work depended on further research, and the second volume was not completed until 1860.

A. D. Waller, *Proceedings of the Royal Society*, **75**, 124, 1905.

J. B. Sanderson, *Nature*, **55**, 230, 1897.

Allgemeine Deutsche Biographie.

E. A. Schäfer (Ed.), *Textbook of Physiology.* 1898–1900.

F. H. Garrison, *History of Medicine.* 1929. (Portrait.)

Dictionary of Scientific Biography.

E A U

DUFAY, CHARLES FRANÇOIS DE CISTERNAY

Born in Paris, 14 September 1698; died there, 16 July 1739. Scientist; recognized the existence of two types of electricity.

Dufay started his career, as family tradition demanded, in the French Army. He was commissioned in 1712 at the age of 14, and had risen to the rank of captain by 1723. He had during this time been studying chemistry, and he left the Army to become Assistant Chemist to the *Académie des Sciences* in Paris. In 1732 he became Superintendent of the *Jardin du Roi* in Paris.

Dufay wrote a number of papers on chemistry, but is best known for his six memoirs on electricity published between 1733 and 1737. He charged a gold leaf with a rubbed glass rod and was surprised to find that rubbed resinous bodies such as amber, silk, and paper attracted it, while other vitreous substances like rock crystal, hair, and wool, when rubbed, repelled it. He concluded that there were two types of electricity, which he called vitreous and resinous, and that they were responsible for the phenomena of attraction and repulsion. He also repeated the work of Stephen GRAY and showed the connection between the ability of a body to conduct away an electric charge and its ability to receive a charge; by suspending a person by silk cords he was able to electrify him and draw sparks from his body.

P. F. Mottelay, *Bibliographical History of Electricity and Magnetism.* 1922.

B. Fontenelle, *Histoire de l'Académie des Sciences.* 1739.

W. Sturgeon, *Lectures on Electricity.* 1842.

J. R. Partington, *A History of Chemistry*, vol. 3. 1962.

Dictionary of Scientific Biography.

B K

DUHAMEL DU MONCEAU, HENRI LOUIS

Born in Paris, 1700: died there, August 1782. A prolific writer who made contributions to several fields of science and technology, especially botany and agriculture.

Duhamel du Monceau studied under C. F. DUFAY and Bernard de Jussieu (1699–1777) at the *Jardin du Roi* in Paris. He undertook a study of the cultivation of saffron in Gatinais and his memoir on the parasitic fungus which attacks the bulb of the plant earned him admission to the *Académie des Sciences* in 1728. In the following decade he made a number of researches in chemistry and in 1736 he published a memoir *Sur la Base du Sel Marin* in which he distinguished between the salts of sodium and potassium by observing that in sea salt and digestive salt the acids were the same but the bases different.

In 1739 Duhamel was appointed *Inspecteur Général de la Marine*, reported to be as a compensation for losing to G. L. L. BUFFON the honour of succeeding Dufay at the *Jardin*. The functions of his office required him to visit the forests, arsenals, and ports of France, and he acquired an extensive knowledge of the arts and crafts of his time. He contributed many articles to the *Descriptions des Arts et Métiers* published by the *Académie des Sciences*, including a study of sugar refining (1764); the craft of the locksmith (1767); and the manufacture of tobacco pipes (1771). In 1752 he published a work directly associated with his office, *Élémens de L'Architecture Navale; ou traité practique de la construction de vaisseaux.*

His agricultural researches involved experiments using husbandry methods developed by the Englishman Jethro TULL and a study of the parasitic diseases of grain. His major contribution in this field, however, concerned the study of the growth and strength of wood, a subject at that time of great military as well as economic importance. In his *Traité des Arbres* (1755) he enumerated the species of trees and in his *chef-d'oeuvre La Physique des Arbres* (1758) he described their structure and physiology.

Nouvelle Biographie Universelle. 1852–66.

A. H. Cole and G. B. Watts, 'The Handicrafts of France' as recorded in the *Descriptions des Arts et Métiers 1761–1788.* 1952. (Portrait.)

Dictionary of Scientific Biography.

M P E

DUJARDIN, FÉLIX

Born at Tours, France, 5 April 1801; died Rennes, 8 April 1860. Celebrated French zoologist, one of the most prominent microscopists of the nineteenth century.

Dujardin, the son and grandson of watchmakers, had a wide-ranging career which included engineering and a professorship of zoology at Rennes (1840–60). His studies were wide ranging in the biological fields, but it was as a protozoologist that he was most eminent.

The success of Dujardin's career was based on his capabilities as a microscopist and he made a number of significant contributions to the development of microscopical technique during the first half of the nineteenth century. His most important biological studies concerned infusoria. Much important work on the subject had been carried out earlier by C. G. EHRENBERG but a great deal of this was mitigated by his attempt to discover in infusoria the same organs as in the higher animals.

Dujardin, in contrast, helped to place the subject on a firmer base. His studies showed that what he called 'sarcode' (protoplasm) was a fundamental constituent of all infusoria, and that it did not contain such organs as a stomach as suggested by Ehrenberg. Dujardin also made important contributions to classification, and his achievements can be seen in his magnificent work *L'histoire naturelle des zoophytes infusoires* (1841).

Dujardin's other contributions to biology included significant studies on parasitology, and his large work *Histoire naturelle des helminthes ou vers intestinaux* (1845) can still be consulted profitably by parasitologists.

P. Huard and J. Théodorides, 'Prélude au centenaire de la mort de Félix Dujardin (1801– 1860)', *Biologie médicale*, April 1959.
W. D. Foster, *A History of Parasitology*. 1965.
Dictionary of Scientific Biography.

J K C

DULBECCO, RENATO Born at Catanzaro, Italy, 22 February 1914. Virologist.

After graduating from the University of Turin in 1936 Dulbecco did his military service as a medical officer until 1938. Postdoctoral work in pathology at Turin was interrupted by the outbreak of war, and he served in the army until wounded in 1942. He then worked for the Italian Resistance as a doctor to the partisans. After the war he returned to Turin as assistant professor of experimental embryology.

In 1947 Dulbecco went to the University of Indiana, Bloomington, at the invitation of S. E. Luria (1912–1991). He moved to the California Institute of Technology in 1949 to join Max DELBRÜCK, and was appointed professor of biology in 1952. With Luria, and later with Delbrück, he worked on bacteriophages. In the mid-1950s he began research on animal viruses. He concentrated on the poliomyelitis virus, developing techniques for studying virus growth in tissue culture. This work contributed to the development of a polio vaccine. In 1959 he moved on to the study of DNA viruses, working on the tumour viruses. With H. M. TEMIN he was able to show that tumour cells transformed by tumour viruses divide indefinitely. He suggested that this process, which he called cell transformation, was caused by a viral gene that had become part of the cellular DNA.

Dulbecco moved to the new Salk Institute for Biological Studies, La Jolla, California as senior research fellow in 1963, and set up a research group to study DNA tumour viruses and cell growth regulation. From 1972 to 1977 he was assistant director of the Imperial Cancer Research Foundation Laboratories in London, directing research on the clinical application of his discoveries relating to tumour viruses. He returned to California in 1977.

In 1986 Dulbecco published an editorial in *Science* urging a national effort to sequence the human genome (all the human genetic material) comparable to the effort that had led to the conquest of space. He argued that this would mark a turning point in cancer research. This led to the start of the Human Genome Project in the USA (see W. F. BODMER.)

Dulbecco shared the Nobel prize for physiology or medicine in 1975 with D. Baltimore (1938–) and H. M. Temin for his discoveries concerning the interaction between tumour viruses and the genetic material of the cell.

R. Dulbecco, *The Design of Life*. 1987.
J. E. Bishop and M. Waldholz, *Genome*. 1990.
R. Dulbecco, *Science*, 7 March 1986.
Tyler Wasson (Ed.), *Nobel Prize Winners*. 1987. (Portrait.)

A P B

DULONG, PIERRE LOUIS Born at Rouen, France, 12 February 1785; died Paris, 18 July 1838. Discoverer (with A. T. PETIT) of Law of Atomic Heats.

Dulong's earliest work was as assistant to C. L. BERTHOLLET. After holding a post at the *École Normale* and the veterinary school at Alfort, he returned to Paris (1820) as professor of physics at the *École Polytechnique*, becoming Director in 1830.

In 1811 he discovered nitrogen chloride, losing an eye in the process. He worked on the oxygen compounds of phosphorus and nitrogen, in the course of which he became an early adherent of the hydrogen theory of acids.

From 1815 onwards he worked closely with Petit, first on accurate comparisons of the mercury and air thermometers, then on the dilatation of solids, liquids, and gases, and on Newton's law of cooling, which they showed was obeyed closely only for small differences of temperature. In 1819 they produced their classic paper incorporating the Law of Dulong and Petit: namely, that the product of the atomic weight and the specific heat of an element approximates to a constant. This was of great value in the controversy then current over criteria for the establishment of a norm for atomic weights.

He collaborated successfully with other colleagues; for example with J. J. BERZELIUS, on the composition of water (1820), with L. J. THENARD on catalysis of reactions (1823); and with D. F. J. ARAGO on the physical properties of steam at high temperatures (1830).

At the end of his life he was exploring the field of thermochemistry. His excellent experimental skill was hampered by inadequate resources, since, unlike some of his contemporaries, he made no fortune out of industrial work.

P. Lemay and R. Oesper, *Chymia*, 1, 171, 1948. (Portrait.)
Dictionary of Scientific Biography.

F G

DUMAS, JEAN BAPTISTE ANDRÉ Born at Alais, France, 14 July 1800; died Cannes, 11 April 1884. Organic chemist.

Dumas was educated at the College of Alais in the classics, and was intended for the Navy, but after the overthrow of Napoleon he began a different career, as an apothecary's apprentice. To improve his prospects he went to Geneva, where he joined the laboratory of A. Le Royer (one of the early investigators of digitalin) in 1816. He concentrated on physiological chemistry for a while, investigating, with J. F. Coindet (1774–1834) the use of iodine compounds as a cure for goitre. He also worked with J. L. Prévost on muscle action and blood corpuscles.

His career was changed by his meeting Alexander von HUMBOLDT, who urged him to develop himself in Paris. In 1823 he became lecture assistant to L. J. THENARD at the *École Polytechnique*. He lectured privately and began work on his important comprehensive *Traité de Chimie*. In 1829 he helped found the *École Centrale des Arts et Métiers*. In 1835 he succeeded Thenard as professor of chemistry at the *École Polytechnique*. He also held professional posts at the *École de Médecine* and at the Sorbonne (1841).

He was an excellent teacher, developing his talent by patient application and by assiduous preparation of lecture demonstrations. He was the first French chemist to give instruction in the laboratory, to a great extent at his own expense. After the revolutionary changes of 1848 he became Minister of Agriculture and Commerce, then Minister of Education. He was appointed Permanent Secretary of the *Académie des Sciences* in 1868.

He isolated anthracene from coal tar, and studied the essential oils, obtaining formulae for camphor, menthol, and other related substances. His principal contribution to theoretical chemistry was his opposition to the dualistic theory of J. J. BERZELIUS. J. L. GAY-LUSSAC had suggested that in bleaching, hydrogen takes the place of chlorine. Dumas had to investigate the emission of choking fumes from candles used at the Tuileries, found they had been bleached with chlorine, and by taking up this clue eventually embarked on a study of the action of chlorine on alcohol. This gave chloroform, for which Dumas derived a correct constitution. From further work on the chlorination of turpentine he showed that for every atom of hydrogen removed from the molecule one atom of chlorine takes its place. He generalized this as a theory of substitution. He showed that the chlorination of acetic acid to form trichloracetic acid was directly opposed to the strict electrical dualism of Berzelius. This brought about a temporary union of effort by Dumas and J. von LIEBIG, but they were incompatible in temperament and did not collaborate for any length of time, although continuing to respect each other's positions.

Early in his career he attempted a redetermination of atomic weights, but used a faulty theory which only further confused an already confused situation. However, he devised for this an excellent method of determining vapour densities. In 1849, assisted by J. G. STAS, he made a masterly determination of the atomic weight of carbon.

A. W. Hofmann, *Proceedings of the Royal Society*, **37**, x, 1884.
J. R. Partington, *A History of Chemistry*, vol. 4. 1964. (Portrait.)
W. Perkin, *Journal of the Chemical Society*, 310, 1885.
Journal of Chemical Education, **28**, 630, 1950.
E. Farber (Ed.), *Great Chemists*. 1961. (Portrait.)
Dictionary of Scientific Biography.

F G

DUNLOP, JOHN BOYD Born at Dreghorn, Ayrshire, Scotland, 5 February 1840; died Dublin, 23 October 1921. Inventor of the pneumatic tyre.

Dunlop practised successfully as a veterinary surgeon in Edinburgh and Belfast. Having considerable skill at working in rubber, in October 1887 he began to experiment with air tubes to reduce shock from the wheels of his 9-year-old son's tricycle. In December of the following year he patented the pneumatic bicycle tyre, consisting of a rubber tube covered by a canvas jacket, the latter having rubber treads and also flaps for attaching the tyre to the wheel-rim with rubber solution. Within a few months its successful use at a bicycle race attracted the attention of W. H. Du Cros, who formed a company with Dunlop for exploiting the tyre. Although difficulties arose from a prior invention by R. W. Thomson in 1845, this grew eventually into the Dunlop Rubber Company with world-wide interests.

The inventor of a device which transformed the bicycle and made the motor-car industry possible derived little profit from it. Having sold his patent rights to Du Cros, Dunlop retired to Dublin, where he lived on for many years with no business interest beyond a local drapery establishment.

Jean McClintock, *History of the Pneumatic Tyre*. 1923.
Dictionary of National Biography.

T K D

DÜRER, ALBRECHT Born at Nuremberg, Bavaria (now Germany), 21 May 1471; died there, 6 April 1528. Remembered as a great painter, engraver, and designer of woodcuts; also one of the earliest writers on scientific principles of pictorial representation.

Dürer was the son of a goldsmith, and worked as his father's apprentice, an experience later to be of great value to him when he pioneered the art of engraving in his own region. At 15 he entered the workshop of the painter Michel Wohlgemuth (1434–1519) and learnt the techniques of painting, drawing, and making woodcuts. From 1490 he travelled through much of western Europe, finally settling in Nuremberg in 1495. In the Netherlands in 1521 he contracted malaria, from which he never fully recovered. He was court painter to the Emperors Maximilian I and Charles V. He died in 1528, by which date his output of work was represented by over seventy paintings, over a hundred engravings, about two hundred and fifty woodcuts, more than a thousand drawings, and three books, on geometry, fortifications, and the theory of human proportions. His artistic genius, the unique revolution that he brought about in the art of engraving and the woodcut, and his remarkable insight into, and articulate expression of, aesthetic principles are dealt with in many publications on his art.

In his books Dürer also made contributions to science. Art theory was evolving in Italy during the Renaissance, but Dürer was the first artist from northern Europe, trained in workshops steeped in late medieval traditions, to attempt to apply scientific principles to pictorial representation. In his treatise on geometry he treated perspective as a mathematical subject. This chapter owed much to Italian influence, for he had visited Bologna to learn the 'secret perspective' and spent two years in Venice (1505–7). The other chapters of the treatise covered linear geometry; two-dimensional geometry; the application of geometry to architecture, engineering, decoration, and typography; and the geometry of three-dimensional bodies. His *Treatise on Human Proportion* (1528) laid the foundations of scientific anthropometry. The *Treatise on Fortification* (1527) was little noted at the time, and has not been thought to compare with such works by Italian contemporaries. Nevertheless, it had some influence locally and the view has been expressed that the 'New Prussian System' of fortification was based on it.

H. T. Musper, *Dürer*. 1952.
E. Panofsky, *The Life and Art of Albrecht Dürer* (4th ed.). 1955. (Portraits.)
F. Winkler, *Dürer*. 1952.
J. L. Coolidge, *The Mathematics of Great Amateurs*. 1949.
Dictionary of Scientific Biography.

N H

DUTROCHET, RENÉ JOACHIM HENRI Born at Château de Néon, Canton Tournou, Indre, France, 14 November 1776; died Paris, 4 February 1847. A founder of plant physiology.

Henri Dutrochet, member of an impoverished noble family, served in the Army and began medical studies in Paris in 1802. After graduating in 1806 he served as a military surgeon with the Army in Spain. He resigned his commission in 1809 and thereafter devoted himself entirely to science. He lived from that time at Château-Renault in Touraine, but spent the winter months in Paris. He became a member of the *Académie de Médecine* in 1823, and of the *Académie des Sciences* in 1831.

Although the process of osmosis had been previously observed, these crude observations had been forgotten, and it was Dutrochet who first studied it exactly (1826). In later years he repeatedly studied its importance in relation to plant physiology, such as the ascent and descent of the sap. He pointed out correctly that respiration in plants is identical with respiration in animals, and he studied plant respiration in relation to the air passages and the stomata. He appreciated that only cells that contain chlorophyll decompose carbon dioxide, and he introduced the method of measuring the rate of decomposition by counting the gas bubbles given off by submerged plants in sunlight. He was one of the first to study successfully the production of heat during the growth of plants, and he advanced the work of T. A. Knight (1759–1838) on geotropism and the movements of plants.

J. von Sachs, *History of Botany*. 1906.
R. J. Harvey-Gibson, *Outlines of the History of Botany*. 1919.
Isis, **37**, 14, 1947.
Dictionary of Scientific Biography.

E A U

DU VIGNEAUD, VINCENT Born at Chicago, Illinois, USA, 18 May 1901; died Scarsdale, New York, 11 December 1978. Biochemist.

Du Vigneaud graduated from the University of Illinois in 1923, and was awarded a PhD by Rochester University, New York, in 1927 for work on the chemistry of insulin. He continued the study of insulin under J. J. Abet at Johns Hopkins University Medical School, in Dresden working with Max Bergmann (1886–1944), in Edinburgh with George BARGER, and at University College Hospital, London, with C. R. Harington (1897–1972). In 1932 Du Vigneaud became professor of biochemistry at the George Washington University Medical School in Washington DC, and worked on sulphur-containing amino acids. In 1937 he demonstrated that the amino acid cystine accounts for the entire sulphur content of insulin.

In 1938 he moved to New York City as head of the biochemistry department at Cornell University Medical School. He succeeded in isolating vitamin H from liver and showed that it was identical to biotin. By 1942 he had determined the structure of biotin. He also worked on the synthesis of penicillin, completed in 1946. He went on to study two pituitary hormones, oxytocin and vasopressin, and determined their structures. This led to the first synthesis of a polypeptide hormone when he synthesised oxytocin in 1954. For this he was awarded the Nobel prize in chemistry in 1955.

Du Vigneaud was professor of chemistry at Cornell University, Ithaca, New York from 1967 until his retirement in 1975.

Du Vigneaud, *A Trail of Research in Sulfur Chemistry and Metabolism and Related Fields*. 1952.
Tyler Wasson (Ed.), *Nobel Prize Winners*. 1987. (Portrait.)

A P B

DYSON, SIR FRANK WATSON Born at Ashby de la Zouch, Leicestershire, England, 8 January 1868; died at sea (on a voyage from Australia), 25 May 1939. Astronomer.

Dyson was the son of a Baptist minister. Educated at Bradford Grammar School and Trinity College, Cambridge, he graduated Second Wrangler in 1889, becoming a Smith's Prizeman and Fellow of his College in 1891. In 1894, he was appointed Chief Assistant at Greenwich Observatory, where he worked at a large cataloguing project. Together with W. G. Thackeray he found the proper motions of over 4000 circumpolar stars, using Stephen Groombridge's data of 1806–19. He became FRS in 1901.

In 1905 Dyson became Astronomer Royal for Scotland. His most important work during this period was the series of observations which showed that J. C. Kapteyn's hypothesis of star-streaming was confirmed by stars of large proper motion. From 1910 to 1933 Dyson returned to Greenwich as Astronomer Royal. He made extensive observations of the spectrum of the corona and chromosphere of the Sun during eclipses, and, in 1919, organized two expeditions, one from Greenwich and one from Cambridge, to observe the solar eclipse at which EINSTEIN's predicted gravitational deflexion of light passing the Sun was observed.

Obituary Notices of Fellows of the Royal Society, 1940. (Portrait.)
M. Wilson, *Ninth Astronomer Royal*. 1951.
Dictionary of National Biography.
Dictionary of Scientific Biography.

J D N

E

EADS, JAMES BUCHANAN Born at Law-renceburg, Indiana, USA, 23 May 1820; died Nassau, Bahamas, 8 March 1887. Hydraulic engineer and bridge builder.

Son of Thomas Eads, a migrant merchant, J. B. Eads left school at 13 and after a variety of jobs became in 1838 a purser on a Mississippi steam-boat. Impressed by the enormous number of wrecks littering the river, he devised a diving bell and at the age of 22 devoted himself to full-time employment as a salvage engineer, making enough money in three years to retire and establish the first glassworks west of the Ohio River. When this failed in 1848 he returned to salvage work on the Mississippi with such success that in 1857 he was able to retire for good.

At the outbreak of the Civil War in 1861 he advised President Lincoln to acquire a fleet of steam-propelled armour-plated gunboats on the western rivers. He himself successfully contracted to build seven such boats without their guns in sixty-five days, and in the course of the war built or converted another eighteen, all by techniques similar to those later to be exploited by Henry Kaiser in the Second World War.

When the war was over he successfully bid for the contract to construct a bridge across the Missis-sippi at St Louis. Owing to his extensive knowl-edge of the currents and of the river bed he fulfilled the exacting conditions of the contract: a 500-foot centre span with a 50-foot clearance.

The 'Eads Bridge', as it is known, was finished in 1874 and was the prelude to further ambitious projects. In 1875 he was commissioned to open one of the mouths of the Mississippi. This he accomplished in 1879 by constructing a number of jetty traps. Subsequent efforts to secure a ship railway across the isthmus of Panama sapped his health. He was the first American to be awarded the Albert Medal of the Royal Society of Arts.

Louis How, *James B. Eads*. 1900.

C. B. Boynton, *History of the Navy through the Rebellion*. 1868. (Portrait.)

Dictionary of American Biography.

W H G A

ECCLES, WILLIAM HENRY Born near Ulverston, Lancashire, England, 23 August 1875; died Oxford, 29 April 1966. Pioneer of wireless telegraphy and radio science.

Childhood illnesses interrupted Eccles' edu-cation, which took place mainly at home, but he graduated BSc (London) from the Royal College of Science in 1898 with first class honours in physics. In 1899 he became one of the assistants of G. MAR-CONI. For his work on coherers, used in early wire-less receivers, he was awarded a DSc (London) in 1901. He also worked on the design of towers for use in transatlantic experiments.

In 1901 Eccles became head of the physics department at the South West Polytechnic, Chel-sea, and in 1910 was appointed reader in Graphic Statics at University College, London. He suc-ceeded Silvanus Thompson (1851–1916) in the chair of Applied Physics and Electrical Engineer-ing at the City and Guilds College, Finsbury in 1916. While at Finsbury he worked on the thermi-onic triode and developed the Eccles–Jordan cir-cuit in 1919. He was elected FRS in 1921.

During the First World War he was on several advisory committees on wireless telegraphy, advis-ing army and Admiralty officials. In 1919 he became vice-chairman of the Imperial Wireless Committee which was working on the establish-ment of an Imperial chain of wireless stations, and he helped to design the first long-wave radio station. He became involved in the organisation of public broadcasting, and played an important role in the early years of the BBC after it became a public corporation in 1926.

In 1926 Eccles retired from his chair to become a private consulting engineer, acting as technical advisor on recording and broadcasts for EMI from 1926 until 1958. He published *Wireless* for the Home University Library in 1933.

Biographical Memoirs of Fellows of the Royal Society. 1971. (Portrait.)

Dictionary of National Biography.

A P B

ECKERT, JOHN PRESPER Born in Philadelphia, Pennsylvania, USA, 9 April 1919. Electrical engineer who jointly developed one of the first modern computers.

Eckert graduated in 1941 from the Moore School of Electrical Engineering at the University of Penn-sylvania, where he remained for another five years as a research associate. During that time he was engaged on calculations for artillery ranging tables, a slow process with the mechanical calculators then available. From 1942 to 1946 he worked with John W. MAUCHLY, first on improvements to the uni-versity's existing differential analyser, and then on the development of what became the world's first electronic digital computer, known as ENIAC (Electronic Numerical Integrator and Computer). ENIAC had more than 0.5 million hand-soldered connections, required more than 150 kW of power, weighed 30 tons, and filled a 30 ft × 50 ft room.

In 1948 the Eckert-Mauchly Computer Corpor-ation was formed, and in the following year BINAC (Binary Automatic Computer) was launched, using magnetic tape to store data instead of the punched cards of ENIAC. Further research resulted in UNIVAC I (Universal Automatic Computer) which contained many of the elements of today's most sophisticated machines, such as built-in automatic checking and the ability to store programs. Eckert became a vice-president of UNIVAC in 1955; in 1961 he and Mauchly received the John Scott Medal for 'adding to the comfort, welfare and happiness of mankind'. In 1969 he was awarded the National Medal of Science by US President Lyndon Johnson.

> *Modern Scientists and Engineers.* McGraw-Hill. (Portrait.)
>
> *Technology and Culture*, **23**, 569, 1982.

R M B

EDDINGTON, SIR ARTHUR STANLEY Born at Kendal, Westmorland, England, 28 December 1882; died Cambridge, 22 November 1944. Pioneer of stellar structure and the General Theory of Relativity.

Arthur Stanley Eddington, the son of the headmaster and proprietor of a Kendal school at which John DALTON had once taught, was educated at home and at Brymelyn School, Weston (1893–8). At 16 he won a scholarship to Owens College, Manchester, graduating in physics (1902). He then went to Cambridge, where he was successively Senior Wrangler (1904), Smith's Prizeman, and Fellow of Trinity (1907). After minor research on thermionic emission (1905), he succeeded Sir Frank DYSON as Chief Assistant at Greenwich. There he initiated an immense programme of observations on latitude variation, at the same time gaining much practical experience. In 1906 he began, concurrently, his theoretical studies of stellar movements (especially by statistical methods), his first book being on this subject (1914). In the same year he was made Director of the Cambridge Observatory, and elected FRS.

Eddington was now led to make a theoretical study of the internal constitution of the stars, and at the same time, a little reluctantly, he was drawn into the discussion of the General Theory of Relativity of EINSTEIN. The report he prepared for the Physical Society (1918), expanded finally into his *Mathematical Theory of Relativity* (1923), gave the English-speaking public a chance to learn the mathematical details not only of Einstein's theory of gravitation but of Eddington's own fine generalization of H. Weyl's (1885–1955) theory of the electromagnetic field. Eddington drew attention to a tendency of extragalactic nebulae to recede from our own Galaxy. He was the first to realize the full implications of some work by his one-time pupil, Georges LEMAÎTRE, namely that the Einstein Universe is unstable. This provided a new theoretical approach to the law of nebulae recession found by E. P. HUBBLE and others shortly before.

In 1928 P. A. M. DIRAC had introduced relativistic ideas into quantum theory, in his famous paper giving the wave equation of the electron. Eddington now tried to unify general relativity and quantum mechanics. His later writings, published posthumously, and known as his 'Fundamental Theory', have been the source of much admiration and much hostility, the latter on the grounds that they are rationalistic. He attempted to prove gravi-

tation to be a consequence of the exclusion principle.

The subject of stellar structure is largely one of Eddington's creation. His *Internal Constitution of the Stars* appeared in 1926. Although seemingly withdrawn from the world, he had a great ability to convey complex mathematical ideas to the layman.

> A. Vibert Douglas, *The Life of Arthur Stanley Eddington*. 1956. (Portrait.)
>
> C. W. Kilmister, *Sir Arthur Eddington*. 1966.
>
> L. P. Jacks, *Sir Arthur Eddington*. 1949.
>
> *Obituary Notices of Fellows of the Royal Society.* 1945. (Portrait.)
>
> H. Oxbury (Ed.), *Great Britons: 20th Century Lives.* 1985.
>
> *Dictionary of Scientific Biography.*

J D N

EDGEWORTH, RICHARD LOVELL Born at Bath, Somerset, England, 31 May 1744; died Edgeworthstown, Co. Longford, Ireland, 13 June 1817. Inventor and educationist.

R. L. Edgeworth came from a landed but impoverished Anglo-Irish family, with estates at Edgeworthstown. After six months at Trinity College, Dublin, he went to Oxford in 1761; within two years he married, and left the University. He decided to become an inventor and designed improved carriages, an umbrella for covering haystacks, a turnip-cutter, a carriage with sails, and an odometer. These inventions won him gold and silver medals from the Society for the Encouragement of Arts. He also constructed over a hundred unsuccessful models of a robot wooden horse with caterpillar tracks. In the late 1760s he made the first practical demonstration of a mechanical telegraph. Edgeworth was a man of engaging personality, and in 1766 he became a popular member of the Lunar Society of Birmingham, being particularly friendly with Thomas Day (1748–89), Erasmus DARWIN, James KEIR, and William Small (1734–75)

Edgeworth returned to Ireland in 1782 to look after his estate. Apart from short visits, he remained there, still inventing, for the rest of his life. In 1783 he contributed his classic paper on the air resistance of projectiles to the *Philosophical Transactions* of the Royal Society, of which he became a Fellow in 1781. Another of his papers showed that good springs would not only make carriages more comfortable but also reduce tractive effort and road wear. He tried to convince the military of the advantages of his mechanical telegraph. He wrote a treatise on road construction (1813), advocating a method better than that later proposed by J. L. MCADAM whose name has, however, become attached to Edgeworth's method.

Edgeworth married four times and had twenty-two children, so it is not surprising that he was concerned about education. He had a particular interest in the ideas of Rousseau, whom he met in France. His three-volume work *Practical Education* (1798) – written in collaboration with his daughter Maria, herself a distinguished author – had great success, and the ideas put forward were widely adopted.

> D. Clarke, *The Ingenious Mr. Edgeworth*. 1965. (Portrait.)
>
> R. L. and Maria Edgeworth, *Memoirs of Richard Lovell Edgeworth* (3rd ed.). 1844.

R. E. Schofield, *The Lunar Society of Birmingham.* 1963.

Dictionary of Scientific Biography.

Dictionary of National Biography.

D G K-H

EDISON, THOMAS ALVA Born at Milan, Ohio, USA, 11 February 1847; died West Orange, New Jersey, 18 October 1931. Inventor.

Edison came of Dutch and Scottish immigrant stock. His great-grandfather fled from the newly formed United States as a loyalist to Canada; his father fled back again as a rebel against the Canadian Government in 1837. The family prospered in Ohio and Michigan, where Thomas received a rudimentary education from his mother because he was slow at school and inept in mathematics. At 10 he divided his time chiefly between private experiments in chemistry and the sale of vegetables and newspapers; at 12 he was employing other boys.

Though handicapped by increasing deafness, attributable to an accident, Edison profited by the shortage of trained men during the Civil War to become a telegraph operator, in which capacity he roamed the country in 1863–8, living very roughly. The chance acquisition of the works of Michael FARADAY then gave him a less purely empirical knowledge of electricity, with the result that he patented his first invention, an electrographic vote-recorder, in which Congress showed a disappointing lack of interest. In the same year (1869) Edison arrived in New York, with no job or money, but armed with a strong determination to direct his inventive talents into some more profitable channel. Having already interested himself in the improvement of stock-ticker apparatus, he quickly made his services indispensable to the Gold Indicator Company; there he had direct experience of the value of up-to-date telegraphic equipment during the notorious attempt of James Fisk and Jay Gould to organize a corner in gold on 24 September 1869.

Within a week he had joined forces with a friend to set up a firm of 'electrical engineers' (said to be the first professional use of the term), which improved the stock-ticker in various ways; Edison eventually held forty-six patents in this field. Next year the firm was disposed of at a large profit, and at the age of 23 Edison became the proprietor of a business of his own, employing a staff of about fifty in the manufacture and improvement of telegraphic and other apparatus. This was the first 'invention-factory', the forerunner of the vast research organizations of modern industry. In a sense it was itself the most significant of all Edison's inventions, expanding into specially designed premises at Menlo Park in 1876 and at his final home at West Orange ten years later. Edison developed a remarkable gift for pursuing several wholly different lines of research at once, and at one period his staff were simultaneously engaged on nearly fifty inventions. But a remarkable run of success was due to at least three main causes. Edison possessed boundless energy and untiring intellectual curiosity; his precocious and varied experience made him a good judge of men as well as a hard taskmaker; and a constant stimulus was provided by the condition of American society, with abundant natural resources, a limited labour

supply, and an insatiable appetite for novelties.

In 1874 Edison made his first major invention – the diplex method of telegraphy which, when combined with the existing duplex method, enabled four messages to pass over a single wire. This was followed by his three contributions to the telephone – the carbon transmitter, a button of compressed lamp-black enabling the voice to be transmitted by high-voltage currents and hence for long distances; a non-magnetic relay; and a loudspeaking telephone receiver. Since the two latter inventions were called for as weapons in an intercompany struggle to secure the right to exploit the original invention of A. G. BELL, the speed with which they were produced clearly demonstrated the hitherto unrealized possibility of inventing to order.

Edison's most original invention was the phonograph (gramophone), which dates from 1877. Although Bell had drawn attention to the problems involved in reproducing speech, no one had suggested the possibility of a machine for placing speech on permanent record. Edison reached it by way of an automatic recording telegraph, making embossed marks that could be used to retransmit Morse messages at very high speed. He noticed that the rattle of the lever employed in this operation sometimes rose to a musical note, and reasoned from this that a diaphragm could be employed to reproduce sounds recorded from another diaphragm. The method of embossing by needle on a cylinder covered with tinfoil proved to be mechanically successful, but for at least a decade the whole contrivance was both too crude and too delicate to be launched commercially for any of the ten practical uses listed beforehand by the inventor.

Instead, Edison's main interest was for a time transferred to perfecting the incandescent electric lamp, of which the construction was now being rapidly advanced by Sir Joseph SWAN. After researches involving the examination of thousands of alternatives, he devised the cotton thread filament which, when joined with bulb patents, made the 'Ediswan' lamp a commercial success. These investigations were marked by his only first-rate scientific discovery, namely the fact that the vacuum lamp could act as a valve, permitting the passage of negative electric currents only. This Edison Effect was duly patented, but it was left to J. A. FLEMING, at that time a consultant of the Edison Electric Light Company in London, to conduct independently the research which led to the thermionic valve.

Edison's construction of the first central power station at Pearl Street, New York, in 1881 further illustrates his concentration upon immediate usefulness to society. Ten years later he made the first commercial motion pictures, using 35 mm celluloid film, forty-six pictures a second, and four perforations to align each picture. In April 1894 he opened his first Kinetoscope Parlor, but fell behind in this particular race through not realizing quickly enough that the need would arise for projection to large audiences. It would be unreasonable to expect that each of the 1097 patents issued in his name should prove a winner, and, in fact, he lost the whole of his fortune at the turn of the century when an elaborate investigation of the magnetic separation of iron ore was rendered unprofitable by new ore finds. Undismayed, he turned his attention to cement manufacture and new uses for concrete; to a highly successful electric storage battery; and to the growing vogue for office machinery. In the First World War he conducted research for the US Navy on torpedo mechanisms, flame-throwers, and periscopes.

The career of Thomas Edison was not that of a great man of science, nor even that of an inventive genius whose path is illuminated by flashes of inspiration. He made his discoveries mainly by a process of trial and error, at which he was prepared in his most productive years (1876–84) to work for as much as twenty hours a day. Yet no other inventor has shown practical talents ranging over so wide a field: the United States Congress hardly exaggerated when it claimed that the inventions of Edison had 'revolutionized civilization'.

W. A. Simonds, *Edison: His Life, His Work, His Genius.* 1935.

T. P. Hughes, *Thomas Edison: Professional Inventor.* 1976.

M. Josephson, *Edison.* 1959.

Dictionary of American Biography.

T K D

EHRENBERG, CHRISTIAN GOTTFRIED Born at Delitzsch, Germany, 19 April 1795; died Berlin, 27 June 1876. A founder of protozoology.

Ehrenberg studied zoology at Leipzig, and other sciences and medicine there and at Berlin. He spent six years in Egypt and North Africa as the naturalist to an expedition, and in 1829 accompanied Alexander von HUMBOLDT on his expedition to Russia. He was then appointed to a chair at Berlin. He was elected a member of the Berlin Academy of Sciences in 1827, and he served as its Secretary for many years.

Ehrenberg's main interest was microscopical research on the lowest forms of life, the animalcules of the organic infusions of earlier workers. These embraced protozoa, bacteria, and plant forms such as diatoms, and they were collectively described as Infusoria, i.e. infusion animalcules. In 1838 he published a large work on this subject. To it was appended an atlas of sixty-four magnificent plates, drawn by himself and reproduced in colour. In his experiments he fed living infusoria with dyes, and the particles of the dyes appeared in their contractile vacuoles. These he took to be stomachs, and he figured them and other organs. He therefore erroneously regarded all infusoria – including bacteria – as multicellular animals. Despite this error his work continued to exert great influence. Ehrenberg also demonstrated that certain earth-strata were formed by the calcareous shells of infusoria.

W. Bulloch, *History of Bacteriology.* 1938.

Parasitology, **15**, 320, 1923. (Portrait.)

Dictionary of Scientific Biography.

E A U

EHRLICH, PAUL Born at Strehlen, Silesia, 14 March 1854; died Bad Homburg, Hessen, Germany, 20 August 1915. A pioneer of scientific haematology and of immunology, and the founder of chemotherapy.

Ehrlich studied medicine in the Universities of Breslau, Strasbourg, Freiburg-im-Breisgau, and Leipzig, and graduated at Leipzig (1878). He then engaged in research and also became chief assistant to the physician F. T. von Frerichs (1819–85) at the *Charité* in Berlin. In 1887 he became Reader in Medicine in the University of Berlin. In 1890 Robert KOCH provided him with a laboratory in the Institute for Infectious Diseases. The excellent results obtained with diphtheria antitoxin induced Althoff, the Prussian Minister of State, to found at Steglitz (Berlin) an institute for serology and serum-testing, and Ehrlich was appointed its Director (1896). Three years later the scope of this institute was broadened and it was transferred to Frankfurt-am-Main as the Royal Institute for Experimental Therapy; to it was affiliated in 1906 the Georg Speyer Institute for Chemotherapy. Ehrlich was Director of these establishments until his death. On the foundation of the University of Frankfurt he was appointed a full professor. Ehrlich received many honours. He shared the Nobel prize with Ilya METCHNIKOFF in 1908. In 1910 he was elected a Foreign Member of the Royal Society, to which he had delivered the Croonian Lecture in 1900. In 1911 he was honoured with the title 'Excellenz'.

While still a student Ehrlich began investigations on the aniline dyes. With their aid he discovered (1877–81) all the different types of white blood corpuscles; he distinguished the leucaemias according to the prevalent type of cell; and he introduced his tri-acid stain for blood.

The staining of bacteria was then very difficult, and in 1881 Ehrlich introduced the highly satisfactory methylene blue stain. Much of Koch's work was done with this stain, and with it, by laborious staining over a prolonged period, he discovered the tubercle bacillus. On the day following Koch's announcement of his discovery, Ehrlich evolved a rapid method for staining the organism. This method is essentially that now known as the Ziehl-Neelsen method (after Franz Ziehl (1857–1926) and Friedrich Neelsen (1854–94)). In 1882 Ehrlich introduced his diazo-reaction for the diagnosis of typhoid fever, and in 1885 his work on the oxygen affinities of the tissues led to vital staining.

In 1891 Ehrlich discovered that the injection of poisons such as ricin induced the production of antibodies in the blood, and in the same year he discovered the latent period in the development of active immunity. In 1892 he illuminated the distinction between active and passive immunity. About this time many unsuccessful attempts had been made to provide standards for the dosage of diphtheria antitoxin. In 1897 Ehrlich published his classic paper on this subject. The method that he recommended was long employed in practice, and the scientific principles laid down in this paper are still fundamental. In 1897 also he evolved his well-known 'side-chain' theory of immunity. In 1899–1900 Ehrlich, with Julius Morgenroth (1871–1924), made fundamental advances in the study of haemolysis, and introduced the terms 'complement' and 'amboceptor'.

Ehrlich had meanwhile been interested in the production of a chemical substance which would be lethal for a particular organism, but harmless to its host. In 1891 he had used methylene blue for the treatment of malaria, and he tested other aniline dyes. In Liverpool, 'atoxyl' (a synthetic organic arsenic compound) had been tried in experimental trypanosome infections. Ehrlich repeated this work, but found that the organisms could become drug-resistant. He therefore set his chemists the task of producing successive modifications of this compound, and each was tested against trypanosomes as it was produced. In 1905 Fritz SCHAUDINN discovered the organism of syphilis. Ehrlich now also tested his compounds against this organism, and he found that compound No. 606 in the series was active and specific. It was named salvarsan, and was first used in the treatment of human syphilis in 1911. The science of chemotherapy – Ehrlich's term – was born.

R. Muir, *Journal of Pathology and Bacteriology*, **20**, 350, 1915–16.
W. Bulloch, *History of Bacteriology*. 1938. (Portrait.)
H. J. Parish, *History of Immunization*. 1965.
M. Marquardt, *Paul Ehrlich*. 1949.
Dictionary of Scientific Biography.

E A U

EIJKMAN, CHRISTIAAN Born at Nijkerk, Gelderlands, Netherlands, 11 August 1858; died Utrecht, 5 November 1930. A pioneer in the recognition and study of vitamins.

Eijkman, son of a schoolmaster, was educated at Zaandam, and then trained as a medical officer for the Army of the Dutch East Indies. He graduated in medicine at Amsterdam in 1883. For a period he worked with R. KOCH in Berlin, and he was then appointed as assistant to the Dutch Commission to study beriberi in Batavia. When the Commission returned to Europe in 1887 their laboratory was continued and Eijkman was made Director. He retained this post from 1888 to 1896. In 1898 he was called to the Chair of Hygiene and Forensic Medicine at Utrecht. In 1907 he was appointed a member of the Royal Academy of Sciences of the Netherlands, and in 1929 he shared a Nobel prize with Sir Frederick Gowland HOPKINS.

When Eijkman went to Batavia there had been many severe outbreaks of beriberi in the Dutch East Indies. This disease is characterized by ascending paralysis (due to a polyneuritis), cardiac symptoms, and oedema. In some outbreaks the death-rate was over 80 per cent. Many workers, including Eijkman, tried unsuccessfully to find a causative organism. The civilian research laboratory of which Eijkman was Director was situated in a military hospital at Batavia. It happened that a disease broke out among the chickens kept in the laboratory. The condition was characterized by an ascending paralysis ultimately affecting the respiratory muscles. There was no evidence that the disease was due to an infection. Eijkman discovered that the laboratory attendant had, for a short period, fed the birds on cooked rice obtained from the hospital kitchen. Then a new cook arrived, and he refused to allow rice from the military hospital to be given to the civilian laboratory. This latter event coincided with the disappearance of the disease in the chickens. Eijkman then showed that the disease could be produced at will by feeding chickens on polished rice instead of on unmilled rice, and that the bran removed by polishing would cure the disease if administered with the polished rice. Eijkman's work soon led to experiments by others on the feeding of prisoners in the Far East, and to the prevention and cure of human beriberi.

Eijkman misinterpreted his results; he thought that the bran contained a special protein or salt, or alternatively a protective substance against some poison. Later workers in Batavia and in British India demonstrated that the bran contained an essential food factor, now known as Vitamin B_1 (thiamine).

L. G. Stevenson, *Nobel Prize Winners in Medicine and Physics, 1901–1950*. 1953. (Portrait.)
Tyler Wasson (Ed.), *Nobel Prize Winners*. 1987. (Portrait.)
Dictionary of Scientific Biography.

E A U

EINSTEIN, ALBERT Born at Ulm, Württemberg, Germany, 14 March 1879; died Princeton, New Jersey, USA, 18 April 1955. Theoretical physicist, whose major contribution was the theory of relativity.

Einstein's father was a chemical engineer whose business was in continual difficulties, resulting in the family's moving frequently, with consequent irregular education for his son. At 17, Albert entered the *Eidgenössische Technische Hochschule* in Zürich, after some delay because of his inadequacy in mathematics. In 1901 he completed his studies, became a Swiss citizen, and hoped to become a school teacher. He was unable to get a post because he was a Jew, and he accordingly worked in a fairly junior position in the Patent Office in Berne. His first contribution to theoretical physics was made by 1901, but 1905 saw the appearance of three remarkable papers (which are described below). After teaching in the University of Berne he became successively a professor in Zürich in 1909; in the German University of Prague in 1910; and in the ETH Zürich in 1912. In 1913 he agreed to settle in Berlin as a member of the Royal Prussian Academy of Sciences, a research institute. In 1915 his fundamental paper on general relativity appeared. He received a Nobel prize for his work on quantum theory in 1922.

By a fortunate chance Einstein had arranged to spend the winter of 1932 at the California Institute of Technology. By January 1933 Hitler had come to power, and Einstein never returned to Germany. He resigned his position in Berlin, and in the autumn of 1933 accepted a position in the Princeton Institute of Advanced Study, which he held until his death, by which time he had become an American citizen.

One of Einstein's 1905 papers dealt with the Brownian movement, that is, the irregular motion of tiny particles in fluid resulting from their bombardment by molecules. He was the first to show that, by making measurements of the way that the visible particles move, one could infer the number of molecules of liquid per unit volume. Subsequent measurements verified Einstein's calculations completely and as a result the Brownian movement is one of the most direct pieces of evidence for the existence of molecules. The second 1905 paper dealt with the basis of quantum mechanics; this subject then consisted of little more than the ingenious arguments advanced by Max PLANCK for deriving the observed spectrum of radiation. Einstein was able, from the known results on radiation, and from the connection between thermodynamics and probability, to prove that radiation consisted of particles (photons) each carrying a discrete amount of energy. Although much remained to be done in quantum mechanics, this paper was a typical Einsteinian contribution, taking mathematical results which were known already and clothing them in physical understanding so that they were capable of much wider application. This situation is even more apparent in the third paper in 1905, on the special theory of relativity.

A number of difficulties had arisen in the late nineteenth century about optics. The best theory of optics was the electromagnetic theory of light, based on the theories of electricity and magnetism of J. Clerk MAXWELL. This suggested that light was a wave motion of a certain specified velocity and that this velocity was independent of the motion of the source and of the motion of the receiver. This fact seemed irreconcilable with the fact that uniform motion ought to make no difference to physical theory, but ought to add a constant velocity to that of light. By the end of the nineteenth century various subtle optical experiments had been devised for measuring the speed of light in special circumstances. In 1904 H. A. LORENTZ and J. H. POINCARÉ found a new way of altering Maxwell's equations under uniform motion so as to leave the speed of light unchanged. From the point of view of understanding, however, no progress had been made; the equations had been fixed up to give the right answers, without anyone knowing why. It was in these circumstances that Einstein made what was perhaps his greatest single contribution to physics. He had spent many years puzzling about how to measure the speed of light from one point to another point, since all the methods usually employed involve the reflection of a light signal and its reception again at the starting-point, that is a two-way determination of velocity. It was in 1905 that Einstein realized that a one-way determination of velocity was impossible, that the knot had to be cut by a convention, and that this convention at the same time did away with all the difficulties in the Maxwell theory without the *ad hoc* mathematical juggling of Lorentz and Poincaré.

This convention leads at once to the special theory of relativity, and to a resolution of the paradoxes concerning the velocity of light. It proved necessary to modify mechanics slightly in conformity with the convention and, when Einstein did this, he was able to find his famous equation $E = mc^2$ relating energy and mass by means of the square of the velocity of light; this is the basis of atomic energy.

Although the general principles of mechanics were straightforward to amend, one part of mechanics defeated Einstein's efforts for ten more years, that of gravitation. It turned out that for this a completely new outlook on it was required. Until 1915 the main emphasis was on the fact from which NEWTON started, that the gravitational field of a body falls off inversely as the square of the distance. The theory based on this was then further specialized by assuming that the acceleration produced in a body by gravitation was independent of its mass, a fact known already to GALILEO. The general theory of relativity put forward by Einstein in 1915 exactly reverses this approach. The resultant theory agrees very closely with Newton's theory of gravitation in many circumstances, in particular, in the orbits of the planets. A more accurate investigation, however, shows that in the case

of the planet Mercury a small but observable difference arises. The orbit of Mercury is roughly an ellipse with the Sun at one focus, but because of the effect of the other planets this ellipse would be expected to rotate through an angle of 5557 secs of arc per century; the observed advance is 5600 secs of arc per century. The general relativity calculation of the orbit of a planet round a stationary Sun gives, not an ellipse, but an ellipse rotating through an angle of 43 secs arc per century, in close agreement with the discrepancy arising in the Newtonian theory.

P. A. Schilpp (Ed.), *Albert Einstein: Philosopher-Scientist.* 1949. (Portrait.)

G. J. Whitrow (Ed.), *Einstein: the Man and his Achievement.* 1973.

P. Frank, *Einstein; His Life and Times.* 1947.

Tyler Wasson (Ed.), *Nobel Prize Winners.* 1987. (Portrait.)

Dictionary of Scientific Biography.

R. and R. Schulmann (Eds), *Albert Einstein and Mileva Marić: the Love Letters.* 1992. (Trans. from German).

C W K

EINTHOVEN, WILLEM Born at Samarang, Java, 21 May 1860; died Amsterdam, Netherlands, 28 September 1927. Inventor of clinical electrocardiography.

The son of a Dutch physician who practised in the East Indies, Einthoven qualified in medicine at Utrecht in 1885 and was appointed professor of physiology at Leiden the following year, aged 25. He had received some early training in physics; his first papers were on the physiology of the eye, on the bronchial musculature, and on the physics of the capillary electrometer. Thereafter he constructed a string galvanometer and applied it to record the electrical activity of the contracting heart muscle (electrocardiography), as well as for graphic registration of the heart sounds (phonocardiography). The 'electromotive changes accompanying the heart beats' had been demonstrated in 1887 by A. D. Waller (1856–1922), but the inertia of the capillary electrometer did not allow more than a demonstration that there was 'a true electrical variation of the human heart'.

Einthoven recorded electrocardiograms not from the chest wall but from two limbs of the subject in three different combinations (I, right arm to left; II, right arm to left leg; III, left arm to left leg), and these have remained the standard recordings. He also described the main deflections of the tracing and devised a nomenclature. His few classical papers on this topic between 1903 and 1908 touched on the possibilities of using the method in the diagnosis of diseases of the heart, but were concerned mainly with physical principles.

The main clinical application of electrocardiography lies in the diagnosis of coronary artery disease, the definitive accounts of which came from Sir William Osler (1849–1919) and James Herrick (1861–1954) a few years after (and independent of) Einthoven's discoveries. The correlation of electrocardiographic tracings and of clinical data was achieved between 1910 and 1935 by the school of Sir Thomas Lewis (1881–1945) in London and by F. N. Wilson and his colleagues in the United States.

Einthoven continued to perfect the sensitivity of

his string galvonometer and was engaged in attempting to record nerve impulses at the time of his death, but this was achieved successfully only later by others who used the cathode ray oscilloscope. However, the delicacy of the string in Einthoven's later galvanometers made him propound a physical theory of the nature of shadows cast by minute objects.

Electrocardiography is second in importance only to the discovery of x-rays by W. K. ROENTGEN among the physical methods used in clinical medicine. Einthoven received the Nobel prize for medicine or physiology in 1924.

> J. Fulton, *Boston Medical and Surgical Journal.* **197**, 687, 1927. (Portrait.)
> *Lancet,* **2**, 763. 1927.
> Tyler Wasson (Ed.), *Nobel Prize Winners.* 1987. (Portrait.)

EHJ

ELKINGTON, GEORGE RICHARDS Born at Birmingham, England, 17 October 1801; died Pool Park, Denbighshire, Wales, 22 September 1865. Pioneer of electroplating.

Elkington entered the Birmingham small-wares trade in 1815 as an apprentice in the family business and became, in due course, sole proprietor. With his cousin, Henry Elkington (1810–52), he investigated the alternatives to silver plating by rolling or soldering, from about 1832. Following trials of chemical methods, they took out a patent in 1838 for the application of current electricity to gilding, and from 1840 used the cyanide plating bath method discovered by John Wright (*d.* 1844). They established a large plating works in Birmingham in 1841, and eventually made the process a commercial success. With Sir Josiah Mason (1795–1881) – founder of Mason College, Birmingham (later Birmingham University) – Elkington established a copper-smelting works, together with model housing, at Pembrey, Glamorganshire, but the Birmingham business remained his chief concern.

Dictionary of National Biography.

WNS

ELLET, CHARLES Born at Penn's Manor, Pennsylvania, USA, 1 January 1810; died Cairo, Illinois, 21 June 1862. A versatile engineer who has been called 'the Brunel of America'.

Ellet was the son of a Quaker farmer who strongly opposed his wish to become an engineer; he made his own way in canal work before attending the *École Polytechnique* in Paris and making a study tour in Europe. In 1842 he built the first important suspension bridge in the United States, the Fairmount Bridge over the Schuylkill at Philadelphia, and in 1849 the Wheeling Bridge over the Ohio, with a then record span of 1010 feet: the cable was made on the superseded French system of bundles of small wires, but the towers and anchorages have survived two reconstructions.

Ellet was the author of forty-six published works, mainly on transportation economics and military problems; his *Mississippi and Ohio Rivers* (1853) contained flood-control proposals of sufficient importance for the book to be reissued by order of Congress in 1927–8. At the outbreak of the American Civil War he remodelled a flotilla of nine river-boats for ramming, and sustained fatal injuries during their employment for the capture of Memphis on the Mississippi.

Dictionary of American Biography.

TKD

EMPEDOCLES Born in Akragas (Agrigentum), Sicily, *c.*494 BC; according to legend died leaping into crater of Mount Etna, *c.*434 BC. Presocratic philosopher.

Born into a wealthy and distinguished family, Empedocles grew up in a centre of Greek culture. Stories about his life suggest that he travelled around the Peloponnese teaching, and he may have been exiled from Sicily for his political activities. His ideas have been preserved in fragments of his poems *On Nature* and in his religious poem *Purifications*, passed down by later writers. His ideas were the result of philosophical speculation rather than empirical investigation.

Empedocles was concerned with the nature of change. Rejecting the view of Parmenides (*c.*515–*c.*450 BC) that change cannot occur he developed his theory of the elements. He thought that the world and everything in it was made up of four immutable and eternal elements – Earth, Air, Fire and Water – and these could produce change through the actions of two opposing forces, Love and Strife, which mixed and separated the elements in different proportions to form different substances. This theory of the elements, developed by Plato and ARISTOTLE, was dominant until the 17th century.

Empedocles also demonstrated that invisible air could occupy empty space, using his famous example of the movement of liquid in a clepsydra. From this he developed a tidal theory of the circulation of the blood which remained accepted until HARVEY.

Empedocles anticipated DARWIN in his biological speculations. He thought that the Earth had earlier produced a much greater variety of living things, with monsters emerging from random combinations of limbs and organs, but many had been unable to survive and reproduce and so had died out. He is mentioned in the preface to the *Origin of the Species* (1859).

> D. O'Brien, *Empedocles' Cosmic Cycle.* 1969
> M. R. Wright, *Empedocles: The Extant Fragments.* 1981.
> G. E. R. Lloyd, *Early Greek Science: Thales to Aristotle.* 1970.

APB

ENGELMANN, THEODOR WILHELM Born in Leipzig, Germany, 14 November 1843; died Berlin, 21 May 1909. Physiologist.

Engelmann was professor of physiology at Utrecht and later in Berlin. In animal physiology he is remembered, with A. Rollett (1834–1903), for his work on the striation of muscle. In 1881 he discovered the chemotactic effect of oxygen on certain bacteria and used this to detect traces of free oxygen. In investigations of simple animals he showed (1883) that *Vorticella* is able to assimilate oxygen by means of chlorophyll, just as green plants do. In other researches on photosynthesis (1882) Engelmann showed that the chloroplasts of plant cells are activated mainly by red and blue

light and very little by the intermediate parts of the spectrum.
Dictionary of Scientific Biography.

T I W

ENGLER, HEINRICH GUSTAV ADOLF Born at Sargans, Lower Silesia, 25 March 1844; died Dahlem, Berlin, 10 October 1930. German botanist.

Engler's life-long interest in systematic botany began while a pupil at the Magdalenen-Gymnasium in Breslau, when he acquired a remarkable knowledge of the flora of the neighbourhood. In 1863 he matriculated at the University of Breslau and studied botany under H. R. Goeppert (1800–84); three years later he gained his doctor's diploma for a dissertation on the *Saxifraga*, a genus presenting taxonomic problems which interested him throughout life. After graduation he taught natural history at his former school, but in 1872 he moved to Munich to become Custodian of the Botanical Collections under K. W. von NÄGELI. While there he published (1872) his *Monographie der Gattung Saxifraga*. In 1878 he was appointed professor of botany in the University of Kiel. During his six years there he founded (1880) the *Botanische Jahrbücher*, which he edited until his death. When Goeppert died Engler succeeded him at Breslau, and he undertook the reconstruction of the associated Botanic Garden, which he planned on original phyto-geographical lines. In 1887 appeared the first part of his *Die Natürlichen Pflanzenfamilien* – the outcome of an ambition to publish an encyclopaedia of the plant kingdom. For the Phanerogams, the work was completed within twelve years. In 1887 Engler was appointed professor of botany in Berlin, then an exceptionally important and responsible post. He successfully transferred the Botanic Garden from Schöneberg to Dahlem, and he promoted the study of the flora of Germany's colonies, particularly those in Africa. Within a few years appeared many contributions to the *Botanische Jahrbücher* on African floras. In 1891 he communicated his great memoir, *Über die Hochgebirgs-flora des tropischen Afrika*, to the Berlin Academy of Sciences. His activities as a fieldworker led him to visit nearly all European countries, Africa, India, China, Japan, and the USA. His botanical interests covered systematic, evolutionary, and geographical aspects of the plant kingdom. He retired from his professorship and from the direction of the Botanic Garden at Dahlem in 1921. The Linnean Society of London elected him a Foreign Member in 1888 and in 1913 awarded him the Linnean Gold Medal.

Proceedings of the Linnean Society of London, 125 Session, **45**, 1912–13; *143 Session,* 171, 1930–31.

Berichlt der deutschen botanischen Gesellschaft, **48**, 146, 1930. (Portrait.)

A P G

EÖTVÖS, ROLAND Born in Budapest, 27 July 1848; died there, 8 April 1919. Remembered for his measurements of gravitational and magnetic fields.

Roland Eötvös was the son of the celebrated Hungarian poet, novelist, and statesman, Josef von Eötvös (1813–71). On completing his school studies he proceeded to the University of Heidelberg where he received his doctorate in 1870 *summa cum laude*. On his return to Budapest he became *Dozent* at the University of Budapest in 1871 and was made ordinary professor of theoretical physics there in 1872. In 1878 he became professor of experimental physics, a post which he retained until his death. After being Minister of Public Instruction (1894–5) he resigned in order to devote himself entirely to research and teaching.

Eötvös's earliest researches lay in the field of capillarity in which he established the law relating surface tension with temperature. He subsequently carried out a long series of researches into gravitation and magnetism employing extremely delicate torsion balances for measuring variations in the magnitude and direction of gravitational and magnetic fields. These instruments proved of great practical use in geological surveys. He established with great accuracy that gravitational attraction depends only on the mass of bodies, being entirely independent of their nature. He also demonstrated experimentally that bodies moving to the east suffer a loss in weight.

R. Eötvös, *Collected Works*. 1953. (Includes portrait, and memoir in German.)
D. Pekár, *Naturwissenschaften*, 7, 1919.
Dictionary of Scientific Biography.

J W H

EPICURUS Born, probably at Samos, 342/1 BC; died Athens, 271/70 BC. Philosopher; apostle of atomism.

Epicurus came of a noble Athenian family settled in Samos. He taught at Mytilene and Lampsacus and in 306 BC he established a philosophical school ('the Garden') in Athens, where he spent the rest of his life. His writings survive only in part; his philosophy is immortalized in the Latin poem *De rerum natura* of LUCRETIUS.

In the fifth century BC Democritus of Abdera, (d. 361 BC), following his master Leucippus, (*fl.* 480 BC), had taught that the universe consisted of innumerable atoms, indestructible, differing only in size, shape, and position, and moving at random in an infinite void. Physical objects consisted of transient aggregations of atoms, whose configuration determined what we should call the 'secondary qualities' of these objects. Souls, or minds, existed but differed from gross bodies only in the greater subtlety and refinement of their constituent atoms.

Epicurus revived Democritean atomism, but he introduced the conception of 'atomic swerve' thus mitigating blind necessity with an element of spontaneity. For Epicurus all knowledge was based upon sense perceptions common to all mankind. Such perceptions are produced by thin films, or simulacra, continually thrown off by material things and impinging upon our organs of sense.

Atomism had no place in Aristotle's all-prevailing cosmology; and Jewish and Christian teachers, discerning its atheistic implications, drove it underground, to re-emerge only in the seventeenth century and to enter upon its true scientific development in the nineteenth.

C. Bailey, *The Greek Atomists and Epicurus.* 1928.
B. Farrington, *The Faith of Epicurus.* 1967.
Dictionary of Scientific Biography.

A A

ERASISTRATUS Born at Iulis, on the island of

Ceos, Greece, c.300 BC. Regarded as the father of physiology.

Erasistratus studied at Athens, and later taught at Alexandria, where he was a younger contemporary of HEROPHILUS. He made important anatomical observations, but he was more interested in physiology. He excelled Herophilus in his description of the brain, noted the greater complexity of the cerebral convolutions in man as compared with those in animals, traced the nerves into the brain substance, and distinguished more clearly between motor and sensory nerves. He first described the valves between the atria and the ventricles of the heart, and that on the right, the tricuspid, owes its name to him. He gave a clearer description of the lacteals than Herophilus had done.

Erasistratus conceived of the tissues of the body as being composed of a web formed by the ultimate branches, beyond the limits of vision, of the veins, arteries, and nerves. He reverted to the old view that during life the arteries contain air, i.e. vital spirit. He appreciated that during life blood flows from a cut artery. He explained this by assuming that when the artery is cut the vital spirit escapes: but, as nature abhors a vacuum, blood is sucked into the artery from a vein through minute intercommunicating channels. He thus postulated the existence of capillaries, and some believe that he nearly discovered the circulation of the blood.

C. Singer, *The Evolution of Anatomy*. 1925.
T. C. Allbutt, *Greek Medicine in Rome*. 1921.
J. F. Dobson, *Proceedings of the Royal Society of Medicine (Section of the History of Medicine)*, **18**, 19, 1924–5.
Dictionary of Scientific Biography.

E A U

ERATOSTHENES OF CYRENE Born at Cyrene, North Africa, c.273 BC; died Alexandria, c.192 BC. Geographer and polymath; determined the size of the Earth and the obliquity of the ecliptic.

Educated in Athens, Eratosthenes became the chief librarian of the Alexandrian Museum. His measurement of the Earth involved ascertaining both the difference of latitude and the distance apart of two places supposedly located on the same meridian: he selected Alexandria and Syene in Upper Egypt. The circumference of the Earth was thence deduced by proportion. Eratosthenes did not originate this procedure; he was content with round numbers, and how near he came to the true value is affected by uncertainty as to the units he employed. His value is commonly accepted as 29 000 miles, compared with the modern value of a little less than 25 000 miles. He also established the obliquity of the ecliptic (its inclination to the celestial equator) from determinations of the respective meridian altitudes of the Sun at the summer and the winter solstices.

The geographical memoirs of Eratosthenes, surviving only in fragments, seem to have comprised a history of geographical ideas; a section on mathematical geography, establishing the division of the globe into zones and delimiting its inhabited portion; and a concluding account of descriptive geography with crude attempts at map-making. In mathematics Eratosthenes gave his name to the 'sieve' for distinguishing prime from composite numbers, and he proposed a solution of the problem of duplicating the cube. He sought to harmonize and unify the diverse chronological systems of his day; and he was famous in his time as a man of letters.

G. Sarton, *A History of Science: Hellenistic Science and Culture in the last three Centuries BC. 1959.*
T. L. Heath, *A Manual of Greek Mathematics.* 1931.
Dictionary of Scientific Biography.

A A

ERCKER, LAZARUS Born (date unknown) at Annaberg, Bohemia; died 1593. Mining engineer.

Very little is know of the life of this early writer on ores and assaying. He was described in the second and later editions of his famous work as Chief Superintendent of Mines of the Holy Roman Empire and Bohemia. In the foreword he states his place of origin as Saint Annen Bergk, Bohemia (now Annaberg). He served under Emperor Rudolf II, a patron of arts and science who found places in his court for among others, Tycho BRAHE and Johannes KEPLER. The Emperor sent him to the mines of Bohemia as adviser, and he had the reputation of being the best-informed and most careful observer among mining engineers of the time.

His influence lay in a single work first published in 1574, yet still being translated and published in the mid-eighteenth century, and quoted over an even longer period. This book was *Beschreibung allerfürnemisten Mineralischen Ertzt und Bergkwerksarten* ... After its first Prague edition of 1574 it was republished in 1580, 1598, and 1629. An enlarged edition under the title *Aula Subterranea* ... was published in 1672, and reissued in 1684, 1703, and 1736. In 1683 it had been translated into English by Sir John Pettus (1613–90), Deputy Governor of the Royal Mines under Cromwell, under the title *Fleta Minor: the Laws of Art and Nature in Knowing Judging Assaying Fining and Refining* ... *Metals*. According to Pettus, Ercker 'stands for a renowned Assay Master, a Good Chymist, and one that understood but was not a sophisticating Alchemist'.

The work is set out in five books, the first and longest of which deals with silver ores, and the design of apparatus for assaying them. The second and third books cover gold and copper respectively; the fourth embraces lead, tin, bismuth, antimony, mercury, and iron; and the fifth describes methods of purifying saltpetre. It was written in a candid style and always from a practical standpoint.

P. R. Beierlein, *Lazarus Ercker, Bergmann, Hüttemann, und Müntzmeister im 16. Jahrhundert.* 1955.
Dictionary of Scientific Biography.

N H

ERICSSON, JOHN Born at Färnebo, Sweden, 31 July 1803; died New York, 8 March 1899. Inventor and engineer.

The son of a mines inspector, Ericsson served from 13 to 17 as an engineer in training on the Gotha Canal works; was commissioned in the Swedish Army, where he did cartographical surveys; and in 1826 moved to London to exploit a new type of heat engine. He did not succeed with this, but in the next twelve years he launched a major invention annually, including a locomotive to rival the *Rocket*, a self-regulating lead (1836), and finally the screw propeller. The use of the helicoidal screw had already been canvassed by marine engineers, but Ericsson, who realized that the paddle-wheel engine was incapable of further improvement and was specially interested in getting warship engines located below the waterline, played a leading part in the development. His patent (1836) and his first screw-propelled ship (1839) are contemporaneous with those of Sir Francis Smith (1808–79), whose four-bladed screw was adopted by the British Admiralty for the *Rattler* in 1841.

Having crossed the Atlantic to build a screw-driven steam frigate for the US Navy, Ericsson in 1848 became an American citizen. The Civil War brought him his chief fame, through the building of the turreted ironclad *Monitor* with low freeboard and heavy guns; it was built according to plans which Ericsson had previously offered to Napoleon III. Its victory at Hampton Roads on 9 March 1862 marked an epoch in naval design. Ericsson continued to design warships, torpedoes, and (less successfully) a 14-inch gun, but never lost his interest in heat engines. In 1870–88 much of his time and fortune was devoted to the designing of a solar engine and to exploring the possibilities of solar energy, gravitation, and tidal forces as sources of power.

W. C. Church, *Life of John Ericsson* (2 vols). 1891.
Dictionary of American Biography.

T K D

ERLANGER, JOSEPH Born at San Francisco, California, USA, 5 January 1874; died St Louis, Missouri, 5 December 1965. Physiologist; made important observations about the transmission of electrical impulses in nerves.

Joseph Erlanger received his early scientific education at the University of California, and his medical training at Johns Hopkins University, where after graduating MD in 1899 he held various posts in physiology. He became professor of physiology, successively at Wisconsin University (1906), and at Washington University, St Louis (1910). He remained at St Louis until his retirement in 1946, and during this period published more than a hundred papers on neurophysiological topics, including notable contributions on the function of the synapse. His most important work was done in collaboration with H. S. GASSER, with whom he devised new techniques for the amplification and recording of electrical impulses in nerves. They showed that nerve fibres conduct electricity at rates proportional to their diameter. The results of their work was published in 1937 under the title *Electrical Signs of Nervous Activity*, which has become a physiological classic. Erlanger and Gasser were jointly awarded the Nobel prize for physiology or medicine in 1944 for their 'discoveries concerning the functional differentiation of particular nerve fibres'.

Erlanger was a gifted experimentalist with great manual dexterity. He was of shy and retiring disposition, and said that 'communion with nature' was his chief recreation and hobby.

J. Erlanger, *Annual Reviews of Physiology*, **26**, 1, 1964.
Tyler Wasson (Ed.), *Nobel Prize Winners*. 1987. (Portrait.)

C M

ERNST, RICHARD R Born in Winterthur, Switzerland, 14 August 1933. Chemist; made major contributions to development of high resolution NMR spectroscopy.

Ernst is a graduate (1956) of the *Eidgenössische Technische Hochschule* (ETH), Zürich. After five years as a research scientist with Varian Associates, Palo Alto, California, he returned to ETH in 1968, where in 1976 he was appointed professor of physical chemistry.

The phenomenon of nuclear magnetic resonance (NMR) was investigated in the 1940s, notably by F. BLOCH and E. M. PURCELL in the USA, who shared a Nobel prize in 1952. Briefly, it was discovered that certain atomic nuclei have a magnetic moment and so will orientate themselves in a strong magnetic field. They can, however, take up only certain discrete orientations, corresponding to different energy levels. The application of radiofrequency radiation causes them to resonate between these possible positions. The resonance frequency relates to the environment of the nucleus and can thus give valuable information on molecular structure.

In 1956 Ernst – together with W. A. Anderson – discovered that the sensitivity of NMR spectroscopy could be increased enormously, up to a hundredfold, if the slow radiofrequency sweep then in use was replaced by short, intense pulses of radiofrequency radiation. The resulting signal was then measured as the time-lapse after the pulse. This signal is not immediately interpretable but can be converted to a normal NMR spectrum by means of a computer. This new technique was designated FT NMR, and was soon widely adopted. In the 1970s Ernst and his co-workers increased both resolution and sensitivity by using sequences of pulses rather than a single pulse (2DFT NMR). This and further (multidimensional) developments have made it possible to apply the technique to polymers and large natural molecules such as proteins. It is now a very widely used technique of chemical analysis.

Ernst was elected a Foreign Member of the Royal Society in 1993 and was awarded the Nobel prize for chemistry in 1992.

Les Prix Nobel en 1992. 1993. (Portrait.)
La Recherche, December 1991. (Portrait.)
New Scientist, 26 October 1991. (Portrait.)

T I W

ESAKI, LEO Born in Osaka, Japan, 12 March 1925. Physicist best known for his discovery of the tunnel diode.

Esaki gained his first degree at Tokyo University in 1947 and joined the Kobe Kogyo Corporation before moving to the Sony Corporation in 1956. While at Sony he investigated 'tunnelling' in semiconductors, a quantum mechanical effect in which a particle like an electron has a small probability of crossing an otherwise insurmountable energy barrier. Esaki observed an increased current due to tunnelling across junctions between p-type and n-type germanium, provided he made the junctions very narrow and used very high concentrations of the 'n' and 'p' charge carriers. He also discovered that still narrower junctions displayed a negative resistance in certain conditions. In other words, the current across the junction would decrease with voltage.

This type of junction is now known as the tunnel or Esaki diode and has found a wide range of applications, in particular where high-speed switching is necessary. In 1973, Esaki was rewarded with the Nobel prize for physics, which he shared with Ivar Giaever (1929–), who had discovered electron tunnelling in superconductors, and Brian JOSEPHSON, who had predicted an additional 'super-current' tunnelling in superconductors.

Esaki gained his PhD from Tokyo University in 1959, while still working at Sony. The following year he moved to the US, to the IBM Thomas J Watson Research Center in New Jersey, where he continues his research into quantum mechanic effects in semiconductors.

Physics Today, December 1973. (Portrait.)

Tyler Wasson (Ed.), *Nobel Prize Winners*. 1987. (Portrait.)

C S

ÉTARD, ALEXANDRE LÉON Born at Alençon, France, 5 January 1852; died Paris, 1 May 1910. Chemist and teacher.

Étard studied chemistry under A. A. T. Cahours (1813–91) at the Sorbonne, and later became professor of physics and chemistry at the School of Industrial Physics and Chemistry in Paris. He first worked mainly in inorganic chemistry, but later became interested in natural products. He is remembered by the 'Étard reaction' (1880), in which toluene is oxidized to benzaldehyde by chromyl chloride, but the reaction has never attained much practical importance.

J. C. Poggendorff, *Biographisch-Literarisches Handwörterbuch*. 1883–1903.

W V F

EUCLID Flourished in Alexandria, *c*.300 BC. Mathematician; author of the *Elements*.

Euclid was probably educated in Athens and trained at the Academy; later he taught at Alexandria. The contents of the *Elements* did not all originate with Euclid, though the arrangement and certain of the proofs may be attributed to him, together with the establishment of the classic form of a geometrical proposition. Earlier geometers had already established the practice of selecting the basic propositions and setting them forth concisely in logical sequence, but Euclid's collection superseded all previous ones. Of the thirteen Books of the *Elements*, the first six cover the familiar ground of elementary geometry as still taught; they illustrate the 'geometric algebra' of the followers of PYTHAGORAS – e.g. the use of geometrical techniques to solve simple and quadratic equations – and they embody the generalized theory of proportion, traditionally attributed to EUDOXUS OF CNIDUS and applicable to incommensurable as well as to commensurable quantities. Books VII-IX deal with the theory of numbers; Book X is a geometrical treatment of surds; Books XI-XIII are concerned with solid geometry, culminating in the construction of the five regular solids and of their circumscribed spheres.

Geometers early recognized in Euclid's Fifth Postulate (the 'Parallel Postulate') a proposition calling for proof. Yet the needed proof could never be provided; and it was discovered in the nineteenth century that self-consistent systems of geometry could be founded upon the rejection of the 'Parallel Postulate', which thus came to be recognized as implicitly defining the character, or 'metric', of the particular kind of space that Euclid was proposing to study. Such non-Euclidean geometries have assumed an added significance since recent physical theories raised the question of whether the space of our experience can be regarded as a strictly Euclidean one.

In a radical reappraisement of the Euclidean tradition, M. Jean Itard of the Sorbonne has suggested that the *Elements* is a composite work created by a school of geometers working under the direction, or continuing in the teaching, of a founder who may even have been Euclid of Megara (5th cent. BC), a disciple of Socrates (5th cent. BC), with whom, indeed, the author of the *Elements* was frequently identified prior to the sixteenth century.

Of several physical treatises attributed to Euclid, the *Optics*, at least, is accounted genuine. It deals with elementary problems of perspective treated on the ancient assumption that light proceeds in straight lines from the eyes to the object seen.

T. L. Heath, *A History of Greek Mathematics*, vol. 1. 1921.

The Thirteen Books of Euclid's Elements, translated with Introduction and Commentary by T. L. Heath (2nd ed. 3 vols). 1926.

J. Itard, *Les Livres Arithmétiques d'Euclide*. 1961.

Dictionary of Scientific Biography.

A A

EUDOXUS OF CNIDUS Born at Cnidus, Asia Minor, *c*.408 BC; died *c*.355 BC. Mathematician and astronomer; generalized the theory of proportion, invented the 'method of exhaustion', and proposed the hypothesis of homocentric planetary spheres.

Eudoxus studied under Plato (*c*.427–*c*.347 BC). and travelled in Egypt and Asia Minor.

The Pythagorean theory of proportion applied only to commensurable magnitudes; Eudoxus removed this limitation, and he established a classic test for the equality of two ratios. He is also credited with the 'method of exhaustion' which, as applied, say, to finding the area of a circle, consisted in drawing an inscribed polygon and repeatedly doubling the number of its sides, the area of the polygon thus steadily approximating towards that of the circle.

Eudoxus sought to represent the apparent motion of a planet by imagining the planet to be attached to the equator of an ideal sphere rotating uniformly about two opposite poles and having the Earth at its centre. These poles were embedded in the surface of a second sphere, concentric with the first but external to it and itself in uniform rotation about an axis inclined at a constant angle to that of the first sphere. This second sphere was similarly related to a third one, and so on to the number of spheres required to give the planet a compound motion similar to that with which it was observed to move round the Earth. This system of 'homocentric spheres' was adopted, and given a material embodiment, in the cosmic scheme of ARISTOTLE.

T. L. Heath, *A History of Greek Mathematics*, vol. 1. 1921.

J. L. E. Dreyer, *A History of Astronomy from Thales to Kepler*. 1953.

Greek, Roman, and Byzantine Studies, **4**, 83, 1963.

Dictionary of Scientific Biography.

A A

EULER, LEONHARD Born at Basle, Switzerland, April 1707; died St Petersburg, 18 September 1783. The most prolific mathematician of all time.

Euler was the son of a Calvinist pastor, himself an amateur mathematician. Educated first by his father, he attended the University of Basle, where he met the BERNOULLIs. Apart from mathematics, he studied theology, Oriental languages, and physiology. In 1727 he settled in St Petersburg at the invitation of Catherine I. Daniel Bernoulli was already there, and in 1733 Euler succeeded him as professor of mathematics. Invited to Berlin in 1741 by Frederick the Great, he returned to St Petersburg in 1766. Having lost the sight of one eye in 1735, he became totally blind, but continued to write copiously in mathematics, dictating to his servant.

A straightforward list of Euler's works would occupy perhaps seventy pages of this volume. Taking the subjects he studied in roughly chronological order, his first great achievement was the introduction of analytic methods into mechanics from 1736 and the quasi-axiomatic use of the principle of virtual work. Like P. L. M. de MAUPERTUIS, Euler used minimal principles for the expression of natural laws, and not for more than a century was it appreciated that maxima of the definite integrals might also serve. In connection with the problem of minimizing integrals, Euler deduced the differential equation called after him (1744). His work was invariably more general than that of his predecessors. An ingredient of his success was his well-known 'rule of the undetermined multiplier'. After 1764 Euler adopted the new symbolism of J. L. LAGRANGE.

In analysis, as in mechanics, he minimized reliance on geometrical methods. He published three monumental works on analysis (1748, 1755, 1768–70). Some of their results are well known, including Euler's theorem of homogeneous functions and his theory of convergence.

One of Euler's first books dealt with arithmetic (1738), and he occupied himself for much of his life with number theory. He was the first great exponent of Diophantine analysis after DIOPHANTUS and Pierre FERMAT, although his methods were unsystematic. Many of his results were, even in his lifetime, found to be special cases of theorems more easily obtained by different methods. In algebra he is remembered for many results, as for example his determinantal expression for the eliminant of a set of linear equations, his reduction of the biquadratic equation to a cubic, and the theorem that the difference between the sum of the reciprocals of the first n natural numbers and log n tends to a finite limit ('Euler's constant') as n tends to infinity. He published a widely used textbook of algebra.

Some of his best work was in hydrodynamics. He was the first to explain adequately the part played by pressure in fluid flow. He formulated the equations and many of the concepts of fluid motion, and even the so-called Bernoulli theorem was first rigorously derived by him.

When blind, Euler spent a lot of time trying to improve the theory of the Moon's motion, introducing new inequalities in the process. He seems to have been the first to work from the supposition that it is the centre of mass of the solar system, and not the Sun, which is at the centre of the Kepler ellipse. He established many classical principles of perturbation theory.

Euler's first love was geometry, a subject to which he contributed much of value, from the solution of isolated problems, as in his analysis of the hypocyloid, to new methods of developing whole branches of geometry, as when he made his transformation formulae for the general rigid motion in space one of the foundations of his differential geometry of curves and surfaces. One of his best-known results is the formula relating the number of faces, vertices, and edges of polyhedra.

Euler had a very wide general knowledge, and his scientific range can be judged from the three volumes which he wrote at the request of the Princess of Anhalt-Dessau – *Lettres à une princesse* (1768–72). Although the treatment of optics, acoustics, the theory of heat, and physical astronomy is now outmoded, Euler's penetrating style of exposition is as much in evidence now as it was to the Princess.

O. Spiess, *Eulers Leben und Wirken*. 1929. (Portrait.)

E. T. Bell, *Men of Mathematics*, vol. 1. 1937.

Dictionary of Scientific Biography.

J D N

EULER, ULF SVANTE VON Born in Stockholm, 7 February 1905; died there, 10 March 1983. Made outstanding discoveries in neuropharmacology especially in the field of receptor action and function.

His father, Hans von Euler-Cheplin (1873–1964), was awarded, with Arthur HARDEN, the Nobel prize for chemistry in 1929. His mother, Astrid Cleve-Euler, was a scientist of some note. Both parents worked together for some time before their marriage was dissolved in 1912.

Ulf studied medicine in Stockholm and while still a student undertook research with C. Ahlgren on tissue respiration at the University of Lund. In 1930 he came to London to work with Sir Henry DALE at the National Institute for Medical Research. Then began his studies of neurotransmission, which ultimately led to the isolation and identification in 1946 of noradrenaline in the sympathetic nervous system. While in Dale's laboratory he collaborated with J. H. Gaddum (1900–65) in studies of the neural role of acetylcholine; it was also at this time that he began identification and isolation of Substance P.

The role of noradrenaline as a major neurotransmitter was elucidated by von Euler, B. Katz (1911–) and J. Axelrod (1912–), for which they shared the Nobel prize in 1970. An overview of the functions and activities of adrenaline and noradrenaline was given by von Euler in his Sherrington Lecture of 1978 (published 1980).

Von Euler also elucidated the identity and role of the prostaglandins in the mid-1930s. It was his close contact with Sune BERGSTROM that led to the isolation of a pure prostaglandin and thence the sharing of the Nobel prize for physiology or medicine by Bergstrom, Bengt Samuelsson (1934–) and John Vane (1927–) in 1982.

U. S. von Euler, Annual Review of Pharmacology, **11**, 1–12, 1971.

Nobel Lectures: Physiology or Medicine 1963–70. 1972.

Biographical Memoirs of Fellows of the Royal Society, 1985. (Portrait.)

Tyler Wasson (Ed.), *Nobel Prize Winners*. 1987
(Portrait.)

C L

EUSTACHI(O), BARTOLOMEO Born at San Severino, near Ancona, Italy, *c*.1513; died *en route* to Fossombrone, near Pesaro, 27 August 1574. Distinguished anatomist.

Little is known of Eustachio's life. He became physician to the Duke of Urbino and later to Cardinal della Rovere. In 1562 he was professor of anatomy at the Papal College of the *Sapienza* at Rome. About this period he was in straitened circumstances, and he later suffered from gout. Illness caused him to resign his chair, and he died while on a journey to attend della Rovere.

During Eustachio's lifetime he published only three works. Two of these deal respectively with the kidneys and the teeth and are short works; the third, his *Opuscula anatomica* (1564), contains these two works and four other tracts. Eustachio had, however, long been working on a comprehensive anatomical treatise, never completed; but the forty-seven plates, designed to illustrate it, were finished by 1552. After Eustachio's death they passed into the hands of relatives. In 1714 they were recovered by G. M. LANCISI, and published by him. In 1744 the Dutch anatomist B. S. ALBINUS republished them, with full descriptions and notes. Had Eustachio himself published these plates, he would have been regarded as almost the equal of VESALIUS; but by the time of their ultimate publication many of his new observations had been made independently by others.

Eustachio's main purpose was to defend Galen against the attacks of the new anatomists. His defence was based on his very careful dissections, and he corrected not only GALEN, but often Vesalius and the newer anatomists. He introduced the study of anatomical variations. His work on the muscles was accurate, and he showed the nerve supply – which Vesalius had not done. He described the thoracic duct about a century before Jean PECQUET and also the azygos vein. His figure showing the base of the brain and the sympathetic system is very important. His figures of the larynx are in advance of his time, and he described the structure of the teeth at different ages, and a rudimentary valve in the heart. The auditory tube, joining the tympanic cavity to the pharynx, was well described by him and bears his name, but it had previously been described by Alcmaeon *c*.500 BC.

C. Singer, *The Evolution of Anatomy*. 1925.
C. Singer and C. Rabin, *A Prelude to Modern Science*. 1946.
A. Castiglioni, *History of Medicine*. 1947.
(Portrait.)
Dictionary of Scientific Biography.

E A U

EVANS, OLIVER Born near Newport, Delaware, USA, 13 September 1755; died New York, 15 April 1819. Builder of the first high-pressure steam engine in America.

Son of Charles Evans, a farmer, Oliver Evans left school at 14 to be apprenticed to a wagon-maker. By the age of 21 he was involved in making teeth for carding wool (in which he effected some improvements), and at 25 he joined his two brothers in Wilmington, applying water power to conveyors, drills, elevators, and so on, in flour mills; at the same time he tried to adapt Watt's engine to a wagon. As early as 1792 he was working on internally fired boilers for steam engines, but was not successful until 1802.

Having successfully petitioned the legislatures of Pennsylvania and Maryland in 1786 and 1787 for exclusive rights to profit from his inventions, he got a high-pressure engine working at 30 rpm. He concentrated on manufacturing such engines, applying one – at the request of the Board of Health in Philadelphia – to a dredger on the Schuylkill River. This amphibian, *Orukter Amphibole*, was the forerunner of some fifty or so steam engines which he built in the next fifteen years. He proposed the construction of a steam frigate *Columbia* in 1814. In 1807 he established the Mars Iron Works. His main works were destroyed by a fire kindled by a revengeful apprentice on 11 April 1819, and this disaster probably hastened his death a few days later.

His work was certainly known in England – where Richard TREVITHICK was following similar lines – as early as 1807, being mentioned in Olinthus Gregory's (1774–1841) *Treatise of Mechanics* (1807). He himself claimed in the *National Intelligencer* (18 March 1815) to have had the intention of constructing steam carriages as early as 1773 and steam paddle boats as early as 1778.

Greville and Dorothy Bathe, *Oliver Evans, a Chronicle of American Engineering*. 1925.
(Portrait.)
Greville Bathe, *Transactions of the Newcomen Society*, **18**, 87, 1937–8.
Dictionary of American Biography.

W H G A

EWING, WILLIAM MAURICE Born in Lockney, Texas, USA, 12 May 1906; died New York, 4 May 1974. Marine geologist.

After graduating in geology at the Rice Institute in 1926, Ewing did research there and at LeHigh University. In 1944 he was appointed Higgins Professor of Geology in Columbia University, NY, contributing greatly to the prestige of the Lamont-Docherty Geological Observatory. From 1959–61 he was associated with NASA as an adviser on lunar exploration. He is, however, remembered primarily for his investigation of the Earth's upper mantle beneath the oceans, especially using seismic techniques. In 1935 he carried out the first seismic measurements at sea and four years later took the first deep-sea photographs. His research established that the Earth's submarine crust is much thinner than its continental one. He mapped the principal mid-ocean ridges and showed that marine sediment increases in thickness as it becomes more distant from them. His results supported the theory of sea-floor spreading advanced by H. H. HESS in 1962.

Allen G. Debus (Ed.) *World Who's Who in Science*, 1968.
Dictionary of Scientific Biography, Supp. II.

T I W

EWINS, ARTHUR JAMES Born at Norwood, Middlesex, England, 3 February 1882; died Leigh-on-Sea, Essex, 24 December 1957. Chemist, prominent in the pharmaceutical industry.

After leaving school, Ewins began work as a 'research apprentice' in the Wellcome Physiological Research Laboratories. As his experience increased he published papers on alkaloid chemistry (mostly with G. BARGER). and in 1914 (with Sir Henry DALE), isolated acetyl-choline from ergot. During the war of 1914–18 he worked in the Central Research Institute of the Medical Research Council, on the manufacture of pharmaceuticals (notably salvarsan) formerly obtained from Germany. When the war was over he went to the firm of May and Baker as head of their research department, a position from which he retired in 1952.

Ewins played a large part in the discovery and development of sulphapyridine (M and B 693), which was one of the first of the sulphanilamides to be of real use in medicine. He was elected FRS in 1943.

Chemistry and Industry, **77**, 224, 1958. (Portrait.)
Biographical Memoirs of Fellows of the Royal Society, 1958. 1959. (Portrait.)
Dictionary of National Biography.

W V F

EYDE, SAMUEL Born at Arendal, Norway, 29 October 1866; died Aasgaardstrand, 21 June 1940. A founder of the Norwegian electrochemical industry.

Eyde took his diploma in constructional engineering at the Charlottenburg High School, Berlin, and worked for some years in Hamburg and elsewhere in Germany. With a German partner, C. O. Gleim, he undertook important railway-station and harbour works in the three Scandinavian countries, but became increasingly absorbed in the potentialities of electrochemical industries in his native land.

In 1901, while studying the problem of the fixation of nitrogen, he came into contact with Kristian BIRKELAND. They set up a small laboratory where they worked together to establish the conditions necessary for the economic combination of nitrogen and oxygen in an electric arc, as a route to nitric acid. Eyde had already secured rights over some waterfalls, and in 1904 he became administrative director of an electrochemical company, financed partly from Swedish sources, which exploited the Birkeland-Eyde process. In the following year he obtained extensive support from French capital, and started the well-known firm, *Norsk Hydro-Elektrisk Kvaelstofaktieselskab*, which he conducted with great acumen down to his retirement from active participation in 1917.

Eyde was concerned with other electrochemical enterprises in Norway, became a member of the Norwegian Parliament, and was in 1920 appointed Norwegian Minister in Poland. Shortly before his death he published an interesting autobiography, *Mitt liv og mitt livsverk.*

S. Mortensen and P. Vogt (Eds), *One Hundred Norwegians.* 1955.

T K D

F

FABRICIUS, HIERONYMUS (GIROLAMO FAB-RIZI) Born at Aquapendente, near Orvieto, Italy, c.1533; died Bugazzi, near Padua, 21 May 1619. Distinguished anatomist and a founder of scientific embryology.

Fabricius ab Aquapendente, as he is always called, studied humanistic subjects and then medicine at Padua, where he was taught anatomy and surgery by FALLOPPIO. After graduating (c.1559) he practised surgery and taught anatomy privately. Falloppio died in 1562, but it was not until 1565 that Fabricius was appointed to succeed him; in 1600 he was reappointed to the chair for life. In 1609 the chairs of surgery and anatomy were separated; Fabricius remained supra-ordinary in anatomy, and he delegated the surgical work to his pupil and successor, Casserius (1561–1616). Because of ill health Fabricius finally retired from the chair in 1613, after having held it for fifty years. Between then and his death he published eight new works and several new editions. About 1577 he married Violante Vidali, of Padua. About 1596 Fabricius began to acquire an estate at Bugazzi, and there he spent his last years.

Fabricius's greatest work in anatomy was his detailed description of the valves in veins. Previously seen, and even crudely illustrated, by others, Fabricius in 1579 publicly demonstrated them in the veins of the limbs. Not until 1603 did he publish his finely illustrated account in his *De venarum ostiolis* ('On the valves in the veins'). Unfortunately, he misunderstood their true function. In addition to various surgical works Fabricius also wrote treatises on the anatomy of the larynx, the lens of the eye, the mechanics of respiration and the action of muscles.

The most important original work of Fabricius was in the field of embryology. His treatise *De formato fœtu* ('On the formed foetus', 1600) is a comparative study of the late stages of the foetus in different animals, and is the first work of its kind. His other embryological work, *De formatione ovi et pulli* ('On the development of the egg and the chick', 1604), elevated the subject to an independent science. From the sixth day of development onwards his descriptions and illustrations are excellent.

Fabricius was actively concerned with the construction of the permanent anatomical theatre in the University of Padua, the first of its kind. This magnificent structure still exists, much as in his day. It was in this theatre that Fabricius demonstrated the valves in veins to his pupil, William HARVEY; and it was the teaching of Fabricius which first interested Harvey in the problem of the circulation of the blood.

H. B. Adelmann, *The Embryological Treatises of Hieronymus Fabricius.* 1942.
K. J. Franklin, *De Venarum Ostiolis 1603 of Hieronymus Fabricius.* 1933. (Portrait.)
E. A. Underwood, *Annals of Science,* **19**, 1, 1963.
Dictionary of Scientific Biography.

E A U

FABRIZI, GIROLAMO See FABRICIUS.

FAHRENHEIT, GABRIEL DANIEL Born in Danzig, 14 May 1686; died Netherlands, 16 September 1736. Remembered for the temperature scale bearing his name.

Having had little success as a shopkeeper, Fahrenheit turned instead to physics and worked as a glass blower and physical instrument-maker in Holland. By 1714 he had constructed two thermometers containing alcohol which agreed exactly in their reading of temperature. His first announcement of his methods of making thermometers was published in the *Philosophical Transactions* of the Royal Society in 1724. Around 1714 he changed over from alcohol to mercury, following the investigations by G. Amontons (1663–1705) on the expansion of mercury. He used many scales. At last he settled on one ranging between 0° and 212° in which 0° was the temperature given by a mixture of ice, water and cooking salt; 32° that given by a mixture of water and ice; and 212° that corresponding to the boiling-point of water. In 1724 he described the super-cooling of water, and he also observed the variation in the boiling-point of water with air pressure, suggesting its use as a barometer in a paper in the *Philosophical Transactions* of 1725. He was elected FRS in 1724.

A. Wolf, *History of Science, Technology and Philosophy in the 18th Century.* 1938.
W. E. Knowles Middleton, *A History of the Thermometer and its Use in Meteorology.* 1967.
Dictionary of Scientific Biography.

J W H

FAIRBAIRN, SIR WILLIAM Born at Kelso, Roxburghshire, Scotland, 19 February 1789; died Moor Park, Surrey, England, 18 August 1874. Engineer.

Son of Andrew Fairbairn, a farmer who migrated to Newcastle upon Tyne in 1803, William Fairbairn was apprenticed to a millwright at 15, and studied in his spare time. At the Shields Library he became a friend of George STEPHENSON. He went to London in 1811, and joined the Society of Arts; he devised a steam excavator and a sausage machine, neither of which were remunerative. By 1817 he had set up as a manufacturer of machinery in Manchester and in thirteen years was employing 300 people. He became a Member of the Institution of Civil Engineers, in 1830, and extending his interests to the sectional building of ships, opened a works at Millwall in 1835 which was soon employing 2000 people. To counter a strike amongst his Manchester employees he devised a riveting machine for building boilers.

His commitments were wide: water-wheels for Zürich, ferry boats for the Forth and Clyde Company, drainage works for Holland and machinery for the Turkish Government. But perhaps his most impressive memorial is the tubular bridge over the Menai Straits, constructed in association with Stephenson. This enabled him to claim, by 1870, that he had built nearly a thousand bridges.

He took an active part in the ventilation of engineering ideas. He published many papers in the *Philosophical Transactions of the Royal Society*; spoke often, and well, at meetings of the British Association (of which he was President in 1861); and served as a juror for the Exhibitions of 1851, 1855 and 1862.

Fairbairn was elected to Fellowship of the Royal Society in 1850, and was awarded its Gold Medal ten years later. He was created baronet in 1869.

W. Pole (Ed.), *Life of Sir W. Fairbairn.* 1877.
Dictionary of National Biography.

W H G A

FALLOPPIO, GABRIELLO Born at Modena, Italy, 1523; died 9 October 1562. Distinguished anatomist.

Falloppio studied at Modena to become a priest, but abandoned the Church for medicine. He now studied at Ferrara, where he had Antonio Musa Brassavola (1500–55) as one of his teachers. After graduating he studied in other universities, and in 1548 became professor of anatomy at Ferrara. As opportunities there were limited, he soon accepted the anatomy chair at Pisa. In 1551 he was called to the chair of anatomy at Padua. For a short period in 1560 he was physician to the Venetian embassy at Paris. His early death from tuberculosis cut short his brilliant tenure of his chair at Padua, in which he was followed by his pupil FABRICIUS.

As a teacher Falloppio seems to have been equally outstanding in botany, in surgery and in anatomy, but it is as an anatomist that his fame chiefly rests. He was in charge of the famous botanical garden at Padua, which had been recently founded. He left no botanical treatise, but his teaching is known from notes made by his pupils and from observations in his own works.

The anatomical discoveries of Falloppio were published in his *Observationes anatomicae* (1561), which embraces the whole of anatomy. In it he acknowledges the greatness of the *Fabrica* of VESALIUS, whose pupil he had been; but in the book Falloppio corrected and extended the work of Vesalius in many directions. His best-known discovery is that of the uterine tubes and the round ligaments of the uterus, both of which structures bear his name. In other ways he added to our knowledge of the generative organs. His description of the skeleton is excellent, and he gave good descriptions of previously unknown structures in the skull, such as the foramen ovale in the sphenoid. He described the facial canal (aqueduct of Fallopius) in the temporal bone that transmits the facial nerve. He was the first to describe the cochlea, the vestibules, and the semicircular canals of the internal ear, and also the chorda tympani nerve. He gave important descriptions of the cerebral vessels, and he was the first to describe the muscles of the soft palate. In general his account of the cranial nerves was the best up to his time.

C. Singer, *The Evolution of Anatomy.* 1925.
M. Neuburger and J. Pagel, *Handbuch der Geschichte der Medizin*, vol. 2. 1903.
F. H. Garrison, *History of Medicine.* 1929. (Portrait.)
Dictionary of Scientific Biography.

E A U

FARADAY, MICHAEL Born at Newington, Surrey, England, 22 September 1791; died London, 25 August 1867. Discoverer of benzene; inventor of the dynamo; main architect of classical Field Theory.

Michael Faraday was the son of a journeyman blacksmith. His education consisted of the rudiments of reading, writing and arithmetic, which he received as a member of the Sandemanian sect, a dissenting group which left a permanent mark on his approach to science. The Book of Job, with its emphasis on human frailty, especially on the inevitability of human error, was the part of his Bible most marked by him. Throughout his life, he insisted upon the provisional nature of the conclusions he drew from his experiments, yet testified to his faith in them by pursuing their implications to the furthest reaches of his imagination.

At the age of 14 he was apprenticed to a London bookbinder and bookseller, a Mr Riebau, whose shop was at 2 Blandford Street, just off Baker Street. There, he was introduced to the world of books and read omnivorously. Purely by chance he picked up a copy of the *Encyclopaedia Britannica* which had been brought in to be re-bound, and discovered the article on 'Electricity'. He was captivated and, from that moment on, sought to devote himself to the study of science. Entrance to the scientific world was no easy matter in 1812, but, again, chance intervened. Sir Humphry DAVY, at the peak of his fame in London, was temporarily blinded in the laboratory of the Royal Institution, and Faraday was recommended to him as an amanuensis by one of Mr Riebau's customers. Thus began Faraday's scientific career.

His education in science was acquired as assistant to Davy at a crucial point in the latter's career. In 1810 Davy had proved, at least to his own satisfaction, that one major point of LAVOISIER's chemical revolution was wrong. Lavoisier had insisted that chemical qualities accompanied a chemical element wherever it went. Thus he saw oxygen as the carrier of the quality of acidity, hence its name. Muriatic acid, however, as Davy proved, contained no oxygen, but a new element, which Davy christened chlorine. To explain the origin of chemical qualities, Davy turned to an atomic theory which was to be of primary importance in Faraday's later theories. This theory, devised by R. J. Boscovich (1711–87), depicted the atom as a mathematical point with 'shells' of attractive and repulsive force surrounding it, varying with the distance from the centre. Chemical qualities, then, were the result of the patterns of attractive or repulsive forces created by the union of two or more of these primitive atoms. For Davy, this was the way out of what seemed to be an insoluble theoretical impasse; for Faraday, much later, it was the theoretical foundation of some of his most daring speculations.

Faraday's scientific apprenticeship was spent as an analytical chemist, and it was as an analytical chemist that he discovered and described benzene in 1825. In these same years he discovered the first compounds of chlorine and carbon to be described in the history of chemistry.

It was, however, in the field of electricity and magnetism that he did his most important work. Unlike his contemporaries (excepting Davy), he did not believe in the existence of separate, imponderable fluids of positive and negative electricity, or of boreal and austral magnetism. Rather, he was convinced of the unity of all the forces of nature; this fitted in well with his growing belief in the reality of Boscovichean atoms. Thus, electricity, magnetism, light, heat and chemical affinity were merely different manifestations of the attractive and repulsive forces of which the Boscovichean point-atoms were composed, revealing themselves in different guises under different conditions. More specifically, Faraday saw, in his mind's eye, the transmission of such a force as electricity not as the flow of a material fluid from one point to another but as a vibration of a particular kind involving the point-atoms and their 'shells' of force. When this vibration (through a conducting wire) was propagated through the medium surrounding the wire, should it not be detectable as, say, magnetic force? In 1831 Faraday wound an iron ring with two coils; one, connected to a voltaic battery, was to create the primary vibration – the iron ring was to concentrate the lateral vibrations from this – and another coil on the opposite side of the ring was to convert these secondary vibrations into another electric current. Thus, on 29 August 1831, Faraday discovered electromagnetic induction.

But what was vibrating? The analogy with a violin string is useful here. The string, by itself, hangs limp; under tension, it can vibrate. So, the essential element was the tension. Point-atoms, intimately connected to one another, could be put under tension by the application of force at both ends of the tensile line. Following this idea, Faraday was led to a series of epoch-making discoveries. Suppose, for example, that you have two lines of tension in which one line tends to move one way and the other in an opposite direction; further suppose that there are connections between one element in one line and another element in the other. For the motion in opposite directions to take place, the attractions between the elements in the separate lines must be broken. Since these attractions will be specific for specific 'lines', a specific amount of force will have to be applied to break them. In 1834 Faraday announced his two laws of electrolysis which made explicit the amount of force required; for a given amount of electrical force, chemical substances in the ratio of their chemical equivalents were released at the electrodes of an electrochemical cell. Put another way, chemical affinity was electrical force acting on the molecular level.

This is a strange kind of vibration; it is not like the undulation of a stretched string, but more like the bobbing up and down of a loaded spring, with the difference that the spring here constantly breaks and a new load is imposed. This view led Faraday to another discovery. How far can you stretch a spring until it breaks? This depends on the material from which it is made. If of steel, it can be stretched very far; if of paper, it breaks easily. Thus, the capacity for strain will depend upon the material of which the spring is made. Should not the same be true of the capacity for bodies to take on electrical strain? The answer was the discovery of specific inductive capacity in 1837. In 1838 and 1839 came a radically new definition of the electric current; it was the vibration caused by the rapid build-up and break-down of strain in the molecules of good conductors. Insulators were bodies which did not break down easily; conductors could not take much intermolecular strain; electrolytes broke down under strain and also were decomposed by it. Thus, a unitary theory of electricity was proposed, based solely on the existence of intermolecular forces. It was immediately rejected by Faraday's contemporaries.

The reason for the rejection was easy to see. There was no evidence forthcoming of the strain. No matter how he tried, Faraday was unable to detect the intermolecular strain on which his theories rested. In 1845, however, at the urging of a young Scot, William THOMSON, later Lord Kelvin, he turned from electrostatic strains to electromagnetic ones – these latter being much more powerful. This time he was successful; plane-polarized light passed through a specimen of borate or lead glass in an intense magnetic field had its plane of polarization rotated – a clear indication of the strain for which Faraday had been searching for so long. There was only one problem; the strain was not polar, as he had assumed, in electrostatics. The magnetic line of force was a closed curve which went forth from the magnet and returned to it. This line of force, Faraday showed, was conducted by all matter. Those which conducted it well he christened paramagnetics; those which conducted it poorly he named diamagnetics. But the basic fact was the line of strain. The magnet, for example, was not a centre of force; it was an object which concentrated the lines of magnetic force through it. Without the surrounding medium, there could be no magnetism. Thus, the real energy of the magnet was in the space around it, not in the iron bar. This was the fundamental idea of Field Theory. It was immediately rejected by most of Faraday's contemporaries – with one significant exception, James Clerk MAXWELL. It was Maxwell who was to take this fundamental idea and make it respectable to the mathematical physicists of his day. Faraday died before this could be done.

In his personal life, Faraday was a recluse devoted to his duties at the Royal Institution and to his wife. He was one of the great popularizers of science in the nineteenth century; the Friday Evening Discourses at the Royal Institution are even today an important channel of communication between the scientist and the general public, and it was Faraday who created them in 1826. His juvenile lectures became classics in his own time. *The Chemical History of a Candle* is still in print.

Faraday gradually sank into senility after 1860, and died in 1867. He is buried in Highgate cemetery.

Henry Bence Jones, *The Life and Letters of Faraday* (2 vols). 1870.

L. Pearce Williams, *Michael Faraday, a Biography.* 1965.

John Meurig Thomas, *Michael Faraday and the Royal Institution.* 1991. (Portraits.)

G. N. Cantor, D. Gooding and F. A. J. C. James, *Faraday.* 1991.

G. N. Cantor, *Michael Faraday: Sandemanian and Scientist.* 1991.

B. Bowers, *Michael Faraday and the Modern World.* 1991.

I. M. McCabe and J. M. Thomas, *Endeavour* (New Series), **15**, 126, 1991. (Portraits.)

Dictionary of Scientific Biography.

Dictionary of National Biography.

L P W

FERMAT, PIERRE DE Born at Beaumont-de-Lomagne, near Montauban, France, 17 August 1601; died Castres, near Toulouse, 12 January 1665. Mathematician, remembered for his part in founding analytic geometry, the calculus of probabilities, and modern arithmetic.

Fermat was one of the greatest of amateur mathematicians. At the age of 30 he was installed at Toulouse as Commissioner of Requests. Renowned for his legal knowledge, he was promoted to the position of Counsellor in the *Parlement* of Toulouse in 1648, which he occupied until his death. He was an excellent classical scholar and wrote a good deal of poetry.

Much of Fermat's work is known only through his correspondence (in which he had a habit of stating his theorems without proof) or through marginal notes to his books. Some of his theorems were given to the world in the form of challenges to other mathematicians, in the manner of the day. The translation of DIOPHANTUS (1621) by C. G. Bachet (1581–1638) was responsible for stimulating his interest in the theory of numbers. Some of the better known of the numerous important theorems derived by Fermat may be mentioned. (1) A number of the form $4n - 1$ is neither a square nor the sum of two squares, either of integers or fractions. This theorem was conveyed in a letter from M. Mersenne (1588–1648) to DESCARTES (22 March 1638) as having been proved by Fermat. (2) The equation $x^2 - Ay^2 = 1$, where A is any integer not a square, has an unlimited number of solutions in integers. (Letter of Fermat to Frénicle de Bessy (c.1602–75), February 1657). Fermat challenged others to give his or another general rule of solution. Viscount BROUNCKER at length provided a solution, but the fact that the problem had a history of two thousand years speaks for Fermat's genius. (3) He solved the more general equation, $x^2 - Ay^2 =$, but his solution was lost, and J. L. LAGRANGE was the next to supply a proof, more than a century later. (4) Fermat, again, stated that if n is a positive integer not divisible by the positive prime p, then $n^{p-1} - 1$ is divisible by p. The first published proof was that of L. EULER in 1738 (found by him in 1732). Most famous of all, however, was Fermat's 'Last Theorem' which states that there is no solution in integers of the equations $x^n + y^n - z^n$ ($xyz \neq 0$, $n > 2$). Only very recently has there been

an accepted proof of this theorem, which has been of the greatest value in stimulating research in arithmetic and modern algebra, from Fermat's time to ours.

In 1629, or thereabouts, Fermat attempted to supply some of the lost proofs of APOLLONIUS on loci. To do so he used what is essentially Cartesian geometry. The many subsidiary techniques which he devised were published only posthumously (1679), although through his correspondence with G. P. de Roberval (1602–75) and Étienne Pascal (see Blaise PASCAL) many of his methods were known generally by about 1640. Like Descartes, he began by attempting 'Pappus's Problem', to prove that a certain locus is a conic. Starting with what amounted to a transcription into his algebraic terminology (less perspicacious than that later used by Descartes) of a proof by Apollonius, he showed that four specific forms of equation corresponded to conics. He now set himself the new and converse problem of reducing every quadratic equation in two variables which represents a locus (not a pair of straight lines) to one of these fundamental forms. His procedure involved a skilful change of axes – a procedure which Descartes never mastered. In using his new-found analytical geometry to solve the problem of determining maxima and minima, and in his method of finding tangents, Fermat was again in advance of Descartes, and it is known that NEWTON, in laying the foundations of the calculus, considered his debt to Fermat great. HEROshowed that light travelling between two points, and undergoing a reflection in the process, follows the shortest path. Refracted light following the shortest path would, of course, have to travel in a straight line, and therefore Hero's theorem can no longer hold. Fermat showed that in the case of refraction it is the *optical distance* (involving the products of distances and corresponding refractive indices) which is a minimum. The whole of geometrical optics can be logically derived from a suitably modified form of Fermat's principle (maxima as well as minima must be allowed for). Fermat's conception influenced Jean BERNOULLI in founding the calculus of variations, and his principle is the prototype of the so-called 'minimal principles' of modern physics.

With PASCAL, Fermat may be claimed as a founder of the theory of probability. What is often known as his 'principle of conjunctive probability' is as follows: If the probabilities of two events happening are h and k, respectively, then the probability that both events will happen is hk.

No satisfactory explanation has ever been given for Fermat's apparent indifference to public recognition, but it is clear that much of the time he was sufficiently satisfied with the pleasure of discovery itself.

P. Tannery and C. Henry, *Oeuvres de Fermat.* 1891–1922.

Jean Itard, *Pierre Fermat.* 1950.

Dictionary of Scientific Biography.

J D N

FERMI, ENRICO Born in Rome, 29 September 1901; died Chicago, Illinois, USA, 28 November 1954. Responsible for building the first atomic pile.

Fermi received his doctorate at the *Scuola Normale Superiore* at Pisa, and then worked with Max BORN at Göttingen, and with P. Ehrenfest (1880–

1933) at Leiden. From 1924 to 1926 he lectured in mathematical physics at the University of Florence; in 1927 he became professor of theoretical physics at Rome University; and in 1929 was a founder member of the Royal Academy of Italy. He was a Foreign Member of the Royal Society.

While in Rome he worked out the properties of a gas in which the particles obey the Exclusion Principle of W. PAULI; compared with P. A. M. DIRAC's, his methods have been described as inelegant but clear, but his results tallied with those of Dirac. He always showed great skill and instinct for getting good approximations when accurate calculation would have been impossible, or very lengthy. Fermi's calculations made Pauli's neutrino seem more plausible, and less an *ad hoc* hypothesis. His publications on quantum statistics, and on β-decay and the neutrino, made Fermi's name internationally known.

He next took up the discovery by Jean JOLIOT and Irène JOLIOT-CURIE of artificial radio-activity, and he was able to show within a few months that radioactive isotopes of most elements could be produced by neutron bombardment. Further, they found that the intensity of the radioactivity thus induced depended on the surroundings of the specimen undergoing bombardment. A jacket of water or paraffin produced a much greater intensity; and this they interpreted as due to the slowing down of the neutrons in passing through the jacket. This work was to form the basis of the atomic pile, for it indicated how the speed of nuclear reactions might be controlled.

In 1938 Fermi was awarded a Nobel prize. The political state of Italy had made him determined to leave the country, so from the Nobel ceremony in Stockholm he went to Columbia University, New York. There he began building a small pile, which was completed in 1941, but this was not large enough to become 'divergent', or self-sustaining.

At the end of 1941 his group migrated to the University of Chicago and there set about building a larger pile in the squash court of the University. Graphite was employed as the moderator in the pile, to control the rate of the reaction. Fermi apparently enjoyed even the banausic side of the experiment, and carried around the graphite blocks and isotope samples. On 2 December 1942 the pile became operational. It was the first controlled, self-sustaining nuclear reaction – it could be started and stopped at will – and it is the ancestor of all nuclear weapons and nuclear power plants.

It was the first of these uses which was first developed, as everybody knows, and in 1943 Fermi went to Los Alamos, New Mexico, where the Manhattan atomic bomb project was established, and worked there until the end of the war. He then returned to academic work at Chicago, continuing to do research on radioactivity.

It is recorded of him that he was a good lecturer, giving a clear grasp of the problems as well as supplying answers to them. What impressed his colleagues about all his work seems to have been its clarity, and the absence of vagueness and mystery. His most notable personal characteristics were apparently a great joy of living; and great charm which offset a tendency to be provocative or officious.

Biographical Memoirs of Fellows of the Royal Society. 1955. (Portrait.)
Nature, **175**, 18, 1955.

P. de Latil, *Enrico Fermi; the Man and his Theories.* 1965.
E. Segrè, *Enrico Fermi, Physicist.* 1970.
L. Fermi, *Atoms in the Family.* 1954.
Tyler Wasson (Ed.), *Nobel Prize Winners.* 1987. (Portrait.)
Dictionary of Scientific Biography.

D M K

FERNEL, JEAN Born at Clermont de l'Oise, France, 1497(?); died Fontainebleau, near Paris, 26 April 1558. Celebrated as a physician and medical author.

Fernel, the son of a furrier and innkeeper, was a man of wide learning. He received an arts degree from the University of Paris in 1519, but then ardently pursued studies on Aristotle, Plato and other classical authors. When aged 27 he embarked on medical studies, at times supporting himself by teaching philosophy. He later developed a highly successful medical practice and was personal physician to Henry II of France.

Fernel's most important publication was his *Medicina*, the first part of which was published in 1542 under the title *On the Natural Part of Medicine*. This part, which Fernel later entitled *Physiology*, was the earliest treatise systematically setting forth human physiology as an integral subject, although it dealt also with topics outside the present-day scope of the subject. The second part of the *Medicina* dealt with pathology and also broke new ground. Not only did Fernel introduce the term pathology but his systematic method of dealing with each organ in turn was markedly different from the usual approach, which merely enumerated and detailed a series of case histories.

Fernel's studies were characterized by his first-class powers of observation, which led him to reject, for example, astrology as an adjunct to medicine. The influence of the *Medicina* can be partly measured by the fact that it passed through some thirty editions, reprintings and partial translations.

C. L. Sherrington, *The Endeavour of Jean Fernel.* 1946.
R. Hooykaas, *Chymia*, **2**, 65, 1949. (Portrait.)
Dictionary of Scientific Biography.

J K C

FERRANTI, SEBASTIAN ZIANI DE Born at Liverpool, England, 9 April 1864; died Zürich, Switzerland, 13 January 1930. Pioneer of the generation and transmission of electricity at high voltages.

Son of a photographer, Sebastian de Ferranti was educated at a Roman Catholic school at Ramsgate, which he equipped with electric bells of his own design. At the age of 17 he joined the Charlton works of the SIEMENS brothers and attended evening classes at University College, London. Improving a dynamo which he first made at school, he patented it in 1882 and its success at Cannon Street railway station led him to set up his own business. He sold one of his dynamos to the Grosvenor Gallery Electric Supply Corporation, whose engineer he became in 1886. Designing improved equipment led him to consider supplying the whole of London north of the Thames from a high-power station at Deptford, as being more accessible for fuel and water than a central site. The London Electric Supply Corporation was registered in August 1887, with Ferranti as chief electrician. But with its intended coverage limited by the Electricity Lighting Act of 1888, and the possibility of competition from numerous low-power stations, Ferranti had to scale down the original capacity of the station by a factor of four. He designed and built the generators, transformer and cables to provide current at 10 000 volts.

Leaving the London Electric Supply Corporation in 1892 he began to manufacture equipment on his own. From his factory at Hollinwood, near Oldham in Lancashire (established in 1896), he secured contracts for lighting towns and conducted investigations into the application and metering of electricity.

The far-sightedness manifest in his original scheme for Deptford was apparent forty years later when the London Power Company was formed in 1925. In 1910, when President of the Institution of Electrical Engineers, he argued that coal was then being consumed at only 10 per cent overall efficiency and that this could only be improved if it was used to produce electricity. For Ferranti, electricity was the ultimate source of power for the home, the factory, the farm and the road. At Baslow Hall, where he made his home, he put these ideas into practice with electric washers, ironers and driers.

At the time of his death in 1930 he was trying to perfect his invention of tiny air turbines for high-speed flyer-tubes in cotton-twisting frames – a principle that later found application in dentists' drills.

He was elected to Fellowship of the Royal Society in 1927.

G. Z. de Ferranti, *The Life and Letters of Sebastian Ziani de Ferranti*. 1934.
Notes and Records of the Royal Society, **19**, 33, 41, 1964. (Portrait.)
R. H. Parsons, *The Early Days of the Power Station Industry*. 1940.
Dictionary of National Biography.

                                                         W H G A

FERRIER, SIR DAVID Born at Aberdeen, Scotland, 13 January 1843; died London, 19 March 1928. Neurologist and early investigator of brain functions.

Ferrier studied philosophy at Aberdeen, psychology at Heidelberg, and finally medicine at Edinburgh, where he graduated in 1868. He tried his hand at private practice in Suffolk and wrote his MD thesis on comparative anatomy in 1870. Thereafter he worked in London, firstly in physiology and forensic medicine at King's College, and after 1880 at the National Hospital for Nervous Diseases. A chair of neuropathology was created for him at King's College, London, in 1889.

Between 1873 and 1876 he engaged on some experimental work on the cerebral localization of functions 'to put to experimental proof the views entertained by Hughlings Jackson . . . and to follow up the pathology of Fritsch and Hitzig'. By comparative studies he established general principles of functions of the brain from rodents to apes. He investigated the motor and sensory areas of the cerebral cortex, mainly by faradic stimulation. He correlated his experimental work with observations on man and urged his surgical colleagues to practise what was to become neurosurgery. How-

ever, Ferrier was ahead of his time in not pushing the concept of cerebral localization to the limit. In his later years, he was a busy consultant neurologist, but continued his experimental work, and in the 1890s Sir Charles SHERRINGTON worked under him. He was attacked by antivivisectionists and taken to court, but established the case for ethical animal experimentation. In 1878 he founded the journal *Brain* with J. Hughlings Jackson (1834–1911) and others.

Lancet i, 627, 1928. (Portrait.)
W. Haymaker and F. Schiller (Eds), *Some Founders of Neurology*. 1953. (Portrait.)
Dictionary of National Biography.
Dictionary of Scientific Biography.

                                                         E H J

FESSENDEN, REGINALD AUBREY Born in Milton, Quebec, Canada, 6 October 1866; died Hamilton, Bermuda, 22 July 1932. Pioneer of radio transmission.

After studying at Bishop's College, Quebec, Fessenden spent five years (1886–90) with T. A. EDISON before briefly joining G. WESTINGHOUSE. He then held chairs of electrical engineering at Purdue (1892–3) and Pittsburgh (1893–1900) Universities. He then returned to industry as manager of the National Electric Signalling Co., set up by business interests to exploit his inventions.

Throughout these changes his main interest was in radio communication, in which his contemporary G. MARCONI was making rapid progress. One of his major inventions was amplitude modulation, in which the amplitude of a continuous carrier wave responds to the sound waves of voice or music. With this he made, on Christmas Eve 1906, the world's first sound broadcast. He also invented the heterodyne system of reception and the rotary spark gap, and developed radio telephony. In all, he held over 300 patents and had a powerful influence on the early development of radio communication.

Helen M. Fessenden, *Fessenden: Builder of Tomorrow*. 1940.
Dictionary of American Biography, Supp. 1.
Dictionary of Scientific Biography.

                                                         T I W

FEYNMAN, RICHARD PHILLIPS Born in New York City, 11 May 1918; died Los Angeles, California, 15 February 1988. Theoretical physicist.

Feynman, whose father was a maker of uniforms in New York, graduated from Massachusetts Institute of Technology in 1939. This was followed by a PhD from Princeton University in 1942. At Princeton he began working on the Manhattan Project, and moved to Los Alamos in 1943, where he remained until 1946 as part of the team working on the development of the atomic bomb.

He became associate professor of theoretical physics at Cornell University in 1946, moving to California Institute of Technology as professor of theoretical physics in 1950. It was for his work on the interactions between elementary particles and his attempt to merge the special theory of relativity of EINSTEIN with the science of quantum mechanics and the field of electromagnetism into the new theory of quantum electrodynamics (QED) that he was awarded the Nobel prize for physics in

1965, shared with J. S. Schwinger (1918–) and Sin-Itiro TOMONAGA.

Feynman was a popular lecturer and communicator of science, renowned for his practical jokes. His *Lectures in Physics* (3 vols., 1963–5) were very successful with students. After 1986 he was a severe critic of NASA following the loss of the space shuttle *Challenger*, accusing NASA of taking inadequate safety precautions.

R. Feynman, *Q.E.D.: The Strange Theory of Light and Matter.* 1986.
R. Feynman, *Surely you're Joking, Mr. Feynman.* 1985.
Tyler Wasson (Ed.), *Nobel Prize Winners.* 1987. (Portrait.)
J. Gleick, *Genius: Richard Feynman and Modern Physics.* 1992

A P B

FIBIGER, JOHANNES ANDREAS GRIB Born in Silkeborg, Denmark, 23 April 1867; died Copenhagen, 30 January 1928. Pioneer of the experimental production of cancer.

Fibiger, son of a physician, qualified in medicine in 1890. He held a succession of research and academic appointments which included the chair of pathological anatomy at Copenhagen University (1900). He took part in a large number of official commissions and participated in the activities of many scientific societies.

When Fibiger commenced his epoch-making studies in 1907 there were many theories on the cause of cancer, including the view that cancer could be linked with a prolonged irritation. For instance, some cancers, such as those of chimney sweeps, were recognized as being occupational, but all experimental attempts to induce the disease artificially had failed. There had been success with the transplantation of cancerous tissues, but this threw no light on the origin of the disease.

Fibiger's cancer studies commenced with the chance observation that a nematode worm was associated with tumorous growths in the stomachs of three rats. Attempts to link indisputably the nematode worms with the tumours led to a long painstaking research. For one thing he found that the comparative rarity of the condition was because infection only followed the rat's ingestion of a larval stage of a worm, a stage Fibiger finally traced to the striated muscle of a cockroach. Ultimately he was able to show that by feeding healthy rats with larvae-infected cockroaches he could produce, at will, malignant cancerous growths. Fibiger announced these results in 1913 and was awarded a Nobel prize in 1926.

The significance of the work was that it gave an enormous impact to cancer research. By providing a method for producing cancer artificially, it made cancer studies, in part, an experimental science. For instance, by lending support to the view that cancer could be brought about by external influences, it promoted experiments on the long-term effects of irritants. In a short while it was shown that periodic applications of coal-tar on to rabbits and mice could produce skin cancers. Fibiger helped to corroborate this and to extend this type of study (1920). Since that time many carcinogenic chemicals have been discovered. Fibiger's studies also led him to try to combat the disease by immunization treatment, but he was unsuccessful. Simi-

larly his hope that parasitology may have some significance in the genesis of human cancer has so far not been fulfilled. Nevertheless his studies have had a lasting influence on cancer studies.

Nobel Lectures: Physiology or Medicine, 1922–1941. 1965.
Knud Secher, *The Danish Cancer Researcher Johannes Fibiger (1867–1928).* 1947.
Tyler Wasson (Ed.), *Nobel Prize Winners.* 1987. (Portrait.)

J K C

FIBONACCI, LEONARDO (LEONARDO OF PISA) Born in Pisa, Italy, *c.*1170; died there after 1240. Mathematician.

Fibonacci was a member of the Bonacci family of Pisa. His father was Secretary to the Republic of Pisa, and in this capacity was in 1192 entrusted with the management of the Pisan trading colony of Bugia, Algeria. He shortly sent for his son to assist him, and Fibonacci's first introduction to mathematics was in making the everyday calculations of commercial life. However, business took him far afield – to Syria, Egypt and Sicily among other places – and he thus became versed in the Arabic system of numerals, itself derived from India. Returning to Pisa about 1200, Fibonacci was instrumental in introducing this system into general use. While practical considerations were his major concern, he was also keenly interested in theoretical algebra and geometry. A Fibonacci series is one in which each successive term is the sum of its two predecessors (1, 2, 3, 5, 8, 13, 21 etc). His highly original work survives in various writings, notably his *Liber Abacus* (1202, 1228). He is recognized as the first major mathematician of the christian world.

J. Gies and F. Gies, *Leonardo of Pisa and the New Mathematics of the Middle Ages.* 1969.
Dictionary of Scientific Biography.

T I W

FINLAY, CARLOS JUAN Born at Puerto Principe, Cuba, 3 December 1833; died there, 20 August 1915. Physician, noted for his role in identifying the mosquito as carrier of yellow fever.

Carlos Finlay was the son of an English ophthalmologist, Edward Finlay, who joined the army of Simon Bolivar, and remained to practise medicine in Cuba. Carlos was educated in Germany, France and the United States, and eventually followed his father as a medical practitioner in Cuba. As such, he was naturally very familiar with yellow fever, the cause of which was then quite unknown. On 14 August 1881 he read a paper to the International Sanitary Conference in Washington entitled *The Mosquito Hypothetically Considered as the Agent of the Transmission of Yellow Fever.* In 1886 he described in the *American Journal of Medical Sciences* the experimental transmission of yellow fever by the bite of infected mosquitoes. His theory attracted little attention and was indeed received with scepticism, as was its corollary that the way to eradicate yellow fever was to eradicate the mosquito. Not until 1900 did the Fourth US Commission on Yellow Fever (led by W. REED) confirm his views.

Carlos J. Finlay: Obras Completas. 1965–70. (Portrait.)

Carlos E. Finlay, *Carlos Finlay and Yellow Fever*.
1940.
Dictionary of Scientific Biography.

T I W

**FINNISTON, SIR HAROLD MONTAGUE
('MONTY')** Born in Glasgow, Scotland, 15 August
1912; died London, 2 February 1991. Metallurgist
and industrialist.

Son of a haberdashery salesman, Finniston was
educated at Allan Glen's School, Glasgow, Glasgow
University and the Royal College of Science and
Technology, Glasgow, where he lectured 1933–5.
He worked as a metallurgist at the British Coke
Research Institution; then with Stewart and Lloyds,
a steel company; and from 1940 to 1946 in the Royal
Navy Scientific Service, when he was a member of
the Atomic Energy team at Chalk River, Canada. As
Chief Metallurgist with the UK Atomic Energy
Authority, Harwell, 1948–58 he was responsible
for the production of Britain's first plutonium,
before moving back into private industry.

In 1967 Finniston joined the organising committee set up by the Labour government to plan the
nationalisation of the steel industry. He was
Deputy Chairman and Chief Executive of the
British Steel Corporation 1971–3, and Chairman
1973–6 following the death of Lord Melchett, the
first chairman. With Melchett, he was principal
architect of a development strategy, embodied in
the 1973 White Paper, to increase steel output
through a programme of modernisation and investment and a reduction in the number of steel-
making centres, involving massive redundancies.
Bitter clashes with the new Labour government,
elected in 1974, especially with Tony Benn, the
Industry Secretary, over job losses, the recommendations in the Beswick Review that steel closures
should be slowed down, and the collapse of the
world steel market frustrated Finniston's strategy,
and his contract was not renewed in 1976.

As chairman of a government committee of
enquiry into the engineering profession he produced the Finniston Report in 1979, which led to
the formation of the Engineering Council in 1981.
Finniston was elected FRS in 1969 and was
knighted in 1975. He published *Structural Characteristics of Materials* in 1971.

The Times, February 5, 1991.
G. F. Dudley and J. J. Richardson, *Politics and Steel
in Britain, 1967–1988: the Life and Times of the
British Steel Corporation*. 1990.
*Biographical Memoirs of Fellows of the Royal
Society*. 1992. (Portrait.)

A P B

FISCHER, EMIL Born at Euskirchen, near Bonn,
Germany, 9 October 1852; died Berlin, 15 July
1919. Perhaps the greatest of organic chemists.

Against his parents' wishes, Fischer left a business career, and studied chemistry under F. A. KEK-
ULÉ in Bonn; he then worked under J. F. A. von
BAEYER in Strasbourg and Munich. He was professor
successively in Erlangen (1882), Würzburg (1885)
and Berlin (1892, following A. W. von HOFMANN).
His marriage ended with the early death of his wife,
and two of his three sons were killed in the war of
1914–18; his health was affected by chemical
poisoning (mercury and phenylhydrazine).

Like his teacher von Baeyer, Fischer was essen-

tially a practical chemist; the Structure Theory provided him with a sufficient theoretical basis, which
he did not seek to extend. His early discovery of
phenylhydrazine (1875) was important, not only
in itself, but as providing a key to the complex
problems of carbohydrate chemistry. In Munich he
worked with his cousin Otto Fischer (1852–1932)
on the structure of the triphenylmethane dyestuffs.

It was not until he went to Erlangen that he
began the studies for which he is remembered, on
the constitution and synthesis of natural products.
Here he published the first of a long series of papers
on the chemistry of the heterocyclic nitrogen compounds related to uric acid, for which he coined
the name 'purines'. For many years he added to
the very considerable confusion of the subject by
his advocacy of incorrect structures, but by 1897
he and his students had established purine chemistry on a firm footing. In 1898 he synthesized the
parent compound, purine itself.

Fischer's work on carbohydrates dates from his
discovery (about 1884) that phenylhydrazine
forms well-defined crystalline derivatives with
sugars, enabling them to be characterized and separated from otherwise intractable syrups. He synthesized d-glucose and some other sugars from
acrolein dibromide (1890), and discovered 'epi-
merization' in 1891; shortly afterwards he was able
to state the configurations of the sixteen possible
aldohexoses. He studied glucosides and disacchar-
ides; synthesized the first nucleotide (1914); and
using his synthetic sugars, did some fundamental
work on the specificity of enzymes. Knowledge of
the oxide-ring structure of sugars was, however,
due to others.

About 1899 Fischer turned to an even more complex field of natural products, that of polypeptides
and proteins. It had long been known that proteins
could be hydrolysed to amino acids, and he was
able to devise a workable, though laborious,
method for rejoining these amino acids through
amide links. The resulting polypeptides, when
large enough (one containing eighteen amino acids
was made in 1907) bore a general resemblance to
natural proteins, though the synthesis of specific
proteins was still far beyond the technical
resources of the time.

Only brief mention can be made of some of his
other contributions to chemistry, such as the
Fischer indole synthesis (1885), and his late work
on depsides (condensation products of hydroxyb-
enzoic acids) and tannins; he also did a little work
on another great class of natural products, the fats.
His relationship with the important German dyestuffs industry was very close, and he refused
princely offers of industrial posts. During the war
he was active as an adviser to the Government,
especially on such matters as 'synthetic' food.

An austere and hard-working man, he seems to
have been respected rather than loved; his reputation rests on the masterly way in which he put
the growing science of biochemistry on a sound
basis of organic chemistry. He was awarded a
Nobel prize in 1902.

E. Fischer, *Aus meinem Leben*. 1922. (Portrait.)
E. Farber (Ed.), *Great Chemists*. 1961. (Portrait.)
Journal of the Chemical Society, 1157, 1920.
(Portrait.)
M. Engel, *Chemistry in Britain*, **28**, 1106, 1992
(Portrait.)

Tyler Wasson (Ed.), *Nobel Prize Winners*. 1987.
  (Portrait.)
Dictionary of Scientific Biography.
W V F

FISCHER, HANS Born at Höchst-am-Main, Germany, 27 July 1881; died Munich, 31 March 1945. Organic chemist, notable for his work on the pyrrole pigments.

Fischer, whose father was a director of the chemical firm of Kalle and Co., studied medicine and chemistry at Marburg and Lausanne, and became assistant to Emil FISCHER in Berlin (1904). He began his studies of the bile pigments in Munich (1910), but left to take up chairs of medical chemistry in Innsbruck (1915) and Vienna (1918). Little research was possible during the war years, and Fischer's productive period began only with his return to Munich (1921) as successor to H. WIELAND in the *Technische Hochschule*. He was extremely hard-working, secretive about his research – as were many chemists of his generation – but with few interests outside it; nevertheless, he was very popular with his doctorate students. His papers were written in a condensed style which makes them difficult to read. He married late in life, and left no children. During the confused final weeks of the war in Europe he took his own life.

Fischer's work on the pyrrole pigments began with investigations on bilirubin, the main colouring matter of bile. He achieved his first major success, however, with his studies of haemin, the non-protein moiety of haemoglobin, the oxygen-transporting pigment of vertebrate blood. He showed haemin to have a macrocyclic structure (the 'porphin' ring) consisting of four different substituted pyrroles joined by $-CH=$ groups, and having at their centre an atom of iron. This structure he confirmed by a remarkable synthesis in 1929. He later showed that the bile pigments were linear tetrapyrroles formed by oxidative degradation of porphins; he published the synthesis of bilirubin in 1944.

In the 1930s also Fischer took up the problem of the structure of the chlorophylls (the green photosynthetic pigments of plants), which had remained much as R. WILLSTÄTTER left it twenty years before. In over 100 papers he demonstrated that the chlorophylls were substituted porphins with an atom of magnesium at the centre, and paved the way for their eventual synthesis. He was awarded the Nobel prize for chemistry in 1930.

Nature, **160**, 494, 1947.
Angewandte Chemie, **62**, 1, 1950. (Portrait.)
E. Farber, *Nobel Prizewinners in Chemistry*. 1953. (Portrait.)
Perspectives in Biological Medicine, **8**, 419, 1965.
Dictionary of Scientific Biography, Supp. I.
Tyler Wasson (Ed.), *Nobel Prize Winners*. 1987. (Portrait.)
W V F

FISHER, SIR RONALD AYLMER Born at East Finchley, London, 17 February 1890; died Adelaide, Australia, 29 July 1962. Statistician and geneticist.

Fisher was educated at Cambridge, where he studied mathematics and physics. After leaving the University in 1912, he spent some time doing stat-istical work and teaching, before taking a post at Rothamsted Experimental Station in 1919. This situation gave him an opportunity to indulge his interest in biology, especially in the problems of evolution. His time at Rothamsted resulted in two books, *Statistical Methods for Research Workers* (1929) and *The Genetical Theory of Natural Selection* (1930). The first of these was a guide to methods developed by him at Rothamsted, making them available to biologists elsewhere. Its many editions have been very influential in encouraging the use of modern statistical methods in biological research. The second book reconciled Mendelian genetical theories with Darwinian natural selection and put forward Fisher's views on eugenics; it has become a classic of population genetics. This work led to Fisher's appointment as Galton Professor at University College London in 1933, succeeding Karl Pearson (1857–1936). He stayed there for ten years, concentrating his studies on blood groups, before accepting the chair of genetics at Cambridge in 1943. Here he continued his genetical work, publishing *The Theory of Inbreeding* in 1949. After leaving Cambridge in 1957 to go into retirement, Fisher visited Australia and accepted a research fellowship at Adelaide, where he remained until his death.

The Design of Experiments was published in 1935, the first book entirely devoted to this subject, expanding some of the ideas put forward in the earlier *Statistical Methods*. This was followed three years later by *Statistical Tables for Biological, Agricultural, and Medical Research*, written in collaboration with F. Yates. The techniques of experimental design and analysis developed by Fisher have spread from the subject of agriculture, which was the background for their growth, to be used in many other fields that involve experiments on variable material. His last book on this subject was *Statistical Methods and Scientific Inference* (1956).

Fisher's importance in both statistics and genetics was recognized by his election to the Royal Society in 1929. Later he was thrice a Medallist of the Society, and was knighted in 1952.

Biographical Memoirs of Fellows of the Royal Society. 1963. (Portrait.)
J. Neyman, *Science*, **156**, 1456, 1967.
H. Oxbury (Ed.), *Great Britons: 20th Century Lives*. 1985.
Dictionary of National Biography.
Dictionary of Scientific Biography.
S J R

FITTIG, RUDOLPH Born at Hamburg, Germany, 6 December 1835; died Strasbourg, 19 November 1910. Organic chemist and teacher.

Fittig, son of a schoolmaster, taught in a private school, but entered the University of Göttingen in 1856. He studied chemistry under F. WÖHLER and H. F. P. Limpricht (1827–1909), and became *Privatdozent* in 1860. In 1870 he was called to the chair of chemistry at Tübingen; in 1876 he succeeded J. F. A. von BAEYER at Strasbourg. He retired in 1902.

His name is remembered by the 'Fittig reaction', an early piece of work in which he studied the synthesis of alkyl-benzenes by the action of sodium on a mixture of alkyl halide and halobenzene. He and his pupils published an enormous volume of work on organic chemistry, of which only a few topics can be noticed here: the discovery of phenanthrene in coal tar; the 'diketone' structure for benzoquinone; and a long series of studies of unsaturated acids and related lactones.

Fittig was a chemist of Wöhler's type; essentially a practical man, with little interest in theory or speculation, but skilful in laboratory organization and teaching. He had the great (but restricting) virtue of publishing nothing that was not firmly based on experiment.

Berichte der deutschen Chemischen Gesellschaft, **44**, 1339, 1911. (Portrait.)
Journal of the Chemical Society, 1651, 1911. (Portrait.)
Dictionary of Scientific Biography.

W V F

FITZGERALD, GEORGE FRANCIS Born in Dublin, 3 August 1851; died there, 22 February 1901. Theoretical physicist, best known for his hypothesis – the Fitzgerald Contraction – to explain the negative result of the Michelson-Morley experiment on the velocity of light.

Fitzgerald was educated at home under Miss Boole, sister of the mathematician George BOOLE; he was a nephew of the physicist George Johnstone STONEY. At 16 he went to Trinity College, Dublin, and graduated in 1871 as First Senior Moderator in mathematics and experimental science. He then spent six years in the study of mathematical physics, and during this period made his acquaintance with the philosophy of the Irish philosopher George Berkeley (1685–1753), who taught that so-called material things exist only when perceived. He was awarded a Fellowship at Trinity College in 1877; and in 1881 became Erasmus Smith Professor of Natural and Experimental Philosophy there, holding the chair until his death. His publications deal mostly with the development of the theory of electromagnetic radiation elaborated by James Clerk MAXWELL; and he took a leading part in the discussion of electrolysis and of the cathode rays, which he believed to be composed of particles.

He was elected FRS in 1883, and was awarded a Royal Medal of the Society in 1899 for his contributions to theoretical physics. He was at his best in informal discussions and in conversation; in this way he made many of his most important suggestions. He also preferred to pass on ideas to experimentalists rather than test them himself; so that his importance as a seminal figure is perhaps greater than his publications might lead one to suppose. He threw out the suggestion that the oscillatory discharge of a Leyden jar might generate ether waves; and when H. R. HERTZ succeeded in producing 'electric waves', Fitzgerald called attention to the experiment at a meeting of the British Association and ensured that its importance was realized. Also in discussion he suggested the importance of light pressure in astronomy; that streams of charged particles coming from the Sun might cause magnetic storms and aurorae; and that the Michelson-Morley result might be accounted for if bodies moving through the ether were all shortened (see A. A. MICHELSON and E. W. MORLEY). Thus although light propagated forwards from a moving body would, in fact, go slower, only an observer outside the system could know this, because measuring rods would also contract in such a way that

the light would appear to move at the same speed in all directions. The light shone forwards would in reality travel a shorter path, which appeared to be the same length when measured. This hypothesis was taken up by H. A. LORENTZ; and it is a milestone on the road towards the Theory of Relativity formulated by EINSTEIN.

Proceedings of the Royal Society, **75**, 152, 1905. (Portrait.)
Dictionary of National Biography.
Scientific Proceedings of the Royal Dublin Society, No 1. 1952.
J. Lamor (Ed.), *The Scientific Writings of the Late George Francis Fitzgerald.* 1902.
Dictionary of Scientific Biography.

D M K

FIZEAU, ARMAND HIPPOLYTE LOUIS Born in Paris, 23 September 1819; died Chateau de Venteuil, 18 September 1896. Celebrated for his determinations of the velocity of light.

Fizeau's earliest researches concerned the improvement of the Daguerreotype process, in which he substituted bromine for iodine. Through this work he became associated with L. FOUCAULT, with whom he collaborated for a number of years. They were the first to obtain a detailed photographic image of the Sun (1845); they observed the diffraction of heat rays near a diathermous obstacle (1847); and using thin plates they proved that light interference occurs for path differences equal to a half odd integral number of wavelengths. Fizeau was the first to obtain a reasonably accurate determination of the velocity of light (1849), the toothed-wheel mechanical method being employed over a distance of about eight kilometres between Suresne and Montmartre. The following year, in collaboration with L. F. C. Breguet (1804–83), and almost simultaneously with Foucault, he proved that the velocity of light in water is less than that in air, thus lending powerful support to the undulatory as opposed to the corpuscular theory of light. Assuming that light was a vibratory motion in the ether, the problem then arose of what effect the motion of a body would have on the ether through which it moved. To decide between various possible hypotheses, Fizeau devised an ingenious experiment in which a beam of light was split into two halves which traversed tubes containing water moving in opposite directions. The resulting shift of the interference fringes indicated (1851) a partial convection of light in perfect accord with the formula of A. J. FRESNEL.

Apart from his work on the measurement of the velocity of light, Fizeau carried out important experiments on the velocity of electricity in wire conductors; on the utilization of the wavelength of light for the measurement of length; and on the employment of the method of interference for measuring the apparent diameter of stars. He seems also to have been the first to suggest (1848) that the principle of C. J. DOPPLER could be applied equally well to light as to sound waves.

Fizeau became a member of the *Académie des Sciences* in 1860 and was appointed Inspector of Physics at the *École Polytechnique* in 1863. He was elected a Foreign Member of the Royal Society in 1875, receiving the Rumford Medal of the Society in recognition of his scientific work.

Nature, **54**, 524, 1896.

E. Picard, *La Vie et l'Oeuvre d'Hippolyte Fizeau,*
Revue Scientifique, Jan. 1924.
Dictionary of Scientific Biography.
J W H

FLAMSTEED, JOHN Born at Derby, England, 19
August 1646; died Greenwich, near London, 31
December 1719. First Astronomer Royal, and
author of important star catalogues.

John Flamsteed, son of a maltster, was educated
at the Free School in Derby. After an illness, during
which he began to study astronomy, he entered
Jesus College, Cambridge, in 1670. While there he
made the acquaintance of NEWTON and became
widely known as an astronomer. Graduating in
1674, he took orders. On the foundation of the
Royal Observatory at Greenwich, in 1675, Flamsteed became observer there, the first Astronomer
Royal. The Observatory was intended for the
benefit of navigation in general and the computation of lunar tables in particular, but no instruments at all were provided. Flamsteed had to
purchase most of those he needed, and took private
pupils to pay for them. Unable to afford assistance,
he worked single-handed for thirteen years,
recording well over 20 000 observations.

During these years Flamsteed improved existing
tables of star positions and attempted to amend
existing planetary and lunar theory. The observations he could make with his sextant, however,
gave only the relative positions of stars, and
although he repeatedly asked for a transit instrument, fixed in the meridian, and capable of giving
absolute positions directly, he never obtained one.

Flamsteed was one of the select few to cross
swords with Newton. To complete his lunar
theory, Newton needed data which only Flamsteed
could provide, and his demands became increasingly burdensome. Eventually Newton decided
that Flamsteed was deliberately withholding information. Flamsteed regarded his observations as his
own property, but at length he was obliged to
deposit them under seal with the Royal Society, of
which Newton was President. Without Flamsteed's consent, a muddled edition of them
appeared in 1712 under the title *Historia Coelestis
Britannica* (edited by Edmond HALLEY). Flamsteed
later managed to have most copies burnt publicly,
commencing his own edition at his own expense.
He died before printing was complete; it finally
appeared in 1725.

Flamsteed, like Jean PICARD before him, discovered the annual variation by 40″ in the position
of the Pole Star. It was left to James BRADLEY to find
the cause of this, namely aberration. Flamsteed
devised many new techniques for reducing his
data. He was probably the first to use an accurate
timepiece in addition to the usual angle-measuring
instruments. He included the annual equation (see
Tycho BRAHE) in his lunar tables. Perhaps his greatest achievement was his *British Catalogue of 2884
Stars*, with a critique of earlier catalogues from the
time of PTOLEMY. Whereas Tycho Brahe's observations contained errors rarely less than 1′, Flamsteed was usually accurate to 10″.

F. Baily, *Account of the Rev. John Flamsteed.* 1835.
E. F. MacPike, *Hevelius, Flamsteed, and Halley.*
1937.
Dictionary of Scientific Biography.
J D N

FLEMING, SIR ALEXANDER Born at Lochfield,
near Darvel, Ayrshire, Scotland, 6 August 1881;
died London, 11 March 1955. Discoverer of penicillin.

Fleming was a farmer's son and was educated
first at the local village school and then at Kilmarnock Academy. His father having died, he went at
the age of 13 to live with an elder brother, a medical
practitioner, in London. He continued his education for three years at the Polytechnic Institute
in Regent Street, and then spent four years in a
London shipping office. A small legacy made it
possible for him to enter London University as a
medical student in St Mary's Hospital Medical
School, Paddington, where he was to spend the
rest of his working life, save for four years in France
as an officer in the Royal Army Medical Corps
(1914–18). He proved himself an unusually able
student and qualified in 1906, taking his MB, BS,
in 1908 as a gold medallist.

On graduating, Fleming became assistant to the
distinguished bacteriologist, Sir Almroth Wright
(1861–1947), with whom he was to collaborate for
some forty years. From assistant, he was appointed
lecturer in bacteriology and in due course professor (1928). He retired in 1948 as professor emeritus, but continued until 1954 as principal of the
Wright-Fleming Institute of Microbiology that had
been founded in honour of him and his famous
colleague.

Fleming was associated with two major discoveries – lysozyme and penicillin, of which the
latter is by far the better known and, from the practical point of view, the more important. The two
are interrelated, in the sense that the work on
lysozyme paved the way for that on penicillin by
focusing Fleming's attention on natural antibacterial substances that might be therapeutically
useful.

The discovery of lysozyme was made in 1922,
when he showed that the nasal secretion has the
power of dissolving (or lysing) certain kinds of bacteria. Subsequently, he showed that the active
enzyme, lysozyme, was present in many tissues of
the body, but unfortunately its activity was limited
so far as the pathogenic organisms that cause disease are concerned. Nevertheless, lysozyme did
strikingly demonstrate the possibility of the existence of substances harmless to the cells of the
body, but lethal to bacteria – the 'magic bullets'
sought, with only limited success, from the time
of Paul EHRLICH.

The story of the discovery of penicillin is well
known, and exemplifies Fleming's acute power of
observation. Briefly, he noticed in 1928 that a culture of staphylococcus had become accidentally
infected with a mould, subsequently identified as
Penicillium notatum. Around the mould colony
the staphylococci had disappeared, and Fleming
correctly attributed this to the production of an
antibacterial substance by the mould. Carefully, he
isolated the mould and grew it in pure culture in
broth; he found that after a few days the broth had
acquired a high antibacterial activity. He tested the
sensitivity to the broth of a wide range of pathogenic bacteria, and noted that many of them were
quickly destroyed by it. He also showed that white
blood corpuscles were little, if at all, sensitive to
penicillin broth; this was a fair indication that body
cells generally would not be affected by it. He put

the broth to practical use in separating pure strains of bacteria, and in treating local infections.

Fleming did not, however, succeed in making penicillin the immensely valuable and universally used chemotherapeutic agent that it is today; this task was only to be fulfilled some fifteen years later by H. W. FLOREY and E. B. CHAIN and their collaborators at Oxford. The reasons are complex, but certainly a major factor was that the ease with which penicillin was destroyed made its purification exceedingly difficult to effect by the chemical techniques of the time. Lack of purification in turn made it impossible to discover that penicillin combined negligible toxicity with high antibacterial activity in a way then almost beyond imagination. Consequently there was no strong incentive to attempt to overcome the great difficulties involved in purifying penicillin.

At the time Fleming's discovery passed almost unnoticed, but many honours were accorded to him in the fullness of time when its greatness was apparent. In 1945 he shared, with Florey and Chain, the Nobel prize for physiology or medicine. He was elected FRS in 1942 and was knighted two years later. He was honoured by many universities and learned societies throughout the world.

Nature, **175**, 663, 1955.

Biographical Memoirs of Fellows of the Royal Society. 1956. (Portrait.)

R. Hare, *The Birth of Penicillin.* 1970.

Gwyn Macfarlane, *Alexander Fleming: The Man and The Myth.* 1984. (Portrait.)

Tyler Wasson (Ed.), *Nobel Prize Winners.* 1987. (Portrait.)

Dictionary of National Biography.

H. Oxbury (Ed.), *Great Britons: 20th Century Lives.* 1985.

Dictionary of Scientific Biography.

T I W

FLEMING, SIR JOHN AMBROSE Born at Lancaster, England, 29 November 1849; died Sidmouth, Devon, 18 April 1945. Inventor of the thermionic valve.

Fleming was educated at University College, London; the Royal College of Chemistry, London; and St John's College, Cambridge. He was professor of electrical engineering in University College, London, 1885–1926. The Royal Society elected him to Fellowship in 1892 and awarded him their Hughes Medal in 1910.

Fleming was a pioneer in the large-scale application of electricity for lighting and heating, and in the development of radio telegraphy and telephony. In this field he made an outstandingly important invention in the thermionic valve. This was based on an effect noticed by T. A. EDISON in 1884 in connection with his development of the incandescent filament lamp. In 1900 Fleming put this effect to practical use in the simple diode valve. This consists essentially of two electrodes enclosed in an evacuated glass bulb. One (the cathode) is electrically heated so that it emits electrons; the other (the anode) accepts the electrons. Such a device will permit current to flow in only one direction, hence the name valve. Later Lee DE FOREST improved this simple valve by introducing a third electrode, this valve being known as a triode.

For half a century the thermionic valve was an essential part of virtually all radio transmitters and receivers, and of a wide range of other electronic devices such as television sets, electronic computers, and so on. In 1947 its absolute supremacy in this field was challenged by the transistor.

J. A. Fleming, *Memories of a Scientific Life.* 1934.

Nature, **155**, 662, 1945.

Obituary Notices of Fellows of the Royal Society. 1945–8. (Portrait.)

J. T. MacGregor-Morris, *The Inventor of the Valve.* 1954.

Dictionary of National Biography.

T I W

FLEMMING, WALTHER Born at Sachsenberg, Schwerin, Germany, 21 April 1843; died Kiel, Schleswig-Holstein, 4 August 1905. Anatomist and a pioneer of cytology.

Flemming studied medicine at the Universities of Göttingen, Tübingen, Berlin and Rostock, where he graduated in 1868. After a period as assistant in a hospital, he turned to science, and was an assistant in the department of zoology at Würzburg and in the Institute of Physiology at Amsterdam. In 1871 he became lecturer in anatomy at Rostock, and in 1873 associate professor of anatomy at Prague. In 1876 he was called to the chair of anatomy at Kiel.

Flemming published research on the fatty tissues of the body, and on the structure of the lymph nodes. He is, however, best known as a pioneer in cytology. He described the chromosomes in the late 1870s, but the term was not introduced until 1888, by H. W. G. WALDEYER. In 1879 he introduced the term 'chromatin' for the important nuclear substance. R. REMAK had described nuclear division as a relatively simple process. Flemming was among the first to recognize that this type of division is not the rule, and the more complex and common type he called 'mitosis'. The fundamental operation of cell-division, viz. the longitudinal splitting of the chromosomes, was first described by Flemming in 1880. His book *Zellsubstanz, Kern und Zellteilung* ('Cytoplasm, nucleus and cell-division', 1882) is a classic of cytology.

F. von Spee, *Anatomischer Anzeiger*, **28**, 51, 1906. (Portrait.)

E. B. Wilson, *The Cell in Development and Inheritance.* 1896.

H. J. Conn, *Stain Technology*, **8**, 48, 1933.

Dictionary of Scientific Biography.

E A U

FLOREY, HOWARD WALTER (BARON FLOREY OF ADELAIDE AND MARSTON) Born in Adelaide, Australia, 24 September 1898; died Oxford, England, 21 February 1968. Discoverer, with his colleagues, of the chemotherapeutic properties of penicillin.

Howard Walter Florey was an Australian who qualified in medicine at Adelaide in 1921. He was awarded a Rhodes Scholarship at Oxford, where Sir Charles SHERRINGTON suggested to him that the time was ripe for an experimental approach to pathology by someone with a physiological background. In 1924 he went to the Department of Pathology at Cambridge and the following year was awarded a Rockefeller Foundation Fellowship to study techniques of microdissection in the United States. In 1926 he returned to England to work at the London Hospital and then went to Cambridge as Huddersfield Lecturer in Special Pathology and Fellow of Caius College. Four years later he became Joseph Hunter Professor of Pathology at Sheffield. In 1934 he was elected professor of pathology at Oxford and held the chair, together with a fellowship at Lincoln College, for twenty-seven years. It was during this time, at the Sir William Dunn School of Pathology, that his most important work was done.

One of Florey's research interests at Cambridge was in mucus secretion. This led him to an interest in lysozyme, an antibacterial enzyme which had been discovered in 1922 by Alexander FLEMING. In 1930 he studied, with N. E. Goldsworthy, the distribution of lysozyme in the alimentary tract. They noticed that bacterial contaminants of intestinal mucus inhibited the growth of other bacteria and pointed out that the inhibition was an example of an already well known phenomenon.

The desirability of working with chemists then took shape in Florey's mind, but it was not until he went to the Sir William Dunn School of Pathology that this became financially possible. In 1935 E. B. CHAIN came to his Department and a year later was joined by N. G. Heatley (1911–).

Discussions with Florey aroused Chain's interest in lysozyme and thus in other anti-bacterial substances. These discussions culminated in a joint decision to make a systematic study of antimicrobial products of micro-organisms, and in 1939 financial support was obtained from the Medical Research Council and the Rockefeller Foundation. Penicillin, which had been discovered by Fleming in 1929, was among the first substances chosen for detailed investigation, partly because it was active against the staphylococcus and partly because its instability, which had defeated an attempt to purify it in 1932, presented a biochemical challenge.

The first major step forward was made in March 1940. At the suggestion of N. G. Heatley, penicillin which had been extracted from acidified culture filtrate into an organic solvent was re-extracted into an aqueous solution at neutrality. This simple manoeuvre became a key step in subsequent isolation processes.

Florey carried out a chemotherapeutic experiment with impure penicillin in May 1940. Four of eight mice infected intraperitoneally with *Strep. pyogenes* were treated subcutaneously with penicillin and remained well, while the remaining four died within fifteen hours.

Following this remarkable result Florey organized an attempt to produce enough penicillin in the laboratory for a clinical trial. Chain and Heatley were joined by E. P. ABRAHAM and others. Eventually a small supply of material was accumulated, for use by C. M. Fletcher, under Florey's guidance, at the Radcliffe Infirmary, Oxford. The first patient treated, in February 1941, was in the terminal stage of a generalized infection with *Staph. aureus* and *Strep. pyogenes*. After administration of penicillin he showed an astonishing improvement, but supplies of the antibiotic were inadequate and he eventually relapsed and died. In the next three months, however, five more seriously ill patients were treated and all responded well. These results showed that penicillin was effective when the sulphonamides were not, and that it should be produced in larger quantity.

England was then in a critical stage of the war. Florey thus went with Heatley to the United States, where he aroused the interest of pharmaceutical companies. An outstanding effort by the American pharmaceutical industry resulted in the production of enough penicillin to treat all severe battle casualties in Normandy in 1944.

In 1943 Florey went with Hugh Cairns (1896–1952) to North Africa to ascertain how the limited amounts of the antibiotic available could best be used in the field. Following this, he encouraged for some years a study of other antibiotics in his Department. In 1953 Newton and Abraham discovered cephalosporin C among the products of a strain of *Cephalosporium acremonium* isolated by Giuseppe Brotzu in Sardinia. They found that this substance resembled penicillin in some of its properties, but was not destroyed by the enzyme penicillinase from gram positive bacteria. This led Florey to do experiments with mice which showed that cephalosporin C had chemotherapeutic properties and was effective against infections caused by penicillin-resistant staphylococci. He then encouraged the production of cephalosporin C, and further work in England and the United States led to cephalosporins that found clinical use.

Although Florey's active interest in antibiotics spanned some twenty years he was essentially a physiologist who believed that most of the important advances in medicine came from work in the basic sciences and who set out to give pathology 'a good twist away from diagnosis and morbid anatomy'. In his early work he made important contributions to knowledge of the lymphatic system and of Brunner's glands in the duodenum. Later, he returned to research on the vascular system and explored the changes involved in atherosclerosis. After 1958 he made extensive use of the electron microscope to study the way in which substances pass through the endothelial barrier between the intravascular and extravascular spaces. His views and achievements gave a new outlook to experimental pathology.

From 1944 to 1957 Florey was involved in the planning of the John Curtin School of Medical Research at the Australian National University in Canberra, and he was Chancellor of the University from 1965 until his death. In 1962 he was elected Provost of The Queen's College, Oxford, and relinquished the chair of pathology. He was elected to the Fellowship of the Royal Society in 1941 and became the Society's fiftieth President in 1960.

Florey was a man without vanity. He went out of his way to present the discovery of the chemotherapeutic properties of penicillin in its right perspective and to give credit to all those who had played essential parts in the work. His own outstanding contributions to science and medicine were recognised by a Knighthood in 1944; a Nobel prize (with Fleming and Chain) in 1945; and by a life peerage and membership of the Order of Merit in 1965.

In 1926 he married Mary Ethel Hayter Reed, a fellow Australian who had qualified in medicine in 1924. Ethel Florey died in 1966 and he later married Dr Margaret Jennings, who had been his scientific colleague since 1936.

Biographical Memoirs of Fellows of the Royal Society. 1971. (Portrait.)

L. Bickel, *Rise up to Life*. 1972. (Portrait.)

Gwyn Macfarlane, *Howard Florey*. 1979. (Portrait.)

Trevor I. Williams, *Howard Florey: Penicillin and After*. 1984. (Portraits.)

Dictionary of National Biography.

Dictionary of Scientific Biography.

Tyler Wasson (Ed.), *Nobel Prize Winners*. 1987. (Portrait.)

E P A

FLORY, PAUL JOHN Born in Sterling, Illinois, USA, 19 June 1910. Polymer chemist.

Flory was educated at Manchester College, Indiana, and Ohio State University (PhD 1934). Between 1934 and 1938 he worked at the E.I. du Pont de Nemours company with W. H. CAROTHERS on polymer chemistry. He moved to the University of Cincinnati in 1938, to Esso in 1940, and to Goodyear Tire & Rubber Company in 1943. From 1948 he was associated with various universities (Cornell, 1948–56; Mellon Institute 1956–61; Stanford 1961–76).

Flory's work has involved a number of topics within polymer science. He developed the widely used thermodynamic appreciation of the behaviour of polymers in solution in which he was able to account for the large negative deviations from Raoult's Law, phase separation, and swelling of crosslinked polymer networks. He introduced the concept of the θ temperature, which for a given combination of solvent and polymer is the temperature at which polymer molecules behave in a thermodynamically ideal way. In 1949 he demonstrated the surprising result that polymer molecules in the melt, though entangled, exhibit ideal behaviour.

Flory published his influential *Principles of Polymer Science* in 1953, and was awarded the Nobel prize for chemistry in 1974 for fundamental achievements in macromolecular science.

C. H. Bamford, *Chemistry in Britain*, **10**, 461, 1974. (Portrait.)

Les Prix Nobel en 1974. 1975. (Portrait.)

H. Markovitz and E. F. Casassa (Eds), *Polymer Science*. 1976.

Tyler Wasson (Ed.), *Nobel Prize Winners*. 1987. (Portrait.)

J N

FLOURENS, JEAN PIERRE MARIE Born at Maureilhan, near Béziers, Hérault, France, 13 April 1794; died Montgeron, near Paris, 8 December 1867. Discoverer of the functions of the cerebellum and of the semicircular canals.

Pierre Flourens entered medical school at Montpellier in 1809 and graduated as a Doctor of Medicine in 1813. He then went to Paris with a letter of introduction to Baron CUVIER, who befriended him. Flourens gave courses of lectures, and carried out numerous animal experiments. In 1821 he began to present to the *Académie des Sciences* a famous series of reports on his work. In 1828 the *Académie* elected him a member, and Cuvier handed over to Flourens his course of lectures on natural history at the *Collège de France*. In 1832, when Cuvier was dying, he bequeathed to Flourens his post as one of the two Permanent Secretaries of the *Académie*. This appointment was subsequently endorsed by a resolution of the *Académie*. After Cuvier's death Flourens was offered his chair of anatomy at the *Jardin des Plantes*, but he preferred the title of professor of comparative anatomy, and a new chair was created for him. In 1835 he was appointed a professor at the *Collège de France*, and also elected a Foreign Member of the Royal Society of London. Entering politics, he was elected a deputy for Béziers, but he was never active. In 1840 Flourens was elected a member of the French Academy. In 1846 he was elevated to the peerage – abolished by the Revolution of 1848 – and in 1859 he became a *grand officier* of the Legion of Honour.

Flourens' work is in the very highest tradition of French experimental physiology. In 1821 he began a series of epoch-making experiments, many of them reported to the *Académie des Sciences* in 1822. Working at first on pigeons, he showed that vision depends on the integrity of the cerebral cortex. He showed that injury to the cerebellum causes incoordination of movement; he demonstrated the difference between this condition and the effects of alcohol. In 1824 he showed that destruction of the tympanic membrane or the auditory ossicles does not lead to absolute deafness, which is produced only when the nervous connections with the cochlea are destroyed. In 1828 he was the first to show the effect of injury to the semicircular canals individually, and that their function is concerned with balance; and he also showed that stimulation of a canal produces nystagmus in the plane of that canal. He was also the first to show the effects of the experimental crossing of nerves, and his work was important technically in relation to the subsequent practice of nerve suture. In 1812 César Legallois (1770–1814) showed that respiration ceased if the spinal cord was transected at a certain level. In 1824 Flourens confirmed these experiments, and he attempted to localize the 'respiratory centre'. He showed that the centre is bilateral, and he thought that he had localized it (the *noeud vital*) in the medulla. He returned repeatedly to this problem, and showed that different types of respiration are controlled by centres at different levels.

In 1842 Flourens published a revised and extended edition of his earlier book on the nervous system. He had meanwhile studied the doctrine of phrenology enunciated by F. J. Gall (1758–1828) and J. C. Spurzheim (1776–1832), and exploded its scientific merits. He also repeated the experiments of Henri Louis Duhamel du MONCEAU on the growth of bone. Duhamel had shown that the periosteum can form bone, and Flourens confirmed and extended his work and that of John HUNTER, who had shown that simultaneously there is a process of absorption of bone. This problem was later studied scientifically by W. MACEWEN and others.

Ether was first employed in a major surgical operation on 16 October 1846. Very early in 1847 Flourens tried the effects of ether in an experiment on the spinal cord. In a second report shortly afterwards he gave the entire credit for the discovery of the function of the nerve roots to Sir Charles BELL and not to F. MAGENDIE. The result was the bitter and lasting enmity of Magendie. Flourens then tested the anaesthetic effects of various substances on the lower animals, and in March 1847 he reported that chloroform had an anaesthetic effect. This was eight months before J. Y. SIMPSON discovered the anaesthetic effect of chloroform in the human subject.

E. A. Underwood (Ed.), *Science Medicine and History*. 1953. (Portrait.)

J. F. Fulton, *Physiology of the Nervous System*. 1949.

W. Haymaker and F. Schiller (Eds), *The Founders of Neurology*. 1970. (Portrait.)

Dictionary of Scientific Biography.

E A U

FONTENELLE, BERNARD LE BOVIER DE Born at Rouen, France, 11 February 1657; died Paris, 9 January 1757. Outstanding interpreter and popularizer of science.

Fontenelle was the son of a Rouen lawyer; his mother was a member of the Corneille family, distinguished in art and literature. Educated by the Jesuits of Rouen, he qualified as a lawyer, but losing his first case he turned to literature, and after some failures with serious works achieved success with works in lighter style. In his *Entretiens sur la pluralité des mondes* (1686) he aimed to popularize the theories of DESCARTES. He was admitted to the French Academy in 1691, in spite of the opposition of the traditionalist school in the literary controversies which then raged. He became thus a member of the *Académie des Sciences*, and in 1697 he began forty-two years' tenure of the office of Perpetual Secretary.

His outstanding gift was as a popularizer of science in the best sense. The *Histoires* which he wrote for the *Académie des Sciences* summarized and illuminated the work of his contemporaries in all fields. Under his direction the publications of the *Académie* took on the form which fitted them for their leading role in the science of the eighteenth-century.

He did some original work in geometry (*Elémens de la Géometrie de l'Infini*, 1727). Between 1720 and 1740 he wrote a *Histoire de l'Académie* from its foundation in 1666. He instituted the custom of presenting '*Eloges*' of distinguished scientists: addresses or essays in praise of their achievement published after their deaths; these are now valuable historical sources.

A. Laborde-Milan, *Fontenelle*. 1905.

L. Maigron, *Fontenelle, l'homme, l'oeuvre, l'influence*. 1906.

Revue d'Histoire des Sciences et de leurs Applications, **10**, No 4, 1957.

S. Delorme *et al.*, *Fontenelle: Sa Vie et Son Oeuvre*. 1961.

Notes and Records of the Royal Society of London, **12**, 193, 1957.

Dictionary of Scientific Biography.

F G

FORD, HENRY Born at Dearborn, Michigan, USA, 30 July 1863; died there, 7 April 1947. Pioneer of mass production of motor vehicles.

Although Henry Ford's father tried hard to induce him to take up his own occupation of farming, before he left school at 15 he was already a skilled watch-repairer. After working in a machine shop and an engine shop, he became an installer and repairer of farm machines, and in 1887–99 was chief engineer for the Edison Illuminating Company, Detroit. From 1890 onwards his spare time was devoted to the designing of his first car,

which had a twin-cylinder 4 hp engine placed over the rear axle, belt transmission and tiller steering. Having run this for a thousand miles, he started work on an improved model, and in 1899–1902 he served as chief engineer of the Detroit Automobile Company. By 1903 his 80 hp four-cylinder '999' had gained renown for him by winning every race for which it was entered.

Having been interested earlier in the idea of a popular-price farm tractor, Ford naturally thought in terms of a popular-price motor-car. In 1903 he founded the Ford Motor Company, and produced various two-, four- and six-cylinder models while aiming at the eventual production of a light car of maximum strength, simplicity and reliability. When a chance encounter with vanadium steel, not then made in America, solved the problem of a suitable constructional material, he introduced in 1909 his model-T chassis, of which he sold 15 000 000 in nineteen years. It was then replaced by a faster and better-looking car, suited to improved roads and a more mechanically minded public.

Manufacture was based upon rigorous standardization, minute subdivision of labour, and the use of the conveyor belt to extract full efficiency from every worker. Ford paid high wages, but he was not notably successful in human relations. In December 1915 the fiasco of his visit to Europe in the Peace Ship discredited any further attempt at a negotiated settlement of the war. He was from a distance an admirer of Hitler, and his Detroit works were the scene of bitter clashes when he opposed the introduction of trade unionism.

H. Ford, *My Life and Work*. 1925.

H. Thomas and D. C. Thomas, *50 Great Americans*. 1948. (Portrait.)

John B. Rae, *Henry Ford*. 1969.

R. Burlinghame, *Life of Henry Ford*. 1958.

T K D

FORTIN, NICOLAS Born at Mouchy-la-Ville, Île de France, 8 August 1750; died Paris, 1831. An eminent instrument-maker, who gave his name to the portable barometer.

Nicolas Fortin, in his time considered one of the best precision-instrument makers of France, was helped in his early career by A. LAVOISIER. for whom he made a great deal of scientific apparatus. This included a precision balance (1788) with a metre-long beam mounted on steel knife-edges. For the Convention committee on weights and measures (1799) he made a similar balance and a comparator for standardizing weights. He built dividing engines for both circles and rules, and made apparatus for J. L. GAY-LUSSAC in his pneumatic experiments and for D. F. J. ARAGO and P. L. DULONG in their verification of MARRIOTTE's law. Though he does not seem to have made many barometers, his name is linked to that instrument; the inventions of the leather bag, the ivory point, and the glass tube in the cistern, though often ascribed to him, were not his. Nevertheless, he was the first (1797) to use them together in a sensitive portable barometer. This instrument was described and illustrated by J. N. P. Hachette (1769–1834) in his *Programmes d'un Cours de Physique* (1809.) In the later years of his life Fortin turned to the construction of astronomical and surveying instruments, making a 2-metre circle for the Paris Observatory, and a repeating circle for J. B. BIOT and Arago in their triangulations in Spain.

M. Daumas, *Les Instruments Scientifiques aux XVIIe et XVIIIe Siècles*. 1953.

W. E. Knowles, *The History of the Barometer*. 1964.

Dictionary of Scientific Biography.

W N S

FOUCAULT, LÉON Born in Paris, 18 September 1819; died there, 11 February 1868. Celebrated for his demonstration of the rotation of the Earth, and for the first accurate determination of the velocity of light.

Son of a poor bookseller, Foucault at first intended to become a doctor, but later became interested in physical science. From 1845 onwards he edited the scientific section of the *Journal de Débats*. In 1855 he was appointed physicist at the Paris Observatory, and he became a member of the Bureau of Longitudes in 1862. In 1864 he was elected a Foreign Member of the Royal Society of London and in the following year became a member of the *Académie des Sciences*.

Foucault's first account of his experimental demonstration of the rotation of the Earth by means of a swinging pendulum was published in 1850, together with an equation connecting the apparent angular rotation of the plane of the pendulum with the angular velocity of the Earth and the latitude of the position of the experiment. This demonstration aroused enormous scientific and general interest. Many proofs of Foucault's law were given and many repetitions of his experiment made with longer pendulums, including one by Foucault himself in public with a pendulum suspended from the dome of the *Panthéon*. In 1852 he gave an account of experiments performed with his newly constructed gyroscope, including certain laws governing its behaviour. For this work on the rotation of the Earth and on the gyroscope Foucault was awarded the Copley Medal of the Royal Society in 1855.

In 1850 D. F. J. ARAGO informed the *Académie des Sciences* that Foucault had taken over his projected method for comparing the velocity of light in air and water by means of a rotating mirror. In the same year Foucault announced the successful completion of the experiment, showing a diminution of the velocity of light in water compared with air. After surmounting many technical obstacles, he eventually succeeded (1862) in measuring the velocity of light in a confined space by the rotating-mirror method, employing five concave mirrors which increased the path of the light to about 20 metres. The result obtained, 298 000 kilometres per second, was the first reasonably accurate determination of the velocity of light (299 792 kilometres per second).

Among much other work, we may note Foucault's improvements to reflecting telescopes, and to the design of the Watt governor. He also carried out a number of important experiments in collaboration with A. H. L. FIZEAU. In 1849 he anticipated R. W. BUNSEN and G. R. KIRCHHOFF in noting a bright yellow line in the spectrum of an electric arc in exactly the same position as the D line of J. von FRAUNHOFER. At the same time he noted that this line disappeared if a stronger source of continuous radiation were viewed through the electric arc. These results were published in *L'Institut* (1849),

but first became generally known when republished in 1860.

Foucault was an experimenter of genius, of a most original turn of mind with a sure instinct for important subjects for research, and his death from paralysis at the early age of 48 was a severe blow to physical science.

Proceedings of the Royal Society, **17**, 133, 1869.

J. A. Lissajous, *Life*. 1875.

History of European Ideas, **19**, No 3, 1992.

Dictionary of Scientific Biography.

J W H

FOURCROY, ANTOINE FRANÇOIS DE Born in Paris, 15 June 1755; died there, 16 December 1809. Teacher and modernizer of chemistry.

The neglected son of an impoverished apothecary, Fourcroy left school at 15 and earned a meagre living as a copying clerk. Fortunately he met F. Vicq d'Azyr (1748–94), the anatomist, who arranged for him to study medicine (1773). He was helped financially by members of the *Société Royale de Médecine* of which Vicq d'Azyr was Secretary. He became a pupil of P. J. MACQUER and of J. B. M. Bucquet (1746–89). He gained a doctorate in 1780, with academic ease, but only after overcoming administrative and financial obstacles. He soon made a great name as a lecturer, first privately, then at the *Jardin du Roi*. In 1793 he became a member of the National Convention in place of J-P. Marat. He took part in the introduction of the metric system of weights and measures; in the foundation of a national medical school (the *École de Santé* (1795), later to be the *École de Médecine*); and the organization of what became in 1795 the *École Polytechnique*, where he was appointed a professor. He became Consul in 1801, and was Minister of Public Instruction from 1802 until 1808. He was among those who organized new chemical manufactures to help make France self-sufficient. It was once said that he was partly responsible for the death of LAVOISIER, but this cannot be upheld; he was as helpless as anyone else during the trial and he denounced the execution afterwards as an atrocious crime. He died on the very day Napoleon made him a count.

Fourcroy's most important contribution to the progress of chemistry was his advocacy of the views of Lavoisier. At first he was as uncertain as many of his colleagues, but after the establishment of the composition of water and nitric acid by Henry CAVENDISH, he gave it his full support, although he was careful to present a full account of the older view in lectures and textbooks. Fourcroy wrote many works, the one based on his lectures running to many editions in many languages.

Much of his experimental work was done in collaboration with L. N. VAUQUELIN, a man of totally different character, modest and reserved where Fourcroy was eloquent and busy. He established the existence of two series of mercury compounds, studied many constituents of animal and vegetable tissue, discovering that phosphorus could be present other than as phosphate, and developing the chemistry of urea. He made innumerable minor contributions to inorganic chemistry, filling in many gaps in knowledge of salts and so helping to consolidate the edifice of chemistry of which the great theorists had provided only a framework.

W. A. Smeaton, *Fourcroy: Chemist and Revolutionary*. 1962.

W. A. Smeaton, *Endeavour*, **18**, 70, 1959. (Portrait.)

G. Kersaint, *Antoine François de Fourcroy*. 1966.

F G

FOURIER, JEAN BAPTISTE JOSEPH Born at Auxerre, France, 21 March 1768; died Paris, 16 May 1830. Mathematician and mathematical physicist, best known for 'Fourier's series'.

Fourier was the son of a tailor, and was orphaned when 8 years old. A friend arranged his admission to a local military school, where he later taught. After two years (1787–9) as a novice in the Abbey of St Benoît sur Loire, he returned, and in 1795, on its inception, moved to the *École Normale* in Paris, and then to what later became the *Polytechnique*. Scientific adviser to Napoleon in Egypt (1798–1801), there was a time when he virtually governed half of that country. During his subsequent prefecture of Isère (1801–15) he did his best work on the mathematical theory of heat conduction. His career now suffered as many reversals as his country suffered changes of government. In 1826 he at last became a member of the Academy, his election having been previously opposed by Louis XVIII, and in the following year succeeded P. S. LAPLACE as President of the Council of the *École Polytechnique*.

Fourier has a large number of minor results to his credit – as, for instance, his improvement of the method of NEWTON of approximating to the roots of an equation, his use of dimensional analysis, his treatment of statics in terms of the principle of virtual work – but it was through his mathematical analysis of heat propagation that he became undisputed leader of the French analytical school. He began this work in about 1807, presented much of it to the Academy in 1811, and finally published it, as what was to be a famous textbook, in 1822 (*Analytical Theory of Heat*). There he established his law of heat propagation

$$\frac{\delta^2 V}{\delta x^2} + \frac{\delta^2 V}{\delta y^2} + \frac{\delta^2 V}{\delta z^2} = a^2 \frac{\delta V}{\delta t}$$

to integrate which he was driven to develop the so-called 'Fourier series'. Such series, series of the form $\Sigma_n(a_n \sin \frac{n\pi x}{\chi})$, had already been used by Daniel BERNOULLI, J. L. LAGRANGE and L. EULER, but Fourier was the first to recognize that they may be used to represent arbitrary functions. Fourier's methods lacked rigour, and he scarcely even acknowledged convergence requirements, but his physical insight usually won the day. His mathematics provided a starting-point for much later work on the theory of functions of a real variable, his cavalier treatment of concepts of limit and continuity serving to galvanize mathematicians such as P. G. L. Dirichlet (1805–59), G. F. B. RIEMANN, G. CANTOR and K. T. WEIERSTRASS into activity. Likewise Theta functions, which he encountered in the theory of heat flow, were handled with greater precision and taken over into number theory, by such writers as K. G. J. JACOBI and C. Hermite (1822–1901).

Fourier's work on heat served as a useful paradigm for later physics. G. S. OHM found his series useful when dealing with problems of acoustics, and worked by analogy with the equations of heat flow when developing his important theory of the flow of electricity. William THOMSON (Lord Kelvin) and O. HEAVISIDE were also greatly influenced by him.

F. Arago, 'Joseph Fourier', *Smithsonian Annual Report*, 136, 1871.

J. G. Darboux (Ed.) *J. Fourier, Oeuvres*, 2 vols. 1888–90. (Portrait.)

I. Grattan-Guinness and J. Ravetz, *Joseph Fourier 1768–1830*. 1972.

Dictionary of Scientific Biography.

J D N

FOURNEYRON, BENOET Born at St Etienne, France, 31 October 1802; died Paris, 31 July 1867. Devised the outward-flow turbine known by his name.

Son of a mathematician, Fourneyron entered the School of Mines at St Etienne and distinguished himself in mathematics. He left at 17 to work in the steel industry at Creuzot, where power was needed for blowing-engines and forge hammers. Fourneyron's professor, Claude Burdin (1790–1873), wrote a memoir on a new power unit – for which he coined the name turbine – based on the efflux of water outwards from a vertical central rotor. Initially, neither the *Académie des Sciences* nor the *Societé d'Encouragement pour l'Industrie Nationale* accepted Burdin's memoir – though they recognized his achievement later – but it stimulated Fourneyron to make a small 6 hp version. Encouraged and supported by F. Caron, an ironmaster of Fraisans (Doubs), Fourneyron moved to Besançon and produced a successful experimental unit of 50 hp, which in 1833 won him the prize that the *Societé* had offered for a motor of this kind. His turbines were soon in demand throughout the world. The first great hydro-electric installation in the world, at Niagara Falls, used Fourneyron's outward-flow turbines in 1895.

Fourneyron also tried to drive turbines with steam, but neither the materials nor the workmanship existed in his day to make this possible and success was left to Sir Charles PARSONS. His political interests led him to seek election to the Constituent Assembly in 1848, and to write on economic questions of the day.

M. Crozet-Fourneyron, *Invention de la Turbine*. 1924.

F. W. Keatur, *Mechanical Engineering*, **61**, 295, 1939.

Paul N. Wilson, *Transactions of the Newcomen Society*, **31**, 219, 1939.

H. Rouse and S. Ince, *History of Hydraulics*. 1957. (Portrait.)

W H G A

FOWLER, SIR JOHN Born at Sheffield, Yorkshire, England, 15 July 1817; died Bournemouth, Hampshire, 20 November 1898. Civil engineer.

Fowler was the son of a land surveyor, had an early training in railway work, and in 1844 set up as a consulting engineer in London. With Benjamin Baker as his chief assistant, he was mainly responsible for the Metropolitan Railway and, at the end of his career, he was one of the engineers for the first London tube railways. In 1871–9 he was engineering adviser to the Khedive of Egypt. His best-known achievement – again in collaboration with Baker –

was the construction in 1882–90 of the cantilever railway bridge over the Firth of Forth, with its two main spans of 1710 feet. The material was Siemens-Martin open-hearth steel, fabricated on the spot; the amount used was 54 000 tons, a very big margin of safety being allowed in view of the disastrous collapse of the Tay Bridge in 1879.

Fowler received the KCMG for services in Egypt and the Sudan, and was created a baronet on the completion of the Forth Bridge. He became a big landowner in Scotland.

Dictionary of National Biography.

T K D

FOYN, SVEND Born at Tönsberg, Norway, 9 July 1809; died Nötteröy, 29 November 1894. Pioneer of modern whaling techniques.

Foyn went to sea at 11 years of age, and in 1845 invented a special boat for hunting seals. From sealing he turning to hunting whales, especially the rorquals off the north coast of Norway, which moved too fast to be attacked from rowing boats. In 1863 Foyn introduced the steam-driven whaler, and from 1868 onwards he successfully employed a harpoon gun mounted in the bows; attached to the harpoon there was a powerful charge which exploded after penetrating into the animal's body.

Two other innovations of Foyn's, which brought no immediate reward, were the first floating factory (1890–1) and a whaling expedition to the Antarctic in 1893. Strong-willed, industrious and deeply religious, he amassed a considerable fortune, which he bequeathed to missionary work.

T K D

FRACASTORO, GIROLAMO Born at Verona, Italy, in 1478 (?1483); died Incaffi, Garda, 6 August 1553. A pioneer of epidemiology, and a poet who introduced the name 'syphilis'.

Fracastoro studied mathematics, philosophy and medicine in the University of Padua, and he was lecturer in logic there from 1501 to 1507. When Padua was captured by the Austrians (1508) he went to Verona, but on the outbreak of plague he removed to his villa at Incaffi on Lake Garda. He remained there until 1516, when he returned to Verona and practised until 1534. He then retired to devote himself to scholarship. Although Fracastoro was known not only as a physician but also as a geographer, mathematician and astronomer, his fame rests on two books, namely his poem on syphilis and his book on contagion.

From about the end of the fifteenth century a disease, popularly supposed to be venereal, had been epidemic in much of Europe; the name 'morbus Gallicus' (French disease) was soon widely adopted for it and was commonly used for a century. In 1530 Fracastoro published a poem in Latin hexameters entitled *Syphilis sive morbus Gallicus* ('Syphilis or the French disease'), in which he tells of the tribulations of a shepherd named Syphilis who was smitten with the disease by Apollo. It describes the various remedies used for the disease. It went through many editions. The name 'syphilis', coined by Fracastoro, gradually took the place of 'morbus Gallicus'.

Fracastoro's main medical work is his *De contagione et contagiosis morbis* ('On contagion and contagious diseases', 1546). He distinguished three forms of contagion: by direct contact; by indirect contact through the agency of infected articles; and by transmission from a distance. He regarded infection as due to the passage of minute bodies from the infective person to the person infected.

J. J. Abraham, introduction to *Fracastoro, Syphilis* (trans. Wynne-Finch). 1935. (Portrait.)
C. E. A. Winslow, *Conquest of Epidemic Disease.* 1944.
Dictionary of Scientific Biography.

E A U

FRANCK, JAMES Born at Hamburg, Germany, 26 August 1882; died Göttingen, 21 May 1964. A physicist known for his work on the transfer of energy between molecules.

Franck attended school at Hamburg before going to the University of Heidelberg where he studied chemistry and geology. There he met Max BORN, with whom he formed a life-long friendship. He later moved to Berlin, where he studied physics, and in 1906 obtained the degree of PhD for his work on ionic mobility in gases. The following year he became research assistant to Professor H. Rubens (1865–1922). In the First World War he had a distinguished army record, and afterwards he worked under Fritz HABER as a division head at the Kaiser-Wilhelm Institute for Physical Chemistry at Berlin-Dahlem. In 1920 he was appointed to a chair at Göttingen and he retained that post until Hitler came to power; in 1933 he resigned and went to Copenhagen. Shortly afterwards (1935) he went to the United States, where he secured an appointment at the Johns Hopkins University. Later he went to the University of Chicago as professor of chemistry. During the Second World War he worked there with the team of American physicists who developed the atom bomb. He attempted, together with other scientists, to prevent its use, and suggested instead an explosion over an unpopulated area to demonstrate its power. These views were submitted in the Franck Report six days before the New Mexico atom bomb test (16 July 1945).

Throughout his life Franck's work was concerned almost entirely with research on one topic, the interchange of energy between molecules. While he was at Göttingen he carried out research on the transfer of energy in molecular collisions, and in 1926 he was awarded a Nobel prize, jointly with G. HERTZ, for this work. He showed that the energy loss of electrons in mercury vapour changed sharply at particular levels, and this provided direct evidence in support of the quantum theory of Max PLANCK. He discovered a method for determining the heat of dissociation of diatomic molecules from their band spectra, and this led him to put forward, together with E. U. CONDON, the principle known as the Franck-Condon Principle, which accounted for the change observed in the vibrational quantum number during an electronic transition. In the latter part of his life he was concerned with elucidating the reactions occurring during photosynthesis.

Franck was elected a Foreign Member of the Royal Society in 1964.

L. Meitner, *Nature,* **203**, 916, 1964.
Biographical Memoirs of Fellows of the Royal Society. 1965. (Portrait.)
O. Oldenberg, *American Journal of Physics,* **41**, 39, 1971.

B B K

FRANKLAND, SIR EDWARD Born at Churchtown, near Lancaster, England, 18 January 1825; died (on holiday) in Norway, 9 August 1899. His work in chemistry was notable for introducing the concept now known as valency.

After leaving Lancaster Grammar School, Frankland was apprenticed to a local apothecary as the first step towards a medical career. He was advised, however, to become a chemist, and went to London in 1845 to study under Lyon PLAYFAIR. Here he met A. W. H. KOLBE, and together they worked under R. W. BUNSEN at Marburg. Another year was spent with Justus von LIEBIG at Giessen, followed by various teaching posts in England. In 1851 Frankland became the first professor of chemistry in the newly founded Owen's College, Manchester, but left to occupy chairs successively at St Bartholomew's Hospital, London (1857), the Royal Institution, London (1863), and finally the Royal School of Mines, London (1865), as successor to A. W. von HOFMANN. He retired in 1885, but continued to be an adviser on problems of water supply and sewage.

Frankland's first researches aimed at the isolation of the 'compound radicals' of which (according to the theories of the day) organic substances were composed, just as inorganic substances were composed of the chemical elements. This led him (1849) to study the action of zinc on alkyl iodides, and so into the field of organozinc compounds. These very reactive substances were of great value at that time in preparative organic chemistry. This pioneer work in organometallic chemistry was later extended to derivatives of mercury, the alkali metals, tin, and boron. The nature of the 'radicals' produced was a matter of dispute, and Frankland was not entirely convinced even when C. W. Schorlemmer (1839–92) showed in 1864 that 'methyl' was, in fact, ethane.

In 1852 Frankland noted that nitrogen and phosphorus often formed compounds containing three or five atoms of other elements, and suggested that there was 'a tendency or law' for the 'combining power of the attracting element' to be always satisfied by the same number of atoms. This number he called the 'atomicity', an unsatisfactory name which was followed by several others, until 'Valenz' was coined by H. Wichelhaus (1842–1927) in 1868. The concept of valency, under whatever name, was fundamental to the Structure Theory (1858).

Frankland was always interested in chemical technology, especially in coal gas and in the problems of water supply and purification; his later work was largely in these fields. His work with Sir Norman LOCKYER on solar spectra in 1869 should not be forgotten, however, as it led to the discovery of helium.

Frankland was twice married, and had several children, including the chemist P. F. Frankland (1858–1946). He was elected FRS in 1853, and knighted in 1897.

Journal of the Chemical Society, **574**, 1905.
Sketches from the life of Sir Edward Frankland; edited and concluded by his two daughters, M. N. W. and S. J. C. 1902. (Portrait.)
Berichte der deutschen Chemischen Gesellschaft, **33**, 1847, 1900. (Portrait.)
Colin A Russell, *A Lancastrian Chemist: The Early Years of Sir Edward Frankland*.1986. (Portrait.)

Dictionary of National Biography.
Dictionary of Scientific Biography.

W V F

FRANKLIN, BENJAMIN Born at Boston, Massachusetts, USA, 17 January 1706; died Philadelphia, Pennsylvania, 17 April 1790. One of the great founders of the science of electricity.

The tenth son of an emigré English soap-boiler, Franklin was a founder of republican America and one of her greatest sons. After some wandering abroad, he settled as a newspaper proprietor in Philadelphia, becoming the centre of an intellectual group from which emerged the American Philosophical Society. A prolific writer, he was 'America's first man of letters' (David Hume), and his *Autobiography* is still read in US schools. From 1757 he devoted himself to the struggle for independence, representing American colonial interests in London (1757–75), and becoming one of the first sponsors of the federal ideal and one of the five who drafted the Declaration of Independence (1776). His diplomatic mission to France (1777–85) brought substantial French aid to America and the involvement of France in the war with Britain. He played an important part in the 1787 Convention (from which the US Constitution emerged) and held high government office until his death.

His electrical experiments began in 1746. A study of frictional electricity convinced him that a transfer of 'electric fluid' took place, leaving surfaces 'positive' or 'negative'. This 'one-fluid theory', in contradistinction to the 'two-fluids theory' of C. F. de C. DUFAY and others, led to an understanding of the recently invented Leyden jar, and to his invention of 'Franklin's pane', the first planar condenser (glass between lead sheets).

Scientifically he is most famed for his proof (though not the suggestion) that lightning is electrical in nature. In his famous kite experiment (1752), atmospheric electricity was conducted from a kite down a wet string, and made to charge a Leyden jar, produce sparks, etc. Earlier experiments on discharges from pointed objects led to his invention of the lightning conductor. He investigated the charges on thunder-clouds, speculated on other atmospheric phenomena, and suggested further electrical experiments.

Franklin's 'one-fluid theory' gave a permanent unity to electrical studies, and in a pre-Voltaic age 'he found electricity a curiosity and left it a science' (C. van Doren).

He was interested in radiant heat, thermal conduction, hydrodynamics, meteorology and much else. On returning from France at 79 he kept careful records of winds, drifting seaweed, and temperatures. He invented the efficient 'Pennsylvanian Fireplace'.

Franklin was honoured by the Paris *Académie*, was elected FRS (1756), and was made an honorary graduand of Oxford. In 1824 the Franklin Institute, Philadelphia, was founded in his memory.

C. van Doren, *Benjamin Franklin*. 1938.
E. N. da C. Andrade, *Nature*, **177**, 60, 1956.
Proceedings of the American Philosophical Society, **100**, No. 4, 1956. (Portraits.)
Bern Dibner, *Benjamin Franklin, Electrician*. 1976.
J. W. Draper, *Life of Franklin*. 1977.
Endeavour (New Series), **14**, 1, 1990.

V. W. Crane, *Benjamin Franklin and a Rising People*. 1954.
Dictionary of American Biography.
Dictionary of Scientific Biography.

C A R

FRANKLIN, ROSALIND ELSIE Born in London, 25 July 1920, died there, 16 April 1958. X-ray crystallographer; molecular biologist.

Rosalind Franklin came from a professional family with no scientific leanings, but chose to study chemistry at Cambridge after winning an exhibition from St Paul's School, London, in 1938. After postgraduate research on gas-phase chromatography with R. G. W. NORRISH, she joined the British Coal Utilisation Research Association in 1942 to study the physical structure of coal and subsequently continued this interest in Paris (1947–50) in the *Laboratoire Central des Services Chimique de l'Etat*. In this research she made a close study of the graphitization of carbon at high temperatures. In the course of this she became skilled in the technique of x-ray crystallography and this led her to research on the structure of DNA and viruses, first at King's College, London (1951–53) and subsequently at Birkbeck College, London.

At King's College, M. H. F. Wilkins (1916–) and R Gosling had obtained diffraction images of DNA indicating a high degree of crystallinity. The sharpness of the image depended on the ambient humidity and Franklin embarked, with Gosling, on a detailed study of this phenomenon. She established in 1951 that DNA exists in two forms (A and B) in dynamic equilibrium. This seemed to be consistent with a helical structure for DNA proposed by Wilkins a year earlier; at high humidity water could penetrate the A form between the helices, causing the observed change in structure. Nevertheless she was not entirely convinced that the helical structure was the right one and she sought further experimental evidence to resolve the issue. Meanwhile, however, J. D. WATSON and F. CRICK - partly on the basis of some of Franklin's x-ray pictures - had confirmed and identified the double helix structure for DNA.

For the remaining five years of her life - sadly, she died of cancer at the early age of 37 - she rounded off her DNA work and turned to the structure of tobacco mosaic virus (TMV).

Dictionary of Scientific Biography.
J. D. Watson, *The Double Helix*. 1968. (Portrait.)
A. Klug, *Nature*, **219**, 808, 843, 1968.
The Times, 19 April 1958.

???

FRASCH, HERMAN Born at Gaildorf, Württemberg, Germany, 25 December 1851; died Paris, 1 May 1914. Chemical engineer remembered for his method of winning sulphur.

Following schooling at Halle and a pharmaceutical apprenticeship, Herman Frasch emigrated in 1868 to Philadelphia. With an improved chemical knowledge, he had by 1873 established an industrial laboratory and found local clients. After taking out a patent for refining paraffin-wax in 1876, he joined the Standard Oil Company at their Cleveland laboratories. Oil claimed him in the next years but he remained active in other fields of chemical technology. In 1885 he left Standard Oil and launched out as an oil-master near London,

Ontario, but the oil from this field was poor. Establishing that these properties were due to sulphur, Frasch found that the element could be removed with copper oxide. He set up a commercial plant for the removal of sulphur and the recovery of spent oxide. Following the discovery of similar defects in the Ohio oilfield, Frasch rejoined Standard Oil as chief chemist. In 1891 he turned to the winning of a Louisiana sulphur deposit overlain by quicksand through which shaft-sinking had proved impossible. Adapting an old method devised for mining salt as brine, Frasch pumped superheated water down a borehole to the sulphur and recovered a mixture of molten sulphur and water from a pipe concentric with the first. A third pipe acting as heat jacket completed the invention, which broke the Sicilian monopoly for the supply of sulphur. In later years Frasch retired to France.

The National Cyclopaedia of American Biography, **19**, 347, 1926. (Portrait.)
Proceedings of the American Academy of Arts and Sciences, **79**, 15, 1950–1.
Journal of the Society of Chemical Industry, **79**, 168, 1912.
E. Farber (Ed.), *Great Chemists*. 1961. (Portrait.)
Wyndham D. Miles (Ed.), *American Chemists and Chemical Engineers*. 1976.

W N S

FRAUNHOFER, JOSEF VON Born at Straubing, Bavaria, Germany, 6 March 1787; died Munich, Bavaria, 7 June 1826. Remembered for his investigation of the dark lines in the solar spectrum known by his name, and for his development of the spectroscope.

The son of a poor glazier, Fraunhofer spent a period as apprentice to a mirror-maker and glass polisher before entering the Mechanical-Optical Institute of J. von Utzschneider (1763–1840) at Benediktbeuern in 1806. In 1809 he became a partner and after his transfer to Munich in 1819 he was appointed Director of the Physical Cabinet there and a member of the Bavarian Academy of Sciences.

Fraunhofer's early work convinced him that the performance of achromatic object glasses suffered greatly from the uncertainty about the dispersive powers of different kinds of glasses. He first tried to measure the dispersive power of a given glass by the length of the spectrum it produced, but found this impossible owing to the absence of sharp edges. The refractive power of a certain type of glass for a given colour could equally not be used owing to the impossibility of fixing the position of the colour exactly in the spectrum. At this point he noted the characteristic sharp yellow line between red and yellow in the spectrum of many oils and salts, and was thus enabled to plot fixed positions in the spectrum. He then rediscovered the dark lines in the solar spectrum observed previously by W. H. WOLLASTON. By means of an improved apparatus he was able to distinguish 574 such lines with fixed positions. The same lines were also observed in the light of Venus and that of many stars. In 1821–2 Fraunhofer announced that a solar spectrum produced by a grating contained the same lines, thus proving them to be an intrinsic feature of sunlight. Fraunhofer was now able to measure with great precision the wavelengths of the dark lines.

Through Fraunhofer's improvements, the spectroscope was transformed from a scientific toy into a precision instrument of fundamental importance. He was a committed follower of the wave theory of light to which his work largely contributed, but he had little interest in theoretical considerations.

A. Seitz, *Josef Fraunhofer und sein optisches Institut.* 1926.
P. Lenard, *Great Men of Science.* 1933. (Portrait.)
Günter D. Roth, *Joseph von Fraunhofer.* 1976.
Naturwissenschaften, **14**, 522, 1926.
Dictionary of Scientific Biography.

J W H

FREDHOLM, ERIC IVAR Born in Stockholm, 7 April 1866; died there, 17 August 1927. Mathematician who founded the modern theory of integral equations.

Fredholm was educated at the University of Uppsala, receiving a doctorate there in 1898. After working as an actuary he was, in 1906, appointed professor of theoretical physics at Stockholm. His main work was concerned with the theory of integral equations, on which he first published a paper in 1903.

Particular cases of integral equations had previously been studied and Vito Volterra (1860–1940) had treated the general theory. Fredholm considered the equations which bear his name:

$$\int K(x,y)\phi(y)dy = \varrho(x)$$

(equation of first type)

$$\phi(x) - \lambda \int K(x,y)\phi(y)dy = \varrho(x)$$

(equation of second type)

$$\phi(x) - \lambda \int K(x,y)\phi(y)dy = o$$

(homogeneous equation)

Fredholm achieved a solution of the second type by treating the equation as a limiting form of a system of linear algebraic equations with the number of unknowns becoming indefinitely large. He overcame the difficulty which had faced Volterra in the fact that the determinant of the equations approaches singularity.

Fredholm published, with his pupils, definitive works on the general theory of integral equations. He received the Wallmark prize of the Swedish Academy and the Poncelet prize of the *Académie de France.*

Nils Zeilon, *Acta Mathematica*, **54**, 1, 1930.
S. Lindroth, *Swedish Men of Science 1650–1950.* 1952.
Dictionary of Scientific Biography.

D N

FRESNEL, AUGUSTIN JEAN Born at Broglie, Eure, France, 10 May 1788; died Ville d'Avray, near Paris, 14 July 1827. Distinguished in wave-theory of light and in applied optics.

Fresnel was the son of an architect who withdrew from the disturbances of the Revolution and educated his children himself on a small estate near Caen. The young Fresnel showed little aptitude for literary studies, but was exceptionally skilled in practical matters. He went to school in Caen at the age of 13 and made such good progress in mathematics that he entered the *École Polytechnique* three years later, where ill health did not hinder his gaining high distinction. He qualified as an engineer at the *École des Ponts et Chaussées,*

serving in this capacity in the Department of La Verdie and La Drome until March 1815.

During the Hundred Days he adhered to the Royalist cause, and was consequently suspended. He spent the enforced leisure in Normandy and began his great research on light, in which he had shown some interest, but confessed to little knowledge.

On learning of the recent work on polarization he carried out experiments with simple apparatus and soon developed a wave-theory of light, in which the longitudinal waves which had been assumed by previous adherents of wave-theory (like C. HUYGENS and T. YOUNG) were replaced by transverse waves. This bold theory eventually affected not only all considerations of the geometrical and photometric aspects of light but also consideration of its relation to space and matter.

Fresnel was indebted to the encouragement of D. F. J. ARAGO. He became a member of the *Académie des Sciences* in 1823, and a Foreign Member of the Royal Society in 1825. In 1827 the Royal Society awarded him its Rumford Medal. He died within a few days of receiving the news.

His other great achievement arose from his profession and followed a request to consider the distribution of light from lighthouses. Hitherto metal reflectors had been used to concentrate the rays from the illuminant, but these were recognized as inconvenient and inefficient. Lenses had been tried, but seemed impracticable. Fresnel, however, followed up a suggestion of G. L. L. BUFFON for reducing the thickness of the lens by grinding out steps in concentric zones (1748). The Marquis de Condorcet (1743–94) (1773) and D. BREWSTER (1811) had suggested an aggregate of separate rings. Fresnel went much further, building up a lens from annular rings, the centres of curvature of which varied progressively so as to eliminate spherical aberration. Other designs led him eventually to a totally reflecting system which eliminated the need for metal reflectors. He also devised means of periodically increasing the intensity of the beam, so as to combine a fixed and flashing light. Fresnel's calculations still form the basis of lighthouse design.

Nouvelle Biographie Générale, vol. 18. 1857.
P. Lenard, *Great Men of Science.* 1950. (Portrait.)
Dictionary of Scientific Biography.

F G

FREUD, SIGMUND Born at Freiberg, Moravia, (now in Czech Republic), 6 May 1856; died London, 24 September 1939. Founder and creator of psychoanalysis.

Freud, the son of Jewish parents, entered the University of Vienna as a medical student in 1873, and graduated MD 1881. There followed distinguished neurological research under E. W. von Brücke (1819–92), F. S. Exner (1849–1922), and other well-known figures. The year 1885 marked a turning-point in Freud's life. For four and a half months he studied under the great French neurologist, J. M. CHARCOT. Charcot's work convinced him of the genuineness of hysterical phenomena, and determined him to abandon laboratory researches into the anatomy of the nervous system for clinical work on nervous disorders. Returning to Vienna, he set up in practice, but soon became dissatisfied with the available methods for treating nervous disorders, electrotherapy and hypnotism. The outcome was the development of the psychoanalytic method, based on free association and dream analysis. For a time Freud worked in collaboration with J. Breuer (1842–1925), and the first psychoanalytic work, *Studies in Hysteria* (1895), was written jointly. Freud's increasing conviction of the role of sexual impulses in the aetiology of the neuroses, however, alienated Breuer. From 1895 to 1906 he worked single-handed, largely reviled by the medical profession and ostracized professionally. By 1906 he was beginning to attract followers, C. G. JUNG and A. ADLER among others. In 1908 the first psychoanalytic congress was held in Salzburg, with forty-two members present. The International Association of Psychoanalysis was founded in 1910, and continues to flourish, particularly in America. In 1936 the Royal Society elected him a Foreign Member. The Nazi occupation obliged Freud to leave Vienna in 1938, and he spent the last year of his life in London.

Psychoanalysis is at once a psychotherapeutic technique, a theory of the mind and its disorders, and a philosophy of man and society. Therapeutically, it depends on the slow breaking down of the resistances against self-knowledge in a long series of analytic sessions. An important therapeutic factor is the emotional relationship, or transference, between the patient and the analyst.

The most important doctrine of psychoanalytic theory is the Freudian distinction between two levels of mental functioning, the more primitive primary level, marked by symbolic thinking, as in dreams and myths, and the pleasure principle; and the secondary level marked by logical thinking, critical self-awareness and the reality principle. The primary level is never outgrown, but is a permanent feature of the human mind, revealing itself not only in dreams and fantasies but in imaginative literature, in works of art, and in neurotic and psychotic symptoms. This basic distinction is sketched in Freud's *Interpretation of Dreams* (1900), perhaps his most original and important work. The more primitive level of the mind, which Freud came to term the 'Id', is the source of the basic drives, the libido or sex impulse, and the destructive or death impulse. This primitive level comes into conflict with the demands of society, internalized as the 'super-ego', and the 'ego' or self is thus torn by internal strife. It is in these conflicts that neurotic disturbances originate, and various mechanisms have been evolved to handle conflict situations. Among the more important are repression into the unconscious regions of the mind, reaction formation, projection, and sublimation. Among the more controversial features of psychoanalytic doctrine are the great stress laid by Freud on the role of sex in the aetiology of neurotic disorders, and his elaborate theory of the development of the sexual impulses during human childhood. Freud believed that the relations between a child and its parents were basically of a sexual nature, and that the so-called Oedipus complex predominated in the formation of character.

Freudian theories have illuminated many dark places of the human mind, and have had a profound influence on our understanding of man and society. Freud himself applied his theories to the study of primitive thought, mythology, religion, art, literature, the errors and witticisms of everyday life, and the malaise of civilized society. His theories have always been controversial, and he has been attacked both for his unscientific methodology and for the uncritical speculativeness of his theories. Nevertheless he was a man of great integrity and courage, and undoubtedly a rare genius.

Ernest Jones, *Sigmund Freud, Life and Work* (3 vols). 1953–7. (Portraits.)

S. Freud, *An Autobiographical Study*. 1935.

S. Freud, *An Outline of Psychoanalysis*. 1949.

P. Gay, *Freud: Une Vie*. 1991.

Obituary Notices of Fellows of the Royal Society. 1941. (Portrait.)

Dictionary of Scientific Biography.

L S H

FREUNDLICH, HERBERT MAX FINLAY Born in Berlin-Charlottenburg, 28 January 1880; died Minneapolis, Minnesota, USA, 30 March 1941. Colloid chemist.

Freundlich was the son of a German-Jewish father and a Scottish mother. He studied chemistry at Munich and Leipzig, where he was assistant to W. F. OSTWALD until 1911. After a few years in Brunswick, he spent the 1914–18 war in the *Kaiser Wilhelm Institut*, Berlin-Dahlem, working on gas masks. From 1919 he held a permanent position there, and made the *Institut* a world centre for the study of colloid chemistry and physics. For racial reasons he left Germany in 1933; he took up posts first in University College, London, then in the University of Minnesota, where he died.

Freundlich was the author of a large volume of work on all aspects of colloid science, especially its relationship to industrial chemistry and to biology. His studies of the 'zeta potential' and of thixotropy were of particular importance.

Journal of the Chemical Society, 646, 1942. (Portrait.)

Obituary Notices of Fellows of the Royal Society. 1942. (Portrait.)

Dictionary of Scientific Biography, Supp. I.

W V F

FREYSSINET, MARIE EUGÈNE LÉON Born at Objat, near Périgueux, France, 13 July 1879; died St. Martin-Vésubie, 8 June 1962. Civil engineer, pioneer in the design and construction of prestressed concrete structures.

A graduate of both the *École Polytechnique* and the *École des Ponts et Chaussées* in Paris, Eugène Freyssinet worked from 1905 to 1913 as an engineer for local roads and bridges at Moulins, and already during those years displayed his talent for the intuitive and innovative design of reinforced concrete bridges. He invented what became known as the Freyssinet flat jack, which he incorporated horizontally at mid-span in many of his flat arched bridges, enabling him to raise the arches for de-centering, and also to counteract any sag that would have resulted from progressive creep in the concrete.

In 1918 he joined the building firm of Limousin in Paris, for whom he designed some of the most elegant reinforced concrete bridges in the world, including the largest at Plougastel, near Brest, with three 180 m span arches, completed in 1930. At about this time his studies of the creep of concrete convinced him that its performance in structures could be dramatically improved by the introduction of an overall compressive force, which would counteract the tensile stresses developed in resisting applied loads; thus the concept of pre-stressing concrete was born.

He set up a factory to produce prestressed con-crete electricity transmission poles in 1929, but it was not a commercial success. In 1935, however, he was able to demonstrate the potential of his prestressing technique when he used it to under-pin the foundations of the Ocean Terminal at Le Havre, saving it from imminent collapse. The same year he joined the firm of Campenon-Bernard, for whom he designed six bridges over the R. Marne, three 150 m span arch bridges in Venezuela, the Orly bridge completed in 1958, and many others. It was largely due to his efforts, and those of a few other pioneers, that prestressed concrete became accepted as an important new structural material.

Macmillan *Encyclopedia of Architects*. 1982.

(With list of major works, and bibliography).

R M B

FRIEDEL, CHARLES Born at Strasbourg, France, 12 March 1832; died Montauban, 20 April 1899. Chemist, remembered mainly for the 'Friedel-Crafts reaction'.

Friedel was educated at Strasbourg (PASTEUR was one of his teachers) and at the Sorbonne, where he studied under C. A. WURTZ. In 1856 he was made Curator of the Mineral Collections at the *École des Mines*, and in 1876 professor of mineral-ogy. On the death of Wurtz in 1884, Friedel suc-ceeded him as professor of organic chemistry in the Sorbonne, and held this post until his own death.

Friedel was active in two very different fields of chemistry, which were linked to some extent by his work on silicon compounds. As a mineralogist, he studied the synthesis of minerals by reaction in water under heat and high pressure. As an organic chemist, he first worked on problems of interest to the school of Wurtz (the synthesis of ketones and of secondary propanol, among others), but his most fruitful work was done later in collaboration with the American, J. M. CRAFTS. This included exten-sive studies of organosilicon chemistry, but they are immortalized by their joint discovery (1877) of the alkylation and acylation of aromatic hydrocarbons catalysed by aluminium chloride. This reaction has both academic and industrial importance, which continues to increase, especially since the rise of the petrochemicals industry.

Friedel held religious views then somewhat unpopular in France (he was a fervent Protestant), but he was a modest and much-liked man. He was twice married and had six children.

Journal of the Chemical Society. 993, 1990. (Portrait.)

Bulletin de la Société Chimique de France, **23**, 1990, (supplement).

Journal of Chemical Education, **26**, 3, 1949. (Portrait.)

G. Olah, *Friedel-Crafts and Related Reactions* (ch. I.). 1963. (Portrait.)

American Mineralogist, **19**, 329, 1934.

W V F

FRIES, ELIAS MAGNUS Born at Femsjö, Små-land, Sweden, 15 August 1794; died Uppsala, 8th

February 1878. Swedish botanist, regarded as the founder of modern systematic mycology.

Fries's career was remarkably similar to that of LINNAEUS. His father, a rector and rural dean, imparted a wide knowledge of native flowering plants, and allowed him to converse only in Latin; he learnt Latin before Swedish. His interest in mycology began at the age of 12 with the finding of the tooth-fungus, *Hericium coralloides*. He entered the University of Lund in 1811 and took his Phil.D degree three years later. After serving as lecturer in botany, he was appointed professor regius at Lund in 1824, but moved to the University of Upp-sala in 1835 to become professor of rural economy, and, in 1851, professor of botany also when the two chairs were combined. He retired from teaching in 1859.

In 1816 he began detailed investigations of fungi and worked out a system of classification based on stages of development and morphological relation-ships. This resulted in the publication (three vol-umes), of *Systema Mycologicum* (1821–30). He extended his knowledge of lichens whilst on a visit to North Germany, and in 1831 published *Lichen-ographia Europaea Reformata*. Amongst his best-known contributions to mycology is a series of coloured engravings of the higher fungi entitled *Icones selectae Hymenomycetum nondum deline-atum*, sponsored by the Royal Academy of Science in Stockholm, of which he was admitted a member in 1847. Fries began the publication of this large work in 1867, and it was posthumously completed in 1884 by his two sons. In addition to being an expert mycologist, he also had detailed knowledge of Phanerogams and published Floras (*Novitiae Flora Sueciae* and *Botaniska Notiser*) covering the whole of Scandinavia. He was elected a Foreign Member of the Linnean Society of London in 1835, and of the Royal Society in 1875.

English translation of autobiography, *Historiola studii mei mycologici*, in *Friesia. Nordisk mykologisk Tidsskrift*, **141**, 1955. (Portraits.)

Proceedings of the Royal Society, **28**, vii, 1878–9.

Swedish Men of Science. 1952.

Dictionary of Scientific Biography.

A P G

FRIESE-GREENE, WILLIAM Born in Bristol, Eng-land, 7 September 1855; died London, 5 May 1921. A pioneer of cinematography.

Educated at the Blue Coat School, Bristol, Friese-Greene became interested in photography and opened a portrait studio in Bath *c.*1875. In the early 1880s he became acquainted with J. A. R. Rudge, a mechanic for whom he made movable lantern slides for the 'dissolving lantern'. This contact aroused Friese-Greene's interest in animated screen pictures and led to his collaboration in 1888 with Mortimer Evans, an engineer in London, where Friese-Greene had opened a studio in 1885. In 1889 they patented a motion-picture camera to take photographs in rapid succession on a roll of sensitized paper, which was replaced by celluloid film the following year. However, it took only ten pictures per second, whereas sixteen per second is required to produce a satisfactory effect of move-ment. Nor were Friese-Greene's films of sufficient length to constitute a film in the accepted sense. This apparatus was therefore of little consequence in the development of cinematography, and improved cinematographic apparatus patented by him in 1895 and 1896 could not compete with the *cinématographe* of the LUMIÈRE brothers.

Friese-Greene was a prolific inventor: his numerous patents include a two-colour additive method of colour cinematography; stereoscopic cinematography; rapid printing and processing machines, and a three-colour camera.

Ray Allister, *Friese-Greene, Close-up of an Inventor.* 1948 (Portraits.)
Dictionary of National Biography.

H and A G

FRISCH, KARL RITTER VON Born in Vienna, 20 November 1886; died Munich, Germany, 12 June 1982. Ethologist: studied behaviour of the honeybee.

Karl von Frisch spent his childhood at the family summer home at Brunnwinkel on Lake Wolfgang in Austria. He was educated at the Schottengymnasium, a Benedictine school in Vienna, and entered the medical school of the University of Vienna in 1905. When his interests turned to zoology he transferred to the Zoological Institute of the University of Munich in 1908 and studied under K. W. T. R. von Hertwig (1850–1937). In 1910 he was awarded a DPhil. by the University of Vienna for his work on the ability of minnows to mimic the colour of their surroundings. This led to a long controversy with Karl von Hess, director of the Munich Eye Clinic, who believed that fish and all invertebrates were colour blind. As a result of this dispute von Frisch began experiments on the visual abilities of honeybees in 1912.

He held a post at the University of Munich from 1912, and during the First World War worked in a military hospital in Vienna after being invalided out of the army in 1914 because of poor eyesight.

In 1919 von Frisch was appointed assistant professor at the Zoological Institute in Munich, and after holding posts elsewhere he replaced von Hertwig as director in 1925, remaining there until 1946.

Von Frisch became widely known for his work on the organization and communications systems of the honeybee. He discovered that bees communicated the distance and direction of food supplies to other members of the colony by rhythmic movements. He showed that bees used the Sun as a compass even when it was partially obscured by clouds, communicating the source of food by a tail-wagging dance, dancing at the angle to the sun of the food source.

Von Frisch returned to the rebuilt Zoological Institute as director in 1950 with a chair at the University of Munich. He was made emeritus professor in 1958. In 1973 he shared the Nobel prize for physiology or medicine with Konrad LORENZ and Niko TINBERGEN.

Karl von Frisch, *The Dancing Bees.* 1954; *The Dance Language and Orientation of Bees.* 1967; *A Biologist Remembers.* 1967. (Portrait.)
Biographical Memoirs of Fellows of the Royal Society. Vol. 29. 1983. (Portrait.)

A P B

FRISCH, OTTO ROBERT Born in Vienna, 1 October 1904, died Cambridge, England, 22 September 1979. Physicist. Co-author with Lise MEITNER of the explanation of uranium fission. First to observe the fission fragments.

He was educated in Vienna, and very early showed great ability in mathematics and in music, both encouraged by his aunt, Lise Meitner, a nuclear physicist of distinction. He obtained his DPhil. in physics at the University of Vienna in 1926. After a year in the private laboratory of an inventor, and three years in a junior position at the *Physikalisch-Tecnische Reichsanstalt* (the German National Physical Laboratory) in Berlin, he went in 1930 to Hamburg to work with Otto STERN on beams, including the first quantitative work on the diffraction of atomic beams by crystals.

In 1933 the Nazi racial laws forced Frisch (as well as Stern and others) to leave, and after a year at Birkbeck College, London, under Patrick BLACKETT, where he learnt nuclear counting techniques, he was invited to Niels BOHR's Institute in Copenhagen. At this time neutron physics was developing rapidly, and he made many important contributions to it. About Christmas, 1938, he was visiting Lise Meitner, then in Sweden, when she heard from Otto HAHN of his surprising results on uranium. The two discussed this puzzling situation, and came up with an explanation. Frisch then set up an experiment to look for the fission fragments, and in a very simple apparatus demonstrated their existence.

In 1939 he felt unsafe in Copenhagen, because of the proximity of the Nazi army and the likelihood of war, and looked for a job in England. The outbreak of war prevented his return to Copenhagen, and he stayed in a temporary teaching post in Birmingham. In March 1940 he wrote, with Rudolf PEIERLS, a memorandum pointing out that separated uranium isotope 235 would have quite a small critical mass for a fast-neutron chain reaction, and would make a very powerful explosive. This led to a rapid expansion of work on atomic energy, in which Frisch participated, mainly in Liverpool with James CHADWICK and after December 1943 in Los Alamos.

After two years as the head of the nuclear physics division at AERE, Harwell, he was elected to the Jacksonian Chair of Natural Philosophy and a fellowship at Trinity College, Cambridge, from which he retired in 1972.

He was distinguished by great clarity of thought and expression, and this also made him a very effective popularizer of science. He was a pianist of professional standard.

O. Frisch *What Little I Can Remember.* 1979.
Who was Who. Vol VII. 1981
Biographical Memoirs of Fellows of the Royal Society. 1981. (Portraits.)
Dictionary of Scientific Biography, Supp. II.

R P

FRITSCH, GUSTAV THEODOR Born at Cottbus, near Berlin, 5 March 1838; died Berlin, 12 June 1927. Anatomist and anthropologist.

As a student Fritsch received training in medicine and in a wide range of the natural sciences. In 1867 he was an assistant – and in 1874 was appointed professor – at the Institute of Anatomy in Berlin; later he was in charge of the Department of Physiology and Histology. He received the title of Honorary Professor of the Institute of Berlin in 1900. Fritsch is best known for his many extensive travels, which were undertaken in order to study current problems in anthropology, ethnography, zoology and astronomy. He was on an anthropological expedition to South Africa from 1863 to 1866, the results of which he published in 1872 under the title *Die Eingeborenen Südafrikas ethnographie und anatomie*. He observed an eclipse of the Sun while at Aden in 1868, and the transit of Venus while in Persia in 1874. He visited Egypt and the Middle East in 1881, mainly to study the electric organs of fishes. He was more particularly interested in anthropology during the later part of his life, and in 1900, with R. VIRCHOW, founded the Anthropological Society of Berlin. During the nineteenth century anthropologists became increasingly interested in persistent differences of feature in human hair as a physical criterion of race, and consequently Fritsch set out on a world-wide expedition in 1904 to collect samples of different types. His studies of these specimens made a notable contribution to anthropology, and in 1912 he published one of his best-known works, entitled *Das Haupthaar und sein Bildungsstätten bei Menschen.*

Neue Deutsche Biographie, vol. 5. 1960.

Anatomie Anzeiger, **64**, 257, 1927. (Portrait.)

Journal of the History of Medicine, **18**, 125, 1963.

A P G

FUCHS, KLAUS EMIL JULIUS Born at Russelsheim, Germany, 1911; died East Germany, 1988. Physicist: spy.

The son of a Protestant pastor, Fuchs early and openly embraced a sect known as Christian Communism. He was educated at the Universities of Kiel and Leipzig. In 1933 he went to Britain to escape Nazi persecution, studying theoretical physics at the universities of Bristol and Edinburgh. In May 1940, in accordance with general wartime policy, he was among those interned and sent to Canada. Less than a year later his exceptional ability led to his being released and he went to Birmingham University to work with R. PEIERLS on the development of the atomic bomb. In 1943 he went to the USA, working first on the gaseous diffusion project and later on weapons research at Los Alamos. In 1946 he returned to Britain to become head of the theoretical physics division in the newly created UK Atomic Energy Authority, Harwell. He was not a specialist and his remarkable all-round competence led to his membership of a large number of key research and policy committees. In August 1949 it became apparent that there had long been a leak of highly confidential information to the Russians and in January 1949, after several weeks of interrogation, Fuchs admitted his guilt. The scale of his betrayal proved even greater than had been suspected and did much harm to Anglo-American relations. He was tried, convicted, and sentenced to 14 years imprisonment. He was released in 1959 and became an East German citizen.

Alan Morehead, *The Traitors.* 1952.

Margaret Gowing, *Independence and Deterrence: Britain and Atomic Energy 1945–52.* 1974.

T I W

FUCHS, LEONHART Born at Wemding, Bavaria, Germany, 17 January 1501; died Tübingen, Baden-Würtemberg, 10 May 1566. Botanist and physician.

After schooling in Heilbronn and Erfurt, Fuchs entered, at a very early age, the Arts Faculty of the University in the latter town. He obtained a bachelor's degree and then opened a private school in his home town. He entered the University of Ingolstadt, Bavaria, in 1519, where he received a master's degree in classics. He next turned to the study of medicine and took a doctor's degree there in 1524; influenced by the works of Martin Luther, he became a Protestant. For religious reasons he moved to Munich and practised as a physician, but was back again at Ingolstadt in 1526 as professor of medicine. In 1528 he became private physician to the Margrave of Brandenburg in Ansbach. In 1535 he became professor of medicine at the University of Tübingen, where he remained for the rest of his life.

At Tübingen, Fuchs gained fame for his successful treatment of victims of a serious epidemic plague which swept over Germany from 1529 onwards, and he also gathered renown as a botanist. In 1548 he refused an invitation from the Duke Cosimo dei Medici to become Director of the Botanic Gardens in Pisa. Fuchs and two other herbalists of the sixteenth century, Otto Brunfels (1464–1534) and Hieronymus Bock (1498–1554), have been designated 'the German Fathers of Botany'. All three wrote notable herbals, but that of Fuchs, *De historia stirpium* – published in 1542 and followed by the author's German translation, known as the *New Kreüterbuch*, in 1543 – is pre-eminent for the accurate detail and artistic merit of its woodcuts. Fuchs's masterpiece, strictly a herbal making no original contribution to the science of botany, lists about four hundred native and one hundred foreign plants and includes an admirable glossary of botanical terms. Fuchs produced no works on medical science, but he was an enlightened physician: he sought to purge medicine from unsound dogma of Arabic origin, and he supported VESALIUS in challenging the textual authority of GALEN. The Fuchsia, named after him, is his fitting memorial.

Agnes Arber, *Herbals, their origin and evolution.* 1912. (Paperback 1986). (Includes reproduction of woodcut portrait from frontispiece to *De historia stirpium.*)

Neue Deutsche Biographie, vol. 5. 1960.

Dictionary of Scientific Biography, Supp. I.

A P G

FUKUI, KENICHI Born in Nara, near Kyoto, Japan, 14 October 1918. Japanese physical chemist and Nobel Laureate.

Fukui trained as a chemical engineer at the University of Kyoto where, in 1943, he joined the Physical Chemistry department, becoming a professor in 1951. He retired in 1982 to direct an Institute for Fundamental Chemistry. Fukui's theoretical interests arose both from work on fuels in the Second World War and from the agricultural chemical interest in finding more efficient nitrogen fertilisers. In the field of inorganic coordination chemistry Fukui's exploration of the binding of nitrogen to transition metal complexes gave rise to an interest in the molecular orbital theory developed at Oxford by Charles COULSON and Christopher Longuet-Higgins (1923–). In the 1960s Fukui further developed their quantum mechanical mathematical calculations in a theory of 'frontier orbitals' in which organic chemical reactions were explained by the geometry and relative energies of the highest recipient molecular orbital of one reactant and the lowest molecular orbital of the other. Fukui's work was ignored by English-speaking chemists until its translation in the 1970s. By then, a similar theory had been developed to explain certain photochemical reactions in natural products chemistry by R. B. WOODWARD and R. Hoffmann (the 'Woodward-Hoffmann rules'). In 1981, following Woodward's death, Fukui and Hoffmann shared the Nobel prize in chemistry, Fukui being the first Japanese chemist to gain this particular award.

Nature, 294, 114, 1981.
Les Prix Nobel en 1981. 1982. (Portrait.)
Tyler Wasson (Ed.), *Nobel Prize Winners*. 1987. (Portrait.)

                                                                        W H B

FULTON, ROBERT Born at Little Britain, Pennsylvania, USA, 14 November 1765; died New York, 24 February 1815. Steamboat pioneer.

Fulton's father, a farmer, died when his son was three. The boy was educated at a private school in the small-arms town of Lancaster, where he cultivated his interest in painting, design mechanics, and mathematics. At 14 he devised a manually operated paddle boat for fishing on Conestoga Creek, at 17 he went as a designer to Philadelphia, and at 21 he left for London.

Here he made friends with those two innovatory peers, the Duke of Bridgewater and Lord Stanhope. He inspected the former's canal projects and devised a power dredger to facilitate the construction of others, together with a device for raising and lowering boats in them. To propel the boats he approached the firm of Boulton and Watt in 1794 for a steam engine. His *Treatise on the Improvement of Canal Navigation* (1796) was a remarkably prescient assessment, and was followed by a scheme for cheap cast-iron aqueducts, subsequently adopted over the River Dee. Supported by a fellow American, he obtained French patents for his canal inventions, and proposed a canal from Paris to Dieppe. The years 1797–1806 he spent in France, when he drafted plans for a submarine, *Nautilus*, and torpedoes which, though rejected by the Directory, were given a trial in 1800–1 by Napoleon, who commissioned him to operate them against British ships, This came to the ears of his British friends, who secured his return to England, but the British Admiralty, in spite of a successful demonstration, rejected both submarine and torpedoes.

This second official rebuff confirmed Fulton's wish to return permanently to America and improve communications on its inland waterways. Since the new American Ambassador to France, Robert R. Livingston (1746–1813), possessed the monopoly of navigating state waters by steamboats, Fulton had been able, while in France, to experiment with a steamboat on the Seine. When he returned at the end of 1806 he had a Boulton and Watt steam engine installed in a 133-foot boat to drive two 15-foot paddle-wheels. So successful was the experiment that the *Clermont* sailed from New York to Albany and back in sixty-two hours in August 1807. A month earlier he had also demonstrated the potential of his torpedo.

At his third attempt a steamboat Fulton had succeeded in convincing not only European governments but the American people. He built nineteen boats and his skills were requisitioned by the Russian Government and by the US Congress, which commissioned him to build a 156-foot frigate with a 16-foot paddlewheel, carrying thirty 32-pound guns. Known as *Fulton the First*, it was unfinished when he died.

Fulton was not the first successful operator of a steam-propelled ship: in 1783 the paddle-steamer *Pyroscaphe*, built by the Marquis Claude de Jouffroy d'Abbans (1751–1832), ascended the Saône. He was, however, the first to demonstrate that steam propulsion was a practical business proposition.

H. W. Dickinson, *Robert Fulton, Engineer and Artist. His Life and Work*. 1913.
W. B. Parsons, *Robert Fulton and the Submarine*. 1922.
C. Matschoss, *Die Entwicklung der Dampfmaschine*. 1908. (Portrait.)
Dictionary of American Biography.

                                                                        W H G A

G

GABOR, DENNIS (GÁBOR DÉNES) Born in Budapest, 5 June 1900; died London, 8 February 1979. Scientist, engineer, inventor of holography.

Dennis was the first of three sons of Bertalan and Adrienne (Kálmán) Gabor. His father, director of the Hungarian General Coalmining Company, the largest industrial enterprise in Hungary, helped inspire his son to become an inventor by telling him about T. A. EDISON and introducing him to the Museum of Technology in Budapest.

Following his discharge from the Hungarian artillery in November 1918, Gabor enrolled in the Technical University, Budapest. By 1924 he received a diploma in electrical engineering from the *Technische Hochschule*, Berlin. The thesis for his doctorate (1927) was on a high-speed cathode ray oscillograph for recording transient phenomena on a 100-kV transmission line. Gabor was a research engineer with Siemens & Halske from 1927 to 1933.

A brain drain occurred in the 1930s when thousands of intellectuals fled Nazi Germany, Gabor among them. The British Thomson-Houston Company overcame the difficulty of a work permit for a foreigner and hired Gabor as a research engineer in consideration of one of his early inventions, a plasma lamp. In the autobiographical note he wrote on the occasion of his 1971 Nobel award, Gabor included under Honours 'married since 1936 to Marjorie Louise, daughter of Joseph Kennard Butler and Louise Butler of Rugby'. He remained at BTH from 1934 to 1948. He has recounted how, on Easter morning 1947, while waiting his turn for a tennis court, the idea of holography as a way of improving the electron microscope 'came out of my unconsciousness'.

To produce a hologram (Greek: whole + message) one beam of monochromatic light or electrons illuminates an object and is reflected from it to a photographic plate or film. A second reference beam goes directly to the film. The two beams set up an interference pattern which is recorded in the photographic emulsion. After development, a person holding the film between his eyes and a monochromatic light source can see a 3-dimensional image of the original scene. He can even 'look around' objects by moving his head. Oddly, even a fragment of the film contains information which allows him to view the entire scene.

Early holograms were crude; available light sources lacked intensity. The invention of the laser in 1963 provided an ideal source for improved holography. New applications followed: information storage; component testing; 3-D movies; microwave radar; seismic exploration; and electron micrographs to 2.5Å revealing internal structure of a virus. Gabor invented an ultrasonic version of 3-D holography, called sonography, and applied it to medical diagnosis. He was amused by applications of holography in advertising and as an art form, notably by Salvador Dali. Gabor was made Member No.1 and honorary chairman of the Museum of Holography, New York. 'I was one of the lucky physicists who have been able to see one of their ideas grow into a sizeable chapter of physics' – and an industry earning hundreds of millions of pounds annually.

From 1949 to 1958 Gabor held a Mullard Readership in Electronics at Imperial College, London. His work on problems of aberrations in magnetic lenses led to development of an interference microscope for viewing objects in three dimensions. From 1958 to 1967 he occupied the chair of Applied Electron Physics at Imperial College. His inaugural address 'Electronic Inventions and their Impact on Civilization' was expanded in 1962 to the book *Inventing the Future*. He wrote: 'For the social inventor the engineering of human consent is the most essential and the most difficult step'. Long influenced by Aldous Huxley, Gabor said on retirement (1967) 'I have acquired a new hobby, writing on social matters'. In *The Mature Society*, 1971, he advocated – first for pupils at an early age and then for those at university level – two educational branches, one for the gifted minority, the other to prepare the less-gifted majority for entrance into the permissive society. He led a study group of the Club of Rome in writing *Age of Waste* (1978).

During this period of nominal retirement, Gabor was staff assistant of CBS Laboratories, Stamford, Connecticut, whose president, Peter C. GOLDMARK, was a fellow Hungarian and a life-long friend. Here they worked on new schemes of communication and display.

Gabor was a relatively short and sturdy man with a grey moustache, who was meticulous in dress. He spoke in a soft, heavily-accented voice. Although he did not have children of his own, he was fond of young people whom he encouraged by his warm-hearted interest in their work. In his lifetime he received many honours, including Fellowship of the Royal Society (1956) and the Nobel prize for physics (1971).

Biographical Memoirs of Fellows of the Royal Society. 1980. (Portrait.)

Science, **174**, 674, 1971.

Dictionary of National Biography.

Dictionary of Scientific Biography, Supp. II.

Tyler Wasson (Ed.), *Nobel Prize Winners*. 1987. (Portrait.)

R L W

GABRIEL, SIEGMUND Born in Berlin, 7 November 1851; died there, 22 March 1924. Organic chemist, noted for studies of heterocyclic compounds containing nitrogen.

Gabriel studied chemistry in Berlin (under A. W. von HOFMANN) and at Heidelberg (under R. W. BUNSEN). In 1874 he returned to Berlin University, successively as assistant, *Privatdozent*, and professor (1886); he retired in 1921. He was a great friend of Emil FISCHER.

Gabriel's work was almost entirely in the field of the heterocyclic compounds of nitrogen. He discovered isoquinoline, and is remembered particularly for 'Gabriel's synthesis' of primary amines from potassium phthalimide and alkyl halides, followed by hydrolysis (1887).

Berichte der deutschen Chemischen Gesellschaft, **59**, 7A, 1926. (Portrait.)

W V F

GADOLIN, JOHAN Born at Abo (now Turku), Finland, 5 June 1760; died Wirmo, 15 August 1852. Notable as the first chemist to have an element (gadolinium) named in his honour.

Gadolin was the son of Jacob Gadolin (1719–1802), a professor of physics (1753) and theology (1762) at Abo University. He studied under T. O. BERGMAN at Uppsala (1778) and travelled widely in Europe. From 1785 he taught at Abo, and on the death of P. A. Gadd (1727–97) succeeded to the chair of chemistry, a post which he held from 1797 until 1822.

He wrote papers in Latin, Swedish and German on such diverse topics as metals, minerals, fossils and heat. In memoirs of 1784 and 1792 he criticized the work of A. Crawford (1748/9–1795), (who was the first to determine specific heats of gases); published a table of specific heats, some of which were the results of his own experiments; and showed that specific heats were not independent of temperature.

The black mineral ytterbite was first discovered in the porcelain feldspar quarry at Ytterby, near Stockholm, and an account of the ore appeared in 1788. In 1794, Gadolin extracted a new substance, yttria (Y_2O_3, though probably a mixture with other oxides) from the ore, which later became known as Gadolinite. Gadolinium, isolated by J. C. G. de MARIGNAC in 1880 and P. E. L. de Boisbaudran (1838–1912) in 1886, was named in honour of Gadolin by its discoverers.

As early as 1789 Gadolin is said to have taught the antiphlogistic doctrine, and in 1798 he became the first author to publish a textbook in Swedish incorporating the new chemistry.

E. Hjelt and R. Tigerstedt, *Johan Gadolin 1760–1852: In Memoriam, Wissenschaftliche Abhandlungen Johan Gadolins in Auswahl.* 1910.

V. Ojula and E. R. Schierz, *Journal of Chemical Education,* **19**, 161, 1937.

G R T

GAJDUSEK, DANIEL CARLETON Born in Yonkers, New York, 9 September 1923. Virologist.

Gajdusek graduated first in physics (University of Rochester) and then in medicine (Harvard). Thereafter his interest turned increasingly to virology, with a special concern with infections of the nervous system. He held a succession of appointments in the USA and abroad-including the Institut Pasteur, Iran (1954–5) and the Walter and Eliza Hall Institute, Australia (1955–7) – before taking up in 1958 a permanent appointment at the Laboratory of Central Nervous System Studies, National Institutes of Health, Bethesda, USA.

During an active life he published more than 500 research papers on neurobiology, genetics, anthropology and related topics. He is particularly remembered, however, for his investigation of kuru, a protracted and usually fatal disease formerly very prevalent among the Fore people of Papua New Guinea. It is possibly transmitted through cannibalistic rituals involving eating the brains of the dead. This led in the late 1950s to the discovery of a new class of slow virus infections, including scrapie in sheep and Creutzfeldt-Jacob disease in man. For this Gajdusek shared a Nobel prize in 1976.

A. Hammond (Ed.) *A Passion to Know.* 1984.
Les Prix Nobel en 1976, 1977. (Portrait.)
Who's Who. 1992.
Tyler Wasson (Ed.), *Nobel Prize Winners.* 1987. (Portrait.)

T I W

GALEN (GALENOS) Born at Pergamum, Asia Minor, AD 129; died Rome, AD 199(?). Physician, anatomist and experimental physiologist.

Galen studied at Pergamum, Smyrna, Corinth and Alexandria. In AD 157 he became surgeon to the gladiators at Pergamum. In 162 he settled in Rome. Four years later he returned to Pergamum, but was soon called by the Emperor, Marcus Aurelius, to deal with plague in the Army. Galen then settled permanently in Rome, became physician to Marcus Aurelius, and also to the three succeeding emperors.

When aged 30 Galen produced paralysis of the larynx experimentally by tying the recurrent laryngeal nerve, and similarly he demonstrated the respiratory action of the thoracic muscles. Later he proved that the arteries contain blood and not air. In pigs he showed that if the spinal cord is transected between the second and the third vertebrae, or above that level, the animal dies at once. If the cut is between the third and fourth, respiration ceases and the body below the level of section is paralysed. If the section is between the sixth and seventh, the thoracic muscles are paralysed, but respiration is carried on by the diaphragm alone. These important experiments were forgotten until modern times.

Galen was an expert dissector and teacher of anatomy. He dissected the pig, the dog, and especially the rhesus monkey. There is some evidence that he had also dissected human subjects. His anatomical work is described in his *De anatomicis administrationibus* ('On anatomical procedures') and in his *De usu partium* ('On the functions of the parts of the body'). His descriptions of the bones and the muscles were especially good. After his death all anatomical research ceased, and during the next 1200 years Galen's statements were regarded as infallible.

Galen tried to found a universal system, applicable to physiology, pathology and clinical medicine. The system depended upon a development of the Hippocratic doctrine of the humours, and postulated the production of natural spirit (in the liver); of vital spirit (in the left ventricle); and of animal spirit (in the brain). It postulated also the presence of minute pores in the septum separating the two ventricles of the heart. These non-existent pores inhibited physiology for 1400 years.

Galen was a great clinician. In his therapy he leaned heavily on drugs, and he travelled widely in search of new ones. He was a voluminous writer, in Greek, on philosophy as well as on medicine. His works were later translated into Arabic, and they first reached western Europe about the twelfth century in the form of Latin translations of the Arabic versions.

A. J. Brock, *Galen, On the Natural Faculties.* 1925.
C. Singer, *Galen, On Anatomical Procedures.* 1956.
G. Sarton, *Galen of Pergamon.* 1954.
Annals of Medical History, **13**, 209, 1931; **8**, 61, 1926.
Dictionary of Scientific Biography.

E A U

GALILEO (GALILEO GALILEI) Born at Pisa, Italy, 18 February 1564; died Arcetri, near Florence, 8 January 1642. A principal founder of classical physics and an outstanding representative of the movement which transformed medieval natural philosophy into modern science.

Galileo was the eldest son of the Florentine musician Vincenzio Galilei (1520–91). At the age of 17 he entered the University of Pisa as a medical student, but soon turned to mathematics, and in 1585–7 wrote his first small tracts (on the centre of gravity, and on an ingenious beam balance for determining specific weights). In 1587 he began lecturing in Siena and Florence and visited the mathematician C. Clavius (1537–1612) in Rome. In 1589 he was appointed to a chair of mathematics in Pisa moving in 1592 to a better position at Padua, where for eighteen years he displayed an enormous creative activity. Among other things, he invented a machine for raising water; an air thermoscope; and a computing device for geo-metrical and ballistic purposes described in his first printed work, *Le operazioni del compasso geometrico e militare* (Padua, 1606). His research in pure science led him about 1602 to the dis-covery of the isochronism of the pendulum and to a preliminary (but wrong) discussion of the laws of falling bodies. In 1609 he was the first to apply the newly invented telescope to astronomical observations, revealing the mountains in the Moon; numerous stars invisible to the naked eye; the nature of the Milky Way; and four of Jupiter's satellites (named the Medicean Stars). This was described in *Sidereus Nuncius* (Venice, 1610) which almost at once made Galileo famous all over Europe.

In 1610 he gave up his chair at Padua and accepted an honorary professorship in Pisa. Moving to Florence, he lived there for the rest of his life, devoting his entire energy to scientific research under the benevolent protection of the court of the Medicis. He now discovered the phases of Venus; the composite structure of Sat-urn; and the existence of Sun Spots, described in the *Istoria e dimostrazioni intorno alle macchie solari* (Rome, 1613). An almost triumphal journey to Rome in the spring of 1611 confirmed his grow-ing fame. He became a member of Prince Cesi's very active *Accademia dei Lincei* and was more and more audacious in pointing to the incompati-bility of the new celestial phenomena with traditional astronomy. He openly confessed his Copernican conviction (see COPERNICUS), already stated (1597) in a letter to KEPLER, at the same time as he successfully attacked current views on hydrostatics in his *Discorso intorno alle cose che stanno in su l'acqua* (Florence, 1612).

From the beginning of this period Galileo had to defend his discoveries and opinions against numerous attacks from scientific opponents and jealous academic enemies. A conspiracy among the latter aiming at Galileo's downfall led first to an abusive sermon against him in Florence 1614, and next to a process (1615–16) before the Holy Office in Rome which ultimately (23 February 1616) condemned the Copernican system as hereti-cal and incompatible with Holy Scripture. Galileo was not personally involved, but nevertheless Car-dinal Bellarmine admonished him not to defend the Copernican theory in public.

The following years marked a certain decline in Galileo's activity. He mainly occupied himself with computing tables of the motions and eclipses of the moons of Jupiter with a view to a new method of determining the longitude at sea which he in vain tried to sell to the Spanish and Dutch Govern-ments. In 1618 he was involved in a bitter strife concerning the nature of comets, and lost the sym-pathy of his former supporters, the Roman Jesuits. A result of this controversy was the polemical work *Il Saggiatore* (Rome, 1623), in which Galileo expressed his thoughts on epistemological and methodological questions, stressing the necessity of quantitative experiments and observations and the strength of hypothetical-deductive reasoning.

In 1623 his former protector, Cardinal Maffeo Barberini, became Pope Urban VIII, and after a fourth journey to Rome 1624 Galileo felt himself encouraged to begin the composition of a major work on astronomy, planned many years before and finally published as *Dialogo sopra i due Mas-simi Sistemi del Mondo* (Florence, 1632). It was a highly technical account in the form of a dialogue between a supporter of the Aristotelian-Ptolemaic tradition (Simplicio); a youthful, inquiring mind (Sagredo); and an advocate of the new astronomy (Salviati). Galileo had tried to safeguard himself by letting Simplicio win the battle, and the book was published with the imprimatur of the ecclesiastical authorities. Nevertheless, the strength of Salviati's arguments was so evident that the Holy Office found that Galileo had exceeded the limits set by the admonition of 1616. He was summoned to Rome, imprisoned, and forced solemnly to abjure his Copernican conviction before the Congre-gation. A sentence of imprisonment for life was so executed that Galileo was confined to his home at Arcetri.

Here he engaged in new research, but was ham-pered both by his ill health, ending with complete blindness, and by the constant supervision of the Inquisition. Yet he succeeded in finishing his final and most important work, the *Discorsi e Dimostra-zioni matematiche intorno a due nuove scienze* (Leiden, 1638), significantly published outside Italy. Containing among other things the proof of the laws of the fall in vacuum, the principle of the independence of forces, and the complete theory of parabolic ballistics, it was destined to become one of the cornerstones upon which C. HUYGENS and NEWTON one generation later built classical mechanics. The laws of fall made it possible to study accelerated motion.

Galileo had a versatile mind and was deeply interested in art and literature. Furthermore he was an inspired teacher. He occupied himself with almost every branch of physics, but is chiefly remembered for the example he gave of the efficacy of the hypothetical-deductive method combined with quantitative experiments. In general history, too, he occupies an important place because of his personal fate.

A. Favaro (Ed.), *Le Opere di Galileo Galilei* (20 vols.). 1890–1909. (2nd ed. 1929–39.)
A. Koyre, *Études galiléennes*. 1939.
Giorgio de Santillana, *The Crime of Galileo*. 1958.
E. McMullin (Ed.) *Galileo, Man of Science*. 1967.
Colin A. Ronan, *Galileo*. 1974. (Portrait.)
Stillman Drake, *Galileo, Pioneer Scientist*. 1991.
M. A. Finocchiaro (Ed.), *The Galileo Affair: A Documentary History*. 1991.
Dictionary of Scientific Biography.

O P

GALTON, FRANCIS Born at Birmingham, England, 16 February 1822; died Haslemere, Surrey, 17 January 1911. Founder of eugenics.

Galton, the son of a Birmingham businessman, was half-cousin of Charles DARWIN, his grandmother having been the second wife of Erasmus DARWIN. He began to study medicine, but read mathematics at Cambridge; his father's death soon after he graduated in 1844 left him with independent means which enabled him to travel in the Sudan, Syria, and South West Africa; he published *Tropical South Africa* and *The Art of Travel* on his return.

He then turned his attention to meteorology, and discovered the importance of anticyclones in weather systems, publishing his *Meteorographica* in 1863; he played a large part in establishing the Meteorological Office, and the National Physical Laboratory. Meantime his interest in heredity, especially the inheritance of physical and mental characters in man, increasingly engaged his attention. He saw that advancement of the subject was hampered by the lack of quantitative information, and started anthropometric researches which resulted finally in the setting up of the Biometric Laboratory at University College, London. Arising from this work, he developed the system of identification by fingerprints now in universal use. He also turned his attention to experimental psychology, to which he applied quantitative methods.

Through a consideration of the inheritance of mental ability as well as of physical characters, and by applying statistical analysis to problems of heredity, he advocated the application of scientific breeding to human populations. He realized the difficulties of getting such ideas adopted practically, but strongly advocated that seriously defective individuals should be restrained from reproducing. He invented the term 'eugenics', and by his energy ensured that the subject became widely discussed. By his will he endowed the Chair of Eugenics at University College London.

Galton was elected FRS in 1856, and received many honours from scientific bodies; he was knighted in 1909.

F. Galton, *Memories of my Life*. 1908.
D. W. Forrest, *Francis Galton*. 1974.
Karl Pearson, *The Life, Letters and Labours of Francis Galton*. 4 vols. 1914–30.

L H M

GALVANI, LUIGI Born at Bologna, Italy, 9 September 1737; died there, 4 December 1798. Discoverer of animal electricity.

On completing his university studies at Bologna, Galvani was appointed lecturer in anatomy (1762) for a thesis on the human skeleton mainly concerned with the development of bone. In 1775 he was appointed professor of anatomy and gynaecology following a remarkable treatise on the semicircular canals in birds. He also did much research on the excitation of nerves. The first announcement of his electrical researches was in a paper *De viribus electricitatis in motu musculari commentarius* of 1791 which contained an account of the famous chance observations of the twitchings of a frog laid out for dissection on a table bearing an electrical machine. Galvani was himself at first not interested in this phenomenon, the effect of electricity on animals being in any case already well known. Later, however, he subjected the phenomenon to a series of careful investigations and proved that convulsions were produced if a frog were connected either to an electrical machine or to a lightning conductor during stormy weather or under troubled atmospheric conditions. More significant, he found that frogs being prepared for dissection by drying out of doors experienced convulsions if the metal skewers through their marrow bone were put in contact with an iron fence. On repeating these experiments indoors he found that in the absence of an electrical machine, and even in the most settled atmospheric conditions, convulsions were produced in a frog when it formed part of a circuit containing one or more pieces of metal. A motion of the nerve juices appeared to accompany these convulsions, and not unnaturally Galvani was led to suppose that they were produced by electricity residing in the animal, the muscle fibre and the enclosed nerve acting very much in the manner of a Leyden jar. These findings led to a lively controversy between those who favoured Galvani, those who regarded Galvanic electricity as different from other electricity, and those who followed A. VOLTA in supposing the electricity in Galvani's experiments to have originated in the metal part of the circuits. This controversy was ultimately settled in Volta's favour by his announcement of the discovery of the voltaic cell in 1800.

At the setting up of the Transalpine Republic in 1797 Galvani refused to swear an oath of allegiance and was dismissed from his office. He died in the following year, overcome by domestic bereavement aggravated by poverty and criticism of his scientific views.

W. Bergin, *Luigi Galvani*. 1912. (Portrait.)
W. Majorana, *Commemorazione di Luigi Galvani, Nuovo Cimento*, **14**, 1937.
P. Lenard, *Great Men of Science*. 1933. (Portrait.)
Bern Dibner, *Luigi Galvani*. 1971.
Dictionary of Scientific Biography.

J W H

GAMBEY, HENRI-PRUDENCE Born at Troyes, France, 8 October 1787; died Paris, 28 January 1847. Eminent French instrument-maker.

After spending some years at the *Écoles des Arts et Métiers* at Compiègne and Châlons-sur-Marne, Gambey set up in business in Paris as a scientific-instrument maker. The excellence of his work was very much dependent on the equipment in his workshop and the machine tools which he designed showed advances in both technique and accuracy over his contemporaries. His lathes had toolposts with movements along and across the bed controlled by micrometer screws, and the tool was tilted by a toothed sector with helical gearing and a vernier graduation. He made dividing engines for marking both circles and rules, and astronomical and surveying instruments of all descriptions. He built equatorial and meridian telescopes, and made a 2-metre wall circle of great accuracy in 1840 for the Paris Observatory. He gained a gold medal at the Paris Exhibition of 1819, in which his exhibit of scientific instruments surpassed the work of Jesse RAMSDEN in England, and George Reichenbach (1772–1826) or Joseph von FRAUNHOFER in Germany. He considered emigrating to America at one time, but was persuaded to remain in France by D. F. J. ARAGO. He was a member of the French longitude board and became a member of the *Académie Française* in 1837.

F. Arago, *Notices Biographiques.* 1847.

Maurice Daumas, *Scientific Instruments of the 17th and 18th Centuries and their Makers.* 1972.

Dictionary of Scientific Biography.

W N S

GAMBLE, JOSIAS CHRISTOPHER Born near Enniskillen, Ayrshire, Scotland, 1776; died St Helens, Lancashire, England, 27 January 1848. Industrial chemist.

Gamble's parents were staunch Presbyterians, who moved from Ayrshire to Ireland for religious reasons. His parents wished him to enter the ministry, and after graduating at Glasgow University (1797) he returned to Enniskillen (1799) as minister of the Presbyterian church. While at Glasgow, Gamble attended the chemical lectures of William Cleghorn (1754–83) and the knowledge so gained he put to practical account when he went to Belfast (1804) as minister. He became interested in the manufacture of bleach for the local flax-growers, and eventually gave up the ministry to establish himself as a chemical manufacturer in Dublin. There, in 1820, he married Hannah Gower, daughter of a solicitor in the city.

For the manufacture of bleach he at first purchased sulphuric acid from Charles TENNANT of Glasgow, but he soon began to manufacture his own. In 1828 he moved to Liverpool, and for two years was in partnership with James MUSPRATT, a pioneer of soda manufacture by the process of Nicolas LEBLANC. In 1836 he entered into partnership with Joseph (1792–1844) and James (1787–1852) Crosfield, soap manufacturers, to manufacture Leblanc soda. Difficulties arose as a result of litigation with local landowners, arising from the objectionable waste products, and in 1838 the Crosfields insisted on introducing absorption towers of a type devised by William GOSSAGE. Gamble objected and a quarrel ensued, which led to the dissolution of the partnership in 1845.

Gamble was not a great innovator, but he played a leading role in establishing the British chemical industry.

J. Fenwick Allen, *Some Founders of the Chemical Industry.* 1907. (Portrait.)

A. E. Musson, *Enterprise in Soap and Chemicals, Joseph Crosfield & Sons Limited 1815–1965.* 1965.

Dictionary of National Biography (Missing Persons). 1993.

T I W

GARROD, SIR ARCHIBALD EDWARD Born London, 15 November, 1857; died Cambridge, 28 March, 1936. Physician, geneticist and molecular biologist.

Garrod was educated at Christ Church, Oxford and St Bartholomew's Hospital, London. Succeeded Sir William Osler (1849–1919) as Regius Professor of Medicine, Oxford, in 1920. Garrod developed the concept of genetic faults as the cause of certain rare diseases. Noting that alcaptonuria (black urine) occurred in certain members of the same families, he suggested that an enzyme was missing due to a genetic error, causing an inborn metabolic block that made the organism incapable of a particular step in normal metabolism. In his Croonian lectures of 1908 and his book, *Inborn Errors of Metabolism* (1909, 2nd edition, 1923) Garrod described other diseases caused by similar genetic errors, including phenylketonuria, galactosaemia, fructosuria and glycogen storage disease. His work coincided in the 1920s with that of Frederick Gowland HOPKINS on vitamin deficiency diseases.

Garrod was Director of the Medical Unit and consulting physician to St Bartholomew's Hospital and was also consulting physician to the Great Ormond St Hospital for Sick Children. A member of numerous medical societies, he delivered various important lectures including the Harveian Oration at the Royal College of Physicians in 1924. In 1925 he was awarded the Osler Memorial Medal. As consulting physician to HM Forces in the First World War Garrod was twice mentioned in despatches. He was awarded the CMG in 1916 and was knighted in 1918.

Obituary Notices of Fellows of the Royal Society of London, vol. 2 (1936–9). (Portrait.)

British Medical Journal, i, 731, 1936.

Lancet, i, 807, 1936.

Dictionary of National Biography.

Dictionary of Scientific Biography, Supp. II.

A. G. Bearn, *Archibald Garrod and the Individuality of Man.* 1993.

N G C

GASKELL, WALTER HOLBROOK Born at Naples, Italy, 1 November 1847; died Great Shelford, Cambridge, England, 7 September 1914. Physiologist, and a pioneer in our knowledge of the autonomic nervous system.

Gaskell, the son of a barrister, was born while his parents were temporarily resident in Italy. Educated at Highgate, London, he entered Trinity College, Cambridge (1865), read mathematics, and graduated in 1869. He then decided to study medicine, and soon became a pupil of Michael Foster (1836–1907). After a year working under Carl LUDWIG at Leipzig, he qualified in medicine, but decided to devote himself to physiology. In 1878 he graduated as a doctor of medicine at Cambridge, and in 1883 he was appointed university lecturer in physiology, a post which he retained until his death. He was elected (1889) to a fellowship at Trinity Hall. In 1882 Gaskell was elected a Fellow of the Royal Society, to which he delivered the Croonian Lecture in the same year, and by which he was awarded a Royal Medal in 1889. He received honorary degrees from the University of Edinburgh and from McGill University, Montreal.

During his year in Leipzig Gaskell was set by Carl Ludwig to work on the problem of the control of the circulation in voluntary muscles. Gaskell continued this work after his return to Cambridge, devised a method of observing the flow of blood in a frog's muscle during stimulation of its nerve, and showed that vasomotor fibres run in motor nerves (1877). He then studied the action of the heart and showed that the nerve ganglia in the sinus venosus play an important role in the heartbeat. He also did much to demonstrate that the heart's action is essentially myogenic. This classical paper was published in 1882.

Gaskell next turned to investigation of the 'sympathetic nervous system', a subject on which he worked for the rest of his life. When he started his work the view currently held was that of Xavier BICHAT, who taught that in all vertebrates there were two nervous systems, an 'animalic' system, concerned with locomotion and the sense organs, and an 'organic' system, concerned with the regulation of the nutrition of the body. Each system had its own central nervous system, the cerebrospinal system and the chain of sympathetic ganglia respectively. The two systems were regarded as mutually independent. Gaskell decided to discover whether there was a reciprocal communication between the two systems. He showed that the sympathetic non-medullated fibres that entered a spinal nerve root did not, in fact, enter the spinal cord itself, but supplied the blood-vessels of the meninges. He had previously shown that the vagus nerve of the frog contained two sets of fibres which had opposite effects on the heart, and which differed in their place of origin in the central nervous system. He then extended his research to other viscera, and found that they were all supplied by motor and inhibitory nerves, which were entirely of spinal origin and arose from special sections of the central nervous system. He was thus able to define the 'thoracolumbar outflow' in 1882, and in 1886 he added the bulbar and sacral outflows. He finally included all these sympathetic nerves and their ganglia under the term 'involuntary nervous system'.

Most of Gaskell's early work was done using serial sections stained with osmic acid. When the silver-impregnation method of C. GOLGI and S. Ramón y CAJAL came to be used, it was found that some of his observations were incorrect. But the fundamental importance of his work has never been questioned, and it was later extended by J. N. LANGLEY. Gaskell's final, posthumous, work, The Involuntary Nervous System (1916), is a classic of physiology.

In the course of his researches Gaskell had to consider the phylogenetic evolution of the nervous system of animals, and this led to his book The Origin of the Vertebrates (1908). The soundness of many of Gaskell's contentions in this much-debated work is still undecided, but it contains a mass of observations of the greatest interest.

J. N. Langley, Proceedings of the Royal Society, B, 88, xxvii, 1915.
W. Haymaker and F. Schiller (Eds), The Founders of Neurology. 1953. (Portrait.)
Dictionary of National Biography.
Dictionary of Scientific Biography.

E A U

GASSENDI, PIERRE Born at Champtercier, near Digne, France, 22 January 1592; died Paris, 24 October 1655. A philosopher remembered for his interest in the atomic theory.

Gassendi taught rhetoric in Digne from the age of 16 years. In 1611 he went to Aix, where he taught and studied before becoming a lecturer in theology. In 1615 he travelled to Paris, where he continued his studies and in 1616 obtained the degree of Doctor of Theology. In the following year he was ordained and returned to teach at Aix, where he remained until 1624, when he was appointed Provost of Digne Cathedral. In 1645 he became professor of mathematics in the Collège Royale in Paris.

Gassendi was interested in astronomy, and wrote biographies of G. von Peurbach (1423–61), REGIOMONTANUS, COPERNICUS and Tycho BRAHE. He made a number of important observations, which included a comet (1618); the aurora borealis (1621), which he was responsible for naming; a lunar eclipse (1623); and the transit of Mercury (1631). This last observation was particularly important, for it revealed an error in the observations of Longomontanus (1562–1647), the Danish astronomer.

Early in his career Gassendi became dissatisfied with the current philosophy, and in 1624 he published a criticism of Aristotle entitled Exercitationes Paradoxicae adversus Aristotelos. Only the first volume was printed; the rest was probably suppressed owing to a parliamentary decree which forbade the holding or teaching of doctrines opposed to Aristotle. Gassendi is best known for his atomic theory, which he put forward after a careful study of the works of EPICURUS, of whom he published a biography in 1647. Two years later he published Animadversiones in Decimum Librum Diogenis Laertii (Lyons, 1649); this had an appendix, Philosophiae Epicuri Syntagma, which put forward his own interpretation of Epicurus's views on matter. He considered that the prima materia was represented by atoms whose different properties were due to differences in size, shape and weight; that combination occurred not because of attractive forces between atoms but by a simple hook-and-eye mechanism; and that movements of the atoms were by God's will.

After his death, Gassendi's collected works were published by his pupil, S. Sorbière, (1615–70), under the title Opera Omnia (Lyons, 1658).

P. Rochot, Pierre Gassendi: sa vie et son oeuvre (1592–1655). (Portrait.) 1944.
L. Thorndike, A History of Magic and Experimental Science, vol. 7. 1958.
G. B. Stones, Isis, 10, 460 1928.
R. H. Kargon, Atomism in England from Hariot to Newton. 1966.
Dictionary of Scientific Biography.

B B K

GASSER, HERBERT SPENCER Born at Platteville, Wisconsin, USA, 5 July 1888; died New York, 11 May 1963. Made fundamental discoveries about the functions of nerve fibres.

Herbert Gasser was educated at Platteville Normal School and at the University of Wisconsin, where he received his BA in 1910. He graduated in medicine at Johns Hopkins University in 1915. From 1916 to 1931 he taught pharmacology at the Washington University, St Louis, being professor there from 1921. Whilst at St Louis he collaborated with Joseph ERLANGER in a series of investigations into the physiology of nerve fibres, which culminated in the publication of *Electrical Signs of Nervous Activity* (1937). They adapted the low-voltage cathode-ray oscillograph to provide new techniques of electrical recording from nerves. They showed that groups of nerve fibres conducted electrical impulses at different rates and related these functional differences to the different diameters of fibres. Thicker fibres conveyed impulses faster. Gasser and Erlanger demonstrated that nerve trunks contained fibres of various sizes, subserving different functions. For this work they received the Nobel prize for medicine in 1944. He was elected a Foreign Member of the Royal Society in 1946.

Gasser left St Louis to become professor of physiology at Cornell Medical College and in 1935 was appointed Director of the Rockefeller Institute in New York. He continued his studies into the physiology of nervous transmission and after his retirement in 1953 extended his interests into the electron microscopy of nerve.

He was a tall, spare man whose rather frail appearance was associated with a reedy, high-pitched voice. His health was never robust, and he suffered from migraine throughout his life.

Journal of the American Medical Association, **184**, 911, 1963. (Portrait.)
Biographical Memoirs of Fellows of the Royal Society. 1964. (Portrait.)
Les Prix Nobel en 1940–1944. 1946. (Portrait.)
Dictionary of Scientific Biography.
W. Haymaker and F. Schiller (Eds), *The Founders of Neurology.* 1970.
Tyler Wasson (Ed.), *Nobel Prize Winners.* 1987. (Portrait.)

C M

GATLING, RICHARD JOHN Born in Hertford Country, North Carolina, USA, 12 September 1818; died New York, 26 February 1903. Inventor.

As a boy Richard Gatling helped his father, a well-to-do planter, to perfect a machine for sowing cotton seed. In 1839 he invented a screw propeller, but was anticipated by John ERICSSON; and he patented and manufactured sowing machines and other widely used forms of agricultural equipment. At the time of his death he was organizing the manufacture of a motor-driven plough.

The Civil War having turned his attention to armaments, Gatling patented a marine steam ram and, only two months later (November 1862), the rapid-fire gun known by his name. This comprised a ring of ten gun barrels rotated by hand crank around a central shaft; each barrel was loaded by gravity feed during one half-revolution, followed by firing, extraction, and ejection of the cartridge during the other half. The initial firing capacity was 250 shots a minute, which was increased

eventually to 1200. The gun was adopted for the US Army in 1866, and was widely used until the end of the century. In 1886 Gatling invented a new alloy of steel and aluminum; he also experimented with the production of a cast-steel cannon.

Dictionary of American Biography.

T K D

GATTERMANN, LUDWIG Born at Goslar, Lower Saxony, Germany, 20 April 1860; died Freiburg, 20 June 1920. Organic chemist, remembered for several synthetic reactions, and for a famous textbook.

Gattermann studied chemistry at Göttingen, and became assistant to Victor MEYER; he moved with Meyer to Heidelberg, and stayed there from 1889 to 1900. At the end of this period he became acting head of the department, after Meyer's sudden death. From 1900 until his death he was professor in the University of Freiburg-im-Breisgau.

Apart from a study of the highly dangerous compound nitrogen trichloride, Gattermann's work was all in the field of organic chemistry, and usually had a strong industrial bias; he collaborated closely with the German dyestuffs industry. His name is associated with two important reactions; the synthesis of aldehydes by formylation with a mixture of hydrogen cyanide and hydrogen chloride (with or without a catalyst); and the facile replacement of the diazonium group by certain other groups in presence of copper powder. He also worked on liquid crystals, anthraquinone derivatives, and electrochemical reduction. His *Praxis der organischen Chemie* (universally known, even to its author, as the '*Kochbuch*') ran into many editions, and was widely translated.

Considering the conventional nature of his research, Gattermann seems to have had an unconventional and speculative mind. His marriage was unhappy, and ended in separation; he left one daughter.

Berichte der deutschen Chemischen Gesellschaft, **54**, 115A, 1921. (Portrait.)
J. R. Partington, *A History of Chemistry,* vol. 4. 1964.

W V F

GAUSS, KARL FRIEDERICH Born at Brunswick, Germany, 30 April 1777; died Göttingen, 23 February 1855. Mathematician, astronomer and physicist, with few peers – and none in the theory of numbers.

Karl Gauss was the son of a poor gardener and bricklayer. His genius was evident at an early age; he was one of the few great mathematicians to have had a facility for highly involved mental computation. Attending the Collegium Carolineum in Brunswick (1792), he mastered works by NEWTON, L. EULER and J. C. LAGRANGE, and there, unaided, he found the law of quadratic reciprocity and the method of least squares (published independently by A. M. Legendre (1752–1833), in 1806). He moved to the University of Göttingen in 1795. His years there (to 1798) were perhaps the most inventive of his life. During this time he prepared his finest work, *Disquisitiones arithmeticae* (publication delayed to 1801). On the death of his patron, the Duke of Brunswick, he was given the post of Director of the Göttingen Observatory. He lived there until his death, publishing much of his work in the journals of the Royal Society of Göttingen. From 1821 to 1848 he was scientific adviser to the Hanoverian and Danish Governments in a geodetic survey. He spent much time and thought on establishing, with the help of Wilhelm WEBER, a geomagnetic observatory at Göttingen from 1833.

In his book of 1801, Gauss developed Lagrange's theory of arithmetical forms, in particular that of the binary quadratic. His treatment so swept the field of Diophantine analysis (see DIOPHANTUS) that not until the end of the century was it realized that it had not entirely superseded earlier methods. His new concept of congruence enabled him to simplify the proof of, and to generalize, many earlier theorems on arithmetic divisibility (e.g. the theorem of FERMAT). Notable, too, is the proof of his theorem of reciprocity between the pair of congruences $x^2 \equiv p(\text{mod } q)$ and $x^2 \equiv p(\text{mod } p)$, where p and q are both prime. The congruences are either both solvable or both unsolvable, unless both p and q are congruent to 3(mod 4), in which case one of the original congruences is solvable and the other not. He also investigated the cyclotomic equation, connecting it with the condition for inscribing regular polygons in a circle. He found that a regular polygon of 17 sides can be so inscribed by Euclidean methods, and that, more generally, a regular m-gon can be inscribed when m is of the form $2^k P$, where P is a product of different odd primes, each of which is of the form $2^n + 1$.

In 1809 Gauss published a second remarkable work, *Theoria motus corporum coelestium*, in which is a thorough discussion of the determination of cometary and planetary orbits from observational data, and the best account then available of the analysis of perturbations. He had first put his methods (including the method of least squares) into effect after the discovery of the minor planet Ceres, in 1801, by G. PIAZZI. Gauss determined the elements of the planet's orbit from the earliest meagre observations. Afterwards it was lost for the best part of a year, and when found was in almost precisely the position predicted by Gauss.

Gauss made several important contributions to mathematics which he made known only after others had covered the same ground. Although he failed to carry his researches into non-Euclidean geometry as far as J. BOLYAI and N. I. LOBACHEVSKI had done, his correspondence shows that he had anticipated some of their ideas whilst yet a boy. Again, in 1811, he sent a letter to F. W. BESSEL which contained the fundamental theorem discovered independently by A. L. CAUCHY in 1825: The line integral of a function of a complex variable round a contour is zero if the function is uniform and monogenic (regular) at all points inside and on the curve. Many of his unpublished papers turned out to contain discoveries which made later mathematicians famous – W. R. HAMILTON, N. H. ABEL, K. G. J. JACOBI, all had occasion to feel annoyed.

In connection with his geodesic work he was led to the study of differential geometry, and the concepts of curvilinear coordinates, parametric representation, line-element, Gaussian curvature, conformal mapping, and the applicability of surfaces are all owed primarily to him. Much mathematical physics of the later century, and EINSTEIN's

Theory of Gravitation, would hardly have been possible without Gauss's work.

Gauss refused to draw a hard and fast line between pure and applied mathematics; even in what amounts to a theory of knots, which he might be taken to have founded, and which is only now coming into its own, he used an electrodynamic definition of some of his terms. Many of his terms of electromagnetism are, in fact, well known, including his so-called 'proof' of the inverse square law and his theorem equating the surface integral of normal force over a surface with $4\pi \times$ the enclosed electric charge.

In stature, Gauss bears comparison with ARCHIMEDES and Newton, but in range he probably outstripped both.

E. T. Bell, *Men of Mathematics*, vol. 1. 1937.

C. W. Dunnington, *C. F. Gauss, Titan of Science*. 1955. (Portrait.)

H. Wussing, *C. F. Gauss*. 1974.

Sartorius von Waltershausen, *Gauss zum Gedächtnis*. 1856. (Published in English as *Gauss, a Memorial*. 1966.)

Dictionary of Scientific Biography.

J D N

GAY-LUSSAC, JOSEPH LOUIS Born at Saint-Léonard, Haute Vienne, France, 6 December 1778; died Paris, 9 May 1850. Distinguished for work on laws of gases and properties of iodine and cyanogen.

Gay-Lussac was the son of a judge, and grandson of a physician. He was educated at the *École Polytechnique*, and became assistant to C. L. BERTHOLLET in 1800, working at the latter's house at Arcueil. In 1805–6 he travelled with Alexander von HUMBOLDT, making measurements of terrestrial magnetism. He was elected to the *Institut* in 1806, becoming professor of chemistry in the *École Polytechnique* and of Physics in the Sorbonne in 1809; Superintendent of the Government gunpowder factory in 1818; and Chief Assayer to the Mint in 1829. His last appointment was as professor of chemistry in the *Jardin des Plantes*. He worked too hard, providing for a large family, to produce important theoretical work in his later years, but his early work was brilliant.

In 1802 he published (independently of John DALTON) a law of the expansion of gases by heat (which later became known as Charles' Law (see J. A. C. CHARLES). In 1804 he made a daring balloon ascent to 23 000 feet above sea-level to bring down samples of air, which, on analysis, proved to have the same composition as air at ground-level.

In 1808 he published his most influential work, the law of combining volumes of gases: that gases combine among themselves by simple integral proportions by volume. This was to be of great importance in consolidating the atomic theory, but Dalton refused to accept it.

Gay-Lussac had excellent experimental technique. He devised an apparatus for determining vapour densities of liquids (1811). In collaboration with L. J. THENARD he produced the alkali metals in quantity by the action of fused alkalis on red-hot iron.

He investigated (1813–14) in detail the chemistry of iodine, discovered in 1811 by B. Courtois (1777–1838). (There was an unhappy controversy with Humphry DAVY over priority in iodine work.)

From his study of Prussian blue he developed the chemistry of cyanogen and the cyanides.

He developed several volumetric methods, the most important of which was his titration of silver with chloride; this was the first effective alternative (1832) to the ancient method of assaying silver by cupellation. In the course of this study he established many of the essential disciplines of accurate volumetric analysis. He invented the tower (named after him) which recovered oxides of nitrogen in the chamber-process for the manufacture of sulphuric acid.

He was a clear and informative lecturer, a good linguist (he taught his wife, so that she could help him), and an orderly organizer of laboratory routine. He was honoured (although reluctantly by some who thought he worked too much with his hands to be a gentleman) by being created a Peer of France.

J. B. Biot, *Proceedings of the Royal Society*, **5**, 1013, 1850.
M. Crosland, *The Society of Arcueil.* 1967. (Portrait.)
Endeavour (New Series), **2**, 52, 1978.
K. R. Webb, *Endeavour*, **9**, 207, 1950. (Portrait.)
M. Daumas, *Revue d'histoire des sciences*, **3**, 335, 1950.
Dictionary of Scientific Biography.

F G

GEBER (JABIR IBN HAYYAN) Born at Tus, near Meshed, Persia, 721 or 722; died Kufa (probably), *c.*815. Alchemist.

Geber was the son of an Arabian druggist, Abu Musa Jabir ibn Hayyan (*fl.* early 8th cent.), who lived in Kufa and was a supporter of the powerful Abbasid family. The latter hoped to depose the Caliph, and Abu Musa was sent on a political mission through Persia to prepare the way for revolt. In the course of this he visited Tus, where his son was born, but shortly afterwards he was captured by the Caliph's agents and beheaded.

The fatherless boy was sent to study in Arabia, and became attracted to the Shiite sect. He appears to have studied virtually all branches of contemporary Eastern learning, including medicine. Meanwhile the Abbasids had been successful in their revolution, and Geber became attached to the court of the famous Caliph Haroun-al-Rashid, probably as physician. He was befriended by the Caliph's ministers, the Barmecides, and was expelled with them when they fell from power in 803, and found refuge in Kufa. Thereafter his fate is uncertain, though it is possible that he returned to court on the accession of the Caliph al-Mamun in 813.

A very considerable number of alchemical works – about a hundred in all – are attributed to Geber, and five of the most important were translated from the Latin (the Arabic originals being lost) by Richard Russell in 1678 (new edition 1686); others have been translated since, but several still await scholarly investigation. Of them *The Sum of Perfection*, included in Russell's volume, is perhaps the most interesting, for Geber claims that in it he summarizes the alchemical content of all his other works.

There is, however, some doubt about the authenticity of many of the works attributed to Geber (who in this respect resembles HIPPOCRATES), and some may be the work of disciples or even (as some allege) Western forgeries fathered on him to give them authority. However, E. J. Holmyard (1891–1959), a leading authority on Arabic alchemy, concluded 'we know of no other chemist, Muslim or Christian, who could for one moment be imagined to have written them'.

Geber was a firm believer in the possibility of the transmutation of metals, notably, of course, the transmutation of base metals into gold. In this, he was not illogical according to the generally accepted ideas of his time. The conception of a chemical element had yet to be formed and it was considered that all metals were derived from sulphur and mercury. Absolutely pure sulphur and mercury, combined in ideal proportions, yielded gold; a slightly less favourable combination yielded silver; and so on. It was clear to Geber that some idealized form of sulphur and mercury was involved, for he was aware that the ordinary forms of these elements combine readily to give not a metal but the red sulphide of mercury known as cinnabar.

In searching for the secret of transmutation Geber mastered many basic chemical manipulations – such as sublimation and distillation – and transformations, and became familiar with the preparation and properties of a considerable range of simple chemicals.

E. J. Holmyard (Ed.), *The Works of Geber, Englished in the year 1678 by Richard Russell.* 1928; *Alchemy.* 1957.
H. J. J. Winter, *Eastern Science.* 1952.
Dictionary of Scientific Biography.

T I W

GEER, CHARLES DE *See* DE GEER.

GEER, GERARD JACOB DE Born in Stockholm, 2 October 1858; died there, 24 July 1943. Geologist, noted for his contribution to geochronology.

Baron Gerard Jacob de Geer, the noble son of a Swedish Prime Minister, studied at Uppsala University, where in 1878 he began an unsupervised study of quaternary geology. He was impressed by the regular light and dark bands (varves) exhibited by the recent clays in the Stockholm region and, with their similarity to tree rings in his mind, suggested in 1882 that they, too, might represent annual cycles. In 1884 he measured exposures of varves on a Stockholm canal and showed that, over very short distances, correlations could be made from one to another. He realized that here was a possible basis for a time scale of the glacial period, but he let the matter rest.

In 1889 he suggested that the many small frontal moraines around Stockholm might represent the limit of winter re-advance in the ice sheet. Behind each moraine lay a mound of gravel, and it was in 1897, the year of de Geer's election to the chair of geology at Stockholm University, that he showed these mounds to be deltas formed at the edge of a glacial lake, and that they merged into the locally lowest varve. The annual nature of the varves was thus established. In 1904, seeing a freshly cut section of varves a kilometre from the site of his 1884 measurements, he realized that correlation was possible over larger distances. Further measurements showed the lowest varves to disappear stepwise, indicating the gradual retreat of the ice.

Having at last realized the potentiality of his discovery, he set out to exploit it and made the necessary measurements over 200 km of southern Sweden.

In the next ten years the chronology thus established was extended from local station to local station, and by 1915, he had established correlation over a distance of some fifty miles. In 1920 investigations showed that varve patterns in North America could be related to those of Sweden, and since then similarities have been established among patterns throughout the world. In 1920 de Geer was awarded the Wollaston Medal of the Geographical Society; in 1924 he became the first director of the Stockholm Geochronological Institute; and in 1930 was elected to Foreign Membership of the Royal Society. He was a prolific author of geological papers, and much of his work is available in English in his *Geochronologica Suecica: Principles* (1940).

Obituary Notices of Fellows of the Royal Society. 1943. (Portrait.)
Nature, **152**, 209, 1943.
Dictionary of Scientific Biography.

W N S

GEIGER, HANS WILHELM Born at Neustadt, Rhein-Pfalz, Germany, 30 September 1882; died Potsdam, 24 September 1945. Pioneer in nuclear physics and inventor of the 'Geiger counter'.

Geiger studied under E. E. G. Wiedemann (1852–1928) at Erlangen, gaining a doctorate in 1906 with a thesis on electrical discharges through gases. He then became assistant to A. Schuster (1851–1934), professor of physics at Manchester and an authority on these phenomena. After Schuster's retirement a year later Geiger continued his work under his successor, E. RUTHERFORD, applying his experience of gaseous ionization to the study of radioactive disintegration. In 1908 Rutherford and Geiger devised a counter for α-particles, each particle causing a gas to ionize and conduct a current whose passage was registered by an electrometer. With this device they showed that α-particles have two units of charge. The results agreed with those obtained by a scintillation counter devised in the same year. In 1909 Geiger and E. Marsden demonstrated the occasional but large deflection of α-particles by gold leaf. This discovery led to Rutherford's nuclear theory of the atom, and in 1913 they published confirmatory evidence in further scattering experiments, showing that the nuclear charge was about half the atomic weight.

Meanwhile, Geiger's work on α-particles included the discovery (with Rutherford, 1910) that two α-particles appear to be released when uranium disintegrates, and (with J. M. Nuttall (1890–1958), 1912) that this is due to two uranium isotopes. In 1910 Geiger showed that the range of an α-particle is proportional to the cube of its velocity, and, with Nuttall in 1911, reported a linear relationship between the logarithms of the range and the radioactive constant (the Geiger-Nuttall rule). Amongst the disintegration products he identified actinium-A (with Marsden, 1910) and thorium-A (with Rutherford, 1911).

In 1912 Geiger became Head of the *Physikalisch-Technische Reichsanstalt*, Berlin, joined later by W. W. G. Bothe (1891–1957), J.CHADWICK, and others. He improved his ionization counter and in 1925 used it to confirm the Compton effect (see A. H. COMPTON), making simultaneous observations on the scattered radiation and the recoil electron.

Appointed professor of physics at Kiel in 1925, Geiger improved still further the sensitivity of his counter, and, with W. Müller, produced essentially the modern form of the apparatus (1928). As head of the physics department at the Technical University at Charlottenburg from 1936 he worked on cosmic rays, artificial radioactivity, and nuclear fission, and edited *Zeitschrift für Physik*. Dogged by illness during the war, he lost his home and possessions in the occupation of June 1945, and died shortly afterwards.

J. R. Partington, *A History of Chemistry*, vol. 4. 1964.
Science, **124**, 166, 1956. (Portrait.)
A. S. Eve, *Rutherford.* 1939.
Dictionary of Scientific Biography.

C A R

GEIKIE, SIR ARCHIBALD Born in Edinburgh, 28 December 1835; died Haslemere, Surrey, England, 10 November 1924. From 1882 to 1912 the leading figure in British geology.

After leaving Edinburgh High School, Archibald Geikie started to study banking, but his enthusiasm for geology and literature took him among the Scottish rocks and to the classical department of Edinburgh University. The combination of these two subjects, each completely mastered and perfectly blended, became the great feature of his career. His geological observations as a boy attracted the attention and friendship of Hugh Miller (1802–56) and were brought to the notice of Sir Roderick MURCHISON, then head of the Geological Survey, who appointed him in 1855 as a member of the Scottish branch. He became Director for Scotland in 1867 and Director-General for Great Britain in 1882, retiring in 1901. From 1871 to 1881 he also held the newly founded professorship of geology in Edinburgh.

Up to 1882 he had written several memoirs on the districts of Scotland he had surveyed, but his reputation rested chiefly on his papers published with the Royal Society of Edinburgh, particularly that on the Old Red Sandstone (1879). He had also published, in 1865, the first of his books, *The Scenery of Scotland*. The most important work carried on by the Survey under his directorship was the research in the north-west Highlands which culminated in the publication of the great memoir of 1907.

Geikie was deeply concerned with the work of the learned societies. Of the Geological Society he was President from 1890 to 1892, and again for the centenary celebrations, (1906–8), and foreign secretary from 1908 to the time of his death. He was foreign secretary of the Royal Society (1889–93), one of the two general secretaries (1905–8), and President (1908–12). In 1910 he was President of the Classical Association. Among several educational appointments he was a trustee of the British Museum.

His writings are great literature on great themes. His monumental works are two: the *Textbook of Geology* (1882, fourth edition 1903) and *The Ancient Volcanoes of Great Britain* (1897). Among the others his biographies are the most notable, especially those of Sir Roderick Murchison (1875) and Sir Andrew Ramsay (1814–91) (1895); also *The Founders of Geology* (chief edition 1905). His penetrating short studies are packed with interest; for instance, *Charles Darwin as Geologist* (1909). The vigour and charm of his writing are undiminished in his autobiography (see below) written shortly before his death at the age of 89.

Geikie was knighted in 1891, created KCB in 1907, and awarded the Order of Merit in 1913. He held honorary degrees from nearly every British university and from many abroad.

A. Geikie, *A Long Life's Work.* 1924. (Portraits.)
Proceedings of the Royal Society, B, 99, i, 1926. (Portrait.)
J. S. Flett, *The First Hundred Years of the Geological Survey of Great Britain.* 1937. (Portrait.)
Dictionary of National Biography.
Dictionary of Scientific Biography.

J C

GERARD, JOHN Born at Nantwich, Cheshire, England, 1545; died Holborn, London, February 1612 (exact date unknown). Herbalist.

John Gerard is perhaps the best known of the great herbalists whose work, false though it was in many particulars, laid the foundations of botany and pharmacology as sciences. He was attracted to medicine as a young man and travelled to Scandinavia, Russia and the Mediterranean countries, probably as a ship's surgeon. By 1577, however, he had settled in London and begun the study of plants, especially those possessing medicinal properties, that became his life's work. He superintended the magnificent gardens of Lord Burghley and cultivated an extensive garden of his own in Holborn. A catalogue of the latter, published in 1596, listed over a thousand different kinds of plant; it is the earliest extant catalogue of a single garden.

His main work was his great *Herball* of 1597, illustrated with 1800 woodcuts of native and imported plants. Though by no means original, being clearly derived from *Stirpium Historiae Pemptades Sex* (1583) of R. Dodoens (1517–85), it is an important survey of botanical knowledge and outlook at the end of the sixteenth century. It includes original work of his own as well as accounts of discoveries made by his contemporaries. A greatly enlarged and improved edition, describing 2850 plants, was brought out by Thomas Johnson, an apothecary, in 1633, and reprinted three years later.

Agnes Arber, *Herbals.* 1912 (paperback 1986). (Portrait.)
R. H. Jeffers, *The Friends of John Gerard (1545–1612).* 1967.
Dictionary of National Biography.

T I W

GERHARDT, CHARLES FRÉDÉRIC Born at Strasbourg, France, 21 August 1816; died there, 19 August 1856. Chemist, notable for his attempt to systematize organic chemistry under the Theory of Types; his reputation is inseparable from that of Auguste LAURENT.

Gerhardt (the name is pronounced in the French manner) studied chemistry in Karlsruhe and Leipzig. As a result of family financial troubles, and a quarrel with his father, he became a soldier, but

was bought out by an unknown friend. He returned to chemistry under Justus von LIEBIG at Giessen, and in 1838 became lecture assistant to J. B. A. DUMAS in Paris; there he met Laurent. In 1844 he was appointed to a professorship at Montpellier, but he had no laboratory facilities, and his desire to do research made him unpopular. He began to spend long periods in Paris, working with Laurent, sometimes with permission from Montpellier, sometimes without; his appointment was terminated in 1851. For a few years he and Laurent taught chemistry privately in Paris, but after Laurent's death he returned to his birthplace, Strasbourg, as professor of chemistry and of pharmacy (1855). His first year was happy and successful, but he died suddenly, following a chill, just before his fortieth birthday. His career was dogged by ill health (partly due to overwork) and by quarrels (not all of his own seeking), but he achieved a great deal under difficult circumstances.

Gerhardt published many papers on the preparation and analysis of organic compounds, but his reputation rests on his attempts to rationalize the increasing confusion of organic chemistry. His theoretical views are separable only with difficulty from those of his collaborator, Laurent. In contrast to the 'dualistic' theory of J. J. BERZELIUS, which regarded all molecules as composed of two parts of opposite electrical charge, Gerhardt considered a molecule as a unity (the 'unitary theory') held together by undefined chemical attraction. These unitary molecules had, no doubt, a definite structure; but this would be disturbed in unpredictable fashion during chemical reactions, so that attempts to discover this structure would be futile. A purely formal classification was therefore the only way of reducing chemistry to order; and to this end Gerhardt took over the concept of 'types' from A. W. HOFMANN and others, and elaborated it into a theory. All compounds were to be referred to one (or more) of four types (hydrogen, hydrogen chloride, water, ammonia) by replacing one or more of the hydrogen atoms in the type by radicals; the resulting formulae were not structural, but were intended to be a summary of all the reactions of which a compound was capable. The Theory of Types was admired and influential, but the later success of the Theory of Structure showed it to have been oversubtle and needlessly agnostic.

J. R. Partington, *A History of Chemistry*, vol. 4. 1964. (Portrait.)
E. Grimaux and C. Gerhardt jr., *Charles Gerhardt, sa Vie, son Oeuvre, sa Correspondance, 1816–1856.* 1900.
C. de Milt, *Journal of Chemical Education*, **28**, 198, 1951.
Dictionary of Scientific Biography.

W V F

GESNER, CONRAD Born at Zürich, Switzerland, 26 March 1516; died there, 13 December 1565. The greatest of the 'Encyclopaedic Naturalists' and a founder of bibliography.

Gesner was the son of a Protestant furrier who was killed at the battle of Cappel (1531). Thereafter Gesner was helped by friends, and for a time he studied the classics with the theologian Fabricius Capito (1478?–1541) at Strasbourg. Then he studied classics, science and medicine at Basle, Paris and Montpellier. He was for a time professor of Greek at Lausanne, and then graduated in medicine at Basle (1541). He settled in practice at Zürich, and was appointed to a chair of philosophy in the University there; in 1554 he became Chief Town Physician of Zürich. Gesner travelled widely – to Augsburg, Vienna, the Alps, and to Italy – in connection with his studies on natural history. He was one of the first to express a feeling for mountains, and he made many ascents in the Alps. His health seems to have suffered as a result of the work which he carried out during the epidemic of plague in Zürich in 1564. In the following year the plague returned, and he succumbed to it.

Gesner was a polyhistor. His *Bibliotheca universalis* (1545–9), a bibliographical study of all writers in Latin, Greek and Hebrew, made him one of the founders of bibliography. His *Pandectae universales* was an index to all the knowledge published in books; and his *Mithridates* (1555) was an attempt at comparative philology embracing very many languages.

Gesner's only substantial scientific work was his *Historia animalium* (1551–8), a fifth volume of which was published after his death. In this vast work the various animals are arranged alphabetically, though allied forms are sometimes grouped around a type animal. His method is distinctly reminiscent of PLINY, each animal being described under eight headings, including its habits and instincts, the means of its capture and domestication, and its uses as food and in medicine. The work is copiously illustrated, most of the illustrations being borrowed. But the work includes many valuable new observations by Gesner himself and by naturalists with whom he corresponded. This work is regarded as the beginning of modern zoology.

Gesner's greatest work, a *Historia plantarum*, was never written. For this he had collected 1500 illustrations, many finely drawn by himself, 400 of which had been cut in wood. This collection was handed down after his death, and the illustrations were engraved and published between 1751 and 1759. His botanical correspondence, the contents of much of which would have appeared in his book, was partly published, posthumously. From this it is seen that Gesner appreciated that flower, fruit and seed are better indications of botanical affinity than are leaves. He recognized genera, species, and even varieties. Gesner also wrote a small book on fossils.

C. Singer, *History of Biology*. 1959.
W. Osler, *The Evolution of Modern Medicine*. 1921. (Portrait.)
Papers of the Bibliographical Society of America, **10**, No 2, 53, 1916.
Hans Fischer, *Library*, **21**, 269, 1966.
E. W. Gudger, *Isis*, **22**, 21, 1939.
Dictionary of Scientific Biography.

E A U

GESS, GERMAN IVANOVICH See HESS.

GIAUQUE, WILLIAM FRANCIS Born at Niagara Falls, Ontario, Canada, 12 May 1895; died at Berkeley, California, USA, 28 March 1982. Physical chemist.

After beginning a commercial course at Niagara Falls Collegiate and Vocational Institute, Giauque turned to electrical engineering. To gain experi-

ence and raise money for the course he took a job with the local Hooker Electro-chemical Company and this diverted him again, to chemical engineering. He eventually enrolled in the University of California at Berkeley, graduating brilliantly in 1920. He remained there for the rest of his life, becoming professor of chemistry in 1934.

Professionally, his main interest was in chemical thermodynamics, especially in relation to the third law of thermodynamics. This led to research on entropy and low-temperature processes. He invented the adiabatic demagnetization process for attaining temperatures near absolute zero: he attained 0.53 K in 1933, eventually achieving 0.004 K. In other research he discovered two rare natural isotopes of oxygen, ^{17}O and ^{18}O. He also discovered the ortho and para forms of hydrogen. He was awarded the Nobel prize for chemistry in 1949.

Les Prix Nobel in 1949. 1950. (Portrait.)
In Memoriam (Berkeley). 1985.
Dictionary of Scientific Biography, Supp. II.
Tyler Wasson (Ed.), *Nobel Prize Winners*. 1987. (Portrait.)

T I W

GIBBS, JOSIAH WILLARD Born at New Haven, Connecticut, USA, 11 February 1839; died there, 28 April 1903. Chemist; responsible for much of the basic work in modern chemical thermodynamics and statistical mechanics.

Born into a family with long and distinguished academic, but not scientific, connections, Gibbs early excelled in classics. After turning to the study of mathematics and allied subjects, he gained in 1863 the first Yale PhD awarded for an engineering thesis; (his work dealt with the design and manufacture of gears). He was at once appointed a tutor at Yale, teaching first Latin and then natural philosophy. He retained his interest in engineering, and in 1866 obtained a patent for an improved design in railcar brakes.

In this same year he decided to widen his academic horizons and made a protracted visit to Europe, attending courses at Paris (1866–7), Berlin (1867–8), and Heidelberg (1868–9), after which he returned permanently to America.

Gibbs, though then almost unknown outside New Haven, was appointed professor of mathematical physics at Yale. Private means enabled him to accept the unsalaried appointment and he retained this post till his death. He was not thought a good teacher and few students could understand his work. His reputation rested almost wholly on his written works, but nevertheless he had offers of well-paid academic posts at Bowdoin College (1873) and the new Johns Hopkins University (1884).

Gibbs wrote numerous valuable papers on mathematics (particularly on quarternions), and physics, but is best known for his papers *Graphical Methods in the Thermodynamics of Fluids*(1873), *A Method of Geometrical Representation of the Thermodynamic Properties of Substances by Means of Surfaces* (1873), and *On the Equilibrium of Heterogeneous Substances* (1876–8). All were published in the *Transactions of the Connecticut Academy of Sciences*. There was also his work on statistical mechanics (1902). The second of these papers caught the attention of James Clerk MAXWELL who, in 1875, became the first international figure to appreciate Gibb's work. The 1876−8 papers included the new concept of chemical potential which later gave rise to the celebrated 'Phase Rule' and established Gibbs as a major scientist.

His great importance lies in his comprehensive application of mathematics to chemical subjects, and though some parts of his work were unwittingly duplicated in Europe, his overall grasp of chemical thermodynamics, which he can reasonably be said to have founded, was unrivalled in his time. In statistical mechanics, his ensemble method is particularly interesting. His numerous honours included a Copley and a Rumford Medal of the Royal Society.

L. P. Wheeler, *Josiah Willard Gibbs, the History of a Great Mind*. 1951. (Portraits.)
The Collected Works of J. Willard Gibbs. 1928.
Dictionary of American Biography.
E. Farber (Ed.), *Great Chemists*. 1961. (Portrait.)
M. Ruckeyser, *Willard Gibbs*. 1942.
Wyndham D. Miles, *American Chemists and Chemical Engineers*. 1976.
Dictionary of Scientific Biography.

G R T

GIFFARD, HENRI Born in Paris, 8 February 1825; died there, 14 April 1882. French aeronautical engineer.

Son of a poor family, Giffard studied at the *Collège Bourbon* and joined a railway company in 1841, studying engineering at the *École Centrale*. Becoming interested in aviation, he devoted himself to constructing a light steam engine of 3 hp, to drive an 11-foot screw propeller at 110 rpm. With this he succeeded in 1852 in propelling a 143-foot balloon at some 5.5 mph over a distance of 17 miles from the Paris Hippodrome to Trappes. As it had a rudder for steering, he can be credited with the construction of the first really navigable balloon, and the pioneer of the semi-rigid type of airship. A second airship was built in 1855.

After patenting a steam injector in 1858 that proved successful in locomotives, ships, and in industry, he became wealthy enough to devote all his time to building even larger balloons. These were at first captive: one for the Paris Exhibition in 1867, another for London in 1868, and the third for the Paris Exhibition of 1878. His wealth was bequeathed to the state for humanitarian and scientific purposes. His younger brother, Paul, helped him in his work, specializing in gas technology.

Louis Figuier, *Les Merveilles de la Science*. 1860−70. (Portrait.)
E. Moignan, *L'Inventeur Paul Giffard*. 1888. (Portrait.)

W H G A

GILBERT, WALTER Born at Boston, Massachusetts, USA, 21 March 1932. Molecular biologist.

Gilbert began his scientific career as a theoretical physicist. He graduated from Harvard University in 1953, majoring in physics, and was awarded a PhD by Cambridge University in 1957 for work in mathematics under A. SALAM. He returned to postdoctoral work at Harvard, working as research assistant to J. S. Schwinger (1918−) until his appointment as assistant professor of physics in 1959, a post he held until 1964.

From 1960, under the influence of James WAT-SON, Gilbert's interests moved towards biochemistry and molecular biology, and in 1964 he was appointed assistant professor of biophysics. From 1968 to 1972 he was professor of biochemistry. He held the American Cancer Society chair for molecular biology at Harvard 1972−82 before leaving the academic scene for two years to become chairman of Biogen, an international biotechnology corporation specializing in genetic engineering which he had helped to found in 1978. He returned to Harvard in 1984.

In the 1960s Gilbert worked on isolating and identifying the repressor substances which J. L. MONOD and F. Jacob (1920−) had suggested might regulate gene activity. With B. Muller-Hill he succeeded in producing large quantities of one of the repressor substances, and after isolating and purifying it he was able to identify it as a large protein molecule in 1966. He published *Genetic Repressors*, with Mark Ptashne, in 1970.

By 1975 Gilbert had developed a method for determining the sequence of bases in DNA. He wanted to start a project to sequence the 3000 million chemical bases in DNA that make up the entire human genome. Having failed to raise enough capital to start a private corporation, in 1986 he pressed for a national effort, declaring that 'the total human sequence is the goal of human genetics'. The idea was taken up by R. DULBECCO and the US Human Genome Project was started (see W. R. BODMER).

Gilbert shared the Nobel prize in chemistry in 1980 with Paul BERG and Frederick SANGER for his work in developing a method for determining the sequence of bases in DNA.

Joel Davis, *Mapping the Code. The Human Genome Project and the Choices of Modern Science*. 1990.
Robert Shapiro, *The Human Blueprint*. 1992. (Portrait.)
Tyler Wasson (Ed.), *Nobel Prize Winners*. 1987. (Portrait.)

A P B

GILBERT, WILLIAM Born at Colchester, Essex, England, 24 May 1544; died there, 10 December 1603. Early investigator of magnetic and electrical phenomena.

Gilbert had a conventional training in medicine. Entering the University of Cambridge, he graduated in arts and medicine; in 1561 he was elected a Fellow of St John's College. He then went to London and established himself in practice there with such success that in 1599 he was elected President of the College of Physicians. The following year he was appointed physician to Queen Elizabeth, and he subsequently served James I in the same capacity.

Despite this success in medicine, it is as an original investigator of magnetism and electricity that Gilbert is most deservedly remembered. His *De Magnete* (1600) is one of the outstanding classics of experimental science, and took the subject far beyond the stage represented by the *Epistola de Magnete* (1269) of Petrus PEREGRINUS. The outstanding importance of Gilbert's book was immediately recognized by, among others, GALILEO.

In assessing Gilbert's contribution it must be remembered that the most powerful magnets then available were still natural loadstones (magnetic iron oxide) which were rare and expensive. He showed how their strength could be increased by 'arming' them with soft-iron pole pieces. He devised and carefully described methods for magnetizing steel rods by stroking them with loadstones. He discovered that iron bars left lying in the direction of the Earth's magnetic field gradually became magnetized, and that this effect can be greatly accelerated by hammering them. He discovered, too, that magnetism is destroyed by heating to red heat. He investigated the Earth's magnetic field using a dip-circle of a still familiar design. He concluded that the Earth behaves as a giant magnet with its poles near the geographical poles. So comprehensive were Gilbert's studies that as late as 1822 Sir John Robinson (1778–1843) asserted that *De Magnete* 'still contains almost everything we know about magnetism'. Not until William STURGEON made the first electromagnet in 1825, and Michael FARADAY made the field so much his own, was substantial new progress made. Today, the unit of magneto-motive force is called the gilbert.

Gilbert also investigated electrical phenomena, showing that many substances other than amber could be electrified by friction. He also carried out chemical experiments, and rejected the alchemical belief in the transmutation of metals.

S. P. Thompson, *Gilbert of Colchester: an Elizabethan Magnetizer*. 1891.

S. Chapman, *Nature*, **154**, 132, 1944.

Dictionary of Scientific Biography.

T I W

GILCHRIST, PERCY CARLYLE Borne at Lyme Regis, Dorset, England, 27 September 1851; died 15 December 1935. Collaborated with S. G. THOMAS in the basic process for dephosphorizing steel.

From Felsted Grammar School, Gilchrist studied at the Royal School of Mines, London, where he became Murchison Medallist. He became associated with the work of S. G. THOMAS, his cousin, after taking a post in 1875 as chemist at Cwm Avon works in South Wales. He agreed, though pessimistic as to the outcome, to carry out tests in his spare time for smelting phosphoric iron ores in a converter lined with a basic material such as magnesia. Despite the poor finances of the partners, patents for the process were taken out in 1877 and 1878. These were practical only because of Gilchrist's work first at Cwm Avon and then at Blaenavon ironworks. A further collaborator was Edward Martin, manager at Blaenavon, who provided equipment for pilot tests, first with a 6 lb converter with basic lining, then with others eventually holding 12 cwt. Since dephosphorizing had by then proved practicable, Gilchrist undertook operations on a larger scale at the Bolckow Vaughan works at Middlesbrough. Here a manager, W. Richards, aided him in his attempts to improve the process in a 30 cwt converter. Considerable difficulties in securing adhesion of the basic lining to the converter during the 'blow' were overcome, while an 'afterblow' was introduced to remove some residual phosphorus. After the death of S. G. Thomas in 1882, Gilchrist took over full supervision of the rights granted to their joint interests.

Gilchrist added many further improvements, and he extended the basic process to the open-hearth furnace. No greater benefit to the European iron industry of the period can be found than the Gilchrist-Thomas process which opened to exploitation the vast Lorraine and Luxemburg ore fields.

Journal of the Iron and Steel Institute, 640–2, 1936.

Gilchrist-Thomas Jubilee Book. 1929.

J. C. Carr and W. Taplin, *History of the British Steel Industry*. 1962.

The Times, 18 December 1935.

Obituary Notices of Fellows of the Royal Society, **19**, 2, 1936. (Portrait.)

M S

GLASER, DONALD ARTHUR Born in Cleveland, Ohio, USA, 21 September, 1926. Inventor of the bubble chamber.

After gaining his first degree at the Case Institute of Technology in Cleveland in 1946, Glaser moved to the California Institute of Technology where he was awarded a PhD in 1950. For this, Glaser studied under Carl ANDERSON, who had used the cloud chamber to discover two elementary particles – the positron and the muon. In the cloud chamber, the tracks of charged particles appear as trails of droplets in a vapour. However, the device has limitations when it comes to studying the production and subsequent decay of high-energy particles.

After Glaser moved to Michigan University in 1949, he began to search for a new technique, and eventually decided to utilize boiling. Under appropriate conditions, bubbles will form along the tracks of charged particles passing through a superheated liquid.

Glaser's first bubble chamber, built in 1952, contained 3 centilitres of diethyl ether. However, by 1960 bubble chambers had grown to 2 m in size, in particular under the direction of Luis ALVAREZ at Berkeley.

Glaser moved to the University of California at Berkeley in 1959, and in 1960 was awarded the Nobel prize for physics for the invention of the bubble chamber. His research at Berkeley initially concentrated on studies in high-energy particle physics, but later it turned to molecular genetics and neurobiology, and in 1989 Glaser became professor of molecular and cell biology as well as professor of physics at Berkeley.

Nobel Lectures, Physics, 1942–1962. 1964.

Tyler Wasson (Ed.), *Nobel Prize Winners*. 1987. (Portrait.)

C S

GLASHOW, SHELDON LEE Born in New York, 5th December 1932. Theoretical physicist known for his work on elementary particles.

Educated in the same class at school as Steven WEINBERG, Glashow, like Weinberg, graduated from Cornell University in 1954. Glashow then went to Harvard University, gaining his PhD in 1959. His supervisor, Julian SCHWINGER (1918–), had suggested that the electromagnetic force and the weak nuclear force should be treated together if a self-consistent theory of the weak force was to be achieved. Then in 1960, while at the Niels Bohr Institute in Copenhagen, Glashow realised what the mathematical group structure of such a theory should be. However, his theory was incomplete and he effectively abandoned it. Later in the 1960s, Abdus SALAM and Weinberg independently developed a unified 'electroweak' theory with the same group structure but with an added ingredient to account for the differing strengths of the weak and electromagnetic forces. The resulting theory predicted the existence of weak 'neutral currents', which were discovered in 1973, and in 1979 Glashow, Salam and Weinberg shared the Nobel prize for physics.

After a period from 1961–7 at the University of California, Berkeley, Glashow returned to Harvard as professor. Here in 1971, he and J. Iliopoulos and L. Maiani showed how a theory of weak interactions between quarks could be made if there were four types of quark, rather than the three known at the time. This quark, to which Glashow gave the name 'charm', was found in new particles discovered in 1974.

Physics Today, December 1979. (Portrait.)
Les Prix Nobel en 1979. 1980. (Portrait.)
A. Hammond (Ed.), A Passion to Know. 1984.
Tyler Wasson (Ed.), Nobel Prize Winners. 1987.
  (Portrait.)

C S

GLAUBER, JOHANN RUDOLPH Born at Karlstadt, Franconia, Germany, 1604; died Amsterdam, Netherlands, (early) March 1670. Chemist.

Glauber was the son of a barber, and was orphaned at an early age. As a youth and young man he wandered widely through Europe. In 1625 he contracted what appears to have been typhus; apparently miraculously, he was saved by drinking the waters of a mineral spring issuing near Neustadt. This led him to a career in iatrochemistry, in which he modelled himself on PARACELSUS, to whose grave in Salzburg he made pilgrimage. After many years, Glauber settled in Amsterdam about 1655, and there he died, possibly from the effects of slow poisoning by the compounds of mercury, arsenic and antimony with which he experimented freely in investigating their medicinal qualities.

Although Glauber made himself very familiar with the chemical knowledge of his time, and acquired great manipulative skill in preparing a wide range of chemicals, he was nevertheless something of a charlatan. Certainly, he ascribed quite excessive virtue to his sal mirabile (Glauber's salt, sodium sulphate) which he identified with the sal-enixum of Paracelsus.

Glauber was a prolific writer, in German, and some forty works are attributed to him. The most important was his Opera omnia Chymica, a general chemical treatise, which first appeared in seven volumes at Amsterdam in 1658; it was subsequently reprinted widely elsewhere in various forms. His Furni Novi Philosophici (1651) was a useful treatise on furnaces and their use in chemical operations.

E. Pietsch, Johann Rudolph Glauber; Der Mensch, sein Werk und seine Zeit. 1956.
E. Farber (Ed.), Great Chemists. 1961. (Portrait.)
F. Greenaway, Endeavour, 29, 67, 1970. (Portrait.)
Dictionary of Scientific Biography.

T I W

GLISSON, FRANCIS Born at Rampisham, Dorset, England, 1597; died London, 16 October 1677. Famed for his anatomical research on the liver; for his description of rickets; and for his physiological doctrine of irritability.

Glisson graduated as a bachelor (1621) and a master (1624) of arts at Cambridge. He was a Fellow and Dean of Caius College, and he also lectured on Greek. He then studied medicine and became a doctor of medicine of Cambridge (1634). In 1635 he was elected a Fellow of the Royal College of Physicians where he was Anatomy Reader (1639) and Gulstonian Lecturer (1640). Glisson had been appointed Regius Professor of Physic at Cambridge in 1636, and he resided and lectured there until about the outbreak of the Civil War. He then removed to Colchester, and during the siege of that city by Fairfax in 1648 he played a prominent part. Afterwards Glisson removed to London, where he practised successfully. Also active in the College of Physicians, he was a Censor in 1656 and President from 1667 to 1669. He was one of the small band of 'philosophers' who formed the Royal Society, and he was named as an Original Fellow in the second charter. Although he now never visited Cambridge, he held the Regius professorship for forty years, but latterly he had to appoint a deputy.

The first medical description of rickets was given by Daniel Whistler (1619–84) in his 1645 thesis for the MD degree of Leiden. In 1649 Arnold Boot (or Boate) (1600?–1653?) published a brief account of the disease. Meanwhile, rickets was being studied by a small circle of Glisson's friends, two of whom were supposed to collaborate with him in writing up the material. Having completed his own section, Glisson then wrote up the sections allocated to his collaborators, who desired him to take all the credit. The resulting book, De rachitide, (1650), was published under his name and is generally regarded as his work. It is by far the best of the earlier writings on rickets, and little was added to his clinical descriptions until the twentieth century.

In 1654 Glisson published his work Anatomia hepatis, in which he gave a very clear and original account of the anatomy of the liver, both normal and pathological. He was the first to describe the fibrous covering of the duct and vessels entering the liver, which accompanies them into the organ, and since then this covering has been called 'Glisson's capsule'.

In 1672 Glisson published his Tractatus de natura substantiae energetica, in which he propounded his theory of the 'irritability' of living tissues. In a muscle, irritability was that property of the muscle fibre which perceived irritation and reacted to it. This view was further developed in his De ventriculo et intestinis (1677), in which he showed that a muscle does not experience a change in volume when it contracts. These views had an important influence on the work of Albrecht von HALLER.

W. Munk, Roll of the Royal College of Physicians. 1878.
H. D. Rolleston, The Cambridge Medical School. 1932. (Portrait.)
W. Langdon-Brown, Some Chapters in Cambridge Medical History. 1946.
Dictionary of National Biography.
Dictionary of Scientific Biography.
G. Wolstenholme (Ed.), The Royal College of Physicians of London: Portraits. 1964.

E A U

GMELIN, LEOPOLD Born at Göttingen, Germany,

2 August 1788; died Heidelberg, 13 April 1853. The first great systematizer of chemistry.

Gmelin came of a family of great intellectual distinction; a family tree is given in the first reference below. He studied chemistry, medicine and mathematics in Tübingen, Göttingen and Vienna before settling down in Heidelberg; he also spent a year with L. N. VAUQUELIN in Paris. In 1817 he became Heidelberg's first full professor of chemistry, a post which he held until his retirement (through ill health) in 1851. Besides his academic work he was the owner and manager of a paper-mill.

Although distinguished both as a teacher (F. WÖHLER was his pupil) and as a research worker, Gmelin is mostly remembered for his *Handbuch der Chemie*, the first edition of which appeared in 1817, and whose successors are current today. Gmelin devoted himself to a complete and objective collection of the whole corpus of chemical knowledge, still in a chaotic state after the Lavoisier revolution. He committed himself to the minimum of theory compatible with a workable classification; for this reason his adoption of the atomic theory in the fourth edition (1843) was of great importance. He was the inventor of several now common chemical terms, including 'ester' and 'ketone'.

Gmelin's most significant research work was on the physiological chemistry of digestion, in which, partly with his colleague F. Tiedemann (1781–1861), he discovered several of the constituents of bile. He also studied the complex cyanides, and discovered (1825) the remarkable synthesis of croconic acid (hexahydroxybenzene) from potassium carbonate and coal. He published little original work after about 1830.

Berichte der deutschen Chemischen Gesellschaft, **72**, 5A, 1939. (Portrait.)

E. Farber (Ed.), *Great Chemists*. 1961. (Portrait.)

P. Walden, *Journal of Chemical Education*, **31**, 534, 1954.

Dictionary of Scientific Biography.

W V F

GODDARD, ROBERT HUTCHINGS Born at Worcester, Massachusetts, USA, 5 October 1882; died Baltimore, Maryland, 10 August 1945. Physicist, pioneer of modern scientific rocket propulsion.

Goddard graduated BSc from the Worcester Polytechnic Institute in 1908, and PhD from Clark University in 1911. He taught briefly at Princeton but returned in 1914 to Clark, where he remained for almost 30 years. From the age of 17 he devoted his whole life to the development of bigger and better rockets, working either alone or in a small group in semi-isolation, virtually ignored by the US government during his life-time. After the end of the Second World War it was discovered that many of his published results had been utilised by the Germans in their V-2 rocket missile research at Peenemunde (see W. M. M. VON BRAUN).

His first aim had been to build a rocket powerful enough to carry research instruments into the upper atmosphere, and with financial support from the Smithsonian Institute he succeeded in carrying aloft, on a liquid fuel rocket, a number of instruments and a recording camera on 17 July 1929. This achievement attracted the support of the Guggenheim Foundation, and he was able to set up a rocket experimental station in New Mexico

where in 1935 he launched the first gyroscopically controlled rocket, and in 1937 set a new altitude record with a height of 3 km.

In the course of this work he introduced the use of liquid oxygen and paraffin (kerosene) as the propellant fuel, designed efficient combustion chambers, and patented multi-stage rocket launchers. At the time of his death he held more than 200 patents, but it was not until 1960 that the US government admitted it had frequently infringed many of them in its missile and satellite development programmes, and awarded his widow, jointly with the Guggenheim Foundation, one million dollars in compensation. His collected papers were published in three volumes in 1970.

M. Lehman, *This High Man: the Life of Robert H. Goddard*. 1963.

Journal of the British Interplanetary Society, **35**, 530, 1982.

Dictionary of American Biography.

R M B

GOEPPERT MAYER, MARIA Born at Kattowitz, Upper Silesia, 28 June 1906; died San Diego, USA, 20 February 1972. Co-discoverer of the shell structure of the atomic nucleus.

Maria Goeppert was the only child of Friedrich Goeppert, a professor of paediatrics, and his wife Maria. The family moved to Göttingen in 1910, where the younger Maria later attended university, gaining a doctorate in theoretical physics in 1930. She married Joseph Mayer (1904–), a visiting American chemist, in 1930 and returned with him to the US. In 1946, Goeppert Mayer became a professor of physics at Chicago University, where she worked with Edward TELLER and Enrico FERMI.

Her most important work was in developing the shell model of the atomic nucleus to explain the occurrence of 'magic numbers'. These are the numbers of nucleons (protons or neutrons) in particularly stable nuclei. In the shell model the nucleons move within a nucleus with only certain values of angular momentum, and nucleons with the same orbital angular momentum are said to be in the same 'shell'. Some of the magic numbers correspond to shells full of nucleons, while others correspond to full 'half-shells' with nucleons spinning in only one direction.

In 1963, Goeppert Mayer shared the Nobel prize for physics with J. Hans D. Jensen, (1907–73), who had independently arrived at the same theory of nuclear shells. (Eugene WIGNER also shared the prize in 1963 for his work on symmetry in the nucleus and elementary particles.)

Nobel Lectures: Physics, 1963–1970, 1972.

Physics Today, May 1972. (Portrait.)

Joan Dash, *A Life of One's Own; Three Gifted Women and the Men they Married*. 1973.

Dictionary of Scientific Biography. Supp. II.

L. Haber, *Women Pioneers of Science*. 1979

Tyler Wasson (Ed.), *Nobel Prize Winners*. 1987. (Portrait.)

C S

GOLD, THOMAS Born in Vienna, 22 May 1920. Astronomer: proponent of the steady-state theory of the origin of the Universe.

An Austrian emigré, Gold was educated at Zuoz College, Switzerland, and Trinity College, Cambridge, where he gained a BA in Mechanical

Sciences in 1942 after spending a year at the beginning of the Second World War interned as an enemy alien. He was a fellow of Trinity from 1947 to 1951, working at the Cavendish Laboratory and the MRC Zoological Laboratory until 1952.

In 1948 Gold, Herman BONDI and Fred HOYLE proposed the steady-state theory of the origin of the Universe, challenging the 'Big Bang' theory. They argued that the Universe had no beginning and no end, but was in a steady state with new matter continually being created from empty space as the Universe expanded. This theory was discredited in 1965 after A. A. PENZIAS and R. W. Wilson (1936–) discovered the cosmic microwave background which was thought to be the remains of the radiation generated in the original Big Bang.

After working at the Royal Greenwich Observatory as chief assistant to Martin RYLE from 1952 to 1956, Gold emigrated to the USA, first to Harvard University, and then to Cornell University, where he was Director of the Center for Radiophysics and Space Research 1959–81 and professor of astronomy 1971–86. There he became interested in pulsars, first discovered by A. HEWISH and S. J. Bell (1943–) in 1967. Gold suggested in 1968 that the source of the regular pulsating radio emissions was a rapidly rotating neutron star, called a pulsar, emitting a beam of radio waves.

From the late 1950s onwards Gold developed the controversial 'deep-earth gas' theory to explain the origins of petroleum and natural gas. He believed that the Earth contained large quantities of hydrocarbon fuel generated at the time of the formation of the planet, when hydrocarbons became trapped deep inside the Earth. In the 1980s he became involved in a Swedish project to drill deep into the granite bedrock in the hope of finding deep-earth gas. He published *Power from the Earth* in 1987.

Y. Terzian and E. A. Bilson (Eds), *Cosmology and Astrophysics. Essays in Honor of Thomas Gold.* 1982. (Portrait.)

A P B

GOLDMARK, PETER CARL Born in Budapest, 2 December 1906; died Rye, New York, 7 December 1977. Physicist and electrical engineer who developed the first practical colour television system, and the long-playing microgroove record.

After gaining his BSc and PhD at the universities of Vienna and Berlin, Goldmark went to the USA where in 1936 he became chief engineer of the Columbia Broadcasting System's new television research laboratories in New York. Under his direction colour television was transmitted for the first time by CBS in August 1940. Although his field-sequential system has been superseded for high-quality commercial TV transmissions, it is still widely used for closed-circuit and industrial TV cameras.

In 1948 Goldmark and his associates at the CBS laboratories introduced the long-playing microgroove 33 1/3 rpm (LP) record, which on one disc gave listeners the equivalent of six 78 rpm records, as well as much improved sound quality. He was particularly interested in the development of educational technology, believing that teachers at all levels from primary schools to universities should have access to equipment for storing, processing

and displaying the ever greater amounts of information available to them. To this end he developed electronic video recording (EVR) as a versatile means of storing moving or still images on film, to be viewed on conventional television monitors.

In 1954 he became president of CBS Laboratories, and for some years served as visiting professor of medical electronics at the University of Pennsylvania Medical School. He was elected to the National Academy of Engineering in 1966, and was awarded the 1976 National Medal of Science.

Current Biography, 339–40 1940; 177–9, 1950. (Portraits.)
Modern Scientists and Engineers. McGraw-Hill. (Portrait.)

R M B

GOLDSCHMIDT, JOHANN (HANS) WILHELM Born in Berlin, 18 January 1861; died Baden-Baden, 21 May 1923. Inventor of the 'Thermit' process.

Goldschmidt's family were the owners of a metallurgical firm in Essen. He studied chemistry in Berlin, Leipzig and Heidelberg (under R. W. BUNSEN) and in 1888 became a partner in the family business. His first success was a process for recovering tin from tinned iron scrap; but in 1894 he discovered the reduction of metallic oxides with aluminium powder, a discovery which in the next few years he developed into a very versatile industrial process. It became known as the 'Thermit' process, and was of importance not only for producing some of the carbon-free metals required for alloy steels, but as a technique for producing local high temperatures for otherwise intractable welding operations. The hard form of aluminium oxide produced (corundum) was a useful by-product.

With the Thermit process an assured financial success, Goldschmidt retired from active work in industry in 1917.

Berichte der deutschen Chemischen Gesellschaft, **56**, 77A, 1923. (Portrait.)

W V F

GOLDSCHMIDT, VICTOR MORITZ Born in Zürich, Switzerland, 27 January 1888; died Vestre Aker, Oslo, Norway, 20 March 1947. Founder of modern geochemistry.

Goldschmidt's family emigrated to Oslo in 1900. He entered the University of Christiania in 1905, studying geology and mineralogy. In 1907 he began a pioneering study relating the chemistry of regionally thermally altered rocks to the systematic evolution of distinct mineralogical assemblages. Obtaining his PhD in 1911, after two years as a lecturer he was appointed Director of the University's Mineralogical Institute in 1914. He became Director of the Government's Raw Materials Laboratory in 1917, where, charged with finding Norwegian sources of previously imported chemicals, Goldschmidt investigated factors governing the distribution of elements in nature. Adopting x-ray crystallography in 1923, he and his assistants measured atomic and ionic radii in simple compounds and by 1928 demonstrated the importance of ionic size, polarizability, charge, and interatomic distance in controlling the physical properties and constitution of minerals.

At the University of Göttingen (1929–35) he pioneered the use of semi-quantitative spectrographic methods to investigate the distribution of elements in igneous and sedimentary rocks and the biosphere. Forced by growing anti-Semitism to return to Norway, he resumed work at the University of Oslo until imprisoned in a concentration camp during the German occupation in 1942. Escaping to Britain in poor health, he began to work on his classic book *Geochemistry*, but died, following his return to Norway in 1946, as a result of wartime deprivations.

Biographical Memoirs of Fellows of the Royal Society, 1948–9. (Portrait.)
Dictionary of Scientific Biography.

R J H

GOLDSTEIN, EUGEN Born at Gleiwitz, Upper Silesia, 5 September 1850; died Berlin, 25 December 1930. Discoverer of the so-called 'canal rays' produced in discharges of electricity through gases at low pressures.

Goldstein studied at the Universities of Breslau (1869–70) and Berlin, where he became a student of and later co-worker with H. L. F. von HELMHOLTZ. In 1878 he became a physicist at Berlin Observatory, gaining promotion ten years later on the basis of his publications on electrical discharges through gases. From 1890 to 1896 he was able to work at the *Physikalisch-Technische Reichsanstalt*, and after this he had a laboratory with one assistant in a rented house in Berlin. He worked intensively there until 1927, and eventually became head of the astrophysical section of the Observatory at Potsdam.

With Helmholtz, Goldstein worked on electric discharges through gases at low pressures, producing his first paper in 1876. In several respects this anticipated the findings reported by Sir William CROOKES in his Bakerian Lecture of 1879, particularly in the discovery that objects in the path of the emanation from the cathode could throw a shadow. This emanation, which had been noticed by several earlier workers, was termed by Goldstein 'cathode rays'. He examined the influence of applied magnetic fields and variation in tube dimensions upon the character of the discharge. Like his German colleagues, E. E. G. Wiedemann (1852–1928) and H. HERTZ, Goldstein believed that cathode rays were waves like light. In Britain, however, they were usually regarded as particulate, and J. J. THOMSON identified them as 'electrons'.

In 1886 Goldstein discovered the 'canal rays'. During an examination of the yellow light near the cathode he devised a perforated cathode to divide the tube into two parts. On the side opposite to the anode he observed straight yellow beams of rays streaming through the holes in the cathode; he called these *Kanalstrahlen*. They moved in a direction opposite to that of the cathode rays, and appeared to be little deflected by a magnetic field. However, in 1898 deflection was observed by W. WIEN in a manner that indicated that the canal rays were positively charged particles. From Goldstein's discoveries came the developments that led to the identification of the electron (cathode rays) and more particularly to the use of positive ray analysis and mass spectroscopy (canal rays).

Other work by Goldstein included investigations of the complex phenomena around the anode. He thought that the aurora borealis consisted of cathode rays emanating from the Sun. He studied spark

spectra from simple ionizing atoms, and the band spectrum of helium. In 1908 he was awarded the Hughes Medal of the Royal Society.

Proceedings of the American Academy of Arts and Science, **78**, 29, 1950.
Nature, **127**, 171, 1931.
Neue Deutsche Biographie.
Naturwissenschaften, **8**, 715, 1920. (Portrait.)
Dictionary of Scientific Biography.

C A R

GOLGI, CAMILLO Born at Corteno, Lombardy, Italy, 7 July 1844; died Pavia, Lombardy, 21 January 1926. Histologist; a pioneer of the minute structure of the nervous system.

Golgi graduated in medicine at Pavia (1856), and was then a physician in a Pavia hospital for seven years. He then became chief physician in the hospital of the small town of Abbiategrasso. In 1875 he was appointed professor of histology at Pavia, but in the same year he went to Siena as professor of anatomy. In 1876 he returned to Pavia as professor of histology, and in 1881 he transferred to the chair of general pathology there.

While at Abbiategrasso, Golgi devised his silver impregnation method of staining nervous tissue (1873). This method revolutionized the histology of the nervous system. In 1880 he first described the neurotendinous spindle ('organ of Golgi') found near the junction of a tendon with a muscle. He classified nerve cells, and described that type in which the main process (axon) does not become a nerve fibre, but divides repeatedly to form an arborescence ('Golgi cells'). These researches were published in 1885 in his book on the histology of the nervous system. Golgi's method of staining enabled individual nerve fibres to be followed through much of their course. In 1898 he described a peculiar reticular formation in the cytoplasm of cells ('the Golgi apparatus').

The real discoverer of the malaria parasite was Alphonse LAVERAN (1880). In 1884–5 Ettore Marchiafava (1847–1935), Golgi, and other Italians cleared up much of the asexual cycle of the parasite in the erythrocytes. In 1885 Golgi differentiated between the parasites of the tertian and the quartan types of malaria, and he showed that the beginning of a bout of fever was synchronous with that stage of the life-cycle of the parasite when numerous young parasites burst out of their containing erythrocytes into the blood stream. In 1892 he showed that, whereas in intermittent types of malaria (tertian and quartan fever) the parasite passes through its life-cycle in the blood, in the pernicious type of malaria the parasites develop mainly in the organs of the body, and especially in the brain.

Golgi's work on the nervous system inspired that of RAMÓN Y CAJAL. They were jointly awarded a Nobel prize in 1906. But whereas Cajal was a strong adherent of the neurone theory, Golgi was – incorrectly – an equally strong opponent.

C. Da Fano, *Journal of Pathology and Bacteriology*, **29**, 500, 1926.
W. Haymaker and F. Schiller (Eds), *The Founders of Neurology*. 1953. (Portrait.)
E. Macorini (Ed.) *Scienziati e Tecnologi*, vol. 2. 1975. (Portrait.)

E A U

GOODYEAR, CHARLES Born at New Haven, Connecticut, USA, 29 December 1800; died New York, 1 July 1860. Invented the sulphur vulcanizing process for rubber.

Goodyear began his commercial activities in partnership with his father, an inventor and hardware manufacturer. After examining a rubber lifebuoy in a shop, Goodyear sought to improve the valve, but was advised to find some curing process for rubber as a more urgent need. Unsuccessful in business and in poor health, he made many empirical experiments while kneading his 'gum elastic' with various additives, such as magnesia. After meeting Nathaniel Hayward (1808–65), who had experimented with rubber treated with a sulphur solution (as Alexander PARKES did in Britain), Goodyear in 1839 made his well-known accidental discovery. He dropped a rubber mix containing sulphur and white lead on to a hot stove and noted that the rubber became tough and its tackiness disappeared. Meanwhile C. MACINTOSH and T. HANCOCK in Britain had also been seeking methods of overcoming the tendency of natural rubber to become tacky when hot, and hard and brittle when cold. Only two months before Goodyear sought to patent his invention in Britain they had taken out key patents for the use of sulphur to vulcanize rubber. Consequently, Goodyear had to come to terms with the British interests. Hancock prospered and was included in the Rubber Hall of Fame at Akron, but Goodyear was less fortunate. Although awarded the Legion of Honour by Napoleon III, he became heavily in debt and died a pauper.

Charles Goodyear, *Gum Elastic*. 1855. (Reprinted by the *India Rubber Journal* in 1937.)

Dictionary of American Biography.

Rubber Journal and International Plastics, 972, 1960. (Portrait.)

A. C. Regli, *Rubber's Goodyear*. 1941.

Wyndham D. Miles, (Ed.), *American Chemists and Chemical Engineers. 1976.*

M S

GORDAN, PAUL ALBERT Born at Breslau, (Wroclaw) (then in Germany), 27 April 1837; died Erlangen, 21 December 1912. Algebraist.

Paul Gordan was educated at the University of Giessen, taking his doctorate in 1862 and becoming professor of mathematics there in 1867. In 1875 he was appointed to the chair of mathematics at the University of Erlangen, and remained there until his death.

Gordan's first notable work was a book on Abelian functions (1866) (see N. H. ABEL) written with Rudolph Clebsch (1833–72). The authors provided geometrical interpretations for the functions. Gordan's best-known work, however, is in the theory of algebraic invariance. In his 'theorem of finiteness' (1868) he proved the existence of a finite fundamental system of invariants and covariants for all binary quantics, and two years later he showed that all covariants and invariants of a finite number of binary quantics are rational integral functions of a finite number of covariants and invariants of the system. Though his proofs were later replaced by the more elegant proofs of D. Hilbert (1862–1943) and A. B. Kempe (1849–1922), Arthur CALEY gave high praise to Gordan's fundamental theorem.

Late in life Gordan took up the suggestion of

J. J. SYLVESTER that there is more than a superficial resemblance between the formulae of chemistry and those of the algebra of quantities, and his reputation suffered as a result.

Proceedings of the London Mathematical Society, **12**, li, 1913.

C. Fischer, *Archive for History of Exact Sciences*, **3**, No 2, 137, 1966.

Dictionary of Scientific Biography.

J D N

GORGAS, WILLIAM CRAWFORD Born at Toulminville, Alabama, USA, 3 October 1854; died London, 3 July 1920. Celebrated for his work in preventive medicine, especially in combating yellow fever.

Gorgas, son of a confederate soldier, studied medicine at Bellevue Medical College, New York, and entered the United States Medical Corps in 1880. After many army postings he became, in 1898, Chief Sanitary Officer in Havana. In the hope of eliminating the fearful scourge of yellow fever and other diseases he turned his remarkable administrative talents to cleansing the horrifying filth of Havana. But yellow fever still appeared. It was only when he applied the results obtained by the United States Army Yellow Fever Commission (see W. REED) – that the disease was transmitted by mosquitoes – that he was successful. His success also provided valuable support for the Commission's results. Gorgas systematically destroyed watery mosquito breeding-grounds – ranging from household utensils to small pools – either by emptying or covering them with kerosene.

His fame rests, however, on his triumph in ridding the Panama Isthmus of yellow fever and other diseases during the building of the Canal (1904–14). Yellow fever, especially, had wrecked earlier efforts. The story of Gorgas's activities is full of details of his ingenuity in locating and destroying mosquito breeding-grounds and of overcoming opposition and lack of understanding by the administration. The success of his brilliant administration was perhaps the most important factor behind the completion of the Canal.

Gorgas spent his last years dealing actively with disease in South Africa and South America and as Surgeon-General from 1914 to 1918.

M. D. Gorgas and B. J. Hendrick, *William Crawford Gorgas*. 1924. (Portraits.)

Dictionary of American Biography.

J K C

GOSSAGE, WILLIAM Born at Burgh-in-the-Marsh, Lincolnshire, England, 1799; died Bowdon, Cheshire, 9 April 1877. Industrial chemist.

At the age of 12, Gossage – the youngest of thirteen children – assisted his uncle, a chemist and druggist in Chesterfield. For a short time he ran a similar business of his own at Leamington, but very soon gave it up to start a salt and alkali works at Stoke Prior, Worcestershire. In 1850 he moved to Widnes, Lancashire, and established himself as a manufacturer of both alkali and soap. In its day, his mottled soap was famous, and in the period 1862–87 over 200 000 tons of it were manufactured.

Gossage made an exceedingly important improvement in the soda process invented by N. LEBLANC. In that process, which dominated the industrial chemical scene for a century, vast quantities of hydrochloric acid were generated. At first this was discharged straight into the atmosphere, causing great annoyance and involving the manufacturers in litigation. Gossage solved this problem by introducing towers (1836) in which ascending hydrochloric acid was absorbed in a descending stream of water. This paved the way for the Alkali Act (1863), requiring British manufacturers to absorb 95 per cent of the hydrochloric acid evolved. Henry DEACON devised a process for oxidizing hydrochloric acid to chlorine, for the manufacture of bleaching powder.

For a time Gossage became interested in copper-smelting, establishing works in both Widnes and Neath, South Wales, but his main interest was in the chemical industry. He was of a most inventive turn of mind, and over a period of some forty years registered a remarkable series of industrial chemical patents.

> J. Fenwick Allen, *Some Founders of the Chemical Industry*. 1907. (Portrait.)
> D. W. F. Hardie, *A History of the Chemical Industry in Widnes*. 1950. (Portrait.)
> *Dictionary of National Biography (Missing Persons)*. 1993.

                                                              T I W

GOUDSMIT, SAMUEL ABRAHAM Born at The Hague, Netherlands, 11 July 1902; died Reno, Nevada, USA, 4 December 1978. Co-discoverer of electron spin.

While they were students at the University of Leiden in 1925, Goudsmit and G. E. Uhlenbeck realized that the fourth quantum number Pauli introduced in his exclusion principle could be interpreted as a new degree of freedom of the electron. By assigning a spin 1/2 and a magnetic moment of one Bohr magneton to the electron, they explained both why hydrogen has double the number of spectrum lines previously expected and also the behaviour of the spectrum lines in a magnetic field. It was soon recognized that spin is also a property of protons, neutrons and most elementary particles. For their discovery Goudsmit and Uhlenbeck received Research Corporation awards (1953) and Max Planck medals (1964). 'Why they never received a Nobel prize will always be a mystery to me', said I. I. RABI.

After he received a PhD from Leiden in 1927, Goudsmit, with Uhlenbeck, joined the physics department of the University of Michigan where he helped develop the renowned Physics Summer School. During the Second World War (1941–5) Goudsmit worked first on radar at the Massachusetts Institute of Technology and in England, and then headed an intelligence effort known as *Alsos* (Greek: groves, after Major General Leslie R. Groves) to learn of German progress in development of an atomic bomb. Some of Goudsmit's conclusions about what had hindered progress in nuclear science in Germany were later disputed by protagonist Werner HEISENBERG. During the *Alsos* mission Goudsmit had the devastating experience of seeing ruins of his childhood home in The Hague and of learning that his parents had been deported to an extermination camp.

In 1946 Goudsmit joined Northwestern University and in 1948 went to Brookhaven National Laboratory, where he remained until his retirement in 1970. He was influential as editor of the *Physical Review* 1951–62, and as editor-in-chief of all publications of the American Institute of Physics to 1974. He founded *Physical Review Letters* in 1958, a much imitated letter journal. He wrote *The Structure of Line Spectra* with Linus PAULING (1930), *Atomic Energy States* with R. F. Bacher (1932), and two popular books, *Alsos* (1947) and *Time* (1966).

Goudsmit enjoyed teaching physics, especially to 'humanists', which he did at Rockefeller University while at Brookhaven. Interest in puzzles prompted him while still an undergraduate to take a course in detective techniques and as an amateur Egyptologist he could read hieroglyphs. He was noted for friendliness and concern for human problems. He also was a man who stood up for his convictions, as he did in resisting the McCarthy Committee's repeated 'investigations' of the Signal Corps Engineering Laboratories at Fort Monmouth.

> *McGraw-Hill Modern Men of Science*. 1966. (Portrait.)
> *Physics Today*, **32**, 71, 1979. (Portrait.)
> *Dictionary of Scientific Biography*, Supp. II.

                                                              R L W

GOULD, JOHN Born at Lyme Regis, Dorset, England, 14 September 1804; died London, 3 February 1881. Producer of elaborately illustrated bird books.

John Gould was the son of an under-gardener who obtained a post as foreman of gardeners at Windsor Castle when John was 14 years old. Here the boy learned bird-stuffing in addition to his trade of gardener, and in 1827 became taxidermist to the Zoological Society of London. In 1830 he received a collection of bird-skins from the Himalayas containing many rarities; these were described in a folio volume beautifully illustrated by his talented wife, and was an immediate success. He followed this with the *Birds of Europe* (five volumes 1832–37) and a monograph of the toucans (1834).

The financial returns on these works enabled him and his wife to spend two years in Australia, where he made large collections of birds and mammals. On his return he produced the *Birds of Australia* in seven volumes, followed by the *Mammals of Australia* in three. He accumulated an enormous collection of humming birds and produced five volumes figuring them (1849–61). Many monographs on various families of birds; on kangaroos; and on the birds of Great Britain, Asia and New Guinea appeared during the rest of his life.

Gould, although possessed of great energy and tenacity, had very mediocre artistic talents, and after his wife's death employed others to draw many of his plates – among them Joseph Wolf (1820–99), who said he was 'the most uncouth man I ever knew' – and was not above fixing his signature to their pictures. He was elected FRS in 1843. In total, he published forty-one folio volumes illustrated by 2999 coloured plates, which are highly prized by collectors.

> R. B. Sharpe, *An Analytical Index to the Works of the late John Gould*. 1893. (Contains biographical memoir and portrait.)
> A. H. Palmer, *The Life of Joseph Wolf*. 1895.
> *Dictionary of National Biography*.

                                                              L H M

GRAAF, REGNIER DE *See* DE GRAAF.

GRAAF, ROBERT JEMISON VAN DE *See* VAN DE
GRAAFF.

GRAEBE, KARL JAMES PETER Born at Frankfurt-am-Main, Hessen, Germany, 24 February
1841; died there, 19 January 1927. Organic chemist, important in the synthetic dyestuffs industry.

At his father's wish, Graebe began to study engineering, but soon turned to chemistry; his teachers
were R. W. BUNSEN in Heidelberg and A. W. H. KOLBE
in Marburg. In 1864 he started work with Meister,
Lucius and Co. in Höchst, but had to leave the next
year because exposure to organic vapours was seriously impairing his health. He went to Berlin as
assistant to J. F. A. von BAEYER, and in 1870 became
professor in Königsberg. In 1875 he had a nervous
breakdown, from which he recuperated in Switzerland; in 1878 he was appointed professor in Geneva.
He retired in 1906 to Frankfurt, his birthplace; he
was ruined by the postwar inflation, and died forgotten and in poverty.

Nearly all Graebe's work was connected with
coal-tar and dyestuffs, and throughout his career he
collaborated closely with the German dyestuffs
industry. He is most famous for his discovery in
1868 with C. Liebermann (1842–1914) that alizarin
is a derivative of anthracene, and for the rapid devising of a commercially practicable synthesis, on
which the fortunes of the German dyestuffs industry was built. It was Graebe also who introduced the
terms ortho, meta and para into aromatic chemistry,
to indicate the positions of substituents, and
extended the benzene formula proposed by F. A.
KEKULÉ to naphthalene. He studied extensively the
minor constituents of coal-tar (phenanthrene,
pyrene, acridine, carbazole, etc.) partly in collaboration with H. Caro (1834–1911) in Ludwigshafen.
With Caro also he did important work on triphenylmethane dyestuffs. His retirement was
devoted partly to studies in the history of chemistry.

Berichte der deutschen Chemischen Gesellschaft,
    61, 9A, 1928. (Portrait.)
Nature, **119**, 500, 1927.

                                                            W V F

GRAHAM, THOMAS Born in Glasgow, Scotland, 21
December 1805; died London, 16 September 1869.
Chemist; first President of the Chemical Society of
London.

Graham was the son of a Glasgow manufacturer,
who hoped that he would enter the ministry. He
was, however, determined on an academic career
and entered Glasgow University in 1819, at the
early age of 14. It was, however, at Edinburgh that
he graduated (1824), having worked and studied
under T. C. HOPE. He returned to Glasgow to teach,
first privately and then at the Mechanics' Institute,
established in 1823 by Professor George Birkbeck
(1776–1841) to provide scientific training for
working men. In 1830 he was appointed professor
of chemistry at Anderson's College, Glasgow (a
chair once held by Birkbeck), and four years later
was elected FRS. The Society accorded him the
unusual distinction of twice awarding him a Royal
Medal (1837, 1863) as well as its Copley Medal
(1862). He left Scotland on being appointed to the
chair of chemistry at University College, London.
Robert Warington (1807–67) was at that time can-
vassing support for a national chemical society in
Britain. Such a society – the Chemical Society of

London – was founded in 1841, and Graham was
its first President. Although this was by no means
the first chemical society, it was the first firmly
established on a national basis. Similar societies
were in due course founded elsewhere, notably in
France (1857), Germany (1867), and the United
States (1876). Graham remained at University College for twenty years, and was then appointed
Master of the Mint, a post once held by NEWTON.

In modern terminology, Graham was primarily
a physical chemist: that is to say, he was primarily
interested in the physical factors relevant to chemical reactions. Within this field, he had a particular
interest in gases: his name is remembered in Graham's Law, which governs the rate at which gases
of different densities will diffuse through small
apertures. He investigated also the adsorption of
gases by charcoal, a process now of great industrial
importance. He investigated the solubility of gases
and observed that the law formulated by William
HENRY is not true for very soluble gases. He also
made intensive investigations of the colloid state
(for example, emulsions and foams) and made
important contributions in this then comparatively
new field. He noted, for example, the mutual precipitation of sols whose disperse phases bear opposite electrical charges, and the relatively high
viscosity of emulsions compared with that of the
pure solvent.

In 1829 he became interested in the glow of
phosphorus, and noted its extinction by certain
organic vapours. This led him on to a study of
phosphorus compounds, including phosphine and
certain inorganic phosphates. In the latter field he
distinguished between ortho-, pyro- and meta-
phosphates.

In 1866 he began a series of investigations into
the occlusion of hydrogen by metals – evidence of
his continuing interest in gases – in the course of
which he made the remarkable observation that
heated palladium is freely permeated by hydrogen,
whereas at somewhat lower temperatures the
metal absorbs very large volumes of the gas.

E. Farber (Ed.), *Great Chemists*. 1961. (Portrait.)
T. S. Moore and J. C. Philip, *The Chemical Society
    1841–1941*. 1947. (Portrait.)
A. C. Munro, *The Philosophical Journal*, **9**, 30,
    1972.
E. Frame, *The Philosophical Journal*, **7**, 116, 1970.
Dictionary of Scientific Biography.
Dictionary of National Biography.

                                                            T I W

GRAM, HANS CHRISTIAN JOACHIM Born in
Copenhagen, 13 September 1853; died there, 11
November 1938. Physician who invented an
important standard staining method for the differentiation of bacteria.

Christian Gram studied medicine at the University of Copenhagen, and graduated in 1878. During
the next five years he held junior hospital posts. He
then spent two years (1883–5) in postgraduate
study in Berlin, Strasbourg and Marburg. In 1883
he was officially recognized as a lecturer in the
University of Copenhagen, and in 1891 he was
called to the Chair of Pharmacology. In 1900 he
was appointed to the Chair of Pathology and Therapeutics, which he held until his retirement in 1923.
In 1892 he had been appointed Director of the
medical department of the Frederick's Hospital at

Copenhagen, and this post also he held until 1923.

Gram's most important contribution to science was his research, carried out while he was working with C. Friedländer (1847–87) in Berlin, which led to the empirical introduction of a new method of staining bacteria. The method was derived from the use by P. EHRLICH of a solution of gentian-violet in aniline water. Gram found that if bacteria were stained in this way and then treated with a solution of iodine in potassium iodide, the colour could be discharged from some bacteria ('Gram negative'), but not from others ('Gram positive'). This method was published in 1884, and it was soon found that it was applicable to all bacteria. Although numerous modifications have been introduced, the method remains essentially as Gram devised it. The Gram method is essential in classifying, and, to some extent, in identifying micro-organisms.

W. Bulloch, *History of Bacteriology*. 1938.

H. Bailey and W. J. Bishop, *Notable Names in Medicine and Surgery*. 1959. (Portrait.)

Dictionary of Scientific Biography.

E A U

GRASSI, GIOVANNI BATTISTA Born at Rovellasca, Como, Italy, 27 March 1854; died Rome, 4 May 1925. Distinguished malariologist.

Grassi studied medicine in the Universities of Pavia and Catania, and graduated as a doctor of medicine at Pavia in 1878. He then spent some time in Heidelberg, where he studied under C. Gegenbaur (1826–1903) and O. Bütschli (1848–1920). In 1883 he was appointed professor of zoology and comparative anatomy in the University of Catania, and in 1895 he was called to the chair of comparative anatomy in the University of Rome.

Grassi's most important work was in the realm of parasitology. In 1873 Friedrich Lösch discovered *Entamoeba histolytica* in dysenteric stools. He did not regard it as the cause of the disease, but believed that it prevented the healing of the ulcers. Grassi (1879–88) and other Italians studied this question, but, as their available material contained only the non-pathogenic *Entamoeba coli*, which they failed to distinguish from *E. histolytica*, they erroneously concluded that all intestinal amoebae are harmless.

In 1878 it was shown by Grassi and the brothers Ernesto (1849–1902) and Corrado (1848–1922) Parona that the finding of hook-worm ova in human faeces indicated the presence of hookworms in the intestine. This important finding was utilized in the interests of hygiene in 1880 during the construction of the St Gothard tunnel. In 1883 Grassi showed that flies can carry the eggs of intestinal worms.

By the autumn of 1898, as a result of the work of, *inter alia*, A. LAVERAN, Ettore Marchiafava (1847–1935), and C. GOLGI, the asexual life cycle, in human blood, of the main species of malaria parasites had been worked out very completely. Ronald ROSS had seen the fertilized oocyst projecting through the stomach wall of an anopheline mosquito. Owing to unavoidable circumstances Ross was unable to carry his researches farther in relation to human malaria. He now turned to the very similar bird-malaria, and he worked out the sexual cycle of that parasite in the mosquito, ending with the migration of the sporozoites to the mosquito's salivary gland. By allowing infected mosquitos to feed on healthy birds he proved that transmission was by the bite of the mosquito. Again owing to unavoidable circumstances he had at that time no opportunity of carrying out the crucial test in relation to human malaria, namely, allowing an anopheline mosquito to feed on malarious blood and then observing whether it could transmit the infection to a healthy volunteer by its bite.

In November and December 1898 Grassi, in collaboration with Amico Bignami (1862–1929) and Giuseppe Bastianelli (1862–1959), carried out this experiment and showed that the mosquito does transmit the infection to man by its bite. In 1900 Grassi published his studies on malaria, in a book which contained very fine illustrations of the parasite.

H. H. Scott, *History of Tropical Medicine*. 1939.

J. Jaramillo-Arrango, *The Conquest of Malaria*. 1950. (Portrait.)

A. Neghme, *Experimental Parasitology*, **15**, 260, 1964.

E A U

GRAY, ASA Born at Sauquoit, Oneida County, New York State, USA, 18 November 1810; died Cambridge, Massachusetts, 30 January 1888. Plant taxonomist.

After studying medicine at Fairfield Academy, Gray became a science instructor in 1831 at Bartlett's High School, Utica, New York. In 1834 he assisted John Torrey (1796–1873) in the Chemical Laboratory of the Medical School, New York; the two men formed a lifelong friendship as a result of their common interest in botany, and collaborated in the *Flora of North America* (1838–43). In 1835 Gray was appointed Curator and Librarian of the New York Lyceum of Natural History, where he found the opportunity to write the first of a series of standard botanical textbooks, *Elements of Botany* (1836). He was appointed botanist to the Wilkes Exploring Expeditions in 1836, but because of delays in sailing he resigned the following year. He made his first visit to European herbaria in 1838 in order to examine American type specimens, and became friends with many distinguished European botanists. In 1842 he succeeded to the professorship of natural history at Harvard University. There he created the Gray Herbarium and Library, and trained a whole school of American botanists.

Like his friend Sir Joseph HOOKER, he was a pioneer plant geographer, particularly of the North American flora and its East Asian affinities. He was the founder of systematic botany in the United States – his *Manual of the Botany of the Northern United States* (1848) went through several editions – and many institutions in America and Europe honoured him with academic awards and distinctions. In 1857 Charles DARWIN outlined in a letter to Gray his theory of the origin of species; subsequently Gray became Darwin's chief advocate in North America.

J. L. Gray (Ed.), *Letters of Asa Gray*. 1893.

A. Hunter Dupree, *Asa Gray, 1810–1888*. 1959. (Portrait.)

A. D. Rodgers III, *American Botany 1873–1892*. 1944.

Dictionary of American Biography.

R G C D

GRAY, STEPHEN Born c.1670; died London, 25 February 1736. Remembered for his electrical experiments.

Observing that corks in the end of a glass tube exhibited electrical properties when the glass is rubbed, Gray found that a pine stick inserted in the cork transmitted the influence to its end, and that this was also the case with threads hanging vertically. Transmission in a horizontal direction proved unsuccessful until the thread was supported by silk. In this way he was able to transmit electrical influences to a considerable distance. He also used indifferent conductors such as hair, glass and silk to store electricity on bodies for a considerable time, observing that two spheres of the same size, one hollow, one solid, had an equal capacity for storing electricity. Gray's electrical investigations published in the *Philosophical Transactions* for the years 1731–2 and 1735–6 exerted a considerable influence on C. F. DUFAY.

Dictionary of National Biography.
Dictionary of Scientific Biography.

                                                               J W H

GREGOR, WILLIAM Born at Trewarthenick, Cornwall, England, 25 December 1761; died Creed, Cornwall, 11 June 1817. First recognized the existence of titanium as a new element.

Gregor was educated at Cambridge; he was a classical scholar, and became a Fellow of St John's College. In 1793 he became Rector of Creed, where he remained until his death. The influence of John Warltire (1739–1810) made him an amateur chemist and mineralogist.

In 1791 Gregor published his analysis of a black sand found in Menacchan, Cornwall (now spelt Manaccan), and showed that it contained the oxide of a new element, which he was unable to isolate; he proposed the name Menacchanine. M. H. KLAPROTH (1785) independently obtained a new oxide from a German mineral called *schorl*, and two years later showed it to be identical with Gregor's material. However, Klaproth's suggested name 'titanium' was preferred to Gregor's.

Gregor also published sermons and pamphlets. His later years were clouded by severe ill health.

Dictionary of National Biography.
Annals of Philosophy, **11**, 112, 1818.

                                                               W V F

GREGORY, DAVID Born at Aberdeen, Scotland, 24 June 1661; died Maidenhead, Berkshire, England, 10 October 1708. Mathematician.

The nephew of James GREGORY, David Gregory was made professor at Edinburgh in 1684, and, at the recommendation of NEWTON and J. FLAMSTEED (with whom he later fell out) Savilian Professor of Astronomy at Oxford in 1691. In 1692 he was elected FRS. His *Exercitatio Geometria de Dimensione Figurarum* (1684) is based on his uncle's notes, and contains, *inter alia*, an extension of the method of quadrature by infinite series. The closing remarks of his work (1695) on optics suggests the idea of achromatic lenses made from two different media (see J. DOLLOND); his model was the eye. Gregory is remembered less for original work than for his part in spreading the doctrines of Newtonian physics, on which he was one of the first to lecture publicly; in 1702 he published his *Astrono-*

miae Physicae et Geometricae Elementa, the first textbook on gravitational principles.

C. Hutton, *A Mathematical and Philosophical Dictionary.* 1795.
Dictionary of National Biography.
Dictionary of Scientific Biography.

                                                               R P L

GREGORY or **GREGORIE, JAMES** Born at Drumoak, near Aberdeen, Scotland, November 1638; died Edinburgh, October 1675. A leading contributor to the discovery of the differential and integral calculus.

After graduating from Marischal College, Aberdeen, Gregory wrote the *Optica Promota* in 1663; this included a description of the first plausible reflecting telescope, and also the suggestion that the transits of Mercury and Venus be used for calculating the distance of the Sun. He lived in Italy from 1664 to 1668, and there began his mathematical work. He became professor of mathematics at St Andrew's University, Scotland, in 1668, and was appointed to the first chair of mathematics at Edinburgh University in 1674. He died suddenly at the height of his career.

While in Italy he wrote the *Vera Quadratura,* which included basic ideas of functionality, convergence, and the distinction between algebraic and transcendental functions. He attempted to prove the transcendence of π and e; observed the relation between circular and hyperbolic functions; and discussed elliptic functions. Appended to this work was the *Geometricae Pars Universalis,* which contained the earliest proof of the fundamental theorem of calculus (1667). His *Exercitationes Geometricae* (1668) supplied a geometrical proof of Mercator's series for log $(1 + x)$ and demonstrated the logarithmic properties of the rhumb line.

His correspondence with John Collins (1625–83) in 1670–1 shows him to have made discoveries in analysis well ahead of his contemporaries, even including NEWTON. Among these were the formulae known as the binomial series, Newton's interpolation formula, and the series discovered by Brook TAYLOR.

H. W. Turnbull (Ed.), *James Gregory Tercentenary Memorial Volume.* 1939.
Dictionary of National Biography.

                                                               J M D

GREW, NEHEMIAH Born in Warwickshire, England, 1641; died London, 25 March 1712. Plant anatomist and physician.

Nehemiah was the only son of Rev. Obadiah Grew, a parliamentary divine, but his activities were apparently little affected by the troublous times in which he lived. He was educated at Pembroke Hall, Cambridge, graduating in 1661, and then at the University of Leiden, where he studied medicine and received the degree of MD in 1671. He settled in London and in 1680 was admitted to Honorary Fellowship of the College of Physicians. Grew records that his interest in plant life arose from his conception that plants and animals must possess similar structures, as they are both 'Contrivances of the same Wisdom'. He wrote an essay on this theme which was read to the Fellows of the Royal Society. It was approved, and Grew was elected FRS in 1671. On the death of Henry

Oldenburg (*c.*1615–77), Grew (with Robert HOOKE) became Secretary of the Royal Society and edited the *Philosophical Transactions* for a year. He resigned in 1679, probably because of the demands of his prospering medical practice, but he drew up a catalogue of the specimens in the Society's museum. This was published in 1681 under the title *Musaeum Regalis Societatis*, and had appended *The Comparative Anatomy of Stomachs and Guts Begun*, being several lectures read before the Royal Society in 1667. Grew's studies on comparative anatomy – he himself introduced the term in 1665 – brought a revival to botany, which had been in decline. He is deservedly best known for his work (1682) entitled *The Anatomy of Plants*, which was accompanied by numerous excellent engravings. The first three parts were revised versions of earlier works: *The Anatomy of Vegetables Begun*, *The Anatomy of Roots*, and *The Comparative Anatomy of Trunks*. The fourth part, dedicated to Robert BOYLE, was entitled *The Anatomy of Leaves, Flowers, Fruits and Seeds*. He used the term 'parenchyma' to describe soft tissues, which he considered sponge-like with interwoven fibres. He noted the tubular nature of the vascular tissue, accounting correctly for its different distribution in roots and stems. He speculated, but never tested by experiment, that flowering plants exhibit sexuality and that their sexual organs are borne in the flowers. Stamens he curiously called the 'attire' and was uncertain of their primary purpose. Grew's piety is particularly evident in his last work, *Cosmologia Sacra* (1701), which was chiefly composed 'to demonstrate the truth and excellence of the sacred writings'. It is recorded by his contemporary John Shower that 'he was grave and serious in his conversation; yet affable and courteous'.

Philosophical Transactions of the Royal Society, 6, 660, 1671.
Dictionary of National Biography.
W. Carruthers, *Journal of the Royal Microscopical Society*, **129**, 129, 1902.
Dictionary of Scientific Biography.

A P G

GRIESS, PETER JOHANN Born at Kirchhosbach, near Cassel, Germany, 6 September 1829; died (on holiday) Bournemouth, England, 30 August 1888. Industrial chemist; discovered diazonium salts and azo dyestuffs.

Griess came of a farming family, which, although not wealthy, supported him through a long student career at the Kassel *Technische Hochschule* and the Universities of Jena and Marburg; this was interrupted by military service, rustication for rowdy behaviour, and a period in a tar distillery. In 1858 A. W. HOFMANN visited Marburg and chose Griess to be his assistant in the Royal College of Chemistry, London. Four years later he went to Allsopp's brewery at Burton-on-Trent as a chemist, and remained there for the rest of his life. He married at the age of forty, and left several children.

The firm of Allsopp allowed Griess ample freedom to pursue his own interests in research matters. While still at Marburg he had discovered the important class of diazonium salts, made by the action of cold nitrous acid on aromatic amines. He continued the study of the chemistry of these reactive substances both in London and Burton-

on-Trent, and in 1861–2 discovered their reactions with amines and phenols to give a new class of colouring matters, the azo dyestuffs. This was perhaps the greatest single discovery ever made in dyestuffs chemistry, but Griess took little part in the development of the dyestuffs industry, although he later patented (1884) the first direct cotton dyes (i.e. dyes needing no mordant).

He also discovered choline in hops; studied the reactions between amines and sugars; and published a number of other papers on topics connected with his work at the brewery, but none of these was of major importance.

E. Fischer, *Berichte der deutschen Chemischen Gesellschaft*, 24, 1007R, 1891. (Portrait.)
Chemistry and Industry, **77**, 616, 1958. (Portrait.)
Journal of Chemical Education, 35, 187, 1958. (Portrait.)
Dictionary of National Biography (Missing Persons). 1993.

W V F

GRIGNARD, FRANÇOIS AUGUSTE VICTOR Born at Cherbourg, France, 6 May 1871; died Lyons, 13 December 1935. Discovered the versatile organomagnesium compounds which bear his name.

Grignard, whose father was a sailmaker, went to the University of Lyons with the intention of becoming a teacher of mathematics. He was later persuaded to study organic chemistry, and when he began research was advised by P. A. Barbier (1848–1922) to investigate organomagnesium compounds. Magnesium was soon found to react with many organic halides in ether solution, to give compounds, stable in solution, which are now known as Grignard reagents. These reagents have immense potentialities for organic and organometallic syntheses, which are even now not exhausted, and Grignard spent much of the rest of his career working out some of the implications of his discovery. He also worked on organic compounds of aluminium and mercury, and on terpenes.

His tenure of a chair at Nancy, which began in 1909, was interrupted by the First World War, during which he worked on several chemical projects for the French Government. In 1919 he returned to his old university, Lyons, on the retirement of Barbier, and remained there until his death. In his later years he was busy with his great *Traité de Chimie Organique*, whose volumes began to appear in 1935, but which had to be completed by other hands.

Among other honours, he shared the Nobel prize for chemistry in 1912 with Paul SABATIER, and was elected in 1926 to the *Académie des Sciences*.

Bulletin de la Société Chimique de France, 3, 1433, 1936.
Journal of the Chemical Society, 171, 1937. (Portrait.)
Journal of Chemical Education, 27, 476, 1950. (Portraits.)
E. Farber (Ed.), *Great Chemists*. 1961. (Portrait.)
Dictionary of Scientific Biography.
Tyler Wasson (Ed.), *Nobel Prize Winners*. 1987. (Portrait.)

W V F

GRIMALDI, FRANCESCO MARIA Born at Bologna, Italy, 2 April 1618; died there, 28 December 1663. Discoverer of the diffraction of light.

Grimaldi entered the Society of Jesus at the early

age of 14 and thereafter led the quiet life of a Jesuit scholar and teacher. He had his first scholastic education at his Order's houses at Parma, Ferrara and Bologna, to which city he returned in 1637 to remain for the rest of his life. In 1645 he completed his theological studies and in 1648 took over the chair of mathematics at the Society's *Collegio di Bologna*, where for some years he had already taught rhetoric, at the same time acting as assistant to Father Giovanni Riccioli (1598–1671), who occupied the chair of astronomy at the college. During this period Riccioli was engaged in the long series of researches in astronomy which he published in his *Almagestum novum* in 1651. Grimaldi, among other things, helped with geodetical measurements; with the determination of the length of the seconds pendulum; with the verification of GALILEO's laws of falling bodies; and with observations of the Moon. Grimaldi drew a detailed map of the Moon (*Almagestum novum* I, 204) from which all later selenographic terminology stems.

This experience made Grimaldi a good experimental scientist and prepared him for his own researches, which led to two important discoveries. In physiology Grimaldi was the first to observe the weak sounds produced by contracting muscles, and in physics he is remembered for his fundamental experiments in optics. In one of these Grimaldi let sunlight into a dark room through a narrow hole and placed in the path of the rays a diaphragm with another narrow hole. When these fell on a white screen the illuminated part of the latter proved to be larger than was to be expected from the law of the rectilinear propagation of light in geometrical optics. In another experiment he placed thin, opaque objects in the rays and observed bright lines on the screen inside the geometric shadow. This proved that 'Light is propagated or diffused not only directly, by refraction, and by reflection, but also in still a fourth way – by diffraction'. These discoveries were set forth in a copious volume published posthumously under the title *Physico-mathesis de lumine* (Bologna, 1665), in which Grimaldi also tried to establish a theory of light and colours compatible with the new phenomenon. He was here led to regard light not as an accidental quality but as a substantial entity with certain undulatory properties. The book was known to NEWTON, who repeated the experiments in a quantitative way and confirmed Grimaldi's discovery, although he did not realize the strength of his proofs that neither reflection nor refraction is able to explain the phenomenon.

V. Ronchi, *Histoire de la lumière*. 1956.

V. Busacchi, 'F. M. Grimaldi', *Actes du VIIIe*
Congrès International d'Histoire des Sciences,
Florence-Milan. 1958.

W. F. Magie, *Source Book of Physics*. 1935.

Dictionary of Scientific Biography.

O P

GROSSETESTE, ROBERT Born at Stradbrook, Suffolk, England, *c*.1168; died Buckden, Buckinghamshire, 9 October 1253. A great statesman and philosopher, who caused many English Franciscans to study mathematics and natural philosophy.

Born of humble parents, Robert Grosseteste was educated probably at Lincoln, and certainly at

Oxford. After being a member of the household of William de Vere, it is likely that he taught at Oxford before 1209 and took his mastership in theology there, or at Paris. For a period of perhaps six years, ending in 1221, he was Master of the Oxford schools, (i.e. Chancellor). After holding several ecclesiastical appointments, he lectured in theology to the Franciscans, newly arrived in Oxford. He left there only on being appointed in 1235 to the See of Lincoln, where he died in office.

Grosseteste's commentary on ARISTOTLE's *Posterior Analytics* was one of the earliest and most influential medieval commentaries on this work. He also wrote a commentary on Aristotle's *Physics*. Original works include a treatise on the calendar, which, like his *Compendium Spherae*, discussed the possibility of its reform. The latter work is related to the famous treatise on the sphere by Sacrobosco (otherwise John Holywood, d. 1256), but the exact connection has not yet been established. Grosseteste's work contains the erroneous doctrine of the trepidation of the equinoxes, taken from Islamic astronomy. Other Islamic ideas – in addition, of course, to those of PTOLEMY – were evident in his writings on comets and on the generation of stars.

Even allowing for the apocryphal nature of many of the texts ascribed to him, Grosseteste was a prolific author. Apart from commentaries on Scripture and translation of Greek works and commentaries, he wrote at length on sound, heat, and on optics or 'perspective'. In particular he wrote on the subject of the rainbow. The study of light was of more than physical interest for Grosseteste. Following Augustine, he held that physical light was analogous to that spiritual light by which the mind received certain knowledge of unchanging forms, or essences. He accepted the Aristotelian distinction between the fact (*quia*) and the reason for the fact (*propter quid*), and argued that in natural philosophy such reasons could be provided only in terms of mathematics and, ultimately, on the fundamental corporeal substance, namely light. Light was the first form to be created in prime matter. It propagated itself from a point into a sphere, giving rise to both spatial dimensions and to everything contained therein, all in accordance with immanent natural laws. Optics was thus, for him, the fundamental science. If this metaphysics of light may appear to have had no lasting importance, it was nevertheless associated with a theory of experimental method which, through Roger BACON, passed into the Western scientific tradition.

A. C. Crombie, *Robert Grosseteste and the Origins of Experimental Science*. 1953. (Portrait.)

D. A. Callus (Ed.), *Robert Grosseteste*. 1955.

Dictionary of National Biography.

Dictionary of Scientific Biography.

J D N

GROVE, SIR WILLIAM ROBERT Born in Swansea, Wales, 11 July 1811; died London, 1 August 1896. Electrochemist.

After graduating at Oxford (1832) Grove embarked on a legal career, becoming a barrister in 1835. Ill health led him to abandon law for science, with a particular interest in the rapidly developing field of electrochemistry. This resulted in the development of an improved (Zn/Pt) cell, which was widely adopted. R. W. BUNSEN improved it by replacing the platinum with carbon. This cell is not to be confused with his more important 'gas battery', in effect the first fuel cell (1842). This consisted of two platinum strips, the lower halves dipping into dilute sulphuric acid, the upper in gaseous oxygen and hydrogen respectively.

From 1841 to 1846 Grove was professor of experimental philosophy at the London Institution. In later life he reverted to legal practice – especially patent infringement – and became a QC in 1853. In this capacity he was a member of the legal team which in a sensational trial unsuccessfully defended William Palmer, the notorious 'Rugeley Poisoner' in 1856.

Dictionary of National Biography.
Dictionary of Scientific Biography.
Nature, 54, 393, 1896.
Journal of the Royal Institute of Chemistry, 85, 291, 1961.

T I W

GUERICKE, OTTO VON

GUERICKE, OTTO VON Born at Magdeburg, Saxony, Germany, 20 November 1602; died Hamburg, 11 May, 1686. Inventor of the vacuum pump.

From 1617 to 1625 Guericke studied at Leipzig, Helmstadt and Jena, completing his studies in jurisprudence at Leiden where he also occupied himself much with mathematics, mechanics, and fortifications. In 1646 he was elected one of the four burgomasters of Magdeburg for his services to that town during its siege by Tilly (1631). But he found time from his official occupations to pursue his scientific researches first published in his famous New Experiments concerning Empty Space (1672). Most of the researches described in that book had been carried out many years previously, some having been published already by Kaspar Schott (1608–66) in 1657 and 1664. Guericke was finally released from his position as burgomaster in 1678. He died in the home of his son in Hamburg.

His first attempt to settle the ancient question of the existence of empty space was made with a barrel filled with water which he attempted to evacuate with a pump. But finding that the air penetrated through the walls of the barrel he tried instead an experiment on a stout metal sphere connected to a pump by a pipe containing a stopcock. His success in evacuating the air from the sphere resulted in a number of striking demonstrations of atmospheric pressure, especially the famous experiment carried out before the Reichstag at Regensburg on 8 May 1654, in which sixteen horses were unable to separate the two halves of an evacuated hollow sphere. He also constructed a water barometer.

Guericke performed a number of famous experiments to show the properties of a vacuum, including the muffling of a bell and the extinguishing of flames. He also performed various experiments to demonstrate the elasticity of air. He carried out electrical experiments using a rotating sphere of sulphur as an electrical machine, noting that objects attracted to the sulphur when it was rubbed were repelled once they had touched it. In magnetism, he made the interesting observation that iron hammered in a north-south direction became magnetized (see W. GILBERT).

F. W. Hoffmann, Otto von Guericke. 1874.

P. Lenard, Great Men of Science. 1933. (Portrait.)
Alfons Kauffeld, Otto von Guericke. 1968.
Dictionary of Scientific Biography.

J W H

GUILLAUME, CHARLES EDOUARD

GUILLAUME, CHARLES EDOUARD Born at Fleurier, Switzerland, 15 February 1861; died Sèvres, near Paris, 13 June 1938. Physicist, known for his work on alloys of iron and nickel.

Guillaume's father was a watchmaker, and his early interest was in this field. He attended school at Neuchâtel and in 1878 entered Zürich Polytechnic; on completing his course he joined the Army as an artillery officer. In 1883 he obtained the degree of DPhil., and entered the Bureau International des Poids et Mesures. His main work was, at first, concerned with thermometry, and in 1889 he published his Traité Pratique de la Thermométrie de Précision, which became a standard work for metrologists. His comparative work on the thermal expansion of standards of length led him to the investigation of various alloys. In 1896 he found that the thermal expansion of a steel alloy containing about 30 per cent nickel was only half that of pure iron. It was this discovery that initiated his research on ferronickels, pursued with the help of the Imphy steelworks, that led to the discovery of the alloy invar, having an extremely small coefficient of expansion. This is used in surveyors' tapes, clock pendulums, and various accurate instruments. Another alloy containing about 40 per cent nickel was found to expand at about the same rate as glass. It is called platinite, and is commonly used where a metal has to be sealed into glass. In 1915 Guillaume became Director of the Bureau International des Poids et Mesures, and retained this post until his retirement in 1936. In 1920 he received the Nobel prize for his work on ferronickels.

Proceedings of the Physical Society, **I**, 971. 1938.
Nature, **142**, 322. 1938.
Les Prix Nobel en 1919–20. 1922. (Portrait.)
Robert L. Weber, Pioneers of Science: Nobel Prize Winners in Physics. 1980. (Portrait.)
Tyler Wasson (Ed.), Nobel Prize Winners. 1987. (Portrait.)

B B K

GUINAND, PIERRE LOUIS

GUINAND, PIERRE LOUIS Born at Brenets, Switzerland, c.1744; died there, 1824. Inventor of an improved method of making optical glass.

Guinand began his career as a maker of clock cases. In addition he cast bells for clocks and it was while thus engaged that he made an important discovery in a quite different field. He had become interested in the making of optical glass after examining an English telescope and noting the superiority of its lenses over those he had previously seen. In 1775 he built a furnace, and carried out some experiments in glass-making, but had little success. The main problems in the making of fine-quality optical glass were to reduce distortion and to eliminate air bubbles. These were interrelated: the stirring necessary to produce a homogeneous melt introduced air bubbles which would not rise to the surface because of the viscosity. Just after 1800 Guinand related his knowledge of bell-founding to his new problem. Homogeneity of the molten material, also critical in bell-founding, was ensured by a continuous stirring process, using a vertical hollow cylindrical stirrer of fireclay; this was an outstanding success and was later widely adopted.

In 1805 Guinand was invited to move to Bavaria to make lenses for J. von Utzschneider (1763–1840), the German manufacturer. There he worked with J. von FRAUNHOFER, who was the manager of the firm at the time. Together they made improvements in the stirring process which remained a secret until well after Guinand's death. In 1814 he returned to Switzerland, where he died in 1824.

H. C. King, *The History of the Telescope*. 1955.

Charles Singer, E. J. Holmyard, A. R. Hall and Trevor I. Williams (Eds), *A History of Technology*, vol. 4. 1958.

Biographie Générale. 1859.

N H

GULDBERG, CATO MAXIMILIAN Born at Christiania (Oslo), Norway, 11 August 1836; died there, 14 January 1902. Known for his work with P. WAAGE on the Law of Mass Action.

Guldberg was first a teacher at the Royal Military School (1860), then professor of applied mathematics in the Royal Military Academy at Christiania (1862). He entered the university in that city as a lecturer (1867), and became professor of applied mathematics in 1869.

He wrote several papers on what is now called chemical thermodynamics, including (1870) a discussion of the relationship between lowering of vapour pressure and depression of freezing point. Guldberg's Law (1890) relates critical temperature to boiling-point on the absolute scale; it was discovered independently by P. A. Guye (1862–1922). He also wrote a work entitled *Études sur les mouvements de l'Atmosphère* (with H. Mohn) 1876, but is best known for the Law of Mass Action, resulting from work performed in collaboration with Peter Waage, his brother-in-law.

According to their first paper (1864), Guldberg and Waage were led to study chemical equilibrium by the work of M. BERTHELOT and L. P. de Gilles (1832–63), who had given a mathematical expression for the velocity of the forward reaction between alcohol and acid to give ester plus water (1862). Guldberg and Waage were able to extend this work to cover both forward and reverse reactions, and cited some 300 quantitative experiments as evidence of the manner in which mass, concentration and temperature affected reaction rates.

The original work was in Norwegian and despite a later more finished attempt in French (1867), their work was little known at first. Consequently the Law, foreshadowed by C. F. WENZEL in 1777 and L. F. Wilhelmy (1812–64) in 1850 was independently discovered by A. G. Vernon HARCOURT and W. Esson (1839–1916) at Oxford (1864–66).

J. R. Partington, *A History of Chemistry*, vol. 4. 1964. (Portrait.)

Grande Larousse Encyclopédique, vol. 5. 1962. (Portrait.)

F. W. Ostwald (Ed.), *Klassiker der exacten Wissenschaften*, No. 104, 1889, and No. 139, 1903.

E. W. Lund, *Journal of Chemical Education*, **42**, 548, 1965.

G R T

GULLSTRAND, ALLVAR Born at Landskrona, Sweden, 5 June 1862; died Uppsala, 30 August 1930. Ophthalmologist.

Gullstrand, the son of a physician, studied medicine at the universities of Uppsala, Vienna and Stockholm, and obtained his doctorate of medicine in 1890. When aged 32 he was appointed professor of ophthalmology at Uppsala, and in 1913 was given the chair of physiology and physical optics, which he held until 1927.

Gullstrand made many notable contributions to ophthalmology and in 1911 he was awarded a Nobel prize for medicine 'for work on the diffraction of light by lenses as applied to the eye'. His most notable achievement was the discovery of intracapsular accommodation. H. L. F. von HELMHOLTZ had made significant contributions to the theory of the accommodation of the eye by showing that the refractive power of the lens is altered by changes in its surface curvature, changes which are controlled by the ciliary muscles. But these studies were based on the view that the eye was an entirely homogenous medium and it was Gullstrand who showed that this was not so. He demonstrated that the refractive power is only about two-thirds dependent on the surface curvature and that the remaining third is due to other factors, which he called the 'intracapsular mechanism of accommodation'.

Gullstrand's work extended into many areas. For example, he improved methods for estimating astigmatism and for locating paralysed muscles (in 1889 he introduced a photographic method for locating the paralysed ocular muscle). He also introduced spherical lenses for corrective glasses after cataract operations. Such successes were in part due to his skill as an experimenter and as an inventor of many instruments. His best-known diagnostic instrument is the slit-lamp, which he first demonstrated in 1911. The lamp supplies a thin beam of light on the area to be examined, the rest of the eye being in darkness. With the aid of the corneal microscope, which allows relatively high magnifications, parts of the eye can be closely examined. This led to many advances in knowledge of the structure of the eye in both normal and diseased conditions.

Gullstrand's influence also stemmed from his large number of publications, such as his *Allgemeine theorie der monochromatischen aberrationen* (1900).

S. Lindroth (Ed.), *Swedish Men of Science, 1650–1950*. 1952.

C. Snyder, 'Allvar Gullstrand', *Archives of Ophthalmology*, **68** (I), 139, 1962. (Portrait.)

Dictionary of Scientific Biography.

Tyler Wasson (Ed.) *Nobel Prize Winners*. 1987. (Portrait.)

J K C

GUTENBERG, JOHANN Born in Mainz, Rhineland-Palatinate (now Germany), between 1395 and 1400; died 3 February 1468. Generally accepted as the inventor of printing in Europe from movable types.

Gutenberg was born Gensfleich, but assumed his mother's family name; he was the third child of a patrician family of Mainz. He learned the trade of a goldsmith in that city, but while still a young man his family was exiled (1428) after strife between the patricians and the popular factions of the city council and guilds. Between 1430 and 1444 he is known to have been in Strasbourg. His experiments into printing began during this period, and by 1450 he had a printing plant. Two years later he took Johann Fust (c.1400–66) into partnership, and also employed Peter Schoeffer (c.1425–1502). Fust sued Gutenberg for 2,000 guilders, a figure representing loans and interest previously made to him. The court found against Gutenberg and Fust thereby acquired Gutenberg's materials and set up in partnership with Schoeffer. Under these circumstances provenance of printed works of this period is very difficult, especially since there is no printed work bearing Gutenberg's name. The famous '42-line Bible' which left the press of Fust and Schoeffer in 1457 was in all probability begun by Gutenberg; while the 31-line Indulgences of 1454, the 'Paris Donatus', and the 'Fragment of the World Judgement' were almost certainly the work of his press. The '36-line Bible' and the *Catholicon*, both printed about 1460, are strongly believed to be Gutenberg's work. Apart from the internal evidence of the printed works themselves, the strongest evidence for assigning the invention of printing to Gutenberg (nowhere proven beyond possibility of error) is among the writings of contemporaries,

where he is often so described, and in the fact that his most serious rivals for the title, Fust and Schoeffer, never themselves made such a claim.

The mid-fifteenth century was ready for the introduction of printing. Printing from blocks (one block to a page) incorporating illustrations and text had appeared earlier in the century, having been practised in the Far East (China, Japan, Korea) from the 14th century. Bookbinders used single-letter punches either alone or clamped together to make words for the purpose of blind stamping on leather. An ink suitable for printing was available, as was an abundant supply of paper. An alloy from which types might be cast was also in use. All that was required was the incorporation of these elements into a process which also involved individual types whose shanks were so accurately squared off as to clamp uniformly together, and a device for holding a large area or series of areas of assembled types perfectly rigid and flat. There is the strongest evidence that it was Johann Gutenberg who had the immense skill and vision to marshal all into an invention of the most fundamental importance in the history of Europe and of the world.

A. Ruppel, *J. Gutenberg*. 1947.

D. C. McMurtrie, *The Book*. 1943.

N H

HABER, FRITZ Born at Breslau (Wroclaw), Silesia, 9 December 1868; died Basle, Switzerland, 29 January 1934. Synthesized ammonia from the elements.

Fritz Haber was the only son of a prosperous drysalter, and after an indifferent university career took his doctorate in chemistry in 1891. He taught himself the then new subject of physical chemistry, and for the rest of his life his scientific work centred on that discipline. He became *Assistent* at the *Technische Hochschule* of Karlsruhe in 1894, where his first investigations concerned pyrolysis. Haber wrote a textbook on electrochemistry, and in 1905 published *Thermodynamik technischer Gasreaktionen.*

Sir William CROOKES had warned that the exhaustion of the Chilean nitrate deposits would be followed by hunger, since there would be insufficient nitrogenous fertilizers to raise crop yields and so feed the growing world population. Haber was aware of the work then being done to fix nitrogen by the cyanamide and the arc processes; he was familiar with metal nitrides and in 1904 turned to the determination of the ammonia equilibrium. He found that the concentration of ammonia was very low. Independently of him, W. H. NERNST was also studying this problem and was indeed the first to apply considerable pressure to the gases, but again the yields were negligible. Haber, nevertheless, persisted, and after two years' work, 1907–9, was able to demonstrate that the reaction $N_2 + 3H_2 \leftrightarrow 2NH_3$ was industrially practicable at a pressure of 150 to 200 atm and with a suitable catalyst, first osmium and later uranium. The apparatus devised by Haber and R. Le Rossignol pumped the gas mixture continuously through the converter, whence ammonia was withdrawn, while the unreacted gases were recirculated. This system has remained unchanged in its essentials to the present day. By 1913 C. BOSCH had translated the laboratory equipment to the industrial scale, and the Haber-Bosch process had solved the nitrogen problem.

Haber held the chair of physical chemistry at Karlsruhe from 1906 to 1911, when he accepted the post of director of the newly formed *Kaiser Wilhelm Institut für Physikalische Chemie & Electrochemie* at Dahlem on the outskirts of Berlin. The Institute was opened in 1912, and for the next two years he occupied himself with the application of the quantum theory of Max PLANCK to chemistry.

The outbreak of the Great War transformed Haber's life and gave full scope to his organizing ability. The work of the Institute was entirely subordinated to Germany's military needs: he became chief of the country's chemical warfare service, and as such directed the introduction of poison gases as well as the development of defensive measures, notably gas masks. He was also concerned with the supply and allocation of essential raw materials for the war effort. Defeat in 1918 came as a bitter blow to him, and his health suffered.

During the 1920s he devoted his energies principally to the Institute. It was enlarged, and Haber attracted many scientists, including a high proportion of foreigners, who were later to enrich the physical sciences. The research workers met fortnightly for discussions at which Haber's guidance and inspiration gave new meaning to the German tradition of scientific scholarship. He took an active part in several major investigations, the most spectacular being the search for gold in the sea. He eventually convinced himself that the amounts were too small for commercial extraction, and so this attempt to pay off Germany's reparations failed. More satisfying were the results of his later studies on pyrolysis and autoxidation.

Haber's work at the Institute, as well as his many other academic activities, ended abruptly in 1933. As a patriotic German he could not reconcile himself to the life of a second-class Jewish citizen. In a dignified letter to the Nazi Minister of Education he resigned his post and went into exile. He was offered the hospitality of the Cavendish Laboratory and spent the last few months of his life in Cambridge.

Haber's outstanding achievements were recognized by the chemistry Nobel prize for 1918, awarded in 1919. He was a Rumford Medallist of the Royal Society and an honorary fellow of the Chemical Society of London.

F. Haber, *Fünf Vorträge.* 1924.
F. Haber, *Aus Leben und Beruf.* 1927.
J. E. Coates, *Journal of the Chemical Society*, 1642, 1939.
E. Farber (Ed.), *Great Chemists.* 1969. (Portrait.)
M. Goran, *The Story of Fritz Haber.* 1967.
L. F. Haber, *Endeavour*, **27**, 150, 1968 (Portrait.); *The Poisonous Cloud.* 1986. (Portrait.)
Tyler Wasson, (Ed.), *Nobel Prize Winners.* 1987. (Portrait.)

L F H

HADFIELD, SIR ROBERT ABBOTT Born at Attercliffe, Yorkshire, England, 28 November 1858; died Kingston, Surrey, 30 September 1940. Metallurgist and industrialist.

Sir Robert Hadfield was the son of a Sheffield steel manufacturer, a pioneer of steel casting in Britain. Robert was educated at the Collegiate School, Sheffield, and took an early interest in science. He chose to enter the steel industry rather than go to university, and joined the family business. At 24 he had to take over the firm because of his father's ill health, and in 1888, when his father died, a limited company was formed of which he was chairman and managing director.

His most notable work was on the development of manganese steel, for which the firm took out a patent in 1883. Such steels had been previously made, for example by R. F. MUSHET, but although hard they were too brittle. Hadfield overcame this by increasing the manganese proportion to one-eighth. The remarkable qualities of this tough steel were seen by Hadfield to be of great significance and prompted a lengthy series of researches. He next worked on silicon alloys, though it was not until Sir William Barrett (1844–1925) – professor of physics at the Royal College of Science, Dublin – combined with him (1899) that the important magnetic properties of this alloy were recognized. Both these steels were developed commercially by his firm. Hadfield also worked on steel containing other additives and his firm extensively produced armour-piercing and heat-resisting steels, though details of the composition and processes were not disclosed.

He was keenly interested in the history of metals and metalworking, both recent and ancient, and he was a generous supporter of education in his native city. He was knighted in 1908; elected FRS in 1909; and created baronet in 1917.

Obituary Notices of Fellows of the Royal Society.
    1941. (Portrait.)
Dictionary of National Biography.
C. S. Smith (Ed.). *The Sorby Centennial
    Symposium on the History of Metallurgy.* 1965.
                                                    N H

HADLEY, JOHN Born 16 April 1682; died East Barnet, near London, 14 February 1744. Mathematical instrument maker.

John Hadley was the son of a High Sheriff of Hertfordshire. He was elected FRS in 1717, and there is evidence that he knew considerably more mathematics than was usual in those without a university training. His first important achievement was to produce, through the use of new grinding techniques for both mirrors and lenses, a large reflecting telescope of unusually high quality (f/12; aperture 6 inches.) S. Molyneux (1689–1728) and James BRADLEY were only too glad to be schooled in these techniques. The reflector, made in 1721, was tested and praised by both Bradley and Edmond HALLEY.

In 1730 Hadley designed the 'reflecting quadrant' (ancestor of the modern sextant) independently of NEWTON, who described to Halley exactly the same modification of the octant of Robert HOOKE, and independently of Thomas Godfrey (1704–49) of Pennsylvania, who arrived at precisely the same design later the same year. A pamphlet war over the question of priority ensued. In fact, there were at least six different designs of reflecting quadrant currently on sale and the crucial step to the new form was not very great. The convenience for use on board ship of Hadley's portable instrument was nevertheless of the first importance to navigators, and it was sold in large numbers both in England and abroad until the last years of the nineteenth century. The names 'octant'

and 'quadrant' were applied almost indifferently to it, the former referring to the actual length of the scale, the latter referring to the maximum measurable angle. It was Captain John Campbell (*c.*1720–90) who first suggested extending this arc to 120 degrees, in the sextant.

In 1732 Hadley fitted an ordinary Davis quadrant with a bubble-level, for use when the horizon was not visible. Later he added this refinement to his own instrument, which can be regarded as the ancestor of the 'bubble sextant' still used in air navigation.

Hadley was a Vice-President of the Royal Society. Some of his instruments are exhibited in the Science Museum, London.

E. G. R. Taylor, *The Mathematical Practitioners of
    Hanoverian England.* 1966. (Portrait.)
H. C. King, *The History of the Telescope.* 1955.
Dictionary of National Biography.
                                                    J D N

HAECKEL, ERNST HEINRICH Born at Potsdam, Germany, 16 February 1834; died Jena, Saxony, 8 August 1919. Propounder of the 'biogenetic law' and the 'gastraea' theory.

Haeckel was intended for the medical profession, and studied medicine and science at Würtzburg, Vienna, and Berlin, graduating in 1857. He was not interested in medical practice, and in 1862 became a professor of comparative anatomy and Director of the Zoological Institute of the University of Jena, where he spent the rest of his life; after 1865 as professor of zoology. He had wide interests in zoology and showed immense industry in pursuing them, completing many elaborate systematic and descriptive monographs on various invertebrate groups. He adopted the views of Charles DARWIN on evolution, and was the main instrument of their dissemination and ultimate acceptance by German zoologists, and by a wider public through his semi-popular writings.

Haeckel's researches on embryology produced the 'biogenetic law' or theory of recapitulation, stating that ontogeny repeats phylogeny; it was widely accepted, but has since been much criticized – W. Garstang (1868–1949) pointed out that ontogeny does not recapitulate phylogeny but creates it. Haeckel followed this with an attempted genealogical tree of the animal kingdom showing the descent and relationship of the different types. He thought that all animals pass through a gastrula stage in their development, and traced the metazoa back to a common ancestor, a hypothetical 'gastraea'. His enthusiasm for his theories led him into attempts at forcing observed facts to fit into his schemes of evolution, rather than allowing the facts to test and if necessary modify them; nature, however, refuses to conform to neat universal patterns. Haeckel's wanderings into psychology led him to put forward peculiar views such as those about the 'cell-soul' of protozoa which although unacceptable might make some sense if translated into terms of molecular biology – but nebulous philosophical speculations were fashionable in his time. Haeckel's literary production, both scientific and popular, was enormous; he was also an accomplished artist, and sometimes allowed his artistic skill to replace scientific accuracy in the illustration of his monographs.

W. May, *Ernst Haeckel.* 1909.

E. Nordenskiöld, *History of Biology*. 1928. (Portrait.)

E. W. MacBride, *Nature*, **133**, 198, 1934.

Dictionary of Scientific Biography.

L H M

HAHN, OTTO Born in Frankfurt-am-Main, Hessen, Germany, 8 March 1879; died Göttingen, 28 July 1968. Pioneer in radiochemistry and a co-discoverer of nuclear fission.

Hahn was the youngest son of a glazier. Encouraged by his parents to prepare for a career in architecture he stayed at the local *Realschule* until he was 19, his elder brothers having entered the family business. Like F. A. KEKULÉ before him, however, his architectural aspirations became displaced by an increased liking for chemistry. Accordingly he entered the University of Marburg, to pursue chemical studies under E. C. T. Zincke (1843–1928). These concluded with a piece of research on the bromine derivatives of *iso*-eugenol.

Following a year's military service, Hahn returned to Marburg to become Zincke's lecture-assistant, a post that seemed to be a good stepping-stone to the German chemical industry which was now his goal. However, events took a quite different turn in 1904. Zincke was informed that the firm of Kalle & Co. had a vacancy for a chemist proficient in French and English. He suggested that Hahn might be suitable, following a short period abroad, and arranged for him to spend six months with Sir William RAMSAY at University College, London. It was in this way that he began his acquaintance with the new subject of radiochemistry, to which he was to make such outstanding contributions.

Hahn's first task was to extract the traces of radium from a sample of an impure barium salt, using the fractional crystallization method of Marie CURIE. As the fractions became progressively richer in radium it began to be obvious that another radioactive substance was present as well, and the new 'element' was named 'radiothorium'. This process changed the direction of Hahn's career once more. Determined now to pursue academic research in radiochemistry he was recommended by Ramsay to Emil FISCHER, at the University of Berlin. But further overseas experience was first necessary, and in 1905 Hahn joined the group led by RUTHERFORD at Montreal. Again rapid success followed. Others had suggested that radioactive materials could be characterized by their α-particle emissions and Rutherford invited Hahn to examine the α-radiation from his own sample of 'radiothorium', as well as other sources. Within a short time, Hahn had identified two further new radioelements: 'thorium-C' and 'radio-actinium'.

The following year he returned to Germany. His work in Berlin began in a converted woodworking shop in the basement, no radiochemistry laboratory being in existence. Shortly afterwards he was joined by a young theoretical physicist, Lise MEITNER, who by virtue of her sex was denied access to the all-male laboratories upstairs. Thus began 30 years of fruitful scientific collaboration, Hahn contributing his skills from chemistry, Meitner hers from physics. Early achievements included the recognition of mesothorium 1 and 2 and a phenomenon termed 'radioactive recoil'.

As a manifestation of pre-war German chemical prestige the Kaiser Wilhelm Institute for Chemistry was opened in 1912. Shortly afterwards Hahn was appointed head of a department of radioactivity. Taking advantage of the absence of radioactive contamination, he began a study of the very weak β-emitters potassium and rubidium. Subsequently, he showed that the latter could offer a means for establishing geological ages of minerals.

During the war of 1914–1918, Hahn was re-enlisted and became involved in the technical development of chlorine and phosgene as wargases. Some radiochemical work was still possible and, with Lise Meitner, he discovered protoactinium. Following the war his work on uranium disintegration led to the recognition of nuclear isomerism. Less successful were his attempts to correlate the degree of radioactive emanation from a given substance with its physical properties (particularly its surface-area). Rules governing precipitation of radio-elements and absorption of ions by precipitates were worked out in connection with this research.

The years of Hahn's greatest triumph came immediately before the Second World War. In 1934 he and Meitner had learned of the work by Enrico FERMI on the bombardment of atoms by slow neutrons in which neutron-capture appeared to occur, so forming the next heavier element. Like many others, Hahn and Meitner pursued the matter further and concluded that the bombardment of uranium did in fact produce new, 'trans-uranic' elements. They were soon joined by F. Strassmann (1902–80). In 1938 Meitner, whose Jewish ancestry made it unsafe for her to remain in Germany, left for Holland, finally settling in Stockholm.

Unable to account for some radioactivity observed in a similar neutron bombardment by I. JOLIOT-CURIE and P. Savitch, Hahn and Strassmann postulated a new isotope of radium as the cause. Towards the end of 1938 experiments made this increasingly unlikely, and the chemical evidence pointed clearly to the 'radium' being in fact barium. Yet they hesitated 'to take this big step which contradicts all previous experience of nuclear physics', for such a small atom could have come only if the nucleus had split. Within weeks the probability became a certainty, and Meitner and O. R. FRISCH (her nephew) postulated that 'nuclear fission' had taken place.

During the Second World War, Hahn and his colleagues were spared the agony of consummating their discovery with the development of an atomic bomb. They were chiefly concerned with chemical investigations of the fission products. In 1944, Hahn (with other German nuclear scientists) was taken to England, returning to Germany in 1946 to become President of the Max Planck Society and to assist in the post-war rehabilitation of German science. He was active in the cause of nuclear disarmament. In 1960 his only son died in a car accident and Hahn's declining years were given to the care of his grandson and invalid wife.

Hahn's achievements won him the 1944 Nobel prize for chemistry and he was widely honoured by many universities and learned societies. His name is commemorated in the Hahn-Meitner Institute for Nuclear Research in Berlin; the Otto Hahn Institute for Chemistry at Mainz; and in West Germany's first nuclear vessel, the *Otto Hahn*.

The Times, 29 July, 1968. (Portrait.)

Biographical Memoirs of Fellows of the Royal Society, 1970. (Portrait.)

Otto Hahn, *Scientific Autobiography*, (trans. and ed. W. Ley). 1967.

Otto Hahn, *My Life*, (trans. E. Kaiser and E. Wilkins). 1970.

W. R. Shea (Ed.), *Otto Hahn and the Rise of Nuclear Physics*. 1983.

Dictionary of Scientific Biography.

                                                                    C A R

HALDANE, JOHN BURDON SANDERSON Born in Oxford, England, 5 November 1892; died Bhubaneswar, India, 1 December 1964. Geneticist.

Haldane was educated at Eton and Oxford, where he studied mathematics, classics, and philosophy. After spending the years of the First World War in the army, he returned to Oxford to carry on his work in genetics and human physiology, before going to Cambridge as reader in biochemistry in 1923. To this post he added those of supervisor of genetical research at the John Innes Horticultural Research Station in 1927, and Fullerian Professor of Physiology at the Royal Institution, London, in 1930. In 1933 he became professor of genetics at University College London, changing to the professorship of biometry in 1937. He stayed there for twenty years, before going to India to join the Biometry Research Unit in Calcutta in 1957. He became an Indian citizen in 1961, and a year later went to direct the Laboratory of Genetics and Biometry at Bhubaneswar, Orissa, where he stayed until his death.

Haldane's work, with that of R. A. FISHER and Sewall Wright, formed the basis of the mathematical study of population genetics. Through his other studies in physiology and biochemistry he was also able to bring together information from other subjects relevant to genetics, as, for example, in *The Biochemistry of Genetics* (1954). *The Causes of Evolution* (1932) examined the theory of natural selection in the light of modern work on heredity, and was part of Haldane's major contribution to the quantitative study of the subject.

His physiological work, often using himself as a subject, began in collaboration with his father, J. S. HALDANE, studying human respiration and the effects on it of changes in pressure or the composition of the atmosphere. At Cambridge he carried on research into other human physiological and biochemical problems. As a biochemist, his book *Enzymes* (1930) was perhaps his most important contribution.

Many papers in a great variety of periodicals show Haldane's influence as a popularizer of science. His first book in this field was *Daedalus, or Science and the Future* (1924) and it was followed by several others.

Haldane was elected a Fellow of the Royal Society in 1932, and received the Society's Darwin Medal twenty years later. In spite of his unpopular political beliefs, his position was recognized by the award of many other honours from several countries.

Biographical Memoirs of Fellows of the Royal Society. 1966. (Portrait.)

H. Oxbury, (Ed.), *Great Britons: 20th Century Lives*. 1965.

Science Reporter (Delhi), **2**, 1965. (Special number.)

L. K. Haldane, *Friends and Kindred*. 1961.

Ronald Clark, *J. B. S.* 1968.

Dictionary of National Biography.

Nature, **206**, 239, 1965..

                                                                    S J R

HALDANE, JOHN SCOTT Born in Edinburgh, 3 May 1860; died Oxford, England, 14/15 March 1936. Eminent physiologist, and authority on respiration and the effects of high and low atmospheric pressures on the organism.

Haldane, a younger brother of Viscount Haldane of Cloan, was educated at Edinburgh Academy, studied in the Universities of Edinburgh and Jena, and graduated in medicine at Edinburgh (1884). He then became demonstrator of physiology at University College, Dundee. After a few months in Berlin he became in 1897 demonstrator at Oxford under his uncle J. S. Burdon Sanderson (1828–1905) who held the chair of physiology. He was elected a Fellow of New College in 1901, and reader in Physiology in 1907, but he resigned the latter post in 1913. In 1912 he became the Director of a mining research laboratory near Doncaster. This laboratory was transferred to Birmingham in 1921, and he was then made an honorary professor of mining in the University of Birmingham. He was President of the Institution of Mining Engineers from 1924 to 1928. For his work in human physiology Haldane was elected (1897) a Fellow of the Royal Society which awarded him a Royal Medal in 1916 and the Copley Medal in 1934. In 1928 he was appointed a Companion of Honour.

In 1892 Haldane, with James Lorrain Smith (1862–1931), showed that the increased depth of respiration caused by breathing vitiated air was very probably due to the excess of carbon dioxide in the air, and not to lack of oxygen. Then for several years he studied 'black damp' in mines and 'choke damp' in wells. In 1896 he reported to the Government that most deaths in colliery explosions are due to carbon monoxide poisoning, and in 1897 he investigated for them the causes of ill health in Cornish tin-mines.

In 1894 Haldane paid a visit to the laboratory of Christian Bohr (1855–1911) in Copenhagen, and he there learned of Bohr's suggestion that there might be an active secretion of oxygen in the lungs. During the following years he perfected methods for the estimation of gases in the blood. In 1905, in collaboration with John Gillies Priestley (1880–1941), Haldane published his important observations which showed that while an individual is at rest his breathing is automatically regulated to maintain a constant partial pressure of carbon dioxide in the alveoli. Their evidence also pointed to the fact that regulation of normal breathing depends solely on the partial pressure of carbon dioxide in the respiratory centre in the brain. It was later shown that this regulation is effected by the regulation of the hydrogen-ion concentration of the blood.

In the period before the First World War there was much interest in acclimatization to high altitudes. In 1911 Haldane led an expedition to Pike's Peak, Colorado, and from it much scientific information was obtained on cyanosis at high altitudes and on acclimatization. Haldane's work confirmed his belief that, in an acclimatized individual performing muscular work, oxygen is secreted by the alveolar wall. This conflicted with the diffusion theory, supported by (Sir) Joseph BARCROFT, whose work had many interrelationships with that of Haldane. Barcroft had at about the same time been on similar expeditions, and ten years later he led a final expedition to the Andes, partly with the question of oxygen secretion in mind. The work of August KROGH was also important in disproving the secretion theory.

Haldane was invited by the Admiralty to investigate the problem of 'caisson disease' in deep diving. Hitherto the method of slow decompression to avoid the 'bends' caused by bubbles of nitrogen in the tissues had been a lengthy process. Haldane showed by experiments on animals and man that it was safe immediately to halve the alveolar air pressure to which the diver had been exposed, and then to return more gradually to a normal pressure by 'stage decompression' (1907). He also showed that in the regulation of body-temperature in deep mines the crucial instrument is the wet-bulb thermometer.

C. G. Douglas, *Obituary Notices of Fellows of the Royal Society.* 1936–8. (Portrait.)
The Times, 16 March 1936.
J. B. S. Haldane, *Nature*, **187**, 102, 1960.
J. S. Haldane, *The Philosophy of a Biologist.* 1935.
Dictionary of National Biography.
H. Oxbury (Ed.), *Great Britons: 20th Century Lives.* 1985..

E A U

HALE, GEORGE ELLERY Born in Chicago, Illinois, USA, 29 June 1868; died Pasadena, California, 21 February 1938. Discovered magnetic fields in sunspots.

As a boy, Hale was provided with woodworking and machine tools, and a laboratory with microscope and telescope, which combined to give him an interest in mechanics and astronomy. He was educated at Oakland Public School, the Adam Academy, Chicago, and the Massachusetts Institute of Technology, where he studied mathematics, physics, and chemistry. By then he had his own 12-inch reflector, and before he graduated (1890) he had made one of his first important contributions to astronomy, namely the spectroheliograph. In this instrument the light of one spectral line, selected by a slit, is used to photograph, by continuous scanning, either the whole Sun, or (for example, when prominences are being observed) only the limb of the Sun. This is clearly a modification, simple in principle but complex mechanically, of the method devised by P. J. C. JANSSEN and N. LOCKYER more than twenty years before. By isolating a fraction of a broad line (e.g. of hydrogen or ionized calcium) it was later found possible to photograph several layers of the solar atmosphere.

After being appointed professor of astrophysics at Chicago in 1892, Hale both founded the *Astrophysical Journal* and planned the new University Observatory, named after its benefactor, C. T. Yerkes (1837–1905). Shortly after, he established a solar observatory at Mount Wilson (near Pasadena), thanks to the benefaction of Andrew CARNEGIE. From 1904 to 1923 he was director of this observatory, which was to house the largest telescope in the world, of 100-inch aperture. In 1928 he obtained funds from the Rockefeller Foundation for the famous 200-inch reflector on Mount Palo-

mar; this cost 6 million dollars and took twenty years to complete. Without it, modern cosmology could not have developed as it has.

In 1905, Hale and his collaborators, by comparing the spectra of sunspots with those of laboratory sources, showed the presence of certain ions in spots, and also showed their temperature to be lower than that of the surrounding photosphere. Later he proved the existence of strong magnetic fields in sunspots, working from the effect discovered by P. ZEEMAN. This was a prelude to what was probably his greatest discovery (1919, in collaboration with W. S. Adams (1876–1956)), namely the twenty-three-year cycle of reversal of polarity of the magnetic fields of sunspots.

The National Research Council, the National Academy of Sciences, the California Institute of Technology and the International Astronomical Union all owe a great deal to his organizing ability. He was honoured by many learned societies and universities.

W. S. Adams, *National Academy of Science, Biographical Memoirs*, vol. 21. 1941.
Helen Wright, *Explorer of the Universe: a Biography of George Ellery Hale.* 1966.
Astrophysical Journal, **87**, 369, 1938.
Dictionary of Scientific Biography..

J D N

HALES, STEPHEN Born at Bekesbourne, Kent, England, 17 September 1677; died Teddington, near London, 4 January 1761. Chemist and plant physiologist.

Hales entered Corpus Christi College, Cambridge (then Bene't College), in 1696, studying theology, and in 1709 became perpetual curate of Teddington. There he remained until his death more than half a century later, refusing preferment on the ground that it would interfere with his scientific investigations, which extended to both the physical sciences and biology. In his day he was highly regarded: he was elected to Fellowship of the Royal Society in 1718, and the Society twice awarded him its Copley Medal (1718, 1739).

It is not without significance that Hales entered Cambridge in the year that NEWTON left to become Master of the Mint. The University was still powerfully influenced by Newton's thoughts, and it is not surprising that in investigating chemical and biological phenomena Hales sought to use essentially physical methods. While this was in some respects rewarding, in that Hales's approach to his problems was quantitative – he was among the first to stress the importance of weighing and measuring in chemical experiments – he often failed to see the essential chemical differences between the various substances he investigated. This limitation is particularly apparent in his researches on gases. He much improved the then very primitive technique for collecting and handling gases and it is clear from his descriptions of his experiments that he isolated several distinct species of gas, including carbon dioxide (from mineral waters) and oxygen (from nitre). Yet he never clearly realized these distinctions and supposed that, regardless of the source, he was dealing only with ordinary air, perhaps slightly modified. Not until the time of Joseph PRIESTLEY, a century later, was it clearly recognized that there were many chemically different kinds of air.

Hales became greatly interested in the respiration of plants and animals, and like John MAYOW recognized the similarity of this process to combustion. He carried out elaborate experiments on the absorption of water and air by growing plants and demonstrated that it is the leaves that absorb air. He also recognized, though somewhat obscurely, that light plays a vital role in the growth of plants. He summarized his conclusions in his *Vegetable Staticks* (1727). He also investigated the circulation of the blood in animals and was probably the first to measure blood pressure, by inserting a glass tube into veins and arteries and observing the height to which the blood rose. He also made observations on the rate of flow of blood. These investigations he described in his *Statical Essays, containing Haemastaticks, etc.* (1733).

A. E. Clark-Kennedy, *Stephen Hales, D.D., F.R.S. an Eighteenth Century Biography.* 1929. (Reprinted 1965.)

D. G. C. Allen and R. E. Schofield, *Stephen Hales: Scientist and Philanthropist.* 1980.

Notes and Records of the Royal Society, **3**, 53, 1940.

Dictionary of National Biography.

T I W

HALL, CHARLES MARTIN Born at Thompson, Oregon, USA, 6 December 1863; died Daytona, Florida, 27 December 1914. Discovered independently of P. L. S. HÉROULT the electrolytic process for manufacturing aluminium.

At Oberlin College, Hall was influenced by Professor F. F. Jewett, a former pupil of F. WÖHLER who developed the first commercial process for manufacturing aluminium, but at a cost too high for success. Hall made protracted experiments on heating alumina with various reducing agents, but turned to electrolysis as the most practicable process. He built his own batteries, and in a home laboratory studied the electrolysis of aluminium compounds in molten fluorspar and other fluorides; eventually cryolite (sodium aluminium fluoride) proved superior. Hall's professor was surprised when, in 1886, his young student showed him aluminium buttons he had prepared, buttons now preserved as 'Aluminium Crown Jewels'.

In contrast to Héroult's use of large carbon anodes, Hall adopted several small anodes. After his first success came difficulties in getting the process adopted industrially. The original company of Alfred Cowles took an option for a year, but the fused electrolyte baths proved inefficient in operation after a few days. Then the Pittsburgh Reduction Company, parent of the Aluminium Company, built commercial units using 2000 ampère cells, which required no external heating during the working. In Britain the Hall process was used in a pilot plant at Patricroft in 1890 by the Metal Reduction Company.

J. D. B. Hobbs, *Aluminium.* 1938. (Portrait.)

Journal of Chemical Education, 233, 1930.

Science, **83**, 175, 1936.

Dictionary of Scientific Biography.

Dictionary of American Biography.

M S

HALL, JAMES Born at Hingham, near Boston, Massachusetts, USA, 12 September 1811; died Bethlehem, New Hampshire, 6 August 1898. Famous for work on the geology and palaeontology of New York State.

James Hall was of English parentage; the family was poor, but the young James showed such promise and determination that he was able to enter the newly founded scientific Rensselaer School (later the Rensselaer Polytechnic Institute) at Troy, New York State, under the teaching of Amos Eaton (1776–1842); from this he graduated in 1832. After geological work on his own initiative in the nearby mountains, he returned to Troy, now as an instructor. In 1837 he began his great career as investigator of the geology of New York State, being given charge of one (the western) of the four districts apportioned by the geological survey of the state (part of the newly-established official Natural History Survey). In 1843 Hall produced the result of his field work; his massive report is one of the classics of American geology. This was, however, but the prelude to an even greater work, on which he was engaged for the next fifty years, the palaeontology of the whole of the richly fossiliferous rocks (Silurian and Devonian) of the state. This was issued in thirteen great quarto volumes, 1847 to 1894.

He was president of the American Association for the Advancement of Science in 1856; director of the New York State Museum (in Albany) in 1871; and first president of the Geological Society of America, founded in 1888. In 1858 he was awarded the Wollaston Medal by the Geological Society of London.

Hall's geological work was vast in output and of the utmost value. Unfortunately there was ruthlessness in his character and his vigour and strength of will were so great that he allowed nothing, and no person, to stand in his way. This led to serious official disagreements and private enmities.

J. M. Clarke, *James Hall, Geologist and Palaeontologist.* 1921. (Portraits.)

G. P. Merrill, *The First One Hundred Years of American Geology.* 1924. (Portrait.)

Bulletin of the Geological Society of America, **61**, 425, 1895.

Dictionary of American Biography.

Dictionary of Scientific Biography.

J C

HALL, MARSHALL Born at Basford, near Nottingham, England, 18 February 1790; died Brighton, Sussex, 11 August 1857. A pioneer of the study of reflex action.

Hall was apprenticed to a druggist in Newark (1805). In 1809 he became a medical student at Edinburgh University. He graduated as a doctor of medicine (1812), and then held resident posts in the Edinburgh Royal Infirmary until 1814, when he studied at Paris, Göttingen, and Berlin. He then practised at Bridgwater (1816) and settled in Nottingham (1817). In 1825 he was elected physician to the Nottingham General Hospital, but in 1826 he removed to London, where he practised until his last illness. Hall was never on the staff of any London hospital, but he soon built up a lucrative consulting practice. In 1832 he was elected a Fellow of the Royal Society, with which he frequently had serious differences because it declined to publish some of his communications. He was not elected to its Council until 1850. His scientific work received few other marks of recognition at home, but abroad it was regarded with the greatest respect.

In London, Hall began experiments, especially on the capillaries and on hibernation. Some of these papers were published in the *Philosophical Transactions*. While carrying out such experiments he noted a reflex action in the amputated tail of a newt. The first studies of reflex action were those of Stephen HALES (*c*.1730), Robert WHYTT, J. A. Unzer (1727–99) and others. Previous to Hall a reflex had been observed in relation to the segment of the cord to which the stimulated nerve passed. Hall sectioned the cord of a snake behind its head, and found that a stimulus applied to the body surface produced writhing movements, which continued until external stimuli were blocked by wrapping it in cotton wool. This response to stimuli ceased after the cord was destroyed. Hall argued that the cord consists of a chain of units, each functioning as an independent reflex arc, but that these arcs are interconnected and interact with one another, and with the higher centres, to produce co-ordinated movement. In a crucial experiment he stimulated an intercostal nerve in a decapitated tortoise, and thus produced movements of both the fore and hind limbs. He concluded that the spinal cord has a 'diastaltic' action, a life of its own. This view was much in advance of his time, and was not greatly extended until the work of C. S. SHERRINGTON.

C. Hall, *Memoirs of Marshall Hall*. 1861.

A. Keith, *Menders of the Maimed*. 1919. (Portrait.)

E. A. Underwood (Ed.), *Science, Medicine and History*, vol ii. 1953.

Dictionary of National Biography.

E A U

HALLER, VICTOR ALBRECHT VON Born in Bern, Switzerland, 16 October 1708; died there, 12 December 1777. One of the outstanding biological scientists of the eighteenth century.

Haller studied medicine under the great Dutch physician, H. BOERHAAVE, at Leiden and became his favourite pupil. He received the MD degree in 1727, and in 1736 was called to the newly founded University of Göttingen as professor of anatomy, botany, and medicine. Here he spread the teaching of Boerhaave and helped to establish an important school of medicine. After seventeen years' labour he refused other academic appointments and returned to Bern, where he spent the last twenty-four years of his life engaged mainly in writing, bibliographical research, and municipal and state duties.

One of Haller's main fields of activity was that of anatomy and physiology. Together with a sequence of students he studied the form and function of many organs and systems of the animal and human body. He is not only the initiator of anatomy as an experimental science, but he also extended the work of the seventeenth-century investigators in applying dynamic principles to the problems of physiology. The latter is best illustrated by his fundamental and painstaking investigation of the irritability of muscle and of the sensibility of nerves. In so doing he gave due acknowledgement to Francis GLISSON, who had discussed the problem some fifty years previously,

but unlike Glisson, Haller substantiated each of his claims and advances with experimental evidence. He thus introduced one of the basic concepts of biology.

He also made important contributions to the physiology of the circulation and studied the circulation time and the automatic action of the heart. He gave the first correct and adequate discussion of the mechanism of respiration, although the lack of contemporary chemical knowledge limited his endeavours here as it did in the field of the physiology of digestion. In 1747 he published what was to be the first textbook of physiology, and his *Elementa physiologicae* (1757–66) is a remarkable repository of data which can be thought of as initiating the modern science of physiology. His work in anatomy was equally extensive, but less original, although his anatomical textbooks were very popular. The action of drugs was also of great interest to him and he recorded auto-observations on the action of opium.

As important as his biological research was his teaching of students and his general influence, which in eighteenth-century intellectual activity is said to have been exceeded only by that of Voltaire. He possessed a pleasant personality, but at the same time made many enemies and this may account for his premature departure from Göttingen. Throughout his life he wrote poetry, and it has been acknowledged that these contributions had an important effect on the development of German verse. He devoted the last few years of his life to bibliography and he published remarkable collections of references to the literature of botany (1771–2), surgery (1774–5), anatomy (1774–7), and medicine (1776–88) which today are still invaluable source-books.

J. C. Hemmeter, *Johns Hopkins Hospital Bulletin*, **19**, 65, 1908.

S. D'Irsay, *Albrecht Haller*. 1930. (In German.) (Portrait.)

L. S. King, Introduction to reprint of *First Lines of Physiology* (1786). 1966.

O. Klotz, *Annals of Medical History*, **8**, 10, 1936.

Dictionary of Scientific Biography.

E C

HALLEY, EDMOND Born in London, 8 November 1656; died Greenwich, near London, 14 January 1742. Discovered proper motions of the stars and periodicity of comets.

Halley was the son of a wealthy London businessman. After attending St Paul's School he went up to Queen's College, Oxford, in 1673. Even then he was an experienced astronomical observer. While yet at school he determined the variation of the magnetic needle at London to be 2° 30′ W, and as an undergraduate he devised an improved method of determining the elements of planetary orbits. The errors he found in the available star tables convinced him that a more accurate description of the positions of stars was vital to the progress of astronomy and, as John FLAMSTEED and Hevelius (1611–87) were engaged in cataloguing stars of the Northern Hemisphere, Halley took upon himself the task of cataloguing those of the Southern. In 1676 he left Oxford without taking a degree and went to St. Helena, where he succeeded in determining the co-ordinates of 360 stars.

With the publication of his *Catalogus Stellarum*

Australium in 1679 his reputation was made. Flamsteed named him the 'Southern Tycho' (though Halley had the advantage of the telescope, unknown to Tycho BRAHE); he was granted his MA by royal mandate and elected FRS. In 1682 he settled at Islington, London, engaging upon a series of lunar observations designed to solve the problem of finding longitude at sea. The problem of gravity also occupied him, and failing a satisfactory explanation from Robert HOOKE and Christopher WREN, he travelled to Cambridge to consult NEWTON. A friendship was established that was to survive through many vicissitudes. Halley persuaded Newton to publish his *Principia* through the Royal Society, of which he was Clerk and Editor. Unfortunately, the Society was in financial straits, and the arduous task of financing the work and seeing it through the press fell entirely on Halley. The great work finally appeared in 1687.

Through Newton's influence, Halley was appointed Deputy Comptroller of the Mint at Chester in 1696. From 1698 to 1702 he made expeditions to observe the variation of terrestrial magnetism and survey the tides and coasts of the English Channel. In 1703 he became Savilian Professor of Geometry at Oxford.

Halley's greatest contribution to astronomy was his study of comets, finally published in his *Synopsis Astronomiae Cometicae* (1705). After observing the great comet of 1680, in Paris, Halley computed the orbits of twenty-four comets. Noting the similarity of four orbits traversed by the comets of 1456, 1531, 1607, and 1682, he deduced that they represented one periodic comet and correctly predicted its return in 1758. This confirmed the belief that comets were celestial bodies and not, for example, meteorological phenomena, and permitted Newton's theory of gravitation to be applied to them in due course. The comet later bore Halley's name, though he could not live to see it.

Halley greatly reduced the margin of error in calculating the solar parallax. Observation of the transit of Mercury across the Sun at St Helena suggested that observations of the transit of Venus would prove of value in determining the Sun's distance, although his predictions for the transit of Venus in 1761 were less well confirmed than N. L. de LACAILLE's, by expeditions at the time. Up to Halley's time it was generally believed that the fixed stars never changed their relative positions. Observations of Sirius, Procyon, and Arcturus in 1718 convinced Halley that they had motions over and above those previously recognized (including precession). This discovery of the 'proper motions' of the stars was followed by some careful measurements of them. Less well known is Halley's discovery that the aurora borealis is magnetic in origin.

In 1720 Halley succeeded Flamsteed as Astronomer Royal. He undertook to observe the Moon through the eighteen-year revolution of her nodes and thereby discovered the secular acceleration of the Moon's mean motion, later explained by P. S. LAPLACE.

A. Armitage, *Edmond Halley.* 1966. (Portrait.)

E. F. MacPike (Ed.), *Correspondence and Papers of Edmond Halley.* 1932.

C. A. Ronan, *Edmond Halley: Genius in Eclipse.* 1969. (Portrait.)

E. Bullard, *Endeavour,* **17**, 189, 1956. (Portrait.)

G. L. Huxley, *Scripta Mathematica,* **24**, 265, 1959.

H. Spencer Jones, *Nature,* **149**, 69, 1949.

Dictionary of National Biography.

Dictionary of Scientific Biography.

J D N

HAMILTON, SIR WILLIAM ROWAN Born in Dublin, 4 August 1805; died Dunsink, Ireland, 2 September 1865. Mathematician; predicted the existence of conical refraction, but is better known for his invention of quaternions and for 'Hamilton's principle'.

William Rowan Hamilton was the son of a solicitor. His intellectual ability was soon evident from the ease with which he acquired languages, and by the age of 13 he could boast thirteen, including Malay, Sanskrit, Hindustani, Arabic, and Persian. Hamilton was one of the few great mathematicians with a facility for involved mental calculations (K. F. GAUSS was another). By this time he had mastered Euclid, and was beginning NEWTON's *Arithmetica universalis.* Soon he had read the *Principia* and Laplace's *Mécanique céleste.* He entered Trinity College, Dublin in 1823, where he made such an impression that, without ever taking his degree, he was appointed Andrews Professor of Astronomy (1827), which involved his installation at the Dunsink Observatory. In 1835 he was secretary to the British Association meeting, at which he was knighted. Unhappily, he acquired intemperate habits, and the last twenty years of his life were spent as a recluse, and most of this time he spent in elaboration of quaternion theory. He was honoured by many foreign societies, including the St Petersburg Academy. The National Academy of Sciences of America made him their first foreign member shortly before he died.

From the age of 17 Hamilton had been in possession of some results in optics which he was advised to simplify, and develop further, before publishing. This he did under the title *Theory of Systems of Rays* (1828, with large supplements later). Discussing A. J. FRESNEL's construction of wave surfaces, he noticed (paper of 1833) that the surface defined by the Fresnel equations has four conical points, at each of which there is an infinite number of tangent planes. A ray intercepting one of these points from within the crystal will thus be divided on emergence into an infinite number of rays, forming a conical surface. He also showed that a similar thing could happen to rays coming into the crystal. His prediction was confirmed experimentally afterwards by Humphrey Lloyd (1800–81).

Hamilton made what was probably his most useful discovery in about 1827, when applying his optical methods to dynamics. He showed that the equations of motion formulated by J. L. LAGRANGE may be replaced by a set of first-order differential equations (the so-called canonical form of the equations of motion). The advantage of these equations over Lagrange's second-order equations is largely illusory, as K. G. J. JACOBI showed (1842–3) when he developed a procedure for finding solutions, and yet Hamilton's formulation has been found to supply a useful basis for statistical and quantum mechanics. Celestial mechanics profited more immediately from Hamilton's study, as instanced by Jacobi's work on the three-body problem (1844). In both optics and mechanics Hamilton made great use of what is now known as 'Hamilton's Principle', which he referred to as the principle of varying action. The optical principles of both P. FERMAT and C. HUYGENS were comprised in this, when applied to optics, namely by equating to zero the variation of the integral known as 'action' – namely the integral of the optical path. In Newtonian mechanics the action is the integral of the Lagrangian function with respect to time. The principle is encountered throughout modern theoretical physics.

The latter part of Hamilton's life was mostly given over to the study of pure mathematics, not only quarternions, but also an investigation of the solution of algebraic equations of the fifth degree. In 1835 he published a paper on complex numbers regarded as ordered pairs of real numbers, in which the application to geometry was uppermost in his mind, but where he used a rather peculiar explanation in terms of 'sets of time steps'. There was little new, and his ideas go back in part to J. R. Argand (1768–1822), the Abbé Buée (1804), and even to John WALLIS. G. Peacock (1791–1858) and A. De Morgan (1806–71) had broached these ideas in their double algebra, but Hamilton was soon led to study the properties of triplets, and then of quadruplets (i.e. of *quarternions*) in 1843. Some of his more elementary results had been found in another connection by L. EULER, and A. F. MÖBIUS (1790–1868) had even followed the same path some little way before being daunted by the apparent need to reject the commutative law of multiplication. The overwhelming importance of Hamilton's theory, in the long run, was its introduction of a law of non-commutative multiplication, which although introduced in connection with a theory of rotations and stretched in 3-space, inspired other algebraists to reject it from their axiom sets. To this extent his bears comparison with that of George BOOLE in mathematical logic, and that of the founders of non-Euclidean geometry. Quaternions were soon related to A. CAYLEY's matrices and the theory of invariants to the theory of numbers, and many applications were found in physics. More general than vectors, they have been eclipsed by vector and tensor methods in physics. At the end of the century there was a protracted controversy over their relative merits.

P. G. Tait, *North British Review*, September 1866.
A. Macfarlane, *Lectures on Ten British Mathematicians of the Nineteenth Century*. 1919. (Portrait.)
C. Lanczo, 'William Rowan Hamilton; an Appreciation', *American Scientist*, **55**, 129, 1967.
E. Whittaker, *Scientific American*, **190**, 82, 1954.
Dictionary of National Biography.
Dictionary of Scientific Biography.

J D N

HANCOCK, THOMAS Born at Marlborough, Wiltshire, England, 8 May 1786; died Stoke Newington, London, 26 March 1865. Inventor of processes in rubber manufacture.

Thomas Hancock was the son of a timber merchant and cabinetmaker, and was the elder brother of the pioneer of steam road carriages. In April 1820 he patented the application of indiarubber springs for articles of clothing; this interest led on in the same year to his prime invention, the rubber masticator. In order to get his raw material into a convenient form for manufacture, he experimented with a shredding machine, in which the material was torn up by revolving teeth, but found to his surprise that the end product was not shreds but a homogeneous mass of solid rubber. He therefore began to make large cylinder-shaped pieces of rubber by feeding scraps of raw material into an annular space having a revolving spiked roller at its centre; when the outer frame was reopened, the cylinder of rubber could be cut off and afterwards pressed in iron moulds into the shape required.

The sixteen patents secured by Hancock between 1820 and 1847 also covered the cutting of rubber into sheets and square thread; its blending with other substances, including pitch and tar; and its application to various manufactures. In November 1843 he took out the first English patent for vulcanization, after examining and slightly improving upon the hard rubber already produced in the United States by heating with sulphur. With the help of his four brothers, Thomas Hancock manufactured rubber products in London, while also acting as a partner to Charles MACINTOSH in Manchester. In 1828 he supervised the introduction of his methods at a works in Paris.

T. Hancock, *Personal Narrative of the Origin and Progress of the India-Rubber Manufacture*. 1857.
Dictionary of National Biography.

T K D

HANTZSCH, ARTHUR RUDOLF Born in Dresden, Saxony, Germany, 7 March 1857; died there, 14 March 1935. Pioneer of physical organic chemistry.

Hantzsch studied chemistry at the Dresden *Polytechnikum* and the University of Würzburg. He became a *Privatdozent* in Leipzig, and was appointed professor successively in Zürich (1885), Würzburg (1893), and Leipzig (1903); he retired in 1927. He was twice married, and had several children.

The earliest work of Hantzsch was in pure organic chemistry ('collidine' synthesis; chemistry of thiazoles), but, especially after coming under the influence of F. W. OSTWALD at Leipzig, he became more interested in the relation between chemical and physical properties of organic compounds. He was a severe critic of the work of others, and since his own arguments were intuitive rather than logical (though often correct), he was led into one controversy after another. He and A. WERNER made their reputations with their explanation (1890) of the isomerism of the oximes as due to the non-planar distribution of the valencies of the nitrogen atom; much of his later career was devoted to seeking experimental support for the extension of this principle to the isomerism of the industrially important diazo-compounds. This involved him in a bitter controversy with E. Bamberger (1857–1932), which, however, had the happy result that Bamberger made important discoveries in organic chemistry, while Hantzsch was forced to invent some of the basic techniques of modern physical-organic chemistry. These included studies of conductivity and of absorption spectra; he published a long series of papers on the relationship between spectra and constitution. His work on 'pseudo-acids' and 'pseudo-bases' was also outstanding in its day.

Journal of the Chemical Society, 1051, 1936. (Portrait.)

E. Farber (Ed.), *Great Chemists*. 1961. (Portrait.)

F. Hein, *Berichte der deutschen Chemischen Gesellschaft*, **68**, 65, 1935; **74**, 147, 1941. (Portrait.)

Dictionary of Scientific Biography.

W V F

HARCOURT, WILLIAM VERNON Born at Sudbury, Derbyshire, England, June 1789; died Nuneham, Oxfordshire, 1 April 1871. Chemist; a principal founder of the British Association for the Advancement of Science.

After being educated at home, Harcourt served for five years in the Royal Navy before going up to Christ Church, Oxford, in 1807, with the intention of becoming a clergyman. There he became a friend of John Kidd (1775–1851), who lectured in chemistry and imparted to Harcourt an interest in the sciences. In 1811 he began clerical duties at Bishopsthorpe, Yorkshire – his father, Edward Harcourt (1757–1847), was Archbishop of York – and set up there a chemical laboratory, taking advice from Humphry DAVY and W. H. WOLLASTON. In 1824 he was elected FRS.

In 1821 the Kirkdale cavern was explored and described by the geologist William Buckland (1784–1856), and the fossils discovered there were taken to found a museum connected with the Yorkshire Philosophical Society, of which Harcourt became first President. In 1831 he organized the inaugural meeting of the British Association for the Advancement of Science at York, and drew up plans for its future which were embodied at the meeting in the constitution of the British Association. In contrast to the Royal Society, which was becoming increasingly restricted and professional in its membership, and was under attack for its apathy, the British Association was to be open to all interested in the sciences and would, at its annual meetings in different places in the United Kingdom, point out promising lines of research and problems which needed to be solved.

Dictionary of National Biography.

Proceedings of the Royal Society, **20**, xiii, 1871/2.

O. J. R. Howarth, *The British Association for the Advancement of Science*. 1922. (Portrait.)

I. B. Cohen and H. M. Jones (Eds), *Science before Darwin*. 1962. 1963.

D M K

HARDEN, SIR ARTHUR Born in Manchester, England, 12 October 1865; died Bourne End, Buckinghamshire, 17 June 1940. Biochemist, noted for studies of alcoholic fermentation.

Harden studied chemistry at Manchester and Erlangen, and in 1888 was appointed demonstrator at Owens College (now Manchester University). Here his work with H. E. ROSCOE on the papers of John DALTON led to the writing of their historical study, *A New View of the Genesis of Dalton's Atomic Theory*. In 1897 he joined the Jenner (later Lister) Institute for Preventive Medicine, where from 1907 to his retirement in 1930 he was head of the biochemistry department. During the war of 1914–18 he was acting head of the Institute, and did notable work on nutrition.

Harden is chiefly remembered for his work (with a series of collaborators, notably, W. J. Young (1878–1942) and R. Robison (1883–1941) on the alcoholic fermentation of sugars. E. BUCHNER had shown that this fermentation would occur in the presence of a cell-free extract of yeast, which he supposed to contain an enzyme, 'zymase'. Harden proved 'zymase' to be a complex mixture of enzymes, each component of which catalysed one stage in the stepwise degradation of sucrose to ethanol. He also showed that the essential first step was the phosphorylation of the sucrose, and that carbohydrate phosphates were key intermediates in the process. Related studies were also made on the conversion of glycogen to lactic acid in muscle. For this work, Harden received the Nobel prize for chemistry in 1929 (jointly with H. von EULER). Among other honours, he was made FRS in 1909 and knighted in 1936. He was Joint Editor of the *Biochemical Journal* 1913–37.

Ida Smedley-Maclean, *Biochemical Journal*, **35**, 107, 1941. (Portrait.)

Obituary Notices of Fellows of the Royal Society. 1942. (Portrait.)

Dictionary of National Biography.

Les Prix Nobel en 1929. 1930. (Portrait.)

J. R. Partington, *A History of Chemistry*, vol. 4, 1964.

Tyler Wasson (Ed.), *Nobel Prize Winners*. 1987. (Portrait.)

A. Findlay and W. H. Mills (Eds), *British Chemists*. 1947. (Portrait.)

W V F

HARE, ROBERT Born at Philadelphia, Pennsylvania, USA, 17 January 1781; died there, 15 May 1858. Inventor of the oxyhydrogen blowpipe.

Hare was brought up in Philadelphia, where his father, an Englishman, had a brewery. An early interest in chemistry led him to join the Philadelphia Chemical Society, which James Woodhouse (1770–1809) had founded in 1792. Here he came into contact with Joseph PRIESTLEY, who had settled in the United States after his unhappy experiences in Birmingham. It was apparently to Priestley that Hare, then only 20 years of age, first demonstrated his oxyhydrogen blowpipe, which gave an intensely hot flame capable of melting platinum. The necessary oxygen and hydrogen, fed through two platinum orifices, was obtained by electrolysis of water. His invention was recognized by the award of the Rumford Medal of the American Academy of Boston.

For some forty years, until his death in 1858, Hare was professor of chemistry in the medical school of Pennsylvania University, of which his father was a trustee. While there he extended his high-temperature work by developing an electric furnace in which he prepared calcium carbide, phosphorus, and graphite.

Important though it was to prove, Hare's invention was little used in his lifetime. Then, in 1857, Henri DEBRAY and Henri Ste-Claire DEVILLE took out patents for a platinum-melting device based on the oxyhydrogen torch. This immediately attracted the interest of the platinum-fabricating industry, which was making increasingly large platinum vessels for industrial use, especially for purifying sulphuric acid. The torch made possible strong welds in place of the old gold-soldering.

Edgar Fahs Smith, *Life of Robert Hare, An American Chemist* (1781–1858). 1917.

E. Farber (Ed.), *Great Chemists*. 1961. (Portrait.)
Dictionary of American Biography.
Endeavour, **17**, 59, 1958.

T I W

HARGREAVES, JAMES Born at Oswaldtwistle, near Blackburn, Lancashire, England, 1720–1; died Nottingham, April 1778. Textile engineer.

James Hargreaves was a handloom weaver at Stanhill, Blackburn, probably making Blackburn Checks or Greys from linen warps and cotton weft. An invention ascribed to him doubled production in the preparatory carding process before spinning. Two or three cards were nailed to the same stock and the upper one was suspended from the ceiling by a cord and counterpoise weight. In 1762 Robert Peel (1750–1830) asked his assistance in constructing a carding engine with cylinders, but this was not successful.

In 1764, inspired by seeing a spinning wheel which continued to revolve after it had been knocked over accidentally, he invented his spinning jenny. The first jennies had horizontal wheels and could spin eight threads at once, but as the drawing was done by hand the yarn produced was coarse and lumpy. He sold two or three of these machines, possibly to Peel, but then, in 1768, local opposition and a riot forced him to flee to Nottingham. Here he entered into partnership with Thomas James and established a cotton mill. In 1770 he followed Arkwright's example and sought to patent his machine; this he was unable to enforce because he had sold jennies before leaving Lancashire. Arkwright's 'water twist' was more suitable for the Nottingham hosiery trade than jenny yarn, and in 1777 Hargreaves replaced his own machines with Arkwright's. He died, comparatively poor, in the following year.

W. A. Hunter, *Transactions of the Newcomen Society*, 28, 1951–3.

A. P. Wadsworth and J. de L. Mann, *The Cotton Trade and Industrial Lancashire*. 1931.

Dictionary of National Biography.

R L H

HARIOT (or HARRIOT), THOMAS Born at Oxford, England, 1560; died near Isleworth, London, 25 July 1621. English algebraist, astronomer, and physicist.

Having attained his BA at Oxford in 1580, Hariot was sent by Sir Walter Raleigh in 1585 to accompany Sir Richard Grenville in his expedition to the New World. On his return (1587) Hariot wrote his *Brief and True Report of the New-Found Land of Virginia* (1588), which was many times reprinted. His work on algebra, *Artis Analyticae Praxis*, which he probably wrote in 1610, was not printed until 1631. It includes such topics as the formation of equations from given roots; the relation of roots to coefficients; the solution of numerical equations; and 'Hariot's Law' on the number of roots of an equation. He showed the equivalence of any nth degree equation to the product of n linear equations. Like many contemporary mathematicians, he improved the notation of algebra, introducing $<$ and $>$ for 'greater than' and 'less than' respectively. There was an extended dispute between the French and English mathematicians about possible plagiarism by DESCARTES from Hariot. His astronomical work was only really known when Baron von Zach

(1754–1832) drew attention to it in 1788. There is evidence that he used a telescope for astronomical purposes and discovered sunspots independently of GALILEO. It is generally admitted that he had the refraction law before either W. SNELL or DESCARTES, but failed to publicize the discovery. Hariot's unpublished material is mostly in the British Museum.

R. H. Kargon, *Atomism in England from Hariot to Newton*. 1966.

C. Hutton, *A Mathematical and Philosophical Dictionary*. 1795.

Dictionary of National Biography.

F. Johnson, *Astronomical thought in Renaissance England*. 1937.

J. W. Shirley (Ed.), *Thomas Harriot*. 1974.

M. Rukeyser, *The Traces of Thomas Hariot*. 1970.

Dictionary of Scientific Biography.

R P L

HARRIOT, THOMAS *See* HARIOT.

HARRIS, JOHN Born in Shropshire(?), England, 1667; died Norton Court, Kent, 7 September 1719. Lecturer and scientific encyclopaedist.

Harris was educated at St John's College, Cambridge (1684–8) and took holy orders. He was incumbent of several parishes in Sussex, Kent, and in the City of London, and was a prebendary of Rochester Cathedral. He took an interest in science and was elected FRS in 1696. He gave the Boyle lectures in St Paul's Cathedral in 1698, and became DD of Lambeth in 1706. He was a member of the Council of the Royal Society for some time, and was Secretary for one year (1709–10). From about 1698 to about 1704 he gave public lectures on mathematics, founded by Charles Cox, MP. He wrote a number of works on notable travels; on a variety of theological topics; and on the use of the globes, the latter in the form of a series of dialogues between a lady and a gentleman.

His distinctive contribution to science was a *Dictionary of Arts and Sciences*. It explained over 8000 scientific terms and was the first of its kind.

Dictionary of National Biography.

D. McKie, *Endeavour*, **4**, 53, 1945. (Portrait.)

Dictionary of Scientific Biography.

F G

HARRISON, JOHN Born at Foulby, Yorkshire, England, 1693 (baptized 31 March); died London, 24 March 1776. Horologist.

Harrison was the son of a carpenter, and himself followed this trade for a time. He became increasingly interested, however, in the construction of clocks and watches, with a view to improving their accuracy and reliability and it is in this field that he made his name. In 1726 he devised the grid-iron pendulum, constructed of two metals having different coefficients of expansion such that one compensated for the other if there was any change of temperature.

The position of a ship at sea is determined by its latitude and longitude. The former is fairly readily determined with the necessary accuracy by astronomical observations, but the determination of longitude depends, in effect, upon knowing the local time relative to some agreed longitude (in practice, now that of Greenwich). In the early eighteenth century the increasing demands of navigation made urgently necessary a solution to the problem of determining longitude at sea. To encourage inventors, the British Government in 1714 set up a Board of Longitude empowered to give a prize of £20,000 – a very large sum indeed for those days – to anybody devising and demonstrating a method of determining longitude with an accuracy of thirty minutes. Lesser, but still substantial, prizes were offered for less precise solutions.

The real problem was to devise a clock that would keep accurate time for long periods. This presented no great difficulty on land, where pendulum-controlled clocks could be used. These proved useless at sea, however, except under virtually calm conditions; the normal pitch and roll at sea made them unreliable even when gimbals and other devices for mounting them were used.

In 1728 Harrison took to London designs for a marine chronometer that he hoped would meet the conditions of the award. He showed these to George Graham (1673–1751), a leading horologist, who saw their promise and lent him money to continue. Not until 1735, however, did Harrison complete his first timepiece and submit it for the award. Preliminary trials were promising, but were not completed, as Harrison had meanwhile constructed two improved versions in 1739 and 1757. In the event, however, he rested his claim not on any of these but on another timepiece small enough – only 5 inches in diameter – to be described as a watch. This was Harrison's famous No. 4 Marine Chronometer. All these instruments are preserved, in perfect order, at the National Maritime Museum, Greenwich. They include many very ingenious innovations, but none of these are included in modern chronometers, which are of simpler design and construction.

Harrison's No. 4 was rigorously tested on two voyages to Jamaica, and in 1763 he received an award of £5,000. He did not receive the full amount until 1773, however, after Larcum Kendall (1721–95), at the instruction of the Board of Longitude, had independently constructed a duplicate to Harrison's specification.

Harrison was never a Fellow of the Royal Society, but received its Copley Medal in 1749.

Dictionary of National Biography.

R. T. Gould, *The Marine Chronometer: its History and Development.* 1923.

H. Spencer Jones, *Endeavour,* **14**, 212, 1955. (Portrait.)

H. Quill, *John Harrison, the Man Who Found Longitude.* 1966.

Dictionary of Scientific Biography.

T I W

HARRISON, ROSS GRANVILLE Born at Philadelphia, Pennsylvania, USA, 13 January 1870; died New Haven, Connecticut, 30 September 1959. Famed for his pioneering work on tissue cultures.

Harrison, the son of an engineer, began studying zoology while a student at Johns Hopkins University. In 1899 he became Associate Professor of Anatomy there, the same year as he received his MD degree from the University of Bonn, where he had undertaken several periods of study. In 1907 he went to Yale University as Bronson Professor of Comparative Anatomy.

He was led to his momentous discovery of tissue culture through his interest in the development of

nerve fibres. When he published his first relevant paper on nerve fibres in 1901 the topic was a controversial one. There were three main theories: that the nerves were formed by the same cells that gave rise to the Schwann sheath (see Theodor SCHWANN); that they were differentiated from a preformed set of protoplasmic 'bridges'; that the fibres grow out of the nerve cells situated in the central nervous system or in the ganglia. Harrison proved the correctness of the third theory by carefully conducted experiments. In a series of papers he reported many fundamental facts; for example, that nerve fibres do not develop after the removal of embryonic nervous systems and that nerve fibres can be observed developing, towards the periphery, from severed nerves in the tadpole tail fin.

However, his most invincible evidence was his observation of nerve fibres actually developing from nerve cells which were growing in his new technique of tissue culture. In devising this new technique he placed fragments of neural tissue from a frog embryo in drops of nutrient fluid on the underside of the cover slip of a special microscope slide. After early difficulties, because he did not realize the need for a solid substrate for cell movement, he was successful by using frog lymph of suitable consistency. This first tissue culture was made in the spring of 1907 and his results soon achieved wide publicity. The technique made a tremendous impact on science and medicine – the cultivation of poliomyelitis virus for the preparation of polio vaccine is just one example.

Harrison himself did not pursue his tissue culture studies; for the remainder of his scientific career he was preoccupied with polarity and symmetry in embryonic organs and the control of organ growth. Not only his contributions to science but also his influence as a teacher arose from his laboratory work. He was Managing Editor (1906–46) of the influential *Journal of Experimental Zoology.* He was a Foreign Member of the Royal Society (1940), to which he delivered the Croonian Lecture in 1933.

Biographical Memoirs of Fellows of the Royal Society. 1961. (Portrait.)

J. S. Nicholas, *Yale Journal of Biological Medicine,* **32**, 407, 1060.

Dictionary of Scientific Biography.

J K C

HARVEY, WILLIAM Born at Folkestone, Kent, England, 1 April 1578; died Roehampton, Surrey, 3 June 1657. Discoverer of the circulation of the blood; investigated formation of the embryo.

William Harvey was the son of Thomas Harvey, a yeoman-farmer. He was one of 'a week of sons whereof this William, bred to learning, was the eldest'; the other brothers became merchants in London. The whole Harvey family showed a remarkable lifelong unity and mutual support. William was educated at the King's School, Canterbury, and Caius College, Cambridge. After a serious illness, he went to Padua in 1600, studying under FABRICIUS ab Aquapendente, whose Aristotelian outlook and interest in the formation of the foetus and the valves of the veins influenced Harvey's future researches. In 1602, having graduated as a Doctor of Medicine, Harvey returned to England. In 1604 he married Elizabeth Browne, daughter of

Lancelot Browne (d. 1605), Physician to Elizabeth and James I; they had no children. His professional success was rapid. By 1618 he had been elected a Fellow of the College of Physicians; appointed physician to St Bartholomew's Hospital, London; and later Physician Extraordinary to James I. Though he was physician and friend to Charles I throughout his tragic reign, Harvey was not knighted. Dying during the Cromwellian Protectorate, he was not buried in Westminster Abbey but in the family vault at Hempstead, Essex.

Harvey's greatest work was his *Anatomical Treatise on the Movement of the Heart and Blood in Animals* (1628). In this and two supplementary letters written some twenty years later, he described his experimental analysis of the movements of the heart and blood, establishing that in systole the heart actively contracts in all dimensions, expelling its contained blood as a muscular pump. Cardiac diastole or dilation he found to be passive, not active as GALEN had held. Cardiac systole Harvey likened to 'blowing into a glove and producing simultaneous distension of all its fingers.' By dividing arteries he showed that each systole of the heart pumped out blood in jets, the expansion of the arteries being felt as pulses in the limbs. Having demonstrated that the right ventricle is responsible for the pulmonary circulation, Harvey showed that the left ventricle supplied the rest of the body through its arteries. That blood flows towards the heart in the veins he demonstrated experimentally by cutting them; by obstructing them with ligatures; and by observing the action of their valves in preventing blood from moving to the periphery. Here again he contradicted Galen. Estimating that the quantity of blood expelled from the heart was far greater than that ingested as food in the same time he concluded, 'therefore the blood must circulate'. Thus Harvey founded systematic, quantitative, experimental physiology.

Though Harvey's work *On the Generation of Animals* did not appear until 1651, he was working on it for most of his professional life. Clearly based on the similar work on generation by ARISTOTLE, Harvey's study demonstrated that the developing embryo differentiates its organs and limbs as it grows by a process called epigenesis. In this book Harvey also deals broadly with many biological problems; it is as much an expression of his philosophy as a scientific work.

Though at first violently opposed, Harvey's work on the heart found general acceptance in his lifetime. That on the generation of animals was rapidly superseded on the observational level by microscopic studies of the embryo, which led to the theory that this was from the first performed in miniature. The theory of epigenesis was not finally rehabilitated until K. E. von BAER made his embryological studies in the nineteenth century.

D'Arcy Power, *William Harvey*. 1897. (Portrait.)
Kenneth D. Keele, *William Harvey: the Man, the Physician and the Scientist*. 1965. (Portrait.)
Endeavour (New Series), **2**, 104, 1978.
Geoffrey Keynes, *The Life of William Harvey*. 1966. (Portraits.)
W. Pagel, *William Harvey's Biological Ideas*. 1967.
H. P. Bayon, *Annals of Science*, **3**, 59, 1958; **4**, 65, 329, 1939.
Dictionary of Scientific Biography.

L. Chauvois, *William Harvey: His Life and Times*. 1957.
K. J. Franklin, *William Harvey, Englishman*. 1961.
K D K

HAUKSBEE, FRANCIS Born in (?)Colchester, Essex, England, *c*.1666; died London, April 1713. Physicist.

Little is known of Hauksbee's life. He was a student of Robert BOYLE, with whom he worked on the design and construction of the air-pump for experimental work. He was responsible for introducing the double-cylindered pump. Using this pump and an electrical machine in which amber was rotated against a woollen pad in an evacuated vessel, he showed that air glows at a low pressure when excited by an electric discharge. Such experiments he illustrated in his *Physico-Mechanical Experiments* which appeared first in 1702 and in an enlarged edition in 1719; it appeared also in French and Italian translation. Again using the vacuum pump, he carried out experiments on the transmission of sound through air, confirming its dependence on pressure, an effect first observed by O. von GUERICKE. He determined the density of water relative to air, recording a value of 855.

In 1705 Hauksbee was elected to Fellowship of the Royal Society, to whose *Philosophical Transactions* he made many contributions. The instrument-maker and writer on science, Francis Hauksbee the younger (1687–1763), was probably his son.

Dictionary of National Biography.
A. Wolf, *A History of Science, Technology, and Philosophy in the 16th and 17th Centuries*. 1935.
E. G. R. Taylor, *Mathematical Practitioners of Tudor and Stuart England*. 1967.
Dictionary of Scientific Biography.
T K D

HAWKING, STEPHEN WILLIAM Born at Oxford, England, 8 January 1942. Mathematician and theoretical physicist.

Stephen Hawking was the son of a research biologist in tropical diseases. Educated at St. Alban's School and University College, Oxford, where he read physics, graduating in 1962, Hawking moved to Cambridge to work for a PhD on relativity theory at the department of Applied Mathematics and Theoretical Physics. After four years as a research fellow at Gonville and Caius College, Cambridge, he was elected a Fellow in 1969. In 1979 he became Lucasian Professor of Mathematics at the University of Cambridge. The onset of motor neurone disease in 1962 and its increasingly debilitating effects brought Hawking much public attention.

Hawking's research on general relativity led to the investigation of anomalies in space-time known as singularities, breakdowns in the space-time continuum when the classic laws of physics no longer apply. In particular, Hawking investigated the properties of black holes. A black hole, the final form of a collapsed star, is a prime example of a singularity. He later studied the behaviour of matter in the immediate vicinity of a black hole. In *The Large Scale Structure of Space-Time* (1973) Hawking argued that a space-time singularity must have occurred at the beginning of the Universe, that this was the Big Bang, and that the Universe has been expanding from this point ever since.

Hawking's best-known and most popular book is *A Brief History of Time* (1988), on the best-seller list for a record number of weeks. Written for the non-mathematical layman, it is about the origin and future of the Universe.

Included among Hawking's many honours and awards are his election as a Fellow of the Royal Society in 1974 and his appointment as Companion of Honour in 1989.

John Boslough, *Stephen Hawking's Universe.* 1985.

Michael White and John Gribbin, *Stephen Hawking, a Life in Science.* 1992.

Stephen Hawking (Ed.) (prepared by E. Stone), *Stephen Hawking's A Brief History of Time: A Reader's Companion.* 1992.

                                                          A P B

HAWORTH, SIR WALTER NORMAN Born at
Chorley, Lancashire, England, 19 March 1883; died Birmingham, 19 March 1950. Pioneer of carbohydrate chemistry.

Haworth went to school in Chorley and Preston and then studied chemistry at Manchester under W. H. PERKIN, jun. A scholarship then took him to Göttingen for a year, working under O. WALLACH. He returned to England as senior demonstrator in chemistry at Imperial College, London; then (1912–20) he was reader in chemistry at St Andrews University. By then his reputation was growing, and he held chairs successively in the Universities of Durham (1920–5) and Birmingham (1925–48). Initially, his interests were in the chemistry of the terpenes, but at St Andrews he joined J. C. IRVINE in the investigation of carbohydrates and this important group of natural products became his lifelong interest. Irvine and T. Purdie (1843–1916) had begun to characterize sugars by converting them first into their methyl ethers. Haworth made very effective use of this powerful new technique, particularly in identifying the point at which ring-closure occurs in sugar molecules. In 1926 he and E. L. Hirst (1898–1975) recognized that methyl glucoside must normally exist as what is now called (following Haworth) a pyranose ring. Later, he established that it may also exist with a furanose-ring structure. His book *The Constitution of the Sugars* (1929) rapidly became a standard work. Growing knowledge of the simpler sugars made it possible to grapple with the polysaccharides, and to this field, too, he and his collaborators made notable contributions, especially in investigating the chain structures of cellulose, starch, and glycogen. His 'end-group' method was a useful general method for determining the nature of the repeating unit in polysaccharides generally.

Haworth's interest in sugars led him to investigate Vitamin C, which has a fairly simple molecule chemically not unlike that of a sugar. He and his colleagues at Birmingham elucidated the structure of the vitamin and subsequently synthesized it. This work was not only of great scientific importance but paved the way to the industrial synthesis of Vitamin C for medical purposes.

Haworth's outstanding work earned him many honours, chief among them a Nobel prize for chemistry in 1937. The Royal Society elected him to Fellowship in 1928 and subsequently awarded him their Davy (1934) and Royal (1942) Medals. He was President of the Chemical Society 1944–6, and recipient of their Longstaff Medal (1933). He was an honorary member of many foreign academies, and was knighted in 1947.

Les Prix Nobel en 1937. 1938. (Portrait.)

E. L. Hirst, *Nature*, **165**, 587, 1950.

S. Peat, *Journal of the Chemical Society*, 2790, 1951.

Obituary Notices of Fellows of the Royal Society. 1951. (Portrait.)

Dictionary of National Biography.

Tyler Wasson (Ed.), *Nobel Prize Winners.* 1987. (Portrait.)

                                                          T I W

HEATHCOAT, JOHN Born at Duffield, Derby, England, 7 August 1783; died Tiverton, Devon, 18 January 1861. Inventor of the bobbin-net machine.

Heathcoat was the son of a small farmer who became blind, obliging the family to move to Long Whatton, near Loughborough. He was apprenticed to a local hosiery-machine maker and later joined William Caldwell of Hathern, whose daughter he married, in the machine trade. A lace-making apparatus they patented jointly had already been anticipated, so Heathcoat turned to the problem of making pillow lace.

He began by analysing the complicated hand-woven lace into simple warp and weft threads and found he could dispense with half the bobbins. The first machine he developed in 1808 made narrow lace an inch or so wide, but in the following year he made much broader lace on an improved version. Called the 'Old Loughborough', it was acknowledged the most complicated machine so far produced. The fifty-five frames in his factory at Loughborough were destroyed by Luddites in 1816. Heathcoat was awarded damages of £10,000, but he determined to move away from the area and refused the money. In a water-powered mill at Tiverton he built frames of greater width and speed and, by continually making inventions and improvements till he retired in 1843, his business flourished.

He patented a silk cocoon-reeling machine and also a steam plough for developing agriculture in Ireland which was said to be the best in its day. From 1832 to 1859 he represented Tiverton in Parliament, and among other benefactions he built a school for his adopted town.

A. Barlow, *History of Weaving.* 1878.

W. Felkin, *Hosiery and Lace Making.* 1867. (Portrait.)

Dictionary of National Biography.

                                                          R L H

HEAVISIDE, OLIVER Born in London, 18 May 1850; died Torquay, Devon, 3 February 1925. A founder of the theory of cable telegraphy, and discoverer of the 'Heaviside layer' in the upper atmosphere.

Heaviside was the son of an artist and a nephew (by marriage) of Sir Charles WHEATSTONE. Lacking a university education, in 1870 he was appointed as a telegraph operator with the Great Northern Telegraph Company at Newcastle upon Tyne. Forced by deafness to retire, and never marrying, from 1876 he lived with his parents until they died. In 1889 they moved from London to join his brother at Paignton, and Heaviside lived the rest of his life in Devonshire. Although poverty was relieved by a Civil List pension, his remaining years were spent in loneliness and eccentric seclusion. He died in a Torquay nursing home.

Despite his lack of formal education, Heaviside's years of solitary study enabled him to master much mathematical and physical theory, though his approach to academic studies was rarely orthodox. His first technical articles, in the early 1870s, included proposals for multiplex telegraphy. His contributions to telegraphy theory had a significance far beyond their immediate technical importance. To the theories of W. THOMSON (Lord Kelvin) he added his own new concept of inductance, or self-induction. He also introduced ideas of impedance and conductance, and regarded telegraphy by a cable or by radio-waves as being essentially the same. He was concerned with the shape of transmitted waves in cables, and showed how to produce waves that, though attenuated, were not distorted. In his view, electric waves were propagated along a wire chiefly by surface conduction. His understanding of electric conduction owed much to the electromagnetic theory of J. Clerk MAXWELL, and in many respects he forms a bridge between Maxwell and H. R. HERTZ, whose work he anticipated in a number of instances. He also advocated reform of electrical units. His interest in radio waves led him to suggest in 1902 that something in the upper atmosphere was responsible for reflecting them back to ground. This atmospheric feature, called the Heaviside layer in 1911, was suggested at about the same time, but independently, by A. E. KENNELLY.

Much of Heaviside's early work attracted little attention, but Kelvin's reference to him in his Presidential Address to the Institute of Electrical Engineers in 1889 seems to have brought him to prominence. He was elected FRS two years later. In 1908 he was elected an Honorary Member of the Institution of Electrical Engineers (having formerly been struck from their roll for his inability to pay his annual subscription).

Journal of the Institution of Electrical Engineers, **63**, 1152, 1925.
A. Russell, *Nature,* **115**, 237, 1925.
G. Lee, *Oliver Heaviside.* 1947.
Proceedings of the Royal Society, 110A, xiv, 1926.
Dictionary of National Biography.
I.E.E., The Heaviside Centenary. 1950.

C A R

HEILBRON, SIR IAN MORRIS Born in Glasgow, Scotland, 6 November 1886; died London, 14 September 1959. An organic chemist distinguished for his work with natural products.

Heilbron, whose father was a Glasgow wine merchant, studied chemistry at the Royal Technical College, Glasgow (now University of Strathclyde), and in 1909 returned there as a lecturer after two years at Leipzig. He served as an officer during the war, becoming Assistant Director of Supplies at Salonika. Then, following a few months with the British Dyestuffs Corporation in Manchester, he became professor of chemistry at Glasgow in 1919, later being appointed to chairs in organic chemistry at Liverpool (1920), Manchester (1933), and Imperial College, London (1938). During the Second World War he also became scientific

adviser to the Ministry of Production, and was a powerful advocate of the agricultural use of DDT. In 1949 he was appointed the first Director of the Brewing Industry Research Foundation.

Heilbron's first research, at Glasgow, was on terpenes. After studies on isomerism, O-heterocyclics, and other topics, he returned in 1926 to the natural product field with an investigation into squalene, vitamins A_1 and A_2, and other constituents of fish-liver oils. In the related steroid field he used spectroscopic criteria to demonstrate the connection between ergosterol and vitamin D_2, whose structure he helped to determine by oxidation methods. Examination of the constituents of seaweed led to further work in both terpene and steroid fields, and the synthesis of vitamin A was begun, but owing to other wartime demands this could not be completed.

Following H. W. FLOREY's work on the production of penicillin, Heilbron commenced a study of its chemistry in 1941. His contributions included a recognition of the importance of *p*-hydroxy-benzyl penicillin, studies of degradation products, and a general enrichment of the chemistry of the azoles.

Heilbron worked also on dyestuff chemistry and in other applied fields. Perhaps his most significant contribution to organic chemistry lay in his use of physical methods of structure determination, especially spectroscopy, and his employment of the relatively new techniques of chromatography and organic micro-analysis. He is remembered also for his *Dictionary of Organic Compounds,* compiled jointly with H. M. Bunbury and first appearing in 1934-7. For his services in the two wars he received a DSO in 1918 and a knighthood in 1946. He was elected FRS in 1931, and gained its Davy (1943) and Royal (1951) Medals. The London and American Chemical Societies also honoured him. He was a man of much culture, an able administrator, and an experimenter of great care and precision.

Nature, **184**, 767, 1959.
E. R. H. Jones, *Proceedings of the Chemical Society,* **242**, 1962. (Portrait.)
Biographical Memoirs of Fellows of the Royal Society. 1960. (Portrait.)

C A R

HEISENBERG, WERNER KARL Born in Duisberg, Germany, 5 December 1901; died Munich, 1 February 1976. Philosopher, physicist, founder of quantum mechanics.

Heisenberg studied theoretical physics under Arnold SOMMERFELD at the University of Munich, receiving his PhD degree in 1923. He advanced from assistant to lecturer, first under Max BORN at Göttingen, and then under Niels BOHR at Copenhagen, 1924-6. He then returned to Germany as professor of theoretical physics at Leipzig, 1927-41. From 1941 to 1945 he was director of the Max Planck Institute and professor at the University of Berlin; after 1958 he held a similar dual appointment in Munich.

The Bohr theory had not received better confirmation from experiment, Heisenberg felt, because it was based on things not directly observable, such as the picture of electrons moving in orbits. Making use of matrix algebra, Heisenberg in 1927 developed a system called matrix mechanics. This consisted of an array of quantities which when appropriately manipulated gave the observed frequencies and intensities of spectral lines. The wave mechanics of Erwin SCHRÖDINGER, published only months later, was shown by J. von Neumann (1903–57) to be equivalent to Heisenberg's theory.

The alternation of strong and weak lines in the spectrum molecular hydrogen, Heisenberg concluded, was due to the existence of two forms: orthohydrogen, in which the spins of the two separate hydrogen nuclei (protons) are in the same direction, and parahydrogen, in which they are in opposite directions. Heisenberg's discovery of the allotropic forms of hydrogen was specifically mentioned in the citation for his Nobel prize (1932).

An engaging, and perhaps philosophically disturbing, consequence of Heisenberg's work is his principle of uncertainty (*Unbestimmtheit*). If we accept the view that a particle is represented by ('guided by') a de Broglie wave, then it is impossible to make an exact and simultaneous determination of both the position x and the momentum mv of any body. By asserting that the premise is impossible, Heisenberg negates the Laplacian view that the entire history of the Universe, past and future, could in principle be calculated if the position and velocity of every particle in it were known for any one instant in time. EINSTEIN found Heisenberg's replacement of complete predictability by a statistical probability uncomfortable; they had numerous discussions.

During the Second World War, Heisenberg was the man most feared by the US atomic bomb experts as they raced to perfect that weapon. The facts are not clear, but perhaps Germany's interest in developing, under Heisenberg's leadership, atomic energy for industrial purposes was not diverted into a weapons programme because of the higher priority assigned by the government to aeroplanes and flying bombs.

From about 1950 Heisenberg courageously worked on unified field theory, publishing over twenty papers, some with collaborators, especially his close colleague H. P. Dürr. Heisenberg tried the extreme view that the phenomena of physics can be explained by assuming only a single field with four components. Definitive assessment of this work has not yet been achieved. It may be related to the 'gauge theories' of weak interactions which also involve treating several seemingly disparate fields as part of the same entity.

A. Hermann, *Werner Heisenberg 1901–1976.* 1976.

Biographical Memoirs of Fellows of the Royal Society. 1977 (Portrait.)

Dictionary of Scientific Biography, Supp. II.

E. Heisenberg, *Inner Exile: Recollection of Life with Werner Heisenberg.* 1984.

Tyler Wasson (Ed.), *Nobel Prize Winners.* 1987.(Portrait.)

D. C. Cassidy, *Life and Science of Werner Heisenberg.* 1991; *Uncertainty.* 1992.

R L W

HELMHOLTZ, HERMANN LUDWIG FERDINAND VON Born at Potsdam, Germany, 31 August 1821; died Charlottenburg, 8 September 1894. Celebrated for his contributions to physiology and theoretical physics.

A delicate child, like J. Clerk MAXWELL, Helmholtz early displayed a passion for understanding things, but otherwise developed slowly, having no capacity for parrot learning and no marked early talent for mathematics. Although he wished to study physics, he was persuaded by his father to take up the study of medicine, entering the Friedrich Wilhelm Medical Institute at Berlin in 1838. Pupils at this institute attended lectures at the University of Berlin where Helmholtz came under the influence of J. P. MÜLLER, the foremost physiologist of the day, and of H. G. Magnus (1802–70), the professor of physics. In 1848, through the influence of F. H. A. von HUMBOLDT, he was relieved of his military duties and became assistant at the anatomical museum and Extraordinary Professor of Physiology at the Albert University. In 1849 he was appointed to the chair of physiology and general pathology at Königsberg. He moved to Bonn in 1855 and in 1858 to Heidelberg where he continued professor of physiology until his appointment to the chair of Magnus in Berlin in 1871. In 1887 he became director of the newly founded Physico-Technical Institute at Berlin Charlottenburg, on which the National Physical Laboratory in Britain was modelled.

Helmholtz's thesis of 1842 on the connection between nerve fibres and nerve cells was followed by a study of animal heat which provided a natural introduction to his investigations into conservation of energy, culminating in the publication in 1847 of his celebrated *Über die Erhaltung der Kraft* (on the conservation of force). His researches into physiological optics commenced around 1850 with the invention of the ophthalmoscope (1851) followed by investigations into colour, including the problem of colour blindness. He also made fundamental contribution to the understanding of the structure and mechanism of the human eye, especially of the process of accommodation in which his ophthalmometer played a vital part. His classic *Handbuch der physiologische Optik* appeared in parts between 1856 and 1866 (complete edition 1867).

In physiological acoustics he published important papers on combination tones (1856); on vowel tones (1857); and on organ pipes (1859), followed in 1860 by a work on the mechanism of the bones of the middle ear, with particular attention to the shape and mechanism of the drumhead. In 1863 there appeared the first edition of his masterly *Die Lehre von den Tönempfindungen als physiologische Grundlage für die Theorie der Musik*.

Among other physiological researches particular mention should be made of Helmholtz's investigations into the speed of propagation of nervous impulses, which he showed to be of the order of one-tenth the velocity of sound (1850). He improved this result in subsequent experiments, returning to the same subject again some twenty years later when he published several papers on it.

Helmholtz's first, and most celebrated, paper in theoretical physics was that on the conservation of force, in which he proved the conservation of total energy of a system of particles interacting through central forces depending only on the masses and separations of the particles. Applications of this principle were then made to different branches of experimental science. Among a large number of contributions to electricity and magnetism, special mention should be made of the paper setting up an analogy between a magnetic field and the flow of an incompressible fluid in which vortex filaments corresponded to electric currents (1858), and of the suggestion of a method (later taken over by H. A. LORENTZ) for satisfying the boundary conditions in Maxwell's equation in the case of reflection or refraction (1870). Other important work in theoretical physics included the famous paper on vortex motion (1858), and the application of the principle of least action to electrodynamical problems.

Helmholtz was undoubtedly the most versatile of nineteenth-century scientists. From 1871 onwards he was perhaps more famous as a theoretical physicist than as a physiologist. But it seems probable that apart from his work on the conservation of energy he will ultimately be remembered more for his epoch-making researches in physiological optics and acoustics in which full scope was provided for the simultaneous exercise of his talents as a physiologist, a physicist, a mathematician, and an experimentalist of genius.

Helmholtz was elected a Foreign Member of the Royal Society of London (1860), being awarded its Copley Medal in 1873; in 1892 he was elected a Foreign Associate of the *Académie des Sciences*.

J. G. McKendrick, *Hermann Ludwig Ferdinand von Helmholtz*. 1899.

L. Königsberger, *Hermann von Hemholtz*. 1902. (Abridged English trans. by F. A. Welby, 1906.)

Dictionary of Scientific Biography.

D. Cahan (Ed.), *Hermann von Helmholtz and the Foundation of Nineteenth-Century Science*. 1993.

J W H

HELMONT, JOANNES BAPTISTA VAN *See* VAN HELMONT.

HENRY, JOSEPH Born at Albany, New York, 17 December 1797; died Washington, DC, 13 May 1878. Famous for experiments on electromagnetic induction.

Henry was a student at Albany Academy, where, after a spell as a teacher, he was appointed professor of mathematics in 1826. Six years later – at the invitation of John Maclean (1800–86), later President of Princeton University – he became professor of natural philosophy at Princeton. In 1846 he was appointed secretary and first director of the Smithsonian Institution (see James SMITHSON). He became a founder member of the National Academy of Sciences and its first president (1868–78). He played an active part in establishing the American Association for the Advancement of Science (1848).

From his first appointment at Albany, Henry became interested in electricity and magnetism. He improved the electromagnet of William STURGEON, and made, as 'a philosophical toy', one of the earliest electromagnetic motors. In 1830 he discovered the phenomenon of self-induction, but through his failure to publish, priority was given to Michael FARADAY, to Henry's great mortification. Today, the unit of electrical inductance is named after him. With Stephen Alexander (1806–83), his brother-in-law, he carried out an investigation of sunspots and solar radiation. At the Smithsonian, he introduced a weather-forecasting system based on meteorological information received by the electric telegraph.

N. Reingold (Ed.), *Science in Nineteenth Century America*. 1966.

Dictionary of American Biography.

Nathan Reingold (Ed.), *The Papers of Joseph Henry*. 1972– .

T. Coulson, *Joseph Henry: His Life and Work*. 1950.

C. L. Andrews, *Physics Teacher*, **3**, 13, 1965.

Dictionary of Scientific Biography.

T I W

HENRY, WILLIAM Born at Manchester, England, 12 December 1774; died there, 2 September 1836. Chemist and physician.

William Henry was the son of Thomas Henry (1734–1816), a physician who became secretary (1781) and president (1807) of the Manchester Literary and Philosophical Society. He was educated at Manchester Academy (a Dissenting institution) and at Edinburgh University (1795–6 and again in 1805–7), where he graduated MD. An accident as a child made him short of stature, and left him a legacy of ill health, which forced him to give up the practice of medicine and led to his eventual suicide. The example of his friend John DALTON turned him to research in chemistry; he also gave chemical lectures and wrote a successful textbook, *Elements of Experimental Chemistry* (11th ed., 1829).

His most important work was a study of the solubility of gases in water under different conditions of temperature and pressure; this led him to the generalization (1803) which became known as Henry's Law.

Henry was elected FRS in 1808. He married, and his son, W. C. Henry, also became a chemist.

Memoirs of the Manchester Literary and Philosophical Society (second series), vol. 6. 1842.

J. R. Partington, *A History of Chemistry*, vol. 3. 1962.

Dictionary of National Biography.

Royal Institute of Chemistry Reviews, **4**, 35, 1971.

Dictionary of Scientific Biography.

W V F

HENSEN, VICTOR Born at Schleswig, Schleswig-Holstein, Germany, 10 February 1835; died Kiel, 5 April 1924. Physiologist and marine biologist.

Hensen studied science and medicine in the Universities of Würzburg, Berlin, and Kiel. He graduated at Kiel in 1859, became an assistant in the department of physiology and embarked on research in embryology and histology. He was thereafter appointed to the chair of physiology in Kiel. Although continuing to hold this chair, he later devoted much of his time to marine biology. In 1877 he was Rector of the University of Kiel.

In 1857 Hensen published important work which has been largely forgotten. He knew from the work of Claude BERNARD that the liver may contain large amounts of sugar, and he investigated and identified the source of the sugar. In the same year Bernard published his own research on this substance, which he named 'glycogen'. To Hensen is due the credit of having discovered glycogen simultaneously with, and independently of, Claude Bernard. In 1866 Hensen, jointly with K.

Voelckers (1836–1914), showed that in accommodation the lens of the eye recedes, and they tended to confirm the theory of vision enunciated by L. H. F. von HELMHOLTZ. In 1893 Hensen published an important paper on the sense of touch, and for testing this he introduced his hair-aesthesiometer and other methods. He also published research on the physiology of hearing and of reproduction.

Hensen's work in marine biology was related to the fishing industry. He introduced the term 'plankton' for the population of drifting organisms in the sea, including the lower forms of plants. (Forms of life which were fixed to, or crawled on, the sea-bed were excluded.) In 1889 he was a member of the German Plankton Expedition, and he edited its reports. He devoted his own research on this subject especially to micro-plankton, the microscopic plants which form the food of animal plankton.

E. A. Schäfer, *Text-book of Physiology*. 1898–1900.

C. Singer, *History of Biology*. 1959.

Muenchener Medizinische Wochenschrift, **102**, 1205, 1960. (Portrait.)

R. Porep, *Der Physiologe und Planktonforscher Victor Hensen (1835–1924)*. 1970.

Dictionary of Scientific Biography.

E A U

HERO OF ALEXANDRIA Dates uncertain, but probably flourished, in Alexandria, *c*.AD 60. Mathematician and mechanician.

Hero's *Metrica* is a treatise on the mensuration of the simpler plane and solid figures, with proofs of the formulae involved. It established the (approximate) areas of triangles, quadrilaterals, regular polygons, the circle and ellipse, the parabolic segment, the sphere, cylinder, and cone (Book I), and the volumes of the parallelopiped, cone, cylinder, sphere, the pyramid and its frustum, the anchor-ring, and the five regular solids (Book II). It treats of the division of plane and solid figures in stated proportions (Book III). It contains what is known as 'Hero's Formula' (though probably discovered by ARCHIMEDES) for calculating the area of a triangle given its three sides, and a method (anticipated by the Babylonians) of approximating to the square root of a non-square number.

Hero's treatise *On the Dioptra* describes an instrument designed to serve the purposes of the modern theodolite and depending upon a refined screw-cutting technique. He explains its application to engineering problems such as boring a tunnel through a mountain from both ends. He also describes a hodometer for indicating the distance travelled by a wheeled vehicle.

Hero's *Mechanics*, preserved in Arabic, enunciates the parallelogram of velocities; extends the law of the lever to bent or irregular levers; estimates (incorrectly) the force required to support a weight on an inclined plane; determines simple centres of gravity; and discusses the mechanical powers and gearings by which a small force can be used to lift a large weight, with some anticipation of the principle of 'virtual work'.

Hero's *Catoptrics*, on the reflection of light from mirrors, demonstrates that the equality of the angles of incidence and reflection at a mirror follows from the principle that reflected light travels by the shortest path from its source to the observer's eye.

Hero's *Pneumatics* may be largely derived from the writings of CTESIBIUS and Philo of Byzantium (*fl.* 150 BC). The mechanical contrivances described are mostly operated by the pressure of the atmosphere or of heated gases; they include the siphon, the fountain, the pump, the 'steam engine' (operated by the reaction of escaping steam), the organ (driven by water-power or by a windmill), the thermoscope, the coin-in-the-slot machine, and automata in human or animal forms.

T. L. Heath, *A History of Greek Mathematics* vol. 2. 1921.

C. Singer, E. J. Holmyard, A. R. Hall, and T. I. Williams (Eds), *A History of Technology* vol. 2. 1956.

A. G. Drachmann, *Ktesibios, Philon and Heron*. 1948.

Dictionary of Scientific Biography.

A A

HEROPHILUS Born at Chalcedon, Bithynia, about the end of the fourth century BC. Regarded as the father of human anatomy.

Herophilus studied at Alexandria and afterwards taught there. He was probably the first to make public dissections of human subjects. He distinguished the cerebrum from the cerebellum, described the meninges, the optic nerve and the retina, and several minor anatomical features of the brain, one of which still bears his name. He was the first to distinguish nerves from tendons, and he knew that they were connected to the brain, which he considered to be the seat of intelligence. He appreciated that there are motor and sensory nerves. He also distinguished between arteries and veins, and rightly held that arteries during life contain blood, and not air, as had previously been thought. His description of the genital organs contains new features, and he was the first to describe the duodenum. His pioneer work on the lacteals was extended by ERASISTRATUS.

Important also as a clinician, Herophilus was the first to study the pulse systematically. He thought that pulsation was entirely involuntary and caused by the contraction and dilatation of the arteries. He also wrote a textbook for midwives and a work on dietetics, and he introduced some new drugs. The writings of Herophilus have all been lost, and their contents are known only from the works of GALEN.

C. Singer, *The Evolution of Anatomy*. 1925.

T. C. Allbutt, *Greek Medicine in Rome*. 1921.

J. F. Dobson, *Proceedings of the Royal Society of Medicine (Section of the History of Medicine)*, 18, 19, 1924–5.

Dictionary of Scientific Biography.

E A U

HÉROULT, PAUL LOUIS TOUSSAINT Born at Thury-Harcourt, Normandy, France, 10 April 1863; died near Antibes, 9 May 1914. Discovered independently of C. M. HALL electrolytic process for aluminium.

While a student at the *St Barge Institut* in Paris, Héroult read of H. E. St C. DEVILLE's work on the preparation of aluminium by sodium reduction of aluminium chloride. After a year at the Paris School of Mines, Héroult began experimenting on the electrolysis of aluminium compounds. He was fortunate in acquiring a small power-driven dynamo from his father's tannery at a time when reliable direct current sources were rare. He used his dynamo for the electrolysis of alumina dissolved in fused salt baths, cryolite (sodium aluminium fluoride) proving most promising. By maintaining a shift system with his associates, Héroult kept his furnace going for 56 hours, using as cell a graphite crucible with a central carbon electrode.

The struggle to commercialize aluminium, by the process first patented in 1886, was only successful when Héroult added alumina from time to time to keep the fused baths at a constant composition as aluminium was removed, and when Swiss and German interests at Neuhausen joined in large-scale working. After some fifteen years' litigation with Hall regarding priority, agreement was reached. Aluminium alloys were introduced at an early stage, Héroult's patent being adopted in 1888 by Aluminium Industrie A. G.

Apart from Héroult's work on aluminium, his designs of electric furnaces brought him fame in the electrometallurgy of steel.

J. D. B. Hobbs, *Aluminium*, 1938. (Portrait.)

C. J. Gignoux, *Histoire d'une Enterprise Française*. 1961.

Centenaire Paul Héroult, *Revue d'aluminium et de ses applications*. (May 1963.)

M S

HERSCHEL, SIR JOHN FREDERICK WILLIAM Born at Slough, near London, 7 March 1792; died Hawkhurst, Kent, 11 May 1871. Mathematician, physicist, and astronomer.

The only son of Sir William HERSCHEL, J. F. W. Herschel went to St John's College, Cambridge, in 1809. He graduated in 1813 as Senior Wrangler and was elected to a Fellowship at his College. He was a friend of William Whewell (1794–1866), George Peacock (1791–1858), and Charles BABBAGE, and with the last two formed the 'Analytical Society of Cambridge'. The three young mathematicians upgraded English mathematical analysis by the introduction of the continental 'd-ism'.

In 1814 Herschel began to study law, but was persuaded by W. H. WOLLASTON and Sir James South (1785–1867) to turn to science. Some optical researches performed in his father's house at Slough yielded valuable results: for example, he showed that the distinction between left-handed and right-handed rotation of the plane of polarization in quartz is associated with a difference of spirality of crystalline form. He later correctly argued that an electric field should rotate the plane of polarization, but it was left to FARADAY to show this experimentally (1845).

From about 1816 Herschel took an active part in assisting his father with observations and the reduction of data. Like his father, he constructed his own telescopes. By the end of 1833 he had re-examined all his father's double stars and nebulae, adding many more to the lists. He resolved to do for the Southern Hemisphere what he and his father had done for the Northern Hemisphere. He and his family arrived at the Cape in 1834, where they stayed for four years; he carried out almost every type of astronomical observation. Especially noteworthy was his photometric work on the Sun,

and his tireless 'gauging' of the skies on his father's principles. He decided against his father's simple disk theory of the Milky Way, in favour of an annulus of stars, but his work is open to many of the same objections as his father's.

John Herschel had much geophysical work to his credit, and in particular he drew up very detailed instructions for the expedition of Sir James Ross (1800–62) to the Southern Hemisphere (1839–43) for the purpose of making geomagnetic observations. He is remembered, too, as the inventor of the photographic application of sensitized paper, and the use of hypo as a fixing agent. He even made some crude attempts at colour photography. In 1850 Herschel was made Master of the Mint, as Newton before him. Honours were showered upon him. He was knighted in 1831, and almost every learned society in the world made him a member.

Living as he did in the shadow of his father's fame has tended to obscure the fact that of the two he contributed much more to science as a whole.

A. M. Clerke, *The Herschels and Modern Astronomy*. 1895.

C. A. Lubbock, *The Herschel Chronicle*. 1933. (Portrait.)

Günther Bultmann, *The Shadow of the Telescope: A Biography of John Herschel*. 1974.

David S. Evans *et al.* (Eds), *Herschel at the Cape*. 1969.

C. A. Ronan, *Endeavour* (New Series), **16**, 178, 1992.

Dictionary of National Biography.

Dictionary of Scientific Biography.

J D N

HERSCHEL, SIR WILLIAM Born in Hanover, Germany, 15 November 1738; died Slough, near London, 25 August 1822. Discoverer of the planet Uranus, the intrinsic motion of the Sun, and the form of the Milky Way.

William Herschel was the son of a musician in the Hanoverian Guards, which he himself entered at the age of 14. After the hardships of campaigning during the Seven Years War he came to England in 1757, where he made a living as organist and musician. He secured a fashionable appointment as organist at Bath in 1766 and began to study mathematics and astronomy seriously; by 1774 he had made his own 5½-foot Gregorian reflector. This was the beginning of a lifetime devoted to the construction and use of larger and larger telescopes. By 1781 he had discovered the planet Uranus, which he at first took for a comet (see also J. E. BODE). As soon as its planetary character was known he named it 'Georgium Sidus', in honour of the King, who shortly afterwards appointed him Court Astronomer with a salary of £200 a year.

In 1787 Herschel found two satellites of Uranus by the device of omitting the small mirror of his 20-foot telescope and pointing his eyepiece directly at the speculum. This, the so-called Herschelian arrangement, was subsequently favoured where light was at a premium. In particular it was used with his greatest telescope, which was almost 40 feet long and which had an aperture of nearly 50 inches. This was slung on scaffolding which moved on circular rails, and was therefore of little use for astronomical work. This instrument was last used in 1811, and Herschel was never able to repolish the mirror adequately, but it remained the largest in existence for half a century. However, his most valuable observations were carried out with the less cumbersome instrument of 20-inch aperture.

Herschel's first major discovery in stellar astronomy was that of the intrinsic motion of the Sun through space (1783). Tobias Mayer (1723–62) had tried unsuccessfully to detect this by analysing lists of stellar proper motions. Herschel carefully observed the proper motions of seven bright stars which had been painstakingly observed by N. MASKELYNE and showed them to converge towards a fixed point which he interpreted as the solar antapex. He confirmed the theory to his own satisfaction by many further observations.

For many years Herschel catalogued double stars, and issued extensive catalogues (1782 and 1785), in the first of which he hinted that many of them might be in relative orbital motion. In 1793 he remeasured the relative positions of many double stars, and found he had been justified. For the first time in the history of astronomy, KEPLER's laws could be applied outside the solar system.

Hoping to measure annual parallaxes through the relative displacements of 'optical' double stars, he was led, as explained, to the conclusion that many of the double stars were true binaries. They contained, nevertheless, stars of disparate brightness, thus showing that he had earlier been wrong to assume all stars to have the same intrinsic luminosity. With this hypothesis, however, and the hypothesis that the stars are uniformly distributed in space, his star-counts had led him to a remarkable picture of the overall form of the Milky Way. Whether this 'island universe' was comparable with the nebulae external to it, he could not decide. He managed to resolve into stars many nebulae, including some globular clusters, galactic clusters, and true galaxies. (His catalogue of 5000 new nebulae appeared in 1820.) This last aspect of his work was not given its proper recognition until this century.

Herschel is remembered also for his discovery of infra-red radiation in the light of the Sun and for some remarkable conjecture as to the properties of this radiation (1800). He may be said to have created the subject of astronomical colour-photometry. His son J. F. W. HERSCHEL – with whom some of his work was done – was also an astronomer of great distinction.

C. A. Lubbock, *The Herschel Chronicle*. 1933.
M. A. Hoskin, *William Herschel and the Construction of the Heavens*. 1964.
A. Armitage, *William Herschel*. 1962. (Portrait.)
J. B. Sidgwick, *William Herschel*. 1953.
C. A. Ronan, *Endeavour* (New Series), **12**, 189, 1988. (Portrait.)
Dictionary of National Biography.
Dictionary of Scientific Biography.

J D N

HERSHEY, ALFRED DAY Born at Owosso, Michigan, USA, 4 December 1908. Bacteriologist.

Educated at public schools in Owosso and Lansing, Michigan, Hershey graduated with BS in chemistry from Michigan State College in 1930, and was awarded a PhD in 1934 for work in bacteriology. He taught at Washington University School of Medicine, St. Louis, Missouri, from 1934 to 1950. Here he worked under J. J Bronfenbrenner

(1883–1953), one of the first bacteriologists in the USA to study bacteriophages. In 1943 he met M. DELBRÜCK, and with S. Luria (1912–1991) was one of the founding members of the American Phage Group. His discovery in 1946 of the existence of the exchange of genetic material in phage was the first laboratory demonstration of genetic recombination in viruses.

Hershey moved to the Genetics Research Unit of the Carnegie Institute at Cold Spring Harbor, New York, in 1950, and was director from 1962 until 1974. Here, in 1952, with Martha Chase, a geneticist, he conducted the famous Hershey-Chase experiment which confirmed the hypothesis put forward by O. T. AVERY in 1944 that genes were made of DNA. The experiment demonstrated that viruses which infected and replicated in bacterial cells did so by injecting their DNA into the cells. This convinced the other members of the Phage Group that DNA was the genetic component of viruses, and influenced F. H. C. CRICK and J. D. WATSON in Cambridge to try to find the structure of DNA.

Hershey continued to investigate the biochemical structure of bacteriophage DNA for the remainder of his career. In 1969 he shared the Nobel prize for physiology or medicine with Luria and Delbrück for their discoveries concerning the replication mechanism and the genetic structure of viruses.

J. Cairns, G. S. Stent, and J. D. Watson (Eds), *Phage and the Origins of Molecular Biology*. 1966.
F. H. Portugal and J. S. Cohen, *A Century of DNA. A History of the Structure and Function of the Genetic Substance*. 1977. (Portrait.)
Tyler Wasson (Ed.), *Nobel Prize Winners*. 1987. (Portrait.)

A P B

HERTZ, GUSTAV LUDWIG Born in Hamburg, Germany, 22 July 1887; died East Germany, 30 October 1975. Physicist: confirmed with J. FRANCK that energy can be absorbed by an atom only in definite (quantized) amounts.

In the original Franck-Hertz experiment (1914) electrons with variable energy were made to collide with mercury atoms in a vapour. Spectroscopic measurements gave the wavelength of radiation corresponding to a transition between the ground state and the first excited state of mercury as 2536Å. This is equivalent to a photon energy for excitation of 4.88 electron volts. Franck and Hertz found that electrons bombarding mercury atoms must have kinetic energy of at least 4.88 eV before the atoms accepted any energy, and that when they did the mercury atoms emitted radiation of 2536Å. Thus by an electrical experiment Franck and Hertz confirmed the hypothesis of Niels BOHR that the electrons in an atom exist in definite energy levels. They obtained numerical values for these levels as well as for the energy needed to ionize the atom. Hertz shared the Nobel prize for physics with Franck in 1925.

Gustav Hertz, a nephew of Heinrich HERTZ, studied at Göttingen, Munich, and Berlin where he obtained his doctorate in 1911 with a thesis on infrared absorption. He was severely wounded in the First World War and when he returned to Berlin in 1917 the only available position was that of an unpaid *Privatdozent* at the University. From

1920 to 1925 he worked in the laboratory of the Philips Company in Holland, one of the first industrial laboratories to support basic research. There he began important experiments on the separation of isotopes by diffusion cascade, starting with neon.

Hertz was appointed professor of physics at Halle University in 1925 and in 1928 became a professor at the *Technische Hochschule* in Berlin-Charlottenburg. There he continued his work on isotope separation. Since he was of Jewish descent, Hertz was forced to leave the Hochschule in 1934, after Hitler came to power. But he remained in Germany and became director of Research Laboratory II of the Siemens Corporation.

After the fall of Berlin in 1945, Hertz was one of a group of physicists who went to work in the Soviet Union. His hope that he and his family could integrate into Russian life was unfulfilled. He was segregated from society in a laboratory complex in Sukhumi on the Black Sea where some 200 Russian and German scientists worked on radar, atomic energy, and supersonics.

When the German scientists returned from the Soviet Union at the end of their ten-year contracts, Hertz became a professor and director of the Physics Institute, University of Leipzig, 1954–61. Upon retirement, he moved to East Berlin. Hertz was an excellent photographer and recorded colleagues and events during his long career.

Physics today **29**, 83, 1976. (Portrait.)
Tyler Wasson (Ed.) *Nobel Prize Winners*. 1987. (Portrait.)
R. L. Weber, *Pioneers of Science: Nobel Prize Winners in Physics*. 1980. (Portrait.)

R L W

HERTZ, HEINRICH RUDOLPH Born in Hamburg, Germany, 22 February 1857; died Bonn, 1 January 1894. Experimental demonstrator of electric waves.

Hertz was attracted to optical and mechanical experiments while still at school in Hamburg. In 1878 he went to Berlin and worked under Hermann von HELMHOLTZ. Two years later he became *Privatdozent* at Kiel. In 1885 he became Professor of Physics at Karlsruhe, where his principal work was done. Finally, in 1889, he succeeded R. J. E. CLAUSIUS as professor at Bonn, but died less than five years later.

One of the major scientific problems of the nineteenth century was whether forces act at a distance regardless of an intervening medium or whether the latter plays an essential role. On the whole, Continental physicists favoured the former view, while the English school favoured the latter. James Clerk MAXWELL, in his classic treatise on *Electricity and Magnetism* (1873), showed that all known electric and magnetic phenomena could be interpreted in terms of stresses and motions of a material medium. If the medium is the same as that required for the propagation of light the velocity of light in a vacuum should be numerically the same as the ratio of the fundamental electromagnetic and electrostatic units. In fact, this proved to be so. In spite of this and much other evidence, many of his contemporaries found difficulty in accepting Maxwell's views until their direct experimental verification by Hertz.

In his first important experiment Hertz bent a piece of copper wire into the form of a rectangle, leaving a short gap between its ends. When this was connected to a circuit through which an induction coil was discharged, a spark jumped the gap. Hertz found that a spark could be induced in the open circuit even without connection to the oscillating circuit, provided the dimensions of the two circuits were substantially the same. Such simple tuned circuits enabled him to detect electric waves at a distance from their source. Using 24-centimetre waves, he established that electric waves are essentially the same as those of light. They travel in straight lines with the same velocity as light waves; they can be reflected and refracted; they can be polarized; and analogues of optical interference phenomena can be demonstrated.

Hertz's results were not only of great scientific significance but entitle him to be regarded as a pioneer of radio communication. His own equipment allowed detection of electric waves over a distance of only some 60 feet – quite sufficient for his purposes – but by 1901 Guglielmo MARCONI had bridged the Atlantic.

R. Appleyard, *Pioneers of Electrical Communication*. 1930. (Portrait.)
P. Lenard, *Great Men of Science*. 1933. (Portrait.)
M. Planck, *Verhandlungen der Physikalischen Gesellschaft zu Berlin*, **13**, 9, 1894.
Charles Susskind, *Endeavour* (New Series), **12**, 84, 1988. (Portrait.)
Dictionary of Scientific Biography.

T I W

HESS, HARRY HAMMOND Born in New York, 24 May 1906; died at Woods Hole, Massachusetts, 25 August 1969. Geophysicist.

Hess entered Yale University in 1923 with the intention of becoming an electrical engineer, but soon transferred to geology, graduating in 1927. After two years as a field geologist in Rhodesia he returned to the USA to do postgraduate research at Princeton, where most of his working life (1934–66) was spent, latterly as professor of geology. After Pearl Harbor he served in the US Navy, commanding an attack transport in the Pacific. This gave him an opportunity to make many deep-sea soundings, during which he discovered a number of submerged sea mounds, which he named guyots, after the Swiss geologist A. H. Guyot (1807–84). This led to interest in oceanic ridges. To explain these he postulated that magma welled up from the mantle and then spread out horizontally. At the continental margins this relatively heavy material would be pushed under the lighter crust. Similar ideas were independently developed by F. J. VINE and D. H. MATTHEWS with whom Hess collaborated 1964–6.

Geological Society of America Memorials, **1**, 18, 1970.
Year Book of the American Philosophical Society, pp. 126–9, 1970.
Dictionary of Scientific Biography, Supp. II.

T I W

HESS, GERMAIN HENRI (GESS, GERMAN IVANOVICH) Born in Geneva, 7 August 1802; died St Petersburg, Russia, 30 November 1850. A pioneer of thermochemistry.

Hess went to Russia with his parents while still a child. He studied medicine, chemistry, and geology at Dorpat from 1822 to 1825; then worked briefly with J. J. BERZELIUS with whom he always remained on friendly terms. After a geological expedition to the Urals, he practised medicine in Irkutsk for some years, but on being made an Academician in 1830 he returned to St Petersburg and devoted himself to chemistry. He held the chair of chemistry in the Technological Institute, and taught also in other academies; he wrote a textbook of chemistry in Russian (1834) which became a standard work.

His early work was concerned with the analysis of minerals, and later he studied the natural gas of Baku; he also discovered the oxidation of sugars to saccharic acid. He is chiefly remembered, however, for his work in thermochemistry, a field in which few accurate measurements had hitherto been made. He established (1838–40) the law of constant heat summation (often called Hess's Law), which states that the heat developed in a chemical change is constant, whether the change occurs in one or several stages. This is, in fact, a consequence of the principle of Conservation of Energy, but at that time this general principle had not been clearly formulated. In 1842 he put forward the 'law of thermoneutrality', which states that no heat changes occur when neutral salts react in solution; this is not always entirely true. After this date he published little, being occupied with public duties; his health failed in 1848.

H. M. Leicester, *Journal of Chemical Education*, **28**, 581, 1951. (Portrait.)
Dictionary of Scientific Biography.

W V F

HESS, VICTOR FRANZ (FRANCIS) Born at Waldstein, Styria, Austria, 24 June 1883; died New York, 18 December 1964. The discoverer of cosmic rays.

Hess was educated at Graz, first at the Gymnasium and then at the University, where he was awarded his PhD in 1906. For the next four years he worked at the Vienna Physical Institute, studying the phenomena of radioactivity. From 1908 to 1920 he lectured at the Veterinary Academy in Vienna; and from 1910 to 1920 he was an assistant at the Institute of Radium Research of the Viennese Academy of Sciences. In 1920 he was appointed to an extraordinary professorship at Graz. From 1921 to 1923 he was on leave of absence in America, as first director of the research laboratory of the US Radium Corporation, at Orange, New Jersey. In 1925 he was appointed to an ordinary professorship at Graz, and in 1931 to the chair of physics at Innsbruck. In 1938 he again went to America, to Fordham University; he became an American citizen in 1944.

The research for which Hess was awarded the Lieben prize in 1919, and the Nobel prize in 1936, was his discovery and investigation of cosmic rays. In the early studies of radioactivity, it was found impossible to exclude all background radiation from apparatus, even when it was enclosed in lead boxes. It seemed that there must be somewhere a powerful extraneous source of radiation. To see whether this source was in the Earth, somewhat inconclusive experiments were performed at various heights above sea-level; they showed that some at least of the rays were extraterrestrial in origin.

Hess took up the investigation, and made a series of balloon ascents in 1911 and 1912, measuring the ionization produced in hermetically sealed vessels at different altitudes. He found that the intensity fell to a minimum at about 1000 metres, and then increased again until at about 5000 metres it was twice as powerful as on the surface of the Earth. He made one ascent during the nearly total solar eclipse on 12 April 1912, and found no difference in the intensity of radiation; this showed that the rays did not come from the Sun, but must have their origin in outer space. Later studies by A. H. COMPTON indicated that their source is outside our galaxy.

The study of cosmic rays has proved extremely valuable in investigating subatomic particles; for example, the investigation of cosmic-ray tracks in a cloud chamber led to the identification of the positron, by C. D. ANDERSON.

T. W. MacCallum and S. Taylor (Ed.), *The Nobel Prize Winners and the Nobel Foundation, 1901–1937.* 1938. (Portrait.)
Nobel Lectures, Physics. 1965.
J. G. Wilson, *Nature*, **207**, 352, 1965.
Robert L. Weber, *Pioneers of Science: Nobel Prize Winners in Physics.* 1980. (Portrait.)
Dictionary of Scientific Biography.
Tyler Wasson (Ed.), *Nobel Prize Winners.* 1987. (Portrait.)

D M K

HEVESY, GEORG VON Born in Budapest, 1 August 1885; died Freiburg, Germany, 5 July 1966. Inventor, with F. A. PANETH, of the technique of isotopic labelling.

Georg von Hevesy was educated at Budapest and Freiburg. After a short time with F. HABER, he joined E. RUTHERFORD who asked him to separate radium-D from a sample of lead. A year's fruitless work at Manchester convinced him that separation was impossible. In fact, the two are isotopes, chemically indistinguishable, though this term was not then employed. Utilizing their inseparability, Hevesy mixed some pure radium-D with lead and followed the reactions of the latter by the radioactivity of its contaminant. Early in 1913 a few weeks were spent at Vienna with F. A. Paneth, and together they used 'labelled' lead and bismuth to determine the solubilities of their salts and other properties. This work laid the foundation of modern tracer techniques.

In 1913 Hevesy went to Budapest, where he continued to work on lead compounds. After the war he moved to the Institute of Physics at Copenhagen. By now the concept of isotopes was clearer, and Hevesy took part in some early attempts to achieve isotopic separation. In 1922 (with J. N. BRØNSTED) he effected a partial separation of the isotopes of mercury by fractional distillation at very low pressures. He also obtained isotopic enrichment of chlorine and potassium, showing that the naturally radioactive potassium was the heavier isotope. With D. Coster, in 1923, he examined zirconium minerals in a search for the missing element No. 72. The x-ray spectra of the minerals had six unaccountable lines which they attributed to this element, calling it 'hafnium' and then separating it chemically from the zirconium. At about this time he initiated the biological use of radioactive tracers by using radioactive lead to examine the adsorption and distribution of that element in plants.

In 1926 Hevesy moved to Freiburg; in 1934 back to Copenhagen; and in 1943 to Stockholm. With a gift of heavy water sent by H. UREY, its discoverer, Hevesy studied water-exchange between goldfish and their surroundings and within the human body, the first use of stable isotopes in biology (1934). He then used radioactive phosphorus to study exchange in the skeleton, blood, brain, and malignant tissue. In the same year (1935) he invented the technique of activation analysis.

The author (or co-author) of several books on radioactive indicator techniques, he was widely honoured for this work. Elected Foreign Member of the Royal Society in 1939, he received its Copley Medal; the Nobel prize for chemistry (1943); and the Atoms for Peace Prize (1959).

Physics Today, **19**, 95, 1966. (Portrait.)
R. Spence, *Chemistry in Britain*, **3**, 527, 1967.
G. von Hevesy, *Adventures in Radioisotope Research*. 1962.
Hilde Levy, *George de Hevesy*. 1985.
Biographical Memoirs of Fellows of the Royal Society. 1967. (Portrait.)
Tyler Wasson (Ed.), *Nobel Prize Winners*. 1987. (Portrait.)
Dictionary of Scientific Biography.

C A R

HEWISH, ANTONY Born at Fowey, Cornwall, England, 11 May 1924. Astrophysicist and radio astronomer, largely responsible for the discovery of pulsars.

Hewish's studies at Cambridge University were interrupted by war service from 1943 to 1946 at the Telecommunications Research Establishment, Malvern, where he met Martin RYLE. After graduating in 1948 he joined Ryle's research team at the Cavendish Laboratory and was awarded his PhD in 1952. He subsequently became lecturer, reader, and in 1971 professor of radio astronomy in the University of Cambridge until his retirement in 1989.

His first important discovery came in 1964, when he began to investigate the phenomenon of interplanetary scintillation (IPS), an irregular fluctuation, similar to the 'twinkling' of the visible stars, in the intensity of radio waves emanating from very small radio sources such as distant quasars. He quickly realised that this line of research required radio telescopes of greater sensitivity than any then available, and in 1967 he completed a high-resolution dipole array covering an area of 18 000 m^2, with which he and his student Jocelyn Bell (1943–) began a survey of all such sources. Within two months Bell's painstaking analysis of the results caused her to draw Hewish's attention to a source exhibiting larger IPS fluctuations than expected, and by November 1967 it had been established that the signals were not only larger but also remarkably regular, with a period measurable as 1.33730109 seconds. The source was a new type of celestial object, a pulsating radio star or 'pulsar', and several hundred have since been found. Intense speculation as to the nature of pulsars continued until Thomas GOLD suggested that they could be spinning neutron stars, an explanation now widely accepted. For their work in radio astronomy generally, and in the case of Hewish for his discovery of pulsars in particu-

lar, he and Ryle shared the 1974 Nobel prize for physics.

Robert L. Weber, *Pioneers of Science: Nobel Prize Winners in Physics*, (2nd ed.) 1988. (Portrait.)
Modern Scientists and Engineers, McGraw-Hill. (Portrait.)
Tyler Wasson (Ed.), *Nobel Prize Winners*. 1987. (Portrait.)
Physics Today, December 1974.

R M B

HEYROVSKY, JAROSLAV Born in Prague, 20 December 1890; died there, 27 March 1967. Inventor of polarography.

Heyrovsky was the son of Leopold Heyrovsky, professor of Roman law at the Charles University of Prague, where he himself studied chemistry, physics and mathematics. In 1910 he came to London to work at University College under Sir William RAMSAY and F. G. DONNAN, who aroused his interest in electrochemistry. During the war of 1914–18 he served in a military hospital, and afterwards was appointed assistant in the Institute of Analytical Chemistry at Charles University. He was subsequently appointed associate professor (1922) and professor (1926) of physical chemistry in the University. In 1959 he was awarded the Nobel prize for chemistry. From 1950 onwards he was director of the Polarographgic Institute, incorporated (1952) in the Czechoslovak Academy of Sciences. He was honoured by universities and learned societies of many countries; the Royal Society elected him a Foreign Member in 1965.

Heyrovsky's great claim to fame is as inventor of the electrochemical method of analysis known as polarography. This is widely used throughout the world and is applicable to ionic or molecular species, both organic and inorganic, capable of electrolytic oxidation or reduction in solution.

R. Belcher, *Nature*, **214**, 953, 1967.
Les Prix Nobel en 1959. 1960. (Portrait.)
Biographical Memoirs of Fellows of the Royal Society. 1967. (Portrait.)
Dictionary of Scientific Biography.
Z. Zuman and P. J. Elving, *Journal of Chemical Education*, **37**, 572, 1960.

T I W

HIGGINS, WILLIAM Born at (?) Collooney, Co. Sligo, Ireland, in 1763; died, probably Dublin, 1825 (precise date unknown). Early enunciator of a chemical atomic theory.

Although a capable professional chemist – he was elected FRS in 1806 – Higgins would have had no lasting fame but for his claim to have anticipated John DALTON in formulating a chemical atomic theory. As a young man he came to London to work with his wealthy uncle, Dr Bryan Higgins (c.1741–1818), who had a laboratory in Soho. After a year or two he went to Pembroke College, Oxford, to study chemistry. He returned briefly to London, but apparently quarrelled with his uncle over matters of chemical theory and in 1792 went to Dublin to be chemist to the Apothecaries Hall of Ireland. From 1795 to 1822 he was chemist to the Irish Linen Board.

Scientifically, Higgin's reputation rests on his *Comparative View of the Phlogistic and Antiphlogistic Theories*, published in 1789 when he was only 26. This certainly contains the elements of a chemical atomic theory, but he did nothing to develop it. Nevertheless, from 1814 onwards, after Dalton's clear enunciation of his own ideas, Higgins claimed to be the originator of the theory. He gained some measure of support from Humphry DAVY and many subsequent writers up to the present time. Higgins did not advance his own cause by overstating his case nor by his quarrelsome nature. The argument is controversial and difficult, but today the consensus of informed opinion is that the credit for originality must go to Dalton. At the end of a most detailed and closely reasoned survey (see below) J. R. PARTINGTON and T. S. WHEELER (1899–1962) concluded: 'Higgins has an honourable place in the history of chemical theory, but he does not stand on the same level as Dalton.'

J. R. Partington and T. S. Wheeler, *The Life and Work of William Higgins, Chemist* (1763–1825). 1960.

T. S. Wheeler, *Endeavour*, **11**, 47, 1952.

Dictionary of National Biography.

F. W. Gibbs, *Chemistry in Britain*, **1**, 60, 1965.

T I W

HILDITCH, THOMAS PERCY Born in London, 22 April 1886; died Birkenhead, 9 August 1965. Pioneer of chemistry of natural fats.

A graduate of University College London, Hilditch studied further at Jena and Geneva. His early interest was in optical activity and the chemistry of organic sulphur compounds and it was largely by chance – an appointment to the research laboratories of Joseph Crosfield and Sons Limited, soap makers, at Warrington in 1911 – that he entered the field of fat chemistry to which he contributed so much. His taking up of this appointment corresponded closely with the development of industrial interest in the hardening of fats by hydrogenation in presence of a nickel catalyst.

In 1926, Hilditch was appointed professor of industrial chemistry at Liverpool University, which he held until retiring in 1951. There he established an internationally recognized school of fat chemistry. His textbook *The Chemical Constitution of Natural Fats* ran to four editions in his lifetime; he also wrote several other chemical textbooks including *A Concise History of Chemistry*. He was elected Fellow of the Royal Society in 1942.

Chemistry in Britain, **2**, 117, 1966.

Biographical Memoirs of Fellows of the Royal Society. 1966. (Portrait.)

F. D. Gunstone, *Journal of the American Oil Chemists' Society*, **42**, 474A, 530A, 1965.

Dictionary of National Biography.

T I W

HILL, ARCHIBALD VIVIAN Born at Bristol, England, 26 September 1886; died Cambridge, 3 June 1977. Physiologist, principally engaged in biophysical studies of nerve and muscle. Did much pioneering work on energy exchanges during nerve and muscular activity.

Hill went to Blundell's School at Tiverton, Devon, and in 1905 proceeded as a Scholar to Trinity College, Cambridge, three years before E. D. ADRIAN. He took mathematics, finishing as Third Wrangler in 1907. Under the influence of W. M. Fletcher (1873–1933), his interests changed to physiology and he took a first in Part II of the Natural Sciences Tripos in 1909. He then joined the Physio-logical Laboratory under J. N. Langley (1852–1925), and after a brief period of important theoretical and experimental work on drug and enzyme kinetics, began to develop methods for the study of mechanical and thermal energy exchanges during muscular contraction and their relation to the chemical process in muscle tissue. This work was interrupted by the First World War, during which Hill served in the Army as a major, founding and directing an Anti-aircraft Experimental Section.

In 1919, Hill returned to Cambridge and resumed his experiments on the heat production of muscle. In 1920 he accepted appointment to the chair of physiology at Manchester University and three years later moved to University College, London, first as Jodrell Professor of Physiology, and later, from 1916 till his official retirement in 1951, as Foulerton Research Professor appointed by the Royal Society. Even after 1951 Hill was actively engaged in his experiments on nerve and muscle, until he and his wife Margaret (sister of John Maynard Keynes, the economist) finally retired to Cambridge in 1967, where he continued to write on scientific and general subjects.

Hill was one of the great scientific leaders of his generation. He is remembered by many colleagues, including more than 100 personal pupils, not only for his great scientific discoveries, but for bringing physico-chemical ideas and high-precision measurements to bear on biological problems, and above all for his personal example in inspiring and encouraging his young colleagues and for the lead he took during the Nazi period in helping those who had been driven from their laboratories by political or racial persecution.

He gave distinguished public service of many different kinds. In 1935 he was one of the three members of the Tizard Committee who initiated radar for the defence of Britain. During the Second World War, he became an independent Member of Parliament (for Cambridge University); helped early on to establish scientific liaison between Britain, Canada, and the United States; joined the new Scientific Advisory Committee to the Cabinet in his capacity as Biological Secretary of the Royal Society; and in 1943–4 paid an important visit to India and advised the Indian Government on vital matters of scientific and medical postwar reconstruction. In 1952, as President of the British Association, he delivered a notable address in which he pointed very lucidly to the scientific and ethical problems of over-population, long before wide popular interest became focused on it.

Hill received many scientific and public honours in his own country as well as abroad: they include a Nobel prize (1923); the Copley Medal (1918) of the Royal Society, to which he was elected in 1918; the Companion of Honour (1946); the USA Medal of Freedom (1947); Chevalier of the *Légion d'Honneur* (1950); and scores of honorary degrees and academic memberships.

Nature, Lond., **268**, 777, 1977.

Biographical Memoirs of Fellows of the Royal Society, 1978. (Portrait.)

Dictionary of National Biography.

H. Oxbury (Ed.), *Great Britons: 20th Century Lives*. 1985. (Portrait.)

Tyler Wasson (Ed.), *Nobel Prize Winners*. 1987. (Portrait.)

B K

HILL, ROBERT (ROBIN) Born 2 April 1899; died
Cambridge, England, 15 March 1991. Biochemist.

After entering Emmanuel College, Cambridge,
Hill served briefly (1917–8) in the anti-gas department of the Royal Engineers. In 1922 he joined
the newly created department of biochemistry in
Cambridge under F. G. HOPKINS, intending to do
research on plant pigments. Instead, he was set to
work on the blood pigment haemoglobin, though
he contrived to maintain also a subsidiary interest
in dye plants such as madder. In his home the
walls became adorned with water-colours painted
with natural pigments which he prepared himself
and the garden was rich in 'biochemical' plants.
Hill used a simple spectroscopic technique to
measure the oxygen dissociation curve of haemoglobin and in 1937 used this to measure the production of oxygen by an illuminated suspension
of chloroplasts. He showed that, contrary to a generally held view, isolated chloroplasts can dis-
sociate water when illuminated but cannot
produce sugar from carbon dioxide. This led to the
formulation of the so-called Hill reaction, involving reaction of electrons derived from water not
with carbon dioxide but with some other acceptor
such as ferricyanide. This research gained him the
first award for photosynthesis given by the Society
of American Plant Physiologists (1963).

Hill was an acutely shy man and never held a
formal university appointment, his research being
supported by grants from various sources, including the Agricultural Research Council (1943–66).
The Royal Society elected him to Fellowship in
1964 and awarded him its Copley Medal in 1987.
He was elected a Foreign Associate of the US
National Academy of Sciences in 1975.

The Independent, 21 March 1991. (Portrait.)
Who's Who, 1991.

T I W

HINSHELWOOD, SIR CYRIL NORMAN Born in
London, 19 June 1897; died there, 9 October 1967.
Physical chemist, noted for contributions to reac-
tion kinetics.

Hinshelwood, the son of a chartered accountant,
was educated in London at Westminster City
School. The war of 1914–18 interrupted his
studies, and in 1916 he went as chemist to an
explosives factory at Queensferry, Scotland. There,
despite his youth and lack of formal qualifications,
his talent for chemical research was apparent and
after the war he went with a scholarship to Balliol
College, Oxford, where he was elected a Fellow
immediately on graduation (1920). Subsequently
he was made a Fellow of Trinity College, Oxford
(1921–37). In 1937 he was appointed Dr Lee's Professor of Chemistry in the University of Oxford –
following F. SODDY – a post he held until his retirement in 1964. He was then made a Senior Research
Fellow at Imperial College, London, a post he held
at the time of his death.

Hinshelwood's chosen field of research was the
kinetics of chemical reaction, and in this he established an international reputation for incisive
experiment and clear and rigorous exposition. His
classic work *Kinetics of Chemical Change* first
appeared in 1926, and reached its fourth edition
in 1940. Later, he sought to apply the laws of inani-
mate chemical systems to the processes of bacterial
growth. His results and opinions were summarized

in *The Chemical Kinetics of the Bacterial Cell*
(1946). Inevitably, his ideas excited controversy
and no doubt some will not stand the test of time;
nevertheless, the originality of his approach, and
the characteristic lucidity with which he advanced
his arguments, provided a valuable stimulus to
new thought over the whole field.

Hinshelwood's scientific work was internationally recognized. He was elected to Fellowship of the Royal Society in 1929, and was foreign
secretary 1950–5 and president 1955–60. He was
also president of the Chemical Society 1946–8. He
was an honorary graduate of many foreign universities, and was a member of learned societies
throughout the world. The seal was set on his
scientific reputation with the award of a Nobel
prize in 1956. He was knighted in 1948 and elected
to the Order of Merit in 1960.

Hinshelwood's talents were by no means limited
to chemistry. He was a gifted linguist and shared
with A. GEIKIE the unique distinction of being simultaneously President of the Classical Association
and of the Royal Society. He was knowledgeable
on Chinese ceramics, of which he was a collector.
His approach to science was philosophic as well
as practical, as exemplified in his *Structure of
Physical Chemistry* (1951).

Les Prix Nobel en 1956. 1957. (Portrait.)
The Times, 12 October 1967. (Portrait.)
*Biographical Memoirs of Fellows of the Royal
    Society*. 1973. (Portrait.)
Dictionary of National Biography.
J. Oxbury (Ed.), *Great Britons: 20th Century Lives*.
    1985.
Tyler Wasson (Ed.), *Nobel Prize Winners*. 1987.
    (Portrait.)

T I W

HIPPARCHUS OF RHODES Born at Nicaea, Bithynia, and flourished in the late second century
BC. Astronomer, mathematician, geographer; discovered the precession of the equinoxes; constructed the first known star catalogue; founded
trigonometry.

Hipparchus carried out his observations at
Rhodes. All his important works are lost; his astronomical achievements were preserved and
developed, but not always clearly demarcated, by
PTOLEMY.

Hipparchus probably invented or employed
astronomical instruments involving graduated
circles. He used them to catalogue the celestial co-
ordinates of some 800 stars, indicating their brightness on a conventional scale of 'magnitudes' that
still provides the basis for stellar photometry. A
comparison of his own with earlier Alexandrian
determinations of star places revealed to him a progressive shift suggesting a slow eastward rotation
of the sphere of stars. In consequence, the recur-
rence of an equinox precedes the expiry of the sidereal year; hence the term 'precession of the
equinoxes'. Hipparchus evaluated the annual
amount of the precession and the durations of the
sidereal and the tropical years.

Hipparchus improved upon earlier estimates of
the sizes and distances of the Sun and Moon, and
he established a method of determining the Sun's
distance that was adopted in succession by Ptolemy and by COPERNICUS. He rejected the hypothesis,
already proposed by ARISTARCHUS, of a Sun-centred

planetary system. He represented the observed revolutions of the Sun and Moon by means of ideal eccentric and epicyclic motions, and he classified and supplemented existing observations of the five planets later to be utilized by Ptolemy.

Hipparchus reviewed the geography of ERATOSTHENES and he strove to render the science more precise by fixing the positions of places on the Earth's surface. He tried to estimate latitudes from the ratio of the shortest to the longest day, and he suggested determining differences of longitude by comparing the local times of selected eclipses observed at widely separated stations. In a lost commentary quoted by Strabo (63 BC–c.21 AD), Hipparchus criticized inaccuracies and inconsistencies in the positional geography of Eratosthenes, and he put forward proposals for a mathematical geography to be based upon astronomical data.

Hipparchus computed a table of the chords of angles ranging from 0° to 180° and serving the purpose of a table of sines; he is credited with discovering the theorems required for its construction.

T. L. Heath, *A History of Greek Mathematics*, vol. 2. 1921.

P. Tannery, *Recherches sur l'Histoire de l'Astronomie Ancienne*. 1893.

D. R. Dicks (Ed.), *The Geographical Fragments of Hipparchus*. 1960.

Dictionary of Scientific Biography, Supp. I.

A A

HIPPOCRATES Born on the Greek island of Cos, *c*.460 BC; died near Larissa, *c*.377 BC. Venerated for over 2000 years as the ideal physician and the Father of Medicine.

Hippocrates was an Asclepiad, that is, a member of a family practising medicine for generations. Instead of practising and teaching in his native island, he travelled throughout Greece and possibly also in the Near East. In his lifetime he was regarded as a great clinician. He was buried near Larissa. That is virtually all that is known of his life, since any further particulars are derived from biographies written centuries after his death.

Equally unsatisfactory is the position regarding his writings. From early times certain works then extant were ascribed to him. These were all supposedly contemporary, and mainly emanated from the School at Cos, though some were admittedly from the rival School at Cnidos. At an early period they became known as the *Corpus Hippocraticum* (the Hippocratic Collection). It was early recognized that only some of these were by Hippocrates. Modern research suggests that the Collection consisted of the writings of the Hippocratic period that were in the Library at Alexandria. It is now recognized that, of the sixty or seventy books regarded as forming the Collection, a few – such as *Epidemics*, Books I and III; the *Aphorisms; Prognostic; The Sacred Disease; Airs Waters Places*; and the surgical works – are characterized by such acute observation, broad humanity, rational treatment, and similarity in style, that they were possibly written by one man, who may have been Hippocrates. Some scholars believe that no single extant work is by Hippocrates himself. It is certain that at least 100 years separated the earliest from the latest work in the Collection.

In the Hippocratic works there are about forty clinical descriptions of illnesses from which the diseases can be diagnosed, such as malaria, mumps, pneumonia, and phthisis. There is a memorable description of the 'Hippocratic facies' – the countenance before death in certain diseases. In the writings on epidemics, Hippocrates correlated the prevalence of certain diseases with climatic, dietetic, racial, and environmental factors. The *Aphorisms* contain many profound dicta which are still true today. The surgical works abound with clear descriptions of instruments and practical directions. The Hippocratic doctrine of the four humours, further developed by GALEN, dominated medicine until the eighteenth century. The so-called Hippocratic Oath is now regarded as of much later date than the Hippocratic School.

H. E. Sigerist, *A History of Medicine*, vol. 2. 1961.

W. H. S. Jones and E. T. Withington, *Hippocrates*, 4 vols. 1923–31.

C. Singer, *Greek Biology and Greek Medicine*. 1922.

L. Edelstein, *The Hippocratic Oath*. 1943.

C. Singer and E. A. Underwood, *Short History of Medicine*. 1962. (Portrait.)

Wilder Penfield, *The Torch*. 1960.

Dictionary of Scientific Biography.

E A U

HIROHITO, HIS MAJESTY, EMPEROR OF JAPAN Born in Tokyo, 29 April 1901; died there, 7 January 1989. The Showa Emperor. Biologist, collector, systematist, ecologist.

Prince Michi Hirohito, son of Emperor Taisho (d. 1926) and grandson of the Meiji Emperor Mutsuhito (d. 1912), was educated at the Peers' School (Gakushuin), Tokyo, and then at the special institute, Gogakumonjo, Akasaka Palace, Tokyo. He became Prince Regent in 1921 and was crowned Emperor in 1928. In the UK he was invested Knight of the Garter in 1929; the banner of his Arms was removed in 1941 and restored in 1971. He was elected Honorary Member of the Linnean Society of London in 1931 and FRS in 1971. His interest in wildlife began at the age of 12 and was fostered by his teacher Hirotaro Hattori (1875–1965), who became chief of the Biological Laboratory established in 1925 in the Imperial Palace Domain and re-built in 1928. Hirohito devoted most of his spare time to collecting plants and animals in the Imperial Estates and in Sagami Bay south of Tokyo. In so doing he amassed large collections of marine animals, especially invertebrates, higher plants, and slime-moulds, all meticulously labelled in regard to habitat and identified with the help of Japanese specialists. His concern was to discover how these organisms lived together, and thus he became a conservationist. The result was the publication from 1935 onwards of many zoological monographs and floristic works, all beautifully illustrated in colour and line, with the description of many new species and Japanese records. Hirohito specialized in Hydrozoa and became the international authority on these Coelenterata.

His new genus and species *Pseudoclathrozoon cryptolarioides* provided the design for the medal which accompanies the International Prize for Biology, established in 1985 in his honour through the Japan Academy. He not only promoted biology with his own research but stimulated the subject in Japan. His scientific interest is revealed in such works as his *The hydroids of Sagami Bay* (1988) and his part-authorship of *The crabs of Sagami Bay* (1965), *Nova flora Nasuensis* (1972) and *Flora sedis Imperatoris Japoniae* (1989).

Biographical Memoirs of Fellows of the Royal Society. 1990. (Portrait.)

E J H C

HIS, WILHELM Born at Basle, Switzerland, 9 July 1831; died Leipzig, Germany, 1 March 1904. Anatomist and physician.

After qualifying as Doctor of Medicine in 1855, His was *Privatdozent* for histology before his appointment in 1857 as professor of anatomy and physiology at the University of Basle. In 1872 he moved to Leipzig to become professor of anatomy and director of the Institute of Anatomy. One of the pioneers of modern medicine, he is known best for his researches on the embryology of the nervous system; the mode of origin of nerve fibres; and his very detailed studies of the developing human embryo. He was one of the first embryologists to make great use of the microtome for cutting serial sections. In 1875 he founded *Die Zeitschrift für Anatomie und Entwicklungsgeschichte.*

His son Wilhelm (1863–1934) was director of the first medical clinic and (1907–25) professor of internal medicine at the University of Berlin. He investigated the innervation of the heart, and the Bundle of His, composed of muscle-fibres connecting cardiac auricles with ventricles, is named after him.

Dictionnaire Historique et Biographique de la Suisse. 1928.

W. A. Locy, *Biology and its Makers.* 1936. (Portrait.)

R. Fick, *Anatomischer Anzeiger*, **25**, 161, 1904.

Dictionary of Scientific Biography.

A P G

HITTORF, JOHANN WILHELM Born in Bonn, North Rhine-Westphalia, 27 March 1824; died Münster, Westphalia, 28 November 1914. Best known for his work on the migration of ions during electrolysis.

After studying mathematics, Hittorf turned to physics and chemistry. During researches on the allotropic forms of selenium and phosphorus he discovered the important fact that crystalline selenium conducts electricity (1851). In an important series of papers (1853–9) he investigated the variations in the concentrations of electrolytes during electrolysis. Assuming these variations to be due to the differing mobilities of the positive and negative ions, he was able to work out the ratio of the ion velocities by measuring the concentrations at the cathode and the anode. On the basis of this work, in conjunction with the notion of limiting values at infinite dilution, F. W. G. KOHLRAUSCH later calculated the absolute values of drift of the anions and cations. In collaboration with J. PLÜCKER (1865), Hittorf found two distinct types of discharge-tube spectra for a number of gases, the first a faint continuous type produced by the passage of a discharge from an induction coil at low pressure, and the second consisting of bright lines between dark spaces produced by the passage of a discharge from a Leyden jar. In 1869 he published a fundamental paper containing a careful description of the change in the nature of the discharge in vacuum tubes with

lowering of pressure, including the spreading of the cathode glimmer across to the anode. He also described the casting of shadows by obstacles near the cathode, proving that the so-called cathode glimmer was produced by rays. The absence of phosphorescence on parts of the tube within the shadow proved this phosphorescence to be due to the same rays, whose heating effects and deviation in a magnetic field he also investigated.

Hittorf was elected a Foreign Associate of the *Académie des Sciences* in 1910.

G. C. Schmidt, *Johann Hittorf.* 1924.

P. Lenard, *Great Men of Science.* 1933. (Portrait.)

Dictionary of Scientific Biography.

J W H

HITZIG, EDUARD Born in Berlin, 6 February 1838; died St Blasien, Germany, 28 August 1904. Neurophysiologist, chiefly remembered for his work with G. T. FRITSCH on cortical localization in the brain.

Eduard Hitzig graduated from Berlin University in 1862 and turned immediately to the practice of psychiatry. In 1875 he was appointed professor of psychiatry and director of the Burghölzi mental asylum in Zürich. Four years later he accepted the same appointments at Nietleben and in 1885 established an independent neuro-psychiatric clinic in near-by Halle. He retired in 1903.

Working under primitive conditions and in collaboration with Fritsch, he investigated the electrical excitability of the cerebral cortex of the dog. Their classical paper of 1870 (*Archiv für Anatomie und Physiologie*) gave conclusive proof that cortical localization of function exists and thus confirmed earlier suspicions which had, however, been based like those of J. B. Bouillaud (1796–1881), S. A. E. Auburtin (1825–?1893), and of J. Hughlings Jackson (1834–1911) upon clinical evidence and hypothesis. From these and other experiments on cerebral localization, which included a careful delineation of the motor region of the cortex, a direct line of investigation extends to us today. Hitzig strove to obtain precise data in his physiological work and he attempted a more scientific approach to the treatment of mental patients. He was thus a typical product of the German school of physiology which dominated the world in the second half of the nineteenth and at the beginning of the twentieth centuries.

Hitzig was a rigid, unfriendly, arrogant Prussian and he delighted in controversy. In later life he became blind and was impelled reluctantly to cease his polemics.

R. Wollenberg, 'Eduard Hitzig', *Archiv für Psychiatrie und Nervenkrankheiten*, **43**, iii, 1908.

W. Haymaker and F. Schiller (Eds), *The Founders of Neurology.* 1953. (Portrait.)

Dictionary of Scientific Biography.

E C

HODGKIN, SIR ALAN LLOYD Born at Banbury, Oxfordshire, England, 5 February 1914. Neurologist.

Educated at Gresham's School, Holt, Hodgkin graduated from Trinity College, Cambridge in 1936, and began research on the electrical properties of nerve impulses, using single nerve fibres from the shore crab *Carcinus maenas* for his experiments. After a year at the Rockefeller Institute, New York, and the Woods Hole Marine Biological Laboratories, Massachusetts 1937–8, Hodgkin returned to Cambridge and began his collaboration with A. F. Huxley (1917–) using axons of the squid *Loligo forbesi*. During the Second World War he did radar research for the Air Ministry, developing airborne radar to be used at night to intercept enemy bombers.

Hodgkin became a lecturer in the department of physiology at Cambridge in 1945, assistant research director in 1952, and was Foulerton Research Professor from 1952 until 1970. With Huxley he continued to investigate the way in which nerve impulses move along individual nerve fibres. Their work led to the ionic theory of nerve conduction and contributed significantly to the understanding of the nervous system and the medical treatment of nervous disorders.

Hodgkin was awarded the Nobel prize for physiology or medicine in 1963 jointly with J. C. Eccles (1903–) and A. F. Huxley for his discoveries in nerve conduction. He was elected President of the Royal Society 1970–5. He held the chair of biophysics at Cambridge 1970–81, and was Master of Trinity College, Cambridge 1978–81. Hodgkin was knighted in 1972, and was awarded the OM in 1973.

A. L. Hodgkin, *The Conduction of the Nerve Impulse*. 1963.
A. L. Hodgkin, *Chance and Design: Reminiscences of Science in Peace and War*. 1992. (Portrait.)
Tyler Wasson (Ed.), *Nobel Prize Winners*. 1987. (Portrait.)

A P B

HODGKIN, DOROTHY MARY CROWFOOT Born in Cairo, Egypt, 12 May 1910. Chemist; pioneer of x-ray crystallographic analysis.

Dorothy Hodgkin, née Crowfoot, spent much of her early childhood in the Sudan, where her father was Principal of Gordon College, Khartoum, having left the Egyptian Ministry of Education. She was educated at the Sir John Leman School in Beccles, Suffolk, and was awarded first class honours in chemistry at Somerville College, Oxford in 1932. She then joined J. D. Bernal (1901 –1971) in his new crystallographic laboratory in Cambridge from 1932 to 1934. Bernal was exploring the possibility of determining the three-dimensional structure of complex biological molecules. She took the first x-ray diffraction photograph of the protein pepsin in 1934, and this helped to establish that proteins were molecules whose structure could be analysed by the methods of x-ray crystallography.

She returned to Oxford in 1934 as a research fellow at Somerville, and became Fellow and Tutor in chemistry in 1936. In 1937 she married Thomas Hodgkin (died 1972), an expert on African affairs, who was director of the Institute of African Studies at the University of Ghana in the 1960s. They had three children.

From 1942 Dorothy Hodgkin worked on the structure of penicillin. This was announced in 1949, and she then turned her attention to vitamin B-12, crucial in the treatment of pernicious anaemia. This analysis was completed in 1957. Her third important discovery was the chemical structure of insulin, revealed in 1969. From 1960 to 1977 she was Wolfson Research Professor of the Royal Society.

Elected a Fellow of the Royal Society in 1947, Dorothy Hodgkin became the third woman to receive the Nobel prize for chemistry, for the determination by x-ray techniques of the structure of important biochemical substances, and, in 1965, the first woman since Florence Nightingale to be awarded the Order of Merit.

The Times, 21 April, 1975.
W. A. Campbell and N. N. Greenwood (Eds), *Contemporary British Chemists*. 1971. (Portrait.)
Tyler Wasson (Ed.), *Nobel Prize Winners*. 1987. (Portrait.)

A P B

HODGKINSON, EATON Born at Anderton, Cheshire, England, 26 February 1789; died Higher Broughton, Manchester, 18 June 1861. Engineer.

Son of a farmer, Eaton Hodgkinson was destined for the Church, but had to leave school to return to the farm because of his father's early death. With his mother he set up a pawnbroking business in Manchester in 1811 and, stimulated by the members of the Manchester Literary and Philosophical Society – of which he became President 1848–50 – and later by opportunities to experiment in the works of Sir William FAIRBAIRN, he made such a name for himself as an authority on the strength of materials that in 1841 he was elected to the Royal Society and in the same year was awarded its Royal Medal. In 1847 was appointed professor of mechanical engineering at University College, London. As a consultant he advised Robert STEPHENSON on the tubes for the Conway and Britannia Bridges. He was a member of the Royal Commission on the application of iron to railways (1847–9).

Dictionary of National Biography.

W H G A

HOE, RICHARD MARCH Born in New York, 12 September 1812; died Florence, Italy, 7 June 1886. Inventor of the rotary printing press.

Son of Robert Hoe (1784–1832), a Leicester-born printer who improved the cylinder press developed by David Napier, Richard Hoe entered his father's firm at 15; fifteen years later he took full control of it. Richard Hoe was among those who recognized that substantially to increase the speed of printing some alternative had to be found to the reciprocating movement of the heavy flat bed of traditional machines. In 1846 he successfully introduced a strictly rotary press in which the type was set on a central cylinder and the sheets of paper were fed through smaller impression cylinders grouped round it. First used for the *Philadelphia Public Ledger*, by 1857 *The Times* had a ten-feeder Hoe press capable of making 20 000 impressions an hour.

Speed was still limited by the fact that printing was done on single sheets. In 1865 William Bullock (1813–67) of Philadelphia introduced for the *Philadelphia Inquirer* a rotary machine that printed on a continuous roll of paper. In the following year *The Times* introduced the Walter machine, but by 1871 Hoe had devised one embodying all the main advantages of its rivals.

Hoe established a free evening school for his apprentices, as well as numerous welfare ventures.

He had five daughters by two marriages, and his business successor was his nephew Robert Hoe (1839–1909), who developed colour printing.

Robert Hoe, *A Short History of the Printing Press*. 1902.
Dictionary of American Biography.

W H G A

HOFFMANN, FRIEDRICH Born at Halle, Germany, 19 February 1660; died there, 12 November 1742. Distinguished physician, and propounder of a famous medical 'system'.

Hoffmann's father, a well-known physician of Halle, and his nearest relatives all died within a few days, so that Hoffmann was left to his own resources at the age of 15. He studied medicine at Jena (1678–9) and then at Erfurt, and graduated as a doctor of medicine at Jena in 1680. In 1682 he did postgraduate study in Holland, and then went to England, where he became intimate with Robert BOYLE and other philosophers. He was appointed physician to the garrison at Minden (1685) and to the Principality of Minden (1686). Two years later he became physician to the Halberstadt area. In 1693 he was invited by the Kurfürst Frederick III (later Frederick I of Prussia) to be the first professor of medicine at the newly founded University of Halle. He lectured on chemistry, physics, anatomy, surgery, and the practice of medicine. At Hoffmann's request G. E. STAHL was invited to fill the other chair at Halle, and Stahl lectured on botany, physiology, pathology, and materia medica. At Halle, Hoffmann's success as a teacher was phenomenal; his lectures were eagerly attended by students, practising physicians, and even professors. In 1709 he left Halle to became body-physician to Frederick I of Prussia. But court life was distasteful to him, and in 1712 he returned to his old activities at Halle.

Hoffmann was a voluminous writer, and his collected works give a very complete idea of the medicine of his time. He lived in the age of 'systems', such as those of John Brown (1735–88) and William Cullen (1710–90). Hoffmann's system is reminiscent of the ancient views of Asclepiades (*c.*124–*c.*40 BC). He conceived of life in terms of movement, under the influence of force and counterforce, by which contraction and extension were produced. Health is normal movement and disease is disturbed movement. He conceived also of the body being kept in a state of health by a partial contraction of the muscles ('tonus'), which was produced by an ether-like fluid that flowed to them from the brain by way of the nerves. If the 'tonus' was excessive, spasm resulted; if deficient, atony. He also agreed with the old view that imbalance of the humours, and faulty evacuation, might cause some diseases. His treatment was therefore based on the use of sedatives, tonics, alternatives, and evacuants, according to which condition was responsible for the disease.

Apart from his system, Hoffmann was an excellent physician. Contrary to current practice at the time, his prescriptions contained few drugs. He was one of the first to give good descriptions of appendicitis (1716), chlorosis (1730), and rubella (1740). He was also one of the first writers on medical ethics.

Allgemeine Deutsche Biographie.
F. H. Garrison, *History of Medicine*. 1929.

R. H. Major, *History of Medicine*, vol. 2. 1954. (Portrait.)
Dictionary of Scientific Biography.

E A U

HOFMANN (later VON HOFMANN), AUGUST WILHELM Born at Giessen, Hesse, Germany, 8 April 1818; died Berlin, 2 May 1892. One of the major organic chemists and most influential teachers of the nineteenth century.

Hofmann studied philosophy and law in Giessen, turning to chemistry in 1843, when he became Justus von LIEBIG's assistant. After two years, he was appointed (on Liebig's recommendation to Prince Albert) professor in the new Royal College of Chemistry in London. His twenty years there were vital to the development of chemistry in Britain; but, perhaps disappointed at its slowness, he returned to Germany in 1865 as successor to E. MITSCHERLICH in Berlin, where he remained until his death.

Predominant in Hofmann's character was an unquenchable enthusiasm for chemistry. This quickly overrode the inevitable differences of opinion, and his writing display none of the jealousy and nagging polemics of some of his contemporaries. He was a fine lecturer, both in English and German, but as an experimenter his eagerness often outran his technique, and most of the work was actually done by his assistants. His private life was a chequered one; he was four times married, and only eight of his eleven children survived him.

Hofmann published hundreds of papers. Most of his work is based on the compounds obtained from coal tar, their derivatives and reactions. His pupils (W. H. PERKIN, C. B. Mansfield, E. C. Nicholson, and P. GRIESS among them) were responsible for the commercial exploitation of coal-tar distillates, and for the brief flowering of the British dyestuffs industry in his time. In particular, his school studied aniline and its reactions, and its relationship to phenol and benzene. This study was extended to the alkylamines, and it was Hofmann who discovered the quaternary ammonium salts. He was thus led to classify all amines as formal derivatives of ammonia, in which one or more hydrogen atoms were replaced by 'compound radicals'. This idea of the 'ammonia type' (to which further types were soon added by other chemists) was the foundation of the later 'Theory of Types'; (see C. F. GERHARDT); it was Hofmann's only contribution to chemical theory, for he was essentially a discoverer. The extension of the 'ammonia type' to alkyl phosphines and phosphonium salts gave him deep satisfaction.

Hofmann was one of the first to accept and use in his lectures the revised atomic weights of S. CANNIZZARO, but he was slow to avail himself of the insight afforded by the Theory of Structure. However, the important compounds discovered or first properly investigated by him include allyl alcohol, ethylenediamine, formaldehyde, styrene, the isonitriles, and the rosaniline dyestuffs. His discovery of the 'benzidine rearrangement' raised problems which are still not fully solved. He is remembered by the 'Hofmann rearrangement' of amides by hypobromite, to give amines containing one carbon atom less; and by 'Hofmann's exhaustive methylation', which was at one time a valuable tool in the study of the structures of alkaloids.

Hofmann was one of the founders of the German Chemical Society. He wrote a little on historical chemistry, and the long obituary notices of some of his friends (*Zur Erinnerung an vorangegangene Freunde*, 1888) have become a classic. Among other honours, he was elected FRS in 1851.

Chemical Society Memorial Lectures, 1893–1900. (Portrait.)
Berichte der deutschen Chemischen Gesellschaft, 35, 1902. (Portrait.)
J. R. Partington, *A History of Chemistry*, vol. 4. 1964. (Portrait.)
A. S. Travis, *Endeavour* (New Series), **16**, 59, 1992. (Portrait).
E. Farber (Ed.), *Great Chemists*. 1961. (Portrait.)
J. Bentley, *Ambix*, **17**, 153, 1970.

　　　　　　　　　　　　　　　　　　　　W V F

HOFMEISTER, WILHELM FRIEDRICH BENE-DICT Born at Leipzig, Saxony, Germany, 18 May 1824; died Lindenau bei Leipzig, 12 January 1877. Botanist. Hofmeister, who was the son of a music dealer and bookseller, never attended a university, but entered his father's business. His scientific achievements were all the more impressive since he was a completely self-taught botanist. He attracted attention when only 27 years old with his investigations on the development and structure of the archegoniate plants – that is to say, mosses and ferns.

Up to the middle of the last century an imperfect knowledge of the Cryptogams had prevented the formulation of any unifying concept of the plant world. Botanists still believed that the Phanerogams and Cryptogams were widely separated. Certain facts had been discovered, but it was Hofmeister in his *Vergleichende Untersuchungen* (1851) who revealed the relationship between the groups of Cryptogams and established the position of the Gymnosperms between the higher Cryptogams and the Angiosperms. His work removed the barriers between the lower and higher plants and enabled a phylogenetic relationship of the entire plant world eventually to emerge.

In 1863 his exceptional abilities were recognized by appointing him to a professor's post and the directorship of the Botanic Garden at Heidelberg. Many of the students he taught were to achieve distinction as botanists. The two most important books to emanate from Heidelberg were his *Die Lehre von der Pflanzenzelle* (1867) and *Allgemeine Morphologie* (1868). In 1872 he succeeded Hugo von Mohl (1805–72) at Tübingen.

A man of unquestionable genius, his greatest achievement was his discovery of the regular alternation of generations in the plant kingdom. His discoveries broadened the horizons of botanical research, and encouraged others in the study of comparative morphology.

K. von Goebel, *Wilhelm Hofmeister*. 1926. (Royal Society Publication No 111.) (Portrait.)
Plant World, **8**, 291, 1905. (Portrait.)
Dictionary of Scientific Biography.

　　　　　　　　　　　　　　　　　　　　R G C D

HOHENHEIM, THEOPHRASTUS BOMBASTUS VON *See* PARACELSUS.

HOLLERITH, HERMAN Born in Buffalo, New York

State, USA, 29 February 1860; died in Washington, DC, 17 November 1929. Inventor.

After graduating from Columbia University School of Mines in 1879, Hollerith joined the US Census Bureau as a statistician. The Bureau was then organising itself to analyse the 1880 census, a laborious manual task not completed until seven years later, only two years before the next census was due. Hollerith set about mechanizing the process, using the punched card device incorporated in the loom designed by J. M. JACQUARD in 1801. The cards were read by using a pin press containing a small cup of mercury below each position where a hole – corresponding to a specific item of statistical information – might occur. If the pin passed through, an electrical contact was made and registered. Using this technique, the 1890 census was completed in 2½ years, although the population had grown from 50 million to 63 million. In 1896 Hollerith founded the Tabulating Machine Company to exploit his invention more widely and this was eventually (1924) incorporated in International Business Machines (IBM). The UK government used the Hollerith system for the 1911 census.

W. J. Eckert, *Punched Card Methods in Scientific Computing*. 1940.
A. G. Debus (Ed.) *World Who's Who in Science*. 1968.
Dictionary of American Biography.

　　　　　　　　　　　　　　　　　　　　T I W

HOLMES, ARTHUR Born at Hebburn, near Newcastle upon Tyne, England, 14 January 1890; died London, 20 September 1965. Physical and petrological geologist; measurer of geological time.

Arthur Holmes graduated at the Imperial College of Science, London, in 1910 and undertook an expedition to Mozambique in 1911. He returned to Imperial College in 1912 as a member of the staff until 1920. He then joined the Yornah Oil Company in Burma as chief geologist, but returned in 1924 to become head of the newly created department of geology in the University of Durham. In 1943 he was appointed professor of geology in the University of Edinburgh; from this he retired in 1956, remaining in Edinburgh as emeritus professor until 1962.

His researches and textbooks have had a profound influence. His particular field was petrology, his *Petrographic Methods and Calculations* (1921) being a particularly well known book. He went deeply into the major questions concerning igneous rocks and their origins, largely in association with his wife, Doris Reynolds, herself an eminent geologist. However, his outstanding contributions were in the employment of radioactivity methods in the determination of the absolute ages of rocks, thus leading to a time-scale for the geological record and an estimate of the age of the Earth. His first paper of all was on this subject, published by the Royal Society in 1911, and more than fifty further contributions on the same topic culminated in his latest revision in the *Transactions of the Edinburgh Geological Society* in 1959.

Holmes's name is associated not only with these specialized (though fundamental) problems. He dealt with almost all branches of physical geology, always on the grand scale, in their broad philosophical aspects. His *Principles of Physical Geology* was first published in 1944 and was immensely successful; a completely rewritten and greatly enlarged edition was published in 1965, the year of his death. This fine work by Holmes himself and the symposium volume on the geological time-scale, dedicated to him, are fitting memorials.

In addition to his Fellowship of the Royal Society he held many degrees, was elected into membership of numerous scientific societies in Europe and America, and was awarded some of the most prized medals, including the Wollaston Medal of the Geological Society.

It is said of him that he was a quiet man of extraordinary charm and unfailing kindness.

F. H. Stewart, Appreciation in *The Phanerozoic Time-scale* (Geological Society symposium). 1964. (Portrait.)

S. I. Tonkeieff, *Proceedings of the Geologists' Association*, **78**, 374, 1967.

L. Cahen, *Bulletin of the Geological Society of America*, **77**, 127, 1966.

Biographical Memoirs of Fellows of the Royal Society. 1966. (Portrait.)

Dictionary of National Biography.

J C

HOLMES, OLIVER WENDELL Born in Cambridge, Massachusetts, USA, 29 August 1809; died Boston, Massachusetts, 7 October 1894. Physician; showed puerperal fever to be contagious.

Holmes was the son of Abiel Holmes (1763–1837), a well-known Congregational minister and historian, and the father of the jurist Oliver Wendell Holmes (1841–1935). He was educated at Phillips Academy, Andover, Massachusetts, and at Harvard College, graduating in 1829. He then spent a year reading law but decided his true vocation was medicine, and entered Harvard Medical School. He qualified in medicine in 1836, having spent three years in Paris studying under P. C. A. Louis (1787–1872), for whom he formed a profound regard.

After qualifying he set up in practice in Boston. In 1843 he made a notable contribution to medicine with his essay on *The Contagiousness of Puerperal Fever*. In this he established that puerperal fever is contagious and may be carried from one patient to another by the physicians attending them. This view was strongly contested by obstetricians, but was independently confirmed five years later by I. P. SEMMELWEIS in Vienna. From 1847 to 1882 Holmes was Parkman Professor of Anatomy and Physiology at Harvard.

When Holmes was a young man W. T. G. MORTON was carrying out his well-known experiments on the use of ether in surgery. Holmes (in a letter to him of 21 November 1846) suggested the name anaesthesia – now universally used – for this powerful new method of treatment.

Holmes made a reputation as a literary man as well as a physician. He first became famous with his *Autocrat of the Breakfast Table* (1857/8), quickly followed by *The Professor at the Breakfast Table* (1858/9) and later by *The Poet at the Breakfast Table* (1872). He wrote also many novels, including *Elsie Venner* (1861), and poems, including *The Deacon's Masterpiece or the Wonderful One-Hoss-Shay*.

Dictionary of American Biography.

E. M. Tilton, *Amiable Autocrat*. 1947.

T I W

HOOKE, ROBERT Born at Freshwater, Isle of Wight, England, 18 July 1635; died London, 3 March 1703. One of the most brilliant and versatile of seventeenth-century English scientists.

On completing his schooling at Westminster School, Hooke acquired a place as chorister at Christ Church Oxford, later becoming assistant to Robert BOYLE, especially in the construction of the improved version of the air pump of Otto GUERICKE described in Boyle's *New Experiments Physico-Mechanicall* (1660). In 1662 he was appointed curator to the newly founded Royal Society, being responsible for the experiments performed at its weekly meetings. As curator of the Society he had rooms in Gresham College, where he was professor of geology and carried out astronomical observations. In 1677 he became one of the secretaries to the Royal Society. Of a sickly constitution, he was in broken health from 1696 onwards.

Hooke put forward an undulatory theory of light in his *Micrographia* (1665), comparing the spreading of light vibrations to that of waves in water. He even suggested (1672) that the vibrations in light might be perpendicular to the direction of propagation. He investigated the colours of membranes and of thin plates of mica, establishing the variation of the light pattern with the thickness of the plates. But this theory of colours was inadequate, being based on two colours only, red and blue.

In his *Attempt to Prove the Motion of the Earth* (1674), he put forward a theory of planetary motion based on the correct principle of inertia and a balance between an outward centrifugal force and an inward gravitational attraction to the Sun. In 1679, in a letter to NEWTON, he finally suggested that this attraction would vary inversely as the square of the distance from the Sun. Hooke's theory was qualitatively correct, but lacking the necessary mathematical powers he was inevitably precluded from giving it an exact, quantitative expression.

If Hooke's work in optics and gravitation were dwarfed by the transcendent contributions of Newton, he was unrivalled in the seventeenth century as an inventor and designer of scientific instruments. Thus among a host of other inventions he invented the spring control of the balance wheel in watches; the compound microscope; a wheel barometer; and the universal, or Hooke's joint. He also made important contributions to astronomical instruments, being the first to insist on the importance of resolving power, and the advantage of using hair lines in place of silk or metal wire. He constructed the first reflecting telescope, observed the rotation of Mars, and noted one of the earliest examples of a double star.

Hooke's reputation suffered greatly in his own lifetime and beyond from his many controversies with other scientists over questions of priority, such as that with Christian HUYGENS over the spring regulator, and more especially those with Newton, first over optics (1672) and secondly over his claim to priority in the formulation of the inverse square law of gravitation (1686). These unhappy controversies no longer obscure Hooke's genius, and he appears today as the most versatile and brilliant English scientist of the seventeenth century with the exception of Newton, and without exception the member who contributed most in the seventeenth century to the transformation of the Royal Society from a band of scientific virtuosi to a professional body of scientists.

Posthumous Works of Robert Hooke (including life by R. Waller). 1705.

R. T. Gunter, *The Life and Work of Robert Hooke.* (4 vols). 1930–5.

M. 'Espinasse, *Robert Hooke.* 1956.

E. N. de C. Andrade, *Proceedings of the Royal Society,* **201A**, 439, 1950.

Dictionary of National Biography.

Dictionary of Scientific Biography.

J W H

HOOKER, SIR JOSEPH DALTON Born at Halesworth, Suffolk, England, 30 June 1817; died Sunningdale, Berkshire, 10 December 1911. Plant taxonomist, phytogeographer, and explorer.

After studying medicine at Glasgow University, Hooker became Assistant Surgeon and Naturalist on the HMS *Erebus* and *Terror* expedition to Antarctica, (1839–43). His subsequent botanical narrative of the expedition – *Flora Antarctica* (1844–7), *Flora Novae-Zelandiae* (1853–5), and *Flora Tasmaniae* (1855–60) – placed him in the front of taxonomic botanists. In 1847 he departed for India, where he spent three years collecting plants in Bengal, Sikkim, eastern Nepal, and Assam. His *Himalayan Journals* (1854) closely observe the fauna and ethnography as well as the flora of the region, and later travellers have testified to the accuracy of his surveying. The *Rhododendrons of the Sikkim-Himalaya* (1849) appeared while he was still out there, and his love for India culminated in his seven-volume *Flora of British India* (1872–97). Further expeditions that he later undertook were to Syria and Palestine (1860), to the Atlas Mountains in Morocco (1871), and to the western United States with Asa GRAY in 1877.

In 1855 he was appointed assistant director at the Royal Botanic Gardens, Kew, and ten years later he succeeded his father, Sir William J. Hooker (1785–1865), as director. Sir William Hooker had created Kew Gardens and established its main departments, and it was his son who developed it as an international centre of scientific research. Joseph Hooker's major contributions to Kew before his retirement in 1885 were the Jodrell Laboratory for investigations into plant anatomy and physiology (1876); an extension to the Herbarium (1877); the Marianne North Gallery (1882); and the Rock Garden (1882). The Kew Herbarium is still arranged according to a plant classification devised by Hooker and George BENTHAM, and published as the *Genera Plantarum* (1862–83).

Hooker first met Charles DARWIN in 1839 and they became lifelong friends. Although Hooker was aware of Darwin's researches, they worked independently towards the evolutionary theory. In 1858 he and Sir Charles LYELL were responsible for presenting the joint communication of Charles Darwin and A. R. WALLACE on the origin of species to the Linnean Society. Sir Joseph cautiously approved the theory of natural selection in his celebrated introductory essay (1860) to the *Flora Tasmaniae*, but he soon became a vigorous advocate of evolution.

As the leading botanist of his day, Hooker

received many honours, including the Order of Merit (1907); he was President of the Royal Society 1873–8.

L. Huxley, *Life and Letters of Sir Joseph Dalton Hooker.* (2 vols.) 1918. (Portrait.)

W. B. Turrill, *Joseph Dalton Hooker.* 1963. (Portrait.)

M. Allan, *The Hookers of Kew.* 1967. (Portrait.)

Dictionary of National Biography.

Dictionary of Scientific Biography.

R G C D

HOPE, THOMAS CHARLES Born in Edinburgh, 21 July 1766; died there, 13 June 1844. Chemist.

T. C. Hope was the third son of John Hope (1725–1786), Regius Professor of Botany at Edinburgh, and a grandson of Archibald Hope, Lord Rankeillor (1639–1706), a Scottish law lord. He studied medicine at Edinburgh University, and in 1787 was appointed professor of chemistry at Glasgow; in 1791 he was appointed professor of practical medicine. In 1795, when the health of Joseph BLACK began to fail, Hope was appointed joint professor with him at Edinburgh. In 1797 he succeeded Black, and held the chair for nearly fifty years, until 1843.

Although Hope was not of the calibre of Black, he carried out important researches. In physics he conclusively confirmed seventeenth-century observation, in his day regarded with scepticism, that water expands as it nears its freezing point. Hope recorded the temperature of maximum density as 39.1 °F; the accepted modern value is 39.2 °F (3.98 °C). In 1793, in a paper to the Royal Society of Edinburgh, he identified the mineral strontian (from a village of that name in Argyll, Scotland) as containing a new 'earth' (oxide of strontium). His preparation (1791) of the hydroxide of the corresponding new element (strontium) is still preserved at Edinburgh. An independent discovery was made by M. KLAPROTH, also in 1793.

Hope was a remarkably successful teacher; between 1797 and 1825 average attendance at his lectures rose from 225 to 575. This was particularly significant in view of the fact that he was the first professor in Britain – from 1789 onwards – to teach the new chemistry of LAVOISIER.

James Kendall, *Endeavour,* **3**, 119, 1944. (Portrait.)

R. H. Cragg, *Medical History,* **11**, 186, 1967.

Dictionary of National Biography.

Dictionary of Scientific Biography.

T I W

HOPKINS, SIR FREDERICK GOWLAND Born at Eastbourne, Sussex, England, 20 June 1861; died Cambridge, 16 May 1947. Biochemist; discovered tryptophan and glutathione; did work leading to discovery of vitamins.

After a lonely and unhappy childhood, Hopkins was articled for three years to a consulting analyst in the City of London. He became an analytical assistant at Guy's Hospital, meanwhile taking a part-time degree in chemistry in London University. In 1888 he became a medical student, and qualified six years later. He left Guy's in 1898 to become lecturer in chemical physiology at Cambridge, where he remained for the rest of his life, becoming professor of biochemistry in 1914, and retiring in 1943. It was not until 1924, when the Dunn Institute of Biochemistry was founded, that he had adequate laboratory facilities.

Hopkins's first publication (1878) was a note in an entomological journal. This interest led him to a study of the pigments of butterflies' wings, which he believed to be related chemically to uric acid, an intuition which was not confirmed for many years. He soon distinguished himself at Cambridge by devising a method for obtaining crystalline proteins, and by his classical paper (with Morley Fletcher (1873–1933), in 1907) on the chemistry of muscle contraction. A student's failure to obtain the Adamkiewicz colour reaction for proteins led Hopkins to identify glyoxylic acid as the impurity in commercial acetic acid which caused the test to succeed; and to isolate (with S. W. Cole, 1910) the important amino acid tryptophan from protein hydrolysates, as the fragment reacting with glyoxylic acid.

Already by 1906 studies of the relationship between growth and diet had brought Hopkins to the concept of 'accessory food factors' (now called vitamins). He based his ideas on experiments in which addition of small quantities of milk to 'synthetic' diets restored normal growth in rats. Attempts to isolate these substances were both laborious and fruitless, and were followed by a nervous breakdown in 1910, caused by disappointment and overwork. For his part in the development of the concept of vitamins, Hopkins shared the Nobel prize for medicine in 1929 with C. EIJKMAN.

It is now clear, however, that the experiments with milk were not so decisive as Hopkins had supposed. Other biochemists could not repeat his results; the amounts of vitamins in the milk were later shown to be too small to affect growth significantly; and the matter is complicated by the metabolic activities of the bacterial flora in the gut of the experimental animal.

After the war, Hopkins resumed his search for vitamins among the sulphur-containing constituents of proteins. This resulted in the discovery, not of a vitamin, but of the important tripeptide glutathione. This substance (for which an incorrect structure was proposed) plays a major role as a hydrogen carrier in biochemical oxidations, though some of the functions once ascribed to it are now known to be due to cytochrome. Hopkins's later work was largely a development of his glutathione studies, especially among other oxidizing enzymes, such as xanthine-oxidase.

Perhaps Hopkins's greatest contribution to biochemistry was his insistence that biological problems could be solved in chemical terms, as against the vitalistic ideas still much in vogue when he began his research.

He married, and had three children. Among his many honours were the Presidency of the Royal Society (1930), a knighthood (1925), and the Order of Merit (1935).

Dictionary of National Biography.
Obituary Notices of Fellows of the Royal Society. 1948. (Portrait.)
Journal of the Chemical Society, 713, 1948. (Portrait.)
E. N. da C. Andrade, *Endeavour,* **15**, 128, 1956).(Portrait.)
E. Baldwin and J. Needham (Eds), *Hopkins and Biochemistry.* 1949.
E. Baldwin, *Gowland Hopkins.* 1961.
Dictionary of Scientific Biography.

H. Oxbury (Ed.) *Great Britons: 20th Century Lives.* 1985.

W V F

HOPPE-SEYLER, ERNST FELIX IMMANUEL

Born at Freyburg, Thuringia, Germany, 26 December 1825; died Wasserburg-am-Bodensee, Germany, 10 August 1895. A founder of modern physiological chemistry.

Ernst Hoppe was early left an orphan, and was brought up by his brother-in-law, Dr Seyler, whose name he assumed in later life. He studied medicine in Halle and Berlin, where he practised for a short time, and also carried out research in the institute of R. VIRCHOW. Here he published his great *Handbuch der physiologischen und pathologischen Analyse.* From 1861 to 1872 he was professor of applied chemistry in Tübingen; in the latter year he was called to the newly Germanized University of Strasbourg as professor of physiological chemistry, where he remained until his death.

His work covered almost the whole range of physiological chemistry. He investigated the colouring matter of the blood and its reaction with carbon monoxide; oxidation processes in the animal body; the chemistry of fermentation and rotting; and the analysis of milk and urine. He was the first to obtain lecithin in a pure state, and his interest in what would now be called geochemistry led to some studies on the formation of dolomite. His main importance, however, is not as a discoverer, but in the single-minded way in which he established physiological chemistry as an academic discipline in its own right. To this end he developed analytical techniques drawn from physics, chemistry, and medicine, and founded in 1877 the *Zeitschrift für physiologische Chemie,* often known by his name. This journal he edited in an able but extremely high-handed manner, sometimes with unfortunate consequences. At the time of his death he was studying the dissolved gases at various depths in Lake Constance, and correlating them with plant life.

Zeitschrift für physiologische Chemie, **21**, 1, 1895–6. (Portrait.)
Berichte der deutschen Chemischen Gesellschaft, **28**, 2333, 1895.
E. Baumann and A. Kossel, *Hoppe-Seyler's Zeitschrift für physiologische Chemie,* **21**, i, 1895.
Dictionary of Scientific Biography.

W V F

HOUDRY, EUGENE JULES

Born at Domont, Paris, on 18 April 1892; died Upper Derby, Pennsylvania, USA, 18 July 1962. Chemical engineer and industrialist.

Known to Americans as 'Mr Catalysis', Houdry was trained as a mechanical engineer at the *École des Arts et Métiers* in Paris, where he graduated in 1911. After war service, he rejoined his father's steel business, taking up automobile racing as a hobby. Following the introduction of octane numbers as a standard for rating fuels in 1927, Houdry became interested in French attempts to produce petrol from lignite by catalytic hydrogenation – a technique then being exploited in the margarine industry. Although he succeeded in developing a process in 1929, it was uneconomic. When further experiments with a hydrated aluminium silicate catalyst looked promising, Houdry emigrated to America to obtain finance from oil companies. In 1931 he formed the Houdry Process Corporation and after backing by several oil companies to the tune of three million dollars, full commercial production of high octane petrol was achieved in 1936–7. Houdry's process of catalytic cracking meant that 100 octane aviation fuel was available to the Allies during World War 2, giving planes at take-off a manoeuvring advantage denied to German aircraft.

In 1942 Houdry became an American citizen. While working on the wartime synthetic rubber programme, he developed a single-step catalytic process for the dehydrogenation of butane to butadiene. He continued to perfect cracking processes until retirement in 1948. Two years later he formed Oxy-Catalyst Inc. with a view to reducing air pollution caused by car exhaust fumes. The holder of 70 patents, Houdry received the American Chemical Society's Award for Industrial and Engineering Chemistry in 1962.

Chemistry and Industry, 1962, p. 1870. (Portrait.)
Journal of Chemical Education, **61**, 655, 1984.
Dictionary of American Biography, Supplement 7, 1981.

W H B

HOUNSFIELD, SIR GODFREY NEWBOLD Born at Newark, England, 28 August 1919. Electrical engineer, inventor of computerised axial tomography (CAT) for x-ray diagnostic investigations.

After studying at the City and Guilds of London College and the Faraday House Electrical Engineering College, he served in the RAF during the Second World War and in 1951 joined Electrical and Musical Industries (EMI). There he led the design team that built the UK's first large solid-state computer, the EMIDEC 1100, completed in 1959.

Later he began to investigate the possibility of utilising the image processing power of the computer to enhance the quality and versatility of x-ray photography. The principle of tomography, by which a radiograph can be made of a thin layer of an internal organ, was discovered in 1915 by André Bocage, but had obvious limitations in practice. Working independently of the South African-born American physicist Allan M. CORMACK, Hounsfield devised a technique involving the computer processing of the continually changing image of any part of the body obtained by an x-ray detector as it was rotated round the patient. It thus became possible to build up a picture of a 'slice' of the patient with much better resolution than static x-ray photography, and with the added ability to magnify selected areas for detailed examination.

By 1972 the EMI-scanner system was able to screen the whole body at one time, an achievement which gained the 1972 MacRobert Award, and a Gold Medal for EMI. He later became senior staff scientist at the Thorn-EMI Central Research Laboratories, and in 1978 was appointed Professorial Fellow in Imaging Sciences at the University of Manchester. He was awarded, jointly with Cormack, the 1979 Nobel prize in physiology or medicine, 'for the development of computer assisted tomography', and was knighted in 1981.

C. Süsskind, *History of Technology*, **6**, 39, 1981.

Physics Today, December 1979.
Tyler Wasson (Ed.), *Nobel Prize Winners*. 1987. (Portrait.)
Les Prix Nobel en 1979. 1980. (Portrait.)

R M B

HOUSSAY, BERNARDO ALBERTO Born in Buenos Aires, Argentina, 10 April 1887; died there, 21 September 1971. Physiologist, endocrinologist.

The son of a French lawyer, Houssay studied first pharmacy and then medicine in Buenos Aires. His MD thesis (1911), on the hypophysis, epitomized his lasting scientific interest but in 40 years of research there were few fields of physiology which he did not explore. In 1919 he was appointed professor of physiology in the University of Buenos Aires and quickly established an Institute of Physiology of international repute. He was stripped of his academic appointments during the political troubles of 1943–5 and 1946–55 but in his last years directed the Argentine National Council for Scientific and Technical Research.

His outstanding success was in relating the function of endocrine glands to nutritional processes. In particular, he established that it was the anterior, rather that the posterior, lobe of the hypophysis which regulated carbohydrate metabolism. He also investigated the complex relationship between the different endocrine glands – thymus, thyroid and adrenals. He was awarded a Nobel prize in 1947.

Les Prix Nobel en 1947. 1948. (Portrait.)
Dictionary of Scientific Biography, Supp. I.
C. F. Cori *et al* (Eds), *Perspectives in Biology*. 1963.
SBiographical Memoirs of Fellows of the Royal Society. 1974. (Portrait.)
Tyler Wasson (Ed.), *Nobel Prize Winners*. 1987. (Portrait.)

T I W

HOWE, ELIAS Born at Spencer, Massachusetts, USA, 9 July 1819; died Brooklyn, New Jersey, 3 October 1867. Inventor of a sewing machine.

Son of Elias Howe, a farmer, he acquired his mechanical knowledge in his father's mill. He left school at 12, and was apprenticed for two years in a machine shop in Lowell, Mass., and later to an instrument-maker, Ari Davis, in Boston, where his master's services were much in demand by Harvard University.

Fired by a desire to invent a sewing machine, he utilized the experience gained in Lowell to devise a shuttle carrying a lower thread and a needle carrying an upper thread to make a lock-stitch. His attempts were so rewarding that he left his job, sustained first by his father, then by a partner. By 1845 he had built a machine that worked at 250 stitches a minute, and in the following year patented an improved machine.

William Thomas, a London manufacturer of shoes, umbrellas and corsets, secured the British rights and persuaded him to come to England to apply it to the making of shoes. This he did, but he quarrelled with Thomas after less than a year, and returned to America to face – with his partner G. W. Bliss – a bigger fight over his patent, which was being widely pirated; not till 1854 was the case settled in his favour. The patent was again renewed in 1861, and with his royalties he organized and equipped a regiment during the Civil War.

When the war ended he founded the Howe Machine Company of Bridgeport, Connecticut.

N. Salamon, *History of the Sewing Machine from the year 1750*. 1863.

Karl Werckmeister, *Das neunzehnte Jahrhundert in Bildnissen*. 1900. (Portrait.)

Frederick G. Harrison, *Biographical Sketches of Pre-eminent Americans*. 1892–3.

Dictionary of American Biography.

W H G A

HOYLE, SIR FRED Born at Bingley, Yorkshire, England, 24 June, 1915. Astronomer, astrophysicist, cosmologist and writer.

Hoyle was educated at Emanuel College, Cambridge. After war service with the Admiralty (1939–45) he returned to Cambridge as university lecturer in mathematics. In 1948 with Herman BONDI and the astronomer Thomas GOLD, Hoyle announced the steady state theory of the Universe in which the expansion of the Universe and the continuous creation of matter were held to be interdependent. Elected FRS in 1957, Hoyle was Plumian Professor of Astronomy and Experimental Philosophy at Cambridge (1958–72); director of the Institute for Theoretical Astronomy (1967–73); and concurrently professor of astronomy at the Royal Institution, London (1969–72). He was also a staff member of the Mount Wilson and Palomar Observatories (now the Hale Observatories), USA, (1957–62) and held visiting professorships in astrophysics and astronomy at California Institute of Technology and Cornell University. He was knighted in 1972. Since the late 1950s the steady state theory has fallen out of favour with cosmologists; forced to modify his views, Hoyle has tried hard to make the theory consistent with new evidence.

Hoyle is a prolific writer of technical, general and popular works in science and cosmology. His first book was *The Nature of the Universe* (1951); since then he has become well-known as a writer of science fiction. His first novel *The Black Cloud* was published in 1957; *A for Andromeda* (1962) was adapted for television. He has also written a play and several children's stories.

F. Hoyle, *The Small World of Fred Hoyle*. 1986

N G C

HUBBLE, EDWIN POWELL Born at Marshfield, Missouri, USA, 20 November 1889; died San Marino, California, 28 September 1953. Chiefly remembered for his work in nebular astronomy.

Hubble graduated at the University of Chicago in 1911, and was subsequently a Rhodes Scholar at Queen's College, Oxford, where he graduated in jurisprudence. He abandoned law when he was invited to carry out research at Yerkes Observatory, astronomy having previously been his pastime. Returning home after a short period in the American Army in the First World War, he was appointed to the staff of the Mount Wilson Observatory. There he continued studies of nebulae begun at Yerkes, and showed that some nebulae are illuminated by stimulating radiation from embedded stars. In 1923–4 he managed to resolve the outer parts of one or two large nebulae (including that in Andromeda) into distinct stars, among which he was soon able to identify cepheid variables. Using the period-luminosity relation, he found distances for these nebulae in tolerably good agreement with values deduced from novae. In this way he helped to establish once and for all the view that spiral nebulae lie outside our own stellar system.

Hubble used the information already obtained to evaluate the absolute magnitudes of the brightest super giants of extragalactic nebulae, and found the total absolute magnitude of the average nebula. He was thus able to state distances for most visible nebulae. In 1929, with his first distance estimates, he stated that the majority of extragalactic nebulae were receding from our own galaxy with velocities proportional to their distances (Hubble's Law).

Hubble remained an active observer until his death. His work is perhaps best seen from his two books, *The Observational Approach to Cosmology* (1937) and *The Realm of the Nebulae* (1936).

Nature, **172**, 793, 1953.

W. S. Adams, *Observatory*, **74**, 32, 1954.

M. L. Homason, *Monthly Notices of the Royal Astronomical Society*, **114**, 291, 1954.

A. S. Sharov and I. D. Novikov, *Edwin Hubble, the Discoverer of the Big Bang Universe* (Trans. V. Kisin). 1993.

Dictionary of Scientific Biography.

J D N

HUBEL, DAVID HUNTER Born at Windsor, Ontario, Canada, 27 February 1926. Neurophysiologist, specializing in the physiology of visual perception.

Both of Hubel's parents were American, but he was born and educated in Canada, graduating from McGill University, Montreal, in 1947. He then entered McGill University Medical School, and qualified in 1951. His clinical training in neurology from 1951 to 1955 included two years at the Montreal Neurological Institute. In 1955 he was drafted into the US Army, but his assignment to the Neurophysiology Division of the Walter Reed Army Institute of Research in Washington DC enabled him to begin research on nerve-cell activity in the brains of cats. Discharged from the army in 1958, he spent 1958–9 at Johns Hopkins Hospital, Baltimore, working in the laboratory of V. B. Mountcastle (1918–) and later with S. W. Kuffler (1913–1980). When Kuffler moved to Harvard Medical School in 1959, Hubel went too, and in 1968 became professor of neurobiology.

Using electrodes implanted in the visual cortex of cats, Hubel recorded the spontaneous nervous activity of nerve cells in the brain while responding to different stimuli. With T. Wiesel (1924–) at Harvard he discovered that single brain cells fire with the movement of the eye in a certain direction. They experimented with projecting simple visual shapes on to a screen in front of the cat's eyes, and found that some cells fired only when the shape was presented at a certain angle. Some cells responded only to movement, and movement in only one direction. These discoveries contributed significantly to the study of the visual cortex, by showing that there are specific mechanisms in the brain which select certain features of objects.

The results of Hubel's research had an important effect on clinical ophthalmology, and especially on the treatment of congenital cataracts, as he showed that the ability to decode messages from the retina is developed immediately after birth and that therefore cataracts should be removed early in the patient's life in order to preserve vision.

Hubel shared the Nobel prize for physiology or medicine in 1981 with R. W. SPERRY and Wiesel.

D. H. Hubel and T. Wiesel *Scientific American,* September 1979.

J. Y. Lettvin, *Science,* 30 October 1981. (Portrait.)

Tyler Wasson (Ed.), *Nobel Prize Winners.* 1987. (Portrait.)

A P B

HUGGINS, SIR WILLIAM Born in London, 7 February 1824; died there, 12 May 1910. Pioneer of astrophysics.

After attending the City of London School, Huggins was privately educated. Having built an observatory at Tulse Hill, South London (1856), he made routine observations until learning of the findings of G. R. KIRCHHOFF in spectroscopy. Investigating stellar spectra, with the help of W. A. Miller (1817–70) of King's College, London, he published his first important results in 1863, listing numerous stellar emission lines. In 1864 he discovered two green lines in the spectrum of the Great Nebula in Orion, and attributed them to an unknown element, 'nebulium' (cf the genuine discovery of helium by N. LOCKYER). Not until 1928 was it shown, by I. S. Bowen, that the lines were so-called 'forbidden' lines of ionized oxygen and nitrogen.

In 1869, Huggins showed that Lockyer's method of observing prominences could be modified by opening the spectroscope slit fully to show a much larger field. The method soon showed that prominences were of at least two sorts, quiescent and otherwise.

During 1866, 1867, and 1868 Huggins repeated the observations made by G. B. Donati (1826–73) in 1864 on cometary spectra. He showed that the bands in the spectrum of a comet coincided with those in the spectrum of a hydrocarbon flame. He also showed, later, that meteors emitted similar spectra, thus emphasizing the known connection between meteor streams and comets.

From 1863 Huggins had been using photographic recording of spectra, but not until he applied the dry-plate process in 1875 was he really successful. In 1879 he recorded ultraviolet spectra, and before long he was recording cometary and nebular spectra photographically. He contributed to the understanding of the nature of the different sorts of nebula. He received many academic honours, and was knighted (1897) and awarded the Order of Merit (1902).

Nature, **64**, 225, 1901. (Portrait.)

Sir W. and Lady Huggins, *Atlas of Representative Stellar Spectra.* 1899. (Much biographical material.)

Proceedings of the Royal Society, **86**, 1911–12.

Dictionary of National Biography.

Dictionary of Scientific Biography.

J D N

HULL, ALBERT WALLACE Born at Southington, Connecticut, USA, 19 April 1880; died Schenectady, New York, 22 January 1966. Physicist, best known for his work on thyratron and magnetron electron tubes.

After studying classics at Yale University and teaching modern languages at Albany Academy, Hull became increasingly interested in physics and

returned to Yale where he obtained his doctorate in 1909. He taught for five years at Worcester Polytechnic Institute in Massachusetts, then on the recommendation of Irving LANGMUIR joined the General Electric Research Laboratory at Schenectady.

One of his first areas of research was in x-ray crystallography, where in 1917 he discovered, independently of P. J. W. DEBYE and P. SCHERRER, the possibility of using the technique on powdered samples. In 1921 he published his classic paper *The Effect of a Uniform Magnetic Field on the Motion of Electrons between Coaxial Cylinders,* in which he first used the name 'magnetron' for this type of valve. His later work on the improvement of diodes and triodes led to his invention of the thyratron, a high-power gas-filled electron tube originally intended as a power supply rectifier, but more widely used in the electronic control of industrial electric devices.

In the 1930s he broadened his range of interests to include metallurgy and glass science, resulting in his discovery of new alloys, one of which had elastic and thermal properties sufficiently close to those of glass to allow strain-free glass-to-metal vacuum seals to be made, with great benefit to the electrical industry. He was elected President of the American Physical Society in 1942, and was a member of the National Academy of Sciences.

Biographical Memoirs of the National Academy of Sciences, **41**, 215, 1970

National Cyclopedia of American Biography, **53**.

Dictionary of Scientific Biography.

R M B

HUMBOLDT, FRIEDRICH HEINRICH ALEXANDER, BARON VON Born in Berlin, 14 September 1769; died there, 6 May 1859. Traveller and natural historian.

Humboldt was the son of a Prussian officer who intended him to enter politics. While studying at Göttingen in 1789 and 1790 he met J. G. A. Forster (1754–94), the naturalist who had accompanied Captain James COOK on his second voyage round the world 1772–5, and who encouraged his 'ardent desire held from my earliest youth' to travel and explore distant regions. With Forster he made excursions to different parts of Europe, and spent six years in study to prepare himself in all branches of science. He was disappointed when a French expedition to explore the South Pacific, to which he had been attached, was cancelled because of the war in Italy. With his friend A. J. A. Bonpland (1773–1858), the botanist of the expedition, he went to Madrid after an abortive attempt to visit North Africa. He was presented to the King and obtained passports and permission to travel in Spanish America, and the two friends sailed from Corunna early in June 1799. They investigated the geology and botany of the Canary Islands on their way, and arrived at Cumana in the middle of July. Then followed an extensive series of journeys and explorations from which they returned to Europe with immense collections of specimens and observations after more than five years. Their travels included a journey up the Orinoco, a sojourn in Cuba, a journey up the Magdalena and across the Cordilleras to Quito and Lima, visiting the sources of the Amazon, and residence of a year in Mexico. Their industry in surveying, mapping, collecting geological, zoological, and botanical material, and in studying the economics and inhabitants of the countries through which they passed was enormous.

On returning to Europe, Humboldt set himself to working out and publishing his results; after several years in Berlin he removed in 1808 to Paris, where he expected his work would take two years – it was not complete at the end of twenty. The results, which finally occupied thirty volumes, brought him enormous prestige through the wide range of subjects they covered; and the personal narrative, or *Relation historique*, remains one of the most fascinating of travel books. He was summoned for various duties from time to time by the King of Prussia, and sent on diplomatic missions to France after he returned permanently to Berlin in 1827. He later organized a scheme of international magnetic and meteorological observations throughout Russian and Asia and the English colonies.

In 1845, when he was 76 years of age, he started writing his *Kosmos*, which he had long been preparing in his mind, summarizing his experience and philosophy. In this crowning work he describes and illustrates the history and the physical state of the world, and attempts to show a unity amid the complexities of nature. The main part of the task was completed in a couple of years and published in two volumes, to which he added further volumes from time to time until his death in 1859.

Humboldt's literary output was immense, both as separate works and as contributions to the journals of the learned societies. He was held in universal esteem, and was particularly cultivated at the Prussian court; he was honoured by most of the universities and academies of Europe and America, including the Royal Society (1815).

K. Bruhns, *Life of Humboldt*. (English trans. by Lassell.) 1873.

F. H. A. von Humboldt and A. J. A. Bonpland, *Narrative of Travels*. (English ed. 3 vols.) 1818–19. (Reprinted 1894–1900.)

C. Kellner, *Alexander von Humboldt*. 1963. (Portrait.)

H. de Terra, *Humboldt: the Life and Times of Alexander von Humboldt*. 1955.

Dictionary of Scientific Biography.

L H M

HUNTER, JOHN Born at Long Calderwood, East Kilbride, Lanarkshire, Scotland, 13 February 1728; died London, 16 October 1793. Anatomist, biologist, and founder of scientific surgery.

The youngest brother of the anatomist William Hunter (1718–83), John's education was neglected. After a period as a cabinetmaker, at 20 years of age he began to assist William with his dissections in London. He also studied surgery under W. Cheselden (1688–1752) and Percivall Pott (1714–88), and in 1754 he entered St George's Hospital as a surgeon pupil, and also helped William with his lectures. From 1760 to 1763 he served as staff-surgeon with the expedition to Belleisle and the Army in Portugal. On his return he began to practise as a surgeon, and in 1767 he was elected Fellow of the Royal Society. In 1768 he became surgeon to St George's Hospital, and in 1776 surgeon-extraordinary to George III. He married Anne

Home, a minor poet, in 1771. Hunter died of a chronic disease, contracted as a result of an experimental inoculation self-administered twenty-six years before his death. In 1859 his remains were removed to Westminster Abbey.

John Hunter's original work was on comparative anatomy and physiology, and on scientific aspects of surgery which gave rich results later. His treatise on the natural history of the human teeth (1771–8) laid the foundations of dental anatomy and pathology. In 1772 he introduced his important vitalistic views. In 1785 he demonstrated the collateral circulation experimentally, and was the first to use these results practically in the ligation of an artery for aneurysm. He showed that digestion is neither fermentation nor chemical solution. His *Observations on Certain Parts of the Animal Oeconomy* (1786) contains also his experiments on heat production and the mechanism of hibernation in animals, and his description of air-sacs in birds. Of his papers to the Royal Society, one deals with his dissection of the electric organ of certain fishes. Hunter's last work, published posthumously, dealt with the process of inflammation and the effects of gunshot wounds, and incorporated observations and experiments made during the Belleisle Expedition. He correctly regarded inflammation as, firstly, a defensive mechanism, and, secondly, a process of repair.

Hunter's most lasting monument is his museum. He early envisaged the formation of a collection to illustrate comparatively the structure and function of organs throughout the animal kingdom. To this end he spent many hours daily dissecting and preparing his exhibits. Latterly his collection was housed at his home at Earl's Court and in his great establishment in Leicester Square, where he had a surgical school with resident pupils. Among the famous men who trained there, the greatest was Edward JENNER. After Hunter's death his museum was purchased by the nation and was entrusted to the newly founded Royal College of Surgeons, under the supervision of a board of Hunterian Trustees. This very famous collection suffered serious damage through enemy action on 10 May 1941.

S. Paget, *John Hunter*. 1897. (Portrait.)

G. C. Peachey, *Memoir of William and John Hunter*. 1924. (Portrait.)

V. Robinson, *Medical Life*, **36**, 119, 1929.

A. Keith, *Nature*, **121**, 210, 1928.

G. G. Turner, *The Hunterian Museum*. 1946. (Portrait.)

Dictionary of Scientific Biography.

E A U

HUNTSMAN, BENJAMIN Born at Barton-on-Humber, Lincolnshire, England, 1704; died Sheffield, Yorkshire, 21 June 1776. Maker of improved steel.

Benjamin Huntsman, of Dutch descent, was apprenticed to a clockmaker in Epworth, Lincolnshire, and in 1725 set up business in Doncaster, making clocks, locks and roasting-jacks. He was of an inventive nature and designed new tools for his trade, but the poor quality of steel then available limited improvements. He carried out research into producing a better steel and about 1744 moved to Handsworth, near (now part of) Sheffield, where conditions for steel-making were more promising. His aim was to produce a uniformly high-quality steel ingot after melting and purifying crude steel with various fluxes in a crucible. The fuel, the flux, and the composition of the crucibles were critical factors in these experiments, the nature of which he did not disclose, and excavations on the site of Huntsman's works have produced abundant evidence of unsuccessful mouldings. Between 1745 and 1750 he succeeded in producing a crucible steel of a quality far higher than was available elsewhere, but found himself thwarted by the conservatism of the Sheffield cutlers, who rejected his new material as too hard to work.

He sought outlets for his steel abroad and soon was selling his entire output – which was not large, as he was working a batch process – to the French, who in turn found a ready market in England for knives and razors made from Huntsman's new steel. An unsuccessful attempt was made by Sheffield cutlers to prevent him by law from exporting his steel. About 1750 his closely guarded secret process was disclosed. Details of the method were obtained by Samuel Walker, a competitor who made very large profits from its exploitation. Huntsman, however, survived the competition on the basis of quality, and was able to expand his business on a new site in 1770. He died six years later and was buried at Attercliffe, near his new works.

E. N. Simons, *Metallurgia*, **51**, 181, 1955.
Mary Walton, *Sheffield*. 1949.
E. W. Hulme, *Transactions of the Newcomen Society*, **24**, 37, 1943–5.
Dictionary of National Biography.

N H

HURTER, FERDINAND Born at Schaffhausen, Switzerland, 15 March 1844; died near Widnes, Lancashire, England, 5 March 1898. Industrial chemist.

Hurter worked for a short time in the textile industry, then studied chemistry at Zürich Polytechnic and at Heidelberg. He came to Manchester in 1867, and was shortly afterwards appointed chemist to the alkali works of Gaskell and Deacon at Widnes, which was working the soda process of N. LEBLANC. He played a large part in developing the chlorine process devised by Henry DEACON; made important physico-chemical studies of gas-liquid interactions; and devised an unsuccessful variant of the ammonia-soda process using salt-cake as raw material. Hurter became widely known as an authority on every aspect of the Leblanc system; it was perhaps unfortunate that so much of his talent should have been used to defend an industry being made obsolete by the improved ammonia-soda process of E. SOLVAY. When the United Alkali Co. was formed in 1890 by the union of the major UK Leblanc manufacturers, Hurter was appointed Chief Chemist, and set up the first real industrial research laboratory in Britain. In his limited leisure he carried out, with his friend V. C. Driffield (1848–1915), some important research on the fundamentals of photography; for many years the speed of photographic plates and film, was expressed in terms of their 'H & D' number. Although he spent his working life in Britain, Hurter always retained his Swiss nationality.

Journal of the Society of Chemical Industry, **17**, 406, 1898.

D. W. F. Hardie, *A History of the Chemical Industry in Widnes*. 1950. (Portrait.)
Dictionary of National Biography (Missing Persons). 1993.

W V F

HUSSEY, OBED Born in Maine, New England, USA, 1792; died (after a fall from a railway train between Baltimore and New England) early 1859. Inventor of one of the first successful grain-reaping machines.

Obed Hussey came of a cultured Nantucket Quaker family, and after a full education settled down to a life spent in the invention of small machines for agriculture and light engineering. His only important invention was a reaping machine. It embodied a reciprocating saw-toothed cutter sliding within double guard bars which protected the blade. The grain fell on to a platform from which it was raked and bagged by hand. The first public trial was made near Carthage, Ohio, in July 1833, and Hussey obtained a patent for the machine in December 1833. He began manufacture of the machines in Cincinnati, and in 1834 sold them in Illinois, New York, and Missouri. In 1836 he established a factory in Baltimore, Maryland, and devoted all his time to the manufacture and sale of his reapers. The originality of his invention was questioned by C. H. MCCORMICK, who had gained a patent for a similar machine in 1834, and the two became bitter rivals. Over the years Hussey made further improvements to the machine, and both his and McCormick's reapers were demonstrated in London at the Great Exhibition of 1851. McCormick originally gained the gold medal, but on a retrial the jury decided that Hussey's machine was better. Nevertheless, it was in the end of McCormick's firm that emerged as the leader of the American industry. The last years of Hussey's life, before an untimely death, were spent in the further development of the reaper.

F. L. Greeno (Ed.), *Obed Hussey*. 1912. (Portrait.)
L. Rogin, *The Introduction of Farm Machinery, Etc.*, University of California Publications in Economics, **9**, 1931.
Dictionary of American Biography.

W N S

HUTTON, JAMES Born in Edinburgh, 3 June 1726; died there, 26 March 1797. The chief founder of geology as a science.

James Hutton was educated in Edinburgh at the High School, and at 14 followed an Arts course at the University. At 17 he was apprenticed in a lawyer's office, but chemical experiments made in his spare time so engaged his interest that he returned to the university to take up medicine. After three years he went on the Continent to complete his training and took the degree of MD at Leiden in 1749. He now turned to agriculture as his vocation, living on a farm in Norfolk for two years and making a tour in Flanders. In 1754 he settled down on a small paternal estate in Berwickshire. This he farmed energetically, but the questions posed by the rocks beneath the soils already engaged his highly philosophical mind. The success of a sal-ammoniac manufacture enabled him, about 1768, to settle in Edinburgh and devote himself to various scientific pursuits. One of his intimate associates was Joseph BLACK, the chemist.

Observations and speculations on geology, however, became his dominant occupation, inspired by the striking phenomena in and around Edinburgh itself and encouraged by journeys to different parts of Scotland and into England and Wales. A general, reasoned theory grew in his mind and he communicated an account of it to the recently founded Royal Society of Edinburgh in 1785; it appeared in the first volume of the Society's *Transactions* in 1788. This paper was reprinted with much additional material to form the two volumes of his *Theory of the Earth* (1795). (A portion of a third volume was rescued and published in 1899.) Whereas previous geological knowledge had been a matter of scattered observations, and theorizing had been mostly wild fantasy, here at last was the first co-ordination and rationalization; the foundations of geology, as a proper science, were laid. He formulated the two main principles: the geological cycle, by demonstrating igneous intrusion and stratigraphical unconformity in the field; and uniformitarianism, by insisting on continuity of process. These two volumes suffered from prolixity, and it remained for John PLAYFAIR to put them in a more convincing and readable form in his *Illustrations of the Huttonian Theory* (1802).

Hutton united to a strong intellect a gentle and kindly nature, and was very sociable.

J. Playfair, *Transactions of the Royal Society of Edinburgh*, **5**, 39, 1805. (Reprinted in *The Works of John Playfair*. 1822.)

A. Geikie, *The Founders of Geology* (2nd edition). 1905.

Proceedings of the Royal Society of Edinburgh, **63**, 351, 1950. (Portrait.)

E. B. Bailey, *James Hutton – The Founder of Modern Geology*. 1967.

G. Y. Craig, *Endeavour* (New Series), **11**, 88, 1987. (Portrait.)

Dictionary of National Biography.

Dictionary of Scientific Biography.

J C

HUXLEY, HUGH ESMOR Born at Birkenhead, England, 25 February 1924. Physiologist; produced sliding-filament theory of muscle contraction.

Huxley, (not a member of the Huxley family descended from T. H. Huxley), was educated at Park High School, Birkenhead, and Christ's College, Cambridge. After taking Part 1 of the Natural Sciences tripos in 1943 he worked as a radar officer for RAF Bomber Command and at the Telecommunications Research Establishment, Malvern, until 1947. Returning to Cambridge he sat Part 2 of the tripos in physics in 1948. From 1948 to 1952 he was a research student at the MRC Unit for Molecular Biology in Cambridge, and was awarded a PhD in 1952 for a thesis on x-ray diffraction of muscle.

He spent 1952–4 at Massachusetts Institute of Technology learning the technique of electron microscopy in the laboratory of F. O. Schmitt (1903–) in order to apply it to the study of the structural basis of muscle contraction. With E. Jean Hanson (1919–1973) he developed the sliding-filament theory of muscle contraction in 1953, suggesting that thick and thin protein filaments slide past each other in muscle contraction and that this is regulated through changes in the calcium ion concentration. Huxley and Hanson continued to collaborate for several years, producing a joint paper in 1954. At the same time a group under Andrew Huxley (1917–), working independently, reached similar conclusions and published their conclusion also in 1954.

Huxley worked in the biophysics department at University College, London from 1956 until his return to Cambridge in 1961 to the MRC Laboratory of Molecular Biology. In 1977 he became deputy director. He moved to the USA in 1987 as professor of biology at the Rosenstiel Basic Medical Sciences Research Center, Brandeis University, Boston, Massachusetts, and was director from 1988.

He was elected FRS in 1960, and won the Royal Medal in 1977.

H. E. Huxley, 'The mechanism of muscular contraction', *Science*, vol. 164, 1969.

Who's Who. 1993.

A. G. Debus (Ed.), *World Who's Who in Science*. 1968.

A P B

HUXLEY, THOMAS HENRY Born in Ealing, London, 4 May 1825; died Eastbourne, Sussex, 29 June 1895. Remembered as 'Darwin's Bulldog', but a most distinguished scientist in his own right.

T. H. Huxley was seventh of the eight children of Rachel and George Huxley, an unsuccessful schoolmaster. He had only two years' schooling, from the age of 8 to 10, but read widely and taught himself French, Latin, German, Italian, and Greek. In 1842 he obtained a free scholarship to Charing Cross Medical School, but never completed his degree and, in 1856, enrolled as assistant surgeon in the Royal Navy.

He served on 4-year cruise to the South Seas in HMS *Rattlesnake*, studying marine life so successfully that, on his return to England, he was almost immediately (1851) elected FRS because of his brilliant researches. He was given three years' leave of absence to continue his researches, but he was eventually struck off the Navy list. He was appointed Lecturer at the School of Mines, London (which eventually became the Royal College of Science), in 1854. In Australia he had met Henrietta Heathorn, whom he married in 1855, having an ideal married life with seven children.

Huxley produced over 150 research papers, dealing with an immensely wide range of subjects, mainly zoological and palaeontological, but also geological, anthropological, and botanical. He also produced ten scientific textbooks, each quite novel in approach, as well as several books of essays and innumerable controversial articles on education, religion, etc. One reason for his great influence was his beautifully clear and rich literary style.

His researches established the Coelenterata (two-layered jelly-fish etc.) group; reorganized classification of Ascidians (sea squirts etc.) and Cephalous Mollusca (squids etc.); regrouped vertebrates into Ichthyopsida (fish and amphibia), Sauropsida (reptiles and birds), and Mammalia; divided Mammalia into Prototheria (egg-laying), Metatheria (marsupial) and Eutheria (placental); divided birds into the Saururae (fossil Archaeopteryx), Ratites (ostrich etc.) and Carinates (most modern species); and brought order into other confused fields. He also made important conceptual and/or methodological contributions to geology and anthropology.

Some idea of Huxley's influence may be gained from the fact that at various times he was president of the Geological, Ethnological, Palaeontographical, Microscopic, and Royal Societies; of the British Association for the Advancement of Science and the International Geological Congress; Dean of the Government School of Science; Rector of Aberdeen University; Governor of University College, London, Owens College, Manchester, London Medical School, Eton College, and International College; Hunterian Professor at the Royal College of Surgeons and Fullerian Professor at Royal Institution; member of ten Royal and other Commissions; member of the first London School Board; opened John Hopkins University Baltimore, Josiah Mason College (later University of Birmingham) and Owens College (later University of Manchester) Medical School. He was especially active in working-class education.

Huxley was the main supporter of Darwin and did more than anyone else to break down religious and obscurantist opposition to the theory of evolution. He coined the word 'agnostic' to describe his lack of belief in revealed religion. He engaged eminent theologians in essay duels, in which he nearly always came out best. Despite this, he was known as an exceptionally charming man and was very widely loved as well as respected.

Leonard Huxley, *Life and Letters of T. H. Huxley* (2 vols). 1900.

Cyril Bibby *T. H. Huxley; Scientist, Humanist and Educator.* 1959.

Gavin de Beer (Ed.), *Charles Darwin and T. H. Huxley.* 1974.

P. Chalmers Mitchell, *Thomas Henry Huxley,* 1900.

M. Foster, *Proceedings of the Royal Society of London,* 59, 46, 1896.

Dictionary of National Biography.

Dictionary of Scientific Biography.

C B

HUYGENS, CHRISTIAAN Born in The Hague, Netherlands, 14 April 1629; died there, 8 June 1695. Celebrated for his contributions to dynamics and optics.

Son of Constantin Huygens (1596–1687), one of the most brilliant figures of the Renaissance in Holland, Huygens grew up in the intellectual atmosphere of a home which numbered Réne DESCARTES among its visitors. Like NEWTON, the young Huygens seems to have been remarkable for his interest in drawing and in mechanical models. After completing his studies in Jurisprudence at Leiden and Breda he spent a period in travel before settling down at home to study mathematics and science. His first published paper (1651) was on the quadrature of various curves. The period 1655–6 witnessed his first major scientific discovery, that of the rings of Saturn. During a visit to London in 1661 he demonstrated his laws of collision before various members of the newly founded Royal Society, of which body he himself became a Foreign Member in 1663. In 1666 he was elected a foundation member of the *Académie des Sciences.* From 1666 onwards he resided mostly in Paris until his final return to Holland in 1681. In 1672 he met G. W. LEIBNIZ, to whom he gave lessons in mathematics, and whose first paper on the differential calculus he transmitted to the *Académie des Sciences* in 1674. From 1681 onwards Huygens was mostly in indifferent health and lived quietly at home, apart from a visit to London in 1687 during which he met Newton and lectured on gravitation at the Royal Society. He died after a long and distressing illness.

In dynamics, Huygens first treated the problem of colliding bodies, obtaining a correct solution for the case of elastic bodies as early as 1656, although his results remained unpublished till 1669. Basic to his treatment was the employment of a relativity principle, the law of falling bodies formulated by GALILEO, and the assumption that the centre of gravity of an isolated system of bodies could not rise above its original level after release. This principle was later employed by Huygens in his definitive solution to the problem of the compound pendulum, for which he calculated the equivalent simple pendulum length in his celebrated *Horologium Oscillatorium* (1673), which Florian Cajori (1859–1930) ranked second to Newton's *Principia.* In the appendix to this treatise he enunciated the laws of centrifugal force for uniform motion in a circle, the proofs of which were first published in the posthumous works. Outstanding, too, was his proof of the isochronous property of a body rolling on the vertical arc of a cycloid, and his ingenious derivation of the formula of the period of oscillation of a simple pendulum.

Huygens's first account of his undulatory theory of light was in a communication (1678) to the *Académie des Sciences.* He had intended to follow this with the publication of a treatise on the subject, but his *Traité de la Lumière* appeared only in 1690. For Huygens, light was a vibratory motion in the ether spreading out from any source and producing the sensation of light when impinging on the eye. The position of the 'wave front' at any time was given by the principle (Huygens's Principle) that every point of the wave front at any instant was the source of a secondary spherical wave, the wave front at any later instant being the envelope of all such secondary fronts. By the use of this principle, Huygens was then able to give simple explanations of the laws governing the reflection and refraction of light. For refraction it followed that the velocity of light in a dense medium was directly proportional to the sine of the angle of refraction, as opposed to Newton's theory in which the proportionality was inverse rather than direct. A decision between the two theories on the point had to await the experiments of A. H. L. FIZEAU and J. B. L. FOUCAULT in 1851. The most brilliant triumph of Huygens's wave theory was its explanation of double refraction in Iceland Spar, based on the assumption that the secondary wave fronts of the ordinary and extraordinary rays were spherical and spheroidal, respectively. Defects of Huygens's theory of light were the absence of a theory of colour and its inability to explain polarization effects, due to the assumption of longitudinal as opposed to transverse vibrations.

Apart from optics and dynamics, Huygens made many important contributions to mathematics and to the improvement of telescopic lenses and clocks.

Huygens was, after Newton, the greatest scientist of the second half of the seventeenth century, and the only one of Newton's contemporaries capable of proceeding in dynamics beyond the point reached by GALILEO and Descartes to the solution of the problem of centrifugal force. He would undoubtedly have been equally capable of finding a solution to the problem posed by the Laws of Planetary Motion formulated by KEPLER, but was necessarily precluded from doing so by his Cartesian belief in the necessity of action by contact.

Oeuvres Complètes de Christiaan Huygens (22 vols). 1888–1950. (Includes portraits and biography in vol. 22.)

J. Bosscha, *Christiaan Huygens*. 1895.

A. E. Bell, *Christian Huygens and the Development of Science in the Seventeenth Century*. 1947.

E. J. Dijksterhuis, *Christiaan Huygens*. 1951.

Dictionary of Scientific Biography.

J W H

HYATT, JOHN WESLEY Born at Starkey, New York State, USA, 28 November 1837; died Short Hills, New Jersey, 10 May 1920. Inventor.

J. W. Hyatt, who moved at the age of 16 to Illinois to be a printer, early developed into an inventor and occupied most of his life in this way. His first patent was for a knife sharpener in 1861, and eight years later he patented a new method of making dominoes and draughts. Trifling in itself, this invention led him to investigate the problem of producing a cheap substitute for ivory, which was used on dominoes, and more, particularly, for making billiard balls. With his brother, Isaac Smith Hyatt, he discovered in 1868 a method of mixing nitrocellulose with camphor under pressure to produce a substance with the properties requisite for his purpose; this substance he called celluloid. The potentialities of celluloid in sheet form and its key part in the development of photography and cinematography had to wait another twenty years for their appreciation and exploitation, but the 'Hyatt billiard ball' appeared as early as 1875.

Despite the potential of celluloid, Hyatt's inventions in this field were modest in scope. In 1892, however, he invented the 'Hyatt roller bearing' and established the Hyatt Roller Bearing Company in Harrison, New Jersey. The range of inventions under his name suggest an ingenious dilettante, but his technical judgment showed in all the devices with which he was concerned; this is exemplified in the work which he and his brother put into the perfecting of celluloid, and their patient development of special machinery for its production. Though others, notably Alexander PARKES, were working with greater basic scientific knowledge in the same field, it was Hyatt who made the key discovery. Other inventions included a multiple-stitch sewing machine; an improved mill for sugarcane; and a machine for rolling and straightening steel shafts. He was awarded the Perkin Medal of the Society of Chemical Industry in 1914.

Dictionary of American Biography.

N H

I

IABLOTCHKOV, PAVEL NIKOLAIEVITCH *See* JABLOCHKOFF.

INGENHOUSZ, JAN Born at Breda, Netherlands, 8 December 1730; died Bowood, Wiltshire, England, 7 September 1799. Demonstrated the process of photosynthesis in plants.

Ingenhousz studied medicine, physics, and chemistry at the universities of Louvain and Leiden. He first visited London in 1765, before going on to Vienna in 1768, where he became surgeon to the royal family and inoculated them against smallpox using the method of Edward JENNER. His skill in this operation made his name known, and his services were in great demand. He remained in Vienna for some years, but returned to England in 1779 and spent most of the rest of his life here, devoting his time to scientific work. He was elected a Fellow of the Royal Society in 1769, and contributed papers on a variety of subjects to the *Philosophical Transactions*. He died during a visit to the Marquis of Lansdowne's estate at Bowood.

Ingenhousz's frequent travels in Europe brought him into contact with the work of contemporary scientists, including Joseph PRIESTLEY, whose *Experiments and Observations on different kinds of Air* (1774) had shown that plants gave off oxygen. Ingenhousz's own work on plants, *Experiments upon Vegetables, Discovering Their Great Power of Purifying the Common Air in the Sunshine and of Injuring it in the Shade and at Night*, was published in London in 1779; in Leipzig, Delft, and Paris in 1780; and in Vienna in 1786–90, with a second French edition, revised, enlarged, and translated by the author, appearing in 1787–9. It showed that the green parts of plants, in light, absorb carbon dioxide from the air and release oxygen, but that this process is stopped by darkness, during which the plants release carbon dioxide only.

According to Charles Singer (1876–1960) Ingenhousz's discoveries were 'the foundation of our whole conception of the economy of the world of living things', as animal life depends on that of plants, whose substance is made from a mixture of the carbon dioxide from the air and the products of the decomposition of dead animals and plants.

Ingenhousz continued his work on plant physiology and published several more papers on the subject, including *An Essay on the Food of Plants and the Renovation of Soils*, which appeared in 1796 as an additional appendix to a report of the Board of Agriculture. His many other publications are about electricity (he had met Benjamin FRANKLIN in Paris), magnetism, and other aspects of physics, as well as medical topics and the relationship between animals and plants.

H. S. Reed, *Jan Ingenhousz: Plant Physiologist. Chronica Botanica*, II, No. 5–6. 1949. (Portraits.)

J. Wiesner, *et al.*, *Jan Ingen-Housz: sein Leben und sein Wirken als Naturforscher und Arzt*. 1905. (Portraits.)

Dictionary of National Biography.

Dictionary of Scientific Biography.

S J R

IPATIEFF, VLADIMIR NIKOLAIEVICH Born in Moscow, 21 November 1867; died Chicago, Illinois, USA, 29 November 1952. Chemist, whose work is fundamental to the petrochemical industry.

Destined for the Army, Ipatieff was educated in a military academy, in which he later became an instructor. He picked up a good knowledge of chemistry, and soon began to publish papers on organic chemistry; in 1896 he spent a year with J. F. W. A. von BAEYER in Munich. On his return to Russia he began to work in the field with which his name will always be associated, that of high-temperature catalytic reactions. In this period he studied particularly dehydrogenations with metal catalysts, and dehydrations with oxide catalysts. He discovered many reactions which are now used extensively in the petrochemical industry, including some early work on 'cracking'. Although the Russian petroleum industry was interested, it was not then advanced enough to make much use of his work.

When war broke out Ipatieff was made chairman of the 'Chemical Committee' which was to co-ordinate the efforts of chemists for the war effort. In the difficult years after 1917 he spent most of his time in high administrative posts in the chemical industry; but as the result of growing tension with the Soviet Government, he left Russia for good in 1930. For the rest of his life he worked for the Universal Oil Products Co. of Chicago, as an honoured research worker and consultant. Here, with many collaborators, he was able to broaden and deepen his studies of catalytic reactions, especially in the liquid phase, and to help the petrochemical industry at a critical phase in its growth.

E. Farber (ed.), *Great Chemists*. 1961. (Portrait.)

Journal of Chemical Education, **30**, 110, 1953. (Portrait.)

X. J. Eudin *et al.* (Eds), *The Life of a Chemist: Memoirs of Vladimir N. Ipatieff*. 1946. (Portrait.)

Wyndham D. Miles, (Ed.), *American Chemists and Chemical Engineers*. 1976.

W V F

IRVINE, JAMES COLQUHOUN Born in Glasgow, Scotland, 9 May 1877; died St Andrews, Fife, 12 June 1952. Famous for researches in carbohydrate chemistry.

Irvine studied chemistry at Glasgow, St Andrews, and Leipzig. Returning to St Andrews, he became lecturer in the department of T. Purdie (1843–1916), then successively professor (1909), dean (1912), principal (1920), and vice-chancellor (1921).

Applying Purdie's methylation technique to carbohydrates, Irvine obtained methylated derivatives which became reference compounds for degradation studies of polysaccharides. Unable to repeat the claim of A. PICTET to have synthesized sucrose, he synthesized instead iso-sucrose. During the First World World War he supervised production of rare carbohydrates and novocaine. Out of Irvine's work arose the great school of carbohydrate chemistry at St Andrews, associated particularly with W. N. HAWORTH, which passed eventually to Birmingham.

As vice-chancellor, Irvine guided his university through thirty years of great expansion. He also served on the Carnegie and Pilgrim Trusts, on bodies for higher colonial education, and many other organizations. He was elected FRS (1918); knighted (1925); and made KBE (1940).

Journal of the Chemical Society, 476, 1954.
Obituary Notices of Fellows of the Royal Society.
   1953. (Portrait.)
Dictionary of National Biography.
                                                      C A R

ISAACS, ALICK Born in Glasgow, Scotland, 17 July 1921; died London, 26, January 1967. Virologist; discoverer of interferon.

Isaacs studied medicine at Glasgow, graduating in 1944. After a short period of research at Sheffield University, a Rockefeller Travelling Scholarship enabled him to develop his growing interest in the nature of viruses at the Walter and Eliza Hall Institute, Melbourne – a leading centre for research in this field – under Sir Macfarlane BURNET. He returned to England to join the Virology Division of the National Institute for Medical Research, becoming head of the Division in 1961.

Isaacs's particular interest was in the study of the interaction of different viruses – why cellular infection with one virus inhibits secondary infection by another. To an extent, this may be regarded as analogous with antibiosis (the inhibition of the growth of one micro-organism by another), study of which led to the discovery of penicillin and a wide range of antibiotics. His researches led him to the discovery of a specific agent, which he named interferon, responsible for interference in the growth of one virus by another. This he published in 1957, in a paper written jointly with J. Lindemann. The direct medical value of the discovery remains to be assessed, but there is no doubt of its outstanding importance in relation to our understanding of the nature of viral infection and the body's response to them. This was recognized in 1966, when he was elected FRS. He was an honorary graduand (1962) of the University of Louvain.

The Times, 28 January 1967. (Portrait.)
Biographical Memoirs of Fellows of the Royal
   Society. 1968. (Portrait.)
Nature, **213**, 555, 1967.
Dictionary of National Biography.
                                                      T I W

JABLOCHKOFF (IABLOTCHKOV), PAVEL NIKOLAIEVITCH Born at Serdobsk, Russia, 14 September 1847; died Saratov, 19 March 1904. Inventor of the electric candle.

Jablochkoff studied at the electrotechnical military school in St Petersburg, and became engineer-in-chief for the Moscow-Kursk railway telegraph. In 1876, while residing in Paris, he invented the 'Jablochkoff candle', an efficient and cheap low-current arc lamp. Small parallel carbon rods, mounted vertically and insulated by kaolin, were bridged at the apex by a strip of graphite; this was consumed when the current was switched on, leaving an arc which burnt down gradually. The invention was used in Paris and London within a year, and by 1881 there were said to be four thousand in service, in spite of disadvantages which included restriction to alternating current, not then widely available: direct current caused the rods to burn away unevenly. The inventor lived for a time in London, returning to Russia only shortly before his death.

Encyclopaedia Britannica. 1947.

T K D

JACOBI, CARL GUSTAV JACOB Born in Berlin, 10 December 1804; died there, 18 February 1851. Mathematician.

Jacobi was the son of a Berlin banker – in his day overshadowed by his brother Moritz (1801–74), who made early experiments in electricity. He studied in Berlin, receiving a doctorate in 1825 for a thesis on partial fractions. After lecturing there he moved, in 1826, to Königsberg. In this period he produced important work on elliptic functions. He based his theory on four theta functions defined by their series expansions. Their quotients led to the doubly periodic functions sn, cn, dn, the fundamental properties of which logically followed.

In 1832 Jacobi treated successfully the problem of hyper-elliptic integrals by inverting them to form the hyper-elliptic function. This led him to the theory of Abelian functions of p variables ($p2$): such a function has $2p$ periods.

In 1841 his theory of determinants was formulated in the paper *De formatione et proprietatibus determinantium*, a work which founded the determinant and established its basic properties. At the same time he broke new ground in applying function theory to the theory of numbers when he used elliptic functions to prove the assertion of P. FERMAT that any integer is the sum of the squares of no more than four integers.

In 1843 he fell ill and went to Italy for a cure. He returned as professor to Berlin, where he taught until he contracted smallpox in 1851, from which

he died. His investigations of first-order partial differential equations were published posthumously in his treatise on dynamics. His variation principle of mechanics contained in his work foreshadowed relativistic mechanics.

Leo Königsberger, *C. G. J. Jacobi.* 1904.
Wilhelm Ahrens, 'Ein Beitrag zur Biographie C. G. J. Jacobi', *Bibliotheca Mathematica*, vol. 7. 1906.
E. T. Bell, *Men of Mathematics.* 1937.
Dictionary of Scientific Biography.

D N

JACQUARD, JOSEPH MARIE Born at Lyons, France, 7 July 1752; died Oullines, 7 August 1834. Developed the Jacquard loom for weaving complicated patterns.

Jacquard was apprenticed to bookbinding and then to type-founding and cutlery. His parents, who had some connection with weaving, left him a small property on their death; he made some experiments with figure weaving, but lost all his inheritance and returned to type-founding and cutlery. In 1790 he formed the idea for his machine, but it was forgotten amidst the excitement of the Revolution, in which he fought for the Revolutionists in the defence of Lyons.

The machine he completed in 1801 combined inventions of Bouchier, Falcon, and Jacques de VAUCANSON, and was for weaving net. He was sent to Paris to demonstrate it, and in 1804 received a medal and a patent. A small pension enabled him to study and work at the *Conservatoire des Arts et Métiers* to perfect his mechanism for pattern weaving. He was not entirely successful and later modifications by Breton in 1815 and Skola in 1819 were needed before it functioned reliably. Some machines that were brought into use aroused bitter hostility. Jacquard suffered physical violence and his machines were burnt by weavers at Lyons, but by 1812 they began to be generally accepted and soon 11 000 drawlooms of his type were in use in France. In 1819 Jacquard received a gold medal and a Cross of Honour for his invention. His machines reached England around 1816 and remain the only way of weaving complicated patterns.

A. Barlow, *History of Weaving.* 1878.
W. English in *A History of Technology*, Charles Singer, E. J. Holmyard, A. R. Hall, and Trevor I. Williams (Eds), vol. 4. 1958.
Nouvelle Biographie Universelle. 1852–66.

R L H

JANSKY, KARL GUTHE Born in Norman, Oklahoma, USA, 22 October 1905; died Red Bank, New

Jersey, 14 February 1950. Pioneer of radio astronomy.

After graduating in physics at the University of Wisconsin, Jansky joined Bell Telephone Laboratories in 1928. In 1931 he was assigned the task of identifying the cause and cure of 'static', the crackling background noise that can seriously interfere with radio reception. Its origins include thunderstorms and electrical equipment. Using a directional aerial he detected a new source of radio emission which appeared at approximately the same time each day. By 1932 he had identified its source as lying within the constellation of Sagittarius, in the direction of the centre of our galaxy. Although Jansky did not pursue his observations, being more interested in his practical radio engineering, this observation was in fact the birth of radio astronomy. The amateur astronomer G. REBER discovered further sources in the Milky Way, using a dish aerial, but radio astronomy did not emerge as a distinct discipline until after the Second World War, notably in the hands of M. RYLE.

Archives Internationales d'Histoire des Sciences, **8**, 215, 1955.

T I W

JANSSEN, PIERRE JULES CÉSAR Born in Paris, 22 February 1824; died there, 23 December 1907. Pioneer of solar physics and photography.

Janssen studied mathematics and physics at the Faculty of Sciences in Paris, after which he taught at the Lycée Charlemagne and the School of Architecture. In 1857, between these two appointments, he went to Peru to determine the magnetic equator, and after returning he spent long periods in Italy and Switzerland studying absorption in the received solar spectrum due to the Earth's atmosphere. While at the School of Architecture (1867) he went on an expedition to the Azores, studying magnetic and astronomical phenomena. He observed two transits of Venus, that of 1874 in Japan, and that of 1882 at Oran, Algeria. He went on all major eclipse expeditions from France between 1867 and his death; he left the besieged city of Paris by balloon to see the eclipse of 1870 from Algiers.

Janssen's principle discovery was made with the Indian eclipse expedition of 1868. There he devised the same means of observing the prominences as N. LOCKYER had invented, independently, in England. The Janssen-Lockyer method was to be modified by Sir William HUGGINS, G. E. HALE, and Henri Deslandres (1853–1948) later in the century, and was of the first importance in obtaining knowledge of the chromosphere.

Throughout Janssen's investigations there is concern with the disadvantages of atmospheric absorption, which he proved to be mainly due to oxygen and water vapour (1865). Hence his decision to establish an observatory at the top of Mont Blanc, in order to reduce the thickness of the air through which observations were made. The observatory was completed 1893, when Janssen, then aged 69, made the ascent, and spent several days working there. In 1875 he became director of a new astrophysical observatory at Meudon, and began, in 1876, a remarkable collection of solar photographs, published in 1904. Some of these have scarcely been bettered since. Janssen, in fact, is usually regarded as one of the great pioneers of photography. Using newly developed sensitive plates, together with a 'photographic revolver' with focal plane shutter, he took a rapid sequence of photographs of the transit of Venus in 1874. His technique, developed by E. MUYBRIDGE and J. MAREY was one of the first steps on the road to the cinematograph. Janssen did important work on solarization, and perhaps his greatest achievement in photography was the discovery of reciprocity law failure.

A. M. Clerke, *A History of Astronomy during the Nineteenth Century*. 1903.

H. Macpherson, *Astronomers of Today*. 1905.

G. Bigourdan, *Bulletin astronomique*, **25**, 49, 1908.

A. de la Baume Pluvinel, *Astrophysical Journal*, **28**, 88, 1908.

J D N

JEANS, SIR JAMES HOPWOOD Born at Ormskirk, Lancashire, England, 11 September 1877; died Dorking, Surrey, 16 September 1946. Remembered for his work in statistical mechanics, stellar dynamics, and the scientific aspects of music.

Jeans was educated at Merchant Taylors' School (1890–6) and Trinity College, Cambridge. He was Second Wrangler (1898), Smith's Prizeman (1900), and Fellow of his College (1901). After lecturing for a time there he wrote, whilst convalescing from an illness, his *Dynamical Theory of Gases* (1904). He was appointed to a chair of applied mathematics at Princeton in 1905 and was elected FRS in 1906. Returning to Cambridge as Stokes Lecturer (1910–12), he soon relinquished formal teaching for research. In 1914 he published a useful *Report on Radiation and the Quantum Theory*, and in 1917 he obtained the Adams Prize for what was probably his best work, *Problems of Cosmogony and Stellar Dynamics* (1919).

Jeans's first important result was his detailed demonstration of the classical formula for the partition of radiant energy in an enclosure, previously proposed by Lord RAYLEIGH in 1900, and subsequently known as the Rayleigh-Jeans law. His treatment of stellar dynamics yielded many new results, especially in regard to the stability of equilibrium of rotating masses. It was known that, with increasing angular velocity, the form assumed by an incompressible mass passed through spheroid ('Maclaurin's spheroid') to ellipsoid with three unequal axes ('Jacobi's ellipsoid'). The stability of the latter, when under no constraint, was doubtful, Sir George Darwin (1845–1912) and A. M. Liapounoff (1905) having come to opposite conclusions. Jeans introduced new and powerful analytical techniques, confirming A. M. Liapounoff's findings. This result he published in his 1919 essay, together with numerous other problems, especially concerning the evolution of stars, of double-star systems, and of spiral nebulae. He showed that the Kant-Laplace hypothesis of the origin of the solar system was untenable, as it stood, and gave much attention to the problem of disruption of the parent star by tidal encounter. Many of these problems are dealt with again in *Astronomy and Cosmogony* (1928), but nuclear physics was still in its infancy, and his conclusions concerning internal stellar structure were short-lived. He made the interesting suggestion that an important source of stellar energy might be the mutual annihilation of protons and electrons.

Jeans wrote many popular expositions of astronomy and cosmogony. He was mainly responsible for making the 'heat-death of the Universe' a heated talking-point. His knowledge and love of music was considerable. He became a director of the Royal Academy of Music in 1931, and his book *Science and Music* (1938), written with his second wife, is probably the best on its subject.

> E. A. Milne, *Sir James Jeans*. 1952. (Portrait.)
> *Obituary Notices of Fellows of the Royal Society*, vol. 5, 1945–8.
> *Dictionary of National Biography*.
> *Dictionary of Scientific Biography*.
> H. Oxbury (Ed.), *Great Britons: 20th Century Lives*. 1985.

> J D N

JENCKS, WILLIAM PLATT Born at Bar Harbor, Maine, USA, 15 August 1927. Biochemist.

After schooling in Baltimore, Jencks studied medicine at Harvard Medical School and the Peter Bent Brigham Hospital from 1944 to 1952. He held pharmacological posts in the Army Medical Graduate School in Boston before doing chemical research with Fritz Lipmann (1899–1986) and R. B. WOODWARD at Harvard University from 1956 to 1957. In 1957 he joined the Biochemistry department at Brandeis University in Maine, where he has been a Professor since 1963.

Jenck's principal interest has been the mechanism of catalysis in solutions and its application to the study of enzyme reactions in living systems. By studying and measuring the lifetimes of unstable intermediates, Jencks developed models that accounted for the sensible differences in rates of catalysis of different acids and bases. In living systems, he suggested that rate accelerations are achieved because enzymes exploit binding links with non-reactive parts of substrates. Jencks has summarized his work in *Catalysis in Chemistry and Enzymology* (1969) and coauthored a textbook on biochemistry in 1992. He was elected a member of the National Academy of Sciences in 1971.

> *McGraw-Hill Modern Scientists and Engineers* (1980). (Portrait.)

> W H B

JENNER, EDWARD Born at Berkeley, Gloucestershire, England, 17 May 1749; died there, 24 January 1823. Pioneer of vaccination.

Jenner was the son of the vicar of Berkeley, and at the age of thirteen was apprenticed to a surgeon at Chipping Sodbury. Then, in 1770, he became for three years the pupil of the great naturalist and surgeon John HUNTER, who remained his lifelong friend. Returning to Berkeley, Jenner set up as a medical practitioner. As a boy, he was probably familiar with the local tradition that those who had had cowpox – a disease not generally familiar to the medical profession because it is localized and irregular in its appearance – were immune to smallpox. Jenner tested this experimentally. Firstly, he inoculated a healthy boy with cowpox and found that it was not subsequently possible to infect him with smallpox. Secondly, he showed that ten people who were known to have had cowpox naturally were likewise immune to smallpox. Thirdly, he showed that cowpox could be trans-ferred from person to person, carrying immunity to smallpox with it. In 1798 Jenner published his important memoir *An Inquiry into the Causes and Effects of the Variolae Vaccinae, a disease discovered in some of the Western Counties of England, particularly Gloucestershire, and known by the name of the Cow Pox.*

Although this publication excited much controversy, both in parts of the medical profession and among clerics, the general success of vaccination with humanized lymph soon led to its general adoption. When failure occurred it could often be attributed to faulty technique. It is estimated that by 1800 some 100 000 persons had been vaccinated, and the practice had spread throughout Europe and to the Americas. In 1807 Bavaria made vaccination compulsory and other countries gradually followed suit. In the United States, where Dr Benjamin Waterhouse (1754–1846) of Harvard medical school pioneered the technique, President Thomas Jefferson became not only interested but an active practitioner.

In 1806 Jefferson wrote to Jenner, 'Future generations will know by history only that the loathsome smallpox existed and by you has been extirpated.' Although this was over-optimistic, for it was nearly two centuries before this goal was achieved, the effect on the incidence of smallpox was dramatic. In the United Kingdom the death-rate fell from 3000-4000 per million in the eighteenth century to 90 per million after 1872, when vaccination was generally enforced; it had been made compulsory in 1853, but was not strictly enforced. In 1850 the hazardous process of variolation – immunization with smallpox material – was made illegal.

In 1802 Parliament awarded Jenner £10,000, to which a further £20,000 was added five years later. Oxford and Harvard gave him honorary degrees. He was elected FRS in 1788, partly for observations on the cuckoo; this reflected his keen interest in natural history, and his last published work (1823) was *On the Migration of Birds.*

> W. R. LeFanu, *A Bio-Bibliography of Edward Jenner*. 1951. (Portrait.)
> John Barnes, *The Life of Edward Jenner*. 1827.
> G. Wolstenholme (Ed.), *The Royal College of Physicians of London: Portraits*. 1964. (Portrait.)
> *Dictionary of Scientific Biography*.
> John Baron, *The Life of Edward Jenner*. 1827.

> T I W

JOLIOT, JEAN-FRÉDÉRIC Born in Paris, 19 March 1900; died there, 14 August 1958. Renowned for his discoveries in nuclear science.

The son of a Paris merchant, Frédéric Joliot studied at the Paris *École de Physique et Chimie*. After a few months as production engineer with a steel company, he entered the Radium Institute at Paris as *préparateur* in 1925. The following year he married Irène Curie (see Irène JOLIOT-CURIE), and in 1930 he gained his doctorate with a study of the electrochemistry of the radio elements.

The discovery of artificial radioactivity by Joliot and his wife earned them the Nobel prize in chemistry in 1935. As Joliot noted later, they might have also discovered the neutron in this work if they had read the prophecy made by E. RUTHERFORD in his 1920 Bakerian Lecture.

After two years at the Sorbonne, Joliot was appointed to a new Chair of Nuclear Chemistry at the *Collège de France.* Here he became leader of France's atomic energy programme and was appointed Director of the new atomic synthesis laboratory of the *Centre National de la Recherche Scientifique* (CNRS). He equipped the new establishment with a cyclotron and other essential apparatus.

Following the suggestion by Otto HAHN and F. Strassman that fission of the atomic nucleus was a possibility, Joliot within a few days obtained decisive proof of this (just after O. R. FRISCH had independently obtained other evidence). With great rapidity, Joliot then determined the number of neutrons emitted per fission and showed that a nuclear chain reaction was possible. With the onset of the war, in October 1939 Joliot deposited a sealed letter with the *Académie des Sciences*, revealing his knowledge of the conditions necessary to obtain a divergent nuclear chain reaction, that is, one capable of sustaining itself. The letter was opened in 1949.

During the war Joliot remained in France, pursuing scientific work on biological aspects of isotopes and playing an active part in the French Resistance Movement. The heavy water which he had procured from Norway was sent secretly to England with two of his colleagues. After the war, Joliot's energies were largely devoted to the reorganization of French science and establishment of a French atomic energy industry. However, in 1950 he was relieved of his post of High Commissioner for Atomic Energy on account of his political activities (he had joined the Communist Party during the war). He returned to the *Collège de France*, and, following his wife's death in 1956 he succeeded to her chair at the Sorbonne.

Like that of his wife, Joliot's devotion to science was accompanied by an outspoken dislike of many traditional institutions (clerical and political) and deep concern for world peace. He was first President of the World Federation of Scientific Workers and of the World Council for Peace. He also played an active part in the formation of the UN Atomic Energy Commission and in UNESCO.

P. Biquard, *Frédéric Joliot-Curie.* 1965. (Portraits.)

Louis de Broglie, *La vie et l'oeuvre de Frédéric Joliot.* 1959.

M. Goldsmith, *Frédéric Joliot-Curie: A Biography.* 1976.

Tyler Wasson (Ed.) *Nobel Prize Winners.* 1987. (Portrait.)

Biographical Memoirs of Fellows of the Royal Society. 1960. (Portrait.)

C A R

JOLIOT-CURIE, IRÈNE Born in Paris, 12 September 1897; died there, 17 March 1956. Famous, with her husband, for the discovery of artificial radioactivity.

Irène, daughter of Pierre and Marie CURIE, learned science from her mother and her colleagues at the Sorbonne. During the 1914–18 war she assisted Marie Curie as a radiographer, and was appointed as her *préparateur* at the Radium Institute in Paris. Her doctoral thesis was a study of the α-rays from polonium. In 1926 she married Frédéric JOLIOT and thereafter worked in close collaboration with him.

A little earlier (1919–21) E. RUTHERFORD and J. CHADWICK had shown that nuclei of most light elements could be disrupted by fast α-particles, with ejection of protons. In order to test for production of γ-rays, a polonium source was necessary, since this, unlike the usual radium-C source, is only a weak γ-emitter. In this way W. Bothe and H. Becker (1930) detected from beryllium a penetrating radiation ten times stronger than from any other light element. This result was confirmed and extended by Irène Joliot-Curie, having use of the largest supply of polonium in the world. With her husband, she showed that this radiation could eject protons from paraffin wax and other hydrogen-containing substances. The so-called 'radiation' was shown by Chadwick to be the neutron in 1932; the Joliots came to within an ace of discovering this particle themselves. However, they went on to make important studies of the materialization of photons and the annihilation of positrons on encounter with electrons.

Meanwhile, they worked with α-particles for another two years, and in 1933–4 observed that aluminium continued to emit positrons after the α-particle bombardment had ceased. They concluded, rightly, that a new, unstable isotope (of phosphorus in this case) had been produced in the laboratory – the discovery of artificial radioactivity. For this work and its development they were jointly awarded the Nobel prize in chemistry in 1935.

In the late 1930s much interest was centred on the nuclear bombardment by slow neutrons. Irène Joliot-Curie and her collaborators submitted uranium to this treatment, and in 1938 she and P. Savitch analysed the products and reported one very similar to lanthanum. This led O. HAHN and F. Strassman to their epochal work from which they drew the reluctant conclusion that the uranium atom had undergone nuclear fission.

In 1936 Irène Joliot-Curie was appointed Under-Secretary of State for Scientific Research. From 1946 to 1951 she was one of the four scientific commissioners for the French atomic energy project.

She had inherited the expertise, single-mindedness, and scientific insight of her parents. Her early death from leukaemia resulted from prolonged exposure to intense radiation.

Nature, **177**, 964, 1956.

The Times, 19 March 1956. (Portrait.)

Nuclear Physics, **4**, 497, 1957. (Portrait.)

Eugénie Cotton, *Les Curie.* 1983.

R. McKown, *She Lived for Science.* 1961.

Tyler Wasson (Ed.), *Nobel Prize Winners.* 1987. (Portrait.)

Dictionary of Scientific Biography.

C A R

JOLY, JOHN Born at Offaly, Ireland, 1 November 1857; died Dublin, 8 December 1933. Geologist and physicist.

Joly was the son of a clergyman, and received his education at Trinity College, Dublin. After two appointments as demonstrator (civil engineering (1882) and experimental physics (1893)), he became professor of geology and mineralogy in 1897. He was elected FRS in 1892, and in 1901 became one of the Editors of the *Philosophical Magazine.*

Joly made notable contributions in both physics and geology. In the first, he devised a constant volume gas thermometer; a photometer; and a differential steam calorimeter to measure the specific heats of gases at constant volume. In geology he became interested in deducing the age of the Earth, and revived a method devised by E. HALLEY, based on the salinity of the oceans. The basic assumption in such methods is that the amount of salt delivered to the seas by rivers flowing into them has remained constant throughout geological time. In 1898 he put forward a value of 80–90 million years, increasing this to 100 million years shortly afterwards. In the event, however, accretion of salt has not proved a very reliable timekeeper.

Turning his attention to the radioactive constituents of the Earth's crust, Joly estimated the contribution of radioactive decay to its heat content. He also investigated the minute 'pleochroic haloes' that surround radioactive nuclei in certain rocks, and used these to measure the age of the rocks themselves. Again in the same field, he devised a method of radium extraction and did pioneer work on its use for the treatment of cancer.

Proceedings of the Geological Society of America, 2, 251, 1934.
Quarterly Journal of the Geological Society of London, **90**, lv, 1934.
Nature, **133**, 90, 1934.

T I W

JONES, SIR HAROLD SPENCER Born in London, 29 March 1890; died there, 3 November 1960. Tenth Astronomer Royal.

As a child, Spencer Jones showed great interest in mathematics, which in due course he read at Cambridge, where he was a Wrangler (1911) and Smith's Prizeman (1913). In 1913 he was appointed chief assistant at Greenwich Observatory (to which he returned as Astronomer Royal in 1933) and ten years later was appointed HM Astronomer at the Cape of Good Hope.

At the Cape, he initiated an important new determination of the solar parallax, based on the favourable opposition of the planet Eros in 1930–1. This involved collating observations at twenty-four observatories, six in the southern hemisphere. The necessary co-operation was organized by the International Astronomical Union, who appointed Spencer Jones President of its Solar Parallax Commission (1928). Reduction of the observations took many years, and the result – giving a mean value of $8._{7904}\pm0.0010$ – was not published until 1941. He also determined the reciprocal of the mass of the Moon; the oblateness of the Earth; and the constant of nutation. For this achievement he was awarded a Royal Medal (1943) of the Royal Society, to which he had been elected in 1930, and the Gold Medal of the Royal Astronomical Society. He was knighted in 1943.

Observational difficulties at Greenwich led Spencer Jones in 1938 to initiate the moving of the Observatory to Herstmonceux Castle, Sussex, away from the atmospheric pollution of London. This move was not completed until some years after the war. (The observatory has now been closed and the castle has lately been sold.) He also greatly improved the accuracy of time measurement at Greenwich by introducing quartz-crystal clocks.

Biographical Memoirs of Fellows of the Royal Society. 1961. (Portrait.)

Dictionary of Scientific Biography.
H. Oxbury (Ed.), *Great Britons: 20th Century Lives.* 1985.

T I W

JORDAN, ERNST PASCUAL Born in Hanover, Germany, 18 October 1902; died Hamburg, 31 July 1980. Theoretical physicist.

Jordan studied physics at the *Technische Hochschule*, Hanover, and the University of Göttingen. From there he moved to Rostock, first as associate professor (1928–35) and then full professor (1935–44). He then moved on to Berlin (1944–51) and finally to Hamburg (1951–80). He was one of the founders of the new physics. In the 1920s he was associated with M. BORN and W. HEISENBERG in developing quantum mechanics: with Born he wrote *Elementare Quantenmechanik* (1932). Later – with W. E. PAULI, E. P. WIGNER and O. B. Klein (1894–1977) – he was closely involved in the development of quantum electrodynamics. His interests extended also to cosmology, geophysics, and gravitational problems. He was awarded the Max Planck Medal (1942) and the Gauss Medal (1955) of the German Physical Society.

Allen G. Debus (Ed.) *Who's Who in Science*, 1968.
E. P. Jordan, *Begegnungen: Albert Einstein, Karl Heim, Hermann Oberth, Wolfgang Pauli, Walter Heitler, Max Born, Werner Heisenberg, Max von Laue, Niels Bohr*, 1971.

T I W

JOSEPHSON, BRIAN DAVID Born in Cardiff, Wales, 4 January 1940. Theoretical physicist: discoverer of tunnelling superconductors.

Josephson graduated in physics at Cambridge in 1960 and – with the exception of a year at the University of Illinois (1965–6) – has done research there ever since. In 1974 he was appointed professor of physics in the Cavendish Laboratory. While still a research student (1962) he discovered the Josephson Effect. If two superconductors are separated by a very thin layer of insulator a current can 'tunnel' between them even if no voltage is applied. If, however, a potential V is applied an alternating current will flow with frequency 2Ve/h. This phenomenon has found practical application in the development of high-speed switching devices for computers and similar equipment. Later, he developed a deep interest in the basic phenomena of intelligence.

He was elected Fellow of the Royal Society in 1970 and in 1973 shared a Nobel prize with L. ESAKI and I. Giaevar (1929–).

Les Prix Nobel en 1973. 1974. (Portrait.)
Robert L. Weber, *Pioneers of Science: Nobel Prize Winners in Physics*, 1980. (Portrait.)
N. Cousins, *Nobel Prize Conversations*. 1985.
Tyler Wasson (Ed.), *Nobel Prize Winners*. 1987. (Portrait.)

T I W

JOULE, JAMES PRESCOTT Born at Salford, near Manchester, England, 24 December 1818; died Sale, Cheshire, 11 October 1889. Celebrated for experimental establishment of the mechanical theory of heat.

Joule studied for a time with his brother under John DALTON, from whom he learned mathematics, chemistry, and scientific method. In 1839 he commenced the series of experiments which ultimately led to his establishment of the mechanical theory of heat. The year 1847 was memorable for his meeting with William THOMSON (Lord Kelvin) and for the latter's recognition of the importance of Joule's work. He was elected a Fellow of the Royal Society the following year. Between 1853 and 1862 he published a series of important papers in collaboration with Thomson. After the death of his wife in 1854 he led a very retired life, and from 1872 until his death in 1889 he was in poor health and did little further work.

In 1840 Joule transmitted to the Royal Society a paper *On the Production of Heat by Voltaic Electricity*. First published in full in the *Philosophical Magazine* (1841), this paper contained clear indications of the notion of the equivalence of mechanical work and heat, as in the observation of the diminution of the heat produced in an electrical circuit on the introduction of an electrical motor performing mechanical work. A paper *On the Calorific Effects of Magneto-electricity and on the Mechanical Value of Heat* read at the 1843 meeting of the British Association, contained a first determination of the mechanical equivalent of heat corresponding to a rise in temperature of 1° Fahrenheit of 1 lb of water for the expenditure of 838 ft lb of work. In 1845 Joule announced his first paddle-wheel experiment, later repeated with additional refinements and resulting in a mean value of 781.8 for the mechanical equivalent of heat, the figure adopted in his paper read at the meeting of the British Association at Oxford in June 1847. His final value (1850) was 772.692. In 1849 his definitive paper, *On the Mechanical Equivalent of Heat*, was read to the Royal Society.

Joule collaborated with William Thomson in an important series of experiments from 1852 onwards to verify various predictions of the new science of thermodynamics developed independently by Thomson and R. J. E. CLAUSIUS on the basis of Joule's mechanical theory of heat and the theorem of Sadi CARNOT. Of these experiments the most famous were on the so-called Joule-Thomson effect which had been predicted by Thomson on the basis of a small deviation from ideality observed by H. V. REGNAULT in his experiments on gases. Mention must finally be made of Joule's epoch-making paper on the kinetic theory of gases which contained the first estimate of the velocity of gas molecules (1848).

Joule combined great patience, experimental skill, and ingenuity in avoiding errors, with extraordinary accuracy. As Lord Kelvin said of him (*Nature*, **26**, 619, 1882), 'His boldness in making such large conclusions from such very small observational effects is almost as noteworthy and admirable as his skill in extorting accuracy from them'.

O. Reynolds, *Memoirs and Proceedings of the Manchester Library and Philosophical Society*. 4th Series, **6**, 1892.

H. J. Steffens, *James Prescott Joule and the Concept of Energy*. 1979.

D. S. Cardwell, *James Joule: A Biography*. 1989/ *Dictionary of Scientific Biography*. *Dictionary of National Biography*.

J W H

nacht, near Zürich, 6 June 1961. The founder of analytical psychology, an off-shoot of Freudian psychoanalysis with distinctive features of its own.

After qualifying in medicine at the University of Basle, Jung turned to psychiatry, and obtained his first post in 1900 at the Burghölzli Hospital near Zürich as assistant to Eugen Bleuler, an authority on schizophrenia. It was while there that he devised his word-association test, and propounded his theory of 'complexes', or emotionally toned, and partially repressed, groups of ideas. In 1907 Jung, who had already become interested in psychoanalysis, first met Sigmund FREUD. Several years of close association followed. Jung became one of Freud's chief lieutenants, and in 1911 was president of the International Psychoanalytic Association. A break with Freud, which became complete, occurred in 1913, following the publication of Jung's *The Psychology of the Unconscious* (1912). Jung came to believe that both the sexual theory of Freud and the inferiority theory of A. ADLER were partial and inadequate. Both these theories dealt one-sidedly with the infantile origins of neurosis; neither dealt adequately with the striving of the individual to realize his whole personality. The differences between the theories of Freud and Adler were in part the result, Jung considered, of differences in temperament, and he came to lay increasing stress on the basic type differences of extroversion and introversion. *Psychological Types* (1923), in which he describes these differences, is one of Jung's most widely recognized contributions to psychology.

In his studies of the unconscious and its symbolisms Jung turned more and more to anthropological and esoteric material. He himself carried out field studies among primitive peoples, and he searched the writings of alchemists and Orientalists. He believed he had found a universal symbolism, a set of archetypes, resident in the collective unconscious, linking present-day humanity with ancestral beginnings. The demands and pressures of society impose restrictions on human development: the 'persona' (or conventional mask we present to the world) excludes the 'shadow' (the undeveloped and unrevealed aspects of the self); the male 'animus' represses the female 'anima', and vice versa. The task of the psychotherapist is to strive for an integration of opposites, and this involves a process of individuation, or deeper self-realization. This process of individuation, Jung held, is in the last resort a religious process, best described as finding the god within. The strongly mystical element in much of Jung's writing does not appeal to everyone, but must not obscure his solid contributions both to the practice and theory of psychology, and his profound insights into the deep needs of the human soul.

Herbert Reed, Michael Fordham, *et al*. (Eds), C. G. *Jung: Collected Works*. 1953– .

A. M. Dry, *The Psychology of Jung – a Critical Interpretation*. 1961.

G. Wehr, *The Psychology of Jung – An Illustrated Biography*. 1971.

Dictionary of Scientific Biography. *The Times*, 7 June 1961. (Portrait.)

L S H

JUNG, CARL GUSTAV Born at Kesswil, Canton Thurgau, Switzerland, 26 July 1875; died Kues-

JUSSIEU, ANTOINE LAURENT DE Born at

Lyons, France, 12 April 1748; died Paris, 17 September 1836. Plant taxonomist.

The Jussieu family dominated plant taxonomy in France for nearly a hundred and fifty years. Antoine completed his medical studies in 1770 under the guidance of his uncle Bernard de Jussieu (c.1699-1777), who was in charge of the *Jardin du Roi*. He published little in the next few years; in his monograph. *Examen de la Famille des Renoncules* (1773) he first proposed the principle of the relative value of characters. This principle was extended to other families in his *Exposition d'un nouvel ordre de Plantes* (1774).

In 1778 he succeeded Bernard as subdemonstrator of Botany at the *Jardin du Roi*. Bernard's system for the arrangement of plants in the Trianon was incorporated, with improvements, in Antoine's *Genera Plantarum* (1789). This great work retained the three primary divisions of John RAY: Acotyledons, Monocotyledons, and Dicotyledons, the last being subdivided into Apetalae, Monopetalae, Polypetalae, and Diclines Irregulares. Altogether Jussieu formed fifteen classes, which were further subdivided into about a hundred 'natural orders' or families, to which he assigned distinctive characters. The excellence of the *Genera Plantarum* is attested by the fact that seventy-six of the one hundred family names are now conserved in the *International Code of Botanical Nomenclature.*

The *Genera Plantarum* was followed by the publication of numerous valuable monographs on different families in the *Mémoires* of the *Muséum d'Histoire Naturelle* in which Jussieu became professor of botany in 1793. He resigned his professorship to his son Adrien (1797–1853) in 1826. The *Muséum* was considerably reorganized when Antoine subsequently became its director and treasurer.

J. von Sachs, *History of Botany (1530–1860).* 1890.
Annales des Sciences Naturelles. Botanique, **7(2)**, 5, 1837. (Portrait.)
Dictionary of Scientific Biography.

R G C D

K

KANE, SIR ROBERT JOHN Born in Dublin, 24 September 1809; died there, 16 February 1890. Chemist and educationist.

Kane was the second son of a Dublin chemical manufacturer, John Kane (originally Kean). He himself became interested in chemistry, and at the age of 20 characterized the natural arsenide of manganese, since known as kaneite. After studying pharmacy in Paris and arts at Trinity College, Dublin, he was appointed professor of chemistry in the Apothecaries Hall, Dublin, in 1831, becoming known as the 'Boy Professor'. Only a year later he was elected to the Royal Irish Academy. He founded the *Dublin Journal of Medical and Chemical Science* (later the *Irish Journal of Medical Science*). In 1840 he became editor of the *Philosophical Magazine*.

In 1833, a year before an independent discovery by Justus von LIEBIG, he identified the ethyl radical. In 1837, partly as a result of work done in Liebig's laboratory at Giessen, he synthesized mesitylene by treating acetone with sulphuric acid; this is an important example of transition from straight-chain to ring structure. In the 1840s there appeared the three volumes of his *Elements of Chemistry*, generally acknowledged as the best and most comprehensive chemical textbook of its day.

A later book, his *Industrial Resources of Ireland*, was to change the course of his career. It attracted the attention of Sir Robert Peel (1788–1850), and led to Kane's becoming an adviser to the Irish Government and taking an active part in the development of education and industry. Besides being president of Queen's College, Cork, he helped to found the Royal College of Science for Ireland, of which he became Dean. In his later years he was vice-chancellor of Queen's University.

Kane was knighted in 1846. In 1849 he was elected FRS. His wife, a botanist of distinction, was a niece of Francis Baily (1774–1844), the astronomer, who described the solar eclipse phenomenon still known as Baily's beads.

T. S. Wheeler, *Endeavour*, **4**, 91, 1945. (Portrait.)
D. Reilly, *Sir Robert Kane*. 1942.
Journal of Chemical Education, **32**, 404. 1955.
Dictionary of National Biography.

T I W

KAPITZA, PIOTR LEONIDOVICH Born in Kronstadt, Russia, 8 July 1894; died Moscow, 8 April 1984. Physicist and engineer, particularly famous for his work in low temperature physics.

Kapitza studied at the St Petersburg Polytechnical Institute and started research under A. F. Joffé (1880–1960) at the newly established Physicotechnical Institute in Petrograd (as St Petersburg became in 1914). He soon acquired a reputation for his skill and originality and joined a Soviet commission in 1921 to renew scientific relations with the West after the Revolution and the Civil war. In Cambridge, RUTHERFORD agreed to have Kapitza spend the winter in the Cavendish Laboratory to gain experience of nuclear physics, but was so impressed by his abilities that he encouraged him to extend his stay, which eventually lasted 13 years. To pursue his studies of α-particles, Kapitza developed new methods of producing very high magnetic fields of short duration but soon abandoned nuclear physics for the study of magnetic properties of metals at these high fields. He then realized that these properties become more interesting at low temperatures and developed ingenious new methods of liquefying hydrogen and helium. The Royal Society Mond Laboratory was built specially for him in 1933 thus laying the foundations of a new school of low temperature and solid state physics in Cambridge. He was elected a Fellow of Trinity College in 1925 and of the Royal Society in 1929.

However, his work in Cambridge came to an abrupt end in 1934 when after a visit to the Soviet Union he was denied permission to return to Cambridge and eventually, in 1936, a new Institute for Physical Problems was created for him in Moscow. Once again, Kapitza changed direction and took up two new lines of research. One was the study of liquid helium below its λ-point, which led to his most important achievement, the discovery of superfluidity in 1938. The other was the development of a new and more efficient turbo-expander method of air liquefaction, which proved important during the War in providing bulk oxygen for the steel industry, and for which he received high government decorations.

In 1946 his fortunes changed yet again, essentially for political reasons. He was abruptly dismissed and retired to his dacha (country house). There he set up a small laboratory and took up various new problems. He invented a new technique for generating high power electromagnetic microwaves and when he was reinstated in his Institute soon after Stalin's death in 1953, he used his microwave source to heat plasma to very high temperatures. This work continued to the end of his life, but although he produced interesting plasma physics, he did not succeed in achieving the goal of nuclear fusion. Late in life, his contributions to low temperature physics were recognized by the award of the Nobel prize in 1978. He became a kind of elder statesman of Soviet science and did much to promote improvement of scientific education and research in the Soviet Union, as well as intervening courageously on behalf of unjustly repressed colleagues such as L. D. LANDAU and A. D. SAKHAROV.

Biographical Memoirs of Fellows of the Royal Society. 1985. (Portrait.)

J. W. Boag, P. Rubinin, and D. Shoenberg (Eds), *Kapitza in Cambridge and Moscow.* 1990.

L. Badash, *Kapitza, Rutherford, and the Kremlin.* 1985.

Tyler Wasson (Ed.), *Nobel Prize Winners.* 1987. (Portrait.)

                                                        D S

KARRER, PAUL Born in Moscow, 21 April 1889; died Zürich, Switzerland, 18 June 1971. Organic chemist; made important contributions to chemistry of natural products, especially carotenoids, vitamins, alkaloids, and co-enzymes.

Paul Karrer was the son of Swiss parents; his father was a qualified dentist. They brought him back to Switzerland, at the age of three, to live in a small rural community. After schooling at Wildegg, Lensburg, and Aarau, he went in 1908 to Zürich University to study under Alfred WERNER. Three years later he was awarded his DPhil. for a thesis on nitrosopentamminocobalt salts. After a further year at Zürich he went to the Georg-Speyer-Haus (for chemotherapy) in Frankfurt (1912–18) to work with Paul EHRLICH on organic compounds of arsenic. In 1918, he returned to Zürich as professor of chemistry and a year later succeeded Werner as director of the Chemical Institute, a post he held until his retirement.

In his first years at Zürich he directed his attention mainly to the chemistry of sugars and polysaccharides, his techniques including enzymatic splitting of the macromolecules to elucidate their structure. In 1925 he published an important monograph *Polymere Kohlenhydrate.* His experiments on the amination of cellulose fibres threw new light on the nature of dyeing processes. He became interested also in various other natural products, including glucosides; alkaloids such as ricin (from castor oil seeds); tannins; and phosphatides such as lecithin. The last of these he showed to be a mixture of α- and β-lecithin.

In 1926, Karrer turned his attention to plant pigments and thus began the classic researches for which he is best remembered and which were in due course to earn for him a Nobel prize for chemistry (1937, with W. N. HAWORTH). He contributed to knowledge of the chemistry of anthocyanins – pioneer work on which had been done by R. WILLSTÄTTER and his school (1913–17) – notably by degradation experiments which identified the points of attachment of sugar residues. His greatest achievements, however, were in the field of the hydrocarbon plant pigments – particularly carotene and lycopene ($C_{40}H_{56}$) which contain conjugated systems of double bonds – and the closely related oxygen-containing xanthophylls. These fat-soluble pigments were, of course, already well-known; carotene had been isolated as long ago as 1831 by H. W. F. Wackenroder (1798–1854), and M. S. TSWETT had demonstrated their ease of separation by chromatography. Nevertheless, their structural chemistry was at that time still obscure. By 1930 Karrer had established the structures of α- and β-carotene and lycopene, partly by degradation and partly by synthesis of the perhydro derivatives. It became clear that the carotenoid pigments are basically constructed from eight isoprene units arranged end-to-end, with a reversal at the centre of the chain.

In 1931, Karrer turned his attention to Vitamin A, the fat-soluble vitamin found in large amounts in the livers of salt-water fish, such as cod and halibut. Deficiency causes, among other symptoms, defects of vision and keratinisation of mucous membranes. In 1931, Karrer established the structure of Vitamin A_1, ($C_{20}H_{29}OH$) and showed it to be an oxidation product of one half of the carotene molecule. He elucidated the structures of other vitamins also – including Vitamin B_2 (riboflavin) (1935), Vitamin B_{12}, Vitamin E (tocopherol) (1938) – and confirmed them by synthesis. Later, he diverted his attention to the curare alkaloids and alkaloids of horse-tails (Equisetaceae). Karrer freely used the organic chemical techniques of his day but made particular use of bromine succinimide for bromination and lithium aluminium hydride as a reducing agent.

It is a measure of the speed with which chemical technique has advanced that today the elucidation of the structures of such molecules would be virtually a matter of routine. In the 1930s, however, the task demanded a high measure of chemical knowledge and manipulative skill, great patience, and – above all – a rare kind of chemical intuition that allows its possessor quickly to discard the unfruitful possibilities and discern the true solution.

Karrer's interest in natural products led him to investigate also the chemical nature of co-enzymes, the relatively simple organic substances that are necessary for the proper functioning of the large, highly complex, enzyme molecules. In this field, too, he made important contributions.

Karrer has a lasting memorial in his well known *Lehrbuch der organischen Chemie,* a conspectus of the whole of organic chemistry that became a standard reference book and had considerable influence on the training of generations of organic chemists. It first appeared in 1927, and ran through no less than twelve editions. Originally in German, it was translated into English, French, Spanish, Italian and Japanese. In 1948 he published his *Monographie über Carotinoide.*

Biographical Memoirs of Fellows of the Royal Society. 1978. (Portrait.)

Dictionary of Scientific Biography, Supp. II.

Tyler Wasson (Ed.), *Nobel Prize Winners.* 1987. (Portrait.)

                                                        T I W

KEELER, JAMES EDWARD Born at La Salle, Illinois, USA, 10 September 1857; died San Francisco, California, 12 August 1900. Remembered for his pioneer contributions in observational astrophysics.

James Edward Keeler's ancestors came from New England. Early in his life he showed interest in astronomy, establishing the Mayport Astronomical Observatory between 1875 and 1877. There he observed the Moon, planets, and stars. In 1881 he graduated AB from Johns Hopkins University, and became assistant in the Allegheny Observatory. He spent 1883–4 studying and travelling in Europe. When Lick Observatory was completed in 1888, Keeler was appointed Astronomer; with the large spectroscope, constructed mainly from his designs, he carried out a number of highly successful research programmes in spectroscopy. In 1891 he left Lick to become director of the Allegheny Observatory and professor of astrophysics in the Western University of Pennsylvania. In 1898 he was appointed to the position of director of the Lick Observatory. Unfortunately, his early death cut short a most promising career.

Keeler was an outstanding observer and experimenter, designing many of the instruments with which he made his researches. With the Allegheny spectroscope he investigated the nature of the Orion nebula and the stars associated with it, showing that the majority of the bright lines in the nebular spectrum corresponded to dark lines in the stellar spectra, thus demonstrating that nebulae and stars are closely related. He also obtained spectra of Saturn and its rings that verified the classic mathematical researches of Clerk MAXWELL on the ring structure. The Doppler displacements (see C. J. DOPPLER) obtained photographically by Keeler showed that each point in the ring system moved with the velocity a satellite of Saturn would have at that distance.

As director of the Lick Observatory he made use of the Crossley reflecting telescope. After modifying it extensively, he began the task of photographing the brighter Herschel nebulae. At the time of his death more than half of the objects had been successfully photographed. The plates taken revealed many thousands of nebulae hitherto undiscovered and established their essentially spiral structure. In modern terms, Keeler had obtained images of tens of thousands of galaxies outside our own galaxy.

Keeler was evidently a stimulating man to work with; his work ably demonstrated the immensely powerful astronomical research tool a large telescope, a camera, and a spectroscope provide in combination. He was a fellow and associate of many societies and was given the Rumford Medal of the American Academy of Arts and Sciences (1898) and the National Academy of Sciences' Henry Draper Medal (1899).

W. W. Campbell, *The Astrophysical Journal*, 12, 239, 1900. (Portrait.)

Biographical Memoirs of the National Academy of Sciences, 5, 231, 1905. (Portrait.)

C. D. Perrine, *Popular Astronomy*, 8, 409, 1900.

A E R

KEILIN, DAVID Born in Moscow, 21 March 1887; died Cambridge, England, 27 February 1963. Biochemist; discoverer of cytochrome.

Keilin was the son of a Polish businessman, and was educated in Warsaw at the Gorski Gymnasium. Later he studied at the University of Liège with the object of qualifying in medicine, but the asthma that troubled him throughout his life led him to seek a less arduous course. Eventually his interest settled in biology, especially entomology, which he studied in Paris. In 1915 he went to Cambridge, where he remained for the rest of his life. In 1921 he and his colleagues moved into the new Molteno Institute, of which he became director in 1931, succeeding G. H. F. Nuttall (1862–1937) – who had originally invited him to Cambridge – as Quick Professor of Biology. He was a gifted linguist, speaking Russian, French, and English fluently in addition to his native Polish.

Keilin is particularly remembered for his discovery of the widely distributed respiratory pigment, cytochrome. His classic paper *On Cytochrome, a Respiratory Pigment Common to Animals, Yeast and Higher Plants* appeared in 1925. This pigment, readily followed because of its distinctive spectrum, has subsequently been shown to play a key role in cellular respiration. He investigated also a range of other pigments – including haemoglobin (mammals), haemocyanin (molluscs), and haemerythrin (worms) – and made a comparative study of them. He carried out also important work on a variety of enzymes, especially the plant-peroxidase system (1936).

He was widely honoured in his lifetime. The Royal Society elected him to its Fellowship in 1928 and awarded him its Royal (1939) and Copley (1951) Medals. He was a corresponding member of the French Academy (1947) and later *membre associé étranger* (1955). He was an honorary graduand of several universities, including Liège.

Biochemical Journal, **89**, 1, 1963.

Comptes rendus de l'Académie des Sciences, 258, 399, 1963.

Biographical Memoirs of Fellows of the Royal Society. 1964. (Portrait.)

Dictionary of National Biography.

Dictionary of Scientific Biography.

T I W

KEIR, JAMES Born in Edinburgh, 29 September 1735; died West Bromwich, Staffordshire, England, 11 October 1820. A pioneer in industrial chemistry.

James Keir came from a prosperous Edinburgh family and was educated at Edinburgh High School and University, where he studied at the medical school and met Erasmus DARWIN. He never took his degree, and instead joined the Army because of 'a strong desire to see foreign countries'. After service in the West Indies during the Seven Years War, he retired with the rank of captain about 1768; in 1770 he married and settled near West Bromwich, where he remained for the rest of his life. He joined Darwin's circle of scientific friends and became a popular member of the Lunar Society of Birmingham. Keir was an agreeable man, of sturdy common sense, a valued friend and collaborator of Matthew BOULTON, James WATT, Josiah WEDGWOOD, and Joseph PRIESTLEY.

In 1771 Keir became manager of a glass-making company at Stourbridge, and he also started manufacturing chemicals on his own. In 1780 he founded the Tipton alkali works, which is often regarded as marking the birth of the scientific chemical industry. It was there that Keir succeeded in making caustic soda from waste sulphates on a commercial scale, by an ingenious method using dilute solutions; his process was working in 1781, some years before the process of Nicolas LEBLANC was devised. Keir's other contributions to science were varied. His annotated translation of the *Dictionary of Chemistry* (1771), by P. J. MACQUER, was widely used as a reference book. In 1780 he patented an alloy known as 'Keir's metal', of virtually the same composition as the 'Muntz metal' developed fifty years later. Keir was elected a Fellow of the Royal Society in 1785 and contributed three papers to the *Philosophical Transactions*, of which the most important is *On the Crystalliza-tions Observed in Glass* (1776).

Amelia Moilliet (née Keir) and James Keir Miolliet, *Sketch of the Life of James Keir.* 1868. (Privately printed.)

R. E. Schofield, *The Lunar Society of Birmingham.* 1963.

Notes and Records of the Royal Society, **21**, No. 2, 1966. (Portrait.)

J. L. Moilliet, *Endeavour* (New Series), **9**, 129, 1985. (Portrait.)

Dictionary of National Biography.

D G K-H

works are his *Antiquity of Man* (1915), *Engines of the Human Body* (1919), and his *Autobiography* (1950).

Sir Arthur Keith, *An Autobiography.* 1950. (Portraits.)

Annals of the Royal College of Surgeons, **20**, 38, 1966. (Portrait.)

William Le Fanu, *A Catalogue of the Portraits in the Royal College of Surgeons of England.* 1960. (Portrait.)

Biographical Memoirs of Fellows of the Royal Society. 1955. (Portrait.)

Dictionary of National Biography.)

K D K

KEITH, SIR ARTHUR Born at Persley, near Aberdeen, Scotland, 5 February 1866; died Downe, Kent, England, 8 January 1955. Anatomist and anthropologist.

Keith was the son of a farmer. He was educated at Robert Gordon's College and Marischal College, Aberdeen; he graduated MB in 1888 and MD in 1894. In later life he was made LLD and Rector of Aberdeen University.

After graduation, Keith went into general practice for a short while at Mansfield, whence he answered the call of adventure to go to Siam as medical officer to a gold-mining company. Here he commenced his studies on the anatomy of monkeys. Returning to Europe, he studied at University College, London, and briefly under W. HIS at Leipzig, after which (1894) he obtained his Fellowship of the Royal College of Surgeons. He was appointed senior demonstrator of anatomy at the London Hospital Medical School in 1896, and there he made his reputation as a teacher. While at the London Hospital he became interested in the anatomy of the heart through contact with Sir James Mackenzie (1853–1925). Keith laid stress on the usefulness of anatomy to medicine and he demonstrated this by his discovery, with the aid of Martin Flack (1882–1931), of the sino-atrial node (pacemaker of the heart).

In 1908 Keith became conservator of the Museum of the Royal College of Surgeons and Hunterian Professor. Here his skill and enthusiasm brought to him specimens of skeletons from many parts of the world for his opinions on their significance in the anthropological story of man. It was during these years he entered into lively controversy with other anthropologists over the interpretation of 'Piltdown Man' – a controversy only solved by the later discovery that this was a forgery, a revelation which for Keith meant 'a loss of faith in the testimony of man'. In 1913 he was knighted, made a Fellow of the Royal Society, and a member of the *Societé d'Anthropologie de Paris*.

In 1932 he suffered from an exacerbation of pulmonary tuberculosis, following which he resigned his post at the College in Lincoln's Inn Fields, becoming Master of the Buckston Browne research farm at Downe in Kent, the site of the home of Charles DARWIN. This was very appropriate, as Keith, a fervent Darwinian, had himself appealed for the preservation of Darwin's home. Keith lived in a cottage close to the farm, and actively continued to maintain his interest in anthropology and farming until the day of his death.

Keith's publications were many. He made a point of writing for students and the general public as well as anthropologists. Perhaps his best-known

KEKULÉ (later KEKULÉ VON STRADON-ITZ),FRIEDRICH AUGUST Born at Darmstadt, Germany, 7 September 1829; died Bonn, 13 July 1896. The founder (with A. S. COUPER) of structural organic chemistry, and the author of the cyclic formula for benzene.

Kekulé began his career as a student of architecture, but was attracted to chemistry by hearing Justus von LIEBIG give evidence in a sensational murder trial. He studied in Giessen (1848–51), and for a year in Paris; then for a short time he worked in a private laboratory in Switzerland. His creative period really began with a stay in London (1854–5) as assistant to J. Stenhouse (1809–80) at St Bartholomew's Hospital; here he became friendly with A. W. WILLIAMSON and W. ODLING, and was able to compare their views with those of the Parisian chemists J. B. A. DUMAS, C. F. GERHARDT, and C. A. WURTZ. From 1855 to 1858 he was *Privat-dozent* in Heidelberg, where his theoretical ideas were made more robust by discussions with the intensely practical J. F. W. von BAEYER. He then became professor successively at Ghent (1858) and Bonn (1867).

Kekulé was a mediocre chemist at the bench, and not, it would seem, an outstanding teacher. Although he had some distinguished pupils, his main contributions to chemistry were theoretical and speculative. When he began research most organic chemists thought (following Gerhardt) that although molecules were no doubt built up of atoms arranged in some quasi-permanent structure, this structure was unknowable, for chemical reactions (the only conceivable source of information) would disturb the structure unpredictably. Williamson at least was beginning to dissent from this; and Kekulé later told of a 'waking dream' on a London omnibus, in which he had seen the atoms grouping themselves in patterns in space. His paper of 1858 (almost simultaneous with Couper's) laid the foundation of structural organic chemistry. He made two explicit postulates: firstly, that carbon atoms can combine directly with one another to form chains of any length and complexity; secondly, that the valency of carbon is invariably four; and a third tacit postulate that a study of reaction products can give valid information about structure (though he also urged, for the first time, the value of physical methods). The way was then clear for organic chemists, led by von Baeyer, to embark on their proper task of assigning structures to the large and ever-growing number of organic compounds.

Compared with Couper, however, Kekulé was a faint-hearted revolutionary. It was long before he could free himself from the philosophical scruples of the Type Theory, and he hampered himself with a clumsy and misleading symbolism. The development of the Structure Theory was largely left to other hands. The exception was his brilliant solution to the problem of the structure of benzene; a regular hexagon with alternate single and double bonds, in rapid oscillation (1865). The consequences of this solution were worked out in great detail by his pupil W. Körner (1839–1925). Kekulé's great *Lehrbuch der organischen Chemie*, which began to appear in 1859, but was never finished, was very influential in spreading his ideas.

Kekulé's brief first marriage (1862) ended with the death of his wife in childbirth. His second marriage (1876), which gave him three more children, was less than happy. In the same year he suffered a severe attack of measles, after which his health was never good, and he seems to have aged prematurely. In his last twenty years he did little work of note.

R. Anschütz, *August Kekulé*. 2 vols. 1929. (Portraits.)

E. Farber (Ed.), *Great Chemists*. 1961.

Journal of the Chemical Society, **73** 97, 1898. (Portrait.)

N. Fisher, *Ambix*, **21**, 29, 1974.

Dictionary of Scientific Biography.

J. H. Wotiz (Ed.) *The Kekulé Riddle*. 1992.

W V F

KELLNER, KARL Born in Vienna, 1 September 1851; died there, 7 June 1905. Chiefly remembered for his part in developing, with H. Y. CASTNER, the electrochemical manufacture of caustic soda from brine.

Karl Kellner practised in Vienna as a consulting engineer and was associated with a number of enterprises, especially in connection with pulp; the latter included the Kellner-Partington Pulp Company. Developing an interest in electrochemistry, he realized the possibilities of a mercury cathode in preparing caustic soda from brine. Patenting the process in 1894, he formed his own organization – the *Konsortium für Electrochemische Industrie* – to work it near Salzburg; the other European rights he assigned to the *Societé Solvay et Cie* of Brussels, who were then very actively engaged in manufacturing sodium carbonate by the ammonia-soda process. Kellner's patent conflicted with ones sought by Castner, but eventually an amicable agreement was reached between the conflicting interests; Kellner became, for a short time, a director of the Castner-Kellner Alkali Company in Britain.

Österreichisches Biographisches Lexikon (14th ed.). 1964.

Trevor I. Williams, *Fifty Years of Progress: the Story of the Castner-Kellner Alkali Company*. 1947. (Portrait.)

T I W

KELLY, WILLIAM Born at Pittsburgh, Pennsylvania, USA, 21 August 1811; died Louisville, Kentucky, 11 February 1888. Inventor of the air-boiling process of steel-making.

William Kelly was the son of a rich landowner and married the daughter of a wealthy tobacco merchant. He acquired land in Eddyville, Kentucky, containing iron ore, and there worked a Cobb furnace.

He launched a company, the Sewanee Ironworks and Union Forge, for making sugar-boiling kettles; these were manufactured from pig-iron converted into wrought-iron by a simple charcoal process. During experiments to reduce costs he discovered that excess carbon could be burnt out of molten iron by subjecting this to an air blast; moreover, the heat generated in the process diminished the need to supply this from an outside source, resulting in a great saving of fuel.

Realizing the potentialities of his discovery, he worked from 1851 to 1856 in secret on the construction of converters. In 1856 he heard that Henry BESSEMER had successfully applied for a US patent for the Bessemer process. Kelly submitted his own application, claiming priority of discovery of his essentially identical process, which he asserted Bessemer had learned from American workmen. The United States patent office accepted his appeal and granted a patent in June 1857, and the first steel made in accordance with it was produced in 1864. The patent was renewed after fourteen years, while that of Bessemer was not.

In the year that he was granted a United States patent he became bankrupt and sold the patent to his father, who in turn left it in his will to Kelly's sisters. On his father's death Kelly applied to his sisters for the return of the patent, but they refused on the grounds of his incompetence; the patent rights did, however, descend to his children. Kelly continued experiments with steel-making at the Cambria Iron Works in Pennsylvania and his eighth converter produced soft steel of a kind suitable for the economic production of rails and bars.

J. N. Boucher, *William Kelly*. 1924. (Portrait.)

Dictionary of American Biography.

N H

KELVIN, LORD *See* THOMSON, WILLIAM.

KENDALL, EDWARD CALVIN Born South Norwalk, Connecticut, USA, 8 March 1886; died Princeton, New Jersey, 4 May 1972. Hormone biochemist.

Kendall trained as a chemist at Columbia University, New York, where he gained a doctorate in 1910. After disillusioning experiences with a pharmaceutical company, which stimulated his interest in the chemistry of the thyroid gland, and in a hospital, he became director of biochemistry at the all-graduate school of the Mayo Foundation in Rochester – part of the University of Minnesota. Following retirement in 1951, he continued research as a visiting professor of biochemistry at Princeton University.

Kendall made his name in 1914 by isolating an iodine-containing compound, thyroxine, from thyroid glands, which he and others showed was part of a hormone, thyroglobulin, responsible for controlling metabolic rate. During the 1920s, Kendall's interest in the general metabolic problem of cell oxidation led to the successful crystallization of the tripeptide, glutathione, a component of most animal cells. In 1935–36, following up a suggestion by a postdoctoral visitor, A. SZENT-GYORGYI, Kendall's research group isolated several steroids from the cortex of the adrenal gland, including the compound later named cortisone. War-time research on steroids was catalyzed by rumours that German pilots were using cortical extracts as stimulants. By 1943 Kendall's group had isolated and synthesized over twenty corticosteroids. His co-worker, Philip S. Hench (1896–1965) showed, in 1949, that this had anti-inflammatory properties and that it was useful in the treatment of rheumatoid arthritis. It was for their work on adrenal hormones that he and Hench, together with the Swiss-Pole, Tadeus Reichstein (1897–), were awarded the Nobel prize for physiology or medicine in 1950.

E. C. Kendall, *Cortisone. Memoirs of a Hormone Hunter*, 1971. (Portrait.)

Nobel Lectures Physiology or Medicine 1942– 1962. 1964.

Biographical Memoirs of the National Academy of Sciences, **47**, 249, 1975.

Dictionary of Scientific Biography, Supp. I.

W H B

KENDALL, HENRY W Born in Boston, Massachusetts, USA, 9 December 1926. Particle physicist.

Kendall is a graduate of the Massachusetts Institute of Technology (MIT) where he has been professor of physics since 1967.

Investigations of atomic structure in the 1930s revealed an apparently very simple state of affairs – a dense nucleus consisting of neutrons and protons, surrounded by a cloud of electrons. It soon became clear, however, that these three fundamental units were inadequate to explain all the properties of atoms. The discovery of a new class of nuclear particle, hadrons, led to a new interpretation and the introduction of three new units called quarks. Experimentally, however, these proved elusive and came to be regarded as mathematical abstractions rather than real entities.

This situation changed with the availability of a very high energy linear particle accelerator, two miles long, at the Stanford Linear Accelerator Center in California. In the late 1960s and early 1970s dramatic results were obtained. Unexpectedly large deflections of electrons fired deep into the structure of nuclei led to the conclusion that quarks do in fact exist as centres of inelastic scattering and constitute the basic building blocks of protons and neutrons. The quarks are bound together by an electrically neutral 'glue' of gluon.

This dramatic fulfilment of theoretical predictions was the result of collaboration between two research teams. One, led by H. W. Kendall and J. I. Friedman, was from MIT. The other, headed by R. E. Taylor, was from SLAC. All three shared the Nobel prize for physics in 1992.

Les Prix Nobel en 1992. 1993. (Portrait.)

T I W

KENDREW, JOHN COWDERY Born in Oxford, England, 24 March 1917. Molecular biologist. Elucidated structure of myoglobin using x-ray diffraction techniques.

Kendrew's father was reader in climatology in the University of Oxford. After the Dragon School, Oxford, and Clifton College, he read natural sciences at Trinity College, Cambridge. During the Second World War he worked on radar research for the Ministry of Aircraft Production.

Back in Cambridge he joined Max PERUTZ in 1946 and began to investigate the structure of myoglobin

using x-ray diffraction techniques. He was elected a fellow of Peterhouse College, Cambridge in 1947 and with Perutz set up the Medical Research Council Unit of Molecular Biology (later the MRC Laboratory for Molecular Biology) in the Cavendish Laboratory in 1947. He was deputy chairman 1947–75. He was awarded a PhD in 1949 and a DSc in 1962. Kendrew incorporated heavy atoms into the myoglobin molecule and with the help of a computer produced a three-dimensional model in 1957. He had determined the complete structure by 1960. His work, and that of Perutz, on myoglobin and haemoglobin was very significant for later developments in the study of the nucleic acids by others, and they were also responsible for many improved techniques which simplified the process of x-ray diffraction.

Kendrew founded the *Journal of Molecular Biology* in 1959 and remained Editor-in-chief until 1987. He left Cambridge in 1975 to become director-general of the newly founded European Molecular Biology Laboratory at Heidelberg, a post he retained until 1982. He was President of St. John's College, Oxford 1981–7.

Elected a Fellow of the Royal Society in 1960, Kendrew shared the Nobel prize for chemistry with Perutz in 1962 for determining the structure of myoglobin. He was knighted in 1974. In 1966 he published *The Thread of Life*.

R. C. Olby, *The Path to the Double Helix*. 1974.

F. H. Portugal and J. S. Cohen, *A Century of DNA*. 1977.

J. C. Kendrew, *Scientific American*, **216**, 141, 1967.

Tyler Wasson (Ed.), *Nobel Prize Winners*. 1987. (Portrait.)

W. A. Campbell and N. N. Greenwood (Eds), *Contemporary British Chemists*. 1971. (Portrait.)

A P B

KENNELLY, ARTHUR EDWIN Born near Bombay, India, 17 December 1861; died Boston, Massachusetts, USA, 18 July 1939. Notable contributor to the theory of alternating currents.

The son of an Irish naval officer, Kennelly received his early education in Europe, spending four years at University College School, London. In 1874 he became office boy to the London Society of Telegraph Engineers (later the Institution of Electrical Engineers), leaving two years later to gain experience of practical telegraphy overseas. This was to include service as an electrician in Malta and as chief electrician in a cable engineering ship. From 1887 to 1894 he was assistant to T. A. EDISON in America, becoming also in 1893 a consultant electrical engineer in Philadelphia. Appointed professor of electrical engineering at Harvard in 1902, he held this post until his retirement in 1930, but from 1913 to 1925 was also professor of electrical communication at Massachusetts Institute of Technology.

Kennelly's chief contributions were to the theory of alternating currents. He defined the term 'inductance speed', which, together with resistance, determined the impedance of a conductor. His treatment used the theory of complex numbers developed by J. R. Argand (1768–1822), and he produced charts and tables of hyperbolic functions to facilitate routine calculations. He also studied heat losses in transmission lines and the rise in temperature of cables buried in the earth. At a time when this was of great importance he did valuable work on standards of illumination.

In 1902, independently of O. HEAVISIDE, he explained the new trans-Atlantic wireless communication as a reflection of the waves back to earth by some layer of the upper atmosphere. The existence of this Kennelly-Heaviside layer was verified by Edward APPLETON in 1924.

Kennelly was a great scientific administrator. He represented the United States at the Electrical Congresses of 1900, 1904 (when he was also general secretary), and 1932. He was a member of the International Commission of Weights and Measures, attending its meeting at Sèvres in 1933. He took part in the International Radio Conference at Washington in 1927, when the international allocation of radio-transmission frequencies was made. He was president of the American Institute of Electrical Engineers (and chairman of its Units and Standards Committee); president of the Illuminating Engineering Society; and president of the Metric Association, being influential in introducing the metric system into American athletics. A member of many other societies, he loved to travel, and lectured in France, Japan, and other countries. He was awarded by the French Government the Cross of the *Légion d'Honneur*.

American Journal of Physics, **29**, 246, 1961. (Portrait.)

Nature, **144**, 64, 1939.

Journal of the Institution of Electrical Engineers, **85**, 777, 1939.

Biographical Memoirs of the National Academy of Sciences, **22**, 83, 1943.

Dictionary of American Biography.

Dictionary of Scientific Biography.

C A R

KEPLER, JOHANNES Born at Weil, Württemburg, 27 December 1571; died Ratisbon, Bavaria, 15 November 1630. Mathematician, physicist, and astronomer, famous in particular for his laws of planetary motion.

Kepler's father was a soldier of fortune, who at length deserted his family. The young Kepler was educated at both the German and Latin schools in Württemburg, at convent schools (Adelberg and Maulbronn), and at the University of Tübingen (1588). At Tübingen he was taught by Michael Maestlin (1550–1631), a follower of Copernican astronomy, although he still intended to enter the Church. In 1594, Kepler became mathematics teacher at the Protestant Seminary, Graz. He fled the country in 1598, when Archduke Ferdinand issued an edict against Protestant teachers, and later joined Tycho BRAHE in Prague, in 1600. On Tycho's unexpected death in October 1601, Kepler was appointed Imperial Mathematician in his stead, with the duty of finishing the 'Rudolphine' Tables begun by Tycho Brahe and giving astrological advice. In 1611, Kepler lost his wife and child, whilst Bohemia lost its ruler. Rudolph's usurper, his brother Matthias, retained Kepler as Court astronomer, but he was also given the post of District Mathematician in Linz (1612–26). Civil, religious, and financial difficulties at length drove him from Linz, and he moved to Ulm. An arrangement whereby he entered the service of Wallenstein, Duke of Friedland, who promised (in vain)

to meet the Emperor's debt of 12,000 florins owed to Kepler, meant another move, to Sagan in Silesia (1628). He died on a journey to Ratisbon (Regensburg).

Kepler's scientific writings are conveniently grouped into three, written at Graz, Prague, and Linz. At Graz he sought the reasons underlying existing planetary distances, and after much mystical speculation he conceived the idea that each planetary orbit is circumscribed by a regular solid, and has inscribed in it the solid of the next planet below. This, and similar *a priori* conceptions of the nature of the Universe, were contained in his *Mysterium Cosmographicum* (1597), which led to a correspondence with Tycho Brahe and a polite exchange of letters with GALILEO whom he entreated to join him in support of COPERNICUS.

Kepler's best work was done at Prague, where he published his *Ad Vitellionem Paralipomena* (1604), a work on optics notable for a good approximation to the law of refraction; an important section on vision, which for the first time clearly separates the physical and the physiological problems; and for the mathematical treatment accorded to most of the optical systems then known. Kepler's most important work at Prague, however, originated with the difficulty he had experienced in fitting Mars into his cosmological schemes. After an immense amount of labour, he was led to his laws of elliptical orbits and of equal areas, these appearing in his *Astronomia Nova* of 1609. The book also contains an attempt to explain his first two planetary laws in terms of magnetic forces: here he was influenced by William GILBERT. In 1610 Kepler was given a Galilean telescope, and within a year he had published his *Dioptrice*, which carried his theory of refraction a stage further, and which contains the principle of the so-called 'astronomical' telescope (i.e. the inverting refractor).

At Linz he published a work on the gauging of casks, which contains the solutions to a large number of problems by methods resembling those used by ARCHIMEDES and Nicholas of Cusa (1401–64). This book, together with parts of the earlier *Astronomia Nova*, appears to have been very influential in the evolution of the infinitesimal calculus.

Kepler never abandoned the train of thought evident in his first work, and in 1619 he published *De Harmonice Mundi*, a fantastic collection of supposed harmonies in nature. The work also contains his third law of planetary motion. This states, in effect, that the squares of the periodic times of the planets are proportional to the cubes of their mean distances from the Sun.

The Rudolphine Tables were not ready for publication until 1627, long after Tycho's death. The immense amount of calculation involved makes it clear why the logarithms of John NAPIER had been so avidly greeted by Kepler, as was evident in his *Chilias Logarithmorum* (1624).

Max Caspar, *Kepler* (trans. C. Doris Hellman). 1959.

G. Holton, *American Journal of Physics*, **24**, 350, 1956.

A. Armitage, *John Kepler*. 1966. (Portrait.)

Dictionary of Scientific Biography.

J D N

KERR, JOHN Born at Ardrossan, Scotland, 17 December 1824; died Glasgow, 18 August 1907. Remembered for the two effects bearing his name.

A student at Glasgow University (1841–9), Kerr later became one of the first research students of William THOMSON (Lord Kelvin). In 1857 he was appointed a lecturer in mathematics at a training college in Glasgow, remaining there for the rest of his life. In 1875, in the first of a series of papers, he announced the birefringence caused in glass and other insulators when placed in an intense electric field. At the Glasgow meeting of the British Association in the following year he announced various effects produced in polarized light by reflection from a polished pole of an electromagnet. Kerr was elected to the Royal Society in 1890, and was awarded a Royal Medal in 1898.

Dictionary of National Biography, 1901–11.

Proceedings of the Royal Society, **82A**, i, 1909.

C. G. Knott, *Nature*, **76**, 575, 1907.

J W H

KHORANA, HAR GOBIND Born at Raipur, Punjab, India, 9 January 1922. Deciphered the genetic code.

Khorana, the son of a Hindu tax clerk working for the British government, was educated in a village outdoor school and then at the DAV High School, Multan, Punjab. He studied chemistry at Punjab University, Lahore, graduating in 1943. Moving to England on a Government of India fellowship he was awarded a PhD in organic chemistry by the University of Liverpool in 1948. He then spent 1948–9 at the *Eidgenossiche Technische Hochschule*, Zürich, working with V. PRELOG on the chemical structure of certain alkaloids. It was as a Nuffield Fellow at Cambridge University, working under A. R. TODD that he became interested in the biochemistry of nucleic acids.

In 1952 Khorana moved to the University of British Columbia, Vancouver, Canada, as director of the organic chemistry section of the British Columbia Research Council. Here he studied the chemical structure of nucleotide coenzymes, and with J. G. Moffatt (1930–   ) he synthesised acetyl coenzyme A in 1959. The method they devised made the coenzyme available for research on the breakdown of sugar molecules to release energy.

Moving to the University of Wisconsin, Madison, in 1960 as co-director of the Institute for Enzyme Research, he published *Some Recent Developments in the Chemistry of Phosphate Esters of Biological Interest* in 1961. He was appointed professor of life sciences in 1964. During the 1960s he worked on the synthesis of protein molecules, and in 1970 he was the first to synthesise a DNA gene of yeast. He subsequently synthesised a DNA gene of *E.coli*. He became professor of biology and chemistry at Massachusetts Institute of Technology in 1970.

In 1968 Khorana shared the Nobel prize in physiology or medicine with M. W. Nirenberg (1927–   ) and R. W. Holley (1922–   ) for his interpretation of the genetic code and its function in protein synthesis.

Les Prix Nobel en 1968. 1969. (Portrait.)

Tyler Wasson (Ed.), *Nobel Prize Winners*. 1987. (Portrait.)

A P B

KHWARIZMI (MUHAMMAD IBN MUSA AL-) Born before 800; died after 847. Mathematician, astronomer.

Of al-Khwarizmi's life we know little but his scientific achievements are known through surviving versions of his written works and references to others. He became attached to the 'House of Wisdom', a scholarly academy in Baghdad. His *Algebra* (829) was a strictly practical work, designed to simplify the solution of everyday problems. It was the first book on algebra to be written in Arabic, and draws heavily on Hindu and Greek sources. A work on Hindu (Arabic) numerals is lost but is known through Latin translations. It was important in introducing this notation to Islam, whence it found its way to the west through L. FIBONACCI. His book on astronomy (*Zij*) is the earliest extant work on this subject in Arabic: it is largely a collection of astronomical tables. His *Geography* is essentially a catalogue of the latitude and longitude of major geographical features. The work of al-Khwarizmi shows little originality; its significance lies in its powerful influence in conveying Hindu and Greek scholarship to Islam and thence to the west.

Dictionary of Scientific Biography.

Seyyed Hassein Nasr, *Islamic Science: An Illustrated Study*. 1976.

T I W

KIPPING, FREDERIC STANLEY Born at Higher Broughton, Manchester, England, 16 August 1863; died Criccieth, Wales, 1 May 1949. Pioneer of the organic chemistry of silicon.

F. S. Kipping was one of the seven children of a Manchester bank official. He was educated at Manchester Grammar School, and in 1879 entered Owens College, Manchester (now Manchester University). He took a London University external degree in 1882, and then obtained a post as chemist to Manchester Gas Department. In 1886 he went to Munich, where he was fortunate enough to work under W. H. PERKIN, jnr. in the laboratory of J. F. W. A. von BAEYER. Returning home, he accepted a post as demonstrator at the Heriot-Watt College, Edinburgh, again under Perkin, who had been appointed Professor there. During this time they began to collaborate in writing a textbook of *Organic Chemistry* (1899), which, in successive editions, was widely used for more than half a century. In 1890 he was appointed chief demonstrator in chemistry at the City and Guilds of London Institute (under H. E. ARMSTRONG). He was elected FRS in 1897 and in the same year moved to University College, Nottingham (now Nottingham University), as Professor of Chemistry. Initially, his facilities there were very limited, but in 1928 new buildings were opened, endowed by Sir Jesse Boot, later Lord Trent (1850–1931), a wealthy local chemical manufacturer. He retired in 1936.

Kipping's main research interest was in optically active compounds; that is, compounds having asymmetric molecules affecting the angle of rotation of a beam of polarized light. Initially (1890–6), he was interested (with W. J. POPE) in camphor derivatives, but later (1900–5) he experimented also with compounds of quinquevalent nitrogen. Simultaneously, however, he was developing (from 1900) the research on organic compounds of silicon for which his name is now internationally remembered. Again, his interest was mainly in the preparation of optically active substances in this rather intractable group – made rather less so by the discovery of a widely applicable method of synthesis by F. A. V. GRIGNARD in 1900 – but he lived long enough to see widespread interest in silicones (as they are now called) because of their exceptional properties of water repulsion and high temperature stability. Today, silicones – ranging from free-flowing liquids to heavy greases and rubbery solids – are manufactured at the rate of thousands of tons annually.

Kirchhoff made important contributions to theoretical physics, especially in analytical dynamics; in the theory of vibrating plates; in the propagation of sound in tubes; and to the theory of light diffraction. His remarkable solution to the generalized Poisson equation (see S. D. POISSON) was of central importance in later work in electromagnetic theory.

Kirchhoff was one of the outstanding physicists of the century, rivalled in Germany for the importance and influence of his work only by R. J. E. CLAUSIUS, H. L. F. von HELMHOLTZ, and Max PLANCK.

Obituary Notices of Fellows of the Royal Society. 1950. (Portrait.)

E. Farber (Ed.) *Great Chemists.* 1961. (Portrait.)

Dictionary of National Biography.

T I W

W. Voigt, *Zum Gedächtnis von Gustav Kirchhoff.* 1888.

A. S. Everest, *Physics Education*, **4**, 341, 1969.

Proceedings of the Royal Society, **46**, vi, 1889.

Dictionary of Scientific Biography.

J W H

KIRCHHOFF, GUSTAV ROBERT Born at Königsberg, Prussia, Germany, 12 March 1824; died Berlin, 17 October 1887. Celebrated for his contributions to spectrum-analysis and theoretical physics.

On completion of his studies at Königsberg, and after a period as *Privatdozent* at Berlin, Kirchhoff was appointed extraordinary professor of physics at Breslau (1850). Here he made the acquaintance of R. W. BUNSEN, whom he followed to Heidelberg on his appointment there as ordinary professor of physics in 1854. He remained at Heidelberg till 1875 when he was finally persuaded to accept the chair of mathematical physics at Berlin, a position he retained until his death.

Kirchhoff's first researches were on the conduction of electricity. In 1845 he gave the laws for closed circuits, extending these to general networks (1847) and to solid conductors (1848). In 1859 there appeared his fundamental paper explaining the production of the Fraunhofer lines (see J. von FRAUNHOFER) by the absorption of the corresponding spectral wavelengths in the atmosphere of the Sun. He proceeded next to advance his celebrated law stating that the ratios of the emissive to the absorptive powers were the same for all bodies at a given temperature for radiation of a given wavelength. His first proof of this result was based on certain special assumptions which he was able to remove in a paper of 1861.

The first announcement of the fundamental work of Kirchhoff and Bunsen on spectrum-analysis appeared in a paper of 1860. If most of the results presented were already known, they were now for the first time subjected to constant laws. Kirchhoff and Bunsen showed that for a very wide variety of compounds, and for various temperatures, a given metal gave a characteristic series of spectral lines, and that conversely the appearance of a given series of lines indicated the presence of the metal in question. In 1860 they announced the discovery of a fourth metal, caesium, in the series of alkaline earths, and the following year a new metal, rubidium, was discovered by Bunsen. They also made important improvements in the construction of spectroscopes, adding a third tube with a scale and a reflection prism to provide a standard spectrum to compare against an unknown spectrum. By means of a spectroscope employing four prisms Kirchhoff obtained (1861) a much broadened solar spectrum in which he was able to identify a large number of terrestial elements.

KIRWAN, RICHARD Born at Cloughballymore, Galway, Ireland, 1 August 1733; died Dublin, 22 June 1812. Chemist.

Kirwan was one of the best-known scientists of his day, partly because of his important contributions to chemistry and partly because of his eccentricity. As a young man he was a Catholic – he was a Jesuit novitiate in 1764 – but in later life he was a Protestant. He studied law in France, England and Germany, and was called to the Bar in 1766, but was not a notably successful practitioner in either London or Dublin. The years 1777–87 he spent in London – he was elected FRS in 1780 – and carried out some important work in his private laboratory. He returned to Dublin in 1787 and two years later was elected president of the Royal Irish Academy, holding this office until his death. His recorded eccentricities include the habitual wearing of topcoat and hat indoors, and subsistence on a diet of ham and milk.

During his most active years Kirwan was a convinced believer in the phlogiston theory, and identified hydrogen with phlogiston. He set out his views in his *Essay on Phlogiston* (1st ed. 1784), which was soon translated into French (1788). Unlike some of his contemporaries – for example, Joseph PRIESTLEY – Kirwan changed his views (1791) when confronted with the evidence of LAVOISIER that combustion does not involve loss of phlogiston, an intangible essence, but rather combination with oxygen. He investigated the combining properties of acids and alkalis and developed a theory of chemical affinity.

Kirwan was a knowledgeable mineralogist and his *Elements of Mineralogy* (1784) – the first systematic treatise on the subject – enhanced his reputation; a French edition appeared in 1785. On chemical grounds – developed in his *Geological Essays* (1799) – he found himself in conflict with the views of the geologist James HUTTON. He measured the specific heats of a number of substances and published a table of them (not all original) in 1780; he also made some gas density measurements (1789).

J. Reilly and N. O'Flynn, *Isis*, **13**, 298, 1930.

C. J. Brockman, *Journal of Chemical Education*, **4**, 1275, 1927.

F. E. Dixon, *Dublin Historical Records*, **29**, 53, 1971.

Dictionary of Scientific Biography.

T I W

KITASATO, SHIBASABURO Born at Kumamoto, Japan, 20 December 1852; died Nakanocho, Azabu, Japan, 13 June 1931. Bacteriologist; discoverer of the plague bacillus, and joint discoverer of antitoxic immunity.

Kitasato began his medical studies at the newly founded medical school at Kumamoto, and continued them at the Imperial University of Tokyo, where he graduated in 1883. In 1885 he went to Berlin to work with R. KOCH. He did very important work during his period in Berlin, and in 1892 the title of professor was conferred on him. In the same year he returned to Japan and founded a private laboratory near Tokyo. In 1899 this laboratory was taken over by the State, and he continued as its director. Against his wishes this institute was amalgamated with the Imperial University, and he therefore resigned his directorship and founded the Kitasato Institute. He had many distinguished pupils. In 1917 he became a Member of the Upper Chamber in Tokyo, and he was ennobled in 1924. Kitasato was elected a Foreign Member of the Royal Society in 1908.

The tetanus bacillus was discovered by Arthur Nicolaier (b. 1862) in 1884, but neither he nor anyone else was able to grow it in pure culture. In 1889 Kitasato employed anaerobic methods, and succeeded in obtaining a pure culture.

In December 1890 Kitasato and Emil von BEHRING announced their discovery that the serum of animals injected with increasing non-lethal doses of tetanus toxin developed the power of neutralizing the toxin. This was the very important discovery of antitoxic immunity. In 1894, after his return to Japan, Kitasato discovered the plague bacillus in Hong Kong, where he had been sent by the Japanese Government to investigate a plague epidemic. This organism was discovered independently, and almost at the same time, by Alexandre YERSIN.

W. Bulloch, *History of Bacteriology*. 1938.

H. J. Parish, *History of Immunization*. 1965. (Portrait.)

H. Fox, *Annals of Medical History*, **6**, 491, 1934.

Dictionary of Scientific Biography.

E A U

KJELDAHL, JOHAN GUSTAV CHRISTOFFER THORSAGER Born at Jaegerspris, Denmark, 16 August 1849; died (on holiday) Tisvilde, 18 July 1900. Inventor of a well-known method for the rapid estimation of nitrogen.

Kjeldahl, the son of a medical officer, studied chemistry at the Royal Polytechnic and Royal Agricultural College in Copenhagen. In 1875 he went as a chemist to the famous Carlsberg brewery in that city. A year later Jacobsen, the owner, founded the Carlsberg Laboratory, financed by the profits of the brewery, to carry out independent research; Kjeldahl was made head of the chemistry department. In connection with his studies of the protein content of biological materials, he required a method for determining nitrogen more rapid and convenient than the combustion-tube methods then in use. He found such a method in digestion of the sample with hot sulphuric acid, followed by estimation of the ammonia produced (1883). Now known by the name of its inventor, this method is still widely used, though improved and modified.

Kjeldahl published other work on the hydrolysis of starch and the estimation of reducing sugars; but his life was clouded by ill health, both physical and mental, and in his last years he did little. He never married.

R. E. Oesper, *Journal of Chemical Education*, **11**, 457, 1934. (Portrait.); **26**, 459, 1949. (Portrait.)

W. Johannsen, *Berichte der deutschen Chemischen Gesellschaft*, **33**, 3081, 1900. (Portrait.)

H. Lund, *Selecta chimica*, **12**, 3, 1953.

W V F

KLAPROTH, MARTIN HEINRICH Born at Wernigerode, Harz, Germany, 1 December 1743; died Berlin, 1 January 1817. A founder of analytical chemistry, and discoverer of several elements.

Klaproth was apprenticed to a local apothecary, and followed his calling in Hanover, Berlin – where his teachers included A. S. MARGGRAF – and Danzig. He returned to Berlin in 1771 to manage the pharmacy of the well-known Rose family. In 1780 he set up his own laboratory, and gave up the practice of pharmacy in 1787. From 1792 he taught chemistry in the Berlin Artillery School; in 1810 he became the first professor of chemistry in the newly founded University of Berlin.

Klaproth was one of the earliest German converts to the antiphlogistic theories of LAVOISIER. At his insistence the Berlin Academy repeated Lavoisier's experiments on combustion, and he was influential enough to ensure that the new chemistry was widely taught. His other great contribution to chemistry was that he founded (with his contemporaries L. N. VAUQUELIN, J. L. PROUST and W. H. WOLLASTON) the science of analytical chemistry. Many methods and techniques which are now standard, such as the ignition of precipitates to constant weight, have their explicit origin in Klaproth's work, though he was, of course, drawing on the experience of generations of unnamed assayers and apothecaries.

Almost as an accidental by-product of his interest in analysis, Klaproth discovered, or confirmed the discovery of, several new elements. In 1789 he isolated a new 'earth' (zirconia) from zircon; and in the same year 'uranium' from pitchblende, though much later the supposed element was shown to be uranium oxide. He confirmed, independently of T. C. HOPE, that strontia was a new 'earth' different from baryta; he discovered titanium (1795) independently of W. GREGOR; and chromium (1797) independently of Vauquelin. His announcement of the new element tellurium (1798) occasioned a courteous priority dispute with the Hungarian chemist P. Kitaibel (1757–1817). He analysed innumerable minerals, discovered mellitic acid in honeystone, and made a start on the chemistry of the rare earths; he also applied analytical chemistry to the study of antiquities. Many of Klaproth's publications appeared (1795–1815) in a collected edition entitled *Beiträge zur chemischen Kentniss der Mineralkörper*. A. W. HOFMANN described Klaproth as 'possessed of a modesty devoid of all conceit, filled with appreciation of the merits of others, though mindful of their weaknesses, but implacably strict in the appraisal of his own work . . . the model of a true natural scientist'.

G. E. Dann, *Martin Heinrich Klaproth*. 1958.

E. Farber (Ed.), *Great Chemists*. 1961. (Portrait.)

Earle R. Caley, *Journal of Chemical Education*, **26**, 242, 1949.
Dictionary of Scientific Biography.)

W V F

KLEIN, CHRISTIAN FELIX Born at Düsseldorf, North Rhine-Westphalia, Germany, 25 November 1849; died Göttingen, 22 January 1925. Geometer and algebraist.

After studying at Bonn, Göttingen and Berlin, Klein became assistant to J. PLÜCKER in Bonn, where he did research in geometry. In 1870 he met M. S. LIE and together they worked on transformation groups. He was appointed professor at Erlangen in 1872. In his inaugural address he formulated the *Erlangen Programm*, a description of the unification of mathematics in terms of group theory. Every geometry is essentially the theory of invariants of a particular transformation group – Euclidean geometry to the metrical group of transformations, projective geometry to linear transformations, topology to continuous point transformations, and so on. The *Erlangen Programm* was received enthusiastically and its influence was felt over all branches of geometry. Klein enabled the non-Euclidean geometries, as conceived by F. BOLYAI and N. I. LOBACHEVSKI to be accepted as geometries with a particular type of metric. He showed that projective geometry had complete independence of the parallel postulate of Euclid.

Klein and his pupils applied the group concept in many other fields of mathematics; a study of rotation groups of the regular bodies (1884) received special attention. In his studies of axiomatic geometries he extended projective geometries to *n*-dimensional space.

Klein was professor from 1872 onwards at Göttingen which became a world centre of mathematical research. He initiated the mathematical *Encyklopädie* in 1895.

G. Prasad, *Some Great Mathematicians of the Nineteenth Century: Their Lives and Works*, vol. 2. 1954.
R. Fricke and A. Ostrowski (Eds), 'C. F. Klein', *Gesammelte Mathematische Abhandlungen*. 1921–3. (Portrait.)
Dictionary of Scientific Biography.

D N

KLINGENSTIERNA, SAMUEL Born at Linköping, Sweden, 18 August 1698; died Stockholm, 26 October 1765. Mathematician and scientist.

Klingenstierna was the son of a major in the Army of Charles XII. He lost his father at the age of 9 and his later education was supervised by the Bishop of Linköping (both Klingenstierna's grandfathers were bishops).

He studied law at Uppsala with the intention of becoming a civil servant, but soon found that his real interest was in mathematics and physics. In 1720 he was appointed secretary to the Swedish Treasury, but was given leave of absence to continue his studies at Uppsala. In 1727 he was given a scholarship to travel in Europe. He visited Marburg, where he studied under Christian Wolff (1679–1754), the German mathematician and philosopher; Basle, where he worked with J. BERNOULLI; and Paris, where he met many of the leading French scientists of the day, especially B. le B. de FONTENELLE. During this tour he learnt that he had been appointed professor of mathematics at Uppsala, probably on the recommendation of Wolff. In 1750 he was appointed to a newly created chair of physics. In 1756 his wide knowledge and experience led to his appointment (until 1764) as tutor to the Crown Prince (later Gustav III).

While professor of physics at Uppsala, Klingenstierna perceived that some of the conclusions of NEWTON on the refraction of light were incorrect. This was a discovery of great practical importance, for according to Newton's theory it would be impossible to construct an achromatic lens. In October 1755, at the suggestion of a pupil of his in London, Klingenstierna communicated his results to John DOLLOND, the optical instrument maker. There is no doubt that this communication was a major factor in Dollond's ultimate success in constructing achromatic compound lenses, though he never acknowledged it. Dollond's achievement aroused great interest in scientific circles and in 1762 the Russian Academy of Science offered a prize for the best method of constructing optical instruments free of chromatic and spherical aberration. This was won, appropriately, by Klingenstierna.

Nouvelle Biographie Universelle. 1852–66.
S. Lindroth (Ed.), *Swedish Men of Science, 1650–1950*. 1952.
H. C. King, *The History of the Telescope*. 1955.
Dictionary of Scientific Biography.

T I W

KOCH, ROBERT Born at Clausthal, Hanover, Germany, 11 December 1843; died Baden-Baden, 27 May 1910. The greatest of all pure bacteriologists.

Koch studied mathematics and science at Göttingen, but soon transferred to medicine and graduated in 1866. He was in general practice in Niemegk (1868) and in Rakwitz (1869), and served with the army throughout the Franco-Prussian War. In 1872 he was appointed as *Kreisphysicus* (district medical officer) at Wollstein, a small town in Polish Prussia, and he now started bacteriological research in his own small house. After publication of his early researches he was appointed to the Imperial Health Office at Berlin (1880). Here he was soon joined by Georg Gaffky (1850–1918) and Friedrich Loeffler (1852–1915), the first two of his famous line of pupil-assistants. In 1885 he became professor of hygiene in the University of Berlin, and director of the newly founded Institute of Hygiene in the University. In 1891 a new Institute for Infectious Diseases was founded for him, and he was director until 1904, when he relinquished the administrative responsibility. He continued to be active in research, especially in Africa.

The anthrax bacillus, seen in the blood of infected cattle in 1849, was shown in 1868, by C. J. DAVAINE, to be the cause of anthrax. But no advance was made in treatment or prevention, and the anthrax mortality of cattle in France and Germany was very high. Fields that had contained infected cattle many years before were found to be still infectious. At Wollstein, Koch tackled this problem in his primitive laboratory. Shortly before, Ferdinand COHN had first observed the formation of spores by a bacillus. Koch now found that in certain conditions, which he studied exhaustively, the anthrax bacillus forms spores that can survive in the earth for years. He passed anthrax bacilli, from the blood of an infected animal, from one mouse to another through twenty generations, and found that they bred true. He showed conclusively that the anthrax bacillus is the cause, and the only cause, of anthrax, and he worked out its life-history. He demonstrated his results to Cohn, and the latter was so impressed that he published Koch's paper at once in his new journal, *Beiträge zur Biologie der Pflanzen*.

Koch next investigated, while still at Wollstein, the causes of infective diseases following wounds. He showed that the injection of putrid material into animals could produce various septic diseases differing clinically. In 1878 aniline dyes were first used to stain bacteria by Carl Weigert (1845–1904). Koch greatly improved Weigert's methods, and his masterly memoir on these researches was published in 1878.

After he went to Berlin, Koch introduced his new methods for obtaining pure cultures, utilizing gelatine, agar-agar, and other substances as solid media. This step (1881–3) revolutionized bacteriology. In 1882 he announced his greatest discovery, the tubercle bacillus, and almost immediately Paul EHRLICH described his definitive method of staining that organism. In 1883 Koch was a member of the German Cholera Commission to Egypt, and there and in India he discovered the causative organism, the cholera vibrio. While his pupils were discovering the organisms of other diseases, Koch returned to tuberculosis. In 1890 he announced that he had prepared from cultures of the tubercle bacillus a substance, tuberculin, which could be used for diagnosis and treatment. Tuberculin was hailed enthusiastically, and was widely used in treatment – often with disastrous results. It is still occasionally used in the treatment of special conditions. But tuberculin, original or in some modified form, is still widely used to ascertain whether a subject has experienced infection with the tubercle bacillus. In 1890 Koch laid down the three conditions – 'Koch's postulates' – that must be satisfied before an organism is accepted as the cause of a disease.

After 1891 Koch headed various expeditions to study malaria, rinderpest, plague, and other tropical diseases. In 1901 he stated his new view that human tuberculosis cannot be transmitted to cattle, and that bovine tuberculosis cannot be transmitted to man. If this statement was true, it rendered unnecessary the enormous efforts then being made to prevent the consumption of milk infected with tubercle bacilli. Koch's statement was later completely disproved by the British Royal Commission on Tuberculosis, appointed in 1911.

Among Koch's many honours was his election as a Foreign Member of the Royal Society (1897); he was awarded a Nobel prize in 1905. As a pure bacteriologist he remains unequalled, and the techniques devised by him are the basis of all modern methods.

C. J. Martin, *Proceedings of the Royal Society*, **83**, xviii, 1910–11.
M. E. M. Walker, *Pioneers of Public Health*. 1930.
M. Kirchner, *Robert Koch*. 1924.
D. C. Knight, *Robert Koch: Father of Bacteriology*. 1961.
Dictionary of Scientific Biography.
Tyler Wasson (Ed.), *Nobel Prize Winners*. 1987. (Portrait.)

E A U

KOCHER, EMIL THEODOR Born in Berne, Switzerland, 25 August 1841; died there, 27 July 1917. Surgeon, noted especially for his work on the thyroid gland.

Kocher, the son of an engineer, after graduating in Berne continued his studies in Berlin, London, Paris and Vienna. In Vienna he studied under the famous surgeon Theodor Billroth (1829–94). In 1872 he became professor of clinical surgery at Berne University and for forty-five years was head of the University Surgical Centre.

Kocher made innumerable contributions to techniques in a wide range of surgical operations such as those on the lungs, the stomach, and the gall bladder. Especially important was his pioneering of ovariotomy and the application of the antiseptic surgery of Joseph LISTER. His surgical success also depended a great deal on the many improvements he made in appliances and instruments.

His surgical skill made a marked impact on his contemporaries, particularly, of course, his many students and assistants. Further, Kocher published numerous studies, including a celebrated *Textbook of Operative Surgery*, which was translated into many languages. He published other important books on diseases of the male generative system and of the spinal cord.

Kocher's most celebrated work however, was his studies on the thyroid gland, investigations for which he received a Nobel prize for medicine in 1909. His studies arose out of his operations – of which he performed over 5000 during his career – for removing the thyroid. Prior to Kocher, this operation had frequently been fatal, but his application of Lister's antiseptic surgery brought him great success.

In 1883 Kocher announced that the complete removal of the thyroid gland led to a characteristic disease pattern, but that where a portion of the gland had been left and had grown, the disease pattern was modified. The disease symptoms described by Kocher (operative myxoedema) were recognized as being analogous to those of the naturally occurring myxoedema, and Kocher's work did a great deal to co-ordinate and relate studies on malfunctions of the thyroid. For instance, the fact became significant that for centuries there had been descriptions of cretinism, a form of idiocy and dwarfism accompanied by the general symptoms of myxoedema.

Kocher also made other important observations, such as the fact that hypothyroidism also resulted from such conditions as goitre. He gave a tremendous general stimulus to studies on the thyroid, particularly in the search for therapeutic treatment. This led to the introduction of such valuable drugs as thyroid and thyroxin.

E. Bonjour, *Theodor Kocher*. 1950. (Portrait.)
E. R. Wiese and J. E. Gilbert, *Annals of Medical History*, **3**, 521, 1931. (Portrait.)

J K C

KOHLRAUSCH, FRIEDRICH WILHELM Born at Rinteln-on-Weser, Lower Saxony, Germany, 14 October 1840; died Marburg, 17 January 1910. Physicist, remembered for his researches on electrical conductivity of solutions.

Kohlrausch was the son of a well-known physicist, R. H. A. Kohlrausch (1809–58), who became, in 1857, a professor at Erlangen. He himself was educated at Erlangen, where he studied under his father's friend and colleague, Wilhelm WEBER, and at Göttingen, where he obtained his PhD in 1863. In 1866 he became an associate professor of physics at Göttingen, and in 1870 professor of physics at the *Technische Hochschule* at Frankfurt-am-Main. In 1871 he moved to the Polytechnic at Darmstadt; in 1875 to the University of Würzburg; and in 1888 to the University of Strasbourg. In 1895 he succeeded H. von HELMHOLTZ as president of the *Physikalisch-Technische Reichsanstalt* at Charlottenburg, a post which he retained until 1905. In 1895 he was elected a member of the Academy of Sciences in Berlin.

Kohlrausch carried out several research projects connected with the measurement of electrical and magnetic quantities, including the determination of an absolute value for the horizontal component of the Earth's magnetic field and the absolute measurement of an electric current. He also attempted to find the absolute value of the 'Siemens unit' of electrical resistance. He is, however, best known for his researches on electrical conductivity of solutions. In 1871 he introduced a method for measuring the electrical resistance of electrolytes, using an alternating current, which almost entirely removed the disturbing effect of the polarization of the electrodes. Using this method, he carried out a whole series of investigations into the conducting powers of electrolytic solutions at different concentrations. He found that molecular conductivities rose with increased dilution and tended to reach a maximum in a very dilute solution, and showed that under these conditions the molecular conductivity consisted of two parts, one due to the anion, and the other due to the cation. This led to what is known as Kohlrausch's Law of the independent migration of ions.

Kohlrausch was one of the first teachers to prepare a systematic course of laboratory instruction for his students, under the title of *Leitfaden den praktischen Physik*. It was first published in 1870, and was quickly translated into English.

G. C. Foster, *Proceedings of the Royal Society*, **85**, xi. 1911; *Nature*, **82**, 402. 1910.
Dictionary of Scientific Biography.

B B K

KOLBE, ADOLPH WILHELM HERMANN Born near Göttingen, Germany, 27 September 1818; died near Leipzig, 25 November 1884. A founder of modern organic chemistry, but committed to outmoded theoretical ideas.

The eldest of fifteen children of a Lutheran pastor, Kolbe studied chemistry under F. WÖHLER and R. W. BUNSEN, then became (1845) assistant to Lyon PLAYFAIR in London, where he began a life-long friendship with Edward FRANKLAND. After a few years with a publishing house in Brunswick, he became successor to R. W. Bunsen at Marburg in 1851. Some of his best work was done there, but his not having been a *Privatdozent* caused animosity; he was glad to move to Leipzig after the death of Justus von LEIBIG in 1865.

Both as teacher and experimenter, Kolbe was outstanding. His published research covered a vast field, including the first 'total synthesis' of an organic compound (acetic acid) from truly inorganic materials; the formation and hydrolysis of nitriles (with Frankland), enabling all the possible fatty acids to be synthesized; the electrolysis of fatty acid salts, giving the supposed 'radicals' (e.g. methyl), later shown to be ethane; the synthesis of salicylic acid from phenol and carbon dioxide, and its use in disinfection. The last two reactions are both known as 'Kolbe's synthesis'. He also played a part in Frankland's work which led to the concept of valency.

Kolbe's theoretical ideas were based on those of J. J. BERZELIUS, whom he much admired. He evolved an elaborate system in which all organic compounds were formally derived from carbon dioxide by substitution, conjugation, etc.; this system had both predictive successes and failures. It involved a denial of the possibility of knowing the real structures of compounds, and Kolbe engaged in abusive polemics against the structure theorists, notably J. F. A. von BAEYER and J. H. VAN'T HOFF; he was given a fine platform by his editorship (1869) of the important *Journal für praktische Chemie*. His ill-tempered writings were not reflected in his private life, however, where he seems to have been genuinely liked. His son Carl also became a chemist.

G. Bugge, *Das Buch der grossen Chemiker*, vol. 2. 1930. (Portrait.)
E. von Meyer, *Journal für praktische Chemie*, **30**, 417. 1884. (Portrait.)
Journal of the Chemical Society, **47**, 323, 1885.
J. P. Phillips, *Chymia*, **11**, 89, 1966.

W V F

KOLLER, CARL Born at Schüttenhoffen, Bohemia (now in Czech Republic), 3 December 1857; died New York, 22 March 1944. Known for his discovery of the local anaesthetic properties of cocaine.

Koller studied medicine at the University of Vienna, obtaining his MD degree in 1882, whereupon he became house surgeon in the general hospital. There he developed a firm friendship with Sigmund FREUD, who, in the spring of 1884, became intensely interested in cocaine – an alkaloid obtained from the coca plant. At the suggestion of Freud, Koller experimented with the substance and soon observed a numbing effect on his tongue. It occurred to Koller that cocaine might therefore be a suitable local anaesthetic for ophthalmological work. He quickly confirmed his idea on frogs, rabbits, and man, finally announcing his discovery on 15 September 1884. Koller, unlike many others who had noticed the anaesthetic effect on the tongue, had previously searched unsuccessfully for a suitable local anaesthetic for ophthalmology and was prepared to take advantage of such an observation.

The importance of Koller's discovery was rapidly appreciated and put into practice, not only in ophthalmology but also in nose and throat, and dental surgery. Cocaine became the subject of a great deal of research, and it has been said that the loneliest doctor in the world was the ophthalmologist who had not written on cocaine.

Koller left Europe for the United States in 1888. He established himself as an ophthalmologist in New York, where he remained in practice and carried out research in his chosen field for the rest of his life.

H. K. Becker, *Psychoanalytic Quarterly*, **32**, 309, 1963.

Chauncey D. Leake, *Isis*, **23**, 253, 1935.

J K C

KOLLIKER, RUDOLPH ALBERT VON *See* VON
KÖLLIKER.

KOPP, HERMANN FRANZ MORITZ Born at
Hanau, Prussia, Germany, 30 October 1817; died
Heidelberg, 20 February 1892. Chemist and his-
torian of chemistry.

Kopp, the son of a physician, studied chemistry
in Heidelberg, Marburg, and Giessen; in the latter
University he became a *Privatdozent*, then (1843),
extraordinary professor. When Justus von LIEBIG
moved to Munich (1852), Kopp succeeded to his
chair, jointly with H. Will (1812–90), but resigned
after one year. He continued to live and work in
Giessen until 1863, when he was appointed professor in Heidelberg; he remained there until his
death.

Kopp's research work was almost entirely concerned with the connection between physical and
chemical properties of elements and compounds.
He carried out hundreds of accurate measurements
of such constants as boiling-point, thermal expansion, specific gravity, and especially specific heat;
his study of the latter, in conjunction with the law
of P. L. DULONG and A. T. PETIT, led him to some
interesting speculations about the nature of the
elements.

He is, however, more often remembered as an
historian of chemistry. His great *Geschichte der
Chemie* appeared in 1843–7; all his life he was
collecting material for a second edition, but this
was never completed. Some of this material was
published as minor works (for example, his *History
of Alchemy*), but a great mass remained unpublished at his death. After the death of J. J. BERZELIUS,
Kopp (with the nominal help of Liebig) continued
the annual *Jahresbericht* for many years; he was
also one of the editors of Liebig's *Annalen*.

E. Farber (Ed.), *Great Chemists*. 1961. (Portrait.)
Journal of the Chemical Society, **63**, 776, 1893.
(Portrait.)
Julius Ruska, *Journal of Chemical Education*, **14**,
3, 1937.
M. Speter, *Osiris*, **5**, 392, 1938. (Portrait.)
Dictionary of Scientific Biography.

W V F

KORNBERG, ARTHUR Born in Brooklyn, New
York, 3 March, 1918. Biochemist and physician.

Kornberg was educated at the City College, New
York and the University of Rochester. He worked
at the National Institutes of Health, Bethesda,
Maryland, (1942–53), becoming head of the
enzyme and metabolic section in 1947. His
research on enzymes and intermediary metabolism
led to the discovery of chemical reactions in the
cell that result in the formation of the coenzymes
flavine adenine dinucleotide (FAD) and diphos-
phopyridine nucleotide (DPN), important hydrogen carriers in biological oxidations and
reductions. As professor and head of the department of microbiology at Washington University,
St Louis, Missouri (1953–59), he continued to
investigate nucleotide formation in the living cell.
In 1956 with his co-workers he discovered the
pathway for the biosynthesis of deoxyribonucleic
acid (DNA) using an enzyme (DNA polymerase)

which, with certain nucleotides, could produce
replicas of short DNA molecules, known as pri-
mers, *in vitro*. For this work he shared the Nobel
prize for medicine with Severo Ochoa (1905–)
in 1959. He was chairman of the department of
biochemistry at Stanford University, Palo Alto,
California, USA (1959–69).

DNA polymers are the components of chromosomes which carry and transmit the genetic information required for the orderly synthesis of
specific cell constituents. Kornberg's work clarified the way in which DNA chains are built up and
replicated in the cell. His discoveries are of basic
importance to genetics, to the study of viruses, to
cell and tissue differentiation, and to the understanding of the synthesis of specific proteins.

American Men and Women of Science, vol. 4,
1989–90.
Les Prix Nobel en 1959. 1960. (Portrait.)
Tyler Wasson (Ed.), *Nobel Prize Winners*. 1987.
(Portrait.)

N G C

KOROLEV, SERGEI PAVLOVICH Born at Zhito-
mir, Ukraine, 30 December 1906; died Moscow,
14 January 1966. Engineer closely identified with
Russian space research programme.

Not until after his death was Korolev, son of a
Ukrainian schoolmaster, identified by the Russians
as chief designer for their space research programme. He was responsible for the design of the
satellite in which Yuri Gagarin (1934–68) made
the first space flight in April 1961, and of the first
rocket to orbit the Moon and take photographs of
its reverse side.

In 1927, Korolev began work in the aircraft
industry, but continued his studies at the Moscow
School of Aviation; in 1930 he graduated from the
aeromechanics department of the Bauman Higher
Technical School. His interest in rocketry was
stimulated by Konstantin Tsiolkovskii (1857–
1935), and in 1933 he helped to found a rocket
research group which over the years trained many
of the men responsible for the great early Russian
achievements in space. His success is attributed to
an unusual combination of personal and professional qualities. His official obituary stated that
inexhaustible energy and talent as a research
worker, splendid intuition in engineering, and
great creative boldness in solving the most complicated scientific and technical problems were combined with great organizational abilities and high
personal qualities. In 1953, Korolev was elected
Corresponding Member of the USSR Academy of
Sciences; he also received the Lenin Prize. He was
buried in the Kremlin Wall, an honour reserved
for Russians of exceptional distinction.

Official Obituary, *Soviet News* (London), 19
January 1966.

T I W

**KOSSEL, KARL MARTIN LEONHARD
ALBRECHT** Born at Rostock, Germany, 16 September 1853; died Heidelberg, 5 July 1927. Pioneer
of physiological chemistry.

Kossel studied medicine at the Universities of
Strasbourg and Rostock, but never practised. His
interests tending more towards chemistry, he
became assistant to E. F. HOPPE-SEYLER in Strasbourg, and later (1881) *Privatdozent*. Two years

later he was made director of the chemical division of the Berlin Physiological Institute; he was then successively professor in Marburg (1895) and Heidelberg (1901), retiring in 1924. His son Walther became a well-known physicist. For over thirty years Kossel was editor of the *Zeitschrift für physiologisches Chemie* of Hoppe-Seyler.

Kossel's mainly analytical work on the chemistry of natural products was in many ways complementary to the synthetic work of his contemporary Emil FISCHER. He opened up the study of the recently discovered 'nuclein' (nucleic acids), and identified many of the purine and pyrimidine bases which are formed on hydrolysis; he recognized the existence of the sugar moiety, but could not identify it. Considering the ill-defined and intractable nature of his crude 'nuclein', this work was for its period (1880–1900) a masterpiece of technique. During the later part of his career he worked mainly on the composition of a class of simple proteins, the protamines of fish-roe; these are rich in basic amino acids, for which he devised a scheme of quantitative separation. This gave the first real knowledge of the gross constitution of a natural protein.

He was awarded the Nobel prize for medicine in 1910.

E. Farber (Ed.), *Great Chemists*. 1961. (Portrait.)
Berichte der deutschen Chemischen Gesellschaft, **60**, 159A, 1927.
E. Kennaway, *Annals of Science*, **8**, 393, 1952.
Dictionary of Scientific Biography.
Tyler Wasson (Ed.) *Nobel Prize Winners*. 1987. (Portrait.)

W V F

KOVALEVSKY, ALÈXANDRE ONOUFRIEVITCH

Born at Dünaburg, Latvia, 19 November 1840; died St Petersburg, 22 November 1901. Russian embryologist.

Kovalevsky, after studying engineering in St Petersburg for three years, turned to biology and in 1861 he continued studying it in Heidelberg and Tübingen. At this time he was very much influenced by Darwin's *Origin of Species* (1859) and he developed a keen interest in the embryology of animals.

Some of his most important work was on Amphioxus, and he showed that the main features in the development of its organs were analogous to those in the vertebrates. Although many important details remained to be discovered by later investigators, Kovalevsky's work drew attention to the importance of Amphioxus for the study of vertebrate embryology. He also created great interest by his study of ascidiacea, which demonstrated that many develop in a very similar way to Amphioxus. Kovalevsky's work, by revealing that such fundamental processes as germ-layer formation and gastrulation were common to all animal phyla, had a tremendous influence on embryology. Much of his work was also acclaimed as strong evidence for the theory of evolution.

But he had other interests. For the remainder of his life from 1890 (when he was made a Member of the Academy of Sciences of St Petersburg) he studied the application of physiological methods to problems of comparative anatomy. He was particularly interested, for example, in problems of secretion and he carried out many first-class experiments.

C. Davydoff, *Revue d'Histoire des sciences et de leurs applications*, **13**, 325, 1960.
E. Ray-Lankaster, *Nature*, **66**, 1712, 1902.
Dictionary of Scientific Biography.

J K C

KRATZER, NICOLAS

Born in Munich, Bavaria, Germany, 1486; died, probably at Oxford, England, 1550. Instrument-maker and astronomer.

Little is known of Kratzer, who studied at Cologne and Wittenberg, but he played an important role in introducing into England the techniques of instrument-making developed on the Continent at Nuremberg, Augsburg, Louvain, and elsewhere. His first appointment appears to have been as tutor in the household of Sir Thomas More (1478–1535), Lord Chancellor of England and author of *Utopia*; it is perhaps not without significance that More visited Louvain in 1508 and on several subsequent occasions, and he may have met Kratzer there.

Kratzer later became astronomer and horologer to Henry VIII and lectured on astronomy at Oxford, where he was a Fellow of Corpus Christi College (1517); he graduated MA in 1523. He made many fine astronomical instruments, a number of which are represented in Holbein's well-known painting 'The Ambassadors'. A sundial made by him for Cardinal Wolsey is preserved at Oxford.

Derek J. Price, 'Some Early English Instrument Makers', *Endeavour*, **14**, 90, 1955. (Portrait.)
Dictionary of National Biography, XXXI.

T I W

KREMER, GERHARD See MERCATOR.

KREBS, EDWIN G

Born in Lansing, Iowa, USA, 6 June 1918. Biochemist.

Krebs graduated at the University of Illinois in 1940 and then took a medical degree at Washington University, Seattle. There he held a succession of academic appointments, latterly (1983–88) as professor in the department of pharmacology and biochemistry. From the 1950s, in close collaboration with Edmond G. Fischer (1920–) he investigated the role of reversible protein phosphorylation as a regulator of cell metabolism.

In the 1940s G. T. CORI and C. F. Cori (1896–1984) isolated phosphorylase, a key enzyme in mobilizing glycogen to produce glucose fuel. This discovery, for which they were jointly awarded a Nobel prize in 1947, opened up new fields of research in cell physiology, in particular the highly complex way in which proteins interact within cells. It became clear that phosphate ions play a key role in regulating protein interactions. The processes of phosphorylation and dephosphorylation are regulated by specific enzymes. This line of progress was actively pursued by Krebs and Fischer, particularly with regard to the mechanism of muscle contraction. Together, they demonstrated that phosphorylase can be activated by transfer of phosphate to the protein from the energy-rich compound ATP. The reaction is catalysed by a protein enzyme kinase. The reverse process is controlled by a phosphatase enzyme. Thus the glycogen-catabolizing phosphorylase is regulated by two enzymes – a kinase and a phosphatase – acting in different directions. This reversible process has very far-reaching implications in relation, for example, to the immune response, the onset of cancer, and the release of hormones.

For this research, Krebs and Fischer were jointly awarded a Nobel prize in 1992.

Les Prix Nobel en 1992. 1993. (Portrait.)

T I W]

KREBS, SIR HANS ADOLF Born at Hildesheim, Germany, 25 August 1900: died Oxford, England, 22 November 1981. Biochemist, notable for his elucidation of metabolic pathways, especially those concerned with energy utilisation.

Krebs was the son of a surgeon and, following the German practice of the day, studied at several universities – Göttingen, Freiburg, Munich, Berlin, and Hamburg. He gained his MD degree at Hamburg in 1925 and for the next five years did biochemical research under Otto Warburg (1883–1970) in the Kaiser Wilhelm Institute for Biology, Berlin-Dahlem. Under Warburg he familiarised himself with the powerful technique of investigating metabolic reactions with the aid of tissue slices and manometers. He moved to Freiburg in 1930 to take up a clinical appointment in biochemistry as *Privatdozent*. Despite his hospital responsibilities he managed to continue research, with the support of the Rockefeller Foundation. With the rise to power of the Nazis, Krebs' position became intolerable, but Sir Frederick Gowland HOPKINS invited him to continue his work at Cambridge. He arrived virtually penniless, but he was able to bring much of his apparatus with him and he continued to enjoy the support of the Rockefeller Foundation. Two years later he took up an appointment as lecturer in pharmacology (subsequently in biochemistry) in the University of Sheffield. In 1945 the University appointed him to a newly created chair of biochemistry and he also became director of a cell metabolism research unit established by the Medical Research Council.

From Sheffield, Krebs moved to Oxford in 1954, to take up the Whitley Chair of Biochemistry, which he held until his retirement in 1967. Retirement meant little, however, for he returned enthusiastically to full-time research in the Nuffield Department of Clinical Medicine in Oxford; he was also appointed visiting professor of biochemistry at the Royal Free Hospital, London.

Krebs was a man of wide interests but throughout his long research career it was the investigation of metabolic pathways that particularly fascinated him. In this field his name is particularly associated with three major developments. The first, while he was still in Germany, was the ornithine cycle of urea synthesis in the liver. The second was the tricarboxylic acid cycle (now generally known as the Krebs Cycle) for the oxidation of pyruvic acid to carbon dioxide and water. This cycle is now recognized – though it had not been immediately – as a major source of energy in animals. Much of this work was done at Sheffield and the crucial paper, written jointly with W. A. Johnson, appeared in *Enzymologia* in 1937. Thirdly, in association with Hans KORNBERG – with whom he wrote *Energy Transformations in Living Matter* (1957) – he uncovered after the war the glyoxalate cycle, important in fat metabolism.

Krebs's original work gained him many honours.

He was elected Fellow of the Royal Society in 1943 (Royal Medallist 1954) and in 1953 shared the Nobel prize for medicine with Fritz Lipmann (1899–1986), another pioneer of metabolic processes. He was knighted in 1958. He married Margaret Cicely Fieldhouse in 1938, and they had two sons and a daughter.

The Times 23 November 1981.
Hans Krebs, *Reminiscences and Reflections.* 1981.
Biographical Memoirs of Fellows of the Royal Society. 1984. (Portrait.)
Dictionary of Scientific Biography, Supp. II.
Tyler Wasson (Ed.), *Nobel Prize Winners.* 1987. (Portrait.)
Dictionary of National Biography.

T I W

KROGH, SCHACK AUGUST STEENBERG Born at Grenaa, Jutland, Denmark, 15 November 1874; died Copenhagen, 13 September 1949. Distinguished worker on the control of the capillaries.

August Krogh, son of a shipbuilder and brewer, loved the sea. In 1889 he joined the Danish navy, but after his first cruise he went back to school, the Gymnasium at Aarhus. In 1893 he entered the University of Copenhagen to study physics but changed to zoology and physiology. In 1899 he graduated in zoology, and in 1903 obtained his doctorate. By this time he was specializing in marine biology, and he continued to write on this subject all his life. In 1902 he went on a scientific expedition to northern Greenland to study the metabolism of Arctic animals. In 1908, with his wife, the scientist Marie Krogh, he made a second expedition to Greenland to carry out metabolic studies in relation to the nutrition of the Eskimos. In that year also a special lectureship in zoophysiology was created for him in the University of Copenhagen. Two years later the Laboratory of Zoophysiology was founded, and in 1916 his lectureship became a professorship, from which he retired in 1945.

It is in the realm of human physiology – the physiology of respiration and the distribution of blood to the tissues – that Krogh's work is very important. In 1904 Christian Bohr (1855–1911) had shown that the oxygen dissociation curve of haemoglobin differs in its shape from that of blood. In the same year, with K. A. Hasselbalch and Krogh, he made the important discovery that the dissociation curve of haemoglobin is greatly influenced by the partial pressure of carbon dioxide present. As the blood takes up carbon dioxide in the capillaries, there is an increased liberation of oxygen from oxyhaemoglobin. About 1908 Krogh developed his micro-aerotonometer, so that the gaseous exchange between a single bubble of air and blood flowing round it could be easily determined. At that time there was much scientific controversy – led by J. S. HALDANE – as to whether under certain conditions oxygen was actually secreted in the lung. Using his aerotonometer Krogh, with his wife, Marie Jørgensen, showed that the arterial oxygen pressures were always below the oxygen pressures in the alveolar air, and he concluded that gaseous exchange in the lungs is always due to diffusion. Part of the argument for secretion had been based on the sequence of events in the swim-bladders of fishes. In 1911 Krogh, working on lower marine forms which also maintained their relative positions despite changes in water pressure, showed that there is no secretion of oxygen into their air-sacs. In man, Krogh calculated the quantity of oxygen which should theoretically diffuse across the walls of the pulmonary alveoli, and he showed that this amount was equal to the exchange of gas actually found, and that this correspondence applied even when there was an extreme demand for oxygen. These results were effectively the death-blow to the secretion theory. In 1912 Krogh, in collaboration with Johannes Lindhard (1870–1947), worked out the nitrous oxide method of measuring the circulation rate in man.

Krogh next turned his attention to the capillaries. By ingenious calculations he showed that the oxygen tension in muscle is only slightly below that in the capillaries, even when the muscle is intensely active. He then confirmed his theories by experiments on the frog's tongue and in other ways. He found that when a muscle is at rest the number of capillaries seen on examination is relatively small. But as soon as the muscle is stimulated many hitherto unseen capillaries open up, become filled with blood, and then disappear on the cessation of activity. He showed that such effects are not due to increased pressure in the vessel supplying the capillary field; on the contrary, the capillaries are in a constant state of tonus, which keeps them constricted. But as soon as there is a demand for more blood to the part, such as on the stimulation of a muscle, the tonus is relaxed, the capillary opens up and is filled with blood. For these researches, published in 1918–19, Krogh received the Nobel prize for medicine in 1920. He was elected a Foreign Member of the Royal Society in 1937, and in 1945 he delivered its Croonian lecture. In 1945 also he was awarded the Baly Medal of the Royal College of Physicians of London. He held honorary doctorates from eight foreign universities.

Obituary Notices of Fellows of the Royal Society. 1950–51. (Portrait.)
E. Lundsgaard, *Experientia*, **6**, 39, 1950.
Dictionary of Scientific Biography.
Tyler Wasson (Ed.), *Nobel Prize Winners.* 1987. (Portrait.)

E A U

KRUPP, ALFRED Born at Essen, Germany, 26 April 1812; died Bredeney, near Essen, 14 July 1887. Technologist.

Alfred Krupp left school at 14 on the early death of his father, Friedrich (1787–1826), who had left the tiny cast-steel firm at Essen, founded by him in 1811, virtually insolvent. But the expansion of the *Zollverein* in 1834 gave Krupp a chance to increase output, and by 1843 he employed about a hundred men, making steel springs and machine parts. In 1848 he was able to buy out his co-heirs, and in the next year he secured his first major railway contract. He showed a flawless 2-ton ingot of cast steel in London at the Great Exhibition of 1851; developed a highly profitable weldless steel railway tyre (which gave the firm its emblem of three rings); and took up the manufacture of steel equipment for other railway uses, and for steamships.

Although Krupp produced successively a musket-barrel (1843), a 3-pounder cannon (1847),

a 6-pounder (1851), and a 12-pounder (1855), all made of steel, he did not sell his first guns – to the Khedive of Egypt – until 1857, and two more years elapsed before he received his first big order, 312 6-pounders for the Prussian Government. But William I, Bismarck, and their military entourage became his firm supporters, and the growth of competitive armaments enabled Krupp to become the biggest steel-producer on the continent. Prussia's victory over France in the great artillery battle of Sedan in September 1870 finally proved the superiority of his steel breech-loaders.

Krupp introduced the Bessemer process (see H. BESSEMER) to Germany in 1862, and during the trade-boom of the early 1870s he expanded his business to secure control of German coal and Spanish iron-ore supplies. An important later development was the manufacture of heavy artillery, including a 17-inch 'built-up' gun, for which he instituted a famous testing-ground near Osnabrück. Alfred Krupp earned for his firm a name for social benefits, which kept his 21 000 workers loyal and satisfied, as well as for stern discipline and autocratic control. His will prescribed that ownership should never be divided.

P. Batty, *The House of Krupp.* 1966.
(Bibliography.)
G. von Klass, *Krupps: The Story of an Industrial Empire* (English trans.). 1954. (Portraits.)

T K D

KÜHNE, WILHELM (WILLY) FRIEDRICH Born in Hamburg, Germany, 28 March 1837; died Heidelberg, 10 June 1900. Physiologist; introduced the term enzyme.

Kühne studied at Göttingen, Jena, Berlin, Paris, and Vienna; his teachers included such outstanding men as Claude BERNARD and R. VIRCHOW. He graduated in medicine at Berlin in 1862. For a short time he worked as assistant to Virchow and was then (1868) appointed professor of physiology in Amsterdam. In 1871 he was appointed to a corresponding chair at Heidelberg, which he occupied until his retirement in 1899; among his research students there was R. H. CHITTENDEN, with whom he investigated the nature of proteins and the way in which they are digested. They elucidated (1883) the important role of trypsin in the pancreatic secretion.

In the third quarter of the nineteenth century there was much controversy about 'formed' and 'unformed' ferments. The formed ferments appeared to be inseparable from the living cell; the unformed, such as invertase, diastase, and pepsin, could be extracted from cells. To obviate this awkward distinction, Kühne in 1878 proposed the word enzyme (*Gr.* in yeast) – now universally used – to cover all types of ferment activating chemical changes in living organisms. This proposal found its justification in 1898 when E. BUCHNER prepared a cell-free ferment ('zymase') from yeast.

Kühne's main interest remained in the protein field. In 1864, in an investigation of egg albumen, he discovered that the coagulation temperature varied considerably according to the source of the material, and he used this to separate different forms of albumen. In a study of post-mortem changes in muscle he identified myosin as the cause of rigor mortis. In 1876 Franz Boll (1849–79) discovered a photosensitive pigment (now known to be a protein conjugated with a carotenoid pigment) in the retina of the frog. Kühne carried out a careful investigation and named the pigment visual purple (*Sehpurpur*).

R. H. Major, *A History of Medicine*, vol. 2. 1954.

F. Hofmeister, *Berichte der deutschen chemischen Gesellschaft*, **33**, 3875, 1900.
Dictionary of Scientific Biography.

T I W

L

LACAILLE, NICOLAS LOUIS DE Born at Rumigny, France, 15 May 1713; died Paris, 21 March 1762. Revived the study of positional astronomy in France.

Left destitute when his father died, Lacaille was educated in theology at the Collège de Lisieux, in Paris. After taking deacon's orders, he turned to astronomy, and through the friendship of G. D. CAS-SINI found a place at the observatory. Shortly afterwards he helped in a coastal survey, and in 1739 joined the party measuring the French meridian. This work, which involved correcting Cassini's results, earned him membership of the Academy and a chair at the Mazarin College (now the Institute of France). Here he compiled an enormous number of positional observations of the Sun and stars. He continued this work on a voyage to the Cape (1750–4), where he also determined the lunar parallax with the simultaneous help of J. J. le F. de Lalande (1732–1807) in Berlin, and compiled a catalogue of southern stars (over 10 000), much more extensive than that of Edmond HALLEY but less accurate. On this voyage, in addition, he carried out the first measurement of a South African meridian arc. His figure of 10″.2 for the solar parallax, obtained by trigonometrical methods, was somewhat worse than Cassini's value of 9″.5.

J. Delambre, *Histoire de l'Astronomie au XVIIIème siècle.* 1827.

David S. Evans, *Discovery*, Oct. 1951.

Angus Armitage, *Annals of Science*, **12**, 165, 1956; *Nature*, **193**, 1018, 1962.

Dictionary of Scientific Biography.

J D N

LA CONDAMINE, CHARLES-MARIE DE Born in Paris, 27 January 1701; died there, 4 February 1774. Explorer and geophysicist.

La Condamine was impelled throughout his life, and to the very moment of his dramatic death, by a vivid curiosity. Although he saw some military action while still only 18 years old, he believed that a career in the army would be slow and dull; he turned to science and was admitted to the *Académie des Sciences* as a chemist. After some Mediterranean voyages studying the African coast, he joined an *Académie* expedition to Peru for investigating the figure of the Earth, accompanying L. Godin (1704–60) and P. Bouguer (1698–1758). He observed the variation of the length of a seconds pendulum over a wide area. By observing a star against the vertical thread of a plumb-line near and away from a mountain mass (the Cordilleras) he showed that the mountains exerted an attraction on the plumb bob (an observation later verified by N. MASKELYNE).

La Condamine ascended the Amazon some hundreds of miles. One memento of his voyage was the discovery (1736) of caoutchouc, of which he sent the first specimen to the *Académie*, describing it in 1751. He conducted a controversy with Bouguer over the seconds pendulum observations and gained sympathy by his gay rebuttal of Bouguer's ill-tempered attacks. He attempted to establish, by a study of Roman remains, the dimensions of Roman linear measure. He experimented with smallpox vaccination.

He became extensively paralysed, and finding a surgeon who claimed to be able to treat him, insisted on preparing to observe all the details of the operation, with a view to publication. He did not survive. He was a Fellow of the Royal Society (1748) and of the Academies of Berlin, St Petersburg, and Bologna.

He wrote verses, not great, but confident and gay, like his whole life.

Nouvelle Biographie Générale, vol. 33. 1859.
Dictionary of Scientific Biography, Supp. I.

F G

LAËNNEC, RENÉ THÉOPHILE HYACYNTHE Born at Quimper, Brittany, France, 17 February 1781; died Kerlouanec, Brittany, 13 August 1826. Physician: invented the stethoscope.

Laënnec, son of a lawyer, was a pupil of J. N. Corvisart (1755–1821) at the *Charité* hospital in Paris, receiving his doctor's degree in 1804. He became particularly interested in pathology. In 1814 he was appointed physician at the Necker Hospital. Ill health due to pulmonary tuberculosis – very probably contracted from his patients – obliged him to retire for a time to Kerlouanec, but he was able to return to Paris for a time as professor at both the *Charité* and the *Collège de France* and physician to the Duchess of Berry. His health failed again, however, and he died in 1826.

In 1816, walking in the courtyard of the Louvre, Laënnec noticed two children with their ears close to the ends of a long stick; they were amusing themselves by tapping lightly on the stick and listening to the transmitted sound. He immediately realized the diagnostic possibilities, and quickly developed an instrument – essentially a hollow wooden tube some twelve inches long – for listening to sounds within the human body. As it was particularly useful for sounding the heart and lungs he called it a stethoscope (Greek *stethos*, the chest). He quickly developed its use as an adjunct to the study of diseases of the chest and described his work in his *De l'auscultation médiate* (1819). This is much more than a book on the use of the stethoscope: it is also an important treatise on diseases of the heart, lungs and liver. It appeared in a much-extended edition in 1826 under the title *Traité de l'auscultation médiate et des maladies des poumons et du coeur*.

R. Kervran, *Laënnec: his Life and Times*. 1960.
L. F. Flick, *Medical Life*, **33**, 543, 1926.
Dictionary of Scientific Biography.

T I W

LAGRANGE, JOSEPH LOUIS Born in Turin, Italy, 25 January 1736; died Paris, 10 April 1813. Mathematician famous for his work on theoretical mechanics.

Lagrange came from a family, mainly of French descent, which had settled in Turin; his father was at one time quite wealthy, but frittered his money away. He became interested in mathematics at the age of 17 after seeing the memoir (1693) by E. HALLEY on the use of algebra in optics, though he was not much impressed by the Greek geometers, whom he also read. At 19 he solved the isoperimetric problem, and sent his work to L. EULER, who was so impressed by the greater generality of the proof over his own that he withheld publication until Lagrange could publish his work. In 1755 he was made professor of mathematics at the Artillery School at Turin, and in 1758 he established with the help of some of his abler pupils a society, in whose transactions (*Miscellanae – Turinensia*) appeared most of his earlier publications. In 1759 Euler got him elected as a Foreign Member of the Berlin Academy, and by 1761 he was recognized as the foremost mathematician of his time. Unfortunately his health broke down through overwork, and thereafter he suffered intermittently from attacks of acute depression. In 1766 he was invited to Berlin by Frederick the Great at the instigation of Euler and H. LE R. D'ALEMBERT. Shortly after his arrival in Berlin, where he was professor at the Academy, he married. At the death of Frederick in 1787 he was invited to Paris by Louis XVI. During the Revolution he feared for his life; needlessly, as he was well treated by the new régime, at whose instigation he perfected the metric system. In 1795 he became a member of the French Academy; in 1797 he was appointed professor of mathematics at the new *École Normale*, where he promoted the thorough training of teachers – hitherto rather neglected; he also organized the mathematics department at the new *École Polytechnique*. In two books (1797, 1801) he tried to establish the calculus using neither infinitesimals nor Newton's limits; though he failed, he inspired the work of A. L. CAUCHY. He became increasingly prone to melancholy, and turned away from mathematics to study such subjects as metaphysics; history of languages; chemistry (he knew LAVOISIER well), and botany. His first wife, Vittoria Conti, died in 1783, and he remarried. He was a very modest man: the only portraits we have of him were sketched without his knowledge.

Lagrange'e masterpiece, *Mécanique Analytique*, found an unwilling publisher in 1788, though he said in a letter to LAPLACE that he had almost finished it in 1782. The first part is on statics: in section II he states the principle of virtual velocities in terms of infinitesimals, which he then converts to the more convenient form involving partial derivatives in section III; the remainder is on applications, to both rigid and fluid mechanics. The second part is an approximately parallel development of dynamics (rigid and fluid): in section IV he derives the equivalent of 'Lagrange's Equations'. Lagrange took pride in the fact that the book contained no diagrams, no constructions, no geometrical nor mechanical reasoning – just 'algebraic operations'. W. R. HAMILTON described the work as 'a scientific poem'.

He contributed many results on number theory, mostly in the 1770s: he proved Wilson's theorem relating to prime numbers and many results stated by P. FERMAT. He also published a great number of papers on astronomy, and made advances in the theory of equations, showing how his predecessors' many results could be replaced by a uniform procedure – his work facilitated the formulation of group theory. He systematized the study of partial differential equations.

Oeuvres Complètes. (Contains biography by J. B. J. Delambre.) 1867–92.
E. T. Bell, *Men of Mathematics*. 1937.
D. J. Struik, *Concise History of Mathematics*. 1954. (Portrait.)
Nature, **137**, 141, 1936.
Dictionary of Scientific Biography.

R P L

LAMARCK, JEAN BAPTISTE PIERRE ANTOINE DE MONET Born at Bazantin, France, 1 August 1744; died Paris, 18 December 1829. Evolutionist.

Lamarck, son of an impecunious lord of the manor and one of several brothers, was intended for the Church and educated at the Jesuits' college at Amiens. At the age of 16, on his father's death, he left and joined the army in the Low Countries; he was injured after peace was restored and giving up a military career went to Paris to study medicine. His interest in science turned to botany, and in 1778 he published his *Flore française*, arranged as a dichotomous key for the determination of species, which was much valued and went through several editions. In 1781 he was appointed botanist to the king, and in the following years travelled widely in Europe on botanical excursions; on his return he wrote voluminous botanical contributions for the *Encyclopédie Methodique* published in 1785. In 1788 he was posted to the *Jardin du Roi*, but when it was reorganized in 1793 he was given a chair of zoology, and although he had a wide contemporary reputation as a botanist, it is the work done after this change of subject by which his name is mainly known today.

His attention was turned particularly to the invertebrates – a term of his invention – and in 1815 he began publication of his *Histoire naturelle des animaux sans vertèbres*, in the first volume of which he amplified the views on the evolution of animals that he had already stated in 1809 in his *Philosophie Zoologique*. Others, such as G. L. L. BUFFON and Erasmus DARWIN, had already expressed opinions favouring the theory of the evolution of animals, but Lamarck crystallized his ideas in four 'laws' under which evolution takes place. The essential part of his theory is contained in his second law, that 'the production of a new organ in an animal body results from a new need which continues to make itself felt'. This has been misinterpreted; and discussion has concentrated on his fourth law, which postulates the inheritance by an individual's progeny of characters acquired during its lifetime.

For fifty years Lamarck's views received little attention, particularly in England, and when they were examined after the publication of the *Origin of Species* by Charles DARWIN they were misunderstood and ridiculed. Lamarck's reputation suffered through the misunderstanding of what he had written, and through few of his critics taking the trouble to consult his writings themselves, most of them swallowing unverified the second-hand opinions of others. Lamarck said that new needs are satisfied by the development of new structures; the word *besoin* was mistranslated as meaning 'want' in the sense of 'desire', and critics who had not read the original ridiculed the suggestion that the giraffe got its long neck because it wished for it instead of, as Lamarck said, because it needed it. Furthermore, the inheritance of characters acquired during the lifetime of an individual has never been proved, and thus Lamarck's fourth law has been cast aside with the belief that it alone was the essence of Lamarckism. It is strange that Lamarck's name should be universally known through ideas rejected with scorn by those imperfectly acquainted with them.

A. S. Packard, *Lamarck, the Founder of Evolution.* 1901.

H. G. Cannon, *Proceedings of the Linnean Society of London*, **168**, 71, 1957.

E. Nordenskiöld, *History of Biology.* 1928. (Portrait.)

Dictionary of Scientific Biography.

L H M

LANCHESTER, FREDERICK WILLIAM Born at Lewisham, London, 23 October 1868; died Birmingham, 8 March 1946. Pioneer of the British motor-car industry.

Lanchester, who was the son of an architect, was educated at Hartley College, Southampton, and the National School of Science, South Kensington; he joined T. B. Barker's gas-engine works at Saltley, Birmingham, in 1889. He soon reorganized it, and improved the product by developing a pendulum governor and a starter. After five years he set up his own small motor-car firm, building a five-seater one-cylinder 5 hp model with a chain drive, that first took the road one night in February 1896, at a time when such trials were illegal. Its ten-mile run so encouraged him that a second model, with a twin-cylinder 8 hp engine at the rear, was built and tested in 1898; this won the Gold Medal of the Royal Automobile Club. A third model followed quickly, and led to the formation of the Lanchester Engine Company in 1899. From his own works at Sparkbrook emerged some three to four hundred 10 hp cars, cantilever sprung. But four years later the firm was bankrupt, and though a new company bearing Lanchester's name was formed in 1905 he had little to do with it.

His interest in flight bore fruit in *Aerial Flight* (1907 and 1908) – an expansion of work he had done over the previous twelve years in the vortex theory of sustentation of flight. Its importance was recognized by his appointment first to the Advisory Committee on Aeronautics in 1909, under Lord RAYLEIGH, and then as consultant to the Daimler Motor Company in 1910. In both capacities he helped foster the rise of what is now called operational research. In 1925, Lanchester Laboratories Ltd was founded, as a subsidiary of Daimlers, to undertake development and research work, and he purchased the Daimler interest in this after terminating his consultancy with them in 1929. When his health broke down in January 1934 the firm closed down. He consoled himself with poetry (published under the pseudonym of Paul Netherton-Herries), education and music. He was awarded an honorary doctorate by the University of Birmingham in 1919; the Alfred Ewing Gold Medal of the Institution of Civil Engineers in 1941; and the James Watt International Medal of the Institution of Mechanical Engineers in 1945. His closing years were clouded by illness, blindness, and financial difficulties. He had no children.

Obituary Notices of Fellows of the Royal Society. 1948. (Portrait.)

P. W. Kingsford, *F. W. Lanchester: A Life of an Engineer.* 1960. (Portrait.)

G. H. Lanchester, *Transactions of the Newcomen Society*, **30, 221**, 1955–7.

Dictionary of National Biography.

W H G A

LANCISI, GIOVANNI MARIA Born in Rome, 26 October 1654; died there, 21 January 1720. A pioneer in the morbid anatomy of cardiac lesions, and a prophet in relation to the cause of malaria.

Lancisi began the study of theology, changed to the physical sciences, and finally studied medicine at the *Sapienza* in Rome. At the age of 18 years he graduated as a Doctor of Medicine (1672). Four years later he was assistant physician to the San Spirito Hospital. He then spent five years (1678–83) studying the medical classics in the *Collegio San Salvatore*. In 1684 he was appointed to the chair of anatomy at the *Sapienza*, and in 1696 he became professor of the practice of medicine. He was body-physician to three successive popes.

In his two works *De subitaneis mortibus* ('On sudden death', 1707) and *De motu cordis et aneurysmatibus* ('On the motion of the heart and on aneurysms', 1728, posthumous), Lancisi laid the foundations of cardiac pathology. Dilatation of the heart he called 'aneurysm of the heart', and he knew the relation of one type of aneurysm to syphilis. He also distinguished enlargement of the heart due to dilatation from that due to hypertrophy of the heart wall. He understood the relationship between hypertrophy and lesions of the cardiac valves, and he described some excellent cases of thickening of the valve cusps. He was also the first to distinguish between true and false aneurysms.

Lancisi also wrote works on fevers epidemic in the Campagna. In his book *De noxiis paludum effluviis* ('On the noxious effluvia of marshes', 1717) he seems from the title to be a supporter of the miasmatic theory. Despite this, however, the text shows that he held that malaria is transmitted, and he suggested that the mosquito might play a part in the transmission. Lancisi had also seen in the tissues of malaria patients a grey-black pigment. This was the pigment produced by the malaria parasite, which was itself not discovered until 1880 (by A. LAVERAN).

Lancisi acquired the neglected and unpublished plates of the great anatomical work by Bartolomeo EUSTACHI, and he published them in 1714.

E. R. Long, *History of Pathology.* 1928.

H. H. Scott, *History of Tropical Medicine.* 1939.
R. H. Major, *History of Medicine*, vol. 2. 1954.
    (Portrait.)
Dictionary of Scientific Biography.

                                                    E A U

LANDOLT, HANS HEINRICH Born in Zürich,
Switzerland, 5 December 1831; died Berlin, 15
March 1910. Pioneer in physical chemistry.

Landolt studied at Zürich, and held appointments there and at Breslau, Berlin and Heidelberg
before going to Bonn in 1857, where he eventually
became professor. After posts at Aix-la-Chapelle
(1869) and Berlin (1880), he became in 1891 director of the second chemical institute of Berlin University.

In the early 1850s Landolt worked on trimethyl
antimony and triethyl arsenic. At Bonn he began
a study of the relation between optical refraction
and chemical constitution, and at Aix-la-Chapelle
extensive work on polarimetry led to the enunciation of his law and publication of a comprehensive treatise.

Landolt also investigated vapour pressures; the
iodic acid/bisulphite reaction; melting-point determinations; and the law of conservation of mass.
The care and precision of his work is reflected in
his *magnum opus*, jointly produced with R. Börn-
stein in 1883, the Landolt-Börnstein *Zahlenwerte
und Funktionen*, now published as *Physikalisch
chemische Tabellen*.

Journal of the Chemical Society, **99**, 1653, 1911.
    (Portrait.)
Dictionary of Scientific Biography.

                                                    C A R

LAND, EDWIN HERBERT Born at Bridgeport,
Connecticut, USA, 7 May 1909; died Cambridge,
Massachusetts, 1 March 1991. Inventor of Polaroid
system of instant photography.

Edwin Land's father ran a scrap iron business.
While still a student at Harvard University, Land
developed a process for the manufacture of cheap
polarising materials, patented in 1932. In order to
manufacture and market his inventions he set up
the Polaroid Corporation in 1937, remaining chairman until 1982. Early applications of the new process included polarising materials for sunglasses
to reduce reflected glare. During the Second World
War Land worked on gun sights and aerial sur-
veillance.

He also began to work on an instant picture
system. The chemical principle of diffusion transfer by which an image formed on one surface could
be transferred to another in contact with it had
been discovered by research workers at Agfa and
Gevaert, 1939–40, but Land was able to develop
materials which gave images of far better quality.
The world's first instant camera, the model 95
Polaroid-Land camera, which produced sepia-
toned prints in one minute, went on sale in 1948.
Land continued to work on the quality of the pictures, and by 1950 black and white pictures could
be produced. The new camera was so successful
that by 1956 one million had been sold. Further
developments included the introduction of the first
instant colour films in 1962, marketed as Polacolor,
and the first pocket sized instant camera able to
deliver dry colour prints, the SX-70, in 1971.

Not all Land's ideas were as successful. Plans

for three-dimensional movies failed in the 1950s;
attempts to eliminate glare from car headlights in
bad weather foundered; he was overtaken by the
more advanced system of Xerox in the field of
photocopying; and his instant movie system,
Polarvision, invented in 1977, proved less appeal-
ing than home video systems.

Nevertheless, his personal fortune was estimated
at between 500 and 1000 million dollars. He was
Founding Director of the Rowland Institute for Science, Cambridge, Massachusetts, 1981–91, and
gave it substantial financial support. He was a
visiting professor at Massachusetts Institute of
Technology, 1956–91.

The Independent, 6 March 1991.

                                                    A P B]

LANDAU, LEV DAVIDOVICH Born in Baku, Azer-
baijan, 22 January 1908; died Moscow, 1 April
1968. Theoretical physicist; developed a theory of
condensed matter and explained the properties of
superfluid helium.

Landau received his early training at the Universities of Baku, Leningrad and Moscow (1922–27).
From 1929 to 1931 he studied with N. H. D. BOHR
in Denmark, the man he regarded as his only
teacher in theoretical physics. Returning to the
USSR, Landau headed leading theoretical physics
groups in Kharkov (1932–37) and at the Institute
of Physical Problems in Moscow (1937–68). His
theoretical work encompassed quantum mechanics, ferromagnetics, plasma physics, hydrodynamics and particle physics. However, his most
important contribution, for which he was awarded
the Nobel prize in physics in 1962, was to develop
the theoretical understanding of the properties of
helium: liquifying at 4.2 K, below 2.2 K ^{4}He
becomes superfluid, behaving as though it has no
viscosity at all and exhibiting an exceptionally
high thermal conducivity. Working with the
experimentalist P. L. KAPITZA, in 1940–45 Landau
developed a quantum mechanical explanation for
this behaviour, predicting that sound would travel
in superfluid ^{4}He as both pressure and heat waves,
and that superfluid ^{3}He would exhibit a unique
oscillatory behaviour. By 1966 all of these properties had been proved experimentally. Landau's
career was essentially terminated as a result of a
car crash in 1962. His multi-volume *Course in
Theoretical Physics*, written with E. M. Lifshitz
(1917–69) has become a standard work.

Dictionary of Scientific Biography.
*Biographical Memoirs of Fellows of the Royal
    Society*, 1969. (Portrait.)
Tyler Wasson (Ed.), *Nobel Prize Winners.* 1987.
    (Portrait.)
I. M. Khalatnikov (Ed.), *Landau: The Physicist and
    the Man.* 1989.
Les Prix Nobel en 1962. 1963. (Portrait.)

                                                    R J H

LANDSTEINER, KARL Born in Vienna, 14 June
1868; died New York, 26 June 1943. Famed for his
pioneer work on blood grouping.

Landsteiner graduated in medicine from the University of Vienna in 1891 and spent the next five
years studying chemistry in various European universities – an excellent training for his later studies
in physiology and immunology. He left Europe in

1923 to work at the Rockefeller Institute for Medical Research.

Landsteiner's scientific career is difficult to summarize in a short notice, for his curiosity led him into many fields – for example, morbid anatomy, syphilis, infantile paralysis, goitre, scarlet fever and typhus, to name but a few. His main interest, however, was immunology, of which he studied many facets, such as the chemistry of immunizing agents, the union of antigen and antibody, and allergies.

Landsteiner was awarded a Nobel prize in 1930 for his work on blood groups. In 1898 J. J. B. V. BORDET had noticed that foreign red blood corpuscles, injected into animals, disintegrated and liberated haemoglobin. Landsteiner, studying this phenomenon further, discovered that the blood serum of one person sometimes agglutinated the red blood cells of another (1900). It soon became clear that human beings could be separated into groups according to the different antigens and antibodies in their red cells and serum. In 1909 he devised a classification scheme which has remained in use ever since (the four main blood groups are A, B, AB and O).

Landsteiner, with co-workers, later found many subgroups within these major groups, and, in 1940, the discovery of the rhesus factor in the red cells of certain individuals was announced. Knowledge of this led to ways of preventing miscarriages, and deaths of babies of rhesus negative mothers and rhesus positive fathers.

A wider practical application of his work was in connection with blood transfusion. Early in his work Landsteiner discussed its significance for blood transfusion which at the time was only rarely carried out because of the problems due to blood incompatibilities. It was not until 1907 that the first matching of blood was performed, and only in the First World War that this necessary precaution became widespread.

One other practical application of Landsteiner's work deserves mention – the significance of blood grouping in questions of paternity. Again Landsteiner's early recognition of this, like his views on blood transfusion, lay dormant for a number of years, but nevertheless became established in his own full, extremely hard-working lifetime.

Obituary Notices of Fellows of the Royal Society, 1945–8. (Portrait).

Biographical Memoirs of the National Academy of Sciences. 1969.

G. R. Simms, *The Scientific Work of Karl Landsteiner.* 1975.

Dictionary of Scientific Biography.

Tyler Wasson (Ed.), *Nobel Prize Winners.* 1987. (Portrait.)

P. Speiser and F. Smekal, *F. Karl Landsteiner.* 1975.

J K C

LANGEVIN, PAUL Born in Paris, 23 January 1872; died there, 19 December 1946. Physicist.

Langevin was a student at the *École de Physique et de Chimie.* As a young man he studied for a short time under J. J. THOMSON at Cambridge, when the Cavendish Laboratory first admitted foreign students, and then returned to Paris to work with Pierre CURIE, taking his PhD degree in 1902. In 1904 he was appointed professor of physics in the *Col-*lège de France* and in 1909 at the Sorbonne. In the First World War he sought to develop submarine detectors, based on ultrasonic waves. During the second he was imprisoned by the Nazis, but escaped to Switzerland. Returning to Paris after the War, he became particularly concerned with educational reform. In 1928 he was elected a Foreign Member of the Royal Society, which awarded him its Hughes Medal.

Langevin is particularly remembered for his early work on magnetism, to which he applied electron theory. He developed a formula relating the paramagnetic movement of a molecule to (among other parameters) the absolute temperature, confirming (1905) Curie's experimental observations that paramagnetic susceptibility varies inversely with the temperature. From his formula Langevin predicted the phenomenon of paramagnetic saturation, observed experimentally by Kamerlingh ONNES in 1914 in gadolinium sulphate. He investigated also the behaviour of ionized gases and in 1903 developed recombination theory for electric discharges at both high and low pressures. He also studied Brownian movement in gases. He was a warm advocate of EINSTEIN's theory of the equivalence of mass and energy – which conclusion he apparently reached independently himself – and did much to make this generally known and accepted in France.

Obituary Notices of Fellows of the Royal Society, 1951.

André Langevin, *Paul Langevin, mon père.* 1972.

J. D. Bernal, *Nature*, **159**, 798, 1947.

Pensées, **165**, 3, 1972. (Centenary issue.)

Dictionary of Scientific Biography.

T I W

LANGLEY, JOHN NEWPORT Born at Newbury, Berkshire, England, 2 November 1852; died Cambridge, 5 November 1925. Physiologist; a pioneer of our knowledge of the autonomic nervous system.

Langley entered St John's College, Cambridge, in 1871. He read mathematics and history, with the intention of entering the Indian Civil Service, but in 1873, influenced by Michael Foster (1836–1907) the praelector of physiology at Trinity College, he transferred to the natural science tripos, and graduated with first-class honours in 1874. In 1875 Foster appointed him as his Demonstrator. In 1877 Langley became a Fellow, and in 1884 a lecturer, at Trinity College, and also university lecturer in histology. In 1900 he became deputy professor to Foster, and in 1903 succeeded him in the chair of physiology, which he held until his death. Langley was elected Fellow of the Royal Society in 1883, was awarded its Royal Medal in 1892, and was its vice-president in 1904–5 and its Croonian lecturer in 1906. He received several honorary degrees and other honours.

Before he graduated Langley worked, at Foster's suggestion, on the action of pilocarpine on the heart (1875). This led to his work on secretion, carried out on mammalian salivary glands. He showed that during the resting stage granules accumulate in the gland cells, but that these granules are discharged from the cells as the gland secretes. His investigations were carried out not only on fixed and stained glandular material, but also on living gland cells. He showed also that these effects were produced by changes in the blood-supply to the gland.

In 1889 Langley, in collaboration with W. Lee Dickinson (1862–1904) showed that, if a sympathetic ganglion were painted with nicotine, the passage of nerve impulses across it was blocked. W. H. GASKELL, also working in Foster's laboratory, had shown that the sympathetic ganglia were connected segmentally to certain sections of the spinal cord. Langley now employed his method of nicotine blocking to investigate systematically the pathways from and to each ganglion. He showed that there is only one sympathetic ganglion on each sympathetic pathway, and that the ganglia are found only on different paths. He also demonstrated that the current view that true reflexes could be elicited from sympathetic ganglia was erroneous, and he explained the phenomena by his concept of axon-reflexes. He introduced the terms 'preganglionic' and 'postganglionic' fibres (1893), and in 1898 he applied the term 'autonomic nervous system' – instead of 'involuntary nervous system' – to cover the nervous system of the involuntary muscles and also of the glands. From about 1907 he investigated the endings of nerves in tissues such as muscle, and he concluded that the excitation of one cell by another was due to the presence under the nerve endings of specific receptive substances. After the First World War he worked on vasomotor reflexes and the control of the capillaries, and thereafter he wrote his final major work, *The Autonomic Nervous System*, the first part of which – all that was published – appeared in 1921.

In 1894 Langley saved the *Journal of Physiology* from extinction by becoming both its editor and its owner. For thirty years he edited this journal in a manner which had a permanent influence on scientific writings in English.

W. M. Fletcher, *Journal of Physiology*, **61**, 1, 1926.
W. Haymaker and F. Schiller (Eds), *Founders of Neurology*. 1953. (Portrait.)
Proceedings of the Royal Society, **101B**, xxxiii, 1927.
Dictionary of National Biography.
Dictionary of Scientific Biography.

                                                                                    E A U

LANGLEY, SAMUEL PIERPONT Born at Boston, Massachusetts, USA, 22 August 1834; died Aiken, South Carolina, 27 February 1906. Astronomer and pioneer of flying machines.

Langley possessed a boyhood passion for astronomy, but received only high-school education. In 1867 he became professor of astronomy in the Western University of Pennsylvania and Director of the Allegheny Observatory, where he invented the bolometer and mapped the infrared region of the solar spectrum. From 1887 onwards he continued his studies of solar radiation while holding office as Secretary of the Smithsonian Institution, Washington.

In the same decade he became interested in the possibilities of heavier-than-air flying machines, and in 1896 his large steam-powered model craft achieved flights of 3000 and 4200 feet: these were the most important flights of their kind then on record. But Langley died a disappointed man when his full-sized machine – undertaken with Charles Manley (1876–1927) – which had a 53 hp engine

twice failed to leave the ground (1903) and he was unable to find funds for further experiments.

Dictionary of American Biography.
Cyrus Adler, *Bulletin of the Philosophical Society of Washington*, **15**, 1, 1907.
Biographical Memoirs. National Academy of Sciences, **7**, 247, 1917.
Dictionary of Scientific Biography.

                                                                                    T K D

LANGMUIR, IRVING Born in Brooklyn, New York, 31 January 1881; died Falmouth, Massachusetts, 16 August 1957. Physical chemist, remembered for his work on surface chemistry and thermionic emission.

Langmuir received his elementary education in Brooklyn, before moving with his parents to Paris where he spent three years at a suburban boarding school. In 1895 the family returned to Philadelphia and after a year at Chapel Hill Academy he went to the Pratt Institute in Brooklyn, graduating in 1898. He continued his studies at the University of Columbia School of Mines, where he obtained a degree in metallurgical engineering (1903), and then went to Göttingen, where he studied under W. H. NERNST, and obtained his PhD (1906) for a dissertation on the *Partial Recombination of Dissociated Gases during Cooling*. He returned to America, and became a teacher at the Stevens Institute of Technology at Hoboken, New Jersey. In 1909, he was appointed to the research laboratories of the General Electric Company, at Schenectady, and he remained there until his retirement in 1950. From 1932 to 1950 he was Associate Director of the laboratories.

In over forty years as an active scientist Langmuir produced over two hundred papers, covering a wide range of interests, and became internationally famous. When he started work at the General Electric Company he carried out an investigation into the thermal conduction and convection of gases, using the recently developed tungsten filaments of W. D. Coolidge. He showed that the blackening of an incandescent filament lamp was due solely to the evaporation of the filament, and that this could be reduced by introducing nitrogen into the bulb instead of using high vacuum. However, the heat losses that resulted caused a decrease in efficiency, and a new filament coiled in a tight helix had to be developed before a high-efficiency gas-filled lamp could be produced (1913). Langmuir also carried out work on electrical discharges in gases at very low pressure, and this led to the discovery of a new effect known as the space-charge effect; further development led to the improvement of electronic tubes so that they became useful in broadcasting. Offshoots of this research were the high-vacuum condensation pump (1916), and the atomic hydrogen blowpipe (patented 1934).

Langmuir was also interested in the properties of liquid surfaces; he recognized the concept of mono-molecular layers (monolayers), and using this was able to obtain some idea of the shape and size of molecules. This led to the idea of monolayer adsorption on solids and to the general theory that chemical reactions occurred between adjacently adsorbed substances on a given surface. Langmuir received a Nobel prize in 1932 for his work in this field. He extended the work of G. N. LEWIS on atomic theory and valency, and in 1919 put forward the octet theory. He coined the terms electrovalence and covalence; electrovalence was to describe the bonding which occurred in simple salts, and covalence the bonding which involved the sharing of a pair of electrons. He visualized a static atom, which particularly appealed to the chemist.

During the two world wars Langmuir carried out important research work. In the first war he developed a submarine detection device, and during the second war he was concerned with V. J. Schaeffer in the improvement of smoke-screens, by using particles of the optimum size to scatter light. He continued to be associated with Schaeffer in his work on the production of artificial rain by seeding cumulus clouds with solid carbon dioxide and silver iodide.

Biographical Memoirs of Fellows of the Royal
   Society. 1958. (Portrait.)
A. W. Hull, Nature, **181**, 148. 1958.
Biographical Memoirs, National Academy of
   Sciences. 1974.
A. Rosenfeld, The Quintessence of Irving
   Langmuir. 1966.
Dictionary of Scientific Biography.
Tyler Wasson (Ed.), Nobel Prize Winners. 1987.
   (Portrait.)

                                        B B K

LANKESTER, EDWIN RAY Born in London, 15 May 1847; died there, 15 August 1929. Distinguished zoologist.

Lankester, son of Edwin Lankester, MD, FRS (1814–74), was educated at St Paul's School, London; Downing College, Cambridge; and Christ Church, Oxford, where he read zoology and geology. On graduating in 1868, he studied in Vienna and Leipzig, and at the newly opened Stazione Zoologica at Naples. He returned to Oxford, where he taught for two years until he was elected to the Jodrell Professorship of Zoology at University College, London. Here he made a great reputation as a teacher, his clear and incisive manner and skill in illustration firing his audience with enthusiasm for his subject. He was elected FRS in 1875, and in 1884 was largely concerned in founding the Marine Biological Association, and the establishment of its now world-famous laboratory at Plymouth.

In 1891 Lankester returned as Linacre Professor of Comparative Anatomy to Oxford, where, in addition to teaching, he reorganized the University Museum as a teaching aid and educational amenity. His experience was invaluable when in 1898 he was appointed Director of the British Museum (Natural History), where, however, he was frustrated in many of his plans for improvement by the opposition of the Trustees. He was knighted when he retired from the Museum in 1907.

Lankester's wide interests and inquiring mind led him into researches covering almost the whole field of zoology, as is shown by the large number of papers he published breaking new ground. His early work dealt with fossil fishes, and was followed by researches on protozoa and blood parasites. His most important contributions were probably those on the structure and embryology of invertebrates, in which he studied the germ layers, and elucidated the nature of the coelom in many forms, inventing numerous new technical terms to describe his discoveries. His wide-ranging interests were reflected in his popular writings, in which he admirably conveyed scientific matters to the layman. For many years he was the editor of the Quarterly Journal of Microscopical Science, of international repute, and of the Treatise on Zoology, never completed.

E. S. G. [Goodrich], Proceedings of the Royal
   Society, B, **106**, x, 1930. (Portrait.)
Dictionary of Scientific Biography.

                                        L H M

LAPLACE, PIERRE SIMON Born at Beaumont, Normandy, France, 22 March 1749; died Paris, 5 March 1827. Mathematician; remembered for his fundamental contributions to mathematical physics and celestial mechanics.

Pierre Simon Laplace came of poor farming people, but showed such scholastic promise that neighbours sent him to school in Caen. From there he became a teacher in the Beaumont Military School. Having mastered applied mathematics by the time he was 18, he went to Paris with a letter of introduction to J. LE R. D'ALEMBERT. None the less, he did not succeed in meeting the great mathematician until he had written him a letter on the principles of mechanics. This so impressed D'Alembert that he found him a post at the Paris Military School. From then on Laplace lived in Paris, occupying a number of official posts, writing numerous papers on astronomy (mainly celestial mechanics) and mathematics. Between 1799 and 1825 he published in five volumes his great work, the Mécanique Céleste, which incorporated all that had been done in celestial mechanics since the time of NEWTON, including his own brilliant researches. In 1796 he published the Exposition du Système du Monde, a popular account of the universe as revealed by astronomy, beautifully written, eschewing the use of mathematical formulae. In 1812 there appeared his Théorie Analytique des Probabilités, on which nearly all subsequent developments in the theory of probability are based, and in 1819 he published a more popular work on the same subject.

Throughout the dangerous years of the French Revolution, the Napoleonic era, and the return of the Bourbons, Laplace managed to survive and prosper, being at various times member of the Commission for Weights and Measures, of the Bureau des Longitudes, and professor at the École Normale. During the Empire, he became Member of the Senate, Grand Officer of the Legion of Honour, Count of the Empire – Napoleon even discussed astronomy with him on the field of battle. The returning Bourbons made him a Marquis and in 1816 he was elected one of the Forty Immortals of the Académie Française.

In importance Laplace's scientific work was second only to that of Newton. His nearest rival, J. L. LAGRANGE, also produced work of first-rate importance, and indeed the two men, for almost thirty years, produced the vast majority of the era's advances in astronomical theory. They kept up a continuous correspondence, each utilizing the discoveries made by the other.

Laplace spent much time on lunar theory; his most notable discovery was the cause of a hitherto unexplained acceleration in the Moon's mean motion, first detected by E. HALLEY from a study of ancient and modern eclipses. Laplace's researches, inspired by his own analysis of the motions of Jupiter's satellites, showed that due to the slow decrease in the Earth's orbital eccentricity, the month would shorten in length, a process that would be reversed after some 24 000 years. More recently J. C. ADAMS showed that it was not possible to explain the whole of the acceleration in this way. Laplace also found a value for the figure of the Earth from an analysis of irregularities in the Moon's motion; he contributed to tidal theory, taking into account the effect of the Earth's rotation. He also explained satisfactorily a variation in the orbital velocities of the great planets Jupiter and Saturn which had long puzzled astronomers and which seemed in contradiction to the law of gravitation. Laplace showed that the near-commensurability in mean motions of the two planets was responsible (twice Jupiter's mean motion is very nearly five times Saturn's) and is in point of fact a triumphant verification of Newton's law of gravitation.

One of Laplace's most important pieces of research concerned the long-term stability of the Solar System. His work was inspired by Lagrange's famous paper of 1766, in which he formulated the method of the variation of orbital elements (the six numbers that describe the size, shape and orientation of an orbit). In 1773, Laplace proved that in the case of any planet perturbed by any other, the perturbed planet's mean distance from the Sun could not have altered appreciably in millenniums. Two years later Laplace applied a method used by Lagrange to show that the eccentricity of a planetary orbit had upper and lower bounds. In 1784, in the same paper that contained his explanation of the great oscillation in the orbits of Jupiter and Saturn, Laplace proved two extremely important theorems involving the mean distances and eccentricities of the planetary orbits, also the angles between the orbital planes and a fixed reference plane through the Sun. The first theorem stated that if the mass of each planet was multiplied by the square root of the mean distance and this product by the square of the eccentricity, then the sum of these quantities was a constant, apart from small oscillations. The second theorem replaced the square of the eccentricity by the tangent of the orbital plane's inclination. Within the reasonable assumptions made by Laplace, the relations prove the stability of the Solar System. Subsequent work has shown, however, that tidal effects modify the picture to some degree.

Laplace also demonstrated the existence of an invariable plane in the Solar System about which the whole system oscillates; he worked on the shape and rotation of Saturn's rings, investigated the figure of a rotating fluid in equilibrium, and introduced the immensely useful concepts of the potential function and the Laplace coefficients. He suggested the well-known nebular hypothesis concerning the origin of the Solar System which produced much fruitful work in the nineteenth century.

These intricate fields of study show Laplace to have been a worthy successor to Newton. Indeed, the list of Laplace's work reminds one irresistibly of the contents of the *Principia*. His two great astronomical works, also his treatise on probability

theory, inspired most of the great mathematicians of the nineteenth century. In his old age, Newton said: 'I seem to have been . . . like a boy playing on the seashore, . . . finding a smoother pebble or a prettier shell than ordinary, whilst the great ocean of truth lay all undiscovered before me.' Laplace, on his death bed, echoed his words: 'What we know is minute; what we are ignorant of is vast.'

Peter Doig, *A Concise History of Astronomy*. 1950. *Endeavour*, **8**, 49, 149.

A. Pannekoek, *A History of Astronomy*. 1961.

M. Crosland, *The Society of Arcueil*. 1967

E. T. Whittaker, *American Mathematical Monthly*, **56**, 369. 1949; *Mathematical Gazette*, **33**, 1, 1949.

H. Andoyer, *L'oeuvre scientifique de Laplace*. 1922.

S. Lilley, *Nature*, 163, 468, 1949.

Dictionary of Scientific Biography, Supp. I.

A E R

LAPWORTH, ARTHUR Born at Galashiels, Selkirkshire, Scotland, 10 October 1872; died Manchester, England, 5 April 1941. Organic chemist.

Lapworth was the son of Charles LAPWORTH, first professor of geology in the University of Birmingham and a pioneer of stratigraphy. He was educated at King Edward's School, Birmingham; at Mason College (later University of Birmingham); and at the City and Guilds of London Institute, where he came under the influence of H. E. ARMSTRONG and F. S. KIPPING. He held a succession of senior academic posts and in 1913 was appointed professor of organic chemistry at Manchester, in succession to W. H. PERKIN, *Jr*; in 1922, primarily to make it possible to offer a chair to R. ROBINSON, he was appointed to the chair of physical and inorganic chemistry, a remarkable transition. He was elected FRS in 1910, and was awarded the Davy Medal in 1931.

He made notable contributions to classical fields of chemistry, notably in investigating the structures of camphor and related compounds, and of the active principles of ginger. It is, however, for his enunciation of the electronic theory of organic chemical reactions (1920) that he is likely to be best remembered. In this he worked closely with but independently of (Sir) Robert Robinson. Briefly, this postulated the existence of alternating electrical polarity along a chain of atoms, creating anionoid and cationoid centres of reactivity which would be attacked by corresponding reagents. This theory, quickly followed by more sophisticated versions put forward by others, was very successful in explaining the occurrence of many known types of organic chemical reaction and in predicting the possibility of others.

A. Findlay and W. H. Mills (Eds), *British Chemists*. 1947. (Portrait.)

Obituary Notices of Fellows of the Royal Society, 1945–8.

Dictionary of National Biography (Missing Persons). 1993.

T I W

LAPWORTH, CHARLES Born at Faringdon, England, 20 September 1842; died Birmingham, 13 March 1920. Geologist; famed for his work on graptolites and the Lower Palaeozoic rocks.

Charles Lapworth was educated at Buckland,

near Faringdon, and Culham, near Oxford; in 1864 he became a schoolmaster in Scotland, first at Galashiels and later, in 1875, at St Andrews. Developing a passion for geology, he worked intensively during holidays on the Lower Palaeozoic rocks of the Southern Uplands, unravelling their stratigraphy and structure chiefly by means of the graptolites they contained, thus opening the way for similar research not only in Britain but throughout the world. This great work culminated in memoirs on the Moffat and Girvan regions, published by the Geological Society in 1878 and 1882.

In 1881 he was appointed to the newly established chair of geology in Birmingham University and made important contributions to the geology of the Midlands, notable papers being published by the Geologists' Association in 1894, with W. W. Watts (1860–1947), and 1898. He made excursions to Scotland and worked out by detailed survey the main features in the structure of the far north-west (*Geological Magazine*, 1883). Unfortunately, under physical stress and the excitement of discovery his health broke down and he never fully recovered. In 1879 he had shown convincingly (*Geological Magazine*) that a distinct stratigraphical system, which he named Ordovician, should be placed between the redefined Cambrian and Silurian. His study of graptolites as fossil organisms, as well as guides to stratigraphical horizons, led to the compilation of the *Monograph of British Graptolites* (1901–18) by Gertrude Elles and Ethel Wood under his guidance.

Lapworth received the highest honours from his fellow workers, including the Wollaston Medal of the Geological Society and a Royal Medal of the Royal Society, to whose Fellowship he was elected in 1888.

Geological Magazine, **38**, 289, 1901. (Portrait.)
Proceedings of the Geological Society, **77**, iv, 1921.
Proceedings of the Royal Society, **92B**, xxxi, 1921.
Proceedings of the Geologists' Association, **50**, 235, 1939.
Advancement of Science, 7, 433, 1951.
Dictionary of Scientific Biography.
Dictionary of National Biography (Missing Persons). 1993.

J C

LATOUR, CAGN(I)ARD DE Born in Paris, 31 May 1777; died there, 5 July 1859. Versatile experimental physicist, discoverer of critical state.

Cagniard, Baron de Latour, was trained at the *École Polytechnique*. His life is distinguished only by a succession of ingenious experiments, the results of which were of considerable theoretical importance, although he did not himself make any considerable contribution to theory.

In acoustics he invented the perforated-disc siren, in which a disc with equidistant holes on its periphery rotates against a jet of air, producing a sound of which the pitch is regulated by speed of rotation. He contributed to ore-dressing by his invention of a rotary washing-machine for cleaning the copper ores of Chessy (1821).

He studied the physics of voice production by means of experiments on a human subject having a hole in the trachea; invented a dynamometer; imitated the formation of minerals; estimated the forces involved in the flight of birds; and tried unsuccessfully to convert carbon to diamond.

His most memorable discovery was that of the critical state. Alcohol and other liquids were heated in sealed glass tubes; at a certain temperature and pressure the meniscus disappeared and the contents became homogeneous.

He was elected a Member of the *Académie des Sciences* in 1850.

Nouvelle Biographie Générale, vol. 29. 1859.

F G

LAUCHEN, GEORG JOACHIM VON See RHETICUS.

LAUE, MAX THEODOR FELIX VON Born at Pfaffendorf, near Coblenz, Germany, 9 October 1879; died Berlin, 24 April 1960 (as a result of a motoring accident). Theoretical physicist whose most widely known achievement – the conclusion that x-rays would be diffracted by a crystal – was proved experimentally with W. Friedrich and P. Knipping.

Laue was brought up on classical studies, but at an early age became interested in physics. Later he studied mathematics, chemistry and mineralogy, but did not devote himself much to crystallography.

He was assistant to Max PLANCK at the Institute of Theoretical Physics in Berlin (1905–9). He wrote papers on applications of the special theory of relativity. He then transferred to Munich, where he continued work on relativity, but also lectured and wrote about wave-optics. As a result of this and a thesis by P. P. Ewald (1888–1985) which he examined he conceived the idea that the short wavelength electromagnetic radiation, which x-rays were suspected to be, should give rise to diffraction phenomena by interaction with a crystal having particles arranged in patterns which repeated with periodicities comparable with the wave length of the radiation.

His assistants Friedrich and Knipping performed the experiment. They showed that the diffraction effects obtained were related to the symmetry of the crystal and Laue produced his theory of diffraction by a three-dimensional grating.

Laue had no part in the two immediate developments. W. H. BRAGG and W. L. BRAGG used the discovery immediately to found the science of crystal structure determination based on a simplified view of Laue's theory, and K. M. G. Siegbahn (1886–1978) and others developed x-ray spectroscopy, the measurement of x-ray wavelengths. Crystal structure work has developed ever since with profound effects on chemistry in particular, but also on physics and the sciences of metals, minerals and biology. X-ray spectroscopy came at the right time for the development of atomic theory, especially in relation to chemistry. The work of H. G. J. MOSELEY on the characteristic x-ray spectra of the elements was one of the first of these advances. The number of elements was settled and their identification made certain. The Periodic Table was understood and its gaps made clear. Until the end of his life Laue made further additions to theories of diffraction of x-rays and electrons by the crystal, this work being based on mathematical methods of which he was a polished master.

After periods in Zürich and Frankfurt am Main, Laue became professor of theoretical physics in Berlin. Here he devoted his thought to the phenomenon of superconductivity and some aspects of relativistic dynamics.

He was awarded the Nobel prize for physics in 1914.

Biographical Memoirs of Fellows of the Royal Society. 1960. (Portrait.)

Nature, **187**, 738, 1960.

Dictionary of Scientific Biography.

Tyler Wasson (Ed.), *Nobel Prize Winners*. 1987. (Portrait.)

H M P

LAURENT, AUGUSTE Born at La Folie, near Langres, France, 14 September 1808 (or 14 November 1807); died Paris, 15 April 1853. A great organic chemist, whose achievements were limited by difficult circumstances.

Laurent was the son of a wine merchant. His date of birth is commonly given as 14 November 1807, but L. E. Grimaux (1835–1900) gives it as 14 September 1808. Grimaux deserves respect; he was a biographer of LAVOISIER and also contributed to the *Life* of C. F. GERHARDT, Laurent's close associate. Laurent studied for three years at the *École des Mines* before becoming assistant in 1830 to J. B. DUMAS in the *École Centrale des Arts et Manufactures*. In 1833 he became chemist to the porcelain factory at Sèvres, but he found the work uncongenial, and left (1835) to engage in private teaching. He also worked for a perfumier, on whose premises he had a laboratory, but only occasionally drew any salary. After receiving his doctorate in 1837, he had another period in a porcelain factory in Luxembourg, but was appointed professor in Bordeaux in 1838. His arrears of salary from the perfumier were lost in an industrial venture. Dissatisfaction with conditions in Bordeaux, especially after a visit to Justus von LIEBIG in 1844, led him back to Paris in 1846, where he lived precariously until he was made Assayer to the Mint in 1848. During these years he was collaborating closely with Gerhardt. He failed to obtain an expected chair in the Collège de France, fell seriously ill, and had to abandon practical work (1850); he was able, however, to finish his *Méthode de Chimie*, which was published posthumously (1854). His family were left almost destitute.

It is very difficult to summarize Laurent's work, and to separate his later contributions from those of Gerhardt. He had an abundance of ideas which his meagre resources seldom allowed him to follow up adequately. His generalizations were put forward with so little experimental support that a lifetime of controversy was inevitable; though it is clear that, within his means, he was a fine experimentalist. His extensive studies of naphthalene and its chlorination products led him to propose a 'nucleus theory' which enshrines primitive structural ideas; the work also influenced Dumas in his 'theory of types', as Dumas belatedly acknowledged. In the hands of Gerhardt the 'Theory of Types' acquired a positivist philosophy of which Laurent would probably not have approved.

Laurent is also noteworthy for his attempt to devise a systematic nomenclature for organic chemistry. This was adopted by the influential Leopold GMELIN, but was short-lived because of its insecure theoretical basis. He wrote numerous papers on minor topics, including anthracene, phthalic acid, indigo and hydrobenzamide.

Clara de Milt, *Journal of Chemical Education*, **28**, 198, 1951. (Portrait.); *Chymia*, **4**, 85, 1953.

Satish C. Kapoor, *Isis*, **60**, 477, 1969.

Dictionary of Scientific Biography.)

W V F

LAVAL, CARL GUSTAF PATRIK DE See DE LAVAL.

LAVERAN, CHARLES LOUIS ALPHONSE Born in Paris, 18 June 1845; died there, 18 May 1922. Discoverer of the malaria parasite.

Alphonse Laveran, the son of a distinguished Army physician, was with his parents in Algeria from 1850 to 1855, and thereafter attended schools in Paris. He studied medicine at Strasbourg, and after graduating (1867) he served in hospitals in Lille and Paris. During the Franco-Prussian War he served in Metz throughout the siege of that city. From 1874 to 1878 he was a professor of military medicine at the *Val-de-Grâce*, the famous military medical school. Posted to Algeria in 1878, Laveran at once began to study the problem of malaria. After six years in Algeria he was appointed professor of military hygiene at the *Val-de-Grâce* (1884–94). During the next two years the army gave Laveran no opportunities for laboratory research. He therefore resigned his commission in 1896, and spent the next twenty five years in research at the Pasteur Institute in Paris. He was elected a Foreign Member of the Royal Society in 1916, and in 1907 he was awarded the Nobel prize in physiology or medicine.

From at least 1847 several workers had described granules of a black pigment in the blood and organs of patients suffering from malaria, but in later years research was concentrated on the discovery of a bacterial cause of the disease. It was generally held that the pigment was a degeneration product of the blood. In Algeria, Laveran confirmed this work, and found that the pigment granules were often contained in hyaline cysts within the blood cells. He suspected that these cysts were protozoa, but he had no proof. On 6 November 1880, while studying such a cyst in malarial blood, he saw long flagella extruded from it; they moved actively in the blood. He published short notes on these observations on 23 November and on 28 December 1880. Further papers followed, and definitive publication appeared in his books of 1884 and 1892. Many malariologists were sceptical of Laveran's findings, especially the Italians. It was not until 1884 that E. Marchiafava (1847–1935) was convinced that the hyaline bodies showed active amoeboid movement and were therefore protozoa; and even Ronald ROSS did not see the parasite until 1894. The asexual cycle of the parasite was soon elucidated by Marchiafava, C. GOLGI and others.

Laveran studied leishmaniasis for many years, and he showed (1917) the identity of two forms of that disease, Indian and Mediterranean kala-azar. With Felix Mesnil (1868–1938), he published in 1904 an important work on trypanosomiasis.

L. W. Hackett, *Malaria in Europe*. 1937.

H. H. Scott, *History of Tropical Medicine*. 1939.

M. E. M. Walker, *Pioneers of Public Health*. 1930. (Portrait.)

M. Phisalix, *Alphonse Laveran*. 1923.
Proceedings of the Royal Society, **94B**, xlix. 1923.
EAU

LAVOISIER, ANTOINE LAURENT Born in Paris, 26 August 1743; executed there, 8 May 1794. The founder of modern chemistry.

Lavoisier studied law in Paris, and became a Bachelor in 1763 and a Licentiate in 1764. Concomitantly he studied geology (under J. E. Guettard (1715–86)), chemistry (under G. F. ROUELLE), astronomy, mathematics, and botany. Having qualified in law, Lavoisier assisted Guettard for three years in the preparation of the geological map of France. In 1764 he submitted his first memoir to the *Académie Royale des Sciences*, and other memoirs followed. In 1768 he was elected a member of the *Académie* and he decided to devote himself to science. To supply the funds he became in 1768 an assistant farmer in the private tax-farm used to collect the Government's taxes; he ultimately rose to be a farmer-general. In 1771 Lavoisier married Marie Anne Pierrette Paulze, who assisted him greatly in his scientific work. In 1775 he was appointed Inspector of Gunpowder for the Government, and until 1792 they lived at their famous house at the Arsenal. He was also practically interested in agriculture, education and prison reform. In 1788 he was elected a Fellow of the Royal Society. After the Revolution the tax-farm and the Academy were suppressed. On 14 November 1793 Lavoisier and the other twenty-seven farmers-general were arrested on wrongful charges. At the trial on 8 May 1794 they were all convicted and guillotined on the same day.

Apart from his books, most of Lavoisier's researches were published in the *Mémoires* of the *Académie*. In 1770 he showed that the 'earth' produced by the prolonged heating of distilled water came from the glass. In 1772 he proved that a diamond can be burned, and that the product of combustion is 'fixed air'. He now began to study the results of combustion, then dominated by the phlogiston theory. On 1 November 1772 he deposited a sealed note with the *Académie*. This showed that his experiments proved that when phosphorus and sulphur burned their gain in weight was due to their combination with atmospheric air, and he suggested that the increase in weight on the calcination of metals was due to the same cause. In 1774 he published his *Opuscules physiques et chymiques*, which dealt with combustion, calcination and 'elastic fluids' (gases). He found that the gas produced by the heating of a calx with charcoal was identical with the 'fixed air' of Joseph BLACK. He had already envisaged that such studies must involve not only combustion but also respiration. This work indicates that Lavoisier had concluded that in the burning of phosphorus the substance which combines with the phosphorus is either air itself or another gas found in a certain proportion in atmospheric air.

On 1 August 1774 Joseph PRIESTLEY obtained from mercuric oxide a gas which vigorously supported combustion. He did not recognize its respirability until 1 March 1775, the date of his discovery of it as 'dephlogisticated air'. Late in August 1774 Priestley told Lavoisier in Paris about his new 'air'. Lavoisier saw that he now had a clue to his problem. He repeated Priestley's experiments, and in 1775 he communicated to the *Académie* his conclusion that the 'principle' which combines with metals during calcination and increases their weight is purified air, not a particular constituent. Before publication in 1778 Lavoisier changed the 'principle' to 'eminently respirable air', and he realized that common air consists of eminently respirable air and an inert *mofette*. By 1777 he had shown that 'eminently respirable' air is converted into 'fixed air' by combustion and respiration, and he thought that it was a component of acids. In that year he called it *oxygine*.

In 1783 Lavoisier explained the composition of water according to his new chemical doctrine. The old ideas no longer fitted the facts, and in 1783 he launched his great attack on the phlogiston theory. In 1787, in collaboration with C. L. BERTHOLLET, A. F. de FOURCROY and L. B. Guyton de Morveau (1737–1816), Lavoisier published the *Méthode de nomenclature chimique*, which swept away all the outdated fanciful names and substituted new names in accordance with known facts. In 1789 Lavoisier published his *Traité élementaire de chimie*, in which he gave a table of the thirty-three elements then known, and set out the lines along which chemistry must develop in the future.

Meanwhile Lavoisier had been concerned with the process of respiration. With LAPLACE he designed an ingenious ice-calorimeter, using which they studied respiration in small animals and concluded that it is very slow combustion. They gave the first definition of the basal metabolic state. In 1785 they showed that during respiration the air breathed extracts something from the lung, and that this substance combines with vital air to form carbon dioxide. Lavoisier deduced that this substance could only be carbonaceous matter (i.e. carbon), and that good air consists of about twenty-five parts of vital air (oxygen) and seventy-five parts of azote (nitrogen).

In 1789 Lavoisier, in collaboration with Armand Séguin (*c.*1765–1835), communicated his first memoir on respiration to the *Académie*. The contents of this, and of his subsequent memoirs on respiration and transpiration (not published till long after his death), are very complex (see E. A. Underwood, below). Very briefly, they showed that, in a confined atmosphere, whether it is of vital air or common air, the amount of vital air consumed by a guinea-pig under static conditions is always the same, and that this amount is increased during digestion or movement. In man they showed that the amount of vital air absorbed is a function of three factors, temperature, digestion, and work performed. Lavoisier's stated view was that the inspired oxygen was consumed in the lungs, but he seems to have had an idea that the process may possibly take place in the tissues. He laid the foundations of the study of metabolism in man.

D. McKie, *Antoine Lavoisier*. 1952. (Portrait.)
E. A. Underwood, *Proceedings of the Royal Society of Medicine*, **37**, 247, 1944.
P. Hartog, *Annals of Science*, **5**, 1, 1941.
T. E. Thorpe, *Essays in Historical Chemistry*. 1894.
E. Grimaux, *Lavoisier, 1743–1795*. 3rd ed. 1899.
M. Daumas, *Lavoisier*. 1941.
L. Velluz, *Vie de Lavoisier*. 1966.
Dictionary of Scientific Biography.
EAU

LAWES, SIR JOHN BENNET Born at Rothamsted, Hertfordshire, England, 28 December 1814; died there, 31 August 1899. Agricultural scientist.

Lawes was educated at Eton; at Brasenose College, Oxford; and then for a short time as a chemist at University College, London. Succeeding to his family estate at Rothamsted in 1834, he devoted the remainder of his life to the development of agricultural science. In this his close collaborator from 1843 was J. H. Gilbert (1817–1901), who had been a fellow student with him in London and had later spent a short time with Justus von LIEBIG at Giessen; for six years (1884–90) Gilbert was Sibthorpean Professor of Rural Economy at Oxford.

Traditional agricultural practice made farmers familiar with the idea that land becomes impoverished by repeated cropping, and methods of obviating this were devised. Of these, the most important was treating the soil with animal manure, to which other fertilizers, including bone meal, came to be added. Up to the beginning of the nineteenth century the use of fertilizers was largely empirical, and it was not until the time of Humphry DAVY and Liebig that some correlation began to be established between soil composition and the growth of crops.

At the beginning of the nineteenth century superphosphate – bones treated with sulphuric acid – began to be introduced as an agricultural fertilizer. The first to have manufactured it on an industrial scale seems to have been a Dublin physician, James Murray (1788–1871), who patented his process in 1842. It was not a commercial success, however, and the real founder of the synthetic fertilizer industry was Lawes, who established a large factory for superphosphate near London in 1843, using imported mineral phosphate in place of bone; by the early 1870s production had risen to 40 000 tons annually. He sold the business in 1872.

Alongside his industrial interests, Lawes conducted at Rothamsted long and careful field trials – backed by careful chemical analysis – to determine the mineral requirements of a variety of important crops. In 1854 his services to agriculture were recognized by a substantial public subscription, which he devoted to the provision of a new laboratory. When he sold the superphosphate business he received £300,000, of which £100,000 was used to establish a trust to ensure the continuation of the work at Rothamsted. Over the years, Lawes and Gilbert established Rothamsted as an internationally famous agricultural research station; among its later directors was Sir John RUSSELL.

Lawes received many honours. The Royal Society elected him Fellow in 1854 and awarded him its Royal Medal in 1867 (with Gilbert) and in 1893 its Albert Medal. He was created baronet in 1882 and was awarded honorary degrees by the Universities of Oxford (1892), Cambridge (1894) and Edinburgh (1877).

Dictionary of National Biography.
Dictionary of Scientific Biography.
E. Grey, *Rothamsted Experimental Station: Reminiscences, Tales, and Anecdotes 1872–1922.* 1922.
Proceedings of the Royal Society, **75**, 228, 1905.
Nature, **62**, 467, 1900/
Journal of the Royal Agricultural Society, **61**, 511, 1900.

LAWRENCE, ERNEST ORLANDO Born at Canton, South Dakota, USA, 8 August 1901; died Palo Alto, California, 27 August 1958. Inventor of the cyclotron.

Lawrence was a son of the president of a teachers' college and studied at the universities of South Dakota, Minnesota and Yale. From 1927 until his death he was on the staff of the University of California, and was director of its Radiation Laboratory from 1936.

After early work on photo-electricity, in 1929 he began working on the suggestion of A. S. EDDINGTON that nuclear reactions might occur at very high energies, as in the stars. The new linear accelerator of R. R. Wideroe was not powerful enough, and in 1931 Lawrence and D. H. Sloan employed up to thirty tubes giving mercury ions acceleration corresponding to 1.26 million volts. As this device was still not effective enough for light ions, he evolved the scheme of acceleration in a spiral path between two D-shaped electrodes. The resultant apparatus, designed by M. S. Livingston and himself, was termed a cyclotron, and acted rather like an electric motor with the armature replaced by the revolving stream of ions. The first apparatus gave protons accelerations equivalent to over 1 million volts, with energies high enough for nuclear reactions to be probable. Later versions gave considerably higher performances.

The cyclotron was used by Lawrence to initiate and study nuclear reactions of many kinds. An important example was the bombardment of sodium by deuterium, in which radio-sodium was obtained in fairly high yield and with an activity equivalent to 1 mg of radium (1934). Other radio-isotopes included tritium, carbon-11 and uranium-233. Some of the important applications of these discoveries were pioneered by Lawrence and his collaborators. He and his brother John explored medical uses for both neutrons and radio-isotopes from the cyclotron. Neutrons were used to destroy malignant tissues and were shown to be more effective than x-rays (1936). Radioactive iron was employed in tracer studies of iron metabolism in dogs (1939).

Plutonium and neptunium were isolated in his laboratory in 1940, followed later by other synthetic elements. Plutonium played an important part in the American atomic-bomb project, with which Lawrence became deeply involved. The Radiation Laboratory attracted nuclear scientists from many countries and its research became a model of organized teamwork. Lawrence himself, already a Nobel Laureate in Physics for 1939, was widely honoured. In 1961, in the laboratories which he had directed, element No. 103 was detected, and named in his memory lawrencium (Lw).

Nature, **144**, 859, 1939; **182**, 1058, 1958.
A. H. Compton, *Atomic Quest: A Personal Narrative.* 1956. (Portraits.)
Herbert Childs, *An American Genius: The Life of Ernest Lawrence.* 1968.
J. L. Heilbron et al., *Lawrence and His Laboratory.* 1981.
Dictionary of Scientific Biography.
Tyler Wasson (Ed.), *Nobel Prize Winners.* 1987. (Portrait.)
Biographical Memoirs. National Academy of Sciences. 1970.

LEAKEY, LOUIS SEYMOUR BAZETT Born at Kabele, Kenya, 7 August 1903; died en route from Kenya to London, 1 October 1972. Archaeologist, anthropologist and palaeontologist, known for his discoveries of early fossil hominids in East Africa.

The child of missionaries, Leakey recorded his youth in Kenya in *White African* (1937). The First World War prevented his travelling to school in England but in 1919 he made this journey to Weymouth College before going on to St John's College, Cambridge. There he began reading modern languages (French and Kikuyu) but changed to archaeology and anthropology, gaining a first-class degree in 1926. By then he had already been a member of an expedition to Tanganyika in 1924, hunting for dinosaur fossils. Four more expeditions to East Africa followed in the next ten years, yielding material for books on *The Stone Age Cultures of Kenya* (1931), *Stone Age Races of Kenya* (1935) and *Stone Age Africa* (1936), the last published at the end of six years as a research fellow at St John's, following the award of a PhD degree in 1930. The first edition of *Adam's Ancestors* also appeared in 1934, its fourth in 1953. J. B. S. HALDANE borrowed his name in 1937 for the magician who is the hero of the book he wrote for children, *My Friend Mr Leakey*.

Leakey returned to Kenya before the Second World War, taking an active part in the political life of the country. After the war he was appointed Curator of the Coryndon Memorial Museum, Nairobi, a post he held until 1961. Early in the 1950s he published two books about the Mau Mau disturbances, but his large study of the Kikuyu remained unpublished until after his death.

In 1942, working in the Rift Valley with his second wife Mary, he found the skull of *Proconsul africanus*, one of the earliest apes known, but their later excavations in the Olduvai Gorge, which started in 1951, produced discoveries of hominid remains that had a major effect on theories of the development of man, though Leakey's views of human origins in Africa were not accepted without question. In 1959 *Australopithecus (Zinjanthropus) boisei* was first described, followed by *Homo habilis* (dated to 1.7 million years old) and *H. erectus*. Reports of the Olduvai work began to be published in 1951 and the series continues, for Leakey's widow Mary and their son Richard kept on the archaeological and anthropological work he had started. He also founded the Pan-African Congress on Prehistory, acting as its secretary from 1947 to 1951 and its president from 1955 to 1959.

He received honorary doctorates from the universities of Oxford in 1953 and California in 1963, was elected a Fellow of the British Academy in 1958, and received a Royal Medal from the Royal Geographical Society in 1964. The Louis Leakey Memorial Institute for African Prehistory in Nairobi and the Californian Leakey Foundation commemorate his name.

Sonia Cole. *Leakey's Luck: The Life of L. S. B. Leakey.* 1975.
Mary Leakey. *Disclosing the Past* (autobiography). 1985.
Dictionary of Scientific Biography.

S J R|

LEAVITT, HENRIETTA SWAN Born in Lancaster, Massachusetts, USA, 4 July 1868; died Cambridge, Massachusetts, 12 December 1921. Astronomer.

Henrietta Leavitt was born into a strict New England family. After graduating in astronomy at Radcliffe College she became a volunteer worker at Harvard College Observatory. In 1902, despite severe deafness, she received a permanent appointment and became head of the photographic photometry department. In this capacity she worked closely with E. C. PICKERING in compiling the great Harvard photographic library recording all stars down to the eleventh magnitude. The Southern Observatory at Arequipa, Peru, made possible inclusion of stars of the southern hemisphere.

Her main task was to classify this monumental collection. She noted that in the case of Cepheid variable stars the brighter variables have longer periods. More specifically (1912), she discovered that the apparent magnitude decreased linearly with the logarithm of the period. Harlow SHAPLEY, at Mount Wilson Observatory, used this observation to calibrate the absolute magnitudes of the variables and hence to calculate the size of the Milky Way Galaxy and the distances to other galaxies.

Dictionary of Scientific Biography.
Popular Astronomy, **30**, 197, 1922. (Portrait.)

T I W

LEBEDEV, PYOTR NIKOLAEVICH Born in Moscow, 24 February 1866; died there, 1 March 1912. Physicist; measured the pressure of light.

Lebedev was unable to enter a Russian university, but studied physics in Strasbourg and Berlin from 1887 to 1891, graduating with a thesis on the Mosotti-Clausius theory of dielectrics. On his return to Russia, he became assistant in the physics laboratory in Moscow University, and was made professor in 1900. With other members of the staff, he resigned his chair in 1911, as a protest against the policies of the Ministry of Education. He declined an invitation to work with S. ARRHENIUS in Stockholm, and died shortly afterwards.

He is best remembered for his work on the pressure of light, which arose from studies of the radiometer of W. CROOKES (in which the apparent effect of light-pressure is really due to traces of gas in the apparatus). Using a more perfect vacuum, Lebedev was the first actually to measure the pressure of light, and to show that it was twice as great for reflecting as for absorbing surfaces.

Bol'shaya Sov'etskaya Entsiklopedia, vol. 24. 1954. (Portrait.)
Dictionary of Scientific Biography.

W V F

LE BEL, JOSEPH ACHILLE Born at Pechelbronn, Alsace, France, 21 January 1847; died Paris, 6 August 1930. One of the founders (with J. H. VAN'T HOFF) of stereochemistry.

Le Bel was educated at the *École Polytechnique*. His family owned an oil well and refinery at Pechelbronn, which he partly managed for some years; he then sold his share, and went to study chemistry at the Sorbonne, becoming assistant to C. A. WURTZ. Here he met Van't Hoff, though their acquaintance seems to have been slight. Le Bel held no academic post, but worked as an industrial consultant, and carried out independent research on his private estate.

In 1874 Le Bel published his theory that the optical activity of organic compounds was due to the presence in their structures of an 'asymmetric' carbon atom, that is, a carbon atom bound to four different groups. If these groups are arranged at the apices of a tetrahedron, then the compound will exist in two forms, related as object and mirror image. At almost exactly the same time Van't Hoff published the same idea independently; in 1893 they were jointly awarded the Davy Medal by the Royal Society, who elected Le Bel to Fellowship in 1911.

Le Bel worked out a method of resolving mixtures of optical isomers which depended on the selective destruction of one isomer by microorganisms. Using this method, he claimed to have resolved a quaternary ammonium salt, but he was probably mistaken. In his private laboratory his research encompassed not only chemistry (petroleum chemistry and problems of fractional distillation) but also biology (the conversion of nitrogen into ammonia by algae) and cosmic physics. Little of this work, unfortunately, was published.

He never married, and appears to have been a rather solitary figure, full of unconventional speculative ideas.

W. J. Pope, *Journal of the Chemical Society*, 2789, 1930. (Portrait.)

Bulletin de la Société Chimique de France, **47**, 1344, 1930.

M. Delépine, *Vie et oeuvres de J-A. Le Bel*. 1949.

Dictionary of Scientific Biography.

W V F

LEBLANC, NICOLAS Born at Ivoy-le-Pré (or at Issondon, near Orléans), France, 6 December 1742; died Paris, 16 January (or February) 1806. Industrial chemist.

As a young man Leblanc was apprenticed to an apothecary. He then studied surgery, and in 1780 he became surgeon to the household of the (future) Duke of Orléans (Philippe Égalité). The Duke was interested in chemical processes (corresponding with Joseph BLACK), and it was doubtless through this that Leblanc became interested in the prize offered in 1775 by the French Academy of Sciences for a process for making alkali from a non-vegetable source. At that time virtually the only source of soda was wood ash, and it was becoming an increasingly scarce and expensive commodity. In 1783 Leblanc was awarded the prize for a process that was widely worked for well over a hundred years. It consisted in treating salt with sulphuric acid to form sodium sulphate. This was calcined with chalk and charcoal, and soda was extracted from the resulting 'black ash' with water. A patent was awarded in 1791, and the Duke of Orléans built a works at St Denis, where production rose to 320 tons per annum. Leblanc was to prove unlucky, however, His patron was executed in 1793, the factory was confiscated, and the process became public property; he never received the prize awarded him. In 1802 Napoleon returned the works to him, but he was then destitute and unable to operate it. Desperate, he died by his own hand in 1806. In 1855 belated reparation was made to his heirs by Napoleon III.

Although Leblanc's process was not entirely novel, in that other chemists were thinking along similar lines, it was nevertheless the one that came to be generally adopted. It was displaced (by the ammonia-soda process perfected by E. SOLVAY), in the last quarter of the nineteenth century. In 1885 world production of soda was 800 000 tons, more than half of it still made by the Leblanc process.

J. Fenwick Allen, *Some Founders of the Chemical Industry*. 1907.

A. Anastasi, *Nicolas Leblanc, sa vie, ses travaux, et l'histoire de la soude artificielle*. 1884.

C. C. Gillispie, *Isis*, **48**, 152, 1957.

R. E. Oesper, *Journal of Chemical Education*, **19**, 567, 1942.

T I W

LEBON, PHILIPPE Born at Bruchey, near Joinville, France, 29 May 1767; died Paris, 2 December 1804. Pioneer of gas illumination.

Son of an officer in the King's household, Philippe Lebon was brought up in the charcoal-burning area of Brackay and was educated at Chalon-sur-Saône and the *École des Ponts et Chaussées*; on graduating in 1792 he served for a time in Angoulême and then, after 1800, in Paris. There he taught at the *École* and discussed with A. F. FOURCROY experiments he had been making on the production of gas from sawdust and for which he was given a patent on 21 September 1799. To publicize his 'Thermolamp' he hired the Hôtel Seignelay, where he exhibited a large model for several months; this attracted favourable notice notwithstanding the resinous smell which it emitted. Gregory Watt wrote from Paris to his father James WATT of Birmingham in 1801 urging that efforts be made to patent similar work which one of Watt's employees, Richard MURDOCK, was conducting at Redruth.

Lebon also devised an engine to work by gas, one of many such projects before his time and after. He was granted a lease of part of the pine forest at Rouvray near Le Havre. He was robbed and stabbed in the *Champs Elysées* on 30 November 1804, just before the celebrations attending Napoleon's elevation to Imperial rank, and died two days later. He had then anticipated most of the applications of gas during the next century.

Louis Figuier, *Les Merveilles de la Science*. 1860–70. (Portrait.)

Shelby T. McCloy, *French Inventors of the Eighteenth Century*. 1952.

A. Fayol, *Philippe Lebon, et le gaz d'éclairage*. 1943.

W H G A

LE CHATELIER, HENRI LOUIS Born in Paris, 8 October 1850; died Miribel-des-Echelles, Isère, 17 September 1936. Enunciator of an important principle in chemical thermodynamics.

Le Chatelier, whose father was Inspector-General of Mines, was educated at the *École Polytechnique* in chemistry, physics and engineering, and for some years worked as a mining engineer. In 1877 he became a professor in the *École des Mines*, and thereafter, until his retirement in 1919, held several teaching appointments (sometimes simultaneously) in the University of Paris and its related institutions. He was married, and had seven children; he lived to become the doyen of French chemists.

His early work was on the physics and chemistry

of the setting of cements, but his interests broadened to cover most aspects of the application of science to processes of industrial importance. His most substantial contribution was a long series of studies on the structure of alloys, but he is remembered for his enunciation in 1884 of what became known as 'Le Chatelier's Principle'. This states that 'If to a system in equilibrium a constraint be applied, a change will take place in the equilibrium tending to nullify the effect of that constraint' (though the original was not so neatly worded). Le Chatelier found that he had been anticipated, in abstract mathematical fashion, by Willard GIBBS, and did much to spread knowledge of Gibbs's work in French translation. This principle had many applications in the growing concern of the chemical industry with high-pressure gas reactions. It would be impossible to detail all of Le Chatelier's industrial contributions; towards the end of his active career he became fascinated by the problems of industrial efficiency and labour relations, and wrote widely on this topic.

C. H. Desch, *Journal of the Chemical Society*, 139, 1938. (Portrait.)

E. Farber (Ed.), *Great Chemists*. 1961. (Portrait.)

R. E. Oesper, *Journal of Chemical Education*, **8**, 442, 1931.

Revue de Métallurgie, **34**, 1, 1937.

Dictionary of Scientific Biography.

A. Silverman, *Journal of Chemical Education*, **14**, 555, 1937.

W V F

LECLANCHÉ, GEORGES Born in Paris, 1839; died there, 14 September 1882. Engineer, remembered for the Leclanché electric cell.

Leclanché was educated in Paris at the *École Centrale des Arts et Manufactures*, and in 1860 he joined the *Compagnie du Chemin de l'Est* as an engineer. By 1866 he had developed his cell, which consisted of zinc and carbon electrodes and a solution of ammonium chloride as electrolyte. To prevent polarization the central carbon electrode was surrounded with manganese dioxide, which oxidized to water the hydrogen released. In 1867 he gave up his job to devote himself to the cell's improvement, and in the following year saw it adopted by the Belgian telegraphic service. It rapidly came into general use wherever an intermittent electric supply was needed, and was later developed into the familiar dry cell, of which countless millions have been used, and still are, throughout the world.

Towards the end of his life Leclanché worked on a system for the electrical distribution of the true time.

Revue Générale de l'Électricité, **8**, 161, 1920.

Athenaeum, **2**, 469, 1882.

B B K

LEE, TSUNG DAO Born in Shanghai, China, 24 November 1926. Theoretical physicist who has made many contributions to elementary particle physics.

Lee attended the National Checkiang University and the National Southwest Associated University in China. In 1946 he was awarded a scholarship and went to the University of Chicago to work under Enrico FERMI. There he completed his PhD on white dwarf stars in 1950. Lee spent from 1951–

3 at the Institute for Advanced Study at Princeton where he renewed his relationship, begun in Chicago, with C. N. YANG. In 1953, Lee moved to Columbia University in New York, but continued to work with Yang through weekly visits to each other's institution.

Lee and Yang made their best known contribution to physics in 1956 when they proposed that 'parity' (symmetry under spatial inversion) is violated in the weak interactions of particles. The following year, experiments by C. S. WU and others proved the theory correct, and Lee and Yang were rewarded with the Nobel prize for physics in 1957.

Lee became the youngest professor in the faculty at Columbia in 1956, and was made Enrico Fermi Professor of Physics in 1963. He has continued to make many contributions to the theory of the high-energy interactions of elementary particles, his work having what Robert OPPENHEIMER has described as 'remarkable freshness, versatility and style'.

Nobel Lectures, Physics, 1942–1962. 1964.

H. A. Boorse, L. Motz and J. H. Weaver, *The Atomic Scientists, a Biographical History*. 1989. (Portrait.)

Tyler Wasson (Ed.), *Nobel Prize Winners*. 1987. (Portrait.)

C S

LEEUWENHOEK, ANTONY VAN Born at Delft, Netherlands, 24 October 1632; died there, 26 August 1723. Microscopist.

Leeuwenhoek received no formal training in science, and was apprenticed at the age of 16 to a linen-draper in Amsterdam. Six years later he returned to Delft, where he bought a house and shop; set up in business as a draper; and remained for the rest of his life. He also served as chamberlain to the sheriffs of Delft 1660–99. His researches followed no scientific plan and were made, for the most part, with the aid of microscopes constructed by himself. All his microscopes consisted of a single, very small, biconvex magnifying-glass of remarkable clarity, mounted between small apertures in two thin oblong metal plates (usually of brass) riveted together. The instrument was held close to the eye, and the object, mounted on a silver needle on the other side of the lens, was adjusted to correct focus by means of thumb-screws. Liquids to be observed were contained in glass capillary tubes.

Leeuwenhoek's long association with the Royal Society, of which he was elected a Fellow in 1680, began in 1673 with a letter of introduction written by R. de GRAAF, a friend and fellow townsman. Most of his discoveries were communicated in letters to the Society written in Nether-Dutch, as he knew no other language; some 120 extracts in English, or occasionally in Latin, were printed in the *Philosophical Transactions* between 1673 and 1723. In 1668 he confirmed the discovery of blood-capillaries by M. MALPIGHI, six years later gave an accurate description of the oval red blood-corpuscles in fishes, frogs and birds, and the disc-shaped corpuscles in man and other mammals. The first written account of free-living ciliate protozoa appeared in a letter of 1674, and of bacteria found in water 'wherein pepper had lain infused', in a celebrated letter (No. 18) of 1676, which is of special interest to protozoologists. His finding of entozoic protozoa in the gut of the frog, and of bacteria in the human mouth, was described in 1683. Observations of the life-history of Rotifers (which he discovered), of insects (fleas, aphids and ants); and of marine and fresh-water mussels confirmed his disbelief in spontaneous generation. Concerning this, he wrote (1702): 'Can there even now be people who still hold to the ancient belief that living creatures are generated out of corruption? ' Among his miscellaneous discoveries were spermatozoa of dogs and other animals, *Hydra, Volvox,* and the globular nature of yeast. He was also one of the first to study the structure of opaque objects by means of sections cut by hand with a sharp razor.

At his death, Leeuwenhoek left 247 finished microscopes and 172 lenses. He bequeathed to the Royal Society a cabinet containing twenty-six instruments and extra lenses. Before their unfortunate loss, their optical properties were ascertained; they were found to have magnifying powers ranging from 50 to 200. Since he kept his 'method for seeing the smallest animalcules' for himself alone, there has been speculation as to what his jealously guarded secret could have been. C. Dobell (see below) has expressed the view that Leeuwenhoek discovered some method of darkground illumination, and B. Cohen (see below) found that the effectiveness of lenses similar to those employed by Leeuwenhoek can be augmented by utilizing the optical properties of spherical drops of fluid containing the objects under observation. During his lifetime Leeuwenhoek became famous; was visited by royalty; and corresponded with such savants as G. W. LEIBNIZ, C. HUYGENS, and A. Magliabechi (1633–1714).

Clifford Dobell, *Antony van Leeuwenhoek and his Little Animals.* 2nd ed. 1958. (Portraits.)

The Collected Letters of Antoni van Leeuwenhoek (edited, illustrated, and annotated by a committee of Dutch scientists). 1939–52.

Dictionary of Scientific Biography.

B. J. Ford, *The Leeuwenhoek Legacy.* 1991.

A P G

LEIBNIZ, GOTTFRIED WILHELM Born at Leipzig, Saxony, Germany, 1 July 1646; died Hanover, 14 November 1716. Polymath, remembered for his part in the foundation of the calculus and attempts at mathematical logic.

Leibniz was the son of a professor of moral philosophy at Leipzig, who died when the boy was 6. His father's library helped to form his wide interests, especially in history and classical literature. At 15 he entered the University at Leipzig and studied law. He was refused a Doctorate in Law, 1666, on account of his youth, but there he also began the study of mathematics. He declined a professorship at Altdorf (Nuremberg) at the age of 20. In 1667 he entered the service of the Elector-Archbishop of Mainz. On visits to Paris and London he met many leading scientists. In Paris he studied geometry under C. HUYGENS, and in London he was elected Fellow of the Royal Society (1673). On the death of his patron (1676) he took the post of librarian to the Duke of Brunswick. From Hanover he helped in the institution of the Berlin Academy (1700), and carried on a large correspondence with scholars throughout Europe. After the Elector of Hanover became George I of

England, Leibniz appears to have lost favour, perhaps as a result of the influence of the supporters of NEWTON, who were angered by the claims of Continental mathematicians that Leibniz was the originator of the calculus. He died broken by illness and dogged by controversy.

From his youth it was Leibniz's ambition to reform all science by the use of a universal scientific language and a calculus of reasoning. *De arte combinatoria* is a remarkable essay on this theme, written before he was 21. He devised a symbolism for such concepts as 'and', 'or', 'class inclusion, ' 'implication', and 'class equivalence'. Although his logic has many shortcomings, it is notable as perhaps the first historical example of abstract mathematics, in the sense of mathematics without concern for space or number.

Leibniz's writings were for the most part never published. They deal with projects that were seldom brought to fruition. If they can be given any unity, it is through the doctrine of substance, which Leibniz managed to introduce into the most diverse subjects. His doctrine of monads – simple, percipient, autonomous beings, the constituent units of all things – had implications not only for his metaphysics but also for his physical views. This can be seen, for example, in his correspondence with Samuel Clarke (1675–1729), conducted in the last two years of his life. This important correspondence helped to clarify many important issues in science and philosophy. Quite apart from theological matters, gravity, the vacuum, the nature of space ('The order of coexistent phenomena') and time ('the order of successive phenomena'), and the measurement of force (should it be measured through momentum or through kinetic energy?), were all discussed.

Leibniz appears to have begun to work towards the differential and integral calculus about 1673, some years after Newton, but independently. Both were led to the subject by the works of ARCHIMEDES, F. B. CAVALIERI, P. FERMAT, B. PASCAL, I. BARROW, and others, in which, with hindsight, the beginnings of the calculus are discernible. Both Newton and Leibniz, nevertheless, can be regarded as founders of the subject in a way which would not be reasonable with their precursors. Both worked out complete algorithms which, except in their foundation, are substantially those used today. Leibniz's notation was that now generally adopted. He gave an interesting early treatment of the notion of the curvature of geometrical curves, although his first article on this (1686) contains mistakes. He also made a useful early contribution to the theory of envelopes.

Besides writing on psychology, international law, historical method, and genealogy, Leibniz found time to write copiously on geology and the formation of the Earth and planets. In his *Protogaea* (1749, posthumously published) he explains the probable passage of the Earth from vapour, through a molten globular state, to its present form. He went on to account for the geological irregularities of the Earth's crust as well as stratified organic remains. In cosmological respects, his views are an interesting anticipation of those of LAPLACE.

The publication of Leibniz's scattered writings, projected in forty volumes, had scarcely begun when interrupted by the last war.

B. A. W. Russell, *A Critical Exposition of the Philosophy of Leibniz* (new ed.). 1937.

R. W. Meyer, *Leibniz and the Seventeenth-Century Revolution.* 1952.

R. Kauppi, *Ueber die leibnizsche Logik.* 1960.

R. L. Saw, *Leibniz.* 1954.

Dictionary of Scientific Biography.

J D N

LEICESTER, EARL OF *See* COKE.

LEISHMAN, SIR WILLIAM BOOG Born in Glasgow, Scotland, 6 November 1865; died London, 2 June 1926. The discoverer of the parasite of kala-azar.

Leishman was a son of the Regius Professor of Midwifery in the University of Glasgow. Educated at Westminster School, he studied medicine at Glasgow University and graduated in 1886. He was then gazetted to the Royal Army Medical Corps, in which he spent the remainder of his life. After seven years in India he was posted to the Army Medical School at Netley, where he soon became assistant professor of pathology under (Sir) Almroth Wright (1861–1947). When the School was transferred to Millbank, London, in 1903 he succeeded Wright as professor. In 1914 he became the War Office expert in tropical diseases on the Army Medical Advisory Board. On the outbreak of war he joined the Expeditionary Force as adviser in pathology, and in 1919 he became the first director of pathology at the War Office. Four years later he was appointed director-general of the Army Medical Services, a post which he retained until his death. Leishman was knighted in 1909, and elected Fellow of the Royal Society in 1910 and a Fellow of the Royal College of Physicians in 1914; he received many other honours.

Leishman assisted Wright in the latter's research on antityphoid inoculation, which proved beneficial in the South African War, and which prevented many thousands of deaths from typhoid fever in the British Army during the First World War. In 1901 he published his modification of the Romanowsky stain for blood and protozoa which bears his name. By its aid he had already (1900) discovered the protozoal parasite of kala-azar (dum-dum fever). The discovery was made using material from the spleen of a soldier who had died from the disease at Netley. Leishman did not publish his results until 1903, and in that year Charles Donovan (1863–1951), of the Indian Medical Service independently discovered the parasite, which was therefore called the Leishman-Donovan body (*Leishmania donovani*). Related species of these bodies were later shown to be the cause of other tropical diseases, now grouped under the name 'Leishmaniases'. Leishman also did important work on the life-history of *Spirochaeta duttoni*, the causal organism of African tick fever.

H. H. Scott, *History of Tropical Medicine.* 1939.

M. E. M. Walker, *Pioneers of Public Health.* 1930. (Portrait.)

E A U

LEMAÎTRE, GEORGES ÉDOUARD Born at Charleroi, Belgium, 17 July 1894; died Louvain, 20 June 1966. Astrophysicist and cosmologist; originator of the basic hypothesis of the 'big bang'.

Having trained as a civil engineer, Lemaître

served in the Belgian army during the First World War, then entered a seminary and was ordained priest in 1923. He nevertheless maintained his interests in science, which were strengthened by periods spent at the University of Cambridge, where he met A. S. EDDINGTON, and the Massachusetts Institute of Technology, where he was influenced by the 'expanding universe' theories of E. P. HUBBLE and H. SHAPLEY. On his return to Belgium he was appointed professor of astrophysics at the University of Louvain in 1927, and remained there for the rest of his career.

He became increasingly absorbed in the problem of the origin of the Universe, and in 1933 published his *Discussion on the Evolution of the Universe*, in which he enunciated his theory of the 'big bang'. This was followed in 1946 by his *Hypothesis of the Primal Atom*, a concept he had actually first proposed in 1931: he saw the primal atom as a single entity containing the sum of all the material in the Universe, within a sphere only thirty times larger than the Sun. The big bang was simply the explosion of this atom, at some time between 20 and 60 billion years ago, resulting eventually in the expanding Universe we now live in. Strong support for this theory has been put forward by George GAMOW and others, with most of the observational evidence now pointing in the same direction.

A. Berger (Ed.) *The Big Bang and Georges Lemaître.* Proceedings of a Symposium in his honour, October 1983.

Revue des Questions Scientifiques, **155**, 139, 1984.

McGraw-Hill *Encyclopedia of World Biography.*

R M B

LÉMERY, NICOLAS Born at Rouen, France, 17 November 1645; died Paris, 19 June 1715. Chemist and writer of an important popular textbook.

Lémery, son of the Procurator of the Parliament of Normandy, studied under an apothecary at Rouen, before moving to Paris, where he worked under C. Glaser (d. *c.*1675). He disliked Glaser's secretive attitude and after six months moved to Montpellier, where his lectures attracted attention. In 1672 he settled in Paris, and shortly afterwards opened a manufacturing laboratory in a basement in the Rue Garland, and began the courses of experimental lectures which made him famous. In 1675 he published his *Cours de Chymie*, which by 1756 had gone through thirty-one editions and been translated into Latin, English, German, Dutch, Italian and Spanish. The first English edition came out in 1677 and a second translation in 1698. Lémery's lectures were very popular with foreign students; forty Scottish students are reputed to have attended one session.

Lémery lectured in a clear and concise style; he rejected alchemical beliefs and avoided mysticism. His work was mainly of a practical nature, and he had himself carried out most of the experiments he described. His book reflected his early training and was almost entirely concerned with pharmaceutical chemistry. His preparations became fashionable, and he is reputed to have been able to live comfortably on the profit from the sale of his cosmetic products.

Lémery adopted an atomic theory, which explained the properties of substances in terms of the shape of their fundamental particles. He assumed that acids were composed of sharp particles which pricked the tongue, and therefore caused a sour taste, and that metals contained pores into which the acid particles could insinuate themselves and tear the metal apart. His recipe for the preparation of sulphuric acid involved the burning, in a closed vessel, of sulphur and salt-petre, and was probably the basis of the commercial manufacture established by Joshua WARD at Richmond.

In 1684 Lémery received his MD from Caen, and began to practise in Paris. As a Protestant, he had, however, been unpopular for some years, and with the revocation of the Edict of Nantes in 1685 he had to go into hiding. The following year he became a Catholic and was returned to favour, and in 1699 became a pensioner of the Academy of Sciences. His son Louis (1677–1743) was a physician and also lectured on chemistry.

E. Farber (Ed.), *Great Chemists*. 1961. (Portrait.)
Chemistry and Industry, **54**, 347. 1935.
M. Leroux, *Isis*, **7**, 430. 1925.
Journal of Chemical Education, **9**, 15. 1932. (Portrait.)
P. Dorveaux, *Revue d'histoire de la pharmacie*, **19**, 208, 1931.
Dictionary of Scientific Biography.

         B B K

LENARD, PHILIPP EDUARD ANTON Born at Pozsony, Hungary, 7 June 1862; died Messelhausen, Baden-Württemberg, Germany, 20 May 1947. Famous for work on photoelectricity and cathode rays.

Lenard studied physics at Budapest, Vienna, Berlin, and Heidelberg. He then became assistant to Heinrich HERTZ at Bonn (1893), and taught at Breslau (1894), Aachen (1895) and Heidelberg (1896). He was professor of experimental physics at Kiel from 1898 and at Heidelberg from 1907 to 1931.

Lenard's most notable work was stimulated by the paper of W. CROOKES in 1879 on cathode rays, from which he conceived the idea of examining these rays outside the discharge tube. After several unsuccessful attempts, he found that they would pass through a thin aluminium window in the tube (1892), utilizing a discovery by Hertz that thin metal sheets could be permeable to such rays. He showed that they could penetrate about 8 cm of air (which became conducting) and that absorption depended upon the density of the material and the velocity of the rays. From the permeability of matter by cathode rays, Lenard concluded that most of it must be empty space, suggesting that the material part of an atom consists of neutral doublets ('dynamids') of positive and negative electricity (1903). This was an important anticipation of the model of the atom proposed by E. RUTHERFORD.

During this period Lenard also studied photoelectricity, and showed that ultraviolet light can disengage negative electricity from a metal plate. The charge/mass ratio of this electricity was shown to be the same as for cathode rays (electrons), and its velocity depended upon the charge of the plate. He explained this in terms of vibrations within the atom in resonance with the light, producing eventually emission of a cathode ray. He denied materiality to this unit ('quant') of electricity.

Other work by Lenard included a study of phosphorescence in which it was shown that small amounts of impurities were responsible, and that there was an optimum concentration at which phosphorescence was at a maximum (1904). He also examined the electrification of falling water-drops; devised the 'grid' to control electron flow in a thermionic valve; and introduced the concept of ionization potentials.

Lenard was unfortunate in just failing to discover x-rays and in the eclipse of his nuclear theory by that of Rutherford. Oversensitive about his own reputation, he was not happy in his personal relationships. His book *Great Men of Science* (1934) was criticized for its omission of several eminent contemporaries, for example W. K. RÖNTGEN, with whom he quarrelled over the discovery of x-rays. He believed that in this research Röntgen had used a tube which he himself had sent him. Infected by anti-Semitism, he opposed EINSTEIN also (he did not accept relativity) and became a Nazi supporter. Yet his scientific merit was justly acknowledged by the Nobel prize for physics in 1905.

Nature, **160**, 895, 1947.
Dictionary of Scientific Biography.
Tyler Wasson (Ed.), *Nobel Prize Winners*. 1987. (Portrait.)

         C A R

LENOIR, JEAN JOSEPH ETIENNE Born at Mussy-la-Ville, Luxemburg, 12 January 1822; died La Varenne-Saint-Hilaire, Seine, France, 14 August 1900. Inventor of the first effective gas engine.

Lenoir, who moved to France in 1838, was a self-taught engineer whose interests extended over many fields: railway signals, electric motors, and the telegraphic transmission of pictures. He brought to a successful conclusion two centuries of experiment to harness the energy resulting from an explosion in a closed cylinder; this began with Christian HUYGENS and Denis PAPIN, and continued with John BARBER and Philip LEBON. The principle employed was that of the double-acting steam engine. Instead of steam, gas and air were successively admitted at each end of the cylinder, enabling induction, explosion, and expansion to alternate with exhaustion on either side of the piston. Patented in 1860, Lenoir's engines varied from ½ to 3 hp and met such a need among small industrialists that in five years he had sold some 300. It was the first internal-combustion engine made in numbers for general use, but it had the defects of lack of compression, excessive heat loss and incomplete expansion. Later he modified his engine to work on heated oil mixed with air, but the heavy competition forced him to bring out a compression engine.

In 1883 he made a two-crank four-cylinder engine with enclosed crank chamber for marine work, and in the same year a four-stroke engine – of which Nicolas OTTO was the real pioneer – which was not a commercial success.

Lenoir suffered from the enterprise and forceful business methods of the Otto Motor Company, and died poor and unhonoured in the country of his adoption.

B. Donkin, *Gas, Oil and Air Engines*. 1911.

L. J. Kastner, *Proceedings of the Institution of Mechanical Engineers*, **169**, 303, 1955.

P. H. Smith, *The High Speed Two-Stroke Petrol Engine.* 1965.

P. Magôt Cuvrii, in *Les inventeurs célébres.* 1950.

W H G A

LENZ, HEINRICH FRIEDRICH EMIL Born at Dorpat, Russia, 12 February 1804; died Rome, 10 February 1865. Remembered for law giving the direction of an induced current.

After studying theology, Lenz turned to physics and became professor at the University of St Petersburg and director of the Academy of Sciences in that city. In 1834 he enunciated the so-called Law of Lenz, stating that the direction of the current induced in a conducting circuit by its motion in a magnetic field is such as to produce an effect opposing the actual motion of the circuit. Lenz also confirmed Peltier's phenomena (see J. C. A. PELTIER) by showing that water could be frozen by the Peltier Cold. He performed experiments attempting to produce a combination of hydrogen and oxygen under great pressure through the increased action of molecular forces, but without success. He also worked on the setting up of standard units of resistance.

W. M. Stine, *The Contributions of H. F. E. Lenz to Electro-magnetism.* 1923. (Portrait.)

Dictionary of Scientific Biography.

J W H

LEONARDO DA VINCI Born at Vinci, near Florence, Italy, 15 April 1452; died Amboise, Indre-et-Loire, France, 2 May 1519. Painter, military engineer, inventor and anatomist.

Leonardo was the illegitimate son of Ser Piero da Vinci, who became official notary to the Signoria at Florence, and of Caterina, a girl of a neighbouring village. From his early years he showed promise in drawing and model-making. He became a pupil of Andrea del Verrocchio (1435–88) at Florence, and was enrolled in the painters' guild. About 1483 he went to Milan. His first anatomical drawings date from about 1487. In 1499 he left Milan, and in 1503 he was back in Florence; in 1506 he returned to Milan, where he was engaged in engineering work for the Lombard canal system. Much of his anatomical work was done during this period. In 1513 he worked for Leo X and was quartered in the Belvidere at Rome. About 1516 he was invited by Francis I to go to France and live on the royal bounty. He was quartered in the castle of Cloux near Amboise until his death.

Leonardo's scientific investigations are recorded in his notebooks, extant in various libraries. He seems to have had a good idea that the Earth moves round the Sun, and COPERNICUS may have heard of his views. He had sound ideas on the cause of the saltness of the sea, and on the origin of seas and rivers. He invented instruments for measuring wind-force and the speed of ships. He was always very interested in the flight of birds, and he studied the subject in great detail. On these studies he designed a machine for human flight, to be strapped to a man, who would be able to control the flapping wings of the machine by the movement of his arms and legs. Leonardo designed numerous interesting mechanical appliances, though many of them were not capable of realis-

ation with the materials and techniques of his time, and made beautiful drawings of flowers and plants.

Our knowledge of Leonardo's work on anatomy is derived from his anatomical notebooks, now in the Royal Library, Windsor. In his earlier period he studied anatomy as an artist, but in his second period at Milan he was dissecting as an anatomist. It was long stated that Leonardo's interest in anatomy was largely due to his friendship with Marcantonio della Torre (1478 (?1481)–1511), professor of anatomy at Pisa and then at Padua. It was also believed, on the testimony of G. Vasari (1511–74), that the two men had planned to publish an anatomical work, for which della Torre would supply the text and Leonardo the illustrations. This view now seems improbable, but della Torre may have stimulated Leonardo to continue with his work. Leonardo never drew a complete skeleton, but many of his drawings of bones are excellent, and his illustrations of the spinal column are beautiful and accurate. His drawings of muscles are very fine. He was particularly interested in the actions of muscles, and he constructed models to enable him to study these actions. His studies of the heart are in advance of his time, and he drew certain structures in which were not known to others until much later, but his drawings of the vessels are of no great value. He devised a method of obtaining casts of the ventricles of the brain. His drawings of the foetus in the uterus are accurate and in themselves very beautiful studies. Leonardo's anatomical studies had no influence on his successors, as they remained quite unknown until centuries after his death.

E. MacCurdy, *The Notebooks of Leonardo da Vinci.* 1938. (Portrait.)

C. D. O'Malley and J. B. de C. M. Saunders, *Leonardo da Vinci on the Human Body.* 1952.

I. B. Hart, *The Mechanical Investigations of Leonardo da Vinci.* 2nd ed. 1963.

C. D. O'Malley (Ed.), *Leonardo's Legacy – an International Symposium.* 1969.

E. M. Almedingen, *Leonardo da Vinci: A Portrait.* 1969.

L. Reti, *The Unknown Leonardo.* 1974.

V. P. Zubov, *Leonardo da Vinci.* 1968.

Dictionary of Scientific Biography.

E A U

LESSEPS, FERDINAND MARIE, VICOMTE DE Born at Versailles, France, 19 November 1805; died La Chênaie, Indre, France, 7 December 1894. Diplomat and promoter of the Suez Canal.

The son of an important and well-connected figure in the French consular service, Lesseps followed the same profession from 1826 to 1849, when he resigned on account of unjust official censure of the failure of a mission in which he was sent to negotiate with Giuseppe Mazzini's short-lived Roman Republic (1849). But in 1854 the succession of his old friend, Mohammed Said, as Khedive of Egypt enabled him to reopen the project for a canal across the Isthmus of Suez which he had formed while resident in Egypt as a consular official in 1832–6. He had then read the report of J. B. Le Père (1761–1844) made for Napoleon in 1798, and was also aware of the ideas of the followers of the Comte de Saint-Simon (1760–1825) on the same subject.

Although the first canal concession was granted

by the new Khedive in November 1854, the subscription lists could not be opened until 1858, and the Ottoman Sultan did not finally give his approval until 1866. Lesseps made his greatest personal contribution by the unwearying persistence and diplomatic skill with which he circumvented British opposition, won the support of Napoleon III, and raised the capital in France and elsewhere for a scheme which cost twice the estimate made by an international technical commission in 1856. Digging was begun with forced Egyptian labour near the site of Port Said in April 1859, but proceeded slowly until the accession of a new Khedive in 1863 led to the cancellation of the labour contract. The French engineers engaged by Lesseps, P. Borel and A. Levalley, then introduced up-to-date engineering methods, especially the use of suction dredgers armed with chisel-pointed rams. The canal was opened by the Empress Eugénie in November 1869, and this last triumph of the Second French Empire made Lesseps a national hero.

In 1879, however, he became involved at the age of 74 in a parallel project for building a canal across the isthmus of Panama. De Lesseps lacked knowledge of the geological and climatic difficulties involved, and although he was shown the mountain and stream which obstructed his chosen route, he insisted that no locks were needed. After six years' work, marked by mounting costs, slow progress, and countless deaths from yellow fever, the public lost confidence; it was impossible to raise more capital, and in December 1888 the Panama Canal Company suspended payment. Political support having been bought on a large scale, Lesseps, whose mind was failing, received a five-year sentence for bribery; it was quashed on technical grounds, and he himself was never aware that it had been passed.

C. R. L. Beatty, *Ferdinand de Lesseps*. 1956.
J. A. Hamilton, *Concise Universal Biography*. (Portrait.)
G. E. Bonnet, *Ferdinand de Lesseps*. 2 vols, 1951, 1959.

T K D

LEUPOLD, JACOB Born at Planitz, near Zwickau, Germany, 25 July 1674; died Leipzig, 12 January 1727. Mechanical engineer and designer of a high-pressure steam engine.

Son of a craftsman, Jacob Leupold studied at Zwickau and at the Universities of Jena and Wittenberg. He abandoned the study of theology to teach masons and carpenters and opened a workshop in Leipzig in 1699. Here his improvements to the air pump earned him the post of Councillor for Mines under the Prussian Government and membership of the Berlin Academy of Sciences. Four years before his death he began to publish what was to be the nine-volume *Theatrum Machinarium generale* (Leipzig, 1723–39), of which the last two volumes were published posthumously. J. E. Scheffler added to it in 1741.

The importance of this vast work of 1764 pages, with 472 full-page copper engravings, lay in its value to craftsman in enabling them to get up-to-date information on new machines and engineering methods. It can be regarded as the first systematic treatment of mechanical engineering. Of particular interest is the inclusion of a design

for a high-pressure non-condensing steam engine. Although it does not appear that such a machine was ever built – and the limited techniques and materials of the day probably precluded this – it foreshadowed the introduction of high-pressure steam early in the nineteenth century.

C. Matschoss (trans. H. S. Hatfield), *Great Engineers*. 1939. (Portrait.)

W H G A

LEVENE, PHOEBUS AARON THEODOR Born at Sagor, Russia, 25 February 1869; died New York, 6 September 1940. Biochemist, notable for pioneer work on nucleic acids.

Levene (originally Fishel Aaronovich Levin) graduated MD from the St Petersburg Imperial Medical Academy in 1891. The same year, fearing anti-Semitism, the whole family emigrated to New York. He practised medicine on the East Side, at the same time studying chemistry at Columbia University. Overwork was followed by tuberculosis in 1896 and a long period of recuperation, during which he decided to leave medicine for chemistry. Further study in Germany was followed by a post in a New York hospital, before he joined (1905) the newly formed Rockefeller Institute for Medical Research, from which he retired shortly before his death.

Levene's studies embraced almost every class of compound of biological importance, including cerebrosides, chondroitin-sulphuric acid, the hexosamines, the sugars and their phosphate esters. He also worked on the purely chemical problem of the Walden Inversion (see P. WALDEN). His most valuable contribution, however, was his work on nucleic acids, substances whose importance was not then apparent, but is now being ever more clearly realized. Although himself a highly original worker, he owed much to the firm foundations of structural organic chemistry laid by Emil FISCHER. From the mild hydrolysis of nucleic acids he isolated the 'nucleotides' (base-sugar-phosphate fragments) and with R. S. Tipson explored their structures by methylation. He first discerned that nucleic acids were of two kinds, distinguished by their sugar moiety; he isolated and identified the sugars as D-ribose (1909) from the type now known as ribonucleic acid, and its 2-deoxy derivative (1929) from deoxyribonucleic acid. A man of remarkable energy, Levene's habit of rapid and fragmentary publication (over 700 papers, all in the *Journal of Biological Chemistry*) made his work difficult to assess during his lifetime, and perhaps denied him due honour.

R. Stuart Tipson, *Advances in Carbohydrate Chemistry*, **12**, 1, 1957. (Portrait.)
E. Farber (Ed.), *Great Chemists*. 1961. (Portrait.)
Wyndham D. Miles (Ed.), *American Chemists and Chemical Engineers*. 1976.
Biographical Memoirs. National Academy of Sciences. 1944. (Portrait.)

W V F

LE VERRIER, URBAIN JEAN JOSEPH Born at St Lô, Normandy, France, 11 March 1811; died Paris, 23 September 1877. Principally remembered for the discovery of Neptune.

Le Verrier was the son of a local government official. His career at the *École Polytechnique* (1831–5) was distinguished, and he accepted a position in the public service. He did chemical research under J. L. GAY-LUSSAC, but abandoned chemistry when a lecturing post at the *École Polytechnique* fell vacant. He turned to celestial mechanics, continuing a strong French tradition which had begun with LAPLACE. He performed some remarkable work (1838–9) on the effect on the stability of the solar system of varying slightly the elements of the planetary orbits. This led him to investigate the perturbations of comets. Prompted by D. F. J. ARAGO, he studied the apparently incompatible groups of observations made on the planet Uranus. In November 1845 he brought up to date the theory of Uranus of A. Bouvart (1767–1843). He first mentioned the possibility that its irregularities were caused by the perturbing effect of an unknown planet in the abstract of a memoir which appeared in the following June. Although J. C. ADAMS had completed very similar calculations some nine months before, Le Verrier was more fortunate in obtaining observational confirmation of his prediction. On 18 September 1846 he wrote to J. G. Galle (1812–1910) at the Berlin Observatory, and on the 23rd Galle found the new planet within a degree of the position indicated. French jubilation was soured by the announcement that Adams had anticipated Le Verrier, and the controversy still rankled at the beginning of this century. The Royal Society gave Le Verrier alone the Copley Medal, its highest honour, and he was twice given the Gold Medal of the Royal Astronomical Society, on one occasion being presented with it by Adams. His own nation honoured him abundantly, and a chair of astronomy was created for him at the Faculty of Sciences. He now entered politics, being successively a member of the Legislative Assembly (1849) and Senate (1851), when he was Inspector-General of Education.

Succeeding Arago as director of the Paris Observatory in 1854, Le Verrier began an uncompromising rule of reform, which ended in his dismissal (1870). He was reinstated after the death of his successor, C. E. Delaunay, (1816–1872), but with restricted powers. His most monumental work was likewise carried out in two corresponding periods (1855–61 and 1874–77). This amounted to a reworking of much of Laplace's planetary theory, in particular the theory of secular inequalities. It was he who first appreciated the secular motion of the perihelion of Mercury (confirmed by S. NEWCOMB in 1882), of crucial importance in the development of EINSTEIN's General Theory of Relativity. He was even able to deduce a figure for the solar parallax from the inequalities of lunar and terrestrial motions. His result of 8″.95 is to be compared with the figure now accepted of about 8″.80.

F. Tisserand, *Annales de l'Observatoire de Paris*, **15**, 1880.

N. R. Hanson, *Isis*, **53**, 359, 1962.

M. Grosser, *The Discovery of Neptune*. 1962.

Dictionary of Scientific Biography.

J D N

LEVI-MONTALCINI, RITA Born at Turin, Italy, 22 April 1909. Neurophysiologist; discovered nerve growth factor.

Rita Levi-Montalcini was awarded a degree from the University of Turin medical school in 1936, and went on to get a degree in psychiatry and neur-

ology in 1940. Until 1943 anti-Semitic laws barred her from an academic career, forcing her to pursue her research on chick embryos in her bedroom at her home in the countryside. When the Germans occupied northern Italy she moved to Florence, and in 1944 worked as a doctor in an Italian refugee camp.

From 1945 to 1947 she worked at the University of Turin Institute of Anatomy as an assistant professor, developing her theory that the death of nerve cells played a role in the development of the nervous system. In 1947 she was invited by V. Hamburger (1900–) to the Institute of Zoology, Washington University, St. Louis, USA to join him in his work on the embryonic nervous system. She went to Brazil in 1952 to learn the technique of tissue culture in order to discover what stimulated the growth of nerve cells. She went on to discover the stimulating substance, which she called the nerve growth factor (NGF), involved in the growth of all kinds of nerves. With S. Cohen (1922–) she established that NGF was a protein. They discovered that male mouse saliva was a good source of NGF and went on to make antibodies to NGF, which inhibited the action of NGF. Their discoveries were important in the study of serious neurological disorders such as Alzheimer's disease.

As well as holding the position of professor of neurobiology at Washington University 1958–77, she set up a laboratory in Rome at the *Istituto Superiore di Sanità* which was involved in a joint research programme on NGF with Washington University from 1961 to 1969. In 1969 she founded the Laboratory of Cell Biology in Rome, and was its director until 1979.

Levi-Montalcini shared the Nobel prize in physiology or medicine in 1986 with Stanley Cohen for identifying nerve growth factor.

R. Levi-Montalcini and P. Calissano, *Scientific American*, June 1979.

Science, 31 October, 1986. (Portrait.)

Tyler Wasson (Ed.), *Nobel Prize Winners*. 1987. (Portrait.)

A P B

LEVINSTEIN, IVAN Born at Charlottenburg, near Berlin, 4 July 1845; died Hale, Cheshire, England, 15 March 1916. Industrial chemist.

After studying chemistry at the University and at the *Technische Hochschule* of Berlin, Levinstein emigrated to Manchester in 1864, and at the early age of 19 set up a small works to manufacture synthetic dyestuffs in Blackley, a few miles to the north of the city. This soon became the largest establishment of its kind in Britain, though small compared with its German competitors; it later formed the nucleus of the Dyestuffs Division of Imperial Chemical Industries. Levinstein campaigned vigorously for reform of the patent laws, which he felt were unfairly hampering the British chemical industry; the Patents Act of 1907 owed much to his influence. This campaign earned him the hostility of Continental dyestuffs manufacturers.

Journal of the Society of Chemical Industry, **35**, 458, 1916; *Special Jubilee Number*. 1931.

S. Miall, *A History of the British Chemical Industry*. 1931. (Portrait.)

W V F

LEWIS, GILBERT NEWTON Born at Weymouth, Massachusetts, USA, 25 October 1875; died Berkeley, California, 24 March 1946. A contributor to chemical thermodynamics and the electronic theory of valency.

Lewis studied in the Universities of Nebraska and Harvard (under T. W. RICHARDS), graduating PhD in 1899. He worked in Leipzig and Göttingen (under W. F. OSTWALD and W. H. NERNST); returned briefly to Harvard as an instructor; then went to Manila as chemist to the Bureau of Science. From 1905 to 1912 he was at the Massachusetts Institute of Technology; in the latter year he became Chairman of the Chemistry Department of the University of California, where (except for war service, 1917–18) he remained until his death. He married, and left three children.

Lewis's early work in chemical thermodynamics mainly concerned the experimental determination of free energies. This bore fruit in his important book (with M. Randall, 1923) *Thermodynamics and the Free Energy of Chemical Substances*. During the same period he published papers on the special theory of relativity. His studies on the electronic theory of valency began in 1916, when (simultaneously with Walther Kossel (1888–1956)) he postulated that the atoms of all elements of atomic weight higher than helium have inner shells of electrons with the structure of the preceding inert gas; and that the 'valency electrons' lie outside these shells, and may be lost or gained relatively easily. This explains ionic compounds (electrovalency), but Lewis later went further than Kossel with his concept of the shared electron-pair, giving what came to be known as a covalent bond. This work was published (1923) as *Valence and the Structure of Atoms and Molecules*. Lewis's ideas were further developed by N. V. SIDGWICK.

Lewis is increasingly remembered for his definition of acids and bases, more generalized than that of J. N. BRØNSTED and T. M. LOWRY; an acid is a substance which can accept, and a base one which can donate, an electron-pair. The term 'Lewis-acid' is now in common use. His later work was on such topics as deuterium chemistry, photochemistry and fluorescence. He is recorded as 'quiet and unassuming in manner, with a wide and philosophic outlook and a most engaging and attractive personality'.

Obituary Notices of Fellows of the Royal Society, 1945–8. (Portrait.)
Biographical Memoirs. National Academy of Sciences. 1958.
Dictionary of Scientific Biography.

                                                                    W V F

LEWIS, TIMOTHY RICHARDS Born at Hafod, Carmarthenshire, Wales, 31 October 1841; died Netley, Hampshire, England, 7 May 1886. A pioneer discoverer in relation to filariasis.

Lewis was educated at Hafod and was then apprenticed to an apothecary. He next served as dispenser at the German Hospital in London. While there he attended lectures at University College, London. He then studied medicine in the University of Aberdeen, where he qualified with distinction in 1867. In 1868 he entered the Army Medical School, from which he passed out with first place, and was commissioned (1868) as Assistant Surgeon. The Government was then concerned about

the ravages of cholera in India, and various erroneous theories as to the causes of the disease, such as a fungus, and the ground-water theory of Max von PETTENKOFER, were being studied. Late in 1868 the Government appointed Lewis and D. D. Cunningham (1843–1914) to investigate these subjects in India. In 1883 Lewis returned to England to take up the post of assistant professor of pathology at the Army Medical School.

In his first report on his cholera researches Lewis gave the first account of amoebae in the human intestine. This was probably *Entamœba coli*. In 1863 J. N. Demarquay (1811–75) had found threadlike worms in the urine of a case of chylous hydrocoele. This observation passed unnoticed, but in 1870 Lewis independently discovered these filaria embryos in the urine in a case of chyluria, but was unable to find them in the blood. In 1872 Lewis by chance saw this same patient again; he made a more detailed examination of his blood and found the embryos. They were named *Filaria sanguinis hominis*. Lewis made prolonged searches for the adult worm, and in August 1877 he found it in a patient suffering from elephantiasis. It then transpired that Joseph Bancroft (1836–94) had independently discovered the adult worm in Australia in 1876. The parasite was therefore called *Filaria bancrofti*. In 1878 Lewis found that the embryos underwent developmental changes in the thoracic and abdominal tissues of a mosquito. These discoveries of Lewis enabled Sir Patrick MANSON to work out the method of transmission of the disease by a mosquito.

Infection of the lower animals by trypanosomes had been known for about a century, and in 1878 Lewis described trypanosomes in the blood of rats.

C. Dobell, *Parasitology,* **14**, 413, 1922.
H. H. Scott, *History of Tropical Medicine.* 1939.
M. E. M. Walker, *Pioneers of Public Health.* 1930. (Portrait.)
Dictionary of Welsh Biography. 1959.
Dictionary of National Biography (Missing Persons). 1993.

                                                                    E A U

LHUYD, EDWARD Born at Loppington, Cardiganshire, Wales, 1660; died Oxford, England, 30 June 1709. Botanist, palaeontologist, philologist.

Lhuyd was the natural son of Edward Lloyd of Oswestry – reputedly descended from the ancient Princes of Powys – and Bridget Pryse of Tal-y-bont, Cardiganshire. After schooling at Loppington he proceeded to the grammar school at Oswestry and thence (1682) to Jesus College, Oxford. Soon after matriculation he was appointed assistant to Robert Plot (1640–96), Keeper of the Ashmolean Museum and professor of chemistry, whom he succeeded in 1691.

Like most natural philosophers of his day, he had catholic interests. His compilation of the plants of Snowdonia was incorporated in the *Synopsis methodica Stirpium Britannicarum* (1690) of John RAY who called it 'the greatest adornment' of his book. At the Ashmolean he was called on to catalogue its collection of fossils and this led him to speculate on how they had been formed (taphonomy). He was sceptical of the general belief that they were the aftermath of a global Deluge, pointing out that some fossils found in Britain are of an exotic nature corresponding to organisms no longer found in the surrounding sea. He postulated that in some way 'seeds' of marine organisms were wafted inland and then buried deep in the earth. There they grew in petrified form to their normal stature. Through his correspondence with Ray these views became widely known, though not generally accepted.

About 1895 he accepted an invitation to write a comprehensive two-volume natural history of Wales, describing not only its flora and fauna but its geology, history and language. In pursuit of this he travelled widely in Wales, Ireland, Cornwall, Scotland and Brittany – the so-called Celtic Fringe. The first volume of his *Archaeologia Britannica* appeared in 1707 and contains the first comparative study of the Celtic languages. Sadly, his early death left the second volume unfinished, though he made many contributions to the *Philosophical Transactions of the Royal Society*: he was elected Fellow in 1708.

Dictionary of National Biography.
Dictionary of Welsh Biography.
Dictionary of Scientific Biography.

T I W

LIBAVIUS, ANDREAS Born at Halle, Saxony, Germany, 1540/50; died Coburg, Bavaria, 25 July 1616. Chemist and physician.

Very little is known of Libavius's early life. He was reputedly the son of a weaver, but even the year of his birth is uncertain. He studied at Jena, where he later returned (1586–91) as professor of history and poetry. He then moved to Rothenburg, Bavaria, where he was appointed town physician and Inspector of the Gymnasium. After a quarrel with the Rector there, he established his own Gymnasium at Coburg in 1605, remaining there until his death. He was widely read in chemistry, of which he was an accomplished practitioner with several original discoveries to his credit, and was himself a prolific writer on the subject.

Libavius was a bitter opponent of PARACELSUS, even though he lived in an age permeated by Paracelsian doctrine, with its extravagant claims for the chemical treatment of disease. His approach to chemistry was essentially analytical: he regarded the prime role of the chemist as being to resolve substances into their component parts and to put to practical use the pure substances so obtained. He is credited with having prepared a number of chemicals for the first time by putting these precepts into practice. Among them are stannic chloride, antimony sulphide, succinic acid and ammonium sulphate; he observed also the intense blue colour resulting (from formation of the cuprammonium ion) when ammonia is added to solutions of copper compounds.

Libavius's major work was his *Alchymia Andreae Libavii* (Frankfurt, 1597), which is often regarded as the first real textbook of chemistry in the modern sense. It is a summary, rather uncritical, of the chemical knowledge and preparative methods of his time.

J. R. Partington, *A History of Chemistry*, vol. 2. 1961. (Portrait.)
E. Farber (Ed.), *Great Chemists*. 1961.
Dictionary of Scientific Biography.

T I W

LIBBY, WILLARD FRANK Born at Grand Valley, California, USA, 17 December 1908; died Los Angeles, 8 September 1980. Developed technique of radiocarbon dating.

Libby grew up on the family fruit ranch near Sebastopol, California. He graduated from the University of California at Berkeley in 1931, and was awarded a PhD in 1933. From 1933 until 1941 he was on the faculty at Berkeley, before moving to Columbia University in 1941 to join the Manhattan Project to develop the atomic bomb, working on a method for separating uranium isotopes in order to produce fissionable uranium-238, essential in constructing the first bomb.

After the war, in 1945, Libby became Professor of Chemistry at the Institute for Nuclear Studies at the University of Chicago, and it was there that he worked on carbon-14, the radioactive isotope of carbon, discovered at the beginning of the war by Serge Korff. In 1946–7 he developed a technique for dating archaeological specimens of biological origin up to 40 000 years old by measuring the amount of carbon-14 they contained. As a result of cosmic radiation some nitrogen atoms transform into carbon-14 atoms and find their way into living trees and plants through photosynthesis. Photosynthesis stops when the tree dies; the carbon-14 then disintegrates at a fixed rate, and the ratio of radiocarbon atoms to carbon atoms falls. Libby was able to calculate the time that had elapsed since the tree or plant died to within two hundred years – this was tested on ancient Egyptian specimens whose age was already known.

In 1954 Libby was appointed by President Eisenhower to be the first chemist to serve on the US Atomic Energy Commission. He moved to the University of California at Los Angeles as professor of chemistry in 1959, and also became director of the Institute of Geophysics. In 1960 he was awarded the Nobel prize for chemistry for developing the method for using carbon-14 to determine age.

W. F. Libby, *Radiocarbon Dating*. 2nd edition, 1955.
Ruth Moore, *Man, time, and fossils. The story of Evolution*. 1962.
Physics Today, February 1981.
Tyler Wasson (Ed.) *Nobel Prize Winners*. 1987. (Portrait.)

A P B

LIE, MARIUS SOPHUS Born at Nordfjordeid, near Bergen, Norway, 17 December 1842; died Christiania (Oslo), 18 February 1899. Eminent mathematician, contributing to the theory of continuous transformation groups.

Educated at the University of Christiania (Oslo) in 1869 Lie visited Paris, where he met and collaborated with C. F. KLEIN in producing papers on transformation groups. Henceforth Lie was to concentrate on continuous transformation groups and contact transformations, with their applications in dynamics. Partial differential equations can be classified in these terms and most of the classical methods can be reduced to a single principle: transformation groups provide the means of deducing from their structure the type of auxiliary equations which are needed in the integration.

After his return to Norway, Lie became professor at Christiania and published a number of standard works: *Theorie der Transformationsgruppe*

(1888–93); *Differentialgleichungen* (1891); and *Kontinuierliche Gruppen* (1893).

Allgemeine deutsche Biographie, vol. 51. 1906.
E. T. Bell, *The Development of Mathematics*. 1945.
Dictionary of Scientific Biography.
M. Noether, *Mathematische Annalen*, **53**, 1, 1900.

D N

LIEBIG, JUSTUS, BARON VON Born at Darmstadt, Hessen, Germany, 12 May 1803; died Munich, Bavaria, 18 April 1873. An outstanding figure in chemical education, and the greatest chemist of his time.

The son of a dealer in chemicals, Liebig decided at an early age to become a chemist, and graduated PhD at Erlangen when only 19. Two years were spent in Paris, partly in association with J. L. GAY-LUSSAC in the Arsenal; this was made possible by the influence of HUMBOLDT, who later secured him a professorship at Giessen (1825). In this tiny University, Liebig built up a great school of chemistry, based on laboratory instruction, though this was not (as he claimed) the first teaching laboratory. He became bored, however, with practical teaching, and moved to Munich (1852), where he had a fine laboratory built, but confined himself to lecturing.

Liebig's extensive researches fall into two periods. His early work is classical organic chemistry; but by about 1840 he had become mainly interested in the wider and more difficult problems of the chemistry of living things, and of agriculture.

His first important work (1826) confirmed, after much confusion, that silver cyanate and fulminate had the same elementary analysis. This, the first well-founded case of isomerism, raised questions which could not then be answered. It impressed upon Liebig, however, the need for reliable analytical methods, and he devised (1830) what is essentially the modern combustion tube for the determination of carbon and hydrogen. Using this method, he and his students analysed hundreds of new organic compounds. This work led to redetermination of the atomic weight of carbon (with J. Redtenbacher, 1841).

With his friend F. WÖHLER, Liebig in 1832 discovered the 'benzoyl radical', and launched the fruitful concept of 'the chemistry of the compound radicals'. Later studies of the 'ethyl' radical were less secure experimentally, and led to bitter exchanges with J. B. DUMAS and J. J. BERZELIUS.

It was courageous of Liebig to venture his reputation in the uncharted field of what is now called biochemistry, as he did in his middle age. It must be admitted, however, that his tendency to generalize from meagre experimental results, though always apparent, increased to a dangerous extent. His theory of fermentation postulated some form of molecular vibration communicated to the fermenting solution by the 'putrefying' yeast'; he denied, in face of all the evidence, that yeast was a living organism. He was worsted in his controversy with PASTEUR, though neither was completely right. His forcible advocacy of artificial manures laid the foundation of a new industry, but proved unfortunate in practice. He overstressed the importance of mineral salts, and belittled the use of nitrates (believing that crops obtained sufficient ammonia from rain water) and of organic manures (which give structure to the soil). These ideas had more currency in Germany than in England, where they were opposed by J. B. LAWES and J. H. Gilbert (1817–1901). His views on nutrition were equally contentious; although he showed that 'animal heat' was entirely accounted for by the oxidation of food, he could not free himself from the concept of 'vital force'. He was wrong about the role of proteins in diet, and his 'extract of meat' had less food value than supposed.

Liebig was a copious writer of books, papers and articles; he travelled and lectured all over Europe. He founded the *Annalen der Pharmacie* (1832, now *Liebig's Annalen der Chemie*). He had a complex and difficult character, of which the most public feature was arrogance, from which his friends suffered as much as his enemies. Though he could be generous, he was more often bitterly unfair; he would admit his mistakes only when it was too late to matter. Wöhler alone understood him completely, and remained his lifelong friend.

Liebig received many honours. He was made Baron in 1845, and in 1840 was elected FRS.

W. A. Shenstone, *Justus von Liebig, his Life and Work*. 1901.
J. Volhard, *Justus von Liebig* (2 vols.). 1909. (Portraits.)
Journal of the Chemical Society, 1065, 1875. (Portrait.)
E. Farber (Ed.), *Great Chemists*. 1961. (Portrait.)
I. Strube, *Justus von Liebig*. 1973.
Dictionary of Scientific Biography.

W V F

LILIENTHAL, OTTO Born at Anklam, Prussia, Germany, 24 May 1848; died Berlin, 10 August 1896. Pioneer of heavier-than-air flight.

Lilienthal's interest in flying began at the age of 13, but he served in the Franco-Prussian War and then spent ten years in industry before he was able to devote himself to his lifework. He then made a close study of bird-flight, especially that of the stork, observing the fact that the curved wing permits of horizontal flight even without any angle of incidence to the wind, and establishing the importance of rising air-currents for soaring. In 1889 he published *Der Vogelflug als Grundlage Fliegerkunst*.

In 1881, Lilienthal began gliding experiments with a winged apparatus, wire-braced and provided with a fixed vertical tail-surface, to which he attached himself by his arms, so as to get a running start; he then used his body for balancing. By 1893 his glider had a 7-metre span and a plane surface of 14 square metres, the material being a light fabric stretched on canes and the weight about 20 kilograms. In that year a photograph, showing him in flight from a 15-metre pillar, helped to create a vogue for gliding as a sport, which he did his best to stimulate. Altogether, he made more than 2500 successful flights, many of them from a steep slope at Rhinow, near Berlin.

In 1895 Lilienthal experimented with a biplane, and in 1896 with the introduction of a small motor to flap the wings. But in the summer of that year he was fatally injured, through the upper plane of his glider coming loose in the air. Otto's work was assisted and continued by his brother Gustav, who survived him by nearly forty years.

W. Schwipps, *Lilienthal*. 1966.
F. M. Feldhaus, *Isis*, **2**, 398, 1919.

T K D

LINACRE, THOMAS Born at Canterbury, Kent, England, c.1460; died London, 20 October 1524. Physician; founder of the Royal College of Physicians of London.

Following the tradition of his time, Linacre studied the classics at Oxford, where he was elected a Fellow of All Souls. He then travelled extensively in Italy, graduating in medicine at Padua. Returning to Oxford, he was summoned in 1501 to be tutor to Prince Arthur, eldest son of Henry VII. Following the Prince's death in the following year, Linacre devoted himself entirely to medicine and became the leading physician of the day, numbering Henry VIII and Cardinal Wolsey among his patients. He published extensively, including a translation of GALEN. In 1523 he was again a royal tutor, this time to the Princess Mary, later Queen of England. He recognized that an essential prerequisite to an improvement in the level of medical practice, then low, was the founding of a college that would set standards of qualification, repress unqualified practitioners, and promote the advancement of medical knowledge. With this object he worked to establish (1518) the Royal College of Physicians of London. He was elected its first President, and held this office until his death. In later life Linacre entered holy orders, and received much preferment.

> G. Wolstenholme and D. Piper (Eds), *The Royal College of Physicians of London: Portraits.* 1964. (Portrait.)
> *Dictionary of National Biography.*
> William Osler, *Thomas Linacre.* 1908.
> C. D. O'Malley, *English Medical Humanists: Thomas Linacre and John Caius.* 1965.
> *Dictionary of Scientific Biography.*

T I W

LIND, JAMES Born in Edinburgh, 4 October 1716; died Gosport, Hampshire, England, 13 July 1794. Studied scurvy, and recommended remedies for it.

At 15, Lind was apprenticed to an Edinburgh surgeon, and later became a surgeon in the Navy. He served in the West Indies, Guinea and the Mediterranean, before obtaining his MD in the University of Edinburgh (1748). He lived in the city for the next ten years. *A Treatise on the Scurvy* was published in 1754, with enlarged editions in 1757 and 1772. During his years at sea, Lind made experiments to find a remedy for scurvy, and in his book he recommended oranges and lemons, green food, onions, or lemon juice. Empirically, he found a cure that was later to be put on a logical basis with the discovery of Vitamin C.

In 1758 Lind became physician to the naval hospital at Haslar, and stayed there for the rest of his life. In 1768 he published his *Essay on Diseases incidental to Europeans in Hot Climates*, which went into six editions.

> *Dictionary of National Biography.*
> *Dictionary of Scientific Biography.*
> L. H. Roddis, *James Lind.* 1950.
> H. D. Rolleston, *Journal of the Royal Naval Medical Service*, **1**, 181. 1915/

S J R

LINDE, CARL VON Born at Berndorf, Bavaria, Germany, 11 June 1842; died Munich, 16 November 1934. Refrigeration engineer.

Linde studied engineering at Zürich Polytech-

nic, one of his teachers being R. J. E. CLAUSIUS. After a period in a locomotive works, he taught (1868) in Munich Polytechnic. From 1879 to 1892 he was director of a refrigerating firm, and took out many patents. He then returned to research in the *Technische Hochschule*, Munich, though maintaining his industrial interests. He was now mainly interested in the liquefaction of gases, especially air; in 1895 he devised a large-scale plant for making liquid air, based on the Joule-Thomson effect, which was an immediate commercial success and laid the foundation of a great industry. His later work was concerned with the economic separation of liquefied gases.

> C. von Linde, *Aus meinem Leben und meiner Arbeit.* 1916.
> *Berichte der deutschen Chemischen Gesellschaft*, **68**, 30A, 1935.
> J. H. Awbery, *Nature*, **149**, 630, 1942.
> *Dictionary of Scientific Biography.*

W V F

LINDEMANN, FREDERICK ALEXANDER (VISCOUNT CHERWELL) Born at Baden-Baden, Germany, 5 April 1886; died Oxford, England, 3 July 1957. Known for the Lindemann melting-point formula; the Nernst-Lindemann theory of specific heat; and the recovery of aircraft from spin. Personal scientific adviser to Winston Churchill during the Second World War.

Lindemann's father was an engineer who emigrated to Britain from Alsace, rather than become a German citizen after 1870; his mother was American. From preparatory school in Scotland he went to Darmstadt, and thence to work with W. H. NERNST, with whom he took his PhD in 1910; in Nernst's laboratory he first met H. T. TIZARD. A good tennis player (who later competed at Wimbledon while an Oxford professor), Lindemann was playing in a German tennis tournament in July 1914 and had to leave his first prize behind in order to return to Britain. He joined the brilliant band collected by Mervyn O'Gorman (1871–1952) at Farnborough to study problems of flight and aircraft instrumentation, along with G. P. Thomson, G. I. Tatlor, B. M. Jones, F. W. ASTON, W. S. Farren, E. D. ADRIAN and others. He learnt to fly, and experimentally tested and proved correct his theory of how to get an aircraft out of the near-fatal state of uncontrolled spin.

In 1919, backed by Tizard, he was elected as Dr Lee's Professor of Experimental Philosophy, Oxford, and became head of the Clarendon Laboratory. This he found moribund after fifty years with no research, and he had to build it up almost from scratch. Not all his attention went to the Laboratory; he was socially inclined, and met many public figures, including (1921) Winston Churchill. He found it difficult to convince Oxford of the importance of science, and particularly of physics, and to draw the best physicists to Oxford against the attraction of Ernest RUTHERFORD at Cambridge. He took the opportunity afforded by the exodus of Jewish physicists from Germany after 1933 to strengthen the Clarendon. From that time onwards it grew until at the time of his retirement it was one of the world's most important laboratories. He and Churchill, although in some ways opposites, had much in common, and they fought from 1933 onwards for British rearmament, and particularly for the application of science to air defence. Here he found himself in conflict with his friend Tizard, not so much regarding the objectives, but because there was effectively only one post at the top, and Tizard was appointed to it in circumstances that made Lindemann think he had been forestalled.

When Churchill became Prime Minister in 1940, Lindemann was his scientific adviser. Some of his advice, which covered economics as well as science, was controversial, but it was an outstanding development for a scientist to have earned such confidence that Churchill would readily act on it. He was appointed Paymaster-General in 1942. After the war, when a Labour Government was elected, he returned to Oxford, but came back as Paymaster-General when Churchill again became Prime Minister in 1951, and stayed until 1953. In this period he was the main architect of the UK Atomic Energy Authority. Churchill, when he retired in 1955, took up the campaign of Cherwell and F. E. SIMON for a UK Institute of Technology. This crystallized not in the form they envisaged, but as Churchill College, Cambridge (see J. D. COCKCROFT).

Lindemann's scientific contributions were many. Besides those already mentioned, there were the Lindemann electrometer, Lindemann glass, the Dobson-Lindemann theory of the upper atmosphere, his work on indeterminacy, on chemical kinetics, and with F. W. ASTON as early as 1919, on the separation of isotopes. While Paymaster-General he produced a new proof of the prime number theorem. He might have achieved more in science had his patience been greater, but he contributed illuminating ideas in many fields at the formative stage, and his achievements are to be found not merely in personal scientific work but in his building up of the Clarendon Laboratory and in the help that was so much appreciated by Churchill.

He was made a Privy Councillor in 1943, Companion of Honour in 1953, created Baron Cherwell in 1941, and Viscount Cherwell in 1956. He was elected FRS in 1920, and was awarded the Messel Medal in 1954 and the Hughes Medal in 1956.

R. V. Jones, *Nature*, **180**, 579, 1957.
Biographical Memoirs of Fellows of the Royal Society. 1958. (Portrait.)
R. F. Harrod, *The Prof.* 1959; *A Personal Memoir of Lord Cherwell*. 1959.
Lord Birkenhead, *The Prof. in Two Worlds*. 1961; *The Professor and the Prime Minister: The Official Life of Professor F. A. Lindemann, Viscount Cherwell*. 1962.

R V J

LINNAEUS, CARL (from 1762 **CARL VON LINNÉ**) Born at Råhult, Småland, Sweden, 23 May 1707; died Uppsala, 10 January 1778. Introduced binomial system of nomenclature for scientific naming of species of plants and animals.

The son of a clergyman, Nils Ingemarsson (1674–1748), who coined for himself the surname Linnaeus (referring to a big linden tree or 'linn' on the family property), Carl Linnaeus possessed the thrifty, tenacious, enterprising character traditionally ascribed in Sweden to natives of Småland, and this, together with the poverty of his youth and indeed of his war-impoverished country, is reflected in his numerous economically produced

works, with their concise, effective methods of biological recording and description. He was a medical student at Lund and Uppsala from 1727 to 1733, being there associated with Petrus Artedi (1705–35); he made a journey to Lapland in 1732, lived in Holland from 1735 to 1738, returned to Sweden in 1738, and practised as a physician until he became Professor of medicine and botany at Uppsala in 1741. An extraordinarily industrious and methodical naturalist, Linnaeus felt it his mission to classify, record, and name the products of the three realms of Nature, using methods devised by himself and Artedi. This he achieved in this *Systema Naturae* (1735; 10th ed., 1758–9; 12th ed., 1766–8); *Genera Plantarum* (1737; 5th ed., 1754; 6th ed., 1764); *Flora Lapponica* (1737); *Hortus Cliffortianus* (1738); *Flora Suecica* (1745; 2nd ed., 1755); *Fauna Suecica* (1746); *Species Plantarum* (1753; 2nd ed., 1762–3); and numerous dissertations reprinted or modified in his *Amoenitates Academicae* (1749–69). He explained his methods in *Critica Botanica* (1737) and *Philosophia Botanica* (1751). These are in Latin. He also published, in Swedish, accounts of his travels through Sweden, *Ölandska och Gothländska Resa* (1745); *Wästgöta-Resa* (1747); and *Skånska Resa* (1751).

Linnaeus's works gave his contemporaries the means of identifying the plants and animals then known, and thereby stimulated further collecting and exploration by his correspondents and students. His so-called 'sexual system' of classification of plants was admittedly artificial, but useful. He divided the flowering plants (angiosperms) into twenty-three classes based on the number, situation and relation of the stamens, e.g. *Monandria* with one stamen, *Diandria* with two stamens, etc., and these in turn he divided into orders based mostly on the number of styles or stigmas, e.g. *Monogynia* with one style or sessile stigma, *Digynia* with two styles or sessile stigmas, etc. Such characters sometimes separated plants closely agreeing in others. Linnaeus's major zoological divisions were *Mammalia* (headed by *Homo sapiens*), *Aves* (birds), *Amphibia* (including also reptiles), *Pisces* (fish), *Insects* (including also crustaceans), and *Vermes* (including also molluscs).

Linnaeus's works remain important today on account of their drastic reform of nomenclature. His *Species Plantarum* (1753) and *Systema Naturae* 10th ed., vol. 1 (1758), are the internationally accepted starting-points of modern botanical and zoological nomenclature respectively. Before their publication, the scientific name of an organism was essentially a concise statement in Latin of its distinguishing features, except in genera with only one species for which the generic name alone sufficed. Such a polynomial or phrase-name had thus two functions which became incompatible owing to the continual discovery of new species, i.e. to serve as a designation, for which it became too long and inconvenient, and as a diagnosis, for which it was too short to be adequate. Linnaeus's introduction of binomial nomenclature separated these two functions; under this system an organism had two complementary names, a binomial or two-word specific name, e.g. *Plantago lanceolata*, for everyday use and a descriptive polynomial of several or many words for diagnostic purposes, e.g. *Plantago* foliis lanceolatis, spica subovata nuda, scapo angulato. These diagnostic phrases served as keys and were basic to the Linnaean system. It was the association of binomials with such phrases in Linnaeus's major encylopaedic works which made evident their convenience and led to the general adoption of binomials by the time of his death. They have proved Linnaeus's most lasting contribution to biology, but were simply by-products of his work of classification and description.

At the same time Linnaeus made numerous innovations in terminology and virtually created botanical Latin as a technical language distinct from both classical and medieval Latin. Thus he provided methods of nomenclature and description which still form the basis of taxonomic work.

Linnaeus's work was of such a pioneer character and touched upon so many fields of inquiry that much of it was necessarily superficial, judged according to later standards. He himself was very egotistical, much liked by his students but opposed by many of his contemporaries, who were reluctant to adopt his classification and nomenclature. His widow sold his collections and library in 1784 to an Englishman, James Edward Smith (1759–1828) of Norwich; the Linnean Society of London purchased his botanical and zoological specimens and library from Smith's widow in 1829 and they remain in the Society's care.

K. Hagberg, *Carl Linnaeus*. 1952.
N. Gourlie, *The Prince of Botanists*. 1953.
W. T. Stearn, *An Introduction to the 'Species Plantarum' of Carl Linnaeus* (prefixed to Ray Society facsimile of *Species Plantarum*, vol. 1). 1957; *Three Prefaces on Linnaeus and Robert Brown*. 1962; *Botanical Latin*. 1966.
H. Goerke, *Carl von Linné, Arzt, Naturforscher, Systematiker*. 1966.
S. Lindroth, 'Linné, Legend och Verklighet', *Lychnos*, 56, 1965–66. (With English summary.) 1967.
T. M. Fries, *Linnaeus: The Story of His Life*. 1923.
W. Blunt, *The Compleat Naturalist: A Life of Linnaeus*. 1971.
Dictionary of Scientific Biography.
Tycho Tullberg, *Linnéporträtt*. 1907.

W T S

LINSTEAD, SIR REGINALD PATRICK Born in London, 28 August 1902; died there, 22 September 1966. Chemist; a Rector of Imperial College, London.

Linstead was educated at the City of London School and Imperial College, graduating in chemistry in 1923. Apart from a short period with the Anglo-Persian Oil Company, he remained at Imperial College until 1938, when he was appointed Firth Professor of Chemistry at Sheffield University. Shortly afterwards he was appointed professor of organic chemistry at Harvard, returning to Britain in 1942 as Deputy Director of Scientific Research, Ministry of Supply. After the war he was appointed director of the Chemical Research Laboratory, but in 1949 returned to Imperial College to succeed Sir Ian HEILBRON as professor of organic chemistry. In 1955 he became Rector of the College. He was knighted in 1959.

Linstead's chemical researches covered a wide field, but his most notable contribution was in the field of phthalocyanine dyes. Other interests were in electrochemical synthesis; high-pressure reactions; the stereochemistry of catalysis; and the pharmacology of lactones. In 1940 he was elected Fellow of the Royal Society, which he served as vice-president and Foreign Secretary.

The Times, 24 September 1966. (Portrait.)
Nature, **212**, 978, 1966.
Biographical Memoirs of Fellows of the Royal Society. 1968. (Portrait.)
Dictionary of National Biography.

T I W

LIPPMANN, GABRIEL JONAS Born at Hollerich, Luxemburg, 16 August 1845; died at sea, 13 July 1921. Inventor of a process of colour photography.

In 1868 Lippmann entered the *École Normale*, where he showed great promise as an experimentalist, but failed his examination for the *aggrégation*. He was subsequently sent to Germany to engage in research and to report on German laboratories, especially in Berlin. During a stay in Heidelberg he began researches on electrocapillarity in the laboratory of G. R. KIRCHHOFF. These he continued on his return to Paris in 1875, first at the *École Normale*, later at the Sorbonne, where he became professor of probability and mathematical physics in 1883. He was elected to the *Académie des Sciences* in 1886, and in the same year became director of Laboratories of Physical Research and professor of physics at the Sorbonne in succession to J. C. Jamin (1818–86). This position he occupied until his death. In 1898 he became a member of the *Bureau des Longitudes*. He was awarded a Nobel prize in 1908, in which year he was also elected a Foreign Member of the Royal Society.

Lippmann's researches in electrocapillarity led to the construction of his capillary-electrometer, an instrument of great sensitivity. In his lectures of 1886 he seems first to have referred to a possible process of colour photography based on the idea that light reflected from a flat plate would produce interference planes at characteristic distances from the surface depending on the frequency. In the subsequent year Lord RAYLEIGH advanced the same explanation for the coloured spectrum which had been observed by Edmond Becquerel (1820–91) in 1848. The development of a practical method of realizing this idea was fraught with many difficulties, including the production of a film of material containing no silver granules larger than the wavelength of light, and the realization of an optical contact between the film and the reflecting surface. In 1893 Lippmann finally announced the production of a perfectly orthochromatic colour photograph.

Apart from the capillary-electrometer, Lippmann constructed a number of important instruments including a perfectly astatic galvanometer, a novel type of seismograph, and the coelostat, through which it first became possible to keep a region of the sky under observation for an extended period of time. He also devoted much time to the precise measurement of various units.

Proceedings of the Royal Society, **101A**, i, 1922.
Nature, **107**, 788, 1921.
Dictionary of Scientific Biography.
Tyler Wasson (Ed.), *Nobel Prize Winners*. 1987. (Portrait.)

J W H

LISSAJOUS, JULES ANTOINE Born at Versailles, France, 4 March 1822; died Plombières-Lès-Dijon, Côte d'Or, 24 June 1880. Physicist.

Lissajous studied the transverse vibrations of elastic plates and the superimposition of two or more vibratory motions by an optical procedure in which light was reflected on to a screen via two mirrors attached to each of two bodies vibrating in perpendicular directions. The resulting Lissajous figures were found to depend on the ratio of the frequencies and the differences of the phases of the two vibrations, being closed or open depending on whether the ratio of the frequencies were rational or irrational. These figures were studied in more detail by replacing one of the mirrors with the object glass of a telescope of which the remainder was stationary. This apparatus was the basis of the so-called vibration microscope later employed by H. L. F. von HELMHOLTZ. Lissajous was also instrumental in the introduction in France of a normal A of frequency 870 half vibrations per second.

He was elected corresponding member of the *Académie des Sciences* in 1879.

Dictionary of Scientific Biography.

J W H

LISTER, JOSEPH (FIRST BARON LISTER) Born at Upton, Essex, England, 5 April 1827; died Walmer, Kent, 10 February 1912. Founder of antiseptic surgery.

Lister was the second son of Joseph Jackson Lister, FRS (1786–1869), a wine merchant who was important in the development of the microscope. The Listers were Quakers. Joseph was educated at Tottenham and at University College, London (BA, 1847). While still an Arts student he was present at Robert Liston's (1794–1847) first operation under ether anaesthesia on 21 December 1846. Lister then studied medicine at University College Hospital. He graduated, and also became FRCS, in 1852. He had decided to become a London surgeon, and in 1854 he went to Edinburgh for experience under James Syme (1799–1870), then the leading Scottish surgeon. In 1855 he became assistant surgeon to the Edinburgh Royal Infirmary, and he married Syme's eldest daughter, Agnes. In 1860 he was appointed to the Regius Chair of Surgery at Glasgow University. He succeeded Syme in the chair of clinical surgery at Edinburgh in 1869. In 1877, with a view to disseminating his methods among the apathetic London surgeons, he accepted the chair of surgery at King's College, London. He retired in 1892, by which time his methods had conquered the world and were passing into their next phase. Lister was elected in 1860 a Fellow of the Royal Society, of which he was later President (1894–1900). He became a baronet in 1883, and in 1897 he was raised to the peerage. He was an original member of the Order of Merit (1902), and he received many other honours.

Lister is universally known as the progenitor of the revolution in surgery. After the introduction of general anaesthesia in 1846 operations everywhere increased in number and in scope. But the boon of anaesthesia was offset by the scourge of sepsis, which now rapidly increased in incidence after operations, especially those performed in hospitals. No large hospital in Europe was free from 'hospital fever' or 'hospital gangrene'. The mortality after amputations for compound fractures

was in most British hospitals about 40 per cent, and in some European hospitals it was 60 per cent. This problem had long been studied by Lister, and he worked on it intensively after he went to Glasgow. It was generally held that sepsis might be caused by the entry of air to a wound, and Lister at first acted on this assumption. In 1865 his attention was directed to the demonstration by PASTEUR, that putrefaction is fermentation and that the latter is caused by the entry of 'organized corpuscles' (i.e. living micro-organisms) into the fermentable matter. Lister decided to destroy these organisms in the air and in the wound, and after many experiments he found that crude carbolic acid was a suitable antiseptic. He experimented for years to devise a satisfactory carbolic dressing.

Lister's first real test of his method was on 12 August 1865 in the treatment of a compound fracture. He obtained a perfect result, and in 1866 he had further successes. His results were published in March-July 1867, and they were so good as to constitute a revolution. His method was adopted enthusiastically in Germany and France, where equally good results were obtained. In 1871 Lister began to spray the air of the operating theatre with carbolic acid to destroy any organisms in it, but this procedure was unnecessary and was later abandoned.

Lister was as great a scientist as he was a surgeon. Soon after graduating he published an important paper on the muscles of the iris. Much of his research thereafter dealt with subjects, such as the coagulation of the blood and the early stages of inflammation, that were later to have an important bearing on his 'antiseptic principle'. He was one of the early pioneers of bacteriology, and he was the first scientist ever to grow a micro-organism in pure culture. The last phase of his complex researches dealt mainly with his attempts to prepare satisfactory sterile ligatures.

R. J. Godlee, *Lord Lister* (3rd ed.), 1924. (Portrait.)
D. Guthrie, *Lord Lister*. 1949.
K. Walker, *Joseph Lister*. 1956.
A. L. Turner (Ed.), *Joseph, Lord Lister, Centenary Volume. 1827–1927.*
Dictionary of National Biography.
Dictionary of Scientific Biography.
Proceedings of the Royal Society, **86B**, i, 1912–13.

E A U

LISTER, SAMUEL CUNLIFFE (FIRST BARON MASHAM) Born at Calverly Hall, Bradford, Yorkshire, England, 1 January 1815; died Swinton Park, Yorkshire, 2 February 1906. Invented very successful wool-combing and waste-silk spinning machines.

Lister started work with Liverpool merchants, Turner & Co., who sent him many times to America. In 1837 his father built for him and his brother a worsted mill at Manningham, where Samuel invented a swivel shuttle and a machine for making fringes of shawls. Four years later he turned his attention to wool-combing and developed the Lister-Cartwright 'square nip' comber, but became involved in a dispute with his associate, Isaac Holden (1807–97), over patents. Lister won and made a fortune, and began to open markets in France, where he became involved with Josué Heilmann over patent rights. Lister bought up the Heilmann machine, and afterwards other types, until he obtained a complete monopoly of combing machines before the patents expired. His invention stimulated demand for wool by cheapening the product and gave a vital boost to the Australian wool trade.

Other ideas included a velvet loom; compressed air brakes for railways; and, in 1853 alone, twelve patents for various textile machines. Then he tried to spin waste silk. After Lister lost £250,000 and was deserted by his partner, his machine caught on and brought him another fortune. In later years he had an annual profit from his mills of £250,000, much of which was presented to Bradford city in gifts such as Lister Park. In 1891 he was made First Baron Masham, and afterwards became Deputy Lieutenant in the North and West Ridings and then High Sheriff of Yorkshire.

S. L. Lister (Lord Masham), *Lord Masham's Inventions*. 1905. (Portrait.)

E. M. Sigsworth, *Black Dyke Mills*. 1958.

Dictionary of National Biography.

R L H

LITTLE, ARTHUR DEHON Born at Boston, Massachusetts, USA, 15 December 1863; died North East Harbor, Maine, 1 August 1935. Consulting chemist significant for idea of unit operations.

Little, a pioneer in the promotion of American industrial science, studied chemistry at the Massachusetts Institute of Technology (MIT), where he founded the alumni journal, *Technology Review*, the forerunner of *Chemical Abstracts*. Between 1884 and 1886 he was works chemist at a paper mill at Rumford, RI, where he became an authority on the sulphite paper bleaching process and began the preparation of a monograph, *The Chemistry of Paper Making* (1894), with R. B. Griffin. In 1886 he founded a consultancy in Boston which undertook analysis, plant construction design, and the technical appraisal of processes and products. By 1909, Arthur D. Little Inc. was the largest private chemical research firm in America. Little's abiding interest was in the chemistry of cellulose. By the 1920s, however, he foresaw the significance of a new industrial chemistry based upon petroleum rather than on wood and coal, and he also turned his laboratory's attention to food research.

In 1915, in an important report on MIT's teaching of chemical engineering, Little adopted the views of the English chemist, George Davies (1850–1907), that the subject concerned 'unit operations' – fermentation, distillation, drying, etc. – rather than specific industrial processes like the manufacture of sulphuric acid or alcohol. Little urged that chemical plants should be seen as a series of operations that could be improved and taught independently. Much in demand as a lecturer, Little became the prophet of commercial and industrial progress through chemistry, summed up in DuPont's advertising slogan, 'Better Living Through Chemistry'. He was President of the American Chemical Society (1912–14) and of the Society of Chemical Industry (1928–29).

A. D. Little (Ed.), *The Handwriting on the Wall*. 1928.

W. D. Miles, *American Chemists and Chemical Engineers*. 1976.

Dictionary of American Biography, Supplement I. (1944).

E. Farber (Ed.), *Great Chemists*. 1961. (Portrait.)

Journal of the Society of Chemical Industry, Special Jubilee Number, July 1931. (Portrait.)

W H B

LOBACHEVSKI, NIKOLA IVANOVICH Born at Nizhni-Novgorod, Russia, 2 December 1792; died Kazan, 24 February 1856. A discoverer of non-Euclidean geometry.

Lobachevski's father died when he was six, and his mother, left in straitened circumstances, took the family to Kazan. He there attended the newly founded university, graduating in 1813. He was taught by J. M. C. Bartels (1769–1836), a friend and teacher of K. F. GAUSS. He became assistant professor (1814), extraordinary professor (1816), and ordinary professor of mathematics (1823), which position he held until falling into disfavour in 1846. In 1855, a year before his death, when he was blind, he dictated and had published, in French and Russian, a complete exposition of the system of non-Euclidean geometry which, earlier had been generally ignored.

As early as 1815, Lobachevski was attempting a proof of the parallel postulate of EUCLID, and he incorporated some attempted proofs in his lectures for 1813–17. By 1823 he was convinced of the futility of his attempts, and by 1826 he had developed, quite independently of J. BOLYAI, one of the non-Euclidean alternative geometries (i.e. the hyperbolic). The basic concept peculiar to his geometry is that of angle of parallelism. His approach is more analytical than Bolyai's, and he is more concerned with deducing the formulae of the new plane and spherical trigonometries than with the deductive system as such. His theory involves implicitly the space-curvature concept, and he might be regarded as a pioneer of non-Euclidean cosmology to the extent that he discussed in detail, and quantitatively, the sort of astronomical results one might expect in his non-Euclidean space.

F. Engel, *N. I. Lobatchewsky*. 1899.

E. T. Bell, *Men of Mathematics*, vol. 2. 1937.

R. Bonola, *Non-Euclidean Geometry: A Critical and Historical Study of its Development*. 1955.

Dictionary of Scientific Biography.

J D N

LOCKE, JOHN Born at Wrington, Somerset, England, 29 August 1632; died High Laver, Essex, 28 October 1704. Philosopher.

Locke was the son of a Puritan country lawyer, and was educated at Westminster School and Christ Church, Oxford. Although his interests were primarily philosophic, he was associated with Robert BOYLE in some of his experiments, and to some extent practised as a doctor; thus he operated on Lord Shaftesbury in 1668, the year of his election to the Royal Society. As Shaftesbury's confidential secretary he came to play an important part in Whig politics – advising in science and politics – with intervals of escape to France and Holland; he finally returned to England in February 1689 in the entourage of Queen Mary.

Locke's philosophy is contained in three main works, reflecting the thought and experience of many years, but all of them published in 1689–90. The *Letter on Toleration* and the *Two Treatises of Government* had mainly political applications, whereas the stated purpose of the great *Essay Con-*

cerning Human Understanding was no less than 'to inquire into the origin, certainty, and extent of human knowledge, together with the grounds and degrees of belief, opinion and assent'. He was the first modern writer to treat the phenomena of the human mind as a subject of fully independent study, and his conclusion that all our knowledge is derived from experience became the starting-point for other philosophers.

Locke's later writings included an influential work on education, papers on economic questions, and a commentary on some of St Paul's Epistles. William III was anxious to employ him extensively in public affairs, but his always poor health became rapidly worse and he preferred to remain at the country seat of friends in Essex.

M. Cranston, *Life of John Locke.* 1957.

K. Dewhurst, *John Locke (1632–1704).* 1963.

Isis, **18**, 439, 1933.

Dictionary of Scientific Biography.

Dictionary of National Biography.

R. I. Anson, *John Locke.* (3rd ed.), 1971.

J. D. Mabbott, *John Locke.* 1973.

T K D

LOCKYER, SIR JOSEPH NORMAN Born at Rugby, Warwickshire, England, 17 May 1836; died Salcombe Regis, Devon, 16 August 1920. Pioneer of astrophysics.

Norman Lockyer was the son of a surgeon-apothecary. After a conventional schooling he became a clerk in the War Office. In 1861 he married and settled at Wimbledon, becoming a keen amateur scientist. His first important discovery concerned the darkening of sunspots. Locyker studied these with the aid of a spectroscope attached to his telescope and showed that the absence of bright emission lines proved the darkening to be due to increased absorption and not to the weakness of light from the Sun's interior.

In October 1868 he began observation with a high-dispersion spectroscope. The line spectra he saw, which proved the prominences to be gaseous, had been observed in India, unknown to Lockyer, two months earlier by the French astronomer P. J. C. JANSSEN. Both found the forms of the prominences to be slowly changing.

Still at the War Office, Lockyer joined forces with the chemist Edward FRANKLAND. Unable to find a certain hydrogen line in the chromosphere, they concluded, after much laboratory work, that this was due to the low pressure of the chromosphere, together with the widening of such lines due mainly, if not entirely, to pressure. Because of the smallness of the deduced pressure, the reality of the corona of the Sun was called into question, and for many years Lockyer was involved in controversy.

By 1869 he was applying the principle enumerated by C. J. DOPPLER to the gases within sunspots. The high velocities he found in them led him to speculate on the movements of gases, and heat transfer, in the Sun.

One of Lockyer's greatest achievements, but one which was too much in advance of his time to be very influential, was his dissociation hypothesis. Perplexed by the absence of certain metallic absorption lines in the solar spectrum, in 1873, he suggested that, under appropriate conditions of temperature and pressure, elements may be split up into simpler constituents with unrecognizable spectra. This idea may be regarded as anticipating the electron theory.

Lockyer, early in his career, found spectroscopic evidence for a new element, which he named 'helium'. The discovery of terrestrial helium was made in 1895 by Sir William RAMSAY.

Lockyer had many other results to his credit. His ingenious star classification, involving a division of the spectral sequence into two, was ahead of its time, and of some influence. His 'meteoritic hypothesis', according to which meteorites are the building-blocks of the Universe, was less successful. He was probably the first to notice the correlation of weather conditions with the eleven-year sunspot cycle. He is remembered for the foundation of the prestigious journal *Nature*.

Nature, **106**, 20, 1920.

T. M. and W. L. Lockyer, *Life and Work of Sir Norman Lockyer.* 1928. (Portrait.)

A. J. Meadows, *Science and Controversy: a Biography of Sir Norman Lockyer.* 1972.

Proceedings of the Royal Society, **104A**, i, 1923. (Portrait.)

Dictionary of Scientific Biography.

J D N

LODGE, SIR OLIVER JOSEPH Born at Penkhull, Staffordshire, England, 12 June 1851; died Lake, near Salisbury, Wiltshire, 22 August 1940. Chiefly remembered for his investigations into the propagation of electromagnetic waves.

Lodge was descended on both sides from families remarkable for both learning and fertility, his two brothers distinguishing themselves intellectually, and his father being the twenty-third of a family of twenty-five. He went first to the grammar school at Newport Shropshire, leaving at 14 to enter his father's business of potter's merchant. In 1873 he entered University College, London, where he graduated BSc in 1875 and DSc in 1877. In 1881 he became professor of physics and mathematics at Liverpool. He was elected FRS in 1887 and in 1900 he became the first president of Birmingham University. He was knighted in 1902 and was president of the British Association, which was long an integral part of his life, 1913–14.

Lodge's first paper (1875) was on the shape of equipotential lines and of the lines of flow between two electrodes on a conducting surface. At the same period he wrote a series of papers on thermal conductivity and also provided a modification of H. Mance's method for measuring the resistance of a battery. Inspired by reading *Electricity and Magnetism* by J. Clerk MAXWELL, he then commenced investigations into the propagation of electromagnetic waves in wires, determining their wavelengths in experiments described to the Physical Society in 1888. On learning of the discovery of H. R. HERTZ, he devised a coherer for the detection of the so-called Hertzian waves. He gave a full demonstration of the physical properties of Hertzian waves in 1894, and at the Oxford meeting of the British Association in August of the same year showed that these waves could be used for telegraphic signalling in the Morse code. His patent of 1897, with its insistence on an increased inductance to combat the heavy damping of the Hertzian oscillator, played a vital part in the realization of spark-telegraphy. In 1898 he was awarded the

Rumford Medal of the Royal Society for his researches into electromagnetic waves. Lodge also investigated the dispersal of dust and smoke by electrostatic discharges, and following the experiment of A. A. MICHELSON and E. W. MORLEY he proved the absence of any detectable effect on light passing in the vicinity of a rapidly rotating wheel.

Apart from science, he devoted much time to the investigation of psychical phenomena.

O. J. Lodge, *Past Years*. 1931.

Obituary Notices of Fellows of the Royal Society. 1941. (Portrait.)

Nature, **146**, 327, 1940.

Dictionary of National Biography.

                                                                    J W H

LOEWI, OTTO

LOEWI, OTTO Born at Frankfurt-am-Main, Germany, 3 June 1873; died New York, 25 December 1961. Pharmacologist and physiologist chiefly remembered for his work on the chemical nature of nerve impulse transmission.

Loewi studied at Strasbourg, Munich, Marburg and Vienna and received an excellent training in pharmacology. In 1909 he was appointed professor of this new subject in the University of Graz. Here he remained until the Nazi occupation of Austria in 1938, when he fled to Britain and then to the United States, where he held a post in the Department of Pharmacology at New York University College of Medicine until his death.

He began his work on neurochemical transmission in 1921. It was then known that an electrical component was associated with the passage of the nervous impulse across the gap at the myo-neural junction, but in addition the work of T. R. Elliott (1877–1961), Henry H. DALE and others suggested that in the case of the autonomic nervous system a chemical transmitter such as acetyl choline was also active. Working on an inspiration which occurred to him during sleep, Loewi carried out simple tests which proved experimentally for the first time that a chemical substance was produced at the myo-neural junction. He was able to show that the perfusate of a vagally stimulated heart contained a substance he at first termed *Vagustoff (Pflüger's Archiv für die gesamte Physiologie des Menschen und der Tiere* (1921) and subsequent articles in this journal). This he eventually identified as acetyl choline, the parasympathetic neurochemical mediator.

Otto Loewi was a pioneer in what is now an ever-expanding field of research and his contribution was given recognition in 1936, when he shared a Nobel prize in physiology or medicine with Sir Henry Dale. His work in the biochemistry of metabolism and diabetes and in endocrine function was of less merit.

O. Loewi, in *Perspectives in Biology and Medicine*, **4**, 3, 1961.

Biographical Memoirs of Fellows of the Royal Society. 1962. (Portrait.)

F. Lembeck and W. Giere, *Otto Loewi: ein Lebensbild in Dokumenten*. 1968. (Portrait.)

W. Haymaker and F. Schiller (Eds), *The Founders of Neurology*. 1970.

Dictionary of Scientific Biography. (Portrait.)

Tyler Wasson (Ed.), *Nobel Prize Winners*. 1987. (Portrait.)

                                                                    E C

LOMONOSOV, MIKHAIL VASIL'EVICH

LOMONOSOV, MIKHAIL VASIL'EVICH Born at Mishaninskaya, Archangel Province, Russia, 8 November 1711; died St Petersburg, 4 April 1765. Russian scientist and polymath.

Lomonosov came from a part of Russia that had escaped Tartar domination, and was less feudal and more European-minded than the south. His father was a fisherman and merchant, and he was educated in Moscow for the priesthood. He showed such promise, however, that in 1736 he was sent to the University of St Petersburg; his studies later took him to Marburg and Freiburg before he returned to Russia in 1741. In 1745 he became professor of chemistry, and in 1757 chancellor, in the St Petersburg Academy of Sciences. He played a leading part in the foundation of Moscow University (1755).

He did much to create a literary Russian language; was a competent (though dull) poet; and wrote a controversial *Ancient History of Russia* (1766). Besides lecturing in the Academy on chemistry and other sciences, he built and managed a glass factory, and established the first chemical laboratory in Russia. He was interested also in theories of colour. He is most often remembered for his development of Newtonian atomism, notably in his tacit use of the principle of conservation of mass, and his formulation of a kinetic theory of gases similar to that D. BERNOULLI. Unfortunately, in spite of his great talents, he was little known outside Russia; and even at home his quarrelsome disposition (he was once imprisoned for slander) and dissolute life made him many enemies.

B. N. Menshutkin, *Russia's Lomonosov*. 1952. (Portrait.)

P. L. Kapitska, *Soviet Physics Uspekhi*, **8**, 720, 1926. (In English.)

H. M. Leicester, *Mikhail Vasil'evich Lomonosov on the Corpuscular Theory*. 1970.

Dictionary of Scientific Biography.

                                                                    W V F

LONSDALE, DAME KATHLEEN

LONSDALE, (*née* **YARDLEY**), **DAME KATHLEEN** Born in Newbridge, Ireland, 28 January 1903; died London, 1 April 1971. X-ray crystallographer.

Kathleen Yardley was the daughter of a postmaster. At the age of sixteen she entered Bedford College for Women, and came top in the London University BSc examinations in physics in 1922 with the highest marks for ten years. She was invited by Sir W. H. BRAGG, one of the examiners, to join his research team at University College, London, where he was developing x-ray crystallography. She moved with Bragg to the Davy-Faraday laboratory at the Royal Institution in 1923, and there, with W. T. ASTBURY she worked out the 230 space-group tables, which appeared in the *Philosophical Transactions* of the Royal Society in 1924. In 1927 she married Dr. T. J. Lonsdale of the Silk Research Association, and moved to Leeds for three years. They had three children. While in Leeds she worked out the crystal structure of hexamethylbenzene. She returned to Bragg at the Royal Institution in 1931, developing his methods for discovering the structure of molecules using x-ray diffraction of crystals. In 1931 she solved the structure of hexachlorobenzene. She worked with Bragg until his death in 1942 and after that with Sir Henry DALE until her appointment as reader in crystallography at University College in 1946. From 1946 until 1968 she was professor of chemistry at University College and head of the crystallography department. In 1948 she published *Crystals and X-rays*, and was also general editor of the *International Tables for X-ray Crystallography*.

Kathleen Lonsdale had become a Quaker in 1935, and she spent one month in Holloway Gaol in 1943 for refusing to register for civil defence or pay the fine imposed. After the war she devoted much of her time to writing and lecturing on pacifism and the moral responsibilities of scientists. *Is Peace Possible?* appeared in 1957.

In 1945 she was one of the first two women to be elected Fellows of the Royal Society. She was awarded the Davy medal of the Society in 1957, and was elected President of the British Association for the Advancement of Science in 1968. She became DBE in 1956.

Biographical Memoirs of Fellows of the Royal Society. 1975. (Portrait.)

P. P. Ewald (Ed.), *Fifty Years of X-Ray Diffraction.* 1962.

Dictionary of National Biography.

W. A. Campbell and N. N. Greenwood (Eds), *Contemporary British Chemists.* 1971 (Portrait.)

A P B

LORENTZ, HENDRIK ANTOON Born at Arnhem, Netherlands, 18 July 1853; died Haarlem, Netherlands, 4 February 1928. Made major contributions to electromagnetic theory.

On completing his early education in Arnhem, Lorentz went at the age of 17 to the University of Leiden, returning two years later as a teacher to Arnhem, where he studied alone for his doctorate. His brilliant thesis on *The Theory of Reflection and Refraction of Light* won him the chair of theoretical physics at Leiden at the early age of 24. He occupied this position till 1912, when he moved to Haarlem as director of the Teyler Institute. Awarded the Nobel prize for physics with P. ZEEMAN in 1902, he was made a Foreign Member of the Royal Society in 1905 and received its Copley Medal in 1918.

In his thesis, Lorentz elucidated the correct boundary conditions to be imposed on the equations of J.Clerk MAXWELL at a surface of discontinuity between two materials. He next turned to other defects in the theory of Maxwell, including its lack of a dispersion formula and inability to predict the formula experimentally observed by A. J. FRESNEL for the convection of light in moving media. Lorentz solved these and other problems through his famous Electron Theory (first memoir 1892) in which a medium susceptible to electric or magnetic fields was regarded as made up of electrons embedded in an ether which was the seat of an electromagnetic field obeying Maxwell's equations together with an additional formula for the pondero-motive force exerted by the field on an electron. The form chosen by Lorentz for this force was a natural extension of the known behaviour of charges and currents in electrostatic and magnetic fields, and agreed with that proposed independently by O. HEAVISIDE in 1889. An averaging process then led to macroscopic equations in which the current term included, besides the induction and convection currents, two additional terms, one

corresponding to Maxwell's displacement current, the other a modification of an additional current term which had previously been introduced by H. R. HERTZ. Experiment later confirmed the correctness of Lorentz's form of this term as opposed to that of Hertz.

From his equation Lorentz derived a 'convection' formula agreeing with that of Fresnel to the first order of the ratio of the velocity of the medium to that of light. He also derived the classical formula for dispersion. But his formulae as they stood could not account for the null result of the Michelson-Morley experiment (see A. A. MICHELSON and E. W. MORLEY). Lorentz's attempts to overcome this difficulty then led, in conjunction with the so-called Lorentz-Fitzgerald contraction (see G. F. FITZGERALD) and the notion of local time, to the Lorentz transformation. This brought him (in company with J. H. POINCARÉ and others) to the very threshold of the theory of relativity. But he never ventured beyond, and in particular he could never accept the full implications of the revolutionary view of space and time put forward by EINSTEIN.

On the discovery of the long-sought-for effect of a powerful magnetic field on spectral lines by Zeeman in 1896, Lorentz immediately applied his theory to give an elegant explanation of this effect. One of the greatest theoretical physicists of the late nineteenth and early twentieth century, Lorentz also played a leading part in international symposia and conferences where his clarity of thought and great natural charm joined with his remarkable mastery of foreign languages to make him the inevitable choice for chairman.

A. Einstein, *H. A. Lorentz, als Schöpfer und als Persönlichkeit.* 1953. (Portrait (with Einstein).)

M. Planck, *Die Naturwissenschaften*, **16**, 549, 1928.

Proceedings of the Royal Society, **121**, xx, 1928.

W. H. Bragg *et al.*, *Nature*, **121**, 287, 1928.

G. L. de Haas-Lorentz (Ed.) *H. A. Lorentz: Impressions of His Life and Work.* 1957.

Dictionary of Scientific Biography.

J W H

LORENZ, KONRAD ZACHARIAS Born in Vienna, 7 November 1903; died there, 27 February 1989. A founder of modern ethology.

The son of a famous Viennese orthopaedic surgeon, Lorenz, after leaving the high school in Vienna, studied medicine at Columbia University, New York, 1922–3, and then at the University of Vienna, graduating in 1928. Turning to zoology, he was awarded a DPhil. in 1933 for a thesis on bird flight. It was at this time that he came under the influence of Oskar Heinroth (1871–1945) and became interested in the relationship between animal and human psychology. In 1936 he met Niko TINBERGEN. Their work established modern ethology, bringing biological perspectives to bear on animal behaviour. Lorenz was particularly interested in studying instinctive behaviour patterns.

It was during the 1930s and early 1940s that his most important discoveries were made. Through his observations of greylag geese he first drew attention, in 1935, to the phenomenon of imprinting. In 1940 Lorenz was appointed to the chair of general psychology at the Albertus University in Königsberg, but he was drafted into the army as a doctor in 1941 and sent first to Poland and later to the Eastern front. Captured during the battle of Vitebsk in 1944, he spent four years in a prison-of-war camp before returning to Austria in 1948. Supported by the Max Plank Institute in Göttingen, Lorenz worked at home in Altenberg for three years, and then in 1951 established a comparative ethology department in the Max Plank Institute in Buldern. In 1955 the Max Plank Institute for Research into Animal Behaviour was founded at Seewiesen in Bavaria, and Lorenz was director from 1961 until his retirement in 1973. In 1973 he became director of the department of animal sociology at the Austrian Academy of Sciences Institute for Comparative Ethology based in Altenberg and in the valley of Alm.

As well as scientific papers, Lorenz wrote popular works including *King Solomon's Ring* (1952) and *On Aggression* (1966). He was elected a Foreign Member of the Royal Society in 1964. In 1973 he was awarded the Nobel prize for physiology or medicine jointly with Tinbergen and K. von FRISCH for his discoveries concerning the organization of individual and social behaviour patterns.

R. Harré (Ed.), *Scientific Thought 1900–1960.* 1969.

A. Nisbett, *Konrad Lorenz.* 1976. (Portrait.)

R. I. Evans (Ed.), *Konrad Lorenz: The Man and His Ideas.* 1975

Biographical Memoirs of Fellows of the Royal Society. 1992. (Portrait.)

A P B

LOWELL, PERCIVAL Born at Boston, Massachusetts, USA, 13 March 1855; died Flagstaff, Arizona, 12 November 1916. Carried out detailed observations of the solar system, especially of Mars.

After graduating from Harvard (1876), Lowell devoted many years to travel and business. The announcement of the existence of 'canali' on Mars by F. SCHIAPARELLI stimulated Lowell's interest in astronomy, and he determined to build a planetary observatory in the best possible atmospheric conditions. This he did above the town of Flagstaff, Arizona, at an altitude of 7200 feet. Starting with an 18-inch refractor (1894) and later using a 24-inch, he concentrated on Mars. He took the first good photograph of that planet in 1907, and sent an expedition to Chile to observe it at the zenith. Lowell greatly increased the number of charted 'canals'. From his observations, many of which are now thought to have involved wishful thinking, he concluded that the canals were indeed artificial, and designed to utilize the water resources of the planet.

Observations of the other planets and their satellites provided new and reliable values for their diameters, degree of oblateness, and rotation periods. He found new divisions in Saturn's rings. His observatory became an important centre, first for the study of the solar system, and later for the spectroscopic study of clusters and nebulae.

In later years Lowell interested himself in the problem of a trans-Neptunian planet, and correctly predicted the position of 'Planet X' (later known as Pluto), which was discovered, after many vicissitudes, on 12 March 1930 at his observatory.

Lowell was a popular lecturer and author. He was made a professor of astronomy at the Massachusetts Institute of Technology in 1902.

Percival Lowell (published by the Lowell Observatory). 1917. (Portrait.)

A. L. Lowell, *Biography of Percival Lowell.* 1935.

L. Leonard, *Percival Lowell: An Afterglow.* 1921.

Dictionary of Scientific Biography.

J D N

LOWER, RICHARD Born at Tremeer, near Bodmin, Cornwall, England, in 1631 (baptized 29 January 1632); died London, 17 January 1691. Physician, anatomist, physiologist and a pioneer of blood transfusion.

Lower was educated at Westminster School, and then entered Christ Church, Oxford (1649). He graduated BA (1653) and MA (1655), and then studied medicine. He was a good dissector, and he did many of the dissections for his teacher, Thomas WILLIS, which the latter acknowledged in his *Cerebri anatome* (1664). He graduated MB and MD in 1665. In 1666 Willis removed to London, and Lower followed him almost at once. He soon acquired a good practice. In 1667 he was elected a Fellow of the Royal Society. He was elected a Fellow of the Royal College of Physicians in 1675. In that year Willis died, and Lower acquired much of his practice. However, in 1678, on the occasion of the Titus Oates Plot, he supported the Whig cause and as a result lost much of his practice at court.

Lower's first important experiment was carried out at Oxford. In the infant Royal Society there had been discussion of the experiments of Sir Christopher WREN, who had injected various intoxicating or purging fluids into the veins of animals (1657), and suggestions were now made for the transfusion of blood from one animal to another. Lower had practised such experiments with fluids, and in February 1666 he successfully demonstrated at Oxford the direct transfusion of blood from an artery of one dog into a vein of another. Lower reported his experiments to Robert BOYLE, and they were published in the *Philosophical Transactions* in December 1666. This was the first successful direct transfusion from artery to vein. Suggestions were made that direct transfusion from an animal to man should be tried, but these trials were not done at the time. Meantime, Jean Denys (1625?–1704), a professor at Montpellier, had read of Lower's success, and in June 1667 he transfused a patient with blood direct from a lamb. Thereafter he transfused several other persons. In November 1667 Lower successfully performed the first animal-to-man transfusion in England. One of Denys's patients died later, and as a result of the subsequent legal action the progress of transfusion was held up for 150 years.

Lower's most important publication was his *Tractatus de corde* ('Treatise on the heart', 1669). In this he gave an excellent account of the structure of the heart, emphasizing that its action depended upon its properties as a muscle. He demonstrated that the action of a muscle is not produced by its inflation by 'spirits'. He noted that systole constitutes the active movement of the heart, and that diastole is simply a return to its previous condition. He also reported his experiment of injecting venous blood into insufflated lungs, and noting that the blood which issued was bright red in colour. From this he concluded that the red colour is due to the blood mixing with inspired air. In this work he also reported his experiments on transfusion.

In a work of 1680 Lower demonstrated that the nasal secretion does not arise in the pituitary body. This old Galenic belief had been disproved by C. V. Schneider (1610–80) in 1662, but when Lower wrote it was still widely held.

W. Munk, *Roll of the Royal College of Physicians.* 1878.

F. Gotch, *Two Oxford Physiologists.* 1907.

R. T. Gunther and K. J. Franklin, *Early Science in Oxford*, vol. 9. 1932.

G. Keynes (Ed.), *Blood Transfusion.* 1949.

A. J. Larner, *Endeavour* (New Series), **11**, 205, 1987. (Portrait.)

Dictionary of National Biography.

Dictionary of Scientific Biography.

E A U

LOWRY, THOMAS MARTIN Born at Low Moor, Bradford, Yorkshire, England, 26 October 1874; died Cambridge, 2 November 1936. Chemist, noted for studies of optical rotation.

Lowry, son of an army chaplain, was educated in London at the Central Technical College, South Kensington, and worked as assistant to H. E. ARMSTRONG from 1896 to 1913. He then became head of the Chemistry Department at Guy's Hospital (1913–20), but spent much of this period on wartime duties, being Director of Shell Filling for two years. In 1920 he was appointed first professor of physical chemistry at Cambridge, and held this post until his death. He was married, and left three children. Among other honours, he was elected FRS in 1914.

Most of Lowry's work was in the field of optical rotation, and he confirmed experimentally an equation relating optical rotatory power with wavelength which had been derived theoretically by P. K. L. Drude (1863–1906). He also demonstrated optical activity in a telluronium salt, and did much to clarify the confusing chemistry of the sulphur chlorides. A generalized concept of acids and bases was published simultaneously with that of J. N. BRØNSTED in 1923.

His *Historical Introduction to Chemistry* is a well-known work.

Journal of the Chemical Society, 701, 1937.

A. Findlay and W. H. Mills, *British Chemists.* 1947. (Portrait.)

Dictionary of National Biography.

Obituary Notices of Fellows of the Royal Society. 1938. (Portrait.)

W V F

LUCRETIUS (TITUS LUCRETIUS CARUS) Born *c.*95 BC; died 55 BC. Poet; disciple of EPICURUS, and author of the poem *De rerum natura* ('On the nature of things') a defence of the Epicurean philosophy.

Of the six Books into which *De rerum natura* is divided, the first describes the Epicurean Universe of eternally subsisting atoms moving in an infinite void. Book II deals first with the motions of atoms; then with their various shapes and sizes as determining the 'secondary qualities' (colour, heat, sound, taste, smell) that we perceive in bodies; the world we know is transient and one of an infinite

number. Book III establishes the atomic constitution of the soul and the mortality that it shares with the body, denying a future life and dismissing the fear of death. Book IV treats of the mechanisms of sensation, thought, and sex. Book V makes crude application of evolutionary ideas to explain the formation of the visible world, the emergence of life, the establishment of plants and animals fitted to survive, the ascent of man, the growth of social institutions, the progress of technology. Book VI discusses the causation of various geophysical phenomena such as lightning, clouds and rain, volcanoes and hot springs, magnetic attraction and repulsion (though not direction-finding). The poem closes with a lurid account of a plague at Athens.

Little is known with certainty about the life of Lucretius. He was bitterly anti-religious, and this militated against the early revival of his ideas. When P. GASSENDI defended a Christianized atomism in the mid-seventeenth century he referred back directly to Lucretius.

H. A. J. Munro (Ed.), *T. Lucreti Cari de rerum natura libri sex* (4th ed. 3 vols). 1886, 1928. (Vol. 2 contains an introduction on the *Scientific Significance of Lucretius*, by E. N. da C. Andrade.)

C. Bailey, *The Greek Atomists and Epicurus.* 1928. (Reprint 1964.)

Dictionary of Scientific Biography.

A A

LUDWIG, KARL FRIEDRICH WILHELM Born at Witzenhausen, Hessen, Germany, 29 December 1816; died Leipzig, 23 April 1895. Distinguished physiologist; introduced the graphic method in physiology and advanced our knowledge of the circulation.

Ludwig studied in the Universities of Marburg and Erlangen, and obtained his doctorate at Marburg in 1839. After a period in the anatomical institute there he was officially recognized as a lecturer in physiology in 1842 and made associate professor of comparative anatomy in 1846. In 1849 he was called to the chair of anatomy and physiology at Zürich, and in 1855 to the chair of physiology and zoology at Vienna. In 1865 he was appointed to the chair of physiology at Leipzig. Here he established his famous Institute of Physiology, in which he trained students of many nations. Ludwig ranks with Johannes MÜLLER as the most catalytic influence in physiology in the nineteenth century, and many authorities have regarded him as the greatest of all teachers of the subject. Apart from his great textbook and a few fundamental contributions, he published little under his own name. Nearly every one of his innumerable researches was published under the name of the pupil to whom he had assigned the problem, although Ludwig had not only planned the research, but had also helped to carry it out and written most of the thesis or paper himself. Ludwig was elected a Foreign Member of the Royal Society in 1875 and was awarded its Copley Medal in 1884.

In 1843–4 Ludwig put forward his filtration theory of the secretion of urine. As a result of further work he later modified this theory to the extent that the secretion was regarded as a process of osmosis through a selective semipermeable membrane. In 1847 he revolutionized research on respiration and the circulation by his invention of the kymograph for recording graphically the movement of organs. He was the creator of the graphic method in physiology. Twenty years later he invented the *Stromuhr* for measuring the amount of blood passing through a vessel in unit time. In the same category was his invention of the blood-pump for the sampling of the gases in blood. In his pre-Leipzig period Ludwig discovered the ganglion cells in the interventricular septum of the heart. In 1851 he found the secretory nerves to the submaxillary gland in the lingual branch of the fifth nerve, and in 1856 he showed the secretory activity of the sympathetic. His inaugural address at Leipzig introduced the method of keeping alive excised portions of the organism by perfusing them. At Leipzig he discovered the depressor nerve, and he was the first to localize a vasomotor centre. He and his pupils made during this period many discoveries regarding the circulation. The two volumes of his famous textbook were first published in 1852–6.

J. B. Sanderson, *Proceedings of the Royal Society*, **59B**, i, 1895.

E. DuBois Reymond and P. Diepgen, *Zwei grosse Naturforscher*. 1927.

A. Castiglioni, *History of Medicine*. 1947. (Portrait.)

W. Stirling, *Science Progress*, **4**, 155, 1895.

Dictionary of Scientific Biography.

E A U

LUMIÈRE, AUGUSTE AND LOUIS

Auguste was born at Besançon, France, 19 October 1862; died Lyons, 10 April 1954. Louis was born at Besançon 5 October 1864; died Bandol, France, 6 June 1948. Pioneers of cinematography and colour photography.

The Lumière brothers expanded the dry-plate factory founded at Lyons by their father Antoine in 1882 to the manufacture of photographic paper and roll film (1887). They worked as a team, and contributed several hundred papers on chemical, scientific and photographic investigations. From this multifarious work only the two most important activities can be singled out.

The Lumières constructed in 1895 the first satisfactory cine-camera and projector, and publicly showed a number of motion films, each of several minutes' duration, in June of that year. The design of their *cinématographe*, incorporating an intermittent claw movement with perforated 35 mm film (of their own manufacture) is followed in nearly all modern cine apparatus. The first public cinema performance to a paying audience was given on 28 December 1895 in the Grand Café at 14 Boulevard des Capucines, Paris. Public demonstrations in other European capitals and overseas followed in 1896. At the International Exhibition, Paris, 1900, the brothers introduced the Photorama, a 360-degree panoramic projection device. In February 1935 they presented a stereo-cine process based on the anaglyphic principle.

In 1904, the Lumières patented Autochrome colour plates, coated with starch grains dyed green, red and blue to act as a colour screen, resulting in a transparency composed of small specks of primary colours giving the effect of mixed colours. The Autochrome process, commercially introduced in 1907 after good panchromatic emulsion became available, was the first commercially successful direct colour process.

Auguste was also active in the field of biology. He founded the Clinique Auguste Lumière, and devoted much of his later life to work in the physiological laboratory.

Auguste and Louis Lumière, *Résumé des travaux scientifiques 1887–1914*. 1914.

Bessy and Lo Duca, *Auguste and Louis Lumière*. 1948. (Portraits.)

G. Sadoul, *L'invention du cinéma*. 1946.

H and A G

LUMMER, OTTO RICHARD

Born at Jena, Saxony, Germany, 17 July 1860; died Breslau (Wroclaw), (now in Poland), 5 July 1925. Physicist, noted for study of radiant energy.

Lummer was appointed professor of physics at Breslau in 1905, and is remembered for his contributions to the study of radiation. With W. WIEN he achieved in practice the 'black body radiator' hitherto conceived as a theoretical abstraction in the study of radiant heat. They realized that a small opening in the wall of a hollow sphere, heated to the required temperature, gave an effective equivalent of an ideal black body at the same temperature. This led on to studies of the distribution of energy within a closed evacuated system by Max PLANCK, Wien and others. In 1899 Lummer and E. PRINGSHEIM pointed out anomalies that assisted Planck in formulating the quantum theory in the following year.

Lummer made important contributions to photometry. The well-known Lummer-Brodhun photometer is an improved version of the grease-spot photometer of R. W. BUNSEN. In 1902 he described an improved interferometer for investigating the fine structure of spectral lines. His investigation of solar radiation led him to an estimate of the temperature of the Sun.

C. Schaefer, *Physicalische Blätter*, **16**, 373, 1960.

Dictionary of Scientific Biography.

T I W

LUSK, GRAHAM

Born at Bridgeport, Connecticut, USA, 15 February 1866; died New York, 18 July 1932. Physiologist.

Lusk, the son of a distinguished obstetrician, graduated in chemistry at the Columbia School of Mines in 1887. He then studied experimental physiology under Karl LUDWIG, and thereafter chemical physiology at Munich under Carl Voit (1831–1908), who was the greatest influence in his life. Lusk graduated PhD at Munich (1891), and was then appointed instructor in physiology at the Yale Medical School. He became assistant professor in 1892 and full professor in 1895. Three years later he was appointed to the chair of physiology at Bellevue Hospital Medical College, New York. In 1909 he was called to the corresponding chair at Cornell University Medical College, New York. He retired in 1932, and was elected a Foreign Member of the Royal Society in the same year.

Lusk's earliest work was on glycosuria (phlorhizin diabetes), and this led to a study of the amino acids as potential sources of carbohydrate. Over a long period he tested the conclusion of M. von PETTENKOFER and Voit that, if meat is given in excess, part of the carbon of the protein is converted into fat in the body. He concluded that, when protein is ingested in excess, the deaminized residues of the amino acids are converted into glycogen, and when glycogen saturation is reached, fat is formed instead. He also investigated whether, in the body, fat is converted into carbohydrate, and he concluded that it is not. For years he studied the specific dynamic action of protein. He finally upheld the hypothesis of Max Rubner (1854–1932) that the excess heat set free during metabolism is due to the metabolism of that part of the protein molecule not convertible into carbohydrate. In other experiments Lusk showed that the ingestion of glucose allows mechanical work to be performed at the expense of 5 per cent less energy than when glucose is not ingested.

At Bellevue Hospital, Lusk was instrumental in having constructed the very advanced respiration calorimeter which led to the clinical use of metabolic studies. With E. F. DuBois (1882–1959), Lusk was mainly responsible for the establishment of scientific standards for energy requirements of individuals. His book, *The Elements of the Science of Nutrition* (1906), passed through several editions, and is a model advanced textbook.

Obituary Notices of Fellows of the Royal Society. 1932–5. (Portrait.)

Biographical Memoirs. National Academy of Sciences, vol. 21. 1941.

Dictionary of American Biography.

Dictionary of Scientific Biography.

E A U

LYELL, SIR CHARLES Born at Kinnordy, near Kirriemuir, Forfarshire (Angus), Scotland, 14 November 1797; died London, 22 February 1875. Established and interpreted the principles of geology.

Charles Lyell was the eldest son of a Scottish father and an English mother. His parents moved to Hampshire and he was brought up in the New Forest and at schools in southern England. As a schoolboy he showed no very striking abilities, but was keen on pursuits of his own choosing; one particular hobby was lepidoptery, a lifelong interest. In 1816 he entered Exeter College, Oxford, as a classicist, and, here again, he made no great mark in his formal studies. His interest in geology had, however, already been aroused by reading the *Introduction to Geology* (1813) by Robert BAKEWELL, among his father's books, and at Oxford he attended the lectures of William Buckland (1784–1856), professor of geology. He became more and more taken up with the subject, making, with his family, what amounted to geological tours in England and Scotland in 1817, and on the Continent in 1818, the first of his many travels abroad. In 1819 he began to study law, but his weak eyesight hindered such work and he was more drawn to geology. He became much concerned with the Geological Society, which in 1823 made him its secretary, and in 1826 its foreign secretary. Later, he was twice president, in 1835–7 and 1849–51, and was awarded the Wollaston Medal in 1866. He himself eventually bequeathed the means for instituting the Lyell Medal and Lyell Fund. He was elected a Fellow of the Royal Society in 1826, and was awarded a Royal Medal in 1834, and the Copley Medal in 1858. He presided over the British Association at its 1864 meeting.

Lyell wrote many geological papers, published chiefly by the Geological Society, but his fame rests almost entirely on his great work, *Principles of Geology*. This was first published in three volumes (1830, 1832, and 1833 respectively) and was revised and kept up to date throughout his life, the twelfth and last edition appearing posthumously in 1875. During the first three decades of the twentieth century geology had made great strides as regards the collecting of facts, but the philosophy of the subject had hardly been approached in the same unbiased and truly scientific spirit. The prevailing opinion among the leaders in Oxford, London and Paris (with all of whom Lyell was familiar) was that geological history necessitated successive world-wide 'catastrophes'. Lyell soon perceived that the doctrine which became known as 'uniformitarianism' was much more likely to be true and he devoted his life to proving it. The essence of this doctrine is that geological history is a matter of ordinary forces and unlimited time; that the geological processes have acted, are acting, and will continue to act in a uniformly regular manner, one which, however, does not rule out periodicities, crises, and minor local convulsions. This fundamental, all-embracing, principle of geology, though not new (it had been stated in a general way by James HUTTON and John PLAYFAIR at the turn of the century), was so powerfully argued and so fully illustrated by Lyell that it finally became permanently established.

Lyell's other books were *Elements of Geology*, variously modified, entitled, and edited (1838–1911); two accounts of his travels in North America (1845, 1849); and *Geological Evidences of the Antiquity of Man* (three editions, 1863–73).

Charles Lyell married, in 1832, Mary Horner, daughter of the geologist Leonard Horner (1785–1864). Horner was the first Warden of the University of London and Lyell himself became, for a few years, the first professor of geology in King's College, London (not then a part of the University). Among scientists his most important associate was Charles DARWIN; Lyell's doctrine greatly helped Darwin to his conclusion that the succession of life was due to a 'uniformitarian' evolution.

Lyell was knighted in 1848 and was created baronet in 1864.

J. Evans, *Proceedings of the Geological Society*, **32**, 53, 1876.

Life, Letters, and Journals of Sir Charles Lyell, Bart, Edited by his sister-in-law, Mrs [Henry] Lyell [*née* Katherine M. Horner.] 1881. (Portraits.)

T. G. Bonney, *Charles Lyell and Modern Geology*. 1895. (Portrait.)

E. B. Bailey, *Charles Lyell*. 1962. (Portrait.)

F. J. North, *Sir Charles Lyell*. 1965. (Portrait.)

Dictionary of Scientific Biography.

Dictionary of National Biography.

J C

LYMAN, THEODORE Born at Boston, Massachusetts, USA, 23 November 1874; died there, 11 October 1954. A pioneer in far ultraviolet spectroscopy.

Lyman studied physics at Harvard from 1893, graduating in 1897 and teaching there until 1917. After two years at the Cavendish Laboratory, Cambridge, he returned to Harvard in 1921, becoming Hollis Professor of Mathematics and Natural Philosophy. Retiring from this post in 1926, he remained Director of the Jefferson Physical Laboratory for over twenty more years.

Lyman served as a major in the Signal Corps in 1918. He travelled extensively to improve his health, which was seldom good.

Lyman's first research project became his life interest. Following a suggestion first made by E. SABINE, he developed an instrument to measure wavelengths in the far ultraviolet (below 2000 Å), replacing prisms in the vacuum spectrograph with gratings, first of metal, later of glass. With this apparatus his first discovery (1901) was of the 'Lyman ghosts' – false spectral lines arising from instrumental faults. In 1906 he measured the hydrogen spectrum in the far ultra-violet, discovering the series of lines named after him, analagous to the series in the visible spectrum discovered by J. J. BALMER. Later he examined the lines given by neon and helium and the spectra of aluminium and magnesium in this region.

A search for short-wave components of the Sun's spectrum proved unsuccessful, even from the high altitude of Mount Whitney. (The Solar Lyman α-line was first photographed in 1959, from a rocket.) Lyman also studied sterilization of liquids by ultraviolet light (1910) and in 1926 produced an improved vacuum grating spectrograph.

Journal of the Optical Society of America, **45**, 586, 1955. (Portrait.)"

Science; **121**, 187, 1955.

Biographical Memoirs. National Academy of Sciences, vol. 30. 1957. (Portrait.)

                                                                            C A R

LYSENKO, TROFIM DENISOVICH Born at Karlovka, Ukraine, 17 September 1898; died Moscow, 20 November 1976. Biologist, ideologist and agronomist.

Lysenko was educated at the Kiev Agricultural Institute and came to national attention in the late 1920s when, as a research worker at a plant breeding station in Azerbaidjan, he promoted techniques for the 'vernalisation' of winter wheat – a chilling process intended to protect the wheat harvest from the depredations of the Soviet winter. On the strength of this work Lysenko was transferred to the prestigious Odessa Plant Research Station and allowed to found his own *Bulletin of Vernalisation*. At Odessa he began to expand the concept of vernalization into a vague but wideranging theoretical perspective which, in the short

run, was to eclipse the bright star of Soviet genetics. In doing this he utilized ideas of the horticulturalist Ivan Michurin (1855–1935) who held that the hereditary qualities of plants could be radically altered by subjecting them to suitable environmental treatments, such as grafting.

In 1935, with the philosopher Prezent, Lysenko published *Plant Breeding and the Phasic Development of Plants* which denounced Mendelian genetics as incompatible with the principles of dialectical materialism. In consequence, a meeting of the two schools was called, at which the Lysenkoites subjected the Mendelians, led by N. I. VAVILOV, to heavy abuse. In 1938 Lysenko was made president of the Lenin Academy of Agricultural Sciences. Shortly afterwards, Vavilov was arrested and died in captivity.

The final triumph of Lysenkoism came in 1948. At a session of the Lenin Academy of Agricultural Sciences, Lysenko announced that his views had the support of the Central Committee of the Communist Party. In rapid order a resolution was carried, denouncing Mendelism and praising Lysenkoism. The USSR Academy of Sciences then passed resolutions which, in effect, outlawed Mendelian genetics and gave an official imprimatur to Lysenkoist biology, based heavily on the view that environment might affect heredity radically and rapidly. Lysenko's power outlasted Stalin's rule and he remained influential throughout the rule of Khruschev, who also gave him protection. Lysenko's fall came only in 1965, a year after Khruschev's, at a time when the disastrous consequences of Lysenkoist agrobiology were becoming alarmingly obvious. Lysenko died in retirement 11 years later.

The historiography of the Lysenko Affair is still a matter for debate, but it is generally agreed that the rise of Lysenko cannot be understood in isolation from the crises occasioned by the rapid and forced collectivization of agriculture in the USSR in the 1930s.

D. Joravsky, *The Lysenko Affair*. 1970.

J. Huxley, *Soviet genetics and World science*. 1949. (Portrait.)

Z. A. Medvedev, *The Rise and Fall of T. D. Lysenko*. 1969.

Dictionary of Scientific Biography, Supp. II.

                                                                            B J N

M

MACEWEN, SIR WILLIAM Born at Rothesay, Bute, Scotland, 22 June 1848; died Glasgow, 22 March 1924. A founder of aseptic surgery, and a pioneer in the surgery of the brain and lung, and in orthopaedic surgery.

Macewen graduated in medicine in the University of Glasgow (1869), held various hospital posts, and became a doctor of medicine (1872). In 1875 he was appointed assistant surgeon, and in 1877 full surgeon, to the Glasgow Royal Infirmary. In 1892 he was appointed Regius Professor of Surgery in the University of Glasgow and surgeon to the Western Infirmary. He was elected a Fellow of the Royal Society (1895) and an Honorary Fellow of the Royal College of Surgeons of England (1900). He was knighted in 1902 and received many other honours.

As an undergraduate Macewen was a student of, and a dresser to, Joseph LISTER. In this period antiseptic surgery was born in the Glasgow Royal Infirmary. Even before he became full surgeon there Macewen was evolving the aseptic technique. For his work on bone he designed in 1876 an 'osteotome' made entirely of one piece of steel so that it could be boiled; it thus differed from all previous surgical instruments, which had wooden or bone handles. Very soon he was also boiling the ligatures and then the needles. Before 1880 his routine technique consisted in wearing a sterilized gown and in the chemical sterilization of the patient's skin, and of the hands of himself, his assistants, and nurses. In the early 1880s he started to boil the gauze, thus anticipating the similar practice (1883–5) of G. A. Neuber (1850–1932) of Kiel; but boiled gauze is not satisfactory as a dressing. In 1886 Ernst von Bergmann (1836–1907) and Curt Schimmelbusch (1860–95) of Berlin began to sterilize dressings by superheated steam but their sterilizer was not demonstrated and made available until a Berlin congress of 1890. Macewen brought one back for installation in his theatre.

Macewen was the chief pioneer in brain surgery. In 1876 he diagnosed and localized a cerebral abscess. The relatives refused permission for the operation until after the patient's death, and the abscess was then found as diagnosed. In 1879 he performed two successful cerebral operations, namely, the evacuation of a subdural abscess and the removal of a meningioma. Between 1883 and 1886 he relieved pressure on the spinal cord in five cases. In 1888 he published the results of twenty-one operations for cerebral abscess, with eighteen recoveries. In 1893 his great book, *Pyogenic Infective Diseases of the Brain and Spinal Cord*, was published. He had operated on seventy-four patients suffering from intracranial infections,

of whom sixty-three were cured. In a number of these, diagnosis, localization and operation were successfully performed several years before the tumour cases of Rickman Godlee (1849–1925) in 1884 and of Victor Horsley (1857–1916) in 1887. Macewen was also an early successful operator in the surgery of middle ear disease.

In 1875 Macewen began to devise an operation to correct the serious and common deformity ('knock-knee') following rickets, and in 1877 it was perfected as 'subcutaneous osteotomy'. Its success depended largely on Macewen's confidence in his aseptic technique. In 1880 his brilliant results were fully described in his book, *Osteotomy*. In 1880 also he performed a pioneer transplantation of bone in a boy who had lost practically all one humerus following osteomyelitis. Macewen implanted bone grafts that he had cut from the deformed tibiae of other patients. These grew, and even many years afterwards the arm was still very useful.

This operation depended in part on Macewen's theory that the periosteum played no active part in bone formation. From 1881 he published on this subject many scientific papers for which he was elected FRS, but because of controversy over the role of the periosteum his advances were not then adequately received. His numerous experimental investigations culminated in his work, *The Growth of Bone* (1912). The results of a new approach to his experiments were published later as *The Growth and Shedding of the Antlers of the Deer* (1920).

Macewen was a pioneer in still another field. In 1895 he operated on a patient suffering from tuberculosis and an abscess of the lung. He excised portions of the ribs and then excised the whole lung. The patient was alive and well forty-five years later. This was the first pneumonectomy.

A. K. Bowman, *Sir William Macewen*. 1942. (Portrait.)

British Medical Journal, i, 603, 1924.

C. Singer and E. A. Underwood, *Short History of Medicine*. 1962.

Dictionary of National Biography.

E A U

MACH, ERNST Born at Turas, Moravia (now in Czech Republic), 18 February 1838; died Haar, near Munich, Germany, 19 February 1916. Physicist and philosopher of science.

After studying at Vienna, Mach was in 1864 appointed to a chair of mathematics at Graz; in 1867 to a chair of physics at Prague; and in 1895 he became professor of physics at Vienna. He retired in 1901. The unifying factor behind what appears a very diversified opus was his desire to purge the sciences of metaphysics. He believed that all assumptions which cannot be controlled by experience are superfluous; and that scientists must continually be wary of 'such encroachments of metaphysical methods'. The absolute space and time of Newtonian physics seemed to him metaphysical, and therefore meaningless. Space and time only have a meaning when they refer to observable relations between things; this conclusion was an important step on the way towards Einstein's theory of relativity.

Mach's belief that the sciences should be concerned with relationships between observables led him to reject atomism, because its objective was to explain all phenomena in terms of the hypothetical motions and arrangements of the hypothetical atoms. Mach thought that atoms were simply a 'model' which helped in making certain predictions, and in achieving 'economy of thought'. They were not to be taken more seriously than that, especially as their properties were different from those of ordinary matter. Such views were characteristic of some nineteenth-century chemists, and particularly of Mach's contemporary, W. OSTWALD, who sought to base chemistry on the laws of thermodynamics rather than on atomic and molecular hypotheses.

In his psychological work, Mach espoused sensationalism, the doctrine that all knowledge of the world comes through sensations, and that therefore one's sensations compose one's world. The elements of the world are not 'things', but sense data: colours, spaces, times, and tones. Any questions which go beyond sense-experience are to be ruled out as meaningless.

Mach was prepared to allow teleological explanations in the sciences, at any rate provisionally. He refused to believe in any one scientific method; his historical studies indicated that while most discoveries had been made starting from experience, accidents and metaphysical or theological beliefs had also on occasion played a very important part. But only when such beliefs were given purely empirical content could they become part of science. Mach's views were of extreme importance for the positivist philosophers of the Vienna Circle; his view of hypotheses as no more than aids to economy of thought has been very influential among physicists, leading, for example, to the 'Copenhagen interpretation' of quantum mechanics.

In his experimental work Mach was particularly interested in the flow of air over objects moving at high speeds, and in this context his name is widely known. Projectiles moving at the speed of sound are referred to as having Mach Number 1; at twice the speed of sound, Mach Number 2; and so on.

J. T. Blackmore, *Ernst Mach*. 1972.

R. S. Cohen and R. J. Seeger (Eds.), *Ernst Mach: Physicist and Philosopher*. 1970.

H. W. Pittenger, *Science*, **150**, 1120, 1965.

Dictionary of Scientific Biography.

D M K

MACINTOSH, CHARLES Born at Glasgow, Scotland, 29 December 1766; died Dunchattan, near Glasgow, 25 July 1843. Inventor and manufacturer of waterproof fabrics.

As the son of the well-known and inventive dyer, George Macintosh, Charles had an early interest in chemistry. At 19 he gave up work as a clerk to manufacture sal ammoniac, and developed new processes in dyeing. In 1797 he started the first Scottish alum works, and until 1814 he was connected with the St Rollox chemical works at Glasgow, deserving part of the credit for Charles TENNANT's invention of bleaching powder. He also had some association with J. B. Neilson (1792–1865), who assigned him a share in his hot-blast patent.

In June 1823, as a result of experiments in the possible uses of the naphtha obtained as a by-product from the distillation of coal tar, Macintosh patented his process for water-proofing of fabric. This consisted of the use of naphtha as a solvent for rubber, and the application of the solution to two pieces of cloth, which were afterwards pressed together to form an impermeable compound fabric. After an experimental period in Glasgow, Macintosh commenced manufacture in Manchester, where Thomas HANCOCK became a partner in 1834. By 1836 the waterproof coat was coming to be called a 'mackintosh' (*sic*). Macintosh's business was gradually enlarged to include many other kinds of indiarubber products.

George Macintosh, *Memoir of Charles Macintosh*. 1847.

Dictionary of National Biography.

T K D

MACLAURIN, COLIN Born at Kilmodan, Scotland, February 1698, died Edinburgh, 14 January 1746. Mathematician; developed Newton's work in geometry, fluxions, and gravitation.

Maclaurin entered Glasgow University at the age of 11, obtaining his MA at 15. He held chairs of mathematics at Marischal College, Aberdeen (1717) and at Edinburgh University (1725). He was a strong advocate of the methods of NEWTON and his ability to work with pure geometry and fluxions influenced other less able British mathematicians to ignore the developments in analysis taking place on the Continent.

His most important geometrical work was the *Geometrica Organica* (1720), in which curves of the second, third, fourth, and even general degree were analysed. Probably his major work was *A Treatise of Fluxions* (1742), in which he tried to refute the objections raised by G. Berkeley (1685–1753) to the differential calculus by developing the properties of fluxions on an axiomatic basis. The work contains the series named after Maclaurin, and a result equivalent to the integral test which is used to compute series by a method now known as the Euler-Maclaurin summation formula. (See also L. EULER.)

An article in 1740, which discussed the attraction of an ellipsoid on a particle by geometrical methods, so impressed A. C. Clairaut (1713–65) that he temporarily abandoned his analytical methods for Maclaurin's, in his work on the figure of the Earth.

Maclaurin also wrote papers on astronomy, did actuarial work for insurance societies, improved the maps of Orkney and Shetland, and organized the defences of Edinburgh against the rebels in 1745.

H. W. Turnbull, *Bi-Centenary of the Death of Colin Maclaurin*. 1951.

F. Cajori, *History of Mathematics*. 1919.
C. Tweedie, *Mathematical Gazette*, **8**, 133, 1915.
Dictionary of Scientific Biography.
Dictionary of National Biography.

J M D

MACLEOD, JOHN JAMES RICKARD Born at
Clunie, Perthshire, Scotland, 6 September 1876;
died Aberdeen, 16 March 1935. Celebrated for his
work on the isolation of insulin.

Macleod, son of a clergyman, studied medicine
in Aberdeen, graduating in 1898, whereupon he
undertook various studies in Europe. In 1903 he
became professor of physiology at Western Reserve
University, Cleveland, Ohio, later holding chairs
of physiology at Toronto and Aberdeen.

Long before the discovery of insulin, Macleod,
in common with many other physiologists, was
very interested in carbohydrate metabolism and
diabetes mellitus. He had carefully studied the far-
reaching work of J. von Mering (1849–1908) and
Oskar Minkowski (1859–1931), who, in 1889,
announced the discovery that the removal of the
pancreas in dogs produced fatal cases of diabetes.

By the time of the isolation of insulin in 1921
treatment of human diabetes by careful diet was
well advanced; by regulating sugar intake symptoms could be minimized, although severe cases
were still invariably fatal. But none of the numerous attempts to prepare extracts of the pancreas
for the treatment of diabetes had been successful,
except that they indicated the idea of extraction
was a sound one. In 1920 F. G. BANTING suggested
that the difficulty was the breakdown of the anti-
diabetic principle (insulin) by digestive enzymes.
He also argued that as ligaturing of the pancreatic
duct led to the degeneration of certain pancreas
cells, this technique might lead on to the isolation
of the active principle without breakdown.

On 14 April 1921 he started to follow up these
ideas at the University of Toronto under the direction of Macleod and with the help of Charles Best.
The pancreatic ducts of dogs were tied for seven
weeks and the atrophied pancreas then removed.
A normal saline extract of them was made which
was found to be effective in treating diabetes. There
next followed an intensive effort, much of it under
the direction of Macleod, to obtain purified insulin
without using the ligaturing process. For their
work on insulin Banting and Macleod were quickly
awarded a Nobel prize (1923), a measure of the
undeniable importance of their success not only
for relieving the suffering of mankind but as a
stimulus to physiological research.

Macleod investigated other subjects besides
carbohydrate metabolism, such as air sickness,
electric shock, purine bases, the carbamates, and
the tuberculosis bacterium. He was also an outstanding teacher and director of research work and
many successful scientists were trained in his laboratories. His influence was also spread by his
authorship of a large number of important books.

Nobel Lectures: Physiology or Medicine 1922–
1941. 1965.
British Medical Journal, **1**, 624, 1935. (Portrait.)
Obituary Notices of Fellows of the Royal Society.
1935.
M. Bliss, *The Discovery of Isulin*. 1982.
Dictionary of National Biography.

Tyler Wasson (Ed.), *Nobel Prize Winners*. 1987.
(Portrait.)

J K C

MACQUER, PIERRE JOSEPH Born in Paris, 9
October 1718; died there, 15 February 1784. Influential encyclopaedist of pre-Lavoisier chemistry.

Macquer took his MD degree in Paris in 1742,
and became a member of the *Académie des Sci-*
ences in 1745. He was one of that great body of
chemists who advanced their subject more by their
gifts for organizing and imparting knowledge than
by any remarkable discoveries. His textbooks, *Elé-*
mens de Chymie Théorique (1751, etc.) and *Elé-*
mens de Chymie Pratique (1751, etc.) were
produced at a time when the *Cours de Chymie*
of N. LÉMERY was showing its age and needed an
up-to-date successor. They led the field for a long
time, an important joint edition appearing in 1775,
containing accounts of the important new discoveries in the preceding decade. He offered chemistry as 'a simple science founded on facts'. This
attitude made him an effective teacher of more
than chemistry, as witness the fact that one of his
most understanding pupils was the Marquis de
Condorcet (1743–94), the mathematician. In a
century when the writing of encyclopaedias
developed into a major intellectual activity Macquer produced the first dictionary of chemistry
organized on modern systematic lines (1766).

His teaching was phlogistonist where theory
required it, and he still favoured a four-element
theory in the absence of anything more convincing
as late as 1778, although by this time he knew
about the work of LAVOISIER and was able to give a
full and fair account of it. He was puzzled by the
increase in weight of lead on calcination, but left
it unexplained in the face of conflicting unsatisfactory hypotheses, preferring to use a theory that
phlogiston is the 'matter of light'. It has been said
with some justice that if one substitutes 'energy'
for 'matter' in his arguments they are near to what
we now believe.

Experimentally he studied gypsum, showing it
to be a compound of vitriolic acid and calcareous
earth; Prussian blue (the colour of which he
ascribed to phlogiston), obtaining potassium ferro-
cyanide from it; fermentation; and dyeing. He also
contributed to the development of the Sèvres porcelain industry (about 1765).

L. J. M. Coleby, *The Chemical Studies of P. J.*
Macquer. 1938.
D. McKie, *Endeavour*, **16**, 133, 1957. (Portrait.);
Nature, **163**, 628, 1949.
Dictionary of Scientific Biography.

F G

MAGENDIE, FRANÇOIS Born at Bordeaux,
France, 6 October 1783; died Sannois, 7 October
1855. The father of experimental pharmacology.

Magendie studied medicine at Paris from 1799,
and had considerable experience when he graduated in 1808; while still a student he was an assistant in anatomy. In 1811 he became prosector in
anatomy, but he resigned in 1813 to practise and to
give private lectures on experimental physiology,
continued until 1831. In 1826 he became a substitute physician at the *Salpêtrière*, in 1830 physician
to the *Hôtel-Dieu*, and in 1831 professor of medicine at the *Collège de France*. Magendie was

elected to the *Académie des Sciences* in 1821, and he was president in 1837. He retired from active duty at the *Hôtel-Dieu* in 1845, and three years later he became president of a new advisory committee on public hygiene.

In 1809 Magendie gave to the *Académie des Sciences* an account of experiments on animals carried out by himself with the assistance of a student, using arrow poisons from Java and Borneo. The plants – of the family *Strychnos* – were identified, and the fatal symptoms after injection described. He later showed that the poison reached the spinal cord by the blood stream, and not by the lymphatics. It was not until 1818 that the alkaloid, strychnine, in the arrow poison was isolated by P. J. PELLETIER and J. B. CAVENTOU. In 1813 Magendie showed that the stomach is merely a passive agent in vomiting, and he studied the action of emetics. Four years later, working jointly with Pelletier, he discovered emetine. In 1821 Magendie published his *Formulaire*, which introduced into medicine the use of strychnine, morphine, iodides, and bromides. In the same year he founded the *Journal de physiologie expérimentale*.

Stimulated by experiments made by Sir Charles BELL and demonstrated to Magendie by an assistant of Bell, Magendie published in 1822 his classic paper, in which he proved that in a spinal nerve the ventral root is motor and the dorsal root sensory in function. Bell was induced to claim priority for this discovery, on the basis of experiments printed privately in 1811. Prolonged controversy – lasting into the present century – regarding priority followed. It is now established that the credit for the full discovery must be given to Magendie. Magendie also studied olfaction (1823); the functions of the cerebellum; and the results of section of certain cranial nerves. In 1828 he described the canal (foramen) in the brain which bears his name. From 1830 he worked with J. L. POISEUILLE on the physiology of the circulation, and from 1843 with his assistant Claude BERNARD on animal heat and sugar in the blood.

J. M. D. Olmsted, *François Magendie*. 1944.
  (Portrait.)
J. F. Fulton, *Physiology of the Nervous System*. 1949.
L. Deloyers, *François Magendie*. 1970.
Dictionary of Scientific Biography.

                                                                                        E A U

MAIMAN, THEODORE HAROLD Born in Los Angeles, California, USA, 11 July 1927. Physicist who constructed the first working laser.

After a period of service in the US Navy Maiman studied engineering and physics at Columbia University, graduating in 1949. He went on to postgraduate work at Stanford University, where he gained an MS in electrical engineering in 1951 and a PhD in physics in 1955. From 1955 to 1961 he was employed by the Hughes Research Laboratories, where he worked on masers (Microwave Amplification by Stimulated Emission of Radiation), the prototype of which had been made by C. H. TOWNES in 1953.

Maiman began by devising various improvements in the design of existing masers, then decided to explore the possibility, already discussed in a theoretical paper by Townes and A. L. SCHAWLOW, of constructing an optical maser, or laser (Light Amplification by Stimulated Emission of Radiation). Townes and Schawlow were in fact attempting to construct a working laser themselves, but it was Maiman who succeeded first, in 1960. His experience with masers led him to believe that crystals of ruby could be adapted to the production of visible light, and after several trials and modifications he decided to use a ruby cylinder with the ends carefully ground flat and parallel, coated with silver to act as reflectors, the cylinder surrounded by a helical pulsed xenon lamp. The light emitted by this first laser was, as predicted by the theory, monochromatic and coherent. In 1962 Maiman left Hughes and formed his own company for the manufacture of high-powered lasers, selling out to the Union Carbide Corporation six years later and becoming a consultant. In 1972 he founded the Laser Video Corporation, and in 1976 became vice-president for advanced technology in TRW Electronics.

Modern Scientists and Engineers. McGraw-Hill.
  (Portrait.)

                                                                                        R M B

MAJIMA, RIKO Born in Kyoto, Japan, 13 November, 1874; died Takarazuka, Hyogo, Japan, 19 August, 1962; Organic chemist, educator, and university administrator.

Riko Majima, the son of a medical doctor in Kyoto, was educated in Tokyo and graduated from Tokyo Imperial University in chemistry in 1899. He was first appointed as an instructor and was then promoted to the rank of assistant professor of Tokyo Imperial University in 1903. He then went on to study at the University of Kiel in 1907 and investigated ozonolysis of urushiol (see below) under the guidance of Professor C. D. Harries, an inventor of ozonization. He then moved to Zürich Politechnikum and studied under the guidance of Professor R. WILLSTÄTTER the quantitative determination of quinone and oxidation of aniline, until he moved to the Davy-Faraday Research Institute in London in 1910.

He returned to Japan in 1911 and was appointed as professor at Tohoku Imperial University (until 1932) and became Dean of the Faculty of Science in 1926. During his professorship at Tohoku Imperial University he also had a laboratory at the Institute of Physical and Chemical Research (Riken), as well as an additional professorship at the newly established Tokyo Institute of Technology from 1929; he was made the first dean of the faculty of science of Hokkaido Imperial University in 1930, and Professor of Faculty of Osaka Imperial University in 1932. He was responsible for the establishment of the faculty of science of Hokkaido and Osaka Imperial Universities. He moved to Osaka Imperial University in 1932, became Dean of the Faculty of Science and then President of the University (1943–1946).

He was the greatest mentor of organic chemistry in Japan, especially regarding the chemistry of natural products. He nurtured numerous excellent students who later became leading organic professors and two presidents at major universities in Japan, and formed the main stream of Japanese organic chemistry.

His major, well-known work was the isolation and structural elucidation of urushiol, a constituent of Japanese lacquer, which he initiated in 1905.

He also carried out pioneering work concerning aconitum alkaloids and plant colouring matter, and found a new method to synthesize indole. He also established *Complete Chemical Abstracts of Japan* (1927). He was awarded the Japan Academy prize (1917). He was also decorated with the Order of Cultural Merits (1949) and the First Order of Merit with the Grand Cordon of the Rising Sun (1962) from the Japanese Government. He was selected to be an emeritus member of the Dutch Chemical Society and German Academy.

Berichte der Deutschen Chemischen Gesellschaft, **43**, 1171, 1910; **57**, 1456, 1924.

Biographical Memoirs of Professor Riko Majima 1970. (Portrait.) (Publication Committee for Professor Majima's Memoirs).

T. Nozoe, *Seventy years in Organic Chemistry*. 1991. (Portrait.)

H S

MALPIGHI, MARCELLO Born at Crevalcore, near Bologna, Italy, 1628 (baptized 10 March and probably born on the same day); died Rome, 29 November 1694. Discoverer of the capillaries, and a very distinguished pioneer in embryology, plant anatomy, histology, and comparative anatomy.

Malpighi graduated at Bologna in philosophy, and then in medicine (1653). One of his teachers was Bartolomeo Massari (1603–55), founder of the *Coro Anatomico*, an academy of nine members for discussion and dissection. Malpighi was elected a member, and he afterwards married Massari's sister. In 1655 he became a lecturer in the University of Bologna, at first in logic.

In 1656 he was called to the chair of theoretical medicine in the University of Pisa. There, at the *Accademia del Cimento*, he associated with Francesco REDI, and more especially with G. A. BORELLI. In 1659 Malpighi was appointed an extraordinary lecturer in theoretical medicine at Bologna.

In 1662 he was elected, by the influence of Borelli, to the Primary Chair in Medicine in the University of Messina, but in 1666 he accepted the chair of medicine at Bologna.

On 2 October 1667, Henry OLDENBURG, Joint Secretary of the Royal Society, requested Malpighi to communicate to the Society anything of interest in his work or in that of others. Thus began a fruitful correspondence which led to the Society publishing many of Malpighi's books; Malpighi was elected a Fellow in 1668.

Malpighi remained at Bologna for twenty-five years. In 1684 a fire at his house destroyed his instruments, books, and his personal manuscripts. Soon after Innocent XII ascended the papal throne he pressed Malpighi to become his personal physician. Malpighi reluctantly agreed, and in 1691 he migrated finally to Rome.

The first and greatest experiments of Malpighi began in September 1660 and were completed by the summer of 1661. All were carried out after Malpighi's return to Bologna from Pisa, and they were described in two letters to Borelli, who published them in 1661. At that time virtually nothing was known of the structure of the lung. It was a fleshy parenchyma in which the finest branches of the blood-vessels and the windpipe were lost, and therefore blood and air mixed freely in the parenchyma. Working mainly on the lungs of dogs, Malpighi showed by December 1660 that the lung consists solely of membranous vesicles filled with air. In January 1661 he was looking elsewhere in the body for the possible anastomosis of arteries with veins, but until March he still conceived that in the lung the minute branches of arteries and air-tubes opened into the vesicles; after the mixing of blood and air in a vesicle, the blood somehow entered the terminal opening of a minute vein. After March he used the lungs of frogs, which are more transparent. Then, using a microscope, he saw that the blood was always contained within anastomosing 'tubules'. In the frog's distended bladder he observed the same phenomenon. The capillaries had been described for the first time.

In a small tract (*De omento*) of 1665 Malpighi described how he had seen red globules of fat in blood vessels. These were probably red blood corpuscles, which he had seen for the first time without appreciating their significance. In two further tracts of 1665 he first described the papillae of the tongue, the rete mucosum (the Malpighian layer of the skin), and the dermal papillae, which he recognized as the organs of touch.

In a fourth tract (*De cerebro*) of 1665 he showed that the white matter of the nervous system consists of bundles of fibres, arranged in tracts connecting the brain with the spinal cord. He also noted the grey nuclei in the white matter of the brain.

Malpighi's *De viscerum structura* (1666) contained his fundamental observations on histology. He showed microscopically that the liver is structurally a secreting gland, and must therefore have a duct, the bile-duct. The bile was therefore not secreted, as had been thought, by the gall-bladder. These conclusions he proved by an animal experiment. In the kidney he showed that the tubules, previously discovered by Lorenzo Bellini (1643–1704), opened into the apices of the pyramids. He found that each tubule began in the cortex in association with a sphere of blood-vessels (the Malpighian tuft). This terminal association, the glomerules, has since been called the Malpighian body. He suspected that it played a part in the secretion of urine. In the spleen he first described the Malpighian corpuscles, and showed that it is a contractile vascular organ, and not a gland.

Malpighi's memoir on the silkworm moth, *De bombyce* (1669), was the first full account of the structure of an insect. He first observed the spiracles and air-tubes, the multi-chambered heart, the nerve cord with its ganglia, and the silk glands. The organs of generation are very accurately described. He noted the movements of the last three segments in the larva, but could not decide whether they were respiratory. In embryology Malpighi published two pioneer memoirs, *De formatione pulli in ovo* ('On the formation of the chick in the egg', 1672, though dated 1673) and *De ovo incubato* ('On the incubated egg', 1675). In the first of these he was misled, by using an egg that had been heated by the sun, into thinking that he saw an embryo in an unincubated egg. This false observation gave rise much later to the theory of preformation. Malpighi described the vascular area, the development of the heart and the gill-arches, the dorsal folds, the developing brain, the mesoblastic somites, and the amnion and allantois. These observations, the first made using the microscope, related to earlier stages of the embryo than any previously made.

In 1675 Malpighi published the first part of his *Anatome plantarum*, and the second part in 1679. It contains many fine illustrations, and he frequently shows the plant cell ('utriculus') with its wall, and the ducts called tyloses. He discovered and illustrated the annular rings of the dicotyledonous stem and the scattered bundles of the monocotyledons. He knew that the material required for growth is formed from the sap by the leaves. He did not describe the movement of the sap as comparable to the circulation of the blood, though this idea has often been attributed to him. He discovered stomata in leaves, though he had no idea of their function. He dealt comprehensively with the structure of the flower. His description of the development of the plant-embryo is very important. He knew the difference between the development of monocotyledons and dicotyledons. He first described the tubercles on leguminous roots. This work is a classic of plant anatomy.

H. B. Adelmann, *Marcello Malpighi and the Evolution of Embryology*. 1966. (Portrait.)

L. C. Miall, *The Early Naturalists*. 1912.

F. J. Cole, *History of Comparative Anatomy*. 1944.

Dictionary of Scientific Biography.

E A U

MALTHUS, THOMAS ROBERT Born at Dorking, Surrey, England, 17 February 1766; died Bath, Somerset, 23 December 1834. Pioneer of population science and economics.

Thomas Malthus was the son of a small landowner. After a successful career at Cambridge – Ninth Wrangler in 1788 and Fellow of Jesus College – he became curate of Albury, Surrey. In 1804 he married Harriet Eckersall, of Bath, and became professor of political economy at Haileybury College.

He is best known for his *Essay on the Principle of Population* which first appeared (anonymously) in 1798 and, in a greatly enlarged edition, in 1803. Malthus argued forcibly that population has a natural tendency to increase faster than the means of sustaining it. This applies throughout the animal and vegetable kingdoms; it is true also of the human race, even though there moral restraint exercises some measure of control. Although this was by no means an original idea, having been advanced by both Plato (427–347 BC) and ARISTOTLE and nearer Malthus's own time by Benjamin FRANKLIN and David Hume (1711–1776), his cogent exposition of it brought him into conflict with the ideas of Rousseau and his followers. Today, the importance of his arguments is generally accepted; Charles DARWIN gained from Malthus the idea of the inevitability of animal mortality resulting from the discrepancy between rate of population increase and quantity of food-supply.

Although reputed to have been of a gentle scholarly nature, Malthus seemed destined for dispute. His contributions to general economics – notably his *Inquiry into the Nature and Progress of Rent* (1815) and *Principles of Political Economy* (1820) – brought him into conflict with David Ricardo (1772–1823), with whom he engaged in a prolonged correspondence. Nevertheless, he was recognized by a number of foreign academies and

the Royal Society elected him to Fellowship in 1819.

J. M. Keynes, *Essays in Biography*. 1933.

P. James (Ed.), *The Travel Diaries of Robert Malthus*. 1966.

J. Bonar, *Malthus and His Work*. 2nd ed. 1924.

Dictionary of National Biography.

Dictionary of Scientific Biography.

H. J. Habakkuk, *Notes and Records of the Royal Society of London*, **14**, 99, 1959.

T I W

MANNESMANN, REINHARD Born at Remscheid, Bleidinghausen, Germany, 13 May 1856; died there, 22 February 1922. Metallurgical engineer.

Son of the founder of a Remscheid engineering works, Reinhard – with his four brothers Otto, Max, Alfred, and Karl – developed it into the firm that long bore their name.

He devised, with his brother Max, the method of extruding seamless tubes. Patented in 1885, the process was shown at the Chicago World Exhibition in 1893; T. A. EDISON described it as the most remarkable of all the exhibits. To produce them factories were established 1886–8 at Remscheid, Bous in the Saar district, Komotau in Bohemia, and Landore, Wales. All except the Welsh factory were consolidated in 1893 into the Mannesmannröhren-Werke AG, with its headquarters at Düsseldorf. After travelling in Morocco in 1906, Mannesmann obtained extensive concessions of land and mining rights from the Sultan, and to exploit these the Morocco-Mannesmann Company was founded in 1908, with headquarters at Hamburg and fourteen branches in Morocco. Such massive German infiltration seemed to threaten French interests in Morocco, and contributed to the Moroccan crisis, as a result of which the Mannesmanns concentrated on their home interests, soon to be massively expanded during the First World War. After the war was over they extended their interests in Bulgaria and, especially, in Czechoslovakia. After Reinhard's death the firm became a constituent part of the Hermann Goering-Werke.

R. M. Kautisch, *Deutsches Biographisches Jahrbuch*. 1929.

C. H. Mannesmann, *Die Unternehmungen der Bruder M. in Morokko*. 1931.

Ruthilt Brundt-Mannesman, *Max Mannesman, Reinhard Mannesmann Dokumente aus dem Leben der Erfinder*. 1964. (Portraits.)

W H G A

MANSON, SIR PATRICK Born at Oldmeldrum, Aberdeenshire, Scotland, 3 October 1844; died London, 9 April 1922. Pioneer in tropical medicine; chiefly remembered for his studies on the role of insect-borne diseases, notably malaria.

Shortly after qualifying in medicine (1865), Manson became Medical Officer for Formosa. He lived in the Far East for twenty-three years, becoming a popular and respected medical practitioner. Not only did he convert many Chinese to Western medicine but he was also one of the first to introduce vaccination.

In addition to his busy medical practice, Manson undertook researches which led him to the conception of insect-borne diseases. During 1876–83 he studied filarial infection in man. After obtaining a clear idea of the life history of the invading parasite, he correctly conjectured that an insect – a common brown mosquito – transmitted the disease. He fully discussed this work in *The Filaria Sanguinis Hominis, and Certain New Forms of Parasitic Diseases* . . . (1883).

Manson successfully studied other parasitic infections, for example, the fluke parasite, ringworms, and guinea worm (*Schistosoma mansoni*). But his name is best remembered for his part in the discovery of the life-history of the malarial parasite, for which he was nicknamed 'Mosquito Manson'. He intermittently studied malaria while he was in the Far East and continued his studies in England in 1892, when he became associated with the Seamen's Hospital Society. By studying living malarial organisms in the blood Manson discovered thought-provoking changes in the interior of the parasite. By analogy with his studies of filaria he developed the hypothesis that malaria was also spread by a mosquito. He first expounded his idea in the *British Medical Journal* on 8 December 1894. The ideas expressed in this paper as well as Manson's active encouragement were the main stimuli to the important work of Sir Ronald ROSS in elucidating the role of the mosquito in malaria. See also C. GOLGI, C. L. A. LAVERAN.

Manson made another lasting contribution to tropical medicine – the founding of the School of Tropical Medicine in London (opened 1899). This developed, in part, out of his annual course of lectures to St George's Hospital Medical School, which he first delivered in 1894, and his campaign for education in tropical medicine. For the remainder of his life Manson spent much of his time developing this now famous school. He was elected FRS in 1900 and knighted in 1903.

P. H. Manson-Bahr and A. Alcock, *The Life and Work of Sir Patrick Manson*. 1927. (Portraits.)

P. H. Manson-Bahr, *Patrick Manson, the Father of Tropical Medicine*. 1962. (Portrait.)

R. Ross, *Memories of Sir Patrick Manson*. 1930.

Dictionary of National Biography.

Dictionary of Scientific Biography.

Proceedings of the Royal Society, **9A**, xliii, 1922.

H. Oxbury (Ed.), *Great Britons: 20th Century Lives.* 1988.

                                                    J K C

MARCONI, GUGLIELMO Born at Bologna, Italy, 25 April 1874; died Rome, 20 July 1937. Radio inventor and entrepreneur.

The son of a wealthy Italian father by his second wife, Annie Jameson (daughter of a well-known Dublin whiskey distiller), Marconi was educated by private tutors and at the Technical Institute in Leghorn. In 1894, the year in which H. R. HERTZ died, he came across an account of the possibilities of the Hertzian waves in a technical periodical. He embarked on a series of experiments at his father's country house near Bologna, and within twelve months established wireless communication over a distance of more than a mile.

On 2 June 1896 Marconi took out in the United Kingdom the first patent for wireless telegraphy based on Hertz's discoveries, though exploiting radiations of a much longer wavelength. His apparatus consisted of a tube-like receiver or 'coherer' connected to an earth and an elevated aerial; its signals were at first transmitted over one hundred yards, a satisfactory demonstration being arranged from the roof of the London General Post Office. Ship to shore communication was established in the following year, when Marconi formed a Wireless Telegraph Company in London for the exploitation of his patents in all countries except Italy; this later developed world-wide affiliations. His first transatlantic signals were made on 12 December 1901 from Poldhu in Cornwall to St John's, Newfoundland.

In 1902 Marconi patented a magnetic detector, and in 1905 the horizontal directional aerial; in 1911 he took over the master patent of Oliver LODGE for a tuning device; and in the following year he introduced the 'timed spark system' for generating continuous waves. In 1916 he began to experiment with very short waves in order to devise a beam system for war purposes; these researches were continued in peacetime and produced results which helped to transform long-distance wireless communication.

Marconi shared the Nobel prize for physics in 1909 with K. F. BRAUN (1850–1918); other distinctions included the Knight Grand Cross of the Royal Victorian Order, and in 1929 an Italian marquisate. His central position in the history of radio development was due to a remarkable combination of inventive talent with a flair for picking out practical features in the inventions of others, and great business capacity.

D. P. Marconi, *My Father, Marconi.* 1962.

O. E. Dunlap, *Marconi, the Man and his Wireless.* 1937.

K. Geddes, *Guglielmo Marconi, 1874–1937.* 1974.

W. P. Jolly, *Marconi: a Biography.* 1972.

Nature, **140**, 182, 1937.

W. J. Baker, *A History of the Marconi Company.* 1970.

                                                    T K D

MARCUS, RUDOLPH A Born in Montreal, Canada, 21 July 1923. Physical chemist.

Marcus graduated from McGill University, Montreal, in 1943 and in 1951 was appointed professor in the Polytechnic Institute of Brooklyn. Subsequently he was professor of physical chemistry in the University of Illinois (1964–78) before taking up his present appointment as A. A. Noyes Professor of Chemistry in the California Institute of Technology.

For much of his working life Marcus has been concerned with the mechanism of electron transfer (redox) reactions, in which one molecule loses electrons (oxidation) and the other accepts them (reduction). In the course of this process the electrons have to surmount an energy barrier, and the size of this determines the speed of reaction, which varies widely. Over the period 1956–65 Marcus published a series of papers on electron transfer reactions and devised a formula for calculating the size of the energy barrier. He deduced a general connection between the electron transfer speed and the free-energy change of the reaction – namely, its 'driving force'. His formula predicted that the larger the driving force, the slower the reaction. This was contrary to the accepted chemical beliefs of the day but its validity was eventually demonstrated convincingly.

Marcus's theory has wide applications, from photosynthesis to chemiluminescence, the electrical conductivity of polymers to corrosion processes.

Among many other honours – including the Wolf Prize for Chemistry (1984) – Marcus was awarded the Nobel prize for chemistry in 1992.

Les Prix Nobel en 1992. 1993. (Portrait.)
Journal of Physical Chemistry, **90**, 3453, 1986.
   (Marcus Commemorative Issue)
Physics Today, January 1993. (Portrait.)

                                                            T I W

MAREY, ETIENNE-JULES Born at Beaune, France, 5 March 1830; died Paris, 15 May 1904. Physiologist and inventor of cine camera; first scientific cinematographer.

On the advice of his father, a wine merchant, Marey studied medicine in Paris, this offering the best combination for his two lifelong interests, animals and mechanics. His first scientific paper, on the sphygmograph in 1860, showed that attention to mechanical detail could produce accurate physiological measurements, for example of the pulse. It was published, like all his subsequent work, in the Comptes rendues of the Académie des Sciences, whose president he became thirty-five years later.

He turned next to the transmission of animal movements from their site of origin, to the recording instrument, the kymograph. He invented the small capsule covered with a rubber membrane, still today called the Marey tambour, from which a small rubber pipe transmitted variations in air pressure to the moving needle on the smoked paper of the kymograph.

Still dissatisfied with the inertia of this system, he saw in photography the ideal, inertialess transmission and recording technique. First, using a rotating photographic glass plate, he introduced his fusil photographique of 1882; he found its twelve frames of flying birds too limited in number to be informative.

His next camera, the chambre chronophotographique, was his final solution and the first modern cine camera. It employed a silver bromide emulsion on a paper ribbon, which was brought intermittently to rest behind a lens, and obscured by a rotating shutter while moved forward for the next exposure. His first scientific films were shown on 29 October 1888 to the Académie.

With this type of camera, Marey not only recorded a very wide variety of animal and human movements, but laid the foundations for all subsequent scientific cinematography. He used high-speed cinematography to slow down rapid movements (first in 1890) and also invented the reverse technique, time-lapse, to speed up slow movements. All his films were analysed frame by frame, the essential step in quantitative measurement of all movements that can be filmed.

Marey was professor of natural history at the Collège de France from 1870 until his death. In 1898 the Institut Marey was founded in Paris with donations from the French Government, the city of Paris, and the Royal Society amongst other Academies, and there his colleagues and pupils continued his work for many years.

A. R. Michaelis, Research Films. 1956; Medical History, **10**, No 2, April 1966. (Portrait.)
Lancet, **1**, 1530, 1904.

Dictionary of Scientific Biography.

                                                            A R M

MARGGRAF, ANDREAS SIGISMUND Born in Berlin, 3 March 1709; died there, 7 August 1782. Chemist known for his analytical work.

Marggraf studied in Berlin under Caspar Neumann (1683–1737), at the schools of Strasbourg and Halle, and finally at the Freiberg School of Mines. He obtained a knowledge of chemistry, pharmacy and metallurgy. In 1738 he became a member of the Academy of Sciences at Berlin, and, in 1754, director of its laboratories. He was a strong proponent of the phlogiston theory throughout his life, even though he showed that phosphorus – still a very rare substance – gained in weight on being burned; by this experiment he explained the production of phosphoric acid. He carried out much work on the composition of substances, and in this his exceptional powers of observation were of value. He introduced the microscope into analytical work, obtaining information from the different crystal structures it revealed. He distinguished potassium and sodium salts by the coloration they imparted to a flame; showed that gypsum, barytes, and potassium sulphate were all derivatives of sulphuric acid; distinguished between alum and magnesia; and used a solution of potassium prussiate to test for iron. In 1747 his research led him to an investigation of the red beet, and in its juice he was able to identify sugar (sucrose). This discovery later became of commercial importance, particularly in Napoleonic France. Most of his papers appeared collectively during his own lifetime in Chemische Schriften (Berlin, 1761–7, 2 vols).

E. Farber (Ed.), Great Chemists. 1961. (Portrait.)
Journal of Chemical Education, **3**, 32, 1926.
   (Portrait.)
J. R . Partington, A History of Chemistry, vol. 2.
   1961.
F. Szabadváry, History of Analytical Chemistry.
   1966.
Dictionary of Scientific Biography.

                                                            B B K

MARIGNAC, JEAN CHARLES GALISSARD DE Born in Geneva, 24 April 1817; died there, 15 April 1894. Chemist, notable for his determinations of atomic weights.

Marignac was educated at the École Polytechnique and the École des Mines in Paris, and spent a year studying mining installations in northern Europe. He then entered Liebig's laboratory at Giessen, where he stayed another year (1840) working on naphthalene and its oxidation to phthalic acid. After a brief period in the Sèvres porcelain factory, which he found uncongenial, he returned to Geneva as professor of chemistry in the Academy (later the University). For thirty years he had only a damp cellar to work in, which may have ruined his health; he retired in 1878, and his last years were spent as a complete invalid. He never married, and lived almost as a recluse; his students found him remote and difficult. Among other honours, he received in 1886 the Davy Medal of the Royal Society, to whose Fellowship he had been elected in 1881.

Most of Marignac's work at Geneva was concerned with problems of atomic weights and was carried out entirely alone. He established the correct formulae for silica (1858) and zirconia (1860), which necessitated a revision of the accepted formulae for almost all known minerals. He spent many years in the tedious and laborious task of separating and characterizing the rare earths; he discovered ytterbium (1878). His careful determinations of the atomic weights of many of the commoner elements were excellent for their time, though inferior to those of J. S. STAS; he is best remembered for his daring speculations which attempted to reconcile the obstinately fractional atomic weights found by experiment with the integral numbers demanded by Prout's Hypothesis. His other work included papers on crystallography and heats of solution.

Bulletin de la Socieété Chimique de France, **11**, 1, 1894. (Portrait.)
Chemical Society Memorial Lectures 1893–1900. 1901. (Portrait.)
W. A. Tilden, *Famous Chemists, the Men and their Work.* 1921.
Dictionary of Scientific Biography.

W V F

MARRIOTTE, EDMÉ Born at Dijon, Burgundy, France, 1620; died Paris, 12 May 1684. One of the founders of experimental physics in France.

In his *Essai sur la Nature de l'Air* (1676), Marriotte announced the so-called Law of Boyle-Marriotte (discovered by Robert BOYLE in 1662) which he then applied in an ingenious attempt to calculate the height of the atmosphere. He also discussed the connection between the variation in barometric height and the motion of the winds. In his *Traité de la Percussion ou Chocq des Corps* (1673) he investigated the collision of bodies experimentally, making use of an ingenious method (later employed by NEWTON) in which two spherical bodies were suspended vertically in contact and then drawn back through measured distances from which their velocities on collision could be calculated. Apart from an unimportant attack on Newton's theory of colour, his *Essai sur la Nature de la Couleur* (1681) contained a suggestive treatment of haloes. He also did useful work on the eye, discovering the blind spot (1660) and discussing the function of the various parts. His most important work was undoubtedly his *Traité du Mouvement des Eaux et des autres Corps Fluides* (published posthumously, 1686) containing a careful experimental investigation of the law of E. TORRICELLI. Also considered was the question of springs, including the problem of their origin. From a rough calculation for the Seine basin he concluded that all spring water originated from rain or snow. The same treatise also contained a discussion of the breaking strength of bodies which was an improvement on that given previously by GALILEO.

A. Wolf, *A History of Science, Technology, and Philosophy in the 16th and 17th Centuries.* 2nd ed., 1950.
B. Davies, *Physics Education*, **9**, 275, 1974.
Dictionary of Scientific Biography.

J W H

MARSH, JAMES Born (birthplace not known), 2 September 1794; died London, 21 June 1846. Devised the 'Marsh test' for arsenic.

Little is known of Marsh's origins or education.

He worked as a chemist at the Royal Arsenal, Woolwich; became assistant to Faraday at the Royal Military Academy there, and was still employed there at his death. His salary was meagre, and his family were left almost destitute.

Marsh worked on electromagnetism, and on problems connected with artillery. He is best known, however, for his studies on poisons and their effects; he devised a test for the presence of traces of arsenic (1836), in, for example, organs removed at autopsy, which made his name famous in many murder trials. A later modification made the test capable of distinguishing between arsenic and antimony.

Dictionary of National Biography.
Gentleman's Magazine, Pt ii, 219, 327, 1846.

W V F

MARTIN, ARCHER JOHN PORTER Born in London, 1 March 1910. Biochemist and pioneer of partition chromatography.

Martin was educated at Peterhouse, Cambridge, receiving MA and PhD degrees. Between 1938 and 1946 he worked at the Wool Industries Research Association in Leeds. While there he and R. L. M. Synge (1897–) became involved in a project to separate mixtures of wool-protein carboxylic acids.

Martin and Synge devised a method in which water adsorbed on to silica gel acted as one separatory phase, while chloroform with a trace of an alcohol (0.5%) acted as the other. The silica gel was finely ground and packed into a column. The amino acid mixtures were introduced by pipette to the top of this column and their separation detected using a coloured indicator. Separation occurs because the amino acids distribute to different extents between the bound water and chloroform phases, this process being called partition chromatography.

Their original account included the mathematical theory of the technique and indicated that a gas could be used as the mobile phase. It also showed that high pressures and small particle column packings would lead to improvements in the process, a concept developed since 1967 as High Performance Liquid Chromatography (HPLC). Martin and Synge shared the 1952 Nobel prize for chemistry for this work.

In 1943 Martin developed paper chromatography, a further refinement of partition chromatography now widely used in biochemistry.

After leaving WIRA, Martin held a variety research posts, mainly in industrial laboratories, before retiring in 1984.

Nobel Lectures: Chemistry 1942–1962. 1964,
L. S. Ettre, *The Analyst*, **116**, 1231, 1991.
W. A. Campbell and N. N. Greenwood (Eds), *Contemporary British Chemists.* 1971. (Portrait.)
Tyler Wasson (Ed.), *Nobel Prize Winners.* 1987. (Portrait.)

J N

MARTIN, PIERRE EMILE Born at Bourges, France, 18 August 1824; died Fourchambault, 23 May 1915. A pioneer of the open-hearth process of steel manufacture.

P. E. Martin was the son of Emile Martin, owner of an iron and steel works at Sireuil near Angoulême. As a young man he became very much interested in improving steel-making, to which the process devised by Henry BESSEMER (and independently in the United States by William KELLY) had given a powerful stimulus. In England, C. W. SIEMENS effected a notable improvement by preheating the air blast by a heat-regeneration process; this gave a substantially higher working temperature. In the Siemens process the excess carbon was removed by adding a calculated amount of iron ore (oxide). Martin applied this heat-regeneration process in 1864 to an open-hearth furnace, built under licence from Bessemer, charged with a mixture of pig-iron and wrought-iron in such proportions that the desired carbon content of the product was attained simply by dilution. Martin exhibited his products at the Great Paris Exhibition of 1867 and won a gold award.

Unfortunately, Martin had great difficulty in establishing patent rights, as it was claimed that his process merely used methods already known. The costs of litigation crippled him financially and, ironically, his later years were spent in comparative poverty while others reaped the benefit of his process, generally known as the Siemens-Martin process. Belatedly, for Martin was then 83, the *Comité des Forges de France* opened (1907) an international subscription for him which was generously supported. Finally, barely a week before his death, the Iron and Steel Institute awarded him its Bessemer gold medal.

Journal of the Iron and Steel Institute, **91**, 466, 1915.
E. Demenge, *Revue Générale des Sciences Pures et Appliquées*, **26**, 427, 1915.

N H

MASHAM, FIRST BARON See LISTER.

MASKELYNE, NEVIL Born in London, 6 October 1732; died there, 9 February 1811. Fifth Astronomer Royal, with many critical observations to his credit.

Nevil Maskelyne was educated at Westminster School and Cambridge, graduating Seventh Wrangler in 1754. He entered the Church, but interest in a solar eclipse caused him to turn to astronomy. On James BRADLEY'S recommendation, he was sent by the Royal Society to observe the transit of Venus of 6 June 1761 from St Helena. He was prevented by the weather and faulty instruments from deducing the solar parallax. He set up a tide gauge in the harbour, later assisted by Charles Mason (*c*.1730–1789) and Jeremiah Dixon (*c*.1741–1771). They calculated a value of the gravitational constant relative to Greenwich by means of a seconds pendulum. On the outward and return voyages Maskelyne calculated longitude at sea by the method of lunar distances. (The error of 1½ degrees was only a quarter of the typical error by the best navigators of the time.) But despite frequent claims to this effect, the method was not of Maskelyne's invention, having already been used by N. L. LACAILLE and A. G. Pingrè (1711–96).

In 1763, Maskelyne went out to Barbados to test the fourth timekeeper of John HARRISON. Two years later he succeeded Nathanial Bliss (1700–64) as Astronomer Royal, and at once initiated the *Nautical Almanac* (1766). Accompanying tables, for seamen's use in determining longitude at sea, sold many thousands of copies and went into three editions. Confining his attentions to observations of the Sun, Moon, planets, and thirty-six fundamental stars, his work served as an invaluable foundation for later researches by J. B. J. DELAMBRE and William HERSCHEL (solar motion). In 1774 he measured the plumb-line deflexion on the mountain of Schiehallion, as a means of determining the absolute value of the gravitational constant.

D. Howse, *Nevil Maskelyne: The Seaman's Astronomer*. 1989.
Dictionary of National Biography.
Dictionary of Scientific Biography.

J D N

MATSUYAMA, MOTONORI Born in Usa, Japan, 25 October 1884: died Yamaguchi, 27 January 1958. Geophysicist.

Matsuyama graduated in physics and mathematics from Hiroshima Normal College (now University) in 1907. After postgraduate study at the Imperial University, Kyoto, he was appointed lecturer there (1913). He then began the research which was to be a lifelong interest, the precise determinations of gravity by pendulum methods. In 1915 he suggested that such measurements could reveal and locate geological substructures. After a brief period in the USA (1919–21), investigating the physics of glacial flow, he returned to Kyoto as professor of theoretical physics (1922). In the following years he carried out extensive gravity surveys, both on land in Korea and Manchuria, and in the Pacific, in submarines, notably in the Japan Trench. Later, in the 1930s, he turned his attention to studying anomalies in the remanent magnetism of rocks. He deduced that the Earth's magnetism has periodically reversed its direction in ancient times. A major reversal, extending from roughly 0.5–2.5 million years ago, is known as the Matsuyama Epoch.

Dictionary of Scientific Biography.

T I W

MATTHEWS, DRUMMOND HOYLE Born 5 February 1931. Marine geophysicist.

After education at Bryanston School, Matthews entered King's College, Cambridge, and graduated in 1954. After postgraduate research he was appointed geologist to the Falkland Islands Dependencies Survey 1955–7. Returning to Cambridge he was successively Senior Assistant in Research in the Department of Geophysics; Reader in Marine Geology; and, since 1982, Scientific Director of the British Institutions Reflection Profiling Syndicate. He was elected FRS in 1974.

With F. J. VINE, Matthews showed in the early 1960s that the remanent magnetism adjacent to mid-ocean ridges is arranged in parallel bands of reversed polarity. This is consistant with the hypothesis advanced by H. H. HESS explaining continental drift as a consequence of seafloor spreading of magma welling up from the mantle. Later he directed his attention to the use of seismic reflection techniques to study the Earth's crust at depths greater than can be attained by drilling.

Who's Who. 1993.

T I W

MAUDSLAY, HENRY Born at Woolwich, near

London, 22 August 1771; died Lambeth, London, 14 February 1831. Engineer.

Son of an artificer in Woolwich Arsenal, Maudslay was apprenticed to Joseph BRAMAH. Leaving at the age of 27, he set up on his own account in London, off Oxford Street, and in 1802 moved to Margaret Street, where he constructed, for M. I. BRUNEL, the machinery for making ships' blocks required for a factory being built at Portsmouth at the then considerable cost of £54,000.

Maudslay was especially interested in engines, though his interests ranged widely and included the purification of water at sea and the elimination of boiler scale. His table engine, patented in 1807, provided a compact power unit that was long used, whilst from his works in Westminster Bridge Road, where he moved in 1810, came a steady number of ever-improving marine engines. The fine machining involved in their construction led to progressive improvements of the lathe, and the slide rest devised for it is attributed to Maudslay by one of his apprentices. Indeed, these apprentices could be described as his great legacy, for a remarkable number of them rose to fame as engineers. They included James NASMYTH, Joseph WHITWORTH, and Richard ROBERTS. With some of these assistants, he devised further refinements, like a screw-cutting lathe and a micro-measuring machine.

By 1826 he was employing nearly 200 men. Amongst his contracts were gun-boring machinery for Brazil, Brunel's shield for the Thames Tunnel, and engines for France and Germany.

Maudslay's two sons, Thomas Henry (1792–1864) and Joseph (1801–61), were themselves able engineers. The first constructed many engines for the Royal Navy for twenty-five years; the second built the engines of the Admiralty's first screw steamship.

C. Matschoss, *Die Entwicklung der Dampfmaschine*. 1908. (Portrait.)

J. W. Roe, *English and American Tool Builders*. 1926.

F. Carnegie, *Transactions of the Newcomen Society*, 11, 168, 1930–2.

Dictionary of National Biography.

W H G A

MAUPERTUIS, PIERRE LOUIS MOREAU DE Born at St Malo, Brittany, France, 17 July 1698; died Basle, Switzerland, 27 July 1759. Mathematician, geodesist.

As a young man (1718) Maupertuis was a captain in the French Army, but he retired to devote himself to mathematics and astronomy. For a time (1745–53) he taught physics in the Berlin Academy, where he was a favourite of Frederick the Great. At Frederick's command he served with the Prussian Army against Austria, and was captured. His remaining years were spent in France.

Maupertuis was elected to the *Académie des Sciences* in 1731 and was chosen to lead an expedition to Lapland to measure the precise length of a meridian degree. The results – published in 1738 as *Sur la figure de la Terre* – indicated that the Earth was not a perfect sphere, but slightly flattened. This confirmed a theoretical prediction made by NEWTON, of whom he was a follower and whose ideas he ardently propagated in France. Voltaire, whose displeasure Maupertuis

had incurred, referred to him sarcastically as the *grand aplatisseur* (the great flattener).

Maupertuis wrote on many mathematical problems, in particular on the properties of curves. He is credited with having formulated the principle of least action, which he developed in his *Essai de Cosmologie* (1751). He was also interested in the formation of species, and his transformist theory to some extent anticipates the modern concept of mutation. He was elected FRS in 1728.

D. E. Smith, *History of Mathematics*, vol. 1. 1923 (Paperback 1958). (Portrait.)

P. Brunet, *Maupertuis: étude biographique*. 1929.

B. Glass, O. Temkin and W. Straus Jr (Eds), *Forerunners of Darwin 1745–1859*. 1959.

Dictionary of Scientific Biography.

T I W

MAURY, MATTHEW FONTAINE Born near Fredericksburg, Virginia, USA, 14 January 1806; died Lexington, Virginia, 1 February 1873. Oceanographer.

Maury, who was of Huguenot descent, entered the US Navy as a midshipman in 1825, and after three extensive voyages published a *Treatise on Navigation* (1836). He was promoted lieutenant, but three years later he was lamed in a stage-coach accident and henceforth served only ashore.

In 1842 he was appointed Superintendent of the Depot of Charts and Instruments at Washington, where he also had the superintendency of the Naval Observatory and Hydrographical Office. Within five years he had issued his *Wind and Current Chart of the North Atlantic* (1847), and his sailing directions resulted in such economy of time that mariners co-operated readily in supplying him with further data. In 1853 Maury was the moving spirit in an international congress at Brussels, where a worldwide system of records was approved. The resulting accumulation of information enabled him to issue revised wind and current charts for the Atlantic and Pacific and to draw one up for the Indian Ocean. He claimed that his charts cut the average passage between New York and California from 183 to 135 days, and between England and Australia from 124 days to 97 days.

In 1853 Maury crowned his work by producing his *Physical Geography of the Sea*, the first textbook of modern oceanography. At about the same time he figured as an important advocate of the transatlantic cable, and received wide recognition at home and abroad.

In later life, however, Maury experienced several reverses. Professional jealousy caused him to be placed on leave of absence from the Navy, but after three years he was reinstated and promoted commander. In the Civil War he sided with his native South, and was sent on a mission to Britain, where he conducted experiments with electrical mines. Having represented the defeated cause in a foreign country, he was unable to return home when the war ended, and had to spend two more years in England, partly on mine experiments and partly on the writing of geography books for schools. A public subscription was raised on his behalf, and Cambridge awarded him a doctorate of laws. For the last four years of his life Maury held a professorship of meteorology in his native state, where he preached the advantage to agriculture of a system of telegraphic reports on weather conditions.

D. F. M. Corbin (his daughter), *Life of Matthew Maury*. 1888.

Dictionary of American Biography.

Frances L. Williams, *Matthew Fontaine Maury: Scientist of the Sea*. 1963.

J. W. Wayland, *Pathfinder of the Seas*. 1930.

C. L. Lewis, *Maury*. 1927.

T K D

MAXIM, SIR HIRAM STEVENS Born at Sangerville, Maine, USA, 5 February 1840; died Streatham, London, 24 November 1916. Inventor of the Maxim machine-gun.

The son of a pioneer farmer and woodturner, at 14 Hiram was employed in carriage-making and he subsequently followed various trades, both in the United States and Canada, with pugilism as a sideline. In 1878, however, he became chief engineer to the first Electric Lighting Company formed in America, for which he invented an improved lamp filament. This was followed by an electric pressure regulator, which he exhibited at the Paris Exhibition of 1881, where he was advised that work on armaments would prove most remunerative.

Setting up a small laboratory in Hatton Garden, London, by 1884 he had completed the invention of the Maxim gun. This was the first fully automatic gun, in which the recoil extracted, ejected, loaded, and fired the cartridges; with a single water-cooled barrel, the rate of fire from the 250-round belt was ten shots a second. Subsequent development produced the Vickers Maxim, which became a standard weapon of the British Army. Maxim was knighted in 1901, the year after his naturalization as a British subject. He was also Chevalier of the Legion of Honour.

Maxim took out 122 United States and 149 British patents for a wide variety of inventions, from mousetraps to automatic spindles. Beside developments in gunnery he had a special interest in flying, and in 1894 produced a steam-driven machine of which the runner-wheels were successfully lifted off the rail-track. Its engine and boiler were remarkably light (6lb per hp), but feed-water for a hypothetical flight of one hour added an insuperable 6000lb handicap.

A striking personality with many of the traits of the self-made man, Hiram Maxim was jealous of other inventors who crossed his path, including T. A. EDISON.

H. S. Maxim, *My Life*. 1915.

P. F. Mottelay, *Life and Work of H. S. Maxim*. 1920.

Dictionary of American Biography.

T K D

MAXWELL, JAMES CLERK Born in Edinburgh, 13 June 1831; died Cambridge, England, 5 November 1879. Creator of the electromagnetic theory of light.

By no means a precocious child, though much given to reading and drawing and the construction of geometrical models, Maxwell failed to distinguish himself at the Edinburgh Academy before the age of about 13, when his intellectual powers suddenly began to develop. In 1847 he entered the University of Edinburgh where he found time for much private reading and research, having the run of the chemical and physical laboratories. He entered Trinity College, Cambridge, in 1850, graduating Second Wrangler and first equal Smith's Prizeman in 1854. In 1855 he became a Fellow of Trinity and in 1856 was appointed professor of natural philosophy at the Marischal College, Aberdeen. In 1856 he was awarded the Adams prize at the University of Cambridge for his essay on the stability of Saturn's rings. In 1860 he became professor of natural philosophy and Astronomy at King's College, London, where he played a prominent part in the drawing up of the 1863 report of the British Association on the determination of an absolute unit of resistance. On the death of his father in 1865 Maxwell resigned from King's College and retired to his estates in Scotland where he devoted himself to research and to the writing of his treatise on electricity and magnetism. In 1871 he became first Cavendish Professor of Experimental Physics at Cambridge where he was responsible for designing the new Cavendish Laboratory. In 1873 his celebrated *Treatise on Electricity and Magnetism* appeared. Incessantly busy in the remaining years of his short life he yet found time to edit the *Electrical Researches of Henry Cavendish* (1879).

In his first paper on electromagnetism *On Faraday's Lines of Force* (1855–56), Maxwell set up partial analogies between electric and magnetic lines of force and the lines of flow of an incompressible fluid. In a series of magnificent papers in 1861–2 he gave a fully developed model of electromagnetic phenomena viewed in the light of the field concept of Michael FARADAY, of whose validity Maxwell had become fully persuaded by 1858. Adopting the belief of William THOMSON (Lord Kelvin) in the rotary nature of magnetism, a magnetic tube of induction was represented by a set of cells rotating about the axis of the tube, interference between the rotations of neighbouring tubes being avoided by rows of intervening cells (in the manner of idle wheels) which corresponded to electric currents. By means of this model Maxwell was able to give an elegant qualitative interpretation of all the known phenomena of electromagnetism. By introducing the notion of elasticity he was then able to give a quantitative description of the propagation of a disturbance in the model. Reinterpreted in terms of the electromagnetic field, this implied that a disturbance in the electromagnetic field should travel with a speed equal to the ratio of the electrodynamic to the electrostatic units of electric force. The value of this ratio as determined by F. W. G. KOHLRAUSCH and W. E. WEBER had been found equal to 3.1×10^{10} cm/sec, very close to the best value for the velocity of light. Maxwell had then no hesitation in identifying light with an electromagnetic disturbance in the ether.

In his *Dynamical Theory of the Electromagnetic field* (1864), Maxwell presented his field equations in a treatment largely stripped of the mechanical model used to derive them in the 1861–2 papers. They then appeared in unmodified form in his great treatise on electricity and magnetism of 1873.

Apart from electromagnetism, Maxwell's most important contributions to theoretical physics were in the kinetic theory of gases. In his first paper, *Illustrations of Dynamical Theory of Gases* (1859–60), he took over R. J. E. CLAUSIUS's notion of mean free path and greatly extended the latter's statistical approach to the subject by allowing for all possible speeds in the gas molecules. There resulted the celebrated Maxwell distribution of molecular velocities, together with important applications of the theory to viscosity, conduction of heat, and diffusion in gases. In his Bakerian lecture of 1866, *On the Viscosity of Internal Friction of Air and Other Gases*, Maxwell turned from the theoretical to the experimental aspects of the subject, showing that the viscosity of a gas was independent of the density and varied directly with its absolute temperature. This latter result was in conflict with the assumption of perfectly elastic gas molecules, and in his next memoir he assumed a central repulsive force between molecules. For the sake of mathematical simplicity he assumed this force to vary inversely as the fifth power of the distance between molecules, and was thus enabled to derive a theoretical explanation of the experimental laws for the viscosity of a gas. Maxwell's approach was then taken over by L. BOLTZMANN, whose somewhat more general treatment was in turn adopted by Maxwell himself in two papers of 1878.

Maxwell possessed all the gifts necessary for revolutionary advances in theoretical physics: a profound grasp of physical reality, great mathematical ability, total absence of preconceived notions, a creative imagination of the highest order. He possessed also the gift to recognise the right task for his genius – the mathematical interpretation of Faraday's concept of the electro-magnetic field. His successful completion of this task, resulting in the field equations bearing his name, constituted one of the great creative achievements of the human intellect, to be compared in pre-quantal theoretical physics only with that of NEWTON in dynamics and of EINSTEIN in relativity.

L. Campbell and W. Garnett, *Life of James Clerk Maxwell*. 1882.

R. T. Glazebrook, *James Clerk Maxwell and Modern Physics*. 1896.

A History of the Cavendish Laboratory 1874–1910. 1910.

Proceedings of the Royal Society, **33**, i, 1882.

C. W. F. Everitt, *James Clerk Maxwell; Physicist and Natural Philosopher*. 1975.

R. V. Jones, *Notes and Records of the Royal Society of London*, **28**, 57, 1973.

Dictionary of Scientific Biography.

Dictionary of National Biography.

D. M. Siegel, *Innovation in Maxwell's Electromagnetic Theory*. 1992.

J W H

MAYBACH, WILHELM Born at Heilbronn, Württemberg, Germany, 9 February 1846; died Constatt, near Stuttgart, December 1929. Motor engineer.

Maybach was the son of a carpenter who died young, leaving him to be cared for by an orphanage from the age of 10. In 1869 he was employed as a draftsman by Gottlieb DAIMLER, whom he had met when they both worked for an engineering firm in Württemberg. He followed Daimler to the firm of Otto and Langen in 1872, and when Daimler set up on his own at Connstatt in 1882 he joined him as a partner in making high-speed motors.

Up to then engines commonly ran at 250–300 rpm; they raised the speed to 900 rpm. By November 1885 the first motorcycle was running at Connstatt and a year later a four-wheeled car and a boat were successfully tried out. Maybach's improvements in carburation, fuel injection, timing, gearing, and steering enabled ever higher speeds to be reached, and in 1894 a Daimler car won the first international motor race. A year later, he became technical director of the firm.

Maybach designed the first Mercédès car, which took the road in 1901, a year after Daimler's death. In 1907 he left the Daimler company and set up a special factory at Frederichshafen to manufacture engines for the airships of Count ZEPPELIN. This factory also built Maybach cars, and was managed by his son Karl.

C. Matschoss, *Great Engineers*. 1939. (Portrait.)

David Scott-Moncrieff, St John Nixon, and C. Paget, *Three-pointed Star. The Story of Mercedes-Benz*. 1966.

W H G A

MAYER, JULIUS ROBERT VON Born at Heilbronn, Württemberg, Germany, 25 November 1814; died there, 20 March 1878. One of those responsible for formulating the Principle of Conservation of Energy.

Mayer studied medicine at Tübingen, and was in 1838 admitted as a physician; he then served for a time as a ship's surgeon. While in Java in 1840 he had occasion to bleed a patient, and noticed that the venous blood was unusually red; his attention was thereby drawn to the whole question of animal heat. The theory of LAVOISIER was by this date generally accepted: namely, that organisms derive their vital heat from a kind of slow combustion, using the oxygen which they breathe. In the lungs the blood absorbs oxygen, acquiring a bright red colour; during the circulation this oxygen is used up to maintain the body temperature, and the blood gradually gets darker in colour. It occurred to Mayer that in the tropics the maintenance of bodily heat was much easier; less oxygen was required for combustion to keep up vital heat, and therefore the blood would naturally appear relatively red, even in the veins. Mayer moved on from this to the conclusion, first as a postulate of the physiological theory of combustion, and then more generally, that a fixed relationship existed between heat and work.

The problem was to determine the quantitive relationship between heat and work; to find how much work a given quantity of heat could produce, and vice versa. Mayer's estimate, in a paper he published in *Liebig's Annalen* (1842), was based on the difference in specific heats of gases. If the specific heat of a gas be measured at constant volume, then the result is always smaller than if it be measured at constant pressure. In the latter case the gas expands, and Mayer argued that the extra heat absorbed is used up as work in expanding against atmospheric pressure. In 1845 he was more explicit about the principle of conservation of energy, and applied it more widely.

Mayer's work seems to have made less impact on his contemporaries than the work of some others following somewhat similar lines; and he suffered a nervous breakdown, apparently on account of his feeling that the scientific community neglected him. Late in life he received numerous honours, among them the Copley Medal of the Royal Society in 1871.

W. F. Magie, *A Source Book in Physics*. 1935.

R. B. Lindsay, *Julius Robert Mayer*. 1973.

S. Friedlander, *Julius Robert Mayer*. 1905.
Dictionary of Scientific Biography.

D M K

MAYOW, JOHN Born at Morval, Cornwall, England, before 21 December 1641 (date of baptism); died London, before 18 October 1679 (date of burial). Physician; recognized similarity between combustion and respiration.

Mayow entered Wadham College, Oxford, in 1658 and studied law and medicine; the latter he practised at some time in London and Bath. In 1660 he was elected a Fellow of All Souls College, Oxford, and most of his scientific work was apparently done there. He was familiar with the research of Robert HOOKE, with whom he probably worked and on whose recommendation he was elected FRS in 1678, less than a year before his early death.

Mayow became interested in the process of respiration, and studied it experimentally. He noted that venous blood when subjected to the vacuum pump (probably Boyle's pump) effervesces only gently; arterial blood (i.e. what we now recognize as oxygenated blood) so treated bubbles freely. Observing a mouse in a sealed glass vessel, he noted that part of the air was consumed as the mouse breathed. He noticed also that air is used up when a lamp or candle burns in a closed space. In these experiments he developed useful new techniques for handling gases.

Mayow conceived that some principle in the air (a nitroaerial spirit) sustained both respiration and combustion, but it was a philosophical rather than a physical principle that he envisaged. Had he lived, he might possibly have discovered oxygen, though this eluded even his successor, Stephen HALES.

W. Bohm, *Ambix*, **11**, 105, 1963.
J. R. Partington, *Isis*, **47**, 217, 1956.
Douglas McKie, *Nature*, **148**, 728, 1941.
Dictionary of Scientific Biography.

T I W

MCADAM, JOHN LOUDON Born at Ayr, Scotland, 21 September 1756; died Moffat, Dumfriesshire, 26 November 1836. Road Engineer.

As a young man, McAdam spent some years (1770–83) in the United States before returning to Britain to develop his interest in road construction. As Deputy Lieutenant of Ayrshire, and a Road Trustee, he freely spent his own money on experimental construction methods. From 1789 he continued this work in the south-west of England, first at Falmouth (1789) – where he was a victualler to the Navy – and then at Bristol, where he was appointed Surveyor-General of the Roads Trust in 1815. From 1827 he was General Surveyor of Metropolitan Roads. The macadamized [*sic*] road – widely adopted after Parliamentary inquiry – is his memorial. By the end of the nineteenth century the majority of the main roads of Europe were built according to McAdam's principles.

Following the French road engineers exemplified by Pierre TRÉSAGUET, McAdam advocated a relatively light construction, making the underlying soil the real load-carrier. This was an important innovation, for it greatly reduced costs. In McAdam's method the important feature was that the soil on which the road was laid should be dry and firm and that the road itself should be impervi-

ous to water, and well drained, so that this state of affairs was maintained. To achieve this, careful grading and compacting of the road material was necessary. In the absence of heavy mechanical rollers – not available until towards the end of the nineteenth century – the necessary compaction was achieved by building the road in layers, usually three, each being compacted by traffic before the next was added. Richard EDGEWORTH advocated making the road surface even more waterproof by washing sand in between the stones, but this McAdam did not accept. Many of the heavier roads constructed by Thomas TELFORD were later reconstructed, as need arose, according to McAdam's method, leaving their original foundations.

McAdam realized that an efficient national road system depended not only on good engineering but on effective organization for construction and maintenance to replace the multiplicity of small local trusts then responsible. The Rebecca Riots in Wales (1843) were evidence of the great public dissatisfaction with the multiplicity of toll-gates. He campaigned rigorously for reform in his *Observations on the Management of Trusts for the Care of Turnpike Roads* (1825). This was the administrative companion to his practical *Remarks on the Present System of Road Making* (1816), which went through many editions in his lifetime.

R. Devereux, *John Loudon McAdam, a Chapter from the History of Highways*. 1936.
R. H. Spiro, *Journal of Transport History*, **2**, 207, 1955.
Dictionary of National Biography.

T. I. W

MCCLINTOCK, BARBARA Born in Hartford, Connecticut, USA, 16 June 1902; died Long Island, New York, 2 September 1992. Geneticist: discoverer of 'jumping genes'.

Although Barbara McClintock came from a medical family there was parental opposition to her seeking higher education. Nevertheless, in 1919 she enrolled at Cornell University to study biology. She soon developed a particular interest in genetics, and particularly that of maize, a crop of great importance in the American economy. Maize was to become her life-long interest. While still a student she developed a method of studying individual chromosomes and relating these to physical characteristics of the corresponding plant. This served as the basis of a PhD thesis in 1927, and a number of important research papers in the next few years.

Nevertheless, she lived in an age of prejudice, and as a woman she found professional advancement difficult. Frustrated, she left Cornell to take up a teaching appointment at the University of Missouri, but fared no better. Not until 1941, when she went to work at Cold Spring Harbor, did she find a sympathetic environment. It was there that she discovered and described the existence of transposable ('jumping') genes. Accepted wisdom was that genes were strung together like beads on a string, and so were fixed in their relative positions. Despite her experimental evidence to the contrary her views were not accepted by fellow geneticists: worse, they were derided. Piqued and disappointed, she continued her research but ceased publication. Then, in the 1970s, the newly rising molecular biologists – with a different approach –

showed her to have been correct: fragments of DNA can indeed relocate themselves on chromosomes. After the long years of neglect, honours were showered upon her, culminating in the Nobel prize for physiology or medicine in 1983.

The Times, 5 September 1992. (Portrait.)

Tyler Wasson (Ed.), *Nobel Prize Winners*. 1987. (Portraits.)

H. Zirin, *Nature, Lond*, **359**, 272, 1992.

N. Fedoroff and D. Bofstein, (Eds), *The Dynamic Genome: Barbara McClintock's Ideas in the Century of Genetics*. 1991.

T I W

McCORMICK, CYRUS HALL Born at Walnut Grove, Rockbridge, Virginia, USA, 15 February 1809; died Chicago, Illinois, 13 May 1884. Agricultural engineer.

Cyrus McCormick was the son of Robert McCormick (1780–1846), who patented a number of agricultural implements, including a threshing machine. In 1831 the father abandoned an attempt to construct a mechanical reaper, but Cyrus took up the task and achieved success almost at once, when he was only twenty-two. His machine employed a knife and cutter-bar, and was pulled by the horse instead of being pushed as in the somewhat earlier machine brought out in 1826 by Patrick BELL. Robert McCormick manufactured the machine under contract from 1837.

At much the same time Obed HUSSEY developed a reaping machine which he patented in 1833; McCormick did not get a patent for his invention until six months later. There was intense rivalry between the two men, and with other manufacturers who came quickly into the field, but McCormick by constant improvement and attention to marketing eventually emerged as the leading manufacturer. He built his own factory in Chicago in 1847 and within a few years had established a national business. His machine excited much interest at the Great Exhibition in London (1851), as did Bell's. His son Cyrus Hall McCormick, jnr. (1859–1936), became president of the International Harvester Company.

Dictionary of American Biography.

H. N. Casson, *Cyrus Hall McCormick: His Life and Work*. 1909.

T I W

McMILLAN, EDWIN MATTISON Born at Redondo Beach, California, USA, 18 September 1907; died El Cerrito, California, 7 September 1991. Nuclear physicist.

The son of a physician, McMillan obtained his BSc at the California Institute of Technology in 1928, and his PhD at Princeton in 1932. He then went to work with Ernest LAWRENCE at the University of California, Berkeley, joining Lawrence's Radiation Laboratory in 1934. In some of his early work there he discovered the isotopes oxygen-15 and beryllium-10. Then in 1939–40, working with the new 60-inch cyclotron, he discovered an element with atomic number 94, the first element heavier than uranium, which has atomic number 93. The new element was given the name 'neptunium'.

McMillan also found evidence for the next heaviest element. However, in 1940 he was called away to work on radar for the Second World War, and

the full discovery of plutonium fell to Glenn SEABORG and his colleagues. McMillan and Seaborg were jointly honoured with the award of the Nobel prize for chemistry in 1951, for their discovery of transuranic elements.

After the war, McMillan made important contributions to the development of particle accelerators, in particular with his discovery of 'phase stability' which would allow the machines known as synchrotrons to go far beyond the energy limit of cyclotrons. After Lawrence's death in 1958, McMillan became director of what is now the multidisciplinary Lawrence Berkeley Laboratory, until his retirement in 1973.

Physics Today, February 1992. (Portrait.)

J. D. Jackson, *Nature, Lond*. **353**, 602, 1991.

Les Prix Nobel en 1951. 1952. (Portrait.)

Tyler Wasson (Ed.), *Nobel Prize Winners*. 1987. (Portrait.)

C S

McNAUGHT, WILLIAM Born at Paisley, Scotland, 29 May 1813; died Manchester, England, 8 January 1881. Inventor of the compound steam engine.

Son of a steam engineer, McNaught was apprenticed to Robert NAPIER at the Vulcan Works, Glasgow, at the age of 14, and attended classes in the Andersonian University. At 19 he went to India as manager of the Fort Gloster Mills on the Hoogly, but returned after three years to Scotland, where he joined his father in the manufacture of steam-engine accessories.

The growing need of industry, especially the textile industry, for more efficient steam engines led to attempts to improve the Watt engine. John McNaught made a simple but important innovation, by introducing a small high-pressure cylinder half-way along one end of the beam. Many existing Watt engines were 'compounded' in this way and it became the standard method of construction for most new ones. Patented in 1845 and first applied to an engine at the Barrowfield Cotton Mills, Glasgow, the demand for his engine became so great that in 1849 he moved his headquarters to Manchester, better to serve his numerous Lancashire customers. In 1859 he helped promote the Boiler Insurance and Steam Power Company, of which he became chairman in 1865; this was a pioneer company in the insurance of steam engines.

The Engineer, 21 January 1881.

Dictionary of National Biography (Missing Persons). 1993.

W H G A

ME(T)CHNIKOV, ILYA (ELIE) Born at Kharkov, Eastern Ukraine, 16 May 1845; died Paris, 15 July 1916. Zoologist, embryologist, and pathologist; noted for discovery of phagocytosis and views on intestinal auto-intoxication.

Educated at Kharkov University, Mechnikov early showed an interest in biology. At 19, he left, to work with R. Leuckhart (1822–98) in Giessen, with whom he soon quarrelled. He then joined his compatriot, A. O. KOVALEVSKY, and studied the embryology of marine invertebrates, writing his degree thesis for Kharkov University on the embryological morphology of the Cephalopoda. In 1867 he obtained a professorship in zoology at St Petersburg, where he married. In 1872 he was appointed to the Faculty of Zoology at Odessa. Soon after, his wife died, following which loss he attempted suicide. His young second wife he married after preparing her for marriage by giving her lessons in zoology, an experiment apparently producing happy results.

At Odessa he became interested in the comparative physiology of digestion, insisting that the endoderm (the lining of the alimentary tract) was formed by cells individually capable of ingesting and digesting food – these he called 'phagocytes'. In 1882 he went to Messina, where he developed the idea that these phagocytes not only digested food but were concerned with the defence of the organism against invasion by parasites and bacteria. With his well-known observations on the effects of the insertion of a splinter of wood in the transparent tissues of a starfish he turned from zoology to pathology, since he saw that the cellular changes produced were those of inflammation. He thus originated the controversy between the cellular (phagocytic) theory of immunity supported by R. VIRCHOW and the humoral theory which saw immunity as arising chemically in the blood, supported by such bacteriologists as Hans Buchner (1850–1902) and G. H. F. Nuttall (1862–1937). This view was further strengthened by the production of antitoxins by E. A. von BEHRING in 1890. Mechnikov replied in 1892 with his *Leçons sur la pathologie comparée de l'inflammation*. Like so many bitter controversies in the history of medicine, this one has been resolved by both views eventually finding their own fields of truth.

After a brief sojourn in Odessa (1885) Mechnikov left Russia for ever, finding sympathy for his phagocytic views, as well as a laboratory, with PASTEUR in Paris (1888); here he remained until his death. About 1898 he conceived the idea that phagocytes might digest not only food and bacteria but the cells of the body-host containing them, thus leading to senile atrophy. This is the earliest concept of auto-immune disease, so fashionable today. To this he added the theory of auto-intoxication by putrefactive bacteria in the intestine, which by weakening the body cells made them suitable for phagocytosis. By eliminating the bacteria and by strengthening the body cells Mechnikov held that man's life could be extended to 120–130 years, its 'normal' cycle or 'orthobiosis'.

In 1906 Mechnikov was awarded the Copley Medal of the Royal Society; in 1908 (with P. EHRLICH) the Nobel prize for medicine or physiology.

Olga Metchnikov, *Life of Elie Metchnikoff*. 1921.

R. B. Vaughan, *Medical History*, **9**, 201, 1965.

Isis, **38**, m 101, 1947.

G. F. Petrie, *Medical Life*, **149**, 547, 1942.

Dictionary of Scientific Biography.

Tyler Wasson (Ed.) *Nobel Prize Winners*. 1987. (Portrait.)

K D K

MÈGE MOURIÉS, HIPPOLYTE Born at Draguignan, France, 24 October 1817; died Paris, 31 May 1880. Inventor of margarine.

In the middle of the nineteenth century the drift from the land to urban industrial areas created a serious problem in the supply of butter for the poorer members of the community and for the large armies of the great European powers. In France, the Government offered a prize for a satisfactory

and economic process for manufacturing a substitute, and this was won by Mège Mouriés, who filed French and British patents in 1869. In the following year he set up a factory at Poissy, near Paris. Production was interrupted by the Franco-Prussian War, but afterwards a new company, the *Société Anonyme d'Alimentation*, was set up to work the process.

Mège Mouriés's original process was to separate a soft yellow fat (oleomargarine) from tallow by macerating it with extract of pigs' stomach. This product resembled butter fat, but was of an undesirably greasy consistency. To render it more palatable, F. Boudet (1872) patented a process for emulsifying it with skim milk and water. The product was chilled with ice-cold water, yielding a granular solid. From its pearly texture this came to be known as margarine (Latin *margarita*, a pearl), though the name butterine was also used for some years. Within a few years margarine manufacture was widely established in Europe and the United States, although it was for a long time banned by many of the big butter-producing countries such as Canada and the Union of South Africa.

T I W

MEITNER, LISE Born in Vienna, 7 November 1878; died Cambridge, England, 27 October 1968. Renowned for her work in radioactivity and nuclear physics.

Lise Meitner, the daughter of a lawyer, earned her doctorate at the University of Vienna in 1905 with a study of thermal conductivity in non-homogeneous bodies. She was especially stimulated by the lectures of Ludwig BOLTZMANN, and worked in his institute for more than a year after receiving her degree. In 1906, she went to the University of Berlin to continue her studies by attending the theoretical lectures of Max PLANCK and by doing experimental work. There she began her research in the new field of radioactivity in collaboration with the chemist Otto HAHN, first at the University and then, in 1913, at the newly established Kaiser Wilhelm Institute for Chemistry in Berlin-Dahlem. She focused her attention on the behaviour of beta radiation from radioactive elements, experimenting with the primitive methods then available for measuring and analysing radioactivity. During her education and early research work she had to surmount cultural and institutional barriers to the participation of women in academic and scientific roles.

At the beginning of the First World War, Meitner and Hahn were searching for the 'parent element' from which actinium was produced. The work was interrupted when Lise Meitner volunteered to serve as a radiologist, or x-ray nurse, in frontline Austrian hospitals, and Hahn was called to military service. However, they were able to return to their laboratories often enough before the war's end successfully to complete their research by discovering protactinium, the rare radioactive element of atomic number 91 which disintegrates into actinium.

In 1917, Lise Meitner was asked to establish and head a department of radioactive physics at the Kaiser Wilhelm Institute. After further work on the properties of protactinium, she launched a series of investigations of the relation between beta and gamma radiation. In 1925 her studies showed that the electron lines were in fact emitted after the radioactive transformation and not before, as suggested by Charles Ellis. A related contribution was her observation and interpretation of electron transitions in which the energy resulting from the change is used in emission of other electrons (later called Auger electrons, after Pierre AUGER's subsequent work on the subject). Another highlight of this period of her work was her use in 1930 of the Geiger-Müller counter in an experimental test of the Klein-Nishina formula regarding the passage of gamma rays through matter. She noted anomalous results in heavy elements, which were attributed by others in 1933 to the formation of an electron-positron pair.

Lise Meitner's work in the 1920s and early 1930s emphasized the physical aspects of radioactivity. The nature of the subject required frequent collaboration between the staff of her physics department and of Hahn's chemistry department. She resumed direct collaboration with Hahn in 1934 to pursue a line of research stemming from results obtained in the neutron bombardment experiments of Enrico FERMI and his collaborators in Rome. Lise Meitner had been concerned with the latest exciting developments in nuclear physics, starting with the discovery of the neutron and the achievement of artificial disintegration of nuclei of light elements by accelerated particles in 1932, and the discovery of artificial radioactivity by Irène JOLIOT-CURIE and Jean-Frédéric JOLIOT in 1934. Fermi's group had shown that when a heavy element is bombarded by neutrons, a heavier isotope of the element is formed. The neutron irradiation of uranium had produced substances which Fermi took to be elements heavier than uranium, called transuranic elements.

Attempts to isolate and identify these elements occupied the attention of Meitner, Hahn, and their collaborator F. W. Strassmann (1902–1980) in Berlin-Dahlem until the spring of 1938. Then the German army occupied Austria. Lise Meitner's Austrian citizenship could not continue to protect her from the Nazi laws which since 1933 had caused the dismissal of large numbers of professors of Jewish descent. Not only would she be subject to dismissal because of the anti-semitic laws, but she also faced the possibility of not being able to leave Germany. At this point scientific colleagues in other countries came to her aid, first helping her to make a hasty exit from Germany to the Netherlands, and then welcoming her in Copenhagen. Her friendship with Niels BOHR and his wife Margrethe had begun in the 1920s and had grown through her frequent participation at the annual informal conferences at Bohr's Copenhagen institute during the 1930s. She soon accepted an invitation to work at Manne Siegbahn's (1886–1978) new Nobel Institute for Physics in Stockholm.

Not long after her arrival in Stockholm she arranged to meet her nephew, the physicist O. Robert FRISCH, at a small town in Sweden where she was spending the Christmas holidays. Frisch had left Germany in 1933 and was working with Bohr in Copenhagen. It was at this reunion that Lise Meitner discussed the now famous letter from Hahn reporting the latest results in his attempt to identify the products of neutron irradiation of uranium. In 1935 Irène Joliot-Curie had reported that she had found one of those products to be

similar in chemical behaviour to thorium, an element lighter than uranium. Subsequent work by Hahn and Strassmann revealed other products with chemical properties similar to actinium and radium, both of them lighter than uranium.

Lise Meitner wrote to Hahn urging him to provide positive identification of these elements. The further work of Hahn and Strassmann showed that the products they had identified as radium were actually barium isotopes, and it was this information that Hahn sent to his former collaborator, who discussed it with Frisch at their meeting in December 1938. Puzzling over these results, Meitner and Frisch applied Niels Bohr's theoretical model of the structure of the nucleus to the new phenomena, and showed that neutron bombardment of a uranium nucleus caused it to divide into two smaller nuclei with a consequent release of great energy, which they calculated. They applied the name 'fission' to this process of nuclear splitting. This interpretation, and subsequent experimental work by Frisch in Copenhagen in January 1939, stimulated extensive research on nuclear fission at research centres in many countries, providing the basis for the subsequent construction of the atom bomb.

Lise Meitner declined to work on the development of the atom bomb, remaining in Sweden throughout the war. At Siegbahn's institute she was concerned with the properties of new radioactive isotopes produced by the cyclotron. However, she had few students and colleagues in this work and was somewhat isolated. After her retirement in 1947 she worked in a laboratory at the Royal Academy for Engineering Sciences, in connection with the Swedish Atomic Energy Committee programme. Although she became a Swedish citizen, she also retained her Austrian citizenship. Her career was illustrious and productive (she published more than 135 scientific papers), but throughout her life she remained a shy person, with a deep interest in music, and an appreciation of her close friendships with such leading physicists as Max Planck, James FRANCK, and Niels Bohr. Her work was recognized through membership of academies in Germany, Sweden, Norway, Denmark, Britain (FRS) and Austria, and a number of prizes from several countries including the Planck Medal, and the Enrico Fermi Award from the United States. In 1960 she moved to Cambridge, England, where she died in 1968.

Lise Meitner, 'Looking Back,' in *Bulletin of Atomic Scientists*, November 1964.
Biographical Memoirs of Fellows of the Royal Society. 1970. (Portrait.)
Dictionary of Scientific Biography.

C W

MELLANBY, SIR EDWARD Born at West Hartlepool, Co. Durham, England, 8 April 1884; died Mill Hill, London, 30 January 1955. Physiologist.

From Barnard Castle School, Mellanby entered Emmanuel College, Cambridge, as an Exhibitioner in 1902 and his future career was greatly influenced by Gowland HOPKINS, who at that time was University Lecturer in Chemical Physiology and his college medical tutor. With a College Research Studentship awarded after graduation he worked, under guidance from Hopkins, on changes produced in certain excretory products (creatin and creatinin) in pathological conditions. He moved to St Thomas's Hospital, London, in 1907 in order to complete his clinical course, and four years later was appointed Demonstrator in Physiology there: in this period he studied some effects of bacterial action in the intestine. In 1913 he became Professor of Physiology, University of London, at King's College for Women (now Queen Elizabeth College), and working in the laboratories in Kensington discovered the antirachitic factor – Vitamin D, later isolated and purified by others. In 1920 he was appointed Professor of Pharmacology at Sheffield University and Honorary Physician at the Royal Infirmary; while there he found in cereals a toxic agent (phytic acid and its salts) which antagonizes the effect of Vitamin D. As facilities were made available to continue his research he accepted in 1933 the invitation to become Secretary of the Medical Research Council and held this administrative post until retirement in 1949. He proved an enlightened and resourceful public official during a period of much expansion of medical research. During the Second World War he rendered valuable service advising on nutritional problems.

GBE, 1948. KCB, 1937. FRS, 1925. Harveian Orator (Royal College of Physicians), 1938. Croonian Lecturer (Royal Society), 1943. Fullerian Professor of Physiology at the Royal Institution, 1935–7. Honorary Fellow, Emmanuel College, Cambridge, 1946.

Biographical Memoirs of Fellows of the Royal Society. 1955. (Portrait.)

H. Oxbury (Ed.), *Great Britons: 20th Century Lives.* 1985.

Dictionary of National Biography.

A P G

MENDEL, JOHANN GREGOR Born at Heinzendorf, Silesia (now Hynčice, Czech Republic), 22 July 1822; died Brünn (now Brno), 6 January 1884. Laid the foundations of genetics.

Mendel, whose parents were peasants, entered the Augustinian Order at Brünn in 1843, after terminating his university studies at Olmütz for lack of funds. His first five years in the monastery were devoted to theological studies, after which he became a deputy teacher at Znaim High School. Despite two semesters spent at Vienna University (1851–3) and two attempts to pass the teachers' qualifying examination (1850 and 1856), he failed, due largely to examination amnesia. His interest in evolution and his skill as a gardener led him to hybridize plants to discover the role of hybrids in evolution. The plan of these experiments was brilliant and revealed the statistical regularities from which Mendel arrived at the famous ratios 3:1 and 9:3:3:1. The seven characters which he studied in the edible pea (*Pisum*) all gave the 3:1 ratio, so he realized that there was a fundamental law. With other plant species, some obeyed the law and some did not. The theory he put forward to explain these results can be summarized thus: (1) The germ cells of hybrids formed between parents differing only in one character are pure, just like those of the parental species. (2) At fertilization all possible combinations of the germ cells are achieved equally, providing a large number of cases are considered. (3) The resulting progeny therefore show statistical regularities between the three classes. (4) All the characters behave in inheritance independently of each other. Mendel went on to postulate hereditary elements, the determinants of the characters, which segregate from each other in the formation of the germ cells. This theory is normally summarized under two laws: the Law of Segregation and the Law of the Independent Assortment of Characters. In an attempt to get other botanists to extend his work he read a very condensed account of his work on the pea to the Brno Natural Scientific Society at two of its monthly meetings in 1865. Although the paper stimulated lively discussion, and was published in the Society's *Verhandlungen*, no one undertook such experiments. Nor did his correspondence with Germany's foremost botanist, K. W. von NÄGELI, bear fruit, for Nägeli doubted Mendel's results and recommended him to pursue further his work on the Hawkweeds (*Hieracium*). Because of the reproductive anomalies in this (apomictic) genus Mendel's efforts were doomed to fail. He ruined his eyesight, and lost some of his confidence. In 1865 he had allowed that there are permanent hybrids, which do not show segregation in their offspring: the Hawkweeds are conspicuous examples. He also realized that characters are not all subject to the simple type of inheritance which he found in the pea. Flower colour in the bean, he suggested, may be a 'Compound Character'.

Little is known of the details of his further experiments, since the manuscripts which he preserved were destroyed around the time of his death. In later life he avoided the subject of his experiments with the pea, but remained an active horticulturist, beekeeper, and meteorologist.

In 1868 he became Abbot of the Monastery, where he remained until his death. In 1900, sixteen years after his death, his results were rediscovered by H. de VRIES, K. E. Correns (1864–1935), and E. von Tschermak (1871–1962). The most important modification of Mendel's work was introduced by T. H. MORGAN between 1910 and 1919, when he showed how linkage and crossing-over alter Mendel's second law.

H. Iltis (trans. E. and C. Paul), *Life of Mendel.* 1932 (reprinted 1966). (Portrait.); *Scientific Monthly,* **56**, 414, 1943.

R. C. Olby, *Origins of Mendelism.* 1966. (Portrait.) *Dictionary of Scientific Biography.*

D. Oldroyd, *Endeavour* (New Series), **8**, 29, 1984.

R C O

MENDELÉEFF, DMITRY IVANOVICH Born at Tobolsk, Siberia, 27 January 1834; died St Petersburg, 20 January 1907. Chemist; formulated the Periodic Table of the elements.

Mendeléeff was the fourteenth, and last, child of the Director of the Gymnasium at Tobolsk. At 16 his father retired prematurely, through blindness, and he was taken by his mother to St Petersburg to seek higher education. There he trained as a teacher at the Pedagogical Institute, where his father had also studied, and on qualification was sent to Odessa. In 1856 he returned to St Petersburg for a course of higher education, and took a degree in chemistry. In 1859 he was sent for two years of further training in Paris and Heidelberg, returning to St Petersburg in 1861 as professor of chemistry in the Technological Institute. In 1866 he joined A. M. BUTLEROV at the University, as professor of general chemistry, but retaining also his appointment at the Technological Institute. He resigned his university appointment in 1890 following an internal dispute that led to his being rebuffed by Count Delyanov, Minister of Education. Three years later, however, he was made Director of the Bureau of Weights and Measures, holding this appointment until his death.

In 1880 Mendeléeff was a candidate for the chair of chemical technology at the Imperial Academy of Sciences. Acknowledged as the leading Russian scientist, he had a strong claim, but in the event the award went to F. K. BEILSTEIN, who was supported by the German faction then strong in Russian academic circles. No doubt Mendeléeff's irascible and impetuous nature was a factor in his failure, for it led him into dispute with Count Tolstoy, then Minister of Education. He was in dispute also with the Church, for his second marriage – contracted within less than the statutory seven years of the dissolution of his first – was technically bigamous, though no action was taken against him, for he had powerful friends as well as powerful enemies.

Mendeléeff was a prolific writer, and nearly three hundred publications are credited to him. Most were chemical, but he was interested also in art, education, and economics. In 1868 he embarked on a great textbook of chemistry, known in its English translation as the *Principles of Chemistry*. In compiling this, he sought some system of classifying the elements – some sixty in all were then known – whose properties he was describing. This led him to formulate the Periodic Law, which earned him lasting international fame. He presented it verbally to the Russian Chemical Society in October 1868 (in a paper read, because of his own illness, by N. A. Menschutkin (1842–1907)) and published in February 1869.

In this paper he set out clearly his discovery that if the elements are arranged in order of their atomic weights, chemically related elements appear at regular intervals. The groups of elements that thus emerge have similar valencies. Evident gaps in Mendeléeff's table made it possible to predict not only the existence of some elements then unknown but the properties of some of their principal compounds. Similarly, the anomalous position of certain known elements suggested that their properties had been inaccurately recorded. Both kinds of prediction were quite quickly fulfilled: thus Mendeléeff's ekaboron was characterized as scandium in 1879 by L. F. Nilson (1840–99). Mendeléeff – who was apparently not aware of the earlier work of J. A. R. NEWLANDS in this field – quickly elaborated his Periodic Table of the Elements, and it rapidly became generally accepted and used. See also J. L. MEYER.

The greatness of Mendeléeff's achievement lies in his having discovered a generalization that not only unified an enormous amount of existing information but pointed the way to further progress. He was honoured abroad in his own time. The Royal Society awarded him (with Lothar MEYER) its Davy Medal in 1882 and its Copley Medal in 1905; he was elected Foreign Member in 1892. The Imperial Academy of Sciences, however, never recognized him.

The Periodic Law was Mendeléeff's great achievement, but he also carried out original research, mostly arising from his interest in the forces between atoms and molecules. In particular, he discovered – independently of T. ANDREWS – that there is critical point at which liquid and vapour become indistinguishable.

E. Farber (Ed.), *Great Chemists*. 1961. (Portrait).
J. R. Partington, *A History of Chemistry*, vol. 4. 1964. (Portrait.)
Nature, **40**, 193. 1889.
Proceedings of the Royal Society, **134A**, xvii, 1910–11.
Daniel Q. Posin, *Mendeleyev*, 1948.
Dictionary of Scientific Biography.

T I W

MENGOLI, PIETRO Born in Bologna, Italy, 1625; died 1686. Mathematician who made early discoveries in the differential and integral calculus.

Pietro Mengoli was professor of mathematics at the University of Bologna. His most important work was concerned with the convergence of series and with integration. In his study of infinite series he established some of the fundamental results concerning their convergence or divergence: e.g. a necessary condition that $\sum A_n$ be convergent is $\lim A_n = 0$; a sufficient condition for the convergence of a series of positive terms is that their partial sums be bounded. He discovered some years before Jacques BERNOULLI, to whom it is usually credited, that the harmonic series $\sum \frac{1}{n}$ is divergent. He produced a series for logarithms some ten years before G. MERCATOR.

His definition of definite integral is similar to that of A. C. CAUCHY a century later. He divides the range of integration up into sub-intervals and considers maximum and minimum co-ordinates for each sub-interval leading to sums which both tend to the same limit, the definite integral.

Archives Internationales d'Histoire des Sciences, vol. 13. 1950.
Dictionary of Scientific Biography.

D N

MERCATOR, GERARDUS (GERHARD KREMER) Born at Rupelmonde, Flanders (Roermond, Netherlands), 5 March 1512; died Duisburg, Germany, 2 December 1594. Mathematical instrument maker and geographer, remembered primarily for his map projection.

Mercator was educated at Bois-le-Duc and Louvain (matriculated 1530; licentiate 1532), where he met Gemma Frisius (1508–55), from whom he learned a great deal about cartography and mathematical instrument making. In 1534 he founded a centre for the study of geography at Louvain, from which he issued a series of maps in the years following. He made two complete sets of surveying instruments at the request of Charles V (the first being destroyed by fire) and terrestrial (1541) and celestial (1551) globes, which achieved some fame, although not the first of their kind. Being a Protestant, he had been persecuted for much of this time, and in 1552 emigrated to Duisburg in the German Duchy of Juliers, continuing to issue maps, especially of Europe. In 1568 he published a chronology of the world, 'from the creation', based on astronomical records, especially of eclipses.

In 1569 appeared his chart of the world using what is now known as 'Mercator's projection'. It is usually said that the mathematical principles on which it is based were first explained by Edward Wright (1558–1615) in 1594, but there is enough information on the margins of the maps themselves for any competent contemporary cartographer or astrologer to have followed Mercator's method.

Biographie Nationale Belgique, XIV. 1897.
Nieuw Nederlandsch biografisch Woordenbock. 1911–37.
Dictionary of Scientific Biography.

J D N

MERCER, JOHN Born at Great Harwood, Lancashire, England, 21 February 1791; died Oakenshaw, Lancashire, 30 November 1866. Pioneer of textile chemistry.

Mercer began work at the age of 9, as a bobbin-winder, and had no formal education in chemistry. Nevertheless, he became the acknowledged 'father of textile chemistry' and the Royal Society elected him to Fellowship in 1850. His name is remembered in connection with the lustrous 'mercerized' cotton which, although not developed commercially until 1890, arose from his discovery, about 1844, of the effect of caustic soda on cotton linters. He discovered also that cotton could be dissolved in a solution of copper oxide in ammonia, a phenomenon later exploited in the manufacture of artificial silk.

As a youth, Mercer experimented at home with dyeing processes, and soon acquired sufficient skill to set up as an independent dyer. Most of his working life was, however, spent with the calico-printing firm of Oakenshaw Print Works – in which he eventually became a partner – and it was there that most of his experimental work was done. The association was a very appropriate one, for it was a member of this firm's staff who first recognized Mercer's potential talent and took the trouble to teach him – in his spare time – reading, writing, and arithmetic. Among his innovations was the chlorination of wool in order to make it as easily printable as cotton; not until many years later was it realized that this treatment also conferred valuable shrink-resisting qualities. Becoming interested in photochemistry, he devised processes for photographic printing on fabric; Queen Victoria was presented with a handkerchief printed in this way when she visited the Great Exhibition of 1851, of which Mercer was a Juror.

A. W. Baldwin, *Endeavour*, **3**, 138, 1944. (Portrait.)
E. A. Parnell, *The Life and Labours of John Mercer, F.R.S.* 1886.
Dictionary of National Biography.

T I W

MERGENTHALER, OTTMAR Born at Hachtel, Germany, 11 May 1854; died Baltimore, Maryland, USA, 28 October 1899. Inventor of linotype.

Son of Johann Georg Mergenthaler, a teacher, Ottmar Mergenthaler was apprenticed to a watch-maker at the age of 14, and to avoid army service emigrated to the United States four years later.

From 1872 to 1876 he worked as an instrument-maker, first in Washington and then in Baltimore, under August Hahl, son of his German employer. While advising on the construction of a machine to eliminate typesetting, devised by James Cle-phane of Washington, the two partners (for so Mergenthaler was to become in 1880) built two such machines – one based on lithographic, the other on stereotypic principles. The first was only partially successful, and the second was abandoned.

Nevertheless, after setting up on his own in 1883, Mergenthaler persevered and was commissioned by Clephane to build another machine. He first tried a paper matrix; then conceived of type bars on which the molten type metal was cast. On 26 August 1884 he obtained his first patent for direct cast 'linotype' (line of type) and Clephane in 1885 organized the National Typographic Company to exploit it. Mergenthaler later made many improvements, including automatic justification of the line. The Linotype machine was first employed, for the *New York Tribune*, in 1886. After the Company had been taken over in 1888 by a consortium of newspaper-owners, Mergenthaler resigned, but continued to effect improvements in the machines. He died of tuberculosis.

Waldemar Kaempffert, *A Popular History of American Invention.* 1926.
Ottmar Mergenthaler (1854–1889), *Der Moderne Buchdrucker.* 1929.
Illustrated London News, **115**, 717, 1899. (Portrait.)
Dictionary of American Biography.

W H G A

MESSEL, RUDOLPH Born at Darmstadt, Hessen, Germany, 14 January 1848; died London, 18 April 1920. Industrial chemist.

Messel, son of a banker, was educated at a Huguenot school in Friedrichsdorf and in 1863 was apprenticed for three years to the chemical manufacturing firm of E. Lucius in Frankfurt. He then studied chemistry at Zürich, Heidelberg, and Tübingen. In 1870 he came to England as assistant to Sir Henry ROSCOE, but on the outbreak of the Franco-Prussian War in the same year was recalled to Germany. Afterwards he returned to London and joined Dunn, Squire & Co., of Stratford, manufacturers of sulphuric acid. Shortly afterwards this firm amalgamated with Spencer Chapman to form Squire, Chapman & Co. In 1878 he became managing director of this firm, subsequently known as Spencer, Chapman & Messel Ltd.

Messel's great contribution to chemical technology was to devise a new process (patented with W. S. Squire in 1875, almost simultaneously with a similar application by C. A. WINKLER in Germany) for sulphuric-acid manufacture. It was based on the earlier, but unexploited, process of Peregrine PHILLIPS and was quite different from that introduced by earlier British manufacturers such as Joshua WARD and John ROEBUCK. The earlier process involved oxidation of sulphur dioxide by oxides of nitrogen. Philips' process involved oxidation of sulphur dioxide to sulphur trioxide by air in the presence of a catalyst. Early attempts to exploit this commercially failed, mainly because the catalyst quickly became 'poisoned' and ineffective. Messel discovered that this could be effectively avoided if the gas was highly purified before being admitted to the catalyst.

This 'contact' process yields directly a highly concentrated form of sulphuric acid known as oleum, which was required in increasing quantities, particularly for the manufacture of dyes, fertilizers, and explosives. The demand for oleum rose enormously during the 1914–18 war. At its beginning, UK production was about 20 000 tons, made mostly by Spencer, Chapman & Messel Ltd; by its end, output – from a number of factories – had reached 450 000 tons.

Messel was elected FRS in 1912, and was president of the Society of Chemical Industry 1911–12 and again in 1914.

Journal of the Society of Chemical Industry,
    Special Jubilee Issue, July 1931. (Portrait.)
G. T. Morgan and D. D. Pratt, *British Chemical
    Industry*. 1938.
*Dictionary of National Biography (Missing
    Persons)*.1993.

                                                                     T I W

MEYER, JULIUS LOTHAR Born at Varel, Oldenburg, Germany, 19 August 1830; died Tübingen, 11 April 1895. Chemist; discovered, independently, the Periodic System of the elements.

Lothar Meyer was the son of a physician, and at first wished to follow his father's profession; he studied in Zürich and Würzburg, and qualified as MD. But an increasing interest in chemistry and physics led him to work at Heidelberg under R. W. BUNSEN and G. R. KIRCHHOFF (where he did important work on the gases of the blood), and to study mathematical physics at Königsberg. In 1859 he became *Privatdozent* at the University of Breslau, where his brother Emil was professor of physics. He was then professor successively at the School of Forestry, Neustadt-Eberswalde (1866), the Karlsruhe Polytechnicum (1868), and the University of Tübingen (1876). During the Franco-Prussian War the Karlsruhe Polytechnicum was converted into a military hospital, and Meyer reverted for the duration to his first profession of surgeon. He was married, and left four children.

Meyer's reputation was made by his book, *Die modernen Theorien der Chemie* (1864), a clear statement of the basic principles of chemistry by one who was, by training, much more than a chemist; it ran into many revised and enlarged editions. This book was stimulated in the first place by S. CANNIZZARO'S advocacy of A. AVOGADRO'S Hypothesis and the elucidation of correct atomic weights at the Karlsruhe Conference of 1860. In it is to be found the first sketch of an arrangement of the elements in order of atomic weight. About 1868, Meyer drew up a much-expanded table, probably for a proposed second edition of his book; this was very similar to the Periodic Table of D. I. MENDELÉEFF published the next year. Meyer himself did not publish his version until 1870, by which time he was fully cognizant of Mendeléeff's work, and made no claim for priority. His own particular contribution was the well-known graph connecting atomic volume with atomic number, exhibiting a clear periodic relationship.

Although Meyer worked in several branches of chemistry, much of his work stemmed from his interest in the classification of the elements. He recalculated (with K. F. O. Seubert (1851–1942)) many atomic weights; he used the Periodic Table to predict and study the chemical properties of related elements; and he campaigned for the use of the Table as a rational basis for the teaching of inorganic chemistry. Education was, indeed, one

of his abiding interests and he wrote widely on this subject.

Chemical Society Memorial Lectures, 1893–1900.
    1901. (Portrait.)
K. Seubert, *Berichte der deutschen Chemischen
    Gesellschaft*, **28**, 1109R, 1895. (Portrait.)
R. Wunderlich, *Journal of Chemical Education*, **27**,
    365, 1950.
Dictionary of Scientific Biography.

                                                                     W V F

MEYER, VICTOR Born in Berlin, 8 September 1848; died Heidelberg, 8 August 1897. Chemist and teacher.

Victor Meyer came of a wealthy Jewish family in the textile trade. He was educated at Heidelberg, and became assistant to R. W. BUNSEN; but the analysis of mineral waters soon bored him, and he went to work under J. F. W. von BAEYER in Berlin. He was professor successively in the Zürich Polytechnic (1872), and the universities of Göttingen (1885) and Heidelberg (1889), as successor to Bunsen. As a teacher, he was brilliant and popular; he wrote (with P. Jacobson (1859–1923)) a well-known textbook. His private life was apparently happy; but he seems to have overworked frantically, and his last years were clouded by neuralgia, insomnia, and depression. He took his own life.

Meyer and his students published over 300 papers, many of great importance; only a few of his research interests can be mentioned here. His early work concerned the orientation of di-substituted benzenes; he discovered nitro-alkanes, and studied their colour reactions with nitrous acid. He also discovered oximes, and worked on their isomerism, though his explanation of this was wrong. The failure of a supposed colour test for benzene led to the finding of thiophen as an impurity, and to pioneer work on thiophen chemistry. Iodoso-compounds and iodonium salts were described for the first time. His well-known apparatus for the determination of vapour density (if necessary, at high temperatures) led to many publications; the results for chlorine gave rise to a flurry of speculation about its possible compound nature, in which Meyer himself did not join. He also worked, rather inconclusively, on gaseous explosions.

Berichte der deutschen Chemischen Gesellschaft,
    41, 4507, 1908. (Portrait.)
Journal of the Chemical Society, **169**, 1900.
    (Portrait.)
E. Farber (Ed.), *Great Chemists*. 1961. (Portrait.)
R. Meyer, *Victor Meyer, Leben und Werke*. 1917.
Dictionary of Scientific Biography.

                                                                     W V F

MEYERHOF, OTTO FRITZ Born in Hanover, Germany, 12 April 1884; died Philadelphia, Pennsylvania, USA, 6 October 1951. Biochemist who studied the glycogen–lactic acid cycle.

Meyerhof studied medicine at Heidelberg, his doctoral thesis being in psychiatry. In 1909, working in L. Krehl's clinic, he began a fruitful collaboration with O. Warburg (1883–1970). In 1913 he was appointed *Privatdozent*, and in 1918 professor, in Kiel; from 1924 to 1929 he worked in the Kaiser Wilhelm Institute in Dahlem, and was then professor in Heidelberg. He sought refuge in Paris in 1938 for political reasons, and had to flee again in 1940. His last years were spent in the University of Pennsylvania.

The unravelling of the complex enzyme systems and intermediate stages of the glycogen–lactic acid cycle in muscle was Meyerhof's most notable achievement. He also discovered the high energy-content of phosphocreatine and adenosine triphosphate, and introduced the concept of 'energetic coupling' between oxidation and phosphorylation. The Nobel prize for physiology or medicine was awarded to him (jointly with A. V. HILL) in 1923.

Science, **115**, 365, 1952.
Biographical Memoirs. National Academy of Sciences, vol. 34. 1960.
Obituary Notices of Fellows of the Royal Society, vol. 9. 1954. (Portrait.)
Dictionary of Scientific Biography.
Tyler Wasson (Ed.), *Nobel Prize Winners.* 1987. (Portrait.)

W V F

MICHELSON, ALBERT ABRAHAM Born at Strelno, Posen (now Poznan), Poland, 19 December 1852; died Pasadena, California, USA, 9 May 1931. Best known for the Michelson-Morley experiment to measure the Earth's motion through the ether.

When he was 2 years old Michelson's parents went to the United States, first to Nevada and then to San Francisco. He was sent to Annapolis Naval Academy, graduated in 1873, and became a midshipman; two years later he returned as instructor in physics and chemistry. Apparently he was not greatly interested in science until he received this appointment. In 1879 he went to the Nautical Almanac Office in Washington, DC; after a year there he went to Europe for two years, to the *Collège de France*, to Heidelberg, and to Berlin. In 1882 he became professor of physics at the Case School at Cleveland, Ohio; in 1889 he went to Clark University; and in 1892 to the new University of Chicago, where he remained until his death.

It was while he was at Cleveland that he co-operated with the chemist E. W. MORLEY on their famous experiment. Light was believed to be a wave motion, and a medium, the ether, was postulated as filling all space. The light waves were regarded as undulations of this ether, for a wave motion cannot be transmitted except through some medium. If a source of light were moving through the ether, then the speed of the light emitted in different directions would be different; the waves propagated forwards, for instance, would apparently go more slowly. In Michelson and Morley's apparatus two beams of light were sent out along equal paths at right-angles, and reflected back. If one were to go faster than the other, the apparatus would reveal this, and the speed of the Earth's motion through the ether could be calculated. In fact, both beams took the same time; and the theory that the Earth was ploughing through the stationary ether had eventually to be given up. The experiment, for which G. F. FITZGERALD proposed a solution, marked a crucial stage on the way towards the Theory of Relativity formulated by EINSTEIN.

Michelson employed similar apparatus for quite different purposes, such as estimating the angular diameters of the satellites of Jupiter, and even of a

star; and for the evaluation of the metre in terms of the wavelength of light from a standard, monochromatic source. He was awarded a Nobel prize in 1907, the first American scientist to be thus honoured, and was elected FRS in 1902. He was a clear lecturer; and while he was impressed by technology, he valued pure science as an end in itself, like painting, poetry, or music.

Obituary Notices of Fellows of the Royal Society, 1932–5. (Portrait.)
J. H. Wilson, *A. Michelson: America's First Nobel Prize Winner.* 1958.
D. T. McCallister, *Albert Abraham Michelson.* 1970.
Biographical Memoirs. National Academy of Sciences, vol. 19. 1938.
Dictionary of Scientific Biography.
Tyler Wasson (Ed.) *Nobel Prize Winners.* 1987. (Portrait.)

D M K

MIDGLEY, THOMAS JR Born in Beaver Falls, Pennsylvania, USA, 18 May 1889; died Worthington, Ohio, 2 November 1944. Chemical inventor.

After graduating in mechanical engineering at Cornell University, Midgley worked for a time in his father's Midgley Tire and Rubber Company. When this failed he joined the Dayton Engineering Laboratories (Delco) of Charles F. Kettering (1876–1958) in 1916. There he was assigned the task of finding the cause and cure of 'knocking' in petrol engines. By empirically testing over 30 000 disparate chemicals Midgley's team eventually discovered in 1921 that tetraethyl lead (TEL) was a very effective anti-knock additive for petrol and it was adopted by petroleum companies world wide. A second major discovery, made in the early 1930s, was that of the chlorofluorocarbons (Freons), developed as cheap, nonflammable refrigerants. These, too, were soon widely used in large quantities. He made many other contributions to science and technology and held over 100 patents.

Midgley died prematurely in 1944 in a tragic accident following a crippling attack of poliomyelitis, He was thus spared the disappointment of seeing both his major inventions fall from grace as a result of their unsuspected long-term damage to the environment.

George B. Kauffman, *Chemtech.*, Dec. 1989, p. 717. (Portraits.)
E. Farber (Ed.) *Great Chemists.* 1961. (Portrait.)
Biographical Memoirs: National Academy of Sciences, Vol.24, 1947.
Dictionary of Scientific Biography.

T I W

MILLIKAN, ROBERT ANDREWS Born at Morrison, Illinois, USA, 22 March 1868; died Pasadena, California, 19 December 1953. Famous for his evaluation of the fundamental physical constants e and h.

The son of a Congregational minister, Millikan studied physics in the United States and Germany. In 1896 he was appointed to Chicago University (professor from 1910), and from 1921 to 1945 was chairman of California Institute of Technology.

After ten years spent teaching and writing textbooks, in 1907 he began measurements of the electronic charge e. Earlier workers had examined the behaviour of clouds of charged droplets, but Millikan studied the effect on single drops of water (1909) and oil (1912) of electrical and gravitational fields. From this he derived the first accurate value of e (and the best for some years), and thereby strengthened the atomistic conception of electricity.

In 1916 Millikan confirmed the photo-electric equation of EINSTEIN according to which the kinetic energy of an electron is proportional to the frequency of the incident radiation multiplied by Planck's constant, h. By varying both energies and frequencies, Millikan obtained an accurate value for h. For his determinations of e and h he was awarded the Nobel prize in physics for 1923.

Millikan did much research on cosmic rays, organizing a world-wide survey in 1934, with results similar to those of A. H. COMPTON. He measured cosmic-ray intensities at great heights and great depths (in mines, at the bottom of lakes, etc.), and observed seasonal variations. His work gave a unity to the study of ultraviolet, cosmic, and x-radiation.

American Journal of Physics, **31**, 868, 1964. (Portrait.)
R. A. Millikan, *Autobiography*. 1950.
Biographical Memoirs. National Academy of Sciences, vol. 33. 1959.
R. H. Kargon, *The Rise of Robert Millikan*. 1982.
Dictionary of Scientific Biography.
Tyler Wasson (Ed.), *Nobel Prize Winners*. 1987. (Portrait.)
Judith R. Goldstein, *Millikan's School: A History of the California Institute of Technology*. 1992.
C A R

MILNE, EDWARD ARTHUR Born at Hull, Yorkshire, England, 14 February 1896; died Dublin, 21 September, 1950. Remembered for his work on solar structure and his 'kinematic relativity'.

Milne was the son of the headmaster of a Church of England school. Educated at Hymers College, Hull, he won a scholarship to Trinity College, Cambridge (1914). He was made a Prize Fellow of Trinity College in 1919, and in the following year was appointed Assistant Director of the Solar Physics Observatory, Cambridge. In 1924, Milne was give a chair of applied mathematics in Manchester, which he left only to take up the newly created Rouse Ball Chair of Mathematics at Oxford. He was elected FRS in 1926.

Milne's earliest researches were into the problems of radiative equilibrium and the theory of stellar atmospheres. He collaborated for some time with R. H. Fowler (1889–1944), on M. SAHA's theory of high temperature ionization, modifying considerably many of its accepted results. Their fixing of a temperature scale for the sequence of stellar spectra marked an enormous advance in the knowledge of the surface condition of stars. Milne investigated the balance of radiation pressure and gravitational forces in the chromosphere, and found conditions of instability which would lead to the ejection of atoms from the Sun with high thermal velocities. At Oxford, he continued his work on stellar atmospheres, and on amending the pioneer work of A. S. EDDINGTON on stellar structure.

In about 1932, Milne's attention turned to the phenomenon of galactic recession – the 'expanding Universe'. His world models, especially those with a statistical character, seemed to some astronomers to offer more than contemporary relativistic homogeneous models. He was, however, severely criticized by many for the rationalism supposedly inherent in his basic 'kinematic relativity'.

Obituary Notices of Fellows of the Royal Society, 1951. (Portrait.)
G. J. Whitrow, *Nature*, **166**, 715, 1950.
Dictionary of National Biography.
Dictionary of Scientific Biography.
J D N

MILSTEIN, CÉSAR Born at Bahia Blanca, Argentina, 8 October 1927. Molecular biologist.

Milstein was educated at the Collegio Nacional, Bahia Blanca, and graduated from the University of Buenos Aires in 1952. He studied at the Institute of Biological Chemistry in Buenos Aires, and was awarded a PhD in 1957 for his work on enzymes. He then went to Cambridge University on a British Council fellowship to work under F. SANGER, gaining a second PhD in 1960. In 1961 he returned to Argentina as head of the molecular biology division of the National Institute of Microbiology in Buenos Aires, but resigned after the military coup in 1962. He returned to Cambridge in 1963 where he joined the staff of the MRC Laboratory of Molecular Biology. In 1983 he became deputy director and head of the Protein and Nucleic Acid Chemistry Division.

In Cambridge, Milstein worked on the structure of an immuno-globulin and then moved on to research into how the body makes antibodies, proteins produced by the immune system to destroy antigens. With G. J. F. Köhler (1946–) he developed a technique for making antibodies with identical chemical structures, which he called monoclonal antibodies. The first monoclonal antibody was made in 1975. It soon became possible to produce antibodies against a wide range of antigens. By the 1980s monoclonal antibodies were also being used for diagnostic tests, and were important in improving the diagnosis and treatment of cancer.

Milstein shared the Nobel prize in physiology or medicine in 1984 with N. K. Jerne (1911–) and G. J. F. Köhler for developing a technique for making monoclonal antibodies.

C. Milstein, *Messing about with Isotopes and Enzymes and Antibodies*. In F. Ahmad *et al.* (Eds), *From Gene to Protein: Translation into Biotechnology*. 1982.
Les Prix Nobel in 1984. 1985. (Portrait.)
Tyler Wasson (Ed.), *Nobel Prize Winners*. 1987. (Portrait.)
A P B

MINKOWSKI, HERMANN Born at Alexotas, near Kaunas, Lithuania, 22 June 1864; died Göttingen, Germany, 12 January 1909. Mathematician who propounded the concept of space-time.

After studying and lecturing at Königsberg, Minkowski was professor at the *École Polytechnique* at Zürich from 1896 to 1902, and then at Göttingen.

His chief work was in the field of relativity. In a paper of 1908 he showed that the differential equations of the electromagnetic field for moving bodies can be derived from the same system of bodies at rest, by using the principle of relativity, as proposed by J. H. POINCARÉ. He proceeded to study those groups of transformations which leave invariant the propagation of electromagnetic waves in free space. He then arrived at a conception of a four-dimensional manifold in which space and time were interlinked. His ideas on this space-time continuum were published in *Raum und Zeit* (1909). His formulation of the continuum as one in which time is not separable from the three space dimensions was not generally accepted; however, his views were invaluable. To quote EINSTEIN: 'His recognition that the four-dimensional space-time continuum of the theory of relativity shows a pronounced relationship to the three-dimensional continuum of Euclidean geometrical space ... Without it the general theory of relativity would have got no further than its long clothes.'

He made contributions in other pure mathematical fields, being responsible for theorems in the theory of quadratic forms, in 1881 receiving the grand prize of the *Académie des sciences* for his memoir on the theory of quadratic forms with integral coefficients. He introduced number theory into geometry by the conception of the lattice point. Apart from *Raum und Zeit*, his main publications were *Geometrie der Zahlen* (1896), *Diophantische Approximationen* (1907), and *Gesammelte Abhandlungen* (1911).

D. Hilbert, *Nachrichten der Gesellschaft der Wissenschaften zu Göttingen*. 1909.
L. L. Woodruff (Ed.), *The Development of the Sciences*. 1923.
Dictionary of Scientific Biography.

D N

MINOT, GEORGE RICHARDS Born at Boston, Massachusetts, USA, 2 December 1885; died there, 25 February 1950. Renowned for introducing liver treatment for pernicious anaemia.

Minot, the son of a physician, graduated in medicine at Harvard University in 1912 and in 1928 was appointed professor of medicine there, and also Director of the Thorndike Memorial Laboratory.

His interest in blood disorders developed while he was a medical student and remained one of the main interests of his life. Early in his studies he became convinced that pernicious anaemia was caused by a deficiency of something in the body. In 1934, along with G. H. Whipple (1878–1976) and W. P. Murphy (1892–1987), he was awarded a Nobel prize for the discovery of liver therapy in anaemias. Whipple, in 1920, began studying the influence of food on blood regeneration in dogs which had been artificially bled. He found that certain kinds of food – liver in particular – were considerably superior to others in stimulating a vigorous formation of blood. Whipple's results gave Minot the idea that certain foods might give favourable results in patients with pernicious anaemia – an idea vastly different from the current methods of treating the disease, which involved, for example, the use of arsenic and splenectomy. In 1926, Minot and his co-worker Murphy published their famous short paper entitled *Treatment of Pernicious Anaemia with a Special Diet*. Their studies included regularly feeding large quantities – up to half a pound daily – of liver to patients. On previous occasions when liver had been tried the

quantities used had been too small for successful results.

After the success of liver therapy had been established Minot – with co-workers – extended anaemia studies by demonstrating the efficacy of certain liver fractions (Vitamin B_{12} is now known to be the active principle), and by devising quantitative methods for assessing the response of the body to haemopoietic factors. The success of the liver/anaemia story – coming only a few years after the discovery of insulin (see F. G. BANTING) – was important not only because of the many lives it saved, but because it stimulated a new physiological approach to problems of haemopoiesis and of gastro-intestinal function.

Minot's general medical interests were widespread. For example, he studied arthritis, cancer, and Vitamin B deficiency. However, much of his far-reaching influence on medical research stemmed from his directorship of the Thorndike Laboratory in Boston, whither, it has been said, young graduates of every nationality journeyed to obtain the training and mental stimulation which were inseparable from an association with Minot.

Ll. G. Stevenson. *Nobel Prize Winners in Medicine and Physics 1901–1950*. 1953. (Portrait.)
Biographical Memoirs. National Academy of Sciences, vol. 45. 1974.
Dictionary of Scientific Biography.
Tyler Wasson (Ed.), *Nobel Prize Winners*. 1987. (Portrait.)

J K C

MITSCHERLICH, EILHARD Born at Neuende, Jever, Germany, 17 January 1794; died Berlin, 28 August 1863. Famous for his discovery of the chemical phenomenon of isomorphism.

Originally intending to enter the diplomatic corps, Mitscherlich studied Oriental languages at Heidelberg and Berlin. Forced to abandon this ambition by changing political circumstances, he went to Göttingen to read medicine and science (1817). Moving to Berlin in 1818 he began to study crystallography. Struck by the similarity between arsenate and phosphate crystals, he learned from the mineralogist G. Rose (1798–1873) how to measure crystal angles and soon embarked on extensive crystallographic studies. Investigations on the sulphates showed that many of them had both similar compositions and identical (or nearly identical) crystal forms.

Late in 1819 BERZELIUS was passing through Berlin, and, learning of this work, invited Mitscherlich to join him in Stockholm. Here a fruitful partnership ensued for one and a half years and Mitscherlich extended his studies from arsenates and phosphates to carbonates, deducing that isomorphism (similar crystal form) implies similar constitutions (1822). He recognized the limitations of his law, and also the existence of dimorphism (two different crystalline forms for one substance).

In 1822 Mitscherlich returned to Berlin as assistant professor of chemistry; from 1825 until his death he was full professor. He continued to do much work on isomorphism, and discovered many further examples, crystallographic data being accompanied by analytical figures. He also worked on a modification of the method devised by J. B. A. DUMAS for determining vapour densities (applying it to many inorganic substances), and developed a combustion method for organic analysis. He introduced 'fusion mixture', a mixture of sodium and potassium carbonates, for treatment of silicates in analysis. He discovered selenic acid in 1827 and always retained a keen interest in mineralogy and geology.

The name benzene ('Benzin') is due to Mitscherlich, who obtained it from benzoic acid and lime. He also prepared nitrobenzene, azobenzene, benzophenone, diphenyl sulphone, benzene sulphonic acid, and various halogenated benzenes. Interested in catalysis, he shared the view of H. DAVY of the catalytic role of the oxides of nitrogen in the 'chamber process' for making sulphuric acid (see J. ROEBUCK). He was one of the first to recognize yeast as a micro-organism (1842) and showed its aqueous suspension could invert sugar.

Mitscherlich maintained a high regard for Berzelius, whose theories he helped to propagate and whose influence is clear in his own work. Berzelius, in his extensive use of the law of isomorphism in correcting atomic weights, gave to Mitscherlich a worthy and enduring memorial.

J. R. Partington, *A History of Chemistry*, vol. 4. 1964. (Portrait.)

W. J. Hughes, *Journal of the Royal Institute of Chemistry*, **87**, 265, 1963.

Dictionary of Scientific Biography.

H. W. Schütt, *Eilhard Mitscherlich: Baumeister am Fundament der Chemie.* 1992.

C A R

MOBIUS, AUGUST FERDINAND Born at Schulpforta, Germany, 17 November 1790; died Leipzig, 26 September 1868. Astronomer and mathematician.

Mobius originally intended to read law at Leipzig University but soon abandoned this in favour of astronomy and mathematics. After studying elsewhere in Germany (1813–16) he returned to Leipzig as extraordinary professor of astronomy. He was appointed full professor in 1844 and director of the observatory in 1848.

In astronomy he published some observational work but his greatest contribution was *Die Elemente der Mechanik des Himmels* (1843) a rigorous treatment of celestial mechanics not invoking higher mathematics. In mathematics his greatest achievement was the development of the barycentric calculus, based on analogy with the physical principle that a system of weights located at various points can be treated as the sum of the weights located at the centre of gravity. This he made public in a classic work *Der Barycentrische Calcul* (1827). He was also interested in topology and his name if perpetuated in the single-sided object known as the Mobius Strip.

Dictionary of Scientific Biography.

Allgemeine deutsche Biographie, Vol XX, 1885.

J. Fauvel, R. Flood and Robin Wilson (Eds), *Mobius and his Band: Mathematics in Nineteenth-Century Germany.* 1993.

T I W

MOHOROVIČIĆ, ANDRIJA Born in Volosko, Croatia, 23 January 1857; died Zagreb, 18 December 1936. Seismologist, meteorologist.

Mohorovičić graduated in mathematics and physics at Prague in 1875. After seven years as a school teacher he was appointed to the Royal

Nautical School in Bakar, teaching among other things meteorology and oceanography: he founded the Bakar Meteorological Station in 1887. In 1892 he became director of the Meteorological Station in Zagreb. In 1900 he succeeded in removing control of this from Budapest and re-establishing it as the Royal Regional Centre for Meteorology and Geodynamics (later (1921) the Geophysical Institute). In 1901, following a powerful earthquake near Zagreb, a seismological observatory was added and this quickly became one of the leading seismological centres in central Europe. He continued in active seismological research until 1926.

Although he was a dedicated and meticulously accurate observer, it is doubtful whether Mohorovičić would have become internationally known but for an event that occurred on 8 October 1909. A powerful earthquake occurred in the Kulpa Valley 50 km south of Zagreb. By careful analysis of all the available records of the resulting P (primary) and S (secondary) waves he identified two distinct pairs of P and S phases travelling at different speeds. He deduced the existence of a well-defined outer layer of the Earth (the crust), some 50 km thick, overlying the mantle: the boundary of the two is now known as the Mohorovičić Discontinuity (popularly the Moho). Later research established that the layer extends worldwide, being comparatively thin (5–8 km) under the oceans. This complemented the discovery (1906) by R. D. OLDHAM of the Earth's central core at a depth of about 3000 km.

Dictionary of Scientific Biography.

T I W

MOHS, FRIEDRICH Born at Gernrode, Saxony, Germany, 29 January 1773; died Agordo, South Tyrol, Austria, 29 September 1839. Geologist and mineralogist.

Mohs studied at the University of Halle, and at the Freiberg *Bergakademie* under the great A. G. WERNER. He was professor-elect in a proposed mining academy (on the Freiberg model) in Dublin, but the venture fell through, and he became a teacher in Graz. In 1817 he was appointed Werner's successor in the *Bergakademie*, though he no longer held to the latter's geological theories; in 1826 he went to Vienna as professor of mineralogy.

Mohs is chiefly remembered today for his widely used scale of hardness of minerals. In his lifetime he was more famous for his system of classification of minerals, which he divided into genera and species, after the style of Linnaeus's *System of Nature*; but though formally impeccable, his system took too little account of chemical composition to satisfy mineralogists for very long.

Allgemeine Deutsche Biographie.

Wilhelm Fuchs *et al.*, *Friedrich Mohs und sein Wirken in wissenschaftlicher Hinsicht.* 1843.

Dictionary of Scientific Biography.

W V F

MOISSAN, FERDINAND FRÉDÉRIC HENRI Born in Paris, 28 September 1852; died there, 20 February 1907. He was the first to prepare fluorine, and also several of the less common metals.

The son of a railway employee, Moissan began life as a pharmacist's apprentice. Then he returned to study under Edmond Frémy (1814–94), professor of chemistry at the *École Polytechnique* and the *Muséum d'Histoire Naturelle*, who was interested in the problem of liberating fluorine. Though Frémy was well aware of the toxic nature of fluorides, which had proved fatal to his Belgian associate, Paulin Louyet (1818–50), he persevered with the electrolysis of fused calcium fluoride. He failed, however, to collect any fluorine, though in Birmingham, George Gore (1826–1908) in 1869 obtained evidence of transient evolution of the gas from the vigorous attack on electrodes and reagents.

It was left to Moissan to isolate this highly reactive element and win the approval of Frémy, who had failed. As the accommodation at the School of Pharmacy was poor, Moissan found other laboratory premises; he was able to devote all his time to the fluorine quest, thanks to an affluent father-in-law. He was able to use the electric battery of Henri Jules Debray (1827–88) for electrolysis of fused fluorides, the only possible means of preparing this exceptionally reactive element. Frémy had found anhydrous hydrogen fluoride to be non-conducting, and addition of water was impracticable. Moissan made the decisive innovation of dissolving potassium fluoride in liquid hydrogen fluoride; his use of platinum-iridium electrodes and fluospar stoppers solved corrosion problems, though later protective fluoride coatings on metals provided alternatives.

Moissan's success in liberating fluorine in 1886 brought him international recognition, but this should not detract from his striking contributions in the field of metallurgy. His name is linked also with artificial diamonds, though the significance of his results has since had to be reassessed. Far more significant was Moissan's work in using the high temperatures attainable in the electric furnace he developed in 1892. He prepared synthetic ruby, and nitrides, borides, and carbides of metals. Since he had access to industrial premises in Paris such as the Edison Works, he was able to prepare a number of less common metals. Long before modern metallurgy made commercially available such metals as molybdenum, tantalum, niobium, vanadium, titanium, tungsten and uranium, he prepared samples in his electric furnace.

Moissan, so practical in applied science, was also an outstanding lecturer, excelling with demonstrations at the Sorbonne, where he was appointed professor of inorganic chemistry in 1900. He received many honours, including Foreign Membership of the Royal Society (1905) and a Nobel prize (1906).

W. Ramsay, Moissan Memorial Lecture, *Journal of the Chemical Society*, **101**, 477, 1912.

A. Stock, *Berichte Der Deutschen Chemischen Gesellschaft*, **40**, 5099, 1907.

E. Farber (Ed.), *Great Chemists*. 1961. (Portrait.)

B. Harrow, *Eminent Chemists*. 1927.

Tyler Wasson (Ed.), *Nobel Prize Winners*. 1987. (Portrait.)

Dictionary of Scientific Biography.

M S

MOIVRE, ABRAHAM DE *See* DEMOIVRE.

MOND, LUDWIG Born at Kassel, Germany, 7 March 1839; died London, 11 December 1909. Chemist and industrialist.

Mond came of a middle-class Jewish merchant family. He studied chemistry at Marburg and Heidelberg, but left in 1858 without taking his doctorate. While working in a series of short-lived jobs in the chemical industry, he invented a process for recovering sulphur from the offensive 'alkali waste' of the soda process invented by N. LEBLANC. In 1862 John Hutchinson (1825–65) of Widnes offered Mond the opportunity of perfecting and working this invention, and for several years he lived a rather unsettled existence, travelling between Lancashire and another project in Holland.

He was impressed, however, by the great possibilities of the new ammonia–soda process, which had no problems of waste-product disposal; and in 1872 (under special agreement with the inventor, E. SOLVAY) he set up his own works at Winnington Hall, Cheshire, in partnership with J. T. BRUNNER. Winnington came into full production only in late 1874, after a long series of formidable engineering and organizational difficulties had been surmounted. This ever-expanding venture posed a threat to the established Leblanc alkali manufacturers of the Widnes district. Despite regrouping as the United Alkali Company, the Leblanc manufacturers were eventually overwhelmed.

With increasing prosperity and leisure, Mond turned to industrial research. A search for cheap ammonia for the Solvay process led him to attempt, and abandon, the fixation of atmospheric nitrogen, finally achieved by Fritz HABER; the burning of coal in a mixture of steam and air, however, gave him not only ammonia but also producer gas, to exploit which he formed the Power Gas Corporation. He was always anxious to utilize waste products, or to avoid their production, but his many attempts to use the chloride wasted in the ammonia–soda reaction were failures. Observation of the corrosion of nickel by gases containing carbon monoxide led to the unexpected discovery (1889) of nickel carbonyl. Mond seized upon this as a novel means of refining nickel, and spent his later years building up the Mond Nickel Company, based on Canadian ore.

Among other honours, he was elected FRS in 1891. Towards the end of his life he lived mainly in Rome, and amassed a valuable collection of paintings, which he bequeathed to the National Gallery in London. Of his two sons, Robert (1867–1938) became an Egyptologist, and was knighted; Alfred, Lord Melchett (1868–1930), went into politics, and was one of the founders, and first chairman, of Imperial Chemical Industries.

J. M. Cohen, *The Life of Ludwig Mond*. 1956. (Portraits.)

Dictionary of National Biography.

Peter J. T. Morris, *Endeavour* (New Series), **13**, 34, 1989. (Portrait.)

Journal of the Chemical Society, **113**, 318, 1918.

F. G. Donnan, *Ludwig Mond F.R.S., 1839–1909*. 1939. (Reprinted from *Proceedings of the Royal Institution*, **30**, 709, 1939.)

W V F

MONGE, GASPARD Born at Beaune, France, 10 May 1746; died Paris, 28 July 1818. French mathematician, the founder of descriptive geometry.

Monge, who was of humble origins, received an

education at the local *lycée*. He then attended, and soon became an instructor at, the military academy at Mézières in 1768. During this period he developed his conception of descriptive geometry. It is to him we owe the methods of modern engineering drawing. Its practical importance led to its being treated as a military secret for a number of years; only in 1795 were Monge's ideas published in his *Géométrie descriptive*. In that year he was appointed director of the newly founded *École Polytechnique*.

He also at this time worked on the application of calculus to curves and surfaces in three dimensions. He is also credited with the first work on operational research concerned with the transportation of materials for fortifications.

In his work in geometry he combined methods of synthetic and analytical geometry: his teaching and published work led to the further development of projective, analytical, and differential geometry – his pupils included J. N. P. Hachette (1769–1834) J. B. BIOT, C. Dupin (1784–1873), and J. V. PONCELET.

In the revolutionary period, Monge was a close friend of Napoleon; he became Minister of the Navy and later was responsible for munitions; his enthusiastic labours earned him the title of Count of Péluse, but after the second restoration of the Bourbons this and all other honours, including his membership of the *Académie* were stripped from him; he died, a poor man, shortly afterwards.

L. de Launay, *Un grand Français: Monge, Fondateur de l'École Polytechnique.* 1933.

E. T. Bell, *Men of Mathematics.* 1937.

P-V. Aubry, *Monge, le savant ami de Napoléon: 1746–1818,* 1954.

E. D. Smith, *Scripta Mathematica,* **1**, 111, 1952.

Dictionary of Scientific Biography.
D N

MONIZ, ANTONIO EGAS Born at Avanca, Portugal, 29 November, 1874; died Lisbon, 13 December 1955. Inventor of cerebral angiography and of psychosurgery.

Moniz qualified in 1899 as Doctor of Medicine at the University of Coimbra, where he had previously taught mathematics and considered a career in engineering. He decided to specialize in neurology and turned to the great French School of Pierre Marie, J. J. Dejerine, J. F. F. Babinski, and J. A. Sicard (the originator of myelography for the radiological demonstration of spinal tumours) for his higher education. In 1911 he was appointed to the new chair of neurology at Lisbon.

He was dissatisfied with the early methods of demonstrating intracranial tumours by the injection of air into the cavities of the brain, introduced by W. E. Dandy (1886–1946), and began to experiment on cadavers by injecting different radio-opaque solutions into the arteries and taking x-ray pictures. After demonstrating the constancy of the position of the main cerebral arteries in the normal brain, he was the first to outline in a patient the size and location of an intracranial (pituitary) tumour by the displacement of the injected arteries in 1927. Although the contrast media first used by Moniz were not as harmless as he thought, the method has become established in diagnosis of brain affections, and has been applied with increasing success to the study of other organs; to

the diagnosis of tumours and of vascular disease throughout the body; and has led indirectly to great advances in treatment. Moniz and his school published 200 papers on normal and abnormal cerebral angiography.

Moniz worked on toxic psychosis early in his medical career (with F. Regis) and wrote in 1935: 'I am convinced that only by an organic orientation can psychiatry make real progress'. In the same year he learnt from J. F. Fulton (1899–1960) and G. F. Jacobsen the effect of frontal leucotomy (i.e. surgical division of the nerves connecting the frontal lobes to the rest of the brain) on the behaviour of two chimpanzees. After operation the animals lost the temper tantrums to which they had been prone when confronted with difficult problems. They remained alert, intelligent, and friendly, and it was no longer possible to induce an experimental neurosis. Moniz and Almeida Lima proceeded to carry out similar procedures on mental-hospital patients, the first attempt to affect the mind by operating on brains which were not organically diseased. This raised ethical problems, but very satisfactory results were obtained; fourteen of the first twenty patients were declared cured or improved, and none had died. Various modifications of the operation were carried out all over the world during the next two decades, until the advent of new psychotropic drugs obviated the need for this kind of operation in a high proportion of cases. However, increased knowledge of brain function has resulted from this vogue and it showed the way to psychosurgical attacks on other parts of the brain.

Moniz was elected to Parliament as a left-wing monarchist in 1900. After the revolution of 1908 he spent a short spell in prison, but was Portugese Minister in Madrid towards the end of the 1914–18 war, and Foreign Minister of Portugal in 1918, leading the delegation of his country at the Paris Peace Conference in 1919. However, a political quarrel led to a duel in 1919, after which he retired from politics. A schizophrenic patient tried to assassinate him some years later. He wrote an operetta and was an accomplished literary critic and historian. He received, with W. R. Hess (1881–1973), the Nobel prize for physiology or medicine in 1949.

F. R. Perino, *Journal of the International College of Surgeons,* **36**, 261, 1961. (Portrait.)

Lancet, ii, 1345, 1955.

E. Moniz, *How I Came to Perform Prefrontal Leucotomy.* 1948.

Tyler Wasson (Ed.), *Nobel Prize Winners.* 1987. (Portrait.)

American Journal of Psychiatry. April 1956.
E H J

MONOD, JACQUES LUCIEN Born in Paris, 9 February 1910; died Cannes, 31 May 1976. Molecular biologist.

Jacques Monod, educated in Cannes and Paris, graduated in natural sciences in 1931. After working with the distinguished microbiologist E. Chatton in Strasbourg in 1932, he returned to Paris to do research at the Sorbonne on the growth of *E. coli*, becoming assistant in the Zoology Laboratory in 1934. He went to work under T. H. MORGAN at the California Institute of Technology in 1936 on a Rockefeller Fellowship, returning to Paris in 1937 and obtaining a PhD in 1941.

In 1943 he explained enzymatic adaptation in bacteria in terms of mutation. With M. Cohn he proceeded to develop the induction theory of enzyme synthesis, using immunological techniques.

In the late 1950s the operon theory elaborated by Monod with F. Jacob (1920–) and A. Lwoff (1902–) introduced the concept of induction and repression in enzyme synthesis as previously suggested by L. Shilard. Their discovery of a class of genes responsible for the regulatory mechanism of the cell and of the messenger role of the RNA molecule in 1961 was built on the work of F. H. C. CRICK, J. D. WATSON, M. PERUTZ and others in the 1950s and led to the elucidation of the chemistry of the transfer of genetic information and established molecular biology as an exact science.

At a meeting in Cold Spring Harbor in 1961, Monod reviewed the state of molecular biology and put forward the theory of allostery whereby the regulator acts on the enzyme at a specific site other than that of the substrate. He was awarded a Nobel prize for physiology or medicine (together with Jacob and Lwoff) in 1965. Soon afterwards he published his classic in the philosophy of biology, 'Chance and Necessity'.

In 1945 he joined the Pasteur Institute under Lwoff, taking charge of the Cellular Biochemistry Laboratory in 1954; he became professor of metabolic chemistry at the Sorbonne in 1959. In 1967 he was appointed to a chair at the Collège de France and became director of the Pasteur Institute in 1971.

He was recipient of many academic and national honours including the Legion d'Honneur.

Biographical Memoirs of Fellows of The Royal Society, 1977. (Portrait.)
Les Prix Nobel en 1965. 1966. (Portrait.)
Dictionary of Scientific Biography, Supp. II.
Tyler Wasson (Ed.), *Nobel Prize Winners*. 1987. (Portrait.)

I M McC

MONRO, ALEXANDER, *primus* Born in London, 8 September 1697; died Edinburgh, 10 July 1767. Distinguished anatomist and a founder of the Edinburgh Medical School.

Monro, son of John Monro (1670–1740), a Leiden-trained surgeon in Edinburgh, was educated there and first assisted his father in his practice. In 1717 he studied anatomy in London under William Cheselden (1688–1752). In 1718 he went to Paris and then to Leiden, where he studied under H. BOERHAAVE. He was admitted a member of the Incorporation of Surgeons at Edinburgh (1719), and in 1720, by the influence of his father and others, he was appointed the first professor of a medical subject – viz. anatomy – in the University of Edinburgh. This marked the formation of the Edinburgh School. In 1723 Monro was elected a Fellow of the Royal Society of London, but it does not appear that he was ever formally admitted. The number of students attending his lectures rose from 57 in 1720 to 182 in 1749. In 1755 his son Alexander MONRO *secundus* was associated with him as Conjoint Professor. In 1756 he was made a Fellow of the Royal College of Physicians

of Edinburgh; he now attended patients in the Edinburgh Royal Infirmary. He resigned his chair in 1764.

Monro's best-known work was his *Anatomy of the Human Bones* (1726). In later editions there was included the *Anatomy of the Human Nerves* and of other parts. This work went through eleven editions. His real influence was as a teacher and a founder of the Edinburgh School.

R. E. Wright-St Clair, *Doctors Monro: A Medical Saga.* 1964. (Portrait.)
University of Edinburgh Journal, **17**, 77, 1953.

J. D. Comrie, *History of Scottish Medicine.* 1932.
A. Miles, *The Edinburgh School of Surgery before Lister.* 1918.
Dictionary of Scientific Biography.
Dictionary of National Biography.

E A U

MONRO, ALEXANDER, *secundus* Born in Edinburgh, 10 March 1733; died there, 2 October 1817. Distinguished anatomist.

In 1745 Monro, the son of Alexander MONRO *primus*, entered the University of Edinburgh at the age of 12. In 1750 he began the study of medicine, and early showed his great interest in anatomy. In 1753 Monro *primus* virtually handed over the evening session of his successful anatomy class to his son. The experiment was so successful that in June 1754 Monro *primus* petitioned the Town Council to appoint his son Conjoint Professor. Monro *secundus* received his commission of appointment in July 1755, although he did not qualify in medicine until later that year. Thereafter he studied in London, Paris, Berlin and Leiden. In 1759 he was elected a Fellow of the Royal College of Physicians of Edinburgh. In the session 1758–9 Monro *primus* delivered only the opening lecture, and his son gave all the others. From then on for fifty years he delivered his famous lectures at Edinburgh. In 1807, on the eve of his retirement, he stated that since he was appointed to the chair, 13 404 students had passed through his hands, and of these 5 831 were from outside Scotland. In 1798 he successfully petitioned the Town Council to have his own son, Alexander MONRO *tertius*, appointed as Conjoint Professor with him.

Monro had an extensive practice as a physician, and he also acted as a surgical consultant, but he was not an operating surgeon. He was also professor of systematic surgery but between 1766 and 1804 the effective teaching of surgery passed from his hands by the creation of other chairs of surgery in the University and the Royal College of Surgeons of Edinburgh.

Monro's most important work was his *Observations on the Structure and Functions of the Nervous System* (1783). This contains his description of the 'foramen of Monro' in the brain, which he had originally described in 1764. Although this structure had been previously mentioned by other anatomists, Monro's description is by far the best. This book also contains good descriptions of the sympathetic ganglia. In 1788 he published an excellent account of the mucous bursae of the body. Of his many other publications mention may be made of *The Structure and Physiology of Fishes*

(1785). In 1767 he was the first to describe and use a stomach-tube.

R. E. Wright-St Clair, *Doctors Monro: A Medical Saga*. 1964. (Portrait.)

J. D. Comrie, *History of Scottish Medicine*. 1932.

A. Miles, *The Edinburgh School of Surgery before Lister*. 1918.

Dictionary of National Biography.

Dictionary of Scientific Biography.

E A U

MONRO, ALEXANDER, *tertius* Born in Edinburgh, 5 November 1773; died Craiglockhart, near Edinburgh, 10 March 1859. Anatomist.

Monro was the son of Alexander MONRO *secundus*. Educated at the University of Edinburgh, he graduated as a doctor of medicine in 1794. In the same year he became a Fellow of the Royal College of Physicians of Edinburgh. On the petition of his father he was appointed Conjoint Professor (with his father), of Medicine, Anatomy, and Surgery in the University of Edinburgh. From 1802 he carried out the greater part of the teaching in anatomy, and from 1808 he was in sole charge. During his tenure of the chair a dispute regarding the creation of a separate chair of systematic surgery in the University came to a head. Although the Crown established a Regius Chair of Surgery in 1831, Monro continued to teach that subject. He was elected a Fellow of the Royal Society of Edinburgh in 1798, and from 1825 to 1827 he was President of the Royal College of Physicians of Edinburgh.

Monro *tertius* was a voluminous writer, but he made no important anatomical discovery. Although it was frequently stated that he was a dull and unimpressive lecturer, men such as Robert Liston (1794–1847), Richard BRIGHT, Thomas ADDISON, and Marshall HALL learned much of their anatomy from him. When Monro retired from his Chair in 1846 he had held it for forty-eight years. The Monro dynasty in Edinburgh now ended, after having lasted for 126 years.

R. E. Wright-St Clair, *Doctors Monro: A Medical Saga*. 1964. (Portrait.)

J. D. Comrie, *History of Scottish Medicine*. 1932.

Dictionary of National Biography.

E A U

MONTGOLFIER, JOSEPH-MICHEL AND JACQUES-ETIENNE Joseph was born at Vidalon-lès-Annonay, France, in 1740; died Balaruc-les-Bains, 26 June 1810. Etienne was born at Vidalon-lès-Annonay, 7 January 1745; died Serrieres, 2 August 1799. Pioneers of lighter-than-air-flight.

The sons of a paper manufacturer, both brothers were employed for a time in the family business, to which they contributed various inventions. Etienne, though he had studied architecture under J-G. SOUFFLOT, was engaged in the concern until his death, and is said to have owed his safety during the Reign of Terror to the loyalty of his workmen. Joseph, who set up in paper manufacture on his own, received the Legion of Honour from Napoleon; and was the chief promoter of the Society for the Encouragement of National Industry, formed in 1802.

The origins of their interest in flight are unknown; according to one version, Joseph was attracted by the problem of penetrating the defences of Gibralter during the famous siege of 1779–83; according to another, Etienne's attention was aroused by the paper *On the Different Kinds of Air* by Joseph PRIESTLEY. Using a mixture of chopped hay and wool burnt under an envelope of taffeta silk, they lifted their first model hot-air balloon to a height of 70 feet (15 November 1782). On the following 5 June they sent up a much larger sphere of paper-covered canvas carrying 400 lb of ballast, in the presence of the local Estates. On 19 September 1783 three animals were successfully lifted in a wicker cage, and finally (21 November 1783) two passengers made a 7½-mile voyage in a *montgolfière*, remaining air-borne for nearly half an hour and reaching a height of about 3000 feet.

Although the hydrogen balloon quickly demonstrated its superiority, the brothers were planning the construction of a hot-air dirigible when the Revolution cut off provision for their experiments.

L. Rostaing, *La famille de Montgolfier*. 1910.

C. C. Gillispie, *The Montgolfier Brothers and the Invention of Aviation*. 1983.

Dictionary of Scientific Biography.

T K D

MOORE, STANFORD Born in Chicago, Illinois, USA, 4 September 1913; died New York, 23 August 1982. Biochemist concerned with analysis of amino acids.

Moore graduated in chemistry from Vanderbilt University in 1935, obtaining his doctorate in biochemistry from the University of Wisconsin in 1938. His entire career was spent in research on proteins at the Rockefeller Institute in New York. Following the onset of an incurable wasting disease, he committed suicide.

In 1940 Moore began a long collaboration with William H. Stein (1911–). Together they made a fundamental breakthrough in protein chemistry by using ion-exchange column chromatography to fractionate the complex of compounds formed during the hydrolysis of proteins. Amino acids were, in this way, identified and sequenced within a protein. A successful technique was announced in 1948, and by 1958 the process was automated by Beckman Instruments to became a standard piece of equipment in biochemical laboratories. The structure of proteins had hitherto been formulated by using the laborious methods of classical organic analysis, as in the method used by F. SANGER for insulin in 1950. Using the chromatographic technique, in 1959 Moore determined the amino acid sequence of ribonuclease, the enzyme which splits ribonucleic acid. This giant 124-amino acid protein was the second protein to be sequenced after insulin. Moore and Stein, together with C. B. Anfinsen (1916–), were jointly awarded the Nobel prize for chemistry in 1972. Together with the methods later developed for DNA sequencing, Moore's technology is a major feature of molecular biology.

The Annual Obituary 1982. 1983. (Portrait.)

McGraw Hill Modern Scientists and Engineers, vol.2, 1980.

Les Prix Nobel en 1972. 1973. (Portrait.)

Tyler Wasson (Ed.), *Nobel Prize Winners*. 1987. (Portrait.)

W H B

MORGAGNI, GIOVANNI BATTISTA Born at Forli, Italy, 20 February 1682; died Padua, 6 December

1771. Anatomist; initiator of the science of morbid anatomy.

Educated at the University of Bologna, where he graduated in philosophy and medicine in 1701, Morgagni became prosector under A. M. Valsalva (1666–1723), whom he admired for the rest of his life. When Valsalva left Bologna for Parma, Morgagni succeeded him as demonstrator of anatomy. His advancing reputation is indicated by his being made president of the *Accademia Inquietorum* at the age of 24, in which office he discouraged speculation in favour of accurate observation. In 1706 he commenced a series of anatomical publications under the title of *Adversaria Anatomica*, which gave him a European reputation as an anatomist. In 1712 he left Bologna for Padua, where, apart from a short unsuccessful trial of medical practice in his native town of Forli, he spent the rest of his life as a professor of anatomy. Shortly after settling in Padua he married Paola Vergieri of Forli, by whom he had fifteen children.

Morgagni was beloved both by his colleagues, who showed no envy of his rapidly increasing stipend, and his students. He basked in the friendship of many distinguished Venetian senators and cardinals and received honours from several successive Popes. His popularity with students is illustrated by his election as patron of those of the German nation at Padua. His international popularity amongst scientific workers was indicated by his election as a member of the *Accademia Naturae Curiosorum* 1708; the Royal Society 1724; the Academy of Sciences, Paris 1731; the Imperial Academy of St Petersburg 1735; and the Berlin Academy 1754.

All these honours came to him before he had produced his greatest work – *De Sedibus et Causis Morborum per Anatomen Indagatis*, published in 1761 when Morgagni was in his eightieth year.

The study of the anatomy of diseased organs was not new, but it could not become a science until normal anatomy had been established. This Leonardo da VINCI, VESALIUS, and their successors at Padua had achieved in the sixteenth century. During subsequent years many collections of abnormal or 'morbid' anatomical findings had been made, the earliest being those of Antonio Benivieni (*c.*1440–1502) in Florence. William HARVEY, too, collected many such observations which remained unpublished. Post-mortem examinations were reported by such men as F. Ruysch (1638–1731) in Holland, by R. de Vieussens (1641–1715) in France, and especially by Theophilus Bonet (1620–89) in his great *Sepulchretum Sive Anatomica Practica* (1679), which was a survey of 3000 autopsies made since classical times. Morgagni saw himself as improving on Bonet's work by adding to it his own 640 post-mortem descriptions. By systematically relating his pathological findings to careful and detailed clinical records of the patients' symptoms he revolutionized clinical medicine. Symptoms were henceforth seen as 'the cry of the suffering organs' and in the hands of men like L. Auenbrugger (1722–1809), who introduced percussion, and R. LAËNNEC who introduced auscultation, methods of detecting abnormalities of organs in the living patient began to be successfully devised. Later, in 1896, x-rays as introduced by W. K. RÖENTGEN provided an even better means of making anatomical diagnosis.

A. Castiglione (trans. E. B. Krumbhaar), *A History of Medicine*. 1941.
H. E. Sigerist, *Great Doctors*. 1933. (Portrait.)
G. R. Cameron, *Notes and Records of the Royal Society of London*, **9**, 218, 1952.
Dictionary of Scientific Biography.

K D K

MORGAN, THOMAS HUNT Born at Lexington, Virginia, USA, 25 September 1866; died Corona del Mar, California, 4 December 1945. Geneticist and embryologist.

Morgan studied biology at the universities of Kentucky and Johns Hopkins. He held three posts: Associate Professor of Zoology, Bryn Mawr (1891–1904); Professor of Experimental Zoology, Columbia University, New York (1904–28); and Professor of Biology, the California Institute of Technology, Pasadena (1928–45). His first studies were in embryology; it was he who showed by a very simple experiment with frog eggs that the Roux-Weismann theory of differentiation is untrue. A visit to H. de VRIES in Amsterdam, where mutant forms of the evening primrose were growing, drew him to the subject of variation. He was doubtful of the orthodox Darwinian theory of variation and like W. BATESON was inclined to rate discontinuous variations as more significant for evolution than continuous variations.

Morgan was also sceptical about the validity of MENDEL's laws. L. Cuénot's (1866–1951) breeding experiments with mice, which involved multiple alleles, increased his doubts. In 1908 he started breeding mice himself, followed by rats and the fruit fly *Drosophila*. At first he tried the effect of various mutagens on *Drosophila*, but without apparent success. His hybridization of these flies, however, instead of invalidating Mendel's laws, confirmed them. At the same time he found deviations from the law of independent assortment of characters. Thus his first mutant ('white eye') was almost completely confined to male flies, which led him to conclude that it is the male which is heterogametic (i.e. male = XY, female = XX). His second mutant ('rudimentary', i.e. rudimentary wings) was also confined to the males. But when he bred a race of the double mutant he obtained in their offspring all assortments of characters, as Mendel's law states, but not quite in the proportions expected if there were completely independent hereditary transmission of wing and eye characters. The initial limitation of these mutants to one sex he interpreted as due to their being determined by genes on the same chromosome. The recombination between them suggested to him that chromosomes had exchanged segments in the manner suggested by F. A. Janssens (1863–1924) in 1909. The departure from Mendelian expectation was not sufficient in this case to clinch the matter. In 1911 he discovered a considerable departure – very low percentage of recombination – between 'white eye' and 'yellow body'. In a short communication to *Science* that year he put forward the chromosome theory of inheritance, according to which the extent of recombination obtained between genes on the same chromosome is a measure of their spatial separation. A. H. STURTEVANT was still an undergraduate in 1911 when, in conversation with Morgan, he realized that variations in the strength of linkage between characters gave an index to their linear sequence on the chromosome. The same night he drew up the first chromosome. The same night he drew up the first chromosome map, which showed five sex-linked genes.

Morgan and his co-workers, Sturtevant, C. B. Bridges (1889–1938) and H. J. MULLER, developed this simple theory with astonishing success, with the result that they were able to interpret the whole range of Mendelian phenomena in terms of it. Morgan was a very active research worker and prolific writer. In his latter years he returned to his embryological studies.

The Royal Society, which awarded him its Darwin and Copley Medals, elected him to Fellowship in 1919. In 1933 he was awarded the Nobel prize for physiology or medicine.

Obituary Notices of Fellows of the Royal Society. 1947. (Portrait.)

Biographical Memoirs. National Academy of Sciences, vol. 33. 1959. (Portrait.)

I. Shine and S. Wrobel, *Thomas Hunt Morgan: Pioneer of Genetics.* 1976.

G. E. Allen, *Thomas Hunt Morgan.* 1978.

Tyler Wasson (Ed.) *Nobel Prize Winners.* 1987. (Portrait.)

Dictionary of Scientific Biography.

                                                                    R C O

MORLEY, EDWARD WILLIAMS Born at Newark, New Jersey, USA, 29 January 1838; died Hartford, Connecticut, 24 February 1923. Chemist and physicist; remembered for his work on the densities of oxygen and hydrogen, and for his development with A. A. MICHELSON of the interferometer and the Michelson-Morley experiment.

After graduating from Williams College in 1860, Morley entered the Congregational ministry before he became professor of natural history and chemistry in Western Reserve College (1869); he retired as Professor Emeritus in 1906. Morley was not only capable of original thought, but had a genius for designing and constructing the necessary experimental apparatus, especially devices for fine and exact measurement, such as a precision eudiometer, two types of differential manometers, and, in collaboration with A. A. Michelson, the interferometer for measuring lengths in terms of wavelengths of light. The latter instrument was used in the famous and crucial Michelson-Morley experiment to measure the relative motion of the Earth and the luminiferous ether. The research that brought Morley world-wide recognition, however, was completed in 1895; the very accurate determination of the densities of oxygen and hydrogen and the ratio in which they combine. The values he arrived at were accepted as definitive for over thirty years. He received many awards from learned societies, including the Royal Society and the American Chemical Society; he also received honorary degrees from a number of universities.

O. F. Tower, *Science,* **57**, 605, 1923.

Smithsonian Contributions to Knowledge, No. 980.

H. R. Williams, *Edward Williams Morley.* 1957. (Portrait.)

                                                                    A E R

MORSE, SAMUEL FINLEY BREESE Born at Charlestown, Massachusetts, USA, 27 April 1791; died New York, 2 April 1872. Artist and inventor.

Morse was the son of a Congregational clergyman, famous for his geography textbooks; he was educated at Phillips Academy, Andover, and at Yale. Until he was over 40 his life was devoted to painting, which he studied in London (1811–15) and in France and Italy (1829–32). He had considerable success as a portrait-painter, becoming the first president of the National Academy of Design and a life professor in the University of the City of New York. His earnings, however, were small, and he was greatly disappointed when Congress rejected his application to take part in the embellishment of the Capitol.

He had been interested in electrical demonstrations given at Yale and later at the New York Athenaeum, and was the inventor of a flexible piston-pump and a machine for cutting marble. But his interest in invention was not effectively aroused until October 1832, when a fellow passenger on the return Atlantic crossing happened to demonstrate some electrical apparatus acquired in Europe. The idea of the telegraph was discussed, and before the end of the year Morse's notebook recorded each of his three basic conceptions. These were respectively a transmitting apparatus, based on interruption of an electric circuit; a very crude receiving apparatus, in which an electromagnet operated a pen to record notches in a track on a moving slip of paper; and a code for translating these signals into numbers and letters.

By 1837, with the help of Joseph HENRY and his friend L. D. Gale (1800–83), Morse had added the use of electromagnetic relays to extend the distance to which a message could be sent and the number of branch lines through which it could be transmitted. He then found in Alfred Vail (1807–59) an assistant with money, but in Europe his invention had been anticipated by that of C. WHEATSTONE and even in America it had no success until 1843. Morse was then allowed to construct for Congress a forty-mile line from Washington to Baltimore, over which he sent the well-known message to Vail (24 May 1844), 'What God hath wrought'.

Although the following years were clouded by litigation and an unfortunate quarrel with Henry, Morse eventually made a fortune from his US patents, and received a modest gratuity from European sources. In 1857–8 he was for a time electrician for the transatlantic cable project of C. W. Field (1819–92). The Morse code, still widely used, is perhaps his chief original contribution to modern communications, yet in American eyes 'he remains the greatest figure in the history of the telegraph'.

C. Mabee, *The American Leonardo.* 1943.

Dictionary of American Biography.

P. J. Staiti, *Samuel F. B. Morse.* 1991.)

                                                                    T K D

MORTON, WILLIAM THOMAS GREEN Born at Charlton City, Massachusetts, USA, 9 August 1819; died New York, 15 July 1868. Dentist; pioneer of anaesthesia.

Little is known of Morton's early life. He is reputed to have been a graduate of the Baltimore College of Dentistry, but this is doubtful. He established himself in practice with Horace WELLS, who was interested in applying the anaesthetic properties of nitrous oxide, first observed by Humphry DAVY. Morton was at the time working for a medical degree at Harvard Medical School and there had as a teacher the chemist C. T. Jackson (1805–80), who suggested to him the local application of ether to deaden pain when stopping teeth. This led Morton to practise ether anaesthesia (a term coined by O. W. HOLMES). This he demonstrated publicly on 16 October 1846, successfully anaesthetizing a patient who was to have a tumour removed from his neck.

Despite uninformed criticism, ether soon became widely established in medical practice, but unfortunately Morton reaped no benefit from his discovery. He fell into violent dispute with Jackson – with whom he had patented his technique – over the question of priority, and engaged in ruinous litigation with him. A fund was raised for Morton in England, but he never received the money, as the offer was eventually withdrawn in the face of bitter opposition by Jackson; likewise, a Bill to make him an award of $100,000 thrice failed to pass Congress (1852/3/4). In the fullness of time Morton was elected (1920) to the American Hall of Fame, but he died bitter and impoverished. Though his claim to be the sole discoverer of ether anaesthesia is questionable, there is no doubt that it was he who secured its wide use in surgical practice.

Dictionary of American Biography.

W. S. Sykes, *Essays on the First Hundred Years of Anaesthesia* (2 vols). 1960–1.

R. H. Major, *A History of Medicine*, vol. 2. 1954.

R. S. Atkinson and T. B. Boulton (Eds.), *The History of Anaesthesia.* 1989.

T I W

MOSANDER, CARL GUSTAV Born at Kalmar, Sweden, 10 September 1797; died Ångsholm, near Drottningholm, Sweden, 15 October 1858. Chemist known for his work on the rare earth elements.

Mosander studied pharmacy and medicine, and eventually became a pupil and friend of J. J. BER-ZELIUS. In 1825 he obtained the degree of MD, and shortly afterwards became curator of the mineral collections of the Academy of Sciences at Stockholm. He also took charge of the chemical laboratory at the Caroline Institute, and in 1832 succeeded Berzelius as professor of chemistry and mineralogy. In 1839 he showed that ceria, which had been independently isolated by Berzelius and M. H. KLAPROTH was not a simple earth but a mixture. He heated cerium nitrate and treated the product with dilute nitric acid. A yellow insoluble residue was obtained, and Mosander called this true ceria. The earth which had dissolved he called lanthana (Greek *lanthano*, to hide). In 1841 he showed that lanthana was a mixture of a colourless substance, which he regarded as true lanthana, and a brown earth, which he called didymia (Greek *didymos*, a twin) because of its close relationship with lanthana. In 1843 he turned his attention to yttria, which had been discovered by J. GADOLIN in 1794. By fractional precipitation with ammonium hydroxide he was able to separate it into yttria and two other earths which were the oxides of new elements, erbium and terbium.

M. E. Weeks and H. M. Leicester, *Discovery of the Elements* (7th ed.). 1968. (Portrait.)

J. E. Jorpes, *Acta chemica scandinavica*, **14**, 1681, 1960.

Dictionary of Scientific Biography.

B B K

MOSELEY, HENRY GWYN JEFFREYS Born at Weymouth, Dorset, England, 23 November 1887; died Gallipoli, Turkey, 10 August 1915. The first to identify experimentally the atomic number and nuclear charge of an element.

Moseley came from a family of long scientific tradition, his father H. N. Moseley, FRS (1844–91), being professor of anatomy at Oxford. His grandfather, also a FRS, was the mathematician H. Moseley (1801–72). He was related also to Benjamin Moseley (1742–1819), the writer on tropical diseases. He studied at Eton and Oxford, where he read natural science, and in 1910 joined E. RUTHER-FORD at Manchester. He was first lecturer in physics and then research fellow. After a successful investigation of the β-emission from radium, he began to examine the bright-line x-ray spectra that had been discovered by W. H. BRAGG and his son, W. L. BRAGG, using his own photographic recording technique. In December 1913 his first results were published. They showed that the frequencies of the K-lines in a series of elements ranged in order of increasing atomic weights changed by a regular increment from one element to the next. From this he inferred the existence of a quality increasing stepwise with each element which, since it was not atomic weight, must be the nuclear charge. A few months previously A. van den Broek (1870–1926) had suggested that the nuclear charge indicated the position of an element in the Periodic Table; Moseley now gave a firm experimental basis for this, equating nuclear charge with what he called 'atomic number'.

During 1913 Moseley moved back to Oxford, where he continued his work under J. S. E. TOWNS-END. Early in 1914 a further paper described his investigations on the x-ray spectra of over thirty other elements, up to gold. Discontinuities in his spectral series led him to predict that some elements were missing, and he was also able to show that elsewhere in his series no new elements remained to discovered. Several of the missing members were shortly brought to light. A connection between nuclear charge and atomic number was now firmly established; Moseley's belief that it was an identification was vindicated in 1920 by J. CHADWICK's experiments on α-particle scattering. As F. SODDY put it: 'Moseley, as it were, called the roll of the elements'.

Later in 1914 Moseley travelled with his mother to Australia to attend the British Association meetings there. On returning home he enlisted in the Royal Engineers, was commissioned, and on 15 June 1915 sailed for Gallipoli. A few weeks later, at the Battle of Suvla Bay, he was killed in action. Considered by Rutherford as 'a born experimenter', Moseley in his brief life established one great fact – the primacy of atomic number. On this basis all later developments in nuclear physics and atomic chemistry have been built.

Dictionary of National Biography.

Journal of Chemical Education, **24**, 482, 1947. (Portrait.)

W. A. Smeaton, *Chemistry in Britain*, **1**, 353, 1965.

J. L. Heilbron, *H. G. J. Moseley*. 1974.

E. Rutherford, *Proceedings of the Royal Society of London*, **93A**, xxii, 1916.

George Sarton, *Isis*, **9**, 96, 1927.

Dictionary of Scientific Biography.

MOSSBAUER, RUDOLF LUDWIG Born in Munich, Germany, 31 January 1929. Physicist.

Mossbauer studied physics at the Munich Institute of Technology and was research assistant at the Max Planck Institute, Heidelberg, 1955–7. Subsequently, he returned to Munich, where he was appointed professor of experimental physics in 1964. On leave from there he was director of the Institut Max von Laue-Paul Langevin at Grenoble 1972–7. He has had a distinguished career, especially in neutrino physics and gamma resonance spectroscopy but is particularly famous for his discovery – while taking his doctorate at Heidelberg – of the Mossbauer Effect. When an atomic nucleus emits a gamma-ray photon it must recoil to conserve momentum. In accordance with the Doppler Effect the consequent movement will affect the frequency of the radiation. However, if the nucleus is firmly anchored in a crystal lattice, recoil is impossible and the momentum is taken up by the lattice as a whole. Thus the absorbed and emitted radiation is of identical wavelength and analysis of it throws light on the electronic configuration of nuclei. In 1961 Mossbauer shared a Nobel prize with Robert Hofstadter (1915–   ), who investigated nuclear structures by electron scattering.

Les Prix Nobel en 1961, 1962. (Portrait.)

Who's Who, 1993.

Tyler Wasson (Ed.), *Nobel Prize Winners*. 1987. (Portrait.)

T I W

MOTT, SIR NEVILL FRANCIS Born Leeds, Yorkshire, England, 30 September 1905. Physicist.

After reading physics at Cambridge (1924–7) Mott was appointed lecturer in physics at Manchester University, under W. L. BRAGG (1929–30), and Fellow and lecturer in mathematics at Gonville and Caius College, Cambridge (1930–33). In 1933 he became professor of theoretical physics at Bristol University where he studied the properties of metals, applying the quantum theory to free electrons in their structures. In 1936 he was elected FRS.

During the war Mott worked on radar, but in 1945 he returned to Bristol as head of the physics department. He also joined the board of Taylor and Francis, scientific publishers, becoming chairman in 1970 and president in 1976.

In 1948 Mott became Director of the H. H. Wills Physical Laboratories at Bristol and in 1954 succeeded W. H. BRAGG as Cavendish Professor of Experimental Physics at Cambridge University. From 1959–66 he was Master of Gonville and Caius College; chaired the Ministry of Education standing committee on the training and supply of teachers (1959–62) and the Nuffield advisory committee on physics education (1961–73). He was knighted in 1962 and retired from the Cavendish Chair in 1971.

Mott received the Hughes (1941), Royal (1953), and Copley (1972) Medals of the Royal Society and in 1977 was awarded the Nobel prize for physics jointly with P. W. ANDERSON and J. H. van Vleck (1899–1980) of the United States, for work on the magnetic and electrical properties of non-crystalline solids, substances widely used in tape recorders, electronic computers, solar energy converters, and other devices.

N. F. Mott, *A Life in Science*, 1986. (Portrait.)

Les Prix Nobel en 1977. 1978 (Portrait.)

Physics Today, December 1977.

Tyler Wasson (Ed.), *Nobel Prize Winners*. 1987. (Portrait.)

N G C

MUDGE, THOMAS Born at Exeter, Devon, England, September 1717; died Newington Place, Surrey, 14 November 1794. Horologist; invented the lever escapement.

Thomas Mudge was the son of Zachariah Mudge (1694–1769), the divine, and brother of John Mudge, FRS (1721–93), physician and astronomer. As a youth (1731) he was apprenticed to a watchmaker and subsequently established his own business in partnership with William Dutton in 1750. He made some exquisite chronometers, including one for Ferdinand VI of Spain. He became particularly interested, after 1770, in the problems of the marine chronometer and made some modifications in the famous chronometer No. 4 constructed by John HARRISON in 1759. He devised a constant-force escapement which was exceedingly accurate, but required such high precision of workmanship that its general use was impracticable. Nevertheless he eventually received an award (1792) for his first marine chronometer after it had been tested by Nevil MASKELYNE during 1776 and 77. He is better remembered for his invention of the lever escapement now widely used in watches. In 1776 he was appointed watchmaker to the king.

Dictionary of National Biography.

T I W

MULLER, HERMANN JOSEPH Born in New York, 21 December 1890; died Indianapolis, Indiana, 5 April 1967. Geneticist.

Muller went to Morris High School, in the Bronx, and then studied biology at Columbia University, and at this early stage made up his mind that he wanted to make genetics his life-study. After a short period at Cornell Medical College, he returned to Columbia (1912–15) as a lecturer and then spent some time with Julian S. Huxley (1887–1975) at the Rice Institute, Houston, Texas. By this time he had developed his interest in the rate at which mutations occur. The years immediately after the First World War saw him back at Columbia, but in 1920 he returned to Texas, where he was appointed professor in 1925. In 1932 he went to Berlin to continue his researches with N. W. Timofeff-Resovsky, and then went on to spend three years in Russia doing genetic research in the Academy of Sciences, first in Leningrad and then in Moscow. The growing intrusion of politics into his field of research, which culminated in the fall of N. VAVILOV, caused him to leave Russia, and he continued his work for a time at Edinburgh (1937–40) and then back in the United States at Amherst College (1942). Finally, in 1945, he took up his last academic appointment, as professor of zoology in the University of Indiana.

Muller's great contribution to genetics resulted from his careful quantitative studies of rates of mutation, under both natural and artificial conditions. He showed temperature to have an effect, and later (1927) carried out classical experiments demonstrating the effects of x-rays, which may increase the mutation rate as much as 150 times. This resulted in his receiving a Nobel prize for physiology or medicine in 1946. His own experience of the far-reaching genetic effect of irradiation of the germ cells, often leading to lethal mutations, led him to campaign against the dangers of such irradiation for the human race.

Nature, **215**, 108, 1967.
Biographical Memoirs of Fellows of the Royal Society. 1968. (Portrait.)
E. A. Carlson, *Canadian Journal of Gentics and Cytology*, **9**, 437, 1967.
T. M. Sonneborn, *Science*, **162**, 772, 1968.
Tyler Wasson (Ed.), *Nobel Prize Winners*. 1987. (Portrait.)
Dictionary of Scientific Biography.

T I W

MÜLLER, JOHANN *See* REGIOMONTANUS.

MÜLLER, JOHANNES PETER Born at Coblenz, Rhineland-Palatinate, Germany, 14 July 1801; died Berlin, 28 April 1858. Great physiologist and comparative anatomist; a founder of modern scientific medicine.

Müller, son of a shoemaker, was educated at Coblenz and then studied medicine at Bonn (1819–22), where he graduated in 1822. He then proceeded to Berlin to take his State Examination. During his eighteen months in Berlin he was much influenced by the anatomist and physiologist C. A. Rudolphi (1771–1832). On his return to Bonn, Müller was recognized as an official lecturer (1824), and was appointed associate professor (1826) and full professor (1830) in the university. In 1833 he was called to succeed Rudolphi in the chair of anatomy and physiology, and in the directorship of the Museum of Comparative Anatomy, in the University of Berlin. Müller occupied this chair until his death. During his tenure he travelled widely abroad in pursuit of his zoological studies. During his rectorship of the University of Berlin in 1848 the revolution broke out, and Müller had to deal with severe disturbances among students and staff. At the end of his term of office he had a breakdown in health, from which his recovery was protracted. He was admitted a Foreign Member of the Royal Society in 1840.

In Berlin, Müller taught human and comparative anatomy, embryology, physiology, and pathological anatomy. In each of these subjects he is regarded as a pioneer, and when he died his chair was replaced by three independent chairs.

In descriptive anatomy Müller described the helicine arteries of erectile tissue (1835–6), and clarified the anatomy of the perineal muscles (1830) and of the otic ganglion (1832). In embryology his best-known discovery was that of the 'Müllerian duct', a significant structure in early embryonic life (1825). In 1830 he was the first to describe the development of the great omentum. In 1842 he redescribed features in the reproduction of the dogfish, known to ARISTOTLE but subsequently forgotten. In histology he described the structure of a series of secreting glands (1830), and he wrote on the minute structure of cartilage and of bone (1830). He clarified our understanding of the types and distribution of connective tissues (1830). In comparative anatomy he discovered the lymphhearts of amphibians and reptiles (1840); and he published a series of classical memoirs on the anatomy of the myxinoid fishes (1836–45); on

Amphioxus (1842); and on the Echinoderms (1846–52). Müller was one of the first to use the microscope in pathology, and in 1838 he published the first part of his unfinished work on the minute anatomy of malignant growths.

In 1826 Müller published his early observations on stimuli applied to the sense organs; and in his textbook (1840) these were generalized into his Law of Specific Nerve Energies. In 1826 also he gave his explanation of the colour sensations produced by pressure upon the eye. In 1831 he confirmed by his experiments on the frog the correctness of the so-called 'Bell-Magendie Law' (see F. MAGENDIE), of the direction of the nerve impulse in the ventral and dorsal spinal-nerve roots, and he contributed to our knowledge of reflex action. Beginning in 1835, he published a series of papers on the mechanism of the vocal cords and the production of tones in the voice. In 1837 he isolated chondrin and glutin, and he also published work on the chemical composition of the blood. In 1834 and 1840 the two volumes of Müller's textbook of human physiology were published. This work was translated into several languages, and it remains one of the great landmarks in physiological research and teaching. Müller's pupils included T. SCHWANN, E. DU BOIS REYMOND, H. L. F. von HELMHOLTZ, R. REMAK, J. Henle (1809–84), K. B. Reichert (1811–84), and Rudolf VIRCHOW.

W. Haberling, *Johannes Müller*. 1924.
H. E. Sigerist, *Great Doctors*. 1933. (Portrait.)
W. Haymaker and F. Schiller (Eds), *The Founders of Neurology*. 1970. (Portrait.)
Dictionary of Scientific Biography.

E A U

MURCHISON, SIR RODERICK IMPEY Born at Tarradale, Ross-shire, Scotland, 19 February 1792; died London, 22 October 1871. Geologist. Founder of the Silurian system.

Roderick Murchison, descended from an old Highland family, entered the army at 15 and served in the Peninsular War, after which he left the army, married, and took up fox-hunting, his means allowing him to choose his own pursuits. After dallying with art and antiquities he at last, at the age of 32, became an enthusiastic scientist, devoting the rest of his life to geology. After some geological exploring in Scotland, France and the Alps, sometimes with Adam SEDGWICK, sometimes with Sir Charles LYELL, he began, in 1831 (the same year that Sedgwick started to tackle North Wales), his great research into the mass of hitherto geologically unknown 'greywacke' rocks (i.e. Lower Palaeozoic) underlying the Old Red Sandstone. Working in South Wales and the Welsh Borderland he made out the sequence of the rocks and their contained fossils, finally producing his monumental work, *The Silurian System* in 1839. In 1839, too, he and Sedgwick together established the Devonian system. In 1841, as a result of explorations in Russia with French colleagues, he proposed the name Permian for yet another world-wide geological system (the uppermost of the Palaeozoic). Further researches into regions of Silurian rocks resulted in his book *Siluria* (1854 and subsequent editions). In 1855 he succeeded Sir Henry de la BECHE as director-general of the Geological Survey, the most important official post in British geology. He was twice president of the Geological Society of London, in 1831–2 and 1842–3, and was awarded its Wollaston Medal in 1864. He himself eventually endowed by bequest the Society's second highest award, the Murchison Medal, and had already helped to establish the Murchison Professorship of Geology at Edinburgh University. He was one of the founders of the British Association; acted as its secretary; and was president in 1846. In that year he was knighted, and was made a baronet in 1866. For many years, from 1844, he was president of the Royal Geographical Society. He was elected FRS in 1826. He held honorary degrees from several British universities and received many foreign honours and distinctions. He was one of the most distinguished geologists of the nineteenth century, and is described as a man of great dignity and kindness.

A. Geikie, *The Life of Sir Roderick I. Murchison.* 1875. (Portrait.)

K. A. von Zittel, *History of Geology and Palaeontology,* 1901. (Portrait.)

Dictionary of National Biography.

Dictionary of Scientific Biography.

J C

MURDOCK, WILLIAM Born at Old Cumnock, Scotland, 21 August 1754; died Soho, Birmingham, England, 15 November 1839. Pioneer of the gas industry.

Of little education, though with high mechanical ability, Murdock was engaged by Matthew BOULTON and sent to Cornwall in 1779 to manage the engine business there. He is reputed to have suggested to Boulton the sun-and-planet gear which he patented in 1781. While at Redruth he began to experiment on coal gas as illuminant, after hearing of the work of Philippe LEBON in Paris. Lebon used wood gas to light his house; Murdock worked from 1792 with coal gas, which proved superior, generated in a retort set up in his back-yard at Redruth. The Birmingham partners were at first apathetic to his gas-making, but they changed their views when Gregory Watt (1777–1804) reported from Paris that Lebon was developing his schemes and no time was to be lost if the firm was to profit from Murdock's experiments.

Back in the Soho works, Murdock was authorized to set up a gas-lighting apparatus, a move which established Birmingham as a centre for gas-producing plant for a period. Murdock devised washing and purifying techniques for coal gas, together with retorts of elliptical cross-section and gas-collecting plant. Gas-lights were instituted at Soho to celebrate the Peace of Amiens in 1802. Murdock's inventiveness enabled the Soho partners to manufacture gas retorts, piping, and burners for lighting mills at Manchester (1806) and Halifax. Murdock described the basic principles in a paper to the Royal Society in 1808. Boulton and Watt abandoned gas manufacture in 1814, being outdistanced by rivals.

Alexander Murdock, *Light Without a Wick.* 1892.

S. Smiles, *Lives of Boulton and Watt.* 1865.

Trevor I. Williams, *A History of the British Gas Industry.* 1981.

Dictionary of National Biography.

J. Griffiths, *The Third Man: The Life and Times of William Murdock 1754–1839, the Inventor of Gas Lighting.* 1992.

M S

MURRAY, SIR JOHN Born at Coburg, Ontario, Canada, 3 March 1841; died Edinburgh, 16 March 1914. Marine biologist and oceanographer.

Although born in Canada, Murray was educated in Scotland, studying medicine and biological sciences at the University of Edinburgh. After a journey to the Arctic seas, he joined the *Challenger* Deep-sea Exploring Expedition, under the direction of Sir Wyville THOMSON, in 1872, taking responsibility for the study of plankton, the deposits of the sea bed, and the formation of coral reefs and islands. On the *Challenger's* return in 1876 he became an assistant in the office of the Commission set up to arrange the results of work on the collections made during the voyage, and in 1882 he succeeded Thomson as director of the Commission. Publication of the fifty volumes of reports was completed in 1895.

Murray led other, shorter, expeditions in the *Knight-Errant* in 1880, and the *Triton* in 1882, and his own research was continued until late in his life, often using his own yacht, *Medusa*; it covered a wide range of biological and geological subjects. He became FRS in 1896, and was knighted in 1898.

Murray's last expedition was in 1910, in the Norwegian boat *Michael Sars*. As well as a series of reports, this journey resulted in *The Depths of the Ocean* (1912), written by Murray and Johan Hjort. It is a popular account of the kind of work carried out on the voyage. Another of Murray's books, *The Ocean* (1913), is a valuable introduction to oceanography.

W. A. Herdman, *Founders of Oceanography and their Work.* 1923. (Portrait.)

Margaret Deacon, *Scientists and the Sea 1650– 1900.* 1971.

A. Shipley, *Proceedings of the Royal Society,* **89B**, vi, 1915–16.

Dictionary of Scientific Biography.

Dictionary of National Biography.

S J R

MUSHET, ROBERT FORESTER Born at Coleford, Gloucestershire, England, 8 April 1811; died Cheltenham, Gloucestershire, 19 January 1891. Pioneer of alloy steels.

Son of David Mushet, ironmaster in the Forest of Dean, and discoverer of the Black Band Ironstone of Scotland, R. F. Mushet developed the Coleford industry and founded the Forest Steelworks. He utilized his father's puddling process, in which iron oxide was added to pig iron to improve the yield. He pioneered alloy steels, containing manganese, tungsten and titanium, for machine tools. He improved 'burnt iron' from the Bessemer process, which contained excess oxygen, by adding his triple compound (Fe-C-Mn) or *spiegeleisen*, for which he was granted a patent. In 1856 he took out further patents for improving iron by air-blowing and adding manganese. These innovations brought him into dispute with Henry BESSEMER though in due course the latter acknowledged the value of Mushet's contribution.

Mushet merited fuller recognition of the alloy steels made by his Titanic Steel Company of 1865. Not until 1867 did Sir William FAIRBAIRN report on the superior strength of 'Titanic steel'. Mushet met much criticism from John Percy (1817–89), the well-known metallurgist, because of the many patents – totalling over fifty – which he took out. Yet this Coleford man awakened British and American interests to the value of alloying elements in preparing special steel for the rapidly growing machine-tool industry. Mushet's two sons moved to Sheffield, to join industries to which licences for his patents had been granted.

F. M. Osborn, *The Story of the Mushets*. 1952. (Portrait.)
Dictionary of National Biography.
J. C. Carr and W. Taplin, *History of the British Steel Industry*. 1962.
Dictionary of Scientific Biography.

M S

MUSPRATT, JAMES Born in Dublin, 12 August 1793; died Seaforth Hall, near Liverpool, England, 4 May 1886. Founder of the British alkali industry.

Muspratt's father, an English immigrant, established himself as a cork-cutter in Dublin. At 14, James was apprenticed to a wholesale chemist and druggist, with whom he remained for some three to four years. Then in rapid succession he lost his father and his mother, and went off to fight in the Peninsular War. After many hardships, he made his way home by enlisting as a midshipman; he deserted when his ship reached Wales and made his way back to Dublin. There he came into a small inheritance, and was able to enjoy the literary, dramatic, and scientific life of the city. Among his friends was the chemist Robert KANE, and no doubt this influenced him in establishing himself as a small chemical manufacturer.

Muspratt must have been well aware of the process invented by Nicolas LEBLANC for manufacturing soda from salt. In 1823 the British Government repealed the duty of £30 per ton imposed on salt and this made the Leblanc process much more attractive. Muspratt seized his opportunity, and set up as a manufacturer of soda and other chemicals in Liverpool, close to the Cheshire salt fields. Originally, his main customers were soap-boilers and he had difficulty in persuading them to use his soda in place of the potash to which they were accustomed. Overcoming this ignorant prejudice, he found the demand far greater than he could supply. To expand his business he joined forces in 1828 with Josias GAMBLE, but the partnership lasted only two years and Muspratt built a new works at Newton, on the St Helens Canal.

The next twenty years were ones of great difficulty, as Muspratt, in a prosperous agricultural district, was constantly involved with local landowners in litigation arising from the vast outpouring of corrosive hydrochloric acid from his works. Even a chimney 400 feet high failed to disperse the pollutant adequately, and Muspratt failed for a long time to realize the value of the absorption towers invented by William GOSSAGE. In despair, he moved from Newton and re-established himself in works at Widnes and at Flint; there he prospered greatly.

In 1837 Justus von LIEBIG came to the meeting in Liverpool of the British Association for the Advancement of Science. He and Muspratt became close friends, and Muspratt sent three of his sons, who also became chemical industrialists, to study at Giessen, which he himself often visited. In 1843

Muspratt tried unsuccessfully to manufacture artificial fertilizers based on Liebig's agricultural chemistry.

J. Fenwick Allen, *Some Founders of the Chemical Industry*. 1907. (Portrait.)
D. W. F. Hardie, *A History of the Chemical Industry in Widnes*. 1950. (Portrait.)
M. D. Stephens and G. W. Roderick, *Annals of science*, **29**, 287. 1972.
D. W. F. Hardie, *Endeavour*, **14**, 29, 1955.
D. Reilly, *Journal of Chemical Education*, **28**, 650, 1951.
Dictionary of National Biography.

T I W

MUYBRIDGE, EADWEARD JAMES Born at Kingston-on-Thames, near London, 9 April 1830; died there, 8 May 1904. Investigator of animal locomotion by photography.

Muybridge, the son of a corn merchant, emigrated to California in 1852. About 1866 he became a professional photographer and assisted the explorer and photographer Carleton A. Watkins in San Francisco. Muybridge's impressive views of Yosemite in 1867 led to his appointment to a Government survey of Alaska. Later he became chief photographer to the US Government. Leland Stanford, ex-Governor of California, following an argument about the gait of the horse, in 1872 commissioned Muybridge to make a photographic investigation at his stud farm. Owing to the slowness of the photographic material, results were inconclusive, and for the next few years Muybridge photographed the Modoc War, and in Central America. In 1877 he returned to the investigation, and proved that a trotting horse at times has all its hoofs off the ground. In renewed experiments 1878–9 he used a battery of up to twenty-four small cameras with electromagnetic shutters set off by clockwork, or by threads stretched across the track which were broken by the running horse. *The Horse in Motion* (1882) exposed the fallacy of the 'rocking-horse' attitude depicted by artists, and Muybridge convinced the sceptical of the correctness of his analysis by projecting drawings based on the photographs in the zoopraxiscope which he devised in 1880. This paved the way for cinematography.

After a European tour lecturing to learned societies (1881–2), Muybridge undertook for the University of Pennsylvania an extensive survey of the movements of human beings and animals (1884–5) using up to thirty-six cameras and the newly introduced rapid gelatine dry plates. *Animal Locomotion* (1887), illustrating over 20 000 figures in motion, remains the most comprehensive publication of its kind. Popular selections from it were published in England under the titles *Animals in Motion* (1899) and *The Human Figure in Motion* (1901).

Helmut and Alison Gernsheim, *The History of Photography*. 1955. (Portrait.)
H. Gurtner, *Ciba Symposium*, (Summit, N.J.), **4**, 1356, 1942.
K. MacDonnell, *Eadweard Muybridge*. 1972.
Dictionary of American Biography.

H and A G

N

NÄGELI, KARL WILHELM VON Born at Kilchberg, Switzerland, 27 March 1817; died Munich, Bavaria, 10 May 1891. Botanist.

Nägeli was the son of a physician, and it was intended that he should follow the same profession, but his own inclination was to a more philosophical career. For a time he studied under the nature-philosopher Lorenz Oken (1779–1851), but then developed a growing interest in botany, which he studied at Geneva under A. P. de CANDOLLE, becoming particularly interested in problems of taxonomy. For a short time he studied philosophy under G. W. F. Hegel (1770–1831) – reflected in his later concern with the laws of thought (See *Über die Aufgabe der Naturgeschichte* (1844)) – but then moved on to resume his botanical studies with M. J. SCHLEIDEN at Jena. Later he became professor successively at Freiburg, Zürich, and Munich. Although afflicted by chronic ill-health, he carried out much original work in a wide range of fields, notably cytology.

As a young man (1842) Nägeli published an important essay on pollen formation, especially in the Liliaceae. He described the process of cell division with then unparalleled accuracy, even observing division of the nucleus. What he recorded as 'transitory cytoblasts' were, in fact, chromosomes. He did not understand the significance of these observations, and when Gregor MENDEL sent him a copy of his now classic paper on inheritance in peas Nägeli dismissed it as unimportant. Indeed, when he himself wrote a work on evolution (*Mechanischphysiologische Theorie der Abstammungslehre* (1884)) some twenty years later he did not even mention Mendel. Not until 1900, long after his death, was the significance of Mendel's work properly appreciated, by H. de VRIES and others. Nägeli's own views on evolution, which differed from those of Charles DARWIN, had something in common with those of J. B. A. A. de LAMARCK. He conceived the process as one of discrete jumps, rather than by extremely gradual variation, and he may be considered to have anticipated the later concept of mutation.

Surprisingly, Nägeli continued to believe in the possibility of spontaneous generation, despite the mounting evidence against it. He did not, however, conceive of the generation of complete organisms, even very simple ones, but rather of much smaller units that might combine together to form a living organism.

In taxonomy he made a detailed study of the complex Hieracium (hawkweed) genus. His investigations of the growth of plants were outstanding. He characterized and described many unicellular algae, and investigated the process of osmosis in them (*Über Endosmose und Exosmose in Pflanzenzelle*, 1855).

E. Nordenskiöld, *The History of Biology*. 1928.
Allgemeine Deutsche Biographie. 1875–1912.

T I W

NAKANISHI, KOJI Born in Hong Kong, 11 May 1925; Organic chemist.

The son of a Japanese banker, Nakanishi spent his childhood in Lyons, London and Alexandria and returned to Japan in 1935. After attending high school in Kobe, he went to Nagoya Imperial University (1944–47). There he joined the research group of Professor F. Egami (1910–1982), a biochemist, and began his undergraduate and graduate studies under the guidance of Professor Y. Hirata (1915–). In 1950 he won a scholarship from the Government Aid and Relief in the Occupied Area (GARIOA) programme, to the chemistry department of Harvard University, where his work concerned quinone oxidation and steroids under the guidance of L. F. Fieser (1899–1977). He returned to Japan in 1952 and was appointed as an instructor of Nagoya University, and then promoted to assistant professor in 1955. His work at Nagoya was concerned with the structure determination of several natural products obtained from plants and fungi, and antibiotics. In 1958 he moved to Tokyo Kyoiku University where he remained as professor until he was invited by Professor T. NOZOE to the Department of Chemistry of Tohoku University, Sendai, in 1963. During his professorship there, he carried out extensive work for six years concerning the isolation and structure determination of complex natural products, such as chromomycins, ginkgolides (constituents of the ginkgo tree), and ecdysteroids. He also devised a chiroptical method, known as the benzoate sector rule, to determine the absolute configuration of secondary alcohols. In 1969 he accepted a chair of organic chemistry in the Department of Chemistry of Columbia University. There he studied diverse problems concerning bioscience based on organic chemistry; his work there concerned the structure determination of nucleic acid minor bases, polyaromatic hydrocarbon-nucleic acid adducts, mitomycin-DNA adducts, as well as the isolation and structure determination of insect hormones. His most notable contributions at Columbia, however, were in the area of retinal proteins. He and his colleagues prepared a number of retinal analogues and studied the mechanism of vision by incorporating them into a variety of rhodopsins. He was a director of research of the International Centre for Insect Physiology and Ecology (ICIPE) in Nairobi (1969–1977) and has been the director of the Sun-tory Institute for Bioorganic Research (Sumbor) in Osaka since 1979. He was awarded the Imperial prize, the highest honour for a Japanese scholar, in 1990.

Tetrahedron Letters, **299**, 30, 309, 315, and 321, 1967.

T. G. Ebrey, H. Frauenfelder, B. Honig, and K. Nakanishi (eds), *Biophysical Studies of Retinal Proteins*. 1987.

Science, **235**, 1204, 1987.

K. Nakanishi, *A Wandering Natural Products Chemist*. 1991. (Portrait.)

H S

NANSEN, FRIDTJOF Born near Christiania (Oslo), Norway, 10 October 1861; died Lysaker, 13 May 1930. Explorer, scientist, statesman, and humanitarian.

Nansen was trained as a zoologist, and took his PhD at Christiania in 1888. Six years earlier a sealing expedition had fired his interest in the exploration of the far north, for which he was particularly well equipped by his marvellous physique and ski-ing technique. With no possibility of survival in the event of failure, he set out with three Norwegian and two Lapp companions to cross the Greenland ice-cap on skis, reaching the west coast in forty days (24 September 1888). He then raised funds to build the *Fram*, a specially strengthened diesel-engined vessel of 402 tons, designed for scientific observation while drifting in the pack-ice, which Nansen reasoned would carry it close to the North Pole.

On 22 September 1893 the *Fram* entered the ice north of the New Siberian Islands; it emerged nearly three years later north of Spitsbergen, after drifting to 87° 57′N. In March 1895 Nansen left the ship with one companion and twenty-eight sledge-dogs in a dash for the Pole but was forced to turn back at 86° 4′N. The scientific results are recorded in *The Norwegian North Polar Expedition* (6 vols). Nansen's later studies of physical and biological conditions in the Norwegian Sea and the North-East Atlantic further contributed to the establishment of oceanography as an exact science.

An ardent nationalist, Nansen played an important part in the separation of Norway from Sweden. He was a leading figure in the League Assembly, where he headed every attempt to mitigate the sufferings of war prisoners, refugees, and famine victims; he received the Nobel peace prize in 1923.

Nansen's autobiographical and scientific writings are mostly available in English; the complete works, edited in part by his son, were published in Oslo (8 vols, 1961–2).

Edward Shackleton, *Nansen the Explorer*. 1959.

Per Vogt (ed.), *Fridtjof Nansen, Explorer-Scientist-Humanitarian*. 1961.

R. E,. Reynolds, *Nansen*. 1932.

M. Langley, *History Today*. **18**, 637, 1968.

T K D

NAPIER, JOHN Born at Merchiston Castle, near Edinburgh, 1550; died Merchiston, 4 April 1617. Inventor of logarithms.

John Napier, eighth laird of Merchiston, was educated first in France (1561) and then at St Andrews (1563). He probably completed his education abroad, returning home and marrying in 1571. Although not in full possession of the family estates until 1608, for many years before then he conducted a large number of agricultural experiments. His leisure was devoted to religious controversy, mathematics, and the invention of somewhat fanciful instruments of war. In 1596, for example, he sent to the statesman Anthony Bacon (1558–1601), a manuscript entitled 'Secret inventions, profitable and necessary in these days for defense of this island, and withstanding of strangers, enemies of God's truth and religion'. This deals with burning mirrors, an artillery piece, and an approximation to a modern tank.

Napier is principally remembered for his invention of logarithms. He began his studies in the appropriate branches of mathematics soon after his first marriage. In fragments first published in 1839 he is seen to have been considering imaginary roots, and to have been struggling with methods for extracting all real roots of any positive number. Theological controversy interrupted his work, but by 1594 he was clearly in the possession of the underlying principle of logarithms. The rest of his life he spent in developing the theory, in simplifying the methods of computing logarithms, and in actually drawing up the tables. In the course of this work he devised the present decimal notation.

Napier's work was given to the public in 1614, when he published his *Mirifici Logarithmorum Canonis descriptio*. This contains the tables; canons for their use, especially in trigonometry; and an explanation of the nature of logarithms. They were explained in terms of the motion of points in a straight line, and in terms of a correspondence of a geometrical and an arithmetical series. An earlier work, the *Mirifici Logarithmorum Canonis constructio*, was not published until two years after his death. Logarithms were there called 'artificial numbers'. This work contains very few clues as to the processes of thought which led Napier to his discovery, and these remain obscure.

The *Descriptio* was received enthusiastically by the mathematicians Edward Wright (c.1558–1615) and Henry BRIGGS, and Wright translated it at once into English (published 1615). Briggs wrote to Napier, and later visited him, suggesting ways in which the base of the logarithms could be more conveniently chosen. Napier had already considered this possibility, which of course, involved re-computing the tables. Eventually compromising, Briggs published tables of decimal logarithms in 1617 and 1624: Napier's logarithms are not the same as those now known as Napierian or natural logarithms. The spread of Napier's ideas on the Continent was considerably helped by Johannes KEPLER, who pressed for the publication of the *Constructio*.

In 1617 Napier published his *Rabdologia*, which explains how numbered rods ('Napier's bones') may be used for performing multiplication and division. The method achieved some popularity, but is mathematically uninteresting. Of immense ingenuity, nevertheless, is the section dealing with 'local arithmetic', in which he explains how multiplication, division, and the extraction of roots may be performed by the movement of counters on a chess-board.

Several rules of spherical trigonometry are known by Napier's name. His 'rules of circular parts' are found in his work of 1614, as is one of the four formulae known as 'Napier's analogies'.

The aim of these formulae was to allow logarithms to be applied more easily to astronomical calculation.

Both in his Calvinism and in his mathematics Napier showed his great resolution. It is astonishing that the computations of his tables, which occupied him for twenty years, were such that no great programme of recalculation was thought necessary for more than a century.

M. Napier, *Memoirs of John Napier of Merchiston.* 1834.

C. G. Knott (ed.), *Napier Tercentenary Memorial Volume.* 1915. (Portrait).

E. W. Hobson, *John Napier and the Invention of Logarithms.* 1914.

Dictionary of Scientific Biography.

Dictionary of National Biography.

J D N

NASMYTH, JAMES Born in Edinburgh, 19 August 1808; died London, 7 May 1890. Engineer; inventor of the steam hammer.

James Nasmyth, son of Alexander Nasmyth (1758–1840), a well-known artist, left Edinburgh High School at the age of 12 and, amongst other things, made model engines that were so successful that he was asked to build a steam carriage for use on the roads. He then joined Henry MAUDSLAY in London for two years before returning to Edinburgh, where he continued as a manufacturing engineer. The demand in Manchester being far greater, Nasmyth migrated there in 1834, and by 1836 began to lay out at Patricroft, near the junction of the newly-built Liverpool to Manchester railway and the Bridgewater Canal, his Bridgewater foundry where machine tools of all kinds were made, together with many steam-powered machines. The most famous of these – his steam hammer devised to forge the driving-shaft for the paddle-wheels (subsequently abandoned in favour of screw propellers) of the *Great Britain* – was designed in 1839 and patented in 1842. The steam hammer was an exceedingly important invention, greatly increasing the size of forging possible, without loss of precision. In 1839 he also began to manufacture steam locomotives for various railway companies, and in fourteen years built 109. He also made many small high-pressure steam engines, as well as donkey pumps, hydraulic presses for making lead pipes, steam hammers, and other machines.

As locomotives now bulked ever larger in the development of Patricroft, Nasmyth at the age of 48 retired to Penshurst in Kent. There he indulged himself more freely in his hobby, astronomy, and applied himself especially to surveying the surface of the Moon, on which his first paper was published in 1846. His lunar cartography received a prize in the Great Exhibition of 1851, where his steam hammer also was shown. Twenty-three years later he embodied the results of his work in *The Moon Considered as a Planet, a World and a Satellite* (1874). He died in 1890, leaving a quarter of a million pounds.

T. S. Rowlandson, *History of the Steam Hammer.* 1875.

James Nasmyth, *An Autobiography* (ed. S. Smiles). 1883. (Portrait.)

J. W. Roe, *English and American Toolbuilders.* 1916.

A. E. Musson, *Economic History Review,* **10**, 121, 1957.

Dictionary of National Biography.

W H G A

NATTA, GIULIO Born at Imperia, Italy, 26 February 1903; died Milan, 1 May 1979. Famous for his discovery of the stereoregular polymerization of propylene and many other olefin and non-hydrocarbon monomers.

Natta was the son of a well known judge, but contrary to the family tradition did not take up law studies. He studied mathematics at the University of Genoa but changed his discipline when he moved to the Milan Polytechnic Institute, where he obtained his 'Dottore' degree in Chemical Engineering at the early age of 21, and his 'Libero Docente' three years later. He was assistant Lecturer in chemistry at Milan before he moved in 1933 to the University of Pavia as professor of general chemistry, and two years later to Rome as director of the Institute of Physical Chemistry. In 1937 he became professor of chemistry in Turin, and finally, from 1938 until he retired in 1973, professor and director of the Milan Institute of Industrial Chemistry. His earlier researches were on the structural chemistry of minerals and inorganic materials used as heterogeneous catalysts for certain important industrial processes. At the same time he investigated processes for the synthesis of methanol, higher alcohols, and formaldehyde, and in 1938 initiated a programme for the production of synthetic rubber. During this period he also investigated the use of petroleum derivatives and in particular olefins and diolefins as raw materials for chemical syntheses.

At his suggestion Montecatini – Italy's largest chemical company, for whom he was a consultant – purchased the rights for the commercial development of the work of Karl ZIEGLER at Mulheim, on the organo-metallic synthesis of aliphatic compounds. Having access to Ziegler's research, Natta commenced work on the polyaddition of ethylene using organo-aluminium compounds, and using the catalysts developed by Ziegler for the polymerization of ethylene. In 1954 Natta made his great discovery of the stereo-regular polymerization of propylene, butene-1, and styrene. Feverish research resulted within a short time in the polymerization of many olefins to stereoregular polymers, and the propylene polymerization commercialized by Montecatini within three years was rapidly taken up by other companies around the world, and polypropylene soon became a major new plastic.

Natta was a quietly dressed, soft spoken man of slight stature, who showed courtesy and consideration to visitors from all over the world who came to Milan out of scientific interest or to pursue the industrial development of his discoveries. He was a keen nature lover and an active mountain climber. His main hobbies were collecting fossils, which he displayed in his home in Milan, and edible fungi – a subject on which he had extensive knowledge.

His work was internationally recognized by awards in many countries, and he was co-winner with Ziegler of the Nobel Prize in Chemistry in 1963.

Angewandte Chemie, **68**, 393, 1956.

Journal of Polymer Science, **51**, issue 156, 1961.
  (Portrait.)
Chemistry in Britain, **17**, 298, 1981.
Dictionary of Scientific Biography, Supp.II.
Tyler Wasson (Ed.), *Nobel Prize Winners*. 1987.
  (Portrait.)

C E H B

NAUDIN, CHARLES Born at Autun, Saône-et-Loire, France, 14 August 1815; died Cap d'Antibes, 19 April 1899. Plant hybridist and horticulturist.

Naudin's father having spent the family's small fortune, he had to earn his own living from an early age and could study only in his spare time. In 1844 he obtained a teaching post in botany, in the *Musée d'Histoire Naturelle*, Paris. During a botanical excursion two years later he was afflicted with deafness so severe that within two years he became stone deaf. Teaching became out of the question, and he was demoted to assistant naturalist. Thus relieved of his teaching duties, he forged ahead with his taxonomic studies.

In 1852, in a speculative paper on evolution, Naudin suggested that species are formed by a selective process and that hybridization plays a part. From 1854 to 1864 he hybridized plants in order to discover how fertile hybrids behave. His experimental technique was far inferior to that of J. A. MENDEL, so he did not discover any statistical regularities, although he grew several generations of hybrids. Nevertheless, perceiving that the hybrid has a twofold nature, he put forward a hypothesis of disjunction between the two natures (or 'specific essences') at reproduction causing the germ cells to be of two kinds. Random unions between them, he held, would account for the various types of hybrid offspring. He corresponded with Charles DARWIN, who showed interest in his work but failed to realize its significance.

E. André, *Revue Horticole*, **71**, 177, 1899.
H. F. Roberts, *Plant Hybridization before Mendel*.
  1929 (reprinted 1965). (Portrait.)
R. C. Olby, *Origins of Mendelism*. 1966.
Dictionary of Scientific Biography.

R C O

NEEDHAM, NOEL JOSEPH TERENCE MONT-GOMERY Born in London, 9 December 1900. Biochemist: historian of Chinese science and technology.

Needham, the son of a Harley Street specialist, was educated at Oundle School and Gonville and Caius College, Cambridge, where he read Natural Sciences. He was elected a Fellow of Caius in 1924, and was awarded a doctorate in biochemistry the following year. Under Professor Frederick Gowland HOPKINS he embarked on research into the chemistry of embryology, studying the chemical changes involved in the development of an individual from a single fertilised egg cell. He published his three-volume *Chemical Embryology* in 1931, and became Sir William Dunn Reader in Biochemistry at the University of Cambridge in 1933, a post he held until 1966. His *History of Embryology* appeared in 1934. As a result of his collaboration with C. H. Waddington (1905–75) during the 1930s he published *Biochemistry and Morphogenesis* in 1942.

Needham's interest in China began in 1936 when a group of Chinese biochemists, including Lu

Gwei-Djen (1904–91), came to work in the department. Needham learned Chinese, and from 1942 to 1946 he was in China as head of the British Scientific Mission, advising the Chinese government on scientific and technical matters, lecturing to scientists, and travelling throughout China collecting information. He was appointed the first director of the department of Natural Sciences, UNESCO, 1946–8.

The first volumes of his monumental *Science and Civilisation in China* appeared in 1954 with the help of Lu Gwei-Djen, and by 1990 sixteen volumes had appeared, twelve written by Needham, with a further sixteen volumes planned. Many other books on Chinese science and technology were published, including *Heavenly Clockwork* (1960), a study of astronomical clocks in medieval China, and *The Grand Titration: Science and Society in East and West* (1969). Needham's central concern was to explain why China, more advanced technologically and scientifically than Europe in 1400, failed to develop a modern scientific culture similar to that developed in Europe from the 16th century onwards. His conclusion was that the power of the civil service prevented the development of a politically powerful merchant class, and this inhibited the development of modern science and technology.

Needham was elected a Fellow of the Royal Society in 1941. He was Master of Gonville and Caius College, Cambridge, 1966–76, and was director of the Needham Research Institute, Cambridge (the East Asian History of Science Library) from 1976 to 1990. His wife, who was also a Fellow of the Royal Society, died in 1987, and he married Lu Gwei-Djen in 1989. He was made a Companion of Honour in 1992.

J. Needham, *Science and Civilisation in China*.
  1954 ff.
M. Teich and R. Young (ed.), *Changing
  Perspectives in the History of Science: Essays in
  Honour of Joseph Needham*. 1973. (Portrait.)
Mansel Davies (ed.), *A Selection from the Writings
  of Joseph Needham*. 1990.

A P B

NÉEL, LOUIS EUGÈNE FÉLIX Born in Lyons, France, 22 November 1904. Physicist noted for his fundamental discoveries relating to antiferromagnetism and ferrimagnetism.

After studying at the *École Normale Supérior* Néel entered the University of Strasbourg, where in 1937 he succeeded to the chair of Pierre Weiss (1865–1940), and continued his research into the magnetic properties of solid materials. In 1945 he moved to Grenoble, which became under his leadership an outstanding centre for scientific research in several different fields. Néel himself was a professor at the university, president of the polytechnic, director of the *Laboratoire d'Electrostatique et de Physique du Métal*, director of the *Centre d'Études Nucléaires de Grenoble*, and largely responsible for the joint Franco-German-British high-flux reactor laboratory established at Grenoble.

At the start of the Second World War he devised a method for the protection of French warships against German magnetic mines. Before that, however, in 1932, he had shown that there was a fourth type of magnetism which he called antiferromagnetism, where two interlaced atomic lattices have magnetic fields acting in opposite directions, so that the net magnetic effect is very small. In 1948 he first gave an explanation for the strong magnetic fields found in ferrite materials such as magnetite; he suggested that in these materials, which he called ferrimagnetic, the lattices were of different strengths, producing a strong resultant magnetic effect.

Néel shared the 1970 Nobel Prize for physics with Hannes ALFVÉN, for his 'fundamental research and discoveries concerning antiferromagnetism and ferrimagnetism which have important applications in solid state physics'. He has also developed techniques for the study of the past history of the Earth's magnetic field.

Modern Scientists and Engineers. McGraw-Hill. (Portrait.)
Robert L. Weber, *Pioneers of Science: Nobel Prize Winners in Physics*, (2nd ed.) 1988. (Portrait.)
Tyler Wasson (ed.), *Nobel Prize Winners.* 1987. (Portrait.)
D. Pestre, *La Recherche*, **22**, 1432, 1991; *Louis Néel, le magnetisme et Grenoble.* 1991.

                                                                                     R M B

NERNST, HERMANN WALTHER Born at Briessen, West Prussia, Germany, 25 June 1864; died Zibelle, on the Silesian-Polish border, 18 November 1941. Discoverer of the Third Law of Thermodynamics, and a pioneer physical chemist.

Nernst was the son of a civil servant. He studied science at the Universities of Zürich, Würzburg, and Graz. At Würzburg he worked for his doctorate under F. KOHLRAUSCH, and at Graz he joined A. von Ettinghausen (1850–1932) in a study of the electrification of heated metals placed in a magnetic field. He then (1887) became assistant to W. F. OSTWALD at Leipzig, and in 1890 moved to Göttingen, first as an assistant and then (1894) as first professor of physical chemistry. In 1904, he succeeded H. H. LANDOLT in the physical chemistry chair at Berlin, where, apart from active service during the war, he remained until 1922, being rector of the University in his last year. He then became president of the *Physikalisch-Technisches Reichsanstalt*, but in 1924 he accepted the chair of physics at Berlin. Out of favour with the Nazis, he retired in 1933 to his country home, spending his remaining years in farming, fishing, and administration of his estate.

Nernst soon became active in electro-chemistry. Before leaving for Göttingen he derived an expression connecting ionic mobilities and temperature with the potential difference between solutions in contact. He devised methods for measuring dielectric constants (1894), degree of ionic hydration (1900), and pH by indicators (1903). In 1889 he developed the idea of solubility product, and in 1903 suggested the use of buffer solutions. Nernst's theories of galvanism, based upon the concept of electrolytic solution pressure and the associated equations, are still basic to electrochemistry today. He also developed theories on decomposition and contact potentials, the behaviour of palladium electrodes, and nerve stimulation (the last involving concentration changes at the protoplasm/liquid interface). He gave a method for determining the ionic product of water and was the first to advocate the hydrogen electrode as an electrochemical standard.

At Berlin, Nernst's greatest contributions were in thermodynamics. In 1905–6 he produced his Heat Theorem, or Third Law of Thermodynamics. This was essentially a derivation from the Helmholtz Equation (see H. L. F. von HELMHOLTZ) and the Thomsen-Berthelot principle of maximum work (see P. BERTHELOT). The latter, Nernst maintained, can be true only near absolute zero. The theorem was first used chiefly in the study of chemical equilibria, but later became connected with quantum theory and statistical mechanics. With his students, Nernst began to collect accurate thermodynamic data. In 1911, with F. A. Lindemann (later Lord CHERWELL) he devised a special calorimeter for determination of specific heats at low temperatures and results led to significant advances in the quantum theory of specific heats.

Nernst made important measurements on the degree of dissociation of gases by following changes in thermal conductivities. He examined ignition points of gases, and studied the hydrogen/nitrogen reaction at high pressures. In 1918 he explained the very high quantum yields in the photochemical reaction between hydrogen and chlorine in terms of a chain mechanism. He advanced a valuable theory on the velocities of heterogenous reactions.

For technical achievements, Nernst is remembered especially for his electric lamp, having a 'glower' of zirconia and other oxides and of greater efficiency than the carbon filament lamp (1897). A useful infrared source, it also had wide general use until supplanted by the tungsten filament lamp. Nernst sold his patent on it for 1 million marks, the proceeds enabling him to become a pioneer motorist. His electronic 'Neo-Bechstein' piano was less successful. He invented a simple but effective apparatus for production of liquid hydrogen, needed for his low-temperature work.

His work, founded on thermodynamics and the atomic theory, was expounded in many books and won for him the 1920 Nobel prize in chemistry, foreign membership of the Royal Society (1932), and many other honours.

Nature, **149**, 375, 1942.
Obituary Notices of Fellows of the Royal Society. 1942. (Portrait.)
K. Mendelssohn, *The World of Walther Nernst.* 1973.
Albert Einstein, *Scientific Monthly*, **54**, 195, 1942.
J. R. Partington (Nernst Memorial Lecture), *Journal of the Chemical Society*, **3**, 2853, 1953. (Portrait.)
E. Farber (Ed.), *Great Chemists.* 1961. (Portrait.)
Dictionary of Scientific Biography.
Tyler Wasson (Ed.), *Nobel Prize Winners.* 1987. (Portrait.)

                                                                                     C A R

NEWCOMB, SIMON Born at Wallace, Nova Scotia, Canada, 12 March 1835; died Washington, DC, 11 July 1909. One of the greatest masters of celestial mechanics in the nineteenth century.

Simon Newcomb became assistant in the American Nautical Almanac office at Cambridge, Massachusetts, at the age of 22, after some years of school-teaching. Subsequently, he was appointed professor of mathematics in the US Navy at the Washington Naval Observatory. In 1877 he became superintendent of the American Nautical Almanac, directing its activities for twenty years until his retirement in 1897. From 1884 to 1894 he was also professor of mathematics and astronomy at Johns Hopkins University, and editor of the *American Journal of Mathematics*.

Newcomb wrote more than 350 papers and a number of books, both popular and specialized. He made a major contribution to our understanding of the movements of the Moon and the planets. He studied the serious differences between the Moon's positions and those given in Hansen's Tables and by exhaustive searches extended the history of the Moon's motion back to 1675, laying a firm foundation for future workers to build on. He also contributed an important series of papers on the planet's effect on the Moon's motion. Twenty-five years were spent deriving improved elements and tables of positions for the eight major planets (Pluto was not known then), the results being published in the *Astronomical Papers of the American Ephemeris*, a series of volumes he founded.

Modest by nature, he received many awards, including the Royal Society's Copley Medal and the Royal Astronomical Society's Gold Medal.

Ormond Stone, *The Astrophysical Journal*, 30, 171. 1909 (Portrait.)

Dictionary of American Biography.

W. W. Campbell, *Science*, **84**, 165, 1936.

A. F. C. Stevenson, *Journal of the Royal Astronomical Society of Canada*, **29**, 180, 1935.

Biographical Memoirs. National Academy of Sciences, vol. 17. 1916.

Dictionary of Scientific Biography.

A E R

NEWCOMEN, THOMAS Born at Dartmouth, Devon, England, and christened there 24 February 1663; died Southwark, London, 5 August 1729. Inventor of the first practical steam engine.

Of Newcomen's early life little is certain. He appears to have come of a small merchant family with a landed ancestry, and to have received his education at the hand of John Favell, a Nonconformist scholar of Bromsgrove. He may have served an apprenticeship with an Exeter ironmonger, and was certainly in that trade – metalworker and toolsmith would be a modern description – in Dartmouth by the end of the seventeenth century. In this trade he was assisted by John Calley or Cawley (d. 1717), plumber and glazier, and both would have been familiar with the metalliferous mines of Devon and Cornwall. Stimulated by the high cost of extracting water from mines, Newcomen set about the creation of a steam-operated pump in the first decade of the eighteenth century. The first well-authenticated Newcomen engine, erected near Dudley, Worcestershire, in 1712, was a mature and practical machine, almost certainly preceded by development models, probably in the Cornish mines. Whilst the claim by John Robison (1739–1805) that Newcomen was directly aided by Royal Society savants has been discredited, the development of the engine certainly required a scientific knowledge of the properties of the atmosphere.

Both Newcomen and Calley were devout Baptists and made considerable use of contacts in Baptist communities for the sale and erection of the machine: perhaps they also made use of these contacts during its development. The engine itself consisted of a brass cylinder (later iron), with one end open to the air and the other connected to a boiler providing low-pressure steam. A piston worked in the cylinder and was connected to one end of a great pivoted beam, at the other end of which were the pump rods. The whole thus resembled a great pump, the piston rod acting upon the pump handle. With the piston at the top of the cylinder, counterbalanced by the pump rods, steam entered the cylinder and swept out any air. The connection with the boiler being closed, the steam was condensed by the injection of cold water and the piston was pushed to the bottom of the cylinder by the weight of the superincumbent atmosphere; this was the workstroke. By the addition of a vertical rod to the great beam to operate the valve gear in its rise and fall, the engine became the second self-acting machine (the clock being the first).

The Newcomen engine was undeniably operated 'by the Impellent Force of Fire' and so infringed the patent held by Thomas SAVERY. Newcomen was thus forced to join Savery in its exploitation. Following Savery's death in 1715, the patent passed into the hands of a syndicate which does not appear to have included Newcomen, but the latter continued to be concerned in the erection of the engines. From the second decade of the century a considerable number were erected, especially on the developing coalfields and in Cornish tin-mines. Though Newcomen's part in the development of the engine seems to have been minimized, his invention, aided by ironfounders at Coalbrookdale and engineers such as John SMEATON, was to be a mainstay of the Industrial Revolution until the expiry of the Watt patents in 1800.

H. W. Dickinson, *A Short History of the Steam Engine*. 1938 (2 ed. 1963).

L. T. C. Rolt, *Thomas Newcomen: The Prehistory of the Steam Engine*. 1963.

M. Hine, *Transactions of the Newcomen Society*, **9**, 105, 1928–9.

Dictionary of National Biography.

W N S

NEWLANDS, JOHN ALEXANDER REINA Born in London, 26 November 1837; died there, 29 July 1898. Chemist; the first to prepare a Periodic Table of the elements.

Newlands studied under A. W. von HOFMANN at the Royal College of Chemistry, London, and later became assistant to J. T. Way, chemist to the Royal Agricultural Society. Then he set up (1864) with his brother as a consulting analyst, but this venture seems not to have been a success, as two years later he became chemist in a sugar factory in the Victoria Docks, London.

About 1860 the researches of S. CANNIZZARO and others were beginning to put the atomic weights of the elements on a firm foundation. Newlands was the first to point out, in papers published from 1863 onwards, that if the elements were arranged in order of atomic weights, similar properties tended to appear after every eighth element; for this reason his idea became known as the Law of Octaves. Perhaps J. W. DOBEREINER had given an inkling of this work with his Triads; groups of three similar elements of which the atomic weight of the middle one was the average of that of the other two.

Newlands published his ideas in the form of a

table of some sixty elements in 1865 and a year later gave an account of his discovery to the Chemical Society in London. Unfortunately, he was in advance of his time and his ideas were at first received with scepticism, even ridicule. The Chemical Society refused to publish Newland's papers. It was not until D. I. MENDELÉEFF – who was apparently not aware of Newland's work – independently put them forward in a somewhat more developed form in 1869 that their importance was generally acknowledged. Today the Periodic Table of the elements – whose underlying principles can be understood in the light of later knowledge of atomic structures – is still the effective basis of their chemical classification, and is used throughout the world. Later, Newlands's claim was formally recognized by the Royal Society, which awarded him its Davy Medal in 1887, though it did not elect him to Fellowship.

J. R. Partington, *A History of Chemistry*, vol. 4. 1964.

W. H. Taylor, *Journal of Chemical Education*, **26**, 491, 1949.

Dictionary of National Biography (Missing Persons). 1993.

J. W. van Spronsen, *Chymia*, **11**, 125, 1966.

Dictionary of Scientific Biography.

T I W

NEWTON, SIR ISAAC Born at Woolsthorp, Lincolnshire, England, 25 December 1642; died London, 20 March 1727. Natural philosopher and mathematician.

Born prematurely, Newton was also a posthumous child, his father, reputed to have been a 'wild, extravagant and weak man', having died in the previous October. In 1645 his mother, Hanna, married the Rev. Barnabas Smith, with whom she then went to live at his rectory in North Witham, leaving the infant Isaac in charge of his grandmother Ayscough. Some scholars have not unreasonably seen the origin of Newton's profoundly neurotic temperament in this early severance from his mother's care. After early education at nearby schools he was sent at the age of 12 to the King's School, Grantham, where he remained for four years, returning home in 1658 to assist his mother who had returned to Woolsthorp on the death of her husband in 1656. But Newton proved a somewhat absent-minded farmer and on the advice of his uncle William Ayscough he was sent back to Grantham to prepare for Cambridge. He entered Trinity College in 1661. His undergraduate studies seem not to have been particularly distinguished and in 1663 he failed in a scholarship examination due to woeful inadequacy in geometry. Owing to the Plague, a great part of the years 1665–6 were spent away from Cambridge, and it was then, in the peace and security of the Lincolnshire countryside, that Newton laid the foundations of his future greatness in optics, dynamics, and mathematics. Returning finally to Cambridge, he became a minor Fellow at Trinity in 1667 and a major Fellow in the following year.

In 1669 he was appointed to the Lucasian Chair of Mathematics vacated by Isaac BARROW. His public lectures in the years 1669–71 contained a detailed account of his discoveries in optics. In 1672 he presented his first paper (on optics) to the Royal Society, of which he became a Fellow in the same year. The years 1672–6 were marred by troublesome controversies over his optical discoveries. Returning to Cambridge in November 1679, following an absence of six months due to his mother's death in June of that year, Newton entered into a correspondence with Robert HOOKE which seems to have led to a renewal of his interest in dynamics, culminating in his solution to the problem of Kepler motion. In 1684, following a visit paid him by E. HALLEY at Cambridge, Newton returned to dynamics, composing the *Principia* between the autumn of 1684 and the spring of 1686. Presented to the Royal Society in June 1686, it was published the following year.

Newton played a prominent part in University affairs, being one of eight Fellows who accompanied the Vice-Chancellor to London in 1687 to answer the University's case in connection with illegal encroachments by James II. At Cambridge he became friendly with the Whig politician Charles Montague, later Lord Halifax, and about the time of Montague's departure from Cambridge in 1688 he seems to have grown weary of academic life, making repeated but unsuccessful attempts to obtain a position in London. Through Montague's influence he was finally appointed to the position of Warden of the Mint in 1696, playing a major part in the successful revision of the coinage in the period 1696–9, in which latter year he was appointed Master of the Mint. In 1701 he resigned both his fellowship and chair at Cambridge, and in the same year was elected one of the Members of Parliament for the University. In 1703 he was elected President of the Royal Society, a position which he held until his death. He was knighted in 1705. He died in 1726, after a painful illness stoically borne. He was given a national funeral and buried in Westminster Abbey.

Begun during the Plague Years, when he gave a complete solution to the problem of colliding bodies and discovered the law of centrifugal force, Newton's researches in dynamics were continued in 1679 and culminated in the *Principia*. Its composition was made possible only by Newton's solution to the problem of Kepler motion (1679) and the wonderful theorem proving that a homogeneous gravitating sphere attracts at points outside it as if all its mass were concentrated at its centre (February 1685). Equally decisive were the tests of the inverse square law of gravitation against the Moon's motion – probably first carried out with inconclusive results in 1666, and then with compelling success in 1679 or 1684, employing the improved measure of the Earth's radius made by Jean PICARD. On the formal side, Newton's most original contribution to dynamics was his precise concept of force enshrined in his second law of motion.

In the *Principia* Newton displayed his consummate mastery in theoretical physics. His optical researches show him an equally great master of precise experiments. Commenced in 1666, when he determined to try the 'celebrated experiments on colours' the superior arrangement of his experiments compared with his predecessors, and his quick eye for the unexpected, soon led him to the revolutionary discovery of the existence in white light of a mixture of distinct coloured rays distinguished by their differing refrangibilities in the prism. His paper of 1672 presented an overwhelming body of evidence in favour of this view. In his 1675 paper he described further experiments on the colour of thin films and plates, and put forward an ingenious corpuscular theory of light involving the notion of easy fits of transmission and reflection bearing a surprising likeness to the modern theory of light quanta. First published in 1704, his *Optics* went through many editions and was the most influential work on experimental science for almost the whole of the century.

Apart from dynamics, optics, and chemistry (in which he published little in spite of a large expenditure of time in thought and experiment), Newton exerted a profound influence on eighteenth century thought through his views on scientific method and the philosophy of science, as found especially in the *Queries* to the *Optics* and in the preface to the second edition of the *Principia* (1713). From Britain these views spread to the Continent, first to Holland, later to France and Germany, so that at the end of the century Newton's influence in science as a whole was as dominant in Europe as it had been in England.

Newton's contributions to science were matched by his great mathematical achievements, especially his discovery of the Binomial Theorem and the direct and inverse method of fluxions.

Newton's genius in science and mathematics was marred by an inordinate intolerance of criticism and an intensely jealous regard for priority in his discoveries in optics, dynamics, and mathematics. Thus his controversies with Hooke, John FLAMSTEED, and G. W. LEIBNIZ were marked by a bitterness remarkable even by the standards of the age. Nevertheless, although modern historical research has tended to lessen our sympathy with Newton in these controversies, it has equally tended to increase our admiration for the marvellous nature of his achievements in science, a feeling expressed by EINSTEIN in a foreword to a new edition of his *Optics*:

'Nature was to him an open book, whose letters he could read without effort. The conceptions which he used to reduce the material of experience to order seemed to flow spontaneously from experience itself, from the beautiful experiments which he ranged in order like playthings and describes with an affectionate wealth of detail. In one person he combined the experimenter, the theorist, the mechanic and, not least, the artist in exposition. He stands before us strong, certain, and alone: his joy in creation and his minute precision are evident in every word and every figure'.

D. Brewster, *The Life of Sir Isaac Newton*. 1831 (enlarged 1855).

L. T. More, *Isaac Newton: a Biography*. 1934.

E. N. da C. Andrade, *Sir Isaac Newton*. 1954. (Portrait.)

J. W. Herivel, *The Background to Newton's Principia*. 1965.

A. R. Hall, *Philosophers at War: the Quarrel between Newton and Leibniz*. 1980; *Isaac Newton: Adventurer in Thought*. 1992.

R. S. Westfall, *Never at Rest: A Biography of Isaac Newton*. 1980; *The Life of Isaac Newton*. 1993.

B. J. T. Dobbs, *The Janus Face of Genius*. 1993.

F. E. Manuel, *A Portrait of Isaac Newton*. 1968.

D. B. Meli, *Equivalence and Priority: Newton versus Leibniz*. 1993.

A. Rupert Hall, *All was Light: An Introduction to Newton's Optics*. 1993.

Dictionary of Scientific Biography.

Dictionary of National Biography.

J W H

NICOL, WILLIAM Born in Scotland, *c*.1768; died Edinburgh, 2 September 1851. Inventor of the Nicol prism.

In 1828 Nicol announced the invention of his prism, consisting of a long crystal of Iceland spar split into two equal parts and rejoined in their original position with Canada balsam. Light entering one of the faces of the prism was divided into the ordinary and extraordinary rays, the ordinary ray being totally reflected at the surface of separation between the two halves of the prism while the extraordinary ray was transmitted. This prism proved of great use in investigating the polarization of light.

Nicol was Professor of Physics at Edinburgh, where he had J. Clerk MAXWELL as a pupil.

Dictionary of National Biography (Missing Persons). 1993.

Dictionary of Scientific Biography.

J W H

NICOLLE, CHARLES JULES HENRI Born at Rouen, France, 21 September 1866; died Tunis, 28 February 1936. Noted for many contributions to the study of infectious diseases especially in identifying the louse as the vector of typhus.

Nicolle, the son of a physician, graduated in medicine in Paris. After general practice and specialized study in microbiology at the Pasteur Institute in Paris, he became (1902) director of the Pasteur Institute in Tunis. There, in 1903, he began studying the spread of typhus, announcing (with associates), in 1909, the successful results of this work. For these studies he was awarded a Nobel prize in 1928. The clue that led to the success came from his careful observations, in a Tunisian hospital, that typhus patients were infectious on entering the hospital, but that once inside the medical ward no cross-infection occurred. This indicated that the cause of infection was removed when the patients were bathed and their clothes disinfected. This suggested to him that the body louse was probably the culprit.

Nicolle began rigorous experimental studies to prove his view. He succeeded in transmitting typhus to various animals ranging from the monkey to the guinea pig. He also showed that the louse was the vector of the causative organism (*Rickettsia prowazetii*), and demonstrated that the louse was infective only after taking in blood from an infected human. Furthermore, he found that the infection is spread via the faeces of the louse.

This work led to a practical method of fighting typhus, which had long been known to spread rapidly under insanitary conditions. Nicolle carried out stern measures to combat the louse and did much to eradicate the disease in Tunis. His methods were particularly beneficial a few years later, during the First World War. Nicolle's prophylactic measures against typhus were part of his activities in developing the role of the Pasteur Institute in Tunis in public health. Additionally, he was the founder of the influential *Archives de l'Institut Pasteur de Tunis*.

Nicolle made a number of other contributions to medicine, for instance studies on Mediterranean fever, Kala-azar, trachoma, and the demonstration that protective antibodies were present in patients convalescing from typhus, influenza and measles. Any notice on Nicolle must also mention that he was a more than competent novelist, poet, and philosopher.

During his last years, from 1932, he held the Professorial Chair at the *Collège de France* and did much to promote experimental medicine.

E. Mesnil, *Bulletin de Académie nationale de médicine*, **115**, 541, 1936.
Dictionary of Scientific Biography.
Tyler Wasson, *Nobel Prize Winners*. 1987. (Portrait.)

J K C

NIÉPCE, JOSEPH NICÉPHORE Born at Châlon-sur-Saône, France, 7 March 1765; died St Loup-de-Varennes, 5 July 1833. Inventor of photography and photomechanical reproduction.

Elder son of a King's Councillor and barrister, Niépce lived quietly on his country estate at St Loup-de-Varennes, devoting himself to scientific pursuits. With his brother Claude he invented the pyréolophore, a combustion engine for boats (1807).

Attempts to fix the images of the *camera obscura* started in April 1816, and Niépce recorded the view from his workroom window on paper sensitized with silver chloride, fixed only partially with nitric acid. He tried, unsuccessfully, to correct the reversal of light and shade by printing through one of his negatives. The first permanent camera photograph was exposed for about eight hours in the summer of 1826 on a pewter plate coated with bitumen of Judaea, the shadow portions not hardened by light being dissolved with lavender oil and white petroleum. At the same time, Niépce copied an engraving by superposition on a similar plate which was etched and paper prints pulled – the first photo-mechanical reproduction process. Both camera photographs and printing plates were called heliography by Niépce.

Visiting England in 1827, Niépce failed to interest George IV and the Royal Society in his invention because he insisted on keeping the method secret. In December 1829 he formed a partnership with L. J. M. DAGUERRE to perfect the process, but died six years before the publication of the daguerreotype which the latter developed from heliography.

Helmut and Alison Gernsheim, *L. J. M. Daguerre: The History of the Diorama and the Daguerreotype*. 1956. (Portrait.)
Helmut and Alison Gernsheim, *The History of Photography*. 1955. (Portrait.)
Dictionary of Scientific Biography.

H and A G

NIEUWLAND, JULIUS ARTHUR Born at Hansbeke, near Ghent, Belgium, 14 February 1878; died Washington, DC, 11 June 1936. Famous for his discoveries in acetylene chemistry.

From early childhood, Nieuwland lived in Indiana, then studied at the University of Notre Dame and did research on acetylene at the Catholic University, Washington. He entered the Roman Catholic priesthood in 1903. From 1904 to 1918 he taught botany at Notre Dame, working on plant classification and editing the *American Midland Naturalist*. From then until his death he was professor of organic chemistry.

Returning to research on acetylene, he showed that this could be converted into divinyl-acetylene and that this in turn could be polymerized to a rubber-like solid. The announcement of this result at an American Chemical Society meeting in 1925 prompted a member of the audience to advise his firm (the du Pont Chemical Company) to acquire rights for the process. This was done, royalties being paid to Nieuwland's religious order as he had himself taken a vow of poverty.

In 1929 Nieuwland discovered that acetylene could be catalytically converted into monovinylacetylene, which with hydrogen chloride gives 'chloroprene' (2-chloro-buta-1:3-diene). Polymerization of this, developed by du Pont in conjunction with Nieuwland, led to 'neoprene', the first commercially successful synthetic rubber, marketed first in 1932.

Nieuwland made other discoveries in the acetylene field, one of which was used by G. N. LEWIS in development of the poison gas lewisite. With R. R. Vogte he wrote *The Chemistry of Acetylene* (1945), which became the standard book on the subject.

Journal of the Chemical Society, 708, 1936.
Dictionary of American Biography.
Dictionary of Scientific Biography.

C A R

NOBEL, ALFRED BERNHARD Born in Stockholm, 21 October 1833; died San Remo, Italy, 10 December 1896. Inventor and philanthropist.

Alfred Nobel received little formal education, but owed much to the training given by his father, a highly talented inventor and entrepreneur, who was bankrupted both in his native Sweden and in Russia, yet made great contributions to both countries, especially in armaments. In 1850–2 Alfred travelled widely, visiting America, where he had dealings with John ERICSSON, and perfecting his knowledge of five languages. In 1863 he made his first big discoveries in a business organized by his father on his return from St Petersburg to Stockholm, but in 1865–73 his headquarters were in the vicinity of Hamburg and in 1873–91 at Paris. The last years of his life were spent mainly at San Remo, though they also covered his development of the Bofors munition works and other interests in Sweden.

Nobel revolutionized the explosives industry. Between 1863 and 1865, in spite of an explosion which killed his youngest brother and four other persons, he successfully developed a detonator, based on mercury fulminate, to make possible the industrial use of nitroglycerine. This was quickly followed by the development of dynamite, in which the admixture of kieselguhr, while reducing the explosive force of the nitroglycerine by one-fourth, provided a blasting substance which was reasonably safe in manufacture and use. From its first patenting in 1867, dynamite enjoyed a world-wide success, and in 1875 Nobel introduced the still more powerful blasting gelatine, in which the nitroglycerine was gelatinized with collodion cotton. Finally, in 1887 he contributed one of the first smokeless powders for military purposes. This was ballistite, a mixture of collodion cotton, nitroglycerine, benzol, and (initially) camphor, and was first used by Italy.

In spite of many battles over patent rights, these inventions earned Nobel a considerable fortune, which was increased from his large holdings in the Baku petroleum industry, organized by his two elder brothers, Robert and Ludvig. The width of the interests of this indefatigable inventor and man of affairs, ranging from international relations to the principal European literatures, was strikingly illustrated by the provisions of his will, establishing the world-famous prizes for chemistry, physics, physiology or medicine, literature of an idealistic tendency, and the promotion of world peace.

H. Schück and R. Sohlman, *The Life of Alfred Nobel*. 1929.

E. Bergengren, *Alfred Nobel: The Man and his Work*, (English translation). 1962. (Portrait.)

Trevor I. Williams, *Alfred Nobel*. 1974. (Portrait.)

J. Schück et al., *Nobel, the Man and his Prizes*. 1962.

Dictionary of Scientific Biography.

T K D

NOBILI, LEOPOLDO Born at Trassilico, near Reggio, Italy, 1784; died Florence, 5 August 1835. Physicist.

Nobili was professor of physics at the Florence Museum. He was a pioneer worker in the field of electrochemistry and in 1828 published an account of experiments in which electricity was generated by immersing platinum plates in solutions of two different chemicals (nitre and potash). To measure current, he devised the astatic galvanometer, which is independent of the Earth's magnetic field. He invented the thermoelectric couple, by which an electric potential is created by the junction of two metals at different temperatures. Using thermocouples joined in series, he created the thermopile, very useful for measuring thermal radiation.

J. R. Partington, *A History of Chemistry*, vol. 4. 1964.

Paolo Cantoni, *Leopoldo Nobili* (Commemorative Lectures). 1874.

Dictionary of Scientific Biography.

T I W

NOLLET, JEAN ANTOINE, ABBÉ Born at Pimprez, Oise, France, 19 November 1700; died Paris, 24 April 1770. Remembered for his electrical researches.

In 1730-2 Nollet collaborated on electrical researches with C. F. de C. DUFAY, whom he accompanied in 1734 to England where he was made a Fellow of the Royal Society. On his return to Paris in 1735 he gave a course of experimental physics, visiting Holland in the following year where he met W. J. S. vans' Gravesande (1688-1742), P. van Musschenbroek (1692-1761), and other Dutch scientists. He was elected to the *Académie des Sciences* in 1739. He played an important part in the popularization of experimental science in France.

Nollet was an indefatigable experimenter, especially in electrical phenomena, which he regarded as due to the movement in opposite directions of two currents of fluid producing repulsion or attraction on the surface of charged bodies. This theory was in vogue for some time before being replaced by that of Benjamin FRANKLIN. He constructed one of the first electrometers (1747) in which the electrical charge of a body was measured by the angle of deflection of the supporting thread of a pith ball.

J. J. Walsh, *Catholic Churchmen in Science*. 1906. (Portrait.)

J. Torlais, *Un physicien au siècle des lumières, l'abbé Nollet 1700-1770*. 1954.

Dictionary of Scientific Biography.

J W H

NORDENSKIÖLD, NILS ADOLF ERIK Born in Helsingfors (Helsinki), Finland, 18 November 1832; died Västerljung, Sweden, 12 August 1901. Arctic explorer and geographer.

Nordenskiöld took his PhD in geology at Helsingfors in 1857, but his anti-Russian sympathies made it necessary for him to move to Sweden, from which his family originally came. In the course of extensive studies of the geology and geography of Spitsbergen, his ship in 1868 achieved a record distance north; he also began the exploration of the Greenland ice-cap (1870, 1883).

On 25 July 1878 he set out from north Norway in the steamer *Vega* to traverse the North-East Passage; he was stopped by ice on 28 September, only 110 miles short of the Behring Straits and finally got through on 18 July of the following year. He was created a baron for achieving the passage first sought by Sir Hugh Willoughby (d. 1554) in 1553, and the scientific results of the voyage were published in five volumes (1882-7). Nordenskiöld's *Facsimile Atlas* (1889) and *Periplus* (1897) made important contributions to the history of cartography.

N. A. E. Nordenskiöld, *Voyage of the Vega* (English translation). 1883.

S. Lindroth (ed.), *Swedish men of science, 1650-1950*. 1952.

J. A. Hammerton, *Concise Universal Biography*. (Portrait.)

Dictionary of Scientific Biography.

T K D

NORRISH, RONALD GEORGE WREYFORD Born in Cambridge, England, 9 November 1897; died there, 7 June 1978. Pioneer of flash photolysis and kinetic spectroscopy.

Norrish was educated at the Perse School, Cambridge, and went on to read chemistry there at Emmanuel College. His studies were interrupted by military service in the First World War, during which he became a prisoner of war. Afterwards he returned to Cambridge as demonstrator (1925), lecturer (1930), and finally professor of physical chemistry (1937) until his retirement in 1965.

Norrish's life work was in reaction kinetics, with a particular interest in photochemical reactions. From 1945 he developed, with George PORTER (now Lord Porter) a new technique of flash photolysis, and for this they were jointly awarded a Nobel Prize for chemistry in 1967. In this, a chemical reaction is initiated by an exceedingly intense flash of light, around 600 000 kilowatts, which creates a number of short-lived radicals. The nature of these is investigated spectroscopically by means of a weaker flash following close on the first. By this means, it has proved possible to investigate the kinetics and energetics of reactions taking place in as little as a ten billionth of a second.

Norrish was honoured by many foreign scientific societies. In Britain, the Royal Society elected him to Fellowship in 1936.

Les Prix Nobel en 1967. 1968. (Portrait.)
Biographical Memoirs of Fellows of the Royal Society. 1980. (Portrait.)
Dictionary of National Biography.
Tyler Wasson (Ed.), *Nobel Prize Winners.* 1987. (Portrait.)

T I W

NORTHROP, JOHN HOWARD Born in Yonkers, New York, 5 July 1891; died Wickenburg, Arizona, 27 May 1987. Biochemist, enzymologist.

Northrop was born into a scientific family, both his parents being biologists. He studied chemistry and biology at Columbia University, graduating in 1912. In 1916 he was appointed to the Rockefeller Institute, where he spent the rest of his working life. Research on the manufacture of acetone by fermentation during the First World War led to a lifelong interest in enzymes. In 1926 J. B. SUMNER succeeded in crystallizing urease and showed it to be a protein. Northrop perceived the importance of this and over the next few years prepared several enzymes, including trypsin and pepsin, in crystalline form. He also crystallized ribonuclease and deoxyribonuclease In 1937 W. M. Stanley (1904–71) first crystallized a virus (tobacco mosaic) and a year later Northrop did the same with a bacterial virus. In 1946 Northrop, Sumner and Stanley shared the Nobel Prize for chemistry.

New York Times, 16 July 1987.
Les Prix Nobel en 1946. 1947. (Portrait.)
Tyler Wasson (ed.), *Nobel Prize Winners.* 1987. (Portrait.)

T I W

NORTON, THOMAS Born at Bristol, England, late fourteenth century; died *c.*1480. Alchemist.

Norton was the author (about 1477) of an important alchemical work, written in verse, entitled *The Ordinall of Alchimy.* Several early manuscript versions are in the British Museum. It was printed at Frankfurt-am-Main in Latin translation in 1618, but its first printing in English appears to have been in 1652, when Elias Ashmole (1617–92) included it in his *Theatrum Chemicum.* Supposedly anonymous, the text contains a simple cipher that reveals the author as:

Thomas Norton of Briseto
A parfet Master ye maie him call trowe.

Norton appears to have learned his alchemy from George Ripley (d. *c.*1490). Like most alchemists of the day, his objectives were the elixir of life and the philosophers' stone (to transmute base metals into gold), but the *Ordinall* contains much practical information on chemical manipulations.

Norton has been identified as a member of a well-known Bristol family, his father having been Sheriff in 1401 and Mayor in 1413. He was a Member of Parliament for the borough in 1436 and became a member of the Privy Chamber of Edward

IV, whom he accompanied to Burgundy in 1470 when he fled.

E. J. Holmyard, *Alchemy.* 1957.
Dictionary of National Biography.
H. Kopp, *Die Alchemie in älterer und neurer Zeit.* 1886.

T I W

NOZOE, TETSUO Born in Sendai, Japan, 16 May 1902; Organic chemist.

Tetsuo Nozoe, the son of an attorney and a politician, was educated in Sendai and graduated from Tohoku Imperial University in chemistry in 1926 under the guidance of Professor R. MAJIMA, a great leader in the history of organic chemistry in Japan. After graduation he went to Formosa (Taiwan) to take a post at the Government Monopoly Bureau Research Laboratories, and was then appointed as an assistant professor of the newly established Taihoku Imperial University (now National Taipei University) in 1929. He was then promoted to the rank of professor in 1937 and began investigating the isolation and structure of saponin, sapogenin, and constituents of Taiwanhinoki, a conifer tree which grows in Formosa. In 1936 he isolated hinokitiol from the essential oil of the conifer. His structural study in 1943–47 led him to propose a then unprecedented cyclic seven-membered α-trienolone structure for the hinokitiol, which was subsequently found to be a novel type of aromatic compound. On the other hand, M. J. S. Dewar (1918–) in Britain independently proposed the α-trienolone structure for stipitatic acid in 1945. He proposed to name these novel seven-membered skeletons 'tropolone'.

Nozoe was asked to remain as a professor in Formosa when the Second World War ended in 1945. He was then invited to Tohoku University in Japan in 1948, where he remained as a professor until his retirement in 1966. At Tohoku University he continued to study natural products, such as triterpenoids as well as structural and synthetic work concerning hinokitiol. He succeeded in synthesizing hinokitiol and its parent tropolone in 1949. He then undertook an extensive investigation of tropolone chemistry. These investigations opened up a wide area of study involving troponoid as well as nonbenzenoid aromatic chemistry. After retiring from Tohoku University he has been enjoying research on the troponoids and non-benzenoid aromatic compounds in the research laboratory of a private company.

He is a recipient of the Japan Academy Award (1953) and the Hofmann Award of German Chemical Society (1981). He was also decorated with the Order of Cultural Merit from the Japanese Government in 1958.

Proceedings of the Japanese Academy, **26(7)**, 38, 1950.
T. Nozoe, 'Tropons and Tropolones' in D. Ginsburg (ed.), *Non-Benzenoid Aromatic Compounds.* 1959.
Heterocycles, **11**, 1, 1978.
T. Nozoe, *Seventy Years in Organic Chemistry.* 1991. (Portrait.)

H S

O

OCCAM, WILLIAM OF See OCKHAM.

OCKHAM (OCCAM), WILLIAM OF Born at Ockham, Surrey, England, c.1285; died probably in Munich, Bavaria, Germany, 1349. Logician and philosopher.

Ockham, the *Doctor invincibilis*, had a profound influence not only on medieval thought but on later philosophers, including Francis BACON. He studied at Oxford, possibly under Duns Scotus (c.1265–1308), and entered the Franciscan order, of which he subsequently became Vicar. He clashed with Pope John XXII as a result of his *Opus nonaginta Dierum* – a systematic refutation of the papal attack on evangelical poverty – and was imprisoned at Avignon; escaping, he made his way to Munich, where he probably spent the rest of his life, under the protection of the Emperor. Later, he became reconciled with the Pope.

He was a distinguished theologian, political theorist, and logician. Scientifically, his claim to fame rests mainly on his enunciation of the so-called 'Ockham's razor', according to which 'entities ought not to be multiplied except of necessity'. Translated into modern terminology, this dictum asserts that when a phenomenon can be interpreted in several ways the preferred explanation is that involving the fewest assumptions.

Gordon Leff, *Medieval Thought: St Augustine to Ockham*. 1958.
Dictionary of National Biography.
Dictionary of Scientific Biography.

T I W

ODLING, WILLIAM Born in London, 5 September 1829; died Oxford, 17 February 1921. Teacher of chemistry.

Odling, the son of a surgeon, qualified in medicine at London University, but was more interested in chemistry. He studied in Paris under C. F. GERHARDT, and in 1863 followed his friend Sir Edward FRANKLAND as professor of chemistry at St Bartholomew's Hospital. On the death of FARADAY he became Fullerian Professor at the Royal Institution (1867), and (1872) Waynflete Professor at Oxford. He retired in 1912.

Although Odling took a vigorous part in the discussions of the 1850s about valency, the theory of types, and the classification of the elements, he had more talent for teaching than for original research. His lectures were highly esteemed, though his writings are disfigured by his free use of ugly neologisms. He was interested in problems of water supply and purification, and their relationship with disease; he also held office in both the Chemical Society and the Royal Society

and the Royal Institute of Chemistry, and was elected FRS in 1859.

J. E. Marsh, *Journal of the Chemical Society*, 553, 1921. (Portrait.)
Proceedings of the Royal Society, **100A**, i, 1922. (Portrait.)
J. L. Thornton and A. Wiles, *Annals of Science*, **12**, 288, 1956.
Dictionary of National Biography (Missing Persons). 1993.
Dictionary of Scientific Biography.

W V F

OERSTED, HANS CHRISTIAN Born at Rudkjöbing, Langeland, Denmark, 14 August 1777; died Copenhagen, 9 March 1851. Discovered magnetic effect produced by electric current.

Oersted was the son of an apothecary. Having completed his studies at the University of Copenhagen with a thesis on Kant's philosophy, he became chemical assistant to the medical faculty in 1799. In 1801–3 he travelled in Germany, Holland and France. In 1806 he was appointed professor of physics at Copenhagen. In 1812–13 he made further travels in Germany and France and in 1822–3 visited England. On his return, he founded the Danish Society for the Promotion of Scientific Knowledge. In 1829 he became director of the Polytechnic Institute in Copenhagen.

According to his own account, Oersted's discovery of electromagnetism was made during a lecture in the spring of 1820. In the summer of the same year he published the result in a paper (in Latin) which he circulated both to scientific academies and to all the leading physical scientists of the day. The resulting explosion of interest, both popular and scientific, was comparable to that produced by the *Siderius Nuncius* of GALILEO or by the announcement of the electric pile by A. VOLTA in 1800. If Oersted's actual discovery was a chance one, nevertheless it was the outcome of long search based on a belief in a connection between electricity and magnetism which he had expressed as early as 1812 in his *View of Chemical Laws*. Oersted's discovery was taken up by many other scientists and led to a rapid development in electromagnetism culminating in the memoir of A. M. AMPÈRE. In 1822, after many fruitless attempts, he was the first to obtain a reasonably accurate value for the compressibility of water by using an ingenious piezometer and by ensuring that increased pressure was exerted both inside and outside the water container. From his researches (1823) into thermoelectric junctions he concluded that such junctions produced a relatively high current at a relatively low potential difference compared with the voltaic cell. He also made important improvements in the torsion balance of C. A. de COULOMB.

Oersted maintained an extensive correspondence with most of the leading scientists of the day. He was a prolific writer, his most widely read non-scientific work being *The Soul in Nature* published in Munich in 1850.

C. M. Harding (Ed.), *Correspondence* (2 vols). 1920.

L. and J. B. Horner (in preface to) *The Soul in Nature.* 1852. (Reprinted 1966.)

P. Lenard, *Great Men of Science.* 1933. (Portrait.)

Kirstine Meyer, in H. C. Ørsted, *Scientific Papers.* 1920.

Dictionary of Scientific Biography.

J W H

OHM, GEORG SIMON Born at Erlangen, Bavaria, Germany, 16 March 1789; died Munich, Bavaria, 7 July 1854. Physicist.

After a short period in 1805 at the University of Erlangen, Ohm took up various teaching positions before returning there for three semesters as a *Privatdozent* in 1811–12. He then held further teaching positions until in 1817 he was made head of the Department of Mathematics and Physics at the Polytechnic Institute in Cologne. It was there in 1826 that he discovered the law bearing his name. During the period 1826–33 he held a position at the Military Academy in Berlin. In 1833 he was appointed professor of physics at the Polytechnic Institute in Nuremberg, where he remained until in 1849 he was appointed Extraordinary Professor of Physics at the University of Munich. He became Ordinary Professor of Physics there in 1852.

Ohm's original discovery of his law was based on the use of a thermoelectric couple employed at the suggestion of J. C. POGGENDORF to avoid the variation of electromotive force encountered with the voltaic cell. But in his epoch-making work *Die Galvanischekette* (1827), in which he set up a suggestive analogy between electric currents and the flow of liquids, he extended his results to the case of a voltaic cell, setting the electromotive force equal to the current flowing multiplied by the sum of the resistance of the circuit plus an equivalent resistance due to the cell itself.

Ohm's work received a rather mixed reception in Germany, and for some years remained largely unknown elsewhere. The great importance of his work was ultimately recognized in Britain by the award of the Copley Medal of the Royal Society in 1841, and by his election as Foreign Member of the Society the following year.

In 1843 Ohm announced the important result that the human ear recognizes only sinusoidal waves as pure tones, automatically performing an analysis of any periodic sound into its component tones. Like his law for electric currents, this law at first received little attention and it was later rediscovered and applied by H. L. F. von HELMHOLTZ. In 1852–3 Ohm carried out some important work on interference phenomena in uniaxial crystals.

P. Lenard, *Great Men of Science.* 1933. (Portrait.)

E. G. Deuerlein, *Georg Simon Ohm.* 2nd ed. 1954.

J. B. Thornton, *Australian Journal of Science,* **17**, 43. 1954.

B. Gee, *Physics Education,* **4**, 106, 1969.

Dictionary of Scientific Biography.

J W H

OLDHAM, RICHARD DIXON Born in Dublin, 31 July 1858; died Llandrinod Wells, Wales, 15 July 1936. Geologist, seismologist.

Oldham was the son of Thomas Oldham (1816–78) who became Director of the Geological Survey of India (1850–76). He himself joined the Survey in 1879, retiring in 1903. He sprang to fame with the publication in 1899 of his very detailed account of the exceptionally violent earthquake of 12 June 1897 in Assam. Examination of seismograms from many stations enabled him to demonstrate the actual existence of P (primary) and S (secondary) ground waves already theoretically predicted. Proceeding to analyse records of other large earthquakes he demonstrated invariable delays in the arrival of P waves at points on the Earth diametrically opposite the epicentre. He showed that this could be explained only by assuming that the Earth has a central core at a depth of about 3000 km. In 1906 A. MOHOROVIČIĆ made the complementary discovery, also by analysis of P and S wave records, that the Earth has a well-defined crust varying in depth from around 50 km to 5 km, being thinnest under the oceans.

Obituary Notices of Fellows of the Royal Society, 1936. (Portrait.)

Nature, **138**, 316, 1936.

Dictionary of Scientific Biography,

T I W

ONNES, KAMERLINGH HEIKE Born at Groningen, Netherlands, 21 September 1853; died Leiden, 21 February 1926. Chiefly remembered for his work on low-temperature physics.

After a period at the University of Groningen, Onnes moved in 1871 to Heidelberg, where he carried out researches under R. W. E. BUNSEN and G. R. KIRCHHOFF. Returning to Groningen, he was awarded his doctor's degree there *Summa cum laude* in 1879 and in 1882 was appointed professor of experimental physics at Leiden. Under the influence of J. D. van der WAALS, he was led to a study of the properties of liquids and gases over a wide range of temperatures and pressures, becoming finally most interested in their properties at low temperatures. In 1894 he founded the famous Cryogenic Laboratory at Leiden. In 1908 he succeeded in liquefying helium which was later first solidified by his pupil W. H. Keesom. He discovered the phenomenon of 'superconductivity' in which the resistance of electrical conductors suddenly disappears near the absolute zero of temperature. He carried out extensive investigations of this phenomenon. Onnes also studied the magneto-optical properties of bodies. For his work on low-temperature physics he was awarded the Nobel prize for physics in 1913. He became a Foreign Member of the Royal Society in 1916, and in 1925 was elected a Foreign Associate of the Académie des Sciences.

E. J. Cohen, *Chemical Society Memorial Lectures,* vol. 3. 1933.

H. A. Lorentz et al., *In Memoriam: Heike Kamerlingh Onnes.* 1926.

Dictionary of Scientific Biography.

Tyler Wasson (Ed.), *Nobel Prize Winners*. 1987. (Portrait.)

J W H

ONSAGER, LARS Born in Oslo, Norway, 27 November 1903; died Oxford, Ohio, USA, 5 October 1976. Theoretical chemist.

Onsager was the son of a lawyer. After a liberal education he entered the *Norges Tekniske Hogskole*, Trondheim, in 1920, to study chemical engineering. Graduating in 1925, he left Norway to be research assistant to P. DEBYE at the E.T.H. in Zurich. The circumstances of the appointment were characteristic of Onsager's unconventional methods. At the end of the nineteenth century S. A. ARRHENIUS had enunciated his theory of electrolytic dissociation, which gave a satisfactory account of the properties of dilute solutions. It failed, however, to describe the properties of strong electrolytes. In 1923 Debye and E. HÜCKEL published the theory which bears their joint names: in effect, it was based on a statistical analysis of a system in which each ion is surrounded by a cloud of ions of opposite charge. The Debye-Hückel theory was not wholly in agreement with experimental observations for strong solutions but Onsager discovered that much closer correlation was possible if account was taken of the Brownian motion of the ion. On the basis of this Onsager introduced himself to Debye and said simply: 'Professor Debye, your theory of electrolytes is incorrect'. Debye was convinced, and offered him an assistantship. From Zurich, Onsager moved on permanently to the United States, initially (1928–33) at Brown University. In 1933 he became a Sterling and Gibbs Fellow at Yale University and in 1945 he was appointed professor of theoretical chemistry there. This appointment he held until 1973 when, on retirement, he was offered a Distinguished Professorship in the University of Miami.

While at Brown, Onsager formulated his theory of Reciprocal Relations in irreversible processes, commonly known as the Fourth Law of Thermodynamics. In 1968 he was awarded a Nobel prize for chemistry. In presenting him, Stig Claesson cited his work on solutions of strong electrolytes and on the quantization of vortexes in liquid helium: 'However, your discovery of the reciprocal relations takes a special place – it represents one of the great advances in science during this century'. It is ironic that when Onsager sent an outline of his views in 1931 to the University of Trondheim as a submission for a doctorate, it was rejected.

Onsager was a man *sui generis*. His brilliance amounted to genius and was both his strength and his weakness. His strength, because it allowed him to understand and solve, with seeming ease, theoretical problems of great complexity. His weakness, because he had a touching faith that others could match him intellectually if only they would try a little, whereas in fact even the keenest minded of his contemporaries found it exceedingly difficult to follow him. He was ahead of his time, and it was really only after the Second World War that his true stature was acknowledged: even then his following was largely among physicists rather than chemists.

Les Prix Nobel en 1968. 1969. (Portrait.)

Biographical Memoirs of Fellows of the Royal Society. 1978. (Portrait.)
Nature, Lond., **264**, 819, 1976.
Dictionary of Scientific Biography, Supp. II.
Tyler Wasson (Ed.), *Nobel Prize Winners*. 1987. (Portrait.)

T I W

OORT, JAN HENDRIK Born at Franeker, Netherlands, 28 April 1900; died Leiden, 5 November 1992. Astronomer.

After schooling in Leiden, Oort gained his doctorate at Groningen University in 1926. He was research assistant at Yale University Observatory (1922–4) and subsequently spent his working life at Leiden Observatory, latterly as Director.

In 1927 he established that our Galaxy is rotating and Galactic dynamics remained a lifelong interest. He was one of the first to appreciate the immense possibilities of radio-astronomy and in 1951 detected the crucial 21-centimetre line, only days later than astronomers at Harvard. He and his colleagues used this to map the spiral arms of the Galaxy, and went on to study its hitherto hidden centre. In 1956 they observed the polarization of light from the remnants of the Crab supernova and deduced that it was synchrotron radiation. He postulated the existence of an 'Oort Cloud' of some 10^{11} comets surrounding the solar system about 50 000 AU from the Sun and gravitationally bound to it. He is widely regarded as Holland's greatest astronomer and one of its greatest scientists.

W. McCrea, *Physics World*, **6**, 61, 1933. (Portrait.)

T I W

OPPENHEIMER, J ROBERT Born in New York, 22 April 1904; died Princeton, New Jersey, 18 February 1967. Known for many contributions to quantum theory and to the development of the atom bomb.

After graduating from Harvard in 1925, Oppenheimer spent some years doing research in various centres in Europe, including Cambridge, Leiden, Göttingen, and Zurich, obtaining his PhD in Göttingen in 1927.

At that time quantum mechanics had become a consistent set of laws, and the way was open for developing its applications. Amongst his contributions at that time was the first treatment of the emission of continuum radiation (*Bremsstrahlung*) and his work with Max BORN on the quantum theory of molecules. He returned to the United States in 1929, and for a time held academic posts both at Berkeley and at the California Institute of Technology, dividing his time between the two institutions. His work during the California period included the recognition that the vacancies in electron states of negative energy, which appeared necessary to make P. A. M. DIRAC's relativistic wave equation consistent, could not be identified with protons, as Dirac had first thought. He thus postulated the existence of the positron, discovered shortly afterwards in experiments by C. D. ANDERSON. He also developed the theory of electron showers, then observed in cosmic radiation. At this time also Oppenheimer's powers as a teacher and interpreter of physics became evident. A large group of young theoretical physicists gathered around him, many of whom filled leading positions in the United States and elsewhere. He had an unusual ability for formulating the results and the significance of modern physics, and the nature of the unresolved problems. His quick and clear mind could grasp, and comment on, the ideas of others in discussion before they had time to explain them fully.

During the Second World War he was one of the first to appreciate fully the implications of the discovery of the fission of uranium, and in 1942 he was asked to set up and take charge of the laboratory at Los Alamos, New Mexico, which had the task of designing and developing atomic bombs. As Director of Los Alamos he was able to get the best out of a large group of scientists to whom work in a military laboratory did not come naturally, and the credit for the smooth and successful co-operation between the scientists and the military belongs very largely to him. He was a member of an advisory committee which was consulted on the decision to use atomic weapons, and he always remained conscious of his share in the responsibility for the consequences. After the war, he returned to California, but he was appointed in 1947 Director of the Institute for Advanced Study at Princeton. He resigned the Directorship in 1966, but remained a professor in the Institute until his death. His breadth of knowledge and interest, and his flair for the use of language, were great assets in this position. He continued to exert a strong influence on the thinking of theoretical physicists both in the Institute and elsewhere.

After leaving Los Alamos he remained an adviser to many government agencies. He was a member of the committee which drafted the Acheson-Lilienthal proposals for the international control of atomic energy. He was Chairman of the Scientific Advisory Committee of the Atomic Energy Commission. His committee advised against an intensive development of thermonuclear weapons, partly because of the effect of this on the international situation, and partly because of the technical prospects. When eventually this project went ahead and, as a result of new inventions, was successful, Oppenheimer's motives were claimed to be disloyal. The subsequent investigation became a *cause célèbre*. As a result, Oppenheimer was barred from all access to secret information, and therefore from all his advisory activities. The Enrico Fermi Award in 1963, recommended by the Atomic Energy Commission and conferred by the President, made some amends.

The Times, 20 February 1967. (Portrait.)

A. Pais, G. T. Seaborg, R. Serber, V. F. Weisskopf, and I. I. Rabi, *Oppenheimer*. 1969.

P. Goodchild, *J. Robert Oppenheimer*. 1980.

Biographical Memoirs of Fellows of the Royal Society. 1968. (Portrait.)

P. M. Stern, *The Oppenheimer Case: Security on Trial*. 1969.

Dictionary of Scientific Biography.

R E P

OSTWALD, FRIEDRICH WILHELM Born at Riga, Latvia, 2 September 1853; died Leipzig, Germany, 4 April 1932. Physical chemist, and man of many-sided intellectual activity.

Ostwald, who came of a German artisan family, studied physics and chemistry at the University of Dorpat. In 1881 he was appointed professor in the Riga Polytechnic; in 1887 he went to the chair of physical chemistry in Leipzig. In 1905, partly as the result of serious differences with the University authorities, and partly because he felt that he was past his best as a chemist, Ostwald resigned his chair; but he spent the year 1905–6 as an exchange professor at Harvard. The rest of his life was spent in literary and philosophical studies. He married in 1880, and his son Wolfgang (1883–1943) also became a chemist of note; his daughter Grete wrote his biography.

Despite the lack of facilities in Dorpat and Riga, Ostwald did much of his most original work there, making the apparatus with his own hands. He studied the course of reactions in solution by following changes in density and refractive index, and related his results to the Law of Mass Action. His work on the kinetics of acid-catalysed hydrolyses marks the beginning of a lifelong interest in catalysis, though his theory, that catalysts act by merely being present, and not by taking any part in the reaction, is now known to be incorrect. He was an early convert to the theory of Ionic Dissociation put forward by S. A. ARRHENIUS, and deduced from it the Ostwald Dilution Law. It was in his Riga period also that he wrote his ambitious *Lehrbuch der allgemeinen Chemie* (two volumes, 1885 and 1887; known to students as the 'grosse Ostwald'), and began the *Grundriss der allgemeinen Chemie* (1889; the 'kleine Ostwald').

In Leipzig, Ostwald had the opportunity to build up a great research school, and used it to the full. Of his numerous students, W. H. NERNST was perhaps the most distinguished. But his influence spread far beyond Leipzig, and he came to be regarded as a sort of 'elder statesman' of physical chemistry, and indeed of science in general. At the beginning of his tenure of the Leipzig chair physical chemistry was a new discipline, and Ostwald, using his two books as a text, forced it into prominence against indifference and even opposition. The journal of the new movement was the *Zeitschrift für physikalische Chemie* founded by Ostwald, Arrhenius and J. H. van't HOFF in 1887; but although these three are looked upon as the founders of modern physical chemistry, the role of Ostwald (though vital) was that of publicist rather than original thinker. In spite of his philosophical strivings, he never produced anything of importance comparable to the Ionic Theory, or VAN'T HOFF's theory of solutions. He was generous in his recognition of others, notably Willard GIBBS.

Ostwald was deeply interested in the history of science, and republished a series of classical papers. In the 1890s, however, philosophy began to get the upper hand. He was at first a positivist, and wished to free chemistry from its dependence on the atomic theory, though later he grudgingly admitted the probable existence of atoms. He attached great importance to the concept of Energy, holding that the whole Universe was a manifestation of Energy in its various forms. Two books were written, and a journal was founded, to propagate this version of *Naturphilosophie*. Later Ostwald wrote extensively on theories of colour, a universal language, the philosophy of Goethe, and other topics. Whatever may be the final judgment on his ideas, they are certainly unfashionable at the present time.

Among other honours, Ostwald was awarded the Nobel prize for chemistry in 1909. He seems to have been a happy and well-liked man, though over-intense and devoid of any sense of humour.

Wilhelm Ostwald, *Lebenslinien*. 1926.

Grete Ostwald, *Wilhelm Ostwald, mein Vater*. 1953.

Journal of the Chemical Society, 316, 1933. (Portrait.)

E. Farber (Ed.), *Great Chemists*. 1961. (Portrait.)

E. P. Hillpern, *Chymia*, **2**, 57, 1949.

Walter Ostwald, *Journal of Chemical Education*, **34**, 328, 1957.

F. E. Wall, *Journal of Chemical Education*, **25**, 2, 1948.

Dictionary of Scientific Biography.

W V F

OTIS, ELISHA GRAVES Born at Halifax, Vermont, USA, 3 August 1811; died Yonkers, New York, 8 April 1861. Inventor of safety mechanism for lifts.

Otis was the son of a substantial farmer, but was forced by ill health to give up his own building and wagon-making businesses and became a master mechanic for a bedstead-maker. When this firm built a new factory at Yonkers he was put in charge of its construction, for which he designed a safety lift. Each side of the shaft was provided with a ratchet, which engaged with pawls on the lift cage by means of springs brought into operation by any failure of tension in the rope. A sensational demonstration was given at the American Institute Fair in New York in 1854.

Otis established a small manufacture of lifts, employing only eight to ten persons, but three months before his early death he patented a new steam-lift, on which his two sons based a great commercial success.

Dictionary of American Biography.

T K D

OTTO, NIKOLAUS AUGUST Born at Holzhausen, Nassau, Germany, 14 June 1832; died Cologne, 26 January 1891. Built first successful four-stroke internal-combustion engine.

Otto, a farmer's son, left school at 16 to work in a merchant's office. Moving to Cologne, he became greatly interested in the gas engine developed by E. LENOIR. In 1861 he built a small experimental gas engine and three years later joined forces with Eugen Langen (1833–95), an industrialist trained at the Karlsruhe Polytechnic, to form a company to market such engines. He received valuable help also from a former fellow student, Franz Reuleaux (1829–1905). At the Paris Exhibition of 1867 the firm's product won a gold medal in competition with fourteen other gas engines. Further capital was raised, and a new factory, the Gasmotorenfabrik, was built at Deutz near Cologne in 1869. Otto concentrated on the administrative side, leaving Langen, with his new recruits Gottlieb DAIMLER and Willhelm MAYBACH to develop the engineering side.

In 1876, Otto described the four-stroke engine for which his name is famous. Unfortunately, his patent was invalidated in 1886 when his competitors demonstrated that Alphonse Beau de Rochas (1815–93) had described the principle of the four-stroke cycle in an obscure pamphlet.

In the period 1860–5 Lenoir sold several hundred of his double-acting gas engines, all small, but technical weaknesses – especially low compression – limited their success. Otto's much more efficient and relatively quiet engine – the so-called 'silent Otto' – was well received and more than 30 000 were sold in the first ten years of manufacture.

A. Nägel, *Zeitschrift des Vereines deutscher Ingenieure*, **75**, 827, 1931; **80**, 1289, 1936.

C. Matschoss (trans. H. S. Hatfield), *Great Engineers*. 1939. (Portrait.)

A. Langen, *Nikolaus August Otto, der Schöpfer des Verbrennungsmotors*, 1949.

L. Bryant, 'The Silent Otto', *Technology and Culture*, **7**, 184, 1966.

W H G A

OWEN, SIR RICHARD Born at Lancaster, England, 20 July 1804; died Sheen Lodge, Richmond Park, London, 18 December 1892. Anatomist.

Owen was recognized as the leading comparative anatomist of his time and a worthy successor to G. L. C. CUVIER, with whom he studied for a short time in Paris. He entered the University of Edinburgh in 1824, but moved the following year to St Bartholomew's Hospital, London, where he completed his medical course. In 1826 he was appointed as assistant, later becoming Curator, of the Museum, and in 1836 the first Hunterian Professor at the Royal College of Surgeons. He became the first Superintendent of the Natural History Departments of the British Museum in 1856 and was subsequently appointed Director when this part of the museum was moved to the present site in South Kensington. His published works included over 360 detailed monographs on recent and fossil invertebrates and vertebrates, the most notable being concerned with the Pearly Nautilus, the birds of New Zealand, the dodo from Mauritius, *Archaeopteryx* from Bavaria, and British fossil vertebrates. Although he first correctly distinguished between the concepts of 'analogy' and 'homology', he was an evolutionist to only a limited degree, believing in the production of many modern species by degeneration from more perfect archetypes. Regrettably, he was very hostile to the views expressed in the *Origin of Species* by Charles DARWIN, and engaged in bitter controversy with T. H. HUXLEY.

He was elected FRS in 1834 and served as Fullerian Professor of Physiology and Comparative Anatomy at the Royal Institution from 1858 to 1862. He was awarded honorary degrees by Oxford, Cambridge, and Dublin, and received many foreign distinctions. On retirement in 1884 he was made KCB.

Richard Owen (grandson), *The Life of Richard Owen*. 1894. (Portrait.)

Dictionary of National Biography.

Dictionary of Scientific Biography.

A P G

P

PALADE, GEORGE EMIL Born in Jassy, Moldavia (Iaşi, Romania), 19 November 1912. Cell biologist.

After taking his baccalaureate at the Al Hasden Lyceum in Buzau, Palade enrolled in the medical school of Bucharest University in 1930. As a student he developed a keen interest in biomedical science and after graduating in 1940 – followed by military service – he went to the USA in 1946 for further medical training. This led to a series of appointments at the Rockefeller Institute for Medical Research and eventually (1973–) to an appointment in the Department of Cell Biology, Yale University. Cell biology – and particularly the structure and function of cell organelles such as mitochondria and ribosomes – has always been his main interest. Two factors contributed to his success. First, the careful maceration of tissue so that organelles could be extracted undamaged; second, their examination with the electron microscope, with which Palade first became acquainted in 1946 through his colleague Albert Claude (1899–1983). Later, in the 1960s, he became interested also in structural aspects of capillary permeability in the pancreas, renal glomeruli, and other tissue. In 1974 Palade shared a Nobel prize with Claude and Christian de Duve (1917–), discoverer of two new organelles, the lysosome and the peroxisome.

Les Prix Nobel en 1974. 1975. (Portrait.)
Tyler Wasson (Ed.), *Nobel Prize Winners.* 1987. (Portrait.)

T I W

PANETH, FRIEDRICH ADOLF Born in Vienna, 31 August 1887; died there, 17 September 1958. Made important contributions to the study of radioactivity.

Paneth, son of a physiologist, was educated at Vienna, Munich, and Glasgow. In 1912 he entered the Radium Institute, Vienna, where he showed that radium-D and lead were inseparable; for some months he worked with G. von HEVESY, who had independently reached the same conclusion, and developed their ideas on radioactive indicators. Paneth held appointments at Prague (1917), Hamburg (1919), Berlin (1922), and Königsberg (1929). The rise of Nazism compelled him to emigrate to England in 1933.

Using radioactive tracers, he demonstrated the existence of unstable hydrides of bismuth (1918) and lead (1920), and using the natural radioactivity of polonium found that this also formed a hydride (1922). In 1929 Paneth and co-workers obtained the first evidence for free radicals of short life. Methyl, and later ethyl, were formed by pyrolysis of lead alkyls and identified by the products they gave when attacking metallic mirrors.

In England, Paneth became Reader at Imperial College, London, and in 1939 professor of chemistry at Durham. Here he continued studies on microanalysis of the rare gases; originally undertaken in connection with radioactivity, they were now turned to atmospheric chemistry. He showed that air has constant composition at least up to 60 km. His measurements of the helium concentrations of meteorites opened up a method for determining their age. During the war (1943–5) he was head of the chemistry division of the joint British-Canadian atomic energy team in Montreal. On returning to Germany from Durham he became Director of the Max Planck Institute for Chemistry at Mainz.

Paneth published *Radioelements as Indicators, A Manual of Radioactivity* (with Hevesy), and several items on the history of science. He was elected FRS in 1947.

G. R. Martin, *Nature,* **182**, 1274, 1958.
Proceedings of the Chemical Society, 103, 1959.
Biographical Memoirs of Fellows of the Royal Society. 1960. (Portrait.)
Dictionary of Scientific Biography.

C A R

PAPIN, DENIS Born at Blois, Loire et Cher, France, 22 August 1647; died London, 1712. Mathematician and physicist; pioneer of the steam engine.

Papin worked under Christiaan HUYGENS at Leiden. He then worked for a time in London, where he was elected FRS in 1682. He assisted Robert BOYLE in his experiments with the air pump, and is credited with having invented the double-acting air pump. He spent some time in Venice, returning to London in 1684, and in 1687 went to Marburg as professor of mathematics. Some ten years later he went to Cassel, finally returning to London in 1707.

Papin's best-known invention is his digester (1679). This makes use of the fact that the boiling-point of water depends on the pressure to which it is subjected; at a pressure of 16 atmospheres, for example, it boils at 200°C, instead of at 100°C as under normal pressure. This principle is widely used: for example, in the familiar domestic pressure-cooker; in the high-pressure boiler for steam engines; and in the sterilization autoclaves used in hospitals. It is, of course, essential not to exceed the desired pressure or the vessel may explode; to avoid this Papin devised a lever-type safety valve.

Of greater significance were his attempts to use steam as a source of power; his interest in this field most probably stems from Huygens's attempt to derive power from the explosion of gunpowder in a tube closed by a piston. Papin's engine of 1690 consisted of a vertical tube, about 3 inches in diameter, at the bottom of which was a little water; the tube was closed by a movable piston. The water was boiled in the tube, causing the piston to rise. The steam was then condensed by cooling the tube, whereupon the atmospheric pressure drove the piston down again. Papin was not sufficient of an engineer to turn his discovery to practical advantage, but he clearly saw the possibilities, for he was associated with Thomas SAVERY about 1705 in an attempt to improve the latter's steam engine. In the end, however, it was Thomas NEWCOMEN who made the first successful steam engine, using Papin's cycle.

H. W. Dickinson, *Nature*, **160**, 422, 1947.
H. W. Robinson, *Notes and Records of the Royal Society of London*, **5**, 47, 1947.
Dictionary of National Biography.
Dictionary of Scientific Biography.

T I W

PAPPUS OF ALEXANDRIA Flourished in Alexandria in the late third century AD. Mathematician.

Pappus was the author of a *Synagoge* ('Collection') in eight Books (Book I and part of Book II are lost) affording a critical and systematic account of earlier achievements in Greek geometry. In this and in other, minor, tracts and commentaries, Pappus dealt historically with the classic problems of squaring the circle, trisecting the angle, and duplicating the cube. He discussed isoperimetrical problems on the areas (or volumes) of figures having different shapes but equal peripheries (or surfaces). He classified problems as plane, solid, or linear according as they could be solved by means of ruler and compasses, conic sections, or curves of higher order. He formally defined analysis and synthesis as they are still commonly applied in the solution of geometrical riders. Pappus stumbled upon the projective invariance of the cross-ratio of four collinear points and other related results reclaimed by modern projective geometry; and he gave the first recorded statement of the focus-directrix property of the three conic sections. He formulated the 'centrobaric' theorems, frequently attributed to Paul Guldin (1577–1643), for calculating the volume and surface generated by a plane figure rotating about an axis in its own plane. He discussed theoretical mechanics, the equilibrium of a heavy body on an inclined plane, the use of the mechanical powers, and the construction of mechanical toys.

With the achievements of Pappus, creative work ceased in the now exhausted field of Greek geometry.

T. L. Heath, *A History of Greek Mathematics*, vol. 2. 1921.
Dictionary of Scientific Biography.

A A

PARACELSUS (THEOPHRASTUS BOMBASTUS VON HOHENHEIM) Born at Maria-Eisenseideln, near Zürich, Switzerland, 17 December 1493; died Salzburg, Austria, 24 September 1541. Alchemist; founder of medical chemistry.

Paracelsus was one of the most remarkable characters of the sixteenth century. His immense conceit is indicated by his self-styled title, indicating his superiority to CELSUS, the 1st century Roman writer on medicine. Like many scholars of his time, he took the whole realm of human knowledge as his province, and acquired it by wide travelling. Little is known of his early life except that his father, Wilhelm von Hohenheim, was a physician who practised first at Maria-Einseideln and later at Villach, Carinthia. In 1514 he went to work in the Tyrol in the mines and workshops of Sigismund Füger, an ardent alchemist, and this experience must have been valuable to him in acquiring a sound knowledge of chemical manipulations. Afterwards, he travelled widely in Europe and possibly also in Russia and the East; during part of this time he may have been an army surgeon in the Venetian service. In 1526 he settled in Strasbourg, and by a fortunate chance effected a notably successful cure of Frobenius, a printer in Basle, who was a close friend of the great Dutch scholar Erasmus (1466–1536) and of Oecolampadius (1482–1531), Professor of Medicine and City Physician at Basle.

Characteristically, he commenced his new appointment by publicly burning the works of AVICENNA and GALEN with sulphur and nitre, at once signifying his contempt for ancient learning and his faith in the curative power of chemicals. Not surprisingly, Paracelsus did not endear himself to the established physicians and apothecaries of Basle and two years later he had to fly from the town, following a tempestuous outburst of libellous comment after some unsuccessful litigation over a professional fee. He wandered through Europe, finally finding refuge at Salzburg under the patronage of Archbishop Duke Ernst of Bavaria, himself a dabbler in alchemy.

It is difficult to assess the significance of Paracelsus in the history of science and medicine. Unkempt, loud-mouthed, drunken, undoubtedly something of a charlatan, he subsisted mostly on the discoveries and ideas of others, often only imperfectly understood. Nevertheless, he had in two separate ways a powerful influence on the thought of his time. Firstly, he gave alchemy a new purpose by deflecting emphasis from the fruitless attempt to transmute base metals into gold into the useful channel of preparing medicinal products. Secondly, his interest in using pure compounds, rather than indeterminate mixtures, paved the way to an understanding that chemical compounds are distinguished by their elemental composition. Despite his unsettled life, Paracelsus was a prolific writer, and well over 300 works – some of doubtful authenticity – are attributed to him, of which perhaps a third are of chemical interest. They were published in Basle 1589–90.

E. Farber (Ed.), *Great Chemists*. 1961. (Portrait.)
W. Pagel, *Paracelsus, an Introduction to Philosophical Medicine in the Era of the Renaissance*. 1958.
J. Maxson Stillman, *Paracelsus, His Personality and Influence*. 1920.
J. Hargrave, *The Life and Soul of Paracelsus*. 1951.
Dictionary of Scientific Biography.

T I W

PARÉ, AMBROISE Born at Bourg Hersent, Mayenne, France, 1509; died Paris, 22 December 1590. Surgeon.

Paré came of a humble family – his father was a valet and baker – and had little formal education; in later life he was very conscious that French was his only language. In 1532/3 he was apprenticed to a barber surgeon in Paris and shortly obtained a junior post at the Hotel Dieu, the largest hospital. He then did service as a military surgeon, a profession that he followed for much of his life; not surprisingly, his writings are much concerned with treating battle wounds. He made his reputation with the publication in 1545 of his *La Méthode de traicter les playes faictes par hacquebutes* (Method of treating wounds inflicted by arquebuses); within two years it was translated into Dutch and it quickly became a standard work in all the European armies. In 1549 appeared his handbook of anatomy for surgeons, the *Briefve collection de l'administration anatomique*; 1563 saw his *Dix livres de la chirurgie*. His collected works, *Les oeuvres d'Ambroise Paré*, appeared in 1575, and he published three subsequent editions before his death at 80. Paré's reputation led to his appointment in 1562 as chief surgeon to Charles IX; he had previously served Henry II and Francois II as surgeon-in-ordinary. It may have been through the interest of Charles IX that Paré, reputedly a Huguenot, survived the massacre of St Bartholomew's Day.

Paré abandoned the brutal cauterization of wounds with hot irons or boiling oil, and used instead a mixture of egg yolk, oil of roses, and turpentine. He introduced the use of ligatures in amputation. He advocated podalic version in difficult labour. He devised new methods in dentistry for extracting teeth, filling cavities, and making artificial dentures. He describes an artificial hand made from iron, and artificial eyes.

Although his writings include many of the superstitions of his time, Paré can fairly be described as the founder of modern surgery.

R. H. Major, *A History of Medicine*, vol. 1. 1954. (Portrait.)

W. B. Hamby, *Ambroise Paré, Surgeon of the Renaissance*. 1967.

B. H. Hill Jr, *Journal of the History of Medicine and Allied Sciences*, **15**, 45, 1960.

F. R. Packard, *Life and Times of Ambroise Paré*. 1921.

Dictionary of Scientific Biography.

T I W

PARKES, ALEXANDER

Born in Birmingham, England, 29 December 1813; died West Dulwich, London, 29 June 1890. A founder of the plastics industry and a versatile metallurgist.

From being an apprentice in the Birmingham art metal trade, Parkes became 'the Nestor of Electrometallurgy' when he joined a leading electroplating firm. He silver-plated such delicate objects as flowers and spiders' webs, which were exhibited. His use of phosphorus in solvents like carbon disulphide for reduction of silver solutions led him to turn his attention to solutions of rubber and of cellulose nitrate for use in waterproofing. More significant was his moulding of xylonite (cellulose nitrate) – the price of which he reduced from twelve shillings to sevenpence a pound – to prepare plastic objects commercially rather than as the laboratory curiosities of C. F. SCHÖNBEIN. Despite the inflammability of celluloid, Parkes's pioneer work – patented in 1855 – was followed up by J. W. HYATT in America, and by other enthusiasts. Hyatt developed celluloid about 1869.

Parkes's place in the history of plastics should not distract attention from his many contributions to metallurgy. Apart from his work in electroplating, he took out many patents relating to alloys of copper, nickel, zinc and silver. The Parkes process for desilverizing lead (1850) is widely known.

M. Kaufman, *The First Century of Plastics*. 1963. (Portrait.)

M. Schofield, *Metallurgia*, 125–6, 1963.

Dictionary of National Biography.

M S

PARSONS, SIR CHARLES ALGERNON

Born at Parsonstown, Ireland, 13 June 1854; died Newcastle upon Tyne, England, 13 February 1931. Invented the steam turbine and developed it for marine use.

Charles was the fourth son of William Parsons, 3rd Earl of Rosse (1800–67), a distinguished astronomer who was President of the Royal Society 1848–54. At the family seat in Ireland, William Parsons constructed in his own workshops a 6-foot reflecting telescope which for many years had no rival and attracted to his household many distinguished astronomers and mathematicians. As his mother excelled at every form of handicraft, including modelling and photography, Charles Parsons had an unusual upbringing. At 17 he went to Trinity College, Dublin, and then to St John's College, Cambridge, where he passed out Eleventh Wrangler in 1877.

After some years engineering experience as a pupil-apprentice, he became junior partner in a firm very much interested in electric lighting, then greatly stimulated by the work of T. A. EDISON and Joseph SWAN on the incandescent filament lamp. Parsons realized the urgent need for a high-speed engine capable of driving dynamos directly. For this a reciprocating engine was inherently unsuitable, and he was led to develop the steam turbine, the first patents for which he took out in 1884. The principle was not new, but unlike earlier inventors he realized that the drop in pressure must take place in stages. His first engine, built in 1884, developed 10 horse-power at 18 000 revolutions per minute. Later, he introduced a condenser to utilize low-pressure steam formerly wasted, and the use of high-pressure superheated steam.

After initial difficulties, Parsons established a successful business of his own, and this made it possible for him to develop the turbine further for use at sea; his knowledge of seamanship stood him in good stead. In 1897 his *Turbinia* created a sensation at the naval review in the Solent marking Queen Victoria's jubilee. He developed reduction gearing which made it possible to use turbines in slow powerful vessels as well as in light fast ones. Within a decade turbines were widely used at sea. In 1906 the British Admiralty installed them in the famous *Dreadnought*; the great Cunarders *Lusitania* and *Mauretania* followed. Later, reverting to his earliest interests, Parsons manufactured large telescopes.

The importance of Parsons's work was widely recognized in his time. His honours included FRS (1898), KCB (1911), and OM (1927). Many regard him as the most original British engineer since James WATT.

It is recorded that although an excellent mathematician, formal calculation interested Parsons very little. He generally reached his results almost instinctively, by obscure mental processes which even he himself did not properly understand.

R. Appleyard, *Charles Parsons: his Life and Work.* 1933.
Proceedings of the Royal Society, **131A**, v, 1931.
Nature, **137**, 314, 1931; **141**, 185, 1938.
Dictionary of National Biography..

T I W

PARTINGTON, JAMES RIDDICK Born at Bolton, Lancashire, England, 20 June 1886; died Weaverham, Cheshire, 9 October 1965. Historian of science.

Partington was a graduate of Manchester University, and after a short period of research there went to work on the specific heats of gases with W. H. NERNST in Berlin. After the First World War he was appointed professor of chemistry at Queen Mary College, London University, continuing his work on gases. As a teacher, he was recognized for his encyclopaedic knowledge and his meticulous attention to detail. He wrote several chemical textbooks, culminating in his great *Advanced Treatise on Physical Chemistry* (4 vols, 1949–54).

It is, however, primarily as an historian of chemistry that Partington will be remembered. In 1935 he published his first major work in this field, an exceedingly well-documented *Origins and Development of Applied Chemistry*, dealing mainly with the practice of chemistry in the ancient civilizations. In 1937 there appeared a book smaller in size, but of wider scope, *A Short History of Chemistry*. This was the prelude to his great four-volume *History of Chemistry*, of which one volume unhappily was uncompleted at the time of his death. This comprehensive survey, crowded with references, will be indispensable to historians of chemistry, and indeed of science generally, for as long ahead as one can foresee. In 1960 he published, in the same characteristic style, a *History of Greek Fire and Gunpowder*.

Partington's reputation was firmly established in his lifetime. In 1961 he received the Dexter Award of the American Chemical Society (History of Chemistry Division), and in 1965 the Sarton Medal of the American History of Science Society.

The Times, 11 October 1965.
H. C. Butler, *British Journal for the History of Science*, **3**, 70, 1966.
Dictionary of Scientific Biography.

T I W

PASCAL, BLAISE Born at Clermont Ferrand, France, 19 June 1623; died Paris, 19 August 1662. Mathematician, physicist and religious thinker.

Pascal was the son of Étienne Pascal (d. 1650), sometime President of the Court of Aids at Clermont. His mother died when he was 4, and his two sisters, Gilberte, Madame Périer, and Jacqueline, later a nun at Port Royal, the centre of the Jansenist movement, had a predominating influence on his life. In 1631 the family moved to Paris where they went through a difficult period, having incurred the enmity of Richelieu. In 1641 they moved to Rouen, where, five years later, they espoused Jansenism – which involved them in fierce opposition to and from the Jesuits. The education of Blaise had been principally obtained within the family circle, despite which he had already written some of his best mathematical work by the time of the

move to Rouen. The intensity with which he worked was perhaps partly caused by, and partly the cause of, ill health. As his health declined, so his religious fervour increased, and one of his less creditable acts was to inform against the supposed unorthodoxy of a Capuchin friar. Shortly after their return to Paris in 1650, Étienne died, and Jacqueline entered a convent. In 1654 Pascal's 'second conversion' took place, and he began to frequent Port Royal. A year later Antoine Arnaud, most outspoken of the Jansenists, was expelled from the Sorbonne. This was the occasion of Pascal's first famous literary work, the *Provincial Letters*, published anonymously at intervals during 1656. His health declined very rapidly after 1658, and in 1662 he died in the home of Madame Périer (who wrote a valuable biography of her brother). Eight years after his death there appeared an edition of his best-known work, his *Pensées*.

About half of Pascal's writings are devoted to mathematical and physical subjects. Beginning with a study of geometry at the age of 12, he astonished his father with his rapid progress. Before the age of 16 Pascal had proved one of the most important theorems of the projective geometry of conics – sometimes known as 'Pascal's mystic hexagram' (the points of intersection of the three pairs of opposite sides of a hexagon inscribed in a conic are collinear). It seems that he first proved this for a circle, and then extended it by projection to conics. The Porisms of Euclid contain the theorem, unproved, for a degenerate conic, and in this form the theorem was finally proved by PAPPUS. The general theorem was later seen to be implicit in the work of G. DESARGUES, and its dual theorem was to be found in 1806 by C. J. Brianchon (1783–1864). In his *Essai pour les coniques*, written in 1640, only a fragment of which was published (the rest is now lost), Pascal used his theorem to derive four hundred propositions, including many from APOLLONIUS and other geometers. G. W. LEIBNIZ is known to have examined a copy of the full *Essai*, and there can be no doubt as to its genuineness.

Pascal may be said to have put the finishing touches to the theory of hydrostatics. In a pamphlet of 1647, *Expériences nouvelles touchant le vide*, he described experiments largely imitative of those of E. TORRICELLI. Appreciating that those could be explained either in terms of the 'limited horror vacui' or of atmospheric pressure, he devised an experiment (in which one barometric column was enclosed within another) in order to support the second hypothesis. Even then he was not satisfied, and he asked his brother-in-law Périer to perform the now well-known experiment with a barometer at different heights on a mountain. (R. DESCARTES had previously suggested this to Marin Mersenne (1588–1648), and, according to him, he had also suggested it to Pascal.) Périer performed the experiments on the Puy de Dôme, a mountain (4000 feet) near Clermont, confirming Pascal's views. His finished *Traité de l'équilibre des liqueurs* was not, however, published until a year after his death. There he shows that in a fluid at rest the pressure is transmitted equally in all directions ('Pascal's Principle'). Although this was not at first accepted generally, it is usually now admitted that with it Pascal provided the essential link between the mechanics of fluids and the mechanics of rigid bodies.

According to his sister, Pascal invented his calculating (adding) machine at the age of 19. It is now known that Guillaume Schickart (1592–1635) had designed a similar machine in 1624, but that it was lost through fire; it seems to have been unknown to Pascal. Although it was said that only one instrument-maker was capable of making machines to Pascal's design (some of the principles of which are still used in mechanical calculators), upward of seventy were made, some for royal gifts. At least seven survive.

Pascal's solitary important contribution to mathematics after his entry to Port Royal is said to have been the result of toothache. To take his mind off the pain, he pondered on problems associated with the cycloid (the curve is sometimes known as the roulette). The curve had been discussed by GALILEO, G. P. de Roberval (1602–75), Descartes, P. FERMAT, and Torricelli, without any of them having managed to evaluate its area. Pascal worked intensively on the problem, and solved it, with many others. He found the centre of gravity of the curve, and of its segments, and the volume and centre of gravity of several different types of solid of revolution derivable from it. Publishing a number of his new theorems without proof, as a challenge to other mathematicians, solutions were sent by J. WALLIS, C. HUYGENS, C. WREN, Roberval, and others. This episode provided an important stimulus in the formulation of the differential and integral calculus.

The mathematical theory of probability and combinatorial analysis can be reasonably dated from the correspondence between Pascal and Fermat (1654). Both agreed on the answer to a problem set by the gamester the Chevalier de Méré (1610–85), although they obtained it in different ways. Pascal gave his methods in a series of tracts written in the same year (published 1665). His starting-point is the so-called 'Pascal triangle'. This can now be simply described – anachronistically – as the triangular arrangement of the coefficients of successive integral powers of a binomial. The '^nC_r' notation used today for coefficients in a binomial expansion should serve as a reminder of the connection between this and the theory of combinations. Pascal was not the first to write down the triangle of numbers, but was the first to use it in a theory of combinations – and subsequently for calculating probabilities.

The volume of Pascal's scientific and mathematical writing is not great, but it is marked by the sort of originality one might hope for, but not expect, in a man who did not receive a conventional education. He managed to preserve the freshness of his approach in almost everything he wrote – and an excellent example of this is his essay on magic squares, which hitherto had been the subject of a few ad hoc rules, but which he now treated attractively, succinctly, and systematically. The secret of his style is perhaps to be found in this quotation from the Provincial Letters: 'I have made this letter longer than usual because I lacked the time to make it short.'

Jean Mesnard, Pascal, his life and works. 1952.

P. Costabel et al., L'œuvre scientifique de Pascal. 1964.

E. Mortimer, Blaise Pascal. 1959.

M. Bishop, Pascal, the Life of Genius. 1936.

R. Hazelton, Blaise Pascal. 1974.

Dictionary of Scientific Biography.

J D N

PASTEUR, LOUIS Born at Dôle, France, 27 December 1822; died Villeneuve l'Etang, 28 September 1895. Celebrated for his work on stereochemistry; the germ theory of fermentation and disease; and the development of vaccines.

Pasteur, the son of a tanner, studied at the famous École Normale Supérieure. His doctorate dealt with crystallographic problems and led him to pioneering studies in what is now known as stereochemistry. He demonstrated the phenomenon of optical isomers and devised a number of methods for separating two such isomers. These ranged from separating, by hand, crystals which had different orientations of their facets to microbiological methods whereby an organism growing in a mixture of the two isomers metabolized one, but left the other unchanged.

In 1854 Pasteur became professor of chemistry and dean of sciences in the University of Lille. It was suggested to him that he interest himself in local industries and before long he was examining the problem as to why vinegar sometimes soured during its production from beet juice by fermentation. Thus began studies on fermentations extending over twenty years which established the role of micro-organisms, such as yeast, in causing these processes. When Pasteur first announced his germ theory of fermentation in 1857 it aroused considerable interest, for, at the time, fermentation was commonly thought to be a chemical decomposition process in which micro-organisms were unnecessary. Even though, in 1857, he had little experimental proof to support his claim, Pasteur himself later confirmed his intuitive theories (which were linked with his earlier work on optical isomers) by studying – and making improvements – in the economically important industries of alcohol, vinegar, wine, and beer production.

Arising from his fermentation studies was his strong opposition to the doctrine of the spontaneous generation of micro-organisms. The controversies over spontaneous generation which raged in France in the early 1860s were largely initiated by support for the doctrine given by F. A. Pouchet (1800–72) in his work Hétérogénie ou traité de la génération spontanée (1859).

Pasteur's main counter attack appeared in his famous paper Mémoire sur les corpuscules organisés qui existent dans l'atmosphère, examen de la doctrine des générations spontanées. This included numerous experimental results to support his view that phenomena sometimes attributed to spontaneous generation could be explained adequately only by the germ theory – that is, that contamination is caused by widely distributed 'organized corpuscles' (micro-organisms).

Two other areas of study developed from his fermentation work, anaerobic life and pasteurization. His discovery of anaerobic life was a chance observation that air (oxygen) inhibited the movements of bacteria that were changing sugar solution into butyric acid. He immediately recognized the importance of the observation and coined the adjective 'anaerobic' to contrast with aerobic organisms living in the presence of air. Pasteurization (a process of partial heat sterilization) arose from his studies on wine, while he was looking for a method for improving its storage properties. His method is now applied to many perishable food substances.

In 1865 an unexpected challenge came to Pasteur, but one illustrating the high regard his scientific colleagues had for him. Although Pasteur knew nothing about silkworms, he was asked to study the disease which was attacking these organisms and devastating the French silk industry. Although he was never able to isolate the causative organism, he recommended a method of controlling the disease, *pébrine*, by selecting eggs free from the characteristic black spots. In a similar way he devised methods to control another silkworm disease, *flacherie*. These studies were not only of great importance to the French economy but were of inestimable value to his later studies on animal and human diseases.

When Pasteur began studying animal diseases in 1877 he was not unprepared for this new venture. Apart from his silkworm studies, he had long been interested in the problems of infectious diseases, some of which were considered analogous to fermentations. From 1877 until his death in 1895 Pasteur studied diseases, notably anthrax, chicken cholera, swine erysipelas, and rabies (hydrophobia). Each study fell broadly into two parts: attempts to isolate the causative organism and grow it in a suitable medium, and devising methods of controlling the infection. His studies were given a dramatic twist in 1879 with a lucky observation that chickens inoculated with old cultures of the chicken cholera organism failed to develop the disease. On repeating his experiment with a fresh culture inoculated into new chickens as well as into those which had resisted the old culture he found that the new chickens died, while the old ones survived.

Pasteur was prepared for such an observation and almost intuitively he developed the idea of attenuation – that the virulence of an infecting organism could be altered and decreased. He was, of course, aided by the fact that smallpox vaccination was well established (see E. JENNER) and by the knowledge that recovery from an infectious disease gave immunity against further attacks. Pasteur introduced a number of vaccines, the most celebrated of which were for anthrax and rabies. It was because of the latter that he became universally famous.

Rabies – caused by the bite of a 'mad' dog – presented unexpected problems, because he failed to isolate the causative organism (now known to be a virus) and culture it in a nutrient broth. However, after conceiving the idea of growing it in living experimental animals, he found that he could attenuate the virus by storing in dry sterile air the infected spinal cords taken from rabbits which had died of the disease. By repeatedly injecting dogs with progressively less attenuated virus it was possible to protect the animal against an inoculation of the most virulent form of the virus. This was because of the formation of protective antibodies, and, owing to the time lag between infection and onset of serious damage, this technique could be used therapeutically as well as prophylactically.

One of the most celebrated incidents in medical history was the first treatment of a human patient, a young, badly bitten boy, Joseph Meister. The successful outcome, as with the young shepherd J. B. Jupille a short while later, immediately established rabies vaccination and crowds of bitten patients flocked to Paris for treatment.

No notice of Pasteur is complete without a reminder of the overall impact of this enormously hard-working and painstaking man of science and medicine. The impact in his lifetime is quite clear if only because of the rapid practical application of his work resulting in tremendous benefits to the French economy. But he opened up fields of study still being actively pursued. The description 'Father of modern bacteriology' is apt, but his fundamental contributions to stereo-chemistry, to immunology, and to the general application of scientific methods to medicine must also be remembered.

R. J. Dubos, *Louis Pasteur: Free Lance of Science.* 1951.

P. Vallery-Radot, *The Life of Pasteur.* 12th ed. 1960. (Portraits.)

E. Duclaux, *Pasteur: The History of a Mind.* 1920.

J. R. Porter, *Science,* **178**, 1249, 1972.

Dictionary of Scientific Biography.

                                                                              J K C

PATTINSON, HUGH LEE Born at Alston, Cumberland, England, 25 December 1796; died Gateshead, County Durham, 11 November 1858. Invented a process for the desilverization of lead.

Pattinson became clerk to a Newcastle upon Tyne soap boiler in 1821, after local schooling and some time spent with his Quaker parents in the retail trade. In 1825 he was appointed assay-master to the Greenwich Hospital Commissioners at Alston. In 1829 he observed that, as a solution of silver in lead cooled, pure lead at first separated, and so conceived a process of mechanical enrichment which allowed the economic working of lean ores. Whilst manager (1831–4) to Wentworth Beaumont, he patented (1833) the process and exploited it, with partners, at Felling, County Durham. He also held patents for the manufacture of white lead through the oxychloride (1841), and magnesia alba (1842). His honours included FRS (1852), and Fellowship of the Geological and the Royal Astronomical Societies.

J. Percy, *Metallurgy: Lead.* 1870.

H. Lonsdale, *Worthies of Cumberland.* 1873. (Portrait.)

Dictionary of National Biography.

                                                                              W N S

PAULI, WOLFGANG ERNST Born in Vienna, 25 April 1900; died Zürich, Switzerland, 15 December 1958. Theoretical physicist, best known for his work on atomic structures and particularly for his Exclusion Principle.

Pauli's father was a professor at Vienna, but he himself went to the University of Munich and studied under A. SOMMERFELD. He was something of a prodigy; when he was only 19, Sommerfeld made him write an exposition of the theory of relativity, and this was recognized everywhere as masterly. His PhD thesis on the hydrogen molecule ion has been described as 'possibly the most ambitious application of the old Bohr-Sommerfeld quantum theory that has ever been attempted'. All his papers impressed contemporaries because of their incisive clarity. After leaving Munich he worked at Göttingen, at Copenhagen, and at Hamburg; the last thirty years of his life were spent at Zürich, except for five years during the Second World War at the Institute for Advanced Studies, Princeton.

In the 1920s quantum mechanics was an unsatisfactory and illogical mixture of old and new elements, and the study of the spectra of the alkali metals under a strong magnetic field (involving the effect discovered by P. ZEEMAN) showed twice as many energy states as the theory predicted. In 1924 Pauli suggested his Exclusion Principle, adding a new degree of freedom for the electron. Two electrons (instead of one), he postulated, could occupy each energy level, but they must differ in a property which was called 'spin'. With the publication of this Principle, much existing knowledge of atomic structure fell into place. Another phenomenon that was little understood was radioactivity involving the emission of β-rays, called β-decay; the electrons given off formed a continuous spectrum where one would have expected to find them emitted with discrete energies. Further, energy did not appear to be conserved in the process. To save the Principle of Conservation of Energy, Pauli proposed the existence of a new particle, the neutrino, with no charge and a very small mass. So that spin might be conserved in β-decay, it was necessary to postulate a spin of ½ for the neutrino. For his work on theoretical physics, Pauli was awarded a Nobel prize for physics in 1945.

Pauli could be a very caustic wit, and seemed rather unapproachable; he was not a good formal lecturer, but shone in discussion. Many of his most important suggestions were made in informal discussion or in letters. He was notoriously bad at experiments.

Nature, **183**, 1089, 1959.
Biographical Memoirs of Fellows of the Royal Society. 1959. (Portrait.)
E. I. Valko, *Journal of Chemical Education*, **27**, 2, 1950. (Portrait.)
M. E. Fierz and V. F. Weisskopf, *Physics Today*, **12**, 17, 1959.
Dictionary of Scientific Biography.
Tyler Wasson (Ed.), *Nobel Prize Winners*. 1987. (Portrait.)

D M K

PAULING, LINUS CARL Born Portland, Oregon, USA, 28 February 1901. Physical organic chemist.

Pauling was educated at Oregon State College and California Institute of Technology. From 1925 to 1927 he worked in the laboratories of A. SOMMERFELD (Munich), N. BOHR (Copenhagen), E. SHRÖDINGER (Zürich) and W. H. BRAGG (London), then returned to California Institute of Technology. He was Director of the Gates and Crellin Chemistry Laboratories (1936–58).

Pauling investigated molecular structures using quantum mechanics, x-ray diffraction, electron diffraction, magnetic effects, and heats of reaction to calculate interatomic distances in molecules and the angles between chemical bonds. He introduced the concepts of hybrid orbitals, directed valency, the partial ionic character of covalent bonds, and resonance whereby the true molecular structure of labile molecules is regarded as intermediate between two or more possible structures. From 1934 Pauling applied his knowledge of molecular structures to complex organic molecules such as

proteins, including those involved in immunological reactions. His work with Robert B. COREY on the structures of amino acids and polypeptides showed that certain proteins have helical structures. Pauling explained his ideas in *The Nature of the Chemical Bond* (1939), perhaps the most influential chemical textbook of the 20th century.

In the late 1940s Pauling identified the cause of sickle-cell anaemia as a molecular abnormality in haemoglobin; in 1961 he proposed a molecular model to explain anaesthesia and later introduced some ideas to explain memory. His chemical work is characterised by bold intuitive guesswork, backed by a phenomenal memory for chemical facts. He was not afraid to suggest unorthodox views to stimulate discussion and argument. He was elected FRS in 1948 and was awarded the Nobel prize for chemistry in 1954.

In 1958 Pauling presented a petition to the United Nations in New York, signed by over 11 000 scientists world-wide protesting against nuclear tests. In 1963 he joined the Center for the Study of Democratic Institutions at Santa Barbara, California, to study the problems of peace and war. In the same year, following the signing of the test-ban treaty, he was awarded the Nobel Peace Prize for 1962 and received the International Lenin Peace Prize in 1972. His pacifist views estranged him from many fellow scientists and although he was impartial in his opposition to nuclear tests, his loyalty to the USA was questioned in some conservative quarters. In 1969 Pauling resigned from the University of California to join the chemistry department at Stanford University.

R. P. Huemer (Ed.), *The Roots of Molecular Medicine: A Tribute to Linus Pauling*. 1986.
E. Farber, *Nobel Prize Winners in Chemistry 1901– 61*. 1963.
M. L. Huggins, *Chemical Engineering News*, **37**, 242, 1955. (Portrait.)
Les Prix Nobel in 1954. 1955. (Portrait.)
Tyler Wasson (Ed.), *Nobel Prize Winners*. 1987. (Portrait.)

N G C

PAVLOV, IVAN PETROVICH Born at Ryazan, Central Russia, 26 September 1849; died Moscow, 27 February 1936. Physiologist remembered chiefly for work on the conditioned reflex and the physiology of digestion.

Pavlov received the MD degree from the University of St Petersburg in 1883 and for two years thereafter he studied in Germany. In 1891 he became Director of Physiology in the St Petersburg Institute for Experimental Medicine and he remained there for forty-five years. In addition he was made professor of pharmacology in the Military Medical Academy in 1891 and was given the chair of physiology there four years later. He was also in charge of the physiology laboratory of the St Petersburg Academy from 1907 and remained head of it for thirty years. Eventually the Soviet Government provided him with a splendid laboratory at Koltushig, about thirty miles from Leningrad.

Pavlov's professional research activities fall into two sections: on digestion and on the conditioned reflex. Concerning the former he discovered the secretory nerves to the pancreas in 1888 and being an ingenious experimenter was able to study the effects of sham feeding by creating gastric pouches.

He thus elucidated the 'psychic' gastric juice produced by the sight or smell of food, the role of the vagus nerve in the secretion of gastric glands, and the constancy of gastric juice acidity; and he was able to enunciate the three phases of digestion; nervous, pyloric, and intestinal. He confirmed the discovery of W. M. BAYLISS and E. H. STARLING that a hormone, secretin, is responsible for inducing pancreatic secretion. Pavlov's ingenious laboratory techniques in these researches were of especial importance and it has been said that he introduced both aseptic surgery and the chronic experiment into physiology. His conclusions on digestion appeared in *Die Arbeit der Verdauungsdrüsen* (1898, English and French versions), and it was for these studies that he was awarded the 1904 Nobel prize in physiology or medicine.

On the whole he was mostly interested in the neural aspects of digestion, and this led him to conditioned reflexes or responses which engaged his attention from 1902 for the rest of his life. His fellow countryman, I. M. Sechenov (1829–1905), had introduced a theory of brain reflexes, having shown that psychic phenomena are akin to the essentially somatic acts which constitute nervous activity. Pavlov's studies sprang from this work and they form the basis of present-day Russian physiology. Food placed in a dog's mouth induces gastric juice flow, an 'unconditioned' response according to Pavlov. If, however, a bell is rung regularly before the food is presented, the response, which may eventually take place in the absence of food, is 'conditioned' and it is dependent upon the integrity of the cerebral cortex. This basic pattern has led to a remarkable proliferation of experimental activity and concepts which have pervaded many parts of physiology other than that of the nervous and digestive systems. It is, however, too early to evaluate adequately the importance of the conditioned reflex in the functioning of the human and animal systems. Some would point to the widespread influence it has had on our knowledge of higher nervous function in the fields of physiology, psychology, psychiatry and education, whilst others would admit only that it provides a valuable experimental technique for the analysis of cerebral function. It is perhaps of significance that whereas the teachings of Pavlov have remained influential only in Russia and in Russia-dominated countries, those of his contemporary C. S. SHERRINGTON concerning the function of the nervous system have been accepted throughout the rest of the world.

B. P. Babkin, *Pavlov. A Biography*. 1949. (Portraits.)

W. Haymaker and F. Schiller (Eds), *The Founders of Neurology*. 1953.

W. H. Gantt *et al.*, (Eds), *Pavlovian Approach to Psychotherapy*. 1970.

Y. P. Frolov, *Pavlov and His School*. 1937.

Obituary Notices of Fellows of the Royal Society. 1936. (Portrait.)

E. A. Astratyan, *Ivan Petrovich Pavlov*. 1953.

J. A. Gray, *Ivan Pavlov*. 1971.

Dictionary of Scientific Biography.

Tyler Wasson (Ed.), *Nobel Prize Winners*. 1987. (Portrait.)

E C

PECQUET, JEAN Born at Dieppe, France, in 1622; died Paris, February 1674. Discoverer of the thoracic duct.

Pecquet studied classics in clerical schools in Dieppe and Rouen. He then taught at Paris in the *Collège de Clermont*, and was awarded the title of Master of Arts at Paris. As a protégé of François Fouquet, Bishop of Agde (Hérault), he studied medicine in Paris, later transferring to Montpellier, where he graduated as a doctor of medicine in 1652. In 1655 he returned to Paris and became a protégé of Bishop Fouquet's brother, Nicolas Fouquet, who was Superintendent of Finances to Louis XIV. Nicolas Fouquet was disgraced and arrested in 1661, and after a trial lasting three years he was imprisoned for life. Pecquet, choosing to share his patron's disgrace, was not liberated from the Bastille until 1665. After his release he was nominated by Colbert as a member of the *Académie Royale des Sciences*.

While Pecquet was still a medical student he published his book entitled *Experimenta nova anatomica* (1651), embodying the results of experiments lasting three years. In 1622 G. ASELLI had discovered the lacteals in the mesentery, but he thought that they conveyed the chyle to the liver. Pecquet discovered in 1647 a milky fluid issuing from a cut venous trunk in the right upper thorax of a dog. On pressing the mesentery this fluid issued abundantly. He deduced that the lacteals could not pass to the liver, and he discovered that they led to the receptaculum chyli, the lower part of the thoracic duct. Pecquet discovered both these structures and described them accurately for the first time. His experiments gave great support to William HARVEY's doctrine of the circulation of the blood.

J. Delmas, in R. Dumesnil and F. Bonnet-Roy, *Les Médecins Célèbres*. 1947. (Portrait.)

Dictionary of Scientific Biography.

E A U

PEDERSEN, CHARLES JOHN Born in Pusan, Korea, 10 March 1904; died Salem, New Jersey, USA, 26 October 1989. Industrial chemist.

After graduating in chemical engineering and organic chemistry at the University of Dayton and at Massachusetts Institute of Technology, Pedersen joined the Du Pont Company in 1927 as a research scientist, (Research Associate 1946) remaining with them until retirement in 1969. He is particularly remembered for his pioneer work on organic compounds known as crown ethers (CE). These are a family of cyclic polymers of ethylene glycol with a unique capacity for absorbing ionic compounds into an organic phase. They do this by retaining the ion by chemical bonds within a circular cage. This is known as a 'host-guest' relationship, the CE acting as host to the coordinately bound cation guest. This led on to the concept of 'molecular recognition', offering an explanation of how biochemical entities find their match. How, for example, does an antibody recognize an antigen, or an enzyme its substrate? For his original research in this fruitful new field Pedersen was awarded a Nobel prize in 1987, jointly with Donald CRAM and Jean-Marie Lehn (1939–   ). He also did research on autoxidation, suppression of metal catalysis, and photochemistry.

Les Prix Nobel en 1987. 1988. (Portrait.)

T I W

PEIERLS, SIR RUDOLF ERNST Born in Berlin, 5 June 1907, Atomic physicist.

Peierls studied physics at the University of Berlin under Max PLANCK, Walther Bothe (1891–1957) and Walther NERNST, wave mechanics with SOMMERFELD at Munich and the electron theory of metal structure with W. K. HEISENBERG at Leipzig. In 1929 he joined W. E. PAULI at the Federal Institute of Technology in Zurich and also visited Rutherford's Cavendish Laboratory at Cambridge, England. At Zurich he applied quantum electrodynamics to investigate electron behaviour in metals. In 1930, during a visit to Holland, Peierls met P. Ehrenfest (1880–1933), H. A. Kramers (1894–1952) and F. Bloch (1905–   ). He also visited N. BOHR in Copenhagen and later worked with E. FERMI (1901–54) in Rome. In 1933 he visited the Cavendish Laboratory at Cambridge again where J. CHADWICK had just discovered the neutron, J. D. COCKCROFT and E. T. S. Walton (1903–   ) had shown how to produce nuclear reactions, the positron had been identified, and P. M. S. BLACKETT was developing the Wilson Cloud Chamber.

Peierls began to study nuclear physics in 1933 with Hans BETHE at the University of Manchester under W. L. BRAGG. He returned to Cambridge in 1935 as research assistant at the Mond Laboratory for magnetism and low temperature physics, but in 1937 he was appointed professor of applied mathematics at Birmingham where he continued to work on nuclear reactions. In 1939 Otto HAHN and Fritz Strassman (1902–80) in Berlin discovered uranium fission. Peierls and Otto FRISCH, in a joint paper, showed that by using uranium 235 a nuclear explosion could be produced. Through Mark Oliphant (1901–   ) this paper eventually reached G. P. THOMSON, chairman of the British MAUD committee concerned with atomic energy, to which Peierls and Frisch were eventually elected after doubts about their German origins had been resolved. Peierls became a naturalised British citizen in February 1940 and began work on the atomic energy project. In 1943 he led the British group on the Manhattan (atomic bomb) project at Los Alamos, California, USA. Elected FRS in 1946, he was awarded a CBE in 1947.

After the war Peierls returned to Birmingham as professor of a new department of mathematical physics. He became active in political efforts by the Atomic Scientists' Association to control the use of atomic energy and nuclear weapons and later at the Pugwash Conferences. In 1961 he was appointed Wykeham Professor of Physics at Oxford and he remained in this position there until his retirement in 1974. He received the Royal and Copley Medals of the Royal Society in 1959 and 1986 respectively and was knighted in 1968.

R. Peierls, *Bird of Passage; Recollections of a Physicist*, 1985. (Portrait.)

N G C

PÉLIGOT, EUGÈNE MELCHIOR Born in Paris, 24 February 1811; died there, 15 April 1890. Applied chemist; isolated uranium.

Péligot studied chemistry under J. B. DUMAS at the *École Polytechnique*, and collaborated with him in his research for many years. He became professor of applied chemistry in the *Conservatoire des Arts et Métiers*; he also worked in the Paris Mint, finally becoming Director of Assays.

His main interest was in applied chemistry, and he wrote important books on silk manufacture (1853) and glass-making (1877); he also worked on agricultural chemistry. He is remembered, however, for his isolation of uranium metal by heating the tetrachloride with potassium (1841); previously uranium dioxide had been mistaken for the element.

Bulletin de la Société Chimique de France, **5**, xxi, 1891.

M. E. Weeks, *Discovery of the Elements*. 1956. (Portrait.)

W V F

PELLETIER, JOSEPH Born in Paris, 22 April 1788; died there, 19 July 1842. The founder (with J. B. CAVENTOU) of alkaloid chemistry.

Pelletier came of a family of pharmacists; he studied in the *École de Pharmacie*, and also taught there until illness forced him to retire in 1840. He also ran his own pharmacy business.

He began research on the chemical constituents of *materia medica* about 1809. The great advance which he made was to use only mild methods, such as solvent extraction, instead of the dramatic, but chemically uninformative, methods of a previous generation, such as destructive distillation. The work of F. W. SERTÜRNER and of certain French apothecaries directed his attention to the new class of 'vegetable bases', later called alkaloids. With the physiologist F. MAGENDIE in 1817 he isolated emetine; and in the same year he began the series of researches with his friend Caventou, in which they discovered the alkaloids colchicine, veratrine, strychnine, brucine, quinine, and cinchonine among others less well defined. For several years Pelletier and Caventou strenuously denied the presence of nitrogen in these compounds; but in 1823, J. B. A. DUMAS and Pelletier published fairly accurate elementary analyses of nine alkaloids, which first put their chemistry on a rational basis. Pelletier also isolated and studied a number of other natural products, including picrotoxin, caffeine, piperine and olivil.

M. Delépine, *Journal of Chemical Education*, **28**, 454, 1951. (Portrait.)

Chemistry and Industry, **56**, 1084, 1937. (Portrait.)

Dictionary of Scientific Biography.

W V F

PELTIER, JEAN CHARLES ATHANASE Born at Ham, Somme, France, 22 February 1785; died Paris, 27 October 1845. Remembered for the discovery of the thermoelectric effect which bears his name.

T. J. Seebeck (1770–1831) had shown that temperature differences could produce electric currents. In 1834 Peltier completed Seebeck's discovery by showing that the passage of electricity through a junction of two different metals (such as antimony and copper) could produce a rise in temperature at the junction when passing in one direction, and a drop in temperature when passing in the contrary direction. He investigated the production of electricity associated with the vaporization of water with a view to explaining the origin of atmospheric electricity. He also attempted to improve the Coulomb balance (see A. C. de

COULOMB) by replacing the arm by a magnetic needle free to rotate on a vertical bearing.
Dictionary of Scientific Biography.

J W H

PENFIELD, WILDER GRAVES Born at Spokane, Washington State, USA, 26 January 1891; died Montreal, Canada, 5 April 1976. Pioneer of physiological neurosurgery, particularly in the treatment of epilepsy.

Penfield's first degree at Princeton University led to a Rhodes Scholarship to Oxford, where he came under the influence of C. S. SHERRINGTON and W. Osler (1849–1919). After war service he completed his medical degree at Johns Hopkins University and from 1921–8 was in the surgical department of Columbia Medical School, being responsible for developing neurosurgery in those pioneering days. He was greatly helped by six months in Madrid under RAMÓN Y CAJAL and Pio del Rio-Hortega (1882–1945). In 1925 began the partnership with William Cone that continued until Cone's death in 1959.

The great opportunity came to Penfield in 1928 with the invitation to develop neurosurgery at McGill University, Montreal. There he remained for the remainder of his life. The establishment of the Montreal Neurological Institute (MNI) in 1934 brought the realization of Penfield's dream to have an Institute with the basic sciences, neurophysiology and neuropathology, in close apposition to clinical neurology and neurosurgery. Until his retirement at the age of 70 he guided the MNI into the path of greatness, making it one of the great neurological institutes of the world. Cone developed neuropathology and Herbert Jasper neurophysiology. Later came neurochemistry, under K. A. C. Elliott. The MNI is the great achievement of Penfield's life. Just before his death in 1976 a large addition to the MNI was named the Penfield Pavilion as a working memorial to his ideals. These are inscribed on the plaque of the MNI: 'Dedicated to relief of sickness and pain and to the study of neurology.'

Penfield's most notable contribution to neurology was on cerebral localization and epilepsy. He followed the method of Otfrid Foerster (1873–1941) in ensuring accurate localization of stimulated points on the exposed brain of patients under surgical treatment for epilepsy. There was a photographic recording and a record of the sensory and motor phenomena evoked from each stimulated point. This mapping was a necessary procedure in searching for the epileptic focus that was to be excised, but Penfield used it scientifically to produce a most valuable topography of the human brain. At the same time there was electrical recording from the brain, the EEG. So the operating theatre was also a scientific laboratory. There were many publications of this wonderful work, both its scientific and its clinical aspects. It was the greatest centre of the world for the surgical treatment of epilepsy.

There were associated important studies on memory. Stimulation of some areas of the cerebral cortex gave to the patient vivid flashbacks of memory of long ago incidents. Brenda Milner very effectively studied the memory deficits resulting from the surgical excisions. So arose the concept that the various types of memory tended to be located in different areas of the cortex. The most significant of these cortical localizations was that of language. Penfield and L. Roberts wrote a classical book *Speech and Brain Mechanisms*, but the justly famous publication was *Epilepsy and the Functional Anatomy of the Human Brain*, by Penfield and H. Jasper (1954).

Penfield was deeply interested in medical education, particularly in the whole field of the neurosciences. He played a notable role with the many neurological injuries in the Second World War. In later life his historical studies led him to write two novels: *No other Gods*, about Abraham, and *The Torch* with his hero Hippocrates as the central figure. He always had a deep religious faith and the mystery of human existence was the theme of his philosophical book *The Mystery of the Mind* (1975). 'To understand man himself and to analyze the means by which man, the creator of science, has done what he had done.'

In 1917 he married Helen Katherine Kermott. Withal, his greatness was manifested in his personal relations to others, in his family life, and in his superb humanity and simplicity. His work brought him many honours, notably Fellowship of the Royal Society (1943); the Order of Merit (1953); and the Companion of the Order of Canada (1967).

W. G. Penfield, *No Man Alone: a Neurosurgeon's Life* (autobiography up to 1934). 1977.
Biographical Memoirs of Fellows of the Royal Society. 1978. (Portrait.)

J C E

PENROSE, ROGER Born in Colchester, Essex, England, 8 August 1931. Mathematician.

Penrose studied mathematics at University College London. After a series of academic appointments in the UK and abroad he was appointed Rouse Ball Professor of Mathematics at Oxford in 1973. He made many important contributions to the theory of gravitational collapse and geometrical aspects of theoretical physics. He discovered in 1965 that a collapsing star would, once it had passed a certain point, end up as a singularity irrespective of the irregularity of its collapse. This conclusion ran against the commonly accepted notions and opened up large new fields of investigation as well as expanding the theory of general relativity (See EINSTEIN). He has continued to make substantial contributions to our understanding of both special and general relativity.

Within the areas of geometry and topology Penrose has made influential contributions, many of which bear his name – such as Penrose diagrams, Newman-Penrose coefficients, and the Penrose process for extracting energy from Black Holes. In recent years his twistor theory has made a significant impact on mathematics. This is an attempt to provide information on a firm foundation for an alternative to conventional spacetime physics. As well as providing some insights into relativity the ideas contained in the twistor theory also relate to complex numbers and complex spaces, corresponding to 'string' theory.

Penrose has also written on artificial intelligence and the analogies between the human brain and computers. His book *The Emperor's New Mind* (1990) challenges the views of the proponents of 'Hard AI' who contend that it is possible to construct a model of the brain using computational analogies and thereby provide insights into the mind-body question. Penrose has proposed that the failure of the Hard AI approach lies in the impossibility of simulating in any satisfactory way the link between the physical action of the brain and consciousness.

Penrose has also worked with Stephen HAWKING since the 1960s and made the very important discovery concerning the presence, if relativity theory is correct, of a singularity at the centre of Black Holes where the laws of physics no longer apply.

Penrose's work on the topology of complex spaces led to innovative 3-dimensional mapping using 'tiling' processes in multidimensional space. This provides clues about the deep structure of matter. The most recent application has been in an understanding of quasicrystals, which have 5-fold quasisymmetric atomic arrangements.

R. Penrose, *The Emperor's New Mind: Concerning Computers, Minds and the Laws of Physics.* 1990. *Who's Who.* 1993.

C L

PENZIAS, ARNO ALLAN Born in Munich, Germany, 26 April 1933. Co-discoverer of the cosmic microwave background radiation.

Having left Germany with his parents when he was four years old, Penzias was brought up in New York City. He gained his first degree in 1954 at City College New York, and then went to Columbia University where he worked under Charles TOWNES. He received his PhD in 1962, having joined AT&T Bell Laboratories in New Jersey in 1961.

In 1964, Penzias and Robert Wilson (1936–   ), a colleague at Bell Labs, began to try to measure radio emissions from the halo of gas that surrounds our galaxy. They discovered a microwave signal that appeared to come uniformly from all directions and which they could not attribute to any source of 'noise'. They turned to astrophysicists at Princeton for an explanation, and together came to the conclusion that the signal was due to radiation from the Big Bang, cooled to 3 K through the expansion of the Universe. Such background radiation had been predicted as a consequence of the Big Bang by Ralph ALPHER and Robert Herman in the 1940s. In 1978 Penzias and Wilson shared the Nobel prize for physics, together with Peter KAPITZA who received his share for work on low-temperature physics.

Penzias became director of Bell's radio research laboratory in 1976, and executive director for research and communications in 1979. In 1981 he became vice president of research and led the formation of the new Bell Communications Research Organization.

Physics Today, December 1978. (Portrait.)
Tyler Wasson (Ed.), *Nobel Prize Winners.* 1987. (Portrait.)

C S

PEREGRINUS, PETRUS (PETER THE PILGRIM) Born *c.*1220. Place and date of death unknown. Scholar and soldier.

Very little is known of the life of Petrus Peregrinus. He was in Paris about 1250, where he was the friend and tutor of Roger BACON, who praised him highly: 'what others strive to see dimly and blindly, like bats in twilight, he gazes at in the full light of day, because he is a master of experiments'.

In 1269 he was at the siege of Lucera, probably serving as an engineer under Charles of Anjou, and it was during this time that he wrote the work *Epistola de Magnete*, which is his lasting claim to fame.

In this first serious work on magnetism Petrus refers to its then being common knowledge that if a piece of iron that had been touched with a lodestone (i.e. magnetized) were floated on a light piece of wood it would always come to rest pointing north. He proceeded to formulate the simple laws of magnetic repulsion and attraction. He asserted that it was not the Pole Star that attracted the magnet but the celestial poles. In pursuit of this idea he sought to construct a magnetic clock that would perpetually turn in phase with the heavens. He constructed practical compasses to assist astronomers in finding the meridian and determining the azimuths of heavenly bodies. The ideas of Petrus were elaborated in the 16th century by William GILBERT in his *De Magnete* (1600).

E. G. R. Taylor, *The Haven-finding Art.* 1956.
Silvanus P. Thompson, *Peregrinus and his Epistola.* 1907.
Dictionary of Scientific Biography.

T I W

PERKIN, SIR WILLIAM HENRY Born at Shadwell, London, 12 March 1838; died Sudbury, Middlesex, 14 July 1907. Chemist; prepared the first synthetic dye, mauve.

Perkin came of a family with some inherent gift for chemistry. His grandfather Thomas Perkin (b. 1757) fitted up a laboratory in his Yorkshire farmhouse; three of his own sons were chemists of distinction. They were respectively W. H. PERKIN, *junior*, A. G. Perkin (1861–1937), and F. M. Perkin (d. 1928). All had musical talent, too, and at one time there was an accomplished family orchestra. W. H. Perkin was expected to carry on his father's trade of boat-building and carpentry, but even as a boy he determined to be a chemist. At 15 he entered the Royal College of Chemistry, London, to study under A. W. von HOFMANN. While there his enthusiasm led him to set up a laboratory in his own home for spare-time research, and here he ambitiously set out in 1856 to synthesize the important drug quinine. Although we now know his attempt to have been foredoomed to failure, it appeared – according to the primitive chemical theory of the day – that quinine might be made from the relatively simple substance toluidine. Perkin obtained no more than a brown precipitate, but fortunately this interested him sufficiently to make him repeat the experiment with aniline, a simple analogue of toluidine. From the black precipitate he prepared with alcohol an intensely mauve solution, and at once he recognized the possibilities of this for the dyeing industry. He sent a sample to the well-known Scottish dyeing house of Pullars of Perth, who immediately reported most favourably on it.

Perkin decided to exploit the discovery himself, despite discouragement by Hofmann. Certain technical problems had to be solved before the test-tube experiments could be worked on a large scale, but Perkin's father shared his son's enthusiasm and committed his life's savings to the venture. Works were established at Greenford Green, a little to the west of London, and there a very successful industry was established – so successful indeed that

Perkin was able to sell out and retire at the age of only 36. Meanwhile, he had added the dye alizarine to his products. In this invention he was unlucky, in that his patent was anticipated by a single day by one taken out in Germany by C. GRAEBE, H. Caro (1834–1911), and C. T. Liebermann (1842–1914). However, a friendly settlement was reached by which Perkin acquired the English licence and he shortly improved the process; in 1873 no less than 435 tons of alizarine were made at Greenford.

Despite its outstanding qualities Perkin at first had difficulty in interesting British dyers in mauve; indeed, it was through the interest of the French fashion houses that his compatriots realized their mistake. Before long mauve became universally familiar to the British public through its use in printing penny stamps.

In his retirement Perkin remained active in chemical research. In 1868 he had succeeded in synthesizing coumarin from acetic anhydride and the sodium salt of salicylaldehyde. From this he developed a general reaction (the Perkin reaction) by which he synthesized cinnamic acid in 1877. He is remembered also for his synthesis, with B. F. Duppa (1828–73), of the amino acid glycine.

Perkin was elected FRS in 1866 and was knighted in 1906; the Society awarded him its Royal and Davy Medal.

E. Farber (Ed.), *Great Chemists*. 1961. (Portrait.)
J. R. Partington, *A History of Chemistry*, vol. 4. 1964.
Robert Robinson, *Endeavour*, **15**, 92. 1956. (Portrait.)
Dictionary of National Biography.
Dictionary of Scientific Biography.
Journal of the Chemical Society, **93**, 2214, 1908.
                                                    T I W

PERKIN, WILLIAM HENRY *Jr* Born at Sudbury, Middlesex, England, 17 June 1860; died Oxford, 17 September 1929. Organic chemist; especially noted for work on the structure and synthesis of natural products.

W. H. Perkin was the son of the industrial chemist Sir William PERKIN; his brother, A. G. Perkin (1861–1937), and his half-brother, F. M. Perkin (d. 1928), were also chemists of distinction. He was educated at the City of London School and then (like his father) entered the Royal College of Chemistry, London, in 1877, under E. FRANKLAND. He was an outstanding student, and was invited to take part in research. On graduating (1880) he went to Würzburg to study for two years under J. A. WISLICENUS and then to Munich to work with J. F. W. A. von BAEYER. Returning to England, he worked for a time at Manchester and was then (1887) offered the chair of chemistry at the newly founded Heriot-Watt College in Edinburgh. There he was joined by F. S. KIPPING, with whom he wrote an extremely successful textbook of *Organic Chemistry* (1894).

From Edinburgh, Perkin went to Manchester in 1892 as professor of organic chemistry, and there built up a research school that became internationally famous. Finally, in 1912, he became Waynflete Professor of Chemistry at Oxford. The outbreak of war shortly afterwards directed his interests into practical industrial problems, especially in connection with the dyestuffs industry; for a time after the war he was a director of the British Dyestuffs Corporation. Not until 1922 was the new laboratory completed at Oxford that Perkin had been promised. In it he instituted an outstanding programme of research, as well as introducing some important reforms in the teaching of chemistry at Oxford.

Perkin's first outstanding discovery was made during his time at Munich. There, confounding the experts of the day, including von Baeyer, he succeeded in making substances containing carbon atoms arranged in rings of four atoms; it was then generally supposed that only five- or six-membered rings could exist. In the years 1890–1903 he took a leading part in investigations that elucidated the structure of camphor; in this field his chief rival was the German chemist Julius Bredt (1855–1937) of Aachen, who was, in fact, the first to set out the exact constitutional formula (1893). Camphor was totally synthesized by G. Komppa (1867–1949) in 1909.

In the early years of this century there was great interest in the chemistry of the terpenes, complex hydrocarbons found in natural oils. Much evidence of their structure has been obtained by breaking them down into simpler substances that could be identified, but Perkin realized that confirmation was required by also synthesizing them. In this field he made numerous contributions, including the synthesis of limonene (dipentene) in 1904, and of carvestrene in 1907.

Pursuing his interests in natural products, Perkin made outstanding contributions to the chemistry of the natural bases known as alkaloids. Among those he investigated were berberine, harmine, harmaline, cryptopine, and protopine; his work, both degradative and synthetic, is acknowledged to be brilliant. At the time of his death he had embarked on an investigation of the alkaloids strychnine and brucine. He investigated, too, the nature of the natural dyes brazilin and haematoxylin contained in Brazilian log-wood; again he initiated a brilliant programme of synthetic work.

Partly because of its intrinsic interest, and partly because of its relevance to the complex natural products in which he was so deeply involved, Perkin was keenly interested in stereochemical problems; that is to say, in the precise arrangement of atoms relative to each other in molecules. In this field he carried out a classic investigation, with W. J. POPE, of a new kind of optical activity not requiring – as was then generally supposed essential – that one carbon atom in the molecule should have four different groups attached to it.

Perkin's talent for organic chemical research was matched by his ability as a teacher. In consequence, he profoundly influenced not only those who worked with him in the laboratory but those who attended his lectures. His influence on the development of organic chemistry was enormous. He was widely honoured in his lifetime. He was elected FRS in 1890; the Society awarded him its Royal (1925) and its Davy (1904) Medals, as it had done to his father. He was a member of many foreign academies, including the American Academy of Arts and Sciences. He was President of the Chemical Society 1913–15.

A. Findlay and W. H. Mills (Eds), *British Chemists*. 1947. (Portrait.)
Robert Robinson, *Endeavour*, **15**, 92. 1956. (Portrait.)
Dictionary of National Biography.

Proceedings of the Royal Society, **130A**, i, 1930.
The Chemical Society, *The Life and Work of
Professor William Henry Perkin.* 1932.

                                                   T I W

PERRAULT, CLAUDE Born in Paris, 1613; died
there, 6 October 1688. Physician and architect.

Intended by his father for a career in medicine,
Perrault took a doctor's degree in this faculty at
Paris, and did important work in comparative anatomy, especially of mammals, of which he made
many dissections. He died of an infection contracted while dissecting a camel. As a good Latin
scholar, however, he was employed by Colbert in
1673 to produce the first complete French version
of VITRUVIUS, with lavish drawings and engravings.
As the translator had never been outside France,
it is not surprising that the rendering was in many
respects imperfect, but one result was the diver-
sion of Perrault to a new vocation.

In 1666 his design was accepted for the façade of
the Louvre, and his colonnade (completed in 1670)
proved to be among the most distinguished architectural achievements of the century. This was followed by his construction of the Paris Observatory,
which was built from very carefully cut stone, without resort to wood. Later, he was a pioneer of the
reinforcement of stone with iron. Perrault was also
selected to design the *arc de triomphe* proposed by
Colbert in honour of Louis XIV, but never completed owing to the uncharacteristic lukewarmness
of the King. He took part, too, in the embellishment
of the palace and park at Versailles.

Perrault's numerous literary works included an
important study of the Five Orders; his *Recueil de
machines*, which retained its usefulness down to
the nineteenth century; a volume of essays, published jointly with his brother Charles, in which
the increased volume of hardened steel is first
recorded; and more ephemeral contributions to
natural history.

Nouvelle Biographie Générale, xxxix. 1862.
E. Nordenskiöld, *The History of Biology.* 1928.
A. Hallays, *Les Perrault.* 2nd ed. 1926.
Dictionary of Scientific Biography.

                                                   T K D

PERRIN, JEAN BAPTISTE Born at Lille, France,
30 September 1870; died New York, 17 April 1942.
Known for his work on cathode rays, and for his
calculation of the Avogadro Number from study of
the Brownian Motion.

Perrin's first important paper appeared in the
Comptes Rendus in 1895. In it he sought to show
that cathode rays were composed of particles, in
opposition to the view, widely held on the Continent, that they were a wave motion. This latter
belief seemed to receive support from experiments
in which cathode rays were shown to penetrate
thin sheets of glass or aluminium. Perrin collected
the rays in a hollow cylinder, and showed that this
acquired a negative charge, and also that the rays
could be retarded by an electric charge. When a
fluorescent screen on which the rays were falling
was given an increasing negative charge, the intensity of fluorescence fell until at a given potential it
was extinguished. These experiments helped prepare the way for the paper by J. J. THOMSON in 1897,
on the ratio of mass to charge of the corpuscles
composing the cathode rays.

Even more important were Perrin's papers on
the Brownian Motion, published in 1909 and translated into English by F. SODDY in the following year.
At the turn of the century there was still considerable doubt as to whether matter was really
composed of atoms. The sceptics, of whom W. F.
OSTWALD was the most important, doubted whether
there was any value in the atomic hypothesis; and
it was Perrin's experiments which finally convinced the world that atoms existed. Robert BROWN,
in the mid-nineteenth century, had observed under
the microscope the rapid motions of pollen grains
suspended in water; Perrin argued that such tiny
particles moved because they were being bombarded unevenly by the water molecules in their
ceaseless motion. He applied the kinetic theory of
gases to the situation, assuming that, despite the
great difference in size between the particles and
the water molecules, they would have the same
mean energy of agitation, and would interdiffuse
like the molecules of different gases. Using two
different approaches – counting the number of particles at two different depths in the liquid at equilibrium, and observing the rate of diffusion of
particles in the liquid – he was able to arrive at
values of the Avogadro Number – the number of
molecules in one cubic centimetre of gas at normal
temperature and pressure – which agreed with
those deduced from quite different evidence. This
seemed as near as one could go towards the actual
observation of molecules, and for this work Perrin
received a Nobel prize for physics in 1926.

Obituary Notices of Fellows of the Royal Society.
   1942–4. (Portrait.)
W. F. Magie, *A Source Book in Physics.* 1935.
Mary Jo Nye, *Molecular Reality.* 1972.
J. S. Townsend, *Nature*, **149**, 494, 1942.
Dictionary of Scientific Biography.
Tyler Wasson (Ed.), *Nobel Prize Winners.* 1987.
   (Portrait.)

                                                   D M K

PERRONET, JEAN-RODOLPHE Born at Suresnes,
Paris, 8 October 1708; died Paris, 27 February
1794. Bridge builder and trainer of civil engineers.

Perronet was the son of a Swiss officer in French
service. In early boyhood he showed great promise
in geometry and was accepted for training as a military engineer, but having to support his widowed
mother he sought employment in architecture
instead. In 1745 he joined the *Corps des Ponts et
Chaussées* as an inspector; the next year he was
put in charge of the district of Alençon, and in
1750 was appointed Inspector-General, with responsibility for the newly established *École des
Ponts et Chaussées*, the first of the great French
polytechnics. From 1763 onwards he held the post
of First Engineer, and in 1757–86 he was also
Inspector-General of Salt Works.

About 350 engineers passed through Perronet's
hands in the course of their training, and he was
consulted by the Russian, Danish and other foreign
governments. Apart from his wide general influence, however, his importance is as the designer
of some thirty bridges, including the Neuilly and
Concorde bridges over the Seine, Sainte-Maxence
over the Oise, and a posthumously constructed
bridge which spanned the Loing at Nemours. His
were the first flat bridges in France, the arches
being made as flat, the arch rings as shallow, and

the piers as thin as was consistent with safety. The arrangement of the collapsible timber centring for arch construction was a weak feature, improved upon by Robert Mylne (1734–1811) as early as 1760.

Nouvelle Biographie Générale, vol. 39. 1862.
J. K. Finch, *Consulting Engineer*, **18**, 128, 1962.
Dictionary of Scientific Biography.

T K D

PETER THE PILGRIM *See* PEREGRINUS.

PETIT, ALEXIS-THÉRÈSE Born at Vesoul, Haute-Saône, France, 2 October 1791; died Paris, 21 June 1820. Physicist, co-discoverer of law of atomic heat.

Petit was educated at the central school at Besançon, where he was outstanding in classics and mathematics. Although it is said he had all the ability necessary to enter the *École Polytechnique* at the age of 10, he did not in fact enter it until 1807, after study in Paris. He left with the highest distinction, and was almost immediately employed in teaching physics at the *Lycée Bonaparte*. He received a doctorate in 1811, and was one of the titular professors appointed to the *École Polytechnique*. He was cut off at the height of his powers by a pulmonary disease.

He worked on changes of refractive index with temperature (with F. ARAGO), on the theory of the utilization of heat in engines and, with P. DULONG, on the measurement of temperature, this latter being the work in which the two men established the constancy of the product of atomic weight and specific heat.

Annales de Chimie et de Physique, **16**, 327, 1821.
W. J. Hughes, *Chemistry in Britain*, **6**, 490, 1970.
R. Fox, *British Journal for the History of Science*, **4**, 1, 1968–9.
Dictionary of Scientific Biography.

F G

PETTENKOFER, MAX JOSEF VON *See* VON PETTENKOFER.

PERUTZ, MAX FERDINAND Born in Vienna, 19 May 1914. Molecular biologist. Elucidated structure of haemoglobin molecule using x-ray diffraction techniques.

Perutz, the son of a textile manufacturer, studied chemistry at the University of Vienna (1932–36) where he became interested in the work of the biochemist F. G. HOPKINS at Cambridge. However it was as research assistant to J. D. Bernal (1901–71), in the crystallography laboratory in the Cavendish Laboratory, that he went to Cambridge in 1936. He had already decided to apply x-ray analysis to the haemoglobin molecule in an attempt to determine its structure when Sir Lawrence BRAGG arrived in Cambridge as Cavendish Professor of Physics in 1938. Bernal had by then moved to Birkbeck College, London and Perutz was appointed as Bragg's research assistant, with a grant from the Rockefeller Foundation to support his haemoglobin research. He was awarded a PhD in 1940. Interned as an enemy alien at the outbreak of war, and sent to Canada in 1940, Perutz managed to resume his work and was joined by John KENDREW in 1946. They were the first members of the Medical Research Council Unit of Molecular Biology,

founded at the Cavendish Laboratory in 1947, with Perutz as director until 1962. The Unit expanded and became the MRC Laboratory of Molecular Biology in 1962. Perutz was chairman 1962–79.

Perutz shared the Nobel prize for chemistry with Kendrew in 1962 for his solution of the structure of the haemoglobin molecule. He had been a Fellow of the Royal Society since 1954, and later became a Companion of Honour (1975) and was awarded the Order of Merit (1988). He was Chairman of the European Molecular Biology Organization 1963–79 and Fullerian Professor of Physiology at the Royal Institution, 1973–79. His publications include *Proteins and Nucleic Acids, Structure and Function* (1962), *Atlas of Haemoglobin and Myoglobin* (1981), and *Is Science Necessary?* (1988).

R. C. Olby, *The Path to the Double Helix*. 1974.
F. H. Portugal and J. S. Cohen, *A Century of DNA*. 1977.
Max Perutz, *Chemistry in Britain*, **6**, 152, 1970.
Tyler Wasson (Ed.), *Nobel Prize Winners*. 1987. (Portrait.)

A P B

PFEFFER, WILHELM Born at Grebenstein, near Cassel, Hessen, Germany, 9 March 1845; died Leipzig, 31 January 1920. Botanist.

Pfeffer, son of a pharmaceutical chemist, matriculated in 1863 at Göttingen, where he studied physics, chemistry and pharmacy. Intending to become a fully qualified pharmacologist, he studied pharmacy further at Marburg and at Würzburg, and at the latter met the plant physiologist, Julius SACHS, who influenced him to follow an academic career. He held several successive appointments: *Privatdozent* at the University and custodian of the Botanical Institute at Bonn (1873), professor of botany at the Universities of Basel (1877), Tübingen (1878), and finally Leipzig (1887), where he remained for the rest of his life. Sachs and Pfeffer were the pioneers of modern plant physiology; the former investigated photosynthesis and respiration in plants, whilst Pfeffer's studies on basic cell metabolism led to his classic work on osmotic pressure and its measurement. In 1877 he published *Osmotische Untersuchungen, Studien zur Zellmechanik*, which provided a foundation for more exact knowledge acquired later by others. His best-known work, *Pflanzenphysiologie*, first published in 1881 (revised 1897), was a standard authority for many years and was translated into English (1900–3). With Eduard STRASSBURGER he became in 1895 joint editor of *Die Jahrbücher für wissenshaftliche Botanik*.

He received honorary degrees from many universities and in 1897 was elected a Foreign Member of the Royal Society.

Nature, **105**, 302, 1920.
F. M. Andrews, *Plant Physiology*, **4**, 285, 1929.
Dictionary of Scientific Biography.
Bericht der deutschen botanischen Gesellschaft, **38**, 30, 1920. (Portrait.)
E. Bünning, *Wilhelm Pfeffer*. 1975. (Portrait.)

A P G

PFEIFFER, RICHARD FRIEDRICH JOHANNES Born at Zduny, Posen, Poland, 27 March 1858; died Bad Landeck, Silesia, 15 September 1945.

Pioneer bacteriologist and discoverer of bacteriolysis.

Pfeiffer, educated as a military surgeon in Berlin, graduated in 1880. He thereafter served in the Army as a bacteriologist until 1889, but from 1887 he worked with R. KOCH at the Institute for Hygiene in Berlin, where he became a professor in 1894. He was thereafter professor of hygiene at Königsberg (1899–1909), and in 1909 he was translated to the corresponding chair at Breslau, which he held until his retirement in 1926. He became a Foreign Member of the Royal Society in 1928.

In 1892 Pfeiffer discovered the 'influenza bacillus'. It is now known that the causal agent of influenza is a virus, though the bacillus affects the course of the disease. In 1896 he discovered the *Micrococcus catarrhalis*, a common organism in the pharynx. He traced the life-cycle of *Coccidium oviforme*, a parasite of rabbits (1892). That part of the life-cycle in man was then well known, but inoculation of volunteers with malarial blood had failed to produce the disease. On the basis of his work on coccidia, Pfeiffer correctly predicted that a then unknown phase of the malaria parasite occurs outside the human body.

In 1894 Pfeiffer found that if a guinea-pig is immunized against cholera, live cholera vibrios can be injected into it without ill effects. He then withdrew a drop of the animal's body fluid and examined it microscopically; he observed that the vibrios became motionless and gradually disintegrated. Other organisms that resembled the cholera vibrio in appearance were not similarly affected. Pfeiffer called this action 'bacteriolysis'. He showed that it took place also *in vitro*, and that the power of the injected animal's serum to produce lysis was abolished by heating. This result, known as 'Pfeiffer's phenomenon', had far-reaching effects on the progress of immunology.

Obituary Notices of Fellows of the Royal Society, 1956. (Portrait.)

W. Bulloch, *History of Bacteriology*. 1938. (Portrait.)

H. J. Parish, *History of Immunization*. 1965.

E A U

PHILLIPS, PEREGRINE Born at Bristol, England, about 1800; date and place of death unknown. In 1831, patented the contact process for the manufacture of sulphuric acid.

Peregrine Phillips's fame rests upon a single invention, but one that eventually proved of major industrial importance. Very little is known of his origins, and nothing whatever of his later life. He was the son of Peregrine Phillips, a Bristol tailor, who became a Burgess of the City in 1790, and in 1824 joined with John Thorne in establishing a vinegar manufactory. His sons George and Peregrine both became members of the firm. In 1832 the vinegar partnership was dissolved; though he must still have been a young man, there is no subsequent record of Peregrine Phillips, junior.

In 1831, the younger Peregrine took out a patent for manufacturing sulphuric acid by passing sulphur dioxide and oxygen over finely divided platinum. The wording of the patent suggests that he had a good technical knowledge, but how he acquired this is unknown. The process was not, in fact, worked until near the end of the century,

when it became of particular importance as a source of oleum (fuming sulphuric acid) for the then rapidly growing synthetic dyestuffs industry. Today, well over half the world's sulphuric acid – one of the most important of all industrial chemicals – is made by what is essentially Peregrine Phillips's process.

E. Cook, *Nature*, **117**, 419, 1926.

Dictionary of National Biography (Missing Persons). 1993.

T I W

PIAZZI, GIUSEPPE Born at Ponte di Valtellina, Italy, 16 July 1746; died Naples, 22 July 1826. Discovered first minor planet.

Piazzi entered the Theatine Order in 1764 and turned to astronomy relatively late in life. Created professor of mathematics at Palermo (1780), he persuaded the Bourbon rulers of Naples to found observatories there and at Palermo. He spent three years at the observatories of Paris and Greenwich, purchasing, while in England (1788), a five-foot vertical circle/altazimuth, made by Jesse RAMSDEN. With this he measured star positions with unprecedented accuracy, and his catalogue of 7646 stars (observed 1792–1813) won him international renown. It proved the existence of proper motions beyond all doubt. He also discovered the very large proper motion of the star 61 Cygni.

In January 1801 Piazzi discovered the first minor planet, which he named Ceres. The planet was subsequently lost until later located by Baron von Zach, (1754–1832) working from the calculations of its position made by K. F. GAUSS based on perturbation theory. Piazzi corresponded with William HERSCHEL on the nature of Ceres, who wrongly tried to persuade him that the object did not have planetary status.

G. Abetti, *The History of Astronomy*, 1954.

Enciclopedia Italiana, 1933.

Dictionary of Scientific Biography.

J D N

PICARD, JEAN Born at La Flèche, France, 21 July 1620; died Paris, 12 July 1682. Astronomer, remembered for his measurements of the French meridian.

Jean Picard turned to astronomy early in life, although he entered the Church, becoming Prior of Rillé, in Anjou. A correspondent of P. GASSENDI from 1645, he replaced him as professor of astronomy at the Collège de France in 1655. Picard was made member of the Academy of Sciences in 1660. In 1671 he was sent to Hveen to determine the geographical position of Uraniborg (see Tycho BRAHE), bringing back with him some of Tycho's manuscripts.

Picard made many small inventions. He applied telescopic sights to the quadrant and other instruments; he introduced the astronomical use of pendulum clocks; he improved the micrometer of William Gascoigne (*d.* 1644) placing cross-wires at the prime focus. In 1680 he stated, as a result of ten years' observation, that the Pole Star varies its position by up to forty seconds of arc annually. Some astronomers tried to explain this in terms of parallax, but the true explanation, in terms of aberration, had to wait for James BRADLEY. His most important work, however, relates to the measurement of the meridian. In 1669 he performed a triangulation between Malvoisine near Paris and Sourdon near Amiens. He found the length of the degree to be 57 060 toises (69.104 miles). This figure, much more accurate than anything previously known, was used by NEWTON in comparing the fall of bodies at the surface of the Earth with what he called the 'fall' of the Moon towards the Earth.

Picard was a pioneer in the standardization of a unit of length. He proposed, as a unit, the length of a pendulum beating one second at sea-level, at a latitude of 45 degrees. His suggestion was not adopted, but it was reconsidered for a time towards the end of the eighteenth century, when the National Assembly appointed the commission which eventually decided upon the present metric system.

D. F. J. Arago, *Notices Biographiques*, vol. 3. 1855.
A. Armitage, *Endeavour*, **13**, 17, 1954.
J. L. E. Dreyer, *Nature*, **106**, 350, 1920.
Dictionary of Scientific Biography.

J D N

PICCARD, AUGUSTE Born at Basle, Switzerland, 28 January 1884; died Lausanne, 25 March 1962. Famous explorer of the stratosphere and ocean depths.

The son of a professor at Basle University and twin brother of Jean Piccard, he was educated at Basle and Zürich. After teaching at Zürich from 1907, in 1922 he became professor of physics at Brussels Polytechnic Institute. During the Second World War he worked in Switzerland, but returned to Brussels afterwards, remaining until 1954.

In 1913 the Piccard brothers made a sixteen-hour balloon ascent from Zürich, and in 1915 joined the balloon section of the Swiss Army. By 1930 Auguste had developed an airtight gondola suspended from a hydrogen-filled balloon. In this he reached record heights of 51 961 feet (from Augsburg, 26–27 May 1931) and 53 139 feet (from Zürich, 18 August 1932). Data were collected on cosmic rays and atmospheric electricity and radioactivity. The ascents gained Piccard a gold medal from the Belgian Aero Club. Further experiments were hampered by lack of money and the deterioration of the balloon.

Turning to submarine research, Piccard devised a bathyscaphe, an airtight chamber which, unlike previous apparatus, had no cable attached, but was suspended from a heptane-filled hydrostat. Following an unsuccessful attempt in 1948, Piccard and his son Jacques reached a record depth of 10 335 feet in this device off Capri in 1953. In 1960 another of Piccard's bathyscaphes descended to 35 802 feet off Guam. Piloted by Jacques and an American submarine officer, the craft regained the record which had meanwhile passed to the French. The US Navy bought a bathyscaphe in 1958.

The Times, 26 March 1962. (Portrait.)
A. Piccard, *In Balloon and Bathyscaphe*. 1956. (Portraits.)
A. Field, *Auguste Piccard.* 1969.

C A R

PICKERING, EDWARD CHARLES Born at Boston, Massachusetts, USA, 19 July 1846; died Cambridge, Massachusetts, 3 February 1919. Astronomer.

E. C. Pickering was educated at Harvard and became professor of physics in the Massachusetts Institute of Technology. In 1877 he was appointed Director of the Harvard Observatory, holding this post until 1919. He was assisted by his brother, W. H. PICKERING.

His major contribution was to introduce the meridian photometer to measure the magnitude of stars. Under his direction a photographic library of 300 000 plates was compiled, recording all stars down to the eleventh magnitude. The precise magnitude of 80 000 individual stars was measured. In 1891 a Southern Observatory was established at Arequipa in Peru so that the stars of the southern hemisphere could be included. He was also a pioneer of stellar spectroscopy.

Proceedings of the American Academy of Arts and Science, **57**, 502, 1922.
H. S. Williams, *Great Astronomers*. 1930. (Portrait.)
Dictionary of American Biography.
Dictionary of Scientific Biography.

T I W

PICKERING, WILLIAM HENRY Born at Boston, Massachusetts, USA, 15 February 1858; died Maudeville, Jamaica, 17 January 1938. Astronomer.

W. H. Pickering was a graduate of the Massachusetts Institute of Technology. In 1887 he joined the Department of Astronomy at Harvard, and became assistant to his brother, E. C. PICKERING. With him he worked on the great Harvard collection of star photographs. He made a notable contribution to stellar spectroscopy by devising a method of recording the spectra of stars in groups instead of individually. For a time he was Director of the associated Southern Hemisphere Observatory at Arequipa, Peru, and then directed a third observatory at Maudeville, Jamaica.

With P. LOWELL he made many observations of Mars. He turned his attention also to Saturn and in 1899 discovered its ninth moon, Phoebe. In 1905 he announced the discovery of a tenth (Themis), but this has not been confirmed.

H. S. Williams, *Great Astronomers*. 1930. (Portrait.)
H. MacPherson, *Astronomers of Today and their Work*. 1905.
E. P. Martz, *Popular Astronomy*, **46**, 299, 1938.
Dictionary of Scientific Biography.

T I W

PICTET, AMÉ Born in Geneva, 12 July 1857; died there, 12 March 1937. Famous for his syntheses of alkaloids.

The son of a banker, Pictet was professor of chemistry at Geneva. After studies of tartrate esters and phenanthridine syntheses, he became interested in alkaloids, on which he wrote a book (1888); he synthesized nicotine (1903), laudanosine (1909), and papaverine (1909). Abandoning this field because of its expense, he became the first to study 'low temperature' coal-tar. Led by this work to attempt pyrolysis of starch and cellulose, he obtained surprisingly large amounts of 'laevoglucosan' (1:6, anhydro-β-D-glucopyranose). This discovery directed him to carbohydrate research, where he achieved further syntheses, including that of maltose. A claim in 1929 to have synthesized sucrose (sugar) was not substantiated by others.

The doyen of Swiss chemistry, Pictet was Secretary of the 1892 Geneva Congress of Organic

Nomenclature, and a founder of the Swiss Chemical Society.

Nature, **139**, 661, 1937.
Journal of the Chemical Society, 1113, 1938. (Portrait.)
Amé Pictet, Souvenirs et travaux d'un chimiste. 1941.

C A R

PICTET, RAOUL PIERRE Born in Geneva, 4 April 1846; died Paris, 27 July 1929. The first to produce liquid oxygen in bulk.

Pictet worked at Geneva, where in 1879 he became professor of physics. He moved to Berlin in 1886 and later to Paris. On 24 December 1877 independent communications from Pictet in Geneva and L. P. CAILLETET in Paris reported the preparation of liquid oxygen, each deducing from the work of T. ANDREWS that cooling as well as compression was necessary for liquefaction of the 'permanent gases' with low critical temperatures. Pictet evaporated liquid sulphur dioxide to reduce the temperature sufficiently to liquefy carbon dioxide; evaporation of this cooled oxygen below its critical temperature and application of pressure produced considerable quantities of liquid oxygen (Cailletet's amounts were much smaller).

Pictet continued to study low-temperature phenomena at Berlin, using his 'cascade method'. He wrote on this subject, on acetylene, and on psychic phenomena.

J. C. Poggendorf, Biographisch-literarisches Handwörterbuch. 1883–1903.
W. R. Woolrich, The Man Who Created Cold. 1967.
Dictionary of Scientific Biography.

C A R

PINCUS, GREGORY GOODWIN Born at Woodbine, New Jersey, USA, 9 April 1903; died Boston, Massachusetts, 22 August 1967. Endocrinologist; developed first oral contraceptive pill.

Pincus was descended from Russian Jewish farmers on both sides of his family, and he graduated in agriculture from Cornell University, New York, in 1924. After obtaining his doctorate in science from Harvard University in 1927 he studied at Cambridge University and at the Kaiser Wilhelm Institute in Berlin before returning to Harvard as a lecturer in biology in 1930. In 1931 he became an assistant professor in the physiology department at Harvard.

During the 1930s Pincus studied fertilization, and working with rabbits demonstrated that ova could be grown in culture and transplanted into host mothers. He became famous as the first person to produce 'fatherless' rabbits. His pioneering work, The Eggs of Mammals, was published in 1936.

In 1944 Pincus and H. Hoagland (1899–) founded the Worcester Foundation for Experimental Biology in Shrewsbury, Massachusetts, with Pincus as research director. The research was devoted mainly to studying the role of steroid hormones in reproduction. It was already known that progesterone prevented ovulation during pregnancy, but no work had been done on using it to control fertility. By the early 1950s Pincus had seen the possibilities for developing synthetic progesterone compounds to be used as oral contraceptives. In 1951 he met Margaret Sanger, founder of the American Birth Control League, who was look-

ing for a foolproof method of contraception. Encouraged by her, and with the backing of G. D. Searle and Company, for which Pincus already acted as consultant, he recruited M. C. Chang (1908–1991) to head a research team to see whether steroid compounds would act as contraceptives when taken orally by animals. From 1953 the wealthy feminist Katharine McCormick gave Pincus large sums of money, which enabled him to enlist the help of John Rock (1890–1984) to organise clinical trials to see if progesterone compounds would prevent pregnancy in women. Large scale trials in Puerto Rico in 1956 were highly successful, and in 1960 Searle marketed the first contraceptive pills, the first new contraceptives to be developed in the 20th century.

G. G. Pincus, The Control of Fertility. 1965.
O. Hechter, Perspectives in Biology and Medicine, **11**, No. 3, 1968. (Portrait.)
James Reed, From Private Vice to Public Virtue. The Birth Control Movement and American Society since 1830. 1978.

A P B

PIXII, HIPPOLYTE Born in France, 1808; died 1835. Constructor of the first practical magnetoelectric machine.

Like his father, Hippolyte Pixii was an instrument-maker. Following FARADAY'S announcement to the Royal Society (24 November 1831) of his discovery of electromagnetic induction and description of the first simple dynamo, Pixii constructed a hand-driven electric generator in which the field magnet revolved with respect to the coils. This machine was exhibited to the Académie des Sciences on 3 September 1832. In its original form it generated alternating current, but soon afterwards he fitted, at the suggestion of A. M. AMPÈRE, a commutator which converted this to direct current, in which there was then much greater interest.

Pixii's machine was brought over to England in November 1833 by Count de Predevalli and placed in the Adelaide Gallery, together with another machine which Saxton had just demonstrated to the British Association at Cambridge.

Though Pixii's machine was little more than a working model, it can fairly be described as the first practical electric generator based on Faraday's principle.

Percy Dunsheath, A History of Electrical Engineering. 1962.

W H G A

PLANCK, MAX CARL ERNST LUDWIG Born at Kiel, Germany, 23 April 1858; died Göttingen, 3 October 1947. Celebrated for his enunciation of the quantum theory.

Planck was descended, like J. Clerk MAXWELL, from a long line of scholars, lawyers, and public servants. He attended the Maximilian Gymnasium at Munich where he received his first scientific inspiration. Deciding on a career in physics as opposed to classical philology or music (a subject to which he remained devoted all his life, becoming an excellent pianist) he studied for three years at Munich before transferring to Berlin, to work under H. L. F. von HELMHOLTZ and G. R. KIRCHOFF, being influenced, however, more by their writings than by their lectures. At this point he began also to be influenced by the thermodynamical papers of

R. J. E. CLAUSIUS, with whom he unsuccessfully tried to establish a correspondence. His doctoral thesis (Munich, 1879) was on the second law of thermodynamics and contained certain criticisms of Clausius's definition of irreversibility. In 1880 he became *Privatdozent* at the University of Munich, but it was not until 1885 that he obtained his first university appointment as Extraordinary Professor of Theoretical Physics at Kiel. On Kirchhoff's death he was appointed professor of theoretical physics at Berlin, being promoted Ordinary Professor in 1892. The remainder of his life was spent in Berlin. He resigned from his chair there in 1928, being succeeded by E. SCHRÖDINGER. He was awarded a Nobel prize for physics in 1918, and became a Foreign Member of the Royal Society in 1926.

From 1880 to 1892 Planck published a series of fundamental papers on thermodynamics later collected together in his celebrated *Vorlesungen über Thermodynamik* (1897), which included a general outline of the theory of chemical equilibrium based on the so-called thermodynamical potentials, together with discussions of dissociation in gases, of osmotic pressure, and of the lowering of the freezing point in solutions.

Planck's interest in the subject of heat radiation was first aroused by experimental work carried out at the *Physikalisch-Technische Reichsanstalt* at Berlin-Charlottenburg. Through this he learnt of the theoretical investigation of black-body radiation in which Kirchhoff had shown that the equilibrium ultimately reached within a heated cavity depended only on the temperature, being independent of the wall material. Attracted by the extraordinary generality of this result, Planck determined (1896) to provide a theoretical explanation, his investigations being carried out in close co-operation with the experimental work at the *Reichsanstalt*.

In a series of great papers from 1897 to 1901, Planck gradually realized his ambition. Since Kirchhoff had proved that the nature of the wall substance was immaterial, Planck made the simplest possible choice of electrically charged linear oscillators with proper frequencies and small damping, expecting to find the resulting exchange of energy by emission and absorption would eventually lead to the required equilibrium. But although the result obtained was independent of the damping of the oscillators, Planck was disappointed in his hope that the oscillators would produce an exchange of energy between the different frequencies. He therefore mounted a new attack based on thermodynamical considerations in which he regarded the internal energy as a function of the entropy rather than the temperature. By an historic interpolation of the radiation law of W. WIEN, valid at high frequency and low temperature, and the formula of Rayleigh-Jeans, valid at low frequency and high temperature, Planck then obtained a new radiation formula in excellent agreement with experiment. A satisfying physical explanation remained however to be found. By applying the relation between entropy and probability enunciated by L. BOLTZMANN, Planck found himself forced to introduce his quantum of action, h, with its correlative of a discrete spectrum for radiation. There resulted his celebrated formula for radiation density as a function of frequency and temperature, from which he was able to calculate Boltzmann's constant and his own quantum of action.

Planck, like Einstein, could never accept the acausality of quantum mechanics as more than a transitory feature in the advance to a more satisfactory theory. He remained intellectually creative up to a great age, attempting a synthesis between undulatory and corpuscular concepts as late as 1940. Through his long life he had to endure many bereavements, of which the most cruel was the loss of his son Erwin, executed by the Nazis in 1944 for his part in the July plot against Hitler. All this he bore with a quiet fortitude in the best traditions of his class and race.

M. Planck, *Autobiography* (English trans. F. Gayner). 1949.

Obituary Notices of Fellows of the Royal Society. 1948.

Lise Meitner, *Naturwissenschaften*, **45**, 406, 1948.

Tyler Wasson, (Ed.), *Nobel Prize Winners*. 1987. (Portrait.)

Dictionary of Scientific Biography.

J W H

PLAYFAIR, JOHN Born at Benvie, near Dundee, Scotland, 10 March 1748; died Edinburgh, 20 July 1819. Mathematician, physicist, geologist.

John Playfair was the eldest son of James Playfair, minister of Liff and Benvie, Forfarshire. At the age of 14 he went to the University of St Andrews to prosecute general studies and qualify for the ministry. Here he at once showed remarkable mathematical ability. In 1769 he left St Andrews for Edinburgh. In 1772 the death of his father necessitated his supporting the rest of the family, and he was presented with the living of Liff and Benvie, which he held for ten years. In 1782 he resigned his living and until 1787 was tutor in a private family. In 1785 he was appointed to a professorship of mathematics in the University of Edinburgh, a post he held for twenty years. He published various biographical, mathematical, and physical papers with the Royal Society of Edinburgh – whose *Transactions* he edited for many years – and his *Elements of Geometry* appeared in 1795.

In 1797 his friend James HUTTON died, and this caused him to devote himself to a careful analysis, clarification and amplification of his work. This resulted, in 1802, in the *Illustrations of the Huttonian Theory of the Earth*, one of the most conspicuous landmarks in the progress of British geology. In 1805 he left the Mathematical Chair in Edinburgh to occupy that of natural philosophy, so that his lectures now embraced physics and astronomy; in 1814 he published his textbook on these subjects, *Outlines of Natural Philosophy*. In the *Encyclopaedia Britannica* in 1816 was published his important essay on the history of mathematical and physical science. Another project was also very much in his mind, the preparation of a comprehensive work on geology, which was to have been a greatly amplified edition of his *Illustrations* of 1802. The peace of 1815 enabled him to make, at the age of 68, an extensive tour through France, Switzerland and Italy, to extend his observations for this purpose; but although we have details of the journey, unfortunately nothing of the projected work was composed.

Dictionary of National Biography.

A. Geikie, *The Founders of Geology*. 1905.
Dictionary of Scientific Biography.

J C

PLAYFAIR, LYON (FIRST BARON PLAYFAIR)
Born at Meerut, India, 21 May 1818; died London, 29 May 1898. Chemist.

Playfair was the son of George Playfair, Chief Inspector-General of Bengal. He was educated in Scotland (St Andrews, Edinburgh) and Germany (Giessen); like many other chemists of his time, his professional qualifications were in medicine. In 1843 he became honorary professor of chemistry in the Royal Institution, Manchester, where he became a friend of John DALTON and J. P. JOULE; for a time he was associated with John MERCER in a textile enterprise. In 1845 he became chemist to the Geological Survey and professor of chemistry in the newly founded School of Mines in London. In 1858 he returned to Edinburgh as professor of chemistry – where A. S. COUPER was for a time his assistant – holding this post for ten years. Increasing interest in political affairs led him to active participation. From 1868 to 1885 he was Liberal MP for the Universities of Edinburgh and St Andrews; from 1885 to 1892 he represented South Leeds. He held various Government offices, including that of Postmaster-General (1873) and Deputy Speaker of the House of Commons (1880–3). In 1892 he was raised to the peerage. He was Vice-President of the Council and Lord-in-waiting to Queen Victoria. He was elected FRS in 1848 and was President of the Chemical Society 1857–9.

Playfair's contributions to chemistry were not inconsiderable. The topics he investigated included blast-furnace reactions (with R. W. E. BUNSEN; catalysis (with Mercer); atomic volumes (with Joule); and the dissociation of nitrogen peroxide (with J. A. Wanklyn (1834–1906)). He made important contributions to the chemistry of nitroprussides, and worked on fatty acids. It is, however, as a statesman of science that Playfair was outstandingly important, and in this respect he resembled Sir Joseph BANKS. His connections with the court (especially with Prince Albert), with all the leading political figures of the day, and with the chief men of science both in Britain and on the Continent gave him unparalleled powers for advancing the cause of science and technology. He played a leading part in organizing the Great Exhibition of 1851 and was among the few who realized that – despite her overwhelming successes – this marked the end of an era for Britain and not the beginning. The Paris Exhibition of 1867, where Britain was conspicuously unsuccessful, showed how right he was. He realized the vital role of science and technology in education – a point already noted by leading Continental rivals, especially Germany – and devoted much effort to bringing about the necessary educational reforms in Britain.

W. Reid, *Memoirs and Correspondence of Sir Lyon Playfair*. 1899.
A. Scott, *Journal of the Chemical Society*, 600, 1905.
H. E. Roscoe, *Nature*, **58**, 128, 1898.
R. G. W. Norrish, *Journal of the Royal Society of Arts*, **99**, 537, 1950.
Dictionary of National Biography.

T I W

PLINUS SECUNDUS, GAIUS *See* PLINY.

PLINY (GAIUS PLINUS SECUNDUS, PLINY THE ELDER)
Born at Como, Italy, AD 23; perished (while watching an eruption of Vesuvius), AD 79. Scientific encyclopaedist; author of a great Natural History.

Pliny was educated in Rome; saw service as cavalry officer, colonial administrator, and naval commander; and practised at the bar.

The *Naturalis Historia* is an encyclopaedic but uncritical compilation derived in the main from a wide range of selected authors often cited with imperfect understanding. Yet it is informed with a keen, unprejudiced curiosity and vivified in places by original observation, and it has preserved for us much valuable information, particularly as to the technical arts of antiquity. The work is divided into thirty-seven Books, each with its list of supporting authorities; the arrangement is briefly as follows:

I Dedication and contents.
II Astronomy and physiography.
III–VI Gazetteer of the inhabited Earth.
VII The nature of man; invention of the arts.
VIII The land animals, both wild and domesticated, and their products.
IX Aquatic animals; their physiology and economic uses.
X Birds and their domestication. Animals in general; their nutritive, sensory, and reproductive physiology, sleep, and social behaviour.
XI Insects, their anatomy, physiology and behaviour; the silk industry. Comparative animal and human morphology.
XII Trees, their varieties, uses and products.
XIII Foreign trees and their products; manufacture of paper. Submarine vegetation.
XIV Vine-growing; the different kinds of wine and their manufacture; beer.
XV The olive; production of olive and other oils. Fruit trees and the storage of fruit.
XVI Forest trees; their uses and products; insect pests and parasitic plants.
XVII Trees as affected by aspect, climate and soil; use of manures; rearing trees from seed; transplanting; grafting and pruning; diseases and medication of trees.
XVIII Cultivation of cereals; history of Roman agriculture; astronomical basis of rules for sowing; weather signs.
XIX Cultivation and processing of flax; textiles. Vegetable gardening.
XX–XXVII Dietetic and medical uses of plants and trees.
XXVIII–XXX Remedies derived from animals. Charms and magic cures.
XXXI–XXXII Remedies derived from aquatic animals. Medicinal waters and salts.
XXXIII–XXXIV Metals, their production and uses. Bronze statuary.
XXXV History of painting. Pigments and earths.
XXXVI Marbles and stones. History of sculpture, architecture, and public works.
XXXVII Gemstones and amber.

Pliny, *Natural History* (Loeb Classical Library, 10 vols). 1938–63.
Dictionary of Scientific Biography.

A A

PLÜCKER, JULIUS
Born at Elberfeld, Wuppertal, Germany, 16 June 1801; died Bonn, North Rhine-

Westphalia, 22 May 1868. Mathematician and physicist.

Plücker became *Privatdozent* in the University of Bonn in 1825 and was appointed professor four years later. In 1833 he became professor in a gymnasium in Berlin, but moved in the following year to take up a professorship in the University of Halle. In 1836 he returned to Bonn, as professor of mathematics; in 1847 he was appointed professor of physics. He was elected Foreign Member of the Royal Society in 1855.

In mathematics, Plücker is remembered for his contributions to analytical geometry. His *Theorie der algebräischen Curven* was published in 1839. Later he made an important contribution to the analytical geometry of space (*System der Geometrie des Raumes in neuer analytischer Behandlungsweise*, 1846). His six equations of higher plane curves are also well known. He contributed to the geometry of space.

In physics he investigated experimentally the luminous effects of electric discharge through gases at low pressures (1858). He observed that the glow was deflected in a strong magnetic field.

A. Dronke, *Julius Plücker*. 1871.

C. I. Gerhardt, *Geschichte der Mathematik in Deutschland*.

R. F. A. Clebsch, *Abhandlungen der kaiserlichen Gesellschaft der Wissenschaften zu Göttingen*, **16**, x, 1871.

W. Ernst, *Julius Plücker*. 1933.

Dictionary of Scientific Biography.

T I W

POGGENDORF, JOHANN CHRISTIAN Born at Hamburg, Germany, 29 December 1796; died Berlin, 24 January 1877. Remembered chiefly for his work in electricity, and as biographer.

Poggendorf began work as a pharmacist in 1812. In 1820 he went to Berlin, where he studied physics and became (1834) Extraordinary Professor. His first paper (1821) describes his invention of the galvanometer. He also devised a magnetometer (1827) and the use of brass screws for making electrical connections (1840.) His 'compensation method' for determining electromotive force appeared in 1841. Other studies included work on diffusion, light vibrations, and thermometry. In chemistry, Poggendorf collaborated with J. von LIEBIG, for whom he invented the word 'aldehyde' and with whom he introduced subscript figures into formulae (as H_2O).

Poggendorf contributed powerfully to the renaissance of post-Napoleonic German science, especially as the Editor of *Annalen der Physik und Chemie* from 1824. His notable *Biographisch-literarisches Handwörterbuch* was begun in 1863 and still continues.

Nature, **15**, 314, 1877.

J. R. Partington, *A History of Chemistry*, vol. 4. 1964.

H. Salié, *Isis*, **57**, 389, 1966.

Dictionary of Scientific Biography.

C A R

POINCARÉ, JULES HENRI Born at Nancy, France, 29 April 1854; died Paris, 17 July 1912. Eminent French mathematician, active in most fields.

Poincaré was educated at the *lycée* in Nancy. In 1873 he attended the *École Polytechnique*, then the *École des Mines*, where he qualified as a mining engineer in 1879 with a thesis on the properties of functions defined by partial differential equations. His interest developed in the work of C. Hermite (1822–1901) and the application of non-Euclidean geometry to the theory of quadratic forms. His recognition came when he published (1880) his work on Abelian functions and the generalization to Fuchsian functions, using JACOBI's theta functions.

In that year he appointed an instructor at Caen University, followed in 1881 by appointment as lecturer at the Paris *Faculté des Sciences*. Each year he lectured on a different subject, ranging over most of applied mathematics. He shed new light on most of these subjects and developed ideas on both mathematical techniques and pure mathematics. He published important work on the properties of integral curves of differential equations and the behaviour of solutions near singular points of such systems.

His lectures in 1893–4 on probability theory formed the basis of the book *Leçons sur le calcul des probabilités* (1895); it contained a fundamental exposition of modern ergodic theory.

His work on celestial mechanics led to investigations of the behaviour of divergent and non-uniformly convergent series, which in turn led to a foundation of the theory of asymptotic expansions, and to the study of integral invariants, quadratic forms, and double integrals of periodic orbits. In the physical sciences he was active in the work on electromagnetic theory; he pictured the Poynting vector (see J. H. POYNTING) as an 'electromagnetic momentum'.

He was the author of a number of more general works, e.g. *La Science et l'Hypothèse* (1906) in which he propounded a relativistic philosophy, it being a matter of convenience in Newtonian mechanics that fixed axes are assumed to exist. 'It is impossible', he said, 'to avoid the impression that the principle of relativity is a general law of nature and that we shall never be able, by any conceivable means, to demonstrate anything but relative velocities.'

Already in 1899 he had declared that absolute motion is indetectable in principle in *Electricité et Optique* (1901). In his lectures in 1904 in the United States he named his thesis *Principle of Relativity*. The Lorentz transformations (see H. A. LORENTZ) constitute the transformation group which describe the electromagnetic laws. In *Aether and Matter* (1900) he remarks that one consequence is that nothing can exceed the velocity of light.

Poincaré's contributions to science were recognized by his appointment as Member of the *Académie des Sciences* in 1887 and of the *Académie Française* in 1909. The Royal Society elected him a Foreign Member in 1894.

E. Lebon, *Henri Poincaré*. 1909.

G. Sarton, *Isis*, **1**, 95, 1913.

J. S. Hadamard, *The Early Scientific Work of Henri Poincaré*. 1922; *The Later Scientific Work of Henri Poincaré*. 1933.

Proceedings of the Royal Society, **91A**, vi, 1915.

Dictionary of Scientific Biography.

D N

POISSON, SIMÉON DENIS Born at Pithiviers,

Loiret, France, 21 June 1781; died Sceaux, 25 April 1840. Celebrated for his theoretical contributions to electricity and magnetism.

Poisson's mathematical powers were first awakened through reading the journal of the *École Polytechnique* which was sent to his father as leader of the local commune. In 1798 he headed the list at the *École Polytechnique*, where his genius for mathematics was quickly recognized by J. L. LAGRANGE, whose course in analysis he attended. In 1800, he was appointed demonstrator at the *École*, and in 1802 became assistant to J. B. J. FOURIER, whose chair he assumed when the latter became *Préfet* at Isère. In 1808 he was appointed astronomer at the *Bureau des Longitudes* and in 1812 became a member of the *Académie des Sciences*. He was appointed mathematician at the *Bureau des Longitudes* in succession to LAPLACE in 1827.

In his fundamental memoir of 1812 Poisson adopted a two-fluid theory of electricity, (cf. J. A. NOLLET) in which like fluids repelled and unlike attracted according to the inverse square law. An equal and uniform distribution of both fluids represented the natural state of a body which became electrified positively or negatively on the disturbance of this distribution. Taking over mathematical results from the theory of gravitational attraction, including Lagrange's potential function, Poisson showed that this function would be constant over the surface of an insulated conductor. Acting on a suggestion of Laplace, he gave an ingenious proof of the formula for the force at the surface of a charged conductor. He also gave solutions to various problems, including the calculation of the surface densities of charge for two spherical conductors placed at any distance apart, his theoretical results being in excellent agreement with those already obtained experimentally by C. A. de COULOMB. In an equally fundamental paper of 1824 Poisson gave a wonderfully complete theory of magnetism based on Coulomb's two-fluid model deriving a general expression for the magnetic potential at any point as the sum of two integrals due to volume and surface distributions of magnetism respectively. He also investigated the problem of induced magnetism.

Apart from his work in electricity and magnetism, Poisson made important contributions to the calculus of variations, to differential geometry, and to probability theory, in which he is remembered by the distribution bearing his name. He contributed also to the theory of elasticity, in which field the ratio of lateral contraction to longitudinal extension is known as Poisson's ratio. He also contributed to the theories of capillarity, heat and dispersion. In astronomy, he wrote many important memoirs, especially that of 1833 on the movement of the Moon.

D. F. J. Arago, *Notice* in *Oeuvres de Poisson*, vol. 2. 1854–62.

Dictionary of Scientific Biography.

J W H

POLHAMMER, CHRISTOPHER See POLHEM.

POLHEM (originally **POLHAMMER**), **CHRISTOPHER** Born at Gotland, Sweden, 18 December 1661; died Stockholm, 30 August 1751. Inventor and industrialist.

Left fatherless at 10, Polhem earned the cost of Latin lessons by clock-making and entered Uppsala University to study mathematics at the age of 26. His design for a water-driven ore hoist brought him into the royal service as a mining engineer, and in 1694–7 he was sent to study engineering techniques in Germany, the Netherlands, France and England. On his return he was given charge of an experimental *laboratorium mechanicum*, which provided a great stimulus to Swedish technology; some of its findings were published by the French Academy of Sciences. One of Polhem's devices conveyed power from a waterwheel across 1½ miles of broken country. In 1712 he constructed the dock at the Karlskrona naval base, and he began the canal link between Gothenburg and the Baltic, on which work was, however, suspended when the sea route was reopened by the treaty of Nystadt (1721). Polhem was employed by George I on a mint and mining works in Hanover; both he and Peter the Great of Russia tried in vain to persuade him to migrate from Sweden, where he was ennobled in 1716.

In 1700 Polhem established his own works at Stjärnsund, where waterpower was used to operate grooved rollers, shearing machines, and other advanced equipment for metal fabrication. Articles were made for agricultural, domestic, military and industrial uses, but the best-known products were clocks and locks. The writings of Emanuel SWEDENBORG, who was a pupil at Stjärnsund in 1715, are believed to express many philosophic ideas which had engaged Polhem's interest. He gave up the works in 1735; became one of the first presidents of the Swedish Academy of Science; and was widely acclaimed as 'the father of Swedish mechanics'.

Works, published in four vols., Uppsala, 1947–54; those connected with the Swedish copper mines, edited (with German summary) by S. Lindroth. 1951.
J. G. A. Rhodin, *Transactions of the Newcomen Society*, **7**, 17, 1926–7.
Svenska Teknologförenigen, *Christopher Polhem, the Father of Swedish Technology*. 1963. (Trans. from the Swedish.)

T K D

PONCELET, JEAN VICTOR Born at Metz, France, 1 July 1788; died Paris, 22 December 1867. Mathematician and hydraulic engineer.

Poncelet was admitted to the *École Polytechnique* in 1807, and left in 1810 for the *École d'application* at Metz before serving on the Isle of Walcheren and in Russia. Left as dead on the battlefield at Krasnoi, he recuperated at Saratov on the Volga, and alleviated the rigours of imprisonment by studying the projective geometry of Gaspard MONGE. His papers from this period, published many years later as *Applications d'analyses et de geometrie* (1862 and 1864), contain (in the preface of the second volume) several revealing biographical asides. On his release in 1814, he returned to Metz, where he prepared the first volume of his *Traité des propriétés projectives des figures* (1822) – the second did not appear until 1866. Recalled to Paris in 1834 on admission to the *Académie des sciences*, Poncelet was, four years later, commissioned to establish a course in applied mechanics. He became colonel in 1845,

general in 1848, and, in the same year, commandant of the *École Polytechnique.*

Poncelet became much interested in the
improvement of waterwheels and turbines, and
applied his mathematical knowledge for the purpose. In 1826 he proposed an inward-flow turbine,
though the first of this design does not appear to
have been constructed until twelve years later (in
New York). In 1827 he described experiments by
which he had more than doubled the efficiency of
the undershot waterwheel.

J. Bertrand, *Éloge historique de Poncelet.* 1875.

E. T. Bell, *Men of Mathematics.* 1937. (Portrait.)

H. Tribout, *Un grand savant: Le Général Jean
Victor Poncelet.* 1936.

Dictionary of Scientific Biography.

W H G A

POPE, SIR WILLIAM JACKSON Born in London,
31 March 1870; died Cambridge, 17 October 1939.
Organic chemist with special interest in stereochemistry.

William Pope came of a Nonconformist London
merchant family. He studied chemistry at Finsbury
Technical College and the City and Guilds College,
London, and in 1897 became head of the Chemistry Department of Goldsmiths' Institute. In 1901
he went to a similar post in the Municipal School
of Technology, Manchester, whose status was later
raised to a chair of chemistry in Manchester University. He was made professor of chemistry in
Cambridge in 1908, and held this post until his
death. He never married.

H. E. ARMSTRONG first interested Pope in problems
of stereochemistry and optical activity. Among his
early successes were resolutions of compounds in
which asymmetry was due to elements other than
carbon: nitrogen (1899), sulphur and tin (1900),
and selenium (1902). He also settled (1914), with
J. Read (1884–1963), the once disputed point that
compounds containing only one carbon atom
could be resolved. An important practical innovation was his use of the camphor-sulphonic acids
for the resolution of bases.

During the First World War, Pope devoted all
his energies to the technological side of the war
effort, especially to chemical warfare; this work
later became the subject of bitter professional
controversy. After the war, he resumed his stereochemical studies, but they were no longer in the
main stream of chemical progress, and the reputation of his school declined.

His numerous honours included FRS (1902) and
a knighthood (1919).

Journal of the Chemical Society, 697, 1941.
(Portrait.)

Nature, **144**, 810, 1939.

Obituary Notices of Fellows of the Royal Society.
1941. (Portrait.)

Dictionary of Scientific Biography.

Dictionary of National Biography.

W V F

**PORTER, GEORGE (BARON PORTER OF LUDDEN-
HAM)** Born at Stainforth, Yorkshire, England, 6
December 1920. Physical chemist.

Porter was educated at the University of Leeds
and Emmanuel College, Cambridge, under R. G. W.
NORRISH. From 1949 to 1954 he continued the
research begun with Norrish at Cambridge,

investigating the equilibrium between free chlorine
atoms and molecules. He became assistant
research director in physical chemistry at Cambridge in 1952. After a short period at the British
Rayon Research Association he went to the University of Sheffield as professor of physical chemistry
in 1955. He worked on flash photolysis and the
photochemistry of very fast reactions and in 1963
became Head of Department and Firth Professor.
In 1966 he was appointed Director and Fullerian
Professor of chemistry at the Royal Institution,
London in succession to Sir Lawrence BRAGG. Here
he continued his research and also maintained the
Institution's tradition for popular science lecture
demonstrations. In 1967, he received the Nobel
prize for chemistry jointly with R. G. W. NORRISH
and Manfred Eigen (1927–).

Elected FRS in 1960, Porter held several honorary and visiting professorships in Britain; he was
Fairchild Distinguished Scholar at the California
Institute of Technology, USA, in 1974 and Hitch-
cock Professor at the University of California,
Berkeley in 1978. Knighted for his contributions
to chemistry and chemical education in 1972, he
was President of the Royal Society of London,
1985–90, and was awarded its Copley Medal in
1992. He became a member of the Royal Order of
Merit and was created a life peer in 1990.

Les Prix Nobel en 1967. 1968. (Portrait.)

W. A. Campbell and N. N. Greenwood (Eds),
Contemporary British Chemists. 1971.
(Portrait.)

Tyler Wasson (Ed.), *Nobel Prize Winners.* 1987.
(Portrait.)

N G C

PORTER, RODNEY ROBERT Born at Newton-le-
Willows, Lancashire, England, 8 October 1917;
died Oxford, 6 September 1985. Protein chemist
and immunologist.

Porter was educated at Ashton-in-Makerfield
Grammar School, and graduated from Liverpool
University in 1939 with a BSc (Hons) degree in
biochemistry. After Army service (1939–45),
where he rose to the rank of Major, he went to
Cambridge where he took his PhD under the supervision of F. SANGER. It was at Cambridge that he
became interested in immunochemistry and
started to investigate the structure of antibodies.
In 1949 he joined the scientific staff of the National
Institute for Medical Research at Mill Hill. His particular interest was in chromatographic methods
of protein fractionation, but he returned to the
study of the chemical structure of antibodies, leading to the finding in 1958–9 of the three fragments
produced by splitting with papain. In 1960 he
became the first holder of the Pfeizer Professorship
of Immunology at St Mary's Hospital Medical
School (University of London), the first chair of
immunology to be created in the United Kingdom,
and continued with his research on the peptide
chain structure of antibodies for which he was
awarded the Nobel prize for medicine (jointly with
G. M. Edelman (1924–)) in 1972. In 1967, he was
appointed Whitley Professor of Biochemistry in
the University of Oxford and a Fellow of Trinity
College, Oxford. During his career he received
many honours, including Fellowship of the Royal
Society (1964), the Royal Medal (1972) and Copley
Medal (1983) of the Royal Society, Foreign

Membership of the National Academy of Sciences USA (1972), and the Companion of Honour (1985).

Dictionary of National Biography.

Les Prix Nobel −1972. 1973.

Tyler Wasson (Ed.), *Nobel Prize Winners.* 1987. (Portrait.)

Biographical Memoirs of Fellows of The Royal Society. 1987. (Portrait.)

J S W

POULSEN, VALDEMAR Born in Copenhagen, 23 November 1869; died there July 1942. Electrical engineer who patented in 1898 an audio 'tape recorder' using a steel wire as the recording medium.

Poulsen became technical adviser to the Copenhagen Telephone Company in 1893, and subsequently wrote a number of works on telephony and telegraphy. In 1903 he invented an arc for the production of high-frequency oscillations suitable for the transmission of high-power radio signals, which became known as the Poulsen arc. By the 1920s it had been developed to the point where it was in use by a number of long-wave radio transmitters at outputs of up to 1000kW.

He is best known for his invention of a device for the recording and reproduction of sounds by means of variations in the magnetic field applied along the length of a metal wire or ribbon, the forerunner of today's audio and video tape recorders. He was awarded the Grand Prix at Paris in 1900 for the prototype of his 'telegraphone', but the sound quality was not as good as EDISON's phonograph, and the machine and its wire 'tapes' were considerably heavier.

The basic theory had been worked out in 1888 by an Englishman, Oberlin Smith (1840−1926), who suggested the use of iron filings bonded to a fabric tape, but these ideas were far in advance of the materials and technology available at the time, and it proved to be impossible to produce a commercially satisfactory machine. It was not until after the Second World War that developments in thin plastic magnetic tapes, electronic amplifiers, and solid state circuitry were finally combined to make the tape recorder a practical proposition.

Current Biography, 671, 1942.

Revue d'Histoire des Sciences et de leurs Applications, **22**, 78, 1969.

D. Clarke (Ed.), *Great Inventors and Discoveries.*

R M B

POWELL, CECIL FRANK Born at Tonbridge, Kent, England, 5 December 1903; died Italy, 9 August 1969. Nobel Laureate; noted for his techniques and discoveries in particle physics.

Powell's parents were poor, and they were determined that their children should get a good education to increase their opportunities for a better life. His father and paternal grandfather were gunsmiths, and his mother was the daughter of a schoolmaster. Powell's family influences and boyhood experiences also stimulated his interest in working with his hands and his appreciation and knowledge of the countryside and its flora. After elementary school, he won a scholarship to the Judd School, Tonbridge, where he benefited from the guidance of an able and devoted physics teacher who exposed him to, among other original

experiments, the delights of home-made crystal sets for the reception of wireless signals.

In 1921 Powell won a scholarship to Sidney Sussex College, Cambridge, graduating in 1925 with first-class honours in science. He was then accepted as a research student in the Cavendish Laboratory by Ernest RUTHERFORD, who arranged for him to work under C. T. R. WILSON, renowned for his invention of the cloud chamber. Powell was asked to study whether operation of the chamber at different temperatures could produce improved photographs of the droplets formed in the gas along the trajectory of charged particles. The aim was to obtain better evidence of atomic phenomena essential for fundamental understanding of nuclear processes, but Powell's study led indirectly to a discovery of importance in practical engineering work. He showed that supersaturation in rapidly expanding steam explained the anomalous discharge rate of steam through nozzles, which was higher than seemed theoretically possible. His findings contributed to improvements in the design of steam turbines.

After gaining his PhD at Cambridge, Powell in 1928 accepted a position as research assistant to A. M. Tyndall (1881−1961), director of the new H. H. Wills Physics Laboratory in the University of Bristol. Powell spent the rest of his career there, advancing to professor in 1948 and director of the laboratory in 1964.

His first work was with Tyndall. They obtained precise values for the mobility of ions in gases, by developing instruments and techniques to reduce and control impurities. In 1935, the Bristol physics laboratory, like many others throughout the world, began to build facilities for experimental work in the rapidly developing field of nuclear physics and Powell started to construct a Cockcroft-Walton generator for acceleration of protons. The aim was to use the proton beam to disintegrate light elements and to study the resulting scattering of neutrons in a hydrogen-filled cloud chamber. Early in 1938, as the generator was being completed and the proton beam was obtained, Powell became concerned with a technique for detecting high-energy particles by the changes they produce in the grains of a photographic emulsion through which the particle moves. The technique had been used successfully by Austrian physicists to detect particles in cosmic radiation, and W. Heitler introduced their method at Bristol. Powell prepared a package of small photographic plates which were taken to the Jungfraujoch in the summer of 1938, where it was subjected to intense high-altitude cosmic rays. Months later, when the plates were retrieved and processed in the Bristol laboratory, the tracks on the plates provided clear evidence of nuclear disintegrations due to collisions of the incoming high energy particles with the nuclei in the emulsion.

The success of this and related experiments spurred Powell to use photographic emulsions to detect particle scattering in experiments with the Cockcroft-Walton generator. Direct recording of particle tracks in photographic emulsions was developed by Powell and his co-workers into a detection technique for the study of nuclear reactions which was simpler, faster, and more precise than the cloud-chamber technique then in general use. When Powell began to develop the photographic method in 1939 he was unaware that earlier workers had explored such possibilities and that most nuclear physicists were convinced that the method was not precise enough for work in nuclear physics.

The full potential of the photographic method was realized by Powell and his co-workers after the Second World War, through the development of new emulsions sensitive to specific nuclear reactions; new techniques of exposing the plates to cosmic rays; and new methods of processing and studying the exposed plates. A major role in this work was played by G. P. S. Occhialini (1907–), the Italian physicist who had collaborated with P. M. S. BLACKETT in the early 1930s to develop new cloud chamber techniques and to use them to discover the pair-production of positive and negative electrons in cosmic radiation. Occhialini joined Powell's group in Bristol in 1945 and soon persuaded Ilford Ltd, leading manufacturers of photographic material, to make efforts to improve the recording properties of emulsions. The new emulsions were exposed in the Pyrenees and, when later developed at Bristol, showed a wealth of clearly visible nuclear disintegrations caused by fast, very high energy cosmic ray particles. At the same time, the group introduced new observing methods involving teams of observers using microscopes systematically to search the plates for tracks that showed evidence of disintegrations of special interest. Such scanning teams were soon employed in high-energy physics laboratories throughout the world to identify particle interactions resulting from cosmic radiation or from radiation produced in the new giant accelerators that were built in the postwar period.

The payoff came in 1947, when Powell's Bristol group identified a new particle in the cosmic radiation as revealed in the myriad tracks recorded on the improved photographic plates with 'nuclear' emulsions. By this time, they had developed methods of measuring and analysing the tracks to provide data on the mass, charge, energy, velocity and range of a known variety of incoming particles and the particles they produced by collisions with the nuclei in the emulsion. Powell, Occhialini, and C. M. G. Lattes discovered the pi meson (pion) and demonstrated that this subnuclear particle was produced directly in nuclear reactions and rapidly decayed in flight, producing the mu meson (muon).

The discovery solved a dilemma and helped open a new era of particle physics. In the late 1930s, American cosmic ray physicists had discovered a new particle which appeared to bear out an earlier theoretical prediction by H. YUKAWA of Japan that there existed a particle having a mass 200 times greater than the electron. Yet, by 1947, experiments showed that this particle, the meson, did not strongly interact with nuclei as theory predicted. Powell's group showed that there were in fact two mesons, and that the one they had discovered (the pi meson) was the theoretically predicted particle that keeps the nucleus together. This understanding provided a great stimulus for theory and for experimental work in the field of meson physics, which grew rapidly after 1947.

Powell continued to develop and apply the photographic method at Bristol and his laboratory became the source of new experimental discoveries in meson physics and an international training centre for physicists of many nations. In 1950 he was awarded the Nobel prize for physics for his development of the photographic method and his meson discoveries. In the early 1950s he organized a system of sending stacks of photographic plates aloft in high altitude balloons to record cosmic ray interactions in the stratosphere, and he developed the project into an intensive and fruitful international collaboration involving a number of institutions in almost every European nation. Powell's concern with European scientific cooperation was also shown in the role he played in the establishment of the European Centre for Nuclear Research (CERN) and, later, on its Scientific Policy Committee.

Deeply concerned with problems relating to the social responsibility of scientists, Powell devoted a substantial amount of thought and effort to this subject during the 1950s and 1960s. He was a leader of the World Federation of Scientific Workers in the mid-1950s and was president from 1956 until his death. He was a founder of the Pugwash Conferences on Science and World Affairs in 1957 and deputy chairman of its Continuing Committee until 1967, when he became chairman. In these roles and in his published articles, Powell stressed the perils of destructive weapons and the need for international cooperation.

Powell was honoured by scientific institutions in his own and other countries. His significant impact on the postwar scientific community was due to his discoveries as well as to his direct approach to scientific problems, his organizational and methodological innovations, and his active social concern.

E. H. S. Burhop, W. O. Lock, and M. G. K. Menon (Eds), *Selected Papers of Cecil Frank Powell*. 1972. (Includes a partial autobiography.)
Biographical Memoirs of Fellows of the Royal Society. 1971. (Portrait.)
Dictionary of Scientific Biography.
Dictionary of National Biography.
Tyler Wasson (Ed.), *Nobel Prize Winners*. 1987. (Portrait.)
H. Oxbury (Ed.), *Great Britons: 20th Century Lives*. 1985.

C W

POYNTING, JOHN HENRY Born at Monton, near Manchester, England, 9 September 1852; died Birmingham, 30 March 1914. Known for his work on the transmission of energy in the electromagnetic field, and for his determination of the gravitational constant.

On graduating at Liverpool, Poynting proceeded to Cambridge in 1872 and was bracketed Third Wrangler there in 1876. Following a period as demonstrator at Owens College, Manchester, under Balfour Stewart (1828–87), he was elected professor of physics at Birmingham in 1880, a position which he held until his death. He was elected Fellow of the Royal Society in 1888, and in 1893 was awarded the Adams Prize at Cambridge.

In 1884 there appeared his paper *On the Transfer of Energy in the Electromagnetic Field*, containing the fundamental (Poynting's) formula connecting mechanical motion with electromagnetic forces. In his work on radiation (*Philosophi-*

cal Transactions, 1904, *Philosophical Magazine*, 1905) Poynting analysed the tangential pressure of radiation and showed on both theoretical and experimental grounds that light behaves like a stream of momentum. Although the resulting radiation pressures were very small, he showed how important their consequences might be, especially in astronomy, in which they provided a method of determining the absolute temperatures of the Sun, the planets, and space.

His determination of the gravitational constant by the very accurate use of an ordinary balance (1891) remains a classic of its kind. Other researches by Poynting were on the solid–liquid change of state, on osmotic pressure, and on the construction of a double-image micrometer and a simple form of saccharometer.

Dictionary of National Biography.
Nature, **93**, 138, 1914.
Philosophical Magazine, **27**, 914, 1914.
Proceedings of the Royal Society, **92A**, i, 1916. (Portrait.)
Dictionary of Scientific Biography.
                                                                            J W H

PREGL, FRITZ Born at Laibach (Ljubljana), Slovenia, 3 September 1869; died Graz, Austria, 13 December 1930. The founder of quantitative organic microchemistry.

Pregl, son of a bank official, studied medicine in the University of Graz, graduating in 1894. He specialized in physiological chemistry, becoming a *Privatdozent* in 1899. In 1910 he went to Innsbruck as head of the Chemistry Department in the Medical School, but returned to a similar post in Graz in 1913 and remained there for the rest of his life.

The early work of Pregl was almost entirely in the field of biological chemistry. Especially after a visit to Germany in 1905, he began to feel that progress in this kind of research was coming to a standstill, because of the necessity of working up large quantities of raw material in order to obtain sufficient amounts of pure compound for elementary analysis. He turned his attention, therefore, to refining the standard methods of combustion analysis so that accurate determinations could be made on milligram (instead of gram) quantities. His fellow Austrian, F. Emich (1860–1940), had already gone a long way in this direction, though mostly in inorganic analysis.

The first requisite was a balance which could weigh 20 g to an accuracy of 0.001 mg; this Pregl achieved in collaboration with the instrument-maker W. Kuhlmann of Hamburg. The rest is a long story of the patient tracking down and elimination of errors. Success was attained by 1917, when Pregl published his book, *Die quantitative organische Mikroanalyse*; in 1923 he became editor of the new journal *Mikrochemie*. Present-day organic chemistry would be impossible without the techniques devised by Pregl and his successors, and his services were recognized by the award of a Nobel prize for chemistry in 1923.

Berichte der deutschen Chemischen Gesellschaft, **64A**, 113, 1931. (Portrait.)
Journal of Chemical Education, **35**, 609, 1958. (Portrait.)
E. Farber (Ed.), *Great Chemists*. 1961. (Portrait.)
F. Szabadváry, *History of Analytical Chemistry*. 1966.

Dictionary of Scientific Biography.
Tyler Wasson (Ed.), *Nobel Prize Winners*. 1987. (Portrait.)
                                                                            W V F

PRELOG, VLADIMIR Born at Sarajevo, Bosnia-Herzegovina, 23 July 1906. Hungarian-Swiss organic chemist and Nobel Laureate.

Prelog was trained as a chemist at the Czech Institute of Technology in Prague from 1924 to 1929 and worked as an industrial chemist until 1935 when he joined the University of Zagreb while also serving as a chemical consultant to a Yugoslavian pharmaceutical company. Following the German occupation in 1941, Prelog escaped to Switzerland, joining his countryman, the organic chemist Leopold Ruzicka (1887–1976), at the famous *Eidgenossische Technische Hochschule* (ETH) in Zürich and becoming a Swiss citizen. He retired in 1976 after a lifetime's work of structural and synthetic studies of terpenes, steroids, alkaloids and antibiotics and what he described as 'chemical topology' – the marriage of chemistry and geometry. He was also a director of Ciba-Geigy in Basel.

Prelog's earliest work concerned the structure and synthesis of natural antimalarial compounds, the *Cinchona* alkaloids, and this introduced him to the problems of stereoisomerism in natural products and their stereosynthesis. In 1967 he synthesized the antibiotic, boromycin. Earlier, in 1964, he identified an unusual form of isomerism in cyclic compounds. This was followed by the elucidation of a new type of reaction in multi-membered ring structures when different sized groups are used as substituents. This had implications for understanding the stereospecificity of certain microorganisms when used as synthetic aids. In 1956, in international collaboration with R. S. Cahn (1899–1981) and C. K. INGOLD, Prelog drew up sequence rules for the unambiguous naming of stereoisomers. In 1975 he shared the Nobel prize for chemistry with the Australian chemist, J. C. Cornforth (1917–) for work on the stereochemistry of organic molecules.

V. Prelog, *My 132 Semesters of Chemistry Studies*. 1991. (Portrait.)
Nature **258**, 96, 1975. (Portrait.)
McGraw-Hill *Modern Scientists and Engineers* (1980), vol. 2, pp. 437–8. (Portrait.)
Les Prix Nobel en 1975. 1976. (Portrait.)
Tyler Wasson (Ed.), *Nobel Prize Winners*. 1987. (Portrait.)
                                                                            W H B

PRIESTLEY, JOSEPH Born at Birstal Fieldhead, near Leeds, Yorkshire, England, 13 March 1733; died Northumberland, Pennsylvania, USA, 6 February 1804. A great experimental chemist, a theologian, educationist, and champion of freedom.

Joseph Priestley came from a family of Yorkshire handloom weavers. After his mother died in 1740 he was brought up by an aunt, a keen Calvinist. In 1752 he went to the Nonconformist Academy at Daventry to study for the ministry. Although he had a serious stammer, Priestley became minister at Needham Market, Suffolk, and then at Nantwich, Cheshire. In 1761 he was appointed tutor in languages and *belles lettres* at Warrington Academy. In 1762 he married Mary Wilkinson, sister of John WILKINSON, the great ironfounder. While at

Warrington, Priestly produced his *Rudiments of English Grammar* and his *Chart of Biography*.

In 1765 he was encouraged by John Canton (1718–72) and Benjamin FRANKLIN to write a history of electricity. Priestley at once displayed the skill and industry which was to characterize all his experimental work, for he tried to verify experimentally the facts he was reporting. In the process he obtained several new results. He was elected FRS in 1766, and his *History of Electricity* was published in 1767.

From 1767 to 1773 Priestley was minister at Mill Hill Chapel, Leeds. The thirty books he wrote while there, although mostly theological and educational, included his works on *Perspective* and on *Vision, Light and Colours*, as well as the important *Essay on Government* (1768), which provided Thomas Jefferson with ideas for the American Declaration of Independence, and Jeremy Bentham (1748–1832) with the phrase 'the greatest happiness of the greatest number'.

From 1773 to 1779 Priestley was in the service of Lord Shelburne, nominally as Librarian. He spent the summers at Calne, Wiltshire, and winters in London, apart from a visit to France with Shelburne in 1774. He wrote over twenty books during these years, including the three volumes of his *Experiments and Observations on Different Kinds of Air*, with the results of his most important work on gases. These experiments began in Leeds when he studied the layer of 'fixed air' (carbon dioxide) over a brewing vat, and had the idea of dissolving it under pressure. His 'soda water' became famous all over Europe. At Calne he devised better techniques for treating gases, by collecting them over mercury instead of water, and by applying heat with a burning glass, which caused no contamination. In 1774 he prepared oxygen by heating mercuric oxide; and he established its properties in a long series of experiments with mice and plants. He went on to discover numerous other gases, such as ammonia, sulphur dioxide, carbon monoxide, hydrochloric acid, nitric oxide and hydrogen sulphide. As Humphry DAVY remarked, 'no single person ever discovered so many new and curious substances'.

From 1780 until 1791 Priestley lived at Birmingham, where he was minister of the New Meeting congregation. In the Lunar Society of Birmingham he found a congenial circle of scientific friends – James WATT, Josiah WEDGWOOD, James KEIR, and Matthew BOULTON in particular – who supplied him with funds, chemical apparatus, and new ideas. His unceasing stream of theological and political pamphlets and books became more vindictive against the Established Church. The Establishment made its reply in July 1791, when organized mobs burnt down dissenting chapels in Birmingham and the houses of some of their ministers, including Priestley's.

Priestley moved to London; but feeling against him ran so strongly that he was unable to express his opinions, and reluctantly he decided to emigrate to America in 1794. His last ten years were spent at Northumberland, Pennsylvania.

Priestley was one of the greatest of experimental chemists; but, as he himself recognized, his deductions were often unsound, and he remained to the end an upholder of the phlogiston theory that his experiments did so much to discredit. As G. L. C. CUVIER remarked, he was the father of modern chemistry, but would never acknowledge his child. Like NEWTON, Priestley considered theology more important than science, and it is as a fearless theologian and political thinker that he was most famous in his own day. He wrote about 150 books, mostly theological or educational.

F. W. Gibbs, *Joseph Priestley, Adventurer in Science and Champion of Truth*. 1965. (Portrait.)

I. V. Brown (Ed.), *Joseph Priestley: Selections from his Writings* (includes autobiography). 1962.

Anne D. Holt, *A Life of Joseph Priestley*. 1931.

R. E. Schofield (Ed.), *A Scientific Autobiography of Joseph Priestley, 1733–1804*. 1963.

Dictionary of American Biography.

Dictionary of National Biography.

Dictionary of Scientific Biography.

D G K-H

PRIGOGINE, ILYA Born in Moscow, 25 January 1917. Russian-Belgian theoretical chemist and Nobel Laureate.

Prigogine emigrated to Belgium at the age of twelve and read chemistry at the University of Brussels, where he has been professor since 1947. He also holds a visiting appointment as Director of the Center for Statistical Mechanics at the University of Texas. Through his Brussels teachers, T. de Donder (1872–1957) and J. Timmermanns (1882–1971), Prigogine was inspired to take a deep interest in thermodynamics and statistical mechanics. Traditionally these subjects had been successfully applied in chemistry to equilibrium reactions and reversible process. Instead, following hints by the Norwegian-American thermodynamicist, Lars ONSAGER in the 1930s, Prigogine devised mathematical models for irreversible, or chaotic, processes, in which (as in the real world) the entropy or disorder increases. Prigogine showed that 'dissipative structures' are created and sustained in conditions of chaos or non-equilibrium. More philosophically, he has drawn out implications for the study of living systems. He was awarded the Nobel prize for chemistry in 1977 for the theory of dissipative structures. He is the author of *Introduction to Thermodynamics of Irreversible Processes* (French ed. 1947; English 1954), *Statistical Mechanics of Irreversible Processes* (1962), *Order out of Chaos* (1979) and many other specialized monographs. His Nobel citation described him as 'the poet of thermodynamics'.

McGraw-Hill *Modern Scientists and Engineers*. 1980. (Portrait.)

Nature, **269**, 745, 1977. (Portrait.)

P. Weintraub (Ed.) *The Omni Interviews*. 1984.

Rice, S. A. (Ed.), *For Ilya Prigogine*. 1978.

Les Prix Nobel en 1977. 1978. (Portrait.)

Tyler Wasson (Ed.), *Nobel Prize Winners*. 1987. (Portrait.)

W H B

PRINGSHEIM, ERNST Born at Breslau (Wroclaw), (now in Poland), 11 July 1859; died there, 28 June 1917. Physicist.

Pringsheim was a student at Berlin University, gaining his PhD degree in 1882. Later he was appointed professor of theoretical physics in Breslau (Wroclaw). He became interested in the effect on chemical reactivity of a total absence of water. In 1887 he recorded that hydrogen and chlorine will not react photochemically if the gases have previously been dried by passage over phosphorus pentoxide. He is, however, better known for his work on the distribution of energy radiation from a hot body. With O. R. LUMMER he demonstrated (1899) that an early formula for 'black body' radiation proposed by W. WIEN and Max PLANCK led to some inconsistencies. This was among the factors that led Planck to reconsider the problem and to put forward his quantum theory at a meeting of the Physical Society of Berlin in October 1900.

J. C. Poggendorf, *Biographisch-literarisches Handwörterbuch*. 1883–1903.
Medicinhistorisches Journal, **5**, 125, 1970.
Dictionary of Scientific Biography.

T I W

PRINGSHEIM, NATHANAEL Born at Wziesko, Silesia, 30 November 1823; died Berlin, 6 October 1895. German botanist; investigated reproduction of the lower plants.

Pringsheim studied at the Universities of Breslau, Leipzig and finally Berlin, where he graduated in 1845. His doctoral thesis concerned growth in thickness of cell walls, a topic much discussed at the time. He found that apposition was from the inside, and not the outside, of cells he studied in the testa of seeds. As an investigator of the structure and life-history of the lower plants, Pringsheim ranks as one of the leaders in the renascence of scientific botany during the second half of the 19th century. His only important teaching appointment was at the University of Jena, where he occupied the chair of botany from 1864 to 1868: his researches were conducted in his private laboratory in Berlin. He made the important discovery of the occurrence of sexuality in the algae, and by observing the fusion of zoospores of *Pandorina* he saw revealed the sexual process in its most primitive form. He found gametangia in more complex algal forms, such as *Vaucheria*, and he gave an account of the life-history of *Oedogonium* in a memoir published in the first number of the *Fahrbücher für wissenschaftliche Botanik*, which he founded in 1858 and edited until his death. From studies on morphological differentiation in a family of marine algae, the Sphacelariaceae, he concluded that, in the course of evolution, natural selection plays a minor part, and that variations are spontaneous and determinate, always tending towards greater complexity. These views coincided with those of the Swiss botanist, Karl NÄGELI. As a result of his observations of cell division in the vegetative and reproductive cells of many algae, and in the pollen-mother cells of Phanerogams, he supported the view that cell multiplication is by division, and not by a process of free-cell formation as advocated by M. J. SCHLEIDEN. His last important morphological work was the observation of alternation of generations in mosses and the search for comparable successive generations in the life-history of Thallophytes. He successfully produced protonemata, and so gametophytes, by growth from the setae of mosses (*Bryum* and *Hypnum*), and thus first demonstrated apospory – the production of a sexual from an asexual generation without the intervention of spores. From 1875 onwards his investigations were confined to plant physiology, but in attempting, in middle age, to explore unfamiliar ground, he was unsuccessful in making any further significant new

contributions to scientific botany. He was one of the founders (1883), and first president, of the German Botanical Society.

F. Cohn, *Bericht der deutschen Botanischen Gesellschaft*, **13**, 10, 1895. (Portrait.)
D. H. Scott, *Nature*, **51**, 399, 1895.
Dictionary of Scientific Biography.

A P G

PRITCHARD, CHARLES Born at Alderbury, Shropshire, England, 29 February 1808; died Oxford, 28 May 1893. Astronomer.

Pritchard was educated at Merchant Taylors' School, and at an academy in Poplar, London. In 1826 he went to St John's College, Cambridge, where he had a distinguished career, and in 1832 was elected a Fellow. In 1833 he became headmaster of a school in London, but in the following year moved to Clapham Grammar School, founded to put his educational principles into practice, where he remained until his retirement in 1862.

He was an active member of the Royal Astronomical Society, being its president from 1866 to 1868. In 1870 he was elected Savilian Professor of Astronomy at Oxford, and was responsible for having a new observatory built and equipped. He pioneered the use of photographic plates for accurate determination of position. He contributed over fifty papers on astronomy, and his work on photometry (in which he invented the wedge photometer) and stellar parallax was particularly valuable. He was elected FRS in 1840.

Proceedings of the Royal Society, **54**, iii, 1893.
Ada Pritchard, *The Life and Work of Charles Pritchard*. 1897.
Dictionary of Scientific Biography.

B B K

PROUST, LOUIS JOSEPH Born at Angers, France, 26 September 1754; died there, 5 July 1826. Chemist; upholder of the Law of Constant Composition.

Proust, the son of an apothecary, studied under G. F. ROUELLE, and practised his profession in the hospital of La Salpétrière, Paris. In his thirties he went to Spain, and taught in several academies there, finally in Madrid, where he had a finely equipped laboratory. This was wrecked in a civil uprising in 1808, and Proust spent the rest of his life in France, sometimes in conditions of near penury, though as an Academician (elected 1816) he received a small annual grant.

As a chemist, Proust was a dedicated analyst, with little interest in theory. His most important work was done, mostly in Madrid, from 1797 to 1809, when he was maintaining, with copious experimental results, the thesis that compounds were of constant and determinate composition. This was in opposition to the influential view of C. L. BERTHOLLET (*Statique Chimique*, 1803) that compounds could vary in composition over a rather wide range. The controversy was conducted with (for the period) unusual urbanity, but ended with Proust clearly in the right. This was important for the establishment of the Atomic Theory. However, Proust entirely failed to discover the Law of Multiple Proportions, though it was (as John DALTON pointed out) implicit in some of his results.

It would seem from his numerous papers that Proust analysed everything within reach, both natural and artificial. He had a project for establishing a sugar industry based on grapes, but for some reason refused the help offered by Napoleon.

J. R. Partington, *A History of Chemistry*, vol. 3. 1962. (Portrait.)

E. Farber (Ed.), *Great Chemists*. 1961. (Portrait.)

W. A. Tilden, *Famous Chemists*. 1921.

Dictionary of Scientific Biography.

W V F

PROUT, WILLIAM Born at Horton, Gloucestershire, England, 15 January 1785; died London, 9 April 1850. Chemist; formulated Prout's Hypothesis, that all atomic weights are whole numbers.

Prout was the son of an old west of England family. Like many chemists of the day, his formal training was in medicine, which he studied at Edinburgh (MD, 1811), following which he established himself in practice in London. He established a private chemical laboratory, and in 1813 began a course of lectures on animal chemistry, then scarcely explored. He investigated many natural products – including urea and uric acid, the gastric juice, cuttle-fish ink, urine, etc. – and taught that excretory products result from breakdown of the tissues.

He made a special study of the atmosphere and made some very precise measurements of the density of air (1832–3). For studying changes in atmospheric pressure he constructed a barometer that served as a model for a national standard barometer constructed by the Royal Society (to which he was elected in 1819).

Prout is most remembered, however, for his (initially anonymous) enunciation in 1815 of the hypothesis that atomic weights are all simple multiples of that of hydrogen. This stimulated precise analytical work which, in fact, indicated that he was wrong. The discovery of isotopes a century later, however, renewed interest in his theory, for it showed that the natural elements in fact consist of mixtures of isotopes, each having approximately a whole-number atomic weight.

G. Wolstenholme and D. Piper (Eds), *The Royal College of Physicians of London: Portraits.* 1964. (Portraits.)

O. T. Benfey, *Journal of Chemical Education*, **29**, 78, 1952.

W. H. Brock, *Medical History*, **9**, 101, 1965.

W. S. C. Copeman, *Notes and Records of the Royal Society of London*, **24**, 273, 1969.

Dictionary of Scientific Biography.

T I W

PTOLEMY OF ALEXANDRIA Probably born in Egypt; flourished in the mid-second century AD. Astronomer and geographer; his *Almagest* and *Geography* dominated astronomy and geography for fourteen centuries.

The *Almagest* of Ptolemy embodies basic observations and techniques derived to a considerable (but not precisely indicated) extent from the lost works of HIPPARCHUS OF RHODES. The contents of its thirteen Books are as follows:

I and II Outline of the Earth-centred Universe; Table of Chords and supporting theorems; trigonometry of the celestial sphere. III Length of the year and motion of the Sun. IV Lengths of months and motion of the Moon; Ptolemy's discovery of the second lunar inequality (the evection).

V Distances and sizes of Sun and Moon.

VI Eclipses.

VII and VIII Star catalogue (the earliest that has survived); precession of the equinoxes.

IX–XIII Motions of the five planets, represented by combinations of circular motions (eccentrics and epicycles); these planetary schemes represent Ptolemy's principal original contribution to the work.

Ptolemy's *Geography*, in eight Books, deals with the mathematical technique of constructing accurate maps (I); it lists the latitudes and longitudes of important places (II-VII); and it originally included an atlas of the known world. Book VIII is an astronomical epilogue. The contents were largely derived from earlier geographical writers, including Hipparchus and Strabo (63 BC–C.AD 21), but particularly from Marinus of Tyre (*fl.* 150 AD). Books II-VIII have sometimes been regarded as a late Byzantine compilation. Ptolemy established the use of terms equivalent to longitude and latitude; he was conversant with orthogonal and stereographic projections of the sphere; but the actual co-ordinates he assigned to places on the map were very faulty, since in his time methods of determining latitudes were crude and there were no effective methods of determining longitudes. He was forced to depend on dead reckonings and travellers' tales, and he greatly exaggerated the extent from east to west of the Eurasian continent.

Other works by Ptolemy are extant in whole or in part. His *Optics* deals with the reflection of light from mirrors and its refraction at the surface of separation of two transparent media. However, his table of refractions (from air to water) appears to have been constructed not, as formerly supposed, on a basis of experimental results but to conform to a crude arithmetical rule.

Ptolemy owed not a little of his medieval fame to a classic treatise that he wrote on astrology.

T. L. Heath, *A History of Greek Mathematics*, vol 2. 1921.

J. L. E. Dreyer, *A History of Astronomy from Thales to Kepler*. 1953.

H. F. Tozer and M. Cary, *A History of Ancient Geography* (2 ed.). 1935.

George Sarton, *Ancient Science and Modern Civilization*. 1954.

Dictionary of Scientific Biography.

A A

PURCELL, EDWARD MILLS Born in Taylorville, Illinois, USA, 30 August 1912. Physicist.

Purcell entered Purdue University, Indiana, in 1929. He graduated in electrical engineering but already his interest had turned to physics. After a year at the *Technische Hochschule*, Karlsruhe, he took a PhD at Harvard. After two further years there he moved to the Radiation Laboratory of the Massachusetts Institute of Technology, then embarking on research and development work for microwave radar. One of his colleagues was I. I. RABI. After the war he returned to Harvard, where he was appointed professor of physics in 1949. He retired in 1980.

Purcell is remembered for two major advances. The first was in the field of nuclear magnetic resonance, a powerful technique for investigating the fine structure of atoms and molecules. Later, the method was developed medically to give a non-invasive technique for imaging the human body. Purcell was also the first to detect (1951) the 21-cm radiation emitted by hydrogen atoms in interstellar space. In 1952 he shared a Nobel prize with Felix BLOCH.

Robert L. Weber, *Pioneers of Science: Nobel Prize Winners in Physics*. 1980. (Portrait.)
Les Prix Nobel en 1952. 1953. (Portrait.)
Tyler Wasson (Ed.), *Nobel Prize Winners*. 1987. (Portrait.)

T I W

PURKINJE, JOHANNES EVANGELISTA Born at

Libochowitz, Bohemia (now in Czech Republic), 17 December 1787; died Prague, 28 July 1869. Pioneer histologist and physiologist.

Purkinje was educated by the Piarist monks, but before ordination he went to Prague to study philosophy. He then studied medicine and graduated at Prague (1818) with a famous thesis, on the subjective aspects of vision, which gained him the friendship of Goethe. After a period as assistant in the Department of Physiology, he was called to the chair of physiology at Breslau (1823). There he founded an institute in which histological researches were carried out by pupils who later became famous, notably G. G. Valentin (1810–83). In 1849 Purkinje was called to the corresponding chair in Prague, where he also founded an institute, which he directed until his death. He was elected a Foreign Member of the Royal Society in 1850.

In his graduation thesis Purkinje described the phenomenon now called after him; if the intensity of the illumination is decreased, different objects of equal brightness but different colour appear unequally bright. In 1820 he studied the vertigo produced by rotating the body in an erect position. He thought that it was due to the inertia of the soft brain substance as compared with the solid cranium. He overlooked the effect of the semicircular canals, but he continued to study this problem. In his dissertation of 1823 he described 'Purkinje's images', a threefold image of one object seen by an observer in the eye of a subject. In 1825 Purkinje was the first to see the 'germinal vesicle' (the nucleus) in the eggs of birds, but this observation was not published until 1830.

In 1832 Purkinje first obtained a compound microscope. Using it, he described (1835) the microscopic structure of the skin of various animals. In the same year, with Valentin, he first described ciliary motion. In 1837 he expressed the main characters of the cell theory before T. SCHWANN had enunciated that theory. In 1837–8 he published his best-known observations; he described nerve cells, with their nuclei and dendrites, and also myelinated nerve fibres. He also described the large flask-like cells in the cerebellar cortex which now bear his name. By 1838 both Purkinje and Valentin had observed cell-division. in 1839 Purkinje described the 'fibres of Purkinje', found below the endocardium in a certain area of the ventricles of the heart, which are important in the conduction of the wave of excitation. In an address of 1839 (published 1840) Purkinje was the first to use the term 'protoplasm' in a scientific sense.

W. Haymaker and F. Schiller (Eds), *The Founders of Neurology*. 1953. (Portrait.)
C. Singer and E. A. Underwood, *Short History of Medicine*. 1962.

V. Robinson, *Pathfinders in Medicine*. 1929.
V. Kruta and M. Teich, *Jan Evangelista Purkyně*. 1962.
H. J. John, *Memoirs of the American Philosophical Society*, **49**, 1949; *Proceedings of the Royal Society of Medicine*, **46**, 933, 1953.
Dictionary of Scientific Biography.

E A U

PYTHAGORAS OF SAMOS Born at Samos, *c*.572

BC; died Metapontium, *c*.497 BC. Founder of the Pythagorean school of natural philosophy; mathematician and astronomer.

Pythagoras is reputed to have wandered extensively through the Middle East before founding his brotherhood (religious, political and scientific) at Croton in southern Italy. No writings of his have survived, and his personal achievements were early confused with those of his disciples. Subject to this uncertainty, he may be regarded as having founded the theory of numbers and as having established the ideal of geometry as a logically connected sequence of propositions. He is credited with the proofs of several familiar Euclidian propositions, including that relating to the squares on the sides of a right-angled triangle; and he was probably acquainted with some at least of the five regular solids.

In astronomy Pythagoras taught that the Earth was a sphere located at the centre of a spherical universe. He analysed the apparent spiral course described by the Sun round the heavens into two uniform circular motions (an annual and a diurnal one) simultaneously described, and he applied this artifice, less eligibly, to represent the motions of the Moon and the planets. This technique was adopted by EUDOXUS OF CNIDUS; and the conviction that all the celestial motions could be resolved into uniform circular motions dominated planetary theory until set aside by J. KEPLER in the seventeenth century.

Pythagoras and his disciples represented numbers by means of points (or pebbles) spaced out to form simple geometrical figures (hence our designation of 'square' numbers). These figures could be built up to form solid bodies, or even to constitute space itself, so that, as the Pythagoreans asserted, 'all things are number'. At a deeper level, this aphorism expressed their conviction, and that of their philosophical descendants down to the mathematical physicists of our own day, that the essential truth about the physical world is contained in the formal statement of the mathematical relations underlying natural phenomena.

There is a tradition that Pythagoras discovered the simple ratios connecting the lengths of the segments of a vibrating lyre string that would give off musical notes blending to form a harmonious chord. They associated such lengths with the distances of the several planets from the central Earth, thus inspiring the belief that the planets in their courses sent forth a tuneful 'harmony of the spheres'.

W. K. C. Guthrie, *A History of Greek Philosophy*, vol. 1. 1962.
T. L. Heath, *A History of Greek Mathematics*, vol 1. 1921.
B. L. van der Waerden, *Science Awakening*. 1963.
Dictionary of Scientific Biography.

A A

R

RABI, ISIDOR ISAAC Born in Rymanov, Austria, 29 July 1898; died Manhattan, New York, 11 January 1988. Physicist, known chiefly for his work with molecular beams.

Rabi was brought up in New York city, after his family emigrated to the USA in 1899 when he was only one year old. In 1919 he graduated in chemistry from Cornell University, and left to work outside academia. However, after three years he became a graduate student at Columbia University, gaining his PhD in 1927 for research on the magnetic properties of crystals. Rabi then travelled around Europe on a scholarship, working at times with the leaders in the field of quantum theory, Niels BOHR, Werner HEISENBERG and Wolfgang PAULI. After meeting Otto STERN, Rabi was invited to work with him in Hamburg for a year, on the molecular beam systems that Stern had pioneered.

On his return to Columbia University, Rabi set up his own molecular beam laboratory. During the 1930s he made many improvements to the technique, in particular developing the molecular beam resonance method. With this he applied an oscillating magnetic field to a beam in which the atoms were in certain quantized orientations with respect to a steady magnetic field. When the varying field oscillated at the correct frequency to flip atoms from a particular orientation to another – the resonance condition – these atoms would no longer reach the detector. Measuring the resonance frequencies gave Rabi a means of determining atomic magnetic moments that was much more precise than previous techniques. He was awarded the Nobel prize for physics for this work in 1944.

During the Second World War, Rabi worked on radar at the MIT Radiation Laboratory, declining to become deputy director at Los Alamos, where scientists were working on the atomic bomb. After the war, he became an active advocate of peaceful uses of atomic energy, and in the 1950s initiated a series of international conferences on this. 'Real peace', he once said, 'is more than the absence of violent war . . . peace must be a condition which permits the release of the latent creative energies of all the people . . .' Rabi also promoted the concept of European collaboration in science, which led in 1954 to the foundation of CERN, the centre for nuclear physics near Geneva.

Physics Today, October 1988. (Portrait.)
H. A. Boorse, L. Motz, J. H. Weaver, *The Atomic Physicists, a Biographical History*, 1989.
Les Prix Nobel en 1940–44. 1946.
J. S. Rigden, *Rabi: An American Physicist*. 1987.
Tyler Wasson (Ed.), *Nobel Prize Winners*. 1987. (Portrait.)

C S

RAINWATER, LEO JAMES Born in Council, Idaho, USA, 9 December 1917; died Hastings-on-Hudson, New York, 31 May 1986. Nuclear physicist.

Rainwater graduated in physics at the California Institute of Technology in 1939. He then moved to Columbia University, initially as a teaching assistant: he was appointed professor of physics in 1952. His research was much facilitated by the installation of a synchrocyclotron in 1950. At that time two theories of nuclear structure prevailed. One was the shell model – associated particularly with Maria GOEPPERT MAYER – according to which the electrons were distributed in concentric spheres; the other was the drop model, so called because of its analogy with a drop of liquid. Neither was wholly satisfactory, in particular through failure to explain the observed asymmetry of electric charge distribution. In 1950 Rainwater postulated a new structure, incorporating elements of both the existing ones, and obtained experimental evidence for it. He developed his ideas in association with Aage BOHR (1922–) and B. R. Mottelson (1926–), with whom he shared a Nobel Prize in 1975.

Physics Today, December 1975.
Les Prix Nobel en 1975, 1976. (Portrait.)
Robert L. Weber, *Pioneers of Science: Nobel Prize Winners in Physics*, 1980. (Portrait.)
Tyler Wasson (Ed.), *Nobel Prize Winners*. 1987. (Portrait.)

T I W

RAMAN, SIR CHANDRASEKHARA VENKATA Born at Trichinopoly, India, 7 November 1888; died Bangalore, 21 November 1970. Physicist, pre-eminent in molecular spectroscopy and in acoustics.

The son of a teacher and lecturer, Raman entered the Presidency College in Madras in 1903 and achieved the highest distinctions in the examinations for BA (1904) and MA (1907). Scientific research being at this time almost completely neglected in India, he then entered the Civil Service by competitive examination, and was appointed to a position in the Finance Department in June 1907. He retained this employment for ten years, mostly in Calcutta but with periods in Rangoon and Nagpur. Having published original optical research in the *Philosophical Magazine* when he was barely eighteen years old, he now continued scientific work in his spare time: some thirty papers – to *Nature*, the *Philosophical Magazine* and the *Physical Review* – testified to his ability and energy and helped to make his name familiar to scientists in Europe and America.

Raman's early work was facilitated by the presence in Calcutta of the Indian Association for the Cultivation of Science and it was through his connection with this body that he came into contact with the Vice-Chancellor of Calcutta University, Sir Asutosh Mookerjee. When, eventually, a science college was established within the University, the Vice-Chancellor offered Raman the professorship of physics, an appointment which he accepted enthusiastically, despite the considerable financial sacrifice which the move entailed. He occupied the chair from 1917 to 1933, the 'golden era' of his working life. From 1919 he also acted as Secretary of the Indian Association for the Cultivation of Science. He carefully built up the resources of both the institutions with which he was involved and brought to Calcutta many aspiring young Indians to undertake research into optical phenomena, acoustics, and other branches of physics.

The inquiries reflected Raman's own interests. A substantial essay *On the Mechanical Theory of the Vibrations of Bowed Strings and of Musical Instruments of the Violin Family* appeared as a bulletin of the IACS in 1918 and a book, *Molecular Diffraction of Light*, was published by the University of Calcutta in 1922. This latter study led Raman, early in 1928, to the discovery of the effect which now bears his name, a discovery announced in the *Indian Journal of Physics*, of which he was the founder and editor. Using very simple apparatus, he found that when a beam of monochromatic light is scattered by a transparent liquid, the scattered light contains frequencies of very low intensity not present in the incident radiation. The frequency shifts are characteristic of the substance effecting the scattering and correspond to energy changes accompanying inelastic collisions between incident photons and the molecules of the compound concerned. Raman spectra have therefore provided much valuable information on molecular rotation and, particularly, vibration, and thus on the shape and symmetry of molecules themselves.

During the years in Calcutta, Raman emerged as a truly international figure. He visited England in 1921 for the Universities' Congress in Oxford, and Canada in 1924 as the guest of the British Association. The Royal Society elected him to its Fellowship in 1924 and in 1930 bestowed on him the Hughes Medal. He was awarded the Nobel prize in physics ('for his work on the scattering of light and for the discovery of the effect named after him') in the same year. Universities and scientific institutions, in America, Russia and Europe as well as in his own country, hastened to honour him. He was knighted in 1929.

From 1933 until 1949 Raman was professor of physics (and for a short time director) of the Indian Institute of Science in Bangalore. Once again he quickly succeeded in creating a first-class laboratory and school of research. At the same time he carried on his own investigations: on x-ray crystallography, on the diffraction of light by high frequency sound waves in a liquid, and on other optical problems. He fathered the Indian Academy of Sciences in 1934, superintended the regular publication of its *Proceedings*, and officiated as its president until his death.

In 1949 Raman moved to an independent scientific institution (now the Raman Research Institute)

which he had helped to establish on the outskirts of Bangalore. His laboratory there was for a time particularly identified with the study of the physics of the diamond. Later he worked on the physiology of vision, publishing a book on the subject in 1968. In this period he was justly venerated as the father of Indian science and the Indian Government bestowed on him the first of its National Professorships.

Biographical Memoirs of Fellows of the Royal Society. 1971. (Portrait.)
Proceedings of the Indian Academy of Sciences (section A), **8**, 243, 1938. (Portrait.)
P. Venkataraman, *Journey into Light: Life and Science of C. V. Raman*. 1990.
Dictionary of Scientific Biography.
Tyler Wasson (Ed.), *Nobel Prize Winners*. 1987. (Portrait.)
Dictionary of National Biography.

ADO

RAMANUJAN, SRINIVASA Born at Tangore, Madras, India, 22 December 1889; died Madras, 26 April 1920. Pure mathematician who achieved distinction with the aid of a single textbook on mathematics.

Ramanujan, son of a Brahman accountant, received education only to the first year at college, failing then in English. With the aid of a textbook *Synopsis of Pure Mathematics*, by G. S. Carr, he worked through the theorems of pure mathematics and succeeded in establishing a large number of original results in function theory, power series, and number theory while working in an office of the Madras Port Trust. One example of his achievement was cited by G. H. Hardy (1877–1947) as a property first discovered by E. Landau (1877–1938), in 1908. Thus Ramanujan, isolated and self-taught, had reached the same stage of development as contemporary European mathematicians. Once he had published some articles, Indian mathematicians began to recognize his genius and he began a correspondence with Hardy in Cambridge. Eventually it was arranged that he should have a research scholarship at Trinity College, Cambridge, where he began collaboration with Hardy. There whilst he received tuition in some of the essential branches of mathematics which had not been adequately covered in his textbook, he was able, by a process involving intuition and induction, to produce discoveries in number theory.

In 1917 Ramanujan fell ill with tuberculosis. He recovered sufficiently to resume work in 1918, in which year he was elected to the Royal Society. At this time his collaboration with Hardy produced the theorem concerning the number of ways in which an integer n can be partitioned into a sum of smaller integers. In 1919 Ramanujan returned home, where he died a year later.

Proceedings of the London Mathematical Society, **19**, xl, 1921.
G. H. Hardy, *American Mathematics Monthly*, **44**, 137, 1937.
Nature, **105**, 494, 1920.
E. H. Neville, *Nature*, **149**, 292, 1942.
Proceedings of the Royal Society, **99A**, xiii, 1921.
Dictionary of Scientific Biography.

D N

RAMELLI, AGOSTINO Born at Maranza, Italy, *c*.1531; died Paris, *c*.1600. Engineer.

Ramelli entered the army on leaving school and had a distinguished career, serving and gaining his captaincy under the Marquis de Marignan (1497–1555), who is believed to have studied under LEONARDO DA VINCI. When Marignan died Ramelli joined the service of the Duc d'Anjou (later Henry III of France), who made him his engineer. As a reward for this service he was granted a generous pension.

His reputation rests on his only book, *Le Diversi et Artificiose Machine*, published in Paris in 1588. This was a finely printed and illustrated book describing examples of machines devised by Ramelli for a variety of purposes. Of the 195 illustrations accompanied by explanatory text, a hundred are of pumps and pumping machinery, while the remainder cover derricks, screw jacks, grinding mills, bridges and engines for military use, sawmills, and so on. Water power is utilized in the majority of cases, by means of overshot, undershot, or horizontal impact waterwheels. Though the power is generally transmitted direct as rotary motion – as in chain, or rag-and-chain pumps – there are also illustrations of devices for converting rotary to reciprocal motion for the driving of pistons. A number of illustrations curiously foreshadow successful developments in later centuries: for example, a continuous bucket conveyor and an amphibious armoured vehicle. The existence in a number of illustrations of a reversing mechanism so direct in its application that a full-scale machine would have been wrecked by its use, suggests that many of Ramelli's machines were projects which existed only as drawings or models. Many of these models could not have been enlarged to full-scale, because this would have demanded a precision of machining not then possible.

It is probably the case that most advances in machine design came from adaptations of existing working plant, rather than from the illustrations and models of such imaginative inventors as Ramelli and Leonardo himself. Nevertheless, Ramelli's book was very influential and was a landmark in technical publishing.

W. B. Parsons, *Engineers and Engineering in the Renaissance*. 1939.

Charles Singer, E. J. Holmyard, A. R. Hall and Trevor I. Williams (Eds), *A History of Technology*, vol. 3. 1957.

Martha T. Gnudi (Trans.), *The Various and Ingenious Machines of Agostino Ramelli*. 1976. (Includes biography.)

N H

RAMÓN Y CAJAL, SANTIAGO Born at Petilla, Navarra, Spain, 1 May 1852; died Madrid, 18 October 1934. Distinguished neurohistologist.

Ramón y Cajal was the son of a country doctor who later became professor of anatomy at Zaragoza. In 1873 Cajal was licensed to practise, and then served in the army in Cuba. In 1877 he graduated as a doctor of medicine at Madrid. He was professor of anatomy at Valencia (1884), of normal and pathological histology at Barcelona (1887), and of both these subjects at Madrid (1892–1922). In 1900 he also became director of the newly founded *Instituto Nacional de Higiene* at Madrid. In 1894 he delivered the Croonian Lecture to the Royal Society, of which he was elected a Foreign Member in 1909. In 1906 he was awarded a Nobel prize

jointly with C. GOLGI, and he received honorary degrees from many universities, including Oxford and Cambridge.

When Cajal graduated, all stains for nervous tissue gave little differentiation between the nervous elements proper and the supporting tissue (neuroglia). Tracking of individual nerve fibres was therefore difficult. In 1873 Golgi discovered his silver impregnation method of staining nervous tissue, which stained nerve cells and their fibres black, while leaving the neuroglia faintly stained. Golgi published his method in 1873 and in 1885, and about 1885 Cajal was shown a section of the cerebral cortex prepared by the Golgi method. He was so fascinated that he did not sleep that night. When Cajal was appointed to Barcelona he worked intensively on the histology of the grey matter, and he improved Golgi's method. He disproved the current theory that the grey matter is a network of anastomosing nerve fibres, and he was able to trace long nerve fibres which never fused with any others during their course. He put forward the theory that fibres that appeared to join nerve cells ended in terminal buttons, which, however closely they might approach the nerve cells, never actually touched them. There was thus no anatomical fusion of the substance of one nerve cell with that of another. Cajal also discovered the collateral branches of the axon.

Wilhelm HIS had suggested that the fundamental unit of the nervous system is the nerve cell, with its branching processes and its axon. Cajal's histological work was establishing this view when W. von WALDEYER in 1891 coined the word 'neurone' for the cell and its processes. Waldeyer did no experimental or other work in this field, to which Cajal devoted the rest of his life. Cajal postulated that the nerve impulse passed from the axon of one neurone to the dendrites of the next neurone, and so to its nerve cell and axon. This postulate that conduction is in one direction only was formalized by A. van Gehuchten (1861–1914) as the law of dynamic polarity.

Cajal proved that the long-accepted theory of the existence of uncrossed fibres in the apparent complete crossing of the optic tracts at the base of the brain was correct, despite a denial of that fact by R. A. KÖLLIKER.

In 1906 Cajal attacked the difficult problem of the degeneration of nerve tracts and the method of regeneration of nerve fibres after they had been cut. Two opposing solutions of the problem of regeneration had long been held, but Cajal proved that the proximal cut end of the nerve grows out to meet the degenerated distal end.

Cajal next turned to the neuroglia, the supporting tissue of the nerve fibres in the central nervous system, and he was able to distinguish in it three different types of cells. He also studied vision in the faceted eyes of insects.

Obituary Notices of Fellows of the Royal Society. 1932–5. (Portrait.)

D. F. Cannon, *Explorer of the Human Brain*. 1949.

H. Williams, *Don Quixote of the Microscope*. 1954.

E. H. Craigie and W. C. Gibson, *The World of Ramón y Cajal*. 1968.

Dictionary of Scientific Biography.

Tyler Wasson (Ed.), *Nobel Prize Winners*. 1987. (Portrait.)

RAMSAY, SIR WILLIAM Born in Glasgow, Scotland, 2 October 1852; died Haslemere, Surrey, England, 23 July 1916. Discoverer of the rare gases of the atmosphere.

The son of an engineer, Ramsay was intended for the Church and received a conventional classical education. Nevertheless, he became one of the leading chemists of his generation, discovering not only one new element but a previously unsuspected family of new elements.

Determined to make chemistry his career, Ramsay made good the deficiencies of his formal education by entering the laboratory of the city analyst in Glasgow. In 1871 he went to Tübingen, where he carried out research in organic chemistry under Rudolf FITTIG. Returning to Glasgow, he took up appointments first at Anderson's College, and then at the University. He continued his research in organic chemistry, investigating the chemistry of pyridine and the quinine alkaloids.

It was, however, as a physical rather than an organic chemist that Ramsay made his reputation. He became interested in the continuity of the liquid and gaseous states, and an appointment as professor of chemistry at University College, Bristol (now Bristol University), in 1880 gave him an opportunity of establishing himself in this field. It is an indication of his all-round ability – he was a good athlete, an accomplished musician, and a gifted linguist – that he succeeded in doing this despite his additional appointment (1881) as principal of the College.

In 1887 he was appointed to succeed A. W. WILLIAMSON as professor of chemistry in University College, London, and it was here that his most famous researches were carried out. His continuing interest in the properties of gases and compounds led him into conversation with Lord RAYLEIGH after a lecture given by the latter to the Royal Society on 19 April 1894. Rayleigh had demonstrated that chemically prepared nitrogen was always slightly less dense than nitrogen derived directly from air. Rayleigh favoured the view that the explanation was contamination of chemical nitrogen with some lighter gas. Ramsay believed that the reason was the presence of some heavier gas in atmospheric nitrogen, and within a few months he had proved this to be correct.

Nitrogen is not a reactive gas, but it will combine with heated magnesium to form a nitride. By the end of May 1894 Ramsay had shown that after treatment in this way atmospheric nitrogen could be made progressively denser. Continuing his experiments through the summer, he produced in early August a gas, apparently unaffected by further treatment with magnesium, having a density of just over 19, compared with 14 for the original atmospheric nitrogen. Sir William CROOKES examined the gas spectroscopically and reported that it was new and quite distinct from nitrogen.

Meanwhile Rayleigh had been following up an experiment made by Henry CAVENDISH in 1785; the latter discovered that when an electric spark was passed through air, causing the nitrogen and oxygen to combine, there invariably remained a small unreactive residue. Rayleigh was able to tell Ramsay that this residue of gas was neither oxygen nor nitrogen. The two immediately joined forces, and on 31 January 1895 announced to the Royal Society the discovery of a new gaseous element,

apparently completely inert chemically, which they called argon. It was immediately suggested (by (Sir) Henry Miers (1858–1942) of the British Museum) that argon might be identical with an inert gas, supposedly nitrogen, that W. F. Hillebrand (1853–1925) had obtained by heating certain uranium minerals. Ramsay prepared this gas and found that it was not argon, but yet another new gas; Crookes identified it as the element helium which spectroscopic examination had revealed in the Sun's spectrum during the eclipse of 1868.

The atomic weights of the new gases confirmed Ramsay's early suspicion that 'there is room for gaseous elements at the end of the first column of the Periodic Table' (1892). With M. W. TRAVERS he sought the remaining gases by fractional distillation of liquefied air. This led to the isolation of neon, krypton and xenon. Finally, with Sir Robert Whytlaw-Gray (1877–1958), he identified, using a minute sample, the last member of the family; this was radon, a product of radioactive decay.

Ramsay's discoveries brought him international fame. In 1904 he was awarded the Nobel prize for chemistry; in the same year Rayleigh received the prize for physics. He was elected Fellow of the Royal Society in 1888 and was knighted in 1902.

M. W. Travers, *A Life of Sir William Ramsay, K.C.B., F.R.S.* 1956. (Portraits.)
Endeavour, **12**, 126, 1952.
Proceedings of the Royal Society, **93A**, xlii, 1917. (Portrait.)
Dictionary of National Biography.
Dictionary of Scientific Biography.
Tyler Wasson (Ed.), *Nobel Prize Winners.* 1987. (Portrait.)

T I W

RAMSDEN, JESSE Born at Salterhebble, Yorkshire, England, 1735 (probably 6 October); died Brighton, Sussex, 5 November 1800. Celebrated instrument-maker.

At first an engraver, Ramsden moved in 1755 to London, where he became apprenticed to a mathematical-instrument maker in 1758. Later he started his own business, and was responsible for constructing a number of important physical instruments, especially of an optical nature. Of these one of the most celebrated was a 5-foot vertical circle constructed for the observatory at Palermo which greatly influenced the replacement of quadrants by divided circles towards the end of the 18th century. He also constructed quadrants, micrometers, and an instrument for measuring the size of lenses. In 1768 he invented an electrostatic machine with glass plates.

Ramsden was elected to the Royal Society in 1786 and was awarded its Copley medal in 1795 for various 'inventions and improvements in philosophical instruments'.

Dictionary of National Biography.
Dictionary of Scientific Biography.
M. Daumas, *Scientific Instruments of the 17th and 18 Centuries and Their Makers.* 1972.
E. G. R. Taylor, *The Mathematical Practitioners of Hanovarian England.* 1966.

J W H

RANKINE, WILLIAM JOHN MACQUORN Born

in Edinburgh, 5 July 1820; died Glasgow, 24 December 1872. Engineer.

Son of David Rankine, an engineer, W. J. M. Rankine was educated at Ayr Academy, Glasgow High School and Edinburgh University, where he was a gold medallist. He spent four years in Ireland on surveys for rail, water, river and harbour works as a pupil of J. B. MacNeill (1793? –1880), one of Telford's assistants, before returning to Edinburgh. As Secretary of the Caledonian Railway, his father was able to employ him on various projects, out of which arose Rankine's early papers for the Institution of Civil Engineers.

Attracted to thermodynamics, he examined the entropy theory of Sadi CARNOT, modifying it in 1849. He investigated also what is now known as metal fatigue, a dangerous cause of failure in metal parts. In addition to a steady output of theoretical papers in this field, he found time to consider many practical projects: cylindrical wheels for railways, refrigeration, air engines, the water supply of Glasgow and the stability of ships. During the war scare of 1860 he commanded a volunteer battalion. Elected professor of civil engineering and mechanics at Glasgow University in 1855, he produced a steady and highly successful stream of papers on physics, and manuals on, among other subjects, applied mechanics (1858), the steam engine (1859), civil engineering (1862), and tables (1866), all of which ran to many editions. He was the first president of the Institute of Engineers in Scotland and was elected to Fellowship of the Royal Society (1853).

P. G. Tait, in *Miscellaneous Scientific Papers by W. J. M. Rankine*. 1880. (Portrait.)
V. V. Raman, *Journal of Chemical Education*, **50**, 274, 1973.
A. Barr, *Proceedings of the Royal Philosophical Society of Glasgow*, **51**, 167, 1923.
Dictionary of National Biography.
Dictionary of Scientific Biography.

W H G A

RAOULT, FRANÇOIS MARIE Born at Fournes, near Lille, France, 10 May 1830; died Grenoble, Isère, 1 April 1901. Physical chemist, noted for work on the theory of solutions.

Raoult studied in Paris, but financial difficulties forced him to leave before completing his course. From 1853 to 1867 he taught science in various French provincial schools; working under great difficulties, he gained his doctorate in 1863. He joined the staff of the University of Grenoble, and in 1870 was appointed to the chair of chemistry, a post which he held until his death.

Raoult's first research (for his doctoral thesis) concerned heat changes in electric cells, and their relation to electromotive force. His first work on the freezing-points of solutions (1878) seems to have stemmed from attempts to estimate the alcoholic strength of wines, but soon broadened into a major study, though it was hindered by his adherence to the 'old' atomic weights. He found that the 'molecular depression of freezing-point' was a constant for a given solvent (Raoult's Law, 1882); this was immediately utilized by chemists as a simple method of determining molecular weights. A series of parallel studies was made of the molecular depression of vapour pressure of solutions. Inorganic salts and strong acids in water, however,

gave anomalous values for molecular weights by these methods, and Raoult's work came into prominence when it was realized how well these 'anomalous' results fitted in with the theory of Ionic Dissociation of S. ARRHENIUS, and with the more general theory of solutions of J. H. VAN'T HOFF.

J. H. van't Hoff, *Journal of the Chemical Society*, **81**, 969, 1902. (Portrait.)
E. H. Getman, *Journal of Chemical Education*, **13**, 153, 1936. (Portrait.)
William Ramsay, *Nature*, **64**, 17, 1901.
Dictionary of Scientific Biography.

W V F

RAY, JOHN Born at Black Notley, Essex, England, 29 November 1628; died there, 17 January 1705. Botanical and zoological systematist.

Ray, son of the village blacksmith, was educated at Braintree School, and at the age of 16 went to Cambridge. After nearly two years at Catherine Hall he migrated to Trinity College, where he was later a Fellow and held successively many college offices. He took Holy Orders at the end of 1660, but had to resign his Fellowship two years later because he refused to subscribe to the 1661 Act of Conformity. Thereafter, until he married in 1673, he was provided for by his close friend and pupil Francis Willughby (1635–72) with whom he travelled through Europe in search of botanical and zoological specimens. Six years after his marriage he returned to Black Notley, where he remained for the rest of his days.

Ray and his friend started work on their collections intending to write a systematic description of the entire animal and plant kingdoms, but were frustrated by Willughby's death in 1672. Willughby left an ichthyology and an ornithology which Ray edited and published, and Ray produced his *Historia Generalis Plantarum* in three volumes. Ray was a prolific writer, his first book, published in 1660, being a flora of the neighbourhood of Cambridge – D'Arcy Thompson (1860–1948), writing in 1922, says he minutely describes localities and 'Cambridge students still gather some of their rare plants in the copses and chalkpits where he found them'. His great contribution to botany, however, was the system of classification that he introduced, which although later superseded, produced order out of unsystematic descriptions. He applied similar principles to the classification of insects, and the classes of the vertebrates. He did not confine himself to natural history, but wrote on English proverbs, obscure words, voyages and travels, and other subjects, the best known of these works being *The Wisdom of God manifested in the Works of the Creation* (1691), many times reprinted. Ray, elected FRS in 1667, was a man of great industry and had a flair for collecting information and arranging it systematically; his writings on natural history earned him the appellations of the 'Father of Natural History' and 'Aristotle of England'.

E. Lankester, *Memorials of John Ray*. 1846.
E. Lankester, *Correspondence of John Ray*. 1848.
C. E. Raven, *John Ray, Naturalist; His Life and Works*. 2nd ed. 1950.
G. Keynes, *John Ray: A Bibliography*. 1951.
J. M. Eyles, *Nature*, **175**, 103, 1955.
Dictionary of Scientific Biography.

L H M

RAYLEIGH, LORD (JOHN WILLIAM STRUTT)
Born at Langford Grove, Essex, England, 12 November 1842; died Terling Place, Essex, 30 June 1919. Mathematical physicist.

John William Strutt became the third Lord Rayleigh in 1873, succeeding to a peerage created in 1821 in favour of Lady Charlotte Mary Gertrude, daughter of the first Duke of Leinster and wife of Colonel J. H. Strutt, Member of Parliament for Maldon, Essex. He was educated first under a private tutor at Torquay and then entered Trinity College, Cambridge (1861). In 1865 he graduated First Wrangler, and also gained the first Smith's Prize. He was elected to a Fellowship of Trinity, which he held until his marriage in 1871. In 1879 he succeeded James Clerk MAXWELL as Cavendish Professor. After 1884 his researches were carried out mainly in a private laboratory at his home at Terling. He was elected FRS in 1873, and to the Order of Merit in 1902. From 1908 to 1914 he was Chancellor of Cambridge University.

While at Cambridge he was conspicuously successful in establishing courses of experimental physics in the Cavendish Laboratory. He himself was an experimentalist of great ability, gaining valuable results from very simple apparatus. Initially, only half a dozen students attended the course, but by the time he retired in 1884 the number had risen to seventy; by 1892 this number had doubled. After retiring from Cambridge, Rayleigh became professor of natural philosophy in the Royal Institution, London, following John TYNDALL. He resigned this position in 1905, in which year he was elected President of the Royal Society.

In 1904 Rayleigh was awarded the Nobel prize for physics; at the same time his collaborator Sir William RAMSAY was awarded the prize for chemistry. The prize was awarded for his exceedingly accurate measurements of the density of the atmosphere and of its constituent gases, which led to the discovery of argon – announced at the Oxford meeting of the British Association in 1894 – and of the other inert gases together forming a new and unsuspected family of chemical elements.

His preoccupation with extreme precision of experiment was reflected also in his work at Cambridge, which was concerned with establishing electrical units of resistance, current, and electromotive force. His researches extended also to surface tension, sound and optics. He was responsible for bringing to general notice the overlooked work of J. J. WATERSTON on the kinetic theory of gases. He developed the electromagnetic theory of light enunciated by Clerk Maxwell, though he found difficulty in accepting the quantum theory of Max PLANCK.

R. J. Strutt, *John William Strutt: Third Baron Rayleigh*. 2nd ed. 1968.
R. B. Lindsay, *Lord Rayleigh*. 1970.
Nature, **103**, 365, 1919.
Dictionary of National Biography.
Dictionary of Scientific Biography.
Tyler Wasson (Ed.), *Nobel Prize Winners*. 1987. (Portrait.)

T I W

RÉAUMUR, RENÉ ANTOINE FERCHAULT DE
Born at La Rochelle, France, 28 February, 1683; died Paris, 18 October 1757. Scientist and technologist.

Although Réaumur is today generally remembered only by a thermometric scale and a station on the Metro in Paris, his contemporaries described him as 'the Pliny of the eighteenth century' and later writers have likened him to Francis BACON. Certainly the record of his achievements make it surprising that he is so little appreciated today; possibly the reason is that he subscribed to the now unfashionable belief that the scientific and the useful are indissolubly linked. He saw no limit to what might be achieved by the systematic application of science to industry.

Réaumur was elected to the Paris Academy of Sciences at the early age of 25 and in an active membership of nearly fifty years was Director twelve times and contributed seventy-five original memoirs to its proceedings. His interest lay almost equally in the biological and physical fields. His *Mémoires pour servir à l'histoire des insectes*, published in six quarto volumes 1734–42, entitles him to be regarded as one of the founders of entomology. His researches on the technology of iron and steel – published in 1722 in his *L'Arte de convertir le Fer forgé en Acier*, etc., and later translated into English – led to the establishment of steelmaking in France. For this the Duke of Orleans, Regent of France, awarded him an annual pension of 12,000 livres. Later, he turned his attention to the manufacture of tinplate, then imported into France from Germany, and here, too, his researches led to the establishment of a new French industry. Other inquiries ranged over such diverse fields as the manufacture of mirrors, the working of slate, the making of porcelain, and the preservation of eggs and their artificial incubation. At the Academy, where he was appointed *pensionnaire mécanicien* in 1711, he was responsible for organizing the great series of books on various industries that ultimately appeared, though not until after his death, as the twenty-seven folio volumes of the famous *Descriptions des Arts et Métiers.*

Réaumur embodied his views on the application of science to industry in a long memorandum prepared for the Academy about 1720. In this he called for the full-time employment of scientists charged with improving the useful arts, and pointed out the danger of relying on part-time enthusiasts. The necessary finance should be derived, he thought, by endowing the Academy with land in much the same way as the Oxford and Cambridge colleges were endowed; a single major discovery might more than defray the whole of the cost.

Endeavour, **16**, 183, 1957.
A. G. Sisco, *Réaumur's Memoirs on Iron and Steel: a translation from the original printed in 1722* (with introduction and notes by C. S. Smith). 1956.
Revue d'Histoire des Sciences. **11**, 1, 1958.
Dictionary of Scientific Biography.

T I W

REBER, GROTE Born in Wheaton, Illinois, USA, 22 December 1911. Radio engineer who built the world's first radio telescope.

Even before Reber began his studies at the Illinois Institute of Technology he was already a qualified and enthusiastic radio 'ham', and when he read of K. G. JANSKY's discovery in 1932 of a faint source of radio waves apparently beyond the limits of the solar system, he was fired with the determination to investigate this hitherto unknown phenomenon. By 1937 he had built, in his own back yard, a 30-ft diameter steerable parabolic radio wave reflector with an antenna at its focus, tuned to a wavelength of 60 cm instead of the 15 m used by Jansky. Since Jansky did not continue with his own observations, for almost a decade Reber was the world's only radio astronomer.

He soon detected a number of points in the sky from which he received signals significantly stronger than the overall background radiation, and he found that these 'radio stars' did not coincide with any of the visible stars. He began to publish his results in the early 1940s, and after the end of the Second World War the technique of radio astronomy rapidly grew in importance, largely through the work of Sir Bernard LOVELL at Manchester and his construction of the 250-ft radio telescope at Jodrell Bank in Cheshire. Reber meanwhile pursued his own lines of research, building several other telescopes in such locations as Hawaii and Tasmania so that he could map different parts of the 'radio sky' at different wavelengths.

Chambers *Biographical Encyclopedia of Scientists*. 1983.
I. Asimov, *Biographical Encyclopedia of Science and Technology*. 1964.

R M B

REDI, FRANCESCO Born at Arezzo, Italy, 18 February 1626; died Pisa, 1 March 1697/8. Physician and biologist.

Redi qualified in medicine and philosophy at the University of Pisa in 1647. He became personal physician to two Grand Dukes of Tuscany, Ferdinand II and Cosimo III. His learning embraced almost every branch of contemporary intellectual activity; he was known as a literary scholar and poet, a linguist, and one of the earliest students of dialect. He was a member of the *Accademia del Cimento*. As a biologist he pioneered the study of helminthology, and his work on the reproduction of insects made a great impression on his contemporaries. By simple but well-planned experiments he showed – defying the teaching of ARISTOTLE – that flies were not spontaneously generated in putrescent meat, but developed from eggs laid by flies of the same species. Although this did not prove that spontaneous generation could never occur, the doctrine could never again be assumed without question, though it was not finally overthrown until the time of PASTEUR.

U. Viviani, *Vita e opere di Francesco Redi*. 1924.
Enciclopedia Italiana, vol. 28. 1936. (Portrait.)
R. Cole, *Annals of Medical History*, **8**, 347, 1926.
Dictionary of Scientific Biography.

W V F

REED, WALTER Born at Belroi, Virginia, USA, 13 September 1851; died Washington, DC, 22 November 1902. Celebrated for studies on yellow fever.

Reed, son of a Methodist minister, studied medicine at the University of Virginia and Bellevue Hospital Medical College, New York. After a short period of medical practice he was commissioned in the United States Medical Corps in 1875. After serving many years amid the pioneering conditions of frontier posts, he embarked on the research

period of his life by undertaking a course of pathology and bacteriology under W. H. WELCH at Johns Hopkins Hospital in 1890. Subsequently (1893) he became Curator of the Army Medical Museum and professor of bacteriology and clinical microscopy at the Army Medical School and in the next few years made significant studies on erysipelas, diphtheria, and typhoid.

Reed's most celebrated work, however, began in 1900, when he became leader of the four-man Commission of the United States Army on yellow fever, stationed in Havana. His leadership and skilful administration were particularly valuable to its success. When the Commission was established there were many theories about the cause of yellow fever and, in the preceding year, Reed had contested one theory – G. Sanarelli's (1865–1940) view that the disease was caused by a bacterium. Reed and the Commission soon considered the possibility that the disease was transmitted by a mosquito. This was not an unexpected idea in view of R. ROSS's work on malaria, the observations of H. R. Carter (1852–1925) on the spread of yellow fever which indicated an intermediate host, and the theory of C. FINLAY which he had held since 1881, that the mosquito spread the disease.

The hypothesis of mosquito transmission was quickly reinforced when two members of the Commission, J. Carroll (1854–1907) and J. W. Lazear (1866–1900), developed yellow fever after being bitten by mosquitoes. Lazear's case was fatal. Reed then established an isolation camp – Camp Lazear – and, with soldier volunteers, carried out convincing experiments to prove that the mosquito transmitted the disease and that infected material such as clothes and bedding played no part in this. Twenty-two cases of experimental fever were produced, fourteen by mosquito bites, six by injections of blood, and two by injections of filtered serum. The latter established that the causative organism is a non-filterable organism, now identified as a virus. The Commission's studies from June 1900 to February 1901 were followed by eradication of yellow fever wherever mosquito breeding-grounds were destroyed.

Reed returned to Washington to resume duties at the Army Medical School and as professor of pathology and bacteriology at the Columbian University, but unfortunately his work was cut short by death from acute appendicitis.

H. A. Kelly, *Walter Reed and Yellow Fever*. 1923. (Portrait.)
A. E. Truby, *Memoir of Walter Reed, the Yellow Fever Episode*. 1943.
Laura N. Wood, *Walter Reed, Doctor in Uniform*. 1943.
Dictionary of American Biography.
Dictionary of Scientific Biography.

J K C

REGIOMONTANUS (JOHANN MÜLLER) Born at Königsberg, Prussia, Germany, 6 June 1436; died Rome, 6 July 1476. Influential astronomer and mathematician.

Johann Müller was, appropriately, the son of a miller. He studied dialectics at Leipzig (from *c.*1448) and astronomy and trigonometry under G. von Peurbach (1423–61) at Vienna (from 1452). Peurbach showed him how incorrect were the Alfonsine tables, and how poor those Latin versions of Greek texts which came from intermediate Arabic translations. Peurbach never lived to complete the task of composing an 'Epitome' of the *Almagest* of PTOLEMY and Regiomontanus finally prepared this for publication (1496).

Regiomontanus learned Greek from Cardinal Bessarion (1395–1472), and in 1462 they travelled to Rome together, and began a search for early manuscripts of Greek scientific works. With Bessarion he travelled to Viterbo, Ferrara, Padua and Venice, meeting with some of the leading astronomers of the day. By now he had written much of his most important work, *De triangulis*. Returning to Rome to transcribe and study further manuscripts, he left for Vienna in 1468. Thence he moved to Nuremberg (1471), where he was befriended by Bernard Walther (1430–1504), a rich amateur astronomer, and where also he published his *Tabulae Directionum* (1475), an astrological work, but containing a valuable table of tangents. Walther provided him with an observatory and workshop, and Regiomontanus was largely responsible for making Nuremberg the leading centre for instrument-making.

In 1475, Pope Sixtus IV called Regiomontanus to Rome, to advise on reform of the calendar, but the astronomer died within a year. His possessions were acquired by Walther, after whose death they passed to the Senate of Nuremberg. For this reason, it was only in 1533 that the *De Triangulis* was given to the world. This did for the West what Nasir ad-Din (1201–74) had done three centuries earlier for the East, namely, provide a systematic basis for the development of trigonometry and thus remove the subject from subservience to astronomy. The comparable work of RICHARD OF WALLINGFORD was probably without much influence on it, although the later work strongly resembled the Latin translation (1342) of a Hebrew text by Levi ben Gerson (1288–1344).

Regiomontanus often uses unnecessarily tedious proofs, and although he had introduced the tangent function into the *Tabulae Directionum*, it was not used in the earlier (but posthumously published) work. He seems to have been first with the trigonometrical formula for the area of a triangle.

Regiomontanus was a great scholar, but his importance in the history of mathematics lies in the compilation and transmission of knowledge. Although not a strikingly original astronomer or mathematician, his work contains many flashes of inspiration, as, for example, when he discusses a problem of maxima and minima in a letter of 1471. Like many famous scientists, he had an undeserved reputation for creating stupendous automata of various kinds.

Allgemeine Deutsche Biographie, vol. 22.

E. Zinner, *Leben und Wirken des . . . Regiomontanus*. revised ed. 1968.

Dictionary of Scientific Biography.

J D N

REGNAULT, HENRI VICTOR Born at Aix-la-Chapelle (Aachen), Germany, 21 July 1810; died Paris, 19 January 1878. Famous for his studies on chlorine compounds and his determinations of the physical properties of gases.

After working as a draper's assistant in Paris, Regnault entered the *École Polytechnique* in 1830, qualifying as a mining engineer two years later and

eventually returning as professor of chemistry (after appointments at Giessen and Lyons) in 1840.

During this time he worked on the composition of alkaloids, some reactions of sulphur trioxide, and other topics. More important were his studies of aliphatic halogen compounds. He examined the chlorination products of ethylene chloride, ethyl chloride, and diethyl ether. By using potash as a dehydrohalogenating reagent he discovered vinyl chloride, dichloroethylene, and trichloroethylene – compounds of great industrial importance today. By chlorination of boiling chloroform and sulphur dioxide respectively, he became the first to obtain carbon tetrachloride and sulphuryl chloride.

For the remainder of his life Regnault's interests centred largely in physics, though later work included a report on the test for arsenic devised by James MARSH and studies on respiration and the composition of air. Shortly after returning to Paris he was appointed to the chair of physics at the *Collège de France*. Having improved the usual technique for specific heat determinations, he applied it extensively to solids and liquids, demonstrating the general validity of the Dulong-Petit Law (see P. L. DULONG and A. T. PETIT). By a method of his own devising he found the specific heats of about thirty-five gases and showed that their specific heats at constant pressure did not vary with temperature or pressure, and were inversely proportional to their vapour densities. He invented the air thermometer and examined vapour pressures of simple and mixed gases. Paying particular attention to water, he redetermined its vapour pressure at different temperatures and its specific and latent heats. Accurate measurements of the coefficients of expansion of gases revealed that the gas laws of John DALTON, J. L. GAY-LUSSAC, R. BOYLE and E. MARIOTTE were only approximately true.

In 1854 Regnault became Director of the porcelain factory at Sèvres, in which capacity he worked on ceramic production. The 1870 war brought him a double tragedy; his second son, Henri, was killed, and his laboratory was wrecked by Prussian troops, with loss of hundreds of experimental results. His last scientific communication was a report of this disaster, and his final years were shadowed by grief and increasing physical disability. He was a member of the *Académie des Sciences* from 1840 and of the *Légion d'Honneur* from 1850.

T. H. Norton, *Nature*, **17**, 263, 1878.

M. E. Weeks, *Discovery of the Elements* (5th ed.). 1945. (Portrait.)

J. H. Gladstone, *Journal of the Chemical Society*, **33**, 235, 1878.

R. Fox, *The Caloric Theory of Gases from Lavoisier to Regnault*. 1971.

Dictionary of Scientific Biography.

C A R

REMAK, ROBERT Born at Posen (Poznan), Poland, 26 July 1815; died Kissingen, Bavaria, Germany, 29 August 1865. A pioneer in neuroanatomy and neuro-embryology.

Remak studied medicine at the University of Berlin, where he was a pupil of Johannes MÜLLER, and graduated in 1838 with a very important thesis (see below). He then became an unpaid assistant to Müller, and supported himself by general practice. From 1843 to 1847 he was assistant to Lucas

Schönlein (1793–1864), the physician at the *Char-ité*. In 1847 he became a *Privatdozent* in the University of Berlin, and in 1859 he was promoted to associate professor.

Remak's rather undistinguished academic career bears no relation to the importance and originality of his work. In 1836 he obtained a compound microscope, and on the basis of work done with it he published two important papers on the nervous system before he obtained his doctorate. His doctoral thesis of 1838 dealt with his microscopical observations on nervous tissue. He described the meduallary or myelin sheath of nerves in the main nervous system, but in the same year (1838) Theodor SCHWANN also described this sheath, and Schwann's name has become associated with it. Remak also showed in this thesis that the axis-cylinder (axon) of a peripheral nerve arises from a nerve cell in the spinal cord, and that it runs continuously from the nerve cell to the terminal branching of the nerve. He showed that fibres of the sympathetic nervous system are grey, and not white, because they are non-myelinated. In 1844 he was the first to describe neurofibrils in nerve cells, and the existence of six distinct layers of cells in the cerebral cortex. In that paper also he was the first to describe the sympathetic ganglion-cells of the sinus venosus of the frog's heart. In 1847 he described the gangliated plexuses of sympathetic nerves in the stomach wall.

In 1851 Remak simplified the conception of germ-layers in embryology by regarding the two middle layers of K. E. von BAER as a single layer, and he showed the significance of the three layers in the development of the organs and tissues of the body. He studied the development of the neural tube. In the same year he gave a good description of the earliest development of vessels in the vascular area of the chick embryo. In 1852 he was one of the first to point out that the proliferation of cells to form tissues is accompanied by cell-division, and though he appears to have seen amitotic division, the process of karyokinesis was unknown to him.

In the clinical field Remak must be regarded as a pioneer of the electrotherapy of nervous diseases, on which he published an important work (1858). He wrote also on ascending neuritis, on lead poisoning, on paralysis of the musculo-spiral nerve, and on other nervous conditions. While he was assistant to Schölein, Remak produced favus (a contagious skin disease) in himself experimentally, and he identified the causative fungus, which he named *Achorion Schöleini* after his chief.

Transactions of the American Philosophical Society, **44**, 251, 1954.
Dictionary of Scientific Biography.
W. Haymaker and F. Schiller (Eds), *Founders of Neurology*. 1953. (Portrait.)
S. A. Kinnier Wilson, *Neurology*. 1940.

E A U

REMSEN, IRA Born in New York, 10 February 1846; died Carmel, California, 4 March 1927. Chemist and teacher.

Remsen qualified in medicine at the New York Free Academy, but in 1867 went to Europe to study chemistry. He visited several German universities, and worked under J. von LIEBIG, J. Volhard (1834–1910), F. WÖHLER, and R. FITTIG. He returned to the United States in 1871, and obtained a post in Williams College (Massachusetts), but had no facilities for research. In 1876 he was appointed to the chair of chemistry at the newly founded Johns Hopkins University, Baltimore; he built up a considerable chemical school, and retired as President in 1913. Later he became a consultant to the Standard Oil Company.

Remsen and his students worked in many fields of organic chemistry, but he is remembered for his discovery (with C. Fahlberg (1850–1910)) of saccharin (1879), the first synthetic non-carbohydrate sweetening agent. He also wrote several textbooks, including *Principles of Theoretical Chemistry* (1877), and founded the *American Chemical Journal*.

Journal of the Chemical Society, 3182, 1927.
F. H. Getman, *Journal of Chemical Education*, **16**, 353, 1939.
E. Farber (Ed.), *Great Chemists*. 1961.
F. H. Getman, *Life of Ira Remsen*. 1940.
Dictionary of Scientific Biography.

W V F

RENNIE, JOHN Born at Phantassie, near Haddington, Scotland, 7 June 1761; died London, 4 October 1821. Civil engineer.

Rennie, who was the son of a freehold farmer, was educated at Dunbar High School and Edinburgh University, where he studied under John Robison (1739–1805) and Joseph BLACK. He was also trained as a millwright by Andrew Meikle (1719–1811), the threshing-machine inventor. A visit to James Watt led to his employment for the erection of the Albion Mills in London, the first to have all-iron plant. In the 1790s he succeeded to the position held by John SMEATON as a general canal-work consultant; undertook to drain part of the East Anglian fens; and built (1799) a handsome bridge over the Tweed at Kelso, with semi-elliptical arches and a level roadway.

Using coffer-dams to ensure the safety of the foundations, Rennie was the author of three famous bridges in London. In 1810–17 he built Waterloo Bridge, distinguished by elliptical arches of unusual width and the extensive employment of granite. This was followed in 1814–19 by Southwark Bridge, composed of three massive cast-iron arches, resting on exceptionally solid masonry piers designed to resist the flow of the river at its narrowest and deepest point. In the last year of his life Rennie designed New London Bridge, 30 yards upstream from the previous one, giving the centre arch a span of 150 feet, which provided a 29½-foot clearance at high tide. The bridge was erected by his son John (1794–1874) in 1824–31.

Rennie's work for London also included the construction of the London and East India Docks, where he provided cast-iron columns and roofs for warehouses and steam cranes on the quays. At Hull in 1804 he introduced a steam-driven dredging machine to reduce the labour of clearing the dock site. Altogether, he was consulted about forty-four harbour improvement schemes in the United Kingdom and others in Malta and Bermuda. At Plymouth he began in 1811 the building of the first big breakwater on the English side of the Channel. The provision of a stable slope of large stone blocks resting upon a gigantic mound of rubble was much interfered with by the southwesterly gales, but by the time of its completion in 1848 experience had confirmed Rennie's forecast that the seaward slope must not be steeper than 1:5.

As an expert engineer, Rennie gave his supervision simultaneously to many different enterprises: in 1805–9, for instance, he built the Bell Rock lighthouse, making half a dozen personal visits and engaging Robert STEPHENSON as resident engineer working to his design. It seems reasonable to attribute the decline of his health in the last nine years of his life to habitual overwork: according to Smiles, he had no relaxations and made business appointments for 5 a.m. Rennie became FRS in 1798; refused a knighthood from the Prince Regent in 1817; and was buried in St Paul's Cathedral.

S. Smiles, *Lives of the Engineers*, vol. 2. (Revised ed.) 1874.

C. T. G. Boucher, *Transactions of the Newcomen Society*, **34**, 1, 1961–2; *John Rennie 1761– 1821*. 1963.

Dictionary of National Biography.

T K D

REYNOLDS, OSBORNE Born in Belfast, Ireland, 23 August 1842; died Watchet, Somerset, England, 21 February 1912. Remembered for pioneering studies of turbulent motion and many theoretical contributions to engineering.

After some workshop experience, Reynolds proceeded to Cambridge where he graduated Seventh Wrangler in 1867 and was elected to a Fellowship at Queens' College. In 1868 he was appointed to the new chair of engineering at Owen's College, Manchester. There he organized an exacting course in mechanical and civil engineering which attracted a number of outstanding students, including J. J. THOMSON. He was elected a Fellow of the Royal Society in 1877, and was awarded a Royal Medal in 1888.

In 1873–5 he published a series of papers on the propulsion of ships, including an explanation of the racing of ships' propellers. He also laid down dynamical conditions for models to give results similar to full-scale ships. In 1877 there appeared the first of his papers on hydrodynamics in which he proved the production of vortices by the motion of flat plates or solid bodies through water. The production of these vortices was demonstrated by the use of filaments of coloured dye, a technique which he used to great effect later. In 1833–4 he published a number of fundamental papers in which he introduced the dimensionless Reynolds Number depending on the viscosity, density and linear dimensions of the flow. This number, with the accompanying notion of two distinct types of fluid flow, natural and turbulent, has played a central role in all subsequent work on viscous fluids. In 1887 he read an important paper to the British Association on the employment of models for the determination of estuary tides. A paper of 1886 on the theory of lubrication laid the foundation for all subsequent investigations in the subject and led to the development of modern thrust bearings. In mechanical engineering, he took out patents for improving pumps and turbines, including the notion of a rotating guide vane for the regulation of hydraulic turbines. He also anticipated some of the subsequent work of C. PARSONS on marine turbines. He built an experimental steam engine

which led to a careful redetermination of the mechanical equivalent of heat.

Reynolds was undoubtedly the most successful and influential English theoretical mechanical engineer of the century.

Dictionary of National Biography.

A. H. Gibson, *Osborne Reynolds*. 1946.

H. Lamb, *Proceedings of the Royal Society*, **88A**, xv, 1913.

D. M. McDowell and J. D. Jackson (Eds), *Osborne Reynolds and Engineering Science Today*. 1968.

Nature, **88**, 590, 1912.

Dictionary of Scientific Biography.

J W H

RHAZES (AL-RAZI) Born at Ray, near Tehran (in modern Iran), *c*.AD 841; died there, AD 925. Physician and scientist.

Rhazes, like many medieval scholars, studied a wide range of subjects, including philosophy, music (on which he wrote an encyclopaedia), poetry and logic. His interest in medicine apparently did not begin until he was in his thirties, and is said to have been aroused by a chance meeting with an apothecary in Baghdad. He quickly established a reputation and was made head of the chief hospital in the city. He was a prolific writer; over 200 works are attributed to him, about half of them on medicine. The most famous is the twenty-five-volume *Al-Hawi*; no original version survives, but it is well known in Latin translations. Another major work – but less original, in that it is mostly derived from Greek authors – is the *Al Kitabu-l-Mansuri* (so called because of its dedication to Prince al Mansur). He wrote a treatise on smallpox, giving precise indications for distinguishing this clinically from measles, and another on stone of the bladder and kidney.

Like many physicians of his time, Rhazes was actively interested in alchemy. Again he wrote widely, and some twenty books are attributed to him, though not all survive. The best known is his *Book of the Secrets*, which contains much practical advice on chemical manipulations. He was a believer in the transmutation of metals and like GEBER believed that metals were derived primarily from two simple, but idealized, elements, sulphur and mercury; to these he seems inclined to have added another, an idealized form of salt. He was himself familiar with a wide range of well-defined chemicals, many of which he no doubt used in his medical work. He attempted an elaborate classification of all known substances, dividing them basically into those of an animal, vegetable or mineral nature.

R. H. Major, *A History of Medicine*, vol. 1. 1954.

G. Gabrieli, *Isis*, **7**, 9, 1925.

Dictionary of Scientific Biography.

T I W

RHETICUS (GEORG JOACHIM VON LAUCHEN) Born at Feldkirch, Tyrol, Austria, 15 February 1514; died Cassovia, Hungary, 4 December 1576. Astronomer and mathematician, a protagonist of the work of COPERNICUS.

Georg Joachim von Lauchen, usually known as Rheticus, must have been brought up in fairly easy circumstances, for at an early age he went with his parents to Italy, afterwards studying at Zürich and Wittenberg (1532). He taught there from 1536, having studied at Nuremberg and Tübingen in the meantime. Having heard reports of the Copernican theory, as yet unpublished, he decided to resign his post, and go to Frauenberg to learn of it from the aged Copernicus himself. After two years (1537–9), he returned to Wittenberg, having written a biography, now unfortunately lost, of Copernicus. He then supervised the separate printing of the trigonometrical parts of Copernicus's great work, the *De revolutionibus* (1542; the whole was published in 1543). He had already put out a short summary of the heliocentric ideas, the *Narratio prima*, printed in the form of a letter to Johan Schöner (1477–1547) in 1540, and reprinted in 1541 by popular demand.

Rheticus now moved to Leipzig, where he stayed for nine years (1542–51). Part of this time he spent working at his own great work on trigonometry, which was not, however, finished at his death. This, published as the *Opus palatinum de triangulis*, was completed by Lucius Valentine Otho (d. 1597), and published by him in 1596. Three out of four books are by Rheticus, and they must be counted his most important original work. Even in his relations with Copernicus however, there was probably a two-way exchange of ideas, Rheticus probably supplying Copernicus with trigonometric knowledge derived from REGIOMONTANUS.

The *Opus palatinum* is a somewhat confusing work, containing as it does a terminology peculiar to itself, with great danger of ambiguity. For example, the word 'basis' can mean cotangent or cosine, according to the type of triangle understood. This was not a retrograde step, however, for it helped to establish the attitude that trigonometric functions are properties of angles, rather than lengths associated with certain configurations in a circle or sphere. But probably the most important part of the work was that containing tables of sines, tangents and secants, and their complementary functions, to ten decimal places. By 1551 Rheticus had published tables to seven places, and a set of tables to fifteen places was completed by the faithful Otho, and published in 1613, after the death of both men. In all cases the intervals are ten seconds of arc. This achievement was possible through his discovery of the formulae for $\sin a/2$ and $\sin a/3$ in terms of $\sin a$. He is said to have had computers working for him for twelve years, and certainly these trigonometrical labours have never been equalled without mechanical help.

E. Rosen, *Three Copernican Treatises* (2nd ed.). 1959.

K. H. Burmeister, *Georg Joachim Rhetikus*, 3 vols. 1967–8.

Dictionary of Scientific Biography.

J D N

RICARDO, HARRY RALPH Born in London, 26 January 1885; died Graffham, Sussex, 18 May 1974. A mechanical engineer who made outstanding contributions to the theory and design of internal combustion engines.

Ricardo's father was an architect and artist, and his mother was the daughter of Sir Alexander Rendel (1829–1918), the civil engineer. At Rugby School and Trinity College, Cambridge, he designed and built small engines, first for motorcycles; one, the Dolphin, became a successful 15 hp high-speed two-stroke petrol engine for cars

and boats. In 1907 Ricardo joined his grandfather's firm, Rendel & Robertson (later Rendel, Palmer & Tritton) where he inspected machinery and designed mechanical equipment. In 1916 he designed a six-cylinder, four-stroke, 150 hp engine for tanks which, by the end of 1917, was being produced at a rate of 100 per week. This success enabled Ricardo to set up his own consulting and design company at Shoreham in 1917. The company's pioneering designs included a sleeve valve engine for the Air Ministry (1923); the Triumph-Ricardo motorcycle engine; a 300 hp sleeve valve diesel engine (1929); and a six-cylinder poppet valve diesel engine of 130 hp for AEC buses.

Ricardo was persuaded by Professor Bertram Hopkinson (1874–1918) to work, as an undergraduate at Cambridge (1903–7), on ignition, combustion and detonation. Even before 1914, Ricardo had differentiated between pre-ignition and detonation; devised an optical indicator for measuring pressures in a detonating engine; and started to measure the effect of fuel type on detonation. In 1918 the Asiatic Petroleum Co. sponsored a three-year research programme on fuels and detonation: this work originated the use of the Octane Number for rating fuels and the design of variable compression engines for testing them.

Research on combustion in side valve engines led to an important patent and a successful action against the Humber-Hillman Co. in 1932, and that on combustion in diesel engines led to world-wide use of Ricardo's designs.

Ricardo was elected an FRS in 1929; he was President of the Institution of Mechanical Engineers 1944–5; and was made a Knight Bachelor in 1948. He received many medals, including the Royal Society Rumford Medal, the James Watt Medal of the Institution of Mechanical Engineers, and the Melchett Medal. His well-known book, *The High-speed Internal Combustion Engine* was published in 1923 (fifth edition 1968).

He married Beatrice Bertha Hale in 1911. He had a happy life in Walton-on-Thames, Lancing, Tottington, and Graffham – sailing, butterfly-collecting and travelling. Three daughters, twelve grandchildren and seven great-grandchildren were born during his lifetime.

Biographical Memoirs of Fellows of the Royal Society. 1976. (Portrait.)

Harry Ricardo, *Memories and Machines. The Pattern of my Life.* 1968.

Proceedings of The Institution of Mechanical Engineers, 152, 1945.

Dictionary of National Biography.

W R H

RICHARD OF WALLINGFORD Born at Wallingford, Berkshire, England, *c*.1291–2; died St Albans, Hertfordshire, 23 May 1336. The leading English astronomer and mathematician of his time and builder of one of the first mechanical astronomical clocks.

Richard was the son of a blacksmith, on whose death the boy was taken into the care of the Prior of Wallingford. On account of his great promise, he was sent to Oxford, where he spent about six years (*c*.1308–14), after which he assumed the monastic habit at St Albans. Returning to Oxford in 1317, he remained there until he was appointed Abbot of St Albans in 1326. Returning from a visit to the Pope, necessary if he was to be confirmed in his office, he found himself stricken with leprosy. His rule was a stern one, and there was some opposition from both within and without the monastery to the idea of a leper as abbot of England's premier abbey. But his administrative skill and his great learning earned him the general admiration of his monks.

A number of works survive that can be attributed with some certainty to him. These include instructions for making and using the instruments known as the rectangulus (cognate with the torquetum) and the albion. The latter is basically an equatorium, for computing planetary positions, combined with an eclipse computer. The albion was apparently well known more than two centuries later: the treatise describing it was made known in southern Germany through versions by John of Gmünden (*fl.* 1430) and REGIOMONTANUS and its influence is evident in the later work of Apian (1531–89).

About 1320, Richard had composed his major mathematical work, the *Quadripartitum* (on trigonometry) in four parts. Although in many respects remarkable, this, like his other writings on trigonometry, does not seem to have prompted other mathematicians to help raise the standard of the subject, which was generally poor by comparison with its Islamic counterpart.

Richard of Wallingford, like almost all contemporary astronomers, wrote on astrology, and there are two works on the subject which may be his. One of these, the *Exafrenon*, which may have been the work of his youth, must have been popular, being translated into Middle English (from Latin) more than once.

What was probably his last scientific work, and one which he left unfinished at his death, contained a set of general precepts for the design of astronomical clocks, and much specific information about the design of the great clock which he began to build at St Albans. This had a mechanical escapement and it is the earliest clock about which we can say this with certainty.

The usual lists of Richard of Wallingford's writings contain two literary ghosts: *De opimetris* and *De diametris.*

Dictionary of National Biography.
R. T. Gunther, *Early Science in Oxford*, vol. 1. 1923. (Portrait.)
J. D. North, *Richard of Wallingford.* 1976.
J. D. Bond, *Isis*, **4**, 459, 1922.
Dictionary of Scientific Biography.
                                                           J D N

RICHARDS, THEODORE WILLIAM Born at Germantown, Pennsylvania, USA, 31 January 1868; died Cambridge, Massachusetts, 2 April 1928. Chemist, best known for his atomic weight determinations.

Richards was educated at home until he was 14, when he was sent to Haverford College. At first his main interest was astronomy, but because his eyesight was poor he turned to chemistry instead. In 1885 he obtained his BSc, at the head of his class, and went on to Harvard, where in the next year he obtained a BA *summa cum laude*, with the highest honours in chemistry. At Harvard he came under the influence of Professor J. P. Cooke (1827–94), who wanted to know what truth there was in the hypothesis of William PROUT – that all atomic weights are whole numbers – and in 1888 set Richards to determine the ratio of oxygen to hydrogen in water to see if it were exactly 16:1. The University recognized the excellence of this work by awarding Richards a travelling fellowship to go to Europe, where he met H. E. ROSCOE, Victor MEYER and Lord RAYLEIGH, among others. In 1895 he was again sent to Europe, to W. F. OSTWALD and W. H. NERNST, to learn the newest developments in physical chemistry. In 1901 he was offered a chair at Göttingen, but Harvard made a better offer and Richards remained there for life.

He had an 'intense desire to know something more definite about the material and energetic structure of the universe'; and atomic weights, which are definite and precise and reveal the Periodic System, seemed one of the great mysteries of nature, in need of more searching investigation. He introduced two new techniques. Firstly, a combined drying and bottling apparatus, so that substances had no chance to absorb water between being dried and being weighed. Secondly, the nephelometer, a device for comparing turbidities and thus determining more accurately end-points in titrations involving silver halides. He now began to detect errors even in the very exact analyses of J. G. STAS. Over the years Richards and his co-workers determined the atomic weights of twenty-five elements with unprecedented accuracy, and workers he had trained determined another thirty. The most dramatic determination was in 1913, when M. E. Lembert was sent by K. FAJANS to Richards's laboratory to measure whether lead found in uranium minerals and thought to be derived from the decay of uranium had the same atomic weight as ordinary lead. They found it was lighter; and this led to the rapid acceptance of the theory of radioactive decay and transmutation.

Richards was a good teacher, presenting subjects clearly and logically. In 1915 he was awarded the Nobel prize for chemistry. In his later years he worked also on atomic volumes, and the compressibility of different elements.

Proceedings of the Royal Society, **131A**, xxix, 1928. (Portrait.)
H. Hartley, *Journal of the Chemical Society*, 1930, 1930. (Portrait.)
Dictionary of American Biography.
Dictionary of Scientific Biography.
E. Farber (Ed.), *Great Chemists.* 1961. (Portrait.)
Biographical Memoirs. National Academy of Sciences. 1974.
Tyler Wasson (Ed.), *Nobel Prize Winners.* 1987. (Portrait.)
                                                           D M K

RICHET, CHARLES ROBERT Born in Paris, 26 August 1850; died there, 4 December 1935. Physiologist.

Charles Richet was the son of Alfred Richet, professor of surgery in Paris. He, too, studied medicine there, graduating in 1877. Ten years later he was appointed professor of physiology in the faculty of medicine, Paris. In the same year he became editor of the *Revue Scientifique*, continuing in this office until 1902.

His earliest researches concerned the mechanisms by which animals maintain a constant body temperature. Later he became interested in the possibilities of treating epilepsy with potassium bromide, and in the dietary treatment of tuberculosis. Interest in tuberculosis led him to enter the field of serum treatment and on 6 December 1890 he gave the first human injection of anti-tuberculosis serum.

The growing use of antisera for the treatment of infectious diseases focused attention on shock reaction to injections (allergy), especially when these were repeated. From 1894 onwards, for example, there were repeated references in the medical literature to reactions to diphtheria toxin. Richet, working with dogs injected with extracts of certain sea anemones, was the first to make a close study of this serious problem of hypersensitivity. He discovered that repeated injections of foreign proteins at long intervals could eventually result in a fatal reaction. He called this anaphylaxis, in contradistinction to prophylaxis. For this work he received the Nobel prize for medicine in 1913.

Tyler Wasson (Ed.), *Nobel Prize Winners*. 1987. (Portrait.)
Proceedings of the Royal Society of Edinburgh, **56**, 276, 1935–6.
Nature, **136**, 1017, 1935.
Dictionary of Scientific Biography.

T I W

RICHTER, BURTON Born in Brooklyn, New York, 22 March 1931. Experimental particle physicist.

Richter graduated from Massachusetts Institute of Technology in 1952, and continued there to take his PhD in 1956, having studied the production of the particles called pions at the MIT synchrotron. During this time he became interested in quantum electrodynamics, the quantum theory of electromagnetism, and he moved to Stanford University with the aim of using the electron accelerator there to study the theory at very small distances. He was invited to join W. K. H. Panofsky (1919–) and G. K. O'Neill (1927–) from Princeton, in building an electron-electron collider at Stanford, which started up in 1965 and become the first collider to carry out a successful programme of experiments.

Meanwhile, in 1963, Richter and David Ritson had proposed an electron-positron collider. The project received funding in 1970, and work on the SPEAR machine began at the Stanford Linear Accelerator Laboratory. SPEAR started up in 1973, and in 1974 Richter's group found a new particle, the J/psi, the first of several discoveries. The particle was discovered independently at the Brookhaven National Laboratory by the group of Sam TING, and in 1976 Richter and Ting shared the Nobel prize in physics.

In 1979 Richter proposed a scheme to convert the 3-km long linear accelerator at SLAC into an electron-positron collider, a project which has proved a valuable testing ground for ideas for future accelerators. He has been director of SLAC since 1984.

Physics Today, December 1976. (Portrait.)
Les Prix Nobel en 1976. 1977. (Portrait.)
Tyler Wasson (Ed.), *Nobel Prize Winners*. 1987. (Portrait.)

C S

RICKETTS, HOWARD TAYLOR Born at Findlay, Ohio, USA, 9 February 1871; died Mexico City, 3 May 1910. Discoverer of the insect vectors of Rocky Mountain spotted fever and of tabardillo.

Ricketts graduated in arts at the University of Nebraska (1894). He then studied medicine at the North-Western University Medical School, and graduated in 1897. He was appointed associate professor of pathology in the University of Chicago (1902). Shortly before his death he was called to the chair of pathology in the University of Pennsylvania.

Ricketts's early researches related to blastomycosis. In 1906 he succeeded in transmitting Rocky Mountain spotted fever to guinea-pigs and monkeys. He discovered that the vector is a tick, and that while larval ticks convey the infection to rodents, which act as a reservoir, only adult ticks convey it to human subjects. The seasonal incidence of the disease was therefore explained. In 1909 he discovered in infected guinea-pigs a minute organism, later named after him. In 1909 also Charles NICOLLE proved that typhus fever is spread by lice. Ricketts then studied the disease known as tabardillo in Mexico. He showed that it is typhus fever, and that it also is spread by the body louse. In the course of these researches he lost his life.

Journal of the American Medical Association, **54**, 1640, 1910.
H. T. Ricketts, *Contributions to Medical Science 1870–1910*. 1911. (Portrait.)
Dictionary of Scientific Biography.

E A U

RIEMANN, GEORG FRIEDRICH BERNHARD Born at Breselenz, Hanover, Germany, 17 September 1826; died Selasca, Lake Maggiore, Italy, 20 July 1866. Originator of Riemannian geometry, and of the theory of Riemann surfaces.

Riemann was the son of a clergyman, from whom he received his early education. After attending a local school, he left in 1840 for the Lyceum at Hanover. In 1846 he entered the University of Göttingen, to study theology and philology, but soon turned exclusively to mathematics. Attracted by the reputation of K. G. J. JACOBI, and P. G. Lejeune-Dirichlet (1805–59), J. Steiner (1796–1863), and F. G. M. Eisenstein (1823–52), all at the University of Berlin, he moved there after only a year at Göttingen. In 1850 he returned to prepare his doctoral dissertation on the theory of functions of a complex variable. His thesis, which owed much to his Berlin teachers, was praised by K. F. GAUSS, and laid the foundations for his work of the next decade, on complex functions and their use in the theory of Abelian integrals and theta functions; on the representation of functions by trigonometric series; and on the foundations of differential geometry. In 1859 he went to Göttingen as successor to Lejeune-Dirichlet, who had succeeded Gauss in 1855. But the long struggle to survive on the casual fees of a private teacher, during the intervening years, had undermined his health; he died of pleurisy at the age of 39.

Riemann's starting-point in the theory of complex functions was the extension of the notion of regularity to many-valued functions. He introduced the intuitive idea of many-leafed Riemann surfaces whose sheets are connected around the branch-points of the function, and on which the function can be defined as single valued. He showed how to treat the function as a conformal map of a simply connected domain, this being described essentially by the point singularities of the function and the shape of the map of the boundary of the domain. The Riemann mapping theorem was a by-product of his theory.

Differential geometry of spaces of more than three dimensions began, in effect, with Riemann's paper 'On the hypotheses which lie at the foundation of geometry' (1854, published posthumously 1868). This contains a generalization of most of the results of a famous memoir on the geometry of curved surfaces (in ordinary space) by Gauss (1827). After presenting arguments for considering quadratic metrics as in a sense fundamental, he gave most attention to those having constant curvature. Amongst other things, he showed how the so-called Riemannian curvature of a space of n dimensions is determined by the metric of its geodesic surfaces. Above all, he laid the analytical foundations for non-Euclidean geometry. Throughout this subject he seems to have been motivated by his studies of mathematical physics, which occupied the last years of a life unhappily cut short before its full promise was fulfilled.

H. Weber (Ed.), *B. Riemann, Collected Works.* 1953. (See introduction by H. Lewy and biography by R. DEDEKIND.)

M. P. Jaggi, *Physics Today*, **20**, 42, 1967.

Dictionary of Scientific Biography.

J D N

RITTER, JOHANN WILHELM Born at Samnitz, Silesia, 16 December 1776; died Munich, Bavaria, Germany, 23 January 1810. A pioneer in electrochemistry.

After working as a pharmacist in Liegnitz (1791–5), Ritter studied medicine at Jena, and taught there and at Gotha until 1804, when he became a member of the Bavarian Academy at Munich.

Like many of his contemporaries, Ritter began the study of electricity in a biological context, and in 1798 wrote on animal galvanism. In 1802 he invented the 'dry' voltaic pile and in 1803 an electrical storage battery. He was one of the first to collect hydrogen and oxygen on electrolysis of water (1800), and concluded that they were compounds of water and electricity. His studies of electrolysis convinced him of the electrical nature of chemical combination. He did much work on galvanic and voltaic electricity, which he explained in chemical terms. He was the first to enunciate an electrochemical series.

Ritter was also interested in the role of light in chemical reactions. In 1800 he examined the effect of nitrogen on the glow of phosphorus, and in 1801 he discovered ultra-violet radiation by its darkening effects on silver chloride. Regarding optical spectra rather like a voltaic pile, he supposed that red rays oxidized and violet rays reduced (1808).

Apart from the importance of Ritter's discoveries, his theories of galvanism and electrolysis played a significant part in early electrochemistry. For example, notebooks of H. DAVY indicate how strongly his own views were influenced by those of Ritter.

J. R. Partington, *A History of Chemistry*, vol. 4. 1964.

J. C. Poggendorf, *Biographisch-literarisches Handwörterbuch.* 1883-1903.

C. von Klinkowstroem, *Mitteilungen zur Geschichte der Medizin, Naturwissenschaften und der Technik*, **32**, 303, 1932.

Dictionary of Scientific Biography.

C A R

ROBERT OF CHESTER Born probably at Ketton, Rutland, England, early in the 12th century. Introduced Arabic alchemy and mathematics to western Europe.

The little that is known of Robert of Chester gives him an assured place in the history of western science. Educated at the then flourishing school of Chester, he studied at the Moorish universities of Spain and introduced to Europe the ideas of the Arabs, then the leaders of scientific thought. His Book of the Composition of Alchemy was the translation in Latin, completed on 11 February 1144 (one of the few precise dates that can be attributed to him), of the alchemical treatise of the Umayyad prince Khalid ibn Yazid (d. *c.*704), who is reputed to have studied under a Christian scholar, Morienus. He made also the first Latin translation of the Koran (1143).

Robert's interest in mathematics led him to translate the treatise on algebra of Mohammed AL-KHWARIZMI. He was the first to use the word sine (*sinus*) in its modern trigonometrical sense. For a time he was Archdeacon of Pamplona, but he returned to England about 1147. There he calculated astronomical service tables for the longitude of London.

E. J. Holmyard, *Alchemy.* 1957.

Gordon Leff, *Medieval Thought; St Augustine to Ockham.* 1958.

T I W

ROBERTS, RICHARD Born at Carreghofa, Montgomeryshire, Wales, 22 April 1789; died Manchester, England, 16 March 1864. Inventor.

Second of four sons of a shoemaker and tollkeeper, Richard Roberts left school early and went to work first on Telford's newly opened Ellesmere Canal and then in a limestone quarry until he was 20. In the general shortage of labour during the Napoleonic wars he drifted to works in the Midlands. His wanderings took him to Liverpool, Manchester and London, where he worked for a time with Henry MAUDSLAY. When the fear of compulsory military service ended with the war, he returned to Manchester, centre of the cotton industry, where he set up on his own in 1814. In 1817 he designed a machine for planing metal. Other inventions included improvements in Maudslay's screw-cutting lathe: a back-geared lathe headstock and improvements to the self-acting slide-lathe are both in the Science Museum, South Kensington.

In 1824 the local cotton manufacturers asked him to build a self-acting mule in order to counter a strike. This was an improvement on that invented by Samuel CROMPTON in 1779 and was perfected in four months at a cost of £12,000.

Offered a partnership by Thomas Sharp in 1828, his scope widened. Not only did the firm manufacture self-acting mules – to which he added a radial arm for winding (1832) – but after the opening of the Liverpool and Manchester Railway (1830) they began to manufacture locomotives for the leading

British and Continental railways, beginning with the *Experiment*. In 1834 they constructed a steam carriage with a differential drive to the back axle.

The death of Thomas Sharp in 1842 led to the dissolution of the partnership. Roberts retained the Globe Works, and the remaining members of the Sharp family continued to manufacture locomotives at the new Atlas Works. Roberts turned his attention to further inventions. In 1848 he devised a machine for punching holes in steel plates. This, like his self-acting mule of 1825, was in direct response to an appeal by employers to beat a strike of workmen, in this case of workmen on the Conway suspension bridge. His fertility of invention seemed to increase as his financial resources diminished. He made an electromagnet and a number of clocks, and was involved in devising improvements for steamships, but he became so poor that just before he died a subscription was being raised to sustain him.

He was a founder member of the Manchester Mechanics' Institute (1824). In 1838, he was elected a member of the Institution of Civil Engineers.

H. W. Dickinson, *Transactions of the Newcomen Society*, 25, 123. 1944, (Portrait.)
Dictionary of Welsh Biography.
Dictionary of National Biography.

W H G A

ROBERTS-AUSTEN, SIR WILLIAM CHANDLER

Born at Kennington, Surrey, England, 3 March 1843; died London, 22 November 1902. Metallurgist.

Roberts-Austen was born William Chandler Roberts, and by Royal Licence added his mother's family name in 1885. He decided early on a career in mining, and at 18 entered the School of Mines in Jermyn Street, London, under Professor John Percy (1817–89). Percy was then a well-known metallurgist and under his influence Roberts-Austen changed to a career in metallurgy. In 1865 he joined the Royal Mint, with which he was to be associated for the rest of his life, as personal assistant to the Master. Here he was able to pursue research into precious metals and their alloys. One of his first important papers was written in 1875 and was concerned with the problem of the segregation of the constituents of alloys of the precious metals during solidification from the molten state, a problem of practical importance in coining. One outcome of this paper was the lead it gave to the development of more accurate means of measuring high temperatures. His interest in ferrous metallurgy, which continued throughout his life, began with an investigation he undertook in 1880 to determine the most suitable steel for coinage dies. He was a President of the Iron and Steel Institute.

In 1882 he was appointed professor of metallurgy at the Royal School of Mines, London, Percy having resigned in opposition to the transfer of metallurgical teaching from Jermyn Street to South Kensington. During his tenure of this chair he wrote *An Introduction to the Study of Metallurgy*, a book which passed through five editions during his lifetime. In 1888 he published in the *Proceedings of the Royal Society* the results of experiments he had carried out into the effect of small amounts of impurities on the mechanical properties of metals. The important points raised by this paper led the Institution of Mechanical Engineers in 1890 to set up a committee to continue the investigation under his direction. He submitted five reports to the Committee during the next ten years, and these were of seminal importance in the later development of physical metallurgy. He was elected FRS in 1875, was knighted in 1899, and received many other honours for his scientific achievements.

S. W. Smith, *Roberts-Austen, a Record of his Work.* 1914; *Metallurgia*, 27, 169, 1943; *Nature*, 151, 350, 1943.
Proceedings of the Royal Society, 75, 192, 1905.
Dictionary of National Biography.

N H

ROBINSON, SIR ROBERT

Born at Rufford, near Chesterfield, Derbyshire, England, 13 September 1886; died Great Missenden, Buckinghamshire, 8 February 1975. Organic chemist, famous for research on natural products.

Robinson was educated at Chesterfield Grammar School and Fulneck School, Leeds, before going on to read chemistry at Manchester University. On graduating he worked with W. H. PERKIN, *Jr* – whom in the fullness of time he was to succeed as Waynflete Professor of Chemistry at Oxford – on dyes (especially brazilin) derived from catechol. Subsequently he held chairs of organic chemistry in Sydney (1912), Liverpool (1916), St Andrews (1921), Manchester (1922), and University College London (1928). For a year in the middle of this long period of academic appointments he was Director of Research for the British Dyestuffs Corporation, later one of the constituent members of ICI (1926): brief though it was, this led to a long association with the chemical industry as a consultant, first with ICI and later (1955) with Shell. After retiring from Oxford he became a director of Shell Chemical Co. Ltd. and had a small laboratory at Egham. This readiness to collaborate with industry, not conspicuous among academics of his generation, perhaps stemmed from the fact that he himself came from a family with interests in textile manufacture.

The almost infinite variety of the chemistry of brazilin was to fascinate Robinson for the whole of his working life (his last papers on this were published in 1974) but was no more than the prelude to a series of brilliant researches on a variety of natural products. These ranged from alkaloids to penicillin, from anthocyanins to steroids. His output was prodigious; his official biography lists more than 700 research papers, some 20 of them published after his 80th birthday. Additionally, his name is on 32 patents.

Robinson was perhaps the last of the great organic chemists in the classical tradition, depending on very simple apparatus. He possessed the sure mark of genius, a highly developed gift of intuition. While he undoubtedly owed much of his success to a keenly analytical mind – shown also in his exceptional qualities as a chess player – some of the steps in the intricate syntheses in which he delighted were surely the result of instinct. As a chemist, he had the analogue of the successful gardener's gift of 'green fingers': it is not surprising, perhaps, that as a gardener too, he triumphed. With, but independently of, Arthur

LAPWORTH he developed an electronic theory of organic reactions which had some success in explaining the course of known chemical reactions and of predicting others. Its development, however, meant invoking quantum theory, for which Robinson had little use: unfortunately, the quantum experts of his generation had little knowledge of chemistry. He also devoted much attention to elucidating the biochemical synthesis of many of the wide range of natural products in which he was interested.

As a man, Robinson had a reputation for irascibility. It is true that he did not suffer fools gladly, and by his standards the threshold of foolishness was set pretty high. Nevertheless, he could show great kindness to those fortunate enough to gain his friendship.

He gained virtually all the honours open to him. He was elected Fellow of the Royal Society in 1920 and was its President 1945–50; he was President also of The Chemical Society 1939–44. In 1947 he was awarded the Nobel prize for chemistry. He was knighted in 1939 and appointed to the Order of Merit in 1949. Universities too numerous to list conferred honorary degrees on him.

Biographical Memoirs of Fellows of the Royal Society. 1976. (Portrait.)

Dictionary of National Biography.

Trevor I. Williams, *Robert Robinson: Chemist Extraordinary.* 1990. (Portrait.)

Robert Robinson, *Memoirs of a Minor Prophet: 70 years of Organic Chemistry.* 1976. (Portraits.)

Natural Products Reports, **4**, No 1, 1987. (Special R. R. Centenary issue.)

Tyler Wasson (Ed.), *Nobel Prize Winners.* 1987. (Portrait.)

T I W

ROEBUCK, JOHN Born at Sheffield, Yorkshire, England, 1718; died Kinneil House, near Linlithgow, Scotland, 17 July 1794. Inventor of the lead-chamber process for vitriol manufacture.

After studying medicine at Edinburgh and Leiden, Roebuck established a successful practice in Birmingham. It was there that chemistry attracted him, and he set up at Steelhouse Lane a chemical consultant's business and, in conjunction with Samuel Garbett (1717–1805), a laboratory for recovering gold and silver from jewellers' sweepings, a recovery calling for sulphuric and nitric acids. Roebuck soon appreciated as essential a more practical process for vitriol-making than using large glass globes as practised by Joshua WARD. Roebuck recalled reading a note by Johann GLAUBER on the resistance of lead to sulphuric acid. Hence came his lead boxes of 1746, small chambers – later to be greatly enlarged – for enclosing the charges of burning sulphur and nitre. This development greatly reduced the price of sulphuric acid and, coming at a time when there was a rapidly growing demand for this product, was of major industrial importance.

Roebuck then established a large lead-chamber works at Prestonpans, near Edinburgh. The main reasons for the move were that the patent situation was uncertain and secrecy was difficult to maintain in Birmingham, and that there was a growing demand for acid by Scottish bleachers. He followed this move of 1749 with other Scottish ventures, taking to salt-making at Borrowstouness, to

coal-mining, and to the making of iron, helping to found, at Carron, Scotland's first ironworks, which subsequently became famous for the manufacture of ordnance (carronade). Roebuck's careful control of raw materials here, his process for malleable iron, and other contributions, added to his reputation as a technologist, though he ultimately failed in business.

Roebuck, a friend and patron of James WATT, was elected Fellow of the Royal Society in 1764.

S. Smiles, *Lives of Boulton and Watt.* 1865.

Dictionary of National Biography.

Chemistry and Industry, **61**, 497, 1942.

A. Clow and N. L. Clow, *The Chemical Revolution.* 1942.

A. W. Roebuck, *The Roebuck Story.*

M S

ROHRER, HEINRICH Born at Buchs, Switzerland, 6 June 1933. Inventor of the scanning tunnelling microscope.

Rohrer was educated at the Federal Institute of Technology in Zurich, and was awarded a PhD in 1960 for research on superconductivity. He then held a post-doctoral fellowship at Rutgers University, USA, from 1961 to 1963.

In 1963 he joined the IBM Research Laboratory in Zurich. He became interested in the behaviour of surface atoms and the problem of how to describe the complexities of surface structures. The electron microscope could not resolve surface structures, and surface atoms were arranged differently from those in the interior of a solid. As Wolfgang PAULI said, 'the surface was invented by the devil'. Building on the work of R. D. Young (1923–) at the National Bureau of Standards in Washington, Rohrer and his colleague Gerd Binnig (1947–) constructed a scanning tunnelling microscope which scanned the surface of a solid in a vacuum with an ultra-sharp needle tip at high voltage, causing electrons to tunnel from the sample to the tip, making it possible to map the surface. By 1981 they were able to produce images of single atoms on the surface.

Rohrer and Binnig shared the 1986 Nobel Prize in physics with E. A. F. RUSKA. Rohrer became an IBM Fellow in 1986.

G. Binnig and H. Rohrer, *Scientific American,* **253**, August 1985.

A. L. Robinson, *Science,* **234**, 14 November 1986. (Portrait.)

Tyler Wasson (Ed.), *Nobel Prize Winners.* 1987. (Portrait.)

A P B

ROKITANSKY, KARL Born at Königgrätz, Bohemia (now in Czech Republic), 19 February 1804; died Vienna, 23 July 1878. Distinguished pathologist.

Rokitansky studied medicine at Prague and at Vienna, where he graduated in 1828. He became Prosector in the Pathological Department of the *Allgemeines Krankenhaus* in Vienna, Associate Professor and Head of the Department in the University (1834), and was created the first full professor in 1844. He was associated with a small group of brilliant clinicians, and under his aegis the New Vienna School was born. Rokitansky developed a new attitude to post-mortem work. He did no clinical work, and the whole of his time and that of his assistants was devoted to pathology.

The number of autopsies performed in his institute was enormous, and the findings in each case were carefully recorded, so that a mass of first-hand information could be produced on any one disease. Rokitansky performed his first autopsy in 1827, and by 1866 he had personally performed 30,000.

Between 1842 and 1846 Rokitansky published his great *Handbook of Pathological Anatomy*. The second and third volumes, dealing with special pathology, were published first, and they constitute an amazing record of methodical observation. When the first volume, dealing with general pathology, appeared in 1846, it was found that Rokitansky had misguidedly attached himself to the blastema element in T. Schwann's theory. On this he had built up a pathological doctrine which regarded most diseases as basically diseases of the blood. In a review of his book the youthful R. VIRCHOW demolished Rokitansky's views, but in the second edition the latter discarded his theories of 'crases' and 'dyscrases'.

Rokitansky had a vast knowledge of congenital abnormalities. He first distinguished between lobar and lobular pneumonia and worked out their pathology in detail. He first described acute yellow atrophy in the liver, and gave excellent accounts of endocarditis, gastric ulcer, and cysts in various organs. His book on the diseases of the arteries (1851) is a classic. Virchow called him 'the Linnaeus of pathological anatomy'.

H. E. Sigerist, *Great Doctors*. 1933. (Portrait.)

E. R. Long, *History of Pathology*. 1928.

E A U

RØMER, OLE CHRISTENSEN Born at Aarhus, Denmark, 25 September 1644; died Copenhagen, 19 September 1710. Discoverer of the finite velocity of light and inventor of astronomical instruments.

Rømer was the son of a shipowner and received his first education at the Cathedral School of his native city before he began his studies at the University of Copenhagen in 1662. Here he assisted Erasmus BARTHOLIN during the period in which the latter discovered the double refraction of light and prepared the observations of Tycho BRAHE for publication. When Jean PICARD left Denmark after his verification of the co-ordinates of Tycho's observatory, Rømer went with him to Paris, where he in 1672 became a member of the French Academy, with lodgings at the new observatory. In the following years he acted as assistant to G. D. CASSINI and teacher of the Dauphin; at the same time he contributed a number of articles to the *Mémoires* of the Academy. Among these was a short paper entitled *Démonstration touchant le mouvement de la lumière* (1676). Rømer here called attention to the fact that the period of revolution of one of Jupiter's moons was not the same when it was determined by a series of immersions into the shadow of the planet as when it was found by means of a corresponding series of emergences from it. He explained the discrepancy by the assumption that light is not propagated instantaneously but with a finite velocity, and computed that light passes along a diameter of the Earth's orbit in twenty-two minutes (which is in fact, too small a value). This was the first proof of the finite velocity of light and Rømer's main scientific achievement. In optics he continued his work, predicting the aberration of light (later found by J. BRAD-

LEY) and giving a geometrical proof of the principle of P. de FERMAT.

Rømer returned to Copenhagen in 1681 as professor of mathematics, and soon also became involved in numerous public duties as member of the Supreme Court, director of the police forces, and scientific adviser to the King. In the latter capacity he reformed the Danish system of weights and measures, and introduced the Gregorian calendar (1700). All this restricted his scientific work, which, nevertheless, became very fruitful. The Royal Observatory at Rundetaarn was equipped with new instruments, and a private observatory was erected outside the city and provided with a meridian circle, the most important among Rømer's many inventions. These also included a micrometer for astronomical use, several planetaria, a levelling instrument, and an alcohol thermometer with fixed points which he showed to G. D. FAHRENHEIT in 1708. The use of epicycloidal teeth in gear wheels must also be ascribed to him. In addition he was a very active observer, and tried in vain to discover the parallax of the fixed stars. Only very few of his observations survived the great fire of Copenhagen in 1728, and no collected edition of his works exists.

Mogens Pihl, 'Ole Rømers videnskabelige liv', *Kongelige Danske Videnskabernes Selskab.* 1944.

Axel V. Nielson, *Ole Rømer*. 1944.

I. Bernard Cohen, *Isis*, **31**, 327, 1940. (Reprinted 1944.) (Portrait.)

Dictionary of Scientific Biography.

O. Lodge, *Pioneers of Science*. 1893.

V. Meisen (Ed.), *Prominent Danish Scientists through the Ages*. 1932.

O P

RÖNTGEN, WILLIAM KONRAD Born at Lennep, Rhineland, Germany, 27 March 1845; died Munich, Bavaria, 10 February 1923. Discoverer of x-rays.

In 1855 Röntgen entered the Polytechnic Institute at Zurich to study mechanical engineering. There he was impressed by the lectures of R. J. E. CLAUSIUS on heat and became interested in physics through A. E. E. Kundt (1839–94). In 1869 he completed his thesis on *States of Gases*, and in 1872 went to the new German university at Strasbourg as assistant to Kundt, becoming *Privatdozent* in 1874. After a period as Professor of Physics and Mathematics at the Agricultural Academy of Hohenheim, he returned to Strasbourg in 1876, and became professor of physics at Giessen in 1879. In 1888 he succeeded F. W. G. KOHLRAUSCH as professor of physics and director of the new Physical Institute at Wurzburg. He worked to revive the chair of theoretical physics at Wurzburg, and was instrumental in having A. SOMMERFELD appointed professor of theoretical physics in Munich. In 1900 he became director of the Physical Institute and professor of physics at Munich. He was awarded the Nobel prize in physics in 1901, the first year in which the prizes were awarded.

On 8 November 1895, while experimenting with a Crookes's tube (see W. CROOKES) covered with an opaque shield of black cardboard, Röntgen noticed that when a current passed through the tube a nearby piece of paper painted with barium platinocyanide fluoresced. In a series of classical papers

(1895–7) he described the properties of the new, so-called, x-rays, but his attempts to detect their interference by crystals were unsuccessful. Apart from his work on x-rays, Röntgen is perhaps best remembered by experiments verifying (1888) a theoretical prediction of O. HEAVISIDE that magnetic effects would be produced by a dielectric rotated rapidly between the plates of a charged condenser. He also made a classical determination of the ratio of specific heats of gases, and investigated pyro- and piezo-electrical phenomena.

Before his discovery of x-rays Röntgen was recognized as one of the most outstanding experimental physicists of his day in Germany, and the conception of him as a second-rate scientist who stumbled by chance on a great discovery is entirely incorrect.

O. Glasser, *William Konrad Röntgen*. 2nd ed. 1958.

W. R. Nitske, *The Life of Wilhelm Konrad Röntgen*. 1971.

A. Hermann *et al.*, *Wilhelm Conrad Röntgen*. 1973.

R. Dibner, *Wilhelm Conrad Röntgen and the Discovery of X-Rays*. 1963.

Tyler Wasson (Ed.), *Nobel Prize Winners*. 1987. (Portrait.)

J W H

ROOZEBOOM, HENDRIK WILLEM BAKHUIS Born at Alkmaar, Netherlands, 24 October 1856; died Amsterdam, 8 February 1907. Physical chemist.

As a young man Roozeboom worked in a butter factory, and then became assistant to J. M. van Bemmelen (1830–1911), professor of chemistry at Leiden. This gave him an opportunity to pursue a formal study of chemistry and he graduated in 1884. Two years later he succeeded J. H. VAN'T HOFF as professor of chemistry at Amsterdam.

Roozeboom made a notable contribution to chemistry by applying the Phase Rule of Willard GIBBS to the study of heterogeneous chemical equilibria, an application made the more valuable by its later extension to the study of alloys. His work on the iron-carbon system, fundamental to an understanding of steel, was outstanding. It is said that his attention was first drawn to the work of Gibbs by J. D. VAN DER WAALS.

J. B. Cohen, *Berichte der deutschen Chemischen Gesellschaft*, **40**, 1541, 1907. (Portrait.)

Dictionary of Scientific Biography.

T I W

ROSCOE, SIR HENRY ENFIELD Born in London, 7 January 1833; died Leatherhead, Surrey, 18 December 1915. Prepared the first sample of vanadium, and collaborated with R. W. BUNSEN in photochemistry.

H. E. Roscoe was the son of a Liverpool solicitor, Henry Roscoe (1800–36), who established a name as a biographer. From University College, London, where he studied under Thomas GRAHAM, he went to Heidelberg and worked on photochemistry under Bunsen. When 24 years old, Roscoe succeeded Sir Edward FRANKLAND as professor at Owen's College, Manchester, subsequently part of Victoria University. Roscoe's popular discourses on science were notable; during a depression in Lancashire his Science Lectures for the People, with T. H. HUXLEY and John TYNDALL collaborating, were a model for public lecturing. Roscoe also

pioneered liberal studies in technical education. He wrote several fine chemistry textbooks, translated into several languages; the classic six-volume 'Roscoe and Schorlemmer' (*Treatise on Chemistry*, 1878–89) was a standard work for many years.

The most important of Roscoe's original work was the isolation of vanadium, already well-known in the form of its compounds. He showed that what BERZELIUS had supposed to be the metal was, in fact, the nitride; Roscoe finally obtained the pure silvery-white metal by reducing its chloride with hydrogen.

Roscoe took an active part in public life. From 1885 to 1895 he was Member of Parliament for South Manchester. He was elected FRS in 1863 and was knighted in 1884.

H. E. Roscoe, *Life and Experiences* (autobiography). 1906.

E. Thorpe, *The Right Honourable Sir Henry Roscoe*. 1916. (Portrait.)

Proceedings of the Royal Society, **93A**, i, 1916.

Dictionary of National Biography.

Dictionary of Scientific Biography.

M S

ROSS, SIR RONALD Born at Almora, India, 13 May 1857; died Putney, London, 16 September 1932. Famous for his pioneering work on the life-cycle of the malaria parasite.

Ross was the son of an Indian Army officer. After an English education, including medical training at St Bartholomew's Medical School, he joined the Indian Medical Service in 1881. Against a background of widespread malaria in India, Ross first studied mosquitoes seriously in 1890, but his investigations were given real direction only after he had discussed the problem with Patrick MANSON in 1894. He was fired by Manson's hypothesis that mosquitoes were malaria carriers and therefore it should be possible to find the malarial parasite inside them.

Ross spent three years, amid the difficulties of everyday medical duties, studying mosquitoes and their parasites. His problem was enormous, for he had to deal with two variables – a variety of mosquitoes and the many different parasites each contained. The question was which mosquito transmitted malaria and which parasite was the malarial parasite.

Although he soon identified one stage of the life-cycle of the malaria parasite in the stomach of mosquitoes that had fed on malarial patients, his most significant step forward was in August 1897, when he noticed 'pigmented cysts' in the mosquito stomach wall. It was clear to Ross that these were a further development stage of the parasite. Unfortunately, owing to regimental duties, he had no facilities to trace the return of the parasite to the human subject. However, he turned his attention to avian malaria, and, by examining mosquitoes which had been fed on infected birds, he followed the various stages of the life-cycle of the parasite into the salivary glands of the mosquito. Thus he showed that the bite of certain mosquitoes transmitted the disease from infected birds to healthy ones. Ross himself did not prove the man-mosquito life-cycle, but he provided the correct key for its elucidation. He was awarded a Nobel prize in 1902 for his malarial studies.

Ross returned to England in 1899 to a varied

career which included a Professorship of Tropical Medicine at the University of Liverpool; physician for tropical diseases at King's College Hospital, London; and consultant on malaria to the War Office. He was also active in measures for eradicating malaria. He died in the Ross Institute, founded in 1926 to promote studies and interest in tropical medicine. A note on Ross must mention also that he published poems, novels, and mathematical studies. He was elected FRS in 1901 and was knighted in 1911.

R. Ross, *Memoirs*. 1923.
John Rowland, *The Mosquito Man*. 1958.
Obituary Notices of Fellows of the Royal Society, **1**, 1932–5. (Portrait.)
R. L Mégroz, *Ronald Ross*. 1931.
Dictionary of National Biography.
Dictionary of Scientific Biography.
Tyler Wasson (Ed.), *Nobel Prize Winners*. 1987. (Portrait.)

J K C

ROSSBY, CARL-GUSTAF ARVID Born in Stockholm, 28 December 1898; died there, 19 August 1957. Meteorologist, oceanographer.

After graduating in mathematics and astronomy at Stockholm University, Rossby joined the Bergen Geophysical Institute under V. F. BJERKNES. He then entered the Swedish Meteorological and Hydrological Service (1921). In 1926 a scholarship took him to the USA and he remained there until 1950, establishing strong departments of meteorology first at the Massachusetts Institute of Technology and later at Chicago University (1941). In the 1940s wartime needs gave meteorology a new significance and correspondingly greater governmental support. In 1950 the Swedish government invited him back to Stockholm to found the International Meteorological Institute; thereafter he divided his time between Sweden and America.

Rossby had wide vision and deep insight, studying on a global basis the dynamics of the atmosphere and the oceans and applying rigid mathematical analysis to the processes involved. In particular, he studied the circumpolar system of long waves (Rossby waves) which flow in the middle and upper troposphere and the jet stream which affects both the weather and high-altitude flight. He powerfully influenced the development of meteorology in the first half of the 20th century.
B. Bolin, *The Atmosphere and the Sea in Motion*, 1959.
Biographical Memoirs of the National Academy of Sciences, 34, 249, 1960.

T I W

ROUELLE, GUILLAUME FRANÇOIS Born at Mathieu, near Caen, Normandy, France, 16 September 1703; died Passy, Paris, 3 August 1770. Teacher and classifier of chemistry.

The two brothers Rouelle (see also H. M. ROUELLE) came from farming stock. G. F. Rouelle studied at Blois, at the University of Caen, and in Paris. He became an apothecary in 1725, and from 1742 to 1768 was demonstrator at the *Jardin du Roi*, during the professional careers of L. C. Bourdelin (1696–1777) and P. J. MACQUER. Many French chemists who later achieved distinction (including LAVOISIER for a short time) were his pupils. His lectures were exciting affairs in which he dispensed

with hat, coat, wig, and waistcoat in turn as he warmed to his task. He published a *Cours d'Expériences Chimiques* and a few other small works. He announced some discoveries in his lectures. He was one of the earliest (although not the first) to teach the phlogiston theory in France. His principal service to theoretical chemistry was to impress upon his contemporaries a satisfactory classification of salts. Earlier work (1666) by Otto Tachenius (d. *c*.1699) and by G. Rothe (1679-1710) (posthumously published 1717) had anticipated him, but Rouelle made this important topic familiar in a useful form.

He became a member of the *Académie des Sciences* in 1744.

D. McKie, *Endeavour*, **12**, 130, 1953. (Portrait.)
R. Rappaport, *Chymia*, **6**, 68, 1960; **7**, 73, 1961.
Dictionary of Scientific Biography.

F G

ROUELLE, HILAIRE MARTIN Born at Mathieu, near Caen, Normandy, February 1718; died Paris, 7 April 1779. Chemist.

H. M. Rouelle, younger brother of G. F. ROUELLE, assisted him and, in 1768, succeeded him as demonstrator at the *Jardin du Roi*.

He was an independent discoverer of urea in urine. With J. P. J. D'Arcet (1725–1801) he made experiments on the heating of diamonds. He also examined salts of tartaric acid and the distillate from sugar of lead, and showed the presence of soda in blood. There is some difficulty in distinguishing his researches from those of his brother.

Observations sur la physique, sur l'histoire naturelle, et sur les arts, **16**, 165, 1780.
Dictionary of Scientific Biography.

F G

ROUS, FRANCIS PEYTON Born at Baltimore, Maryland, USA, 5 October 1879: died New York, 16 February 1970. Pathologist, best known for his discovery of the filterable fowl tumour virus which bears his name, and for other work on cancer.

Peyton Rous obtained his medical degree at Johns Hopkins medical school in Baltimore. He soon decided that clinical medicine was not for him and he went to Ann Arbor, Michigan, to study pathology under A. S. Warthin. His career was interrupted for a time by a tubercular infection but this was successfully overcome. An opportunity arose to work at the Rockefeller Institute in New York: the director, Simon Flexner (1863–1946), was seeking a young man to work on cancer. Though his chiefs discouraged him, he nevertheless accepted, and within a short time had made what proved to be a discovery of the utmost importance. A tumour occurring spontaneously in a Plymouth Rock fowl was successfully transplanted in series by means of cell-grafts. This proved to be a sarcoma, and before long Rous had succeeded in passing it not only by grafts but by means of cell-free filtrates. This was a result completely at variance with current ideas about the nature of cancer, and for some time no one took it seriously. Some authorities denied that the growth was a true tumour, others that the filterable cause was a virus. Rous, with a number of colleagues, then proceeded to show, in a series of very thorough experiments, that the tumour differed in no way from known tumours except in having a demonstrable cause;

also that the filterable agent had properties like those of known viruses. Scepticism, however, remained, and Rous, not a little discouraged, turned for a time to other fields.

It was by then early in the First World War, and Rous, with J. R. Turner and O. H. Robertson, discovered a way of preserving red blood cells so that they could be kept for some weeks and still be useful for transfusions. As a result, the world's first blood bank was soon functioning near the front line in Belgium. This work led on to studies of blood pigments and their fate, and this, in turn, to research on the liver and gall-bladder with special reference to bile pigments.

Cancer research was all the time Rous's true love and in the 1930s came a chance to return to it. A colleague, R. E. Shope, had been studying virus-induced warts in cottontail rabbits, and one of these warts had become malignant. Shope gave the material to Rous, who proceeded to make wonderful use of it during the next twenty years, working in collaboration with J. W. Beard, John Kidd, and other colleagues. They studied in detail the changes taking place when a simple wart acquired the properties of a malignant growth: careful comparisons were made between the virus warts and those elicited by tarring. It was shown that the virus and carcinogenic chemicals could act synergistically, cancer being caused by their combined action more quickly than by either agent acting alone. Out of all this came Rous's proposal, now generally accepted, that carcinogenesis involved two processes, initiation and promotion: carcinogenic agents act in one way or the other, or, as with the fowl-tumour virus, in both ways. This idea helped to explain much that was mysterious about cancer, particularly how cells rendered cancerous could fail to reveal themselves until some promoting agent operated.

Rous spent sixty years, nearly all his working life, at the Rockefeller Institute, now Rockefeller University. He ostensibly retired in 1945 but continued working at the Institute and wrote no less than sixty papers after 'retiring'. Many of these were lectures or reviews dealing with general aspects of cancer causation, in particular the role of viruses. He was adviser to many bodies concerned with cancer research. Rous married in 1915 and had three daughters. He and his wife had many ties with Britain and they spent a sabbatical year (1925–1927) at Trinity Hall, Cambridge.

In the early years at the Rockefeller Institute, Flexner asked him to assist in editing the *Journal of Experimental Medicine* and he subsequently served as editor for 46 years. He took his duties very seriously: work on the journal played a great part in his life.

He received many prizes and honorary degrees. He was elected a Foreign Member of the Royal Society in 1940, and in 1966 he shared the Nobel prize in medicine with Charles Huggins (1901–   ).

Biographical Memoirs of Fellows of the Royal Society. 1971. (Portrait.)

Biographical Memoirs. National Academy of Sciences. 1976.

Tyler Wasson (Ed.), *Nobel Prize Winners*. 1987. (Portrait.)

C H A

ROUX, PIERRE PAUL ÉMILE Born at Confolens, Charente, France, 17 December 1853; died Paris, 3 November 1933. Distinguished bacteriologist.

Émile Roux studied science at Le Puy and medicine at the medical college of Clermont-Ferrand. He then transferred to Paris, and while still a medical student became in 1878 the *préparateur* in the laboratory of PASTEUR. Roux graduated as a doctor of medicine in 1883, and was appointed Sub-Director of Pasteur's laboratory. When in 1888 Pasteur moved to the newly founded Pasteur Institute, Roux became his *chef-de-service*. He was promoted to Sub-Director in 1897, and from 1904 until his death he was Director. In 1889 Roux gave the Croonian lecture at the Royal Society, of which he was elected a Foreign Member in 1913. He was awarded its Copley Medal in 1917. Roux was given a national funeral.

From 1878 to 1881 Roux and C. E. Chamberland (1851-1908), a physicist, were Pasteur's sole co-workers. They published jointly ten papers which cleared up the problem of anthrax, including the discovery of vaccination with the attenuated virus and the famous demonstration of its efficacy. Between 1881 and 1884 the same team solved the problem of rabies, and Roux himself published a paper on the passage of the virus along the nerves (1888). From 1888 to 1890 Roux was associated with Alexandre Yersin (1863–1943). They confirmed and extended Friedrich Loeffler's (1852–1915) discovery of the diphtheria bacillus, and they showed that the bacillus elaborates a toxin which produces the signs of the disease. This was the first bacterial toxin to be discovered. They also investigated the chemical properties of the toxin and showed the existence of non-virulent pseudo-diphtheria bacilli. In 1893, Roux with L. Vaillard (1850–1935), published very important work on the prevention and treatment of tetanus by anti-toxic serum. In 1894 Roux demonstrated for the first time the use of horses for the production of diphtheria antitoxin, and published excellent results from its use in 300 cases of diphtheria. Along with other colleagues he discovered in 1898 the infective agent in the pleuropneumonia of cattle. Between 1903 and 1906 Roux worked with I. MECHNIKOV on the problem of syphilis. They were the first to show that the disease was not confined to man, but could be transmitted to the anthropoid apes. After Fritz SCHAUDINN's discovery of the *Spirochaeta pallida* (1905) they demonstrated this causal organism in eight of their ten infected apes.

W. Bulloch, *Journal of Pathology and Bacteriology*, **38**, 99, 1934; *History of Bacteriology*. 1938. (Portrait.)

H. J. Parish, *History of Immunization*. 1965.

E. Lagrange, *Monsieur Roux*. 1954.

M. Cressac, *Le docteur Roux, mon oncle*. 1950.

E A U

ROWLAND, HENRY AUGUSTUS Born at Homesdale, Pennsylvania, USA, 27 November 1848; died Baltimore, Maryland, 16 April 1901. Physicist remembered chiefly for his development of the concave diffraction grating.

Rowland was trained as an engineer. Following graduation from the Rensselaer Polytechnic at Troy, New York, in 1870 and a year spent as a railway engineer, he turned to a life of teaching and research. After a year as an instructor in natural science at Wooster, Ohio, he returned to Troy, where he became an assistant professor in 1874. During a year spent working under H. L. F. von HELMHOLTZ in Berlin, Rowland made a contribution of great moment for electromagnetic theory. He demonstrated that a moving electric charge is accompanied by a magnetic field, as if it were an electric current flowing in a conductor, of strength equal to the product of quantity and velocity of the charge. In 1876 he took up the chair of physics at the new Johns Hopkins University in Baltimore. There he set about the task of determining constants of nature. His measurement of the unit of electrical resistance (1878) yielded a value close to that accepted today, and his repetition (1879) of the determination of the mechanical equivalent of heat by J. P. JOULE provided a result of high accuracy. Other work included a long series of measurements on magnetic permeability (1873–4) (which relates to electric current flowing through a metal plate at right-angles to a magnetic field) and a discussion of the Hall effect. (See J. HALL.)

Much of Rowland's success in experiments of this kind may be put down to his engineering training: it is said that he had no formal teaching in physics, and that his chief merit lay in the critical design of his apparatus. Rowland's greatest contribution to physics, the creation of the concave diffraction grating in 1882, lies in this category. Certainly the theory behind the grating was his, but the ability to score the required regular rulings stemmed from his manufacture of an almost perfect screw, a problem which he treated as one in precision engineering. The new grating allowed the photography of spectra without the use of prisms or lenses, and with greatly increased resolving power and dispersion. Used by its inventor to map the solar spectrum, the grating has found applications in many branches of spectroscopy. In later years Rowland turned again to engineering, and developed a system of multiple telegraphy which was shown at the Paris Exhibition of 1900.

Nature, **64**, 16, 1901.
Dictionary of American Biography.
S. Rezneck, *American Journal of Physics*, **28**, 155, 1960.
Dictionary of Scientific Biography.

WNS

ROYEN, SNELL VAN *See* SNELL.

RUDBECK, OLAUS (OLAF) Born at Vesterås, Sweden, in 1630; died Uppsala, 17 September 1702. Scientist, best known for his studies on the lymphatic system.

Rudbeck, the son of a bishop who had once taught medicine and science, studied at the University of Uppsala, where he became intensely interested in natural history. Following a period of study in Holland, he held various appointments at Uppsala University until he was made rector in 1660.

Rudbeck is credited with the discovery of the lymphatic vessels, although he was not the first to observe them. In fact, isolated observations had been frequently recorded from the time of Aristotle. His contemporary, Thomas Bartholin (1616–80) also has a claim to be the discoverer, but Rudbeck was the first to make numerous observations and at the same time to appreciate their physiological importance.

His painstaking studies, which he published in 1653, allowed him to map out the extent and the pattern of the lymphatic system and to demonstrate many details clearly. For example, by using ligatures he showed that lymph is carried away from the liver, an observation that led him to conclude that the liver was not a blood-forming organ as was generally thought.

Rudbeck did not continue his studies in anatomy and physiology, but spread his talents widely into university administration and the teaching of a wide variety of subjects, including mechanics, astronomy, chemistry and music. He excelled particularly in botany and was not without influence on LINNAEUS. He is remembered in the generic name *Rudbeckia*.

O. Larsell, *Annals of Medical History*, **10**, 310, 1928. (Portrait.)
S. Lindroth, (Ed.), *Swedish Men of Science, 1650–1950.* 1952.
Dictionary of Scientific Biography.

JKC

RÜHMKORFF, HEINRICH DANIEL Born in Hanover, Germany, 15 January 1803; died Paris, 20 December 1877. Inventor of the Rühmkorff coil.

Little is known of Rühmkorff before 1819, when he became a porter in the Paris laboratory of C. Chevalier (1804–59). Becoming interested in electrical equipment, he soon started to manufacture scientific instruments of his own. Although he eventually gained a European reputation, his factory remained small and, after his death, was auctioned for £42.

In 1844 he invented a thermoelectric battery. After much experimenting, in 1851 he produced the Rühmkorff coil, a simple electrical transformer, gaining awards at several exhibitions. The originality of this work was later contested, as he had been anticipated by C. G. Page (1812–68) in America twenty years earlier.

The Rühmkorff coil made possible many later electrical advances, for example in the experiments of H. Geissler (1814–79) on discharge tubes. Widely respected, Rühmkorff was a member of the *Société Française de Physique*. He made many philanthropic and scientific benefactions.

Nature, **17**, 169, 1877.
Scientific American, **38**, 81, 1878.
Dictionary of Scientific Biography.

CAR

RUMFORD, COUNT (BENJAMIN THOMPSON) Born at North Woburn, Massachusetts, USA, 26 March 1753; died Auteuil, Paris, 21 August 1814. Social scientist; measured relationship between work and heat.

Rumford had a colourful career. At 13 he was apprenticed to a merchant in Salem, but this ended abruptly when he was seriously injured during a firework display celebrating the repeal of the Stamp Act (1766). For a short time he studied at Harvard, then again went briefly into commerce, this time in Boston. For a time he supported himself as an itinerant teacher in New Hampshire and Massachusetts, studying science and medicine in his spare time. In these journeyings he met a wealthy widow, Sarah Walker, whom he married in 1772; she died in 1792. He took a commission in the 2nd New Hampshire Regiment, but the hostility this provoked among his associates led him to cut himself off from the British Forces; nevertheless he finally chose the British side. In 1775 his ambivalent position obliged him to sail for England. There he became an intimate of Lord Germain, Secretary of State for the Colonies, to whom his wide knowledge of American affairs was extremely valuable. He became intimate also with Sir Joseph BANKS, President of the Royal Society; he was elected FRS in 1779, and met the leading scientists of the day. Sensing the imminent fall of Germain (1782), and that the British cause was in any case lost in America, Thompson applied for a fresh commission and returned to New York, where he was given command of a regiment; this clearly identified him with the winning side.

Returning to Europe, he entered the service of the Elector of Bavaria in 1784; in the same year George III conferred a knighthood on him. He was made a Count of the Holy Roman Empire in 1791. In Bavaria he held high office, including that of Minister of War and State Councillor and this made it possible for him to put into practice some social reforms in which he had long been interested; he introduced the potato as a staple food and established a Military Workhouse for rehabilitation of the destitute. As Minister of War, he was responsible for the arsenal at Munich, and had occasion to observe the immense amount of heat generated when cannon were bored. Experimenting quantitatively, by measuring the heat in terms of the time taken to bring a given volume of water to the boil, he deduced that there was a definite relationship between the work done and the heat generated. This fundamentally important conception – which transferred heat from the realm of metaphysics to that of physical science – was developed by J. P. JOULE. Rumford reported his findings to the Royal Society in 1798, as an *Experimental Inquiry concerning the Source of Heat Excited by Friction*; it is one of the classics of science.

In 1798 he returned to London, reputedly as Bavarian Minister, but was refused recognition. The occasion gave him renewed opportunity to develop his idea for applying science to everyday life. The Rumford stove became exceedingly popular. More important, he devoted himself to establishing (1800) the Royal Institution of Great Britain, still an outstanding centre for scientific teaching and research. More important still he introduced Humphrey DAVY as Director of the Laboratory. Regrettably, Rumford's relationship with the Institution was not happy – it terminated formally in 1802 – and in 1801 he resumed his Continental travels, and eventually settled in Paris, where in 1805 he married the widow of LAVOISIER; the marriage was not a success. He established a laboratory and occupied himself in studying the heat generated in combustion, improving Lavoisier's calorimeter for the purpose. He also invented an improved lamp. There in 1813 he was visited by Davy and the then unknown Michael FARADAY; the visit gave him particular pleasure in view of the cold attitude of French scientists towards him.

Despite doubts about where his loyalties lay, Rumford's reputation was high in the United States. Franklin D. Roosevelt rated him with Benjamin FRANKLIN and Thomas Jefferson as 'the greatest mind that America has produced'.

E. Larsen, *An American in Europe*. 1953. (Portraits.)

Dictionary of American Biography.

G. E. Ellis, *Memoir of Sir Benjamin Thompson, Count Rumford*. 1971.

Dictionary of Scientific Biography..

                                                T I W

RUNGE, FRIEDLIEB FERDINAND Born at Billwörder, near Hamburg, Germany, 8 February 1795; died Oranienburg, 25 March 1867. Chemist.

Runge began his career as apprentice to an apothecary at Lübeck (1810). In 1819 he graduated in medicine at Jena and three years later took a PhD degree at Berlin. For a time he lived in Paris and was then appointed associate professor of chemistry at Breslau. From about 1830, however, he forsook academic life and became an industrial chemist.

Runge made a number of important contributions to chemistry. In an investigation of coal-tar he identified aniline (1834), which had first been described by O. UNVERDORBEN in 1826 as a product of the dry distillation of indigo. Runge also obtained from the same source quinoline, phenol, pyrrol, and rosolic acid. He wrote a substantial book on dyes and dyeing; this appeared in three volumes under the title *Farbenchemie* (1834, 1842 and 1850 respectively). The last volume is notable for its description of the separation of substances by capillary action; this is the first formal description of what is now called paper chromatography. A later, very rare work, *Der Bildungstrieb der Stoffe* (1855), is illustrated with actual paper chromatograms laboriously cut out and stuck in by hand. This work gives Runge a strong claim to be regarded as the originator of chromatography, one of the most powerful of all modern methods of chemical analysis (see also M. S. TSWETT). Runge published other chemical works, including a *Grundriss der Chemie* (2 vols, 1847–8).

Trevor I. Williams and Herbert Weil, *Arkiv für Kemi*, **5**, 283, 1953.

T. I. Williams, *The Elements of Chromatography*. 1964.

J. R. Partington, *A History of Chemistry*, vol. 4. 1964.

B. Anft, *Journal of Chemical Education*, **32**, 566, 1955.

S. V. Heines, *Journal of Chemical Education*, **46**, 315, 1969.

V. G. Berezkin, *Chromatographic Adsorption Analysis: Selected Works. M. S. Tswett*. 1990. (Portrait.)

                                                T I W

RUSKA, ERNST AUGUST FRIEDRICH Born in Heidelberg, Germany, 25 December 1906; died Berlin, 27 May 1988. Pioneer of transmission electron microscopy.

Ruska – son of Julius Ruska (1867–1949), an authority on Arabic alchemy – studied physics first in Munich and then in Berlin, specializing in high-voltage and vacuum techniques, leading to the development of high-performance cathode ray oscilloscopes. In 1928, while still a student in Berlin, he built the first electron microscope, with 17× magnification. By 1933 he had increased the magnification to 1200×; the best modern instruments achieve $10^6 \times$. Ruska's ideas were developed by Siemens Halske, with whom he worked 1937–55. From 1957–74 he was Director of the Fritz Haber Institute, Berlin.

Ruska's instruments were based on the transmission of a beam of electrons through a specimen, as light is transmitted in the optical microscope. In the 1970s Heinrich ROHRER and Gerd Binnig (1947–) working with IBM in Zurich, developed the scanning tunnelling electron microscope in which the beam follows the contours of the specimen under examination. It can reveal structure at atomic level.

The electron microscope in its various manifestations has become an outstandingly important scientific instrument. For their various contributions to its development Ruska, Rohrer and Binnig shared a Nobel prize in 1986, by which time Ruska was in his 80th year.

New York Times, 16 October 1986.
Les Prix Nobel en 1986. 1987. (Portrait.)
Tyler Wasson (Ed.), Nobel Prize Winners. 1987. (Portrait.)

T I W

RUSH, BENJAMIN Born near Philadelphia, Pennsylvania, USA, 24 December 1745; died there, 19 April 1813. One of the first teachers of chemistry in America.

In 1760 Rush obtained the degree of BA at the College of New Jersey, and subsequently spent over five years in apprenticeship to a physician, John Redman (1722–1808), a disciple of H. BOERHAAVE. To complete his medical education he went to Scotland, and in 1768 received his MD at Edinburgh after studying under William Cullen (1710–90) and Joseph BLACK. He visited London and Paris before returning in 1769 to America, where he was, at the age of 23 years, elected to the chair of chemistry at the College of Philadelphia. He retained this post until 1789, when he became professor of the theory and practice of physic. As a physician, he was a great advocate of purging and bleeding. He was interested in psychiatry and published Medical Inquiries and Observations upon the Diseases of the Mind in 1812.

The syllabus of his lectures on chemistry was first published in 1770, and is one of the earliest American chemical publications. It shows that his teaching was largely based on the lectures of his own teacher, Black. His course contained no practical work and comparatively few lecture demonstrations. He carried out some research on mineral waters and on sugar, and, during the War of Independence, when there was a shortage of gunpowder, he was appointed to investigate its manufacture and wrote several articles on the manufacture of saltpetre. He was a member of the Continental Congress and a signatory of the Declaration of Independence. From 1797 to 1813 he was Treasurer of the US Mint.

G. W. Corner, The Autobiography of Benjamin Rush. 1948. (Portrait.)
W. Miles, Chymia, 4, 37. 1953. (Silhouette portrait.)
Dictionary of American Biography.
N. G. Goodman, Benjamin Rush, 1746–1813. 1966.
C. Binger, Revolutionary Doctor: Benjamin Rush 1746–1813. 1966.

H. S. Klickstein, Bulletin of the History of Medicine, 27, 43, 1953.

B B K

RUSSELL, SIR EDWARD JOHN Born at Frampton-on-Severn, Gloucestershire, England, 31 October 1872; died Woodstock, near Oxford, 12 July 1965. Agricultural scientist.

Russell was the son of a schoolmaster – whose interests included science – who later became a Unitarian minister. Family financial difficulties and moves seriously interfered with his early education and for a time he worked as assistant in a chemist's shop. With great determination he pursued his objective of graduating in chemistry and eventually did so (1896) with distinction, from Aberystwyth University College and Owen's College, Manchester.

A desire to improve the lot of those who lived in city slums aroused his interest in the possibility of founding an agricultural settlement for them. To acquire the necessary background of agricultural knowledge he took (1901) a post as lecturer at Wye Agricultural College (University of London). Experience there convinced him that dwellers in city slums were ill fitted for agricultural work, but satisfied him that his real interest was in agricultural science. In 1907 he joined A. D. Hall (1864–1942) – his former chief at Wye College – at Rothamsted Experimental Station (see J. B. LAWES). In 1912 Russell succeeded Hall as Director.

Under his guidance Rothamsted became a designated research school of London University, and made many contributions in the field of soil science. Its reputation, already great, was enhanced, and it became one of the leading institutions of its kind in the world, attracting many foreign visitors. It celebrated its centenary in 1943, a few weeks before he retired. He himself travelled widely to familiarize himself with agricultural practice in other countries. Increasingly, he became interested in world problems of food and agriculture and in 1954 published World Population and World Food Supplies. In retirement, he developed also his interest in the history of agriculture, and shortly before his death completed A History of Agricultural Science in Great Britain (1965). These were only two of some twenty books he wrote: outstandingly successful was his Soil Conditions and Plant Growth, which first appeared in 1912 and subsequently went through many editions and was translated into nine foreign languages. In addition, he published many papers on agricultural science.

Russell was internationally recognized in his lifetime. He was elected FRS in 1917, and was knighted in 1922. He was an honorary fellow of many foreign academies of science and received honorary degrees from eleven universities, including Toronto, Vienna, Berlin and Rutgers.

Nature, 207, 1031, 1965.
Biographical Memoirs of Fellows of the Royal Society. 1966. (Portrait.)
E. J. Russell, The Land Called Me. 1956.
Dictionary of National Biography.

T I W

RUTHERFORD, SIR ERNEST (LORD RUTHERFORD OF NELSON) Born near Nelson, New Zealand, 30 August 1871; died Cambridge, England, 19 October 1937. Founder of nuclear physics.

Lord Rutherford was the son of James Rutherford, a wheelwright, who later built and operated a sawmill and a flax mill. Ernest was the fourth child of eleven brought up on the small family farm. After attending local schools he went with a scholarship to school at Nelson College, where he showed great distinction, especially in mathematics. In 1889 he won a scholarship to Canterbury College, Christchurch, where he had a brilliant career.

In his fifth year there he started research on the magnetization of iron under very rapidly alternating magnetic forces. He published two papers on this before leaving New Zealand in 1895 with an 1851 scholarship to research at Cambridge under J. J. THOMSON, where he continued this work. With very simple apparatus he proved that iron would respond to magnetic fields reversing 100 000 000 times a second. He used the demagnetizing effect of such fields in radio waves to make a detector consisting of a bundle of steel needles; with this he detected effects over more than half a mile, then a great achievement. In 1896 he changed to a research with Thomson on the conductivity produced in air by the newly discovered x-rays (see W. K. RÖNTGEN). Their paper laid the foundations for the study of the conduction of electricity in gases, introducing the concepts of recombination and mobility of the 'charged' particles, and explained by them the saturation of the current, which in moderate electric fields ceases to follow Ohm's law, (see G. S. OHM). He followed up this work by measuring mobility by two methods and then went on to study conductivity produced by ultra-violet light striking a zinc plate in the gas. Here he introduced a beautiful method of measuring mobility by finding the range through which the ions oscillate when pulled by an alternating electric field.

Rutherford's third paper at Cambridge was actually published after he had left in 1898 to become professor at McGill University, Montreal. It was the introduction to his life's work. A. H. BECQUEREL had discovered the radioactivity of uranium and G. C. Schmidt that of thorium. Pierre and Marie CURIE and Sir William CROOKES were showing that much of the radioactivity of ordinary uranium is due to small quantities of highly active substances mixed with it, among them radium. Becquerel had used the photographic effect of the radiations, Rutherford studied the conductivity they produced in air. He found that there were at least two kinds of radiation, which he called 'alpha' and 'beta', distinguishable by their penetrating powers. He then went on to study those of thorium. He first found a radioactive gas, thorium 'emanation', then a solid thorium X. Eventually, in 1903, he and F. SODDY put forward the theory of successive transformations. A radioactive atom is rather like a china figure falling downstairs, hitting the steps one after another and losing a piece of itself each time, these pieces being the α and β rays. The atom, however, spends very variable times on the different steps, anything from millions of years to a small fraction of a second. These are average times; for the individual atom the time spent on any one step is a matter of pure chance. An atom which has just arrived is no more and no less likely to break in the next minute than one which has been there a week.

It can readily be seen how revolutionary such an idea was to scientists brought up to consider the permanence of atoms as axiomatic. The discovery of the electron had somewhat shaken this view, but Rutherford's and Soddy's paper of 1903 went much further.

Rutherford went on to study the α-ray as an object and by a brilliant series of experiments satisfied himself that it is an atom of the gas helium that has lost two electrons. The final proof was to send the rays through the very thin glass walls of a tube into an exhausted vessel, in which helium could soon be detected. Thus one of the fragments of the transformation process is itself an atom. The transformation of the elements, at least radioactive ones, had been proved. In the summer of 1907 Rutherford moved to Manchester University.

In the course of the study of α-rays, H. GEIGER and E. Marsden in Rutherford's laboratory found that one ray in about 8000 striking a piece of platinum was deflected through more than a right-angle. Rutherford was amazed by this, and was able to show that collisions with electrons were quite unable to turn even this small fraction. There must be something in an atom that is heavy, small, and has a large electric charge. On this basis Rutherford erected his nuclear theory of the atom which more elaborate and more accurate experiments with different metals fully confirmed. The theory was carried further by Niels BOHR, who spent three months with Rutherford and showed how the electron might perform orbits round the nucleus, determined by the quantum theory, like planets round the sun.

Rutherford then studied the collisions of α-rays with light atoms. For atoms lighter than oxygen he expected some knock-on particles with longer range than the original αs. In hydrogen, the range should be up to four times that of the αs. These were observed, though in larger numbers than the simple theory predicted. But, surprisingly, they also appeared with nitrogen, besides plenty with range only slightly increased as expected. Rutherford concluded, in a paper published in 1919, that the α-ray had driven a proton (hydrogen nucleus) out of the nucleus of nitrogen. The nitrogen atom's nucleus had been broken by the impact of the α-ray, itself a helium nucleus, representing an artificial splitting of atoms. In the same year Rutherford succeeded Thomson at Cambridge. There he continued this line of work with the aid of a number of pupils. They found that the nuclei of most of the lighter elements were split by α-rays giving protons, often with a net gain in kinetic energy, counting all the parts.

Rutherford was an outstanding team leader as well as an individual discoverer. During the last fifteen years of his life, though he continued to publish important work, the most important discoveries at Cambridge were made by his co-workers, notably the discovery by James CHADWICK of the neutron, on which indeed Rutherford had speculated, and of disintegrations produced by particles artificially accelerated by J. D. COCKCROFT and E. T. S. Walton (1903–).

One characteristic of Rutherford's experiments was the extreme simplicity of the apparatus, but the really important thing was his ability to conceive simple ideas that were right. He received the Nobel prize for chemistry in 1908; was knighted in 1914, and was raised to the peerage in 1931. He was awarded the Order of Merit in 1921.

A. S. Eve, *Rutherford.* 1939.

E. N. da C. Andrade, *Rutherford and the Nature of the Atom.* 1964.

T. J. Trenn, *The Self-splitting Atom.* 1977.

Norman Feather, *Lord Rutherford.* 1940.

Obituary Notices of Fellows of the Royal Society. 1938. (Portrait.)

The Physical Society, *Rutherford by Those Who Knew Him.* 1954.

M. Oliphant, *Endeavour* (New Series), **11**, 133, 1987.

Notes and Records of the Royal Society of London, **27**, Aug. 1972.

Dictionary of National Biography.

Dictionary of Scientific Biography.

G P T

RYDBERG, JOHANNES ROBERT Born at Halmstad, Sweden, 8 November 1854; died Lund, 28 December 1919. Renowned for research in atomic spectroscopy.

Rydberg was associated all his adult life with the University of Lund. Entering there as a mathematical student in 1873, he gained his doctorate six years later. After teaching mathematics and physics for over twenty years, he was appointed to the chair of physics in 1901, holding this until a month before his death.

One of Rydberg's abiding interests was the Periodic Table of the elements. He attempted to relate the physical and chemical properties of an element to its position in the table, and assumed that the force between two atoms was a periodic function of their atomic weights. This interest led him to spectrum analysis, and in 1890 he arrived at the formula that bears his name; he was, apparently, unaware of the work of J. J. BALMER. Examination of the emission spectra of certain elements led to his conclusion that the frequency (v) of a line in the Balmer series was given by

$$v = R \left(\frac{1}{2^2} - \frac{1}{n^2} \right),$$

where n is an integer greater than 2, and R is a constant later known as Rydberg's Constant.

Other work by Rydberg included an examination of the red spectrum of argon (1897), and further essays on the periodic table, which he wrote in a spiral form. His great achievement was a simplification of atomic spectra that enabled their origin to be understood. He was elected a Foreign Member of the Royal Society in 1919.

Nature, **105**, 525, 1920.

Chymia, **6**, 127, 1960. (Portraits.)

Sten Lindroth (Ed.), *Swedish Men of Science 1650–1950.* 1952.

Dictionary of Scientific Biography.

C A R

RYLE, SIR MARTIN Born at Brighton, Sussex, England, 27 September 1918; died Cambridge, 14 October 1984. Pioneer of radioastronomy; Astronomer Royal 1972–82.

Martin Ryle was educated at Bradford College and at Christ Church, Oxford. His father, J. A. Ryle (1889–1950), was Regius Professor of Physic at Cambridge, and later professor of social medicine at Oxford. Graduating in 1939, Martin Ryle's amateur interest in radio led him into wartime radar research at the Telecommunications Research Establishment (TRE). From 1940 to 1945 he played a vital part in countermeasures against German radar; his team at TRE also successfully jammed the guidance system of the V2 rockets, and provided a spoof invasion in the Dover Straits to divert attention from the Normandy landings.

Joining J. A. Ratcliffe (1902–87) at the Cavendish Laboratory in Cambridge after the war, he started a new school of radioastronomy; he is now regarded as one of the founding fathers of this subject. He developed interferometer techniques for observing the Sun at metre wavelengths, and extended them to the recently discovered discrete cosmic radio sources. He produced a series of catalogues of radio sources, which became increasingly comprehensive as his techniques improved and his radio telescopes developed in size and sensitivity. His 3C catalogue provided a standard nomenclature which is still in common use.

He invented the technique of 'aperture synthesis', and in 1961 provided a classic demonstration of 'Earth rotation synthesis', which now forms the basis of much of modern observational radioastronomy. The '5 kilometre' radio telescope at Cambridge was the culmination of these developments; it provided images of radio galaxies and supernova remnants with an angular resolution equal to that of the largest optical telescopes.

The discrete radio sources revealed by these telescopes were at first referred to as 'radio stars', although some were identified with extragalactic nebulae. In his 1955 Halley Lecture Ryle showed that most of the discrete sources were galaxies at very large distances, and that their distribution in magnitude had great cosmological significance. Despite serious inconsistencies between the Cambridge and Australian observations of these sources, and despite passionate opposition by some theorists, he was able to show that the 'Steady State' theory put forward by F. HOYLE, H. BONDI, and T. GOLD on 1948 was incorrect; the alternative 'Big Bang' theory has been generally accepted since that time.

Ryle also played an important part in the development of optical astronomy in the UK, encouraging and supporting the construction of major telescopes both in Australia and in the Northern Hemisphere. He was the first holder of the historic post of Astronomer Royal to be appointed in a purely honorary capacity. He was made FRS in 1952, and was awarded the Royal and Hughes Medals of the Royal Society, and the Gold Medal of the Royal Astronomical Society. He was awarded a Nobel Prize in 1974, with A. HEWISH. A serious illness in 1974 interrupted his work in astronomy, and he devoted the rest of his life to his concern with the world's energy problems and especially the dangers of nuclear energy and its relationship to nuclear weapons.

Biographical Memoirs of Fellows of the Royal Society. 1986. (Portrait.)

Les Prix Nobel en 1974. 1975. (Portrait.)

Physics Today, December 1974.

Tyler Wasson (Ed.), *Nobel Prize Winners.* 1987. (Portrait.)

F G S

S

SABATIER, PAUL Born at Carcassone, France, 5 November 1854; died Toulouse, 14 August 1941. Chemist, noted for his discoveries, with J-B. SENDERENS, in the field of catalysed gas-phase reactions.

Sabatier studied chemistry at the *École Normale*, and became assistant to M. BERTHELOT at the *Collège de France*. In 1884 he was appointed professor of chemistry in Toulouse, a post which he held until his retirement in 1930, despite an offer to succeed H. MOISSAN at the Sorbonne. He married, and had four daughters. He had a great reputation as a teacher, and continued to lecture almost to the end of his life.

The early researches of Sabatier were in the field of inorganic chemistry; he studied, among other topics, hydrogen disulphide, metallic nitrides, and heats of reaction. It was not until the 1890s that he turned his attention to the catalytic effect of inorganic compounds (especially finely divided metals) on organic reactions, particularly in the gas phase. In this work he collaborated closely with the Abbé Senderens, who was a teacher in a Catholic college in Toulouse. Their major discovery (1897), made almost at the beginning of the research, was of the ability of finely divided nickel to catalyse the hydrogenation of acetylene and ethylene to ethane, and of benzene to cyclohexane. This work made possible several important innovations in industrial chemistry, in which Sabatier himself played little part, though he took out a few patents. He preferred to broaden his academic studies of catalysis in general, and made valuable investigations of such matters as the specificity of catalysts; the often baffling problem of 'catalyst poisoning'; and the use of heavy-metal oxides for catalysing hydration—dehydration reactions. These studies were epitomized in his book *La Catalyse en Chimie Organique*, (1912), whose theoretical views have, on the whole, stood the test of time.

The value of this work on heterogeneous catalysis was recognized by the award of a Nobel prize for chemistry, shared with F. A. V. GRIGNARD, in 1912. It is, however, so difficult to separate the contributions of Sabatier and Senderens to their fundamental discoveries of 1897 that the award of the prize to Sabatier alone was a little unfortunate. He was also elected the first non-resident member of the *Académie des Sciences* (1913).

Obituary Notices of Fellows of the Royal Society 1942–4. (Portrait.)

Journal of the American Chemical Society, 1615, 1944. (Portrait.)

J. R. Partington, *Nature*, **174**, 859, 1954.

Tyler Wasson (Ed.), *Nobel Prize Winners.* 1987. (Portrait.)

W V F

SABINE, SIR EDWARD Born in Dublin, 14 October 1788; died East Sheen, Surrey, England, 26 May 1883. Geophysicist.

Sabine was educated at the Royal Military Academy, Woolwich, and was commissioned in the Royal Artillery in 1803, rising to major-general in 1859. He developed an early interest in astronomy and geography, and was appointed astronomer on various expeditions, including those of Sir John Ross (1777–1856) and Sir William Parry (1790–1855) in search of the North-west Passage. He spent many years working in the tropics and in Greenland. From 1861 to 1871 he was President of the Royal Society, and became KCB in 1869.

Between 1819 and 1829 Sabine, using the sensitive pendulum devised by H. Kater (1777–1835), at seventeen different stations the world over, investigated, as he thought, the figure of the Earth. His figure for the ellipticity was later found to be too high, as the result of his failing to take into account the variation in density of the Earth's crust, especially as between continents and islands.

Through Sabine's influence magnetic observatories were established in several British colonies. These, with the exception of that at Toronto, were short-lived, but they provided Sabine with data for his greatest discovery: he found that the number of magnetic perturbations, or 'storms', in which the magnetic needle deviates abnormally from its average position (Sabine gave a valuable definition of such perturbations), is subject to a periodic variation with a period of ten or eleven years. The results obtained by S. H. SCHWABE were just becoming known, and Sabine correlated variations in magnetic and solar activity. J. Lamont (1805–79) working in Munich, found the magnetic cycle a few months before Sabine, but failed to correlate it with the solar cycle.

G. C. Wallich, *Eminent Men of the Day.* 1870. (Portrait.)

The Times, 27, 29 June, 1883.

Dictionary of National Biography.

Dictionary of Scientific Biography.

J D N

SACHS, FERDINAND GUSTAV JULIUS VON Born at Wroclaw (Breslau), Silesia, 2 October 1832; died Würzburg, Bavaria, Germany, 29 May 1897. Botanist and eminent plant physiologist.

After leaving his Gymnasium in 1845, Sachs became a private assistant in 1851 to the physiologist J. E. PURKINJE at Prague; there he studied at the University, taking his PhD in 1856, and becoming *privatdozent* for plant physiology. In 1859 he was appointed assistant in physiology at the Agricultural Academy of Tharandy, Saxony, and two years later became director of the Agricultural Academy at Popplesdorf, near Bonn. He was appointed to his first chair of botany in 1867, at the University of Freiburg-im-Breisgau, but moved the following year to become professor of botany at the Bavarian University of Würzburg, where he remained for the rest of his life.

The vast new knowledge of plant physiology gained during the second half of the 19th century is a memorial to Sachs's labours and outstanding achievements. His main investigations concerned the study of plant metabolism by means of the microchemical examination of tissues; the morphological and physiological details of the process of germination; the relative physiological importance for plant nutrition of various minerals, using the method of water-culture; and the formation of starch in chloroplasts and its relation to carbon-assimilation in the foliage leaf. He also conducted researches on phototropism and geotropism, and provided a great deal of experimental evidence on which he based his 'imbibition-theory' of the transpiration-current. Of his many publications, the best known is *Lehrbuch der Botanik* (1868; English translation, 1875 and 1882), which gives a comprehensive account of the botanical knowledge of the time. The work, unusual in a textbook, embodies the results of a good many of the author's original investigations and is, in consequence, the more stimulating; it is further enriched by drawings which bear witness to the author's artistic skill. Sachs exerted a great influence on the botanists of his time, and his lucid exposition and impressive personality made him pre-eminent as a teacher. The King of Bavaria ennobled him and nominated him a Privy Councillor. He was elected a Foreign Member of the Linnean Society of London in 1878, and of the Royal Society in 1888.

Proceedings of the Royal Society, **62**, xxiv, 1898.

E. G. Pringsheim, *Julius Sachs, der Begründer der neueren Pflanzenphysiologie*. 1932. (Portraits.)

R. B. Harvey, *Plant Physiology*, **4**, 155, 1929.

Dictionary of Scientific Biography.

A P G

SAHA, MEGHNAD Born at Seoratali, Dacca, India, 6 October 1893; died New Delhi, 16 February 1956. Physicist; remembered for fundamental researches in astrophysics.

Meghnad Saha's parents were poor shopkeepers; only the generosity of a local doctor enabled the boy to attend school. In 1905 he entered the Government Collegiate School in Dacca. He became a lecturer in the Department of Mathematics of the University of Calcutta College of Science in 1916, transferring in 1917 to the Department of Physics. He was now reading N. BOHR, A. SOMMERFELD, Max PLANCK, and W. H. NERNST, (whom he visited in Berlin in 1921); also the popular books on astronomy by A. M. Clerke (1982–1907); these undoubtedly inspired his epoch-making work on the thermal ionization of elements, leading to the famous Saha equation. His theory of high-temperature ionization and its application to stellar atmospheres influenced every worker in this field so that much of the subsequent work is a development of Saha's ideas. His two fundamental papers appeared in the *Philosophical Magazine* (1920) and the *Proceedings of the Royal Society* (1921). The work enabled the

bewildering abundance of lines of different intensity in stellar spectra to be interpreted with confidence, leading to increased knowledge of the pressure and temperature distributions in stellar atmospheres, also their composition.

Subsequently, Saha became professor of physics (Calcutta 1921, Allahabad 1923–38, Calcutta (again) 1938–53). He was active in research until his death; was a Fellow of the Royal Society from 1927; received many awards; and had an enormous and fruitful influence in building scientific institutes in his native country.

Biographical Memoirs of Fellows of the Royal Society. 1959. (Portrait.)

S. N. Sen (Ed.), *Professor Meghnad Saha.* 1954. (Portrait.)

Science and Culture, **22**, 1, 1956.

F. J. M. Stratton, *Nature*, **177**, 917, 1956.

A E R

SAKHAROV, ANDREI DMITRIEVICH Born in Moscow, 21 May 1921; died there, 14 December 1989. Theoretical physicist well known as an advocate of human rights.

Sakharov joined Moscow University in 1938, but was evacuated during the Second World War to Ashkabad where he graduated in 1942. He joined the Lebedev Institute in 1945, working under Igor Tamm (1895–1971), and gained his PhD in 1947. He remained with Tamm during the early 1950s, working on the Soviet H-bomb project. After the successful test in 1953, he became the youngest ever full member of the USSR Academy of Sciences. Sakharov and Tamm also proposed a technique for confining a plasma in a toroidal magnetic field, which is the basis of the tokamak used in nuclear fusion research.

Sakharov returned to academic research in the 1960s, working on the quark model of elementary particles and on quantum gravity. He also identified the conditions in the early Universe that would give rise to the apparent dominance of matter over antimatter.

In the mid-1960s he began to take a lead in supporting dissidents and monitoring the observation of human rights in the USSR. He was awarded the Nobel Prize for Peace in 1975, but was not allowed to leave the USSR to collect the prize, and in 1980 was sent to the closed city of Gorky. In 1986 President Gorbachev invited Sakharov to return to Moscow and allowed him to travel abroad. He was also elected a Member of the Congress of People's Deputies.

Physics World, February 1990. (Portrait.)

A. Babyonyshev (Ed.), *On Sakharov.* 1982.

S. Le Vert, *The Sakharov File.* 1986.

Tyler Wasson (Ed.), *Nobel Prize Winners.* 1987. (Portrait.)

S. D. Drell and S. P. Kapitza (Eds), *Sakharov Remembered: A Tribute by Friends and Colleagues.* 1991.

J. Trân Thank Vân, *Andrei Sakharov: Facets of a Life.* 1991.

C S

SAKMANN, BERT Born in Stuttgart, Germany, 12 June 1942. Neurophysiologist.

After graduating in medicine at the Universities of Tubingen, Munich and Göttingen, Sakmann became research assistant in the Max Planck Institute for Psychiatry in 1969 and then spent two years in the Department of Biophysics, University College, London. He then returned to Göttingen to work in the Max Planck Institute for Biophysical Chemistry, ultimately as director (1985–7) and professor (1987–9). Since 1989 he has been Director, Department of Cell Physiology, Max Planck Institute for Medical Research, Heidelberg.

It has long been known that the contents of living cells are contained within a cell membrane and that this membrane does not isolate the contents but serves to regulate the passage of chemical agents in both directions. However, this regulatory process is extremely complex and its nature is still imperfectly understood. It has been suspected however, that the channels of communication consist of single molecules, or complexes of molecules, through which charged particles (ions) can pass. How this passage of ions is controlled is evidently of crucial importance to the metabolism of the cell.

Clear experimental evidence of the existence of such channels, and the way in which they function, was first gained by Erwin Neher (1944–) and Bert Sakmann, who in 1991 shared the Nobel prize for physiology or medicine. They developed an extraordinarily delicate technique to measure the exceedingly small electric currents (around one picoamp) that flow through a single channel. Further, they were able to record how the channel alters its shape, and so controls the flow of current, over periods as short as a few millionths of a second. They demonstrated that the process is controlled by a 'sensor' located in the channel wall. These discoveries have not only revolutionized the field of cell biology but are clinically important, for many diseases are related to defective regulation of certain ion channels. These include diabetes, cystic fibrosis and certain neuro-muscular conditions.

Les Prix Nobel en 1991. 1992. (Portrait.)

T I W

SALAM, ABDUS Born in Jhang, Pakistan, 19 January 1926. Theoretical physicist well known for his work on unified theories.

Salam was educated at Punjab University and then at Cambridge University. He received his PhD from Cambridge in 1952, and returned to Pakistan as a lecturer from 1951–4. After two years back at Cambridge, he became professor at Imperial College, London, where he has since remained.

Around 1959 Salam and John Ward (1924–) began working on a theory of the weak nuclear force, and in 1964 they discovered a mathematical group structure in which they could incorporate the weak and electromagnetic forces in a consistent manner. Later, in 1968, Salam saw how to account for the great difference in strengths of the two forces, using the 'symmetry-breaking' mechanism developed by Peter Higgs (1929–) and others. One prediction of this unified 'electroweak' theory was the existence of weak 'neutral currents' – weak interactions with no exchange of electric charge. Such interactions were discovered in 1973, and in 1979 Salam shared the Nobel prize for physics with Sheldon GLASHOW and Steven WEINBERG, who had independently developed similar ideas of electroweak unification.

Salam has made many contributions to the theory of elementary particles, but he has also worked tirelessly to assist physicists from developing countries. In 1964 he initiated the establishment of the International Centre for Theoretical Physics in Trieste, Italy for the benefit of such physicists, and he has been director of the centre since then, dividing his time between London and Trieste.

Physics Today, December 1979. (Portrait.)
Les Prix Nobel en 1979. 1980. (Portrait.)
A. Ghani, *Abdus Salam*. 1982.
Tyler Wasson (Ed.), *Nobel Prize Winners*. 1987. (Portrait.)

C S

SANCTORIUS (SANTORIO SANTORIO) Born at Justinopolis, Venetian Republic, Italy, 29 March 1561; died Venice, 22 February 1636. Founder of quantitative medical research.

Sanctorius graduated in medicine at Padua in 1582 and then practised in Venice. In 1587 he was appointed physician to the King of Poland, where he remained for fourteen years. He then settled in practice in Venice. In 1611 he was called to the chair of theoretical medicine at Padua. In 1629 he resigned to devote himself to practice and research in Venice.

Sanctorius is best known for his researches on the variations of body weight after eating and drinking, during sleep, while at rest or performing active movements, and also in pathological states. His aim was to measure the effect of such conditions on the 'insensible perspiration' by which volatile substances were supposed to leave the body. Over a period of thirty years he spent as much time as possible daily sitting in a chair suspended from a steelyard, so that he could weigh himself frequently. He also weighed all the food and drink that he ingested, and all the excreta that he passed. In this way he obtained numerical values for his 'insensible perspiration'. In 1614 he published his results as aphorisms, in a book entitled *De medicina statica aphorismi*. At least thirty-two editions of this small Latin work are known, the last published at Naples in 1784. There were also many translations to modern languages, the last being the English translation published at Glasgow in 1842. Sanctorius realized that he had introduced a new aspect of medical research – the quantitative aspect. By his experiments he founded the modern study of metabolism.

In the time of Sanctorius the emphasis was on the strength and rhythm of the pulse, and not on its rate. There were then no watches with second, or even minute, hands. In 1602 Sanctorius referred to a method of comparing the rates of pulses. His later description showed that it consisted of a pendulum; the length of the string was adjusted until the beat of the pendulum coincided with that of the pulse. Pulses were compared by comparing the lengths of the string.

In 1612 Sanctorius described a thermometer to measure body temperature, and in 1625 he explained how it was to be used in studying diseases. This, the first clinical thermometer, was a clumsy instrument. He also invented a hygrometer to measure humidity, and a device for bathing a patient in bed.

H. E. Sigerist, *Great Doctors*. 1933. (Portrait.)
A. Castiglioni, *La vita e l'opera di Santorio*

Santorio. 1920; English translation in *Medical Life*, **38**, 729, 1931.

R. H. Major, *Annals of Medical History*, **10**, 369, 1939.

Dictionary of Scientific Biography.

E A U

SANDAGE, ALAN REX Born in Iowa City, USA, 18 June 1926. Astronomer.

Sandage was educated at the University of Illinois and the California Institute of Technology. He has been a staff member of Mount Wilson and Palomar Observatories since 1952, and was Homewood Professor of Physics, Johns Hopkins University, from 1987 to 1989. He has made important contributions to cosmic research, especially in the fields of stellar evolution and the chronology of the Universe. His most significant work has been in the area of quasi-stellar radio sources and the elaboration of extragalactic distance scales.

Working with Thomas Matthews, Sandage found the first quasi-stellar radio source (quasar) in 1960. This discovery was the result of an unusually accurate radio position deduced at the California Institute of Technology's Radio Observatory in the Owen's Valley, together with the use of an optical telescope at the Palomar Observatory. Sandage and colleagues have shown quasars to be highly luminous objects discernible using radio, optical and x-ray devices. They vary in overall intensity in periods of hours, days or weeks indicating that the region of strongest emission must be smaller than light-hours, light-days or light-weeks respectively. They appear to be the furthest objects visible in the Universe.

Sandage also found in the mid-1960s a class of radio-quiet quasars which appear to have much in common with the more visible quasars. Work pioneered by Sandage is important in understanding the age of the Universe and the activities of Black Holes located within quasars. His studies with Gustav Tammann resulted in the derivation of the most generally used Hubble constant.

American Men and Women of Science: Physical and Biological Sciences 1991–2. 1992.

C L

SANGER, FREDERICK Born at Rendcombe, Gloucestershire, England, 13 August, 1918. Molecular biochemist.

Sanger was educated at St. John's College, Cambridge, where he held a Beit Memorial Fellowship for medical research (1944–51). His early work concerned the metabolism of the amino acid lysine, followed by the chemistry of proteins and the molecular structure of insulin. In 1951 he joined the external staff of the Medical Research Council and was later head of the division of protein chemistry. He received the Corday-Morgan medal of the Chemical Society in 1951 and was elected FRS in 1954.

Sanger's research on the beef insulin molecule, the largest protein molecule whose structure had then been elucidated, was completed in 1955. He showed that it consisted of two polypeptide chains linked by disulphide bonds; he determined the order of the amino acids in each chain and the positions of the cross links, showing that a complete structural formula could be written for the insulin molecule. This was an essential prelimi-

nary to the chemical synthesis of insulin; it also led to the determination of other protein structures. Sanger received the Nobel prize for chemistry in 1958 for his work on the structure of insulin.

His subsequent work on the sequence of nucleotides in DNA and RNA brought him a share (with Paul BERG and Walter GILBERT) of the Nobel Prize for chemistry in 1980, making him only the fourth person ever to be awarded a second Nobel prize. He was made a Companion of Honour in 1981.

E. Farber, *Nobel Prize Winners in Chemistry, 1901–61*, 1963. (Portrait.)

Les Prix Nobel en 1980. 1981. (Portrait.)

A. Silverstein, *Frederick Sanger.* 1969.

Chemistry and Industry, 13th December 1958.

Tyler Wasson (Ed.), *Nobel Prize Winners.* 1987. (Portrait.)

N G C

SANGER, RUTH ANN Born in Armidale, New South Wales, Australia, 6 June 1918. Haematologist.

After graduating BSc in the University of Sydney in 1939, Ruth Sanger joined the Red Cross Blood Transfusion Service, Sydney, and remained there until 1946. In that year she was appointed assistant to R. R. Race (1907–84), who had just been appointed director of the new Medical Research Council Blood Group Reference Laboratory, housed in the Lister Institute, London. Previously at Cambridge, he was particularly concerned with research on the Rh (Rhesus) antigen and antibody which had been discovered, in the USA, in 1940. In his new capacity he received blood samples from many parts of the world and was recognized as an international authority on blood group systems, which were becoming increasingly complex. From 1948 he was very closely associated in this research with Ruth Sanger and she was co-author of almost all his major publications. Over the years 1950–75 they published six editions of the widely acclaimed *Blood Groups in Man*. In 1957 they were jointly awarded the Karl Landsteiner award of the American Association of Blood Banks. A major discovery (1961) was that of an antigen carried on the X (sex) chromosome. After the death of his first wife Race married Ruth Sanger (1956) and on his retirement in 1973 she succeeded him for another ten years as director of the MRC Blood Group Unit. She was elected a Fellow of the Royal Society in 1972.

Biographical Memoirs of Fellows of the Royal Society. 1985. (Obit. of R. R. Race)

Who's Who. 1993.

T I W

SANTORIO *See* SANCTORIUS.

SANTOS DUMONT, ALBERTO Born at Palmyra (now Santos-Dumont), East Brazil, 1873; died São Paulo, 23 July 1932. Pioneer of aviation.

Santos-Dumont became interested in lighter-than-air flight on a visit to Paris in 1892, and won at his fifth attempt a prize offered for the completion within 30 minutes of a flight round the Eiffel Tower from St Cloud. He built a number of small pressurized airships; in 1901 he aroused great interest by the successful manoeuvring of a 22 000 cubic foot envelope with a 12 hp engine in a 13 mph wind; on a later occasion he navigated the *Avenue du*

Bois de Boulogne so as to descend at his own front door.

Santos-Dumont also played an important part in the early development of heavier-than-air flying. His first flight was made at Bagatelle, near Paris, on 23 October 1906; three weeks later he made three more flights, the longest of which achieved a distance of 240 yards in 21 seconds. Though his machine – a tail-first pusher biplane with a 50 hp petrol engine – was not copied by later designers, he had initiated the use of the powered aeroplane in Europe.

C. H. Gibbs-Smith, *The Rebirth of European Aviation 1902–1908*. 1979.

T K D

SAUSSURE, HORACE BÉNÉDICT DE Born at Conches, near Geneva, 17 February 1740; died Geneva, 22 January 1799. Geologist and meteorologist.

The son of a Swiss agricultural expert, Saussure became a professor of philosophy in 1762 in Geneva, where he founded the *Société pour l'Avancement des Arts*. In 1768 he began his geological journeys, in the course of which he crossed the Alps fourteen times by eight routes; on 3 August 1787 he climbed Mont Blanc, of which the first known ascent had been made the previous year. He discovered fifteen minerals; made careful measurements of atmospheric humidity; improved the thermometer and anemometer; and developed the hair hygrometer approximately to its modern form.

Saussure resigned his chair at Geneva in 1786; eight years later he became paralysed, but in 1798 he was honoured with a professorship of natural history by the French rulers of Switzerland. His publications included an *Essai sur l'hygrométrie* (1783), much admired by G. L. C. F. D. CUVIER, and the modestly named *Voyages dans les Alpes* (4 vols, 1779–96), which, in fact, covers other mountain ranges as far away as Sicily.

A. Geikie, *The Founders of Geology*. 1897.
D. W. Freshfield and H. Montagnier, *The Life of Horace Bénédict de Saussure*. 1920.
Dictionary of Scientific Biography.

T K D

SAVERY, THOMAS Born at Shilston, Devon, England, *c*.1650; died London, May 1715. Inventor of a partially successful engine for raising water 'by the Impellent Force of Fire'.

Little is known of the first four decades of Savery's life. His appellation 'captain' may imply some involvement in the metalliferous mines of the West of England; other suggestions are that he was a military engineer, or a sea-captain. He appears to have been an improver typical of his time, taking out a number of patents for inventions between 1694 and 1710. He patented his water-raising engine in 1698, the term being extended by Act of Parliament in 1699 to a total of thirty-five years. Protection was extended northwards by an Act of the Scottish Parliament in 1701. The machine was described in *The Miner's Friend* (1702) as especially suitable for raising water from mines, for supplying towns with water, and for working mills. The engine, a steam-operated pump, consisted of a strong cylinder connected to a high-pressure boiler and a rising main. This main descended in one direction to the sump or water source and ascended in the other to the delivery cistern: its operation was as follows. Steam admitted to the cylinder was condensed by an external coolant, and by a suitable valve arrangement atmospheric pressure forced water from the sump into the cylinder or pump barrel. Water so raised was then blown up the rising main by direct contact with live steam from the boiler, and the cycle repeated. No such engine is known to have been erected in a mine; but a few, working at low pressure only, were used to recycle water to the heads of mill-wheels during the eighteenth century. The engine found its chief application in the supply of water to country houses and gardens.

After 1705 Savery seems to have abandoned the development of the engine, despite the establishment of a London workshop in 1702. Following his election as FRS (1705) he was appointed Treasurer to the Sick and Wounded Seamen broken in the Dutch Wars, which post he retained until 1714, when he became surveyor of the waterworks at Hampton Court, near London. His publications include a pamphlet, *Navigation Improved* (1698), and a translation from the Dutch of the *Treatise on Fortification (1705)* by Baron van Coehoorn (1634–1704). Despite the very limited success of Savery's own invention, his patent covered the atmospheric engine developed by Thomas NEWCOMEN, who was forced to join Savery or his executors in its further exploitation.

H. W. Dickinson, *A Short History of the Steam Engine*. 1938 (2 ed. 1963).
R. Jenkins, *Transactions of the Newcomen Society*, **3**, 96, 1922–3.
Dictionary of National Biography.

W N S

SCHAFER, SIR EDWARD ALBERT SHARPEY
See SHARPEY-SCHAFER.

SCHAUDINN, FRITZ RICHARD Born at Rösen-ingken, East Prussia, Germany, 19 October 1871; died Hamburg, 22 June 1906. Distinguished protozoologist and discoverer of the causal organism of syphilis.

Fritz Schaudinn studied Germanic philology in the University of Berlin, but turned to the natural sciences, especially zoology. In 1894 he graduated as a Doctor of Science, and was appointed as an assistant in the Berlin Institute of Zoology. In 1898 he was recognized officially as a lecturer in zoology in the University of Berlin. In 1904 he was appointed head of the Laboratory of Protozoology in the *Kaiserliche Gesundheitsamt* in Berlin, and shortly before his death he became a professor in the Institute for Tropical Diseases in Hamburg.

Schaudinn's investigations covered a wide field. He did important work on the morphology of the Rhizopods and Foraminifera, and he worked out the life-cycle of the Coccidiae. He undertook a scientific expedition to the Arctic, and his reports on the fauna which he investigated were published in six volumes. In 1905, working with the dermatologist Paul Erich Hoffmann (1868–1959), he discovered the *Spirochaeta pallida* (*Treponema pallidum*), the causal organism of syphilis.

A. Castiglioni, *History of Medicine*. 1947. (Portrait.)
J. H. Stokes, *Science*, **74**, 502, 1931.

J. H. Talbott (Ed.), *A Biographical History of Medicine*. 1970.

E A U

SCHEELE, CARL WILHELM Born at Stralsund (then Sweden), 9 (or perhaps 19) December 1742; died Köping, Västmanland, Sweden, 21 (or perhaps 26) May 1786. Famous as the discoverer of oxygen, and for other chemical discoveries.

Scheele, after a good elementary schooling, was apprenticed in 1757 to an apothecary at Gothenburg, who provided him with opportunities to read good books on chemistry and to perform experiments. In 1765 he moved to Malmö, and in 1768 to Stockholm. There he became acquainted with the assistant of J. T. BERGMAN, J. G. Gahn (1745–1818), who introduced him to Bergman when Scheele moved to Uppsala in 1770. Bergman complained that a sample of saltpetre from the shop where Scheele worked gave off red fumes on being treated with acid. Scheele was able to explain this phenomenon, saying that the saltpetre (potassium nitrate) must have been heated, and thereby converted into another salt, potassium nitrite. Bergman was impressed, advised Scheele to investigate pyrolusite (manganese dioxide) – research which led to the discovery of chlorine in 1774 – and thereafter did everything in his power to bring Scheele's work before the scientific community. It has been said that Scheele was Bergman's greatest discovery.

In 1775 Scheele was elected a member of the Royal Academy of Sciences of Sweden, the only apothecary's assistant to be so honoured; soon afterwards he moved to the small town of Köping to take charge of a pharmacy there. Despite tempting offers from Berlin and perhaps from England, he remained there for the rest of his life. He did not care about money, and the disinterested pursuit of truth seems to have been his only object. As regards chemical theory, he was conservative, and adhered to the end of his days to the phlogiston theory. Like his great contemporary Joseph PRIESTLEY, he apparently 'made all kinds of experiments without reference to any system or prearranged plan'. Such statements (this was made by his friend A. J. Retzius (1742–1821)) should never – and particularly in this case – be taken at face value; nevertheless there was a difference in approach between these discoverers and the clear-headed systematizer LAVOISIER, who reasoned with such precision on their labours and expelled phlogiston from chemistry.

By 1773, at least a year before Priestley, Scheele had discovered oxygen, but the work in which he described his experiments, *A Chemical Treatise on Air and Fire*, was not published until 1777. Scheele blamed the publisher and printer for the delay, but the major cause seems to have been the dilatoriness of Bergman, who wrote an introduction to the book. In 1774 Scheele discovered chlorine, manganese and baryta, during his investigations of pyrolusite. Davy thought that Scheele correctly – and unlike Lavoisier – included chlorine (or rather, dephlogisticated marine acid) among the elements; but this would seem to be anachronistic. Scheele also investigated the action of light on silver salts. He discovered hydrogen sulphide; arsenic, molybdic, and tungstic acids; arsine; copper arsenite (Scheele's green); and a whole series of organic acids. He also discovered silicon fluoride; prepared phosphorus from bone ash; and distinguished graphite from the mineral molybdenite (MoS_2) which resembles it in physical properties.

But it is for his work on oxygen that Scheele is remembered: a series of researches in which he began by proving that air is made up of two components, of which only one will support combustion. He called these 'spoiled' or 'foul' air, and 'fire' air respectively. After experiments in which the 'fire' air was consumed, leaving the 'foul', he prepared 'fire' air from saltpetre and sulphuric acid, collecting it in a bladder and absorbing the red fumes with milk of lime.

He died, leaving this impressive opus behind him, at the height of his powers in his forty-fourth year.

E. Thorpe, *Essays in Historical Chemistry*. 1923.

J. R. Partington, *Journal of Chemical Education*, **39**, 123, 1962.

'The Discovery of Oxygen', *Alembic Club Reprints*, VIII. 1952.

W. A. Smeaton, *Endeavour* (New Series), **10**, 28, 1986. (Portrait.)

G. Urdang, *The Apothecary Chemist, Carl Wilhelm Scheele*. 2nd ed. 1958.

Dictionary of Scientific Biography.

D M K

SCHIAPARELLI, GIOVANNI VIRGINIO Born at Savigliano, Piedmont, Italy, 14 March 1835; died Milan, 4 July 1910. Astronomer and historian of ancient astronomy.

After graduating at Turin (1854), Schiaparelli studied astronomy at Berlin under J. F. Encke (1791–1865). He became an observer, first at Pulkova (1859) and then at Brera, Milan (1860), of which observatory he was made director in 1862. His first discovery was of the minor planet Hesperia (1861). In 1866 he showed that meteors pursue cometary orbits, and in particular he identified the comets associated with the Leonid and Perseid showers. This work earned him the Lalande Prize of the Paris Academy of Sciences (1868) and many other honours.

In 1877 he made important observations of the markings of the planet Mars, including the position of the Southern polar cap, the direction of the axis of rotation, and the dark lines criss-crossing the planet which he called 'canali' (see P. LOWELL). The nature of the markings is still a matter of controversy.

On retirement he made a study of the astronomy of the Babylonians and the Jews. He also established some important results in the history of Greek astronomy.

Enciclopedia Italiana, vol. 31. 1936. (Portrait.)

Dictionary of Scientific Biography.

J D N

SCHIFF, MORITZ Born at Frankfurt-am-Main, Hessen, Germany, 28 January 1823; died Geneva, 6 October 1896. A pioneer in the study of the endocrine glands.

After education at the Senckenberg Institute at Frankfurt, Schiff studied at the Universities of Heidelberg, Berlin, and at Göttingen, where he obtained his doctorate (1844). He then studied in Paris, experimental physiology under F. MAGENDIE, and zoology – especially ornithology – in the museum of the *Jardin des Plantes*. He was then appointed director of the Ornithological Division of the Zoological Museum at Frankfurt. In the revolution of 1848 he served as a surgeon in the revolutionary forces. In 1854 he was appointed professor of comparative anatomy in the University of Bern. In 1863 he became professor of physiology at Florence, and in 1876 he was called to the corresponding chair at Geneva.

Schiff was one of the earliest investigators to study the effect of ablation of the cerebellum and of hemisection of the spinal cord (1858). In 1856 he worked on experimental diabetes, and in the same year he showed that excision of the thyroid glands of dogs and guinea-pigs was fatal. These cases of thyroidectomy were reported in a paper on another subject, and they were overlooked for many years. Partial excision of the thyroid in human patients had been practised since the late eighteenth century and the first total thyroidectomy was done in 1869. By 1883 J. L. Reverdin (1842–1929) and his brother had reported a condition resembling myxoedema following some of their thyroidectomies, and T. KOCHER reported that nearly a third of his thyroidectomy cases had developed a condition which he called cachexia strumipriva. It was then suggested that both this condition and myxoedema were due to loss of function of the thyroid gland. Schiff now returned to his experimental work on thyroidectomy, and he found that the life of an animal subjected to the operation could be temporarily saved if part of its excised thyroid was grafted into another part of its body; but this result was only temporary, because the transplanted thyroid tissue was absorbed. Victor Horsley (1857–1916) had similar results. These experiments led George Redmayne Murray (1865–1939) to conclude that myxoedema ought to be improved by the hypodermic injection of a thyroid extract. In 1891 he proved his conclusion by publishing a very satisfactory case.

F. H. Garrison, *History of Medicine*. 1929. (Portrait.)

H. Friedenwald, *Bulletin of the Institute of the History of Medicine*, **5**, 589, 1937.

Dictionary of Scientific Biography.

E A U

SCHIMPER, ANDREAS FRANZ WILHELM Born at Strasbourg, Alsace, 12 May 1856; died Basle, Switzerland, 9 September 1901. Plant ecologist.

Schimper received his doctorate in 1878 at Strasbourg, where his father held the chair of geology. Two years later he impressed the botanical world with his paper on the nature and growth of starch grains. In 1880 a fellowship at Johns Hopkins University took him to America, where he made his first acquaintance with tropical plants. On returning to Europe he was appointed a lecturer and in 1886 professor at Bonn University, remaining there until 1898. During his travels in the West Indies in 1881, and again in 1882–3, Schimper made a special study of the distribution of epiphytes in the American tropics, and explained the significance of their habit and structure in *Über Bau und Lebensweise der Epiphyten Westindiens* (1884).

He widened his understanding of tropical vegetation by visits to Brazil in 1886 and to Ceylon and Java in 1889–90, and as a member of the German

'*Valdivia*' Deep Sea Expedition explored the Canary Islands, Cameroons, East Africa, Seychelles and Sumatra in 1898–9. His keen observation of the distribution of types of vegetation found its consummation in his masterpiece, *Pflanzen-Geographie auf physiologischer Grundlage* (1898), a work which illuminates the relationship between the physiological structure of plants and their environment.

Schimper, who became professor of botany at Basle in 1898, died in his forty-sixth year. During his short life he had, however, laid firm foundations for the new science of plant ecology.

H. Schenk, *Berichte der deutschen botanischen Gesellschaft*, **19**, 54, 1901.

Dictionary of Scientific Biography.

R G C D

SCHLEIDEN, MATTHIAS JAKOB Born at Hamburg, Germany, 5 April 1804; died Frankfurt-am-Main, 23 June 1881. Botanist.

Schleiden studied law at Heidelberg. For a while he practised as a barrister in Hamburg, but in 1831 he began to study botany and medicine at the Universities of Göttingen and of Berlin. He graduated in 1831 at the University of Jena, where he was for many years professor of botany. From 1864 until his death he lived as a private teacher.

Schleiden was prejudiced against the purely systematic Linnean school of botanists, and devoted his attention to the microscopic study of plant growth and structure. His investigations of embryonic cells helped to prepare the way for the development of the 'cell theory' of Theodor SCHWANN. By following further the ideas of Robert BROWN on the nucleus, which he renamed the cytoblast, he arrived at his theory of free-cell formation and the (erroneous) conclusion that cells developed out of nuclei and then became encased in cell walls. He accurately observed other cellular features and activities in plants, such as protoplasmic streaming, but his work was less searching than that of Schwann, who studied mainly animal cells and whose observations were, in consequence, more difficult. Schleiden's views on nucleated cells as the only meristematic constituents of plant embryos were published in a communication, *Beiträge zur Phytogenesis*, that appeared in the *Archiv für Anatomie und Physiologie* of Johannes MÜLLER (1838). Long before the awakening of interest in mycorrhizal associations, Schleiden demonstrated that the roots of some plants are infected by fungi. He was sometimes led into error owing to a certain arrogance and quickness of temper, and an inability to criticize his own hypotheses. He had great ability, however, and by his introduction of improved techniques, and his stimulating ideas, he earned for himself the title of 'reformer of scientific botany'.

M. Moebius, *Matthias Jakob Schleiden. Zu seinem 100 Geburtstage.* 1904.

Karl Werckmeister, *Das 19te. Jahrhundert in Bildnissen.* 1899. (Portrait.)

Dictionary of Scientific Biography.

A P G

SCHMIDT, BERNHARD VOLDEMAR Born at Insel Nargen, Estonia, 30 March 1879; died Hamburg, Germany, 1 December 1935. Designer of an important telescopic camera.

Schmidt was the son of poor parents. In early childhood he lost an arm, but despite this handicap he taught himself the art of lens-grinding, making his own optical instruments. Studying engineering at Göteborg (1900–1), he continued his technical education at the Institute of Mittweida (1901–4). He lived at Mittweida until 1928, working at the manufacture of lenses and mirrors for telescopes and other optical instruments. From 1926 until his death he collaborated with the staff of the observatory at Hamburg-Bergedorf.

Schmidt is remembered for an astronomical camera, developed by about 1931, which is practically free from chromatic aberration. This comprises a spherical mirror, in the focal plane of which the photographic film was placed. A thin aspherical glass corrector plate is placed in front of the mirror and at its centre of curvature. The corrector plate has one plane surface, the other being convex at the centre and concave at the rim. The overall effect is to give a high degree of compensation for spherical aberration and at the same time achieve a high definition over a wide field.

The largest Schmidt telescope yet built is at Mount Palomar, where it is a companion to the 200-inch reflector. The aperture of the mirror is 72 inches; the aperture of the correcting plate 48 inches. To list the achievements of observers equipped with Schmidt telescopes the world over would be to list half the achievements of modern optical astronomy. Instruments of smaller size developed from it include the Maksutov and Baker-Schmidt cameras. All have been particularly useful for the spectrography of very faint objects.

A. A. Wachmann, *Sky and Telescope*, **15**, 4, 1955.
P. C. Hodges, *American Journal of Röntgenology and Radium Therapy*, **15**, 1948.
Dictionary of Scientific Biography.

J D N

SCHMIDT, ERNST JOHANNES Born at Jaegerpris, Denmark, 22 January 1877; died Copenhagen, 22 February 1933. Biologist; elucidated breeding habits of the eel.

Schmidt studied botany at the University of Copenhagen and took a Master's degree in 1898. The following year he went as botanist on a Danish expedition to Siam. A large amount of material was collected, adding to knowledge of the flora of South-East Asia, and in 1903 he received a doctorate for his work on the shoots of Old World mangroves. He had already written a detailed account of Danish Cyanophyceae. In 1901 he became assistant at the Danish Biological Station, and two years later went on the small research vessel *Thor* to investigate the fisheries off the Faroes and Iceland assigned to Denmark by the International Council for the Investigation of the Sea. Schmidt traced out the spawning grounds of the cod and other Gadoid fishes, and in 1904 found a leptocephalus larva of the eel near the surface of the sea westward of Faroe. He followed up this discovery, and as a result of investigations carried out over the North Atlantic finally traced (1922) the breeding place of the eel to an area south-east of Bermuda.

In 1910 Schmidt was appointed director of the Physiological Department in the Carlsberg Laboratory, where he worked on the growth, breeding,

and variation of hops. From 1928 to 1930 he took charge of the Carlsberg Foundation's Oceanographical Expedition round the world on the research vessel *Dana*. Very extensive pelagic collections were made during the expedition, but Schmidt died in the midst of organizing the study of the material and the publication of the results. He was, in turn, botanist, zoologist and physicist, and made valuable contributions to oceanography in his studies of the biology of fishes.

In 1927 he was elected Honorary Fellow of the Royal Society of Edinburgh, and in 1923 he became Vice-President of the International Council for the Investigation of the Sea.

Proceedings of the Royal Society of Edinburgh, **53**, Pt. IV, 1932–3.
Anton Fr. Bruun, *The Life and Work of Professor Johannes Schmidt*. 1934. (Portrait.)
C. Tate Regan, *Journal du Conseil*, **8**, 145, 1933.
Dictionary of Scientific Biography.

A P G

SCHÖNBEIN, CHRISTIAN FRIEDRICH Born at Metzingen, Germany, 18 October 1799; died Baden Baden, 29 August 1868. Noted for studies on ozone, and for early manufacture of cellulose nitrate as a high explosive.

After an apprenticeship in a pharmaceutical factory, Schönbein worked in an Augsburg factory and studied chemistry in his very limited spare time. Further part-time study while at Erlangen improved his chemistry, apart from his 'unconquerable shyness for the organic field'. He became a teacher for a time in schools in Thuringia and at Epsom, England. He benefited much by attending lectures of FARADAY and of French chemists, such as GAY-LUSSAC; later he became a regular correspondent of Faraday, BERZELIUS, and other eminent scientists.

Despite his lack of formal training, Schönbein was elected to the Chair of Chemistry at Basle, which he occupied for forty years. He published more than 300 papers, covering a variety of topics ranging from passive iron to catalysts, enzymes, and the nitrification of organic compounds. His work on ozone – which he originally believed to be a new element – was classic, and T. ANDREWS, another eminent investigator of this gas, gave him high praise for it. Schönbein named the gas from its peculiar odour (Greek *ozo*, smell), and noted its presence in rain water after thunderstorms. In 1860 the formation of ozone by sparking pure dry oxygen proved that it was a condensed form of that element.

In a letter to Faraday, Schönbein visualized the birth of a plastics industry when he described 'beautiful vessels' he prepared from cellulose nitrate. But the outstanding role of this substance (gun-cotton), which he discovered in 1845–6, was to be as a high explosive. His early attempts to manufacture it at Faversham, Kent, ended in disaster, as did many other attempts in Europe. Not until twenty years later did Fredrick ABEL discover how to make gun-cotton safe.

R. E. Oesper, *Journal of Chemical Education*, **6**, 432 and 677, 1929.
Journal of the Chemical Society, **22**, 1869.
J. R. Partington, *A History of Chemistry*, vol. 4. 1964.
E. Färber, *Prometheus*, 29, 413, 1918.

Dictionary of Scientific Biography.

M S

SCHRÖDINGER, ERWIN Born in Vienna, 12 August 1887; died there, 4 January 1961. Founder of wave mechanics and originator of the Schrödinger equation describing the quantum behaviour of electrons and other particles.

Schrödinger's education was entirely in Vienna, where he studied at the University under F. Hasenöhrl (1874–1915). He soon made his mark as a research worker in theoretical physics and from 1910 onwards did notable work in several fields. At that stage his work was not yet concerned with the revolutionary new theories of the atom then being developed by Niels BOHR, A. SOMMERFELD and their pupils. Recognition of Schrödinger's work took the form of his appointment to a professorship first at Breslau and then at the University of Zürich, where EINSTEIN had been one of his predecessors. Schrödinger's most important work was done during his Zürich period. Early in 1926 he published the series of papers which formed the foundation of wave mechanics. The central idea, namely that the description of the behaviour of electrons and other particles requires the use of a wave field, was first expressed by Louis de BROGLIE, who in turn was inspired by Einstein's treatment of light in terms of photons associated with electromagnetic waves. Schrödinger's work took this idea to the stage of a complete theory governed by the fundamental differential equation that bears his name. He also proved that this theory is mathematically equivalent to the matrix mechanics which had been worked out almost simultaneously by W. HEISENBERG, M. BORN and P. JORDAN. Today the contributions of Schrödinger, of the above authors, and of N. Bohr, P. A. M. DIRAC, and W. PAULI are seen as one structure called Quantum Mechanics. In explicit detailed calculations, however, particularly where it is of advantage to fall back on physical intuition and geometrical visualization, the specifically wave mechanical methods due to Schrödinger are especially appropriate. The most direct demonstration of the 'reality' of the de Broglie-Schrödinger wave is provided by the experiments on electron diffraction (C. J. Davisson and L. H. Germer, G. P. THOMSON).

In spite of Schrödinger's vital role in the creation of modern quantum theory and in the revolution of ideas it brought about, he himself soon became a severe critic of the generally accepted interpretation of that theory. In introducing matter waves, Schrödinger had hoped to bring into atomic physics a classical wave description not unlike the electromagnetic theory formulated by James Clerk MAXWELL. The accepted view today is that matter waves cannot be interpreted so directly, but are related to the probability of making observations on the particles. Such a departure from classical thinking was unacceptable to Schrödinger, as it was to Einstein, and it is chiefly as a consequence of this that most of the work published by Schrödinger after 1926, though it contains many valuable contributions to knowledge, was much less central to the development of theoretical physics than was his earlier work.

In 1927 Schrödinger received the great honour of succeeding Max PLANCK at the University of Berlin as a colleague of Einstein and Max von LAUE,
but on Hitler's assumption of power he chose to leave Germany and accepted an invitation to Oxford. He was then tempted back to his native Austria, accepting a chair in Graz in 1936, but again had to leave at the time of the Anschluss, this time for Ireland. He was a central figure at the Institute for Advanced Study in Dublin until 1957, when again he could not resist an invitation to return to his homeland, to a chair in Vienna. Unfortunately his health did not permit him to enjoy this homecoming for long; he died after a prolonged illness.

Biographical Memoirs of Fellows of the Royal Society. 1961. (Portrait.)

E. Schrödinger, *What is Life* (inc. *Mind and Matter* and *Autobiographical Sketches*). 1992.

W. Moore, *Schrödinger: Life and Thought.* 1989.

Dictionary of Scientific Biography.

Tyler Wasson (Ed.), *Nobel Prize Winners.* 1987. (Portrait.)

N K

SCHRÖTTER, ANTON Born at Olmütz, Austria, 26 November 1802; died Vienna, 15 April 1875. Chemist; discovered red phosphorus.

Schrötter, the son of an apothecary, taught chemistry in the Johanneum at Graz (1830) and in the Vienna *Polytechnisches Institut* (1845). In 1868 he became Master of the Austrian Mint, from which he retired in 1874. Of his many publications, he is remembered only for those on red phosphorus (1850). Though H. A. Vogel (1778-1867) in 1813 and others had observed the change of yellow phosphorus into red, Schrötter was the first to prepare red phosphorus under controlled conditions, and to show that it was not an oxide of the element but an allotrope. This inert new form of phosphorus found immediate application in the match industry where the use of yellow phosphorus presented a grave health hazard; A. ALBRIGHT began its manufacture in Birmingham in 1851. This was followed by a great improvement in the health of the match-workers, though in some countries yellow phosphorus was still used into the present century in match manufacture.

M. Kohn, *Journal of Chemical Education*, **21**, 522, 1944.

Berichte der deutschen chemischen Gesellschaft, **9**, 90, 1976.

H. Lagler, *Blätter für Technik-Geschichte*, **29**, 1, 1967.

W V F

SCHULTZE, MAX JOHANN SIGISMUND Born at Freiberg, Dresden, Germany, 25 March 1825; died Bonn, 16 January 1874. Biologist.

Schultze studied at the University of Greifswald, where his father was professor of anatomy. He also studied for a time under J. P. MÜLLER in Berlin. After a short period as a lecturer at Halle, he was appointed professor of zoology at Bonn.

He was a man of wide interests, carrying out important investigations in fields as diverse as the nervous system of vertebrates, the structure of electric organs in fish, and the anatomy of worms and molluscs. He developed a special interest in unicellular organisms, and from this arose the work for which he is best remembered, that on the nature of the living cell, which he clearly identified as consisting of both nucleus and protoplasm, but not necessarily contained by a membrane. His most important contribution in this field is an essay *Über Muskelkörperchen und war eine Zelle zu nennen habe (Archiv fur Anatomie und Physiologie, 1861).*

> T. H. Bast, *Annals of Medical History* (New Series), **3**, 166, 1931.
> *Dictionary of Scientific Biography.*

T I W

SCHWABE, SAMUEL HEINRICH Born at Dessau, Halle, Germany, 25 October 1789; died there, 11 April 1875. Discovered the periodicity and existence of the sunspot cycle.

Samuel Schwabe was an apothecary who turned to astronomy in his late thirties. In 1826 he began a series of observations of the Sun, using a very small telescope, and counting daily totals of sunspots. By this means he hoped eventually to discover an inter-Mercurial planet in transit across the Sun's disk. With commendable patience he kept up this daily task for most of his long life. In 1843, after seventeen years of sunspot counts, he noticed a periodicity of ten or eleven years in sunspot totals. His discovery was ignored at the time, but in 1851, with the help of HUMBOLDT, it was given the recognition it deserved. Terrestrial magnetic disturbances, weather conditions, and plant and animal growth-rates were all subsequently found to be more or less closely connected with the sunspot cycle. (See also G. E. HALE.)

> F. H. A. von Humboldt, *Kosmos* **3**, 401, 1851.
> H. H. Turner, *Astronomical Discovery.* 1904.
> *Dictionary of Scientific Biography.*

J D N

SCHWANN, THEODOR Born at Neuss, Rhenish Prussia, Germany, 7 December 1810; died Liège, Belgium, 11 January 1882. Biologist.

Schwann was educated at the Jesuits' College in Cologne, and then studied medicine at the Universities of Bonn, Würzburg and Berlin, where he graduated in 1834. Most of his important work was done during the next four years while he remained in Berlin as assistant to Johannes MÜLLER at the Museum of Anatomy. In 1838 he became professor of anatomy at the Roman Catholic University, Louvain, and nine years later he moved to the University of Liège, where he occupied a similar chair until his death.

While assisting Müller, Schwann made histological preparations and discovered the delicate sheath surrounding nerve fibres which is named after him; investigating the process of digestion, he found the enzyme he named pepsin. Between 1836 and 1837, Schwann, though not alone in his observation, showed fermentation of sugar solutions to be originated by living and budding yeast. The discovery of this microscopic organism ('*Zuckerpilz*') led him to challenge the doctrine of spontaneous generation, and he repeated, with improved technique, experiments performed in 1765 by Lazzaro SPALLANZANI. Schwann showed that no microorganisms originated, and no putrefaction occurred, in a sterilized broth to which air, previously heated in a coiled glass tube, alone had access: he also showed that air, so sterilized, is fully adequate to support animal respiration. The later works of Louis PASTEUR on fermentation and

spontaneous generation derived from these earlier experiments.

Schwann is famous for his development of a 'cell theory'. He realized that the nucleated units he had seen in preparations of notochord, when working under Müller, were the animal equivalents of plant cells observed by M. J. SCHLEIDEN. Both observers confirmed the resemblance, though neither had priority in the discovery of cells, and thus his 'cell theory' was formulated, and the foundations of modern histology laid, in 1839 with the publication of Schwann's *Mikroskopische Untersuchungen über die Uebereinstimmung in der Struktur und dem Wachstum der Tiere und Pflanzen* (English translation, *Microscopical Researches on the Similarity in the Structure and the Growth of Animals and Plants,* 1847). Commencing with a description of cartilage, the work covers a wide field of histology and describes the cellular nature and origin of even the most highly differentiated tissues. His concluding generalizations were that the entire animal or plant is composed of either cells, or the products of cells, and that cells have an individual life which is subordinated to that of the organism as a whole.

> Karl Werckmeister, *Das 19te. Jahrhundert in Bildnissen.* 1899. (Portrait.)
> M. Florkin, *Bulletin de l'Academie de Médecine de Belgique,* **16**, 445, 1951.
> R. Watermann, *Theodor Schwann: Leben und Werk.* 1960.
> *Dictionary of Scientific Biography.*

A P G

SEABORG, GLEN THEODORE Born Ishpeming, Michigan, USA, 19 April 1912. Chemist.

Seaborg was educated at UCLA and Berkeley, California, under G. N. LEWIS, and worked on the identification of radioactive isotopes of common elements using the cyclotron. In 1940 Seaborg and his associates identified isotopes of plutonium and demonstrated the susceptibility of plutonium 239 to nuclear fission when bombarded with low-energy neutrons. Seaborg led a research group at the University of Chicago investigating the separation of plutonium from uranium irradiated in nuclear reactors. The plutonium extracted was used in the atom bomb exploded at Nagasaki in 1945. Seaborg resumed his research at Berkeley in 1946 as professor of chemistry.

Between 1940 and 1974 Seaborg played an important part in the identification and isolation of nine transuranic elements, from Plutonium (element 94) to Nobelium (element 102). Projections of the chemical properties of these elements and their places in the Periodic Table were based on his prediction of the actinide group in 1944, fourteen related elements heavier than actinium forming a single group of the Periodic Table. In recognition of his work on the transuranic elements Seaborg received the Nobel prize for chemistry in 1951.

He was Chancellor of the Berkeley campus, University of California (1958–61) and Chairman of the US Atomic Energy Commission (1961–71), representing the USA at the 3rd and 4th UN international conferences on the peaceful uses of atomic energy in 1964 and 1971. He returned to Berkeley in 1971 as Director of the Lawrence

Berkeley Laboratory. He was elected FRS in 1985.

E. Farber, *Nobel Prize Winners in Chemistry, 1901–61*, 1963. (Portrait.)

Chemical Engineering News, **26**, 740, 1948. (Portrait.)

Les Prix Nobel en 1951. 1952. (Portrait.)

G. Waltz, *What Makes a Scientist?* 1959.

C. F. Madden (Ed.), *Talks with Social Scientists*. 1968

Tyler Wasson (Ed.), *Nobel Prize Winners*. 1987. (Portrait.)

N G C

SECCHI, ANGELO Born at Reggio, Italy, 29 June 1818; died Rome, 26 February 1878. Spectroscopist and specialist in solar and stellar physics.

Father Secchi was educated and trained from early youth as a Jesuit. He became professor of physics at Georgetown College, near Washington, before being appointed director of the Roman College Observatory in 1850. He rebuilt it completely, equipping it with new instruments specifically designed for astrophysical research, and for almost thirty years carried out fundamental research there. He was among the first to use photography in astronomy, obtaining pictures of the solar eclipse of 1851. He also used a thermoelectric pile to measure differences between the radiation from the edge and the centre of the solar disk. Secchi also observed comets, meteors and the planets, particularly Jupiter, Saturn and Mars. With the Merz 10-inch refractor and a spectroscope, Secchi by 1862 not only obtained useful spectra of the planets and the Sun but of the brighter stars. His work on stellar spectra led him to the discovery of the well-known spectral types. As he put it: 'The stars are very numerous; yet their spectra can be reduced to a few well-defined and distinct forms . . .' By this time he had examined almost 4000 stars. He published voluminously in solar physics and in spectroscopy; was a member of most scientific societies, including the Royal Society (1856), and in 1867 was awarded a French prize of 100,000 francs for his pioneer work.

J. W. Stein, S. J., and J. Junkes, S. J, *Die Vatikanische Sternwarte*. 1952. (Portrait.)

G. Abetti, *The History of Astronomy*. 1954.

Nature, **17**, 370. 1878.

Dictionary of Scientific Biography.

A E R

SEDGWICK, ADAM Born at Dent, Yorkshire, England, 22 March 1785; died Cambridge, 27 January 1873. Geologist; founder of the Cambrian system.

Adam Sedgwick's father was vicar of Dent, and he himself went to the near-by Sedbergh School and then, in 1804, to Trinity College, Cambridge, where he studied chiefly mathematics. In 1810 he became a Fellow of Trinity, his main home for the rest of his life, at once throwing himself energetically into the business of college and university. In 1818 he was appointed Woodwardian Professor of Geology, a post he held for fifty-five years. As was not unusual in those days, this appointment was made not because he knew much about geology but on his general merits; the choice was, however, abundantly justified, as he immediately set about putting geology into its proper place as a subject of university study and made important

field investigations in such diverse regions as the Isle of Wight, Devon and Cornwall, the Lake District, and NE England. In 1818 he was ordained priest. His great abilities, together with the strength and charm of his personality, were recognized by his being made President of the Geological Society in 1829 and President of the British Association at its first meeting, in Cambridge, in 1833. He became a canon of Norwich in 1834.

In 1831 Sedgwick began the geological field work with which his name is always associated: the establishing of an orderly rock-succession and the revealing of a grand structure among the mountains of North Wales, and the consequent founding of the Cambrian system. This was done with wonderful energy and insight, but the results were mostly expounded in verbal discourses, very scantily reported. This persistent reluctance to put his researches into writing was altogether unfortunate, and in this case largely contributed to a regrettable controversy with Sir Roderick MURCHISON over priorities of discovery and nomenclature among these Lower Palaeozoic rocks (as they soon came to be called). However, he did compose some important extended treatises, notably that on the structure of rock-masses (*Transactions of the Geological Society*, 1835). In 1839 he and Murchison reported to the Geological Society the results of their work which founded the Devonian system.

Sedgwick was awarded the Wollaston Medal of the Geological Society in 1851 and the Copley Medal of the Royal Society, to which he was elected in 1821, in 1863. Accounts of him describe him as a man of the most winning personality, with his 'eagle eyes', 'gaiety of spirit', 'kindliness of heart', and his 'overflowing goodness of character'. The Sedgwick Museum of Geology at Cambridge is his lasting memorial.

J. W. Clark and T. McK. Hughes, *The Life and Letters of Adam Sedgwick*. 1890. (Portraits.)

A. Geikie, *The Founders of Geology* (2nd ed.). 1905.

Dictionary of National Biography.

Dictionary of Scientific Biography.

J C

SEGRÈ, EMILIO GINO Born at Tivoli, Rome, 1 February 1905; died Berkeley, California, USA, 22 April 1989. Nuclear physicist.

Segrè went to the University of Rome in 1922 to study engineering, but later changed to physics and became the first graduate student of Enrico FERMI, obtaining his PhD in 1928. He returned to Rome in 1932, and although his work had concentrated on atomic spectroscopy, in 1934 he joined Fermi's group to work in neutron research. In 1936 Segrè moved to the University of Palermo, to become director of the physics laboratory. While there he discovered technetium, the 'missing' element with atomic number 43, which had been formed in discarded parts of a cyclotron he had obtained on a trip to the Radiation Laboratory at Berkeley, California.

On a later trip to Berkeley in 1938, Segrè learned that he had been removed from his post at Palermo, due to Mussolini's anti-Semitic policies. He decided to remain in the USA and sent for his family to join him. He obtained a post at Berkeley, and soon discovered another new element, astatine, with atomic number 85.

During the Second World War, Segrè worked at Los Alamos on the atomic bomb project, afterwards returning to Berkeley where he remained until he retired in 1972. His interests turned to high-energy subatomic particle physics, and in 1955, working with the Bevatron, the new accelerator at Berkeley, Segrè's team discovered the antiproton. Segrè and Owen Chamberlain (1920–) were awarded the Nobel Prize for Physics for this work in 1959.

Nobel Lectures: Physics, 1942–62. 1964
Physics Today, October 1990. (Portrait.)
L. M. Libby, The Uranium People. 1979.
Tyler Wasson (Ed.), Nobel Prize Winners. 1987. (Portrait.)

C S

SEGUIN, MARC Born at Annonay, France, 20 April 1786; died there, 24 February 1875. Bridge builder and engine designer.

Son of a cloth manufacturer and nephew of the celebrated Joseph MONTGOLFIER, who made the first balloon ascent at Annonay in 1783, Marc Seguin was self-taught. In association with the Swiss engineer Henri Dufour (1787–1875) he used wire cables in building the first major suspension bridge of this kind in Europe at Geneva. This was the prelude to a number of other cable suspension bridges which Seguin and his brother Camille (who died in 1852 at Toulon) built in France over the next few years, beginning with that over the Rhône in 1827 between Tain and Tournon.

Seguin's second great achievement was to design and bring into immediate use on the Lyons and St Etienne Railway (the first in France) a new kind of boiler in which the water surrounded the heating element. His multitubular boiler was conceived independently of that designed by George STEPHENSON for the 'Rocket'. His works include Des ponts en fil de fer, 1824; Mémoire sur le chemin de fer de Saint-Etienne à Lyon, 1826; Mémoire sur la navigation à la vapeur, 1828; De l'Influence des chemins de fer et de l'Art de les tracer et de les construire, 1839.

Conrad Matschoss, Die Entwicklung der Dampfmaschine. 1908. (Portrait.)
F. Achard and L. Seguin, Transactions of the Newcomen Society, 7, 97, 1926.
P. E. Marchal and L. Seguin, Marc Seguin 1786–1875. 1957.
Dictionary of Scientific Biography.

W H G A

SEMMELWEIS, IGNAZ PHILIPP Born at Ofen, Hungary, 1 July 1818; died near Budapest, 13 August 1865. A pioneer in the treatment of sepsis.

Semmelweis studied law and then medicine in Vienna; he graduated in medicine there in 1844. He then specialized in obstetrics, and became an assistant in the first obstetric unit of the General Hospital in Vienna (1845). The controversy following his discovery (see below) delayed his admission to the medical faculty, but in 1850 he was appointed to his lecturership. Five days later he left Vienna for Budapest, where he was appointed chief physician to a hospital, and in 1855 to the chair of obstetrics in the University of Budapest. He suffered from mental derangement for some time before his death.

In Semmelweis's time the mortality from puerperal fever was very high in Europe. He found that the mortality from it in the first obstetric unit was 10 per cent of women admitted, and that in the second obstetric unit it was about 3 per cent. In the first unit the women were attended by medical students, whereas the second unit was a training school for midwives, who alone attended the women. In 1847 the pathologist J. Kolletschka (1803–47), a friend of Semmelweis, died as the result of pricking his finger while performing an autopsy. Semmelweis was present at the autopsy of Kolletschka's body, and he noticed that the lesions resembled those that he had seen in patients who had died of puerperal fever. He became convinced that puerperal fever was due to infection introduced from without, probably on the hands of the medical attendants. He then found that the students in the first unit performed dissections and attended autopsies immediately before they came to the wards for clinical instruction, and that they did not wash their hands in between. Semmelweis now issued orders that all attendants must wash their hands in a solution of chloride of lime before they examined pregnant women or attended women in labour. Within two months mortality in the first unit had fallen to 1 per cent, and some months later the mortality was nil.

The observations of Semmelweis were supported by F. Hebra (1816–80) and J. Skoda (1805–81), two great teachers in the Vienna School, and Hebra made the first announcement of the discovery in the journal that he edited. But Semmelweis met with very great opposition. It was not until 1860 that he published his great work on the etiology and prophylaxis of puerperal fever.

W. J. Sinclair, Semmelweis. 1909. (Portrait.)
R. H. Major, History of Medicine, vol. 2. 1954.
F. G. Slaughter, Immortal Magyar. 1961.
G. Gortvay and I. Zoltán, Semmelweis: His Life and Work. 1968.
L. F. Céline, Mea Culpa and the Life and Work of Semmelweis. 1937.
Dictionary of Scientific Biography.

E A U

SENDERENS, JEAN-BAPTISTE (THE ABBÉ) Born at Barbachen, Hautes-Pyrénées, France, 27 January 1856; died there, 26 September 1936. Collaborator with P. SABATIER in the study of catalysed gas-phase reactions.

Senderens, the son of a small farmer, wished to become a monk. His family were, however, impoverished by the phylloxera disease in the vineyards, and the necessity of earning enough to educate his brothers and sisters led him into the teaching profession. He studied chemistry at the University of Toulouse, where he worked with Edouard Filhol (1814–83) and his successor, Paul Sabatier. At the same time he was teaching chemistry in the Institut Catholique, a post which he left in 1911 to work with the brothers Poulenc in their industrial establishment at Ivry. He retired after the First World War to his family home at Barbachen, where Poulenc built him a private laboratory. He was also active in religious affairs, and wrote a book, Création et Evolution (1928).

The most productive period of his career was his collaboration with Sabatier (about 1895–1911) on gas-phase reactions catalysed by finely divided metals. This led notably to the discovery of the

hydrogenation of unsaturated hydrocarbons catalysed by nickel, a reaction which soon found wide
industrial application. It is almost impossible to
separate the contributions of Sabatier and Senderens, and the award of a Nobel Prize to Sabatier
alone (1912) caused, for a time, a certain coldness
between them. Senderens also worked in other
fields of chemistry besides catalysis; his early
experience gave him a lasting interest in the problems of viticulture and pest control.

Bulletin de la Société Chimique de France, **6**, 1,
1939. (Portrait.)

W V F

SERTÜRNER, FRIEDRICH WILHELM ADAM

FERDINAND Born at Neuhaus, near Paderborn,
North Rhine-Westphalia, Germany, 19 June 1783;
died Hameln, 20 February 1841. Discoverer of
morphine.

Sertürner practised as an apothecary, first in
Eimbeck, then (1823) in Hameln. He was the
author of papers on *materia medica*, on 'sulpho-
vinic acid' (ethyl hydrogen sulphate), on the formation of dew, and many other topics. Feeling,
perhaps not unjustly, that his work was being
ignored by the scientific world, for some years he
ran a journal of his own. In 1805 he described the
isolation from extract of opium of a crystalline acid
(meconic acid), and another crystalline substance
which was alkaline to indicators. But this discovery was overlooked until 1817, when a second
paper described a series of salts of the new base,
which he named 'morphium' (later morphine), and
tested on himself. Morphine was the first of the
'vegetable bases' to be recognized, and its isolation
represents the beginning of alkaloid chemistry.

G. Lockemann, *Journal of Chemical Education*, **28**,
277, 1951. (Portrait.)
Dictionary of Scientific Biography.

W V F

SERVETUS, MICHAEL (MIGUEL SERVETO)

Born at Tudela, Navarra, Spain, 29 September
1511; died Geneva, 27 October 1553. Medical practitioner and theological writer; described the lesser
circulation.

The family of Servetus removed to Villanueva,
and he later used the pseudonym 'Villanovanus'.
He studied law at Toulouse, and became a secretary on the staff of Charles V. His theological works
of 1531–2 were bitterly criticized. After studying
mathematics and astronomy at Lyons, Servetus,
who had already published a new edition of the
Geography of PTOLEMY, was by November 1536
studying geography and astronomy, and presumably medicine, at Paris. In 1537 he published a
dialectical treatise on the use of the syrups by the
ancient Greek writers. In 1538 he assisted Johann
Guinther (1505–74) of Andernach in his dissections, but by the end of the year he had to leave
Paris, without a medical degree, because of his het-
erodox views on judicial astrology. He then practised medicine at Charlieu and at Vienne.

While at Vienne, Servetus corresponded with
John Calvin (1509–64) in Geneva. While nominally requesting information, Servetus was really
trying to influence Calvin's theological views.
Calvin soon stopped replying, but Servetus continued to write in ever more insulting terms, and
he sent Calvin an early draft of his theological

work, *Christianismi restitutio*. Early in 1553 Servetus had the book secretly printed in Vienne.

Calvin now communicated with the authorities
at Vienne, who imprisoned Servetus for heresy. He
escaped; but while in Geneva *en route* for Italy he
was recognized, imprisoned, and burnt at the
stake. The copies of the *Christianismi restitutio*
were also burned, but three escaped and are extant
today.

In 1694 William Wotton (1666–1727) noticed
that this work contained a description of the passage of the blood from the right ventricle through
the lungs to the left ventricle. The description
relates to the theological view that the divine spirit
(soul) is in the blood, and the problem concerned
the manner in which the divine spirit reached the
blood from the air, and was then distributed in the
blood from the heart to the body. GALEN postulated
the presence of pores in the septum between the
ventricles, but by 1553 many anatomists doubted
the existence of these pores. The only other possible route from the right to the left ventricle was
through the lungs, and of this route Servetus gave
an elementary description. There is no evidence
that he ever carried out any experiments in support, and he failed to realize that all the blood had
to pass through the lungs.

C. D. O'Malley, *Michael Servetus*. 1953. (Portrait.)
H. P. Bayon, *Annals of Science*, **4**, 69, 1939.
R. H. Bainton, *Hunted Heretic*. 1960.
J. F. Fulton, *Michael Servetus: Humanist and
Martyr.* 1953.
Dictionary of Scientific Biography.

E A U

SHANNON, CLAUDE ELWOOD Born in Gaylord,

Michigan, USA, 30 April 1916. Mathematician and
originator of information theory.

Graduating from the University of Michigan in
1936, Shannon went on to Massachusetts Institute
of Technology (MIT), gaining his MS in 1937 with
a remarkable thesis which used G. A. BOOLE's
algebra to analyse and optimize relay switching
circuits. Obtaining his PhD in mathematics from
MIT in 1940, he joined Bell Telephone Laboratories (BTL) in 1941 as a research mathematician.
Here he studied transmission of information across
networks, pulse code modulation, memory
requirements of switching systems, and cryptana-
lysis. By 1945 he had imported the concept of
entropy from classical thermodynamics to describe
the analogy between the degree of randomness in
a transmission system and freedom of choice in
encoding messages, focusing on interplay between
channel capacity, signal coding, and rate of transmission to minimize errors in received messages.
Subsequent work with W. Weaver (1894–1978)
resulted in publication of *A Mathematical Theory
of Communication* in 1949. Information theory has
subsequently underpinned circuit design, computer technology, and research in phonetics. In
1950 Shannon described how a computer could be
programmed to play chess. His work influenced
subsequent development of artificial intelligence
(the first game was played by the Los Alamos
MANIAC computer in 1956). Shannon joined the
faculty of MIT in 1957, remaining a consultant to
BTL until 1972. Now Professor Emeritus, his
awards include the Alfred Nobel AIEE Prize
(1940), the Medal of Honour IEEE (1966), and

Audio Engineering Society Gold Medal (1985).

J. W. Cordata, *Historical Dictionary of Data Processing: Biographies*, 1987.

McGraw-Hill Modern Scientists and Engineers, 1980. (Portrait.)

V. Pratt, *Thinking Machines: The Evolution of Artificial Intelligence*. 1987.

R J H

SHAPLEY, HARLOW Born at Nashville, Missouri, USA, 2 November 1885; died Boulder, Colorado, 20 October 1972. Astronomer; determined the size and shape of the Milky Way galaxy.

Following his PhD at Princeton on properties of eclipsing binary stars, in 1914 Shapley began at Mount Wilson Observatory a study of variable stars in globular clusters. H. S. LEAVITT had found in 1912 that the period of pulsation and apparent brightness of variable stars were related; Shapley calibrated this for absolute magnitude and hence estimated the distances to nearby star clusters containing variable stars. Assuming more distant clusters would also be similar in size, he used their angular diameters to determine their distances. By 1918 he established that globular clusters must lie in a spheroid about the centre of the Milky Way's galactic plane, hence (contrary to previous assumption) the solar system was located on its outskirts. Unaware at that time of the dimming of variable star brightness by interstellar gas, he revised his original distance estimates in 1930 to show the solar system lies approximately 30 000 light years from the galactic centre. His methods laid the foundation for E. P. HUBBLE's subsequent work on spiral galaxies.

Shapley became Director of Harvard College Observatory (1921–52) and helped to establish UNESCO and the National Academy of Sciences. In 1934 he was awarded the Gold Medal of the Royal Astronomical Society and became President of the American Association for the Advancement of Science in 1946.

Dictionary of Scientific Biography.

Biographical Memoirs of the National Academy of Sciences, **49**, 241, 1978. (Portrait.)

R J H

SHARPEY-SCHAFER, SIR EDWARD ALBERT Born at Hornsey, near London, 2 June 1850; died North Berwick, Scotland, 29 March 1935. A founder of endocrinology, and inventor of a much-used method of artificial respiration.

Schafer, a son of J. W. H. Schäfer, formerly of Hamburg, studied at University College, London, qualified in medicine, and was elected the first holder of the Sharpey Scholarship (1871). Schafer worked and taught under William Sharpey (1802–80), the professor of general anatomy and physiology, to whom he owed much. When Sharpey retired in 1874 he was succeeded by J. S. Burdon Sanderson (1828–1905); Schafer became assistant professor, and in 1883, when Sanderson went to Oxford, Schafer became Jodrell Professor at University College. From 1899, until his retirement in 1933, he was professor of physiology in the University of Edinburgh. Schafer was elected a Fellow of the Royal Society in 1878; he delivered the Croonian lecture in 1909; was awarded a Royal Medal in 1902 and the Copley Medal in 1924. He was knighted in 1913, and received many other

honours. Out of gratitude to his old chief Schafer named one of his two sons Sharpey Schafer, and when both his sons were killed in the First World War he slightly modified his own name from Schäfer and prefixed Sharpey's surname to it (1918). In 1876 Schafer was one of the nineteen men who met under Burdon Sanderson to form the Physiological Society, and at its jubilee in 1926 he was the sole survivor. He wrote the history of the Society (1927).

Schafer's early research was on histology, such as the structure of the wing muscles of insects and the absorption of fat by the intestinal villi. He published two excellent textbooks on this subject, one of which was a volume in the eighth edition of Quain's *Anatomy*. By the eleventh edition (1912) this work had grown into a very large book. Between 1883 and 1893 Schafer's research, alone or with Victor Horsley (1857–1916), mostly related to the effects of stimulation or removal of certain areas of the cerebral cortex in primates.

In 1894 Schafer, working with George Oliver (1841–1915), discovered that, if an extract of the medulla of the adrenal gland was injected into an animal, there followed a rise in blood-pressure, due to vasoconstriction, and also a relaxation of the bronchial muscles. The substance responsible was isolated in 1901 and was named adrenaline. In 1895 Schafer carried out important research on the pituitary and other ductless glands, and in 1916 he published his book *The Endocrine Organs*. In 1898 he founded the *Quarterly Journal of Experimental Physiology*, which he edited until 1933.

In 1903 Schafer introduced his prone method of artificial respiration, a great advance on previous methods. It was subsequently adopted by the Royal Life Saving Society.

Obituary Notices of Fellows of the Royal Society, 1932–5. (Portrait.)

Quarterly Journal of Experimental Physiology, **25**, 49, 1935.

Nature, **135**, 608, 1935.

Dictionary of National Biography.

Dictionary of Scientific Biography.

E A U

SHAW, SIR WILLIAM NAPIER Born in Birmingham, England, 4 March 1854; died London, 23 March 1945. Meteorologist.

Shaw was educated at King Edward's School, Birmingham, and then at Emmanuel College, Cambridge, where he graduated sixteenth Wrangler in 1876. In the following year he was elected a Fellow of his College, and was appointed to a lectureship in experimental physics in the Cavendish Laboratory, which he held until 1899. In that year he was appointed secretary of the Meteorological Council, in London, and in 1905 became director of the Meteorological Office, holding this post until 1920. From then until 1923 he was professor of meteorology at Imperial College, London University.

Shaw did much to establish the young science of meteorology on a sound basis, especially through his writings. His *Manual of Meteorology* (4 vols, 1926–31) is still a standard work, and a successor to his *Forecasting Weather* which first appeared in 1923. In his *Life-History of Surface Air Currents* (1906, with R. G. K. Lempfert) he came very near to the polar front theory of cyclones advanced by J. A. B. BJERKNES. His interest in atmospheric problems extended to air pollution, and in 1925 he wrote (with J. S. Owens) *The Smoke Problem of Great Cities*.

Shaw was widely honoured. He was elected FRS in 1891 and was knighted in 1915. In 1910 the Royal Meteorological Society conferred on him their highest award, the Symons Gold Medal. He was an honorary graduand of many universities, including Aberdeen, Harvard and Athens.

Dictionary of National Biography.

Quarterly Journal of the Royal Meteorological Society, **71**, 187, 1945.

Advancement of Science, **8**, 114, 1951.

Biographical Memoirs of Fellows of the Royal Society. 1945. (Portrait.)

T I W

SHERRINGTON, SIR CHARLES SCOTT Born in

London, 27 November 1857; died Eastbourne, Sussex, 4 March 1952. Physiologist of the nervous system.

After an early training in classics, Sherrington was introduced to physiology as a student in 1881 by Sir Michael Foster (1836–1907), professor of physiology at Cambridge. He qualified in medicine from St Thomas's Hospital, London, in 1885, then travelled on the Continent and worked with the physiologist F. Goltz (1834–1902) at Strasbourg, and with R. VIRCHOW and R. KOCH in Berlin before taking up a lectureship in physiology at St Thomas's Hospital. In 1891 he was appointed superintendent of the Brown Institution, a veterinary hospital of the University of London. His experimental work there led to his appointment as professor of physiology at Liverpool in 1895. From 1913 until his retirement in 1936 he was Waynflete Professor of Physiology at Oxford.

Sherrington's first paper in 1884 (jointly with J. N. LANGLEY) concerned the significance of an experimental excision of an area of cerebral cortex from a dog by Goltz before an international congress of medicine in London in 1881. Goltz held that this had had no effect on the animal and that it confounded the views of D. FERRIER on the localization of function in the brain: Sherrington's and Langley's findings vindicated Ferrier. Almost all of Sherrington's more than three hundred subsequent papers recorded experimental studies of the nervous system. In the 1890s he mapped out the motor nerve supply of the musculature and this was followed by similar work on the sensory roots, and the demonstration that one-third of nerve fibres to muscles carried impulses back to the central nervous system. In 1891 he published his first paper on the knee-jerk, and in 1897 he coined (or possibly took over from Foster) the concept of the synapse and the concepts of reciprocal innervation and active inhibition.

In the first three decades of this century he studied the cortex of the brain in apes and defined motor points for certain movements in the precentral gyrus: he established that the postcentral gyrus had mainly sensory functions. Injuries to the motor pathways some distance below the cortex caused a picture of 'decerebrate rigidity'. Motor impulses eventually travelled along a 'final common path'. The spinal cord was investigated by many experiments which were summarized in *The Reflex Activity of the Spinal Cord*, published with several

distinguished pupils in 1932. The knee-jerk was finally identified as a muscle stretch reflex which reflected the 'central excitatory state' of the spinal motoneuron pool. While I. P. PAVLOV demonstrated facilitation and inhibition of conditioned reflexes in the cerebrum of the whole animal, Sherrington elucidated similar processes in a small group of nerve cells in the spinal cord: these concepts leant to some extent on the 'dynamic polarization of nerve cells' postulated by RAMÓN Y CAJAL. The principle of Sherrington's *Integrative Action of the Nervous System* (1904) probably derived initially from the ideas of J. Hughlings Jackson (1835–1911).

Sherrington was interested in pathology and worked as member of a cholera commission as a young doctor in Italy and in Spain (where he first met Cajal). He was first to use diphtheria antitoxin successfully in Britain, on an apparently moribund nephew. In 1916–17 he helped evaluate the use of antitetanus serum in battle casualties. His interests in public health made him a member or chairman of Government committees on lighting in factories, on industrial fatigue, and on alcoholism during the First World War.

Sherrington played a considerable part in the organization of scientific endeavour in various fields and was President of the Royal Society 1920–5. His own department was extremely popular and many of the eminent neurologists, physiologists and neuro-surgeons of this century worked with him at Liverpool or at Oxford. His scientific writings are not easy reading, although he took great trouble over his style. Some of his poems were published in 1940 as *The assaying of Brabantius*. As a philosopher he was a dualist: he tried to draw attention to the work of the French renaissance physician Jean FERNEL in the books *Man and his Nature* (1938) and *The Endeavour of Jean Fernel* (1946). His last book was an enlarged edition of *Goethe on Nature and Science* (1949).

Sherrington has justly been called the William Harvey of the nervous system. Among many honours he received the Nobel prize for medicine or physiology in 1932.

Obituary Notices of Fellows of the Royal Society. 1952. (Portrait.)

R. Granit, *Charles Scott Sherrington*. 1966.

J. C. Eccles and W. C. Gibson, *Sherrington*. 1979. (Portrait.)

J. F. Fulton, *Journal of Neurophysiology*, **15**, 167, 1952.

Wilder Penfield, *Brain*, **80**, 402, 1957.

H. Oxbury (Ed.), *Great Britons: 20th Century Lives*. 1985.

Dictionary of Scientific Biography.

Dictionary of National Biography.

Tyler Wasson (Ed.), *Nobel Prize Winners*. 1987. (Portrait.)

E H I

SHOCKLEY, WILLIAM Born in London, 13 Febru-

ary 1910; died in Palo Alto, California, USA, 12 August 1989. Co-inventor of the transistor.

Shockley's parents, who were American, returned to the USA in 1913, and he was brought up in California. He studied at the California Institute of Technology, graduating in 1932, and gained his PhD at the Massachusetts Institute of Technology in 1936. He then joined Bell Telephone Laboratories in New York and soon pursued his interest in solid state physics. During the Second World War he was director of the US Navy's Anti-submarine Warfare Operations Research Group and later an expert consultant to the Office of the Secretary of War.

In 1945 Shockley returned to Bell Laboratories and became one of two supervisors of a new semiconductor research group, which aimed to use semiconductors in electronic devices, instead of vacuum tubes with their large size and high power consumption. He soon proposed the idea of increasing the number of mobile electrons in a semiconductor by an electric field at the surface, although this initially proved not to work. However, in 1947, two members of Shockley's group, John BARDEEN and Walter Brattain (1902–87) discovered that an external electrode could cause a current of 'holes' to flow in a semiconductor (that is, movement of a 'missing' electron from one atom to another). They found that they could control the current via metal contacts, and devised the first germanium 'point contact' transistor, with which they demonstrated amplification.

Shockley developed the basic principle into the junction transistor, which was a sandwich of one semiconductor type between two others. This discovery, and related developments, led to the enormous growth of microelectronics from the 1960s onwards, fuelling in particular the development of computers. The importance was seen immediately, and Shockley, together with Bardeen and Brattain, were rewarded with the Nobel prize for physics in 1956.

Shockley left Bell Laboratories in 1956 to set up the Shockley Semiconductor Laboratory of Beckman Instruments in Palo Alto, California. In 1965, he returned to Bell as a consultant. He had by now developed strong ties with Stanford University, where he had been professor of engineering science in 1963. He retired in 1975, and in the latter part of his life aroused controversy with studies of the correlation between race and intellect.

Nobel Lectures, Physics, 1942–62, 1964.
Physics Today, June 1991. (Portrait.)
R. Goodell, The Visible Scientists. 1977
Tyler Wasson (Ed.), Nobel Prize Winners. 1987. (Portrait.)

C S

SHRAPNEL, HENRY Born at Bradford-on-Avon, Wiltshire, England, 3 June 1761; died Southampton, Hampshire, 31 March 1842. Inventor of spherical case shot.

Henry Shrapnel was commissioned in the Royal Artillery in 1779; served in Newfoundland, Gibraltar and the West Indies; and was wounded in the Duke of York's campaign at Dunkirk in September 1793. In 1804 he became first assistant inspector of artillery and was for many years employed at Woolwich Arsenal; he retired as a major-general in 1825, and only missed a baronetcy through the death of William IV.

From 1784 onwards he privately investigated the use of a spherical projectile, filled with bullets and fitted with a small bursting-charge and time-fuse, so that the bullets might be scattered among enemy personnel over a wide radius. Known at first as spherical case shot, his device received official approval in 1803 and was employed in Surinam in the following year. It was used in the Peninsular

War from the Battle of Vimiero onwards, and with great effect in the defence of La Haye Sainte on the field of Waterloo. At a later period the powder-charge was strengthened in order to increase the velocity of the bullets beyond that of the shell at the moment of bursting.
Dictionary of National Biography.

T K D

SIDGWICK, NEVIL VINCENT Born at Oxford, England, 8 May 1873; died there, 15 March 1952. Chemist; made notable contributions to valency theory.

Sidgwick, a devoted Oxford man, was of academic descent. His father had been a Fellow of Merton College, Oxford; his mother, too, came of an academic family. He was educated at Rugby School, where in 1891 he won a scholarship in natural science at Oxford. In 1895 he was awarded a First; two years later he demonstrated his brilliant versatility by gaining a First also in classics. For a time he worked under W. OSTWALD at Leipzig, and then returned to Oxford as a Fellow of Lincoln College (1901), where he lived for half a century. After lesser university appointments, he was made reader in chemistry in 1924, and in 1935 the title of professor was conferred on him.

Although he ultimately achieved an international reputation, Sidgwick published little of major importance until middle life, though he wrote a number of papers on the physical chemistry of organic reactions. His Organic Chemistry of Nitrogen (1910) was to prove of lasting value. A turning point in his career was when, in 1914, he went to the meeting of the British Association in Australia. There he met Ernest RUTHERFORD, with whom he formed a lasting friendship and who stimulated his interest in atomic structure. This interest he pursued after the war of 1914–18, when he developed the notion of the 'hydrogen bond' to explain certain observed anomalies in the properties of organic compounds. Later, he began to interpret chemical reactions in terms of the electronic theory being developed by the physicists; he was influenced by, among others, RUTHERFORD, Niels BOHR, G. N. LEWIS, T. M. LOWRY and A. WERNER. He contributed notably to valency theory – that is, to the explanation of the forces that bind atoms together to form molecules – especially to the conception of the co-ordinate link, in which a bond is formed by two electrons derived from one atom. In 1927 there appeared his outstanding work The Electronic Theory of Valency, which established his reputation internationally. Later, he devoted himself to the systematic collection of evidence in support of his theoretical ideas. In 1933 there appeared another major work, Some Physical Properties of the Covalent Link in Chemistry. Shortly before the last war Sidgwick embarked on another great work, The Chemical Elements and their Compounds; this finally appeared in 1950 when he was 77 and his health was failing rapidly.

Sidgwick was accorded many honours. He was elected FRS in 1922. He was President of the Faraday Society and of the Chemical Society; the latter awarded him its Longstaff Medal in 1945. He was also a Foreign Member of the American Academy of Arts and Sciences.

Obituary Notices of Fellows of the Royal Society. 1954. (Portrait.)

L. E. Sutton, *Proceedings of the Chemical Society*, 310, 1958.
E. Farber (Ed.), *Great Chemists*. 1961. (Portrait.)
Dictionary of National Biography.
Dictionary of Scientific Biography.

T I W

SIEBOLD, CARL THEODOR ERNST VON Born at Würzburg, Bavaria, Germany, 16 February 1804; died Munich, Bavaria, 7 April 1885. Physician and zoologist remembered for his work on the life history of invertebrates.

Siebold was one of a distinguished family of physicians. He studied medicine first at Berlin and later in Göttingen, and during this time discovered an interest in zoology. The first of his many publications was a dissertation on the salamander (1828). He practised medicine for a time in Danzig and in his spare time he made observations on marine life. In 1840, on the recommendation of F. H. Alexander von HUMBOLDT, he was given the chair of zoology, comparative anatomy and veterinary medicine at Erlanger. In 1845 he moved to Freiburg; in 1850 to Breslau; and finally in 1853 to Munich, where he stayed until his death in 1885.

In an obituary he was described as the 'Nestor of German Zoology'. In age and knowledge he earned the appellation, for throughout his long career he was an industrious and critical observer. His major contributions were in the field of invertebrate zoology. In his *Lehrbuch der vergleichen den Anatomie* which he produced with Hermann Stannius (1808–83) between 1846 and 1848 he established and named the unicellular group *Protozoa*. In insect studies he demonstrated that the eggs of some – e.g. drone bees – were parthenogenic. Among his more difficult tasks was his study of the stages in the life cycle of the tapeworm and in the preface to his book on this animal (*Ueber die Band und Blasenwürmer*, 1854) he indicated the importance of such studies to medicine when he observed that a knowledge of the life-cycle will discover the mode of origin and suggest means of attacking the parasite in man.

In 1848 he made a major contribution to the advance of zoological knowledge when, with R. A. von KÖLLIKER, he founded the *Zeitschrift für wissenschaftliche Zoologie*, which he edited until his death.

> E. Ehlers, *Zeitschrift für wissenschaftliche Zoologie*, 42, i, 1885. (Portrait.)
> *Dictionary of Scientific Biography.*
> A. Koelliker, *Zeitschrift für wissenschaftliche Zoologie*, Supp. 30, v, 1978.

M P E

SIEGBAHN, KARL MANNE GEORG Born at Örebro, Sweden, 3 December 1886; died Stockholm, 26 September 1978. Physicist, noted for work on x-ray spectroscopy.

A discovery, made by M. T. F. von LAUE, W. Friedrich and P. Knipping in 1912, that x-rays are diffracted by crystals, opened two avenues in physics – investigation of the structure of matter (on the atomic scale) and the study of the structure of atoms. In the latter investigation, started by H. G. J. MOSELEY just before his untimely death at Gallipoli, Siegbahn was pre-eminent. With typical Swedish thoroughness, he measured as precisely as possible the x-ray spectra of the elements from sodium to uranium. He found complete support for the model of the atom proposed by Niels BOHR and he calculated the orbital energies. His book *Spektroskopie der Röntgenstrahlen* (1924) was translated into English in 1925 and became widely used.

Siegbahn received his MS and DSc (1911) at the University of Lund and remained there on the faculty until 1923. He was a professor at the University of Uppsala 1924–37. In 1937 the Royal Swedish Academy of Science created the Nobel Institute of Physics and appointed Siegbahn as Director (1939). He held this post until his retirement in 1964. During his tenure of office research results were published in more than 600 papers, some 40 of which were DSc theses. In 1939 he became a member of the International Committee for Weights and Measures. He was elected a Foreign Member of the Royal Society in 1954 and received the Hughes Medal in 1934 and the Rumford Medal in 1940.

A surprising result in thesis work by E. Bäcklin, supervised by Siegbahn, was that x-ray diffraction from a glass grating ruled with 220 lines/mm gave a value for the electron charge e not in accord with the then generally accepted value R. A. MILLIKAN had obtained from his oil-drop experiment. Bäcklin suspected that the value for the viscosity of air used in the Millikan calculation was in error. At his polite urging, the viscosity of air was redetermined at the Johns Hopkins University. With the new value the oil-drop and the x-ray values for e were brought into agreement.

To bridge the gap between x-ray spectra and optical spectra, Siegbahn designed a ruling engine to make gratings which would produce both x-ray and optical spectra at a very small angle (2–5°) between the incident rays and the surface of the grating. (Gratings ruled on that engine were later used in the US orbiting solar observatory, OSO, to record extreme ultraviolet radiation from the Sun.) Siegbahn opened for investigation the region from about 20Å to 500Å, or about five octaves. By 1934 work by Siegbahn and his colleagues had yielded rather complete analysis of spectra emitted by the lower elements up to the iron group, including spectra resulting from 16- to 18-fold ionization.

> *McGraw-Hill Modern Men of Science.* 1968. (Portrait.)
> *Dictionary of Scientific Biography*, Supp. II.
> Tyler Wasson (Ed.), *Nobel Prize Winners*. 1987. (Portrait.)
> Robert L. Weber, *Pioneers of Science: Nobel Prize Winners in Physics*. 1980. (Portrait.)

R L W

SIEMENS, SIR CHARLES WILLIAM Born at Lenthe, Hanover, Germany, 4 April 1823; died London, 19 November 1883. Pioneer of the open-hearth steel furnace and of the regenerative principle.

After studying at Göttingen University, Karl Wilhelm (Charles William) Siemens was apprenticed in an engineering works and was aided by his elder brother Werner SIEMENS before coming to England in 1843. Here he found scope to apply his scientific training and systematic researches. At a Smethwick works he tried to apply to the steam-engine his regenerative principle for conservation of waste heat. Although unsuccessful in this, Siemens met at Smethwick the designer E. A.

Cowper, who was to apply his regenerative principle in the Cowper Stove for heating the blast in iron-making. This improved pig-iron production by up to 20 per cent.

By 1861 the initial designs of Charles and his brother Frederick SIEMENS became further improved by incorporating a gas-producer which made it possible to utilize low-grade coal. Hence came the Siemens-Martin open-hearth steel furnace, which by 1900 exceeded H.BESSEMER's converter in steel production throughout the world. The Martins acquired a share in the open-hearth process because they had used at Sireuil a modified reverberatory furnace for heating a steel bath by hot gases derived from an external source.

Sir William Siemens is noted for many other achievements. He designed the cable-laying steamship *Faraday* which laid the Atlantic cable of 1874, and in 1883 was concerned with the building of the Portrush Railway in Ireland, one of the first electric railways in the United Kingdom. He was elected FRS in 1863; was President of the British Association for the Advancement of Science in 1882; and was knighted in 1883.

W. Pole, *Life of Sir William Siemens*. 1888. (Portrait.)
J. C. Carr and W. Taplin, *History of the British Steel Industry*. 1962. (Portrait.)
Dictionary of National Biography.
Georg Siemens, *History of the House of Siemens*. 1957.

M S

SIEMENS, ERNST WERNER VON Born at Lenthe, Hanover, Germany, 13 December 1816; died Charlottenburg, 6 December 1892. Electrical inventor and founder of the Siemens and Halske company.

This eldest of the four Siemens brothers was the most versatile of all. After schooling at Lübeck, he became an army officer; he was imprisoned for duelling, but managed to set up a laboratory in his prison cell. He experimented there on silver and gold plating, and sold patent rights to G. R. ELKINGTON of Birmingham. Independently of John Wright he used cyanide baths and also studied nickel plating. He sent his brother Charles SIEMENS to England to develop electrical and other inventions; hence came Charles Siemens's important paper on electrical generators read before the Royal Society in 1867. Werner ran Siemens in Berlin and was co-founder of the Physical Society; his first paper for it, illustrating the wide field of his interests, was on hot-air engines. Siemens invented the well-known ozone tube; an alcohol meter; an electrical standard of resistance based on mercury; and electrolytic refining processes.

His main work began in 1846, when he set out to make Wheatstone's dial telegraph self-acting with 'make-and-break' circuits. He spent much effort in applying the 'dynamo-electric principle' to electric generators which did not need permanent magnets, but used self-generated electricity to activate electromagnetic field coils. The Berlin works of Siemens and Halske (1847) came after Siemens had collaborated with J. G. Halske (1814–90). Their works made possible a full-scale development of Siemens's genius in invention. He was associated with extensive telegraph systems, laid in Russia and Germany; with electrical traction;

and gutta percha insulation of electric cables.
Recollections of Werner von Siemens (new ed.). 1966. (Portraits.)
S. von Weiher, *Werner von Siemens*. 1970.
Dictionary of Scientific Biography.

M S

SIEMENS, FRIEDRICH Born at Menzendorf, Germany, 1826; died Dresden, 24 May 1904. Collaborated with C. W. SIEMENS in developing the regenerative open-hearth furnace.

From Lübeck School, Friedrich Siemens became a seaman; he then accompanied his eldest brother, Werner von SIEMENS, to Kiel, and aided him in early electrical experiments. In 1848 he came to England to sponsor Werner's telegraph inventions. But the heat-regeneration principle became his chief interest, a patent of his coinciding with H. BESSEMER's early patent. He worked so closely with Charles Siemens in Britain that the Siemens' furnace for steel and glass manufacture is referred to without differentiating between the contributions of the two. His first patent of 1856 was of value also in causing E. A. Cowper to apply the regenerative principle in his hot-blast stove in 1860.

In addition to developing the open-hearth furnace from the reverberatory furnace, with hot gases deflected on to the charge, Frederick Siemens also introduced the use of iron oxide added to assist decarburizing of the molten iron; this idea coincided with the use of scrap by Pierre and Emil MARTIN at Sireuil. The Martins had used a regenerative furnace built by Siemens engineers, but the two interests clashed until agreement was reached over the Siemens-Martin furnace, as it became known universally. After Siemens returned to Berlin in 1864 he directed the development of open-hearth steel-making in Europe, while also benefiting the glass industry. At two Birmingham glassworks the regenerative furnace had proved of considerable benefit, and when Friedrich Siemens inherited a Dresden glassworks in his later period his inventive powers were seen in appliances for glass manufacture.

Journal of the Iron and Steel Institute, 1904.
Recollections of Werner von Siemens (new ed.). 1966. (Portrait.)

M S

SIKORSKY, IGOR IVANOVICH Born in Kiev, Ukraine, 25 May 1889; died Easton, Connecticut, USA, 26 October 1972. Aeronautical engineer; pioneer in the design and construction of aeroplanes and helicopters.

Brought up in a prosperous and cultured family, at an early age Sikorsky read a book on the inventions of Leonardo da VINCI, and when he was 12 he made a small model helicopter which could actually fly, powered by an elastic band. At the age of 14 he entered the Russian Naval Academy, but resigned three years later to take up an engineering career. He studied briefly in Paris, then for a year at the Kiev Polytechnic Institute, but he was essentially a practical man and found theoretical subjects merely a distraction. He therefore built and equipped his own workshop in which he could develop his ideas and put them into practice.

He spent the summer of 1908 in France where he met Wilbur WRIGHT, and on his return to Kiev he began to work out his ideas for a full-scale helicopter which would be able to rise straight up off the ground. In the next two years he built two machines, but structural problems and the lack of an engine of sufficient power-to-weight ratio caused him to abandon his attempts for the time being. Turning his attention to fixed-wing aircraft, he flew his own S2 biplane in 1910, and by 1913 had built *Le Grand*, the world's first four-engined passenger aircraft, which in the First World War was modified as a heavy bomber. For some years after emigrating to the USA in 1919 he found it difficult to pursue a career in aviation, but from 1929 he produced a long series of successful designs, culminating in the S-42 and S-44 flying-boats which in the late 1930s pioneered commercial air services across the Atlantic and Pacific oceans. In 1938 he returned to the problem of direct-lift aircraft, and a year later his VS-300 hovered for the first time a few feet above the ground, with Sikorsky at the controls. In May 1941 it set a world endurance record by staying aloft for 1 hour 32 minutes, and by 1943 his R-4 became the first helicopter to be built in large numbers, mainly for military purposes. Thereafter helicopters rapidly developed in size, power and versatility; by the time he retired in 1957, Sikorsky had more than achieved what he set out to do 50 years before.

I. I. Sikorsky, *The Story of the Winged S.* 1967.

F. J. Delear, *Igor Sikorsky: his three careers in aviation.* 1969.

McGraw-Hill Encyclopedia of World Biography. (Portrait.)

R M B

SILLIMAN, BENJAMIN Born at North Stratford (now Trumbull), Connecticut, USA, 8 August 1779; died New Haven, Connecticut, 24 November 1864. Chemist; founder of the *American Journal of Science and Arts*.

Silliman graduated at Yale in 1796 and proceeded to study law; he was admitted to the bar in 1802. He never practised, however, as in July 1801 Timothy Dwight (1752–1817), President of Yale College, invited him to accept the chair of chemistry and natural history there. The offer, surprising in view of Silliman's lack of appropriate qualifications, arose from the absence of a suitable man for the appointment. Dwight recognized that there was 'no way but to select a young man worthy of confidence and allow him time, opportunity, and pecuniary aid, to enable him to acquire the requisite science and skill'. Silliman accepted the invitation and proceeded to acquire 'the requisite science and skill' at the medical school in Philadelphia, working under Robert HARE. He took up the chair at Yale in 1804 and occupied it with distinction for nearly half a century. His *Elements of Chemistry* (1830–1) indicates his success in mastering and communicating the chemical knowledge of his day. Silliman made no major discoveries, but he nevertheless exercised a powerful influence on the development of science in the United States. In 1819 he launched *The American Journal of Science, more especially of Mineralogy, Geology, and the other Branches of Natural History, including also Agriculture and the Ornamental as well as the Useful Arts*. For many years this was commonly known simply as *Silliman's Journal*, and it was a most important outlet for the

publication of original work by American scientists. After the first year its grandiloquent title was shortened to the *American Journal of Science and Arts*, and the last two words of even this shortened title were eventually deleted. The journal still exists, though now devoted to geology, one of Silliman's major interests. He was the first president (1840) of the Association of American Geologists, which developed into the American Association for the Advancement of Science (1848). In 1863 he became a founder member of the National Academy of Sciences.

At Yale, Silliman helped to organize the medical school (1813) and the Department of Philosophy and the Arts (1847), the latter designed to promote science. He was succeeded as professor of chemistry at Yale by his son, Benjamin Silliman, jun. (1816–85).

Dictionary of American Biography.

E. Farber (Ed.), *Great Chemists.* 1961. (Portrait.)

L. G. Wilson (Ed.), *Benjamin Silliman and his Circle.* 1979.

E. S. Dana *et al.*, *A Century of Science in America.* 1918.

Biographical Memoirs. National Academy of Sciences. 1877.

J. F. Fulton and E. H. Thomson, *Benjamin Silliman 1779–1864.* 1947.

Dictionary of Scientific Biography.

Nathan Reingold (Ed.), *Science in Nineteenth Century America.* 1966.

T I W

SIMON, SIR FRANCIS EUGENE (FRANZ EUGEN) Born in Berlin, 2 July 1893; died Oxford, England, 31 October 1956. Contributed notably to low-temperature physics, to thermodynamics, and to the British atomic energy programme of the Second World War.

Son of a wealthy merchant, Simon went to school in Berlin; his grandfather's insistence that he should take classics, despite the boy's natural inclination to physics, may have stiffened his later attitude to classics. After a year at the University of Munich, he was called up for military service in 1913, and served as a lieutenant in the German artillery, winning the Iron Cross 1st Class and being wounded twice. In 1919 he went to the University of Berlin and gained his DPhil. under W. H. NERNST in 1921. He stayed in Berlin until 1931, when he became professor of physical chemistry in Breslau (Wroclaw). With the advent of Hitler and his anti-Semitic policy, Simon realized that Germany could not remain his home, and he accepted an invitation to join F. A. LINDEMANN (later Lord Cherwell) in Oxford in 1933. Simon, assisted by N. Kurti (1908–   ) and K. Mendelssohn (1906–80), built up an outstanding low-temperature school in the Clarendon Laboratory. He was appointed reader in thermodynamics in 1935; professor of thermodynamics in 1945; and he succeeded Lord Cherwell as Dr Lee's Professor of Experimental Philosophy in 1956. Unhappily, he had had just one month in this post, which carried with it the headship of the Clarendon Laboratory, when he died.

Simon's researches covered many topics, all connected with thermodynamics or low temperatures. He believed his most important work was on the Third Law of Thermodynamics – 'the contribution to the entropy due to each factor in a system which is in internal equilibrium becomes zero at absolute zero' With R. Berman he applied this to the graphite-diamond equilibrium and successfully predicted the conditions necessary for diamond formation. Solid and liquid helium (where with B. V. Rollin he discovered Helium II), high pressures, thermal conductivity, magnetic cooling, nuclear orientation, and the design of expansion liquefiers were all subjects in which he made important advances. In the Second World War he took up work in nuclear energy, and championed the diffusion process of isotope separation.

After the war he campaigned against fuel wastage, and for the setting up of an Institute of Technology in Britain on the model of the great American and Continental counterparts.

He was elected FRS in 1941, made a CBE in 1946 and was knighted in 1955. He was awarded the Rumford Medal of the Royal Society in 1948; the Kammerlingh Onnes Medal in 1950; and the Linde Medal in 1952. In this last year he became also an Honorary Foreign Member of the American Academy of Arts and Sciences.

Biographical Memoirs of Fellows of the Royal Society. 1958. (Portrait.)

Nancy Arms, *A Prophet in Two Countries: The Life of F. E. Simon.* 1966.

Dictionary of Scientific Biography.

R V J

SIMPSON, SIR GEORGE CLARKE Born at Derby, England, 2 September 1878; died Bristol, 1 January 1965. Meteorologist.

Simpson was the son of a successful tradesman in Derby and was educated at the Diocesan School, Derby, and Owen's College, Manchester (later Manchester University). After a tutorship in physics at Dalton Hall, Manchester, he went (1902) to Göttingen for a year to undertake research into the Earth's magnetic field. He spent a further year in Lapland investigating the problem of atmospheric electricity, the results of which were published (1905) in the *Proceedings of the Royal Society.*

In 1905 Professor A. Schuster (1851–1934) decided to set up a small meteorological department in the University of Manchester, and placed Simpson in charge; he thus became the first lecturer in meteorology in a British university. He also worked from this time as a volunteer assistant in the Meteorological Office, investigating the relation between the Beaufort Scale and measured speeds of the wind. At the invitation of the International Meteorological Committee he undertook (1921) to reconcile differences between the sets of equivalents in different countries and arrive at an acceptable international scale. His recommendations of a scale on which the 1905 equivalents were adjusted so as to be relevant to an anemometer freely exposed at a height of 6 m in an open situation were accepted in 1926.

Meanwhile he had spent some time (from 1906) at Simla with the Indian Meteorological Office, and this stimulated his interest, maintained for thirty years, in the generation and distribution of the electricity of thunderstorms. In 1910 he sailed with R. F. Scott (1868–1912) to the Antarctic (he had been previously invited in 1902, but illness had prevented his going), and his meteorological obser-

vations made on that trip were published in three volumes (1919–23). In 1920, when he was in Khartoum as a member of the Egyptian Government's Nile Projects Commission, he was invited to succeed Sir Napier SHAW as Director of the Meteorological Office in London. He considerably improved the functioning of this body and developed and directed its entry into the scope of the Air Ministry. By the time he retired in 1938 he had prepared it to undertake the heavy duties imposed upon it by wartime conditions. On the outbreak of the War in 1939 he returned from retirement to take charge of Kew Observatory.

He was honoured in many ways during his lifetime; he was elected FRS in 1915, and received medals from both the Royal Meteorological Society and the Physical Society. He was knighted in 1935.

Biographical Memoirs of Fellows of the Royal Society. 1965. (Portrait.)

Dictionary of National Biography.

N H

SIMPSON, SIR JAMES YOUNG Born at Bathgate, West Lothian, Scotland, 7 June 1811; died London, 6 May 1870. Physician; introduced chloroform anaesthesia.

Simpson was the son of a village baker. At the early age of 14 he entered Edinburgh University to study medicine, graduating in 1832. Seven years later, when still only 29 years of age, he was appointed Professor of Midwifery. He soon became the leading Scottish obstetrician. In 1847 he was appointed Physician to the Queen in Scotland.

In 1846 ether anaesthesia was introduced by W. T. G. MORTON in the United States. Though this represented a major advance in surgery, ether was not an ideal anaesthetic and this led to a search for other agents. In France, J. P. M. FLOURENS experimented with chloroform, and Simpson – after some preliminary tests – began to use this in his obstetric practice from November 1847. He immediately found himself in conflict with the Calvinists, who were much opposed to the use of any anaesthetic in childbirth and it was not until 1853, when Queen Victoria accepted the use of chloroform for the birth of Prince Leopold, that criticism of Simpson died down.

He himself fell into dispute with Joseph LISTER over the practice of antisepsis. The dispute is surprising in view of the fact that he was keenly interested in the high mortality in hospitals of the day, and attributed this to the prevalence of contagious materials.

Simpson lived to receive many honours, including a baronetcy (1866) and the Freedom of the City of Edinburgh.

J. D. Comrie, *History of Scottish Medicine.* 1932.

M. Simpson, *Simpson the Obstetrician: A Biography.* 1972.

J. A. Shepherd, *Simpson and Syme of Edinburgh.* 1969.

Dictionary of National Biography.

T I W

SINCLAIR, SIR CLIVE MARLES Born at Richmond, Surrey, England, 30 July 1940. Inventor; popularized home computers.

The son of a mechanical engineer, Sinclair was educated at thirteen schools, including Highgate School and St. George's College, Weybridge, but he chose not to go to university because he thought the electrical engineering courses too broad. His first job was as an editorial assistant on *Practical Wireless* magazine. At eighteen he was editor of a series of technical works for radio enthusiasts, and himself wrote thirteen practical manuals with titles such as *Modern Transistor Circuits for Beginners* (1962).

In 1962 Sinclair Radionics was registered, and produced radio and hi-fi equipment. In 1972 Sinclair launched his first pocket calculator, the Sinclair Executive, which won a Design Council Award for Electronics in 1973 and was displayed at the Museum of Modern Art, New York. Other calculators followed, and in 1974 the Cambridge Scientific Calculator won two Queen's Awards for Industry. In 1975 Sinclair Radionics was the biggest manufacturer of calculators in Europe. Other innovations were less successful: the Black Watch, a quartz digital watch (1975) and the Microvision, a pocket television set (1977) had technical problems, and by the late 1970s Sinclair Radionics had also lost its position in the calculator market to the Japanese. The products, although cheaper than those of his competitors, had a reputation for unreliability, and in 1979, following financial crises, Sinclair Radionics split up and was sold.

Sinclair formed Sinclair Research in 1979 and moved into the personal computer market, launching the ZX80 in 1980 and the ZX81 in 1981. By the beginning of 1982 he was producing half a million ZX81s a year. This was followed by the ZX Spectrum in 1982, which was his greatest commercial success. The computers were cheap, and Sinclair was largely responsible for the microcomputing boom of the early 1980s. But he failed to get the contract to supply computers for the BBC series on microcomputers, and then his QL computer, produced in 1984, was a failure. In 1986 he sold his computer range to Amstrad.

Sinclair continued to market new inventions, including the C5 electric tricycle in 1985, a commercial disaster, and the Z88 computer in 1987. Other projects included a cheap portable phone, the development of wafer-scale integrated circuits, and satellite TV aerials. Despite the failure of the C5, he launched a new electric bicycle in 1992. Sinclair, described as 'the Heath Robinson of our time', was knighted in 1983.

R. Dale, *The Sinclair Story*. 1985.

I. Adamson and R. Kennedy, *Sinclair and the 'Sunrise Technology'*. 1986.

A P B

SINGER, ISAAC MERRIT Born at Pittstown, New York, 27 October 1811; died Torquay, Devon, England, 23 July 1875. Sewing-machine inventor.

Singer, who was the son of a millwright, was employed as an unskilled labourer at 12, but he later gained wide experience as a travelling machinist. His first patents were for rock-drilling equipment and machinery for shaping wood and metal.

When engaged to repair a sewing machine at Boston, he built an improved version in eleven days. Although he was compelled at the end of a long lawsuit to pay royalties to an earlier Boston inventor, Elias HOWE, it was the Singer machine, first patented in August 1851, which came into general use all over the world. In the next twelve years Singer secured twenty additional patents, so that his original straight-needle vertical design for lock-stitching came to include such refinements as a continuous wheel-feed, yielding presser-foot, and improved cam for moving the needle-bar. After organizing a merger of manufacturers and pooling of patents, in 1863 Singer retired to Europe.

Dictionary of American Biography.

T K D

SKRAUP, ZDENKO HANS Born in Prague, 3 March 1850; died Vienna, 10 September 1910. Organic chemist, noted for his quinoline synthesis.

Skraup studied chemistry at the *Technische Hochschule* in Prague. He moved to Vienna, where he worked in the Mint; later he worked in the University as assistant to F. Rochleder (1819–74) and A. Lieben (1836–1914). In 1886 he went to Graz as professor in the *Technische Hochschule*, but returned to Vienna in 1906 as Lieben's successor. His career was interrupted in 1878, when he served as an officer in the Austrian Army in action in Bosnia. He married, and had five children.

The work for which Skraup is best remembered is his synthesis of quinoline by heating a mixture of aniline, nitrobenzene, glycerol and sulphuric acid (1880). This reaction was generalized into a synthesis of substituted quinolines; it was, however, only one aspect of his interest in cinchona alkaloids and their breakdown products. In a modified form it is still much used in the pharmaceutical industry. His name is remembered also in the Skraup-Priglinger synthesis of dimethylpyrone by action of sulphuric acid on acetic anhydride. Skraup and his students also worked in the carbohydrate field, but his extensive studies of protein chemistry were less successful.

H. Schrötter, *Berichte der deutschen chemischen Gesellschaft*, 43, 3683, 1910. (Portrait.)

M. Kohn, *Journal of Chemical Education*, **20**, 471, 1943, (Portrait.)

W V F

SMEATON, JOHN Born at Austhorpe, near Leeds, Yorkshire, England, 8 June 1724; died there, 28 October 1792. Engineer and instrument-maker.

The son of a Leeds attorney, John Smeaton was educated possibly at the grammar school, and then entered his father's office to learn the law. But his leisure interests were entirely concerned with mechanics: he met Henry Hindley (1701–71), a leading Yorkshire instrument-maker, and made some tools and clocks. Perhaps with hopes of reviving his interests in the law, Smeaton's father sent him to lectures in London in 1742, but to no avail, for with his father's consent he learnt the instrument-making trade, probably with Hindley. In 1748 he opened a shop of his own in London, and dealt not only in his own products, but also in those of Hindley. Contact with instrument-making in the north, where the emphasis was on precision, led Smeaton to attach importance to accurate measurement throughout his life. Sojourn in London brought contact with the Royal Society, and on the strength of papers mostly read before them in the period 1750–4 he was elected FRS in 1753. His systematic approach to the action of the air pump, brought out in his paper on its improvement (1752), was to be typical of his approach to more complex problems in later years.

After 1752, a growing concern for engineering may be discerned in his designs for water- and windmills; his first experiments on model mills; and his Royal Society paper on the improved Savery engine (1752) (see T. SAVERY). Resolving to become an engineer rather than an instrument-maker, Smeaton travelled through the Low Countries in 1755 in view harbour and drainage works. His first important engineering commission came in that year when, through the Earl of Macclesfield, then President of the Royal Society, he was engaged to rebuild the Eddystone lighthouse. In carrying out the design in Portland stone, Smeaton developed a hydraulic cement in which he again exhibited a highly systematic experimental technique. The story of the erection of the light has been often told, most ably by Smeaton himself (1791); its completion in 1759 brought Smeaton widespread recognition. As early as 1756, the year of his marriage to Hindley's granddaughter, he was asked to prepare a scheme for making navigable the upper Calder in Yorkshire. He carried out a survey in 1757 and acted as superintendent engineer during construction of the works (1760–3). In 1759 he gave a series of lectures to the Royal Society on the natural powers of wind and water, for which he received their Copley Medal. In the following decade his practice as an engineer grew markedly, and he emerged as the first fully professional engineer, his reputation resting on his ability to use judgement founded on experience to provide the best answer to a particular problem at the lowest price compatible with sound construction. In this period he was engineer for the Forth and Clyde Canal, begun in 1768, and was repeatedly consulted by the proprietors of the Carron Ironworks.

From 1768 to 1772, Smeaton spent much time at Austhorpe experimenting with a model steam engine in order to determine the causes of poor performance in an engine made for the New River Company in 1767. His experimental method, in which he varied one component at a time, holding all others constant, led to improvements in engine efficiency. Though he erected many improved engines (1772–84) his advances were overshadowed by those of James WATT. The year 1776 saw a paper for the Royal Society on 'mechanic power' in which he demonstrated a thorough understanding of the concepts of work and power. The next years found Smeaton increasingly in demand as a consulting engineer in work of all kinds. With the emergence of a growing number of outstanding engineers, notably Robert Mylne (1734–1811), James Watt, and his own protégé, William Jessop (1745–1814), Smeaton established an informal group in London in 1771. He proposed to retire in 1785, and spend the last years of his life in writing his memoirs, but death intervened.

S. Smiles, *Lives of the Engineers: Smeaton and Rennie*. 1874. (Portrait.)

G. Bowman, *John Smeaton: Consulting Engineer*. 1966.

T. Turner, *Endeavour*, **33**, 29, 1974. (Portrait.)

B. F. Duckham, *History Today*, **15**, 200, 1965.

Dictionary of National Biography.

Dictionary of Scientific Biography.
                                                        W N S

SMITH, HAMILTON OTHANEL Born in New York City, 23 August 1931. Molecular biologist. Isolated restriction enzymes, enabling development of genetic engineering and DNA sequencing.

After attending public schools in Urbana, Illinois, Smith studied at the University of Illinois before transferring to the University of California at Berkeley, where he graduated in mathematics in 1952. He studied medicine at Johns Hopkins University School of Medicine, obtaining his MD in 1956. Following two years in the US Navy he embarked on research at the Henry Ford Hospital, Detroit, from 1959 to 1962. He spent 1962–4 as a research fellow in microbial genetics at the University of Michigan and 1964–7 as a research associate in the department of Human Genetics at the University of Michigan. In 1967 he moved to a post in the Department of Microbiology at Johns Hopkins University School of Medicine, and was appointed professor of microbiology in 1973.

In the 1960s W. Arber (1929–) predicted the existence of restriction enzymes, which cut genes at precise sites on the DNA molecule in relation to the sequence of bases. Smith verified Arber's work, and in 1970 he was the first to isolate a restriction enzyme, from the bacterium *H. influenzae*. He went on to isolate many other such enzymes from different bacteria in co-operation with D. Nathans (1928–). The gene fragments obtained through the use of restriction enzymes could then be used to study the chemical structure of genes. This opened up the possibility of genetic engineering, using restriction enzymes to cut pieces of DNA out of the genome of one organism and splice it into the genome of another, creating new gene combinations. It became possible to produce unlimited amounts of human proteins previously only available in small quantities by transferring human genes into the genetic apparatus of bacteria, and to use these for medical purposes.

The 1978 Nobel Prize for physiology or medicine was shared between Arber, Nathans and Smith.

S. Linn, *Science*, **202**, 8 December 1978. (Portrait.)

Tyler Wasson (Ed.), *Nobel Prize Winners*. 1987. (Portrait.)
                                                        A P B

SMITH, HENRY JOHN STEPHEN Born in Dublin, 2 November 1826; died Oxford, England, 9 February 1883. Mathematician; specialized in the theory of numbers.

Smith went to school at Rugby and then to Balliol College, Oxford, where he met Benjamin Jowett (1817–93), who became his lifelong friend. He was elected Fellow of Balliol in 1849, Savilian Professor of Geometry in 1860, and Fellow of both the Royal Society and of the French Academy in 1861. In 1874 he was made Keeper of the University Museum, Oxford, and from 1879 he served on various Royal Commissions. Although he had many and diverse talents, he was devoid of ambition. The foremost disciple of K. F. GAUSS, he contributed many papers on the theory of numbers, including *On Systems of Linear Indeterminate Equations and Congruences* (1861) and *On the Orders and Genera of Ternary Quadratic Forms* (1867). He also wrote on geometry and elliptic functions.

J. W. L. Glaisher (Ed.), *The Collected Papers of Henry John Smith, M.A., F.R.S.* (2 vols). 1894. (Contains many memoirs (including one by

Benjamin Jowett), and portrait.); *Monthly Notices of the Royal Astronomical Society*, **44**, 138, 1884.

Dictionary of National Biography.

R P L

SMITH, THEOBALD Born at Albany, New York, 31 July 1859; died Princeton, New Jersey, 20 December 1934. Celebrated for his contributions to knowledge of infectious disease.

Smith, born after his German immigrant parents had been in America for five years, studied medicine at Cornell University and at Albany Medical College, but did graduate research in biology. Later he held posts as director of the Pathological Laboratory at the United States Bureau of Animal Industry; professor of comparative pathology at Harvard University; and director of animal pathology at the Rockefeller Institute.

Most of Smith's work was connected with animal infectious diseases and probably his most notable contribution (with associates) was the discovery that Texas cattle fever is caused by a protozoan parasite which is spread by a cattle tick. These studies (1889–93) were characterized by many carefully controlled experiments, and the results were an important step in the recognition of insect vectors in the transmission of disease.

Another subject to which Smith made important contributions was tuberculosis. Particularly significant was his recognition of human and bovine tuberculosis and the realization of the difference in pathogenicity for man and animals. Throughout his life Smith was also very much concerned with hog diseases. Among his contributions to this difficult field was information on *Salmonella* organisms, and on the differentiation of two of the diseases which had hitherto been confused.

Smith's other numerous studies are difficult to summarize, but some idea of his impact can be gauged by the fact that he wrote more than 250 papers ranging in length from a few pages to his famous long paper of 301 pages on Texas cattle fever in 1893.

P. F. Clark, *Journal of the History of Medicine*, **14**, 490, 1959.

S. H. Gage, *Science*, **84**, 117, 1936.

Obituary Notices of Fellows of the Royal Society. 1935. (Portrait.)

Dictionary of Scientific Biography.

Biographical Memoirs. National Academy of Sciences. 1936.

J K C

SMITH, WILLIAM Born at Churchill, Oxfordshire, England, 23 March 1769; died Northampton, 28 August 1839. The 'Father of English Geology'.

William Smith came of farming stock and was educated at the village school. Losing his father early, he was left much to his own resources. He studied surveying, and collected fossils on his solitary rambles. At 18 he was employed by a surveyor at Stow-on-the-Wold and as part of his work travelled in the surrounding counties; this greatly stimulated his enthusiasm for geology, hardly yet a true science. In 1791 he moved to the coal-mining district of northern Somerset, the scene of his activities during the next eight years and of his most important discoveries. Becoming engaged in superintending the construction of canals, he took

part, in 1794, in a six weeks' tour by post-chaise to the north of England to study excavating methods. This provided a great opportunity for him to see the lie of the rocks over wide stretches of country and he returned to Somerset satisfied that he had discovered the general plan of arrangement of the strata of England. His work in connection with canals and the examination of the various strata went hand-in-hand, each helping the other, and resulted in the momentous discovery that beds of the same kind of stone, but at different levels in the succession, could be distinguished by their characteristic fossils. Encouraged by friends in Bath, he began to record his observations: to draw sketch-sections; to tabulate the strata (chiefly Jurassic, with their now familiar names); and to make geological maps, the first proper maps of the kind ever to be made. The last were detailed for the area near Bath, and on a small scale for England as a whole. Leaving Somerset in 1799, he was employed in many schemes, including land drainage and irrigation, which caused him to travel far and wide throughout the country. During these journeys he was able to gather information for his great enterprise, a large geological map which, after much delay, was published in 1815 with the title *A Delineation of the Strata of England and Wales*, on the scale of five miles to the inch.

Between 1816 and 1824 he published *Strata Identified by Organized Fossils*, in which the fossils characteristic of each formation were depicted; *Stratigraphical System of Organized Fossils*, a descriptive catalogue; several charts of sections; and geological maps of twenty-one counties, part of a projected complete atlas. Smith had had his headquarters in London since 1804, but in 1819 he moved to Yorkshire, where he found congenial company and useful employment. General recognition of his work was slow, but in 1831 it was complete when the Geological Society awarded him, the 'Father of English Geology' (as he was then named), the first Wollaston Medal, ever afterwards the principal award of British geologists.

J. Phillips, *Memoirs of William Smith, LL.D.* 1844. (Portrait.)

T. Sheppard, *Proceedings of the Yorkshire Geological Society*, **19**, 75, 1917 (Reprinted, 1920.) (Portrait.)

L. R. Cox, *Proceedings of the Yorkshire Geological Society*, **25**, 1, 1942. (Portrait. Sketch by W. Smith.)

Dictionary of National Biography.

Dictionary of Scientific Biography.

J C

SMITHSON, JAMES (Earlier known as Louis Macie and as James Lewis.) Born in France, 1765; died Genoa, Italy, 27 June 1829. Scientist; founder of the Smithsonian Institution, Washington.

James Smithson was the natural son of Hugh Smithson Percy, Duke of Northumberland. His mother was Elizabeth Keate Macie, a woman of large fortune by two marriages and a descendant of Henry VII. He was educated at Pembroke College, Oxford, graduating in 1782 as 'the best chemist of his year'; he was probably a contemporary there of William HIGGINS. In 1784 he undertook a geological tour of Scotland with a party which included Faujas de St Fond (1741–1819), and was already becoming known as a mineralogist of some merit;

his later work (1802) on calamines corrected theories held by the Abbé R. J. Haüy (1743–1822), and the natural carbonate of zinc was named Smithsonite after him. In 1787 he was elected a Fellow of the Royal Society, his sponsors including Richard KIRWAN and Henry CAVENDISH. Though never an outstanding scientist, he showed great ability and originality of approach, and he contributed to the scientific literature, notably the *Philosophical Transactions of the Royal Society* (up to 1817). He was acquainted with the leading scientists of Europe, whom he met on his many travels on the Continent.

His considerable wealth, inherited from both parents, was left to a nephew with the provision that if he had no issue or should his issue die intestate or under 21 the whole estate should be placed at the disposal of the United States of America for the purpose of founding at Washington the Smithsonian Institution 'for the increase and diffusion of knowledge among men'. In the event, the estate of £100,000 was made available to the United States Government, which took ten years to decide to accept it. Opposition to its acceptance was led by J. C. Calhoun, but John Quincey Adams was eventually able to persuade Congress to accept the legacy, and a Bill creating the Institution was passed on 10 August 1846 whereby the Smithsonian Institution came into existence. In one of the major scientific institutions of the world is perpetuated the name of a man whose own scientific achievements were modest, but whose farsightedness is amply proved.

P. H. Oehser, *Sons of Science: the Story of the Smithsonian Institution and its Leaders.* 1949. (Portrait.)

W. J. Rhees, *James Smithson and his Bequests.* 1881.

L. Carmichael, *Nature*, **208**, 321, 1965.

Dictionary of National Biography.

N H

SNELL (or SNELL VAN ROYEN), WILLEBRORD
Born at Leiden, Netherlands, in 1591; died there, 30 October 1626. Discoverer of the law of refraction.

Snell was the son of Rudolph Snell (1546–1613), a professor, first of mathematics and then of Hebrew, at Leiden. In 1613 Willebrord himself became professor of mathematics there, and two years later he carried out a determination of the radius of the Earth by means of triangulation. He appears to have been the first to find the distance between two points on the same meridian by triangulation, rather than by simple linear measurement, as the first step in determining the Earth's radius. Styling himself 'the Dutch Eratosthenes', Snell measured his base line on the surface of the frozen meadows near Leiden. His work was recomputed and re-observed by P. von Musschenbroek (1692–1761) in 1729. Snell's result was 1 degree latitude equals 55 100 toises; Musschenbroek's 57 033 toises (one toise equals 1.949 metres).

In his short lifetime Snell wrote several books, including one on navigation, a trigonometry, and a work on the rectification of the circle. Above all, he is remembered for his discovery of the law of refraction in 1621. J. KEPLER had repeatedly sought this, and had managed nothing better than upward of two dozen empirical and approximate laws which he used in his theory of lenses (especially

in *Prolegomena ad Vitellionem*, 1604). Snell gave the law in terms of ratios of lengths, interpretable as a ratio of cosecants, whereas DESCARTES was the first to express the law of refraction directly as a ratio of sines in his *Dioptrique* of 1637. Snell's manuscript containing the law was not published in his lifetime, and it is a matter for conjecture whether Descartes knew of Snell's work. Christian HUYGENS, in his posthumous *Dioptrica* (1703), was perhaps the first to draw attention to Snell's priority, although he remarked that Snell did not appreciate the importance of his discovery.

Nouvelle Biographie Universelle. 1852–66.

P. Lenard, *Great Men of Science.* 1933. (Portrait.)

Dictionary of Scientific Biography.

J D N

SOBRERO, ASCANIO Born at Casale, Piedmont, Italy, 12 October 1812; died Turin, 26 May 1888. The discoverer of nitroglycerine.

Sobrero qualified as a physician and surgeon, but later studied chemistry in Turin, Paris and Giessen. In 1849 he returned to Turin as professor of applied chemistry in the Technical Institute, later becoming professor of pure chemistry as well. He retired in 1882.

His numerous publications cover a wide area of pure and applied chemistry, but he is only remembered for his discovery (1846) of the highly explosive glyceryl trinitrate ('*piro-glicerina*', later 'nitroglycerine'). At the time, the substance was far too dangerous to make on the large scale; but much later, in the hands of Alfred NOBEL, it became the foundation of the modern explosives industry.

J. C. Poggendorf, *Biographisch-Literarisches Handwörterbuch.* 1883–1903.

Enciclopedia Italiana. 1936.

I. Guareschi, *Isis*, **1**, 351, 1913.

E. Macorini (Ed.), *Scienziati e Tecnologi.* 1975.

W V F

SODDY, FREDERICK Born at Eastbourne, Sussex, England, 2 September 1877; died Brighton, Sussex, 22 September 1956. Originator of the concept of isotopes.

In 1898 Soddy headed the honours list in chemistry at Oxford, with Sir William RAMSAY as his external examiner. Four years later he was working with Ramsay at University College, London, and was associated with him in the classic experiment which identified the gaseous product of radioactive decay of radium with helium, which Sir Joseph LOCKYER had discovered in the Sun's chromosphere spectroscopically. Earlier, he had worked in Canada with Ernest RUTHERFORD at McGill, and together they had reached the revolutionary conception that 'radioactivity is at once an atomic phenomenon and the accompaniment of a chemical change in which new kinds of matter are produced'.

In 1904 he was appointed lecturer in physical chemistry at Glasgow and it was while there that he advanced (in a letter to *Nature* published on 4 December 1913) the idea that atoms could be chemically identical and yet have different weights. For such elements he proposed the name isotope, because they occupy the same place (Greek, *isos topos*) in the Periodic Table of the elements. Because of this strict classical derivation, the word isotope has passed unchanged into virtually every language in the world. Although Soddy was undoubtedly the first unequivocally to formulate the idea of isotopes, the thoughts of others had turned in the same direction earlier; the idea was, as it were, in the air ready to be snatched up by a man brilliant enough to see the significance of new discoveries. In particular, Soddy's ideas were, as he himself acknowledged, an extension of some put forward only a little earlier by A. van den Broek (1870–1926). The Polish chemist Kasimir Fajans (1887–1975) reached similar conclusions in the same year (1913).

In 1919 Soddy returned to Oxford as Dr Lees Professor of Chemistry, but hopes that he would establish a British school of radiochemistry there were not fulfilled. A controversial character, he came increasingly to believe that the world had not given him the acknowledgement he deserved; it is hard to see any justification for this, however, for the Royal Society elected him to Fellowship in 1910, at the early age of 33, and he was awarded a Nobel prize in 1921. From chemistry he turned increasingly to political and economic theories that gained no general acceptance, and he resigned his professorship at Oxford in 1936.

A. Kent, *Proceedings of the Chemical Society*, 327, 1963.

M. Howorth, *The Life Story of Frederick Soddy*. 1958.

T. J. Trenn, *The Self-splitting Atom*. 1977.

G. B. Kaufmann, *Frederick Soddy*. 1985.

Biographical Memoirs of Fellows of the Royal Society. 1957. (Portrait.)

E. Farber (Ed.), *Great Chemists*. 1961. (Portrait.)

H. Oxbury (Ed.), *Great Britons: 20th Century Lives*. 1985.

L. Wise, *Frederick Soddy: Money Reformer*. 1982.

Tyler Wasson (Ed.), *Nobel Prize Winners*. 1987. (Portrait.)

T I W

SOLVAY, ERNEST Born at Rebecq, near Brussels, 16 April 1838; died Brussels, 26 May 1922. The first successful manufacturer of soda by the ammonia-soda process.

Although the ammonia-soda process was proposed as early as 1811 by A. J. FRESNEL, Ernest Solvay was the first satisfactorily to solve the engineering problems. The basic reaction between ammonium bicarbonate and salt, yielding sodium bicarbonate, which can be converted to soda by heating, involves extreme difficulties in large-scale operation, due mainly to the volatility of ammonia. H. G. Dyar and J. Hemming at Whitechapel tried it in 1838, as did James MUSPRATT, who lost £8,000 in the process. William GOSSAGE, Henry DEACON and Holbrook Gaskell (1813–1909) were among other industrialists who were defeated by the practical difficulties. Solvay himself, however, claimed to have been unaware of this long history of failure.

After four years of struggle Solvay succeeded, and established works at Couillet (1863) and Dombasle (1873). He was an astute businessman, taking out patents covering every stage of his process and granting licences to other soda-makers the world over. His master invention was the Solvay carbonating-tower, which solved the problem of

reacting carbon dioxide with the ammoniacal brine.

Despite the intrinsic advantages of the Solvay process as compared with that devised by Nicolas LEBLANC – notably freedom from the noxious heaps of alkali waste that were inseparable from the latter and involved its operators in frequent litigation – it was many years before it became dominant, the Leblanc process surviving until well into the 20th century.

Solvay was a member of the Belgian Senate and a Minister of State. His name is perpetuated in the International Institutes of Physics, of Chemistry, and of Sociology.

P. Héger and C. Lefébure, *La Vie d'Ernest Solvay*. 1919.

Industrial and Engineering Chemistry, **14**, 1156, 1922. (Portrait.)

J. I. Watts, *Nature*, **10**, 84, 1922.

E. Farber (Ed.), *Great Chemists*. 1961. (Portrait.)

M S

SOMMERFELD, ARNOLD Born at Königsberg, Prussia, Germany, 5 December 1868; died Munich, Bavaria, 26 April 1951. Famous for contributions to mathematical physics.

The son of a physician, Sommerfeld read mathematics and natural science at Königsberg University. After two years as an assistant at Göttingen, he became, in 1897, professor of mathematics at the *Bergakademie* at Clausthal, and in 1900 professor of applied mathematics at Aachen. From 1906 to 1931 he was professor of theoretical physics at Munich.

In 1894 Sommerfeld started an investigation into the diffraction of light by an edge. Jointly with C. F. KLEIN he began, in 1897, the preparation of a four-volume treatise on gyroscopes that was to take thirteen years to complete. At the same time he launched into mathematical treatments of subjects relating to engineering (friction, lubrication, etc.) and to radio waves.

Sommerfeld's most famous work belongs to his Munich period. Turning to atomic spectra, he began a series of investigations that culminated in the five editions of his *Atombau zur Spektrallinien*, first appearing in 1919. In 1915 Sommerfeld and W. Wilson (1875–1965) independently suggested that the circular orbits of the Bohr atom (see N. BOHR) ought to be replaced by elliptic orbits instead. Working out the consequences of this, he was compelled to postulate a new, azimuthal, quantum number to relate to the ratio of minor to major axes in the ellipse. To explain the Zeeman effect (see P. ZEEMAN) he introduced an additional magnetic quantum number. Consideration of the special theory of relativity led him to predict that precession of fast-moving electrons would occur, giving rise to series of fine-structure lines in the spectra. This was quantitatively confirmed by F. Paschen (1865–1947) in 1916.

Later work by Sommerfeld included a detailed study of wave-mechanics on which he wrote two books, the first in 1929. He also showed how to apply Fermi statistics (see E. FERMI) to electrons in metals, and the resultant theory of electrons agreed with the Wiedmann-Franz law, and the Thomson and Peltier effects.

Sommerfeld appears to have been an inspiring teacher and exerted a strong influence on the development of theoretical chemistry and physics. He was able to endure the political upheavals during his twenty years of retirement because of his dedication to science and preoccupation with writing.

P. P. Ewald, *Nature*, **168**, 364, 1951.
Obituary Notices of Fellows of the Royal Society. 1952. (Portrait.)
U. Benz, *Arnold Sommerfeld.* 1975.

C A R

SORBY, HENRY CLIFTON Born at Woodbourne, near Sheffield, Yorkshire, England, 10 May 1826; died Sheffield, 10 March 1908. Geologist, metallurgist, microscopist.

Henry Clifton Sorby was the only child of a prosperous Sheffield tool manufacturer and descended from a very old Sheffield family. He was educated at the Collegiate School, Sheffield, and by private tutor. He early showed a single-minded interest in science and at 21, on the death of his father, had sufficient means to establish himself as an independent scientific investigator, and to equip an adequate laboratory and workshop at his own home. After a brief interest in agricultural chemistry he turned to geology. He attempted to apply quantitative techniques to geological phenomena, extrapolating by enormous factors from constructed models and small-scale natural processes to explain events in geological history. A parallel interest in the microscope, and a resolute faith in its value as a tool in all sciences, led him, partly by chance, to be the first to make and examine thin slices of rock for geological purposes. His work in this field, lasting with interruptions until his death, earned him the title of 'Father of microscopical petrography'. His investigations of meteoric geology led him to the examination, for comparative purposes, of artificial irons and steels (1853), thereby also founding metallography. Remote from the scientific establishment of London, financially independent, and unmarried, he was free to follow his own scientific fancies and moved from one area of investigation to another without always following up his pioneer work: for example, his interests led him also into microscopic spectrum analysis and marine biology. He was acquainted with most of the leading scientists of the time.

He was elected FRS in 1857, and received a number of important medals for pioneer scientific work, as well as an honorary LLD degree of Cambridge University. His interest in higher education and the opportunities for research was well known and he was during its formative years President of Firth College (now the University of Sheffield), where he endowed a chair of geology and a research fellowship.

N. Higham, *A Very Scientific Gentleman.* 1963. (Portraits.)
C. S. Smith (Ed.). *The Sorby Centennial Symposium on the History of Metallurgy.* 1965.
Proceedings of the Royal Society, **80B**, lvi, 1908.
Dictionary of Scientific Biography.
Dictionary of National Biography.

N H

SÖRENSEN, SÖREN PETER LAURITZ Born at Havrebjerg, Denmark, 9 January 1868; died Copenhagen, 13 February 1939. Biochemist, chiefly remembered for his invention of the pH value as a measure of acidity.

Sörensen was the son of a farmer, and was educated locally and at the high school at Sorö, before proceeding, in 1886, to the University of Copenhagen, where he studied chemistry and medicine. He had a distinguished career there, and won gold medals in 1889 and 1895, and obtained the degree of MSc. Since 1892 he had been teaching at the Royal Technical High School in Copenhagen, and after taking his master's degree he became Consulting Chemist to the Royal Danish Navy. He continued with his researches and in 1899 obtained the degree of PhD for his work on cobalt oxalate. Shortly afterwards (1901) he took up his appointment as director of the world-famous Carlsberg Laboratory, in succession to J. G. C. T. KJELDAHL; he retained this appointment for the rest of his working life. He was elected a member of the Royal Danish Academy and later became its Chairman.

Sörensen became interested in amino acids, the basic units of which proteins are composed, and much of his work was concerned with their synthesis. In 1907 he recognized that it was important for the progress of his research to be able to titrate amino acids, and he devised a method whereby this could be done by first blocking the basic amino group by formaldehyde. He carried out a comprehensive investigation of enzymes, and this was important in elucidating the nature of enzyme reactions. He also made a careful study of proteins, and in this field has a number of important papers to his credit.

Sörensen is, however, best known for his pioneer work on the hydrogen ion concentration, which was of great importance to his biochemical researches. He introduced (1909) the symbol pH, which represented the negative logarithm of the number of gram-ions of hydrogen in each litre of solution. It had the great advantage that while its meaning was precise and clear to the expert it also gave an indication of acidity to the untrained worker; pH values of from 0 to 7 indicate acidity, pH values of from 7 to 14 indicate alkalinity, while a pH value of exactly 7 indicates neutrality. This notation is universally used throughout the world.

A. J. Curtin Cosbie, *Nature*, **143**, 629, 1939.
E. K. Rideal, *Journal of the Chemical Society*, 554, 1940.
E. J. Cohn, *Journal of the American Chemical Society*, **61**, 2573, 1939.
Dictionary of Scientific Biography.

B B K

SOSIGENES OF ALEXANDRIA Flourished in Alexandria, 1st century BC. Astronomer: adviser of Julius Caesar on the reform of the calendar; sometimes identified, or confused, with a peripatetic philosopher of the same name.

Following the conclusion of the Civil War in 46 BC, Julius Caesar set about establishing an official calendar to supersede the unsatisfactory and diverse systems of dating events in force throughout the Roman commonwealth. He embarked on the task in Egypt, where the problem of the calendar had become particularly acute; and it was there that he secured the co-operation of Sosigenes. Following a 'year of confusion' in which accumulated discrepancies were wiped off, the new (Julian) calendar was inaugurated on 1 January 45 BC. It provided for a normal year of 365 days to which, every fourth year, was to be added a single day, initially intercalated after 23 February: this date was chosen because, in an earlier calendar, a whole month had been inserted at that point every second year. Thus the mean length of the Julian year amounted to 365 ¼ days.

The slight excess of the Julian over the true (tropical) year became appreciable with the lapse of the centuries, particularly in relation to the rules for fixing the date of Easter. The discrepancy was removed, for all practical purposes, in the reformed calendar instituted in 1582 by Pope Gregory XIII, who decreed that the intercalary day was to be omitted in those centurial years for which the number of centuries was not divisible by 4 (e.g. in 1700, 1800, 1900, but not in 2000).

G. Sarton, *A History of Science: Hellenistic Science and Culture in the last three Centuries B.C.* 1959.

C. Singer, E. J. Holmyard, A. R. Hall, and T. I. Williams (Eds), *A History of Technology*, vol. 3. 1957.

Dictionary of Scientific Biography.

A A

SOUFFLOT, JACQUES-GERMAIN Born at Irancy, France, 22 July 1713; died Paris, 29 August 1780. Architect.

Soufflot's well-to-do father financed his architectural studies, including a stay in Rome; he again visited Italy in 1780, the year after his admission to the French Academy of Architecture. His earliest work was done in Lyons, including the Hospital with its splendid dome.

In 1757 Soufflot won a competition for the rebuilding of the Church of St Genevieve in Paris, which became the Pantheon. Seven years were spent on the foundations, over which he raised an imposing edifice, distinguished by a single-order portal as high as the church and a dome with triple calotte and colonnaded gallery. The vertical load from the dome was borne on clusters of columns supported by built-in cages of wrought-iron bars, a form of reinforced construction of which he was an important pioneer. By 1770 critics were already expressing justified doubts as to the safety of the structure; these are said to have hastened the architect's death. Within a quarter of a century cracks appeared both in the dome and in its supporting columns; the latter had then to be reinforced by additional stone and iron work which was aesthetically unattractive. Investigation showed, however, that the main fault lay in the work of the stonemasons rather than in Soufflot's use of iron.

The School of Law was the only building erected by Soufflot in the neighbourhood of the Pantheon, for which he had, however, planned the complete setting. His other works included the Grand Sacristy at *Notre Dame*, since destroyed. Soufflot was remarkable for his interest in all the arts; he wrote an epitaph for himself in verse, alluding to the jealousy of rivals.

Nouvelle Biographie Générale, xliv. 1865.

Charles Singer, E. J. Holmyard, A. R. Hall, and Trevor I. Williams, *A History of Technology*, vol. 4. 1958.

T K D

SPALLANZANI, LAZZARO Born at Scandiano, Emilia, Italy, 12 January 1729; died Pavia, 11 February 1799. Famous naturalist and a founder of experimental biology.

Spallanzani was educated at Reggio, and studied law at Bologna. His cousin, Laura Bassi (1711–78), who, although a woman, held a chair at Bologna, persuaded him to follow science, his own inclination. But Spallanzani also took orders, and he is often referred to as the 'Abbate' or 'Abbé' Spallanzani. In 1755 he went to Reggio, and in 1757 he was appointed to the chair of mathematics and physics in the University there. In 1763 he became professor of physics and philosophy in the University of Modena, and he also taught Greek and mathematics. In 1769 he was called by Maria Theresa to the chair of natural history in the University of Pavia, and he held that post until his death. At first he was much occupied in teaching zoology, but in later years he made many journeys – to Switzerland, the Adriatic, and Asia Minor among others – in the pursuit of natural history. He held many academic honours, including Fellowship of the Royal Society (1768).

Spallanzani, one of the greatest of all experimenters, did much of his finest work in his short period at Modena. The age-old belief in spontaneous generation was strongly supported jointly by G. L. L. BUFFON, and by John Turberville Needham (1713–81), who thought that he had performed crucial experiments. In 1765 Spallanzani published a detailed description of his own experiments. He showed that the duration of heat necessary to render an organic infusion sterile varied with the type of animalcule. He corrected a technical error in Needham's work by sealing his own flasks hermetically, and he proved that, if both the infusion and the contained air had been thoroughly sterilized, no animalcules developed. In 1776 Spallanzani showed that hot air was not as effective as boiling water for sterilizing purposes. In these experiments some of his organisms were certainly bacteria, and he showed that some organisms can live for many days in a vacuum. He was therefore one of the discoverers of anaerobiosis.

In his experiments on digestion (published 1780) Spallanzani obtained specimens of gastric juice from many types of animal, including himself. These experiments continued those of R. A. F. de RÉAUMUR. Spallanzani confirmed the solvent action of gastric juice on all kinds of foodstuffs, and he concluded that the mechanical trituration in the stomach is merely a preparation for solution. He gave definite experimental proof of the solvent action of gastric juice on foodstuffs. He showed that this action was not putrefaction, as others had thought, and he suspected that it was not vinous fermentation. He believed that it was acid fermentation, but he was unable to find acid in the mixed gastric juice from the stomach cavity. Had he been able to obtain juice direct from the gastric glands he would have found the acid.

Spallanzani, working mainly with amphibians, made important observations on the general biology of reproduction in animals. He was an ovarian preformationist, holding that all the parts of the embryo already existed in the ovum. He performed important experiments on the artificial fecundation of amphibians, and, lastly, of a bitch (1779). He thus demolished the part played by the mysterious *aura seminalis*, but he was unable to decide on the role of the spermatozoa, although their existence had been discovered long before. His work on the reproduction of plants was almost equally important.

In his late experiments on respiration, published posthumously, Spallanzani proved that the tissues use up oxygen and give off carbon dioxide, and he showed that, when placed in an atmosphere of hydrogen or nitrogen, invertebrates give off carbon dioxide, as they do in common air. Spallanzani also wrote on the electric action of *Torpedo*, the zoology of sponges, and the senses of bats.

W. Bulloch, *History of Bacteriology*. 1938. (Portrait.)

E. Tortonese, *Endeavour*, **7**, 92, 1948.

G. Franchini, *Annals of Medical History*, **11**, 56, 1930.

A. E. Adams, *Scientific Monthly*, **29**, 529, 1929.

Dictionary of Scientific Biography.

E A U

SPEMANN, HANS Born at Stuttgart, Baden-Württemberg, Germany, 27 June 1869; died at Freiburg-im-Breisgau, 9 September 1941. Discoverer of the 'organizer effect'.

Spemann studied medicine at Heidelberg and Munich but then abandoned medicine for zoology, and from 1894 to 1908 he worked at the University of Würzburg. He graduated in 1895, and became lecturer in zoology in 1898. In 1909 he was called to the chair of zoology at Rostock, and in 1914 he became associate director of the Kaiser Wilhelm Institute of Biology at Berlin-Dahlem. He was called to the chair of zoology in the University of Freiburg-im-Breisgau in 1919, from which he retired in 1935.

The study of developmental mechanics had been founded by Wilhelm Roux (1850–1924) and advanced by Hans DRIESCH. They showed that, if after the first cleavage of the egg of an amphibian one of the two resulting cells is removed, the remaining cell grows into a smaller but complete embryo. But if one of the two cells is destroyed but not removed the remaining cell develops into half an embryo. By means of his very skilled technique of micro-dissection Spemann now began to study whether the fate of individual cells in a very young embryo was predetermined from the beginning. He transplanted a definite area from one embryo into a definite area of another, and he used eggs of different species which differed in colour, so that the transplanted areas remained distinguishable as they developed. Sometimes for this purpose he used vital staining. He showed that a portion of tissue normally destined to form epidermis could develop into nervous tissue if it was transplanted to the area where the spinal cord normally develops. He then transplanted that part of the anterior end of an embryo – the blastopore – which was destined to form its nervous system, into the ventral aspect of another embryo, and he found that the latter developed a new central nervous system. This did not develop from the transplanted tissue, but from the ventral cells originally destined to produce epidermis. Hence, the fate of these ventral cells had been changed by the presence of the transplanted blastopore tissue, and Spemann concluded that the blastopore has an 'organizing effect' on its environment. Working on these lines Spemann and his associates also dem-onstrated the existence of secondary organizers. Spemann was awarded the Nobel prize for medicine in 1935.

J. Needham, *Biochemistry and Morphogenesis*. 1942.

L. Saxén and S. Toivonen, *Primary Embryonic Deduction*. 1961.

Dictionary of Scientific Biography.

Tyler Wasson (Ed.), *Nobel Prize Winners*. 1987. (Portrait.)

E A U

SPENCE, PETER Born at Brechin, Forfarshire, Scotland, 19 February 1806; died Manchester, England, 5 July 1883. Industrial chemist.

Spence was apprenticed to a grocer in Perth, and went into business with his uncle. The business failed, however, and Spence found employment in the gasworks at Dundee. During these years he had been learning chemistry in his spare time, and in 1834 he set up in London as a small chemical manufacturer. His financial position was extremely precarious until, after a move to Burgh (near Carlisle) he hit on a much-improved process for making alum from coal shale (1845). He built a works at Pendleton, near Manchester, where the raw materials were readily available, and the scale of his operations grew rapidly to a position of near monopoly. The spent shale was converted into cement. His most profitable product was a very crude alum ('aluminoferric'), which found an ever-growing outlet in sewage treatment in towns newly conscious of sanitation, as well as in the paper industry. As time went on Spence broadened his activities into allied products, though in at least one case (the exploitation of phosphate deposits on the island of Redonda, West Indies) with heavy financial loss.

Spence was an active member of the Manchester Literary and Philosophical Society, to which he read papers on a variety of subjects. A staunch Nonconformist, he campaigned vigorously for total abstinence. He campaigned also against industrial pollution of the atmosphere. However, he was him-self successfully prosecuted for pollution in 1857, and had to move his works from Pendleton to Miles Platting. The firm has been part of Laporte Industries Ltd since 1900. He married, and left eight children.

Fenwick Allen, *Some Founders of the Chemical Industry*. 1907. (Portrait.)

Proceedings of the Manchester Literary and Philosophical Society, 23, 121, 1883–4.

Dictionary of National Biography (Missing Persons). 1993.

W V F

SPENCER, HERBERT Born at Derby, England, 27 April 1820; died Brighton, Sussex, 8 December 1903. Philosopher, social reformer, and an early writer on evolution.

Spencer began his career in 1837 as a railway engineer, but later he turned to journalism, though he retained his interest in mechanical invention. He became Editor of *The Economist* in 1848, a post which enabled him to meet G. H. Lewes (1817–78), George Eliot (1819–80), Thomas Carlyle (1795–1881), T. H. HUXLEY, John TYNDALL and other influential reformers. While editor of *The Economist*, Spencer began to publish the long series of books on philosophy, sociology, education and science that made his influence so widespread. His *Principles of Biology* was published in two volumes in 1864 and 1867, after being checked by Huxley and J. D. HOOKER.

Spencer's *System of Synthetic Philosophy* (1862–93) based on many earlier essays, assumed the existence of evolution well before the publication of *The Origin of Species* by Charles DARWIN, and his writings had a good deal of influence on A. R. WALLACE, who shared with Darwin the first exposition of the theory of natural selection.

D. Duncan, *Life and Letters of Herbert Spencer.* 1908. (Includes bibliography.)
H. S. R. Elliot, *Herbert Spencer.* 1917.
H. Spencer, *Autobiography.* 1904.
J. D. Y. Peel, *Herbert Spencer.* 1971.
Dictionary of National Biography.
G. Sarton, *Isis*, **3**, 375, 1921. (Portrait.)

S J R

SPENCER JONES, SIR HAROLD *See* JONES.

SPERRY, ELMER AMBROSE Born at Courtland, New York State, USA, 12 October 1860; died Brooklyn, New York, 16 June 1930. Inventor and entrepreneur.

Sperry had one year of casual attendance at Cornell University, but claimed that his interest in machinery was chiefly aroused by a visit to the Centennial Exhibition at Philadelphia in 1876. He opened his first factory on his twentieth birthday, for the manufacture of improved dynamos and arc-lamps. He then turned his attention in succession to electrical machinery for coal-mining (1888); to electric street cars and automobiles (1890); to an electrochemical process for the manufacture of caustic soda from salt; to experiments on compound diesel-type engines; and to the production of high-intensity arc searchlights (1918). In each case he made significant improvements. Altogether he held more than 400 patents, and he founded eight manufacturing companies.

Sperry's name is remembered chiefly, however, for the practical development of the gyroscope, whose properties he began to investigate about 1896. His gyroscopic compass was first used tentatively in 1910, in the USS *Delaware*, and his gyroscopic stabilizer for ships was introduced in 1913. In the following year his aircraft stabilizer was awarded a first prize in the French Aero Club contest for safety devices.

Dictionary of American Biography.
T. P. Hughes, *Elmer Sperry.* 1971.
Biographical Memoirs. National Academy of Sciences. 1954.

T K D

SPERRY, ROGER WOLCOTT Born in Hartford, Connecticut, USA, 20 August 1913. Neurophysiologist.

Sperry studied zoology at Oberlin College and the University of Chicago (PhD 1941). After appointments there and at Harvard he was appointed professor of psychobiology at the California Institute of Technology (1954–84). His early research concerned nervous regeneration. While mammals cannot regenerate a severed optic nerve some lower animals, such as frogs, can. He showed that the severed nerve will reconnect with the part

of the brain from which it originally sprang. He explored the nature and function of the commissures which connect the two halves of the brain in higher animals. In general, each half controls the opposite half of the body, and Sperry investigated the working of 'split' brains in which the connecting commissures had been severed, either in experimental animals or in humans after brain surgery. He established that the brain's left hemisphere controls the production and regeneration of speech while the right controls non-verbal processes. He shared a Nobel prize in 1981 with D. H. HUBEL and T. N. Wiesel, noted for their research on visual perception.

Les Prix Nobel en 1981, 1982. (Portrait.)
N. Cousins, *Nobel Prize Conversations.* 1985.
Tyler Wasson (Ed.), *Nobel Prize Winners.* 1987. (Portrait.)

T I W

SPÖRER, GUSTAV FRIEDRICH WILHELM Born in Berlin, 23 October 1822; died Giessen, 7 July 1895. Solar astronomer.

Spörer was educated at the University of Berlin, where his doctoral dissertation was written on the comet of 1723. After spending some years on cometary studies he became (1849) a teacher, and later professor, at the Aachen Gymnasium. From 1875 he worked at the astrophysical observatory at Potsdam, where he became First Observer in 1882. He retired a year before his death.

Spörer is chiefly remembered for his discovery that the outer envelope of the Sun does not rotate as a rigid body, but with an angular velocity which increases from the equator to the pole. This he made independently of the discovery of the same effect by R. C. CARRINGTON in 1859. Carrington had noticed that the mean latitude of sunspots also varies systematically throughout the course of the solar cycle (see S. H. SCHWABE). Spörer charted this variation rather more carefully than did Carrington, and consequently the law of variation is usually known by his name. He found that spots tend to appear in the neighbourhood of solar latitude 35 degrees, and work down to the equator where they congregate at about latitude 5 degrees, at the end of the cycle. The physicist V. Bjerknes (1862–1951) eventually gave a theoretical explanation of Spörer's Law in 1926.

Astronomische Nachrichten, 138, 1895.
O. Lohse, *Vierteljahrsschrift der astronomischen Gesellschaft*, **30**, 208, 1895.
Dictionary of Scientific Biography.

J D N

SPRENGEL, HERMANN JOHANN PHILIPP Born at Schillerslage, Hanover, Germany, 29 August 1834; died London, 14 January 1906. Inventor of the Sprengel vacuum pump.

Sprengel was educated in Hanover, and worked for a time in the laboratory of R. W. BUNSEN. He came to England in 1859 and engaged in chemical research at Oxford. In 1862 he moved to London to work in the laboratories of the Royal College of Chemistry, Guy's Hospital, and St Bartholomew's Hospital. He was particularly interested in the newly introduced high explosives, on the practical use of which he wrote extensively. He also introduced an improved pyknometer. He was elected FRS in 1878.

It is, however, in connection with his vacuum pump that Sprengel is best remembered. The importance of this was very great, for without the attainment of high vacuum much work in atomic physics would have been impossible, nor could electric lamps and thermionic valves be made. It was, for example, the availability of the Sprengel pump that encouraged Sir Joseph SWAN successfully to resume his researches on the incandescent filament lamp, and Swan records that his knowledge of the pump came to him from Sir William CROOKES, for whom it was an essential tool in investigating the rare gases of the atmosphere.

Sprengel's pump – described by him in *On the Vacuum* (1865) – made use of the Torricellian vacuum, and was derived from that of H. Geissler (1814–79). In this the space to be evacuated was connected to the Torricellian vacuum by a tap. After partial evacuation, the tap was closed, the Torricellian vacuum re-created, and the process repeated as often as necessary. The procedure was, however, slow and tedious; Sprengel's important contribution essentially was to mechanize the repeated manual raising and lowering of the heavy mercury reservoir.

K. R. Webb, *Chemistry in Britain*, **1**, 569, 1965.

T I W

STAHL, GEORG ERNST Born at Anspach, Bavaria, Germany, 21 October 1660; died Berlin, 14 May 1734. Chemist; established the phlogiston theory of combustion.

Stahl was the son of a Protestant minister, and studied medicine at Jena. He taught there from 1683 until the foundation of the University of Halle in 1693, when he was appointed a professor of medicine there; he included chemistry in his course of lectures. From 1716 until his death he was personal physician to Frederick I of Prussia in Berlin. Most of his medical writings, which are not of great interest, were published by him as *The True Theory of Medicine* (1708).

It was in the field of chemistry that Stahl made his most important contribution. In particular he developed the theory of phlogiston (from the Greek *phlogos* a flame) adumbrated by J. J. BECHER with his *terra pinguis* or fatty earth, which he supposed to be the active principle of combustion. While Stahl fully recognized Becher's contribution, and was also inspired by J. Kunckel's *Nutzliche Observationes* (1676), it was he himself who developed the idea of phlogiston as a consistent theory to explain what happens in combustion. Briefly, he supposed that when metals or other elements, such as phosphorus, were calcined they lost phlogiston; conversely, when the calx was reduced again to metal, phlogiston was taken up. One of the reduction processes then most familiar to chemists was that occurring in the smelting of metals by heating an ore with charcoal. This was simply explained by the phlogiston theory as transfer of phlogiston from the charcoal to the ore. Carbon appeared to be particularly rich in phlogiston because on burning it left no residue.

According to the phlogiston theory, metals should lose weight when they are calcined, because they lose phlogiston, and the calx should gain in weight when reconverted to the metal. In fact, the reverse is the case, as Stahl knew. He knew, too, that air is necessary for combustion.

Nevertheless, these considerations did not shake his confidence, nor indeed, in the context of the time, is it entirely reasonable to expect that they should have done. Phlogiston had not necessarily to be a specific substance that could be isolated; it could perfectly well be an intangible principle like heat or 'caloric' which could flow from one body to another. Phlogiston might even confer some degree of buoyancy, thus explaining the observation that addition of phlogiston was accompanied by a loss of weight. Almost a century, and a very active century in chemistry at that, was to elapse before the process of combustion was generally recognized as being a combination with atmospheric oxygen.

The phlogiston theory was false, but nevertheless it played an important part in the development of chemical thought. For the first time it offered a logical and consistent theory of one of the most important of all chemical transformations, explaining what was known and pointing the way to further experiment. It deserves more credit than it now commonly commands.

Stahl published extensively and a catalogue compiled in 1726 by J. C. Goetz (1688–1733) lists some twenty-five major publications. Among the most important is his *Fundamentia Chymiae*, published in three parts, of which the third is based on his lectures at Halle.

Stahl is among those bridging the gap between alchemy and chemistry. As a young man (1684) he records, in a letter to Johann Juncker (1679–1759) his belief in the possibility of transmuting base metals into gold, but later his attitude was more cautious.

J. R. Partington, *A History of Chemistry*, vol. 2. 1961. (Portrait.)
R. Rappaport, *Chymia*, **7**, 73, 1961.
C. W. Beck, *Journal of Chemical Education*, **37**, 506, 1960.
H. Metzger, *Newton, Stahl, Boerhaave et la doctrine chimique.* 1930.
Dictionary of Scientific Biography.

T I W

STANLEY, FRANCIS EDGAR Born at Kingfield, Maine, USA, 1 June 1849; died (?)Boston, Massachusetts, 31 July 1918. Inventor and manufacturer of steam cars.

Stanley was the son of a teacher and himself trained for teaching, but he became a portrait photographer and invented the Stanley Dry Plate. This was highly successful, and the rights were eventually sold to Kodak (1905).

In 1897 he and his twin brother, F. O. Stanley (1849–1940), designed a steam car weighing only 7 cwt, with elliptic springs, wire wheels, and pneumatic tyres. It had a two-cylinder engine driving the rear axle, the boiler being heated by a petroleum burner and the feed-water tank operating from the boot. Commercial production was begun in the following year and continued until 1917, in spite of the mounting competition of the model-T made by Henry FORD.

The brothers also invented a process for obtaining gas-lighting from petroleum, and shared a keen interest in the manufacture of violins. Francis Edgar was killed in a motor accident; his twin survived until 1940.

Dictionary of American Biography.

T K D

STARK, JOHANNES Born at Schickenhof, Bavaria, Germany, 15 April 1874; died Traunstein, 21 June 1957. Discoverer of the 'Stark effect'.

From 1894 to 1898 Stark studied physical science at the University at Munich, where for two further years he worked at the Physical Institute. In 1900 he became *Privatdozent* at Göttingen University, and in 1906 professor extraordinary at the *Technische Hochschule*, Hanover. Later he succeeded to chairs at the *Technische Hochschule*, Aachen (1909), the University of Greifswald (1917), and the University of Wurzburg (1920). In 1933 he became president of the *Physikalisch-Technische Reichsanstalt*, Charlottenburg.

Like many other German physicists, Stark concerned himself with the phenomena of the discharge-tube. In 1902 he published *Electricity in Gases* and predicted that the high-velocity atoms of the 'canal rays' (see E. GOLDSTEIN) should exhibit the Doppler effect, that is, the apparent change in frequency of radiation emitted by a moving body (see C. J. DOPPLER). Three years later he demonstrated this with hydrogen 'rays'; the lines of the hydrogen spectrum were shifted slightly to the violet or red ends of the spectrum according to whether the 'rays' were approaching or receding from the observer. Later, extensions of this work helped further to confirm the material nature of 'canal rays'.

In 1913 Stark discovered the effect named after him. This is the splitting of spectral lines by an applied electric field, analogous to the effect discovered by P. ZEEMAN with a magnetic field. Despite many fruitless efforts by others before him, Stark was successful. He applied a very strong electric field in a discharge tube by using a third electrode near the perforated cathode, and observed multiple splitting of the lines due to the hydrogen atoms of the 'canal rays'.

The explanation of this effect by the new quantum theory of Max PLANCK did much to establish the latter. For its discovery, and for his work on the Doppler effect, Stark was awarded the Nobel prize in physics for 1919.

Stark was also concerned with the role of light in chemical reactions, and came near to the law of photochemical equivalence enunciated by EINSTEIN in 1912. He also proposed an electrical model of the atom in which a chemical bond could arise from electron-sharing (1908).

He became a warm admirer of the Nazi party and wrote a book about Hitler. This doubtless stabilized his position at the *Reichsanstalt*, but in 1947 he was sentenced by a German denazification court to four years in a labour camp.

N. H. de V. Heathcote, *Nobel Prize Winners in Physics, 1901–1950*. 1953. (Portrait.)

The Times, 24 June 1957.

Dictionary of Scientific Biography.

Tyler Wasson, (Ed.), *Nobel Prize Winners*. 1987. (Portrait.)

C A R

STARLING, ERNEST HENRY Born in London, 17 April 1866; died on board ship, Kingston Harbour, Jamaica, 2 May 1927. Physiologist.

Starling attended King's College School, London, and entered Guy's Hospital Medical School in 1882. After medical qualification he became first a demonstrator and subsequently

head of the Physiology Department at Guy's. At the time of Starling's appointment the equipment in the Physiology Department was meagre and quite inadequate for research, but he instigated such great improvements that the reconstructed laboratory was one of the best equipped in London when he moved to become Jodrell Professor of Physiology at University College in 1899. All his important researches were carried out at University College, and many, including the investigations leading to the discovery of secretin, were conducted in collaboration with W. M. BAYLISS. His first research concerned the secretion and circulation of lymph and other serous fluids. Starling early proved to be a brilliant experimental physiologist and was the first to point out the significance of hydrostatic pressures in blood capillaries and of osmotic pressures of body fluids (in virtue of their relationship to colloidal content): his explanations for movements of internal fluids rendered untenable the previously held 'vital' theory which attributed glandular secretory functions to the walls of capillaries. After the discovery of secretin in 1902 Starling commenced his pioneer and valuable work on the pumping action of the heart. He used the heart-lung preparation which he modified and greatly improved. In this device the heart of an anaesthetized animal is isolated from all other organs except the lungs, which are left intact with the pulmonary blood-vessels. Artificial respiration is applied and the pressures of the circulating defibrinated and warmed blood is measured by manometers attached to the aorta and inferior vena cava. It was demonstrated that the volume of venous inflow, and hence the muscular tension in the walls, is an important factor in regulating cardiac activities. The findings reached from these experiments led to the formulation of Starling's Law of the heart: the energy of the contraction is a function of the length of the muscle fibres. The First World War interrupted further work he hoped to carry out on the innervated heart. In 1914 he was commissioned in the Royal Army Medical Corps and rendered service in the production of antidotes to poison gases and later acted as a scientific adviser to the Ministry of Food. His best-known publication, *Principles of Human Physiology* (1912), was an important reference in its time. It was very characteristic of Starling that he was happiest when advising and helping others in their work.

He was elected Fellow of the Royal Society in 1899, and was subsequently the Society's Croonian Lecturer (1904), Royal Medallist (1913), and first Foulerton Research Professor (1922). He was Baly Medallist (1907) and Harveian Orator (1923) of the Royal College of Physicians. He was made CMG in 1918.

Proceedings of the Royal Society, 102 B, xvii, 1928.

L. G. Rowntree, *Amid Masters of Twentieth Century Medicine*. 1958. (Portrait.)

Dictionary of National Biography.

A P G

STAS, JEAN SERVAIS Born at Louvain, Belgium, 21 August 1813; died Brussels, 13 December 1891. Chemist, notable for his accurate determinations of atomic weights.

Stas qualified in medicine, but never practised. After some early chemical experiments in his own home (he isolated phloridzin), he went to Paris to become assistant to J. B. DUMAS. Here he continued his work in organic chemistry, but, more significantly, he helped Dumas to determine, very accurately, the atomic weights of carbon and oxygen. These proved to be almost exact whole numbers, and belief in Prout's Hypothesis revived (see W. PROUT).

In 1840 he became professor of chemistry in the École Royale Militaire in Brussels. His salary was meagre, but he was unmarried and his needs were simple. Increasing difficulty in lecturing, due to a throat ailment, compelled him to retire in 1869. A post was found for him in the Mint, but he resigned in 1872 on a matter of monetary policy. The rest of his life was spent in retirement.

Stas devoted most of his career to the determination of atomic weights, and set himself standards of accuracy which none of his contemporaries could equal. His results, published only after years of labour, were all fractional numbers; he lost his original confidence in Prout's Hypothesis, and was led to dismiss it as 'a pure illusion'. These accurate analyses provided a firm starting-point for the eventual discovery of the Periodic System. Among his other work were chemical studies of the potato blight and of nicotine poisoning; he was also adviser to the Belgian Government on military matters relating to chemistry.

Stas was a man of extremely independent opinions, and as an agnostic and anticlerical he was the centre of much controversy, especially regarding the role of the Church in education. He was not personally disliked, however, and his friends included many churchmen.

Chemical Society Memorial Lectures 1893–1900. (Portrait.)
Berichte der deutschen Chemischen Gesellschaft, **25**, 1, 1892.
J. R. Partington, *A History of Chemistry*, vol. 4. 1964. (Portrait.)
J. Timmermans, *Journal of Chemical Education*, **15**, 353, 1938.

W V F

STAUDINGER, HERMANN Born at Worms, Germany, 23 March 1881; died Freiburg-im-Breisgau, Baden-Württemberg, 8 September 1965. The founder of polymer chemistry.

After studying chemistry in the Universities of Halle, Darmstadt and Munich, Staudinger was for a short time *Privatdozent* at Strasbourg, then professor successively in the *Technische Hochschule* of Karlsruhe (1908), Zürich (1912), and the University of Freiburg (1926 to his retirement in 1951). He was awarded the Nobel prize for chemistry in 1953.

Staudinger's early work was in the tradition of classical organic chemistry; he studied, among other topics, the chemistry of ketenes and the compounds responsible for the aroma of coffee. His interest in high polymers began about 1920, in dissatisfaction with the work of C. D. Harries (1865–1923) on the structure of rubber. He soon became known as a skilful advocate of the view that high polymers are true 'giant molecules' held together by ordinary valency bonds. This theory, which is now undisputed, gained ground only slowly against the majority of chemists, who preferred to think of polymers as aggregates of monomer mol-

ecules (micelles) loosely bound by 'partial valencies' or even van der Waals forces. Staudinger made his point by discovering reactions that could alter a polymer chemically, leaving its molecular weight effectively unchanged; for instance, the hydrogenation of rubber to a macromolecular saturated hydrocarbon. His interest in, and knowledge of, polymers, was enormous and extended across the whole range of synthetic and natural products, and he published widely. The 'Staudinger equation' relating viscosity of polymer solutions to molecular weight is, despite reservations, of everyday application in the polymer industry. He was the founder and first editor of the journal *Die Makromoleculare Chemie*.

H. Staudinger, *From Organic Chemistry to Macromolecules*. 1970.
Nature, **208**, 626, 1965.
Journal of Chemical Education, **28**, 120, 1951. (Portrait.)
E. Farber, *Nobel Prize Winners in Chemistry*. 1963. (Portrait.)
V. E. Yarsley, *Chemistry and Industry*, 18 February 1967. (Portrait.)
Dictionary of Scientific Biography.

W V F

STEENSTRUP, JOHANNES JAPETUS SMITH Born at Aalborg, Denmark, 8 March 1813; died Copenhagen, 20 June 1897. Zoologist; discovered the alternation of generations in some animals.

Steenstrup was educated at the University of Copenhagen, where he studied many branches of natural history. After a period of exploration in Iceland, working on fossil plants and volcanic formations, he went to the Seeland Academy at Soroe in 1841 to teach botany and zoology. While there he published his important monographs on the alternation of generations and on hermaphroditism. The first of these appeared in both Danish and German in 1842, with an English translation following in 1845; the second appeared in Danish in 1845, and in German in 1846. Steenstrup demonstrated that 'certain animals, notably jelly-fish and certain parasitic worms, habitually produce offspring which never resemble their parent, but which, on the other hand, themselves bring forth progeny, which return in form and nature to the grandparents or more distant ancestors'. This demonstration attracted much attention, and further investigations carried out by other zoologists, for example, the work of C. T. E. von SIEBOLD on intestinal worms, provided more evidence to support Steenstrup's conclusions.

In 1848 Steenstrup was appointed professor of zoology and director of the Zoological Museum at the University of Copenhagen. His other work was mainly on marine zoology, especially the morphology of Cephalopoda, though he also made important contributions to palaeontology and archaeology. He was elected a Foreign Member of the Royal Society in 1863.

Proceedings of the Linnean Society of London, Session 110, 50, 1897/8.
V. Meisen, *Prominent Danish Scientists Through the Ages*. 1972.
C. Lütken, *Natural Sciences*, **11**, 159, 1897.
Dictionary of Scientific Biography.

S J R

STEFAN, JOSEPH Born at St Peter, near Klagenfurt, Austria, 24 March 1835; died Vienna, 7 January 1893. The first to succeed in connecting radiation with absolute temperature.

Stefan came of peasant stock, his parents being poor, illiterate shopkeepers. After studying at Vienna for four years he took up school-teaching and continued at this for seven more years. In 1863 he became professor of physics at the University of Vienna, remaining there for the rest of his life.

Stefan was concerned with the kinetic theory of gases, particularly diffusion. Working on the diffusion of liquids, he demonstrated the relative rates of this process through jellies and through water (1878). He studied electromagnetic induction and thermomagnetic effects; advanced a theory of magnetism; and worked on optical interference phenomena, capillarity, and the thermal conductivity of gases.

His most famous contribution came in 1879. After examining some measurements of heat losses from a platinum wire made by J. TYNDALL, he pointed out that these results imply that the rate of loss was proportional to the fourth power of the absolute temperature. The proportionality constant (σ) is sometimes known as 'Stefan's constant'. This result (which was only fortuitously correct, as glowing platinum is not a black-body radiator) was given a theoretical foundation by one of Stefan's students, L. BOLTZMANN, a few years later. He showed by a thermodynamic argument that it could be derived from the theory of gases formulated by J. Clerk MAXWELL. The generalization is now termed the Stefan-Boltzmann Law.

Stefan was little known in his lifetime, and he rarely attended scientific congresses. His fame today rests largely upon the work of his distinguished pupil.

P. Lenard, *Great Men of Science*. 1950. (Portrait.)
J. C. Poggendorf, *Biographisch-literarisches Handwörterbuch*. 1883–1903.
Elektrotechnische Zeitschrift, **14**, 31, 1893.
Dictionary of Scientific Biography.

C A R

STEINBERGER, JACK Born in Bad Kissingen, Franconia, Germany, 25 May 1921. Experimental particle physicist.

In 1934 Jack and his elder brother were sent to the US, care of an American Jewish charity which found homes for German refugee children. The two boys went to a family in Chicago, who saw to their education and enabled their parents and younger brother to join them in 1938. Jack graduated in chemistry from Chicago University in 1942 and joined the army after the US entered the Second World War. He was sent to work at the MIT Radiation Laboratory, where he became interested in physics. After the war he returned to Chicago University to take his PhD under Enrico FERMI, and made the first of many seminal discoveries in particle physics.

After two years at other institutions, Steinberger joined Columbia University in 1950 and began a succession of notable experiments, first on Columbia's cyclotron and later on the larger machine at the Brookhaven National Laboratory. Here, in 1962, Steinberger and colleagues performed the first experiment with a high-energy neutrino beam, which revealed two types of neutrino. For this work, Steinberger, Leon Lederman (1922–) and Melvin Schwartz (1932–) were awarded the Nobel Prize for Physics in 1988.

In 1968 Steinberger moved to CERN, the European laboratory for particle physics near Geneva. There he has led major experiments on symmetry violations in weak interactions, on high-energy neutrino interactions, and most recently on LEP, the Large Electron Positron collider.

Physics Today, January 1989. (Portrait.)
K. Kleinknecht and T. D. Lee (Eds), *Particles and detectors, Festschrift for Jack Steinberger*. (1986).
Les Prix Nobel en 1988. 1989. (Portrait.)

C S

STENO, NICOLAUS (NIELS STEENSEN) Born in Copenhagen, 1 January 1638; died Schwerin, northern Germany, 1686. Anatomist and geologist.

Steno, son of a well-to-do goldsmith, studied first in Copenhagen where one of his teachers was Thomas Bartholin (1616–80), the anatomist. In 1660 he began his travels and studies abroad, and while in Amsterdam discovered the parotid salivary duct (ductus Stenorzianus). After four years in Leiden he returned to Copenhagen, but no post was available for him there, so he went to Paris, where he made important observations on the anatomy of the brain. After visiting other centres of learning in France, he arrived in Florence in 1665. While dissecting a shark, the distinctive character of the teeth led him to compare them with certain fossils, found far inland, which he then realized were the remains of sharks of a former period, preserved in rocks once laid down in the sea. These observations and conclusions formed part of his treatise *Canis Carchariae Dissectum Caput* (1667) and was more fully expounded in his *De Solido intra Solidum naturalites contento dissertionis Prodromus* (1669). An English translation by Henry Oldenburg (1615? –77), Secretary of the Royal Society, appeared in London in 1671. In England, at about this time, similar fundamental geological ideas were occurring to scientists, particularly to Robert HOOKE. In 1672 Steno returned to Copenhagen, where he gave anatomical demonstrations; but he abandoned science for religion, and went back to Florence in 1674. He had become a Roman Catholic in 1667, took holy orders in 1675, and was made a bishop in 1677, residing in various towns in northern Germany until his death.

Biography (in English) by Vilhelm Maar in *Nicolai Stenonis: Opera Philosophica*. 1910.
V. A. Eyles, *Nature*, **174**, 8, 1954.
Anne Tjomsland, *Annals of Medical History*, **10**, 491, 1938.
R. Cioni, *Niels Stenson: Scientist-Bishop*. 1962.
G. Scherz, *Nicolaus Steno and His Indice*. 1958.
Dictionary of Scientific Biography.)

J C

STEPHENSON, GEORGE Born at Wylam, near Newcastle upon Tyne, England, 9 June 1781; died Tapton, Chesterfield, Derbyshire, 12 August 1848. Railway engineer, pioneer of steam traction.

Son of Robert Stephenson, a colliery fireman, George Stephenson followed his father's trade. At 17 he was put in charge of a new pumping engine at Water Row, where his father worked. He moved to other pits at Walbottle before going to Black Collerton as brakesman in charge of the winding engine. In 1802 he moved to a similar engine, installed to draw ballast wagons from Willington Quay to the top of a dump, and finally to Killingworth West Moor pit in 1804.

Personal sorrows – he lost his wife and daughter in 1805, and his father was injured – led him seriously to consider following the example of his sister and emigrating. But at Killingworth, through caring for the education of his son, Robert STEPHENSON, he acquired a new interest in life. He rose steadily in the service of the 'Grand Allies' who controlled the pits; he was put in charge of the machinery at all their collieries in 1812, and was allowed to act as a consultant for other owners, too. He built some thirty-nine stationary engines during this period – one of 200 hp – and was responsible for rationalizing coal handling above and below ground by replacing horse-drawn sleds with trains running on rails and drawn by stationary engines. Amongst other mining improvements, he devised a safety lamp in 1815 for which he was thanked three years later with a gift of £1,000 raised by public subscriptions. This brought him into some controversy with Sir Humphry DAVY, who had devised a similar lamp at about the same time, as also had W. R. Clanny (1776–1850).

The mounting cost of horse fodder prompted colliery-owners to experiment with steam-driven locomotives, running on cast-iron rather than wooden rails. A high-pressure locomotive of the Trevithick type was built at Gateshead in 1805, but proved too heavy for the wooden rails of the Wylam Colliery. Two Trevithick-type locomotives with pinion wheels engaging with iron rack rails were successfully built in 1812 to carry coal from the Middleton collieries to Leeds; two more were built, one of which made a brief appearance on Tyneside. William Chapman of Durham also built one in 1813 which employed bogies to soften its impact on the rails, and in the same year William Hedley (1779–1843) built another for a newly laid cast-iron tramway at Wylam. Stephenson's employers commissioned him to build a locomotive for Killingworth at their West Moor workshops. The *Blucher* took to rails on 25 July 1814; it embodied the important innovation of running on flanged wheels. Some subsequent engines had a steam-cushioned suspension for smoother running. As a result of this, and other successes with the *Wellington* and the *My Lord*, he was invited to join the Walker Ironworks in 1815, on a part-time basis, to exploit his inventions, which included the steam-blast. From 1819 to 1822 he built an eight-mile railroad for the Thetson colliery.

Cut off from easy access to the River Tees at Stockton, the Auckland coalfield was severely handicapped in comparison with that on the Tyne. Schemes for linking it by canal had been discussed since 1768, but nothing was done until 1821, when an Act of Parliament approved the laying of a railway between Stockton and Darlington. Appointed engineer, Stephenson recommended a new route, and persuaded Edward Pease (1767–1858), one of the promoters, and Thomas Richardson to join him in establishing a locomotive works at Newcastle – where his son Robert joined him in 1827 as manager – in order to make the locomotives. Begun on

23 May 1823 the Stockton and Darlington Railway was opened on 27 September 1825. The success of Stephenson's *Locomotion*, which hauled the first train on the Stockton–Darlington railroad, added greatly to his reputation. In 1830 the Liverpool–Manchester Railway was opened, the world's first main-line railway to carry passengers, for which he was the engineer; the bogs of Chat Moss presented a particularly serious obstacle. In the previous year the *Rocket*, adopted for this run, achieved a spectacular success in the famous Rainhill trials, reaching a speed of 30 mph.

Thereafter George Stephenson played a leading part in developing the British railway system, as well as some Continental ones. To supervise what was eventually the Midland Railway he moved to Tapton, near Chesterfield. Later he tried to check the 'railway mania' in which so much money was lost.

L. T. C. Rolt, *George and Robert Stephenson, The Railway Revolution*. 1960. (Portrait.)

R. L. Galloway, *The Steam Engine and its Inventors*. 1881.

W. O. Skeat, *George Stephenson: The Engineer and his Letters*. 1973.

Dictionary of National Biography.

M. Jamieson, *The Railway Stephensons*. 1970.

W H G A

STEPHENSON, ROBERT Born at Willington Quay, near Newcastle upon Tyne, England, 16 October 1803; died London, 12 October 1859. Mechanical and civil engineer.

Robert was the only son of George STEPHENSON who expended much care on his education, and sent him for a year (1822) to Edinburgh University, where he made a lifelong friendship with G. P. Bidder (1806–78). Bidder, the 'calculating phenomenon', was later associated with him in building the London–Birmingham Railway. Apprenticed before this at the Killingworth Colliery, where his father worked, he was so close to his father that his absence for three years supervising mines in Colombia from 1824 to 1827 was keenly felt.

Robert returned to manage Robert Stephenson and Company, founded at Newcastle in 1823, with the backing of Edward Pease (1767–1858), to build locomotives. His first engine, the *Lancashire Witch* (1828), had inclined cylinders with direct drive to crank-pins on the wheels, a precursor of the more famous *Rocket* (1829), winner of the Rainhill Trials, and their heavier successors the *Meteor*, *Comet*, *Dart* and *Arrow*, all with nearly horizontal cylinders which made for smoother running and higher speeds. This trend reached its climax with the *Planet* (1830) which had the engine beneath the boiler, with the cylinders directly under the smoke box and the pistons driving a cranked rear axle. Up to 1840 the works sent locomotives to France, Germany, Italy, Belgium and the United States.

Obtaining Parliamentary permission for the London–Birmingham Railway involved him in much work giving evidence to Parliamentary Committees in 1832. Appointed engineer-in-chief in 1833, it marked his emergence as an engineer in his own right. He moved to London, the better to cope with the problems posed by the 112-mile line, from tunnels at Primrose Hill, Watford, to fighting the canal company at Wolverton, and the great four-year battle against subterranean quicksands at Kilsby. The first train ran from London to Birmingham on 24 June 1838.

Robert Stephenson was also drawn into the design of bridges. His first bridge over the Dee collapsed with a train on it, but soon afterwards he embarked on a railway bridge of unprecedented size over the Menai Straits. It was of tubular design, executed in wrought iron. The success of this Britannia Bridge and of another at Conway encouraged him to build others in Egypt, and finally the Victoria tubular bridge over the St Lawrence at Montreal. He also built the High Level Bridge at Newcastle and the Royal Border Bridge at Berwick.

The Britannia Bridge, with two 459-foot spans, was a remarkable achievement; previously the longest wrought-iron span was a mere 31 feet. In executing his design Stephenson carried out elaborate tests, enlisting the help of William FAIRBAIRN and Eaton HODGKINSON.

He was MP for Whitby for many years from 1847. He was President of the Institution of Civil Engineers (1856–7) and was elected FRS in 1849. Oxford awarded him an honorary degree. At his death, he was buried in Westminster Abbey.

L. T. C. Rolt, *George and Robert Stephenson*. 1960. (Portraits.)

Discovery, **20**, 414, 1959.

M. Jamieson, *The Railway Stephensons*. 1970.

Dictionary of National Biography.

W H G A

STERN, OTTO Born at Sorau, Upper Silesia (then in Germany), 17 February 1888; died Berkeley, California, USA, 17 August 1969. Developed the technique of molecular beams.

After gaining a PhD in physical chemistry at Breslau University in 1912, Stern worked with EINSTEIN, first in Prague and then in Zürich, writing important papers on statistical mechanics, thermodynamics and quantum theory. In 1914 he moved to Frankfurt, and later began to develop molecular beams, which he used to verify MAXWELL's law for the distribution of molecular velocities in gases. Then in 1920, Stern and Walther Gerlach (b. 1889) demonstrated spatial quantization – the prediction of quantum theory that the magnetic moment of an atom should take up only certain orientations in space, in particular with respect to an applied magnetic field. Stern and Gerlach passed a beam of silver atoms through an inhomogeneous field and found that the beam was split into two, corresponding to the two orientations of the silver atoms.

Later, in Hamburg, Stern used a hydrogen molecular beam to measure the magnetic moment of the proton, and found a value 2.5 times greater than expected from comparison with the electron. This was the first evidence that the proton has a more complex structure than the electron.

Stern left Germany in 1933, and joined the Carnegie Institute of Technology in Pittsburgh, retiring in 1945. He received the Nobel Prize for Physics for his work on molecular beams in 1943.

Nobel Lectures, Physics, 1942–1962. 1964.

H. A. Boorse, L. Motz, J. H. Weaver, *The Atomic Scientists, a Biographical History*, 1989. (Portrait.)

Biographical Memoirs of the National Academy of Sciences. 1973

Dictionary of Scientific Biography.

Tyler Wasson (Ed.), *Nobel Prize Winners*. 1987. (Portrait.)

C S

STEVINUS, SIMON Born at Bruges, Flanders (now in Belgium), *c*.1548; died at Leiden, Netherlands, or The Hague, *c*.1620. Made important contributions to mechanics and hydrostatics; introduced decimals into common usage.

Little is known of Stevinus's origins, but he is believed to have been a merchant's clerk. As a young man he entered the service of the Dutch Government and after service in Scandinavia, Poland and Prussia rose to be Quartermaster-General to the Army and was responsible as an engineer for some important public works.

His contributions to statics and hydrostatics clearly stemmed primarily from consideration of the practical problems he encountered as an engineer. He investigated, for example, the principles governing the behaviour of single and multiple pulleys. He recognized and formulated the principle of the parallelogram of forces. In hydrostatics, he showed experimentally that the pressure exerted by a liquid is dependent only on its vertical height, and is independent of the shape of the vessel in which it is contained. He clearly recognized that relatively small volumes of liquids could exert enormous pressures if contained in long narrow tubes, thus establishing the principle of the hydraulic press. He showed the conditions necessary for stability in floating objects. He refuted experimentally – by simultaneously dropping two unequal lead weights from a height – the doctrine of ARISTOTLE that heavy bodies fall faster than light ones. In this he probably anticipated the famous experiment of GALILEO at Pisa, which is indeed now commonly believed to be apocryphal.

Stevinus's contributions to mechanics were set out (in Flemish) in his *De Beghinselen der Weeghconst* (1586). This was translated into Latin by W. SNELL and appeared in 1605/8 as *Hypomnemata Mathematica*; a French translation was published in 1634.

Stevinus was responsible also for introducing decimal fractions into common usage, though he was not the originator of the idea and his notation was rather clumsy. His ideas were set out in his book *De Thiende* (1585), which appeared in English translation in the same year and in a French edition in 1608. The true inventor of the decimal notation was possibly Muhammad al-Qushchi (al-Kashi d. *c*.1430), director of Ulugh Beg's great observatory at Samarkand – who gave the value of π to sixteen decimal places – though the basic idea may have been of very much earlier Chinese origin. In Europe, C. Rudolff (*fl.* sixteenth century) described the decimal notation, and how to manipulate it, in his *Exempel-Büchlin* (1530).

D. E. Smith, *History of Mathematics*, vol. 2. 1925. (Paperback, 1958.)

R. Depau, *Simon Stevin*. 1942.

G. Sarton, *Isis*, **21**, 241, 1934.

E. J. Dijksterhuis, *Simon Stevin: Science in the Netherland Around 1600*. 1970.

Dictionary of Scientific Biography.

T I W

STIRLING, ROBERT Born in Cloag, Perthshire, Scotland, 25 October 1790; died Galston, Ayrshire, 6 June 1878. Inventor of the Stirling hot air engine.

Stirling was educated at the Universities of Glasgow and Edinburgh and was ordained in 1816. In 1824 he moved from Kilmarnock, where he was second minister at Laigh Kirk, to become minister of the parish of Galston, Ayrshire, remaining there for the rest of his life, retiring only in 1876. He received an honorary DD from the University of St Andrews in 1840.

An early interest in mechanics led him to experiment with the design of a hot air engine, and with his brother James Stirling (1800–1876), a mechanical engineer, he took out a patent in 1816. Improved versions were patented in 1827 and 1840. The Stirling engine was an external combustion engine with a continuously burning source of heat outside the cylinder. The design involved two pistons facing each other separated by a heat exchanger which alternately absorbed and gave up heat. Stirling was the first to apply the idea of using the circulation of water to cool an engine. In 1818 the first engine was put into use to pump water from a quarry, but it burned out after two years and despite years of work by James Stirling to improve the engine he never solved the problem of the need for very high temperatures to make the engine work efficiently. In 1843 he converted a steam engine at the Dundee Foundry Company to work as a hot air engine driving machinery, but although it used less coal than a steam engine it burned out very soon and after three years was reconverted to steam. Stirling engines continued to be used for powering small pumps until the end of the 19th century, but they were eventually superseded by small electric motors.

However interest revived in the 1960s when research into Stirling engines which had been going on since the 1930s in the Philips laboratories at Eindhoven in Holland led to collaboration with General Motors and later with the Ford Motor Company. In 1985 the French submarine *Saga* was equipped with two Stirling engines.

G. Walker, *Stirling Engines.* 1980. (Portrait.)
J. Zarinchang, *The Stirling Engine.* 1972.
Dictionary of National Biography.

A P B

STOKES, GEORGE GABRIEL Born at Skreen, County Sligo, Ireland, 13 August 1819; died Cambridge, England, 1 February 1903. Physicist; studied the behaviour of fluids and the phenomenon of fluorescence.

Stokes went up to Pembroke College, Cambridge, in 1837. He became Senior Wrangler and Smith's Prizeman, and in 1841 was elected a Fellow of his College; in 1902 he was elected Master. In 1849 he was appointed to the Lucasian Professorship of Mathematics, and held it until his death. Stokes promoted the study of advanced mathematics in Cambridge, but in his work there is an emphasis on the importance of physical ideas, and not simply on abstract mathematics.

In 1845 and 1850 he published memoirs on viscous fluids, and calculated corrections for friction of the air; this led on to work on convergent series. In 1849 came papers on the optical interference phenomenon known as Newton's rings, and in 1849 a paper on

a dynamical theory of diffraction, dealing with the general problem of disturbances from vibrating sources passing through an elastic ether. His more positivistic successors did not find this approach helpful. Stokes's law of falling bodies in viscous media, stating that the rate of fall depends on their weight, dates from this period. In 1849 he published a paper on the variation of gravity over the Earth's surface, making him a pioneer in the science of geodesy.

In 1852 he produced a paper on fluorescence, a name which he originated. It had been discovered that certain solutions, notably those of quinine, were normally colourless, but appeared blue in certain aspects. Stokes showed that this phenomenon, fluorescence, was produced by ultraviolet light, and found other inorganic and organic substances which exhibited the property.

In 1851 he was elected Fellow of the Royal Society and in 1854 became Secretary of the Society, a post he held for over thirty years, until he was elected President (1885–90). While Secretary, he devoted a great deal of attention to improving papers submitted to the Society; but his obituarist noticed that after Stokes took up this post his own output fell off greatly.

In 1854 he made the suggestion that the black lines observed by J. von FRAUNHOFER in the solar spectrum might be due to absorption of light by cooler atoms in the Sun's outer layers. But he never followed this up, and G. R. KIRCHOFF and R. W. BUNSEN receive the credit for applying spectrum analysis to the heavenly bodies.

Stokes possessed a combination of mathematical ability and experimental skill; but he was somewhat overcautious. He was a good administrator, and was MP for Cambridge University from 1887 to 1891. He took a great interest in natural theology.

Dictionary of National Biography.
Lord Rayleigh, *Proceedings of the Royal Society,* **75**, 199, 1905. (Portrait.)
W. F. Magie, *A Source Book in Physics.* 1935.
Lord Kelvin, *Nature,* **67**, 337, 1903.
Dictionary of Scientific Biography.

D M K

STONEY, GEORGE JOHNSTONE Born Oakley Park, King's County, Ireland, 15 February 1826; died London, 5 July 1911. Mathematical physicist; introduced the term 'electron'.

The finances of the Stoney family suffered in the Napoleonic War and in the Irish Famine, and Stoney had to pay his way through Trinity College, Dublin, by coaching. His brother, Bindon Blood Stoney (1828–1909), was a well-known civil engineer. In 1847 G. J. Stoney was Second Senior Moderator in Mathematics and Physics, and in the following year was appointed astronomical assistant to Lord Rosse (1800–67), President of the Royal Society, at Parsonstown (see Sir Charles Algernon PARSONS). He tried unsuccessfully for a Fellowship at Trinity College, Dublin, in 1852 – the last time the examinations were held in Latin – and Lord Rosse got him the Chair of Natural Philosophy at Queen's College, Galway. In 1887 he returned to Dublin as Secretary of the Queen's University, a post involving administration of the scattered colleges of the federal university. In 1893 he moved to London, to enable his daughters to get the benefit of a university education, in accordance with his advocacy of higher education for women. He was elected FRS in 1861.

His researches were on physical optics, in which he followed on from the work of G. G. STOKES, and on molecular physics. He produced papers on the atmosphere of the Sun and planets, showing why hydrogen and helium would have escaped from the Earth's gravitational field, and why moons lack atmospheres. In 1873 he served on the Committee of the British Association which decided to adopt metric units in the United Kingdom. In 1874 he spoke at the British Association Meeting at Belfast of 'an absolute unit of electricity (which) exists in that amount of it which attends each chemical bond or valency'. Later, he proposed the term 'electron' for this unit in place of the term 'corpuscle' proposed by J. J. THOMSON. Stoney's remarks do not seem to have aroused much attention until H. L. F. von HELMHOLTZ said much the same thing in 1881.

Dictionary of National Biography.
Proceedings of the Royal Society, **86A**, xx, 1912. (Portrait.)
F. T. Trouton, *Nature,* **87**, 50, 1911.
Dictionary of Scientific Biography.

D M K

STRASBURGER, EDUARD ADOLF Born in Warsaw, 1 February 1844; died Poppelesdorf, Germany, 19 May 1912. Plant cytologist.

Strasburger was the son of German parents. He was educated at Bonn and Jena, and became professor of botany at Jena in 1869 and director of the Botanical Garden there in 1873. In 1881 he went to Bonn University, where his laboratory became the most important centre for cytological research in the world. His earlier research continued the investigations by W. F. B. HOFFMEISTER on the alternation of generations, and accurately described the embryo sac in gymnosperms and angiosperms.

Gradually his interests turned to the study of the cell and his *Zellbildung und Zelltheilung* (1875) and *Über Befruchtung und Zelltheilung* (1877) were the first of a series of important cytological papers.

He was a particularly good lecturer and sympathetic friend of his students. His most popular work was his *Lehrbuch der Botanik für Hochschulen* (1894), which appeared in subsequent editions and translations.

Proceedings of the Linnean Society of London, **64**, 1911–12.
Genetics, **36**, 1, 1951. (Portrait.)
Nature, **80**, 379, 1912.
Dictionary of Scientific Biography.

R G C D

STRUTT, JOHN WILLIAM *See* RAYLEIGH.

STRUVE, FRIEDRICH GEORG WILHELM Born at Altona, Germany, 15 April 1793; died (probably) Pulkova, Russia, 23 November 1864. Remembered for his contributions to geodesy and double-star astronomy.

In 1811 Struve took a degree in philology at the Russian University of Dorpat before turning to science. Appointed professor of astronomy and mathematics in 1813, he began work at Dorpat Observatory, of which institution he became director. The possession of a superb refractor of over 9 inches aperture and a meridian circle enabled Struve to measure stellar positions with great accuracy, Between 1819 and 1827 he examined 120 000 stars and found 2200 doubles. In the next ten years he measured the position angles, distances, brightness and colours of such systems, the results of which he published in 1837 in his *Stellarum Compositarum Mensurae Micrometricae.* Fifteen years later a second major work was published, extending his observations and giving the stars' movements as calculated from the oldest observations. His work demonstrated the high proportion of all stars that are composite.

In 1835 the Emperor Nicholas entrusted Struve with the erection of Pulkova Observatory. It became the best-equipped observatory in Europe. Struve was made director in 1839, in which post he remained until 1858, when his son Otto (1819–1905) succeeded him.

Apart from his stellar work, Struve left new and accurate determinations of the constants of aberration, precession and nutation. He also carried out fundamental geodetic measurements from the Danube to the Arctic Ocean. His son Otto, grandsons Hermann and Ludwig, and great-grandsons Georg and Otto, all had distinguished astronomical careers.

H. Shapley and H. E. Howarth, *Source Book in Astronomy.* 1929. (Portrait.)
G. Abetti, *The History of Astronomy.* 1954.
E. B. Frost, *Popular Astronomy,* **29**, 536, 1921.
P. van de Kamp, *Journal of the Royal Astronomical Society of Canada,* **59**, 106, 1965.
Dictionary of Scientific Biography.

A E R

STURGEON, WILLIAM Born at Whittington, Lancashire, England, 22 May 1783; died Prestwich, Lancashire, 4 December 1850. Electrician and inventor.

Born in humble circumstances, Sturgeon became a private soldier, but managed to educate himself in languages and natural science. Leaving the Army in 1820, he set up in Woolwich as a bootmaker, but spent much time lecturing and constructing electrical apparatus. In 1824 he was made lecturer in science at the Royal Military College; in 1840 he went to Manchester as superintendent of the Royal Victoria Gallery of Practical Science. When this failed financially, he became an itinerant lecturer, and died in poverty.

Sturgeon was the first to make a workable electric motor; he introduced the soft-iron electromagnet; and invented the commutator. He also worked on thermo-electricity and the improvement of batteries. Essentially a practical man and inventor, his theoretical views are of little interest.

Dictionary of National Biography.
The Electrician, 13 September 1895. (Portrait.)

W V F

STURTEVANT, ALFRED HENRY Born in Jacksonville, Illinois, 21 November 1891; died Pasadena, California, 5 April 1970. Geneticist.

While a student at Columbia University, Sturtevant developed an interest in heredity – initially on the basis of the coat colours of his father's horses – and this was stimulated by reading a book on Mendelism by R. C. Punnett (1875–1967). He wrote up his findings and sent them to T. H. MORGAN who in 1911 had just elucidated the principles of sex-linked inheritance. Morgan gave him a place in his famous 'fly room', where the fruit-fly *Drosophila* was used experimentally, and thus launched Sturtevant on a very distinguished career in genetics. He remained at Columbia until 1928, when he moved to California Institute of Technology – as professor of genetics – to join Morgan in a new laboratory there. He remained at Pasadena for the rest of his life: one of his close colleagues was T. DOBZHANSKY.

Sturtevant's research ranged widely, but he is particularly remembered for his pioneer work on mapping the position of genes on their chromosomes. His basic concept – which by his own account came to him in a flash of inspiration in 1913 while still a student – was that the frequency of crossing-over between genes was a measure of their distance apart. In his later years he took a particular interest in the genetic effects of radiation and in 1954 publicly warned of the potentially serious consequences of atom bomb tests.

G. W. Beadle, *Yearbook of the American Philosophical Society*, 1970.

S. Emerson, *Annual Review of Genetics*, 5, 1, 1971.

T I W

SUGDEN, SAMUEL Born at Leeds, Yorkshire, England, 1892; died Epsom, Surrey, 20 October 1950. Chemist; introduced the 'parachor'.

Sugden, who came from a family concerned with the wool trade, studied chemistry at the Royal College of Science, London. During the First World War he served in the Medical Corps, then as a chemist in the Royal Arsenal, Woolwich. He then joined the staff of Birkbeck College, London, becoming professor of physical chemistry in 1932. In 1937 he was made professor of chemistry in University College, London; during the Second World War he worked for the Ministry of Supply and the US Air Force. About 1943 he suffered a severe breakdown in health from which he never recovered, although after the war he resumed his academic duties.

Most of Sugden's early work was concerned with surface tension and related properties. In 1924 he introduced the 'parachor', a function which in effect permits molecular volumes to be compared at the same internal pressure. This was an additive function, with values empirically determined for atoms and various types of bond. Organic chemists had great hopes of the parachor for structural determinations, but it proved disappointing. On the basis of parachor measurements, Sugden postulated single-electron bonds, but the ensuing controversy convinced him that he was mistaken. His later work concerned magnetochemistry and radioactive tracers. He was elected FRS in 1934.

Obituary Notices of Fellows of the Royal Society, 1951. (Portrait.)

W V F

SUMNER, JAMES BATCHELLER Born at Canton, Massachusetts, USA, 19 November 1877; died Buffalo, New York, 12 August 1955. Biochemist who isolated the first crystalline enzyme.

Sumner, son of a wealthy cotton manufacturer and farmer, was all his life under the disadvantage (especially severe for a practical chemist) of having lost his left arm in a hunting accident in childhood. He studied chemistry and physiology at Har-

vard, graduating PhD in 1914; in the same year he joined the staff of the medical school at Cornell University, where he remained until shortly before his death, becoming professor of biochemistry in 1929. He was three times married, and left seven children.

Heavy teaching duties, and, in the early years, inadequate laboratory facilities, severely limited Sumner's research. It was about 1917 when he embarked on the apparently hopeless project of isolating enzymes as pure chemical compounds. Much of his work was done with the enzyme urease present in the jack-bean, whose activity was easily estimated by ammonia analyses. For several years he worked with amorphous fractions of high, but variable, urease activity, until in 1926 a simple change of procedure (from using aqueous ethanol to using aqueous acetone as a solvent) gave him a crystalline product which he concluded was pure urease. It also gave all the normal reactions for protein, confirming the views of those few biochemists who believed that enzymes were all proteins of special type.

The majority of biochemists, however, including the influential school of R. WILLSTÄTTER, were not disposed to agree with this view, and a rather acrimonious controversy ensued, in which it was implied that Sumner's urease was merely a crystalline protein with a high concentration of enzyme adsorbed upon it. Sumner (who was somewhat embittered by this controversy) was eventually justified by the isolation of an increasing number of other enzymes in crystalline form, notably of pepsin by J. H. NORTHROP in 1930. His work was recognized by the award of a Nobel prize for chemistry in 1946, which he shared with Northrop and W. M. Stanley.

National Academy of Sciences, Biographical Memoirs. 1958. (Portrait.)

Nature, **176**, 859, 1955.

Dictionary of American Biography.

Tyler Wasson (Ed.), *Nobel Prize Winners*. 1987. (Portrait.)

W V F

SWAMMERDAM, JAN Born in Amsterdam, 12 February 1637; died there, 17 February 1680. A founder of comparative anatomy and of minute dissection.

Swammerdam, the son of an apothecary, studied insects from his youth and he continued with this work at home until he was 24. He then studied medicine at Leiden, having Nicolaus STENO and Regnier de GRAAF as fellow students. He graduated doctor of medicine at Leiden (1667). Swammerdam had meanwhile been continuing his brilliant dissections of insects, and, despite repeated protests by his father, he never practised medicine. In 1673 he came under the influence of the Flemish mystic and religious fanatic, Antoinette Bourignon, whom he accompanied as a convert to Schleswig and Hamburg. Swammerdam became increasingly involved in religious controversy, and continued illness led to his early death.

Swammerdam's graduation thesis, on respiration (1667), contains important new observations, such as the correct statement that at the beginning of life the lung of a mammal sinks in water before respiration has been established, but floats once the animal has breathed. His next work was a general history of insects, first published in Dutch (1669). In 1675 he published, also in Dutch, a detailed account of the morphology of the may-fly. His last five years were devoted to dissections of the bee, other insects, the tadpole, the snail, *inter alia*. After his death the manuscripts relating to this great work had a chequered history. Over fifty years later they were bought by H. BOERHAAVE, who published them in two sumptuous volumes entitled *Biblia naturae* (the *Bible of Nature*, 1737). Swammerdam's Dutch text was translated into Latin, and the plates were engraved from his own drawings.

In this monumental work Swammerdam gave the first scientific account of insect transforma-tions. Under each form discussed he gave the life-history and the minute anatomy in great detail. His account of the honey-bee contains the first accurate descriptions of the mouth-parts, the compound eyes, and the sting. His descriptions of certain mol-luscs are equally significant. In the frog he was the first to discover the nucleated red blood cor-puscles, and he demonstrated experimentally that when a muscle contracts its volume does not increase.

L. C. Miall, *The Early Naturalists*. 1912.
F. J. Cole, *A History of Comparative Anatomy*. 1944; *Nature*, **139**, 218, 287, 1937.
A. Schierbeek, *Jan Swammerdam*. 1967. (Portrait.)
Dictionary of Scientific Biography.

E A U

SWAN, SIR JOSEPH WILSON Born at Sunder-land, Co. Durham, England, 31 October 1828; died Warlingham, Surrey, 27 May 1917. Inventor of the Swan incandescent filament lamp.

After a private education, Swan was apprenticed to a chemist. Later he joined, and shortly became a partner of, John Mawson, a chemical supplier. The firm was particularly interested in the supply of fine chemicals for photography and Swan made a number of important contributions in this field. He invented the carbon (autotype) process for making permanent prints (1862) and introduced rapid dry plates, which revolutionized the art of photography. In later life these contributions earned him the Progress Medal and honorary membership of the Royal Photographic Society.

It is, however, in connection with the develop-ment of the incandescent filament lamp that Swan is best remembered. As a young man he had noted an American patent taken out in 1845 by J. W. Starr (*c.*1822–47) for a lamp in which a platinum filament was electrically heated in an evacuated glass container. Starr suggested a carbon filament as an alternative and from about 1848 Swan actively experimented with this. However, the cur-rent state of other fields of technology limited his progress. Firstly, it was difficult to attain the neces-sary degree of vacuum in the bulbs. Secondly, a steady supply of electricity was obtainable only from batteries. By the 1870s, however, both these difficulties were beginning to disappear. The invention of the high-vacuum pump by H. SPRENGEL in 1865 (of which Swan became aware through the researches of Sir William CROOKES) solved the difficulty of evacuation and a little later the dynamo became available as a source of electricity for wide distribution. Swan resumed his work on the carbon-filament lamp and demonstrated it to

the Newcastle upon Tyne Chemical Society on 18 December 1878. By 1881 he established himself as a manufacturer near Newcastle, using filaments made by carbonization of mercerized cotton threads (see John MERCER). Later (1883) he used filaments made by extruding nitrocellulose dis-solved in acetic acid. This gave him a much-improved product and incidentally led him twenty years later to make artificial silk.

Meanwhile T. A. EDISON had been pursuing simi-lar investigations in the United States and, unlike Swan, had systematically patented his inventions. Inevitably, conflict arose, but in 1882 Edison failed in a patent-infringement action against Swan. Dif-ferences were composed, and the Edison and Swan United Electric Light Company Limited was formed in 1883.

Swan's work was widely recognized. Elected FRS in 1894, he was knighted ten years later.

M. E. Swan and K. R. Swan, *Sir J. W. Swan*. 1929 (reprinted 1968).
Proceedings of the Royal Society, **96A**, ix, 1920.
Dictionary of National Biography.

T I W

SWEDENBORG, EMANUEL Born in Stockholm, 29 January 1688; died London, 29 March 1772. Natural philosopher, religious writer, and mystic.

Swedenborg is commonly remembered as the founder of a religious sect which still has a loyal following. His religious experiences came late in life, however, when he had made contributions to mathematics, science and technology which entitle him to a high place in the annals of science. It has indeed been said of him that 'the number of his discoveries that have had to be repeated later before being recognized as such is probably greater than that of any other man' (H. Dingle).

Swedenborg's father was a Lutheran bishop, and he was brought up in Uppsala. As a young man he travelled widely in Europe and met many of the leading scientists of the day. On his return to Sweden in 1715, Charles XII appointing him Assessor Extraordinary at the Board of Mines, an appointment which marked the beginning of a long and deep interest in mining and metallurgy. In 1724 he was given a more formal appointment of the same kind, which he held until 1747, when he settled in London. His *Regnum subterraneum* (1734), a beautifully illustrated work, gives an excellent account of the mining and smelting tech-niques of his day. In the same year appeared his *Opera Philosophica et Mineralia*, a far-reaching survey of the nature of matter and of the laws of motion, which some historians of science have compared to the *Principia* of NEWTON. In his later years he attempted not only a synthesis of all scien-tific knowledge but sought to include within the same framework an understanding of the nature of the soul. Gradually he became more wrapped in mystical experience and lost interest in rational explanations of phenomena.

G. Trobridge, *Swedenborg: Life and Teaching* (4th ed.). 1935.
S. Lindroth, *Swedish Men of Science*, 1650–1950. 1952.
H. Dingle, *Endeavour*, **17**, 127, 1958. (Portrait.)
S. Toksvig, *Emanuel Swedenborg*. 1948.
Dictionary of Scientific Biography.

T I W

SWINBURNE, SIR JAMES

SWINBURNE, SIR JAMES Born at Inverness, Scotland, 28 February 1858; died Bournemouth, Hampshire, England, 30 March 1958. Electrical engineer.

Son of a naval officer, an Inspecting Officer of Coastguard, in Scotland, James Swinburne was educated at Clifton College under William TILDEN. He served his engineering apprenticeship at a locomotive works in Manchester before going to Tyneside, whence Sir Joseph SWAN sent him in 1880 to establish a lamp factory in France, and later another in Boston, Massachusetts. Joining the dynamo-manufacturing works of R. E. B. CROMPTON as an electrical assistant in 1885, he subsequently became its manager.

In 1899 he set up as an engineering consultant in Victoria Street, London, with his own laboratory and workshop; here his exceptional manual dexterity proved very useful. During his lifetime he took out more than a hundred patents, many of them relating to the generation and distribution of electricity and the improvement of the incandescent-filament lamp. Appreciating the potential of a hard resin obtained from phenol and formaldehyde, he formed in 1904 the Fireproof Celluloid Syndicate Ltd, which, by using caustic soda as a catalyst, considerably accelerated production. Though unluckily anticipated by a day by L. H. BAEKELAND when he filed his patent in 1907, he went on to develop the lacquer Damard. The syndicate was absorbed by the Damard Lacquer Company in 1910 and later by Bakelite Ltd, of which company Swinburne remained chairman till 1948. He was in great demand as an expert witness and achieved fame in many important cases.

Elected to the Royal Society in 1906, for his major contribution to dynamo design and electrical theory, he was only the fifth Fellow who lived to be over a hundred years old. He also set a record with his seventy-three years' membership of the Institution of Electrical Engineers. Gifted in many ways, he was an accomplished musician and set two of Tennyson's poems to music. His title was inherited, the baronetcy dating from 1660.

Biographical Memoirs of Fellows of the Royal Society. 1960. (Portrait.)
Dictionary of National Biography.
Journal of the Plastics Institute, July 1958.
Journal of the Institution of Electrical Engineers, May 1958.

W H G A

SWINTON, ALAN ARCHIBALD CAMPBELL Born in Edinburgh, 18 October 1863; died London, 19 February 1930. Electrical engineer.

Alan Campbell Swinton, educated at Edinburgh and Le Havre, was apprenticed in W. G. Armstrong's engineering firm at Elswick-on-Tyne in 1882. He moved to London in 1887 as electrical contractor and consultant. He was responsible for the development of the new electrical industries, notably the installation of electric lighting. Other new inventions and discoveries which engaged his attention included radiotelegraphy and x-rays. In 1896 he opened the first radiographic laboratory in Britain. Since his school days, photography had been his favourite occupation and he had the distinction of having the x-ray photograph of his hand, the first x-ray photograph published, in *Nature* in January 1896. He also collaborated in

research on the steam turbine with C. A. PARSONS and became a director of the Parsons Marine Steam Turbine Co. Ltd, as well as that of Crompton Parkinson Ltd and of W. T. Henley's Telegraph Works.

In 1908 he published his pioneering ideas on an electrical system for television which finally came into fruition nearly 30 years later in preference to J. L. BAIRD's photomechanical system. He wrote prophetically on shortages of energy resources facing mankind and advocated the use of solar energy as well as the need to lower the resistance of conductors. His elegant style of writing on scientific matters, including his autobiographical memoirs and reminiscences of his scientific contemporaries, provides an important record of the science of his time.

In 1915 he had the rare distinction, for an engineer, of being elected a Fellow of the Royal Society, and he served on its council. He was also Vice-President of the Institution of Electrical Engineers, and President of the Röntgen Society as well as of the Radio Society. He was Chairman of the Royal Society of Arts and a Manager of the Royal Institution. He endowed the British Association for the Advancement of Science and the Royal Society.

Proceedings of the Royal Society, 130, xiii, 1931.
A. A. C. Swinton, *Autobiographical and Other Writings.* 1930. (Portraits.)
J. D. McGee, *Nature,* **138,** 674, 1936.

I M McC

SYDENHAM, THOMAS Born at Wynford Eagle, Dorset, England, in 1624 (baptized 10 September); died London, 1689 (?29 December). Celebrated physician, known as 'the English Hippocrates'.

Sydenham, a member of an old Dorset family, entered Magdalen Hall, Oxford, on 1 July 1643, but within two months joined the Parliamentary Army, and served under his elder brother, who was Commander-in-Chief in Dorset. In 1646 Sydenham returned to Oxford. He was created a bachelor of medicine on 14 April 1648, and was elected a Fellow of All Souls College. On 21 April 1651 he rejoined Cromwell's army as a Captain of Horse, was wounded at Worcester and then returned to Oxford. In 1655 he resigned his Fellowship, married Mary Gee, and started practice as a physician in King Street, Westminster. He now began his study of the agues, smallpox, and other fevers then prevalent in Westminster, and this he continued after his removal in 1664 to his final London home in Pall Mall. In 1663 he was admitted a Licentiate of the Royal College of Physicians. During the Great Plague Sydenham removed temporarily to the country with his wife and family. In 1676 he graduated as a doctor of medicine at Cambridge, where his son was then a student.

Sydenham had little faith in the importance of anatomy, pathology and the use of the microscope. He reintroduced the Hippocratic method of accurate observation at the bedside and precise recording of his observations, and he used his records to build up the general clinical description of individual diseases. His simple cooling regimen for smallpox revolutionized the treatment of that disease, and of other fevers also. He was a pioneer in the use of quinine in the treatment of malaria. For the relief of pain he was the first to use laudanum (opium in fluid form), and in the treatment of the blood disease, chlorosis, he was the first to use preparations of iron. Sydenham's most important work is his treatise on gout, from which he himself suffered. He first described 'Sydenham's chorea' (St Vitus's Dance) and recognized the widespread incidence of hysteria. He was one of the founders of epidemiology, but his views, based on the Hippocratic 'epidemic constitutions', had little subsequent influence.

J. F. Payne, *Thomas Sydenham*. 1900. (Portrait.)
K. Dewhurst, *Dr. Thomas Sydenham*. 1966.
Dictionary of Scientific Biography.
Dictionary of National Biography.

E A U

SYLVESTER, JAMES JOSEPH Born in London, 3 September 1814; died there, 15 March 1897. Prominent mathematician.

Sylvester graduated as Second Wrangler from St John's College, Cambridge, in 1837. He held professional appointments at University College, London (1838–41); Virginia University (1841); the Royal Military Academy, Woolwich (1855–70); Johns Hopkins University (1876–83); and Oxford University (1883–94). He also worked as an actuary in 1844 and was called to the Bar in 1850.

He published over three hundred papers on a variety of topics in pure mathematics, including the theory of numbers; matrices and determinants; the theory of equations; elimination; and Sturm's functions. Many of his ideas arose out of his close friendship with Arthur CAYLEY.

While at Johns Hopkins University, he specialized in the study of modern algebra and the theory of invariants. He was the first editor of the *American Journal of Mathematics*.

He was a gifted musician and poet, and wrote *The Laws of Verse* in 1870.

P. A. MacMahon, *Proceedings of the Royal Society*, **63**, ix, 1898; *Nature*, **55**, 492, 1897.
A. Cayley, *Nature*, **39**, 217, 1889. (Portrait.)
Dictionary of National Biography.
Dictionary of Scientific Biography.

J M D

SYLVIUS, FRANCISCUS (FRANZ DE LE BOË) Born at Hanau, Hessen, Germany, 1614; died Leiden, Netherlands, 14 November 1672. Iatrochemist and famous teacher.

Sylvius studied medicine at Sedan, Leiden, and other universities, and graduated at Basle in 1637. He then practised medicine at Hanau, Paris and Leiden, and lectured unofficially at Leiden. From 1641 he practised successfully in Amsterdam. From 1658 until his death he was professor of medicine at Leiden.

Sylvius represents the culmination of iatrochemistry. His system was particularly related to the acids and bases, and he recognized many salts as the products of interaction between acids and alkalis. He taught that disease is the result of an excess of 'acridity' – i.e. of acid or of alkali – and his therapy was largely based on this principle. He rejected the mystical *archaei* of J. B. van HELMONT, but was much influenced by his work on fermentation. This he applied to the fluids of the body, and he taught that digestion was fermentation. Digestion was carried out by the saliva, the bile, and the pancreatic juice (which he knew from the work of

R. de GRAAF). Although Sylvius probably did little chemical research himself, he founded a very important school, and he established at Leiden his 'Laboratorium', the first chemical laboratory in a university.

Sylvius dissected frequently, and here his work is of lasting value. He had an advanced knowledge of the brain, in which two cerebral veins, a major fissure and an aqueduct are all called after him. He made a great advance in pathology by recognizing the constant presence of tubercles, hitherto unknown structures, in the lungs of phthisical patients, and he described their growth and softening to form cavities. He also recognized tuberculosis of the mediastinal and mesenteric glands.

M. Foster, *Lectures on the History of Physiology*. 1901.
J. R. Partington, *History of Chemistry*, vol. 2. 1961.
E. R. Long, *History of Pathology*. 1928.
H. E. Sigerist, *Great Doctors*. 1933. (Portrait.)
C. L. Dana, *Annals of Medical History*, **1**, 422, 1917. (Portrait.)
E. Ashworth Underwood, *Endeavour*, **31**, 73, 1972. (Portrait.)

E A U

SZENT-GYÖRGYI, ALBERT VON Born in Budapest, 16 September 1893; died Woods Hole, Massachusetts, USA, 22 October 1986. Biochemist and Nobel Laureate.

Born into the Hungarian aristocracy, Szent-Györgyi (pronounced St Georgie) graduated in medicine from the University of Budapest in 1911. A lifelong pacifist, he was discharged from war service in 1917 after deliberately wounding himself in order to continue his postgraduate studies. In 1930, following immersion in physiology, pharmacology and biochemistry with the world's leading research workers, including F. G. HOPKINS at Cambridge and E. C. KENDALL at Rochester, he returned to Hungary as a professor of medical chemistry at Szeged. In 1947, after exciting war experiences as an anti-Nazi, he emigrated to America to direct the Institute of Muscle Research at Woods Hole.

Between 1924 and 1934, Szent-Györgyi resolved the dispute between H. WIELAND and O. WARBUR over the mechanism of cellular respiration by demonstrating that dicarboxylic acids such as fumaric acid acted as catalytic 'go-betweens' in releasing oxygen and hydrogen for purposes of energy production. This 'Szent-Györgyi cycle' became one of the elements in H. KREBS's later elucidation of the citric acid cycle of cell respiration. In related work, Szent-Györgyi showed that ascorbic acid (abundantly present in Hungarian paprikas) was identical to vitamin C and that it played a complementary role as an enzyme in cell respiration. It was for these achievements that he was awarded the Nobel prize for physiology or medicine in 1937.

At Woods Hole he tried to develop quantum mechanical explanations of muscle action while simultaneously articulating controversial views concerning the prevention of cancer using vitamin C. A charismatic, flamboyant man, Szent-Györgyi was a witness to and participant in the emergence of classical biochemistry. It was perhaps inevitable that in old age he was unreceptive to the insights offered by molecular biology.

R. W. Moss, *Free Radical. Albert Szent-Györgyi and the Battle over Vitamin C.* 1987. (Portrait.)
Nobel Lectures in Physiology or Medicine 1922– 1941. 1965
Annual Review of Biochemistry, 32, 1, 1963 (autobiography).
Tyler Wasson (Ed.), *Nobel Prize Winners.* 1987. (Portrait.)

W H B

SZILARD, LEO Born in Budapest, Hungary, 11 February 1898; died La Jolla, California, USA, 30 May 1964. Physicist best known for his work on the nuclear chain reaction.

Szilard's further education began in electrical engineering in Budapest, but after the First World War, when he was drafted into the Austro-Hungarian army, continued in Berlin, where he changed to studying physics. He gained his PhD in physics at the University of Berlin in 1922, and continued to work there until 1933, when he fled Nazi Germany, first for Vienna and then for England. While in England, Szilard realised that it might be possible to use neutrons to break up atomic nuclei and give rise to a nuclear chain reaction, with the release of vast amounts of energy.

Szilard moved to Columbia University in New York in 1938. A year later, together with Walter Zinn (1906–) at Columbia, he showed that uranium-235 undergoes a chain reaction when bombarded by neutrons, and in 1942 he joined Enrico FERMI at Chicago University to work on the production of the first controlled chain reaction, established on 2 December 1942.

After the Second World War, Szilard turned to biology, becoming professor of biophysics at Chicago in 1946. In 1956 he joined the Salk Institute of Biological Sciences at La Jolla in California, where he worked until he died, his interests lying with genetics and immunology.

Physics Today, October 1964.
S. R. Weart and G. W. Szilard (Ed), *Leo Szilard: his version of the facts*, 1978. (Portrait.)

C S

TAKAMINE, JOKICHI Born at Takaoka, Japan, 3 November 1854; died New York, 22 July 1922. Biochemist and industrialist.

The son of a physician, Takamine was brought up in the strict Samurai code, but proceeded to the College of Science and Engineering in Tokyo, from which he graduated in 1879. The Japanese Government sent him for postgraduate study to Glasgow, where he spent two years at the University and Anderson's College. On his return to Japan he entered the Department of Agriculture and Commerce, and was soon made head of the chemistry division; he was also head of the patent office. He left Government service in 1887, however, to take charge of his own factory making superphosphate fertilizers. Meanwhile, in his private laboratory, he was developing a process to make (from a fungus grown on rice) a potent and stable preparation of the starch-digesting enzyme, diastase.

Takamine, who had married an American wife, took up permanent residence in the United States about 1890. There he tried to market his diastase preparation to the brewers under the name of 'Takadiastase'; but the venture did not prosper, until in 1894 it was taken up by the firm of Parke, Davis and Co., with which Takamine remained in close association for the rest of his career. He also acted as consultant to the Japanese Government on matters connected with the chemical industry, and played an important part in establishing in Japan the fixation of nitrogen; the extraction of aluminium; and the manufacture of Bakelite (see L. H. BAEKELAND). He was the recipient of many Japanese honours.

His most important scientific work, the isolation of the hormone adrenalin from an extract of suprarenal glands, was done in his private laboratory (1901). This was the first pure hormone to be isolated from natural sources, and it was soon identified by others and synthesised. The isolation was achieved almost simultaneously by T. B. Aldrich. Curiously, adrenalin proved to be similar in structure to ephedrin, a powerful ingredient of traditional Chinese and Japanese medicine.

K. K. Kawakami, *Jokichi Takamine*. 1928.
Dictionary of American Biography.

W V F

TALBOT, WILLIAM HENRY FOX Born at Melbury House, Dorset, England, 11 February 1800; died Lacock Abbey, Wiltshire, 17 September 1877. Inventor of the negative/positive process of photography.

Fox Talbot, only son of William Davenport Talbot, an officer of Dragoons, was educated at Harrow and at Trinity College, Cambridge (Twelfth Wrangler, 1821, MA 1825). Like many others, Talbot used the *camera obscura* for sketching, which led him to experiment from 1834 onward in fixing the images by chemical means. In 1835 he took a one-inch square photograph of Lacock Abbey, his family seat, on paper coated with silver chloride, and fixed with sodium chloride. He also copied botanical specimens, lace, engravings and manuscripts by superposition on the sensitive paper, and made photomicrographs. The announcement of the daguerreotype (see L. J. M. DAGUERRE) caused Talbot to lay his 'Photogenic Drawing' before the Royal Society on 31 January 1839: the method of manipulation was revealed there three weeks later. Talbot next investigated the light-sensitivity of silver bromide and silver iodide, and discovered (September 1840) that a latent image was produced, which could be developed with gallic acid, of whose accelerating function he had been informed. The exposure required for this faster Calotype (or Talbotype) process, patented in February 1841, was reduced to a minute or two. The paper negatives were made transparent by waxing, and positive prints made by contact copying on silver chloride paper – the negative/positive principle on which present-day photography is based. Talbot published *The Pencil of Nature* (1844–6), the first book illustrated with photographs, demonstrating many applications of photography. He pioneered flash photography of fast-moving objects (1851) by photographing by an electric spark a page of *The Times* attached to a rapidly turning wheel.

Having independently discovered the light-sensitivity of bichromated gelatin, Talbot patented photoglyphy (1852), a method of photo-etching on steel or copper plates, and in 1858 an improved process giving fairly good half-tone rendering by initial exposure of the plate under a piece of folded black gauze, forming a half-tone screen.

Talbot's various patents retarded the progress of photography in Britain until the failure (December 1854) of his claim that the collodion process of Frederick Scott ARCHER was covered by his Calotype patent.

Apart from inventing photography on paper and photoglyphy, Talbot was a distinguished mathematician, and decipherer of Assyrian cuneiform inscriptions. He communicated to the Royal Society, to which he was elected in 1831, a total of fifty-nine papers, chiefly on mathematics.

Helmut and Alison Gernsheim, *The History of Photography*. 1955. (Portrait.)
D. B. Thomas, *The First Negatives*. 1964. (Portrait.)
H. Gernsheim, *Endeavour*, **1** (New Series), 18, 1977.

A. H. Booth, *William Henry Fox Talbot*. 1965.
Dictionary of Scientific Biography.
Dictionary of National Biography.
A. Jammes, *William H. Fox Talbot*. 1973.

H and A G

TANSLEY, SIR ARTHUR GEORGE

TANSLEY, SIR ARTHUR GEORGE Born in London, 15 August 1871; died Grantchester, near Cambridge, 25 November 1955. Botanist.

He attended Highgate School from 1886 to 1889, where at the time chemistry was the only science in the curriculum. From school he entered University College, London, and from F. W. Oliver (1864–1951) received his first instruction in botany – the science he was destined to teach so notably in later years. In 1890 he entered Trinity College, Cambridge, and three years later, after graduating, he returned to University College as Oliver's assistant and demonstrator in the Botany Department. In this period he founded *The New Phytologist*, the periodical he edited for thirty years. At the invitation of Professor A. C. Seward (1863–1941) in 1907 he became University Lecturer in Botany at Cambridge and began an unbroken period of teaching lasting for many years. Tansley sought to make the teaching of botany more dynamic: at the elementary level he fostered the study of a wide selection of plants (particularly Cryptogams). His elementary textbook, *Elements of Plant Biology*, published in 1922, was unique at the time. More importantly, he became a pioneer in the teaching of ecology, urging more field work and the study of habitats from every aspect. He published several 'practical guides', such as *Practical Plant Ecology* (1923), which served to aid and encourage the study of ecology in schools, also some very readable 'texts', such as *Britain's Green Mantle* (1949); from 1917 to 1937 he edited the *Journal of Ecology*.

The end of the First World War left him, like many another, very exhausted and unsettled; his interest turned to psychology and in 1920 he published *The New Psychology and its Relation to Life*.

He resigned his University Lectureship at Cambridge in 1923 and travelled to Austria in order to study with Sigmund FREUD. He returned to his home in Grantchester, however, in 1924 and in 1927 was appointed to the vacant post of Sherardian Professor of Botany at Oxford. The appointment also carried a Fellowship at Magdalen College. In this post he remained for ten years until retirement to his home in Grantchester.

Whilst at Oxford Tansley completed in 1939 the work with which his name will long be associated – *The British Islands and their Vegetation*. The work is a masterly and comprehensive survey of Britain's uncultivated habitats and their native flora. Towards the end of his life Tansley was very active in the public interest, serving on advisory committees whose recommendations ultimately led to the establishment of the Nature Conservancy, of which he was Chairman from 1949 to 1953, and of the Council for the Promotion of Field Studies, of which he was President from 1947 to 1953.

Knighted in 1950. Elected FRS in 1915, and member of Council of the Royal Society, 1931–3. Honorary Fellow of Trinity College, Cambridge, 1944. Gold Medal of the Linnean Society, 1941.

Biographical Memoirs of Fellows of the Royal Society. 1957. (Portrait.)
Dictionary of National Biography.

A P G

TARTAGLIA, NICCOLO (TARTALEA)

TARTAGLIA, NICCOLO (TARTALEA) Born at Brescia, Italy, c.1501; died Venice, 13 December 1557. Mathematician and mechanician.

Tartaglia was brought up in poverty and largely self-educated. He assumed the title 'Tartaglia' (Stammerer) from an impediment resulting from his mutilation by French troops at the sack of Brescia in 1512. By 1521 he was teaching mathematics at Verona, leaving there for Venice in 1534. In 1548 he taught geometry at Brescia, but soon returned to Venice, where he spent the rest of his life.

Tartaglia's first published work, *Nuova scienza* (1537), dealt with the theory of gunnery. It gives evidence of more practical than theoretical knowledge, but was one of the first applications of mathematics to gunnery. He dealt with artillery and fortification again in his *Questi et invenzioni diverse* (1546), dedicated to Henry VIII of England. At the end of this Tartaglia contributes to the famous controversy with CARDANO over the discovery of the solution to the cubic equation. It seems that Scipio del Ferro (c.1510) had found the solution to the cubic lacking the square term, perhaps from an earlier source, revealing the solution to a pupil, Antonio Fiorido. Fiorido in turn challenged Tartaglia to solve such a problem (1535), shortly after he had found, as the result of a challenge by Zoanne de Tonini da Coi (1530), a solution of the cubic without linear term. He applied himself to Fiorido's problem, and solved that also. He confided his methods to Cardano (c.1539), under pledge of secrecy, but Cardano amplified them, finding the method of reducing the general case to one of the special cases, and published the methods in 1545. Cardano's contribution was far from trivial, and the mathematical honours, in what was perhaps the most important achievement in European algebra at that time, must be divided.

Tartaglia's biggest publication, his *Trattato generale* (1556), was perhaps the best mathematical compilation of the time. It covered arithmetic, mensuration, geometry and algebra, and was a valuable synthesis of the practical and commercial mathematics of his century. He also published the first translation of EUCLID into Italian (1543), and the first Latin edition (1543) of ARCHIMEDES, translated by William of Moerbeke (d. c.1281).

Tartaglia's writings, although generally prolix, are often penetrating. Worth mentioning, in addition to his algebra, is his treatment of statics, in the *Trattato generale*, which improved on Jordanus Nemorarius (c.1220) at a time when it was the fashion to do the opposite. Remarkable, too, is the rule, given without proof in the same book, for dividing a number into two parts such that the continued product of the numbers and their difference is a maximum.

A. Favaro *Isis*, **I**, 329, 1913.
Ateneo di Brescia, *Quatro Centenario della Morte de N. Tartaglia*. 1962. (Portrait.)
G. Sarton, *Isis*, **2**, 167, 1914.
Dictionary of Scientific Biography.

J D N

TARTALEA, NICCOLO See TARTAGLIA.

TAYLOR, BROOK Born at Edmonton, London, 18 August 1685, died London, 29 December 1731. Mathematician, physicist, philosopher and artist; mainly remembered by 'Taylor's series'.

Taylor entered St John's College, Cambridge, in 1701, graduating LLB in 1709, LLD in 1714. He was elected FRS in 1712, and was Secretary of the Royal Society 1714–18. He was a close friend of E. HALLEY and NEWTON, and strongly defended Newton's claims in the controversy over the priority of invention of the calculus.

He wrote several papers for the *Philosophical Transactions of the Royal Society* on physical subjects, including dynamics, hydrodynamics, magnetism and heat. Among his mathematical writings the major work was the *Methodus Incrementorum Directa et Inversa* (1715). This included the series named after him and some theorems on interpolation; and it introduced the calculus of finite differences. Among the applications of calculus in this work were the problem of the transverse vibrations of strings and the determination of the differential equation of the path of a ray of light passing through a heterogeneous medium.

Taylor was a gifted musician and artist, applying geometrical methods to the problem of perspective. He wrote *Linear Perspective* in 1715 and *New Principles of Linear Perspective* in 1719; the latter included the principle of vanishing points. He also wrote on religion and philosophy.

He published nothing during his last ten years. A short biography by his grandson, Sir William Young (1749–1815), is contained in Taylor's *Contemplatio Philosophica*, published posthumously in 1793.

W. W. R. Ball, *A Short Account of the History of Mathematics*. 1888. *Dictionary of National Biography*.

Dictionary of Scientific Biography.

J M D

TELFORD, THOMAS Born at Westerkirk, Eskdale, Scotland, 9 August 1757; died Westminster, London, 2 September 1834. Civil engineer.

Thomas Telford was the only child of a shepherd who died in the year of his birth; he worked on farms from a very early age, and at 13 was apprenticed to a stonemason. After working in the new town at Edinburgh, in 1782 he moved to London, where his first employment was at Somerset House. He quickly rose to the superintendence of buildings under construction, and in 1787 became surveyor of public works for Shropshire, which led to his appointment in September 1793 (with the support of John WILKINSON) as engineer for the Ellesmere Canal. At one point this involved the construction of nineteen locks in 16 miles, with a total rise of 132 feet, but its outstanding feature was the provision of two aqueducts. At Chirk the Ceriog was crossed by ten 40-foot arches; at Pont-y-Cysylltau the Dee, by nineteen arches carrying the canal for 1007 feet on piers rising 121 feet above the river. In the former case Telford gave the canal an iron bed; in the latter he placed it in a complete trough of iron.

Telford was concerned in the construction or improvement of several other canals in the West Midlands, and from 1804 onwards was employed by the Government to make the Caledonian Canal. By 1822, when the first vessel went through, the scheme had already cost twice the estimated amount, and it was not effectively completed until 1847. However, Telford's high reputation caused him to be engaged to survey and supervise the works for the Gotha Canal, for which he received a Swedish order of knighthood. In Britain he made a greater mark through his survey of Scotland for the Government in 1802. This resulted in his opening up the Highlands with 920 miles of roads and 1200 bridges and improving many of the Scottish harbours.

As a roadmaker in England and Wales as well as Scotland, his influence was second only to that of J. L. MCADAM. He made the bed for the road level, and placed on it a first layer of large stones laid edgeways; this was covered by a layer of smaller stones, about equally thick, but rising at the centre, and a one-inch binding of gravel. The chief drawback was the high cost of the foundation, which was, however, so durable that a macadam surface was often laid on top by way of renovation (see P. TRÉSAGUET).

It was in connection with the greatest of his roads, the reconstructed mail route from London to Shrewsbury and its extension to Holyhead, that Telford built his greatest bridge. He had built five cast-iron road bridges during his service as county surveyor, and in 1801 argued forcibly for the replacement of London Bridge by a single-arch structure in iron. In 1819–26, accordingly, he used wrought-iron chains for his bridge across the Menai Straits, where a double-track timber roadway 579 feet long was successfully suspended from 153-foot piers on either shore.

J. Rickman (Ed.), *Memoirs*. 1838.

S. Smiles, *Lives of the Engineers*, vol. 3 (revised ed.). 1878.

A. Gibb, *The Story of Telford*. 1935.

B. Bracegirdle and P. H. Miles, *Thomas Telford*. 1973.

Dictionary of National Biography.

T K D

TELLER, EDWARD Born in Budapest, 15 January 1908. Theoretical physicist; 'father' of the H-bomb.

The son of a lawyer, Teller studied physics at Karlsruhe, Munich, Leipzig and Göttingen. After brief spells in Copenhagen and London he emigrated to the USA in 1935 (naturalized 1941), holding chairs of physics at George Washington University (1935–41) and Columbia (1941–2). He then became deeply involved in the Manhattan Project to develop an atomic (fission) bomb, working first with L. SZILARD and E. FERMI in Chicago, and later at Los Alamos. After the war he remained there (on leave from Chicago) to develop the hydrogen (fusion) bomb, the first of which was exploded in 1952. His motivation was fierce anti-Communism: having seen his beloved Hungary despoiled he fervently believed that America must arm for a new conflict which then seemed inevitable. Subsequently, he held appointments in the University of California (Berkeley) devoting himself to theoretical aspects of nuclear fusion and its peaceful application.

R. Jungk, *Brighter than a Thousand Suns*. 1958.

Otto Frisch, *What Little I Remember*. 1979.

(Portrait.)

T I W

TEMIN, HOWARD MARTIN Born in Philadelphia, Pennsylvania, USA, 10 December 1934. Virologist: co-discoverer of reverse transcriptase.

Temin graduated from Swarthmore College, Pennsylvania, in 1955. As a student he had worked in the Institute of Cancer Research, Philadelphia, and subsequently worked on animal virology with R. DULBECCO at Caltech, Pasadena. Together they investigated the filterable virus discovered by Peyton ROUS in 1910: in research for his doctoral thesis Temin developed an analytical technique for measuring the growth of the virus. Further research led him to suspect that certain viruses can alter the genetic code of cells they attack, and this idea he developed after moving to the University of Wisconsin in 1960. This led to his provirus theory, postulating that certain viruses catalyse the copying of viral genes into the host cells' DNA. It remained, however, to demonstrate the existence of such a virus. Many doubted this, holding that genetic information could be transmitted only from RNA and DNA to proteins and not vice versa. Nevertheless, Temin persevered and in 1970 isolated the enzyme, which is now known as reverse transcriptase because it transfers genetic information from viral RNA to cellular DNA. Viruses containing this enzyme are known as retroviruses. These are potentially carcinogenic because the viral DNA can be incorporated into the chromosomal DNA of the host. There is evidence that a retrovirus of HTLV (Human T-cell Lymphoma Virus) is responsible for AIDS (Acquired Immune Deficiency Syndrome).

Reverse transcriptase was isolated independently by David Baltimore (1938–) – who had worked with Temin as a student at the Institute of Cancer Research – at Massachusetts Institute of Technology. In 1975 Temin, Dulbecco and Baltimore shared the Nobel prize for physiology or medicine. Since 1969 he has held professorships in oncology in the University of Wisconsin – Madison.

Tyler Wasson (Ed.), *Nobel Prize Winners.* 1987. (Portrait.)
Les Prix Nobel en 1975. 1976. (Portrait.)
Science, 14 November 1975.

T I W

TENNANT, CHARLES Born at Ochiltree, Ayrshire, Scotland, 3 May 1768; died Glasgow, 10 October 1838. Pioneer chemical industrialist.

Tennant was educated at home and at the parish school, and was then apprenticed as a weaver at Kilbarchan. He studied bleaching at Wellmeadow, before setting up his own bleachfield at Darnley, near Paisley. In 1797 he took out a patent for the manufacture of an improved bleach liquor made from chlorine and milk of lime, instead of from chlorine and potash. In 1802, when he took out an infringement action against several Lancashire bleachers, the patent was proved bad, as the process was shown to have been in prior use. His second patent, in 1799, was for the manufacture of a dry bleaching powder from chlorine and solid slaked lime. Although this patent was taken out in Tennant's name, there is evidence to show that the process was originated by one of his partners, Charles MACINTOSH. The bleaching powder produced had the great advantage of being easily transportable, and was soon being sold to neigh-

bouring bleachers. In 1799 the firm moved to St Rollox, Glasgow, and shortly afterwards Tennant gained financial control of it. The business prospered largely due to the great demand for bleaching powder by the rapidly expanding textile industry, and by 1835 the factory occupied 100 acres and was producing bleaching powder, sulphuric acid, alkalis and soap. It was at one time the largest chemical works in the world.

E. W. D. Tennant, *140 years of the Tennant Companies.* 1937.
W. Alexander, *Chemistry and Industry,* **21**, 411. 1943.
Dictionary of National Biography.

B B K

TENNANT, SMITHSON Born at Selby, Yorkshire, England, 30 November 1761; died Boulogne, France, 22 February 1815. Noted for the discovery of osmium and iridium.

After a year at Edinburgh University as a pupil of Joseph BLACK, Tennant went to Christ's College, Cambridge, and read medicine for one year. He travelled widely abroad; later, his work in agriculture, in running his estates, and in designing lime kilns, occupied much of his time. In spite of these preoccupations Tennant was elected FRS in 1785; graduated in medicine in 1788; and even occupied the chemistry chair at Cambridge for a period from 1813. Though a noted agriculturist in Lincolnshire and Cheddar, he resided at the Temple in London for long periods.

Tennant's first chemical experiment of note was his proof that diamond consists solely of carbon, this being proved by combustion in a gold tube. His classic work came when he studied crude platinum before his assistant, W. H. WOLLASTON, became father of a British school of platinum science. In 1803–4 Tennant worked on a black residue left on dissolving crude platinum in diluted aqua regia, a residue hitherto believed to be graphite. L. N. VAUQUELIN and his pupil H. V. Collet-Descotils (1773–1815) had studied this, but it was left to Tennant to show that two new members of the platinum group were present. One he named iridium because of its coloured salts, while the other he christened osmium from the odour (Gr. *osme*) of its volatile oxide.

In 1804 Tennant became Copley Medallist of the Royal Society.

Dictionary of National Biography.
D. McDonald, *A History of Platinum.* 1960.
A. E. Wales, *Nature,* London, **192**, 1224, 1961.
K. R. Webb, *Journal of the Royal Institute of Chemistry,* **85**, 432, 1961.
Notes and Records of the Royal Society of London, **17**, 77, 1962.

M S

TESLA, NIKOLA Born at Smitjan, Lika (in former Yugoslavia), 9 July 1856; died New York, 7 January 1943. Electrical engineer.

After studying mathematics and physics at Graz Polytechnic, and philosophy at Prague University, Tesla turned for a livelihood to electrical engineering. Working in Budapest in 1881 he invented a telephonic repeater. After further work in France and Germany, he emigrated to the United States in 1884, and there became a naturalized citizen. For a few years he worked on motors and generators with T. A. EDISON, and then joined the Westinghouse Company. In 1888 he developed the first alternating current induction motor, and with his improvements in power transmission revolutionized the industry. Able now to finance his own laboratory, for the next ten years he was a prolific inventor, and held a number of useful patents. A recluse in later years, much of his work was directed toward the transmission of energy without wires.

Transactions of the American Institute of Electrical Engineers, **62**, 76, 1943.
Journal of the Institution of Electrical Engineers, **90**, 457, 1943.
I. Hunt and W. W. Draper, *Lightning in His Hand*. 1964.
J. J. O'Neill, *Prodigal Genius*. 1944.
Dictionary of Scientific Biography.
E. J. Holmgren, *Nature*, **178**, 1426, 1956.

W N S

THALES OF MILETUS Born *c*.624 BC; died *c*.548 BC. Founder of the Ionian school of natural philosophy.

The life and achievements of Thales are involved in some obscurity, but he appears to have studied for a time in Egypt, encountering there new ideas which he introduced into Greek thought. He is presented by tradition as a man of shrewd common sense and political responsibility.

Several geometrical theorems, familiar to us from EUCLID, are ascribed to Thales, though his proofs may well have been lacking in rigour and generality. He is credited with having shown how to determine the height of a pyramid from the length of the shadow cast and how to estimate the distance of a ship from the shore. However, the frequently cited tradition that Thales predicted the solar eclipse of 28 May 585 BC. is now authoritatively rejected as incredible.

Thales initiated the quest for a primary substance of which all things might be conceived to consist. He identified this substance with water, representing the Earth as a disc or a short cylinder floating upon an underlying ocean. He was credited with the knowledge that the lodestone attracts iron.

Thales played a pioneer role in establishing the ideal of a naturalistic interpretation of phenomena that was to characterize much subsequent Greek philosophy and to find its fulfilment in modern science.

W. K. C. Guthrie, *A History of Greek Philosophy*, vol. 1. 1962.
T. L. Heath, *A History of Greek Mathematics*, vol. 1. 1921.
C. H. Kahn, *Journal of Hellenic Studies*, **90**, 99, 1970.
Dictionary of Scientific Biography.

A A

THENARD, LOUIS JACQUES Born at La Louptière, near Noger-sur-Seine, France, 4 May 1777; died Paris, 21 June 1857. Chemist.

A peasant's son, Thenard went to Paris when 17 years old and became laboratory assistant to L. N. VAUQUELIN, who, probably because he came of similar stock, befriended him as well as employed him.

With this encouragement, Thenard rose by 1804 to the position of professor at the *École Polytech-*

nique, in succession to Vauquelin. He also held chairs at the *Collège de France* and in the University of Paris. He became a baron in 1824; a peer of France in 1833; and, in the year of his death, Chancellor of the University of Paris.

After establishing the excellence of his technique by showing that a new acid distilled from meat by P. L. BERTHOLLET was only impure acetic acid, he went on to distinguish, with G. Dupuytren (1777–1835), the sugar in diabetic urine from ordinary sugar, and to classify esters and distinguish them from ethyl ether.

His best work was done in collaboration with J. L. GAY-LUSSAC, whose reserved manner contrasted strongly with his own forceful energy. Following Humphrey DAVY's discovery, by electrolysis, of sodium and potassium, they first repeated the preparation, using a huge battery provided by Napoleon. Then they prepared the metals by a direct chemical method, reducing the caustic alkalis with iron heated to bright redness. In the course of this they detected the evolution of hydrogen, so showing that the caustic alkalis were not simple oxides, but were in some way hydrated. In their investigation of the metals they first made new higher oxides. They obtained nearly anhydrous hydrofluoric acid by distilling fluorspar with sulphuric acid in a lead retort.

They made a great advance in the technique of elementary quantitative organic analysis, using potassium chlorate as oxidizing agent, getting good results on many organic compounds, and finding a number (sugars, starch, wood, gum) which had hydrogen and oxygen in the same proportions as water. These they called carbohydrates. Their method was improved on by J. J. BERZELIUS.

Thenard discovered (1818) hydrogen peroxide, by the action of acids on the various peroxides he had made with Gay-Lussac.

The well-known Thenard's blue, produced by fusion of cobalt oxide and alumina, had been observed by J. G. Gahn (1745–1818), but was rediscovered by Thenard in the course of a search, prompted by J. A. C. CHAPTAL, into blue colours for porcelain.

P. Thenard, *Un grand Français. Le Chimiste Thenard 1777–1857*. 1950. (Written by his son *c*. 1859. Published 1950 with introduction and notes by G. Bouchard.)
J. R. Partington, *History of Chemistry*, vol. 4. 1964. (Portrait.)
M. P. Crosland, *The Society of Arcueil*. 1967. (Portrait.)
Dictionary of Scientific Biography.

F G

THEOPHRASTUS Born at Eresus in Lesbos, Greece, *c*.370 BC; died *c*.285 BC (presumably buried in the Lyceum garden at Athens). The father of scientific botany.

Theophrastus became a pupil of Plato at the Academy, where ARISTOTLE was then working. After Plato's death in 347 BC Theophrastus joined Aristotle during the latter's period at Assos and Mitylene. When Aristotle founded the Peripatetic School at Athens, Theophrastus, his favourite pupil and intimate friend, became his chief assistant; on Aristotle's retirement to Chalcis, Theophrastus became head of the School. It is said that there were 2000 pupils at it. Many came from distant parts of Greece, and Theophrastus employed them in making botanical observations near their homes.

Theophrastus was a prodigious worker and a voluminous writer. His most important work, *Enquiry into Plants*, deals with the description and classification of plants, and a less well-known work, *Causes of Plants*, deals with plant physiology. Of his minor works, the treatise on sense-perception is significant for psychology.

The *Enquiry into Plants* is systematically arranged, and contains numerous first-hand observations. Theophrastus was the first to invent botanical terms, thus making scientific botany possible. In his account of germination he shows that he appreciated the difference between monocotyledons and dicotyledons, and he had a good idea of the relation between flower and fruit in different plants. He thought that plant distribution depended on soil and climate, and he was the first to attempt a general classification.

A. Hort, *Theophrastus*, 2 vols. 1916.

C. Singer, *Studies in the History and Method of Science*, vol. 2. 1921. (Portrait.)

Dictionary of Scientific Biography.

E A U

THEORELL, AXEL HUGO THEODOR Born at Linköping, Sweden, 6 July 1903, died Stockholm, 15 August 1982. Pioneer of the study of the structures and mechanisms of redox enzymes requiring non-protein cofactors.

Theorell graduated in medicine from the Karolinska Institutet, Stockholm, in 1924. His first substantial researches were on the isolation and properties of myoglobin, which he showed to be distinct from haemoglobin. In 1933, he was awarded a Rockefeller Travelling Fellowship to work under Otto WARBURG in Berlin on the old yellow enzyme. With his early electrophoresis apparatus he purified it, and then split it into inactive apo-protein and a yellow pigment, identified as flavin mononucleotide. Spontaneous recombination in stoichiometric proportions occurred in alkaline solution, and activity was regained. After this fundamental work, Warburg called Theorell 'Meister der Enzyme-forschung', which aptly describes his subsequent role in biochemistry.

In 1937 the Biochemistry Department of the Nobel Medical Institute was created in Stockholm, with Theorell as Professor and Å. Åkeson (1914–88) as technician. They were to work there together until Theorell's death. He drew together a small permanent group of researchers, and also attracted many foreign scientists.

A common theme of almost all Theorell's work, on the old yellow enzyme, cytochrome c, peroxidases, catalases, liver alcohol dehydrogenase, and myoglobin – most of which he was the first to purify – was to discover the chemical nature of the linkages between the enzyme apo-protein and the cofactor, whether flavin, haem, or nicotinamide adenine dinucleotide. To this end he developed several techniques such as magnetic susceptibility measurements to study haem proteins, and sensitive fluorimetric methods to study the kinetics and equilibria of reactions between apo-enzymes and their cofactors, and of the overall reactions catalysed by the holo-enzymes. He laid the foundations, theoretical and experimental, for kinetic and

mechanistic studies of pyridine nucleotide linked dehydrogenases. Amongst his many discoveries were the chemical nature of the linkages between apo-protein and haem in cytochrome c and its stereochemical structure; the heterogeneity of myoglobin and liver alcohol dehydrogenase; and the green transient intermediate in the reaction of peroxidase with hydrogen peroxide, which attracted B. Chance to visit the Institute with his fast reaction apparatus and begin work on the mechanisms of peroxidase, catalase and alcohol dehydrogenase. With C-I. Brändén, Theorell initiated the discovery of the 3D-structure of alcohol dehydrogenase by x-ray analysis of the crystals.

When very young, Theorell contracted poliomyelitis, and his left leg was paralysed. However, he made no concessions to this disability, and was greatly helped by his wife Margit, who accompanied him on his many travels abroad. She is a professional pianist, and Theorell was a very talented violinist. They were the centre of the musical life of Stockholm. He was a kind man, a convivial companion, child-like in his enthusiasm for the results of a good experiment, or a satisfactory musical interpretation, and a truly inspiring mentor. In 1955 he was awarded the Nobel prize in physiology or medicine, and in 1959 was elected a Foreign Member of the Royal Society.

Biographical Memoirs of Fellows of the Royal Society, 1983. (Portrait.)

Les Prix Nobel en 1955. 1956. (Portrait.)

Tyler Wasson (Ed.), *Nobel Prize Winners.* 1987. (Portrait.)

K D

THIELE, FRIEDRICH KARL JOHANNES Born at Ratibor, Silesia, 13 May 1865; died Strasbourg, France, 17 April 1918. Organic chemist; proposed the idea of 'partial valency'.

Thiele began to study mathematics at the University of Breslau, but when his father's bookselling business failed he moved to Halle to live with relatives. Here he turned to chemistry, graduated PhD in 1890 under J. Volhard (1834–910), and became *Privatdozent*. In 1893 he was made associate professor in Munich, where, in the congenial school of A. von BAEYER, his best work was done. From 1902 until his death he was professor in Strasbourg, following R. FITTIG. He never married. His hobby was ballooning, and he travelled extensively. During the war of 1914–18 he worked on respirators, though under the handicap of failing health.

Thiele worked extensively on organic compounds of nitrogen, including nitroso- and aminoguanidines; hydrazoic acid and its derivatives; nitramide; and aliphatic azo-compounds. He discovered (1898) the Thiele acetylation reaction for converting quinone to 1:2:4 triacetoxy-benzene. He is best remembered, however, for his studies of unsaturated compounds, which led him to the discovery (1900) of the red hydrocarbon, fulvene; and of addition reactions to conjugated systems, which led him to the concept of 'partial valency' (1899). Thiele believed that two double-bonded atoms might each preserve sufficient 'residual affinity' to confer on an adjacent single bond some characteristics of a double bond; this explained the observed 1:4 addition (with double-bond shift) of halogens to butadiene. Such ideas could easily be taken too far, but they represented an important loosening of the rather rigid concepts of valency previously current.

F. Straus, *Berichte der deutschen Chemischen Gesellschaft*, **60**, 75A, 1927. (Portrait.)
J. R. Partington, *A History of Chemistry*, vol. 4. 1964.
Dictionary of Scientific Biography.

W V F

THIOUT, ANTOINE Born near Vesoul, Haute Saône, France, 1692; died Paris, 1767. Clock- and instrument-maker.

Thiout had left his home in eastern France and set up in business as a clockmaker in Paris by 1724. In that year, and again in 1725, his proposed equation clock, showing solar rather than mean time, was approved by the *Académie Royale*, but seems never to have been made. He made a number of curious clocks, including some repeaters. In improving the timekeeping of his clocks he developed an anchor escapement in which some additional freedom was given to the pendulum. He is remembered particularly as a technical writer, and his *Traité de l'Horlogerie* (1741) shows him to have been in the van of machine-tool innovation. He developed one of the earliest fusee engines, and his screw-cutting lathe incorporated the first toolpost with a longitudinal movement. He became clockmaker to Philippe d'Orléans, French Regent, in 1752.

M. Daumas, *Scientific Instruments of the 17th and 18th Centuries and their Makers.* 1972.

W N S

THOMAS, SIDNEY GILCHRIST Born in London, 16 April 1850; died Paris, 1 February 1885. Made possible the manufacture of steel from phosphoric iron ore.

After leaving Dulwich College, this 17-year-old student had to earn a living as police-court clerk for ten years, but during this time he attended lectures at Birkbeck College and experimented at home. At Birkbeck he heard a reference to the need to eliminate phosphorus in the Bessemer process for steel manufacture, thus rendering useful enormous reserves of phosphatic iron ores. Attempts had previously been made to remove phosphorus as the oxide by adding a basic compound during smelting; one idea was to introduce powdered lime blown in with the blast.

The SIEMENS, Lowthian Bell (1816–1904), and other prominent steel-makers found no solution allowing the exploitation of Cleveland ores and the ores of Lorraine, which Germany had annexed from France in 1871. After experimenting with various basic substances, such as magnesia and lime, Thomas developed the modern lining for furnaces, namely calcined dolomite plus a binder. A cousin, Percy Carlyle GILCHRIST, chemist at the Blaenavon steel works, organized the necessary pilot-scale trials. Later, at Middlesbrough, came further trials, using a converter holding 30 cwt.

Thomas resigned his police-court job, to attend to world-wide demands for licences to use his patented process, while his cousin developed the final stages of the process, but German ironmasters sought to evade royalties, but the Thomas-Gilchrist Process and 'Thomas Slag' – a valuable fertiliser – were fully protected; the discovery brought into use vast deposits of ores not previously workable. Thomas travelled abroad in search of health, but unhappily died young.

J. C. Carr and W. Taplin, *History of the British Steel Industry.* 1962. (Portrait.)
W. T. Jeans, *Creators of the Age of Steel.* 1884.
Dictionary of National Biography.
Lilian Gilchrist (Thomas) Thompson, *Sidney Gilchrist Thomas: An Invention and its Consequences.* 1940.
R. W. Burnie, *Memoir and Letters of Sidney Gilchrist Thomas.* 1891.
Dictionary of Scientific Biography.

M S

THOMPSON, BENJAMIN *See* RUMFORD.

THOMSON, SIR CHARLES WYVILLE Born at Linlithgow, Scotland, 5 March 1830; died there, 10 March 1882. Marine biologist; leader of the *Challenger* expedition.

Wyville Thomson studied medicine at the University of Edinburgh, but poor health prevented his taking a degree before leaving in 1850. In spite of this, he taught botany, zoology and geology at Aberdeen, Cork and Belfast. His interest in life in deep seas made him join exploring expeditions sent out by the Admiralty in the years 1868 to 1870, using the ships *Lightning* and *Porcupine*. These expeditions led to his book *The Depths of the Sea* (1872). In 1869 he became a Fellow of the Royal Society, and the following year professor of natural history in the University of Edinburgh.

His idea of a longer exploring expedition was put into practice in the circumnavigational voyage of the *Challenger* from December 1872 to May 1876; this was sponsored by the British Government and the Royal Society. Thomson became director of the expedition's scientific staff, which included H. N. Moseley (1844–91) and John MURRAY, and on his return to England was knighted and awarded the Royal Society's gold medal. He then directed the *Challenger* Expedition Commission in Edinburgh, which published fifty large volumes of reports on collections made during the voyage. His preliminary account of the expedition appeared in *The Voyage of the Challenger – the Atlantic* (1877). He planned to complete his account with a book on the Pacific section of the voyage, but his death occurred before he could do so.

The *Challenger* voyage aroused great interest, and preliminary reports were published during the journey. The final *Results* are one of the classics of marine biology.

W. A. Herdman, *Founders of Oceanography and their Work.* 1923. (Portrait.)
Margaret Deacon, *Scientists and the Sea 1650– 1900.* 1971.
Dictionary of National Biography.

S J R

THOMSON, SIR GEORGE PAGET Born in Cambridge, England, 3 May 1892; died there, 10 September 1975. Physicist.

G. P. Thomson, son of Sir J. J. THOMPSON, was educated at Trinity College, Cambridge and became a Fellow of Corpus Christi College and lecturer in mathematics (1914). In the war he served in France and later at Farnborough, Hampshire, working on aeronautical problems. He returned to Cambridge in 1919 and was appointed professor of natural philosophy at Aberdeen University, Scotland, in 1922. He began research on applications of wave mechanics in 1925 and in 1927 showed that a beam of electrons passing through a thin metal foil was diffracted. Elected FRS in 1930, he succeeded H. L. Calendar as professor of physics at Imperial College, London, where he continued his work on electron diffraction. Thomson shared the Nobel prize for physics with Clinton J. Davisson (1881–1958) (USA) in 1937.

From about 1932 he became interested in nuclear physics and soon realized its practical potential. In 1939 he alerted the Air Ministry to the feasibility of a uranium bomb; as chairman of the British Committee on Atomic Energy he established the wartime atomic energy project in Britain. He was knighted in 1943. After the war he looked ahead to thermonuclear fusion as a source of power and began work on a method of achieving very high temperatures.

Thomson was Master of Corpus Christi College (1952–62), a member of Government committees concerned with nuclear energy, fuel research and scientific administration, President of the Institute of Physics (1958–60) and of the British Association for the Advancement of Science (1960).

Biographical Memoirs of Fellows of the Royal Society, 1977. (Portrait.)

Margaret Gowing, *Britain and Atomic Energy* 1964.

The Times, 12 September 1977.

Dictionary of Scientific Biography. Supp. II.

N G C

THOMSON, JAMES Born in Belfast, Ireland, 16 February 1822; died Glasgow, Scotland, 8 May 1892. Engineer and physicist.

Thomson was educated at home until 1832, when he went to Glasgow University; he matriculated in 1834 and despite his youth obtained a class prize. After graduating, he held various posts as an engineer, and in 1857 was appointed professor of civil engineering at Belfast, and then (1872) at Glasgow, where his more famous brother William THOMSON, Lord Kelvin, was also a professor. He resigned in 1889.

In 1850 he patented the 'vortex' water wheel, a turbine wheel much smaller than the great wooden or iron wheels then in general use. At Belfast he continued work on problems of whirling fluids, and on the improvement of pumps. In 1849 he published a paper on the effects of pressure in lowering the melting-point of ice, which led to an understanding of glacier flow. His researches on critical temperatures were an extension of the work of his Belfast colleague, Thomas ANDREWS.

Nature, **46**, 129, 1892.

Proceedings of the Royal Society, **53**, i, 1893.

E. King, *Lord Kelvin's Early Home.* 1909. (Portrait.)

Dictionary of National Biography.

D M K

THOMSON, SIR JOSEPH JOHN Born at Cheetham Hill, Manchester, England, 18 December 1856; died Cambridge, 30 August 1940. Physicist, discoverer of the electron.

J. J. Thomson was the son of a bookseller specialising in antique books. J. J. at first intended to become an engineer. He went to Owen's College (now the University of Manchester) at the age of 14, but when his father died two years later the family could not afford the premium for training as an engineer, so he stayed on at Owen's, studying mathematics, physics and chemistry, until he won a scholarship at Trinity College, Cambridge; he went up in 1876 and spent most of every term there until his death. He studied mathematics and was Second Wrangler in 1880.

J. J.'s first important paper was an application of the new and not yet fully accepted electromagnetic theory of James Clerk MAXWELL to the motion of a charged sphere. In this he showed that the sphere would have apparent added mass due to the charge and proportional to the electrostatic energy. This was the first step towards EINSTEIN's famous law of the equivalence of mass and energy.

He won his Fellowship at Trinity with a dissertation showing how a number of physical and chemical effects could be predicted from the laws of mechanics without detailed knowledge of the mechanism. An example is the effect of an electric charge in promoting the condensation of water vapour into drops, which is the foundation of the 'cloud chamber' which his pupil C. T. R. WILSON devised to make visible the tracks of fast-moving atoms.

After graduating, Thomson started work in the Cavendish Laboratory, then under Lord RAYLEIGH. He won the Adams Prize with an essay on vortex rings, of which smoke rings are a familiar example. It was then surmised that atoms may be vortex rings in ether. Though untrue, this view caused J. J. to start experiments on the discharge of electricity through gases, a subject which led him to his greatest discoveries. In 1884 he succeeded Rayleigh as Cavendish Professor.

The discovery of x-rays led to increased study of the cathode rays which produce them. The nature of these latter rays had been much disputed. German physicists mostly believed they were some process in the ether, while the British and French thought them particles. One of the strongest arguments against this latter view was an experiment by H. R. HERTZ which appeared to show that cathode rays are not deflected in an electric field, such as should exist between two parallel metal plates each connected to one pole of a battery. Thomson was able to show in 1897 that the failure of Hertz's experiment was due to the 'vacuum' through which the cathode rays passed not being good enough, the residual gas forming charged particles which neutralized the expected field. By improving the vacuum Thomson got deflections which, combined with the long-known deflections by a magnet, determined the ratio of the charge to the mass of the supposed particles. This ratio e/m was over 1000 times larger than the ratio for hydrogen, the lightest atom known. Thomson considered that this was due to the smallness of the mass, and that particles with this small mass were universal constituents of matter, since they were the same whatever the chemical nature of the gas carrying the discharge and the electrodes through which it entered and left. He examined two other cases of the discharge of electricity, namely those from a hot wire negatively charged and from a negatively charged zinc plate illuminated by ultraviolet light. In both he found charged particles with the same e/m ratio as the cathode rays, and in the second was able to measure the actual charge by condensing drops of water on the particles to form a mist, finding the size of the drops from their rate of fall. The result agreed with the supposed value of the charge on a hydrogen atom as far as this was then known. Thomson called these new light particles 'corpuscles', but later adopted the word 'electron', invented a few years before by G. J. STONEY for the charge on a hydrogen atom regarded as a natural unit of charge.

In the next ten years J. J. and his research students discovered many of the properties of these new particles both as conductors of electricity in gases and as components of atoms.

Later he turned to the positively electrified particles in gas discharges and by measuring their e/m ratio showed that they all have masses of atomic magnitude. They are of many kinds and this work was the beginning of the method of analysis now called mass spectrography, extensively used in oil and other technologies. In conjunction with F. W. ASTON, Thomson found strong evidence that the elementary gas neon has atoms of at least two different weights. After the First World War, Aston, with a much-improved apparatus, confirmed the existence of three kinds of neon atoms (isotopes) and further showed that the great majority of chemical elements are complex in a similar way (see F. SODDY).

In 1918, Thomson was appointed Master of Trinity College by the Crown. When peace came he resigned the Cavendish Professorship. The University appointed him to an honorary chair which enabled him to continue to work in the laboratory.

Though Thomson was an excellent mathematician he made his discoveries primarily by an insight into the physical nature of the world, which the mathematics made precise, and by a flair for devising experiments which went straight to the point. He is important in science not only for his own work but as the leader of a group of research workers, who made the Cavendish Laboratory world-famous.

He received the Nobel prize for physics in 1906 and the Order of Merit in 1912, and was knighted in 1908.

J. J. Thomson, *Recollections and Reflections*. 1936.
Lord Rayleigh, *The Life of J. J. Thomson*. 1942.
G. P. Thomson, *J. J. Thomson and the Cavendish Laboratory in his Day*. 1965.
Obituary Notices of Fellows of the Royal Society. 1941. (Portrait.)
Dictionary of National Biography.
Dictionary of Scientific Biography.

G P T

THOMSON, WILLIAM (BARON KELVIN OF LARGS) Born in Belfast, Ireland, 26 June 1824; died Netherhall, Largs, Ayrshire, Scotland, 17 December 1907. Made many contributions to theoretical and experimental physics.

Son of James Thomson (1786–1849), professor of mathematics first at the Academical Institution, Belfast, and then (1832) at the University of Glasgow, William Thomson was an extremely precocious child, matriculating at the University of Glasgow in 1834 at the age of 10. In 1841 he entered Peterhouse, Cambridge, where he graduated Second Wrangler and First Smith's Prizeman

in 1845. In 1846 he was elected a Fellow of Peterhouse and in the same year became professor of natural philosophy in Glasgow, a position he held for the next fifty-three years in spite of many invitations to move elsewhere. At Glasgow he organized one of the first physical laboratories for students in the British Isles. At an historic meeting of the British Association in 1847 Thomson intervened on behalf of J. P. JOULE, the beginning of an extended collaboration between the two. In 1884 he delivered his famous Baltimore lectures on electrodynamics, first published (with additions) in 1904. He became a Foreign Associate of the *Académie des Sciences* in 1877 and was President of the Royal Society from 1890 to 1895. Thomson was knighted in 1866 for his contribution to the laying of the first Atlantic cable, and in 1892 he was made a peer. On retiring from his university chair in 1895 he characteristically had himself enrolled as a research student.

Michael FARADAY and Thomson were jointly responsible for initiating the theory of electromagnetic field. In one of his earliest papers (1842) Thomson compared the distribution of electrostatic force in a region containing electrified conductors with the distribution of heat in an infinite solid. This comparison was important not for its mathematical analogy but for the physical realization that the theory of electrostatics, previously regarded as necessarily based on action at a distance, could be interpreted in a similar way to the theory of heat based on action by contact. This idea was followed by a fundamental paper (1847) setting up an analogy between the electrostatic field and an incompressible elastic solid which suggested the possibility of expressing propositions concerning electricity and magnetism in a manner analogous to those expressing changes of displacement in an elastic solid. This paper seems to have exercised a decisive influence on J. Clerk MAXWELL in his construction of models to represent the electromagnetic field. In a memoir of 1851 Thomson derived the results of POISSON's theory of magnetism from experimental data without using the hypotheses of magnetic fluids, introducing for the first time the vectors later termed magnetic induction and magnetic force by Maxwell. In a fundamental paper, he derived a result expressing the energy of a system of permanent and temporary magnets in terms of a volume integral throughout space. The emergence of the same result for a system of circuits carrying steady currents suggested that in both cases energy could be regarded as stored throughout the field. Other important electrical papers by Thomson included one on the oscillatory discharges of a Leyden jar (1853), the beginning of the theory of electrical oscillations, and a series of papers on telegraphic signalling by wires which played an important part in the successful laying of the first Atlantic cable.

Thomson's contributions to thermodynamics were comparable in importance with those to electricity and magnetism. In 1848 he suggested an absolute scale of temperature based on the theorem of Sadi CARNOT. In 1849 he published a detailed account of Carnot's theorem emphasizing the incompatibility between Carnot's proof and the new mechanical theory of heat. It was not until 1851 that he was able to reconcile the two theorems. There resulted a formulation of the second law of thermodynamics equivalent to, but independent of, that given by R. J. E. CLAUSIUS in the preceding year. In the same year there appeared Thomson's great memoir *On the Dynamical Theory of Heat*, full of ingenious applications of the new laws of thermodynamics, including the definitive introduction of the absolute (Kelvin) scale of temperature. In 1852 there appeared two further important memoirs on available energy and on the dissipation of mechanical energy. During the period 1850–60 he carried out researches on thermoelectric effects which included the discovery of the so-called Thomson Heat Effect. He also made important original contributions to elasticity, hydrodynamics and geophysical questions.

Thomson constructed a large number of instruments, of which the most important were his siphon recorder for telegraphy; a tide predictor; and a mirror galvanometer. He also made important improvements to the mariner's compass. He was the leading member of the British Association Committee on Electrical Standards, whose final system of units was effectively that later adopted by international agreement.

In his own lifetime Lord Kelvin was the acknowledged leader of the physical sciences in the British Isles. If his reputation has diminished somewhat since his death, his early papers on electromagnetism and his papers on heat, especially his great memoir of 1851, provide an enduring proof of his scientific genius.

Kelvin's Collected Mathematical and Physical Papers (6 vols). 1882–1911.
S. P. Thompson, *Life of Lord Kelvin* (2 vols). 1901.
A. Russell, *Lord Kelvin*. 1938.
Nature, **77**, 175, 1907.
Proceedings of the Royal Society, **81A**, iii, 1908.
Agnes King (niece), *Kelvin the Man*. 1925.
Dictionary of Scientific Biography.
Dictionary of National Biography.

J W H

THORPE, SIR THOMAS EDWARD Born near Manchester, England, 8 December 1845; died Salcombe, Devon, 23 February 1925. Chemist, physicist, and historian of science.

Thorpe graduated in chemistry at Owen's College, Manchester, and continued his studies in Heidelberg (with R. W. BUNSEN) and Bonn (with F. A. KEKULÉ). On his return he occupied chairs successively at Anderson's College, Glasgow (1870–4); the newly founded Yorkshire College at Leeds (1874–85); and the Royal College of Science, London (for two periods; 1885–94 and 1909–12). From 1894 to 1909 he was the first Government Chemist. He married, but left no children.

Thorpe began his career by studying, with Sir Henry ROSCOE, the chemistry of vanadium, and most of his later work was in the fields of inorganic and analytical chemistry. He wrote textbooks on both of these subjects, and made accurate determinations of many atomic weights. His interest in applied chemistry led to the compilation of his famous *Dictionary of Applied Chemistry* (first edition, 1893) and to his appointment as Government Chemist, where he was in charge of a laboratory mainly concerned with analytical investigations for revenue purposes. As an historian, he is remembered for his book on Joseph PRIESTLEY

(1906); some of his other writings are collected in *Essays in Historical Chemistry* (1894). He also participated in four eclipse expeditions, and carried out with Sir A. Rücker (1848–1915) a magnetic survey of the British Isles (1884–8).

Thorpe was elected FRS in 1876, and was knighted in 1909, on his retirement from Government service.

P. P. Bedson, *Journal of the Chemical Society*, 1031, 1926. (Portrait.)
Dictionary of National Biography.

W V F

THUNBERG, CARL PER Born at Jönköping, Sweden, 11 November 1743; died Uppsala, 8 August 1828. Botanical explorer; professor of medicine and natural history at Uppsala University.

Thunberg entered the University of Uppsala in 1761 to study medicine. While there he became a pupil of LINNAEUS, forming one of the group of students whose botanical explorations provided material for the work of Linnaeus and other European botanists. After taking the degree of Doctor of Medicine in 1770, he studied in Paris for a year, before travelling as a surgeon to the Dutch colony in Capetown, where he arrived in April 1772. The journey was made as the first stage of a collecting trip that was to lead to Japan, a country still virtually closed to all foreigners except those employed by the Dutch East India Company. During almost three years at the Cape, Thunberg collected over three thousand species of plants, including more than a thousand new to science. On two of his journeys he was accompanied by the English collector, Francis Masson (1741–1805). Thunberg was the first great botanical explorer to work in this region, and he sent valuable collections of both plants and insects back to Europe.

In 1775 he travelled on to Japan, arriving in August at Nagasaki, where the Dutch East India Company had a trading station on the nearby island of Deshima. Although restrictions on the movements of foreigners gave Thunberg no opportunity of making long botanical excursions, he nevertheless formed large collections of plants. These plants were the first to be sent back to Europe from Japan since the collection of Engelbert Kaempfer (1651–1715) in 1690. Thunberg left Japan late in 1776, and spent some time in Batavia, Colombo, Capetown and London on his way back to Sweden, which he reached in March 1779.

In 1778 he had been appointed demonstrator in botany at Uppsala; in 1781 he became an assistant professor, and in 1784, after the death of Linnaeus the younger (1741–83), who had succeeded his father as professor in 1778, he was given the professorship, which he held until his death in 1828. In 1807 the university botanic garden was moved to the grounds of Uppsala Castle, where a museum formed part of the new buildings. This museum housed Thunberg's natural history collections, including his herbarium, which he had given to the University in 1785, a gift that partly filled the gap left by the sale of Linnaeus's collections to Sir James Smith (1759–1828), founder of the Linnean Society of London.

Thunberg's importance as a botanical explorer of both the Cape and Japan is underlined by his publication of floras of both regions: *Flora Japon-*

ica, issued in 1784, with its companion, *Icones Plantarum Japonicarum*, 1794–1805, and *Prodromus Plantarum Capensis*, 1794–1800, followed by *Flora Capensis*, 1807–23, which was finished and edited by the German botanist J. A. Schultes (1773–1831).

Thunberg was never able to carry out his plan of publishing an illustrated flora of the Cape, but he did produce many shorter botanical works dealing with the plants of this and other regions. His travel diaries appeared in four languages: Swedish in 1788–93, German in 1792–4, English in 1794–5, and French in 1794. The English version went into three editions. The published account is supplemented by letters and other manuscripts written during his journeys and sent to correspondents in Europe, including Linnaeus.

H. O. Juel, *Plantae Thunbergianae*. 1918. (Portrait.)

J. H. Verduyn den Boer, *Botanists at the Cape*, vol. 1. 1929.

S. Lindroth (Ed.), *Swedish Men of Science*. 1952.

N. Svedelius, *Isis*, **35**, 128, 1944.

S J R

TIEMANN, JOHANN CARL WILHELM FERDI-NAND Born at Rübeland, Harz Mountains, Germany, 10 June 1848; died Meran, South Tyrol, Austria, 14 November 1899. Organic chemist and teacher.

After a brief apprenticeship to a druggist, Tiemann entered the University of Berlin to study chemistry under A. W. von HOFMANN, whose brother-in-law he later became. Except for service in the Franco-Prussian War, he remained in this department all his life, first as assistant, then *Privatdozent* (1878), and finally extraordinary professor (1882). Worsening health compelled him to spend the winter of 1899 in the South, where he died of a heart attack, leaving a widow and three children.

Tiemann was primarily an organic chemist, though he also did much work on water analysis and purification. He had the reputation of a fine teacher, and his lectures were popular. He and his pupils published many papers on amidoximes and related compounds, and established the constitution of the amino-sugar glucosamine, obtained from lobster-shells. His main research, however, was in the field of plant products, notably essential oils and glucosides. In this connection, he took up and extended a reaction discovered (1876) by C. L. Reimer (1856–1921) (another of Hofmann's assistants); this reaction, in which hydroxy-aldehydes are synthesized by the action of chloroform and alkali on a phenol, is usually known by their joint names. His work was of great importance to the growing synthetic perfume industry, in which he had a financial interest; but his later work on ionone (the perfume of violets) involved him in tedious and exhausting legal proceedings. He was editor of the *Berichte* of the German Chemical Society 1882–97.

O. N. Witt, *Berichte der deutschen Chemischen Gesellschaft*, **34**, 4403, 1901. (Portrait.)

W V F

TILDEN, SIR WILLIAM AUGUSTUS Born in London, 15 August 1842; died there, 11 December 1926. Pioneer of terpene chemistry, teacher, and historian.

After a somewhat irregular education, Tilden was apprenticed to a London pharmacist. His employer encouraged him to attend the lectures of A. W. von HOFMANN, and he was befriended by J. Stenhouse (1809–80), whose influence gained him the post of demonstrator to the Pharmaceutical Society. During this period (1863–72), he was awarded the DSc of London University for his research work. For the next eight years he was senior science master at Clifton College, Bristol, where he continued to do research, under rather difficult conditions, partly in collaboration with his colleague W. A. Shenstone (1850–1908). In 1880 he was appointed professor of chemistry at the newly founded Mason College, Birmingham (later Birmingham University), where he had an uphill task to establish his new department. He left in 1894 to become professor in the Royal College of Science, South Kensington, where he remained until his retirement in 1909.

Tilden's early work at the Pharmaceutical Society concerned alkaloids and the active principles (aloins) of bitter aloes. In 1874, however, he isolated and characterized nitrosyl chloride, and studied its reactions with organic substances. With turpentine it gave a crystalline nitrosochloride, and Tilden realized that he had a key to the complex problems of terpene chemistry, which then became his major research interest. In 1884 he published an important paper on the decomposition of terpenes at very high temperatures, a foreshadowing of the 'cracking' process now so widely used in the petrochemicals industry. Among the products was the unsaturated hydrocarbon isoprene, which Tilden showed (1892) could be polymerized to a synthetic rubber, but the industrial application of this reaction was long delayed.

Tilden also investigated the specific heats of the elements, and their relationship with temperature, and Dulong and Petit's Law (see P. L. DULONG and A. T. PETIT). He was the author of several books, mostly relating to the history of chemistry.

Tilden was twice married, and had one son. Among other honours, he was elected FRS in 1880, and knighted in 1909.

Journal of the Chemical Society, 3190, 1927. (Portrait.)

Proceedings of the Royal Society, **117 A**, i, 1927–8. (Portrait.)

W V F

TINBERGEN, NIKOLAAS Born in The Hague, Netherlands, 15 April 1907; died Oxford, England, 21 December 1988. Co-founder of the discipline of ethology.

Niko Tinbergen, the son of a grammar school teacher, came from a distinguished family which produced two Nobel prize winners (Niko in medicine and his eldest brother Jan in economics), the Director of Energy in The Hague, and another zoologist who died just as a potentially distinguished career was unfolding. He was not a dedicated schoolboy, and spent much of his schooldays studying natural history. On leaving school, influenced by Paul Ehrenfest, the theoretical physicist (1880–1933), he spent several months at Vogelwarte Rossitten, a bird observatory, and as a result decided to study zoology at Leiden University. He was not a distinguished student, spending most of his energy on hockey or his own natural history pursuits. However, he was influenced by a number of amateur and professional natural historians and eventually received the PhD degree for a thesis only 32 pages long. He then went to Greenland, where he studied snow buntings and aspects of Inuit (Eskimo) life. The observations he made during this trip formed the basis of much of his later thinking. He taught at Leiden from 1933 where, after enduring a spell in a hostage camp, he became a full professor in 1947. In 1949 he moved to a lectureship at Oxford, where he built up a very active group of colleagues and students. In 1937 Tinbergen had spent some time with Konrad LORENZ in Austria, and with him is to be regarded as the founder of ethology, the objective study of animal behaviour. Lorenz, Tinbergen and Karl von FRISCH jointly received the Nobel prize in physiology or medicine in 1973.

One of Tinbergen's contributions has been to emphasise the distinction between the four basic questions about behaviour: its immediate causation, its development, its function and its evolution, while at the same time showing how they are interrelated. His first major book, *The Study of Instinct* (1951) contained 127 pages on causation but only 24 on development, 34 on function, and 26 on evolution. Much of his early work on causation concerned the homing of insects (e.g. *Philanthus* species) and the courtship of the three-spined stickleback (*Gasterosteus aculeatus*) and focused on the nature of the stimuli that elicit behaviour and the manner in which behaviour is organised. From the 1950s onwards, however, Tinbergen concentrated on questions of function ('What is this behaviour for? ') and on evolution ('How did it evolve? '). Here he worked primarily with gulls (*Larus* species), and his work was characterized by ingenious field experiments and observation.

Tinbergen was a remarkably unselfish scientist, who put a great deal of his energies into training students and into spreading knowledge of ethological principles amongst scientists and laymen. His influence has been enormous, spreading into the social as well as other biological sciences. He inculcated an extraordinary feeling of common enterprise amongst those who worked with him. He was primarily an experimentalist, but most of his experiments were conducted in the field. Although his partnership with Lorenz is often cited, in fact they were very different men who gave rise to two rather different ethologies. Tinbergen also sponsored a great deal of research in Africa, and devoted considerable attention to the application of ethological principles to human behaviour, the latter concerned especially with the problem of war and with environmental issues.

G. P. Baerends, *Arden*, **77**, 129, 1989.
Biographical Memoirs of Fellows of the Royal Society, 1990. (Portrait.)
Tyler Wasson (Ed.), *Nobel Prize Winners*. 1987. (Portrait.)
Les Prix Nobel en 1973. 1974. (Portrait.)
M. S. Dawkins, T. R. Halliday and R. Dawkins (Eds), *The Tinbergen Legacy*. 1992.

R A H

TING, SAMUEL CHAO CHUNG Born in Ann Arbor, Michigan, USA, 27 January 1936. Experimental particle physicist.

Ting was born in the USA of Chinese parents while his father was studying at the University of Michigan. He was brought up in China and later in Taiwan, but came to the US to study at Michigan himself, where he graduated in 1959 and gained his PhD in 1962. After a year at CERN, the European particle physics laboratory near Geneva, he joined Columbia University in 1964, and then moved to the Massachusetts Institute of Technology in 1969, where he has since remained.

In the early 1970s, Ting and his colleagues proposed an experiment for the proton accelerator at the Brookhaven National Laboratory to measure the production of electron-positron pairs in proton collisions. The experiment began in the summer of 1974, and by early September the team had found a narrow peak in the number of electron-positron pairs they detected. This was interpreted as a new particle, now called the J/psi. The particle was found independently at the same time by Burton RICHTER's team at the SPEAR machine at the Stanford Linear Accelerator Center. Ting and Richter shared the Nobel prize for physics for this discovery in 1976.

Ting has since built important experiments on the PETRA machine at DESY in Germany, where his experiments along with others revealed the gluon that transmits the strong force, and at the Large Electron Positron collider (LEP) at CERN.

Physics Today, December 1976. (Portrait.)
Les Prix Nobel en 1976. 1977. (Portrait.)
New Scientist, 21 October 1976
Tyler Wasson (Ed.), *Nobel Prize Winners*. 1987. (Portrait.)

C S

TISELIUS, ARNE WILHELM KAURIN Born in Stockholm, 10 August 1902; died Uppsala, 29 October 1971. Biochemist.

Tiselius studied chemistry, physics and mathematics at the University of Uppsala. He did his graduate studies for The Svedberg (1884–1971) at the same university and presented his PhD thesis in 1930. He was assistant professor in physical chemistry (1930–37) and subsequently professor in biochemistry 1937–67. His first studies with Svedberg were on certain aspects of ultracentrifugation, but his interest rapidly focused on electrophoresis of proteins. His thesis entitled 'The Moving Boundary Method of Studying the Electrophoresis of Proteins' is a thorough study of the behaviour of proteins in an electric field in the so-called U-tube which he invented. The results demonstrated that such biological 'colloids' as proteins were in fact composed of different species of discrete macromolecules that were homogeneous in the same sense as ordinary low molecular weight compounds. Thus, Tiselius's work with electrophoresis confirmed what Svedberg had earlier found with the ultracentrifuge. In the 1930s, Tiselius introduced several improvements on the electrophoresis technique. An electrophoresis cell was constructed with a rectangular instead of circular cross-section. By this change, the sensitivity of the optical detection system was increased and the Joule heat generated was more efficiently dissipated. Furthermore, the experiments were carried out at a temperature of 0–4°C, at which the solutions used had their density maxima. These improvements eliminated to a great extent convective disturbances and made electrophoresis an exact and powerful analytical tool in biochemistry. Important results from the application of the new technique soon followed. It was, for example, shown by Tiselius and co-workers that blood serum contains at least four classes of proteins, designated albumin and α-, β- and γ-globumin respectively.

Tiselius also made fundamental contributions to our knowledge of adsorption phenomena, particularly by the application of chromatography to proteins. He developed the general techniques of chromatography: for example, elution, gradient, and displacement chromatography. He introduced the use of calcium phosphate as a non-denaturating adsorbent for protein chromatography.

In 1946 Tiselius became head of a new Institute of Biochemistry in Uppsala which has become a very active centre for developing new separation techniques in biochemistry. In 1948 he was awarded the Nobel prize in chemistry for his work on electrophoresis and adsorption analysis, and in particular for his discovery of the complex nature of the serum proteins. He was elected a Foreign Fellow of the Royal Society in 1957.

Tiselius played a very active and important role in Swedish society after the Second World War. He took the initiative in starting the Swedish Natural Science Research Council and a government advisory committee on general research policy. Politicians and government officials listened to him and took his advice seriously; he was thus a very important link in the communication between science and government in Sweden. He also worked in various international scientific organizations. He was President 1951–55 of IUPAC (International Union of Pure and Applied Chemistry) and was one of the founders of EMBO (European Molecular Biology Organization). He also took an active part in the Pugwash movement.

Reflections from Both Sides of the Counter, (autobiographic review), *Annual Review of Biochemistry*, **37**, 1, 1968.
Biographical Memoirs of Fellows of the Royal Society. 1974. (Portrait.)
Dictionary of Scientific Biography.
Tyler Wasson (Ed.), *Nobel Prize Winners*. 1987. (Portrait.)

P-Å A

TIZARD, SIR HENRY THOMAS Born at Gillingham, Kent, England, 23 August 1885; died Fareham, Hampshire, 9 October 1959. Physical chemist; best known for his leadership in bringing together scientists and serving officers to meet the threat of German air attack on Britain.

Tizard's father was Assistant Hydrographer of the Royal Navy; he himself expected to become a naval officer, but this was precluded by an eye defect discovered while he was at preparatory school. Instead, he became an Exhibitioner at Westminster School, London, and there developed a liking for science, especially chemistry. He went to Magdalen College, Oxford, with a demyship (scholarship) in 1904, and took Mathematical Moderations in 1905. He graduated in chemistry in 1908, and went to Berlin to work with W. H. NERNST, in whose laboratory he met F. A. LINDEMANN (later Lord Cherwell). He returned to Oxford in 1909, and started to work on the sensitiveness of indicators. With a Fellow-

ship of Oriel College from 1911 onwards, he appeared to be comfortably set; but his misgivings regarding too much comfort were confirmed by the outbreak of the First World War, most of which he spent as an experimental pilot in the Royal Flying Corps. By 1918 he was a lieutenant-colonel, and Controller (Research and Experiment) for Aircraft at the Ministry of Munitions.

After the war he returned to Oxford, and did notable work with D. R. Pye (1886–1960) on aircraft fuels, one result of which was the modern system of octane rating. He was made reader in thermodynamics in 1920, but left in the same year to be Assistant Secretary of the Department of Scientific and Industrial Research, with special responsibility for co-ordinating research for the three services. In 1927 he became Permanent Secretary, but left in 1929 to be Rector of Imperial College, London. At the same time he was chairman of the Aeronautical Research Committee. He pressed hard for more science to be taught in schools, and was president of the Education Section of the British Association in 1934.

When the Hitler threat crystallized after 1933, Tizard was invited to become chairman of the Committee for the Scientific Survey of Air Defence, and it was here that his greatest work was done. The Committee fostered the development of radar (see R. A. WATSON-WATT), and Tizard's special and vital contribution was to bring scientists and serving officers together in thinking about the many problems, and to insist that it was not enough to have good scientific equipment – you must also have a Service educated to use it. Tizard had enough faith in radar to get the Royal Air Force to work out the organization for using it before the equipment was actually available. This foresight may well have made the difference between victory and defeat in the Battle of Britain in 1940.

Tizard's Scientific Mission to the United States in 1940 provided an intense stimulus to defence science in America. While he suffered in the Second World War from Churchill's preference for Cherwell, he nevertheless did much valuable work before he left Whitehall to be President of Magdalen College, Oxford, in 1942. He was recalled in 1946 to the Ministry of Defence as chairman of the Defence Policy Research Committee and of the Advisory Council on Scientific Policy, from which he retired in 1952.

His many honours included the Air Force Cross (1918); GCB (1949); the Medal for Merit – a direct award from the President of the United States (1947); the Gold Medals of the Royal Society of Arts (1944) and of the Franklin Institute (1946); the Messel Gold Medal of the Society of Chemical Industry (1952); and honorary Doctorates from ten universities. He was elected FRS in 1926, and was a Vice-President of the Society on two occasions (1940–1 and 1944–5). He was President of the British Association for the Advancement of Science in 1948.

Biographical Memoirs of Fellows of the Royal Society. 1961. (Portrait.)
R. V. Jones, *Journal of the Royal Aeronautical Society*, **68**, 789, 1964; *Nature*, **205**, 943, 1965.
R. W. Clark, *Tizard*. 1965; *Minerva*, **4**, 202, 1966.
Dictionary of National Biography.

R V J

TODD, ALEXANDER ROBERTUS (BARON TODD OF TRUMPINGTON) Born in Glasgow, Scotland, 2 October, 1907. Bio-organic chemist.

Todd was educated at the Universities of Glasgow and Frankfurt-am-Main, Germany. He worked on bile acids and anthocyanins at the Dyson Perrins Laboratory, Oxford, under Sir Robert ROBINSON. In 1934 Todd investigated the chemical structure of vitamin B_1 at the University of Edinburgh, continuing in 1936 at the Lister Institute, London. He isolated β-tocopherol, a component of vitamin E, and began work to devise syntheses of both β- and α-tocopherol. He also investigated the active principles of *Cannabis indica*.

In 1938 Todd became Sir Samuel Hall Professor of Chemistry in the University of Manchester, where he completed his work on vitamin E and the synthesis of α-tocopherol and mounted a comprehensive research programme on nucleoside synthesis, the phosphorylation of nucleosides, nucleotide synthesis, co-enzymes, and nucleic acids. He also became a member of the Dyestuffs Division research panel of ICI, with Robinson and I. M. HEILBRON. He was elected FRS in 1942.

Moving to Cambridge as head of the chemistry department in 1944, Todd continued his ambitious research programme. He synthesized the co-enzyme adenosine triphosphate (ATP), investigated polynucleotide synthesis, the chemical structures of blood anticoagulants, penicillin, and the colouring matter of the haemolymph of aphids. In 1951 he announced his results on the structures of the nucleic acids at the 75th Anniversary Meeting of the American Chemical Society. By 1955 he had, with A. W. Johnson (1917–82), elucidated the structure of vitamin B_{12}. He was awarded the Davy (1949), Royal (1955) and Copley (1970) Medals of the Royal Society of London and in 1957 he received the Nobel prize for chemistry.

Todd has been honoured by universities and institutions world wide. He was President of the British Association for the Advancement of Science in 1970 and of the Royal Society of London (1975–80). In 1962 he was created a life peer and became member of the Order of Merit in 1977. His scientific advice has been sought by the Government and other bodies; he served on the Council on Scientific Policy (1947–63), the Chemical Board of the Ministry of Supply (1948–52), and as a trustee of the Nuffield Foundation (1950–79). In 1954 he became a trustee of Churchill College, Cambridge. He was Master of Christ's College, Cambridge (1963–78) and first Chancellor of the University of Strathclyde (1965–91).

A. R. Todd, *A Time to Remember* (autobiography), 1983. (Portrait.)
Les Prix Nobel en 1957. 1958. (Portrait.)
W. A. Campbell and N. N. Greenwood (Eds), *Contemporary British Chemists.* 1971. (Portrait.)
Tyler Wasson (Ed.), *Nobel Prize Winners.* 1987. (Portrait.)

N G C

TOMPION, THOMAS Born at Northhill, Bedfordshire, England, *c.*1639; died London, 20 November 1713. Horologist.

Tompion is said to have been originally a farrier, but the first attested event in his life is his apprenticeship to a London clockmaker from 1664 to 1671. In 1675 he made one of the earliest English balance-spring watches of the type invented by Robert HOOKE, and in the following year provided part of the equipment for the new Royal Observatory, Greenwich, namely two clocks with 13-foot pendulums and a 2-second beat. Fitted with maintaining power and requiring to be wound only once a year, they contained many novel features and were more accurate than those available in other observatories. He also made repeating watches on the basis proposed by Edward Barlow (1639–1719), and shared with him the patent for the horizontal-wheel cylinder escapement which made the construction of flat watches possible. He raised the English clock- and watch-making industry to a new level. Several of his clocks survive, as do the barometer and sundial which he constructed for William III for Hampton Court Palace.

Tompion was Master of the Clock-makers' Company in 1704; had his portrait painted by Kneller; and was buried in Westminster Abbey. He never married: the clock-makers George Graham (1673–1751) and Thomas Tompion the younger were his nephews.

Dictionary of National Biography.

T K D

TOMONAGA, SIN-ITIRO Born in Tokyo, Japan, 31 March 1906; died there, 8 July 1979. Physicist, noted for work in the field of quantum electrodynamics.

Quantum electrodynamics weaves together special relativity and quantum mechanics to form a theory of great generality which unifies such diverse phenomena as radiation, creation and annihilation of particles, solid-state and plasma properties, masers, lasers, optical and microwave spectroscopy, electronics, and chemistry. Toward the end of the Second World War, in isolation from foreign scientists and living in war-damaged housing, Tomonaga achieved a renormalization of the covariant field theory which avoided the absurd predictions (infinite mass and charge) earlier theory gave under boundary conditions.

Tomonaga's family moved to Kyoto in 1913 when his father became professor of philosophy at Kyoto University. He graduated from the renowned Third Higher School and then entered Kyoto Imperial University in 1926 where he met Hideki YUKAWA, who in 1935 predicted the existence of the meson. After graduating in 1929 he continued his study of quantum mechanics in the same office as Yukawa. In 1932 Tomonaga joined the laboratory of Yoshio Nishina (1890–1951) at the Institute of Physical and Chemical Research, Tokyo. They discovered and investigated pair creation and annihilation (1933–5). In 1937 Tomonaga joined the group of Werner HEISENBERG in Leipzig where he worked on nuclear matter and attended seminars on cosmic rays. In 1940 he developed intermediate coupling theory for mesons. In 1941 he was appointed professor at Tokyo Bunrika University (which was absorbed into the Tokyo University of Education in 1949).

During the Second World War Tomonaga solved the motion of electrons in the magnetron and developed theory for a system of wave guides and cavity resonators. During a year (1949) at the Institute for Advanced Study, Princeton, USA,

Tomonaga worked on the nature of collective oscillations in a one-dimensional fermion system. His book *Quantum Mechanics* was published in 1949 and was translated into English in 1963: several hundred thousand copies were sold. Tomonaga led in the establishment of the Institute for Nuclear Study, University of Tokyo, in 1955. The outstanding quality of his work was acknowledged by the award of a Nobel prize in physics in 1965 (with J. Schwinger (1918–)and R. P. FEYNMAN).

Tomonaga served as President of Tokyo University of Education from 1956 to 1962. He occupied important positions in various government committees for scientific research and policy making. His interest in the history of physics led him to write two books. *The Spin is Spinning* tells stories about quantum theory; *What Would Be Physics*, Vol.1, describes underlying ideas in mechanics and thermodynamics. Both are written in colloquial language and display his wit. Sadly, he was unable to finish volume two of the second work, for he died of cancer at the age of 73.

Physics Today, **32**, 67, 1979. (Portrait.)
Science, **186**, 588, 1965. (Portrait.)
Dictionary of Scientific Biography, Supp. II.
Tyler Wasson (Ed.), *Nobel Prize Winners*. 1987. (Portrait.)

R L W

TOPCHIEV, ALEKSANDR VASIL'EVICH Born in Russia, 1907; died Moscow, 27 December 1962. Industrial and organic chemist, administrator and diplomat.

Topchiev graduated from the Institute of Chemical Technology, Moscow, in 1930, and taught there for two years. After working in the Institute of Technology of the Food Industry, he joined the Petroleum Institute, of which he became Director in 1947. He was Deputy Minister of Higher Education from 1947 to 1949; a member of the USSR Academy of Sciences from 1949, and its Scientific Secretary from 1958. Among his honours were a Stalin Prize and the Order of Lenin.

His published work, which included several books, was mainly concerned with the chemistry of aliphatic hydrocarbons; their nitration, halogenation, alkylation, polymerization and radiolysis, usually under conditions of catalysis and high pressure. He played a great part in the building up of the Russian petrochemical industry, especially during the difficult conditions of the 1940s. His knowledge of the chemical, fuel and polymer industries gained him a place on many high-level committees, where he made a reputation as an able administrator. It is probable that he was deeply concerned with the rocket-fuel aspects of the Russian space-programme. In his last few years, he had almost the status of a roving ambassador for Soviet science, and he became a familiar figure at international conferences on such topics as co-operation in space research, and the uses of nuclear energy.

Nature, **197**, 847, 1963.
Encyclopedia of Russia and the Soviet Union. 1961. (Portrait.)

W V F

TORRICELLI, EVANGELISTA Born at (presumably) Faenza, Italy, 15 October 1608; died Flor-

ence, 25 October 1647. Inventor of the mercury barometer.

Torricelli seems to have been an orphan and to have got his early education in Jesuit schools, but in 1627 we find him in Rome as a pupil of Benedetto Castelli (1577–1644), who inspired many of his first works. Towards 1640 he wrote a long treatise (*De motu gravium*) in which he worked out the consequences of laws of falling bodies (also in parabolic ballistics) formulated by GALILEO, and verified them by a number of ingenious experiments. In a particular section Galileo's laws were applied to liquids flowing from apertures in vessels, and what is known as Torricelli's law was stated and experimentally proved. Castelli showed this work to Galileo, who subsequently engaged Torricelli as his personal assistant at Arcetri. This was in September 1641, only a few months before Galileo died; Torricelli then succeeded him as mathematician to the court of Tuscany, and in the years before his untimely death engaged eagerly in scientific activity.

In pure mathematics Torricelli wrote a great number of papers dealing with conic sections, the cycloid, the logarithmic curve and other subjects which made him known to F. B. CAVALIERI, Marin Mersenne (1588–1648), G. P. de Roberval (1602–75), and other mathematicians of his time. His determination of the area of the cycloid and his method of drawing tangents to it are no doubt independent of the works of others, but nevertheless involved him in bitter strife over priority with Roberval.

In the practical field Torricelli succeeded in grinding telescope lenses which – even with a diameter of 80 mm – came near to optical perfection. He also constructed a simple microscope with a small glass sphere as lens. However, his most important work was the invention (1643) of the mercury barometer, communicated in a letter to Michelangelo Ricci (1619–92) in Rome dated 11 June 1644. At the beginning of the century Galileo had constructed thermoscopes using a bottle with a long, narrow neck placed upside down with the aperture under water. Torricelli filled such a bottle with mercury and placed it similarly in a vessel filled with the same liquid. He then discovered that the surface inside the tube adjusted itself to a well-defined level about 76 cm higher than the free surface outside, and realized that this must be due to the pressure of the atmosphere upon the free surface. Thus the pressure of the air was experimentally demonstrated, and the existence of a vacuum on the top of the mercury in the tube was evident. Through Mersenne in Paris the discovery was made known in France and the existence of an atmospheric pressure diminishing upwards was soon afterwards confirmed by a famous experiment made at Puy de Dôme by Blaise PASCAL.

B. Caldonazzo, E. Carruccio, and V. Ronchi, *E. Torricelli*. 1951.
W. E. Knowles Middleton, *The History of the Barometer*. 1964.
G. Vassura and G. Loria (Eds), *Opera di Evangelista Torricelli*, 4 vols. 1919–44.
Dictionary of Scientific Biography.

O P

TOWNES, CHARLES HARD Born at Greenville,

South Carolina, USA, 28 July 1915. Physicist who built the first working maser.

After studying at Furman University in Greenville, Duke University, and the California Institute of Technology, where he took his PhD in 1939, Townes spent the years of the Second World War at the Bell Telephone Laboratories working on the design of radar bomb sights and navigational systems. At the end of the war he was one of three physicists who independently discovered the technique of microwave spectroscopy of gases. He joined the faculty at Columbia University in 1948, and three years later conceived the idea of stimulating ammonia molecules to resonate with and amplify microwaves of the appropriate wavelength. By 1953 he had constructed the first maser (Microwave Amplification by Stimulated Emission of Radiation).

Townes had conceived the maser originally as a means of studying atoms and molecules by microwave spectroscopy, but in the first few years after its invention it found applications also in radio astronomy, in the precise measurement of both time and length, and in the production of extremely intense ultra high frequency sound waves. In 1958, with A. L. SCHAWLOW, he published a paper outlining the possibility of developing the maser to emit radiation in the infrared, visible and ultraviolet regions of the spectrum. This was first achieved by T. H. MAIMAN in 1960, but Townes and many others subsequently made use of masers and lasers (Light Amplification by Stimulated Emission of Radiation) in a great variety of scientific research projects and industrial applications.

In 1964 he shared the Nobel prize for physics with N. BASOV and A. PROKHOROV for 'fundamental work in the field of quantum electronics which has led to the construction of oscillators and amplifiers based on the maser-laser principle'. From 1961 to 1966 he was provost of Massachusetts Institute of Technology, and in 1967 he became University Professor of Physics at the University of California until his retirement in 1986.

Robert L. Weber, *Pioneers of Science: Nobel Prize Winners in Physics*, (2nd ed.). 1988. (Portrait.)
McGraw-Hill, *Modern Scientists and Engineers.* (Portrait.)
T. Berland, *The Scientific Life.* 1962.
Tyler Wasson (Ed.), *Nobel Prize Winners.* 1987. (Portrait.)

R M B

TOWNSEND, SIR JOHN SEALY EDWARD Born at Galway, Ireland, 7 June 1868; died Oxford, England, 16 February 1957. The founder of the kinetic theory of ions and electrons in gases.

Townsend, whose father was professor of civil engineering at Queen's College, Galway, studied at Trinity College, Dublin, and in 1895 became one of the first research students of J. J. THOMSON at Cambridge. Becoming a demonstrator at the Cavendish Laboratory and a Fellow of Trinity College, Cambridge, he worked with such distinction on electrically charged clouds that in 1900 he was appointed Wykeham Professor of Physics at Oxford, where he spent the remainder of his life. Amongst his distinguished students were H. G. J. MOSELEY, R. J. van der GRAAFF and H. TIZARD.

At Cambridge, Thomson set him to work on conductivity in gases induced by the newly discovered x-rays. In 1897 he produced ionized gases by electrolysis with heavy currents; obtained a dense cloud by bubbling these through water; and by measuring the ionic charge of droplets in the cloud he obtained the first value of the elementary charge, showing this to be the same in gases and in liquid electrolytes. Much of his work was concerned with the passage of a weak current through a gas at low pressures, the 'Townsend discharge'. He developed a method for measuring ionic mobilities in such a discharge, using crossed magnetic fields, and was the first to study ionic diffusion in gases. In 1911 he determined the velocity of electrons at low pressures. Townsend's idea of 'hot electron gas' involves the movement of electrons with considerably higher average energy than that of the uncharged molecules through which they are driven in an electric field.

Townsend also examined energy transfers between electrons and molecules, and related the mean free path of electrons to the mean electron energy of swarms. From an extensive study of ionization in gases he showed that loss of electrons from the electrodes may eventually give rise to 'electrical breakdown' in the intervening gas, that is, passage of a spark. He was also concerned with electrochemistry and spectroscopy of ionized gases, and with electrodeless discharges in high-frequency fields.

Other work by Townsend included a study of solar disturbances, magnetization of liquids, and the effects of secondary x-rays. He published several treatises on the subject of electrons in gases, and wrote also on radio transmission and electromagnetic waves. Widely esteemed through his publications, though rarely attending scientific meetings, he was honoured in America and France; elected FRS in 1903; and knighted in 1941.

Nature, **179**, 757, 1957.
The Times, 18 February 1957.
Biographical Memoirs of Fellows of the Royal Society. 1957. (Portrait.)
Dictionary of National Biography.
Dictionary of Scientific Biography.

C A R

TOWNSHEND, CHARLES (SECOND VISCOUNT TOWNSHEND) Born at Raynham, Norfolk, England, 1674; died there, 21 June 1738. Agriculturist; introduced the turnip into general agricultural practice.

Townshend was educated at Eton and King's College, Cambridge. He succeeded to the peerage and family estates in 1687. He had a busy and distinguished political career, in the Whig interest, and in 1713 married the sister of the Whig statesman Sir Robert Walpole, Earl of Oxford (1676–1745). He retired from political life in 1730 and devoted himself to his estates. His great contribution to agriculture was the introduction of the turnip, then commonly only a garden crop, for winter fodder – hence his nickname 'Turnip' Townshend. This, introduced into a four-course rotation system – the Norfolk system – revolutionized the keeping of livestock during the winter, and relieved the farmer of the necessity of keeping one-third of his land as bare fallow every year. In Walpole he found a powerful advocate of his methods.

Dictionary of National Biography.

J. A. Scott Watson and M. E. Hobbs, *Great Farmers*. 1937.

T I W

TRAUBE, MORITZ Born at Ratibor, Silesia, 12 February 1826; died Berlin, 28 June 1894. Biochemist, noted for his studies of enzymes.

Traube studied chemistry at the universities of Berlin and Giessen; he was influenced towards studies of fermentation by his teacher Justus von LIEBIG, and by his elder brother Ludwig (1818–76), who became prominent as a pathologist. He began also to study medicine, but the sudden death of another elder brother made it necessary for him to abandon his career, and to return to Ratibor to run the family wine business. This he did with conspicuous success from 1849 to 1886, moving to a larger concern in Breslau in 1866. After his retirement, he removed to Berlin. He was married and had five children; his two sons both became professors, one of chemistry, the other of mineralogy.

During the whole of his time as a wine merchant Traube was carrying out research, first in his own premises in Ratibor, then in the University of Breslau, though he never held any official position there; he seldom had any assistance, but published fifty papers. His main interest was in fermentation; he showed that Liebig's views were untenable and that fermentation was caused by a non-living 'unorganized ferment' (later called an enzyme) secreted by the vigorously growing yeast cell. He studied and classified enzymes, but was not able to isolate them. Closely related to this work were studies of artificial semipermeable membranes as models of cell walls; of the phenomenon of 'autoxidation', and of the chemistry of hydrogen peroxide.

Berichte der deutschen Chemischen Gesellschaft, **28**, iv, 1085, 1895. (Portrait.)

T. L. Sourkes, *Journal of the History of Medicine*, **10**, 379, 1955.

Dictionary of Scientific Biography.

W V F

TRAVERS, MORRIS WILLIAM Born in London, 24 January 1872; died Stroud, Gloucestershire, 25 August 1961. Collaborator with Sir William RAMSAY in discovery of the rare gases.

Travers was the son of a London physician. He was educated at Blundell's School and then at University College, London. After a short time spent at the University of Nancy, he returned to University College, London, in 1894 to work with Ramsay; he was appointed assistant professor in 1898. In 1904 – in which year he was elected FRS – he was made professor of chemistry at University College, Bristol (which post Ramsay had occupied 1880–7); he played an active part in the movement that eventually led to the college achieving university status in 1909. Before this, however, Travers had gone to India as director of the Indian Institute of Science, Bangalore (1907–14). He returned to England on the outbreak of war and engaged in the manufacture of chemical glassware – hitherto largely imported from the Continent – as a director of Duroglass Ltd (1914–19). In 1922 he was elected president of the Society of Glass Technology. His concern with glass led him to take a special interest in furnaces, and for a time he manufactured one of his own design. From 1927 to 1937 he was

honorary professor and Nash Lecturer in the University of Bristol, retiring in 1937; in the previous year he had been elected president of the Faraday Society. During the Second World War he emerged from retirement to act as consultant to the Ministry of Supply on explosives.

Travers's major researches fall into two separate divisions. In the years 1894–1904 he was associated with Ramsay – and so indirectly with Lord RAYLEIGH – in the great discovery of the rare gases of the atmosphere – argon, helium, neon, krypton and xenon. The excitement of these classic researches he described in his *Discovery of the Rare Gases* (1928). Much later (1956) he published an admirable *Life of Sir William Ramsay*, completed when he was past 80. His second major field of research, pursued while professor at Bristol, was in the study of gaseous and heterogeneous reactions, to which he made useful contributions.

D. H. Everett, *Nature*, **192**, 1127, 1961.

Biographical Memoirs of Fellows of the Royal Society. 1965. (Portrait.)

D. McKie, *Proceedings of the Chemical Society*, 377, 1964.

M. W. Travers, *The Discovery of the Rare Gases*. 1928.

Dictionary of National Biography.

T I W

TRÉSAGUET, PIERRE Born at Nevers, France, 1716; died Paris, 12 March 1796. Civil engineer.

Trésaguet was one of the civil engineers whose work underlay the rebuilding and extension of the European road system in the latter part of the 18th and in the 19th centuries, introducing lighter and cheaper methods of construction than his predecessors had believed to be possible. N. Bergier (1567–1623) and H. Gautier (1660–1713), for example, advocated a construction – based on a foundation of large stones, covered by layers of smaller ones – some 18 inches deep at the centre. Trésaguet believed that if the road was well drained, and the stones more carefully selected, graded, and applied than was then customary, the thickness of the road could be reduced by half, with a corresponding reduction in capital cost. Trésaguet began his road construction work at Limoges in 1764, and was encouraged by A. R. Turgot (1727–81), the French statesman and economist who was Intendant of Limoges 1761–74. Eventually he became *Inspecteur-général des Ponts et Chaussées*. He realized the importance of proper maintenance as well as sound construction. Accordingly, he introduced a regular corps of road repairers instead of relying on casual local labour. He showed that if roads were regularly maintained, instead of being neglected until they fell into serious disrepair, their lives were long. Around Limoges, for example, his roads were as good after ten years as they were when first constructed.

Trésaguet's system was generally adopted by French road engineers and soon spread over most of Europe. In Britain, it was followed by Thomas TELFORD and developed by J. L. MCADAM.

Charles Singer, E. J. Holmyard, A. R. Hall, and Trevor I. Williams (Eds), *A History of Technology*, vol. 4. 1958.

T I W

TREVITHICK, RICHARD Born at Illogan, Cornwall,

England, 13 April 1771; died Dartford, Kent, 22 April 1833. Pioneer of steam traction.

Richard Trevithick was 4 years old when his father, manager of Dolcoath Mine in Cornwall, installed a Newcomen engine there. As he grew older, familiarity with the engineers responsible for the mine engines drew his attention to the need to improve the steam engine to increase its efficiency and to cope with the increasing depth of the mines. When Watt's master patent expired in 1800, Trevithick built a double-acting high-pressure engine for Cook's Kitchen Mine. This engine represented a very important innovation, for Watt was opposed to the use of steam at much more than atmospheric pressure. Its fame spread not only in Cornwall but also in South Wales; by 1804 he had built nearly fifty for sugar mills, ironworks, corn grinding, and pumps, using the high-pressure principle. Trevithick built a steam carriage which on Christmas Eve 1801 carried passengers over short distances on extremely bad roads. His system of diverting waste steam up the chimney to increase the draught was a most important innovation. Going up to London, he was encouraged by his fellow countryman Humphry DAVY and by Count RUMFORD to patent it. A second model made several journeys in the suburbs, but the engine was subsequently removed to drive a mill. He ran a third machine on a railway whilst acting as engineer to the Pen-y-Darran ironworks near Merthyr Tydfil. It was designed to draw ten tons of iron and seventy men in five wagons, but since the railway was imperfectly constructed this engine, too, was applied for other purposes; a copy of this locomotive was built for a colliery near Newcastle in 1805. He built a fifth version which ran for entertainment on a circular track at Euston, but though passengers were charged a shilling a ride, it did not pay. Discouraged, Trevithick abandoned railways, though he had virtually established the major principles of their operation. In particular, he refuted the current belief that friction between smooth iron wheels and rails would be insufficient to permit traction.

Believing in the universal utility of steam, Trevithick designed also a dredger and a threshing machine. He also planned a tunnel under the Thames, which had got only as far as the exploratory stage when it was flooded. Adjudged bankrupt in 1811, he returned to Cornwall.

Leaving England in 1816 for Peru, he remained there for ten years, but the outbreak of the War of Independence led him to Costa Rica, where he considered linking the Atlantic and Pacific Oceans by a railway. Penniless, he met Robert STEPHENSON in Carthagena, who gave him his passage money home. Apart from a visit to Holland, to inspect some pumping engines, he spent the remainder of his life working on various schemes in a Dartford workshop, so poor that when he died the workmen had to raise a subscription for his funeral.

H. W. Dickinson, *A Short History of the Steam Engine*. 1938. (Portrait.)

H. W. Dickinson and A. Titley, *Richard Trevithick, the Engineer and the Man*. 1934.

J. Hodge, *Richard Trevithick*. 1973.

Dictionary of National Biography.

W H G A

TSWETT, MICHEL SEMENOVICH Born at Asti,

Italy, 19 May 1872; died Voronezh, Russia, 26 June 1919. Botanist distinguished for his researches on plant pigments and his contributions to chromatography.

Michel Tswett was the son of a Russian father (Simeon Tswett) and an Italian mother (Maria Dorozza). As a boy, he was brought to Switzerland and educated at Geneva University. In 1897 he went to St Petersburg to do biological research, and five years later received the MSc degree of Kazan University for research on chlorophyll. In 1902 he went to Warsaw University and was appointed professor first at the Veterinary Institute (1907) and then at the Polytechnic (1908). When the Germans occupied Warsaw in 1915 his institute was evacuated to Nizhniy-Novgorod. Later, he was appointed director of the Botanic Garden of Yuriev University, Estonia, but again the German invasion threatened and he had to move to Vononezh, where he died.

Tswett made notable contributions to an understanding of the chemistry of the principal plant pigments, carotene, chlorophyll and xanthophyll, which he isolated by passing them in solution in petroleum ether through a column of powdered chalk. By 'developing' the column with pure solvent the pigments were made to separate in horizontal bands, which could then be isolated mechanically. Although Tswett described this method in publications from 1903 onward, it attracted virtually no attention, partly because he wrote in obscure journals. In the 1930s, however, the method was taken up very successfully by other chemists interested in natural pigments, notably by R. Kuhn (1900–1967). Subsequently, especially during and after the War of 1939–45, this technique of chromatography was developed into one of the most powerful of all methods of chemical analysis. Today, it is routine practice in virtually every chemical laboratory in the world. Basically, chromatography depends on the distribution of desired substances between two immiscible phases. In the case of Tswett's experiments the phases were liquid and solid, but more recently liquid/liquid and gas/liquid systems have been very much favoured. Among the advantages of chromatography are its great sensitivity, its ability to deal with very labile substances, its speed and simplicity, and the fact that little prior knowledge of the chemical nature of the substances sought is required.

The contribution of chromatography to chemistry is hard to overestimate. Not only does it make possible analyses that are difficult or impossible by other methods, but it makes it possible to do them quickly and easily in great numbers. In a sense, chromatography has done for chemical analysis what the computer has done for calculation.

Although modern chromatography certainly stems from Tswett's work, he was not the originator of the method, for in the scientific literature there are many long-forgotten references to similar techniques. Notable among early pioneers are F. F. RUNGE and D. T. DAY.

Charles Dhéré, *Candollea*, **10**, 23, 1943. (Portraits.)

Trevor I. Williams and Herbert Weil, *Arkiv fúr Kemi*, **5**, 283, 1953.

T. Robinson, *Chymia*, **6**, 146, 1960.

V. G. Berezkin, *Chromatographic Adsorption*

Analysis: Selected Works of M. S. Tswett. 1990. (Includes biography.)

L. Zechmeister, *Isis*, **36**, 108, 1946.

V. Heines, *Chemical Technology*, **1**, 280, 1971.

T I W

TULL, JETHRO Born at Basildon, Berkshire, England, 1674 (baptized 30 March); died Prosperous Farm, near Hungerford, Berkshire, 21 February 1741. Pioneer agricultural engineer.

Tull was educated at St John's College, Oxford, and then read for the bar at Gray's Inn, London. About 1701 he farmed an estate at Howberry, near Wallingford, but he later (1709) moved to Prosperous Farm, near Hungerford. His great contribution to agriculture was his seed-drill, invented at Howberry in 1701 and described in his *Horse-Hoing Husbandry* of 1731. This was a major step towards the mechanization of soil cultivation. A typical drill of Tull's design sowed three rows of wheat, and was drawn by one horse. This method of sowing in regularly spaced rows, rather than broadcast, made possible the introduction, also by Tull, of the horse-drawn hoe to destroy weeds in the growing crop. His methods attracted the attention of Voltaire (1694–1778) who practised them on his estate at Ferney, near Geneva, but it was a considerable time before they came into general use. Not surprisingly, in view of the scarcity of labour to cultivate large tracts of land, it was in North America that such mechanical devices first became widely employed.

Dictionary of National Biography.

G. E. Fussell, *Jethro Tull.* 1973.

T I W

TUPOLEV, ANDREI NIKOLAEVICH Born in Russia, 29 October 1888; died Moscow, 23 December 1972. Aeronautical engineer.

As a young man Tupolev entered the Higher Technical School, Moscow, in 1908 and was greatly influenced by the pioneer work in aeronautical engineering of N. E. Zhukovsky. He joined a group interested in gliding and later joined Zhukovsky in establishing the Central Aerodynamic Institute, of which he was deputy director 1918–35. There he supervised the design of the single-seater ANT-1, with a wooden air-frame; its successor, the two-seater ANT-2 (1923), had a duralumin frame, unusual at that time in small aircraft. It was the first Russian all-metal aircraft. Thereafter, he designed a succession of medium and large aircraft for military and civil use, of which 70 went into production, and also some naval torpedo boats. He is best known, however, for the large Tupolev jet transports. The British *Comet* was introduced in 1952, but the original model had to be withdrawn due to structural defects: the revised version was not introduced until 1958. Meanwhile, the Tu-104 was put into service in 1954. It had a cruising speed of 500 mph at 30 000 feet, relying on a pressurized cabin. The larger Tu-114 came into use in 1956: it could carry 170 passengers and had turbo-prop engines. In 1958 he was awarded the Zhukovsky Gold Medal for the best work in aviation theory.

Tupolev's work was widely acclaimed in the USSR. He was elected Academician in 1953 and awarded a Lenin Prize in 1957. He was a Deputy

of the Supreme Soviet during several convocations. He was also acknowledged in the West, to which he was permitted to travel from time to time. He was an honorary member of the Royal Aeronautical Society (1970) and of the American Institute of Aviation and Space Travel (1971).

L. L. Kerber, *Tupolev: Man and Aeroplane.* 1973.

Soviet Encyclopaedia. 1977. (Portrait.)

T I W

TURING, ALAN MATHISON Born in London, 23 June 1912; died Wilmslow, Cheshire, 7 June 1954. Mathematical logician and pioneer in development of computing machines.

Turing's father, a member of the Indian Civil Service in Madras, arranged to have his children brought up in England. Educated at Sherborne School and King's College, Cambridge, Turing was elected a fellow of King's in 1935, and began the work in mathematical logic which was to lead to the publication in 1937 of his paper 'On Computable Numbers, with an Application to the Entscheidungsproblem' in the *Proceedings of the London Mathematical Society*. In this he proved that some mathematical problems cannot be solved by an automatic machine, and he gave a theoretical description of a universal computing machine, soon to become known as a 'Turing machine', which could do anything a human could do if given explicit instructions in advance. After working under Alonzo Church (1903–) at Princeton University from 1936 to 1938, Turing returned to Cambridge. In 1939 he attended Wittgenstein's classes on the foundations of mathematics.

At the beginning of the Second World War he moved to the headquarters of the Government Code and Cipher School at Bletchley Park, where he spent the war breaking enemy codes, notably the German Enigma code. This had a crucial effect on the Allies' ability to attack German U-boats and disrupt their supply system. He was awarded the OBE in 1946.

From 1945 to 1948 Turing worked at the National Physical Laboratory in Teddington on the design of an automatic computing machine (ACE). He moved to Manchester University in 1948 as a Reader, and in 1950 published his paper 'Computing Machines and Intelligence' in which he examined the view that machines might be said to think. This was followed in 1953 by proposals for making a computing machine play chess, producing a defence lasting thirty moves against a weak player. Turing was elected FRS in 1951. Sadly, he took his own life at the height of his powers.

Biographical Memoirs of Fellows of the Royal Society. 1955. (Portrait.)

Andrew Hodges, *Alan Turing: The Enigma of Intelligence.* 1983.

A. Turing, *Mind*, **59**. 1950.

Rolf Herken (Ed.) *The Universal Turing Machine: A Half-century Survey.* 1991.

Dictionary of National Biography.

H. Oxbury (Ed.), *Great Britons: 20th Century Lives.* 1985.

Dictionary of Scientific Biography.

A P B

TURNER, WILLIAM Born at Morpeth, Northumberland, England, *c.*1508; died London, 7 July

1568. 'The Father of English Botany', who also studied the English fauna.

Turner was educated at Cambridge, where he studied medicine, took holy orders, and joined the reformers led by Latimer and Ridley. In 1540 his religious opinions forced him into exile, and during the next four years he travelled in Europe, studying botany in Ferrara and Bologna. In Switzerland he met Konrad GESNER, with whom he later corresponded, contributing information to his *Historia Animalium*. He returned to England in 1547, following the death of Henry VIII, and became physician to the Duke of Somerset. In 1550 he was appointed Dean of Wells, but only three years later Queen Mary's accession exiled him again. After eight years in Germany, her death in 1558 left him free to return. He was reinstated at Wells in 1561, but retired to London in 1564.

Turner's best-known work is his *Herball*, the first in English to include original material, which was published in three parts dated 1551, 1562 and 1568. His first botanical book, *Libellus de Re Herbaria*, appeared in 1538. It is a catalogue of plants in Latin, with the equivalent names in Greek and English sometimes added. *The Names of Herbes* (1548) is a similar, but extended, list in English, with German and French names added. These books contain the first English records of many plants, the results of Turner's own exploration. His book on birds, *Avium Praecipuarum* (1544), includes similar original observations.

As well as theological tracts, Turner's other writings deal with fishes, mineral baths, and the wines of England.

R. Pulteney, *Historical and Biographical Sketches of the Progress of Botany in England*. 1790.

C. E. Raven, *English Naturalists from Neckam to Ray*. 1947.

W. Turner, *Libellus de Re Herbaria*, 1538. *The Names of Herbes*, 1548. (Facsimiles with introductory matter by James Britten, B. Daydon Jackson and W. T. Stearn. 1965.)

A. Arber, *Herbals*. 2nd ed. 1938. (Paperback 1986.)

Dictionary of National Biography.

S J R

TWORT, FREDERICK WILLIAM Born at Camberley, Surrey, England, 22 October 1877; died there, 20 March 1950. Renowned for discoveries in microbiology, especially in relation to bacteriophage.

Twort, the son of a doctor, qualified in medicine in 1900. He was soon appointed assistant in the clinical laboratory at St Thomas's Hospital, London, and he became (1902) demonstrator to William Bullock (1868–1941) at the London Hospital. In 1909 he was appointed Superintendent of the Brown Institution, an animal dispensary. He was elected FRS in 1929.

Twort is probably best known for his observation, published in 1915, of what is now known as bacteriophage. He had, for some years, been trying to grow viruses in artificial media and, by chance, he noticed that colonies of contaminating cocci growing on agar became virtually transparent. He also showed that if colonies which did not undergo this change were touched with a trace of the transparent material they similarly showed the phenomenon (which is due to the action of bacterial viruses). Twort was unable to continue this

work and in 1917 Félix d'Hérelle (1873–1949) independently recognized the phenomenon which is still known eponymously as as the Twort-d'Hérelle phenomenon.

Equally significant was Twort's work on culturing, for the first time, the causative organism of Johne's disease, a serious intestinal ailment of cattle. He had had valuable experience for this study through investigations on cultivating leprosy bacillus with the use of essential 'growth factors'. Twort believed that there was a close relationship between Johne's bacillus and the tubercle bacillus, and as both of them grew in the same animal while only the tubercle bacillus developed on a normal culture medium he argued that the tubercle bacillus could synthesize something of nutritional importance which Johne's bacillus could not. He therefore incorporated dead tubercle bacilli in a culture medium and found that it was suitable for successfully cultivating Johne's bacillus. Further, Twort (with G. L. Y. Ingram (1884–1914)) studied the disease in great detail and opened up a profitable field of research.

Twort made many smaller contributions to bacteriology, such as his studies on the adaptation of organisms to artificial media, but much of his work became highly speculative, being based on the possibility that bacteria were developed from viruses which he thought had in turn developed from other primitive forms. He spent many years trying to cultivate viruses or hypothetical precursors, but unfortunately he did not publish any significant results.

One provocative aspect of Twort's personality was his extreme dislike of the 'nationalization' of scientific research, a view he never failed to impress on his contemporaries.

Obituary Notices of Fellows of the Royal Society, 1950–51. (Portrait.)

A. Twort (son), *In Focus, Out of Step*. 1993.

Dictionary of National Biography (Missing Persons). 1993.

J K C

TYNDALL, JOHN Born at Leighlin Bridge, near Carlow, Ireland, 2 August 1820; died London, 4 December 1893. Best known for his researches on heat.

After working for a time in the Ordnance Survey of Ireland, Tyndall was appointed teacher of mathematics at Queenswood College in 1847. In 1848 he moved to Marburg to study chemistry under R. W. BUNSEN, graduating in 1850. After a period in Berlin under H. G. Magnus (1802–70), he returned to England in 1851, being elected a FRS in 1852 (Rumford Medallist 1864). In 1843 he was appointed professor of natural philosophy at the Royal Institution, succeeding Michael FARADAY as Superintendent in 1867.

His first paper (1850), in collaboration with K. H. Knoblauch, dealt with the behaviour of crystalline bodies in a magnetic field. The authors concluded that the phenomena were due not to the action of altogether new forces, as suggested by J. PLÜCKER and Faraday, but to the modifications in crystals of the known forces of magnetism and diamagnetism. His *Researches on Diamagnetism and Magnecrystalline Action – including the Question of Diamagnetic Polarity* appeared in 1870.

Tyndall's most important work, however, lay in

the field of heat, his first paper on this subject (1854) being concerned with the transmission of heat through organic substances. For various kinds of wood he found three axes of calorific conduction coinciding with the axes of cohesion for the wood in question. In 1859 he communicated to the Royal Society the first of a series of papers on the action of radiant heat on gases and vapours, a subject on which he delivered the Bakerian Lecture in 1861. Tyndall's researches in radiant heat were marked by much ingenuity in the construction of sensitive apparatus and by his skills in removing many different sources of error. Similar experiments carried out independently by Magnus led to results in agreement with those of Tyndall save in one important respect, in which Tyndall was ultimately proved right. He investigated the scattering of light by fine particles suspended in the air, and in this field is remembered by the Tyndall effect.

Tyndall, who was an expert Alpinist – one of the first to climb the Matterhorn – also made useful contributions to the theory of glaciers, and in a series of careful experiments he confirmed the findings of PASTEUR on the impossibility of spontaneous generation. He did much to gain recognition for the work of J. R. von MAYER.

Dictionary of National Biography.

A. S. Eve and C. H. Creasey, *Life of John Tyndall.* 1945. (Portraits.)

E. Frankland, *Proceedings of the Royal Society,* **55**, xviii, 1894.

Nature, **49**, 128, 1894.

D. Thompson, *Annals of Science,* **13**, 9, 1957.

Dictionary of Scientific Biography.

J W H

U

UNVERDORBEN, OTTO Born at Dahme, near Potsdam, Prussia, Germany, 13 October 1806; died there, 27 December 1873. Organic chemist; discovered aniline (1826).

Unverdorben's chemistry seems to have been mostly self-taught, though he studied for a year in the Pharmaceutical Institute in Erfurt; he probably also worked under H. Rose (1795–1864) in Berlin. His main published work is a series of papers (1824–9) on the products obtained by the destructive distillation of various organic substances. Most of these products, for which he invented names, are not now identifiable; but 'odorin' (from bone-oil) is probably a mixture of picolines, and 'crystallin' (from indigo, so-called because it formed crystalline salts) is certainly aniline. These substances were further studied by Carl Reichenbach (1788–1869). About 1830, Unverdorben took charge of the family manufacturing business, and did no more scientific work; he became a lonely and eccentric man.

Zeitschrift für angewandte Chemie, **94**, 31, 1921. (Portrait.)

J. R. Partington, A History of Chemistry, vol. 4. 1964.

W V F

URBAIN, GEORGES Born in Paris, 12 April 1872; died there, 5 November 1938. Chemist, notable for his researches on the rare earths.

Urbain studied chemistry at the Sorbonne; in 1895 he began work on the separation of the rare earths, for which he was awarded a doctorate in 1899. After five years in the electrical industry, he returned to academic life in 1908 as professor of mineral chemistry in the Sorbonne, later (1928) professor of general chemistry.

Although he suffered from poor health, Urbain was a tireless worker in the difficult and tedious field of rare-earth chemistry. He discovered lutetium, and played a part in the discovery of hafnium. Using his new method of characterizing the elements by their magnetic susceptibilities, he was able to show that there were not (as some had supposed) an almost infinite number of practically indistinguishable rare earths, but a small number of very similar ones. This conclusion was confirmed by H. G. J. MOSELEY (using Urbain's specimens) in his classical work on x-ray spectra.

Among other honours, Urbain was elected a member of the Académie des Sciences in 1921.

P. Job, Bulletin de la Société Chimique de France, **6**, 745, 1939. (Portrait.)

G. Champetier and C. H. Boatner, Journal of Chemical Education, **17**, 103, 1940.

W V F

URE, ANDREW Born in Glasgow, Scotland, 18 May 1778; died London, 2 January 1857. Chemist and writer on science and technology.

Andrew Ure studied at the university of Edinburgh and subsequently at Glasgow, where he took the degree of MD; in 1804 he became professor of chemistry at Anderson's College in succession to George Birkbeck (1776–1841). Ure shared Birkbeck's interest in the education of the workers, for whom he introduced popular scientific lectures (c. 1809). In 1830 he moved to London, where he worked for the Board of Customs as an analytical chemist. His achievements in chemistry included work on the specific gravity of solutions of sulphuric acid and the invention of a method of mercury extraction which was in use at Landsberg, Bavaria, in 1847. He became FRS in 1822.

Apart from his Dictionary of Chemistry (1821), Ure is chiefly remembered for the valuable information embodied in his enthusiastic accounts of the new industrial era. His Philosophy of Manufactures; Cotton Manufactures of Great Britain; and Dictionary of Arts, Manufactures, and Mines were published respectively in 1835, 1836 and 1839.

Dictionary of National Biography.

W. V. Farrar, Notes and Records of the Royal Society of London, **27**, 299, 1973.

W. S. C. Copeman, Proceedings of the Royal Society of Medicine, **44**, 655, 1951.

T K D

UREY, HAROLD CLAYTON Born at Walkerton, Indiana, USA, 29 April 1893; died La Jolla, California, 5 January 1981. Discoverer of deuterium and pioneer of isotope-labelling techniques.

Urey's career was notable for the variety of interests he successfully cultivated. He originally graduated from the University of Montana in 1917 with a degree in zoology. After a brief spell in industry as a chemist with the Barrett Chemical Co. he did chemical research in the Universities of Montana and California before going to spend a year with Niels BOHR in Copenhagen (1923–4) as American-Scandinavian Foundation Fellow. Returning to the USA he became successively associate in chemistry at Johns Hopkins (1924–9); associate professor of chemistry, Columbia; and professor of chemistry, Columbia (1934–45). At Johns Hopkins his research was concerned with absorption and Raman spectra (see C. V. RAMAN), and the kinetics of chemical reactions. His academic career was interrupted by the Second World War, during which he was director of the Atomic Bomb Project at Columbia. Freed of this responsibility he went to Chicago (1945–58), again as professor of chemistry. During this time he spent a year (1956–7) in Oxford as George Eastman visiting Professor. The last years (1958–81) of his long and busy working life were spent as professor emeritus in the University of California, La Jolla.

As early as 1919 O. STERN and M. Volmer, in Germany, had sought, unsuccessfully, for a heavy isotope of hydrogen to account for the small departure of the atomic weight from exact unity. In 1927 F. W. ASTON in Cambridge reported that his mass spectrograph indicated only a single isotope, of atomic weight 1.00778 compared with a chemical atomic weight of 1.00777. Two years later F. W. GIAUQUE and H. L. Johnston in the USA found, however, that oxygen contains three isotopes and showed that atomic weights determined by the mass spectrograph should not necessarily be equated with chemical ones. They corrected Aston's value to 1.00751, a significant difference. In 1931 R. T. Birge and D. H. Menzel attributed this to the presence in natural hydrogen of 1 part in 4500 of an isotope of mass 2.

With F. G. Brickwedde and G. M. Murphy, Urey made a determined search for this isotope by the controlled evaporation of liquid hydrogen from 4 litres to 1 ml. Spectroscopic examination of the residue showed a clear line corresponding to the mass 2 isotope (deuterium). Later, with E. W. Washburn (1881–1934), Urey developed a method of preparing deuterium by the electrolytic decomposition of water, based on the fact that the lighter isotope is evolved marginally more rapidly. While this was in progress, it was found elsewhere that water residues in industrial electrolytic cells used for the production of hydrogen and oxygen were significantly denser than ordinary water. This 'heavy water' is relatively rich in deuterium, and when pure has a specific gravity of 1.108. Urey went on to prepare a number of compounds in which deuterium took the place of hydrogen, beginning with deuteromethane. This was the first example of the isotope-labelling techniques that have since proved so valuable in modern chemistry.

Later, Urey turned his attention to the natural distribution of isotopes in relation to the origin of the universe and of life on Earth. This led, in 1952, to his stimulating book *The Planets: Their Origin and Development*. As a chemist, he prided himself in invading the realm hitherto the preserve of physical scientists.

Urey's discovery of heavy hydrogen gained him a Nobel prize for chemistry in 1934. He was elected a Foreign Member of the Royal Society in 1947 (Davy Medal, 1940).

Chemistry in Britain, **17**, 383, 1981.
Biographical Memoirs of Fellows of the Royal Society. 1983. (Portrait.)
H. G. Thode and H. Alfvén, *Physics Today*, **43**, 82, 1981.
Dictionary of Scientific Biography, Supp. II.
Tyler Wasson (Ed.), *Nobel Prize Winners*. 1987. (Portrait.)

T I W

UVAROV, BORIS PETROVITCH Born in Uralsk, Russia, 5 November 1889; died London, 18 March 1970. Entomologist.

Uvarov became keenly interested in entomology while still a boy and improved his knowledge by attending weekly meetings of the Russian Entomological Society while studying at St Petersburg University. On graduating he held a series of government appointments in entomological institutions, latterly in the State Museum of Georgia and the State University of Tiflis. During this time he made his classic discovery that swarming and non-swarming locusts are not distinct species but phases of the same insect.

Political and nationalistic difficulties in Georgia after the Revolution led him to seek refuge in London, where in 1920 he was given an appointment at the Imperial Bureau (later Commonwealth Institute) of Entomology. Although he was concerned with many aspects of entomology, especially taxonomy and biogeography, he rapidly became the world's leading expert on locust research and control. His unit became the Anti-Locust Research Centre in 1945, and he was its Director until 1959. He was knighted in 1961.

Biographical Memoirs of Fellows of the Royal Society. 1971. (Portrait.)
H. Oxbury (Ed.), *Great Britons: 20th Century Lives*. 1985.
Dictionary of National Biography.

T I W

V

VALLISNERI, ANTONIO Born at Tresilico, near Modena, Italy, 3 May 1661; died Padua, 18 January 1730. Physician and naturalist.

After studying medicine under M. MALPIGHI in Bologna, Vallisneri graduated MD in Reggio (1684) and practised in Bologna. In 1700 he was appointed to the chair of practical medicine in the University of Padua, in which post he was succeeded by his only surviving son. He was a Fellow of the Royal Society (1703).

Apart from his medical work, Vallisneri continued the studies of the generation of insects begun by his fellow countryman F. REDI. He showed that insects originate from eggs laid by females of the same species, even in those cases, such as the insects causing oak-galls, in which Redi had been compelled to reserve judgment; consequently his denial of the possibility of spontaneous generation carried more weight than Redi's. He also studied mammalian reproduction in the same spirit, and concluded correctly that the follicles of R. de GRAAF were not the true mammalian eggs, as Graaf and others believed. His observations of the reproduction of a certain aquatic plant led to its genus later being named *Vallisneria*. Among his other works were monographs on the chameleon and the ostrich; he recognized the existence of geological 'faults'.

Vallisneri's speculative views on the relationship between species have led some to think of him as an evolutionist, though he is perhaps more properly regarded as extending the medieval concept of the 'great chain of being'.

Enciclopedia Italiana, vol. 34. 1936.
Dictionary of Scientific Biography.

W V F

VAN ALLEN, JAMES ALFRED Born in Mount Pleasant, Iowa, USA, 7 September 1914. Physicist.

Van Allen studied physics at Iowa Wesleyan College and the University of Iowa, to which he eventually returned in 1951 as professor of physics. During the Second World War he served (1942–6) with the US Navy, with a particular concern for the development and use of proximity fuses (see W. A. S. BUTEMENT). This demanded a combined interest in missile technology and miniaturized electronic devices, which led him on to post-war research on the upper atmosphere – studying cosmic radiation in particular – using instrument-carrying balloons and, later, rockets. In 1958 he discovered the two Van Allen Radiation Belts located in the stratosphere and forming the earth's magnetosphere. The lower belt is at an altitude of 1000–5000 km above the equator: the upper at around 20 000 km. They contain trapped electrons derived from the solar wind. Later, his interest extended to charged particles in space and planetary magnetospheres. He was a member of the Space Science Board of the National Academy of Sciences 1958–70.

Who's Who, 1993.

T I W

VAN BENEDEN, EDOUARD JOSEPH LOUIS-MARIE *See* BENEDEN.

VAN DE GRAAF, ROBERT JEMISON Born at Tuscaloosa, Alabama, USA, 20 December 1901; died Boston, Massachusetts, 16 January 1967. Physicist; inventor of the high-tension generator that bears his name.

Van de Graaff trained as an engineer at the University of Alabama. After a brief spell with the Alabama Power Company, he went to Europe in 1924 to study at the Sorbonne. There, largely influenced by the lectures of Marie CURIE, he became interested in atomic physics, in which he undertook research at Oxford (1925–8) as a Rhodes Scholar in the laboratory of John TOWNSEND. Here his principal topic of research was the mobility of gaseous ions; in 1928 he published an important paper on the mobility of positively charged ions in hydrogen. The necessary ions were generated by means of a Whimshurst electrical machine, and it occurred to him that the efficiency of this could be greatly increased if the generated charge were stored by discharging it inside a large hollow sphere.

Returning to the United States in 1929, he developed this idea at Princeton University, and constructed a simple working model which developed a potential of 80 000 volts. Encouraged by this, he proceeded successfully to construct a 2 000 000 – volt generator. In 1931 he moved to the Massachusetts Institute of Technology to continue the development of this type of generator. After the last war he became a director of the very successful High Voltage Engineering Corporation, which developed his invention on a commercial scale. Today van de Graaff machines are widely used as a source of very high voltage in research laboratories, hospitals and other institutions throughout the world.

Nature, **214**, 217, 1967.
E. A. Burrill, *Physics Today*, **20**, 49, 1967.
S. E. Hunt, *Physics Education*, **2**, 140, 1967.

T I W

VAN DER WAALS, JOHANNES DIDERIK Born at Leiden, Netherlands, 23 November 1837; died Amsterdam, 8 March 1923. Physicist known for his derivation of an equation of state applicable to real gases.

Van der Waals began his career as a teacher of physics at Deventer and at The Hague. It was not until 1873, when he was 35, that he published his dissertation for his doctor's degree, *On the Continuity of the Liquid and Gaseous States*. It received great acclaim and was translated into English, French and German. In 1877 he was appointed to a professorship in the University of Amsterdam. He was a member of the Academy of Sciences of Amsterdam, and from 1896 to 1912 he was Secretary. During the last ten years of his life illness caused him to give up most of his scientific work.

Van der Waals's doctoral thesis provided the foundation for most of his work. The ideal gas equation which related pressure, volume and temperature of a gas was derived from the empirical results of Robert BOYLE and J. A. L. CHARLES, but could also be deduced from the Kinetic Theory by assuming that the molecules of a gas were of negligible size compared to its volume, and that they did not exert any attraction on one another. This ideal gas equation was, however, not accurate, particularly for those gases that could be easily liquefied. Van der Waals modified it by introducing one term to account for the finite size of the molecules, and another to account for their mutual attraction. The result was the van der Waals equation, which is one of the best-known equations of state for real gases. Even with a gas like carbon dioxide it gives good agreement with experimental results. The van der Waals equation is a cubic with regard to the volume. Consequently, for a given temperature and pressure, there are three possible volumes, one of which may be regarded as representing the liquid state, one the gaseous state and one an unstable state. The equation, therefore, holds, at least qualitatively, for the liquid and gaseous states, and supports van der Waals's contention that molecules in the gaseous and the liquid states are identical and exert identical forces. He was awarded a Nobel prize in 1910 for his work on the continuity of state.

J. H. Jeans, *Journal of the Chemical Society*, 3398, 1923.

H. Kamerlingh Onnes, *Nature*, **111**, 609, 1923.

Journal of Chemical Education, **32**, 117, 1955. (Portrait.)

E. Farber, (Ed.), *Great Chemists*. 1961. (Portrait.)

Tyler Wasson (Ed.), *Nobel Prize Winners*. 1987. (Portrait.)

                                                    B B K

VAN HELMONT, JOANNES BAPTISTA Born in Brussels, January 1579; died there, 30 December 1644. Physician, chemist, and originator of the word 'gas'.

Van Helmont came from a noble family, and was educated at the University of Louvain, where he studied philosophy and theology. He was led to the study of medicine by an interest in natural science and a philanthropic disposition, and after a period of ten years during which he studied and travelled extensively in Europe, he took the degree of MD in 1609. The rest of his life was spent in comparative solitude – he was a mystic and believed all knowledge to be the gift of God – either in Brussels or on his estate near by at Vilvorde,

and it was during this time that most of his scientific work was accomplished. An early publication led him into difficulties with the Catholic authorities, and this may account for his seclusion and the limited number of papers published during his lifetime. On his death-bed he handed all his manuscripts to his son, Franciscus Mercurius (1614–99) and ordered him to publish them unchanged. The result was van Helmont's great work, *Ortus Medicinae*, dedicated to Jehovah, which first appeared in 1648. It was published in English in 1662 and French in 1670.

Van Helmont was essentially a physician, and he studied GALEN before becoming a disciple of PARACELSUS. His researches in medicine were important, and he first showed that acid in the stomach was associated with digestion. He also made contributions to the understanding of asthma and bronchial ailments, and made an important gravimetric analysis of urine. His extensive use of the balance gave him a clear insight into the concept of the indestructibility of matter; as a demonstration of this, he showed that a metal could be dissolved in an acid and recovered without loss of weight. He rejected the old idea of four elements (earth, air, fire and water) and Paracelsus's three principles (sulphur, salt and mercury) and postulated that all matter was composed of the two elements water and air. Some evidence for this belief came from his willow-tree experiment. He placed two hundred pounds of dried earth in an earthenware vessel, watered it, and planted in it a willow weighing five pounds. Water was added daily and at the end of five years the willow weighed one hundred and sixty-nine pounds and three ounces, and the earth when dried was shown to have lost a negligible weight. He, therefore, assumed that the willow, and thus presumably all vegetation, was composed only of water, and that water was the primary element. Earth, which could be formed by burning vegetation was, therefore, not an element; besides, it could, van Helmont thought, be prepared directly from water. In another experiment, he burned sixty-two pounds of charcoal and found that only one pound of ash was left. He assumed that the rest had gone off into the air as a spirit which he called *gas sylvestre*. He derived the word gas from the Greek word *chaos*. He recognized that the same gas was obtained by burning alcohol and organic matter, by fermenting beer and wine, by the action of acids on shells and limestone, and from some spring waters. He also recognized different gases, some of which were combustible, but without any apparatus for collecting them his study was limited. Not until the time of Joseph PRIESTLEY did the different species of gas begin to be clearly distinguished. He showed that when a candle burned in an enclosed space some of the air was used up.

In spite of his chemical achievements, van Helmont subscribed to many of the fallacious ideas of the time. He believed, for example, in spontaneous generation; a universal solvent; and transmutation. However, his work was generally in advance of its time and influenced many later scientists, including Robert BOYLE.

F. Strunz, *J. B. van Helmont*. 1907. (Reprinted in E. Farber (Ed.), *Great Chemists*. 1961. (Portrait.))

R. O. Moon, *Proceedings of the Royal Society of Medicine*, **25**, 23. 1931.

H. S. van Klooster, *Journal of Chemical Education*, **24**, 319. 1947.

N. de Mévergnies, *Jean-Baptiste van Helmont*. 1935.

Dictionary of Scientific Biography.

B B K

VAN LEEUWENHOEK, ANTONY See LEEU-WENHOEK.

VAN'T HOFF, JACOBUS HENRICUS Born at Rotterdam, Netherlands, 30 August 1852; died Steglitz, Germany, 1 March 1911. Pioneer of stereochemistry and of theory of solutions.

Van't Hoff, the son of a doctor, early displayed a talent for mathematics, but decided to study chemistry; this he did first at the Delft Polytechnic and later (1871) at the University of Leiden. In 1872 he went to work for a short time with F. A. KEKULÉ at Bonn, but found this uncongenial and joined C. A. WURTZ in Paris. There he met J. A. le BEL, who independently of him published an important theory of optical activity (see below). In 1876 he returned to Holland as lecturer in the Veterinary College at Utrecht; two years later he was appointed to the chair of chemistry at Amsterdam. There he remained until 1896, when he was elected to the Berlin Academy and was appointed professor in the University of Berlin, remaining there until his death.

Van't Hoff's stereochemical work stemmed from some earlier observations on polarized light. Briefly, it was known that tartaric acid existed in two forms chemically indistinguishable but sharply characterized physically by the fact that whereas one rotated the plane of polarization of a polarized beam of light to the left (laevo) the other rotated it to the right (dextro). As a young man, PASTEUR had noticed that these differences were associated with the occurrence of the acid in two crystal forms that were mirror images of each other, as are the left- and right-hand members of a pair of gloves. Van't Hoff realized that this phenomenon could be explained if it was assumed that the four valencies by which a carbon atom links itself with other atoms lay not in a plane but were directed to the four apices of a regular tetrahedron. This was a discovery of great importance for practical as well as theoretical reasons; for example, a great many vital natural products – such as sugars, amino acids amd some drugs – can be utilized by the body in only one of the two possible forms. Although they were both working in Wurtz's laboratory, Van't Hoff and Le Bel seemed to have reached the same conclusion independently. Van't Hoff published his theory in Dutch on 5 September 1874; le Bel presented his as a paper to the Paris Chemical Society exactly two months later.

No less important were Van't Hoff's contributions to the theory of solutions – especially in relation to reaction kinetics and the attainment of equilibrium – much of which was contained in his *Études de Dynamique Chimique* of 1884 (English edition 1896). He established a simple thermodynamic relationship between the osmotic pressure of solutions and their vapour pressure. Sir James WALKER, professor of chemistry at Dundee, summarized Van't Hoff's contribution in the following way. He was 'a man of ideas, a thinker. With no great mathematical experimental attainment, with no striking gift as a teacher, Van't Hoff yet influenced and moulded the current thought, and even much of the practice, of chemistry for decades.' One of the greatest chemists of his day, he was appropriately a Nobel Laureate in 1901, the first year in which the awards were made.

J. Walker, *Journal of the Chemical Society*, 1127, 1913. (Portrait.)

E. Cohen, *J. H. van't Hoff: Sein Leben und Wirken*. 1912.

F. G. Donnan, *Nature*, **86, 84,** 1911; *Proceedings of the Royal Society of London*, **86A**, xxxiv, 1912.

E. Farber (Ed.), *Great Chemists*. 1961. (Portrait.)

Tyler Wasson (Ed.), *Nobel Prize Winners*. 1987. (Portrait.)

T I W

VAROLIO, COSTANZO Born at Bologna, Italy, in 1543; died Rome, 1575. Distinguished anatomist, after whom a part of the brain is named.

Varolio studied at Bologna and became professor of anatomy there. In 1573 he was called to the corresponding chair at the *Sapienza* at Rome, and he also became body-physician to Pope Gregory XIII. In 1573 he published at Padua a work on the optic nerves and other cranial nerves (*De nervis opticis*, etc.). In it he gives a rather immature diagram of the base of the brain. One part is labelled the 'transverse process of the brain, which is called the 'pons'. That part of the brain has since then been called the 'pons Varolii'. Twenty years earlier Bartolomeo EUSTACHIO had made a much better illustration, but his figures were not published until a century and a half after Varolio's death.

J. E. Dezeimeris, *Dictionnaire historique de la médecine*. 1839.

Grazzetta Internazionale di Medicina e Cirurgia, **50**, 70, 1941. (Portrait.)

Dictionary of Scientific Biography.

E A U

VAUBAN, SEBASTIEN LE PRESTRE DE Born at Saint-Léger, Nivernais, France, 15 May 1633; died Paris, 30 March 1707. Military engineer.

Vauban was the son of a country gentleman. He joined the army under Condé in 1651, and transferred his services to the King's side two years later, when he had been taken prisoner. Commissioned as an engineer, he received the support of the Marquis de Louvois, Louis XIV's powerful Minister of War, for whom he drew up in 1669 his *Mémoire pour servir à l'instruction dans la conduite des sièges* (Leiden, 1740). In 1678 Vauban was appointed Commissary-General of Fortifications, in which capacity he ringed France with fortresses, some of which can still be traced clearly from the air. He also conducted a whole series of successful siege operations, ending with the capture of Old Breisach in a fortnight in 1703, the year in which he was created a Marshal of France.

For defence, Vauban designed vast polygonal works of stone and earth, the walls being defensible by flanking fire from musketry as well as from artillery on the ramparts; further protection was provided by carefully sited two-storeyed gun chambers, whose thick walls and roof prevented the cannon from being put out of action. For attacking fortresses he elaborated the use of trenches dug as 'parallels' to bring the besieging forces within striking distance (first at Maastricht in 1673), and invented the ricochet battery (first employed at Philipsburg in 1688).

As a civil engineer Vauban designed two of the three major aqueducts required for the great Languedoc Canal, and the Maintenon aqueduct which conveyed the water of the Eure to Versailles. Still more notable are the statistical studies which grew out of the surveys he made in so many regions for military purposes, posthumously published under the ironical title of *Oisivetés* (or 'leisure affairs'). These provided the background for his famous protest against the system of privilege which was ruining France, *Projet d'une dîme royale* – a plea for a single tax, to be imposed equally upon all classes. The great Marshal died of a broken heart within a few days of Louis XIV giving orders for his book to be suppressed.

P. Lazard, *Vauban 1633–1707*. 1934.

R. Blomfield, *Vauban*. 1938.

M. Parent and J. Verroust, *Vauban*. 1971.

F. J. Hebbert and G. A. Rothrock, *History Today*, **24**, 149, 1974.

H. Guerlac, *Vauban: The Impact of Science of War*. 1943.

                                                    T K D

VAUCANSON, JACQUES DE Born at Grenoble, France, 24 February 1709; died Paris, 21 November 1782. Invented first mechanical loom, but more famous for automatons.

Vaucanson showed considerable mechanical aptitude even as a boy, when he built from wood a clock which kept good time. He went to Paris to study mechanics, and there made his first automaton, a flute player. This was followed by many others, one being a duck which swam, quacked, flapped its wings and even swallowed and digested its food. For this precision work he designed various lathes and drills.

In 1741 he was appointed an inspector of silk factories and introduced improved machines for weaving and dressing silk, and in 1745 made the first important self-acting loom. The cloth was woven by turning a handle connected to a shaft on which tappets were fixed to operate the healds and shuttle. He used a friction roller to wind on the cloth, an idea which did not reappear for another century, but he did not include John Kay's flying shuttle, or it might have been more successful. He made some improvements for weaving figured cloths by dispensing with the draw-boy and putting the pattern-selecting apparatus on top of the loom. Soon after this he succeeded in making the Dutch ribbon loom self-acting. This was probably the first loom capable of being driven by power, and his method of working the shuttles by the wheel-and-rack motion is still in use today. He left his fine collection of automatons and models of his inventions to the Queen, who did not appreciate it and allowed it to be dispersed, although some pieces still exist.

A. Barlow, *History of Weaving*. 1878.

Transactions of the Newcomen Society, **26**, 1948.

A. Doyon and L. Liaigre, *Jacques Vaucanson, mécanicien de génie*. 1967.

                                                    R L H

VAUQUELIN, NICOLAS LOUIS Born at Saint-Andrée d'Hébertut, near Pont l'Eveque, Normandy, France, 16 May 1763; died there, 14 November 1829. Discoverer of chromium and beryllium.

Son of a farm worker, Vauquelin was apprenticed to an apothecary in Rouen, but left for Paris, where after some hardship he was employed as a laboratory boy by A. F. de FOURCROY. The menial assistant became friend and colleague, the two men collaborating for some nine years. Vauquelin became a member of the *Académie des Sciences* in 1791, and professor at the *École des Mines* in 1794.

He published a *Manuel de l'Essayeur* in 1799, and this, with his great analytical skill, earned him the post of Assayer to the Mint in 1802. He was one of the first to be admitted to the Legion of Honour. He succeeded Fourcroy in 1811 as professor at the Faculty of Medicine in 1811. In his Doctorate of Medicine thesis he established the existence of phosphorus compounds in the brain.

His principal work was on the analysis of minerals, many of them specimens given by R. J. Haüy (1743–1822). He prepared many compounds of chromium and isolated the metal in 1798. He showed that beryl was a compound of a hitherto uncharacterized earth. He also discovered a number of organic compounds, among them malic acid and asparagine.

From 1791 he was one of the editors of the *Annales de Chimie*.

Nouvelle Biographie Générale, xlv. 1866.

E. G. Ferguson, *Journal of Chemical Education*, **17**, 555, 1940; **18**, 3, 1941.

Dictionary of Scientific Biography.

                                                    F G

VAVILOV, NIKOLAI IVANOVITCH Born in Moscow, 26 November 1887; died Siberia, 26 January 1943. Geneticist; particularly studied the origins of cultivated plants.

Vavilov, whose father was a wealthy merchant, came to England to study under W. BATESON at Cambridge and at the John Innes Horticultural Institution, having graduated from an agricultural academy near Moscow. Back in Russia he became professor at the University of Saratov (1917–20), then director of the Bureau of Applied Botany, Petrograd. Under his direction, and with the support of Lenin, this Bureau became the centre of over 400 research institutes spread over Russia, with a total staff exceeding 20 000. From 1916 to 1933 Vavilov undertook a vast programme of plant collecting, and the 50 000 varieties of wild plants that he brought back from all over the world were tested in his institutes for suitability as crop plants in Russia. Essentially a man of grand ideas and actions, he synthesized this vast material in his theory of the centres of origin of cultivated plants. By studying the numerous varieties amongst wild species he hoped to throw fresh light on the ancestry and relationships of what we believe are their cultivated descendants. This knowledge should help in the task of forming a rational policy of plant breeding, and should furnish fresh varieties for immediate use.

In 1920 his classic book, *Centres of Origin of Cultivated Plants*, added more to the subject than any other work since A. P. de CANDOLLE. In it he argued that the centre of origin of a cultivated plant is identified with the region in which its wild relatives show their maximum adaptiveness. Reasoning thus, he at first concluded that there are six centres of origin; nine years later he raised this number to eleven or twelve. Like all grand syntheses, this was an oversimplification, and Vavilov's method for discovering the centre of origin is not now given wide credence.

The practical value of his collection of varieties we shall never be able to assess, for a programme conceived on so large a scale required more than a lifetime to complete and Vavilov was given only two decades. Opposition came from the agricultural Communes led by T. D. LYSENKO, who gained the support of political factions within the Party, published violent criticisms of Vavilov in the Press, and attacked him openly at the Plant Breeding Congresses from 1934 to 1939. As Lysenko strengthened his grip on the All-Union Party, Vavilov lost his. He had to cancel his acceptance of the invitation to be President of the International Congress of Genetics at Edinburgh in 1937. In 1940, while plant collecting in Bukowina, he was arrested and taken to Moscow. The winter of 1941–2 saw him in a concentration camp at Saratov, from which he was taken to Magadan by the Sea of Okhotsk, after which nothing was heard of him. All mention of his name was erased from the official records in Russia, including that of the Academy of Sciences; he had been an Academician since 1928. He was made a Foreign Member of the Royal Society in 1942.

Obituary Notices of Fellows of the Royal Society. 1954. (Portrait.)

C. Zirkle, *Death of a Science in Russia.* 1949.

Th. Dobzhansky, *Journal of Heredity*, **38**, 227, 1947.

S. C. Harland and C. D. Darlington, *Nature*, **156**, 621, 1945.

G. L. Stebbins, *Science*, **123**, 721, 1956..

R C O

VENING MEINESZ, FELIX ANDRIES Born at The Hague, 30 July 1887; died Amersfoort, 11 August 1966. Geophysicist, pioneer of submarine gravity determinations.

Vening Meinesz was the son of a burgomaster of Amsterdam. He graduated at Delft in 1910 and five years later was awarded his doctorate for a thesis on 'Contributions to the Theory of Oscillation Observances'. The title indicates his early interest in a field to which he was to make many important contributions. He recognized that systematic measurements of the Earth's gravitational field could yield valuable information about the underlying geological structures. As the variation from place to place is small, however, only very accurate local determinations of the force of gravity would be useful. On land, these are fairly easily obtainable by the classical method of timing the swing of a pendulum, but as this is not normally applicable at sea by far the greater part of the Earth's surface is inaccessible for investigation in this way. Vening Meinesz conceived the idea of carrying out determinations in submarines, which provide a far more stable base than surface craft. With the co-operation of the Royal Netherlands Navy he made important gravitational surveys in the Pacific in the 1920s. A painstaking series of observations enabled him to identify a low-gravity belt extrud-

ing from a point near Sumatra to the Mindanao Deep off the Philippines. On the basis of this he formulated a theory of the origin of mountains which is now generally accepted as being correct in principle.

Much of his work was done while Professor Extraordinary of Geodesy, Cartography and Geophysics at Utrecht (1927–57); he was also Professor Extraordinary in Geodesy at Delft.

The Times, 12 August 1966. (Portrait.)

Nature, **215**, 109, 1967.

B. J. Collette, *Geologie en mijnbouw*, **45**, 285, 1966. (Portrait.)

Dictionary of Scientific Biography.

T I W

VERMUYDEN, SIR CORNELIUS Born on the Island of Tholand (Tholen), Netherlands, *c.*1595; died 11 October (probably) 1677. Drainage engineer.

Son of Cornelius Wastendyk, of St Martensdyk, Vermuyden was commissioned in 1621, through his brother-in-law, Joachim Miens, to embank the Thames between Havering and Dagenham, where it had broken through. In 1626 he was undertaking to drain Hatfield Chase in the Isle of Axholme, Lincolnshire. By 1630 he had bought land at Malvern Chase in Worcestershire, and in the same year contracted to drain 300 000 acres of the Great Level of the Lincolnshire Fens. He was knighted in 1628.

His operations met with opposition from the very beginning. The Essex Commissioners of Sewers declared that he left the lands by the Thames in a worse state than that in which he found them; the commoners of the Chase objected to his Dutch workmen as well as to the scheme in general, for if successful it deprived some of the local inhabitants of fish and ducks and others of existing navigational facilities. Further, while draining some lands, he flooded others previously dry. Attacked in 1641 and interrogated by Parliament, he replied with his long-prepared *Discourse Touching the Draining of the Great Fennes* (1642), a statement of his principles. Essentially, these were based on cutting straight drains, as opposed to his opponents' principle of embanking the existing watercourses. He was involved in much litigation, especially in connexion with lead mines in Derbyshire. Notwithstanding all its shortcomings, the Bedford Level remains as his monument today, but his plans for the drainage of Sedgemoor in Somerset did not materialize. He enjoyed the favour of both Charles I and Cromwell; the latter sent him to Holland in 1653 in an attempt to establish a close alliance.

J. Korthals-Altes, *Sir Cornelius Vermuyden*. 1925.

H. C. Darby, *The Draining of the Fens*. 1940.

L. E. Harris, *Vermuyden and the Fens*, 1953. (Portrait.); *Transactions of the Newcomen Society*, **27**, 7, 1949–51.

Dictionary of National Biography.

W H G A

VERNIER, PIERRE Born at Ornans, near Besançon, France, 19 August 1584; died there, 14 September 1638. Mechanician.

Vernier, mathematician and soldier, spent most of his life in the Spanish service in the Netherlands. He is an example of a man whose claim to fame rests on a single outstanding invention; this was the familiar vernier measuring device, first described in 1631 and still used throughout the world for a wide range of precision instruments. It was derived from the nonius (named after the Portuguese mathematician Pedro Nunez (1492–1577)) used for graduating the scales of mathematical instruments; among the first to use it was Tycho BRAHE. The use of the nonius was, however, complicated and Vernier's device was a notable improvement.

D. E. Smith, *A History of Mathematics.* 1923. (Paperback 1958.)

A. Wolf, *A History of Science, Technology, and Philosophy in the 16th and 17th Centuries.* 1935.

Dictionary of Scientific Biography.

T I W

VESALIUS, ANDREAS Born in Brussels, 31 December 1514; died on the island of Zante, Greece, (?April) 1564. The founder of modern anatomy.

Vesalius, the son of the pharmacist to Charles V, was educated in Brussels, and about February 1530 he entered the University of Louvain. In September 1533 he matriculated at Paris in the medical faculty of the University. He was a pupil of Jacobus Sylvius (1478–1555), a staunch Galenist, and of Johann Guinter (1505–74) of Andernach. From Sylvius he probably learned more animal than human anatomy. Guinter was more interested in philology than dissection, and Vesalius helped him with his human dissections. This help Guinter later acknowledged. At the outbreak of war Vesalius became an enemy alien. In 1536 he returned to Louvain, and graduated in medicine in 1537.

Vesalius next went to Padua, graduated in medicine there in December 1537, and was at once appointed to the chair of anatomy and surgery. He assumed his duties on 5 December. He gave his first public lecture within three weeks, and within three months had introduced two innovations; he put his own hands to the business of dissecting, instead of reading aloud while a demonstrator did the work, and he employed drawings to facilitate his teaching. The drawings (see below) were published in April 1538. Up to this time Vesalius was a Galenist, but he now discovered that GALEN was not infallible, and began to write his *Fabrica*. At Padua there were two chairs of surgery; Vesalius held them both. But Raeldo COLOMBO was anxious to obtain a teaching post in the University, and in August 1541 he was chosen to fill the second chair. In October, the Senate reversed its decision and stated that only Vesalius was to give the lectures. Vesalius chose Johannes Oporinus (1507–68) of Basle as printer of the *Fabrica*. By September 1542 the text was written, the illustrations drawn, and the woodblocks cut and on their way to Basle. Type-setting began before October. Vesalius obtained leave of absence, and Colombo was appointed as his substitute. Before going to Basle, Vesalius may have spent some time in Ferrara; he was in Basle early in 1543 and the book was ready for publication by July 1543.

During his leave Vesalius had possibly sought a post in the imperial service. Early in August 1543 he followed Charles V, who was conducting a campaign, until he obtained an audience. He was appointed 'regular physician to the imperial household'. Late in the year he returned to Padua and found that Colombo had been criticizing him. During 1544 Vesalius demonstrated very successfully at Bologna and Pisa. About this time the University of Pisa sought his release from the imperial service to fill the chair of anatomy, but Charles V would not consent. Although not officially the Emperor's body-physician, he frequently acted as such, and his treatment of Charles with china root is embodied in a famous letter (see below). On the abdication of Charles in 1556 Vesalius was created Count Palatine, retired with a pension, and at once took service with Philip II.

Under Philip, Vesalius had to spend much time in Spain, where he found the Spanish doctors, Galenists to a man, hostile and jealous. Vesalius now had designs on his old chair at Padua, for Gabriele FALLOPPIO had died in 1562 and the chair had not been filled. Vesalius had preferably to consult his friends in Venice, for the appointment to the University of Padua was made by the Venetian Senate. But to leave Spain he had to have Philip's permission, and he probably used a proposed pilgrimage to Jerusalem as an excuse. Permission was granted, in (?March) 1564. Vesalius proceeded to Venice, and the indications are that he was appointed to his old chair. He then went to Jerusalem; in returning he died unbefriended on the Greek island of Zante.

During his early period Vesalius wrote minor works and the so-called *Tabulae anatomicae sex.* This untitled work, published in 1538, consists of six large anatomical plates. The first three, all drawn by Vesalius, represent respectively the portal, venous and arterial systems. Much of the anatomy depicted is Galenic and represents the organs of apes. The first plate contains the first illustration of the prostate gland. The fourth, fifth and sixth plates, drawn by Jan Stefan van Calcar (1499–1546), show three views of the human skeleton. The *Tabulae* were also important with regard to anatomical nomenclature. Two copies of these plates have survived. They were plagiarized both before and after publication.

With his *De humani corporis fabrica* ('On the structure of the human body', Basle, 1543) Vesalius rendered all previous works out of date and elementary. It was supremely important because most of its descriptions set a new standard of clarity and accuracy, seen especially in the first two books dealing with the bones and the muscles. The sternum is now correctly described as consisting of three and not seven parts. The sphenoid, the malleus, and the incus are well described and illustrated for the first time. His description of variations in human head-shapes makes him a pioneer of physical anthropology. The book on muscles gives accurate descriptions of the origin and insertion of each muscle, and attempts to define the mode of action of each. The uterus is erroneously represented as being bifid, but the vermiform appendix is clearly illustrated. Vesalius provided the name 'mitral valve'. He stated that none of the pits in the interventricular septum penetrated it, and he could only wonder how the blood managed to pass through pores which eluded the sight. In Book VII, dealing with the brain, his descriptions are generally excellent. He described and illustrated, for the first time, the corpus callosum, thalamus, caudate nucleus, lenticular nucleus, globus

pallidus, putamen, pulvinar, and the cerebral ped-
uncles. He overlooked the pons, later described by
Costanzo VAROLIO, and he was not convinced of
the non-existence of the *rete mirabile* in human
subjects, or that the infundibulum does not secrete
pituita.

The illustrations in the *Fabrica* vary in quality
and are by different artists. The seventeen full-page
'tabulae', three depicting the skeleton and fourteen
the muscles, are among the greatest examples of
anatomic illustration. Long attributed to J. S. van
Calcar, it now appears that the artists of these 'tabulae', and of the text illustrations, are unknown.

The *Fabrica* was reprinted and plagiarized on
innumerable occasions in the two centuries following its publication, which shows the value of the
work to the contemporaries and successors of
Vesalius.

The book was intended for anatomists and medical men, and simultaneously with its publication
Vesalius published an *Epitome* for the use of students. This work had a larger page than the *Fabrica*
and contained nine full-page 'tabulae', most of
them new. The text of the *Epitome* consisted of
condensed versions of selected passages from the
Fabrica.

In 1555 Vesalius published the second edition
of the *Fabrica*, and a reprint of the *Epitome*. In the
second edition Vesalius now says that he has not
perceived even the most hidden channels by
which the interventricular septum is (allegedly)
pierced. His statement is equivalent to a denial of
the passage of the blood.

Of the other work of Vesalius his *Epistola
rationem modumque propinandi radicis Chynae
decocti*, the China-root Letter (1546) is a product
of his early imperial service, and deals with the
relative merits of china root, guaiac, and other substances as medicaments. It also contains his replies
to the criticisms of Sylvius.

C. D. O'Malley, *Andreas Vesalius of Brussels*.
  1964. (Portrait.)
C. Singer, *Vesalius on the Human Brain*. 1952.
H. Cushing, *Bio-Bibliography of Andreas Vesalius*.
  1943.
Dictionary of Scientific Biography.

                                                    E A U

VIÈTE (or VIETA), FRANÇOIS, SEIGNEUR DE LA
BIGOTIÈRE Born at Fontenay-le-Comte, Poitou,
France, 1540; died Paris, 13 December 1603. The
leading algebraist of the sixteenth century.

Viète studied law at Poitiers and began his career
as an advocate. After 1567 he became a councillor
of the *Parlement* of Brittany, until forced to flee
during the persecution of Huguenots, whose faith
he professed at this time. Only with the accession
of Henri IV, a former Huguenot, was Viète restored
to office, becoming Master of Requests (1580) and
a royal Privy Councillor (1589). His chief political
service was the breaking of the Spanish secret
cipher, enabling the French to master the contents
of all secret dispatches.

Although Viète's algebra, best seen in his major
work *Isagogo in artem analyticam* (1591), is in
many respects superior to what went before, he
overlooks some of the best work of his predecessors. For example, although he generalized the
work of CARDANO on cubic equations, being greatly

helped by his own symbolism, he made no use of
Cardano's notion of negative roots. He was the first
writer to denote quantities by letters of the alpha-
bet on a large scale, choosing to use vowels for
variables and consonants for constants. He also
introduced a great many technical terms into
algebra, many of which survive, e.g. 'coefficient'
and 'negative'. Among his contributions to the
theory of equations are a method of approximation
similar to that put forward by NEWTON in 1669 and
by W. G. Horner (1786–1837) in 1819, and a
method for the solution of particular cubic equations by trigonometrical means. He was aware of
some of the simple relations between the coefficients of an algebraic equation and the symmetric
functions of its roots (when positive). He also
attempted the resolution of a general polynomial
into linear factors, but without much success. It
was Viète more than any other who effected the
substitution of algebraic for geometrical constructions in mathematical proof generally. In plane and
spherical trigonometry he preferred to establish his
fundamental identities algebraically.

Viète's power as a mathematician is evident in
his solution of the 'fourth Apollonian problem'
(1600), namely that of constructing a circle touching three given circles. He may well have found
the solution used by Apollonius himself, this being
now lost. He also has an ingenious infinite product
for the value of π.

Viète knew scarcely any astronomy, a fact which
became painfully evident in his opposition to
Christopher Clavius (1537–1612) over the question of the Gregorian reform of the calendar. By
printing and freely distributing his works he
gained a considerable reputation in his own
lifetime.

A. De Morgan, in the *Penny Cyclopaedia*. 1843.
D. E. Smith, *Portraits of Eminent Mathematicians,
  with Brief Biographical Sketches*. 1946. (Portrait.)
Dictionary of Scientific Biography.

                                                    J D N

VILLEMIN, JEAN ANTOINE Born at Prey, Vosges,
France, 28 January 1827; died Paris, 6 October
1892. Discoverer of the inoculability of tuberculosis.

Villemin's father, a farmer, died when his son
was aged 10 years, and he was assisted by his
father's brother. He studied first at Bruyères, and
after military training at the military medical
school at Strasbourg, he qualified in 1853 as an
Army doctor, and was sent for further study to the
Val-de-Grâce, the military medical school at Paris.
In 1860 he became an assistant in the physiology
department at the Strasbourg school, and in 1863
assistant professor of clinical medicine at the Val-
de-Grâce. Here he carried out his experiments on
tuberculosis. In 1869 he was appointed to the chair
of hygiene and legal medicine at the Val-de-Grâce,
and he was in Paris throughout the siege of that
city (1870); in 1873 he became professor of clinical
medicine. Villemin was elected a member of the
Académie de Médicine in 1874, and was its Vice-
President at his death.

Villemin's belief in the infectiousness of tuberculosis was encouraged by his observation that many
strong, healthy young men from country districts
developed the disease while living in barracks during their military training. He was also impressed

by the known fact that a similar disease, glanders in horses, is transmissible by inoculation. He began his experiments, in very primitive conditions at the Val-de-Grâce, in March 1865. He first inoculated a rabbit with tuberculous material from a fatal human case of tuberculosis, and found that, when killed three months later, it showed widespread tuberculous lesions, from which a control animal was free. He carried this experiment on through six series. He then found that rabbits inoculated with tuberculous material from a cow developed widespread tuberculous lesions and died rapidly. In 1867 Villemin reported his results to the *Académie de Médicine*, but they were received without enthusiasm. The British Government then arranged for J. S. Burdon Sanderson (1828–1905) and John Simon (1816–1904), to repeat the experiments, but they were misled by some accidental occurrences and were not quite convinced regarding Villemin's discovery. About the same time, however, Villemin was completely vindicated by J. COHNHEIM, using a new experimental method. Villemin later obtained similar results on the injection of tuberculous material into cats, sheep, goats and other animals. In the same way he proved by injection that sputum and blood from tuberculous patients can transmit the disease to animals.

S. L. Cummins, *Tuberculosis in History*. 1951.
W. Bulloch, *History of Bacteriology*. 1938.
R. Dumesnil and F. Bonnet-Roy (Eds), *Les Médecins Célèbres*. 1947. (Portrait.)

E A U

VINE, FREDERICK JOHN Born in Brentford, Essex, England, 17 June 1939. Geophysicist, who was important in the development of the theory of plate tectonics.

Vine was educated at Latymer Upper School, London, and St John's College, Cambridge, where he worked with Drummond MATTHEWS before moving to Princeton University as assistant professor in the Department of Geological and Geophysical Sciences, 1967–70. He returned to England in 1970 as reader in the School of Environmental Sciences at the University of East Anglia. He has been professor of environmental sciences there since 1974.

The theory of continental drift had first been put forward by Alfred WEGENER in 1912, but he had been unable to explain why the continents had drifted apart. H. H. HESS (1906–69), building on the work of R. S. Dietz (1914–) developed the theory of seafloor spreading to explain continental drift, arguing that continents moved apart as the oceans grew wider. By applying paleomagnetic studies to the rocks of the ocean floor Vine was able to argue in 1963 that magnetic anomalies in the rocks across mid-ocean ridges showed that the continents must have moved. He discovered that the oceanic crust on either side of a mid-ocean ridge was magnetized alternately in opposite directions. He suggested that as hot molten rocks rising to the surface of the Earth cooled down they were magnetized in the prevailing direction of the Earth's magnetic field, but as this periodically reversed direction the oceanic crust would be magnetized in alternately normal and reversed polarity. Vine used the analogy of a tape recorder on which the history of the reversal of the Earth's magnetic field was permanently recorded.

The Vine-Matthews hypothesis was generally accepted by 1966. This confirmed the earlier hypotheses of continental drift and seafloor spreading and the combination of these led to the development of the theory of plate tectonics, which revolutionised all branches of the earth sciences.

F. J. Vine, *Science*, **154**, 1966.
F. J. Vine, *Nature*, Vol. 266, 1977.
P. Kearey and F. J. Vine, *Global Tectonics*. 1990.
H. E. Legrand, *Drifting continents and shifting theories*. 1988.

A P B

VIRCHOW, RUDOLF LUDWIG CARL Born at Schivelbein, Pomerania, Germany, 13 October 1821; died Berlin, 5 September 1902. Founder of 'cellular pathology'; distinguished pathologist, physical anthropologist, and statesman.

Virchow studied medicine at Berlin, and graduated in 1843. Appointed to a minor post at the *Charité*, in 1845 he gave one of the two first independent descriptions of 'white blood' (leucaemia). In 1846 he was appointed Prosector in Pathological Anatomy at the *Charité*. In 1847 he became *Privatdozent*, and with Benno Reinhardt (1819–52), he founded the *Archiv für pathologische Anatomie*, which Virchow edited alone for fifty years. In 1847–8 he investigated officially 'typhus' in Silesia, and his report was very critical of the Government. As a result the Government suspended Virchow from his post in March 1849, but he was soon partially reinstated.

In November 1849 the University of Würzburg appointed Virchow to the first chair of pathological anatomy in Germany. His seven years there were among the most fruitful in the history of pathology. In 1856 the Berlin chair fell vacant, and Virchow accepted the call on condition that he was given an institute of pathology. He remained at Berlin till the end of his life.

In 1859 Virchow was elected to the Berlin City Council, and he remained a member until his death. He was responsible for many of the social, sanitary and medical reforms carried out there. In 1861 he was elected to the Prussian Diet. Bismarck became Prime Minister in 1862, and his policy was strenuously opposed by Virchow. In the wars of 1866 and 1870 Virchow equipped the first hospital trains and built military hospitals. He was a member of the Reichstag from 1880 to 1893.

In 1869 Virchow founded the Berlin Society of Anthropology, Ethnology and Pre-history, of which he was President until his death. He was instrumental in founding the Berlin Ethnological Museum (1886) and the Folklore Museum (1888). His lasting friendship with H. Schliemann (1822–90), the archaeologist of Troy, was due initially to William Ewart Gladstone. Among Virchow's many honours was that of Foreign Membership of the Royal Society (1884), to which he delivered the Croonian Lecture in 1893.

In the pathological field Virchow demolished the current role of phlebitis (1846), and he introduced the concepts of embolism and of pyaemia. He revolutionized the concept of inflammation. Relative to the role of the cell, Virchow wrote in 1854 that 'There is no life but through direct succession'. In 1855 he published in his journal an article on 'cellular pathology' which contains the famous phrase *omnis cellula e cellula*. In 1858 Virchow gave to Berlin practitioners a series of lectures on this subject, and later in the year he published them as a book with the title *Die Cellularpathologie*. Although others – e.g. J. Goodsir (1814–67) – had claimed that cells arise only from cells, he was the first to apply this doctrine to pathological material, with immediate revolutionary effects on pathology and medicine. Virchow also worked intensively on tumours, and he published a large treatise on this subject. Among his numerous original contributions to pathology, mention may be made of his work on the animal parasites of man, e.g. trichina. Virchow was on the whole antagonistic to the role of bacteria in disease, and he rightly pointed out that the discovery of an organism in a certain disease did not explain how the organism caused the disease. He suggested the production of toxins before their existence was discovered. Virchow's publication in 1875 of his method of conducting post-mortem examinations had important consequences for the study of morbid anatomy. Of his many publications on anthropology and archaeology, mention may be made of his *Contributions to the Topography of Troy* (1879) and of his *Ancient Trojan Graves and Skulls* (1882).

E. H. Ackerknecht, *Rudolf Virchow*. 1953. (Portrait).

G. S. Woodhead, *Journal of Pathology and Bacteriology*, **8**, 374, 1903.

L. Aschoff, *Rudolf Virchow*. 1948.

Proceedings of the Royal Society, **75**, 1898, 1904.

F. Semon, *British Medical Journal*, **2**, 795, 1902.

Dictionary of Scientific Biography.

E A U

VITRUVIUS (VITRUVIUS POLLIO) Flourished (probably) in the latter part of the first century BC. Author of a treatise on architecture.

Nothing is known with certainty of the career of Vitruvius, but he probably held some official position in the Rome of Augustus. His treatise, *De Architectura*, partly based upon his own experience and partly compiled from (mostly Greek) authorities, falls into ten Books made up as follows:

I General principles of architecture; liberal education of young architects; choice of salubrious sites (e.g. by examining the livers of indigenous animals); wind charts; town planning.

II Origin and growth of building techniques; choice of materials.

III Temple architecture; Ionic order.

IV Corinthian and Doric orders; Tuscan temples (preceding Roman adoption of Greek models).

V Architecture of public buildings, harbours, etc., leading on, through problems of acoustics, to a discussion of the nature of sound and music. The voice spreads out circlewise 'as when we throw a stone into standing water ... but while in water the circles move horizontally only, the voice both moves horizontally and rises vertically by stages'. Open-air theatres were to be designed accordingly, to avoid reverberations, echoes, etc. Use of artificial resonators; classical theory of harmony.

VI Planning of private houses with due regard to individual needs and local conditions; influence of climate upon national character.

VII Interior decoration; preparation of stucco; pigments and wall painting.

VIII Water, its discovery from local indications; hot and mineral springs and their curative effects; supplying water by aqueducts or tunnels or by leaden or earthenware pipes; poisonous effect of leaden pipes; levelling instruments; digging of wells; use of lighted lamps to test purity of air.

IX Construction of sundials, with astronomical introduction; phases of the Moon; dialled clocks operated by the inflow of water.

X Mechanical contrivances (developing the inventions of CTESIBIUS and Philo (*fl.* 150 BC); pulleys and levers, machines for raising water; water-wheels, water-driven automata and organs; engines of war.

Vitruvius made no capital discoveries, but he transmitted Hellenistic mechanical inventions to Latin readers and his manual was widely studied by Renaissance scholars. He possessed a sense of history manifested particularly in his treatment of architecture, geometry, astronomy, geography and mechanics.

F. Granger (Ed.), *Vitruvius, On Architecture* (Loeb Classical Library, 2 vols.). 1931, 1934.

G. Sarton, *A History of Science: Hellenistic Science and Culture in the Last Three Centuries B.C.* 1959.

J. G. Landels, *Engineering in the Ancient World*. 1978.

Dictionary of Scientific Biography.

A A

VOGEL, HERMANN WILHELM Born at Dobrilugk, Brandenburg, Germany, 26 March 1834; died Berlin, 17 December 1898. Photochemist and spectroscopist; inventor of the 'orthochromatic' plate.

Vogel was educated in the *Gewerbeakademie*, Berlin, and held several teaching posts in that city before being appointed to a professorship in the *Technische Hochschule*, Charlottenburg. His work was almost entirely concerned with photochemistry and spectroscopy, and with the theory and practice of photography; he took part in several solar eclipse expeditions. He is remembered for his discovery (1874) that certain dyestuffs can sensitize silver bromide plates to light of wavelength similar to their own absorption maxima, so that plates can be made sensitive to the whole range of visible light ('orthochromatic').

Berichte der deutschen Chemischen Gesellschaft, **32**, 1, 1899.

W V F

VOLTA, ALESSANDRO Born at Como, Italy, 18 February 1745; died there, 5 March 1827. Inventor of the electric battery, or voltaic cell.

Volta came from an aristocratic family, and first showed interest in natural philosophy while at school. He learnt French thoroughly, and was thereby enabled to keep abreast of developments in the sciences. His first paper on electricity he wrote when he was 24, and sent it to G. B. Beccaria (1716–81), a well-known physicist. Soon Volta himself began to acquire a reputation in the scientific world. In 1775 he was appointed to a professorship at Como, and three years later became professor of physics at Pavia University. In 1795 he was appointed Rector of the University, but was dismissed in 1799 for political reasons and went to Paris. There he met Napoleon, and when the

French took over northern Italy he was reinstated at Pavia as Rector. He retired in 1815.

Volta's invention of the electric battery – announced in 1800 in a letter to Sir Joseph BANKS, President of the Royal Society – transformed the science of electricity, because it put into the hands of scientists a reliable source of reasonably large electric currents. The frictional electrical machines and Leyden jar condensers previously available generated potential differences but small currents. Volta's discovery made possible the research on electrolysis in which the names of Humphry DAVY and Michael FARADAY are particularly prominent.

In 1786 L. GALVANI had made his famous observation that when an electric discharge took place near the legs of a recently dissected frog, the muscles contracted; and further that when the legs were hung on copper hooks, and touched an iron railing so as to complete an electrical circuit, they also contracted, even though there was no electrical machine in operation in the vicinity. Galvani's experimental results were published in 1791, and aroused great interest; Volta, among others, took up this branch of study. Galvani himself had attributed the effect to the animal matter; he believed that animal bodies were in some way storehouses of electricity, and that this was simply discharged by contact with the metals. In 1792 Volta published a paper in which he disagreed with this view of Galvani's, and suggested instead that electricity was simply an agent of nervous stimulation.

If this were so, then clearly animal matter should not be necessary for the production of electricity. Volta performed various experiments with different pairs of metals, testing them by touching with his tongue two metals in contact, and placing them in an order which we should call an electrochemical series. Until 1799, however, he was unable to demonstrate any electricity except in the presence of some animal matter. In that year he constructed his battery, which consisted of a pile of discs, alternately of silver and zinc, with absorbent materials soaked in water between each disc. This apparatus produced an electric current, and Volta wrote his famous letter to Banks, with the title *On the Electricity Excited by the Mere Contact of Conducting Substances of Different Kinds*. Almost immediately, W. Nicholson (1753–1815) and A. Carlisle (1768–1840) used the battery to decompose water by electrolysis.

Volta himself did little more work of great interest on the pile; it was left to others to establish that a chemical reaction produced the electricity, and that the electricity from Volta's battery was identical to that produced by electrical machines and electric eels.

Grand Larousse Encyclopédique, vol. 10.
(Portrait).
R. Olby (Ed.), *Late Eighteenth Century Scientists*. 1966.
G. Polvani, *Alessandro Volta*. 1942.
E. C. smith, *Nature*, **155**, 473, 1945.
Dictionary of Scientific Biography.

D M K

VON BABO, CLEMENS HEINRICH LAMBERT See BABO.

VON BAER, KARL ERNST See BAER.

VON BAEYER, JOHANN FRIEDRICH ADOLF See BAEYER.

VON BEHRING, EMIL ADOLF See BEHRING.

VON BOLLSTÄDT, ALBRECHT See ALBERTUS MAGNUS.

VON BRAUN, WERNHER MAGNUS MAXIMILIAN
Born in Germany, 23 March 1912; died Germantown, Maryland, USA, 16 June 1977. Pioneer of spaceflight.

Von Braun was educated at the University of Berlin, taking his PhD in 1930. From this time he became deeply interested in rocket propulsion, and particularly in the possibility of spaceflight. To further this, he took a post (1932) as technical assistant to the newly founded German Guided Missile Centre – originally at Kummersdorf but soon moved to Peenemunde on the Baltic – created to develop rockets for military use. Their research was founded primarily on principles expounded by Hermann Oberth (1894–) in his classic *Rakete zu den Planetenräumen* (Rockets into Planetary Space) of 1928. Von Braun was technical director of the Centre from 1937 to 1945, by which time the staff had grown to over 4000. There the liquid-fuel V-1 and V-2 rockets were developed and some 6400 of the latter were launched against London and other targets. They did much random damage but came too late to affect the outcome of the war and in May 1945 Peenemunde surrendered to US forces. With over 100 other specialists, and a vast amount of technical equipment, Von Braun was taken to America and supervised V-2 test firings in New Mexico. In 1950 he was appointed to the Guided Missile Development Division at Redstone Arsenal and became closely involved with the American Space Programme – thus circuitously achieving his early ambition – which culminated in the historic Moon landing on 21 July 1969. Von Braun was Director of the George C. Marshall Space Flight Center of NASA from 1960 to 1970. With Oberth and the Russians S. P. KOROLEV and K. Tsiolkovskii (1857–1935), Von Braun is recognized as a founding father of spaceflight.

J. C. Goodrum, *Wernher von Braun: Space Pioneer*. 1969.
Frank H. Winter, *Rockets into Space*. 1990.
(Portrait.) Paperback, 1993.

T I W

VON FRAUNHOFER, JOSEF See FRAUNHOFER.

VON GUERICKE, OTTO See GUERICKE.

VON HALLER, ALBRECHT See HALLER.

VON HELMHOITZ, HERMANN LUDWIG FERDINAND See HELMHOLTZ.

VON HEVESY, GEORG See HEVESY.

VON HOFMANN, AUGUST WILHELM See HOFMANN.

VON HOHENHEIM, THEOPHRASTUS BOMBASTUS See PARACELSUS.

VON HUMBOLDT, BARON FRIEDRICH ALEXANDER See HUMBOLDT.

VON KÖLLIKER, RUDOLPH ALBERT Born at Zürich, Switzerland, 6 July 1817; died Würzburg, Bavaria, Germany, 2 November 1905. Swiss biologist.

Kölliker studied medicine and science at the University of Zürich before undertaking further studies at Bonn and Berlin. In Berlin he was influenced by the pioneer biologists Johannes MÜLLER and Jacob Henle (1809–84), studying under them histology and comparative anatomy. In 1845 he was created a professor of anatomy and physiology in Zürich and two years later was appointed to a similar chair in Würzburg.

Kölliker's wide-ranging biological work makes his career difficult to summarize. An analysis of his publications, which appeared after his death, recorded 108 on histology, 52 on embryology, 19 on comparative anatomy and zoology, 11 on physiology, 5 on Darwinism, and 2 on anatomy. These include important books, such as the first modern histology textbook *Handbuch der Gewebelehre des Menschen* (1852) and the embryology text-book *Entwicklungsgeschichte des Menschen und der höhreren Thiere* (1861).

That Kölliker's fields of research were mainly dependent on the microscope is not altogether surprising, for he was influenced by the cell theory enunciated by M. J. SCHLEIDEN and T. SCHWANN in 1838–9. He himself made significant contributions to the theory, for he did much to disprove the idea that cells could arise freely – that is, not from existing cells – a view that had been put forward by Schwann. Kölliker, demonstrated for example, the process of cleavage of cells in the eggs of the cuttlefish.

Of Kölliker's other contributions to biology many were of considerable importance: for example, his microscopical work provided evidence connecting nerve fibres with nerve cells, and information on the mode of origin of the spermatozoa. In contrast, he made significant studies on the action of poisons such as curare and strychnine, and also played an important part in the acceptance of the theory of evolution. Although he appreciated the great service to biology rendered by Charles DARWIN, he made valid criticisms of Darwin's theory, especially on the question of the variations on which natural selection acts.

Kölliker's influence was felt not only through his books and research papers but also for his founding of the *Zeitschrift für wissenschaftliche Zoologie* (1849) and his membership of scientific societies. He was also an inveterate traveller, and came to Britain many times, where there is little doubt that he influenced the growing numbers of British biologists. He also had the reputation of being a first-class teacher.

R. A. von Kölliker, *Erinnerungen aus meinem Leben*. 1899.
British Medical Journal, **2**, 1375, 1905.
Dictionary of Scientific Biography.

J K C

VON LAUCHEN, GEORG JOACHIM *See* RHETICUS.

VON LAUE, MAX THEODOR FELIX *See* LAUE.

VON LIEBIG, BARON JUSTUS *See* LIEBIG.

VON LINDE, CARL *See* LINDE.

VON MAYER, JULIUS ROBERT *See* MAYER.

VON NÄGELI, KARL WILHELM *See* NÄGELI.

VON NEUMANN, JOHN [originally **JOHANN**] Born in Budapest, 28 December 1903; died Washington DC, 8 February 1957. Mathematician; pioneer of game theory and computer science.

Von Neumann graduated in chemical engineering from the *Technische Hochschule*, Zurich, in 1925 and obtained his PhD on axiomatic set theory, from the University of Budapest in 1926. Emigrating to the United States in 1930, he joined Princeton University and in 1933 moved to the Institute of Advanced Studies (IAS) as professor of mathematics, where he remained until his death. His early work was mainly concerned with quantum physics, the ergodic theorum, set theory, operator theory, Neumann algebras, logic, topological groups and continuous geometry, although he published the minimax theorum, later to become the cornerstone of his work with O. Morgenstern (1902–77) (1944) on the theory of games, in 1928.

By 1940 his interests had broadened into applied mathematics and statistics. He became a consultant (1940–57) to the US Armed Forces and Atomic Energy Commission atomic and hydrogen bomb development programme, contributing particularly to implosion lens development and hydrodynamics. Enthusiastic to apply computing to solution of related numerical problems, his advocacy of stored program control and use of a single processor in the University of Pennsylvania EDVAC computer (1945) and the IAS ('JOHNNIAC') computer (1951) influenced development of the next generation of computers. In 1956 he received the Medal of Freedom, the Enrico Fermi Award, and Albert Einstein Commemorative Award in recognition of his services to the nation.

W. Aspray, *John von Neumann and the Origins of Modern Computing*, 1990. (Portrait.)
W. Poundstone, *Prisoner's Dilemma: John von Neumann, Game Theory, and the Puzzle of the Bomb*. 1992.
Biographical Memoirs of the National Academy of Sciences, **32**, 437, 1958. (Portrait.)
Cordata, J. W. (Ed.) *Historical Dictionary of Data Processing: Biographies*, 1987.
J. J. Heims, *John von Neumann and Norbert Wiener: From Mathematics to the Technology of Life and Death*, 1980.
N. Stern, *From ENIAC to UNIVAC: An Appraisal of the Eckhert-Mauchly Computers*, 1981. (Portrait.)
Dictionary of Scientific Biography.

R J H

VON PETTENKOFER, MAX JOSEF Born at Lichtenheim, Bavaria, Germany, 13 December 1818; died Munich, Bavaria, 10 February 1901. A founder of modern hygiene.

Pettenkofer, after early attempts at acting, graduated in medicine at Munich in 1843. After research in physiology and chemistry, he was appointed professor of medical chemistry at Munich in 1847, and in 1853 became attached to the medical faculty. During the next ten years he undertook pioneer studies on nutrition and air conditioning. In 1865, through his influence, hygiene became recognized as an independent field of study in the Bavarian universities and he was appointed the first professor of hygiene at Munich.

He was tireless in promoting studies both on the origin of infectious diseases and on the prophylactic measures to combat them. He played a big part in the publication of the *Archiv für Hygiene* and the *Zeitschrift für Biologie*, and was co-author of the great *Handbuch der Hygiene* (1882).

Though Pettenkofer contributed greatly to hygiene and epidemiology, he refused to be converted to the germ theory of disease which became firmly established between 1860 and 1890. He was one of the last to uphold the idea that infectious diseases were spread by poisonous miasmata. In 1892, when aged 74, Pettenkofer swallowed – fortunately without harm – cultures of the causative organism of cholera. He firmly held to his celebrated 'ground-water theory', arguing that certain terrains emitted a poisonous cholera-producing miasma. Despite the incorrectness of the theory, it had important practical consequences, for it led Pettenkofer to a vigorous advocacy of adequate sewage systems. When put into practice this led to an effective reduction of intestinal diseases in Munich and elsewhere – one of the many practical consequences of his work.

O. Neustatter, *Dr. Max Pettenkofer.* 1925. (Portrait.)

C. E. A. Winslow, *The Conquest of Epidemic Disease.* 1943.

J. S. Haldane, *Journal of Hygiene*, **1**, 289, 1901.

British Medical Journal, **1**, 489, 1901.

Dictionary of Scientific Biography.

J K C

VON SACHS, FERDINAND GUSTAV JULIUS *See* SACHS.

VON SIEBOLD, CARL THEODOR ERNST *See* SIEBOLD.

VON SIEMENS, ERNST WERNER *See* SIEMENS.

VON WASSERMANN, AUGUST *See* WASSERMANN.

VON WELSBACH, BARON CARL AUER *See* WELSBACH.

VON WRÓBLEWSKI, ZYGMUNT FLORENTY *See* WRÓBLEWSKI.

VON ZEPPELIN, COUNT FERDINAND *See* ZEPPELIN.

VRIES, HUGO MARIE DE Born at Haarlem, Netherlands, 16 February 1848; died Amsterdam, 21 May 1935. Plant physiologist and hybridist; author of the Mutation Theory.

De Vries, whose father had been a Prime Minister, studied science at Leiden, Heidelberg and Würzburg. His researches into the extension of plant cells won him international repute. Using the technique of plasmolysis, he compared the suction pressures of cells, and showed that they depend on the concentration of the cell sap and the elasticity of the cell wall. He confirmed the theory of osmosis put forward by J. H. VAN'T HOFF, gave evidence for the theory of ionic diffusion, developed by S. ARRHENIUS, and determined the molecular weight of raffinose.

During the 1870s the Prussian Ministry of Agriculture invited de Vries to prepare monographs on cultivated plants. He contributed three: on clover, sugar beet and potatoes respectively. The experience thus gained proved valuable when he turned from physiology to heredity and variation. His first book on these subjects, *Intracellular Pangenesis* (1889), stressed the need to study characters as separate units whose inheritance is determined by elements in the nucleus which he called 'Pangenes'. The term 'Pangenesis' he took from Charles DARWIN, but unlike him he denied that the hereditary elements can move freely from cell to cell, hence the qualification 'intracellular'. This farsighted book had surprisingly little impact.

In 1892 he started breeding plants. Four years later he got clear examples of the 3:1 ratio. After obtaining this ratio with many other species, he announced his results in 1900, referring to the work published by J. G. MENDEL thirty-four years earlier. Within two months of de Vries's publication C. E. Correns (1864–1935) and E. von Tschermak (1871–1962) announced similar results.

De Vries's discovery of Mendelian ratios was only part of a much bigger programme designed to discover how mutant plants behave when crossed with the original species. When he found that mutations are preserved even when outbred, he put forward the view that evolution proceeds by steps as large as the mutations he observed. In his book, *Die Mutationstheory* (1901–3) he put forward his evidence. Later work has shown that his *Oenothera* mutants were due not to gene mutations but to chromosome rearrangements, so his discoveries were not as significant as he imagined. He was honoured by many learned societies (including the Royal Society 1905) and universities.

Almanach der Österreichisch Akademie der Wissenschaften, vol. 85. 1935.

Obituary Notices of Fellows of the Royal Society. 1935. (Portrait.)

A. F. Blakeslee, *Science*, **81**, 581, 1935.

Dictionary of Scientific Biography.

R C O

W

WAAGE, PETER Born at Flekkefjord, Norway, 29 June 1833; died Oslo, 13 January 1900. Known for his work on the Law of Mass Action with C. M. GULDBERG.

Peter Waage, son of Captain Peter Waage of the Norwegian merchant service, entered the University of Christiania (now Oslo) in 1854 to study medicine, but soon turned from this to the natural sciences. In his fourth year he won a gold medal for an essay entitled *The Theory of the Radicals of Oxygenated Acids*. As a further reward, he was appointed to a salaried position on the University staff (*stipendiat*) and while holding this position visited Germany to study under R. W. BUNSEN. In 1862 he returned and succeeded Adolf Strecker (1822–71) as professor of chemistry at Christiania, on the latter's departure for Túubingen. Two years later, in co-operation with his brother-in-law, C. M. Guldberg, he published the first draft of their treatise on chemical affinities. This work, embodying the Law of Mass Action, with a wealth of experimental evidence, was not very influential in its original Norwegian edition, but a French edition, *Études sur les Affinités Chimiques* (1867), brought its authors more prominence.

Waage's interests outside physical chemistry were devoted to the welfare of his country and its youth. He was president of the Norwegian equivalent of the Young Men's Christian Association. He invented an instrument for testing the percentage of alcohol in beer, with the aim of having stronger beer more heavily taxed. This arose from his interest in temperance, which was so great that he is said to have written to Gladstone in 1881 to suggest a similar extension of tax for Great Britain.

Waage was remembered by Sir William RAMSAY who described him in his obituary as 'rough in appearance . . . kindly . . . and . . . having a sense of power to influence people'.

W. Ramsay, *Journal of the Chemical Society*, 591, 1900.
J. R. Partington, *A History of Chemistry*, vol. 4. 1964. (Portrait.)
H. Haroldsen (Ed.), *The Law of Mass Action: A Centenary Volume*. 1964.
Dictionary of Scientific Biography.

G R T

WAKSMAN, SELMAN ABRAHAM Born in Novaya Priluka, Russia, 22 July 1888; died at Woods Hole, Massachusetts, USA, 16 August 1973. Microbiologist.

Waksman was brought up in a strictly orthodox Jewish family and antisemitism in Russia led him to emigrate to the USA in 1909. He studied agriculture at Rutgers College (now University) from 1911 to 1916 and returned there in 1918 to lecture on soil microbiology; he became full professor in 1930. At Rutgers he had a fruitful research career in enzymes; soil and soil organisms; and, later, antibiotics. In the latter field he is particularly identified with the isolation of streptomycin (1944) from *Streptomyces griseus*, jointly with A. Schutz and E. Bugi. However, Waksman alone was awarded the Nobel prize for physiology or medicine in 1952.

Waksman was also keenly interested in marine microbiology, and developed a laboratory for research in this field at Woods Hole Oceanographic Institute (1931). Until 1943 he and some of his research students worked there during the summer vacations. In collaboration with the US Navy important work was done on the fouling of ships' hulls.

S. A. Waksman, *My Life with Microbes*. 1954.
Dictionary of Scientific Biography, Supp. II.
Les Prix Nobel en 1952. 1953. (Portrait.)
Nature, 246, 367, 1973.
Trevor I. Williams, *Howard Florey: Penicillin and After*. 1984.
Tyler Wasson (Ed.), *Nobel Prize Winners*. 1987. (Portrait.)

T I W

WALDEN, PAUL Born in Livonia, Latvia, 26 July 1863; died Tübingen, Baden-Württemberg, Germany, 22 January 1957. Organic and physical chemist; discovered the 'Walden inversion'.

Walden entered the Riga Polytechnic (a mainly German-speaking institution) in 1882, and remained there as student, assistant, professor, and Rector until 1915. The Polytechnic was then evacuated to Moscow for three years; it returned to Riga, but the country was in such turmoil that Walden fled to Germany, where he became head of the Chemistry Department of Rostock University, from 1919 until his retirement in 1934. After his house and library were destroyed in 1942, he found refuge in Tübingen, where he was made guest professor; financial stringency forced him to continue teaching almost to the end of his long life.

Walden began research under W. F. OSTWALD, measuring the conductivity of electrolytes. This was the beginning of his life's work on the electrochemistry of non-aqueous solutions, for which he is remembered by 'Walden's rule', linking conductivity and viscosity. Ostwald's successor, C. A. Bischoff, was, however, an organic chemist; and, partly in collaboration with Bischoff, Walden began another line of research, on stereochemistry, which bore fruit (1896) with what was later called the 'Walden inversion'. This is the conversion of one optical isomer into a derivative of another by the action of certain reagents; it was long before an acceptable explanation was put forward, but it was, and is, of great importance in the theory of reaction mechanisms. Walden was also an historian, and wrote a *History of Organic Chemistry* (1941), and of *Chemistry* (1947).

Proceedings of the Chemical Society, 186, 1960.

Journal of Chemical Education, **28**, 160, 1951. (Portrait.)

D. S. Tarbell, *Journal of Chemical Education*, **51**, 7, 1974.

W V F

WALDEYER-HARTZ, HEINRICH WILHELM GOTTFRIED Born at Hehlen, Brunswick, Germany, 6 October 1836; died Berlin, 23 January 1921. Distinguished anatomist.

Wilhelm Waldeyer (as he is usually called) studied science and mathematics at Göttingen, and medicine there and at Greifswald and Berlin. He graduated in Berlin, and then became assistant in physiology at Königsberg and at Breslau. In 1865 he became associate professor and in 1867 full professor of pathological anatomy at Breslau. In 1872 he was appointed professor of normal anatomy at Strasbourg, and in 1883 he was called to the corresponding chair in Berlin, where he established a famous institute. He retired in 1917.

Waldeyer was the first to use haematoxylin as a histological stain (1863), but his results were not very good. Two years later Böhmer, by adding alum to the haematoxylin, evolved the stain now used. In 1867 Waldeyer published important work on the mode of spread of cancer. He published a notable book on the ovary and the ovum in 1870, and in it he gave the first description of the germinal epithelium. In 1884 he emphasized the true relations of the faucial and pharyngeal tonsils – 'Waldeyer's ring' – and his work was important in relation to the treatment of adenoids. In 1888 he introduced the term 'chromosomes' for the structures previously described by W. FLEMMING. Waldeyer followed closely the work of S. RAMÓN Y CAJAL and others on the connections of nerve cells. In 1891 he coined the term 'neurone theory' in an article which established the use of this term, but he himself did no original work in this field.

H. W. G. Waldeyer, *Lebenserinnerungen*. 1920.

F. H. Garrison, *History of Medicine*. 1954. (Portrait.)

Dictionary of Scientific Biography.

E A U

WALKER, SIR JAMES Born at Dundee, Scotland, 6 April 1863; died Edinburgh, 6 May 1935. Physical chemist and teacher.

James Walker began his career in a business house, but left it to study chemistry under Alexander Crum BROWN in Edinburgh. After a period in Germany, mostly with W. F. OSTWALD, he returned to Edinburgh (1889); went to University College, London (1892) to work under Sir William RAMSAY; and became professor of chemistry successively in Dundee (1894) and Edinburgh (1908). He retired in 1928.

His research was mostly in the field of physical chemistry. He and his students published on such topics as ionization constants, amphoteric electrolytes, and osmotic pressure – all aspects of the new ideas about solutions associated with the names of J. H. VAN'T HOFF, S. A. ARRHENIUS, and Ostwald. He was, however, a skilled organic chemist, and worked on the electrolytic synthesis of dibasic carboxylic acids. His *Introduction to Physical Chemistry* (1899) ran into many editions.

Walker was elected FRS in 1900, and knighted in 1921, in recognition of his services to the chemical industry during the war.

Journal of the Chemical Society, 1347, 1935. (Portrait.)

Obituary Notices of Fellows of the Royal Society. 1935. (Portrait.)

Dictionary of National Biography.

W V F

WALKER, JOHN Born at Stockton-on-Tees, Co. Durham, England, 1780 or 1781; died there, 1 May 1859. Inventor of the friction match.

Walker was articled to a surgeon in his native town, and indeed practised, but an increasing aversion to surgical operations turned his interest to chemistry. He set up in business as an apothecary in Stockton about 1818, and in his leisure worked on means of producing fire. Unlike nearly all his contemporaries in this field, he did not confine himself to preparations of phosphorus; about 1827 he invented, and began to sell, the first friction matches. These were wooden splints coated with sulphur, and tipped with a head made of a mixture of potassium chlorate, antimony sulphide, and gum arabic. The match was struck by gripping the head in a piece of sandpaper (supplied with the matches) and withdrawing sharply; fifty were sold for a shilling.

Although Walker did not patent his invention, and consequently had many competitors, he made a considerable fortune.

Dictionary of National Biography.

W. A. Bone, *Nature*, **119**, 495, 1927.

W V F

WALLACE, ALFRED RUSSEL Born at Usk, Monmouthshire, England, 8 January 1823; died Broadstone, Dorset, 7 November 1913. Naturalist.

After a rudimentary education and a variety of jobs, Wallace in 1844 became a master at the Collegiate School, Leicester, where he made the acquaintance of the entomologist H. W. BATES. Already he was a dedicated naturalist, and persuaded Bates to join him on a collecting expedition to the Amazon in 1848. His readings of the works of F. H. A. von HUMBOLDT and Charles DARWIN had convinced him that in Tropical America he would find the materials for his particular interest, the origin of species. Unfortunately, most of the specimens collected on this expedition were lost during the return voyage, when the ship was destroyed by fire.

In 1854 Wallace went to the Malay Archipelago, spending over eight years there collecting and observing. His essay (written in Sarawak, 1855) *On the Law which has Regulated the Introduction of New Species* was a significant pre-Darwinian contribution to the theory of evolution. It attracted little attention, but its similarity to his own private theories was recognized by Darwin. Wallace was not deterred by this lack of public interest, and while ill with fever in the Moluccas, he recollected the arguments postulated by T. MALTHUS in his

Essay on the Principle of Population. This suggested to him, as it had to Darwin many years earlier, the theory of natural selection which he elaborated in an essay, *On the Tendency of Varieties to Depart Indefinitely from the Original Type*; this he sent to Darwin in 1858 for his comments. Darwin was amazed: 'I never saw such a striking coincidence: if Wallace had my MS. sketch written out in 1842, he could not have made a better short extract! ' With characteristic generosity, Darwin was prepared to concede priority of publication to Wallace, but was persuaded by J. D. HOOKER and C. LYELL to agree to a joint presentation of both papers at a meeting of the Linnean Society on 1 July 1858. Wallace's diffidence led him to the subordinate role of a disciple to Darwin, whose theories he comprehensively considered in relation to the evolution of mimicry, speciation, and human evolution in his book *Darwinism* (1889).

Wallace's line, in spite of subsequent doubts about its validity, still commemorates his abiding interest in the distribution of animals. He observed that the Malay Archipelago is divided into two distinct zoological regions by the strait between Bali and Lombok, with a predominantly Oriental fauna on the western side, and an Australian one on the eastern. It was Wallace who first produced a synthesis of all available evidence on the geographical distribution of animals, and the modern science of zoogeography springs from his magnum opus, *Geographical Distribution of Animals* (1876).

His *Malay Archipelago* (1869) is one of the best travel books of the period. *Island Life* (1880), which described with Wallace's clarity and simplicity the fauna and flora of some of the main islands of the world, excited the admiration of naturalists.

After the publication of *Darwinism*, Wallace was engaged in scientific lecturing, and in publishing his views on spiritualism, which lost him some of the support – but never the respect – of his fellow biologists. He was a socialist and had advanced opinions on land nationalization and women's suffrage.

Academic honours came late in his life. He was elected FRS (against his wishes) in 1893, and received the Order of Merit in 1910. He was half genius, half crank, a very simple man with a kindly nature. His almost total eclipse in public memory is probably due to his innate modesty. Darwin once reproved him: 'You are the only man I ever heard of who personally does himself an injustice, and never demands justice.'

A. R. Wallace, *My Life*. 1905. (Portrait.)

J. Marchant, *Alfred Russel Wallace*. 1916. (Portrait.)

W. George, *Biologist Philosopher*. 1964. (Portrait.)

A. Williams-Ellis, *Darwin's Moon*. 1966. (Portrait.)

Nature **89**, 367, 1912.

H. Lewis McKinney, *Wallace and Natural Selection*. 1972.

Dictionary of Scientific Biography.

Dictionary of National Biography.

L. T. Hogben, *Alfred Russel Wallace: The Story of a Great Discoverer*. 1918.

R G C D

WALLACH, OTTO Born at Königsberg, Prussia, Germany, 27 March 1847; died Göttingen, 26 Feb-

ruary 1931. Organic chemist, remembered for his pioneering studies of the terpenes.

Wallach studied chemistry at Göttingen under F. WÖHLER and also in the University of Berlin. He had to abandon an industrial career for reasons of health, and in 1870 became one of the assistants of F. A. KEKULÉ in Bonn. He was promoted to extraordinary professor in 1876, and in 1889 became professor in Göttingen; he retired in 1915. He never married.

Wallach was a thoroughgoing experimentalist, who made no contribution to chemical theory. His early researches are of little importance, except for the discovery of the 'Wallach rearrangement' (1880) of azoxybenzene into 4-hydroxy azobenzene in sulphuric acid. The gradual withdrawal of the ailing Kekulé from academic duties during the late 1870s meant that Wallach had to take up the teaching of pharmaceutical chemistry. This task introduced him to the unsolved problems of the chemistry of the essential oils, samples of which had lain around the Bonn laboratories for many years.

Although a great deal was known about the essential oils, or terpenes, the knowledge was fragmentary and uncoordinated. Wallach set himself the arduous task of characterizing the main terpenes as chemical individuals; many of the supposedly pure compounds proved to be complex mixtures, and different names had often been assigned to the same compound. Once this matter had been largely clarified, Wallach attacked the problem of the structure of the terpenes, and their often baffling transformations one into another. This work reached its climax in the elucidation of the structure (1895) of the key compound α-terpineol.

For this work on terpenes, Wallach was awarded the Nobel prize for chemistry in 1910. Even after his retirement from the chair at Göttingen he remained attached to the University, and continued to work in the laboratory until shortly before his death.

L. Ruzicka, *Journal of the Chemical Society*, 1582, 1932.

W. S. Partridge and E. R. Schierz, *Journal of Chemical Education*, **24**, 106, 1947. (Portrait.)

E. Farber (Ed.), *Great Chemists*. 1961. (Portrait.)

Tyler Wasson (Ed.), *Nobel Prize Winners*. 1987. (Portrait.)

W V F

WALLIS, BARNES NEVILLE was born at Ripley, Derbyshire, England, 26 September 1887; died at Leatherhead, Surrey, 30 October 1979. An outstandingly innovative engineer.

He was the son of Charles Wallis, who qualified in medicine at Oxford and was a general practitioner first at Ripley and then, despite a crippling illness, at New Cross, London. Barnes did well at Christ's Hospital school, but developed migraine, a lifelong tribulation. Following a marine engineering apprenticeship, he joined H. B. Pratt at Vickers and worked under him on the design of the rigid airship R9. Then Barnes himself designed the airship R80, his favourite. In this he departed from the usual cigar shape to use a streamline form based on wind tunnel tests.

After a slack interval which Wallis used to gain an engineering degree, he was back with Vickers as Chief Designer of the R100. This was notable for the ingenious way in which its framework was manufactured and for the novel network of geodetic wiring that restrained its gas bags.

British airship work was suspended in 1930 after the R101 disaster, and Wallis moved to aeroplane design. Geodetic structures now appeared in the Wollesley and Wellington aeroplanes. They provided a background for the fabric covering then still usual, but the manufacture of the geodetic members required all Wallis' ingenuity.

On the outbreak of war in 1939, Wallis became a successful advocate of bombing Germany's industrial heartland, and invented first his large spinning bombs for the destruction of the great dams in the Ruhr, and then specially penetrating bombs to attack the ships and submarine pens of the German Navy.

After the war, Wallis turned his attention to the design of bridges and commercial submarines, but the times were not ready for his new ideas. He had more success when he helped in the design of a major new radio telescope in Australia. He designed its 210 ft diameter dish and its mechanical operating system.

In his last years, Wallis remembered Christ's Hospital and greatly helped its development at Horsham. His achievements led to many honours: the CBE in 1943; FRS in 1945; a number of honorary doctorates; and knighthood in 1968.

J. E. Morpurgo, *Barnes Wallis, a Biography.* 1972.
Biographical Memoirs of Fellows of the Royal Society. 1981. (Portrait.)

A G P

WALLIS, JOHN Born at Ashford, Kent, England, 22 October 1616; died Oxford, 28 October 1703. Scholar and mathematician, who contributed many results in algebra and analytical geometry; a founder-member of the Royal Society.

In 1632 Wallis entered Emmanuel College, Cambridge, to study medicine and philosophy. He took orders in 1640, and in 1644 was elected to a Fellowship at Queens' College, Cambridge, but left to live in London. In 1643 he published the first of many pamphlets, on a variety of subjects. From 1649 to his death he was Savilian Professor of Geometry at Oxford; Cromwell appointed him, despite his royalist leanings, partly because he used his considerable deciphering skill for the Parliamentarians during the Civil War. He was reappointed in 1660, and became chaplain to Charles II. The well-known controversy with Thomas Hobbes (1588–1679), which started in 1655, was at its most intense when Wallis refuted Hobbes's attempt to square the circle ('Surely their Mercuries are in opposition', said the antiquary John Aubrey (1626–97). The publication of Wallis's *Grammaticae Linguae Anglicanae* (1652), with its appendix on modes of articulation, was the occasion of a dispute with William Holder (1616–98), the divine; Aubrey claims that Wallis plagiarized from Holder, and also from Christopher WREN, Robert HOOKE, and others, because he was 'so extremely greedy of glorie'. He had a prodigious memory for figures.

Wallis's most famous work, *Arithmetica Infinitorum* (1655), which is mainly concerned with series, figurate numbers, and quadrature of geometrical figures by means of series, shows a certain rashness with infinities (he invented the symbol ∞). His treatment of surfaces as actually composed of lines, whose lengths he may add up (using series), to find the area, indicates a dependence on B. CAVALIERI: he says in the preface that his method starts where Cavalieri's (with which he was familiar only through E. TORRICELLI) left off. In proposition CXCI he gives his famous formula:

$$\frac{4}{\pi} = \frac{3 \times 3 \times 5 \times 5 \times 7 \times 7 \times \&c}{2 \times 4 \times 4 \times 6 \times 6 \times 8 \times \&c}$$

the result of an impressive use of interpolation. He was one of the first to consider representing complex numbers on the plane. Wallis's *Algebra*, printed in English in 1685, contains a history of the subject, admired by R. Cotes (1682–1716), but now considered rather too favourable to Englishmen. Wallis wrote many other mathematical works, including *Mechanica* (1669), in which there is a large section on centres of gravity; a work on the pressure of liquids (1674); on conics (1655); on the cycloid (1659); and *Mathesis Universalis* (1657). He also edited and translated many important Greek works, including the *Sand-Reckoner* and *Measurement of the Circle* (1676) of ARCHIMEDES.

J. Wallis, *Opera Mathematica*, 1693–9. (Portraits in vols. 1 and 2.)
Dictionary of National Biography.
J. F. Scott, *The Mathematical Works of John Wallis.* 1938. (Portrait.)
Notes and Records of the Royal Society of London, **25**, 17, 1970.
Dictionary of Scientific Biography.

R P L

WALSCHAERTS, ÉGIDE Born at Malines, Belgium, 21 January 1820; died Saint Gilles, near Brussels, 18 February 1901. Engineer.

As a 15-year-old pupil of the Municipal College at Malines he witnessed the opening of the railway line to Brussels and three years later he exhibited five models at a local exhibition. He left the University of Liège owing to illness without taking his degree, and in 1842 joined the workshops of the State railways at Malines as a mechanic. At the end of two years he was made a shop foreman in Brussels, a post he kept throughout his life. On 5 October 1844, the chief engineer of the Belgian State Railways filed an application for a patent for a new system of steam distribution applicable to both stationary steam engines and locomotives. This was done because the rules of the department did not allow a foreman to exploit a Belgian patent for his own profit. Walschaerts himself took out a patent in France for the same invention. This was the famous radial valve gear that derived its motion from a return crank outside the driving-wheel crank and big-end. It was adopted by many foreign countries and, after initial suspicion, became standard on British locomotives.

A picture of the first British engine to be fitted with this gear is in the *Railway Magazine*, April 1910, p. 268; an 0-4-4 engine built in 1878 and subsequently placed in service on the Swindon, Marlborough and Andover line.

J. Boulvin, *Railway Gazette*, 8 December 1905.
Railway Magazine, May–June, November–December 1943; January–February 1944; cii, 1956. (Portrait.)

A. Vendeghen, *American Society for Testing and Materials, Book of Standards*, **5**, 23, 1944. (Portrait.

Ulysse Lamalle, *Science et Technique*, **5**, 23, 1944. (Portrait.)

W H G A

WALTER, PHILIPPE Born at Cracow, Poland, 1810; died Paris, 9 April 1847. Organic chemist.

Walter studied chemistry in Cracow, but had to leave Poland after taking part in the abortive rebellion against Russia of 1830–1. He went to Paris, joined the school of J. B. DUMAS, and taught analytical chemistry in the *École des Arts et Métiers*. He discovered toluene in the distillate from pine-resin (with P. J. PELLETIER 1838) and distinguished menthol from camphor. From the reaction between camphoric anhydride and sulphuric acid (1842), he obtained 'sulphocamphoric acid' and carbon monoxide. At the time this result was of great significance, as showing that even carbon could be replaced by other elements in organic compounds, and as supporting the 'substitution theory' of Dumas. He also discovered camphorsulphonic acid (1843), and published a book on Polish chemical nomenclature.

J. C. Poggendorf, *Biographisch-Literarisches Handwörterbuch*. 1883–1903.

J. R. Partington, *A History of Chemistry*, vol. 4. 1964.

W V F

WANKEL, FELIX Born at Lahr, Baden-Württemberg, Germany, 13 August 1902; died Lindau, 9 October 1988. Mechanical engineer who invented the eponymous rotary internal combustion engine.

Without the benefit of a university or college education, Wankel was nevertheless a very talented engineer who from about 1930 was determined to solve the problem of designing an internal combustion engine that did not involve the conversion of reciprocating to rotary motion. He first worked for a firm of booksellers in Heidelberg from 1921 to 1926, in order to make enough money to set up his own workshop. He began to investigate the possibility of making radical improvements to internal combustion engines, and from 1934 to 1936 was working under contract to BMW. Thereafter, until the end of the Second World War, he was directed to undertake research for the German Air Ministry.

With the support of NSU and other German motor manufacturers, he set up a research institute at Lindau and by 1957 had built a successful prototype of his rotary engine, which consisted of an epitrochoidal combustion chamber containing a rotor in the shape of an equilateral triangle with slightly convex sides. The Wankel engine is in theory more efficient than those employing either the Otto or Diesel cycles, but an effective method of sealing the rotor at the three points where it is in contact with the internal wall of the combustion chamber has still to be developed, especially for engines of larger size and power.

A twin-chamber Wankel engine was fitted in the NSU RO80 motor car in 1968, and it has since been used in a small number of high-performance sports cars and, with more success, in some motor-cycles. There are, however, continuing problems of high

fuel consumption, exhaust pollution, and long-term reliability, and its early promise has not yet been fulfilled.

The Annual Obituary, 1988.

R M B

WARBURG, OTTO HEINRICH Born in Freiburg-im-Breisgau, Germany, 8 October 1883; died Berlin-Dahlem, 1 August 1970. Biochemist.

Warburg was born into a scientific family; his father was professor of physics at Freiburg and later president of the *Physikalische Reichsanstalt*. He himself studied chemistry at Freiburg and then took a doctorate under Emil FISCHER in Berlin. Later he studied medicine at Heidelberg (1906=N14). During the First World War he served in the Prussian Horse Guards until called – at the instance of EINSTEIN, his father's friend – to be head of the Max Planck Institute for Cell Physiology, Dahlem, from which he retired at the age of 86.

Warburg was a meticulously careful experimentalist and devised novel methods to monitor a variety of biochemical processes. He is particularly remembered for his use of manometry and tissue slices to study cellular respiration. He investigated the metabolism of cancer cells; the catalysis of biological oxidations; and the crystallization of enzymes. He was awarded the Nobel prize for physiology or medicine in 1931, notably for the discovery of the protein ferredoxin, a key factor in photosynthesis.

H. Krebs, *Otto Warburg: Biochemist and Eccentric*. 1981.

Les Prix Nobel en 1931. 1932. (Portrait.)

Biographical Memoirs of Fellows of the Royal Society, 1972. (Portraits.)

Dictionary of Scientific Biography.

Tyler Wasson (Ed.), *Nobel Prize Winners*. 1987. (Portrait.)

T I W

WARD, JOSHUA Born 1685; died London, 21 November 1761. Medical quack; industrial chemist.

Joshua Ward (popularly 'Spot' Ward because of a conspicuous birthmark) was a well-known eighteenth-century quack. His celebrated 'white drops' appear to have contained a dangerous quantity of antimony. In 1717 he tried fraudulently to enter Parliament and had to flee to France. He was pardoned in 1733 and his very successful London practice – established in spite of satire in the newspapers – dates from his return.

For medical preparations he required substantial quantities of sulphuric acid and for this purpose established vitriol works near London at Twickenham (1736) and then at Richmond (1740). His process of making the acid 'by the bell' (*per campanam*) was not new; using nitre and sulphur, it was possibly introduced to Britain by Cornelis DREBBEL and was described by N. LÉMERY. The interest in Ward's process lies in the scale of operation. He used glass vessels of some fifty gallons capacity – no mean feat for the glassblowers of the day – and reduced the price of acid some sixteenfold (to about 2s 6d (12½p) per pound). In due course, sulphuric acid was to become the most important of all industrial chemicals.

A. and N. Clow, *The Chemical Revolution; a Contribution to Social Technology*. 1952.

B. Hill, *Practitioner*, **203**, 820, 1969.

M. H. Nicolson, *Journal of the History of Ideas*, **29**, 177, 1968.
Dictionary of National Biography.

T I W

WASSERMANN, AUGUST VON Born at Bamberg, Germany, 21 February 1866; died Berlin, 16 March 1925. Distinguished immunologist, and inventor of the syphilitic reaction that bears his name.

Wassermann studied in the Universities of Erlangen, Vienna, Munich and Strasbourg, and graduated at Strasbourg in 1888. Two years later he became an assistant in the Institute for Infectious Diseases, of which R. KOCH was Director. In 1906 he was promoted to the directorship of the Department of Experimental Therapy in that Institute. He was ennobled in 1910. In 1913 he was appointed director of the newly founded Institute for Experimental Therapy in Dahlem (Berlin).

Wassermann was one of those who confirmed the discovery, by Emil von BEHRING and S. KITA-SATO, of antitoxic immunity to tetanus and to diphtheria (1894). He later worked on precipitins, and on the complement-fixation test in tuberculosis. In 1906, in collaboration with other workers, he discovered antibodies to a syphilitic antigen in the serum of syphilitic monkeys, and by a similar method he proved that general paralysis of the insane is a late manifestation of syphilis. In the same year also he demonstrated these syphilitic antibodies in the blood serum of syphilitics. This 'Wassermann reaction' is a very specific and sensitive test for previous infection with the causal organism of syphilis, and it has been widely used since its introduction. In 1907 Wassermann was one of the earliest workers to immunize horses to the meningococcus and to inject the resulting immune serum into patients suffering from cerebrospinal fever. With Wilhelm Kolle (1868–1935) he edited (1903–9) a very important multi-volume work on pathogenic micro-organisms, *Handbuch der pathogenen Mikroorganismen*.

W. Bulloch, *History of Bacteriology*. 1938.
H. J. Parish, *History of Immunization*. 1965.
W. A. Pusey, *History of Syphilis*. 1933. (Portrait.)
Dictionary of Scientific Biography, Supp. 1.

E A U

WATERSTON, JOHN JAMES Born in Edinburgh, 1811; died there, 18 June 1883. Physicist; developed early kinetic theory of gases.

Waterston was a graduate of Edinburgh University, in science and medicine. For a time he practised as an engineer in London and Bombay, but then returned to Edinburgh to pursue research in science. He became interested in chemical notation and nomenclature and this brought him into dispute with W. ODLING. More particularly, stimulated by the work of J. P. JOULE on the nature of heat, he turned his mind to the kinetic theory of gases and in 1845 submitted a paper on this subject to the Royal Society. Unfortunately, it was overlooked and received no attention until Lord RAYLEIGH found it in the Society's archives and had it printed in 1892. It was then apparent that Waterston had largely anticipated the kinetic theory put forward by R. J. E. CLAUSIUS in 1857. It is acknowledged that the oversight delayed progress in this field by some fifteen years.

In later life Waterston resumed his interest in medicine and published *Thoughts on the Mental Functions*, an analysis of the physiological basis of mental processes.

R. J. Strutt, *J. W. Strutt: Third Baron Rayleigh*. 1924.
J. S. Haldane, *Collected Scientific Papers of John James Waterston*. 1928.
S. Brush, *American Scientist*, **49**, 202, 1961.
Dictionary of Scientific Biography.
Dictionary of National Biography (Missing Persons). 1993.

T I W

WATSON, JAMES DEWEY Born in Chicago, Illinois, USA, 6 April 1928. Molecular biologist. With Francis CRICK discovered the structure of DNA.

Watson entered the University of Chicago at the age of fifteen, graduating in 1947. He moved to the University of Indiana and studied under the geneticist H. J. MÜLLER, while also working with S. Luria (1912–1991) and M. DELBRÜCK. He was awarded a PhD in 1950 for his work on the effect of x-rays on bacteriophages. With the help of a postdoctoral fellowship he went to the University of Copenhagen 1950–1 to continue his work on viruses.

In 1951 he moved to the Cavendish Laboratory, Cambridge University, and with F. H. C. CRICK set out to discover the structure of DNA in order to find out more about how the gene worked at the molecular level. In 1952 A. D. HERSHEY confirmed the hypothesis of O. T. AVERY that genes are made of DNA. Using the discoveries by E. CHARGAFF that nucleic acids contain four different organic bases and A. R. TODD that they contain sugar and phosphate groups, Crick and Watson built a series of molecular models. In 1953 they succeeded in building a model that incorporated all the known features of DNA and confirmed the x-ray diffraction pattern discovered by M. H. F. Wilkins (1916–   ) and Rosalind FRANKLIN (1920–1958) in London. The model showed that the DNA molecule has the form of a double helix, consisting of two parallel chains of alternate sugar and phosphate groups linked by pairs of organic bases. It showed how genes replicate and carry information. They reported their discovery in *Nature* in April, 1953. Crick and Watson shared the Nobel prize for physiology or medicine with Wilkins in 1962.

Watson returned to the USA in 1953, first to Caltech and then in 1956 to Harvard University, where he set up a Molecular Biology research laboratory. He was appointed professor of molecular biology in 1961. In 1968 he became director of the Cold Spring Harbor Laboratory of Quantitative Biology, Long Island, New York, and resigned from his Harvard chair in 1976. He also became director of the Office of Human Genome Research at the National Institute of health, which funds and coordinates the American effort to map the human genome, in 1989.

His publications include *The Molecular Biology of the Gene* (1965, 4th edition 1987); *The DNA Story: a Documentary History of Gene Cloning* (with J. Tooze, 1981); *The Molecular Biology of the Cell* (1983, 2nd edition 1989); and *Recombinant DNA: a Short Course* (with J. Tooze and D. T. Kurtz, 1984, 2nd edition 1992).

J. D. Watson, *The Double Helix: a personal account of the discovery of the structure of DNA*. 1968.

(New critical edition including text, commentary, reviews, and original papers, ed. G. S. Stent, 1981). (Portrait.)

R. C. Olby, *The Path to the Double Helix*. 1974.

H. F. Hudson, *The Eighth Day of Creation. Makers of the Revolution in Biology*. 1979.

Tyler Wasson (Ed.), *Nobel Prize Winners*. 1987 (Portrait.)

A P B

WATSON, SIR WILLIAM Born in London, 3 April 1715; died Lincoln's Inn Fields, London, 10 May 1787. Physician, best known for his work on electricity.

Watson attended Merchant Taylors' School, London, from 1726 to 1730, and was then apprenticed to an apothecary. In 1738 he set up in business for himself, and three years later was elected a Fellow of the Royal Society. In 1756 he became a trustee of the British Museum. He was admitted Licentiate of the Royal College of Physicians in 1759, and began to practise medicine. In 1762 he was appointed physician to the Foundling Hospital, a post which he retained to the end of his life. In 1768 he published an account of experiments concerning inoculation against smallpox. The Royal Society awarded him its Copley Medal in 1745. He was knighted shortly before he died.

Watson's main interests were natural history (making the work of LINNAEUS known in Britain), electricity, and medicine, and he published over fifty papers on these subjects. He is best known for his work on electricity; from 1745 onwards he published a series of papers entitled *Experiments on the Nature of Electricity*. He made numerous experiments with a Leyden jar, and noticed that moist air was a conductor; this explained the failure of electrical experiments in a humid atmosphere. In 1747–8 he attempted to determine the velocity of electricity, but his experiments seemed only to show that it was 'instantaneous', his method being insufficiently sensitive. He also worked on electrical discharges in gases at low pressures and showed that rarified air was a conductor (see also F. HAUKSBEE). He successfully advocated the use of lightning conductors, as described by Benjamin FRANKLIN, for a new powder magazine at Purfleet.

P. F. Mottelay, *Bibliographical History of Electricity and Magnetism*. 1922.

Gentleman's Magazine, **1**, 454. 1787.

Dictionary of National Biography.

Dictionary of Scientific Biography.

B B K

WATSON-WATT, SIR ROBERT ALEXANDER Born at Brechin, Scotland, 13 April 1892; died Inverness, 5 December 1973. Pioneer of radar development.

Watson-Watt was educated at Brechin High School and then went as an engineering student to University College Dundee, then part of St Andrews University. On graduating, he became assistant to the professor of natural philosophy at Dundee, until the First World War took him to London (1915) as a member of the staff of the Meteorological Office. There he applied himself, because of their potential danger to the growing number of aviators, to the radio location of thunderstorms; by the end of the war, storms could be located at distances up to several hundred miles. Although his interest in radar stemmed from this research it was, in fact, somewhat different in principle. The radio location of storms depended upon detection of random signals generated at the storm centre; in radar, a radio pulse is directed at the object to be located and the echo from it is then recorded at the transmitting station. On the basis of his wartime experience, Watson-Watt was appointed (1921) superintendent of the radio research station at Aldershot and Slough run by the Department of Scientific and Industrial Research. Later he was appointed head of the radio department of the National Physical Laboratory at Teddington, with a special responsibility for radio beacons and direction-finding.

Watson-Watt put forward his first proposals for locating enemy aircraft by means of a radio pulse technique in February 1935; by the summer of that year sufficient success had been achieved in practice to indicate the immense potential of the method. Within two years a major policy decision had been taken by the British government, to organize a comprehensive national network of radar stations to give advance warning of the approach of hostile aeroplanes (see H. T. TIZARD). When war broke out in 1939 this system was virtually complete and in 1940, when Britain stood alone in the face of apparently overwhelming German superiority in the air, it proved dramatically effective not merely in shattering German hopes of immediate invasion but turned the tide from defeat to victory.

The principle of radar (from radio detection and ranging) is quite simple. Bursts of radio energy, covering the airspace to be explored, are transmitted. If the airspace explored contains an aircraft a very small proportion of the energy (about 10^{-17}) is reflected back to the transmitter and can be displayed on a cathode-ray oscillograph. The aircraft is represented by a break in the time-base line and the position of the break indicates its distance. Each burst, of about a million watts at 30 000 megacycles per second, lasts approximately ten millionths of a second. Since the waves travel at the speed of light, a time lapse of one millionth of a second between transmission of the signal and receipt of the echo corresponds to about 500 ft or there-and-back distance to the target. In point of fact, great precision could be achieved largely with conventional radio components and at quite an early stage targets could be pinpointed with an accuracy of about one foot in a mile at ranges in excess of 100 miles.

No new principle was involved in radar: Watson-Watt's genius lay in devising a comprehensive system that could be operated by non-specialists under wartime conditions. Initially restricted to fixed ground stations, it was quickly extended to mobile ground units and to ships (1938) and aircraft (1939). Before long, radar was coupled to guns to give automatic ranging. Ground-scanning devices made it possible to detect major features on the ground below a high-flying aircraft. In the post-war years, radar has of course been immensely valuable as a general navigational aid.

The concept of radar was envisaged in an American science fiction novel of 1911 ('Ralph 124 c 41', by Hugo Gernsback); the author proposed the use of a pulsating polarized wave the reflection of which was detected by an 'actinoscope'. At a more practical level, MARCONI (1922) proposed the use of short radio waves in a collision-avoiding device. In 1924 E. V. APPLETON, who later was to make important contributions to radar, used the principle to detect and locate ionized layers in the upper atmosphere. Elsewhere, other inventors were following similar lines. In the United States, G. BREIT and M. A. Tuve (1901–82) were also exploring the upper atmosphere by reflected radio waves and this led on to development of military radio-location equipment there. In Germany, Rudolf Kuhnhold demonstrated a simple radar device in 1933; until the end of the war, however, German radar limited its success by continuing to use too long wavelengths. Despite the uniqueness of his own contribution Watson-Watt never failed to recognize the contributions of others in the same field.

Watson-Watt's researches earned him many honours. He was elected to Fellowship of the Royal Society in 1941 and was knighted in the following year; he was an honorary graduate of the universities of St Andrews, Toronto, and Laval. From 1943–46 he was deputy chairman of the Radio Board of the War Cabinet. The immense practical importance of his invention to the Allied war effort – it was perhaps the greatest single contribution to victory – was recognized with an award of £50,000, the biggest payment to an individual recommended by the Royal Commission on Awards to Inventors.

The Times, 5 December 1973.

R. A. Watson-Watt, *The Pulse of Radar: The Autobiography of Sir Robert Watson-Watt.* 1959. (Published in Britain as *Three Steps to Victory.* 1957.)

R. M. Page, *The Origin of Radar.* 1962.

Biographical Memoirs of Fellows of the Royal Society. 1975. (Portrait.)

Dictionary of National Biography.

T I W

WATT, JAMES Born at Greenock, Scotland, 19 January 1736; died Heathfield, Birmingham, England, 25 August 1819. Inventor of the improved steam engine, and perhaps the greatest of British engineers.

James Watt's father was a carpenter and merchant at Greenock, and as a boy Watt spent a good deal of time in his father's workshop. After leaving the local grammar school, he went to London in 1755, to learn the craft of mathematical instrument-making. After a gruelling year of work in a shop at Cornhill, he was appointed mathematical instrument-maker to Glasgow University. In 1759 he went into partnership with John Craig, and the business thrived. One of Watt's early inventions was his perspective machine (1763) for drawing three-dimensional objects. At this time Watt also made several useful friends, including Joseph BLACK, James Lind (1736–1812), John Robison (1739–1805) and John ROEBUCK. In 1764 Watt married his cousin, Margaret Miller.

In the spring of 1764 Watt was asked to repair a model of a Newcomen steam engine. He pondered over the deficiencies of this engine and in May 1765 arrived at his famous idea of keeping the cylinder hot and leading the spent steam to a separate condenser. The development of this idea into a full-scale engine was taken up by Roebuck at Kin-

neil; but poor craftsmanship, particularly trouble with the piston packing, made progress painfully slow. Watt travelled to England in 1767, and confided the secret of his invention to Erasmus DARWIN and William Small (1734–75) at Birmingham: both were enthusiastic for its development, and communicated this enthusiasm to their friend, the great Birmingham manufacturer Matthew BOULTON, who met Watt in 1768. Boulton tried to negotiate with Roebuck, but without success.

Watt's undeveloped invention did not earn his living, and in the years 1767–74 his main occupation was canal surveying in Scotland, where his work included surveys for the Caledonian Canal from Inverness to Fort William.

In 1773 Roebuck became bankrupt and in 1774 Boulton acquired the patent of Watt's engine. Watt's first wife died in 1773, and in 1774 he moved to Birmingham. In 1775 Boulton succeeded in obtaining an extension of Watt's patent for twenty-five years, and the illustrious partnership of Boulton and Watt began. Their first engine began working in March 1776, but it took another five years of development to produce reliable and economic engines, and the firm did not show a profit until the 1780s.

From 1775 until the 1790s Watt worked hard on the development of his engine, and made several important improvements: the double-acting engine, the rotative engine with sun-and-planet mechanism, parallel motion, the governor, and the idea of measuring output in 'horse-power'. He and Boulton made many journeys to Cornwall and other places where their engines were being installed. Watt also devised a chemical method for copying documents which became the standard office copying machine for a century.

In 1776 Watt was married again, to Ann MacGregor of Milngavie, near Glasgow. He took a prominent part in the activities of the Lunar Society of Birmingham: after meeting James KEIR and Joseph PRIESTLEY at Lunar gatherings, Watt took more interest in chemistry, and in 1783 he suggested in a paper submitted to the Royal Society that water was not a simple substance but a compound of hydrogen and oxygen (to use the modern terminology). This led to the complicated 'Water Controversy' (see H. CAVENDISH). Watt was elected FRS in 1785.

In the 1790s Boulton and Watt began to hand over some of the business to their sons, and in 1794 a new firm, Boulton, Watt and Sons, was formed. By 1800 Watt had virtually retired, though he continued inventing to the end of his life, devoting much attention to the development of sculpturing machines.

In temperament Watt was inclined to be despondent and pessimistic, and Boulton's hearty overoptimism made him an ideal partner. Watt's invention of the improved steam engine was epoch-making in two senses: firstly, it gave man better sources of power and is the very foundation-stone of the modern technological world; secondly, it led to the idea of control over Nature, as opposed to waiting for the operation of natural forces.

H. W. Dickinson, *James Watt.* 1936. (Portrait.)

L. T. C. Rolt, *James Watt.* 1962.

J. P. Muirhead, *The Origins and Progress of the Mechanical Inventions of James Watt* (3 vols). 1854.

R. E. Schofield, *The Lunar Society of Birmingham*. 1963.

E. H. Robinson and A. E. Musson (Eds), *James Watt and the Steam Revolution*. 1969.

Dictionary of National Biography.

Dictionary of Scientific Biography.

D G K-H

WEBER, WILHELM EDUARD

WEBER, WILHELM EDUARD Born at Wittenberg, Halle, Germany, 24 October 1804; died Göttingen, 23 June 1891. Famous for his work in electrodynamics.

Weber was the son of a professor of divinity, and brother of the anatomists Ernst Heinrich (1795–1878) (with whom he published a treatise on wave motion) and Eduard Friedrich (1806–71) (with whom he studied the mechanism of walking). After a period at Halle as student and then teacher, he became professor of physics at Göttingen but, with six others, was ejected in 1837 for his opposition to royal interference with the Constitution. After a temporary retirement he accepted the chair of physics at Leipzig in 1843, where a non-magnetic laboratory was built for him. He returned to Göttingen in 1849.

The Webers' joint researches on wave motion (1824) and walking (1833) came early in Wilhelm's career. At Göttingen he collaborated with K. F. GAUSS, professor of mathematics, in various magnetic studies. In 1833 they connected Gauss's observatory with Weber's physics laboratory with an electric telegraph – one of the earliest examples of telegraphic communication.

In the 1840's Weber's work, especially at Leipzig, included several technical innovations. His electrodynamometer for the absolute measurement of an electric current was an improvement of the version of the tangent galvanometer devised by H. L. F. von HELMHOLTZ and did not require a knowledge of the local value of H (the horizontal component of the Earth's magnetic field). In 1849 he devised the mirror galvanometer.

Weber's main work was done on his return to Göttingen. In 1851 he expounded the principles for systematization of electrical units, analogous to, and inspired by, the work of Gauss in magnetism. Then, with R. H. A. Kohlrausch (1809–58) he determined the ratio of the electrostatic and electromagnetic units of electrical quantity by discharging a condenser through a ballistic galvanometer. The ratio, Weber's constant, turned out to be the velocity of light, so providing a link between optics and electricity and anticipating the unification of them achieved by J. Clerk MAXWELL. At Leipzig he also determined resistance in absolute terms, and found it to have the dimensions of velocity.

Weber thought an electric current consisted of the opposite movements of positive and negative electricity. Following A. M. AMPÈRE, he regarded magnetism in terms of molecular magnets. He became the first to regard electric currents in terms of elemental units of electricity, each with a definite charge and mass. Weber is reported to have been of a contented nature (despite a certain lack of recognition), generous, and fervently patriotic. He was unmarried.

Nature, **44**, 206, 229, 272, 1891.

P. Lenard, *Great Men of Science* (English trans.). 1950. (Portrait.)

Dictionary of Scientific Biography.

C A R

WEDGWOOD, JOSIAH

WEDGWOOD, JOSIAH Born at Burslem, Staffordshire, England, July 1730; died Etruria, Staffordshire, 3 January 1795. A great potter, whose success in simultaneously advancing art, science and industry is probably unequalled.

Josiah Wedgwood came from a family long established as potters in Staffordshire, and began work at the age of 9. From 1744 until 1759 he worked first for his brother Thomas and later for another potter, Thomas Whieldon. In 1759 Wedgwood set up his own pottery business at Burslem.

From then on improvement was Wedgwood's watchword. He experimented endlessly to improve the quality of his pottery; he sought better methods of transporting his wares; he developed new ways of running his factory and marketing products; he continually improved his own knowledge and taste.

In 1764 he began a campaign for a 'Grand Trunk Canal', to link Staffordshire with ports on the east and west coasts. He was greatly helped by Thomas Bentley (1731–80), a Liverpool merchant of wide interests, and by Erasmus DARWIN and his scientific friends in Birmingham. A Parliamentary Bill for the canal was passed in 1766.

By entering the circle of the Lunar Society of Birmingham, Wedgwood also became friendly with Matthew BOULTON, James KEIR, Joseph PRIESTLEY, and William WITHERING, and their advice about chemistry and mineralogy greatly helped him in devising new ceramic processes. Boulton, at first a rival, became Wedgwood's most important industrial collaborator: Wedgwood's cameos, set in metalwork by Boulton, were, and still are, greatly admired.

In 1767 Bentley became Wedgwood's business partner; Wedgwood produced the pottery, while Bentley looked after its marketing, especially in London, where they established a warehouse and showrooms. In 1768 Wedgwood's right leg was amputated; but, undaunted, he moved his business in 1769 from Burslem to a new factory at Etruria, beside the Grand Trunk Canal. Here Wedgwood turned out the fine new forms of pottery that made his name a household word. Earlier he had developed 'green glaze', and a new type of creamware, known as 'Queen's Ware'. As he became more skilled in blending new minerals, he created various black basalts, caneware, and jasper, a white stoneware of great fineness. Jasper could be tinted to any colour and polished like stone: it was particularly good for cameos, portraits, and other *bas relief*. Probably Wedgwood's finest works were his copies in black jasper of the Portland Vase, perfected in 1790 after years of trials.

Wedgwood's main scientific interests are shown by his five papers in the *Philosophical Transactions* of the Royal Society, of which he was elected a Fellow in 1783. Two of these papers are on mineralogy and the other three describe his pyrometers for measuring high temperatures.

E. Meteyard, *The Life of Josiah Wedgwood* (2 vols). 1865–6. (Portrait.)

A. H. Church, *Josiah Wedgwood, Master-Potter*. 1903.

R. E. Schofield, *The Lunar Society of Birmingham*. 1963; *Chymia*, **5**, 180, 1959.

Dictionary of Scientific Biography.

Dictionary of National Biography.

D G K-H

WEDGWOOD, THOMAS Born at Etruria, Staffordshire, England, 14 May 1771; died Eastbury Park, near Blandford, Dorset, 10 July 1805. A pioneer of photography.

The fourth and youngest son of Josiah WEDGWOOD, Thomas gained much of his education at home under Alexander Chisolm, his father's chemical assistant. An active interest in chemistry would be stimulated by the Lunar Society, frequently meeting at Etruria. After studies at Edinburgh (1786–8), he spent a few working years at Etruria, where he became familiar with the use of the camera obscura for copying designs. But ill health intervened, and he travelled much in search of relief. His photographic experiments were made between 1797 and 1802 and published in 1802 by Humphry DAVY – with whom he had formed a lasting friendship from the latter's days at the Pneumatic Institute in Bristol, which the Wedgwood family supported. Exposing paper or leather impregnated with silver nitrate, Wedgwood obtained prints of leaves and silhouettes, but was unsuccessful with the camera obscura, owing to the very low sensitivity to light of his material. Having no fixing agent, he was unable to make his work permanent; it was left to J. N. NIÉPCE to take this essential final step.

R. B. Litchfield, *Tom Wedgwood, the First Photographer*. 1903. (Portrait.)

H. and A. Gernsheim, *The History of Photography*. 1955.

Journal of the Royal Institution, **1**, 170, 1802.

R. E. Schofield, *The Lunar Society of Birmingham*. 1963.

Dictionary of National Biography.

W N S

WEGENER, ALFRED LOTHAR Born in Berlin, 1 November 1880; died Greenland, November 1930. Meteorologist and geophysicist, remembered for his theory of continental drift.

Wegener was educated at Heidelberg, Innsbruck and Berlin, from which latter university he gained a doctorate in 1905 with an astronomical thesis. His first visit to Greenland was made as a meteorologist with a Danish expedition of 1906–8. On his return, he settled at Marburg, where he worked on his Greenland material and ably lectured in astronomy and meteorology. After a second visit to Greenland in 1912–13 his studies were disrupted by the First World War, in which he saw active service. In 1919 he joined the Meteorological Research Department of the *Deutsche Seewarte* in Hamburg, where he combined academic work with a Civil Service function. In 1924 he was appointed to a newly created chair of meteorology and geophysics at the University of Graz. In the next few years plans were matured for a major expedition to Greenland in 1930–1, which was preceded by a short visit in 1929. During his fourth visit to Greenland, in attempting to cross from a camp on the central ice-cap to the base at Kamarujuk on the west coast, Wegener lost his life.

Though he wrote a few not unimportant papers on meteors, most of Wegener's life was spent in a study of conventional meteorology, and his work *Thermodynamik der Atmosphäre* (1911) was a standard textbook. Though his contributions to meteorology and scientific exploration were recognized in those fields, Wegener is most widely remembered for his theory of continental drift. Unable to reconcile palaeoclimatological evidence with a fixed spatial relation between the continents and the geographical poles, he postulated that the continents were once closer together than they are at present. He suggested that until Mesozoic times the light material of the Earth's crust formed one continental block floating upon a dense core, and that since this time relative movement has occured. The theory was first published in 1912 and appeared in book form as *Die Entstehung der Kontinente und Ozeane* (1915); It was later translated into English (1924) and other languages. There were many objections to the theory, especially over sources of power, and it long remained discounted, but recent work based on new information has led to a general acceptance of the idea (see F. J. VINE).

H. Benndorf, *Beiträge zur Geophysik*, **31**, 337, 1931. (Portrait.)

E. Wegener, *Alfred Wegener*. 1960.

S. K. Runcorn (Ed.), *Continental Drift*. 1962. (Portrait.)

Dictionary of Scientific Biography.

W N S

WEIERSTRASS, KARL WILHELM THEODOR Born at Ostenfelde, Münster, North Rhine-Westphalia, Germany, 31 October 1815; died Berlin, 19 February 1897. Mathematician who made important contributions to analysis.

Weierstrass studied law at Bonn without enthusiasm and then took a teacher's certificate. He then worked as a schoolmaster and, isolated from outside mathematical contacts, produced original work which eventually was recognized in 1854 when he published a paper in *Crelle's Journal* on Abelian integrals. He was then appointed lecturer at Berlin *Gewerbeakademie* and later (1856) at the University, at which time he was also elected to the Berlin Academy.

His contribution to mathematics was primarily in his insistence on maximum rigour of analytical argument. In doing so he clarified many of the current ideas on the meaning of the concepts of function, derivative, and maximum. He discovered the distinction between uniform convergence and non-uniform convergence. His approach to function theory was based on the power series expansion of analytic function valid in the neighbourhood of a point, which is then extended by 'analytic continuation'. If the original series is convergent in the whole complex plane, it represents an entire transcendental function; $\frac{1}{\Gamma(x)}$ is such a function, for example. He was responsible for the definition of irrational numbers in terms of a process for calculating them.

In 1871 he created a considerable stir by his demonstration that there exist continuous functions in an interval which have derivatives nowhere in the interval.

E. T. Bell, *Men of Mathematics*. 1937.

G. Prasad, *Some Great Mathematicians of the Nineteenth Century: Their Lives and Works*, vol. 2. 1954.

Dictionary of Scientific Biography.

D N

WEINBERG, STEVEN Born in New York, 3 May 1933. Theoretical physicist known especially for developing the unified electroweak theory.

Weinberg was educated in New York, graduating from Cornell University in 1954. He received his PhD from Princeton University in 1957, and joined Columbia University for two years. After a year at the Lawrence Berkeley Laboratory he joined the University of California at Berkeley, where he remained until 1969. It was here that his work led him towards a unified theory of the electromagnetic force and the weak nuclear force. Although electromagnetism is much stronger than the weak force at everyday energies, it transpires that the only way to devise a self-consistent theory of the weak force is to include the electromagnetic force. In a paper published in 1967, Weinberg was able to show how this could be done, despite the difference in strengths, although it was another four years before Gerard 't Hooft demonstrated that the theory is fully self-consistent. In 1979, Weinberg shared the Nobel Prize for Physics with Abdus SALAM and Sheldon GLASHOW, who had independently worked on similar ideas.

Weinberg became Higgins Professor of Physics at Harvard University in 1973. While there, one of his widely known achievements was to write the book *The First Three Minutes*, a description for a general audience of the early Universe, which received several accolades. In 1982 he moved to the University of Texas at Austin, where he is professor of physics and astronomy.

Physics Today, December 1979. (Portrait.)

Les Prix Nobel en 1979. 1980 (Portrait.)

Tyler Wasson (Ed.), *Nobel Prize Winners*. 1987. (Portrait.)

C S

WEISMANN, AUGUST FRIEDRICH LEOPOLD Born at Frankfurt-am-Main, Hessen, Germany, 17 January 1834; died Freiburg-im-Breisgau, 5 November 1914. Zoologist remembered for his chromosome theory of heredity.

Weismann studied medicine at Göttingen and practised first in Rostock, then in his home town. The two months which he spent in the laboratory of K. G. F. R. Leuckart (1822–98) in Giessen in 1861 drew him to zoological research, and four years later he became associate professor of zoology at the University of Freiburg, becoming full professor in 1873. In 1864 he first noticed pain in his eyes. Microscopical study soon became impossible, but after two years' leave of absence his sight recovered, and he was able to spend the 1870s working out the life history of Daphnia and the origin of the germ cells of the Hydromedusae. A further lapse of his sight compelled him to give up these studies for good. Instead, he threw his energy into building a theory which would relate heredity and variation to processes and structures in the cell.

He began by questioning the hypothesis of pangenesis put forward by Charles DARWIN and went on to launch a full-scale attack on the inheritance of acquired characters. His study of Daphnia and the Hydromedusae had led him to believe that the progenitors of the germ cells are distinguishable from the body cells at a very early stage, so he postulated an unbroken line of descent between the germ cells of successive individuals (the Continuity of the Germplasm).

Weismann held that the chromatic loops (chromosomes) are the hereditary material, and that the halving of the chromosome number in germ-cell formation is Nature's device for counteracting the doubling which results from fertilization. He perceived that the significant event in fertilization is the bringing together of chromosomes from two individuals, and it was to the permutations and combinations of different chromosomes that he attributed variability.

That these ideas should have been put forward with such vigour and clarity in the 1880s is remarkable. Today they are still valid, but on points of detail Weismann has been found wrong. A selection from his numerous publications was translated and published in *Essays upon Heredity and Kindred Biological Problems* (1889).

E. Gaupp, *August Weismann; sein Leben und sein Werk*. 1917.

E. G. Conklin, *Proceedings of the American Philosophical Society*, **54**, iii, 1915; *Science*, **41**, 917, 1915.

Proceedings of the Royal Society, **89B**, xxvii. 1916. (Portrait.)

A. Petrunkevitch, *Journal of the History of Medicine*, **18**, 20, 1963.

Dictionary of Scientific Biography.

R C O

WELCH, WILLIAM HENRY Born at Norfolk, Connecticut, USA, 8 April 1850; died Baltimore, Maryland, 30 April 1934. The pioneer organizer of scientific pathology in the United States of America.

Welch graduated as a doctor of medicine in 1875 at the College of Physicians in New York. He had interrupted his medical course to study chemistry for a year at Yale University, and after graduating he studied in the Universities of Strasbourg, Leipzig, Berlin and Breslau. In 1879 he was appointed professor of pathological anatomy and general pathology in Bellevue Hospital Medical College in New York. After the foundation of the Johns Hopkins University (1876) and Hospital at Baltimore, Welch was called as the first occupant of the chair of pathology, where his chief colleagues were (Sir) William Osler (1849–1919), W. S. Halsted (1852–1922), and H. A. Kelly (1858–1943). Before taking up his post Welch worked at the Universities of Munich, Göttingen and Berlin (with R. KOCH). At Johns Hopkins, Welch built up a world-famous school of pathology. He retired in 1916 and founded, still at Johns Hopkins University, the School of Hygiene and Public Health, of which he was Director until 1926. In that year he became the first occupant of the new chair of the history of medicine. During his tenure (1926–31), he founded the great library which bears his name, and also the Institute for the History of Medicine. In the laboratory of J. COHNHEIM at Breslau, Welch investigated acute oedema of the lungs, and showed that it might be caused by an inequality of the work carried out by the two ventricles of the heart (1878). Two years later he studied glomerulonephritis. He carried out for several years significant work on thrombosis, embolism and infarction. He was much interested in the bacteriology of surgical infections. In 1891 he discovered the *Staphylococcus epidermidis albus* in stitch abscesses following operation wounds. In 1892, in collaboration with G. H. F. Nuttall (1862–1937), he discovered the organism of gas gangrene, *Bacillus [Clostridium] aerogenes capsulatus*. Through his own work, and that of his assistants and pupils, Welch did a great deal to advance the progress of pathology.

S. and J. T. Flexner, *William Henry Welch and the Heroic Age of American Medicine.* 1941 (reprinted 1966). (Portrait.)

H. Rolleston, *British Medical Journal*, i, 874, 1934.

D. Fleming, *William Henry Welch and the Rise of American Medicine.* 1954.

Biographical Memoirs. National Academy of Sciences. 1943.

Dictionary of Scientific Biography.

E A U

WELDON, WALTER Born at Loughborough, Leicestershire, England, 31 October 1832; died Burstow, Surrey, 20 September 1885. Industrial chemist.

Weldon was the son of a Loughborough manufacturer, and it was intended that he should enter the works, but at 22 he went to London to pursue a career in journalism. In 1860 he founded a short-lived monthly literary journal, *Weldon's Register of Facts and Occurrences in Literature, Science, and Art* (1860–4); contributors included G. A. Sala and W. M. Rossetti. With his wife he founded the successful fashion magazine *Weldon's Journal*.

Though having no formal training, he acquired a working knowledge of chemistry. As a result he became interested in one of the great industrial chemical problems of the day, namely the recovery of manganese used up in manufacturing chlorine. To understand the nature of the problem it must be recalled that the manufacture of soda by the process of Nicolas LEBLANC resulted in the production of enormous quantities of hydrochloric acid gas. The chlorine in this was a valuable bleaching agent and it was released by oxidation with manganese dioxide. The manganese, an expensive chemical, was recovered as manganese chloride, but could not be re-used in this form. Weldon visited St Helens – located in Britain's soda-producing area – to develop his ideas for overcoming this difficulty. In the three years 1866–9 he took out six patents covering the famous Weldon process, by which the manganese dioxide was regenerated by treating the manganese salt with milk of lime and blowing air through it. The economic effect was enormous. The cost of bleaching powder, vital for the textile industry, was reduced by £6 per ton and production was quadrupled. By 1885 virtually every chlorine works in the world used Weldon's process. In the words of J. B. A. DUMAS, presenting Weldon with a gold medal on behalf of the *Société d'Encouragement*, 'every sheet of paper and every yard of calico has been cheapened throughout the world'.

Weldon was elected FRS in 1882. He took an active part in founding the Society of Chemical Industry, and was its President 1883–4.

Dictionary of National Biography.

S. Miall, *A History of the British Chemical Industry.* 1931. (Portrait.)

T. C. Barker and J. R. Harris, *A Merseyside Town in the Industrial Revolution: St Helens 1750– 1900.* 1954.

T I W

WELLCOME, SIR HENRY SOLOMON Born in Almond, Wisconsin, USA, 21 August 1853; died London, 25 July 1936. Drug manufacturer and founder of the Wellcome Trust.

Son of a travelling missionary preaching to the Dakota Indians, Wellcome was brought up in Garden City, Minnesota. After working in a local drugstore he graduated from the Philadelphia College of Pharmacy in 1874. In 1880 Wellcome joined Silas M. Burroughs to form Burroughs Wellcome and Co. in London, selling ready-made pills from the USA. From 1884 they manufactured their own drugs, registering the term 'Tabloid'. Following the death of Burroughs in 1895 Wellcome became sole partner, and branches were opened worldwide.

The first of Wellcome's research institutions, the Wellcome Physiological Research Laboratories, was founded in 1894 with Sir Henry DALE as director. In 1896 the Wellcome Chemical Research Laboratories were founded, headed by F. B. Power (1853–1927). Wellcome set up the Wellcome Tropical Research Laboratories in Khartoum in 1901, together with a floating laboratory on the Nile, and appointed Sir Andrew Balfour (1873–1931) as director. In 1913 Balfour became first director of the Wellcome Bureau of Scientific Research in London, set up to investigate tropical diseases.

Wellcome reorganised his pharmaceutical companies and research institutions into the Wellcome Foundation Ltd in 1924. He still established the Wellcome Trust as sole shareholder and directed the trustees to use the profits from the Foundation for research. It became the largest private body in Great Britain financing medical research. During his lifetime he made an enormous collection of medical artifacts and books, now housed in the Science Museum, London, as the Wellcome Museum of the History of Medicine.

In 1932 Wellcome was knighted (he had been naturalised in 1910), and was elected FRS and honorary fellow of the Royal College of Surgeons.

Obituary Notices of Fellows of the Royal Society, 1938. (Portrait.)

Helen Turner, *Henry Wellcome: The Man, his Collection and his Legacy*, 1980.

A. R. Hall and B. A. Bembridge, *Physic and Philanthropy: A History of the Wellcome Trust 1936–1986*, 1986. (Portrait.)

Dictionary of National Biography.

A P B

WELLS, HORACE Born at Hartford, Vermont, USA, 21 January 1815; died New York, 28 January 1848. Discoverer of nitrous oxide anaesthesia.

Educated at private academies in Massachusetts and New Hampshire, Wells began to study dentistry at the age of 19, in Boston. Practising there as a dental surgeon he accepted amongst his students J. M. Riggs (1810–85) and W. T. G. MORTON. In

December 1844, whilst watching an exhibition of the effects of laughing gas (nitrous oxide) in Hartford, Connecticut, Wells noticed that one of the volunteers, having inhaled gas, bruised his legs badly without being aware of pain. Wells then arranged to have his former student Riggs extract his (Wells's) wisdom tooth while he was under the effect of the gas. After the extraction Wells regained consciousness, having felt no pain. After this, Wells repeatedly used nitrous oxide anaesthesia for the extraction of teeth.

In January 1845 Wells went to Boston and discussed his discovery with his former student Morton, and a chemist, C. T. Jackson (1805–80). Wells's claim was brought to the notice of the surgeon at the Massachusetts General Hospital, J. C. Warren (1778–1856), who, though sceptical, gave Wells the opportunity of demonstrating in front of his students. During Wells's demonstration the patient cried out; though afterwards the patient firmly declared he had felt no pain, his cry was taken to confirm the failure expected by the audience, and Wells retired discomfited.

In 1846, following Morton's successful demonstration of the anaesthetic effects of ether in the same operating theatre, Wells became depressed, and in 1847 went to Paris to try to establish his claim, but found that interest in nitrous oxide had now been superseded by the newer anaesthetics, ether and chloroform. After a further year of failure to make his case, he committed suicide. After Wells's death the Paris Medical Society accepted his claim as 'having successfully discovered and applied the use of vapours or gases whereby surgical operations could be performed without pain'. In actual fact, Crawford W. Long (1815–78), in Georgia, had removed a tumour from a patient's neck under ether anaesthesia as early as March 1842.

V. Robinson, *Victory over Pain. A History of Anaesthesia.* 1946. (Portrait.)
M. E. Soifer, *Bulletin of the History of Medicine*, **9**, 101, 1941.
Dictionary of American Biography.
R. S. Atkinson and T. B. Boulton (Eds.), *The History of Anaesthesia.* 1989.

K D K

WELSBACH, CARL AUER, BARON VON Born in Vienna, 1 September 1858; died Treibach, 4 August 1929. Invented the gas mantle.

After studying at the Vienna Polytechnic and at Heidelberg under R. W. E. BUNSEN, Welsbach undertook researches on the rare earths. In 1885 he succeeded in separating didymia into the two earths neodymia and praseodymia, using the double nitrate with ammonium. Welsbach's patent for the incandescent gas mantle appeared in 1885; this invention came from his experimental observation of the bright light emitted when asbestos fibres impregnated with rare earths were strongly heated. He ignited these to leave 99 per cent thoria and 1 per cent ceria as residue, this providing the best light. This invention gave gas a new lease of life as an illuminant in the face of growing competition from electricity. A second major invention came when Welsbach sought some use for all the ceria dumped in factory yards or given away with purchases of thoria. His alloy of 30–35 per cent

cerium with iron (Auer metal) is the everyday flint of cigarette and gas-lighters.

J. C. Poggendorf, *Biographisch-Literarisches Handwörterbuch.* 1883–1903.
Chemical News, 254–6, 1902.
V. Guttmann, *Journal of Chemical Education*, **47**, 209, 1970.
F. Lieben, *Journal of Chemical Education*, **35**, 230, 1958.
O. Smetana and W. Dauschan, *Treibacher chemische Werke: Entstehung und Entwicklung bis 1980.* 1980. (Portrait.)

M S

WENNER-GREN, AXEL LEONARD Born at Uddevalla, Sweden, 5 June 1881; died Stockholm, 24 November 1961. Industrialist and transport pioneer.

Axel Wenner-Gren was educated at the Berlin Commercial Academy, worked for a time in the Laval Separator Company, and in 1912 designed an improved domestic vacuum cleaner. After the war he founded the Electrolux Company to manufacture this cleaner and, from 1925 onwards, the first absorption refrigerator. In Sweden he had widely ramified interests, ranging from wood-pulp production to armaments. During the Second World War he lived successively in the Bahamas and in Mexico, where he reorganized the telephone and telegraph industry. Part of his wealth was given to Swedish institutions for scientific research and for Scandinavian co-operation; he also endowed the Wenner-Gren Foundation for Anthropological Research, which was set up in New York in 1941.

In 1952–4 Wenner-Gren developed the 'Alweg' – a name composed of his initials. This was a new type of railway, with streamlined electric locomotive and passenger coaches operated by remote control and running along a raised monorail laid on a concrete track. In the autumn of 1952 a half-size model showed a speed of 150 kph, and 250 kph was then said to be attainable as soon as an adequate service track could be provided in the Cologne area, which was the scene of the experiment.

T K D

WENZEL, CARL FRIEDRICH Born in Dresden, Saxony, Germany, 1740; died Freiberg, 27 February 1793. Chemist; carried out work on chemical affinity.

Wenzel ran away from his father's bookbinding business, and travelled to Hamburg and Amsterdam, where he studied pharmacy and surgery. Eventually he became a surgeon in the Dutch marine service. He returned to Leipzig and the study of chemistry and metallurgy, and in 1774 his book *Einleitung zur höheren Chemie* was published. In this Wenzel showed that he still retained alchemical ideas. In 1780 he became chemist, and in 1784 was promoted to Chief Assessor to the Freiberg Mines. Although he subscribed to the phlogiston theory, he made a careful study of burning, and noted that many substances increased in weight on combustion. He assumed that this was due to combination with some material substance. His most important work was on chemical affinity, and was embodied in *Lehre von der Verwandschaft der Körper* (1777), which ran to three editions. He determined the relative rates of solution of metals in acids, and used this to determine affinity, which he took to be in the inverse ratio of the time taken to dissolve. He recognized that the concentration of the acid had an important bearing on the reaction velocity. His researches also extended to the composition of salts, and in this field he made a number of very accurate analyses.

R. Winderlich, *Journal of Chemical Education*, **27**, 57, 1950. (Portrait.)

B B K

WERNER, ABRAHAM GOTTLOB Born at Wehrau, Prussian Silesia, 25 September 1749; died Dresden, Germany, 30 June 1817. A great teacher of mineralogy and geology.

Werner was brought up in a family that for generations had held important positions in Silesia, and he himself took the keenest interest from his earliest years in everything to do with mines, minerals, rocks and metallurgy. He spent two years (1769–71) at the Mining Academy at Freiberg and then entered the University of Leipzig, where he studied a wide range of subjects. While there he wrote a work which introduced entirely new methods in the description of minerals (*Von der ausserlichen Kennzeichen der Fossilien*, 1774). The authorities of the Freiberg Academy, impressed by this and other evidences of marked talent, appointed him as lecturer in 1775, and he continued in this appointment for the next forty years. His genius and renown as a teacher became so great that eager students flocked to hear him from every civilized land. Among them there were many who, inspired by him, became the foremost geologists of Europe. His methods were excellent, but unfortunately he was a dogmatic theorist as regards fundamental geological principles, and he indoctrinated his pupils with an erroneous system which was remarkably resistant, even in the minds of highly intelligent men, to the pressure of truth. The essence of his system was that all rocks, including those we now know to be of igneous origin, had been deposited, as sediments or chemical precipitates, in a constant succession from a universal ocean. The geological world came to be split into two camps, the Neptunists, as Werner's followers were called, and the Plutonists, the followers of James HUTTON. Werner wrote two further short treatises (*Kurz Klassifikation und Beschreibung der verschieden Gebirgsarten*, 1787, and *Neue Theorie von der Enstehung der Gänge*, 1791) and a few magazine articles, but he had a great antipathy to writing, his views being propagated almost entirely though the disputations and writings of his disciples.

D. S. G. Frisch and C. S. Weiss,
    Lebensbeschreibung Abraham Gottlob Werners.
    1825.
A. Geikie, *The Founders of Geology* (2nd ed.).
    1905.
R. Beck, *Abraham Gottlob Werner*. 1918. (Portrait.)
F. D. Adams, *The Birth and Development of the
    Geological Sciences*. 1938. (Portrait.)
V. A. Eyles, *History of Science*, **3**, 102, 1964.
K. A. von Zittel, *History of Geology and
    Palaeontology*. 1901. (Portrait.)
Dictionary of Scientific Biography.

J C

WERNER, ALFRED Born at Mulhouse, France, 12 December 1866; died Zürich, Switzerland, 15 November 1919. Founder of the modern theory of coordination compounds.

Werner, son of an ironworker, first had the opportunity to study chemistry in the Karlsruhe *Technische Hochschule* while doing his military service. He continued his studies at the Zürich Polytechnic, where he graduated; after a short time with M. P. BERTHELOT in Paris, he returned to Zürich, becoming professor in 1895. This post he held until his death, though he became seriously ill with arteriosclerosis in 1915, and was unable to do any more useful work. He had the reputation of a brilliant teacher.

Werner made his mark in organic chemistry with his work (with A. HANTZSCH 1890) on the isomerism of the oximes, but his main contribution was in the field of inorganic chemistry. Here the theory of structure had been far less successful than in the organic realm. Painstaking, though sometimes fanciful, attempts had been made to apply it, but the development of the theory of ionic dissociation made most of these efforts seem misconceived. The confused class of 'complex salts' and 'addition compounds' was especially puzzling; the best that orthodox valency theory could suggest were the chain formulae suggested by S. M. Jørgensen (1837–1914). In a series of masterly papers, Werner set up a theory of 'co-ordination compounds' (as they are now called) on an entirely new basis. Besides the ordinary electrovalency of a metal, Werner supposed that there was a secondary binding force which could accommodate a definite number of 'ligands' around the metal atom, thus forming a new complex ion. This coordination number was usually 6, but could be 4, 8, or other small integers. Some of these ligands (water, ammonia), being electrically neutral, did not alter the electrovalency of the central atom; others (chloride or cyanide ion) did alter it, so that a cobalt atom (for example) could function as the centre of either a complex anion or a cation, or even a neutral compound. Ligands were not ionized, and appeared to be bound by bonds similar to the covalent bonds of organic chemistry; consequently co-ordination compounds have a stereochemistry, the ligands occupying the apices of some figure such as a square or an octahedron. Suitable bifunctional ligands (e.g. ethylenediamine) can occupy two adjacent places in these structures. This gives rise to the possibility of several types of isomerism, which Werner showed experimentally to exist; his most notable result was the optical resolution of a complex compound in 1911.

For this work, Werner received the Nobel prize for chemistry in 1913. It has proved immensely fruitful, both theoretically (in the study of valency) and practically, in such widely different fields as mineralogy, analytical chemistry, and the use of mordants in dyeing.

P. Karrer, *Helvetica Chimica Acta*, **3**, 196, 1920.
    (Portrait.)
G. T. Morgan, *Journal of the Chemical Society*,
    1639, 1920.
Journal of Chemical Education, **19**, 153, 1942.
    (Portrait.)
E. Farber (Ed.), *Great Chemists*. 1961.
    (Portrait.)

G. B. Kauffman, *Alfred Werner: Founder of Co-ordination Chemistry.* 1966. (Portraits.)
Dictionary of Scientific Biography.
Tyler Wasson (Ed.), *Nobel Prize Winners.* 1987. (Portrait.)

W V F

WESTINGHOUSE, GEORGE Born at Central Bridge, New York, 6 October 1846; died there, 12 March 1914. Engineer.

Son of a manufacturer of small steam engines and farm implements, George Westinghouse fought for the North in the American Civil War, and left Union College, Schenectady, after three months to join his father's works; there he took out his first patent when he was only 20. This was the first of 400 he was to take out during the next forty-eight years.

His patents mainly concern communications technology, railways, and the transmission of electricity. Following his re-railing device for trucks, he took out in 1869 the first of what were to be over 100 patents for an air brake and formed the Westinghouse Air Brake Company. This enabled all the individual brakes on coaches and trucks to be simultaneously applied by the driver and greatly increased the safe speed of trains. The system of standardized equipment provided for braking he extended to electrically controlled signals. This led him to investigate the transmission of high voltage alternating current, and in 1886 he formed the Westinghouse Electric Company. By skilful purchase of patents and talent, especially that of Nikola TESLA, he developed against much opposition, including that of T. A. EDISON, a single-phase high-voltage alternating current system for light and power. By 1893 he had secured the contracts to illuminate the World Fair at Chicago and develop the power of Niagara Falls.

Westinghouse also pioneered the utilization of natural gas, then being brought into Pittsburgh, site of his works. Building on his early experiments with compressed air, Westinghouse began in 1883 a series of nearly forty patents all concerning its safer transmission.

As well as establishing works all over the world, Westinghouse built in 1889 a model industrial town in the Turtle Creek Valley, east of Pittsburgh. Here he concentrated his Air Brake works and later his Electric Company and Machine Company. But in 1907 he lost control in a financial crisis, and diverted his attention to reorganizing the Equitable Life Assurance Society. He received, ironically enough in view of his advocacy of high-tension alternating current in the face of Edison's opposition, the Edison Gold Medal of the American Society of Electrical Engineers.

F. E. Leupp, *George Westinghouse.* 1918.
H. G. Prout, *A Life of George Westinghouse.* 1921.
J. G. Crowther, *Six Great Engineers.* 1939. (Portrait.)
Dictionary of American Biography.

W H G A

WESTON, SIR RICHARD Born at Sutton, Surrey, England, 1591; died there, 1652 (buried 5 May). Agriculturist.

Richard Weston was one of the small group of English landowners who greatly improved agricultural practice in the first half of the seventeenth century. He was interested also in inland navigation, and during the years 1635–41 made the Wey navigable as far as Guildford, introducing lock gates. His Royalist sympathies caused him to spend the period 1644–9 in the Low Countries.

Weston had ample opportunity to study the ley farming between Antwerp and Ghent, which he described in his *Discours of Husbandrie used in Brabant and Flanders.* On his return to England he introduced, in an appropriately modified form, some of the practices he had observed abroad. In particular, he introduced clover into the English rotation of crops; this was developed by Charles TOWNSHEND into a widely practised four-course system which greatly improved the productivity of the land (see also A. YOUNG).
Dictionary of National Biography.

T I W

WHARTON, THOMAS Born at Winston-on-Tees, Co. Durham, England, 31 August 1614; died London, 15 November 1673. Distinguished anatomist, and discoverer of the duct of the submaxillary gland.

Wharton entered Pembroke College, Cambridge, in 1638; he later migrated to Trinity College, Oxford. On the outbreak of the Civil War in 1642 he removed to Bolton, Lancashire, where he spent three years in study. He then went to London and studied medicine. After the surrender of Oxford (1646) he returned to Trinity College and was created a doctor of medicine in 1647. Wharton again went to London, where he became a Fellow of the Royal College of Physicians (1650), and was Censor on six occasions. He was appointed physician to St Thomas's Hospital in 1659, and he was one of the few physicians who remained in London, treating their patients, throughout the whole of the Great Plague of 1665.

Wharton was universally recognized as a very skilled anatomist. His only published work was *Adenographia, or a description of the glands of the whole of the body* (1656). In this work he carried the anatomy of glands much farther than it had been carried by M. MALPIGHI and others, and he also gave the first account of the duct of the submaxillary gland.

W. Stirling, *Some Apostles of Physiology.* 1902. (Portrait.)
Dictionary of National Biography.
G. Wolstenholme and D. Piper (Eds), *The Royal College of Physicians: Portraits.* 1964.

E A U

WHEATSTONE, SIR CHARLES Born near Gloucester, England, February 1802; died Paris, 19 October 1875. Remembered for contributions to acoustics and electric telegraphy.

In 1834 Wheatstone was appointed to the chair of experimental physics at King's College, London, a position he retained for the remainder of his life, in spite of his unwillingness to lecture. He was elected a Fellow of the Royal Society in 1836 and became a Foreign Associate of the *Académie des Sciences* in 1873. He was knighted in 1868.

Wheatstone's principal contribution to acoustics was a memoir (1833) on the figures of E. F. F. Chladni (1756–1824), but he also contributed important papers on the resonance of columns of air (1828); on the transmission of musical sound through rigid linear conductors (1831); and on the experimental proof of D. BERNOULLI's theory of air vibrations in wind instruments.

Wheatstone's researches in sound led naturally to an interest in light. In 1838 he presented a paper to the Royal Society on binocular vision. Here we find the origin of the notion of visual solidity. In 1852 he presented a second paper on the same subject, supporting his views by the invention of the pseudoscope, in which the usual perspective pictures are presented to the eye reversed. In 1834 he determined the velocity of electric waves in metallic conductors by use of a rotating mirror, the value obtained being in excess of 250 000 miles per second. This method was later employed by J. B. L. FOUCAULT in the first accurate determination of the velocity of light. Wheatstone entered into partnership with W. F. COOKE to develop the electric telegraph commercially, joint patents being taken out for the five-needle and two-needle telegraphs. He was one of the first English scientists to recognize the great theoretical and practical importance of Ohm's law (see G. S. OHM) of which his own (Wheatstone) bridge method for the accurate measurement of resistance was an immediate application.

C. Wheatstone, *Scientific Papers.* 1879.
Dictionary of National Biography.
Proceedings of the Royal Society, **24**, xvi, 1876.
B. Bowers, *Sir Charles Wheatstone.* 1975.
S. Hubbard, *Cooke and Wheatstone and the Invention of the Electric Telegraph.* 1965.

J W H

WHINFIELD, JOHN REX Born at Sutton, Surrey, England, 16 February 1901; died Dorking, Surrey, 6 July 1966. Inventor of Terylene.

Whinfield was educated at Merchant Taylors' School and Caius College, Cambridge, where he read chemistry. For a time he worked as unpaid assistant in the laboratory of C. F. CROSS, who, with E. J. BEVAN, had invented rayon in 1892. Continuing his interest in textile science, he joined the Calico Printers' Association as research chemist. The invention of nylon by W. H. CAROTHERS in 1935 stimulated interest in synthetic fibres and Whinfield became convinced that other classes of chemical substance could be polymerized and manufactured in a fibre form acceptable to the textile industry. In 1941, with J. T. Dickson, he discovered that a polymerized condensate of terephthalic acid and ethylene glycol could be drawn out as a fibre; it is interesting to note that Carothers had considered this form of polyester fibre, but had finally concentrated his attention on polyamides. The new fibre promised to have wartime applications and development work was put in hand by the Ministry of Supply; Whinfield and Dickson submitted a patent application in July 1941, but because of the war the specification was not published until 1946. Industrially, its possibilities were explored by Imperial Chemical Industries in the United Kingdom and by Dupont in the United States. In 1946 Dupont acquired a licence to operate the Calico Printers' Association's patent in America – marketing it first as Fibre V and then as Dacron – and in 1947 ICI purchased manufacturing rights for the rest of the world.

From this discovery has grown a new branch of the textile industry whose annual production is now measured in hundreds of thousands of tons a year, and Whinfield can fairly be described as one of the great inventors of the twentieth century. In spite of this, he was accorded remarkably little recognition outside his own company; he was awarded the CBE in 1954. A reason stated was that he published little, but as he lived to see most of the population of the Western world accepting Terylene for everyday wear it could fairly be said of him, as of Sir Christopher WREN, *Si monumentum requiris, circumspice* ('If you would see his monument, look around').

J. Jewkes, D. Sawers and R. Stillerman, *The Sources of Invention.* 1960.
The Times 7 July 1966. (Portrait).
Chemistry in Britain **3**, 26, 1967.
Dictionary of National Biography (Missing Persons). 1993.

T I W

WHIPPLE, GEORGE HOYT Born at Ashland, New Hampshire, USA, 28 August 1878; died Rochester, New York, 2 February 1976. Pathologist, best known for his work on anaemias, and on disorders of the gastrointestinal tract.

Whipple, who came from a medical family, took his undergraduate degree at Yale University before entering the Johns Hopkins University Medical School in 1901. His interest in medical research was stimulated by J. J. Abel (1857–1938), W. H. WELCH, and other Hopkins teachers, and following graduation (1905) he remained in Welch's Department of Pathology for two years' training and research. It was there that he first described a rare condition characterized by the deposition of fat in the intestinal and mesenteric lymphatic tissues, subsequently known as Whipple's Disease. Following a year in the Canal Zone, studying many tropical diseases, such as amoebic dysentery, filariasis and blackwater fever, he returned to Johns Hopkins, where from 1908 to 1914 his researches centred on the liver, jaundice and abnormal blood coagulation.

In 1914 Whipple became director of the Hooper Foundation for Medical Research and professor of research medicine at the University of California in San Francisco. Despite the difficulties of fitting out a new laboratory in a wartime atmosphere, he continued his studies on bile formation in dogs, gradually extending this to include haemoglobin production and, consequently, experimental anaemia, on which he published over 200 papers. He developed, with Frieda Robbins (later F. S. Robscheit-Robbins) an experimental model whereby fixed quantities of blood were removed from dogs, and the influence of various diets in the regeneration of blood cells was studied. They found that liver, kidney and meat were (in that order) particularly effective in stimulating the bone-marrow to produce new red blood cells. Liver extract had already been suggested by C. W. Hooper in 1918 as particularly effective in the treatment of pernicious anaemia in human beings. Hooper's findings were neglected, but following Whipple's reports, two Harvard physicians, George MINOT and William Murphy (1892–1987) began in 1926 systematically to investigate the use of liver and other foodstuffs in the treatment of pernicious anaemia. For these researches, Whipple, Minot, and Murphy shared the Nobel prize for physiology or medicine in 1934.

The relationship between pernicious anaemia and vitamin B_{12} deficiency was subsequently elucidated by other workers.

In 1922, Whipple left California to become Dean of the newly established medical school at the University of Rochester, Rochester, New York. Here he remained for the rest of his long career, playing a leading role in the development of the medical school, but also continuing his researches on a broad front. The bile pigments were always of interest to him, but he also made important contributions to our knowledge of the blood proteins; to the mechanism of blood-clot formation; and to the pathology of a genetic disorder which leads to anaemia and other sequelae. Found in people of Mediterranean extraction, it was first named thalassemia by Whipple in his classic (1932) description of its pathology.

Whipple's honours and wider responsibilities were many. He was a Trustee of the Rockefeller Foundation, 1927–43 and a member of the Board of Trustees of the Rockefeller Institute, 1939–60. In 1914 he married Katherine Ball Waring; they had one daughter and one son.

Perspectives in Biology and Medicine, **2**, 253, 1959. (Portrait.)

M. M. Wintrobe (Ed.), *Blood, Pure and Eloquent*. 1980.

G. Corner, *George Hoyt Whipple and his Friends*. 1963.

D J. Ingle (Ed.), *A Dozen Doctors*. 1963.

Tyler Wasson (Ed.), *Nobel Prize Winners*. 1987. (Portrait.)

W F B

WHITE, GILBERT Born at Selborne, Hampshire, England, 18 July 1720; died there, 26 June 1793. Naturalist and antiquary.

Gilbert White, the eldest son of John White, of Selborne, and Anne Holt, daughter of the Rector of Streatham, was educated at Basingstoke, and admitted to Oriel College, Oxford, in 1739, graduating in 1743. He was elected Fellow of his College in 1744; took his master's degree in 1746; and was ordained in 1747. He was of unambitious temperament and strongly attached to the pleasures of quiet country life, especially the study of nature; he soon returned to his native village, where he resided all his life, holding curacies in various parishes in the neighbourhood and finally that of Selborne, and enjoying the college living of Morton Pinkney.

He corresponded largely with prominent naturalists about his favourite subjects, and began his natural history 'comprising a journal for a whole year' which culminated in the publication of the famous *Natural History and Antiquities of Selborne* (1798) many times reprinted. This took the form of a series of letters to his naturalist friends Thomas Pennant (1726–98) and Daines Barrington (1727–1800). It is characterized by acute observation set down with unassuming charm that reflects his gentle nature and placid life, which have endeared it to all who care for good writing and rural ways now gone for ever.

R. Holt-White, *The Life and Letters of Gilbert White of Selborne*. 1901. (Portrait.)

W. S. Scott, *White of Selborne*. 1950.

C. S. Emden, *Gilbert White in His Village*. 1956.

A. Rye, *Gilbert White and His Selborne*. 1970.

Dictionary of National Biography.

L H M

WHITEHEAD, ALFRED NORTH Born at Ramsgate, Kent, England, 15 February 1861; died Cambridge, Massachusetts, USA, 30 December 1947. Noted for his work in mathematical logic and philosophy.

Whitehead was the son of a clergyman, headmaster of a private school. From Sherborne School he won a scholarship to Trinity College, Cambridge (1880), where he remained for thirty years. He was Fourth Wrangler in 1883.

Whitehead's first important work, *A Treatise of Universal Algebra* (1898), was an attempt to extend, and to some extent to unify, the work of W. R. HAMILTON on quaternions, of H. G. Grassmann (1809–77) (*Ausdehnungslehre*), and of G. BOOLE on symbolic logic. With his colleague, Bertrand Russell (1872–1970), he learned of the great work of G. Peano (1858–1932) in symbolic logic in 1900. They appreciated the great power of Peano's methods and extended them, especially to the logical foundations of mathematics, advocating the so-called 'logistic thesis'. Their results were published in the three large volumes of *Principia mathematica* (1910–13), a *tour de force* that was never completed. Whitehead was to have been mainly responsible for a fourth volume on the foundations of geometry, but his interests changed in the direction of epistemology and metaphysics.

In 1910 Whitehead moved to London, where he taught at University College (1911–14) and Imperial College (1914–24). During these years he wrote on philosophy and relativity, being particularly critical of the General Theory of EINSTEIN. His *The Principle of Relativity* (1922) was not generally well received, but some of its cosmological ideas were elaborated by J. L. Synge from 1952, and C. B. Rayner from 1954.

From 1924 until he retired in 1937, Whitehead occupied a chair in philosophy at Harvard. His philosophy, which is of a constructive rather than analytical character, has had a substantial following in America.

Obituary Notices of Fellows of the Royal Society, 1948. (Portrait.)

R. M. Palter, *Whitehead's Philosophy of Science*. 1960.

P. A. Schilpp, *The Philosophy of Alfred North Whitehead*. 1951.

E. T. Whittaker and F. I. G. Rawlins, *Nature*, **161**, 267, 1948.

Journal of Philosophy, **7**, 327, 1969–70. (Special issue.)

Dictionary of Scientific Biography.

J D N

WHITEHEAD, ROBERT Born at Bolton, Lancashire, England, 3 January 1823; died Shrivenham, Berkshire, 19 November 1905. Inventor of the torpedo.

The son of the owner of a cotton-bleaching business, Whitehead was apprenticed at 14 as an engineer in Manchester, where he also learnt draughtsmanship at the Mechanics' Institute. He was employed, under an uncle, at an engineering establishment in Marseilles; moved to Milan, where he made improvements to silk-weaving and marsh-draining machinery, and then to Trieste;

and in 1856 started the *Stabilimento Tecnico Fiumano*, which later became a family concern.

In 1866, with the help of his son John, he designed at Fiume a torpedo capable of running 700 yards at 7 knots. To this he added several improvements, including a 'servo-motor' attached to the steering-gear. By 1889 the range had been extended to 1000 yards at 29 knots, but satisfactory accuracy of direction was not achieved until seven years later, when a gyroscope was introduced, together with vertical rudders which acted on the servo-motor so as to correct the steering. During the last thirty years of the century rights of construction were purchased by the governments of Austria-Hungary and the principal naval powers. The efficiency of the Whitehead torpedo in action was shown by the Japanese in their attack upon the Russian fleet off Port Arthur in February 1904.

Dictionary of National Biography, 1901–11.

T K D

WHITNEY, ELI Born at Westboro, Massachusetts, USA, 8 December 1765; died New Haven, Connecticut, 8 January 1825. Inventor of the cotton gin and pioneer in America of manufacture with interchangeable parts.

Whitney began to manufacture nails at the age of 15, in a small metalworking shop attached to his father's farm, but in 1789–92 he studied at Yale and decided to become a lawyer. Having travelled to Georgia with a view to a tutorship, he attracted attention by making various domestic contrivances for his hostess, the widow of General Nathanael Greene, and was told of the urgent need for a machine to clean green-seed cotton. In ten days he completed his design, consisting of a revolving toothed cylinder, brushes, and a revolving air-fan to throw out the cleaned cotton; the result was a fiftyfold increase in the worker's output and the possibility of cropping land formerly considered unprofitable. In May 1793 Whitney formed a partnership with Phineas Miller for its manufacture, but his patent of 14 March 1794 was very widely infringed; and although the courts eventually vindicated his rights (1807), only five years later Congress refused to extend the patent, on which the prosperous cotton culture of the Southern States was largely based.

Meanwhile, in January 1798 Whitney had secured a Government contract for making 10 000 guns, which he planned to do with unskilled labour, each part being made with such precision as to fit with any other. Interchangeable manufacture had been used previously by a gunsmith in Paris, but this was its first use in America: Simeon North (1802–84) used it one year later for pistols. Lacking a nucleus of skilled craftsmen and machine tools and having no previous experience of gunmaking, Whitney took eight years to complete his two-year contract. But in 1812 he received a second Government order, and his methods were adopted in both the Federal armouries.

A small milling machine, with a power-driven table moving horizontally beneath, and at right-angles to, the cutter-spindle, was made by Whitney in 1818. This is all that survives of the equipment with which he launched what became known in Europe as the 'American system' of manufacture.

J. Mirsky and A. Nevins, *The World of Eli Whitney*. 1952.

C. M. Green, *Eli Whitney and the Birth of American Technology*. 1956.

R. S. Woodbury, *Technology and Culture*, **1**, 325, 1960.

Dictionary of American Biography.

T K D

WHITTAKER, SIR EDMUND TAYLOR Born at Southport, Lancashire, England, 24 October 1873; died Edinburgh, 24 March 1956. Mathematician.

Whittaker was educated at Manchester Grammar School, whence he gained a scholarship to Trinity College, Cambridge; he was Second Wrangler in 1895 and First Smith's Prizeman two years later. From 1906 to 1912 he was professor of astronomy in the University of Dublin. In 1912 he was appointed professor of mathematics at Edinburgh until his retirement in 1946. The Royal Society elected him to Fellowship in 1905 and awarded him their Sylvester (1931) and Copley (1954) Medals. He was President of the Royal Society of Edinburgh 1939–44. He was honoured by many learned societies and was an honorary graduand of six universities, including the University of California.

Whittaker was a man of wide interests, and he published extensively in mathematics and theoretical physics. His *Treatise on the Analytical Dynamics of Particles and Rigid Bodies* (1904) quickly established itself as a standard work. *The Calculus of Observations: A Treatise on Numerical Observations* (with G. Robinson, 1924) reflects his long interest in actuarial matters. But perhaps his greatest work was the *History of the Theories of Aether and Electricity*, first published in 1910. At the time of his death he left unfinished the final volume of an extended version of this in which he exhaustively reviewed atomic and electromagnetic theories – to which he himself contributed notably – from the earliest times. This monumental work was only one reflection of his keen interest in the history of science and mathematics, to which he made numerous contributions, especially in the field of scientific philosophy and biography. His many research papers include contributions on quantum theory, planetary theory, special functions, and algebra.

Biographical Memoirs of Fellows of the Royal Society. 1956. (Portrait.)

A. C. Aitken, *Nature*, **177**, 730, 1956.

C. D. Hardie, *Isis*, **34**, 344, 1943.

W. H. McCrea, *Journal of the London Mathematical Society*, **32**, 234, 1957.

Dictionary of National Biography.

T I W

WHITTLE, SIR FRANK Born Coventry, Warwickshire, England, 1 June 1907. Inventor of jet engine.

After leaving Leamington College, Whittle joined the RAF as an apprentice in 1923 and was awarded a cadetship in 1926 at the RAF College, Cranwell. While still at Cranwell he realised that the gas turbine – then being explored as a source of industrial power – could be used to provide jet propulsion for aircraft. Burning fuel continuously, this would allow high-altitude flight at speeds much higher than would be possible with a piston engine, with its intermittent combustion. He took out his first patent for a gas turbine jet propulsion engine in 1930.

Although the Air Ministry refused to finance the development of a working engine, the RAF sent him to Peterhouse College, Cambridge, in 1934 to read for the Mechanical Sciences Tripos. He graduated with first class honours in 1936. From 1937 to 1946 the RAF attached him to Power Jets, a company he had formed in 1935, to develop an aircraft gas turbine for jet propulsion. It was not until 1939 that the Air Ministry placed a contract for an aeroplane in which the engine could be tested. Meanwhile, in Germany, jet propulsion had been developed by Hans von Ohain (1911–) and a Heinkel jet-propelled aircraft first flew in August 1939. The experimental Gloster jet-propelled aeroplane with a Whittle engine made its first flights in May 1941, reaching speeds up to 460 mph, and the Gloster Meteor came into service in 1944. After the war the jet engine made high-speed civil air travel possible.

In 1948 Whittle retired from the RAF on medical grounds with the rank of Air Commodore. He had been elected a Fellow of the Royal Society in 1947, and was knighted in 1948. After he left the RAF he took on consultancies, and became a research professor at the US Naval Academy, Annapolis, in 1977, publishing *Gas Turbine Aero – Thermodynamics* in 1981. He was awarded the Order of Merit in 1986.

John Golley, *Whittle. The True Story* 1987. (Portrait.)

Glyn Jones, *The Jet Pioneers*. 1989.

Sir Frank Whittle, *Jet: the Story of a Pioneer*. 1953.

Frank Whittle, *Proceedings of the Institution of Mechanical Engineers, 152,* 1945.

Christopher Joyce, *New Scientist,* 5 October 1991. (Portrait.)

A P B

WHITWORTH, SIR JOSEPH Born at Stockport, Cheshire, England, 21 December 1803; died Monte Carlo, 22 January 1887. Engineer.

Son of Charles Whitworth, a schoolmaster, Joseph left school at 14 to be apprenticed to his uncle, a Derbyshire cotton-spinner; after serving four years as a mechanic in Manchester, he joined Henry MAUDSLAY in 1825. Here, and later at the workshop of Joseph Clement, he acquired the skill and accuracy in mechanical matters that he was so brilliantly to exploit when he finally set up on his own in Manchester in 1833.

These skills were manifest in his construction of a truly plane surface, and of a number of machine tools capable of turning, planing, drilling, slotting, gear-cutting and shaping that set new standards of micro-measurement. It has been said that in 1830 a workman who could work to $^1/_{16}$ inch was good, but that by 1840 Whitworth made $^1/_{10,000}$ inch a workshop unit. In 1841 he suggested to the Institution of Civil Engineers the establishment of a uniform system of screw threads, which should have a mean angle of 55 degrees with a standard pitch for different diameters. Ten years later, at the Great Exhibition, his machine tools and screws earned universal approval, whilst a visit to its American counterpart in 1853 confirmed his views as to the importance of further standardization of units.

He became a great deal interested in armaments, and in the 1870s manufactured a special steel for heavy artillery. Earlier, from 1854, he conducted some very precise experiments on rifling, and pro-

duced a novel rifle with a hexagonal bore. While this had some advantages over conventional weapons, its tendency to rapid fouling was a serious disadvantage.

To foster mechanical talent Whitworth founded thirty scholarships (at a cost of £100,000). Similar sums to Owens' College (now the University of Manchester) and the Manchester Technical School, and a lesser, but nonetheless substantial bequest to the Stockport Technical School showed that he appreciated the value of identifying and nourishing talent.

His firm became a modified co-partnership in 1874 and amalgamated with that of Sir William Armstrong (1810–1900) in 1893.

Whitworth received many honours. He was elected FRS in 1857 and made a baronet in 1869. He was an honorary graduate of Oxford (1868) and of Trinity College, Dublin (1863).

Transactions of the Royal Society. 1887.

D. A. Low (Ed.), *The Whitworth Book.* 1926.

A. E. Musson, *The Vickers Magazine,* II, Summer, 1966. (Portrait.)

Dictionary of National Biography.

Proceedings of the Institute of Civil Engineers, **9**(i), 1887–8.

Proceedings of the Institute of Mechanical Engineers, Feb. 1887.

W H G A

WHYTT, ROBERT Born in Edinburgh, 6 September 1714; died there, 15 April 1766. A pioneer neurologist; one of the first to investigate reflex action.

Whytt graduated in arts in the University of St Andrews in 1730. He then studied medicine in the University of Edinburgh, especially anatomy under Alexander MONRO *primus*. Thereafter he went to London, studied surgery under W. Cheselden (1688–1752), and attended the London hospitals. Then he studied at Paris, and at Leiden under H. BOERHAAVE and B. S. ALBINUS. Whytt graduated as a doctor of medicine in the University of Rheims in 1736. In 1737 he became a Licentiate of the Royal College of Physicians of Edinburgh. In the following year he was elected a Fellow of that College, and he set up in practice as a physician in Edinburgh. In 1747 he was appointed professor of medicine in the University of Edinburgh. He was elected a Fellow of the Royal Society of London in 1752, and in 1761 the post of first physician to the King in Scotland was created for him. Whytt was elected President of the Royal College of Physicians of Edinburgh in 1763, and he retained the Presidency until his death.

In 1751 Whytt published *An Essay on the Vital and other Involuntary Motions of Animals.* In this work he gave the only account of the work on reflex action by Stephen HALES. Whytt himself thought that the purpose of any involuntary action is to remove anything that is harmful to the body. He showed that the spinal cord is essential for the completion of such an action. He also demonstrated that reflex action does not depend on the integrity of the spinal cord as a whole, as stimulation of the skin will produce a reflex if only a small segment of the cord is intact. Whytt also introduced the modern terms 'stimulus' and 'response'. He proved that the reaction of the pupil to light is a reflex, and that the afferent pathways lie in the optic thalamus and the efferent in the oculomotor nerves. He reported the case of a child in whom the pupil did not respond to light; at autopsy a cyst was found compressing the thalamus, and Whytt deduced that the intactness of the thalamic region is essential for the production of the reflex.

Whytt's *Observations on Nervous, Hypochondriacal, or Hysteric Diseases* (1765) was the first important treatise on neurology after that of Thomas WILLIS. In his posthumous *Observations on the Dropsy of the Brain* (1768) Whytt described tuberculous meningitis for the first time. In 1743 he published a paper on the treatment of vesical calculus by the ingestion of lime-water. In 1752 he published a small book on this method, soap being now added to the lime-water, and he wrote further papers on this subject. In his time these writings were of great interest and some importance.

W. Seller, *Transactions of the Royal Society of Edinburgh*, **18**, 99, 1861–2.
F. H. Garrison, *History of Medicine*. 1954. (Portrait.)
J. F. Fulton, *History of Physiology*. 1931.
Rachel M. Barclay, *Life and Work of Rober Whytt*. 1922.
C. W. Burr, *Medical Life*, **36**, 109, 1929.
Dictionary of National Biography.
Dictionary of Scientific Biography.

E A U

WIELAND, HEINRICH Born at Pforzheim, Germany, 4 June 1877; died Munich, Bavaria, 5 August 1957. Organic chemist, notable for his work on steroids.

Wieland studied in several universities, finally in Munich under F. K. J. THIELE, whose ideas of valency had some influence on his later work. He became *Privatdozent* (1904); then professor in the Munich *Technische Hochschule* (1917) and in the University of Freiburg (1921). When R. WILLSTÄTTER resigned from the University of Munich in 1925 he insisted that Wieland should be his successor; Wieland held this post almost until his death. His son Theodor also became a prominent organic chemist.

Wieland's reputation was made early, with his clarification of the confused field of the addition products of N_2O_3 and N_2O_4 to olefinic double bonds, especially of terpenes. This led him into some interesting work on organic nitrogen compounds, such as nitrile oxides, fulminic acid derivatives, 'diphenyl nitrogen', and diphenyl nitric oxide. His main interests, however, developed in the direction of natural-product chemistry. He began about 1912, with a study of the bile acids; though their structures were quite unknown, he succeeded in proving that the main acids were related to one another, and also to the well-known sterol, cholesterol. Later, in Munich, Wieland and his students worked on such diverse topics as the lobelia alkaloids, the pigments of butterflies' wings (pterins), and a toadstool poison, phalloidine. During this time, the importance of the hitherto disregarded sterols in living organisms was gradually coming to be recognized. Wieland returned to an intensive study of the bile acids and their congeners, and succeeded in deducing (as he thought) the structure of the sterol skeleton. For this work he was awarded the Nobel prize in 1927. Ironically, however, the work of Wieland himself, and that of O. Rosenheim and H. King (1932) made

necessary a drastic revision of this structure to the one now accepted.

Mention should be made of Wieland's long controversy with O. WARBURG and others on whether biological oxidation was really dehydrogenation; although apparently sterile, it led to a great deal of experimental work on both sides. Wieland was editor of LIEBIG's *Annalen* for over twenty years.

R. Huisigen, *Proceedings of the Chemical Society*, 210, 1958. (Portrait.)
E. Farber (Ed.), *Great Chemists*. 1961. (Portrait.)
Biographical Memoirs of Fellows of the Royal Society. 1958. (Portrait.)
Tyler Wasson (Ed.), *Nobel Prizewinners*. 1987. (Portrait.)

W V F

WIEN, WILHELM CARL WERNER OTTO FRITZ FRANZ Born at Gaffken, East Prussia, Germany, 13 January 1864; died Munich, Bavaria, 30 August 1928. Famous for his studies on thermal radiation.

The son of a farmer, Wien studied at several German universities, including Berlin under H. L. F. von HELMHOLTZ. He remained at Berlin until 1896, when he became Professor Extraordinary at the Technical High School at Aachen. After a year at Giessen he moved in 1900 to Würzburg, where he remained for twenty years. His final post was as successor to W. K. RÖNTGEN at Munich.

Wien's work on black body radiation must be seen against that of L. BOLTZMANN, who (1884) had deduced a law expressing the total energy of such radiation. In 1893, after a study of the energy densities, Wien concluded that the wavelength at which maximum energy is radiated is inversely proportional to the absolute temperature of the body. This Displacement Law was tested experimentally by other workers, who confirmed its validity and evaluated the constant in the equation (for example, O. R. LUMMER and E. PRINGSHEIM).

This work marked the end of successful treatments of the problem by classical methods. The difficulty of the distribution of energy levels remained. In 1896 Wien attempted to resolve this by calculations that assumed very large numbers of oscillators in the black body, having all possible frequencies and in thermal equilibrium. He concluded that the energy density in the neighbourhood of a given wavelength varied inversely as the fifth power of that wavelength. The result was immediately tested by several workers who found that, though satisfactory for short wavelengths, it was seriously in error at higher values.

The importance of this work was that it enabled Max PLANCK to develop a treatment valid for the whole range of wavelengths, in his paper of 1900 which introduced the quantum theory.

Wien also worked on hydrodynamics and x-ray measurements. He studied the phenomena produced when electric discharges are passed through gases, and showed that the 'Canal Rays' which passed through a perforated cathode were positively charged particles, deflected by electric and magnetic fields. He edited *Annalen der Physik* from 1906 until his death. He was awarded the Nobel prize in physics in 1911.

Nature, **122**, 736, 1928.
American Journal of Physics, **32**, 301, 1964. (Portrait.)

Karl Wien (Ed.), *Aus dem Leben und Werken eines Physikers.* 1930.
Dictionary of Scientific Biography.
Tyler Wasson (Ed.), *Nobel Prize Winners.* 1987. (Portrait.)

C A R

WIENER, ALEXANDER SOLOMON Born at Brooklyn, New York, 16 March 1907; died New York City, 6 November 1976. Physician and immunohaematologist, best known as the co-discoverer of the rhesus (Rh) blood factor.

Wiener lived all his life in New York. Following an undergraduate education at Cornell University, he entered the Downstate Medical School (Brooklyn) of the State University of New York in 1926. He began his researches on human blood groups and blood transfusion as a medical student, and following a few years of general practice (1932–5), he devoted the rest of his career to the complex biological and clinical problems surrounding the immunology of red blood cells. He was on the staff of the Jewish and the Adelphi hospitals in Brooklyn, and, from 1938, taught at the New York University School of Medicine. In 1939 he became serologist to the Office of the Chief Medical Examiner of New York City, where he brought the techniques of modern immunohaematology to bear on a variety of medicolegal issues, such as blood-testing in cases of disputed paternity, and examination of blood stains in homicide investigations.

Following the discovery by Karl LANDSTEINER in 1901 of the three chief human blood groups (A, B, O), the way was opened for safe blood transfusion, although, for a variety of reasons, blood transfusion did not become common until after the 1930s. In 1939 Landsteiner's pupil Philip Levine described an unusual haemolytic reaction in a woman (type O) transfused with blood taken from her husband (also type O). Earlier, in 1937, Landsteiner and Wiener had produced a new antibody by the immunization of rabbits and guinea pigs with blood of the rhesus monkey. This antibody was found to agglutinate the red blood cells of 85 percent of Caucasians in New York City ('Rh positive'). Wiener went on to demonstrate that sensitization to this rhesus (Rh) antibody was the cause of the haemolytic reactions observed by Levine and others. In 1940 Wiener introduced Rh typing as part of the cross-matching of blood for transfusion, and by 1944 he had developed the technique of exchange transfusions for newborn babies whose blood reacted to that of their mothers. This often fatal condition (erythroblastosis foetalis) could then be treated.

Since the 1930s many other blood factors were discovered by Wiener, including several of clinical importance. He was instrumental in working out the principles of nomenclature for the blood groups and established the primary blood groups of non-human primates (chimpanzees, rhesus monkeys, baboons, etc.), useful in experimental medicine and surgery, especially transplantation research. He also pioneered the use of blood group serology in physical anthropology and in the study of human evolution.

Wiener wrote more than 600 papers and five monographs in his field and received many national and international awards. One of his students, V. J. Freda, was a pioneer in the immuno-prophylaxis of Rh haemolytic disease. Wiener married Gertrude Rodman in 1932; they had two daughters.

Haematologia, **6**, 39, 1972; **11**, 5, 1977. (Portrait.)

W F B

WIENER, NORBERT Born at Cambridge, Massachusetts, USA, 26 November 1894; died Stockholm, 18 March 1964. Mathematician and creator of cybernetics.

Norbert Wiener was the son of Leo Wiener (1862–1939), the brilliant professor of Slavonic languages and literature at Harvard University. The son was a prodigy and the father a hard tutor, determined that his son's brilliance should be disciplined. Norbert appears to have been driven hard as a child, though it was clear that he had enormous capacity for work. He graduated at the age of 14 and completed a Harvard PhD in the philosophy of mathematics at the age of 18. He then studied mathematical logic under Bertrand Russell (1872–1970) at Cambridge, and later under D. Hilbert (1862–1943) at Göttingen. In 1919 he joined the Massachusetts Institute of Technology as Instructor in the Department of Mathematics. His association with MIT lasted until his death, and he contributed to its development from what he described as 'simply an engineering school' to the present major centre of learning. He spent his early time there working, under the influence of the writings of Willard GIBBS, on Lebesgue integration and the Brownian motion. In 1920 he began work on harmonic analysis, in which he was to do some of his most important work throughout his life. By applying to this field the method of Tauberian theorems, previously used on similar problems by G. H. Hardy (1877–1947) and J. E. Littlewood, who had been close colleagues of his in Cambridge, he was able to simplify large areas in the theory of whole numbers.

In the early thirties he worked with R. E. Paley (1907–33) on Fourier transforms and on the basis of this work wrote *Fourier Transforms in a Complex Domain* (1938). About this time he also carried out research on the problem of quasi-analytic functions. In 1940 he became interested in the development of computing machines and his inquiries into their complexities led him to his war work on fire-control apparatus for anti-aircraft guns. In the course of this work he and his colleagues investigated the problem of feedback control and made great advances in relating this to brain processes. From then on he went deeper into the question of brain functions and the application of statistical theories to these. After the war, the new ideas which he was developing concerning control, communication and organization found a sympathetic audience in England, and he decided to write a comprehensive book on the subject. To describe this new subject he chose the name cybernetics (Greek *kubernetes*, a steersman). In this name he sought to suggest most strongly the element of control and its application over a wide range of fields.

N. Wiener, *I am a Mathematician.* 1956.
Nature, **202**, 540, 1964.
Bulletin of the American Mathematical Society, **72**, No 1, pt 2, 1966 (Special issue.)
Dictionary of Scientific Biography.

N H

WIGNER, EUGENE PAUL Born in Budapest, 17 November 1902. Chiefly known for his applications of symmetry principles in physics.

Wigner's first work was in chemical engineering in Berlin, where he gained his PhD in 1925 for calculating reaction rates between colliding atoms. He soon turned to physics, and in 1926 he introduced the theory of groups into quantum mechanics to deal with symmetries between many identical particles. With fellow-Hungarian John VON NEUMANN he applied group theory to energy levels in atoms. In 1930 both Wigner and von Neumann moved to Princeton University, where Wigner remained until retiring in 1971.

In 1928, Wigner introduced the concept of parity symmetry, or symmetry under spatial reflection, into quantum theory, and in 1932 he introduced time-reversal symmetry. Both symmetries have since become important in understanding the fundamental particles of matter and their interactions.

Over the years Wigner has contributed to many areas of physics, ranging from solid-state theory to the workings of nuclear reactors. He was rewarded for his contributions to the theory of the atomic nucleus and the elementary particles with the Nobel prize for physics in 1963, which he shared with Maria GOEPPERT MAYER and J. Hans D. Jensen (1907–73).

Nobel Lectures: Physics, 1963–1970, 1972.
Les Prix Nobel en 1963. 1964. (Portrait.)
A. Pais, *Inward Bound*, 1986.
E. P. Wigner, in *From a Life of Physics*, 1989.
E. H. Whichmann, *Quantum Physics (Berkeley Physics Course, vol 4)*, 1971. (Portrait.)
F. S. Wagner, *Eugene P. Wigner: An Architect of the Atomic Age*. 1981.
Tyler Wasson (Ed.), *Nobel Prize Winners*. 1987. (Portrait.)

                                                                                        C S

WILCKE, JOHAN CARL Born at Wismar, Mecklenburg, Germany, 6 September 1732; died Stockholm, 18 April 1796. Notable for contributions to physics, particularly in relation to specific and latent heats.

The son of a priest (his mother was related to C. W. SCHEELE), Wilcke moved to Sweden with his parents in 1739 and studied at Uppsala before going abroad during the years 1751–7. Part of this time was spent at Rostock, where Wilcke obtained the Mag. Phil. degree (1757), and part in Berlin, where he did important work on static electricity with F. U. T. Aepinus (1724–1802). He pointed out errors in the electrical theories of C. F. DUFAY and showed that two different sorts of electricity were always produced by the rubbing together of bodies; he drew up a table in which substances higher in the series became positively charged when rubbed on bodies lower in the series. From 1759, Wilcke held a physics lectureship at the Military Academy in Stockholm, and was elected a Fellow and later (1784) Secretary of the Academy of Sciences of that city.

Apart from his work in electricity, he designed an anemobarometer (1785) and drew up a chart showing the value of magnetic dip over a large part of the Earth's surface (1768). He is, however, best known for his work on heat. In 1772 he published a paper on the cold produced when snow melts, having noticed that snow constituted an exception

to the rule of G. W. Richmann (1711–53) for computing the temperatures of mixture; he deduced that the equivalent of 72 (Centigrade) degrees of heat were absorbed at the melting-point before snow turned into water. This observation of latent heat was followed in 1781 by a paper including a table of specific heats based on experiments in which various hot substances were mixed with snow. Unlike J. BLACK and H. CAVENDISH, Wilcke published his work and was in consequence regarded as the discoverer of specific and latent heats by many European scientists.

D. McKie and N. H. de V. Heathcote, *The Discovery of Specific and Latent Heats*. 1935. (Portrait.)
A. Wolf, *A History of Science, Technology and Philosophy in the Eighteenth Century* (2nd ed.), vol 1. 1952.
C. W. Oseen, *Johan Carl Wilcke, experimental-fysiker*. 1939. (Portrait.)
S. Lindroth, *Swedish Men of Science, 1650–1950*. 1952.
Dictionary of Scientific Biography.

                                                                                        G R T

WILKINS, JOHN Born at Fawsley, Northamptonshire, England, 1614; died London, 16 November 1672. Mathematician; a founder of the Royal Society.

Wilkins was the son of an Oxford goldsmith and graduated from the University in 1631, afterwards taking Holy Orders. Parliamentary sympathies – he married a sister of Oliver Cromwell in 1656 – led to his appointment as Warden of Wadham College, Oxford, in 1648, his Royalist predecessor being ejected. He held this appointment for eleven years and was then made Master of Trinity College, Cambridge. With the Restoration his career seemed ended, but he succeeded in gaining ecclesiastical preferment and was made Bishop of Chester in 1668.

At Wadham, Wilkins attracted round him the group of philosophers that was ultimately (1660) to form the Royal Society of London. He might well have been its first President, for he took the chair at many of the early meetings, but in the event this honour went – perhaps for political reasons – to William BROUNCKER. Wilkins was, however, a member of Council and one of the Society's two Secretaries. In his will, he left the Society £400.

Wilkins had a great interest in mechanical devices and was an imaginative writer. In 1638 there appeared his *Discovery of a World in the Moon*, an account of a journey to the Moon and a description of its inhabitants. His *Discourse Concerning a New Planet* (1640), argues (with COPERNICUS) that the Earth is a planet. In 1641 his fertile mind turned in another direction, and he produced a learned work on codes and ciphers. His *Mathematical Magick* (1648) is mainly an account of the fundamental principles of machines; despite doubts, he argues that perpetual motion may not be impossible. His last major work, *An Essay towards a Real Character and a Philosophical Language* (1688) formulated in great detail a universal language.

H. Hartley (Ed.), *The Royal Society: its Origins and Founders*. 1960. (Portrait.)
Biographia Britannica.
Dictionary of National Biography.

Dictionary of Scientific Biography.

T I W

WILKINSON, SIR GEOFFREY Born Todmorden, Yorkshire, England,, 14 July 1921. Inorganic chemist and Nobel Laureate.

Wilkinson read chemistry at Imperial College, London, where he obtained his doctorate in 1942. Following wartime work in Canada on the secret uranium project, he practised nuclear chemistry with G. SEABORG at the University of California, Berkeley, from 1946 to 1950. In 1951 he joined the exciting theoretical and experimental research school of R. B. WOODWARD at Harvard. From 1956, and until his retirement in 1988, he was Sir Edward Frankland Professor of Inorganic Chemistry at Imperial College, where he remains a Senior Research Fellow.

In 1951 (result published March 1952), while working with Woodward, Wilkinson realized that it was possible to coordinate two-parallel 5-membered rings of cyclopentadiene above and below a central metal. Because the resulting 'sandwich compound' possessed a sextet of electrons, it followed on theoretical grounds that such compounds would have aromatic properties. The name ferrocene for the iron compound was chosen to suggest its similarity to benzene. Such metallocenes rapidly became the subject of intense theoretical and commercial interest. In 1954 Wilkinson synthesized a rhodium triphenylphosphine complex (Wilkinson's catalyst) which has proved valuable industrially in the hydrogenation of ethene and propene to form aldehydes. In 1973, he and the German coordination chemist, E. O. Fischer (1918–) were jointly awarded the Nobel prize for chemistry. Wilkinson coauthored with a former American pupil, F. A. Cotton (1930–), the outstanding text *Advanced Inorganic Chemistry* (1962, many eds.) and is general editor of the multivolumed *Advanced Coordination Chemistry*. He was knighted in 1976.

Nature, **246**, 3, 1973. (Portrait.)

G. B. Kauffman, *Journal of Chemical Education*, **60**, 185, 1983.

McGraw-Hill Modern Scientists and Engineers, Vol. 3, 1966. (Portrait.)

W. A. Campbell and N. N, Greenwood (Eds), *Contemporary British Chemists*, 1971.

Les Prix Nobel en 1973. 1974. (Portrait.)

Tyler Wasson (Ed.), *Nobel Prize Winners*. 1987. (Portrait.)

W H B

WILKINSON, JOHN Born at Clifton, Cumberland, England, 1728; died Bradley, Staffordshire, 14 July 1808. Ironmaster.

John Wilkinson's father, Isaac, was a farmer who took up iron-furnace work, patented a box-iron (1738), and eventually established a furnace of his own. Soon after 1750 the family leased Bersham furnace, near Wrexham, which later passed into the hands of John and his brother, William; John by 1763 had risen from management to sole control of Broseley furnace, near Coalbrookdale; and in 1770 he set up a third furnace, at Bradley in Staffordshire. He thus became a leading figure in the expanding iron industry, famous for the manifold uses, from barges to chapels and coins to coffins, which he found for his castings, and an important

supplier of armaments for the American and French wars.

Though he later patented the making of lead pipes by extrusion, Wilkinson's most important invention was his boring machine, patented in 1774 and first built at Bersham for use in cannonfounding. The gun barrel was held rigidly in a cradle, while the cutter head moved forward on a rod inside the hollow boring bar, which was supported in a bearing at each end. With little adaptation, this machine gave the necessary degree of accuracy to the cylinders of the steam engines of Boulton & Watt (see Matthew BOULTON and James WATT), who recommended Wilkinson to their customers. Wilkinson, on the other hand, installed for the blast at his Broseley furnace the first Watt engine to be used other than for pumping. By 1780 he had three others in use, and he later erected the first Watt engine in France, to serve the Paris waterworks, for which he supplied the iron pipes.

Wilkinson came generously to the rescue of Joseph PRIESTLEY, his brother-in-law, after the wrecking of his laboratory in Birmingham. But in most respects 'Iron-mad Wilkinson' was an unattractive character. He quarrelled furiously with his brother, William; is supposed to have traded clandestinely with France in wartime; certainly tried to defraud Boulton & Watt of numerous patent premiums; and though married twice, left his fortune to three illegitimate sons, with the result that it was all spent in litigation.

A. W. Dickinson, *John Wilkinson, Ironmaster*. 1914.

Dictionary of National Biography.

T K D

WILLIAMS, EVAN JAMES Born at Cwmsychpant, Wales, 8 June 1903; died Llanbyther, 29 September 1945. Physicist and operational research worker.

Williams, son of a stonemason, was educated at Llandyssul County School. He was particularly fortunate in that his headmaster there, William Lewis, had been Fifth Wrangler at Cambridge and stimulated his latent interest in physics and mathematics. In 1919 Williams entered Swansea Technical College (later a constituent college of the University of Wales). He went on to take a PhD degree first at Manchester (1926) and then at Cambridge (1929) under Ernest RUTHERFORD. From 1930 to 1937 he was assistant lecturer at Manchester and during this time he spent a year in Copenhagen with Niels BOHR. In 1937 he was appointed senior lecturer at Liverpool under James CHADWICK. He was elected FRS in 1939 and in the following year was appointed professor of physics at Aberystwyth. The outbreak of war diverted him from academic to operational research, and unhappily his untimely death prevented his resuming an exceptionally promising research career in physics.

Williams's strength lay in his combining exceptional theoretical ability with first-rate experimental technique; not only could he carry out his experiments quickly and efficiently, but he could discern just what experiments were needed. These skills stood him in good stead in his prewar research, concerned mainly with electronic and atomic collision processes using the cloud chamber of C. T. R. WILSON. His *Correlation of certain Collision Problems with Radiation Theory*, published while he was in Copenhagen, is recognized as brilliant. In 1940 he demonstrated the decay of a cosmic ray meson into an electron.

During the war he turned his talents with equal enthusiasm to military strategy, especially in the vitally important campaign against German submarines. His statistical analysis of various systems of aerial bombardment led to many traditional beliefs being discredited and to a very considerable increase in efficiency. The outstanding importance of his services in this respect to the Allied cause was widely acknowledged. He was Director of Operational Research, RAF Coastal Command 1941–2; Admiralty Adviser on Anti-U-boat Warfare 1943–5; and Assistant Director of Naval Operational Research 1944–5.

Nature, **156**, 655, 1945.
Obituary Notices of Fellows of the Royal Society, 1945–8. (Portrait.)
Dictionary of National Biography (Missing Persons). 1993.
J. Tysul Jones (Ed.), *Yr Athro Evan James Williams D.Sc., F.R.S., 1903–1945*. 1970.

T I W

WILLIAMSON, ALEXANDER WILLIAM Born in London, 1 May 1824; died Hindhead, Surrey, 6 May 1904. Chemist and teacher.

Williamson, while a boy, left England to live with his parents on the Continent. He studied chemistry under L. GMELIN, then spent two years with J. von LIEBIG at Giessen. In 1846 he went to Paris, studied mathematics, attended the lectures of A. M. F. X. Comte (1798–1857), and worked in his private laboratory. He returned to England in 1849 as professor of analytical chemistry at University College, London, where he stayed until his retirement in 1887. A childhood illness left him permanently disabled, and reduced his ability to do practical work. He married in 1855 and had two children.

Williamson is remembered for his ether synthesis (reaction of sodium alcoholates with alkyl iodides) which first clarified the relationship of alcohols and ethers (1850); both were classified as representatives of the 'water type' of compound. His views on many topics (for example, the structural significance of chemical formulae) were in advance of his contemporaries, but unfortunately, after about 1855, he became immersed in university administration, and published little. He was elected FRS in 1855.

G. Carey Foster, *Journal of the Chemical Society*, **87**, 605, 1905.
Nature, **70**, 32, 1904.
J. R. Partington, *A History of Chemistry*, vol. 4. 1964. (Portrait.)
E. Divers, *Proceedings of the Royal Society*, **78A**, xxiv, 1907. (Portrait.)
Dictionary of Scientific Biography.
J. Harris and W. H. Brock, *Annals of Science*, **31**, 95, 1974.

W V F

WILLIAMSON, WILLIAM CRAWFORD Born at Scarborough, Yorkshire, England, 24 November 1816; died London, 23 June 1895. One of the founders of palaeobotany.

Williamson had little formal education, but acquired a knowledge of natural history from his father and his friends, who included William

SMITH, the geologist. He was apprenticed to an apothecary, but a few early publications led to his appointment as curator to the Museum of the Manchester Natural History Society (1835). Here he became acquainted with John DALTON and the members of the Literary and Philosophical Society; he also continued his medical studies in Manchester and London. He began to practise in Manchester in 1841, and continued to do so until over seventy, despite his other appointments.

In 1851, when Owens College was founded in Manchester, Williamson was made professor of natural history, anatomy and physiology. When the Medical School was incorporated in 1872, he dropped the two latter subjects. In 1880 he became professor of botany, and retired in 1892. He was twice married, and had six children.

Williamson's early research concerned such matters as the anatomy of certain invertebrates (such as *Volvox*) and the structure of fish scales; he gained his FRS in 1854. His most important work was done after this, however, in his extensive studies of the fossil plants found in the Coal Measures, which shed much light on the ancestry of modern plant families. This was true pioneering work, and helped to found the new science of palaeobotany, though it was little appreciated until towards the end of his life. This was largely due to old-fashioned terminology and poor presentation, for Williamson remained essentially an amateur in an increasingly professional world.

Dictionary of National Biography.
W. C. Williamson, *Reminiscences of a Yorkshire Naturalist*. 1896.
Nature, **52**, 441, 1895.
Proceedings of the Royal Society, **60**, xxvii, 1897.
Dictionary of Scientific Biography.

W V F

WILLIS, THOMAS Born at Great Bedwin, Wiltshire, England, 27 January 1621; died London, 11 November 1675. English physician, famous for his description of the anatomy of the brain.

Willis entered Christ Church, Oxford, in 1636. He graduated in arts (1639), and then studied medicine. About this time he bore arms in the King's cause, and he graduated as a bachelor of medicine in 1646. He then set up in practice in Oxford, and began to write his treatises. In 1660, shortly after the Restoration, he was appointed Sedleian Professor of Natural Philosophy in the University of Oxford, and in the same year was created a doctor of medicine. Willis had been one of the 'experimental philosophers' who met in the lodgings of William Petty (1623–87), John WILKINS, or Robert BOYLE at Oxford in 1648–9, and when the Royal Society was founded in London he was elected a Fellow on 18 November 1663. In 1664 he was elected an Honorary Fellow of the Royal College of Physicians. On the invitation of the Archbishop of Canterbury, Willis removed to Westminster in 1666. He soon became one of the most popular physicians in London, and when he died was buried in Westminster Abbey.

Willis's most important publications are those dealing with the brain. In 1664 he published his *Cerebri anatome*, which was the most complete and authentic account of the anatomy of the brain hitherto published. In its preparation he had the assistance of Richard LOWER. In this work he gave a new classification of the cranial nerves, which was universally accepted for over a century. He was also the first to describe the eleventh cranial nerve (spinal accessory). Most important was his description of the cerebral circulation. Owing to the softness of the parts, study of this had previously been inaccurate. By injecting the vessels with 'aqua crocata' Willis saw and described for the first time the important ring of vessels at the base of the brain which is universally known as the 'circle of Willis'. In his *Pathologiae cerebri* (1667) he gave the first account of general paralysis of the insane, now known to be a late result of syphilis.

Another very important observation of Willis related to 'diabetes', which then embraced all conditions in which there was excessive excretion of urine. Willis noted that, in those cases in which the urine had a sweet taste, the patients suffered from great wasting and other symptoms. He was thus virtually the first to recognize diabetes mellitus, although it was not proved until 1776 that the sweet taste of the urine was due to the presence in it of sugar. He was the first to suggest that bronchial asthma consists essentially in spasm of the bronchial muscles. His contribution to epidemiology was some excellent descriptions of outbreaks of diseases such as typhus and typhoid fevers. He was the first to describe myasthenia gravis and puerperal fever.

W. Munk, *Roll of the Royal College of Physicians.* 1878.

M. Foster, *History of Physiology.* 1901.

C. Singer and E. A. Underwood, *Short History of Medicine.* 1962.

H. Isler, *Thomas Willis 1621–1675.* 1968.

Dictionary of Scientific Biography.

J. Trevor Hughes, *Thomas Willis.* 1992.

E. Wolstenholme and D. Piper (Eds), *The Royal College of Physicians of London: Portraits.* 1964.

E A U

WILLSTÄTTER, RICHARD Born at Karlsruhe, Baden-Württemberg, Germany, 13 August 1872; died Locarno, Switzerland, 3 August 1942. Organic chemist, notable for studies of natural colouring matters.

Willstätter, son of a textile merchant, studied chemistry at the *Technische Hochschule,* Munich. His doctorate work on the structure of cocaine (under A. Einhorn (1857–1917)), brought him to the notice of the industrialist Carl Duisberg, who supported his work for many years. He became assistant to A. von BAEYER at the University of Munich, and extraordinary professor in 1902. From 1905 to 1912 he was professor in the *Technische Hochschule,* Zürich; then head of the Chemistry Section of the Kaiser Wilhelm Gesellschaft at Berlin-Dahlem; in 1915 he returned to Munich as full professor, but resigned in 1925 in protest against growing anti-Semitism (he was of Jewish descent). He declined all offers of other posts, but supervised a little research by telephone. His last years were spent in Switzerland. He was bereaved by the early deaths of his wife and son, but a daughter survived him.

Apart from some early work on quinones and quinone-imines, all his important research concerned natural products. As a byproduct of his studies of the tropine alkaloids he first prepared

cyclo-octatetraene (1905) which has properties analogous with those of benzene. At Zürich he attacked the formidable problem of the nature of chlorophyll, the photosynthetic pigment of green plants; he showed that it consisted of two closely related compounds (chlorophylls a and b), which contained magnesium, pyrrole residues, and a long-chain alcohol, phytol; and that it was related to the blood pigments. At Dahlem, he made important pioneering studies of two other classes of natural colouring matters, the carotenes and the anthocyanins, but this work, using huge quantities of expensive solvents, had to be abandoned when war broke out, and Willstätter was diverted into designing gas-masks. His later investigations, in Munich, were into the mechanism of enzyme reactions, and of catalysis by metals and colloids; two topics which he felt to be closely connected. He also revived, with great success, the technique of chromatography exploited earlier by M. S. TSWETT.

Willstätter was awarded the Nobel prize for chemistry in 1915.

R. Willstätter, *Aus meinem Leben.* 1949. (Portrait.); translated as *From my Life.* 1965.

E. Farber (Ed.) *Great Chemists.* 1961. (Portrait.)

R. Robinson, *Journal of the Chemical Society,* 999, 1953. (Portrait.)

Obituary Notices of Fellows of the Royal Society, 1953. (Portrait.)

Tyler Wasson (Ed.), *Nobel Prize Winners.* 1987. (Portrait.)

W V F

WILSON, CHARLES THOMSON REES Born at Glencorse, near Edinburgh, 14 February 1869; died Carlops, Peeblesshire, 15 November 1959. Famed for his invention of the Wilson Cloud Chamber.

After the premature death of his father, a Scottish sheep-farmer, Wilson moved to Manchester with his mother, and eventually entered Owens College (now Manchester University) to study biology. Showing at Cambridge an aptitude for physics, he graduated in this (1892) and shortly afterwards joined J. J. THOMSON at the Cavendish Laboratory. He became Fellow of Sidney Sussex College and (1925–34) professor of natural philosophy at Cambridge.

Always a lover of the Scottish Highlands, Wilson joined a temporary, volunteer staff at the Ben Nevis meteorological observatory during the summer holiday of 1894. Having observed the magnificent early-morning cloud effects visible from the summit, he attempted to reproduce them in his laboratory. His intention was to produce an artificial cloud by the adiabatic expansion of moist air. For condensation to occur it was then believed that each droplet required a nucleus of dust. However, Wilson showed that even in the complete absence of dust particles some condensation was possible, and that it was greatly facilitated by exposure to x-rays. He was led to conclude that charged atoms (or ions) were the necessary nuclei (1896–7). After much labour he produced, in 1911, his Cloud Chamber, in which the paths of single charged particles showed up as trails of minute water droplets.

The Wilson Cloud Chamber, sometimes modified or refined, has been an indispensable tool of modern physics ever since. An early application was to observe, and then photograph, tracks of α- and β-particles from radioactive substances. It was used to study artificial radioactivity induced by α-particles (P. M. S. BLACKETT, 1925) and neutrons (N. Feather (1904–78), 1932). With its aid C. D. ANDERSON discovered the positron (1933) and meson (1937) in cosmic rays.

Wilson's other work included the observation in 1900 that a completely insulated electrometer gradually lost its charge due to gaseous ions in the air. He tentatively suggested that radiation from some non-terrestrial source was responsible, anticipating the later discovery of cosmic rays. He also studied atmospheric electricity, stimulated by further sensations received in the Highlands during a thunderstorm. He devised a sensitive electrometer and suggested a mechanism for the generation of electrical charges in the atmosphere.

His publications were not many, but were models of clarity. He was widely honoured, becoming FRS in 1900; Nobel Laureate in physics (with A. H. COMPTON) in 1927; and Companion of Honour in 1936.

Biographical Memoirs of Fellows of the Royal Society. 1960. (Portrait.)

H. Oxbury (Ed.), *Great Britons: 20th Century Lives.* 1985.

Tyler Wasson (Ed.), *Nobel Prize Winners.* 1987. (Portrait.)

Dictionary of National Biography.

                                                                        C A R

WILSON, KENNETH GEDDES Born in Waltham, Massachusetts, USA, 8 June 1936. Theoretical physicist.

The son of a well-known chemical physicist at Harvard University, Wilson graduated there in 1956. He then worked under Murray GELL-MANN, at the California Institute of Technology, and gained his PhD in 1961. After a brief period back at Harvard, Wilson joined Cornell University at Ithaca, New York, becoming professor in 1971.

At Cornell, Wilson encountered Ben Widom and Michael Fisher who were working on the theory of 'critical phenomena' associated with transitions from one phase of matter (eg liquid, ferromagnetic) to another (eg gas, paramagnetic). Wilson brought with him from his work at Caltech the theory of the 'renormalization group' and was able to apply it to develop for the first time a complete theory for critical phenomena. Briefly, the technique enabled him to extend calculations over small scales to successively larger distances, in other words by 'renormalizing'. He published two seminal papers in 1971, with more following in the succeeding years. He was rewarded with the Nobel prize for physics for this work in 1982.

During the 1980s Wilson became a champion of supercomputers, and in 1985 became director of Cornell's Center for Theory, one of five supercomputer centres set up in the USA. In 1988, he resigned as director at Cornell and, with the aim of spending more time on research, moved to Ohio State University, where he is the Hazel G. Youngberg Professor of Physics.

Science, **218**, 763, 1982. (Portrait.)

Physics Today, December 1982.

Tyler Wasson (Ed.), *Nobel Prize Winners.* 1987. (Portrait.)

                                                                        C S

WINDAUS, ADOLF OTTO REINHOLD Born in Berlin, 25 December 1876; died Göttingen, 9 June 1959. Organic chemist, noted for his studies of natural products, especially calciferol (Vitamin D).

Windaus studied medicine in Berlin and Freiburg, but found himself more attracted to chemistry, especially by the lectures of Emil FISCHER. His PhD thesis on cholesterol (under H. Kiliani (1855–1945) at Freiburg) was to set the tone for his life's work. In 1913 he became professor of medical chemistry in Innsbruck; two years later he moved to the chair vacated by Otto WALLACH in Göttingen, where he remained for the rest of his life, finally as Emeritus Professor.

Windaus was interested in all branches of natural-product chemistry; his studies of histidine, of imidazole chemistry, of colchicine, and Vitamin B_1 are all noteworthy. His main work, however, was in the field of sterol chemistry, for which he was awarded a Nobel prize in 1928. His early interest in cholesterol broadened into a demonstration that substances chemically closely related to cholesterol were widespread both in the plant and animal kingdoms, and played an important part in biological processes. In 1919 he converted cholesterol into cholanic acid, the parent substance of the bile acids, which were being closely studied by H. WIELAND. Later, such disparate materials as digitalin, the toad venoms, saponins and sex hormones were all shown to be based on the sterol structure, though the work of Windaus himself played little direct part in the elucidation of this structure. He is best remembered, however, for his solution of the baffling problem of the anti-rachitic Vitamin D (calciferol). It was known that rickets in rats could be prevented either by a hypothetical dietary factor (Vitamin D) or by irradiating the animals with ultra-violet light. In 1925, A. Hess and others showed that irradiation of the rats' food was all that was necessary; it was supposed that cholesterol in the food might be converted into Vitamin D by irradiation, and Hess asked Windaus to investigate the possibility. Windaus soon proved that the 'pro-vitamin' was not cholesterol, but a dehydrocholesterol contained in it as a minor impurity. In 1936, pure Vitamin D was isolated from cod-liver oil, and the whole complex process of its photochemical synthesis from sterol precursors was elucidated.

A. Butenandt, *Proceedings of the Chemical Society,* 131, 1961.

G. Lunde, *Journal of Chemical Education,* **7**, 1767, 1930.

Tyler Wasson (Ed.), *Nobel Prize Winners.* 1987. (Portrait.)

Dictionary of Scientific Biography.

                                                                        W V F

WINKLER, CLEMENS ALEXANDER Born at Freiberg, Germany, 26 December 1838; died Dresden, 8 October 1904. Analytical chemist, discoverer of germanium.

Winkler, the son of a mining chemist, was educated at the famous *Bergakademie* in Freiberg. After holding various industrial posts until 1873, he was appointed professor of chemical technology and analytical chemistry there, where he remained until his retirement in 1902.

Winkler and his pupils published many papers on analytical methods. His great discovery came in 1885, when a routine analysis of a new mineral (argyrodite) from the Freiberg mines failed to add up to 100 per cent. This led to the isolation of a new element, germanium, whose properties were soon found to be remarkably close to those predicted for 'ekasilicon' by D. I. MENDELÉEFF.

M. E. Weeks, *Discovery of the Elements.* 1945. (Portrait.)

O. Brunck, *Berichte der deutschen Chemischen Gesellschaft*, **39**, 4491, 1906. (Portrait.)

Dictionary of Scientific Biography.

W V F

WINSOR (or **WINZER**), **FREDERICK ALBERT** Born at Brunswick, Germany, 1763; died Paris, 11 May 1830. Pioneer of gas-lighting.

Winsor was a company promoter who visited Paris in 1802 to investigate the work of P. LEBON and tried unsuccessfully to buy his thermolamp. In 1804, during what appears to have been his second stay in England, he lectured on gas-lighting at the Lyceum Theatre in London, and showed how gas could be conveyed from room to room. In May of that year he took out the first of four patents for his 'apparatus for extracting inflammable air from all kinds of fuel'. In June 1807 his methods received a great advertisement when he was allowed to illuminate a wall of Carlton House garden in celebration of the King's birthday.

Realizing that gas would have to be supplied from costly generating plants through a system of mains, Winsor worked for six years to promote a chartered National Light and Heat Company. He was bitterly opposed by rival interests, and when the company was eventually formed he was dismissed in the same year (1812) for lack of engineering or administrative capacity. In 1815 he returned to Paris where, although he installed some gas-lighting, the company he formed failed in 1819.

W. Matthew, *An Historical Sketch of the Origin, Progress, and Present State of Gaslighting.* 1827.

Dictionary of National Biography.

Trevor I. Williams, *A History of the British Gas Industry.* 1981.

T K D

WINZER, FREDERICK ALBERT See WINSOR.

WISLICENUS, JOHANNES ADOLPH Born at Klein-Eichstadt, Thuringia, Germany, 24 June 1835; died Leipzig, 5 December 1902. Organic chemist, noted for synthetic work and studies of geometrical isomerism.

While Wislicenus was still a youth, his father's political and religious opinions made it necessary for the family to leave Germany. They emigrated to the United States, where Johannes studied at Harvard for a time. A change in political climate made possible a return to Europe in 1856, and he continued his education at Zürich and Halle; he later occupied chairs successively at Zürich, Würzburg (1872), and Leipzig (1885, following A. W. H. KOLBE).

Wislicenus began research on lactic acid and its isomers, a field confused both by erroneous work and inadequate theoretical ideas. He was able to clarify the problem, though not to solve it; but he took the first steps towards 'chemistry in space', and was generous in his advocacy of the solution later proposed by J. H. VAN'T HOFF and J. A. LE BEL.

His work on synthetic methods based on the reactions of ethyl acetoacetate and diethyl malonate is classical organic chemistry at its best. Finally, in his years at Leipzig, he made an intensive study of 'geometrical isomerism', which is due to the different arrangements of substituents with respect to a non-rotating double bond.

His private life was overshadowed by the mental illness of his wife, and the early death of two of his six children; but two of his sons became prominent in academic life, one as a chemist. All his contemporaries testify to the excellence of his teaching, and his pupils included M. Conrad, L. Limpach, and W. H. PERKIN *Jr.*

E. Beckmann, *Berichte der deutschen Chemischen Gesellschaft*, **37**, 4861, 1904. (Portrait.)

Journal of the Chemical Society, **87**, 501, 1905. (Portrait.)

Dictionary of Scientific Biography.

W V F

WITHERING, WILLIAM Born at Wellington, Shropshire, England, 17 March 1741; died Birmingham, 6 October 1799. Physician, botanist, and mineralogist.

William Withering was the son of an apothecary at Wellington. He received his medical training at the Edinburgh Medical School, graduating MD in 1766, and was physician at the Stafford Infirmary from 1766 until 1775. On the death of William Small (1734–75), one of the founders of the Lunar Society of Birmingham, Erasmus DARWIN invited Withering to take over Small's medical practice at Birmingham. Withering also became a member of the Lunar Society, and several fellow members, including Matthew BOULTON, were among his patients. Withering soon had a flourishing practice, and became physician to the General Hospital at Birmingham. He continued to live at Birmingham for the rest of his life, apart from a journey to Portugal in 1792–3.

In medicine Withering is chiefly remembered for his classic *Account of the Foxglove* (1785), in which he described the proper use of digitalis, in scientifically controlled dosage, for the treatment of dropsy, and hinted at its possible use in heart disease, for which it is still widely prescribed. In botany he is best known for his systematic survey, the *Botanical Arrangement* (1776), which remained a standard work for nearly a century. Withering became a Fellow of the Royal Society in 1785 and contributed five papers to the *Philosophical Transactions*. Of these, three are concerned with mineralogy, another subject on which Withering was an accepted authority. The mineral witherite (barium carbonate) is named after him.

In the last ten years of his life Withering suffered much from pulmonary disease. To combat this ill health he lived in air-conditioned and thermostatically controlled rooms – a way of life that inspired the *bon mot*, 'The flower of Physic is Withering'.

T. W. Peck and K. D. Wilkinson, *William Withering of Birmingham.* 1950. (Portrait.)

R. E. Schofield, *The Lunar Society of Birmingham.* 1963.

Dictionary of National Biography.

D G K-H

WÖHLER, FRIEDRICH Born at Eschersheim, near

Frankfurt-am-Main, Hessen, Germany, 31 July 1800; died Göttingen, 23 September 1882. Chemist, notable for his recognition (with Justus von LIE-BIG) of the benzoyl radical, and for his discovery of the isomerization of ammonium cyanate into urea.

The son of a veterinary surgeon, Wöhler studied medicine at Marburg and Heidelberg; he graduated MD, but never practised, preferring chemistry. A year (1823–4) spent with J. J. BERZELIUS in Stockholm was probably the formative period of his career. After appointments in technical schools in Berlin (1825) and Kassel (1831), he became in 1836 professor of chemistry in Göttingen, and held this until he died. His predecessor, F. Stromeyer (1776–1835), had founded a teaching laboratory in Göttingen (the first in Germany), and Wöhler became one of the great teachers of the century; about 8000 students are estimated to have passed through his hands. His marriage was ended by the early death of his wife, but his cheerful disposition enabled him to maintain lifelong friendships even with difficult men like Liebig. Some of his best work was done in collaboration with Liebig, not always with acknowledgment by the latter.

Wöhler's work on derivatives of cyanogen began when he was still a medical student. He discovered cyanic acid, and in 1828 found that its ammonium salt was readily isomerized into urea. This represented the synthesis of a well-known product of living matter from materials which were available (at least in principle) from non-living matter. As such, it was difficult to reconcile with the then popular doctrine of vitalism, though many years were to pass before this was finally abandoned. Studies of cyanogen compounds led to an interest in bitter almonds, from which hydrocyanic acid can be obtained. Liebig and Wöhler (1832) showed that the pure oil of bitter almonds was non-toxic, and free from hydrocyanic acid; it was, in fact, what we now know as benzaldehyde. The reactions of benzaldehyde were thoroughly investigated, and the analyses of the products indicated that a cluster of atoms (in modern terms C_7H_5O) persisted unchanged through a long series of transformations, behaving rather like a chemical element, though, of course, it could be broken up under severer conditions. This cluster of atoms was named 'benzoyl'; many others were soon discovered, and called 'compound radicals'. The concept of compound radicals brought the beginnings of order into the then dreadful confusion of organic chemistry.

Wöhler was also active in inorganic chemistry; he isolated aluminium (1827) and beryllium (1828) and published numerous analyses of minerals and meteorites. Other research topics included uric acid derivatives (with Liebig, 1838), quinones, mellitic acid, and the alkaloid narcotine. After about 1845 he published little, but continued as a teacher to the end.

J. Valentin, *Friedrich Wöhler*. 1949.
A. W. Hofmann, *Berichte der deutschen Chemischen Gesellschaft*, **15**, 3127, 1882. (Portrait.)
Dictionary of Scientific Biography.
E. Farber (Ed.), *Great Chemists*. 1961. (Portrait.)
J. R. Partington, *A History of Chemistry*, vol. 4. 1964. (Portrait.)

W V F

WOLF, MAXIMILIAN Born at Heidelberg, Baden-Württemberg, Germany, 21 June 1863; died there, 3 October 1932. Pioneer in the application of photography to astronomy.

Max Wolf early showed interest in astronomy, in 1884 discovering a new comet now named after him. After obtaining his doctorate in philosophy at Heidelberg, he spent a year in Stockholm before returning to Heidelberg as *Privatdozent* in astronomy. In 1893 he was appointed extraordinary professor in astrophysics in the same university, also director of the new Königstuhl Observatory near Heidelberg. In 1902 he became ordinary professor of astronomy in Heidelberg, which higher post, as well as the Observatory Directorship, he held to his death.

Wolf specialized in photographic astronomy, applying his cameras in a number of fields, such as the discovery of minor planets and the photographic survey of the sky, in particular the discovery of nebulae, both galactic and extragalactic. He found many hundreds of asteroids, most of them small and very faint. His work on the nebulae ranks of the first importance. During the course of his photographic surveys he established the presence of the dark clouds of interstellar matter that exist in such profusion in our own Galaxy. Many attendant technical problems were solved by him, and he was the first to apply the stereo-comparator to the examination of celestial photographs.

H. Macpherson, *The Observatory*, **55**, 355, 1932.
Monthly Notices, Royal Astronomical Society, **74**, 377, 1941.
Dictionary of Scientific Biography.

A E R

WOLFF, KASPAR FRIEDRICH Born in Berlin, 1733; died St. Petersburg, 22 February 1794. A founder of embryology.

Wolff studied at the *Collegium medicochirurgicum* at Berlin, and also in Halle. He graduated in 1859 with his famous dissertation on *Theoria generationis* (see below). He served for a time as an Army surgeon, and then was granted permission to give private lectures on pathology and medicine in Berlin. These were very successful, but the professorship for which he hoped did not materialize. Wolff therefore accepted in 1767 a call to St Petersburg, where he was appointed Academician for Anatomy and Physiology. There he prosecuted his researches without interruption until his death.

When Wolff wrote his dissertation the preformation theory of development held the field. According to this, the embryo was supposed to contain in miniature all the parts of the adult already formed. Embryonic life was simply a question of the unfolding of the parts. On purely philosophical grounds Wolff adopted the opposite view that all the parts and organs are formed in the embryo from undifferentiated tissue. In the dissertation he showed that the tip of a growing shoot or root consists of such undifferentiated tissue, and he demonstrated the gradual formation of the different parts, such as the leaf and the flower. In later work he proved that the same principle applies in the development of animals. In the chick he described the primitive and transient 'Wolffian body', and he was one of the first to indicate that both plants and animals are made up of cells.

Allgemeine Deutsche Biographie.

Jane M. Oppenheimer, *Essays in the History of Embryology and Biology.* 1967.

Dictionary of Scientific Biography, Supp. I.

E A U

WOLLASTON, WILLIAM HYDE Born at East Dereham, Norfolk, England, 6 August 1766; died London, 22 December 1828. Pioneer of powder metallurgy; discoverer of rhodium and palladium.

After schooling at Charterhouse, Wollaston went to Cambridge and graduated in medicine, which he practised for eleven years. In 1800 he settled in London to give all his time to researches in science. Before his great work on the platinum metals, he had already proved himself a scientist of wide interests in astronomy, physiology and physics. He published over fifty papers, and became Copley Medallist and Secretary of the Royal Society, to which he was elected in 1794.

Too sensitive to be happy as general practitioner, Wollaston decided to abandon medicine and to live on moderate means near Fitzroy Square, where he had a laboratory behind his house. Here, with typical exactness, he carried out painstaking experiments to produce malleable platinum from crude *platina*, at a time when whole cargoes of this obdurate metal lay idle through lack of ability to fabricate it into useful articles. Others, like P. F. Chabaneau (1754–1842), before him had attained some success but Wollaston's work was the first systematic attempt to produce platinum in a malleable and useful form: this success not only brought platinum into general use but initiated the technique of powder metallurgy, in which metal grains are caused to cohere by high compression, annealing and hammering. The metallurgist's success today with such metals as tantalum, niobium, molybdenum and tungsten derive from Wollaston's pilot-scale processing. He used aqua regia to dissolve the platinum and leave the insoluble iridium; he then prepared ammonium platinichloride and decomposed this to yield fine platinum grains from which he made malleable metal by compressing, heating and hammering. His sheet platinum was suitable not only for crucibles but for fabricating large concentrators for vitriol manufacturers, who were prepared to pay very high prices because of the resistance of the metal to corrosion.

Wollaston made £30,000 from his malleable platinum, justifying his decision to abandon medicine. He revealed his whole technique in a Bakerian lecture to the Royal Society just before his death. He also discovered palladium and rhodium. The man himself remains something of an enigma: 'cold and reserved' according to Edward THORPE, but a 'pleasant and polished' man of science in the view of BERZELIUS.

D. Macdonald, *A History of Platinum.* 1960. (Portrait.)

Dictionary of National Biography.

Metallurgia, 137, 1957.

Dictionary of Scientific Biography.

M S

WOOD, ROBERT WILLIAMS Born at Concord, Massachusetts, USA, 2 May 1868; died Amityville, New York, 11 August 1955; Noted experimenter in physical optics.

After studying at Harvard and Berlin, Wood taught physics at Wisconsin from 1897 until 1901, when he was appointed professor of experimental physics at Johns Hopkins University, Baltimore. Here most of his notable work was done.

Wood became interested in the problems of diffraction and interference, and initiated production at Baltimore of blazed echelette gratings for infrared radiation. In spectroscopy, he observed the Zeeman effect (see P. ZEEMAN) on band lines, and showed that atoms could give rise to continuous spectra. He obtained fluorescence and resonance spectra of sodium vapour at low pressures, and of iodine. He described experiments for observing anomalous dispersion; proved that high temperatures are not attained in vacuum discharge tubes; and helped to discredit the imaginary 'n-rays' postulated by some.

Photographs taken of landscape and lunar subjects by both ultraviolet and infrared light demonstrated strikingly the greater clarity resulting from use of the latter, and experiments with a pinhole camera yielded interesting results. He introduced 'Wood's filter' for ultraviolet work, cutting off most of the visible radiation.

An experimenter of great ingenuity, Wood introduced many instrumental improvements; originated an electrical method for thawing frozen water-pipes; and (while serving as a major in the First World War) developed several secret signalling devices.

Wood was also a talented artist, musician and writer. In addition to his *Physical Optics*, he produced a volume of satirical poetry. He travelled extensively and received many honours, including Foreign Membership of the Royal Society, whose Rumford Medal he was awarded in 1938.

Nature, **176**, 488, 1955.

Biographical Memoirs of Fellows of the Royal Society. 1955. (Portrait.)

W. Seabrook, *Doctor Wood – Modern Wizard of the Laboratory.* 1946.

Dictionary of Scientific Biography.

C A R

WOODWARD, ROBERT BURNS Born in Boston, Massachusetts, USA, 10 April 1917; died Cambridge, Massachusetts, 8 July 1979. Organic chemist.

Woodward entered Massachusetts Institute of Technology near his home town of Boston in 1933 and took his BS and PhD degrees in chemistry in the remarkably short span of four years. After a brief spell at the University of Illinois, he obtained a position at Harvard University where he remained until his death. He became a full professor in 1950, Morris Loeb Professor of Chemistry three years later, and Donner Professor of Science in 1960. Woodward was awarded the chemistry Nobel prize in 1965 for the totality of his contribution to chemistry. But for his untimely death, he would probably have shared the 1981 Nobel prize in chemistry with K. FUKUI and Roald Hoffmann (1937–) for his work on the conservation of orbital symmetry (the Woodward-Hoffmann rules).

In the 1940s and 1950s organic chemists still expended considerable effort on the determination of the chemical structures of natural substances, which are often very complex. After taking part in the determination of the structure of penicillin

during the Second World War, Woodward elucidated the structures of several important natural
products including the alkaloids strychnine and
cevine, the antibiotic terramycin, and the puffer
fish poison tetrodotoxin. He proposed the remarkable 'sandwich' structure for ferrocene (with G.
WILKINSON) in 1952. Woodward also contributed to
the development of physical organic chemistry
with the Woodward rules for the ultraviolet spectra
of steroids (1941) and the octant rule (1961; with
C. Djerassi (1923–), A. Moscowitz, and W. Mof-
fitt). A life-long interest in the Diels-Alder reaction
culminated in the formulation of the rules for the
'conservation of orbital symmetry' with the young
theoretical chemist Hoffmann in 1964–5, which
govern this reaction and others like it. Nonetheless,
his greatest contributions were in the field of total
organic synthesis, the construction of complex
natural products from simple man-made compounds. Woodward first made his name with his
synthesis of quinine in 1944. This was followed by
the elegant synthesis of cholesterol and cortisone
(1951); the alkaloids strychnine (1954), lysergic
acid (1954), reserpine (1956), and colchicine
(1963); the green leaf pigment chlorophyll A
(1960); and the antibiotics cephalosporin C (1965)
and erythromycin (posthumously reported in
1981). The peak of his pathbreaking efforts was
undoubtedly the elaborate total synthesis of vitamin B_{12} (with Albert Eschenmoser) in 1976.

Woodward was justly famous for his flamboyant
lectures, often spanning several hours, replete with
numerous chemical structures delicately drawn
with coloured chalks. He was also legendary for
his consumption of coffee, cigarettes and whiskey,
and for his light blue suits. He was the leading
synthetic organic chemist of the post-Second
World War period and one of the greatest chemists
the world has ever known.

*Biographical Memoirs of Fellows of the Royal
　Society*, 1981. (Portrait.)

Mary Ellen Bowden and Theodor Benfey, *Robert
　Burns Woodward and the Art of Organic
　Synthesis* 1992.

P J T M

WREN, SIR CHRISTOPHER Born at East Knoyle,
Wiltshire, England, 20 October 1632; died London,
25 February 1723. Architect and mathematician.

Wren was the son of a clergyman. His mathematical abilities became evident while he was an
undergraduate at Wadham College, Oxford (1646–
50), and even when a boy at Westminster School
he composed short tracts on dialling and spherical
trigonometry. At Oxford he exhibited a series of
ingenious mechanical inventions, as well as a
'hypothesis of the Moon's libration'. After taking
his degree he was made a Fellow of All Souls College, although as late as 1663 he still had rooms at
Wadham, where met members of the Philosophical
Society, nucleus of the Royal Society. In 1657 he
was made professor of astronomy at Gresham College, London, which he quitted on being appointed
to the Savilian Chair of Astronomy at Oxford
(1661). In 1665 he was appointed a commissioner
for the restoration of the old St Paul's Cathedral.
After the Fire of London in the following year,
St Paul's was rebuilt to one of his designs. In 1668,
after being made Surveyor-General of Public
Works, he gave progressively more time to archi-

tecture, and his scientific work effectively ended
when he resigned his Oxford professorship in
1673, the year in which he was knighted. In all,
he designed eighty London buildings, and about
twenty in the provinces. In 1680 he became President of the Royal Society. He twice sat in Parliament, but he was deprived of his public offices a
few years before his death.

Wren had many minor scientific achievements
to his credit. Perhaps his principal mathematical
achievement was his determination of the length
of the arc, and the centre of gravity, of the cycloid.
This is the curve described by a point carried on
a circle that rolls along a straight line. Another
discovery was that of the two systems of generating
lines on a hyperboloid of one sheet (1669). In this
connection, he wrote on the properties and grinding of hyperbolic mirrors. His practical bent, in
fact, is in evidence in most of his writings, yet he
contributed little of moment to theoretical mechanics, except perhaps his paper on the law of collision of bodies. Like Jean PICARD and at about the
same time (*c.* 1671), he proposed as a standard of
length the pendulum with half-second beat.

In astronomy, his most enduring monument is
the Greenwich Observatory. Wren is said to have
anticipated C. HUYGENS in explaining the telescopic
appearance of Saturn (1655), also attempting a wax
model of the planet. Another model was of the
Moon (1661), showing its features in relief, and
carrying a scale of miles. This seems to have been
the first such globe.

J. Summerson, *Sir Christopher Wren*. 1953.
　(Portrait.)

G. Webb, *Wren*. 1937.

J. Lindsey, *Wren: His Work and Times*. 1952.

C. Whitaker Wilson, *Sir Christopher Wren*. 1932.

Dictionary of National Biography.

Dictionary of Scientific Biography.

K. Downes, *Christopher Wren*. 1971.

J D N

WRIGHT, WILBUR AND ORVILLE Wilbur was
born at Millville, near New Castle, Indiana, USA,
16 April 1867; died Dayton, Ohio, 30 May 1912.
Orville was born at Dayton, 19 August 1871; died
there, 30 January 1948. Producers of the first successful aeroplane.

Sons of Milton Wright, a pastor of the United
Brethren, Wilbur and Orville early made mechanical toys and helped their father with his church
magazine, the *Religious Telescope*; later they
started a paper of their own, *West Side News*. Disabled by an accident before entering college,
Wilbur turned to reading, and became interested
in the gliding experiments of Otto LILIENTHAL, who
sought to control his glider by altering its centre
of gravity, and was killed in 1896. The Wrights
decided to build a glider controlled by means of
ailerons, which enabled the centre of gravity to
remain constant. In 1900 they tested their first
glider at Kitty Hawk in North Carolina, and in 1901
their second.

Turning to the scientific theory of flight, they set
up their own wind tunnel at Dayton in 1901 to
measure lift and drag of aerofoils and other problems, so that they could predict the performance of
their machine. In this they tested over 200 models,
some on more than one scale, and their findings
were embodied in their third glider, which was

tested at Kitty Hawk in September 1902 in nearly 1000 gliding flights. This gave them a complete system of control – a movable vertical rudder (absent from earlier models) and adjustable flaps.

In December 1902, having returned to Dayton, they built a petrol engine and mounted it in a larger version of their glider to drive two airscrews. These were mounted in the rear of the mainplane and revolved in opposite directions to offset torque. This machine was tested at Kitty Hawk on 17 December 1903, and so sure were they of its success that the brothers invited the neighbourhood to attend. Only five braved the cold wind to see them make four flights between 10.30 a.m. and noon: two by Orville and two by Wilbur. The first lasted 12 seconds and the last 59; all were made in a 25 mph gale which, when the machine was left unattended after the last flight, blew it over and made further flights impossible. This original machine weighed 750 lb. and the engine was rated at 12 hp.

Later, they made a larger and more powerful machine with which they flew a full circle in the air in October 1905, covering a 24-mile circuit. They offered it to the US War Department, having patented the machine in 1906, but they had to wait for two years before getting a contract for a plane. Meanwhile, they continued a programme of successful and increasingly ambitious flights, making a flight of more than an hour's duration. Later that year Orville was injured in one of their remarkably rare accidents.

In 1908 Wilbur went to Europe and arranged with a French syndicate to make his aeroplane, and in 1909 the American Wright Company was formed.

J. R. McMahon, *The Wright Brothers: Fathers of Flight*. 1930.

Fred C. Kelley, *The Wright Brothers*. 1944.

M. J. B. Davy, *Interpretive History of Flight*. 1948.

Marvin W. McFarland, *The Papers of Wilbur and Orville Wright*. 1953.

Dictionary of American Biography.

C. H. Gibbs-Smith, *The Wright Brothers, A Brief Account of their Work*. 1953. (Portraits.); *The Invention of the Aeroplane (1799–1909)*. 1966.

R. P. Hallion (Ed.), *The Wright Brothers, Heirs of Prometheus*. 1978.

W H G A

WRÓBLEWSKI, ZYGMUNT FLORENTY VON Born at Grodno, Lithuania, 28 October 1845; died Cracow, Poland, 16 April 1888. Made important contributions to the liquefaction of gases.

Wróblewski studied at Kiev, but was exiled to Siberia for six years for his part in the Polish insurrection of 1863. After working with H. L. F. von HELMHOLTZ in Berlin, in 1874 he moved to Strasbourg, where he studied gaseous diffusion.

In 1882 Wróblewski was appointed to the chair of physics at Cracow, but spent his first year in Paris working on aqueous solutions of carbon dioxide. At Cracow, with K. S. Olszewski, the professor of chemistry, he achieved the first large-scale liquefaction of oxygen and then of nitrogen (1883) by an adaptation of the cascade method (1877) devised by R. P. PICTET, using liquid ethylene as a coolant instead of carbon dioxide. In 1884 Wróblewski obtained a mist of liquid hydrogen.

He died in 1888 from burns after a paraffin lamp overturned in his laboratory.

Nature, **38**, 41, 598, 1888.

Dictionary of Scientific Biography.

C A R

WU CHIEN-SUNG Born in Shanghai, China, 31 May 1912. Experimental physicist who discovered the violation of parity (spatial symmetry) in beta-decay.

Wu was educated in China and received her BSc from the National Central University there in 1934. In 1936 she travelled to the USA to work under Ernest LAWRENCE at the University of California, Berkeley. She was awarded her PhD at Berkeley in 1940. After two more years there, she moved for short spells first to Smith College and then to Princeton University, finally joining Columbia University in New York in 1944.

Wu is best known for her work that led to the discovery of the violation of parity, or spatial symmetry, in beta-decay. By 1956 she was already acclaimed as an expert on experimental work with beta-decay, and it was natural that T. D. LEE, a theorist at Columbia, should turn to her to discuss a radical idea that he and his colleague C. N. YANG, from the Institute for Advanced Study at Princeton, were proposing. Lee and Yang were investigating a puzzle in the decays of subatomic particles called kaons, and had found that they could explain the puzzle if spatial symmetry – parity – were not respected in these decays. They wondered if this were true for all weak decays, including nuclear beta-decay. After consulting Wu, they discovered that no one had ever made a measurement that would test the properties of beta-decay under parity symmetry, so that it remained possible that these decays were indeed parity-violating. Wu then suggested a way to test for parity violation using a beta source in which the nuclear spins were aligned in a magnetic field. She contacted experts at the National Bureau of Standards in Washington, and together with Ernest Ambler and colleagues there, performed the crucial experiment with cobalt-60. By early 1957 they had demonstrated that parity is indeed violated in beta-decay.

Later, in 1963, Wu was able to make another important contribution to the study of weak interactions when she demonstrated together with Y. K. Lee (1929–   ) and L. W. Mo (1934–   ) the conservation of the 'vector current' in beta-decay.

Wu retired from Columbia University in 1981, having been made Pupin Professor of Physics in 1972. During her life she has received many honours, including having an asteroid named after her in 1990.

McGraw Hill Modern Men of Science (I), 1966.

Physics Today, April 1975. (Portrait.)

C S

WURTZ, CHARLES-ADOLPHE Born at Wolfisheim, near Strasbourg, France, 26 November 1817; died Paris, 12 May 1884. Outstanding chemist.

Wurtz's father, a French Protestant clergyman, gave his son the choice of studying either theology or medicine. Wishing to be a chemist, Wurtz chose the latter, and graduated MD from Strasbourg in 1843; he had meanwhile spent a year with Justus von LIEBIG in Giessen. In 1844 he went to Paris and became assistant to J. B. A. DUMAS; after a few misadventures (including a post in the short-lived *Institut Agronomique*) he succeeded to Dumas's chair in the *École de Médecine* (1853). He later became Dean of the school, but resigned on his appointment (1874) as professor of organic chemistry at the Sorbonne. His medical training was used actively in the siege of Paris; later he concerned himself with the welfare of his fellow Alsatians who became refugees. He married, and had four children.

Wurtz's early research was concerned with the oxy-acids of phosphorus, and similar topics. He later became an organic chemist, and made his name with the discovery of ethylamine, the first 'compound ammonia' (1849), and with the synthesis of ethylene glycol (1856). This work was extended to the syntheses of such important compounds as glycollic acid, ethylene oxide, ethylene-chlorhydrin and choline. He tended to take his theoretical views from his friend C. GERHARDT, but substances like these strained Gerhardt's Theory of Types to the limit. It was perhaps no accident that the structure theorists A. S. COUPER and A. M. BUTLEROV were both trained in Wurtz's laboratory.

Wurtz, who was a fine teacher as well as an excellent investigator, was largely instrumental (with M. P. E. BERTHELOT) in making the school of chemistry in Paris the only one in Europe which could compete with the German universities in attracting large numbers of outstanding young men. He took a leading part in founding the *Société Chimique de France* in 1858. Among other honours, Wurtz was made a Foreign Member of the Royal Society in 1864, and elected to the *Académie des Sciences* in 1867. He was briefly a Senator before his death.

Proceedings of the Royal Society, **38**, xxiii, 1885.
Berichte der deutschen Chemischen Gesellschaft, **20**, 815, 1887. (Portrait.)
E. Farber (Ed.), *Great Chemists*, 1961. (Portrait.)
Dictionary of Scientific Biography.

W V F

YALOW, (neé SUSSMAN), ROSALYN Born New York City, 19th July 1921. Physicist, distinguished for developing technique of radioimmunoassay.

Rosalyn Yalow studied physics and chemistry at Hunter College, New York City, and then did postgraduate research at the University of Illinois, Urbana. After further research there, and again at Hunter College, she joined the Veterans Administration (VA) Hospital, New York, where she was successively consultant in the Radioisotope Service and Head of the Nuclear Medicine Service. She also became Director of the Solomon A. Berson Research Laboratory (1973). As a nuclear physicist she developed a major interest in endocrinology, especially in relation to diabetes, being awarded the Banting Medal in 1978. From 1950 she developed the technique of radioimmunoassay, clinically significant in the diagnosis and treatment of a variety of diseases, but particularly important for assaying peptide hormones such as insulin. It is based on tagging with a radioactive isotope any substance for which an antibody can be produced. It is highly sensitive, permitting analysis down to as little as one picogram (10^{ms12} gram). For this work she was awarded a Nobel Prize in 1977.

Tyler Wasson (Ed.), *Nobel Prize Winners*. 1987.
(Portrait.)
Les Prix Nobel en 1977, 1978. (Portrait.)
Physics Today, December 1977.
L. Haber, *Women Pioneers in Science*. 1979.

T I W

YANG CHEN NING Born in Hofei, Anwhei, China, 22 September 1922. Theoretical physicist best known as the co-discoverer of parity violation.

The son of a professor of mathematics, Yang gained his BSc in physics in 1942 at the National Southwest Associated University in Kunming. In 1945, he left China for the USA, and attracted by the presence of Enrico FERMI, he joined the University of Chicago in January 1946. It was here that he first worked with T. D. LEE, with whom he was to have a long and fruitful period of collaboration. Yang received his PhD in 1948. The following year he moved to the Institute for Advanced Study at Princeton, where he was to stay until 1965, becoming professor in 1955.

In 1954, Yang made one of his first major contributions to the theory of elementary particles in work with Robert G. Mills (1924–). They devised a theory for the conservation of the property called isospin, with the same symmetry properties ('gauge invariance') as the theory of electromagnetism, in which electric charge is conserved. 'Yang-Mills' theories later had an important role in the development of the present Standard Model of par-ticles and their interactions. In this model, the interactions are all described in terms of theories that exhibit the gauge symmetry that Yang and Mills had explored.

Although Lee had himself come to Princeton in 1951, in 1953 he moved to Columbia University in New York. However, Yang and Lee kept in touch with weekly visits to each other. In 1956 they did the work for which they are best known, when they proposed that 'parity' (symmetry under spatial inversion) is not conserved when particles interact via the weak force, as for example in radioactive beta-decay. Their theory was proved correct in 1957 by the experiments of C. S. WU and others. Later that year Yang and Lee received the Nobel prize for physics for their work. Yang was elected Foreign Member of the Royal Society in 1992.

In 1964, Yang became a US citizen, and in 1965 he moved to the State University of New York at Stoney Brook, to become Einstein Professor and Director of Theoretical Physics. His work has continued to follow his main interests in symmetry principles and in statistical mechanics.

Nobel Lectures, Physics, 1942–1962. 1964.
C. N. Yang, *Selected Papers 1945–1980 with commentary*. 1983.
H. A. Boorse, L. Motz, and J. H. Weaver, *The Atomic Scientists, a Biographical History*. 1989. (Portrait.)
R. P. Crease and C. C. Mann, *The Second Creation*. 1986
Tyler Wasson (Ed.), *Nobel Prize Winners*. 1987. (Portrait.)

C S

YOUNG, ARTHUR Born in London, 11 September 1741; died there, 20 April 1820. An outstanding writer on agriculture, and Secretary to the Board of Agriculture from its inception in 1793 until his death.

After schooling at Lavenham, Suffolk, Arthur Young was apprenticed to a King's Lynn merchant, but the deaths of his father and his principal prematurely ended his commercial career. He began farming in 1763 at Bradfield, Suffolk, married in 1765, and took a larger Essex farm in 1766. On this last he experimented and lost his money, anonymously publishing his experiences as *The Farmer's Letters to the People of England* (1767). While viewing other possibly suitable farms he prepared *A Six Weeks' Tour through the Southern Counties of England and Wales* (1768) in which he set out the Norfolk system (see C. TOWNSHEND). He eventually took a Hertfordshire farm. His income as a writer rose from this time: among works of this period were the *Six Months' Tour* through the North of England (1770); the Farmer's Tour Through the East of England (1771); and the highly successful Political Arithmetic (1774–9). In 1774 he was elected FRS and in 1776 began the Tour of Ireland (1780). Young commenced the Annals of Agriculture (1784–1815), which attracted important contributors. He made three journeys to France (1787–9) where he compiled an unrivalled account of the peasant economy, Travels in France (1792).

Following Pitt's creation of the Board of Agriculture, Young prepared a number of county reports (1794–1809), as well as more general publications. Through these and his private writings he greatly contributed to the wide spread of growing knowledge of agricultural science. He was left spiritless by the death of his daughter in 1797. His declining eyesight finally failed in 1811, and his remaining life was spent in religious contemplation.

M. Bentham-Edwards (Ed.), Autobiography of Arthur Young. 1898. (Portrait.)

A. Defries, Sheep and Turnips. 1938. (Portrait.)

J. G. Gazley, Life of Arthur Young. 1973.

Dictionary of National Biography.

W N S

YOUNG, JAMES Born in Glasgow, Scotland, 13 July 1811; died Wemyss Bay, Ayrshire, 13 May 1883. Founded the Scottish shale-oil industry.

After part-time study at Anderson's College, Glasgow, Young combined his knowledge of chemistry with his skill in constructing apparatus. This attracted the attention of Thomas GRAHAM to whom Young was assistant for seven years. When Graham moved to University College, London, Young followed him, benefiting further from contacts with first-rate research work.

Young's next phase was in industrial chemistry, a prelude to his oil technology. He was first with James MUSPRATT at St Helens, then in 1843 with Tennants in Manchester as what would now be called a chemical engineer. Young met Lyon PLAYFAIR, and from him heard of an oil seepage at Alfreton, Derbyshire; this led him to experiment on oil for industrial use, and he set up a small works in 1848. Although the Alfreton spring petered out, Young gained invaluable experience.

He moved north on hearing that Torbane Hill shale was to be tried for gas manufacture. He pioneered low-temperature distillation of shale, obtaining rich yields of paraffin oil, valuable for lighting and heating, at his Bathgate works, and built larger works when new shale deposits were found. By sponsoring the production of burning and lubricating oils and paraffin wax in a flourishing Scottish industry, Young established a reputation as an early oil technologist. In 1866 he sold his business for a considerable sum. He was elected FRS in 1873; in 1870 he founded the Young Chair of Technical Chemistry at Anderson's College, of which he was President 1868–77.

Chemical News, 245, 1883.

Journal of the Chemical Society, 630, 1884.

Dictionary of National Biography.

M S

YOUNG, THOMAS Born at Milverton, Somerset, England, 13 June 1773; died London, 10 May 1829. Established the wave theory of light.

A precocious child, with a phenomenal memory, especially for languages, Young also very early showed great mechanical ability. After leaving school he studied various Middle Eastern languages, including Syriac and Hebrew, and by the age of 17 he had mastered the Principia and Optics of NEWTON. Under the influence of his great-uncle, R. Brocklesby (1722–97), a distinguished London physician, he took up medicine with a view to taking over his practice. In 1793 he entered St Bartholomew's Hospital and in the following year was elected FRS for an original paper on the action of the ciliary muscles in the accommodation of the eye. After studying at Edinburgh (1794) and Göttingen (1795), he entered Emmanuel College, Cambridge, in 1797, where he resided for two years. At Cambridge he had ample time to pursue scientific researches of which the first account was given in his Outlines of Experiments and Enquiries Respecting Sound and Light (1800). Before this he had entered medical practice in London, his great-uncle having left him a fortune of £10,000 and his London house on his death in 1797. In 1801 Young became professor of natural philosophy at the Royal Institution. As a lecturer to popular audiences he was a failure, and he retired from the Royal Institution in 1803. From 1807 onwards he devoted himself largely to medicine, becoming physician at St George's Hospital in 1811, a position he held until his death. From 1817 onwards he gradually withdrew from private practice, devoting himself increasingly to his duties as Secretary of the Commission of Weights and Measures and Foreign Secretary of the Royal Society.

Young's first published references to the wave theory of light occurred in Section 9 of his Outlines. Comparing the theories of Newton and C. HUYGENS, he demonstrated the many advantages of the wave theory especially in the natural explanation it provided of reflection and refraction. In his 1801 Bakerian Lecture he introduced the principles of superposition and interference and by combining Huygens's wave theory with Newton's view of colours he explained the colours produced by ruled gratings and thin plates. The same explanation was extended in 1803 to the coloured fringes in the shadows of obstacles, the colours of the supernumerary bows of the rainbow, and the fringes of F. M. GRIMALDI. Throughout these papers Young's theoretical arguments were supported by a number of impressive experiments. But there was an increasing number of experimental facts which could not be explained before the assumption of transverse vibrations was introduced by A. J. FRESNEL, and for a number of years Young himself became increasingly doubtful of his own theory.

Apart from his contribution to sound and light, an impressive paper on capillarity and the cohesion of fluids, and many important papers on physiological optics and medical subjects, Young is remembered for his outstanding contributions to the reading of Egyptian hieroglyphics, beginning with his work on the Rosetta Stone.

G. Peacock, Life of Young. 1855.

F. Oldham, Thomas Young. 1933.

A. Wood, Thomas Young, Natural Philosopher. 1954.

Dictionary of National Biography.

Dictionary of Scientific Biography.

J W H

YUKAWA, HIDEKI Born in Tokyo, 23 January 1907; died Kyoto, 8 September 1981. Theoretical physicist who devised the meson theory of nuclear forces.

Yukawa was born Hideki Ogawa and brought up in Kyoto, where his father became professor of geology at the university in 1908. Hideki studied physics at the same university, graduating in 1929. In 1932 he married Sumi Yukawa and in the Japanese tradition became a member of the Yukawa family in Osaka; at the same time he became a lecturer at Osaka University.

In 1935, Yukawa developed his theory of nuclear forces, based on analogy with the quantum field theory of the electromagnetic force in which the force acts through the exchange of massless photons. He recognized that the force between neutrons and protons must be short range, and showed that this implied that the 'carrier' particle must be about 200 times heavier than the electron. In 1937, a particle with such a mass was discovered in cosmic rays, giving credence to Yukawa's theory. The particle (the muon) proved not to have the expected strong nuclear reactions, but in 1947, a second, slightly heavier particle (the pion) was found with the correct properties.

Yukawa was awarded the Nobel prize for physics for this work in 1949. At the time he was at Columbia University in the USA, but in 1953 he returned to Kyoto to become director of the new Research Institute of Fundamental Physics, until he retired in 1970.

Nobel Lectures, Physics. 1942–1962. 1964.

H. Yukawa, *Tabibito, The Traveler.* 1982.

Physics Today, February 1982. (Portrait.)

Dictionary of Scientific Biography. Supp. II.

Biographical Memoirs of Fellows of the Royal Society. 1983. (Portrait.)

Tyler Wasson (Ed.), *Nobel Prize Winners.* 1987. (Portrait.)

C S

Z

ZEEMAN, PIETER Born at Zonnemaire, Netherlands, 25 May 1865; died Amsterdam, 9 October 1943. Famous for his work in magneto-optics; discoverer of the Zeeman Effect.

The son of a Lutheran minister, Zeeman studied at Leiden University under H. A. LORENTZ, remaining as assistant after gaining his doctorate with a thesis on the Kerr effect (see J. KERR). In 1897 he became lecturer, and in 1900 professor of physics, at the State University of Amsterdam.

In 1896, at Leiden, Zeeman started to examine the effect of a magnetic field on light, following up earlier unsuccessful experiments of Michael FARADAY with an improved magnet and high resolution grating. When a magnetic field was applied to light emitted from sodium or lithium flames, the lines in the emission spectrum were slightly widened. A similar effect was noticed with the absorption spectra, indicating that the changed shape of the flame was not responsible. According to Lorentz's theory that light was caused by vibrating electrons, splitting of the lines should also occur, and in 1897 Zeeman was able to demonstrate this, using the narrow blue-green cadmium line. This Zeeman Effect not merely confirmed Lorentz's theory but enabled its discoverer to calculate the ratio e/m for the oscillating particles, in good agreement with the value obtained by J. J. THOMSON for an electron.

Zeeman's further work on these phenomena was greatly hampered by poor experimental facilities for twenty-five years at Amsterdam, and others quickly outpaced him. Study of the Zeeman effect led to important theoretical advances in spectroscopy. While many of the 'triplets' in the spectra were explicable on the Lorentz theory, many anomalous effects were noted. Consideration of these led S. A. GOUDSMIT and G. E. Uhlenbek to the concept of electronic spin and extension of the quantum theory to include it (1926). Earlier, in 1908, G. E. HALE had observed the Zeeman Effect in spectra of light from sunspots, indicating intense magnetic fields in these regions of solar activity.

Zeeman's work on magneto-optics continued at Amsterdam, marked by great thoroughness and care. He also studied the 'light-drag' predicted on relativity theory; Brownian movement; and isotopes. From hyperfine spectra he derived nuclear moments.

He was awarded, jointly with Lorentz, the Nobel prize for physics for 1902; was elected a Foreign Member of the Royal Society in 1921; and received its Rumford Medal in 1922. His great distinction was to have provided almost the first link between light and magnetism, and his great fortune to have done so at the most propitious time.

American Journal of Physics, **33**, 89, 1965. (Portrait.)
Jena Review, 219, 1966. (Portrait.)
Nature **153**, 158, 1944.
Obituary Notices of Fellows of the Royal Society. 1944. (Portrait.)
Tyler Wasson (Ed.), *Nobel Prize Winners.* 1987. (Portrait.)
Dictionary of Scientific Biography.

CAR

ZEISS, CARL Born at Weimar, Thuringia, Germany, 11 September 1816; died Jena, Saxony, 3 December 1888. Founder of the optical instrument firms which bear his name.

After a wide university training, Zeiss completed his education by a seven years' tour of instrument-makers' workshops from Stuttgart to Vienna. He then established a small optical-instrument workshop in Jena in 1846, where he specialized in the production of precision instruments. Aware that the expanding economy of western Europe and the growing research effort in natural sciences would require new and more accurate measuring devices and instruments, he set out to meet that demand. In common with many of his countrymen, he was aware of the need to co-ordinate the advance of technical art with the furtherance of the physical sciences, and he took advantage of the growing mass of university research in theoretical optics. Already recognized as a manufacturer of the finest instruments, Zeiss improved his position in 1866 by taking into partnership Ernst ABBE, lecturer (later professor) in mathematics and physics at Jena University. Under Abbe's technical direction and Zeiss's commercial control the firm went from strength to strength. In his work on optical imaging and image defects; on light intensity in instruments; and his improvements in the microscope Abbe left a permanent mark on both theoretical and technical optics. Many of the new techniques pioneered by the Zeiss concern were made possible by the use of new optical glasses of widely varying refractive indices and dispersions. These were developed to an industrial scale by Otto Schott (1851–1935) in association with Zeiss and Abbe from 1884 at the *Jenaer Glaswerk Schott & Gen.* After the founder's death, control of the firm passed jointly to his son Carl and Abbe and later to Abbe alone.

W. Schuman (Ed.), *Carl Zeiss Jena, Past and Present.* 1962. (Portrait.)
M. von Rohr, *Zur Geschichte der Zeissischen Werkstätte bis zum Tode Ernst Abbes.* 1930. (Portrait.)
Jena Review, vol. 4, 1966 (supplement marking the 150th anniversary of Zeiss's birth). (Portrait.)

WNS

ZEPPELIN, FERDINAND, COUNT VON Born at Constance, Baden, Germany, 8 July 1838; died Charlottenburg, 8 May 1917. Airship pioneer.

Commissioned in the German Army at the age of 20, Zeppelin was so impressed by the military potential of balloons in the American Civil War (in which he served as a volunteer in the Federal Army) and the siege of Paris, that he tried to persuade the German authorities to take them up. But not until he had retired with the rank of general in 1891 was he able to work on an airship of his own. The LZ 1, his first airship, equipped with two 16 hp engines, first flew on 2 July 1900, and attained a speed of 20 mph With the backing of the King of Württemburg and of an aluminium manufacturer, he built a second vessel which was wrecked by a storm. A third, the Z 1, was more successful, and a fourth flew from Frederichshafen to Lucerne and back, but was wrecked on landing.

Forming a company, he built five more before 1914, and carried nearly 35 000 passengers without accident. During the war of 1914–18 his company built eighty-eight more, but at its conclusion they were forbidden to make more, and the Goodyear-Zeppelin company was formed to make them in the United States.

Eine Festgabe zu Seinem 75. Geburtstag von Luftschiffbau Zeppelin. 1913.

M. J. B. Davy, *Interpretive History of Flight.* 1948.

Margaret Goldsmith, *Count Zeppelin.* 1939. (Portrait.)

T. E. Guttery, *Zeppelin: An Illustrated Life.* 1973.

W H G A

ZERNIKE, FRITS Born in Amsterdam, Netherlands, 16 July 1888; died Groningen, 10 March 1966. Inventor of phase-contrast microscopy.

Zernike was a graduate of the University of Amsterdam, obtaining his doctor's degree in 1915. Thereafter he was associated throughout his working life with the University of Groningen, where he was appointed professor of physics in 1920, having previously worked in the Department of Astronomy. His main interest was in optics, and in 1934 he published a theoretical treatment of the Foucault knife-edge test for testing the accuracy of grinding of mirrors for telescopes. This led him on to his important discovery of the phase-contrast microscope. Briefly, this makes it possible to distinguish any structure in a microscopic preparation that differs in refractive index from the surrounding matrix. This is of particular importance in biological research, for it makes it possible to examine the structure, and changes in structure, of living cells, which to direct observation may appear colourless and transparent. Conventional methods of preparing specimens for examination by dehydration, fixation, staining and so on inevitably involve killing the specimen and also the risk of introducing artifacts. Today, phase-contrast microscopy is a standard technique.

Zernike's contribution was twofold: not only did he see the possibility of the phase-contrast principle but he worked out an effective method of applying it. His achievement was widely recognized in his lifetime and he received many honours, including a Nobel prize (1953). In 1946 the Netherlands Academy of Science elected him a member. The Royal Society awarded him its Rumford Medal in 1952, and four years later elected him to its Foreign Membership.

The Times, 16 March 1966. (Portrait.)

Biographical Memoirs of Fellows of the Royal Society. 1967. (Portrait.)

N. G. van Kampen, *Nature,* **211,** 465, 1966.

Tyler Wasson (Ed.), *Nobel Prize Winners.* 1987. (Portrait.)

T I W

ZIEGLER, KARL Born in Helsa, near Kassel, Germany, 26 November 1898; died Mulheim, 11 August 1973. Distinguished for his work on organic free radicals; alkali and aluminium organic compounds; and polymerization. Discovered process for the low pressure polymerization of ethylene.

Ziegler, son of a Lutheran minister, studied chemistry at the University of Marburg, where he obtained his PhD in 1920, and his 'Habilitation' in 1923. After a brief stay as lecturer at Frankfurt he moved to the University of Heidelberg, becoming professor of chemistry there in 1927. He was appointed professor and director of the Chemical Institute Halle-Saale in 1936, and in 1943 became director, until his retirement in 1969, of the Kaiser Wilhelm Institute for Coal Research at Mulheim-in-Ruhr. His scientific contributions were in three major areas: three-valent carbon studies (1923–50); large ring systems (1933–47); and organo-alkali and aluminium compounds and catalysis (1928–69).

Following from the work of his habilitation thesis on triaryl methyl radicals, Ziegler carried out over the next 20 years a systematic study of the effects of substitution in hexaphenyl ethane on the dissociation equilibrium and reaction of the free radicals produced. New radicals were prepared by reactions of alkali metals and organometallic compounds with ethers and organic halides and by a logical series of events he showed that metal alkyls polymerized isoprene and butadiene. His work on lithium alkyls led to the study of analogous organo-aluminium compounds and his elucidation of the reaction of aluminium alkyls established a new branch of organo-metallic chemistry. He succeeded in reacting aluminium alkyls with ethylene to form molecules ranging from C_4 to C_{40} hydrocarbons, but not the higher polymers he envisaged.

Nickel was accidently found to catalyse the displacement of one olefin from trialkyl aluminium by another, and this opened the door to a systematic scrutiny of other metals and compounds. The outcome was that zirconium acetylacetonate added to triethyl aluminium gave a polyethylene of very high molecular weight. The combination of trialkyl aluminium and titanium chloride was so active that it polymerized ethylene at ambient pressure and temperature in the presence of a solvent. This discovery shattered the long established prejudice that ethylene be polymerized only at high temperature and pressure, and gave birth to a new era in the plastics industry.

Ziegler was a great experimental chemist and teacher and 150 students obtained their PhDs under his direction. The industrial application of his work was a major part of his thinking and planning, and he showed extraordinary talent in promoting the economic evaluation of his discoveries. Part of the royalties from the Ziegler polyethylene process were used to create a Ziegler Fund in the Kaiser Wilhelm Institute at Mulheim, which he endowed with a capital of 40 million marks.

He was a modest, kind, and friendly family man, who arranged his career so as to avoid political involvements in the actions of the Hitler regime, with which he had little sympathy.

> *Biographical Memoirs of Fellows of the Royal Society.* 1975. (Portrait.)
> *Rubber Chemistry and Technology,* **38**, 23, 1964.
> *Angewandte Chemie,* **67**, 426, 541, 1955.
> *Dictionary of Scientific Biography,* Supp. II.
> Tyler Wasson (Ed.), *Nobel Prize Winners.* 1987. (Portrait.)

C E H B

ZSIGMONDY, RICHARD ADOLF Born in Vienna, 1 April 1865; died Göttingen, Germany, 29 September 1929. Colloid chemist, inventor of the ultramicroscope.

Zsigmondy studied chemistry at the *Technische Hochschule* of Vienna and Munich, and physics in Berlin. He was a *Privatdozent* in the *Technische Hochschule,* Graz (1893), but in 1897 went to a post in the famous Schott glass factory, Jena. From 1900 he worked in his private laboratory in Jena, until his appointment (1907) as professor of inorganic chemistry at Göttingen. He retired in 1929, a few months before his death.

Zsigmondy's life work was the study of colloids. His first notable research was on the colours of glass, and this broadened into an investigation of colloid solutions of metals (especially gold), both in glass and water. With the help of H. F. W. Siedentopf (1872–1940) he constructed in 1903 the first 'ultramicroscope', which enabled colloid particles to be observed and counted as points of light, by means of powerful illumination from the side, over a dark background. This proved to be a powerful tool in colloid chemistry, though now outmoded by the ultracentrifuge and the electron microscope. Zsigmondy also worked on protective colloids, and introduced the 'gold number' as a measure of this effect; he was able to explain the old puzzle of the nature of 'Purple of Cassius'. In his later years he was much concerned with collodion membrane filters, which are of importance in biochemistry. He was awarded a Nobel Prize in 1925.

> *Berichte der deutschen Chemischen Gesellschaft,* **63**, 171A, 1930. (Portrait.)
> *Nature,* **124**, 845, 1929.
> E. Farber, *Nobel Prizewinners in Chemistry.* 1953. (Portrait.)
> Tyler Wasson (Ed.), *Nobel Prize Winners.* 1987. (Portrait.)

W V F

ZU CHONGZHI Born in China, 429; died there 500. Mathematician, astronomer.

Like many ancient civilisations, the Chinese attached great importance to precise calendrical computations. Basic to this was determining the exact time of the winter solstice. This in turn is necessary for exact calculation of the tropical year, the period between successive solstices. From about 650 BC the winter solstice was determined by observing the moment at which a gnomon's shadow ceased to change in length. This then gave a tropical year of 365.25 days, sufficiently inaccurate to cause serious cumulative errors over long periods. Using improved observational techniques Zu Chongzhi derived a value of 365.2428, very near to that currently accepted (365.242194). On this basis he compiled the Da Ming calendar (462). He also made a very precise calculation of π, as 355/113. This placed it between 3.1415926 and 3.1415927, a value not improved upon for a thousand years, by F. VIÈTE.

Zu Chongzhi is also credited with the building of a 'thousand-*li*' paddle boat, allegedly capable of covering 1000 *li* (1 *li* = 540 m) in a day (though in fact probably no more than 100 *li*).

> Chinese Academy of Sciences, *Ancient China's Technology and Science.* 1983.

T I W

ZWORYKIN, VLADIMIR KOSMA Born at Mourom, Russia, 30 July 1889; died Princeton, New Jersey, USA, 29 July 1982. Electrical engineer who invented the iconoscope, forerunner of the modern television camera, and the electron microscope.

After graduating with a degree in electrical engineering from the St Petersburg Institute of Technology in 1912, Zworykin went to Paris and began some research into x-rays under Paul LANGEVIN at the *Collège de France,* but returned to Russia on the outbreak of war in 1914. He served in the army as a radio officer, then when the war ended in 1918 he travelled widely and eventually decided to settle in the USA (1919). After working as a bookkeeper while learning English, in 1920 he joined the Westinghouse Electric Corporation, and shortly afterwards enrolled at the University of Pittsburgh where he graduated PhD in physics in 1926. He was naturalized in 1924.

Up to this time several systems had been proposed for the transmission of images in the same manner as sounds by wire or wireless: both P. G. Nipkow (1860–1940) in Germany in 1884 and E. C. SWINTON in Britain in 1908 saw the possibilities but could not overcome the practical difficulties. Zworykin realised that the cathode-ray tube (invented by F. BRAUN in 1897) could be developed into an image scanner of much greater sensitivity if it could reproduce the persistence of vision present in the human eye.

He and his colleagues at Westinghouse succeeded in doing this in 1923, but it was not until after he moved to the Radio Corporation of America (RCA) as director of electronic research in 1929 that any real progress was made towards the commercial utilisation of his invention. By the mid-1930s it was clear that the future of television lay with such all-electronic systems, rather than the electro-mechanical scanner pioneered by J. L. BAIRD. Zworykin served as Vice-President and technical consultant to RCA from 1947 to 1954. His other contributions to electron optics included collaboration in the development by James Hillier (1915–) of the electron microscope, the invention during the Second World War of several optical devices to enhance night vision, and his 1957 patent of the ultraviolet colour-translating television microscope, which allowed colour pictures of living cells to be shown on the screen. In 1967 he was awarded the National Medal of Science by the US National Academy of Sciences, and in 1977 he was named to the US National Inventors Hall of Fame.

Modern Scientists and Engineers, McGraw-Hill. (Portrait.)

The Annual Obituary. 1982.

R M B

NOBEL LAUREATES IN SCIENCE 1901–1993

Year	Physics	Chemistry	Physiology or Medicine
1901	W. C. Röntgen (G)	J. H. Van't Hoff (NL)	E. A. von Behring (G)
1902	H. A. Lorentz (NL)	H. E. Fischer (G)	R. Ross (GB)
	P. Zeeman (NL)		
1903	A. H. Becquerel (F)	S. A. Arrhenius (Swe)	N. R. Finsen (D)
	P. Curie (F)		
	M. Curie (F)		
1904	J. W. S. Rayleigh (GB)	W. Ramsay (GB)	I. P. Pavlov (R)
1905	P. E. A. Lenard (G)	J. F. W. A. von Baeyer (G)	R. Koch (G)
1906	J. J. Thomson (GB)	H. Moissan (F)	C. Golgi (I)
			S. Ramón y Cajal (Sp)
1907	A. A. Michelson (US)	E. Buchner (G)	C. L. A. Laveran (F)
1908	G. Lippman (F)	E. Rutherford (GB)	P. Ehrlich (G)
			I. Metchnikov (R)
1909	G. Marconi (I)	W. Ostwald (G)	E. T. Kocher (Swi)
	C. F. Braun (G)		
1910	J. D. van der Waals (NL)	O. Wallach (G)	A. Kossel (G)
1911	W. Wien (G)	M. Curie (F)	A. Gullstrand (Swe)
1912	N. G. Dalén (Swe)	V. Grignard (F)	A. Carrel (F)
		P. Sabatier (F)	
1913	H. Kamerlingh-Onnes (NL)	A. Werner (Swi)	C. R. Richet (F)
1914	M. von Laue (G)	T. W. Richards (US)	R. Bárány (H)
1915	W. H. Bragg (GB)	R. M. Willstätter (G)	Not awarded
	W. L. Bragg (GB)		
1916	Not awarded	Not awarded	Not awarded
1917	C. G. Barkla (GB)	Not awarded	Not awarded
1918	M. K. E. L. Planck (G)	F. Haber (G)	Not awarded
1919	J. Stark (G)	Not awarded	J. Bordet (B)
1920	C. E. Guillaume (Swi)	W. H. Nernst (G)	S. A. S. Krogh (D)
1921	A. Einstein (G/Swi)	F. Soddy (GB)	Not awarded
1922	N. Bohr (D)	F. W. Aston (GB)	A. V. Hill (GB)
			O. F. Meyerhof (G)
1923	R. A. Millikan (US)	F. Pregl (Au)	F. G. Banting (Ca)
			J. J. R. Macleod (Ca)
1924	K. M. G. Siegbahn (Swe)	Not awarded	W. Einthoven (NL)
1925	J. Franck (G)	R. A. Zsigmondy (G)	Not awarded
	G. Hertz (G)		
1926	J. B. Perrin (F)	T. Svedberg (Swe)	J. A. G. Fibiger (D)
1927	A. H. Compton (US)	H. O. Wieland (G)	J. Wagner-Jauregg (Au)
	C. T. R. Wilson (GB)		
1928	O. W. Richardson (GB)	A. O. R. Windaus (G)	C. J. H. Nicolle (F)
1929	L.-V. de Broglie (F)	A. Harden (GB)	F. G. Hopkins (GB)
		H. K. A. S. von Euler-Chelpin	
		(Swe)	
1930	C. V. Raman (In)	H. Fischer (G)	K. Landsteiner (Au)
1931	Not awarded	C. Bosch (G)	O. H. Warburg (G)
		F. Bergius (G)	
1932	W. Heisenberg (G)	I. Langmuir (US)	C. S. Sherrington (GB)
			E. D. Adrian (GB)
1933	E. Schrödinger (Au)	Not awarded	T. H. Morgan (US)
	P. A. M. Dirac (GB)		
1934	Not awarded	H. C. Urey (US)	G. H. Whipple (US)
			W. P. Murphy (US)
			G. R. Minot (US)
1935	J. Chadwick (GB)	F. Joliot (F)	H. Spemann (G)
		I. Joliot-Curie (F)	
1936	V. F. Hess (Au)	P. J. W. Debye (NL)	H. H. Dale (GB)
	C. D. Anderson (US)		O. Loewi (Au)
1937	C. J. Davisson (US)	W. N. Haworth (GB)	A. Szent-Györgyi (H)
	G. P. Thomson (GB)	P. Karrer (Swi)	
1938	E. Fermi (I)	R. Kuhn (G)(	C. J. F. Heymans (B)
1939	E. O. Lawrence (US)	A. F. J. Butenandt (G)	G. Domagk (G)
		L. Ruzicka (Swi)	
1940	Not awarded	Not awarded	Not awarded
1941	Not awarded	Not awarded	Not awarded
1942	Not awarded	Not awarded	Not awarded
1943	O. Stern (US)	G. de Hevesy (H)	E. A. Doisy (US)
			H. C. P. Dam (D)

Year	Physics	Chemistry	Physiology or Medicine
1944	I. I. Rabi (US)	O. Hahn (G)	J. Erlanger (US)
			H. S. Gasser (US)
1945	W. Pauli (Au)	A. I. Virtanen (Fi)	A. Fleming (GB)
			E. B. Chain (GB)
			H. W. Florey (GB)
1946	P. W. Bridgman (US)	J. B. Sumner (US)	H. J. Muller (US)
		J. H. Northrop (US)	
		W. M. Stanley (US)	
1947	E. V. Appleton (GB)	R. Robinson (GB)	C. F. Cori (US)
			G. T. Cori (US)
			B. A. Houssay (Ar)
1948	P. M. S. Blackett (GB)	A. W. K. Tiselius (Swe)	P. H. Müller (Swi)
1949	H. Yukawa (J)	W. F. Giauque (US)	E. Moniz (Por)
			W. R. Hess (Swi)
1950	C. F. Powell (GB)	O. P. H. Diels (FRG)	P. S. Hench (US)
		K. Alder (FRG)	E. C. Kendall (US)
			T. Reichstein (Swi)
1951	J. D. Cockcroft (GB)	E. M. McMillan (US)	M. Theiler (SA)
	E. T. S. Walton (Ir)	G. T. Seaborg (US)	
1952	F. Bloch (US)	A. J. P. Martin (GB)	S. A. Waksman (US)
	E. M. Purcell (US)	R. L. M. Synge (GB)	
1953	F. Zernike (NL)	H. Staudinger (FRG)	H. A. Krebs (GB)
			F. A. Lipmann (US)
1954	M. Born (GB)	L. C. Pauling (US)	J. F. Enders (US)
	W. Bothe (FRG)		T. H. Weller (US)
			F. C. Robbins (US)
1955	W. E. Lamb (US)	V. du Vigneaud (US)	A. H. T. Theorell (Swe)
	P. Kusch (US)		
1956	W. Shockley (US)	C. N. Hinshelwood (GB)	A. F. Cournand (US)
	J. Bardeen (US)	N. N. Semenov (USSR)	W. Forssmann (FRG)
	W. H. Brattain (US)		D. W. Richards Jr. (US)
1957	C. N. Yang (China)	A. R. Todd (GB)	D. Bovet (I)
	T.-D. Lee (China)		
1958	P. A. Čerenkov (USSR)	F. Sanger (GB)	G. W. Beadle (US)
	I. M. Frank (USSR)		E. L. Tatum (US)
	I. J. Tamm (USSR)		J. Lederberg (US)
1959	E. G. Segrè (US)	J. Heyrovsky (Cz)	S. Ochoa (US)
	O. Chamberlain (US)		A. Kornberg (US)
1960	D. A. Glaser (US)	W. F. Libby (US)	F. M. Burnet (Austr)
			P. B. Medawar (GB)
1961	R. Hofstadter (US)	M. Calvin (US)	G. von Békésy (US)
	R. L. Mössbauer (FRG)		
1962	L. D. Landau (USSR)	M. F. Perutz (GB)	F. H. C. Crick (GB)
		J. C. Kendrew (GB)	J. D. Watson (US)
			M. H. F. Wilkins (GB)
1963	E. P. Wigner (US)	K. Ziegler (FRG)	J. C. Eccles (Austr)
	M. Goeppert-Mayer (US)	G. Natta (I)	A. L. Hodgkin (GB)
	J. H. D. Jensen (FRG)		A. F. Huxley (GB)
1964	Ch. H. Townes (US)	D. Crowfoot Hodgkin (GB)	K. Bloch (US)
	N. G. Basov (USSR)		F. Lynen (FRG)
	A. M. Prochorov (USSR)		
1965	S.-I. Tomonaga (J)	R. B. Woodward (US)	F. Jacob (F)
	J. Schwinger (US)		A. Lwoff (F)
	R. P. Feynman (US)		J. Monod (F)
1966	A. Kastler (F)	R. S. Mulliken (US)	P. Rous (US)
			C. B. Huggins (US)
1967	H. A. Bethe (US)	M. Eigen (FRG)	R. Granit (Swe)
		R. G. W. Norrish (GB)	H. K. Hartline (US)
		G. Porter (GB)	G. Wald (US)
1968	L. W. Alvarez (US)	L. Onsager (US)	R. W. Holley (US)
			H. G. Khorana (US)
			M. W. Nirenberg (US)
1969	M. Gell-Mann (US)	D. H. R. Barton (GB)	M. Delbrück (US)
		O. Hassel (N)	A. D. Hershey (US)
			S. E. Luria (US)
1970	H. Alfvén (Swe)	L. Leloir (Ar)	B. Katz (GB)
	L. Néel (F)		U. von Euler (Swe)
			J. Axelrod (US)
1971	D. Gabor (GB)	G. Herzberg (Ca)	E. W. Sutherland (US)
1972	J. Bardeen (US)	Ch. B. Anfinsen (US)	G. M. Edelman (US)
	L. N. Cooper (US)	S. Moore (US)	R. R. Porter (GB)
	J. R. Schrieffer (US)	W. H. Stein (US)	

Year	Physics	Chemistry	Physiology or Medicine
1973	L. Esaki (J) I. Giaever (US) B. D. Josephson (GB)	E. O. Fischer (FRG) G. Wilkinson (GB)	K. von Frisch (FRG) K. Lorenz (Au) N. Tinbergen (GB)
1974	M. Ryle (GB) A. Hewish (GB)	P. J. Flory (US)	A. Claude (B) C. de Duve (B) G. E. Palade (US)
1975	A. Bohr (D) B. Mottelson (D) J. Rainwater (US)	J. W. Cornforth (GB) V. Prelog (Swi)	D. Baltimore (US) R. Dulbecco (US) H. M. Temin (US)
1976	B. Richter (US) S. C. C. Ting (US)	W. N. Lipscomb (US)	B. S. Blumberg (US) D. C. Gajdusek (US)
1977	P. W. Anderson (US) N. F. Mott (GB) J. H. Van Vleck (US)	I. Prigogine (B)	R. Guillemin (US) A. Schally (US) R. Ralow (US)
1978	P. L. Kapitza (USSR) A. A. Penzias (US) R. W. Wilson (US)	P. Mitchell (GB)	W. Arber (Swi) D. Nathans (US) H. O. Smith (US)
1979	S. L. Glashow (US) A. Salam (Pak) S. Weinberg (US)	H. C. Brown (US) G. Wittig (FRG)	A. M. Cormack (US) G. N. Hounsfield (GB)
1980	J. W. Cronin (US) V. L. Fitch (US)	P. Berg (US) W. Gilbert (US) F. Sanger (GB)	B. Benacerraf (US) J. Dausset (F) G. D. Snell (US)
1981	N. Bloembergen (US) A. L. Schawlow (US) K. M. Siegbahn (Swe)	K. Fukui (J) R. Hoffmann (US)	D. H. Hubel (US) R. W. Sperry (US) T. N. Wiesel (Swe)
1982	K. G. Wilson (US)	A. Klug (GB)	S. Bergström (Swe) B. I. Samuelsson (Swe) J. R. Vane (GB)
1983	S. Chandrasekhar (US) W. A. Fowler (US)	H. Taube (US)	B. McClintock (US)
1984	C. Rubbia (I) S. van der Meer (NL)	B. Merrifield (US)	N. K. Jerne (D) G. J. F. Köhler (FRG) C. Milstein (GB/Ar)
1985	K. von Klitzing (FRG)	H. A. Hauptman (US) J. Karle (US)	M. S. Brown (US) J. L. Goldstein (US)
1986	E. Ruska (FRG) G. Binnig (FRG) H. Rohrer (Swi)	D. R. Herschbach (US) Y. T. Lee (US) J. C. Polanyi (Ca)	S. Cohen (US) R. Levi-Montalcini (I/US)
1987	J. G. Bednorz (FRG) K. A. Müller (Swi)	D. J. Cram (US) J.-M. Lehn (F) C. J. Pedersen (US)	S. Tonegawa (J)
1988	L. M. Lederman (US) M. Schwartz (US) J. Steinberger (US)	J. Deisenhofer (FRG) R. Huber (FRG) H. Michel (FRG)	J. W. Black (GB) G. B. Elion (US) G. H. Hitchings (US)
1989	N. F. Ramsey (US) H. G. Dehmelt (US/Ca) W. Paul (FRG)	S. Altman (US) T. R. Cech (US)	J. M. Bishop (US) H. E. Varmus (US)
1990	J. I. Friedman (US) H. W. Kendall (US) R. E. Taylor (Ca)	E. J. Corey (US)	J. E. Murray (US) E. D. Thomas (US)
1991	P.-G. de Gennes (F)	R. R. Ernst (Swi)	E. Neher (FRG) B. Sakmann (FRG)
1992	G. Charpak (F)	R. A. Marcus (US)	E. H. Fischer (US) E. G. Krets (US)
1993	R. Hulse (US) J. Taylor (US)	M. Smith (Can) K. Mullis (US)	R. Roberts (GB) P. Sharp (US)

ANNIVERSARIES

Dates of births and deaths. A dagger indicates a name listed only in the Appendix.

BC

c. 624	Thales of Miletus b.
c. 610	Anaximander of Miletus b.
c. 572	Pythagoras of Samos b.
c. 548	Thales of Miletus d.
c. 545	Anaximander of Miletus d.
c. 515	Parmenides† b.
c. 500	Anaxagoras of Clazomenae b.
5th Cent.	Socrates†
5th Cent.	Euclid of Megara†
c. 497	Pythagoras of Samos d.
c. 494	Empedocles b.
480	Leucippus† fl.
c. 450	Parmenides† d.
c. 434	Empedocles d.
c. 428	Anaxagoras of Clazomenae d.
c. 427	Plato† b.
c. 408	Eudoxus of Cnidus b.
384	Aristotle b.
c. 370	Theophrastus b.
c. 361	Democritus of Abdera† d.
c. 355	Eudoxus of Cnidus d.
342/1	Epicurus b.
350–300	Aristarchus of Samos
322	Aristotle d.
365–350	Menaechmus† fl.
c. 347	Plato d.
c. 300	Erasistratus b.
250–300	Apollonius of Perga fl.
c. 287	Archimedes b.
c. 285	Theophrastus d.
c. 273	Eratosthenes of Cyrene b.
271/70	Epicurus d.
c. 212	Archimedes d.
1st/3rd Cent.	Ctesibius of Alexandria fl.
c. 192	Eratosthenes of Cyrene
150	Philo of Byzantium† fl.
c. 124	Asclepiades† b.
c. 95	Lucretius (Titus Lucretius Carus) b.
63	Strabo† b.
55	Lucretius (Titus Lucretius Carus) d.
c. 40	Asclepiades d.
c. 25	Aulus Cornelius Celsus b.
1st Cent.	Sosigenes of Alexandria fl.
1st Cent.	Vitruvius (Vitruvius Pollio) fl.

AD

1st Cent.	Heliodorus of Narissa† fl.
23	Pliny (Gaius Plinus Secundus, Pliny the Elder) b.
21	Strabo† d.
60–77	Pedanius Dioscorides fl.
78	Heng Chang (Zhang) b.
79	Pliny (Gaius Plinus Secundus, Pliny the Elder) d.
129	Galen (Galenos) b.
139	Heng Chang (Zhang) d.
150	Marinus of Tyre† fl.
199(?)	Galen (Galenos) d.
c. 250	Ptolemy of Alexandria fl.
c. 250	Diophantus fl.
429	Zu Chongzhi b.

500		Zu Chongzhi d.
c. 704		Khalid Ibn Yazid† d.
721 or 722		Geber (Jabir Ibn Hayyan) b.
800		al-Khwarizmi (Muhammad ibn Musa) b.
c. 815		Geber (Jabir Ibn Hayyan) d.
c. 841		Rhazes (Al-Razi) b.
847		al-Khwarizmi (Muhammad ibn Musa) d.
925		Rhazes (Al-Razi) d.
c. 965		Alhazen (Abu 'Ali al-Hasan) b.
980		Avicenna b.
1037		Avicenna d.
c.1038		Alhazen (Abu 'Ali al-Hasan) d.
Early 12th Cent.		Robert of Chester
c.1168		Robert Grosseteste b.
c.1170		L. Fibonacci b.
1193 (or 1206)		Albertus Magnus b.
1206 (or 1193)		Albertus Magnus b.
c.1214		Roger Bacon b.
c.1220		Jordanus Nemorarius† fl.
c.1220		Petrus Peregrinus b.
c.1240		L. Fibonacci d.
1253	9 Oct.	Robert Grosseteste d.
1256		John Holywood (Sacrobosco)† d.
c.1265		Duns Scotus† b.
1280	15 Nov.	Albertus Magnus d.
c.1281		William of Moerbeke† d.
1288		Levi Ben Gerson† b.
c.1291/2		Richard of Wallingford b.
1292	11 June	Roger Bacon d.
Late 13th Cent.		Pappus fl.
c.1300		William of Ockham (Occam) b.
1308		Duns Scotus† d.
1318		Giovanni de'Dondi b.
1336	23 May	Richard of Wallingford d.
1344		Levi Ben Gerson† d.
1349		William of Ockham (Occam) d.
1389		Feb. Giovanni de' Dondi d.
1395–1400		Johann Gutenberg b.
Late 14th Cent.		Thomas Norton b.
c.1400		Johann Fust† b.
1401		Nicholas of Cusa† b.
1404	18 Feb.	Leone Battista Alberti b.
1423		G. von Peurbach† b.
c.1425		Peter Schoeffert† b.
c.1430		Muhammad Al-Qushchi (Al-Kashi)† d.
1430		John of Gmünden† fl.
1430		Bernard Walther† b.
1434		Michel Wohlgemuth† b.
1435		Andrea del Verrocchio† b.
1436	6 June	Regiomontanus (Johann Müller) b.
c.1440		Antonia Benivieni† b.
1450		Pendolfo Petrucci† b.
1452	15 Apr.	Leonardo da Vinci b.
c.1460		Thomas Linacre b.
1461		G. von Peurbach† d.
1464		Otto Brunfels† b.
1464		Nicholas of Cusa† d.
1466		Erasmus† b.
1466		Johann Fust† d.
1468	3 Feb.	Johann Gutenberg d.
1471	21 May	Albrecht Dürer b.

1472	25 Apr.	Leone Battista Alberti *d*.
1473	19 Feb.	Nicolaus Copernicus *b*.
1476	6 July	Regiomontanus (Johann Müller) *d*.
1477		Johan Schöner† *b*.
1478		Fabricius Capito† *b*.
1478		Jacobus Sylvius† *b*.
1478 (?1481)		Marcantonio della Torre† *b*.
1478		Sir Thomas More† *b*.
1478 (?1483)		Girolamo Fracastoro *b*.
c.1480		Thomas Norton *d*.
1480		Vanuccio Biringuccio *b*.
1482		Oecolampadius† *b*.
1486		Nicolas Kratzer *b*.
1488		Andrea del Verrocchio† *d*.
c.1490		George Ripley† *d*.
1492		Pedro Nunez† *b*.
1493	17 Dec.	Paracelsus (Theophrastus Bombastus von Hohenheim) *b*.
1494	24 Mar.	Agricola (Georg Bauer) *b*.
1497		Marquis de Marignan† *b*.
1497(?)		Jean Fernel *b*.
1498		Hieronymus Bock† *b*.
1499		Jan Stefan van Calcar† *b*.
16th Cent.		C. Rudolff† *fl*.
1500		Antonio Musa Brassavola† *b*.
1500		L. Ghini† *b*.
1501	17 Jan.	Leonhart Fuchs *b*.
c.1501		Niccolo Tartaglia (Tartalea) *b*.
1501	24 Sept.	Girolamo Cardano *b*.
1502		Antonio Benivieni† *d*.
1502		Peter Schoeffer† *d*.
1504		Bernard Walther† *d*.
1505		Johann Guinther† *b*.
1507		Johannes Oporinus† *b*.
1508		Gemma Frisius† *b*.
c.1508		William Turner *b*.
1509		Ambroise Paré *b*.
c.1510		Scipio del Ferro† *fl*.
1511		Marcantonio della Torre† *d*.
1511		Pendolfo Petrucci† *d*.
1511		G. Vasari† *b*.
1511	29 Sept.	Michael Servetus (Miguel Serveto) *b*.
1512	5 Mar.	Gerardus (Gerhard Kremer) Mercator *b*.
1513		Bartolomeo Eustachi(o) *b*.
1514	15 Feb.	Rheticus (Georg Joachim von Lauchen) *b*.
1514	31 Dec.	Andreas Vesalius *b*.
1515		Valerius Cordus† *b*.
c.1515		Matteo Realdo Colombo *b*.
1516	26 Mar.	Conrad Gesner *b*.
1517		R. Dodoens† *b*.
1517		Pierre Belon *b*.
1519		Michel Wohlgemuth† *d*.
1519	2 May	Leonardo da Vinci *d*.
1519	6 June	Andrea Cesalpino *b*.
1520(?)		Leonard Digges *b*.
1522		Luigi Ferrari† *b*.
1522	11 Sept.	Ulisse Aldrovandi *b*.
1523		Gabrielle Falloppio *b*.
1524	20 Oct.	Thomas Linacre *d*.
1527		John Dee† *b*.
1528		Daniel Barbaro† *b*.
1528	6 Apr.	Albrecht Dürer *d*.
1531		Apian† *b*.
1531		Oecolampadius† *d*.
c.1531		Agostino Ramelli *b*.
c.1533		Hieronymus Fabricius *b*.
1534		Otto Brunfels† *d*.
1535		Sir Thomas More† *d*.
1536		Erasmus† *d*.
1537		Christopher Clavius† *b*.
1538/9		Vanuccio Biringuccio *d*.
1540		François Viète (or Vieta) *b*.
1540/50		Andréas Libavius *b*.
1541		Fabricius Capito† *d*.
1541	24 Sept.	Paracelsus (Theophrastus Bombastus von Hohenheim) *d*.
1543		Costanzo Varolio *b*.
1543	24 May	Nicolaus Copernicus *d*.
1544		Valerius Cordus† *d*.
1544	24 May	William Gilbert *b*.
1545		John Gerard *b*.
1546		Jan Stefan van Calcar† *d*.
1546(?)		Thomas Digges *b*.
1546		Rudolph Snell† *b*.
1546	14 Dec.	Tycho (or Tyge) Brahe *b*.
1547		Johan Schöner† *d*.
c.1548		Simon Stevinus *b*.
1550		Michael Maestlin† *b*.
1550		John Napier *b*.
1550		Nicholas Kratzer *d*.
1553		Prospero Alpini *b*.
1553	6 Aug.	Girolamo Fracastoro *d*.
1553	27 Oct.	Michael Servetus (Miguel Serveto) *d*.
1554		Hieronymus Bock† *d*.
1555		Antonio Musa Brassaola† *d*.
1555		Gemma Frisius† *d*.
1555		Marquis de Marignan† *d*.
1555		Jacobus Sylvius† *d*.
1555	21 Nov.	Agricola (Georg Bauer) *d*.
1556		L. Ghini† *d*.
1557	13 Dec.	Niccolo (Tartalea) Tartaglia *d*.
1558		Hendrik Goltzius† *b*.
c.1558		Edward Wright† *b*.
1558	26 Apr.	Jean Fernel *d*.
1559		Matteo Realdo Colombo *d*.
1559		Leonard Digges *d*.
1560		Thomas Hariot (or Harriot) *b*.
1561		Casserius† *b*.
1561		Henry Briggs *b*.
1561	22 Jan.	Francis Bacon, Baron Verulam, Viscount St Albans *b*.
1561	29 Mar.	Sanctorius (Santorio Santorio) *b*.
1562		Longomontanus† *b*.
1562	9 Oct.	Gabrielle Falloppio *d*.
1564	18 Feb.	Galileo Galilei *b*.
1564	(?)Apr.	Andreas Vesalius *d*.
1564	Apr.	Pierre Belon *d*.
1565		Luigi Ferrari† *d*.
1565	13 Dec.	Conrad Gesner *d*.
1566	10 May	Leonhart Fuchs *d*.
1567		N. Bergier† *b*.
1568		Johannes Oporinus† *d*.
1568	7 July	William Turner *d*.
1569		Daniel Barbaro† *d*.
1571	27 Dec.	Johannes Kepler *b*.
1572		Cornelis Drebbel *b*.
1574		Johann Guinther† *d*.
1574		G. Vasari† *d*.
1574		Aug. Bartolomeo Eustachi(o) *d*.
1575		Costanzo Varolio *d*.
1576	21 Sept.	Girolamo Cardano *d*.
1576	4 Dec.	Rheticus (Georg Joachim von Lauchen) *d*.
1577		Benedetto Castelli† *b*.
1577		Paul Guldin† *b*.
1577		Pedro Nunez† *d*.
1577	8 Feb.	Robert Burton *b*.
1578	1 Apr.	William Harvey *b*.
1579	Jan.	Joannes Baptista van Helmont *b*.
1580		Pierre Vernier *b*.
1581		C. G. Bachet† *b*.
c.1581		Gaspare Aselli(o) *b*.
1583		William Bourne† *d*.
c.1584		Humphrey Bradley *b*.
1585		R. Dodoens† *d*.
1585		Claude C. Mydorget *b*.

1588		Isaac Beeckman† b.
1588		Thomas Hobbes† b.
1588		Marin Mersenne† b.
1589		Apian† d.
1590	22 Dec.	Ambroise Paré d.
1591		Sir Richard Weston b.
1591		Willebrord Snell b.
1592		Guillaume Schickart† b.
1592	22 Jan.	Pierre Gassendi b.
1593		Lazarus Ercker d.
1593	2 Mar.	Gérard Desargues b.
1594	2 Dec.	Gerardus (Gerhard Kremer) Mercator d.
1595		Thomas Digges d.
c.1595		Sir Cornelius Vermuyden b.
1596	31 Mar.	René Descartes b.
1597		Lucius Valentine Otho† d.
1597		Francis Glisson b.
1598		Bonaventure Cavalieri b.
1599		Dud Dudley† b.
1599		Christopher Rothman† d.
1600(?)		Arnold Boot (or Boate)† b.
c.1600		Agostino Ramelli d.
1601		F. de Beaune† b.
1601	17 Aug.	Pierre de Fermat b.
1601	24 Oct.	Tycho (or Tyge) Brahe d.
c.1602		Frénicle de Bessy† b.
1602		G. P. de Roberval† b.
1602	20 Nov.	Otto von Guericke b.
1603		Bartolomeo Massari† b.
1603	23 Feb.	Andrea Cesalpino d.
1603	10 Dec.	William Gilbert d.
1603	13 Dec.	François Viète (or Vieta) d.
1604		Johann Rudolph Glauber b.
1605	10 May	Ulisse Aldrovandi d.
1608		John Dee† d.
1608		Kaspar Schott† b.
1608	28 Jan.	Giovanni Alfonso Borelli b.
1608	15 Oct.	Evangelista Torricelli b.
1610		C. V. Schneider† b.
1611		Hevelius† b.
1612		Christopher Clavius† d.
c.1612		John Gerard d.
1613		Claude Perrault b.
1613		Sir John Pettus† b.
1613		Rudolph Snell† d.
1614		Franciscus Mercurius† b.
1614		Franciscus (Franz de le Boë) Sylvius b.
1614		John Wilkins b.
1614	31 Aug.	Thomas Wharton b.
c.1615		Henry Oldenburg† b.
1615		F. van Schooten† b.
1615		S. Sorbière† b.
1615		Edward Wright† d.
1616		Thomas Bartholin† b.
1616		Casserius† d.
1616		William Holder† b.
1616	25 July	Andreas Libavius d.
1616	22 Oct.	John Wallis b.
1617		Prospero Alpini d.
1617		Elias Ashmole† b.
1617		Hendrik Goltzius† d.
1617	4 Apr.	John Napier d.
1618	2 Apr.	Francesco Maria Grimaldi b.
1619		Michelangelo Ricci† b.
1619		Daniel Whistler† b.
1619	21 May	Hieronymus Fabricius d.
1620		Theophilus Bonet† b.
c.1620		Simon Stevinus d.
c.1620		William Brouncker (2nd Viscount Brouncker) b.
1620		Edmé Marriotte b.
1620	21 July	Jean Picard b.

1621	27 Jan.	Thomas Willis b.
1621	25 July	Thomas Hariot (or Harriot) d.
1622		Jean Pecquet b.
1623		N. Bergier† d.
1623		Sir William Petty† b.
1623	19 June	Blaise Pascal b.
1624	(baptized 10 Sept.)	Thomas Sydenham b.
1625		John Collins† b.
1625(?)		Jean Denys† b.
c.1625		Humphrey Bradley d.
1625	8 June	Giovanni Domenico Cassini b.
1625	13 Aug.	Rasmus (Erasmus) Bartholin b.
1626		John Aubrey† b.
1626		Pietro Mengoli b.
1626	18 Feb.	Francesco Redi b.
1626	9 Apr.	Francis Bacon d.
1626	24 Apr.	Gaspare Aselli(o) d.
1626	30 Oct.	Willebrord Snell d.
1627		William Ball† b.
1627	25 Jan.	Robert Boyle b.
1628		J Metius† d.
1628	(baptized 10 Mar.)	Marcello Malpighi b.
1628	29 Nov.	John Ray b.
1629		Richard Towneley† b.
1629	14 Apr.	Christiaan Huygens b.
1630		Olaus (Olaf) Rudbeck b.
1630	Oct.	Isaac Barrow b.
1630	15 Nov.	Johannes Kepler d.
1631		Michael Maestlin† d.
1631		Edward Cocker b.
1631		Richard Lower b.
1631	26 Jan.	Henry Briggs d.
1632	29 Aug.	John Locke b.
1632	20 Oct.	Sir Christopher Wren b.
1632	24 Oct.	Antony van Leeuwenhoek b.
1633		A. Magliabechi† b.
1633	15 May	Sebastien Le Prestre de Vauban b.
1633	c.7 Nov.	Cornelis Drebbel d.
1634		P. van Schooten† b.
1635		Guillaume Schickart† d.
1635		Francis Willughby† b.
1635	6 May	Johann Joachim Becher b.
1635	18 July	Robert Hooke b.
1636	22 Feb.	Sanctorius (Santorio Santorio) d.
1637		Isaac Beeckman† d.
1637	12 Feb.	Jan Swammerdam b.
1637	14 Sept.	Pierre Vernier d.
1638		C. G. Bachet† d.
1638		N. Malebranche† b.
1638		F. Ruysch† b.
1638	1 Jan.	Nicolaus Steno b.
1638	Nov.	James Gregory b.
1639		Edward Barlow† b.
c.1639		Thomas Tompion b.
1640		P. de Lahire† b.
1640		Robert Plott† b.
1640	25 Jan.	Robert Burton d.
1641		U. Hjarne† b.
1641		R. de Vieussens† b.
1641		Nehemiah Grew b.
1641	30 July	Regnier de Graaf b.
1641	(baptized 21 Dec.)	John Mayow b.
1642	8 Jan.	Galileo Galilei d.
1642	25 Dec.	Sir Isaac Newton b.
1643		Lorenzo Bellini† b.
1643		Paul Guldin† d.
1644		Benedetto Castelli† d.
1644	25 Sept.	Ole Christensen Rømer b.
1644	30 Dec.	Joannes Baptista van Helmont d.
1645	17 Nov.	Nicolas Lémery b.
1646	1 July	Gottfried Wilhelm Leibniz b.

1646	19 Aug.	John Flamsteed b.
1647		Longomontanus† d.
1647		Claude C. Mydorge† d.
1647	22 Aug.	Denis Papin b.
1647	25 Oct.	Evangelista Torricelli d.
1647	1 Dec.	Bonaventure Cavalieri d.
1648		Marin Mersenne† d.
1650		John Radcliffe† b.
c.1650		Thomas Savery b.
1650	11 Feb.	René Descartes d.
1651		Engelbert Kaempfer† b.
1652		F. de Beaune† d.
1652	(buried 5 May)	Sir Richard Weston d.
1653(?)		Arnold Boot (or Boate)† d.
1653		Bernard Weiss† b.
1654	26 Oct.	Giovanni Maria Lanfisi b.
1654	27 Dec.	Jacques Bernoulli b.
1655		Bartolomeo Massari† d.
1655	24 Oct.	Pierre Gassendi d.
1656		J. P. de Tournefort† b.
1656	8 Nov.	Edmond Halley b.
1657	11 Feb.	Bernard le Bovier de Fontenelle b.
1657	3 June	William Harvey d.
1660		H. Gautier† b.
1660		Edward Lhuyd b.
1660		F. van Schooten† d.
1660	19 Feb.	Friedrich Hoffmann b.
1660	21 Oct.	Georg Ernst Stahl b.
1661		G. F. A. de l'Hopital† b.
1661	3 May	Antonio Vallisneri b.
1661	24 June	David Gregory b.
1661	18 Dec.	Christopher Polhem (Polhammer) b.
1662		Gérard Desargues d.
1662	19 Aug.	Blaise Pascal d.
1663		G. Amontons† d.
1663	(baptized 24 Feb.)	Thomas Newcomen b.
1663	28 Dec.	Francesco Maria Grimaldi d.
1665	12 Jan.	Pierre de Fermat d.
1665	17 Feb.	Rudolph Jacob Camerarius b.
1666		Kaspar Schott† d.
1666		A. M. Valsalva† b.
1666		William Wotton† b.
1667		John Harris b.
1670		John Monro† b.
1667	26 May	Abraham Demoivre b.
1667	7 Aug.	Jean Bernoulli b.
1668		J. J. Rau† b.
1668	31 Dec.	Herman Boerhaave b.
1669		James Pound† b.
1670		S. Sorbière† d.
c.1670		Stephen Gray b.
1670		Hennig Brand fl.
1670		Mar. Johann Rudolph Glauber d.
1672		Francis Willughby† d.
1672	14 Nov.	Franciscus (Franz de le Boë) Sylvius d.
1672		N – – Cassegrain fl.
1672	16 Nov.	John Wilkins d.
1673		George Graham† b.
1673	17 Aug.	Regnier de Graaf d.
1673	15 Nov.	Thomas Wharton d.
1674		Charles Townshend (second Viscount Townshend) b.
1674	Feb.	Jean Pecquet d.
1674	(baptized 30 Mar.)	Jethro Tull b.
1674	25 July	Jacob Leupold b.
1675		Samuel Clarke† b.
1675		Frénicle de Bessy† d.
1675		G. P. de Roberval† d.
1675		Edward Cocker d.
1675	Oct.	James Gregory d.

1675	11 Nov.	Thomas Willis d.
1676		J. F. Riccati† b.
1677		J. Cassini† b.
1677		Louis Lémery† b.
1677		Henry Oldenburg† d.
1677	4 May	Isaac Barrow d.
1677	17 Sept.	Stephen Hales b.
1677	(probably 11 Oct.)	Sir Cornelius Vermuyden d.
1677	16 Oct.	Francis Glisson d.
1678		Abraham Darby b.
1679		Thomas Hobbes† d.
1679		Johann Junckert† b.
1679		G. Rothe† b.
1679		P. van Schooten† d.
1679		Christian Wolff† b.
1679	(buried 18 Oct.)	John Mayow d.
1679	31 Dec.	Giovanni Alfonso Borelli d.
1680		Thomas Bartholin† d.
1680		C. V. Schneider† d.
1680	17 Feb.	Jan Swammerdam d.
1681	Oct.	Johann Joachim Becher d.
1682		Roger Cotes† b.
1682	20 Feb.	Giovanni Battista Morgagni b.
1682	16 Apr.	John Hadley b.
1682	12 July	Jean Picard d.
1683		John Collins† d.
1683		Caspar Neumann† b.
1683	28 Feb.	Réné Antoine Ferchault de Réaumur b.
1684		Dud Dudley† d.
1684		Daniel Whistler† d.
1684	5 Apr.	William Brouncker (2nd Viscount Brouncker) d.
1684	12 May	Edmé Marriotte d.
1685		George Berkeley† b.
1685		Joshua Ward b.
1685	18 Aug.	Brook Taylor b.
1686		Nicolaus Steno d.
1686–1707		John Hawkins† fl.
1686	11 May	Otto von Guericke d.
1686	14 May	Gabriel Daniel Fahrenheit b.
1687		Francis Hauksbee the Younger† b.
1687		Hevelius† d.
1687		Sir William Petty† d.
1688		William Cheselden† b.
1688		J. C. Goetz† b.
1688		W. J. S. van S'Gravesande† b.
1688	29 Jan.	Emanuel Swedenborg b.
1688	6 Oct.	Claude Perrault d.
1689		Theophilus Bonet† d.
1689		Samuel Molyneux† b.
1689	(?)29 Dec.	Thomas Sydenham d.
1690		William Ball† d.
1690		Sir John Pettus† d.
1690		Jan Wandelaar† b.
1691	17 Jan.	Richard Lower d.
1691	30 Dec.	Robert Boyle d.
1692		Elias Ashmole† d.
1692		P. van Musschenbroek† b.
1692		Michelangelo Ricci† d.
1692		Antoine Thiout† d.
1693		John Harrison d.
1693		Bernard Forest de Belidor b.
1693	Mar.	James Bradley b.
1694	29 Nov.	Marcello Malpighi d.
1695		Nicolaus Bernoulli† b.
1695	8 June	Christiaan Huygens d.
1696		L. C. Bourdelin† b.
1696		Robert Plott d.
1697		John Aubrey† d.
1697	24 Feb.	Bernhard Siegfried Albinus b.
1697/8	1 Mar.	Francesco Redi d.

1697	8 Sept.	Alexander Monro (*primus*) *b.*
1698		Pierre Bouquer† *b.*
1698		William Holder† *d.*
1698		Samuel Klingenstierna *b.*
1698	Feb.	Colin Maclaurin *b.*
1698	17 July	Pierre Louis Moreau de Maupertuis *b.*
1698	14 Sept.	Charles François de Cisternay Dufay *b.*
1698	4 Nov.	Rasmus (Erasmus) Bartholin *d.*
1699		C. E. L. Camus† *b.*
c.1699		Bernard de Jussieu† *b.*
1699		Franciscus Mercurius† *d.*
1699		John Muller† *b.*
c.1699		Otto Tachenius† *d.*
1700		Henri Louis Duhamel du Monceau *b.*
1700	9 Feb.	Daniel Bernoulli *b.*
1700	19 Nov.	Abbé Jean Antoine Nollet *b.*
1701		Henry Hindley† *b.*
1701	28 Jan.	Charles-Marie de La Condamine *b.*
1701	27 Nov.	Anders Celsius *b.*
1702	17 Sept.	Olaus (Olaf) Rudbeck *d.*
1703		Chester Moor Hall† *b.*
1703	3 Mar.	Robert Hooke *d.*
1703	16 Sept.	Guillaume François Rouelle *b.*
1703	28 Oct.	John Wallis *d.*
1704		Lorenzo Bellini† *d.*
1704		G. F. A. de l'Hopital† *d.*
1704		Jean Denys† *d.*
1704		Thomas Godfrey† *d.*
1704		L. Godin† *b.*
1704		Benjamin Huntsman *b.*
1704	28 Oct.	John Locke *d.*
1705		Petrus Artedi† *b.*
1705		G. Amontons† *d.*
1705		Robert James† *b.*
1705	17 Jan.	John Ray *d.*
1705	10 Aug.	Jacques Bernoulli *d.*
1706	17 Jan.	Benjamin Franklin *b.*
1706	10 June	John Dollond *b.*
1686–1707		John Hawkins *fl.*
1707		Richard Towneley† *d.*
1707	30 Mar.	Sebastien Le Prestre de Vauban *d.*
1707	Apr.	Leonhard Euler *b.*
1707	23 May	Carl Linnaeus *b.*
1707	7 Sept.	George Louis Leclerc, Comte de Buffon *b.*
1708		J. P. de Tournefort† *d.*
1708	8 Oct.	Jean-Rodolphe Perronet *b.*
1708	10 Oct.	David Gregory *d.*
1708	16 Oct.	Albrecht von Haller *b.*
1709	24 Feb.	Jacques de Vaucanson *b.*
1709	3 Mar.	Andreas Sigismund Marggraf *b.*
1709	30 June	Edward Lhuyd *d.*
1710		William Cullen† *b.*
1710		G. Rothe† *d.*
1710		James Short† *b.*
1710	19 Sept.	Ole Christensen Rømer *d.*
1711		R. T. Boscovich† *b.*
1711		Laura Bassi† *b.*
1711		David Hume† *b.*
1711		A. G. Pingré† *b.*
1711		G. W. Richmann† *b.*
1711	8 Nov.	Mikhail Vasilevich Lomonosov *b.*
1712		Denis Papin *d.*
1712	25 Mar.	Nehemiah Grew *d.*
1712	14 Sept.	Giovanni Domenico Cassini *d.*
1713		A. C. Clairaut† *b.*
1713		H. Gautier† *d.*
1713		John Turbeville Needham† *b.*
1713		Humphry Sibthorp† *b.*
c.1713		Francis Hauksbee *d.*
1713	15 May	Nicolas Louis de Lacaille *b.*
1713	22 July	Jacques-Germain Soufflot *b.*
1713	5 Oct.	Denis Diderot *b.*
1713	20 Nov.	Thomas Tompion *d.*
1714		A. Magliabechi† *d.*
1714		Percivall Pott† *b.*
1714		John Radcliffe† *d.*
1714	6 Sept.	Robert Whytt *b.*
1715		J. E. Guettard† *b.*
1715		Engelbert Kaempfert† *d.*
1715		P. C. Lemonnier† *b.*
1715		N. Malebranche† *d.*
1715		Hugh Smithson Percy, Duke of Northumberland† *b.*
1715		R. de Vieussens† *d.*
1715	3 Apr.	Sir William Watson *b.*
1715	May	Thomas Savery *d.*
1715	19 June	Nicolas Lémery *d.*
1716		Roger Cotes† *d.*
1716		G. B. Beccaria† *b.*
1716		James Brindley *b.*
1716		L. J. M. Daubenton† *b.*
1716		James Lind *b.*
1716		Pierre Trésaguet *b.*
1716	14 Nov.	Gottfried Wilhelm Leibniz *d.*
1717		Samuel Garbett† *b.*
1717		Jean le Rond D'Alembert *b.*
1717	8 Mar.	Abraham Darby *d.*
1717	Sept.	Thomas Mudge *b.*
1718		John Canton† *b.*
1718		William Hunter† *b.*
1718		P. de Lahire† *d.*
1718		John Roebuck *b.*
1718	Feb.	Hilaire Martin Rouelle *b.*
1718	9 Oct.	Pierre Joseph Macquer *b.*
1719		Edward Barlow† *d.*
1719		Jacob Gadolin† *b.*
1719		J. J. Rau† *d.*
1719		Lord Rodney† *b.*
1719	7 Sept.	John Harris *d.*
1719	31 Dec.	John Flamsteed *d.*
c.1720		John Campbell† *b.*
1720	21 Jan.	Giovanni Maria Lancisi *d.*
1720	30 Jan.	Charles de Geer *b.*
1720	13 Mar.	Charles Bonnet *b.*
1720–1		James Hargreaves *b.*
1721		Larcum Kendall† *b.*
1721		John Mudge† *b.*
1721		Charles Valency† *b.*
1721		Bernard Weiss† *d.*
1721	11 Sept.	Rudolph Jacob Camerarius *d.*
1722		R. Brocklesby† *b.*
1722		L. Auenbrugger† *b.*
1722	23 Dec.	Axel Fredrik Cronstedt *b.*
1723		Tobias Mayer† *b.*
1723		A. M. Valsalva† *d.*
1723	25 Feb.	Sir Christopher Wren *d*
1723	26 Aug.	Antony van Leeuwenhoek *d.*
1724		F. U. T. Aepinus† *b.*
1724		U. Hjarne† *d.*
1724		John Michell† *b.*
1724		James Pound† *d.*
1724	8 June	John Smeaton *b.*
1725		Robert Bakewell *b.*
1725		J. P. J. D'Arcet† *b.*
1725		John Hope† *b.*
1725	25 Sept.	Nicholas-Joseph Cugnot *b.*
1726		Nicolaus Bernoulli† *d.*
1726		Thomas Pennant† *b.*
1726		Jedediah Strutt† *b.*
1726	3 June	James Hutton *b.*
1727		Daines Barrington† *b.*
1727		P. A. Gadd† *b.*
1727		A. R. Turgot† *b.*
1727		J. A. Unzer† *b.*
1727		William Wotton† *d.*

1727	12 Jan.	Jacob Leupold *d.*
1727	19 Mar.	Ferdinand Berthoud *b.*
1727	20 Mar.	Sir Isaac Newton *d.*
1728		A. Baumé† *b.*
1728		Samuel Molyneux† *d.*
1728		John Wilkinson *b.*
1728	13 Feb.	John Hunter *b.*
1728	16 Apr.	Joseph Black *b.*
1728	3 Sept.	Matthew Boulton *b.*
1728	27 Oct.	James Cook *b.*
1729		Samuel Clarke† *d.*
1729		Johann Daniell Titius† *b.*
1729	12 Jan.	Lazzaro Spallanzani *b.*
1729	5 Aug.	Thomas Newcomen *d.*
*c.*1730		Charles Mason† *b.*
1730	18 Jan.	Antonio Vallisneri *d.*
1730	July	Josiah Wedgwood *b.*
1730	8 Dec.	Jan Ingenhousz *b.*
1731		L. C. Cadet† *b.*
1731		Thomas Bentley† *b.*
1731		F. Ruysch† *d.*
1731	10 Oct.	Henry Cavendish *b.*
1731	12 Dec.	Erasmus Darwin *b.*
1731	29 Dec.	Brook Taylor *d.*
1732		J. Gaertner† *b.*
1732		J. J. Le F. de Lalande† *b.*
1732	6 Sept.	Johan Carl Wilcke *b.*
1732	6 Oct.	Nevil Maskelyne *b.*
1732	23 Dec.	Sir Richard Arkwright *b.*
1733		J. C. Goetz† *d.*
1733–64		John Kay† *fl.*
1733		Kaspar Friedrich Wolff *b.*
1733	10 Mar.	Alexander Monro (*secundus*) *b.*
1733	13 Mar.	Joseph Priestley *b.*
1733	4 May	Jean Charles (de) Borda *b.*
1733	1 Aug.	Richard Kirwan *b.*
1734		Thomas Henry† *b.*
1734		Robert Mylne† *b.*
1734		William Small† *b.*
*c.*1734		George Walker† *b.*
1734	14 May	Georg Ernst Stahl *d.*
1735		John Brown† *b.*
1735		Petrus Artedi† *d.*
1735	20 Mar.	Torbern Olaf Bergman *b.*
1735	29 Sept.	James Keir *b.*
1735	(probably 6 Oct.)	Jesse Ramsden *b.*
1736		John Arnold† *b.*
1736		Baron Clas Alströmer† *b.*
1736		James Lind† *b.*
1736		Daniel Solander† *b.*
1736	19 Jan.	James Watt *b.*
1736	25 Jan.	Joseph Louis Lagrange *b.*
1736	25 Feb.	Stephen Gray *d.*
1736	14 June	Charles Augustin de Coulomb *b.*
1736	16 Sept.	Gabriel Daniel Fahrenheit *d.*
1737		L. B. Guyton de Morveau† *b.*
1737		Caspar Neumann† *d.*
1737	9 Sept.	Luigi Galvani *b.*
1738	21 June	Charles Townshend (2nd Viscount Townshend) *d.*
1738	23 Sept.	Herman Boerhaave *d.*
1738	15 Nov.	Sir William Herschel *b.*
1739		Israel Lyons† *b.*
1739		John Robison† *b.*
1739		John Warltire† *b.*
1739	16 July	Charles Francois de Cisteincey Dufay *d.*
1740		John Monro† *d.*
1740		Carl Friedrich Wenzel *b.*
1740		Joseph-Michel Montgofier *b.*
1740	17 Feb.	Horace Bénédict de Saussure *b.*
1741		Joseph Huddart† *b.*
*c.*1741		Bryan Higgins† *b.*

*c.*1741		Jeremiah Dixon† *b.*
1741		Linnaeus, the Younger† *b.*
1741		Francis Masson† *b.*
1741		Faujas de St Fond† *b.*
1741		A. H. Tessier† *b.*
1741	21 Feb.	Jethro Tull *d.*
1741	17 Mar.	William Withering *b.*
1741	11 Sept.	Arthur Young *b.*
1742		Benjamin Moseley† *b.*
1742		A. J. Retzius† *b.*
1742		W. J. S. van S'Gravesande† *d.*
1742	14 Jan.	Edmond Halley *d.*
1742	12 Nov.	Friedrich Hoffmann *d.*
1742	6 Dec.	Nicolas Leblanc *b.*
1742	9 (or 19) Dec.	Carl Wilhelm Scheele *b.*
1743		Marquis de Condorcet† *b.*
1743		R. J. Haüy† *b.*
1743		Louis Lémery† *d.*
1743	2 Feb.	Sir Joseph Banks *b.*
1743	24 Apr.	Edmund Cartwright *b.*
1743	26 Aug.	Antoine Laurent Lavoisier *b.*
1743	11 Nov.	Carl Per Thunberg *b.*
1743	1 Dec.	Martin Heinrich Klaproth *b.*
1744		P. J. Desault† *b.*
1744		P. F. A. Méchain† *b.*
*c.*1744		Pierre Louis Guinand *b.*
1744	14 Feb.	John Hadley *d.*
1744	25 Apr.	Anders Celsius *d.*
1744	31 May	Richard Lovell Ovell Edgeworth *b.*
1744	1 Aug.	Jean Baptiste Pierre Antoine de Monet Lamarck *b.*
1745		A. J. Cavanilles† *b.*
1745		J. G. Gahn† *b.*
1745		William Jessop† *b.*
1745		J. H. Schröter† *b.*
1745	7 Jan.	Jacques-Etienne Montgolfier *b.*
1745	18 Feb.	Alessandro Volta *b.*
1745	24 Dec.	Benjamin Rush *b.*
1746		J. B. M. Bucquet† *b.*
1746		Robert R. Livingston† *b.*
1746	11 Jan.	William Curtis *b.*
1746	10 May	Gaspard Monge *b.*
1746	14 June	Colin Maclaurin *d.*
1746	16 July	Guiseppe Piazzi *b.*
1746	12 Nov.	Jacques Alexandre César Charles *b.*
1747(?)		A. Scarpa† *b.*
1747	19 Jan.	Johann Elert Bode *b.*
1748/9		A. Crawford† *b.*
1748		Jeremy Bentham† *b.*
1748		Thomas Day† *b.*
1748		F. Vicq D'Azyr† *b.*
1748	1 Jan.	Jean Bernoulli *d.*
1748	10 Mar.	John Playfair *b.*
1748	12 Apr.	Antoine Laurent de Jussieu *b.*
1748	*c.*19 Apr.	Sir Charles Blagden *b.*
1748	9 Dec.	Claude Louis Berthollet *b.*
1749		Thomas Earnshaw† *b.*
1749		Thomas Godfrey† *d.*
1749		Sir William Young† *b.*
1749	22 Mar.	Pierre Simon Laplace *b.*
1749	13 Apr.	Joseph Bramah *b.*
1749	17 May	Edward Jenner *b.*
1749	29 Aug.	Sir Gilbert Blane *b.*
1749	19 Sept.	Jean Baptiste Joseph Delambre *b.*
1749	25 Sept.	Abraham Gottlob Werner *b.*
1749	17 Nov.	Nicholas Appert *b.*
1750		Abraham Darby III† *b.*
1750		Robert Peel† *b.*
1750		Abraham Bennet *b.*
1750	8 Aug.	Nicolas Fortin *b.*
1751		Marquis Claude de Jouffroy d'Abbans† *b.*
1751		F. A. H. Descroizilles† *b.*

1751		George Graham† *d.*
1751	17 Mar.	Anders Dahl *b.*
1751	30 Aug.	Christopher Polhem (Polhammer) *d.*
1752		William Cheselden† *d.*
1752		Timothy Dwight† *b.*
1752		A. M. Legendre† *b.*
1752	4 May	Thomas William Coke (Earl of Leicester) *b.*
1752	7 July	Joseph Marie Jacquard *b.*
1753		George Berkeley† *d.*
1753		W. Nicholson† *b.*
1753		G. W. Richmann† *d.*
1753	26 Mar.	Count Rumford (Benjamin Thompson) *b.*
1753	3 Dec.	Samuel Crompton *b.*
1754		P. F. Chabaneau† *b.*
1754		William Cleghorn† *b.*
1754		A. L. C. de Tracy Destutt† *b.*
1754		J. G. A. Forster† *b.*
1754		G. C. Morgan† *b.*
1754		J. F. Riccati† *d.*
1754		Benjamin Waterhouse† *b.*
1754		Christian Wolff† *d.*
1754		Baron von Zach† *b.*
1754	21 Aug.	William Murdock *b.*
1754	26 Sept.	Louis Joseph Proust *b.*
1754	27 Nov.	Abraham Demoivre *d.*
1755	15 June	Antoine François de Fourcroy *b.*
1755	13 Sept.	Oliver Evans *b.*
1756		E. F. F. Chladni† *b.*
1756		J. Cassini† *d.*
1756		B. G. E. de la ville Lacepède† *b.*
1756	4 June	Jean Antoine Claude Chaptal (Comte de Chanteloup) *b.*
1756	21 Sept.	John Loudon McAdam *b.*
1757		P. J. G. Cabanis† *b.*
1757		Sir Samuel Bentham† *b.*
1757		John Gough† *b.*
1757		P. Kitaibel† *b.*
1757		Thomas Perkin† *b.*
1757	9 Jan.	Bernard le Bovier de Fontenelle *d.*
1757	9 Aug.	Thomas Telford *b.*
1757	18 Oct.	Réné Antoine Ferchault de Réamur *d.*
1758		Pierre Bouquert *d.*
1758		F. J. Gall† *b.*
1758		H. W. M. Olbers† *b.*
1758		John Sibthorp† *b.*
1759		William Cockerill *b.*
1759		Johann Juncker† *d.*
1759		T. A. Knight† *b.*
1759		P. J. Redouté† *b.*
1759		Sir James Edward Smith† *b.*
1759		Jan Wandelaar† *b.*
1759	27 July	Pierre Louis Moureau de Maupertuis *d.*
1760		L. Godin† *d.*
1760		Comte de Saint-Simon† *b.*
1760	13 Apr.	Thomas Beddoes *b.*
1760	5 June	Johan Gadolin *b.*
1761		J. B. Le Père† *b.*
1761		P. van Musschenbroek† *d.*
1761		Bernard Forest de Belidor *d.*
1761	4 Jan.	Stephen Hales *d.*
1761	3 June	Henry Shrapnel *b.*
1761	7 June	John Rennie *b.*
1761	27 Oct.	Matthew Baillie *b.*
1761	21 Nov.	Joshua Ward *d.*
1761	30 Nov.	Smithson Tennant *b.*
1761	30 Nov.	John Dollond *d.*
1761	25 Dec.	William Gregor *b.*
1762		Tobias Mayer† *d.*
1762	21 Mar.	Nicolas Louis de Lacaille *d.*
1762	13 July	James Bradley *d.*
1763		John Bell† *b.*
1763		Francis Hauksbee, the Younger† *d.*
1763		J. von Utzschneider† *b.*
1763		William Higgins *b.*
1763		Frederick Albert Winsor (Winzer) *b.*
1763	16 May	Louis Nicolas Vauquelin *b.*
1763	25 Dec.	Claude Chappe *b.*
1764		John Abernethy† *b.*
1733–64		John Kay† *fl.*
1765		A. C. Clairaut *d.*
1765		P. Ruffini† *b.*
c.1765		Armand Séguin† *b.*
1765		James Smithson *b.*
1765	7 Mar.	Joseph Nicéphore Niépce *b.*
1765	4 Apr.	Mikhail Vasil'evich Lomonosov *d.*
1765	19 Aug.	Axel Fredrik Cronstedt *d.*
1765	26 Oct.	Samuel Klingenstierna *d.*
1765	14 Nov.	Robert Fulton *b.*
1765	8 Dec.	Eli Whitney *b.*
1766		M. F. P. G. de Birain† *b.*
1766		W. Hisinger† *b.*
1766	17 Feb.	Thomas Robert Malthus *b.*
1766	15 Apr.	Robert Whytt *d.*
1766	21 July	Thomas Charles Hope *b.*
1766	6 Aug.	William Hyde Wollaston *b.*
1766	(about) 5 Sept.	John Dalton *b.*
1766	29 Dec.	Charles Macintosh *b.*
1767		Alexis Bouvart† *b.*
1767		Davies Gilbert (formerly Giddy)† *b.*
1767		Edward Pease† *b.*
1767		Antoine Thiout *d.*
1767	29 May	Phillipe Lebon *b.*
1767	10 July	Alexander Monro (primus) *d.*
1768		J. R. Argand† *b.*
1768		C. E. L. Camus† *d.*
1768		A. Carlisle† *b.*
1768		James Short† *d.*
c.1768		William Nicol *b.*
1768	21 Mar.	Jean Baptiste Joseph Fourier *b.*
1768	22 Mar.	Bryan Donkin *b.*
1768	3 May	Charles Tennant† *b.*
1769(?)		Sydenham Edwards† *b.*
1769		J. M. C. Bartels† *b.*
1769		J. N. P. Hachette† *b.*
1769	23 Mar.	William Smith *b.*
1769	25 Apr.	Sir Marc Isambard Brunel *b.*
1769	23 Aug.	Baron George Léopold Chrétien Frédéric Dagobert Cuvier *b.*
1769	14 Sept.	Baron Friedrich von Humboldt *b.*
1770		G. W. F. Hegel† *b.*
1770		César Legalloist *b.*
1770		T. J. Seebeck† *b.*
1770		James Woodhouse† *b.*
1770		Alexandre Brongniat *b.*
1770	24 Apr.	Abbé Jean Antoine Nollet *d.*
1770	3 Aug.	Guillaume François Rouelle *d.*
1770	9 Sept.	Bernhard Siegfried Albinus *d.*
1771		Jeremiah Dixon† *d.*
1771		Chester Moor Hall† *d.*
1771		Henry Hindley† *d.*
1771		C. A. Rudolphi† *b.*
1771	13 Apr.	Richard Trevithick *b.*
1771	14 May	Thomas Wedgwood *b.*
1771	22 Aug.	Henry Maudslay *b.*
1771	11 Nov.	Marie François Xavier Bichat *b.*
1771	6 Dec.	Giovanini Battista Morgagni *d.*
1772		John Canton† *d.*
1772		John Redman† *b.*
1772		George Reichenbach† *b.*
1772		David Ricardo† *b.*
1772	29 Mar.	Emanuel Swedenborg *d.*
1772	27 Sept.	James Brindley *d.*
1772		Agostino Bassi *b.*

1773		A. J. A. Bonplandt *b.*
1773		H. V. Collet-Descotilst *b.*
1773		J. A. Schultest *b.*
1773		Thomas Thomsont *b.*
1773		Thomas Webstert *b.*
1773	29 Jan.	Friedrich Mohs *b.*
1773	13 June	Thomas Young *b.*
1773	5 Nov.	Alexander Monro (*tertius*) *b.*
1773	21 Dec.	Robert Brown *b.*
1773	27 Dec.	Sir George Cayley *b.*
1774		William Bickford *b.*
1774		A. M. C. Dumérilt *b.*
1774		Olinthus Gregoryt *b.*
1774		K. B. Mollweidert *b.*
1774	4 Feb.	Charles-Marie de La Condamine *d.*
1774	21 Apr.	Jean Baptiste Biot *b.*
1774	Nov.	Sir Charles Bell *b.*
1774	12 Dec.	William Henry *b.*
1775		Joseph Angladat *b.*
1775		Richard Bacont *b.*
1775		William Clift† *b.*
1775		J. N. Corvisartt *b.*
1775		Sir John Graham Dalyellt *b.*
1775		John Kiddt *b.*
1775		Israel Lyonst *d.*
1775		William Smallt *d.*
1775	22 Jan.	André Marie Ampère *b.*
1776		W. R. Clannyt *b.*
1776		George Birkbeckt *b.*
1776		Amos Eatont *b.*
1776		Josias Christopher Gamble *b.*
1776		David Humet *d.*
1776		Robert Jamest *d.*
1776		J. C. Spurzheimt *b.*
1776		F. Stromeyert *b.*
1776	24 Mar.	John Harrison *d.*
1776	21 June	Benjamin Huntsman *d.*
1776	9 Aug.	Amedeo Avogadro *b.*
1776	14 Nov.	René Joachim Henri Dutrochet *b.*
1776	16 Dec.	Johann Wilhelm Ritter *b.*
1777		L. C. Bourdelint *d.*
1777		G. Dupuytrent *d.*
1777		G. L. Duvernoyt *b.*
1777		Bernard de Jussieut *d.*
1777		H. Katert *b.*
1777		Sir John Rosst *b.*
1777		Gregory Wattt *b.*
1777	30 Apr.	Karl Friederich Gauss *b.*
1777	4 May	Louis Jacques Thenard *b.*
1771	31 May	Cagn(i)ard de Latour† *b.*
1777	3 June	Charles Bernard Désormes *b.*
1777	14 Aug.	Hans Christian Oersted *b.*
1777	12 Dec.	Albrecht von Haller *d.*
1778		Laura Bassit *b.*
1778		Thomas Batemant *b.*
1778		Sir John Robisont *b.*
1778		H. A. Vogelt *b.*
1778		J. C. Warrent *b.*
1778	4 Feb.	Augustin Pyramus de Candolle *b.*
1778	10 Jan.	Carl Linnaeus *d.*
1778	7 Mar.	Charles de Geer *d.*
1778	Apr.	James Hargreaves *d.*
1778	18 May	Andrew Ure *b.*
1778	6 Dec.	Joseph Louis Guy-Lussac *b.*
1778	17 Dec.	Sir Humphry Davy *b.*
1779		William Hedleyt *b.*
1779		Nicolas Clément-Désormest *b.*
1779	14 Feb.	James Cook *d.*
1779	7 Apr.	Hilaire Martin Rouelle *d.*
1779	8 Aug.	Benjamin Silliman *b.*
1779	20 Aug.	Jöns Jacob Berzelius *b.*
1779/80		Aeneas Coffey *b.*
1780		Leopold Crellet *b.*
1780		Thomas Bentleyt *d.*
1780		Robert McCormickt *b.*
1780	29 Aug.	Jacques-Germain Soufflot *d.*
1780	15 Dec.	Johann Wolfgang Döbereiner *b.*
1780/81		John Walker *b.*
1781		G. B. Beccariat *d.*
1781		Charles-Marie Boutont *b.*
1781		John Turbeville Needhamt *d.*
1781		M. M. Pontint *b.*
1781		J. B. von Spixt *b.*
1781		F. Tiedemannt *b.*
1781		A. R. Turgott *d.*
1781	17 Jan.	Robert Hare *b.*
1781	17 Feb.	René Théophile Hyacynthe Laënnec *b.*
1781	9 June	George Stephenson *b.*
1781	21 June	Siméon Denis Poisson *b.*
1781	11 Dec.	Sir David Brewster *b.*
1782		Daniel Solandert *d.*
1782	17 Mar.	Daniel Bernoulli *d.*
1782	Aug.	Henri Louis Duhamel du Monceau *d.*
1782	7 Aug.	Andreas Sigismund Marggraf *d.*
1782	21 Nov.	Jacques de Vaucanson *d.*
1783		C. J. Brianchont *b.*
1783		William Cleghornt *d.*
1783		Jean le Rond D'Alembert *d.*
1783		William Huntert *d.*
1783		Linnaeus, the Youngert *d.*
1783	22 May	William Sturgeon *b.*
1783	19 June	Friedrich Wilhelm Sertürner *b.*
1783	7 Aug.	John Heathcote *b.*
1783	18 Sept.	Leonhard Euler *d.*
1783	6 Oct.	François Magendie *b.*
1783	Oct.	Sir Benjamin Collins Brodie *b.*
1784		William Bucklandt *b.*
1784		C. Dupint *b.*
1784		Robert Hoet *b.*
1784		John Mullert *d.*
1784		Leopoldo Nobili *b.*
1784	15 Feb.	Pierre Joseph Macquer *d.*
1784	8 July	Torbern Olaf Bergman *d.*
1784	22 July	Friedrich Wilhelm Bessel *b.*
1784	30 July	Denis Diderot *d.*
1785		Sir William J. Hookert *b.*
1785		Leonard Hornert *b.*
1785		Sir James Southt *b.*
1785	15 Jan.	William Prout *b.*
1784	12 Feb.	Pierre Louis Dulong *b.*
1785	22 Feb.	Jean Charles Athanase Peltier *b.*
1785	22 Mar.	Adam Sedgwick *b.*
1785	26 Apr.	John James Audubon *b.*
1785	21 Nov.	William Beaumont *b.*
1786		J. E. Guettardt *d.*
1786		W. G. Hornert *b.*
1786		Joseph Jackson Listert *b.*
1786		Hugh Smithson Percy, Duke of Northumberlandt *d.*
1786		James Thomsont *b.*
1786		N. Wallicht *b.*
1786	26 Feb.	Dominique François Jean Arago *b.*
1786	25 Mar.	Giovanni Battista Amici *b.*
1786	20 Apr.	Marc Seguin *b.*
1786	8 May	Thomas Hancock *b.*
1786	21 (or 26) May	Carl Wilhelm Scheele *d.*
1786	31 Aug.	Michel Eugène Chevreul *b.*
1786	12 Sept.	William Cotton *b.*
1787		R. J. Boscovicht *d.*
1787		James Crosfieldt *b.*
1787		Henri Dufourt *b.*
1787		Friedrich Kruppt *b.*
1787		P. C. A. Louist *b.*
1787		N. G. Sefströmt *b.*
1787	6 Mar.	Josef von Fraunhofer *b.*
1787	10 May	Sir William Watson *d.*

1787	8 Oct.	Henri Prudence Gambey *b.*
1787	18 Nov.	Louis Jacques Mandé Daguerre *b.*
1787	17 Dec.	Johannes Evangelista Purkinje *b.*
1788		John Brown† *d.*
1788		James Murray† *b.*
1788		Percivall Pott† *d.*
1788		Carl Reichenbach† *b.*
1788	15 Apr.	George Louis Leclerc, Comte de Buffon *d.*
1788	22 Apr.	Joseph Pelletier *b.*
1788	10 May	Augustin Jean Fresnel *b.*
1788	1 July	Jean Victor Poncelet *b.*
1788	2 Aug.	Leopold Gmelin *b.*
1788	14 Oct.	Sir Edward Sabine *b.*
1789		J. B. M. Bucquet† *d.*
1789		Thomas Day† *b.*
1789		Charles Mason† *d.*
1789	19 Feb.	Sir William Fairbairn *b.*
1789	26 Feb.	Eaton Hodgkinson *b.*
1789	16 Mar.	Georg Simon Ohm *b.*
1789	22 Apr.	Richard Roberts *b.*
1789	25 May	Anders Dahl *d.*
1789		June William Venables Vernon Harcourt *b.*
1789	21 Aug.	Augustin Louis Cauchy *b.*
1789	28 Sept.	Richard Bright *b.*
1789	25 Oct.	Samuel Heinrich Schwabe *b.*
1790		John Campbell† *d.*
1790		John Bachman† *d.*
1790		Claude Burdin† *b.*
1790		William Cullen† *d.*
1790		Sir William Parry† *b.*
1790	18 Feb.	Marshall Hall *b.*
1790	12 Mar.	John Frederic Daniell *b.*
1790	17 Apr.	Benjamin Franklin *d.*
1790	25 Oct.	Robert Stirling *b.*
1790	17 Nov.	August Ferdinand Mobius *b.*
1791		Jean Cruveilhier† *b.*
1791		Abraham Darby III† *d.*
1791		J. F. Eucke† *b.*
1791		J. Gaertner† *d.*
1791		George Peacock† *b.*
1791		F. Savart† *b.*
1791	21 Feb.	John Mercer *b.*
1791	27 Apr.	Samuel Finley Breese Morse *b.*
1791	22 Sept.	Michael Faraday *b.*
1791	2 Oct.	Alexis-Thérèse Petit *b.*
1792		J. A. Arfwedson† *b.*
1792	21 May	Gustave Gaspard (de) Coriolis *b.*
1792		Joseph Crosfield† *b.*
1792		Thomas Henry Maudslay† *b.*
1792		J. B. Neilson† *b.*
1792		Lord Rodney† *b.*
1792	17 Feb.	Karl Ernst von Baer *b.*
1792	19 Feb.	Sir Roderick Impey Murchison *b.*
1792	7 Mar.	Sir John Frederick William Herschel *b.*
1792	3 Aug.	Sir Richard Arkwright *d.*
1792	28 Oct.	John Smeaton *d.*
1792	2 Dec.	Nikola Ivanovich Lobachevski *b.*
1792	26 Dec.	Charles Babbage *b.*
1793(?)		Sir John MacNeill† *b.*
1793		John Michell† *d.*
1793		John Mudge† *d*
1793		P. F. O. Rayner† *b.*
1793		Lucas Schönlein† *b.*
1793	27 Feb.	Carl Friedrich Wenzel *d.*
1793	Apr.	Thomas Addison *b.*
1793	15 Apr.	Friedrich Georg Wilhelm Struve *b.*
1793	20 June	Charles Bonnet *d.*
1793	12 Aug.	James Muspratt *b.*
1793	16 Oct.	John Hunter *d.*
1794		Marquis de Condorcet† *d.*
1794		J. G. A. Forster† *d.*
1794		Robert Liston† *b.*
1794		C. F. P. von Martius† *b.*
1794		A. Valenciennes† *b.*
1794		F. Vicq D'Azyr† *d.*
1794		William Whewell† *b.*
1794	17 Jan.	Eilhard Mitscherlich *b.*
1794	22 Feb.	Kaspar Friedrich Wolff *d.*
1794	27 Feb.	Jean-Rodolphe Perronet *d.*
1794	13 Apr.	Jean Pierre Marie Flourens *b.*
1794	8 May	Antoine Laurent Lavoisier *d.*
1794	13 July	James Lind *d.*
1794	17 July	John Roebuck *d.*
1794	15 Aug.	Elias Magnus Fries *b.*
1794	2 Sept.	James Marsh *b.*
1794	14 Nov.	Thomas Mudge *d.*
1795		A. Crawford† *d.*
1795		P. J. Desault† *d.*
1795		Larcum Kendall† *d.*
1795		Sir Josiah Mason† *b.*
1795		H. Rose† *b.*
1795		Ernst Heinrich Weber† *b.*
1795	3 Jan.	Josiah Wedgwood *d.*
1795	8 Feb.	Friedlieb Ferdinand Runge *b.*
1795	19 Apr.	Christian Gottfried Ehrenberg *b.*
1795	30 June	Joseph Bienaimé Caventou *b.*
1795	1 Oct.	Robert Bakewell *d.*
1796		Baron Clas Alströmert† *d.*
1796		J. B. Bouillaud† *b.*
1796		Sir Henry Thomas de la Beche *b.*
1796		K. K. Klaus† *b.*
1796		A. G. Pingre† *d.*
1796		John Sibthorp† *d.*
1796		J. Steiner† *b.*
1796		Johann Daniell Titius† *d.*
1796		John Torrey† *b.*
1796	12 Mar.	Pierre Trésaguet *d.*
1796	18 Apr.	Johan Carl Wilcke *d.*
1796	1 June	Nicolas Léonard Sadi Carnot *b.*
1796	25 Dec.	Hugh Lee Pattinson *b.*
1796	29 Dec.	Johann Christian Poggendorf *b.*
1797		R. Brocklesby† *d.*
1797		P. A. Gadd† *d.*
1797		Adrien de Jussieu† *b.*
1797		John Morgan† *b.*
1797		Humphry Sibthorp† *d.*
1797		Jedediah Strutt† *d.*
1797	26 Mar.	James Hutton *d.*
1797	10 Sept.	Carl Gustav Mosander *b.*
1797	10 Oct.	Thomas Drummond *b.*
1797	14 Nov.	Sir Charles Lyell *b.*
1797	17 Dec.	Joseph Henry *b.*
1798		A. M. F. X. Comte† *b.*
1798		M. Melloni † *b.*
1798		G. C. Morgan † *d.*
1798		Thomas Pennant† *d.*
1798		G. Rose† *b.*
1798		H. W. F. Wackenroder *b.*
1798	4 Dec.	Luigi Galvani *d.*
1799		John Arnold† *d.*
1799		Abraham Bennet *d.*
1799		L. C. Cadet† *d.*
1799		B. P. E. Clapeyron† *b.*
1799		William Gossage *b.*
1799		P. C. Lemonnier† *d.*
1779		Lorenz Oken† *b.*
1799		Geoffroy Saint-Hilaire† *b.*
1799		James Syme† *b.*
1799		J. A. Virzer† *d.*
1799	22 Jan.	Horace Bénédict de Saussure *d.*
1799	11 Feb.	Lazzaro Spallanzani *d.*
1799	20 Feb.	Jean Charles (de) Borda *d.*
1799	Apr.	Patrick Bell *b.*
1799	7 July	William Curtis *d.*
1799	2 Aug.	Jacques-Etienne Montgolfier *d.*

1799	7 Sept.	Jan Ingenhousz *d.*
1799	6 Oct.	William Withering *d.*
1799	18 Oct.	Christian Frederick Schönbein *b.*
1799	6 Dec.	Joseph Black *d.*
1800		Daines Barrington† *d.*
1800		W. Buckland† *b.*
1800		L. J. M. Daubenton† *d.*
1800		L. D. Gale† *b.*
1800		H. R. Goeppert† *b.*
1800		Humphrey Lloyd† *b.*
1800		John Maclean† *b.*
1800		William Pilkington† *b.*
1800		F. A. Pouchet† *b.*
1800		Sir James Ross† *b.*
1800		Lord Rosse† *b.*
1800		George Smith† *b.*
c.1800		Peregrine Phillips *b.*
1800	11 Feb.	William Henry Fox Talbot *b.*
1800	14 July	Jean Baptiste André Dumas *b.*
1800	31 July	Friedrich Wöhler *b.*
1800	22 Sept.	George Bentham *b.*
1800	5 Nov.	Jesse Ramsden *d.*
1800	29 Dec.	Charles Goodyear *b.*
1801		Sir George Airy† *b.*
1801		A. T. Brongniart† *b.*
1801		J. P. J. D'Arcet† *d.*
1801		Moritz Jacobi† *b.*
1801		Joseph Maudslay† *b.*
1801		H. Moseley† *b.*
1801		A. A. de la Rive† *b.*
1801		A. Trousseau† *b.*
1801	1 Feb.	Jean-Baptiste Joseph Dieudonné Boussingault *b.*
1801	5 Apr.	Félix Dujardin *b.*
1801	16 June	Julius Plücker *b.*
1801	14 July	Johannes Peter Müller *b.*
1801	17 Oct.	George Richards Elkington *b.*
1802		F. U. T. Aepinus† *d.*
1802		Jacob Gadolin† *d.*
1802		H. G. Magnus† *d.*
1802		Hugh Miller† *b.*
1802		Simeon North† *b.*
1802		William Sharpey† *b.*
1802	February	Sir Charles Wheatstone *b.*
1802	18 Apr.	Erasmus Darwin *d.*
1802	21 July	Marie François Xavier Bichat *d.*
1802	7 Aug.	Germain Henri Hess *b.*
1802	30 Sept.	Antoine Jerome Balard *b.*
1802	31 Oct.	Benoit Fourneyron *b.*
1802	26 Nov.	Anton Schrötter *b.*
1802	18 Dec.	Johann Bolyai *b.*
1803		James Challis† *b.*
1803		J. Kolletschka† *b.*
1803	15 Jan.	Heinrich Daniel Rühmkorff *b.*
1803	12 May	Baron Justus von Liebig *b.*
1803	31 July	John Ericsson *b.*
1803	16 Oct.	Robert Stephenson *b.*
1803	21 Dec.	Sir Joseph Whitworth *b.*
1804		A. Baumé† *d.*
1804		L. F. C. Breguet† *b.*
1804		A. J. Cavanilles† *d.*
1804		C. Chevalier† *b.*
1804		A. G. Clark† *b.*
1804		M. A. A. Gaudin† *b.*
1804		P. F. A. Méchain† *d.*
1804(?)		Alexis St. Martin† *b.*
1804		Gregory Watt† *d.*
1804	6 Feb.	Joseph Priestley *d.*
1804	12 Feb.	Heinrich Friedrich Emil Lenz *b.*
1804	16 Feb.	Carl Theodor Ernst von Siebold *b.*
1804	19 Feb.	Karl Rokitansky *b.*
1804	5 Apr.	Matthias Jakob Schleiden *b.*
1804	20 July	Sir Richard Owen *b.*
1804	14 Sept.	John Gould *b.*

1804	2 Oct.	Nicholas-Joseph Cugnot *d.*
1804	24 Oct.	Wilhelm Eduard Weber *b.*
1804	2 Dec.	Phillipe Lebon *d.*
1804	10 Dec.	Carl Gustav Jacob Jacobi *b.*
1805		Peter Gustav Dirichlet† *b.*
1805		Samuel Garbett† *d.*
1805		W. S. Henson† *b.*
1805		C. T. Jackson† *b.*
1805		J. Lamont† *b.*
1805		Francis Masson† *d.*
1805		Hugo von Mohl† *b.*
1805		John Robison† *d.*
1805		J. Skoda† *b.*
1805	23 Jan.	Claude Chappe *d.*
1805	10 July	Thomas Wedgwood *d.*
1805	4 Aug.	Sir William Rowan Hamilton *b.*
1805	19 Nov.	Vicomte Ferdinand Marie de Lesseps *b.*
1805	29 Nov.	Christian Doppler *b.*
1805	21 Dec.	Thomas Graham *b.*
1806		G. P. Bidder† *b.*
1806		Alphonse de Candolle† *b.*
1806		Sir William Fothergill Cooke *b.*
1806		A. De Morgan† *b.*
1806		G. B. A. Duchenne de Boulogne† *b.*
1806		John Stuart Mill † *b.*
1806		Eduard Friedrich Weber † *b.*
1806	14 Jan.	Matthew Fontaine Maury *b.*
1806	16 Jan. (or Feb.)	Nicolas Leblanc *d.*
1806	19 Feb.	Peter Spence *b.*
1806	9 Apr.	Isambard Kingdom Brunel *b.*
1806	23 Aug.	Charles Augustin de Coulomb *d.*
1806	13 Oct.	Otto Unverdorben *b.*
1807		Arnold Henry Guyot† *b.*
1807		Isaac Holden† *b.*
1807		J. J. Le F. de Lalande† *d.*
1807		Alfred Vail† *b.*
1807		George Walker† *d.*
1807		Robert Warington† *b.*
1807	28 May	Jean Louis Rodolphe Agassiz *b.*
1807	20 June	Ferdinand Berthoud *d.*
1807	3 Dec.	David Alter *b.*
1808		P. J. G. Cabanis† *d.*
1808		Nathaniel Hayward† *b.*
1808		Hippolyte Pixii *b.*
1808		John Redman† *d.*
1808		Sir Francis Smith† *b.*
1808		Hermann Stannius† *b.*
1808	29 Feb.	Charles Pritchard *b.*
1808	14 July	John Wilkinson *d.*
1808	19 Aug.	James Nasmyth *b.*
1808	14 Sept. (or 1807 14 Nov.)	Auguste Laurent *b.*
1808	24 Dec.	Thomas Beddoes *d.*
1809		L. Auenbrugger† *d.*
1809		J. D. Forbes† *b.*
1809		H. G. Grassmann† *b.*
1809		Jacob Henle† *b.*
1809		R. H. A. Kolrausch† *b.*
1809		J. Stenhouse† *b.*
1809		Robert Bentley Todd† *b.*
1809		James Woodhouse† *d.*
1809	12 Feb.	Charles Robert Darwin *b.*
1809	15 Feb.	Cyrus Hall McCormick *b.*
1809	9 July	Svend Foyn *b.*
1809	18 Aug.	Matthew Boulton *d.*
1809	29 Aug.	Oliver Wendell Holmes *b.*
1809	24 Sept.	Sir Robert John Kane *b.*
1809	16 Dec.	Antoine François de Fourcroy *d.*
1810		Sir William Armstrong† *b.*
1810		Henry Elkington† *b.*
1810		J. M. Riggs† *b.*

1810		G. G. Valentin† b.
1810		Philippe Walter b.
1810		John Warltire† d.
1810	1 Jan.	Charles Ellet b.
1810	23 Jan.	Johann Wilhelm Ritter d.
1810	24 Feb.	Henry Cavendish d.
1810	26 June	Joseph-Michel Montgolfier d.
1810	21 July	Henri Victor Regnault b.
1810	18 Nov.	Asa Gray b.
1810	7 Dec.	Theodor Schwann b.
1811		J. N. Demarquay† b.
1811		Evarist Galois† b.
1811		Robert Mylne† d.
1811		K. B. Reichert† b.
1811		John James Waterston b.
1811	9 Feb.	Nevil Maskelyne d.
1811	24 Feb.	Eugène Melchior Péligot b.
1811	3 Mar.	Arthur Albright b.
1811	11 Mar.	Urbain John Joseph Le Verrier b.
1811	31 Mar.	Robert Wilhelm Bunsen b.
1811	8 Apr.	Robert Forester Mushet b.
1811	5 May	John William Draper b.
1811	7 June	Sir James Young Simpson b.
1811	11 July	Sir William Grove b.
1811	13 July	James Young b.
1811	3 Aug.	Elisha Graves Otis b.
1811	21 Aug.	William Kelly b.
1811	12 Sept.	James Hall b.
1811	27 Oct.	Isaac Merrit Singer b.
1812		A. A. T. Cahours† b.
1812		J. G. Gallet† b.
1812		James Lind† d.
1812		C. G. Page† b.
1812		Charles Valency† d.
1812		L. F. Wilhelmy† b.
1812		H. Will† b.
1812		N. N. Zinin† b.
1812	19 Mar.	Casimir Joseph Davaine b.
1812	26 Apr.	Alfred Krupp b.
1812	22 June	Richard Kirwan d.
1812	12 Sept.	Richard March Hoe b.
1812	12 Oct.	Ascanio Sobrero b.
1813		Frederick Scott Archer b.
1813		William Bullock† b.
1813		Holbrook Gaskell† b.
1813		D. F. Gregory† d.
1813		Robert R. Livingston† d.
1813	19 Jan.	Sir Henry Bessemer b.
1813	8 Mar.	Johannes Japetus Smith Steenstrup b.
1813	10 Apr.	Joseph Louis Lagrange d.
1813	19 Apr.	Benjamin Rush d.
1813	29 May	John McNaught b.
1813	12 July	Claude Bernard b.
1813	21 Aug.	Jean Servais Stas b.
1813	19 Dec.	Thomas Andrews b.
1813	29 Dec.	Alexander Parkes b.
1814		Edward Filhol† b.
1814		Edmond Frémy† b.
1814		H. Geissler† b.
1814		J. Goodsir† b.
1814		J. G. Halske† b.
1814		William Jessop† d.
1814		Edwin Lankester† b.
1814		César Legallois† d.
1814		Sir Andrew Ramsay† b.
1814	2 Apr.	Erastus Brigham Bigelow b.
1814	19 July	Samuel Colt b.
1814	13 Aug.	Anders Jonas Angström b.
1814	21 Aug.	Count Rumford (Benjamin Thompson) d.
1814	3 Sept.	James Joseph Sylvester b.
1814	25 Nov.	Julius Robert von Mayer b.
1814	9 Dec.	Joseph Bramah d.
1814	28 Dec.	Sir John Bennet Lawes b.
1815		H. V. Collet-Descotils† d.
1815		Crawford W. Long† b.
1815		W. Nicholson† d.
1815		R. Piria† b.
1815		Alphonse Beau de Rochas† b.
1815		Sir William Young† d.
1815	1 Jan.	Samuel Cunliffe Lister b.
1815	18 Jan.	Warren De La Rue b.
1815	21 Jan.	Horace Wells b.
1815	22 Feb.	Smithson Tennant d.
1815	24 Feb.	Robert Fulton d.
1815	26 July	Robert Remak b.
1815	14 Aug.	Charles Naudin b.
1815	31 Oct.	Karl Wilhelm Theodor Weierstrass b.
1815	2 Nov.	George Boole b.
1816		Lowthian Bell† b.
1816		C. E. Delaunay† b.
1816		L. B. Guyton de Morveau† d.
1816		F. Hebra† b.
1816		Thomas Henry† d.
1816		Joseph Huddart† d.
1816		Thomas Oldham† b.
1816		J. H. Schröter† d.
1816		Benjamin Silliman, jun.† b.
1816		Sir John Simon† b.
1816	20 July	Sir William Bowman b.
1816	21 Aug.	Charles Frédéric Gerhardt b.
1816	24 Nov.	William Crawford Williamson b.
1816	13 Dec.	Ernst Werner von Siemens b.
1816	29 Dec.	Karl Friedrich Wilhelm Ludwig b.
1817		Timothy Dwight† d.
1817		J. H. Gilbert† b.
1817		Benjamin Jowett† b.
1817		P. Kitaibel† d.
1817		G. H. Lewes† b.
1817		W. A. Miller† b.
1817		John Percy† b.
1817	1 Jan.	Martin Heinrich Klaproth d.
1817	27 Mar.	Karl Wilhelm von Nägeli b.
1817	8 Apr.	Charles Edouard Brown-Séquard b.
1817	24 Apr.	Jean Charles Galissard de Marignac b.
1817	2 June	George Henry Corliss b.
1817	11 June	William Gregor d.
1817	13 June	Richard Lovell Edgeworth d.
1817	30 June	Abraham Gottlob Werner d.
1817	30 June	Sir Joseph Dalton Hooker b.
1817	6 July	Rudolph Albert von Kölliker b.
1817	15 July	Sir John Fowler b.
1817	2 Oct.	Alexander Monro (secundus) d.
1817	24 Oct.	Hippolyte Mège Mouriés b.
1817	30 Oct.	Hermann Franz Moritz Kopp b.
1817	26 Nov.	Charles-Adolphe Wurtz d.
1818		J. G. Gahn† d.
1818		Bryan Higgins† d.
1818		J. C. Jamin† b.
1818		Paulin Louyet† b.
1818		Ludwig Traube† b.
1818	11 Mar.	Henri Étienne Sainte-Claire Deville b.
1818	8 Apr.	August Wilhelm (von) Hofmann b.
1818	21 May	Lyon Playfair (1st Baron Playfair) b.
1818	29 June	Angelo Secchi b.
1818	1 July	Ignaz Philipp Semmelweis b.
1818	28 July	Gaspard Monge d.
1818	12 Sept.	Richard John Gatling b.
1818	27 Sept.	Adolph Wilhelm Hermann Kolbe b.
1818	7 Nov.	Emil Du Bois Reymond b.
1818	25 Nov.	Clemens Heinrich Lambert von Babo b.
1818	13 Dec.	Max Josef von Pettenkofer b.
1818	24 Dec.	James Prescott Joule b.
1819		Alexander Melville Bell† b.
1819		E. W. von Brücke† b.
1819		E. Edlund† b.
1819		Sydenham Edwards† d.

1819		C. W. Field† b.
1819		F. T. von Frerichs† b.
1819		Benjamin Moseley† d.
1819		F. Rochleder† b.
1819		Faujas de St Fond† d.
1819		Otto Struve† b.
1819	28 Mar.	Sir Joseph William Bazalgette b.
1819	29 Mar.	Edwin Laurentine Drake b.
1819	15 Apr.	Oliver Evans d.
1819	2 July	Thomas Anderson b.
1819	9 July	Elias Howe b.
1819	20 July	John Playfair d.
1819	9 Aug.	William Thomas Green Morton b.
1819	13 Aug.	George Gabriel Stokes b.
1819	25 Aug.	James Watt d.
1819	18 Sept.	Léon Foucault b.
1819	23 Sept.	Armand Hippolyte Louis Fizeau b.
1820		Edmond Becquerel† b.
1820		John Bell† d.
1820		C. A. Lamy† b.
1820		Joseph Wolff† b.
1820	21 Jan.	Égide Walschaerts b.
1820	26 Mar.	Sir Charles Blagden d.
1820	20 Apr.	Arthur Young d.
1820	27 Apr.	Herbert Spencer b.
1820	23 May	James Buchanan Eads b.
1820	19 June	Sir Joseph Banks d.
1820	21 June	Alexis-Thérèse Petit d.
1820	5 July	William John Macquorn Rankine b.
1820	2 Aug.	John Tyndall b.
1820	11 Oct.	James Keir d.
1821		Thomas Bateman† d.
1821		G. H. Bissell† b.
1821		J. N. Corvisart† d.
1821		K. Natterer† b.
1821		A. J. Retzius† d.
1821	16 Aug.	Arthur Cayley b.
1821	31 Aug.	Hermann Ludwig Ferdinand von Helmholtz b.
1821	4 Oct.	John Rennie d.
1821	13 Oct.	Rudolf Ludwig Carl Virchow b.
1822		J. R. Argand† d.
1822		R. J. Haüy† d.
1822		C. Hermite† b.
1822		A. K. Krönig† b.
1822		K. G. F. R. Leuckhart† b.
1822		P. Ruffini† d.
1822		H. Schliemann† b.
c.1822		J. W. Starr† b.
1822		Adolf Strecker† b.
1822	2 Jan.	Rudolf Julius Emmanuel Clausius b.
1822	12 Jan.	Jean Joseph Etienne Lenoir b.
1822	16 Feb.	James Thomson b.
1822	16 Feb.	Francis Galton b.
1822	4 Mar.	Jules Antoine Lissajous b.
1822	22 July	Johann Gregor Mendel b.
1822	30 July	Henry Deacon b.
1822	19 Aug.	Jean Baptiste Joseph Delambre d.
1822	25 Aug.	Sir William Herschel d.
1822	23 Oct.	Gustav Friedrich Wilhelm Spörer b.
1822	6 Nov.	Claude Louis Berthollet d.
1822	27 Dec.	Louis Pasteur b.
1823		F. G. M. Eisenstein† b.
1823		L. Kronecker† b.
1823		David Ricardo† d.
1823	3 Jan.	Robert Whitehead b.
1823	8 Jan.	Alfred Russel Wallace b.
1823	24 Jan.	Edward Jenner d.
1823	28 Jan.	Moritz Schiff b.
1823	3 Feb.	Spencer Fullerton Baird b.
1823	4 Apr.	Sir Charles William Siemens b.
1823	7 Apr.	Jacques Alexandre César Charles d.
1823	23 Sept.	Matthew Baillie d.
1823	30 Oct.	Edmund Cartwright d.
1823	30 Nov.	Nathanael Pringsheim b.
1824		E. F. F. Chladni† d.
1824		M. F. P. G. de Birain† d.
1824		Pierre Louis Guinand d.
1824	7 Feb.	Sir William Huggins b.
1824	22 Feb.	Pierre Jules César Janssen b.
1824	12 Mar.	Gustav Robert Kirchhoff b.
1824	27 Mar.	Johann Wilhelm Hittorf b.
1824	1 May	Alexander William Williamson b.
1824	18 May	Wilhelm Friedrich Benedict Hofmeister b.
1824	26 June	William Thomson (Baron Kelvin of Largs) b.
1824	28 June	Pierre Paul Broca b.
1824	18 Aug.	Pierre Emile Martin b.
1824	17 Dec.	John Kerr b.
1825		S. A. E. Aubertin† b.
1825		C. A. Bjerknes b.
1825		F. A. H. Descroizilles† d.
1825		John Gough† d.
1825		William Higgins d.
1825		John Hutchinson† b.
1825		B. G. E. de la ville Lacepède† d.
1825		K. B. Mollweidert† d.
1825		Comte de Saint-Simon† d.
1825		L. J. Troost† b.
1825	8 Jan.	Eli Whitney d.
1825	18 Jan.	Sir Edward Frankland b.
1825	8 Feb.	Henry Walter Bates b.
1825	8 Feb.	Henri Giffard b.
1825	25 Mar.	Max Johann Sigismund Schultze b.
1825	4 May	Thomas Henry Huxley b.
1825	29 Nov.	Jean-Martin Charcot b.
1825	26 Dec.	Ernst Felix Immanuel Hoppe-Seyler b.
1826		G. B. Donati† b.
1826		C. Gegenbaur† b.
1826		George Gore† b.
1826		Z. T. Gramme† b.
1826		John Hope† d.
1826		Friedrich Krupp† d.
1826		Georg Reichenbach† d.
1826		Friedrich Siemens b.
1826		J. B. von Spix† d.
1826		E. F. A. Vulpian† b.
1826	12 Feb.	Moritz Traube b.
1826	15 Feb.	George Johnstone Stoney b.
1826	10 May	Henry Clifton Sorby b.
1826	26 May	Richard Christopher Carrington b.
1826	7 June	Josef von Fraunhofer d.
1826	5 July	Louis Joseph Proust d.
1826	13 July	Stanislao Cannizzaro b.
1826	22 July	Giuseppe Piazzi d.
1826	13 Aug.	René Théophile Hyacynthe Laënnec d.
1826	17 Sept.	Georg Friedrich Bernhard Riemann b.
1826	2 Nov.	Henry John Stephen Smith b.
1826	23 Nov.	Johann Elert Bode d.
1827		J. P. Cooke† b.
1827		Henri Jules Debray† b.
1827		H. F. P. Limpricht† b.
1827		G. D. Liveing† b.
1827	28 Jan.	Jean Antoine Villemin b.
1827	5 Mar.	Pierre Simon Laplace d.
1827	5 Mar.	Alessandro Volta d.
1827	5 Apr.	Joseph Lister (first Baron Lister) b.
1827	26 June	Samuel Crompton d.
1827	14 July	Augustin Jean Fresnel d.
1827	17 July	Sir Frederick Augustus Abel b.
1827	25 Oct.	Pierre Eugène Marcel(l)in Berthelot b.
1828		B. F. Duppa† b.
1828		F. J. Gall† d.

1828		Albrecht von Graefe† b.
1828		Sir J. S. Burdon Sanderson† b.
1828		Sir James Edward Smith† d.
1828		Balfour Stewart† b.
1828		Bindon Blood Stoney† b.
1828	24 Jan.	Ferdinand Julius Cohn b.
1828	8 Aug.	Carl Per Thunberg d.
1828	6 Sept.	Aleksandr Mikhailovich Butlerov b.
1828	31 Oct.	Sir Joseph Wilson Swan b.
1828	22 Dec.	William Hyde Wollaston d.
1829		Theodor Billroth† b.
1829		Thomas Earnshaw† d.
1829		Franz Reuleaux† b.
1829		I. M. Sechenov† b.
1829	10 May	Thomas Young d.
1829	29 May	Sir Humphry Davy d.
1829	27 June	James Smithson d.
1829	5 Sept.	William Odling b.
1829	6 Sept.	Peter Johann Griess b.
1829	7 Sept.	Friedrich August Kekulé b.
1829	14 Nov.	Louis Nicolas Vauquelin d.
1829	18 Dec.	Jean Baptiste Pierre Antoine de Monet Lamarck d.
1830		J. M. van Bemmelen† b.
1830		Robert Peel† d.
1830	5 Mar.	Sir Charles Wyville Thomson b.
1830	5 Mar.	Etienne-Jules Marey b.
1830	9 Apr.	Eadweard James Muybridge b.
1830	10 May	François Marie Raoult d.
1830	11 May	Frederick Albert Winsor (Winzer) d.
1830	16 May	Jean Baptiste Joseph Fourier d.
1830	19 Aug.	Julius Lothar Meyer b.
1831		John Abernethy† d.
1831		Sir Samuel Bentham† d.
1831		Nicolas Fortin d.
1831		G. W. F. Hegel† d.
1831		J. A. Schultes† d.
1831		T. J. Seebeck† d.
1831		P. G. Tait† b.
1831		Carl Voit† b.
1831	15 Feb.	Henry Maudslay d.
1831	13 June	James Clerk Maxwell b.
1831	9 July	Wilhelm His b.
1831	6 Oct.	J. W. R. Dedekind† b.
1831	5 Dec.	Hans Heinrich Landolt b.
1832		Marquis Claude de Jouffroy d'Abbans† d.
1832		Jeremy Bentham† d.
1832		William Cockerill d.
1832		Evarist Galois† d.
1832		Robert Hoe† d.
1832		C. A. Rudolphi† d.
1832		L. Péan de Saint-Gilles† b.
1832		A. Scarpa† d.
1832		J. C. Spurzheim† d.
1832		Baron von Zach† d.
1832	12 Mar.	Charles Friedel d.
1832	13 May	Baron George Léopold Chrétien Fréderic Dagobert Cuvier d.
1832	16 May	Philip Danforth Armour b.
1832	14 June	Nikolaus August Otto b.
1832	17 June	Sir William Crookes b.
1832	30 July	Jean Antoine Claude Chaptal (Comte de Chanteloup) d.
1832	24 Aug.	Nicolas Léonard Sadi Carnot d.
1832	21 Sept.	Louis Paul Cailletet b.
1832	2 Oct.	Ferdinand Gustav Julius von Sachs b.
1832	31 Oct.	Walter Weldon b.
1832	18 Nov.	Nils Adolf Erik Nordenskiöld b.
1833		Joseph Anglada† d.
1833		Rudolph Clebsch† b.
1833		F. Guthrie† b.
1833		A. M. Legendre† d.
1833		F. D. Recklinghausen† b.
1833	7 Jan.	Sir Henry Enfield Roscoe b.
1833	22 Apr.	Richard Trevithick d.
1833	29 June	Peter Waage b.
1833	5 July	Joseph Nicéphore Niépce d.
1833	17 Oct.	Paul Bert b.
1833	21 Oct.	Alfred Bernhard Nobel b.
1833	3 Dec.	Carlos J. Finlay b.
1834		William Bickford d.
1834		H. Caro† b.
1834		F. Goltz† b.
1834		J. N. P. Hachette† d.
1834		J. Hughlings Jackson† b.
1834		A. Rollett† b.
1834		J. Volhard† b.
1834		J. A. Wanklyn† b.
1834		J. W. Wilson† b.
1834	17 Jan.	August Weismann b.
1834	27 Jan.	Dmitry Ivanovich Mendeléeff b.
1834	16 Feb.	Ernst Heinrich Haeckel b.
1834	17 Mar.	Gottlieb Daimler b.
1834	26 Mar.	Hermann Wilhelm Vogel b.
1834	26 June	Sir Gilbert Blane d.
1834	7 Aug.	Joseph Marie Jacquard d.
1834	29 Aug.	Hermann Johann Philipp Sprengel b.
1834	2 Sept.	Thomas Telford d.
1834	23 Dec.	Thomas Robert Malthus d.
1835		Charles-Marie Bouton† d.
1835		G. Dupuytren† d.
1835		L. E. Grimaux† b.
1835		H. Kater† d.
1835		Hippolyte Pixii d.
1835		Armand Séguin† d.
1835		F. Stromeyer† d.
1835	10 Feb.	Victor Hensen b.
1835	12 Mar.	Simon Newcomb b.
1835	14 Mar.	Giovanni Virginio Schiaparelli b.
1835	24 Mar.	Joseph Stefan b.
1835	24 June	Johannes Adolph Wislicenus b.
1835	5 Aug.	Leopoldo Nobili d.
1835	31 Oct.	Johann Friedrich Adolf von Baeyer b.
1835	25 Nov.	Andrew Carnegie b.
1835	6 Dec.	Rudolf Fittig b.
1835	28 Dec.	Sir Archibald Geikie b.
1836		Joseph Bancroft† b.
1836		J. M. C. Bartels† d.
1836		Ernst von Bergmann† b.
1836		A. L. C. de Tracy Destutt† d.
1836		Sir Michael Foster† b.
1836		A. Lieben† b.
1836		K. Voelcker† b.
1836	17 May	Sir Joseph Norman Lockyer b.
1836	10 June	André Marie Ampère d.
1836	11 Aug.	Cato Maximilian Guldberg b.
1836	6 Oct.	Heinrich Wilhelm Waldeyer-Hartz b.
1836	2 Sept.	William Henry d.
1836	17 Sept.	Antoine Laurent de Jussieu d.
1836	26 Nov.	John Loudon McAdam d.
1837		John Ferguson† b.
1837		W. G. Horner† d.
1837		S. M. Jorgensen† b.
1837		A. H. Tessier† d.
1837		C. T. Yerkes† b.
1837	28 Mar.	Willy Kuhne b.
1837	27 Apr.	Paul Albert Gordan b.
1837	23 Nov.	Johannes Diderik van der Waals b.
1837	26 Nov.	John Alexander Reina Newlands b.
1837	28 Nov.	John Wesley Hyatt b.
1838		P. E. L. de Boisbaudran† b.
1838		T. A. Knight† d.
1838		V. V. Markovnikov† b.
1838	29 Jan.	Edward Williams Morley b.
1838	6 Feb.	Eduard Hitzig b.
1838	17 Feb.	Friedrich Konrad Beilstein b.
1838	18 Feb.	Ernst Mach b.

1838	5 Mar.	Gustav Theodor Fritsch *b.*
1838	12 Mar.	Sir William Henry Perkin *b.*
1838	26 Mar.	Alexander Crum Brown *b.*
1838	16 Apr.	Ernest Solvay *b.*
1838	8 July	Count Ferdinand von Zeppelin *b.*
1838	18 July	Pierre Louis Dulong *d.*
1838	10 Oct.	Charles Tennant *d.*
1838	26 Dec.	Clemens Alexander Winkler *b.*
1839		W. Esson† *b.*
1839		Davies Gilbert (formerly Giddy)† *d.*
1839		Robert Hoe† *b.*
1839		W. Körner† *b.*
1839		A. E. E. Kundt† *b.*
1839		C. W. Schorlemmer† *b.*
1839		Georges Leclanché *b.*
1839	11 Feb.	Josiah Willard Gibbs *b.*
1839	7 Mar.	Ludwig Mond *b.*
1839	8 Mar.	James Mason Crafts *b.*
1839	20 July	Julius Cohnheim *b.*
1839	28 Aug.	William Smith *d.*
1839	29 Sept.	Friedrich Mohs *d.*
1839	15 Nov.	William Murdock *d.*
1840		A. Carlisle† *d.*
1840		L. F. Nilson† *b.*
1840		H. W. M. Olbers† *d.*
1840		P. J. Redouté† *d.*
1840		Oberlin Smith† *b.*
1840		J. von Utzschneider† *d.*
1840	23 Jan.	Ernst Abbe *b.*
1840	5 Feb.	Sir Hiram Stevens Maxim *b.*
1840	5 Feb.	John Boyd Dunlop *b.*
1840	15 Apr.	Thomas Drummond *d.*
1840	25 Apr.	Siméon Denis Poisson *d.*
1840	14 Oct.	Friedrich Wilhelm Kohlrausch *b.*
1840	7 Nov.	Alexandre Onoufrievitch Kovalevsky *b.*
1841		E. H. Amagat† *b.*
1841		J. A. Arfwedson† *d.*
1841		George Birkbeck† *d.*
1841		Nicolas Clément-Désormes† *d.*
1841		Olinthus Gregory† *d.*
1841		George Oliver† *b.*
1841		R. Panhard† *b.*
1841		F. Savart† *d.*
1841	20 Feb.	Friedrich Wilhelm Sertürner *d.*
1841	24 Feb.	Carl Graebe *b.*
1841	3 Mar.	Sir John Murray *b.*
1841	1 June	Nicholas Appert *d.*
1841	25 Aug.	Emil Theodor Kocher *b.*
1841	9 Sept.	Augustin Pyramus de Candolle *d.*
1841	31 Oct.	Timothy Richards Lewis *b.*
1842		J. Breuer† *b.*
1842		A. Caton† *b.*
1842		A. M. Clerke† *b.*
1842		P. F. Chabaneau† *d.*
1842		Amos Eaton† *d.*
1842		C. T. Liebermann† *b.*
1842		N. A. Menschutkin† *b.*
1842		J. L. Reverdin† *b.*
1842		H. Wichelhaus† *b.*
1842	31 Mar.	Henry Shrapnel *d.*
1842	29 Apr.	Sir Charles Bell *d.*
1842	11 June	Carl von Linde *b.*
1842	30 June	Thomas William Coke (Earl of Leicester) *d.*
1842	19 July	Joseph Pelletier *d.*
1842	15 Aug.	Sir William Augustus Tilden *b.*
1842	23 Aug.	Osborne Reynolds *b.*
1842	20 Sept.	Charles Lapworth *b.*
1842	20 Sept.	Sir James Dewar *b.*
1842	12 Nov.	Lord Rayleigh (John William Strutt) *b.*
1842	17 Dec.	Marius Sophus Lie *b.*
1843		Alexis Bouvart† *d.*
1843		D. D. Cunningham† *b.*
1843		Theodor Wilhelm Engelmann *b.*
1843		William Hedley† *d.*
1843		T. Purdie† *b.*
1843		Sir John Robison† *d.*
1843		Gaston Tissandier† *b.*
1843		E. C. T. Zincke† *b.*
1843	13 Jan.	Sir David Ferrier *b.*
1843	3 Mar.	Sir William Chandler Roberts-Austen *b.*
1843	21 Apr.	Walther Flemming *b.*
1843	25 July	Charles Macintosh *d.*
1843	19 Sept.	Gustave Gaspard (de) Coriolis *d.*
1843	22 Oct.	Stephen Moulton Babcock *b.*
1843	11 Dec.	Robert Koch *b.*
1844		Sir William Barrett† *b.*
1844		Richard Bacon† *d.*
1844		Joseph Crosfield† *d.*
1844		D. F. Gregory† *d.*
1844		J. B. Le Père† *d.*
1844		E. Levassor† *d.*
1844		H. N. Moseley† *b.*
1844		Thomas Webster† *d.*
1844	1 Feb.	Eduard Adolf Strasburger *b.*
1844	20 Feb.	Ludwig Boltzmann *b.*
1844	15 Mar.	Ferdinand Hurter *b.*
1844	25 Mar.	Heinrich Gustav Adolf Engler *b.*
1844	13 June	Thomas Charles Hope *d.*
1844	28 June	Alexander Macomb Chance *b.*
1844	7 July	Camillo Golgi *b.*
1844	27 July	John Dalton *d.*
1844	3 Oct.	Sir Patrick Manson *b.*
1844	25 Nov.	Karl Benz *b.*
1845		Sir George Darwin† *b.*
1845		N. G. Sefström† *d.*
1845		Carl Weigert† *b.*
1845	9 Mar.	Wilhelm Pfeffer *b.*
1845	13 Mar.	John Frederic Daniell *d.*
1845	27 Mar.	William Konrad Röntgen *b.*
1845	9 May	Carl Gustaf Patrik de Laval *b.*
1845	16 May	Ilya (Elie) Mechnikov *b.*
1845	31 May	Rookes Evelyn Bell Crompton *b.*
1845	18 June	Charles Louis Alphonse Laveran *b.*
1845	4 July	Ivan Levinstein *b.*
1845	16 Aug.	Gabriel Lippmann *b.*
1845	27 Oct.	Jean Charles Athanase Peltier *d.*
1845	28 Oct.	Zygmunt Florenty von Wróblewski *b.*
1845	3 Nov.	Georg Ferdinand Ludwig Philip Cantor *b.*
1845	8 Dec.	Sir Thomas Edward Thorpe *b.*
1846		Robert McCormick† *d.*
1846		Benjamin Waterhouse† *d.*
1846	9 Feb.	Wilhelm Maybach *b.*
1846	10 Feb.	Ira Remsen *b.*
1846	5 Mar.	Edouard Joseph Louis-Marie van Beneden *b.*
1846	4 Apr.	Raoul Pierre Pictet *b.*
1846	21 June	James Marsh *d.*
1846	19 July	Edward Charles Pickering *b.*
1846	6 Oct.	George Westinghouse *b.*
1847		Alexandre Brongniart *d.*
1847		C. Friedländer† *b.*
1847		Pavel Nikolaievitch Jablochkoff *b.*
1847		J. Kolletschka† *d.*
1847		Robert Liston† *d.*
1847		Ettore Marchiafava† *b.*
1847		John Morgan† *d.*
1847		J. Orth† *b.*
1847		J. W. Starr† *d.*
1847	21 Jan.	Joseph Achille Le Bel *b.*
1847	28 Jan.	Henri Prudence Gambey *d.*
1847	4 Feb.	René Joachim Henri Dutrochet *d.*
1847	11 Feb.	Thomas Alva Edison *b.*
1847	3 Mar.	Alexander Graham Bell *b.*

1847	27 Mar.	Otto Wallach *b.*
1847	9 Apr.	Philippe Walter *d.*
1847	15 May	Edwin Ray Lankester *b.*
1847	14 Sept.	William Edward Ayrton *b.*
1847	1 Nov.	Walter Holbrook Gaskell *b.*
1848		P. A. Barbier† *b.*
1848		O. Bütschli† *b.*
1848		V. C. Driffield† *b.*
1848		Corrado Parona† *b.*
1848		Sir A. Rückert† *b.*
1848	14 Jan.	Rudolph Messel *b.*
1848	27 Jan.	Josias Christopher Gamble *d.*
1848	28 Jan.	Horace Wells *d.*
1848	16 Feb.	Hugo de Vries *b.*
1848	6 May	Henry Edward Armstrong *b.*
1848	24 May	Otto Lilienthal *b.*
1848	10 June	Johann Carl Wilhelm Ferdinand Tiemann *b.*
1848	22 June	Sir William Macewen *b.*
1848	27 July	Roland Eötvös *b.*
1848	7 Aug.	Jöns Jacob Berzelius *d.*
1848	12 Aug.	George Stephenson *d.*
1848	8 Sept.	Victor Meyer *b.*
1848	27 Nov.	Henry Augustus Rowland *b.*
1849		Franz Boll† *b.*
1849		William Clift† *d.*
1849		F. S. Exner† *b.*
1849		Rickman Godlee† *b.*
1849		A. B. Kempe† *b.*
1849		J. von Mering† *b.*
1849		Sir William Osler *b.*
1849		Ernesto Parona† *b.*
1849		F. O. Stanley† *b.*
1849		James Thomson† *d.*
1849	24 Mar.	Johann Wolfgang Döbereiner *d.*
1849	1 June	Francis Edgar Stanley *b.*
1849	16 Aug.	Johan Gustav Christoffer Thorsager Kjeldahl *b.*
1849	26 Sept.	Ivan Petrovich Pavlov *b.*
1849	21 Nov.	Johann August Brinell *b.*
1849	25 Nov.	Christian Felix Klein *b.*
1849	29 Nov.	Sir John Ambrose Fleming *b.*
1849	12 Dec.	Sir Marc Isambard Brunel *d.*
1850		Sir Jesse Boot (Lord Trent)† *b.*
1850		K. F. Braun† *b.*
1850		Hans Buchner† *b.*
1850		W. R. Clanny† *d.*
1850		C. Chevalier† *d.*
1850		A. von Ettinghausen† *b.*
1850		C. Fahlenberg† *b.*
1850		Georg Gaffky† *b.*
1850		Richard Hertwig† *b.*
1850		Paulin Louyet† *d.*
1850		G. A. Neubert† *b.*
1850		John Perry† *b.*
1850		Wilhelm Roux† *b.*
1850		W. A. Shenstone† *b.*
1850		L. Vaillard† *b.*
1850		Woldemar Voigt *b.*
1850	3 Mar.	Zdenko Hans Skraup *b.*
1850	8 Apr.	William Henry Welch *b.*
1850	9 Apr.	William Prout *d.*
1850	16 Apr.	Sidney Gilchrist Thomas *b.*
1850	9 May	Joseph Louis Gay-Lussac *d.*
1850	18 May	Oliver Heaviside *b.*
1850	2 June	Sir Edward Albert Sharpey-Schafer *b.*
1850	6 Jun	Karl Ferdinand Braun *b.*
1850	26 Aug.	Charles Robert Richet *b.*
1850	5 Sept.	Eugen Goldstein *b.*
1850	8 Oct.	Henri Louis Le Chatelier *b.*
1850	17 Nov.	Sir George Thomas Beilby *b.*
1850	30 Nov.	Germain Henri Hess *d.*
1850	4 Dec.	William Sturgeon *d.*
1851		C. E. Chamberland† *b.*
1851		Sir John Graham Dalyell† *d.*
1851		John Kidd† *d.*
1851		Lorenz Oken† *d.*
1851		Otto Schott† *b.*
1851		A. Schuster† *b.*
1851		K. F. O. Seubert† *b.*
1851		Silvanus Phillips Thompson† *b.*
1851	14 Jan.	Ludwig Claisen *b.*
1851	27 Jan.	John James Audubon *d.*
1851	18 Feb.	Carl Gustav Jacob Jacobi *d.*
1851	9 Mar.	Hans Christian Oersted *d.*
1851	12 June	Sir Oliver Joseph Lodge *b.*
1851	10 July	Louis Jacques Mandé Daguerre *d.*
1851	3 Aug.	George Francis Fitzgerald *b.*
1851	1 Sept.	Karl Kellner *b.*
1851	2 Sept.	William Nicol *d.*
1851	13 Sept.	Walter Reed *b.*
1851	27 Sept.	Percy Carlyle Gilchrist *b.*
1851	7 Nov.	Siegmund Gabriel *b.*
1851	10 Nov.	Francis Maitland Balfour *b.*
1851	25 Dec.	Herman Frasch *b.*
1852		H. R. Carter† *b.*
1852		James Crosfield† *d.*
1852		F. G. M. Eisenstein† *d.*
1852		Henry Elkington† *d.*
1852		Otto Fischer† *b.*
1852		William S. Halsted† *b.*
1852		W. Hisinger† *d.*
1852		Friedrich Loeffler† *b.*
1852		Thomas Thomson† *d.*
1852		E. E. G. Wiedermann† *b.*
1852	5 Jan.	Alexandre Léon Etard *b.*
1852	1 May	Santiago Ramón y Cajal *b.*
1852	11 Aug.	Harold Bailey Dixon *b.*
1852	15 Aug.	Johan Gadolin *d.*
1852	30 Aug.	Jacobus Henricus Van't Hoff *b.*
1852	9 Sept.	John Henry Poynting *b.*
1852	28 Sept.	Ferdinand Frédéric Henri Moissan *b.*
1852	2 Oct.	Sir William Ramsay *b.*
1852	9 Oct.	Emil Fischer *b.*
1852	2 Nov.	John Newport Langley *b.*
1852	26 Nov.	Aeneas Coffey *d.*
1852	15 Dec.	Antoine Henri Becquerel *b.*
1852	19 Dec.	Albert Abraham Michelson *b.*
1852	20 Dec.	Shibasaburo Kitasato *b.*
1853		Henri Deslandres† *b.*
1853		W. F. Hillebrand† *b.*
1853		Adrien de Jussieu† *d.*
1853		Sir James Mackenzie† *b.*
1853		Sir Flinders Petrie† *b.*
1853		F. B. Power† *b.*
1853		Geoffroy Saint-Hilaire† *d.*
1853	17 Mar.	Christian Doppler *d.*
1853	13 Apr.	Leopold Gmelin *d.*
1853	15 Apr.	Auguste Laurent *d.*
1853	25 Apr.	William Beaumont *d.*
1853	4 July	Ernst Otto Beckman *b.*
1853	18 July	Hendrik Antoon Lorentz *b.*
1853	21 Aug.	Sir Henry Wellcome *b.*
1853	2 Sept.	Friedrich Wilhelm Ostwald *b.*
1853	13 Sept.	Hans Christian Joachim Gram *b.*
1853	16 Sept.	Albrecht Kossel *b.*
1853	21 Sept.	Kamerlingh Heike Onnes *b.*
1853	2 Oct.	Dominique François Jean Arago *d.*
1853	17 Dec.	Pierre Paul Émile Roux *b.*
1854		J. Carroll† *b.*
1854		Dugald Clerk† *b.*
1854		George Eastman† *b.*
1854		Friedrich Krupp† *b.*
1854		Phoebe Marks† *b.*
1854		M. Mellomi† *d.*
1854		Friedrich Neelsen† *b.*
1854		Max Rubner† *b.*

1854		H. W. F. Wackenroder d.
1854		N. Wallich† d.
1854		H. Marshall Ward† b.
1854		Thomas Watson† b.
1854	4 Mar.	Sir William Napier Shaw b.
1854	14 Mar.	Paul Ehrlich b.
1854	15 Mar.	Emil Adolf von Behring b.
1854	27 Mar.	Giovanni Battista Grassi b.
1854	29 Apr.	Henri Poincaré b.
1854	11 May	Ottmar Mergenthaler b.
1854	13 June	Sir Charles Algernon Parsons b.
1854	7 July	Georg Simon Ohm d.
1854	3 Oct.	William Crawford Gorgas b.
1854	3 Nov.	Jokichi Takamine b.
1854	5 Nov.	Paul Sabatier b.
1854	8 Nov.	Johannes Robert Rydberg b.
1855		Christian Bohr† b.
1855		Julius Bredt† b.
1855		Leopold Crelle† d.
1855		G. L. Duvernoy† d.
1855		J. Gibson† b.
1855		H. Kiliani† b.
1855		Sir William Parry† d.
1855	23 Feb.	Karl Friederich Gauss d.
1855	27 Feb.	Bryan Donkin d.
1855	13 Mar.	Percival Lowell b.
1855	15 Mar.	Sir Charles Vernon Boys b.
1855	13 Apr.	Sir Henry Thomas De la Beche d.
1855	29 May	Sir David Bruce b.
1855	7 Sept.	William Friese-Greene b.
1855	7 Oct.	François Magendie d.
1855	4 Nov.	Frederick Orpen Bower b.
1855	11 Dec.	Charles Frederick Cross b.
1856		William Buckland† d.
1856		Hugh Miller† d.
1856		J. E. W. Peary† b.
1856		C. L. Reimer† b.
1856		Sir John Ross† d.
1856		A. D. Waller† b.
1856		J. C. Warren† d.
1856	27 Jan.	Jean-Baptiste Senderens (The Abbé) b.
1856	17 Feb.	Agostino Bassi d.
1856	18 Feb.	Russell Henry Chittenden b.
1856	24 Feb.	Nikola Ivanovich Lobachevski d.
1856	9 Mar.	Edward Goodrich Acheson b.
1856	6 May	Sigmund Freud b.
1856	13 May	Reinhard Mannesmann b.
1856	9 July	Amedeo Avogadro d.
1856	19 Aug.	Charles Frédéric Gerhardt d.
1856	24 Oct.	Henrik Willem Bakhuis Roozeboom b.
1856	11 Dec.	Edward John Bevan b.
1856	18 Dec.	Sir Joseph John Thomson b.
1857		J. J. Abel† b.
1857		E. Bamberger† b.
1857		A. M. F. X. Comte† d.
1857		T. C. Curtius† b.
1857		A. Einhorn† b.
1857		Victor Horsley† b.
1857		John Joly b.
1857		Karl Pearson† b.
1857		K. Tsiolkovskii b.
1857		Franz Ziehl† b.
1857	2 Jan.	Andrew Ure d.
1857	23 Jan.	Andrija Mohorovičić b.
1857	22 Feb.	Heinrich Rudolph Hertz b.
1857	7 Mar.	Arthur Rudolf Hantzsch b.
1857	2 May	Frederick Scott Archer d.
1857	13 May	Sir Ronald Ross b.
1857	23 May	Augustin Louis Cauchy d.
1857	5 July	Andrew Ellicott Douglass b.
1857	8 July	Alfred Binet b.
1857	21 June	Louis Jacques Thenard d.

1857	12 July	Amé Pictet b.
1857	11 Aug.	Marshall Hall d.
1857	10 Sept.	James Edward Keeler b.
1857	15 Nov.	Sir Archibald Garrod b.
1857	27 Nov.	Sir Charles Scott Sherrington b.
1857	3 Dec.	Carl Koller b.
1857	15 Dec.	Sir George Cayley d.
1858		A. J. A. Bonpland† d.
1858		Robert Brown† d.
1858		P. F. Frankland† b.
1858		H. A. Kelly† b.
1858		R. H. A. Kohlrausch† d.
1858		Sir Henry Miers† b.
1858		George Peacock† d.
1858		G. Peano† b.
1858		Edward Pease† d.
1858		M. M. Pontin† d.
1858	15 Feb.	William Henry Pickering b.
1858	28 Feb.	Sir James Swinburne b.
1858	18 Mar.	Rudolf Diesel b.
1858	27 Mar.	Richard Friedrich Johannes Pfeiffer b.
1858	23 Apr.	Max Carl Ernst Ludwig Planck b.
1858	28 Apr.	Johannes Peter Müller d.
1858	15 May	Robert Hare d.
1858	10 June	Robert Brown d.
1858	31 July	Robert Dixon Oldham b.
1858	11 Aug.	Christiaan Eijkman b.
1858	1 Sept.	Baron Carl Auer von Welsbach b.
1858	11 Sept.	Hamilton Young Castner b.
1858	2 Oct.	Gerard Jacob de Geer b.
1858	15 Oct.	Carl Gustav Mosander d.
1858	11 Nov.	Hugh Lee Pattinson d.
1858	18 Nov.	Sir Robert Abbott Hadfield b.
1858	16 Dec.	Richard Bright d.
1859		Florian Cajori† b.
1859		Edmund Husserl† b.
1859		H. Jacobson† b.
1859		P. G. Lejeune Dirichlet† d.
1859		Cyrus Hall McCormick jr.† b.
1859		Oskar Minkowski† b.
1859		Ernst Pringsheim b.
1859		Alfred Vail† d.
1859	19 Feb.	Svante August Arrhenius b.
1859	10 Mar.	Alexander Monro (tertius) d.
1859	1 May	John Walker d.
1859	6 May	Baron Friedrich von Humboldt d.
1859	15 May	Pierre Curie b.
1859	5 July	Cagn(i)ard de Latour d.
1859	31 July	Theobald Smith b.
1859	10 Sept.	David Talbot Day b.
1859	15 Sept.	Isambard Kingdom Brunel d.
1859	12 Oct.	Robert Stephenson d.
1860		A. M. C. Duméril† d.
1860		F. Emich† d.
1860		Paul Gottlieb Nipkow b.
1860		Curt Schimmelbusch† b.
1860		D'Arcy Thompson† b.
1860		Robert Bentley Todd† d.
1860		Vito Volterra† b.
1860		W. W. Watts† b.
1860	27 Jan.	Johann Bolyai d.
1860	29 Feb.	Herman Hollerith b.
1860	8 Apr.	Félix Dujardin d.
1860	20 Apr.	Ludwig Gattermann b.
1860	2 May	Sir William Maddock Bayliss b.
1860	3 May	John Scott Haldane b.
1860	20 May	Eduard Buchner b.
1860	21 May	Willem Einthoven b.
1860	17 June	William Henry Perkin, jun. b.
1860	29 June	Thomas Addison d.
1860	1 July	Charles Goodyear d.
1860	17 July	Otto Lummer b.
1860	12 Oct.	Elmer Ambrose Sperry b.

1861		A. van Gehuchten† b.
1861		James Herrick† b.
1861		Joseph Maudslay† d.
1861		A. G. Perkin† b.
1861		F. Tiedemann† d.
1861		Sir Almroth Wright† b.
1861	18 Jan.	John Heathcote d.
1861	18 Jan.	Johann (Hans) Wilhelm Goldschmidt b.
1861	15 Feb.	Alfred North Whitehead b.
1861	15 Feb.	Charles Edouard Guillaume b.
1861	8 Apr.	Elisha Graves Otis d.
1861	18 June	Eaton Hodgkinson d.
1861	20 June	Sir Frederick Gowland Hopkins b.
1861	8 Aug.	William Bateson b.
1861	10 Oct.	Fridtjof Nansen b.
1861	17 Dec.	Arthur Edwin Kennelly b.
1862		Amico Bignami† b.
1862		V. F. K. Bjerknes† b.
1862		Giuseppe Bastianelli† b.
1862		W. Lee Dickinson† b.
1862		P. A. Guye† b.
1862		D. Hilbert† b.
1862		G. H. F. Nuttall† b.
1862		Sir James Ross† d.
1862		James Lorrain Smith† b.
1862	10 Jan.	Samuel Colt d.
1862	3 Feb.	Jean Baptiste Biot d.
1862	5 June	Allvar Gullstrand b.
1862	7 June	Philipp Eduard Anton Lenard b.
1862	21 June	Charles Ellet d.
1862	2 July	Sir William Henry Bragg b.
1862	30 Aug.	Charles Bernard Désormes d.
1862	12 Oct.	Theodor Boveri b.
1862	19 Oct.	Auguste Lumière b.
1862	21 Oct.	Sir Benjamin Collins Brodie d.
1863		Charles Donovan† b.
1863		P. K. L. Drude b.
1863		Wilhelm His† b.
1863		F. A. Janssens† b.
1863		L. Péan de Saint-Gilles† d.
1863		A. C. Seward† b.
1863		J. Steiner† d.
1863		Alexandre Yersin† b.
1863	6 Apr.	Sir James Walker b.
1863	10 Apr.	Giovanni Batista Amici d.
1863	10 Apr.	Paul Louis Toussaint Héroult b.
1863	21 June	Max Wolf b.
1863	12 July	L. C. A. Calmette b.
1863	26 July	Paul Walden b.
1863	30 July	Henry Ford b.
1863	16 Aug.	Frederic Stanley Kipping b.
1863	28 Aug.	Eilhard Mitscherlich d.
1863	18 Oct.	Alan Archibald Campbell Swinton b.
1863	14 Nov.	Leo Hendrik Baekeland b.
1863	6 Dec.	Charles Martin Hall b.
1863	15 Dec.	Arthur Dehon Little b.
1864		C. J. Brianchon† d.
1864		B. P. E. Clapeyron† d.
1864		K. E. Correns† b.
1864		A. D. Hall† b.
1864		Leonard Horner† d.
1864		K. K. Klaus† d.
1864		Thomas Henry Maudslay† d.
1864		F. W. Oliver† b.
1864		H. Rose† d.
1864		Lucas Schönlein† d.
1864		L. F. Wilhelmy† d.
1864	13 Jan.	Wilhelm Wien b.
1864	16 Mar.	Richard Roberts d.
1864	17 Mar.	Friedrich Wilhelm Bessel d.
1864	9 Apr.	Sebastian Ziani de Ferranti b.
1864	22 June	Hermann Minkowski b.
1864	25 June	Hermann Walther Nernst b.
1864	5 Oct.	Louis Lumière b.
1864	23 Nov.	Friedrich Georg Wilhelm Struve d.
1864	24 Nov.	Benjamin Silliman d.
1864	8 Dec.	George Boole d.
1865		J. F. Encke† d.
1865		C. D. Harries† b.
1865		Nathaniel Hayward† d.
1865		Sir William J. Hooker† d.
1865		John Hutchinson† d.
1865		George Redmayne Murray† b.
1865		J. B. Neilson† d.
1865		F. Paschen† b.
1865		R. Piria† d.
1865		H. Rubens† b.
1865		G. Sanarelli† b.
1865		A. Valenciennes† d.
1865		Pierre Weiss† b.
1865	10 Feb.	Heinrich Friedrich Emil Lenz d.
1865	26 Mar.	Thomas Hancock d.
1865	1 Apr.	Richard Adolf Zsigmondy b.
1865	25 May	Pieter Zeeman b.
1865	13 Aug.	Ignaz Philipp Semmelweis d.
1865	29 Aug.	Robert Remak d.
1865	2 Sept.	Sir William Rowan Hamilton d.
1865	22 Sept.	George Richards Elkington d.
1865	12 Oct.	Sir Arthur Harden b.
1865	6 Nov.	Sir William Boog Leishman b.
1866		L. Cuénot† b.
1866		A. Hutchinson† b.
1866		J. W. Lazear† b.
1866		F. Swarts† b.
1866		William Whewell† d.
1866	10 Jan.	Karl Albert Ludwig Aschoff b.
1866	5 Feb.	Sir Arthur Keith b.
1866	15 Feb.	Graham Lusk b.
1866	21 Feb.	August von Wassermann b.
1866	7 Apr.	Eric Ivar Fredholm b.
1866	17 Apr.	Ernest Henry Starling b.
1866	20 July	Georg Friedrich Bernhard Riemann d.
1866	21 Sept.	Charles Jules Henri Nicolle b.
1866	25 Sept.	Thomas Hunt Morgan b.
1866	6 Oct.	Reginald Aubrey Fessenden b.
1866	29 Oct.	Samuel Eyde b.
1866	30 Nov.	Robert Broom b.
1866	30 Nov.	John Mercer d.
1866	1 Dec.	William Cotton d.
1866	12 Dec.	Alfred Werner b.
1867		William Bullock† d.
1867		J. Goodsir† d.
1867		G. Komppa† b.
1867		P. F. O. Rayner† d.
1867		Lord Rosse† d.
1867		Julius Ruska† b.
1867		Sir James South† d.
1867		A. Trousseau† d.
1867		H. A. Vogel† d.
1867		Robert Warington† d.
1867	25 Mar.	Friedlieb Ferdinand Runge d.
1867	16 Apr.	Wilbur Wright b.
1867	23 Apr.	Johannes Andreas Grib Fibiger b.
1867	31 July	Benoit Fourneyron d.
1867	25 Aug.	Michael Faraday d.
1867	3 Oct.	Elias Howe d.
1867	28 Oct.	Hans Adolf Eduard Driesch b.
1867	7 Nov.	Marie Curie b.
1867	21 Nov.	Vladimir Nikolaievich Ipatieff b.
1867	8 Dec.	Jean Pierre Marie Flourens d.
1867	13 Dec.	Kristian Olaf Bernhard Birkeland b.
1867	22 Dec.	Jean Victor Poncelet d.
1868		William Bullock† b.
1868		J. D. Forbes† d.
1868		W. Garstang† b.
1868		Paul Erich Hoffmann† b.

1868		Wilhelm Kolle† b.
1868		C. F. P. von Martius† d.
1868		Felix Mesnil† b.
1868		C. G. Page† d.
1868		Theodore William Richards b.
1868		George Smith† d.
1868	8 Jan.	Sir Frank Watson Dyson b.
1868	9 Jan.	Sören Peter Lauritz Sörensen b.
1868	10 Feb.	Sir David Brewster d.
1868	11 Feb.	Léon Foucault d.
1868	22 Mar.	Robert Andrews Millikan b.
1868	2 May	Robert Williams Wood b.
1868	22 May	Julius Plücker d.
1868	7 June	Sir John Sealy Edward Townsend b.
1868	14 June	Karl Landsteiner b.
1868	29 June	George Ellery Hale b.
1868	4 July	Henrietta Swan Leavitt b.
1868	15 July	William Thomas Green Morton d.
1868	29 Aug.	Christian Frederick Schönbein d.
1868	26 Sept.	August Ferdinand Mobius d.
1868	23 Oct.	Frederick William Lanchester b.
1868	5 Dec.	Arnold Sommerfeld b.
1868	9 Dec.	Fritz Haber b.
1869		Joseph Jackson Lister† d.
1869		Carl Reichenbach† d.
1869	9 Jan.	Richard Abegg b.
1869	14 Feb.	Charles Thomson Rees Wilson b.
1869	25 Feb.	Phoebus Aaron Theodor Levene b.
1869	8 Apr.	Harvey Cushing b.
1869	22 Apr.	Patrick Bell d.
1869	27 June	Hans Spemann b.
1869	28 July	Johannes Evangelista Purkinje d.
1869	3 Sept.	Fritz Pregl b.
1869	16 Sept.	Thomas Graham d.
1869	23 Nov.	Valdemar Poulsen b.
1870		Albrecht von Graefe† d.
1870		Johannes Lindhardt† b.
1870		H. G. Magnus† d.
1870		W. A. Miller† d.
1870		James Syme† d.
1870		A. Van den Broek† b.
1870	13 Jan.	Ross Granville Harrison b.
1870	7 Feb.	Alfred Adler b.
1870	31 Mar.	Sir William Jackson Pope b.
1870	6 May	Sir James Young Simpson d.
1870	13 June	Jules Jean Baptiste Vincent Bordet b.
1870	27 July	Bertram Borden Boltwood b.
1870	6 Sept.	Frederick George Donnan b.
1870	30 Sept.	Jean Baptiste Perrin b.
1870	7 Dec.	Joseph Edwin Barnard b.
1871		A Hagenbach† b.
1871		Oscar Heinroth† b.
1871		A. De Morgan† d.
1871		Julius Morgenroth† b.
1871		James Murray† d.
1871		Mervyn O'Gorman† b.
1871		Adolf Strecker† d.
1871		E. von Tschermak† b.
1871		Eduard Friedrich Weber† d.
1871	9 Feb.	Howard Taylor Ricketts b.
1871	18 Feb.	Harry Brearley b.
1871	1 Apr.	William Venables Vernon Harcourt d.
1871	6 May	François Auguste Victor Grignard b.
1871	11 May	Sir John Frederick William Herschel d.
1871	15 Aug.	Sir Arthur George Tansley b.
1871	19 Aug.	Orville Wright b.
1871	30 Aug.	Sir Ernest Rutherford (Lord Rutherford of Nelson) b.
1871	18 Oct.	Charles Babbage d.
1871	19 Oct.	Fritz Richard Schaudinn b.
1871	22 Oct.	Sir Roderick Impey Murchison d.
1872		Rudolph Clebsch† d.

1872		C. E. Delaunay† d.
1872		Camille Guérin† b.
1872		P. C. A. Louis† d.
1872		Lafayette Mendel† b.
1872		Hugo von Mohl† d.
1872		H. Moseley† d.
1872		William Pilkington† d.
1872		F. A. Pouchet d.
1872		Bertrand Russell† b.
1872		H. F. W. Siedentopf† b.
1872	23 Jan.	Paul Langevin b.
1872	24 Jan.	Morris William Travers b.
1872	2 Apr.	Samuel Finley Breese Morse d.
1872	12 Apr.	Georges Urbain b.
1872	19 May	Michel Tswett b.
1872	16 July	Roald Engelbregt Gravning Amundsen b.
1872	26 July	Sir Joseph Barcroft b.
1872	13 Aug.	Richard Willstätter b.
1872	10 Oct.	Arthur Lapworth b.
1872	31 Oct.	Sir Edward John Russell b.
1872	24 Dec.	William John Macquorn Rankine d.
1873		Andrew Balfour† b.
1873		Claude Burdin† d.
1873		Constantin Caratheodory† b.
1873		G. B. Donati† d.
1873		C. Dupin† d.
1873		B. F. Duppa† d.
1873		Hans von Euler-Cheplin† b.
1873		W. Morley Fletcher† b.
1873		O. Foerster† b.
1873		John Stuart Mill† d.
1873		A. A. de la Rive† d.
1873		G. Rose† d.
1873		John Torrey† d.
1873		Alberto Santos Dumont b.
1873	27 Jan.	Adam Sedgwick d.
1873	1 Feb.	Matthew Fontaine Maury d.
1873	18 Apr.	Baron Justus von Liebig d.
1873	8 May	Nevil Vincent Sidgwick b.
1873	21 May	Hans Berger b.
1873	3 June	Otto Loewi b.
1873	28 June	Alexis Carrel b.
1873	26 Aug.	Lee de Forest b.
1873	23 Oct.	William David Coolidge b.
1873	24 Oct.	Sir Edmund Taylor Whittaker b.
1873	18 Dec.	Jean Louis Rodolphe Agassiz d.
1873	27 Dec.	Otto Unverdorben d.
1874		John Bachman† d.
1874		W. Buckland† d.
1874		Jean Cruveilhier† d.
1874		A. Debierne† b.
1874		Moritz Jacobi† d.
1874		F. Hasenöhrl† b.
1874		Herbert C. Hoover† b.
1874		B. Hopkinson† b.
1874		Edwin Lankester† d.
1874		F. Rochleder† d.
1874		The Svedberg† b.
1874	5 Jan.	Joseph Erlanger b.
1874	16 Jan.	Max Johann Sigismund Schultze d.
1874	15 Apr.	Johannes Stark b.
1874	25 Apr.	Guglielmo Marconi b.
1874	28 May	Sir Rowland Harry Biffen b.
1874	21 June	Anders Jonas Ångström d.
1874	18 Aug.	Sir William Fairbairn d.
1874	27 Aug.	Carl Bosch b.
1874	7 Sept.	Cyril Henry Desch b.
1874	26 Oct.	Thomas Martin Lowry b.
1874	2 Nov.	Thomas Anderson d.
1874	9 Nov.	Albert Francis Blakeslee b.
1874	13 Nov.	Riko Majima b.
1874	15 Nov.	Schack August Steenberg Krogh b.
1874	23 Nov.	Theodore Lyman b.

1874	29 Nov.	Antonio Egas Moniz b.
1875		J. N. Demarquay† d.
1875		G. B. A. Duchenne de Boulogne† d.
1875		Henri Dufour† d.
1875		Reginald C. Punnett† b.
1875		W. Wilson† b.
1875	22 Feb.	Sir Charles Lyell d.
1875	24 Feb.	Marc Seguin d.
1875	11 Apr.	Samuel Heinrich Schwabe d.
1875	15 Apr.	Anton Schrötter d.
1875	9 June	Sir Henry Hallett Dale b.
1875	9 July	Nikola Tesla b.
1875	23 July	Isaac Merrit Singer d.
1875	26 July	Carl Gustav Jung b.
1875	23 Aug.	William Henry Eccles b.
1875	19 Oct.	Sir Charles Wheatstone d.
1875	25 Oct.	Gilbert Newton Lewis b.
1875	27 Nov.	Richard Christopher Carrington d.
1876		W. S. Adams† b.
1876		A. T. Brogniart† d.
1876		Charles Kettering† b
1876		Charles Manley† b.
1876		A. N. Richards† b.
1876		Charles Singer† b.
1876		Ludwig Traube† d.
1876	23 Jan.	Otto Diels b.
1876	30 Mar.	Antoine Jerome Balard d.
1876	22 Apr.	Robert Bárány b.
1876	27 June	Christian Gottfried Ehrenberg d.
1876	23 July	Henry Deacon d.
1876	6 Sept.	John James Rickard Macleod b.
1876	28 Nov.	Karl Ernst von Baer d.
1876	20 Dec.	Walter Sydney Adams b.
1876	25 Dec.	Adolf Windaus b.
1877		T. R. Elliott† b.
1877		H. G. Grassmann† d.
1877		G. H. Hardy† b.
1877		E. Landau† b.
1877		Sir Robert Whytlaw-Gray† b.
1877	12 Jan.	Wilhelm Friedrich Benedict Hofmeister d.
1877	22 Jan.	Ernst Johannes Schmidt b.
1877	24 Jan.	Johann Christian Poggendorf d.
1877	9 Apr.	William Gossage d.
1877	5 May	Joseph Bienaimé Caventou d.
1877	9 May	James Colquhoun Irvine b.
1877	4 June	Heinrich Wieland b.
1877	27 June	Charles Glover Barkla b.
1877	29 July	Charles William Beebe b.
1877	1 Sept.	Francis William Aston b.
1877	2 Sept.	Frederick Soddy b.
1877	11 Sept.	Sir James Hopwood Jeans b.
1877	17 Sept.	William Henry Fox Talbot d.
1877	23 Sept.	Urbain Jean Joseph Le Verrier d.
1877	21 Oct.	Oswald Theodore Avery b.
1877	22 Oct.	Frederick William Twort b.
1877	19 Nov.	James Batcheller Sumner b.
1877	20 Dec.	Heinrich Daniel Rühmkorff d.
1878		E. F. Armstrong† b.
1878		G. P. Bidder† d.
1878		C. A. Lamy† d.
1878		G. H. Lewes† d.
1878		Crawford W. Long† d.
1878		Thomas Oldham† d.
1878		Ernst Heinrich Weber† d.
1878		W. J. Young† b.
1878	19 Jan.	Henri Victor Regnault d.
1878	8 Feb.	Elias Magnus Fries d.
1878	10 Feb.	Claude Bernard d.
1878	14 Feb.	Julius Arthur Nieuwland b.
1878	26 Feb.	Angelo Secchi d.
1878	20 Mar.	Julius Robert von Mayer d.
1878	4 Apr.	George Barger b.
1878	13 May	Joseph Henry d.
1878	6 June	Robert Stirling d.
1878	23 July	Karl Rokitansky d.
1878	28 Aug.	George Hoyt Whipple b.
1878	2 Sept.	Sir George Clarke Simpson b.
1878	7 Nov.	Lise Meitner b.
1879		Franz Boll† d.
1879		H. Geissler† d.
1879		A. K. Krönig† d.
1879		J. Lamont† d.
1879		Keith Lucas† b.
1879		Sir Francis Smith† d.
1879	22 Feb.	Johannes Nicolaus Brønsted b.
1879	8 Mar.	Otto Hahn b.
1879	14 Mar.	Albert Einstein b.
1879	30 Mar.	Bernhard Voldemar Schmidt b.
1879	25 June	Sir William Fothergill Cooke d.
1879	13 July	M. E. L. Freyssinet b.
1879	5 Oct.	Francis Peyton Rous b.
1879	9 Oct.	Max Theodor Felix von Laue b.
1879	5 Nov.	James Clerk Maxwell d.
1879	6 Dec.	Erastus Bingham Bigelow d.
1880		S. S. Chetverikov† b.
1880		P. Ehrenfest† b.
1880		M. A. A. Gaudin† d.
1880		F. Hebra† d.
1880		C. T. Jackson† d.
1880		Abram Joffe† b.
1880		Sir John MacNeill† d.
1880		John Gillies Priestley† b.
1880		Alexis St Martin† d.
1880		William Sharpey† d.
1880		J. Stenhouse† d.
1880		N. N. Zinin† d.
1880	28 Jan.	Herbert Max Finlay Freundlich b.
1880	19 Apr.	A. W. Hull b.
1880	31 May	Hippolyte Mège Mouriés d.
1880	24 June	Jules Antoine Lissajous d.
1880	9 July	Pierre Paul Broca d.
1880	1 Nov.	Alfred Lothar Wegener b.
1880	3 Nov.	Edwin Laurentine Drake d.
1881		J. B. Bouillaud† d.
1881		Clinton Joseph Davisson† b.
1881		Edward Charles Edgar† d.
1881		W. R. Hesse† b.
1881		P. P. Laidlaw† d.
1881		T. Lewis† b.
1881		Humphrey Lloyd† d.
1881		Sir Josiah Mason† d.
1881		J. Skoda† d.
1881		A. M. Tyndall† b.
1881		Theodor von Karman† b.
1881		E. W. Washburn† b.
1881	8 Jan.	John McNaught d.
1881	31 Jan.	Irving Langmuir b.
1881	3 Feb.	John Gould d.
1881	27 Feb.	Luitzen Egbertus Jan Brouwer b.
1881	23 Mar.	Hermann Staudinger b.
1881	5 June	Axel Leonard Wenner-Gren b.
1881	23 June	Matthias Jakob Schleiden d.
1881	1 July	Henri Etienne Sainte-Claire Deville d.
1881	27 July	Hans Fischer b.
1881	6 Aug.	Sir Alexander Fleming b.
1881	18 Sept.	David Alter d.
1882		James Challis† d.
1882		J. Clay† b.
1882		Sir John Anderson† b.
1882		Harold Delos Babcock† b.
1882		E. F. DuBois† b.
1882		Martin Flack† d.
1882		Pio del Rio-Hortega† b.
1882		J. Timmermanns† b.
1882		Lord Waverley† b.
1882	4 Jan.	John William Draper d.

1882	11 Jan.	Theodor Schwann d.
1882	3 Feb.	Arthur James Ewins b.
1882	10 Mar.	Sir Charles Wyville Thomson d.
1882	14 Apr.	Henri Giffard d.
1882	19 Apr.	Charles Robert Darwin d.
1882	21 Apr.	Percy Williams Bridgman b.
1882	July	Francis Maitland Balfour d.
1882	27 July	Sir Geoffrey de Havilland b.
1882	26 Aug.	James Franck b.
1882	14 Sept.	Georges Leclanché d.
1882	23 Sept.	Friedrich Wöhler d.
1882	30 Sept.	Hans Wilhelm Geiger b.
1882	5 Oct.	Robert Hutchings Goddard b.
1882	14 Oct.	Gasimir Joseph Davaine d.
1882	11 Dec.	Max Born b.
1882	28 Dec.	Sir Arthur Stanley Eddington b.
1883		L. F. C. Breguet† d.
1883		Edward Filhol† b.
1883		W. Friedrich† b.
1883		L. D. Gale† d.
1883		Wolfgang Ostwald† b.
1883		R. Robison† b.
1883		Hermann Stannius† d.
1883		G. G. Valentin† d.
1883	9 Feb.	Henry John Stephen Smith d.
1883	19 Mar.	Sir Walter Norman Haworth b.
1883	13 May	James Young d.
1883	26 May	Sir Edward Sabine d.
1883	18 June	John James Waterston d.
1883	24 June	Victor Francis Hess b.
1883	5 July	Peter Spence d.
1883	8 Oct.	Otto Heinrich Warburg b.
1883	19 Nov.	Sir Charles William Siemens d.
1884		G. H. Bissell† d.
1884		H. R. Goeppert† d.
1884		Arnold Henry Guyott† d.
1884		Jacob Henle† d.
1884		G. L. Y. Ingram† b.
1884		Simeon North† d.
1884		J. Read† b.
1884		K. B. Reichert† d.
1884	6 Jan.	Johann Gregor Mendel d.
1884	28 Jan.	Auguste Piccard b.
1884	24 Mar.	Petrus (Pieter) Josephus Wilhelmus Debye b.
1884	8 Apr.	Sir Edward Mellanby b.
1884	10 Apr.	Otto Fritz Meyerhof b.
1884	11 Apr.	Jean Baptiste André Dumas d.
1884	12 May	Charles-Adolphe Wurtz d.
1884	13 May	Cyrus Hall McCormick d.
1884	15 Aug.	Julius Cohnheim d.
1884	10 Sept.	George Bentham d.
1884	11 Oct.	Friedrich Bergius b.
1884	25 Oct.	Motonori Matsuyama b.
1884	25 Nov.	Adolph Wilhelm Hermann Kolbe d.
1885		F. T. von Frerichs† d.
1885		J. M. Riggs† d.
1885		Benjamin Silliman, jun.† d.
1885		H. Weyl† b.
1885	26 Jan.	Harry Ralph Ricardo b.
1885	1 Feb.	Sidney Gilchrist Thomas d.
1885	7 Apr.	Carl Theodor Ernst von Siebold d.
1885	1 Aug.	Georg von Hevesy b.
1885	23 Aug.	Sir Henry Thomas Tizard b.
1885	20 Sept.	Walter Weldon d.
1885	7 Oct.	Niels Bohr b.
1885	26 Nov.	Thomas Andrews d.
1885	2 Dec.	George Richards Minot b.
1886		M. Bergmann† b.
1886		W. Dandy† b.
1886		F. Guthrie† d.
1886		J. C. Jamin† d.
1886		John Maclean† d.
1886		D. R. Pye† b.
1886	5 Apr.	Frederick Alexander Lindemann (Viscount Cherwell) b.
1886	22 Apr.	Thomas Percy Hilditch b.
1886	4 May	James Muspratt d.
1886	7 May	Timothy Richards Lewis d.
1886	7 June	Richard March Hoe d.
1886	20 June	James Riddick Partington b.
1886	17 Aug.	Aleksandr Mikhailovich Butlerov d.
1886	13 Sept.	Sir Robert Robinson b.
1886	26 Sept.	Archibald Vivian Hill b.
1886	6 Nov.	Sir Ian Morris Heilbron b.
1886	11 Nov.	Paul Bert d.
1886	20 Nov.	K. R. von Frisch b.
1886	3 Dec.	Karl Manne Georg Siegbahn b.
1886	9 Dec.	Clarence Birdseye b.
1887		A. G. Clark† d.
1887		Sir Charles Galton Darwin b.
1887		H. W. Dudley b.
1887		Kasimir Fajans† b.
1887		C. Friedlander† d.
1887		J. S. Huxley† b.
1887		Leopold Ruzicka† b.
1887		Balfour Stewart† d.
1887		John Batcheller Sumner† b.
1887		E. F. A. Vulpian† d.
1887	22 Jan.	Sir Joseph Whitworth d.
1887	8 Mar.	James Buchanan Eads d.
1887	21 Mar.	David Keilin b.
1887	10 Apr.	Bernard A. Houssay b.
1887	11 May	Jean-Baptiste Joseph Dieudonné Boussingault d.
1887	14 July	Alfred Krupp d.
1887	22 July	Gustav Ludwig Hertz b.
1887	30 July	Felix Andries Vening Meinesz b.
1887	12 Aug.	Erwin Schrödinger b.
1887	19 Aug.	Spencer Fullerton Baird d.
1887	31 Aug.	Friedrich Adolf Paneth b.
1887	17 Oct.	Gustav Robert Kirchhoff d.
1887	26 Sept.	Barnes Neville Wallis b.
1887	23 Nov.	Henry Gwyn Jeffreys Moseley b.
1887	26 Nov.	Nikolai Ivanovitch Vavilov b.
1888		Henri Jules Debray† d.
1888		E. Edlund† d.
1888		W. S. Henson† d.
1888		Walter Kossel† b.
1888	27 Jan.	Victor M. Goldschmidt b.
1888	30 Jan.	Asa Gray d.
1888	11 Feb.	William Kelly d.
1888	17 Feb.	Otto Stern b.
1888	21 Feb.	George Henry Corliss d.
1888	16 Apr.	Zygmunt Florenty von Wróblewski d.
1888	26 May	Ascanio Sobrero d.
1888	5 July	Herbert Spencer Gasser b.
1888	16 July	Fritz Zernike b.
1888	22 July	Selman Abraham Waksman b.
1888	13 Aug.	John Logie Baird b.
1888	24 Aug.	Rudolf Julius Emmanuel Clausius d.
1888	30 Aug.	Peter Johann Griess d.
1888	9 Sept.	Sir Alan Wallace Akers b.
1888	29 Oct.	Andrei Nikolaevich Tupolev b.
1888	7 Nov.	Sir Chandrasekhara Venkata Raman b.
1889		C. B. Bridges b.
1889		J. B. M. Bucquett† d.
1889		Ralph Howard Fowler† b.
1889		Walther Gerlach† b.
1889		John Percy† d.
1889		John Alfred Ryle† b.
1889	8 Apr.	Michel Eugène Chevreul d.
1889	19 Apr.	Warren De La Rue d.
1889	21 Apr.	Paul Karrer b.
1889	18 May	Thomas Midgley b.
1889	25 May	Igor I. Sikorsky b.

1889	30 July	Vladimir K. Zworykin *b.*
1889	11 Oct.	James Prescott Joule *d.*
1889	20 Nov.	Edwin Powell Hubble *b.*
1889	30 Nov.	Edgar Douglas Adrian (Baron Adrian of Cambridge) *b.*
1889	22 Dec.	Srinivasa Ramanujan *b.*
1890		J. G. Halske† *d.*
1890		Y. Nishina† *b.*
1890		J. M. Nuttall† *b.*
1890		John Rock† *b.*
1890		Paul Scherrer† *b.*
1890		H. Schliemann† *d.*
1890		H. Will† *d.*
1890	14 Jan.	Arthur Holmes *b.*
1890	16 Feb.	Sir Robert John Kane *d.*
1890	17 Feb.	Sir Ronald Aylmer Fisher *b.*
1890	11 Mar.	Vannevar Bush *b.*
1890	29 Mar.	Sir Harold Spencer Jones *b.*
1890	31 Mar.	Sir William Lawrence Bragg *b.*
1890	15 Apr.	Eugène Melchior Péligot *d.*
1890	7 May	James Nasmyth *d.*
1890	29 June	Alexander Parkes *d.*
1890	18 Dec.	E. H. Armstrong *b.*
1890	20 Dec.	Jaroslav Heyrovsky *b.*
1890	21 Dec.	Hermann Joseph Muller *b.*
1891		Walther Bothe† *b*
1891		A. A. T. Cahours† *d.*
1891		Edmond Becquerel† *d.*
1891		E. J. Holmyard† *b.*
1891		L. Kronecker† *d.*
1891		H. N. Moseley† *d.*
1891		Sir Andrew Ramsay† *d.*
1891	19 Jan.	Robert Forester Mushet *d.*
1891	26 Jan.	Nikolaus August Otto *d.*
1891	26 Jan.	Wilder Graves Penfield *b.*
1891	15 Mar.	Sir Joseph William Bazalgette *d.*
1891	10 May	Karl Wilhelm von Nägeli *d.*
1891	23 June	Wilhelm Eduard Weber *d.*
1891	5 July	J. H. Northrop *b.*
1891	20 Oct.	Sir James Chadwick *b.*
1891	14 Nov.	Sir Frederick Grant Banting *b.*
1891	21 Nov.	A. H. Sturtevant *b.*
1891	13 Dec.	Jean Servais Stas *d.*
1892		Sir George Airy† *d.*
1892		C. W. Field† *d.*
1892		W. P. Murphy† *b.*
1892		C. W. Schorlemmer† *d.*
1892		Samuel Sugden *b.*
1892		E. W. Von Brücke† *d.*
1892	21 Jan.	John C. Adams *d.*
1892	16 Feb.	Henry Walter Bates *d.*
1892	20 Feb.	Hermann Franz Moritz Kopp *d.*
1892	29 Mar.	Sir William Bowman *d.*
1892	18 Apr.	E. J. Houdry *b.*
1892	3 May	Sir George Thomson *b.*
1892	2 May	August Wilhelm (von) Hofmann *d.*
1892	8 May	James Thomson *d.*
1892	15 Aug.	Louis de Broglie *b.*
1892	6 Sept.	Sir Edward Victor Appleton *b.*
1892	10 Sept.	Arthur Holly Compton *b.*
1892	6 Oct.	Jean Antoine Villemin *d.*
1892	5 Nov.	John Burdon Sanderson Haldane *b.*
1892	6 Dec.	Ernst Werner von Siemens *d.*
1892	18 Dec.	Sir Richard Owen *d.*
1893		Alphonse de Candolle† *d.*
1893(?)		S. A. E. Aubertin† *d.*
1893		Benjamin Jowett† *d.*
1893		Alphonse Beau de Rochas† *d.*
1893	7 Jan.	Joseph Stefan *d.*
1893	4 Feb.	Raymond Dart *b.*
1893	24 Mar.	W. H. W. Baade *b.*
1893	29 Apr.	Harold Clayton Urey *b.*
1893	28 May	Charles Pritchard *d.*
1893	2 July	Sir Francis Eugene (Franz Eugen) Simon *b.*
1893	16 Aug.	Jean-Martin Charcot *d.*
1893	16 Sept.	Albert von Szent-Györgyi *b.*
1893	6 Oct.	Meghnad Saha *b.*
1893	13 Nov.	Edward A. Doisy *b.*
1893	4 Dec.	John Tyndall *d.*
1894		Theodor Billroth† *d.*
1894		Joseph Bancroft† *d.*
1894		Satyendra Nath Bose *b.*
1894		J. P. Cooke† *d.*
1894		Edmond Frémy† *d.*
1894		Pavel Nikolaievitch Jablochkoff *d.*
1894		Oskar B. Klein† *b.*
1894		Hendrik A. Kramers† *b.*
1894		A. E. E. Kundt† *d.*
1894		Friedrich Neelsen† *d.*
1894		Hermann Oberth† *b.*
1894		Warren Weaver† *b.*
1894	1 Jan.	Heinrich Rudolph Hertz *d.*
1894	1 Apr.	Charles Edouard Brown-Séquard *d.*
1894	15 Apr.	Jean Charles Galissard de Marignac *d.*
1894	28 June	Moritz Traube *d.*
1894	8 July	Piotr L. Kapitza *b.*
1894	17 July	Georges Lemaître *b.*
1894	8 Sept.	Hermann Ludwig Ferdinand von Helmholtz *d.*
1894	7 Oct.	Oliver Wendell Holmes *d.*
1894	26 Nov.	Norbert Wiener *b.*
1894	29 Nov.	Svend Foyn *d.*
1894	7 Dec.	Vicomte Ferdinand Marie de Lesseps *d.*
1895		Curt Schimmelbusch† *d.*
1895		Igor Tamm† *b.*
1895	26 Jan.	Arthur Cayley *d.*
1895	21 Feb.	Carl Peter Henrik Dam† *b.*
1895	11 Apr.	Julius Lothar Meyer *d.*
1895	23 Apr.	Karl Friedrich Wilhelm Ludwig *d.*
1895	12 May	William F. Giauque *b.*
1895	23 June	William Crawford Williamson *d.*
1895	29 June	Thomas Henry Huxley *d.*
1895	7 July	Gustav Friedrich Wilhelm Spörer *d.*
1895	10 Aug.	Ernst Felix Immanuel Hoppe-Seyler *d.*
1895	28 Sept.	Louis Pasteur *d.*
1895	6 Oct.	Nathanael Pringsheim *d.*
1895	30 Oct.	Gerhard Domagk *b.*
1896		Hugh Cairns† *b.*
1896		Lester H. Germer† *b.*
1896		Philip Showater Hench *b.*
1896	14 Feb.	Edward Arthur Milne *b.*
1896	8 Mar.	Edward C. Kendall *b.*
1896	27 Apr.	Wallace Hume Carothers *b.*
1896	13 July	Friedrich August Kekulé *d.*
1896	1 Aug.	Sir William Grove *d.*
1896	10 Aug.	Otto Lilienthal *d.*
1896	15 Aug.	Gerty Cori *b.*
1896	18 Sept.	Armand Hippolyte Louis Fizeau *d.*
1896	6 Oct.	Moritz Schiff *d.*
1896	5 Dec.	Carl Cori† *b.*
1896	10 Dec.	Alfred Bernhard Nobel *d.*
1896	26 Dec.	Emil du Bois Reymond *d.*
1897		D. W. Bronk† *b.*
1897		C. R. Harington† *b.*
1897		Odd Hassell† *b.*
1897		Isaac Holden† *d.*
1897		E. Levassor† *d.*
1897		Tadeus Reichstein† *b.*
1897		R. L. M. Synge† *b.*
1897	19 Feb.	Karl Wilhelm Theodor Weierstrass *d.*
1897	15 Mar.	James Joseph Sylvester *d.*
1897	27 May	Sir John Douglas Cockcroft *b.*
1897	29 May	Ferdinand Gustav Julius von Sachs *d.*
1897	19 June	Sir Cyril Norman Hinshelwood *b.*

1897	20 June	Johannes Japetus Smith Steenstrup d.
1897	7 July	Jacob Aall Bonnevie Bjerknes b.
1897	8 Aug.	Victor Meyer d.
1897	12 Sept.	Irène Joliot-Curie b.
1897	9 Nov.	Ronald George Wreyford Norrish b.
1897	17 Nov.	Patrick Maynard Stuart Blackett (Baron Blackett of Chelsea) b.
1898		E. L. Hirst† b.
1898		K. G. F. R. Leuckhart† d.
1898		F. Z. Zwicky† b.
1898	11 Feb.	Leo Szilard b.
1898	25 Feb.	William Thomas Astbury b.
1898	5 Mar.	Ferdinand Hurter d.
1898	15 Mar.	Sir Henry Bessemer d.
1898	29 May	Lyon Playfair (1st Baron Playfair) d.
1898	26 June	Ferdinand Julius Cohn d.
1898	29 July	John Alexander Reina Newlands d.
1898	29 July	Isidor Isaac Rabi b.
1898	6 Aug.	James Hall d.
1898	17 Sept.	Trofim Denisovich Lysenko b.
1898	24 Sept.	Howard Walter Florey (Baron Florey of Adelaide and Marston) b.
1898	11 Oct.	Hamilton Young Castner d.
1898	5 Nov.	Boris Petrovitch Uvarov b.
1898	20 Nov.	Sir John Fowler d.
1898	26 Nov.	Karl Ziegler b.
1898	17 Dec.	Hermann Wilhelm Vogel d.
1898	28 Dec.	Carl-Gustav Rossby b.
1899		L. F. Fieser† b.
1899		J. F. Fulton† b.
1899		Fritz Lipmann† b.
1899		L. F. Nilson† d.
1899		Gaston Tissandier† d.
1899		J. H. van Vleck† b.
1899		T. S. Wheeler† b.
1899		Joseph Wolff† d.
1899	18 Feb.	Marius Sophus Lie d.
1899	8 Mar.	John Ericsson d.
1899	2 Apr.	Robert (Robin) Hill b.
1899	15 Apr.	Clemens Heinrich Lambert von Babo d.
1899	19 Apr.	Charles Naudin d.
1899	20 Apr.	Charles Friedel d.
1899	14 May	Pierre Victor Auger b.
1899	14 July	Gregory Breit b.
1899	9 Aug.	Sir Edward Frankland d.
1899	16 Aug.	Robert Wilhelm Bunsen d.
1899	31 Aug.	Sir John Bennet Lawes d.
1899	3 Sept.	Sir Frank Macfarlane Burnet b.
1899	28 Oct.	Ottmar Mergenthaler d.
1899	14 Nov.	Johann Carl Wilhelm Ferdinand Tiemann d.
1900		Sir William Armstrong d.
1900		L. E. Grimaux† d.
1900		V. Hamburger† b.
1900		R Kuhn† b.
1900		J. W. Lazear† d.
1900	13 Jan.	Peter Waage d.
1900	25 Jan.	Theodosius Grigorievich Dobzhansky b.
1900	6 Mar.	Gottlieb Daimler d.
1900	19 Mar.	Jean-Frédéric Joliot b.
1900	25 Apr.	Wolfgang Ernst Pauli b.
1900	28 Apr.	Jan Hendrik Oort b.
1900	5 June	Dennis Gabor b.
1900	10 June	Willy Kuhne d.
1900	3 July	Arthur Albright d.
1900	18 July	Johan Gustav Christoffer Thorsager Kjeldahl d.
1900	12 Aug.	James Edward Keeler d.
1900	14 Aug.	Jean Joseph Etienne Lenoir d.
1900	25 Aug.	Hans Adolf Krebs b.
1900	9 Dec.	N. J. T. M. Needham b.
1901		J. D. Bernal† b.
1901		J. H. Gilbert† d.
1901		Z. T. Gramme† d.
1901		C. Hermite† d.
1901		K. Natterer d.
1901		Mark Oliphant b.
1901		P. G. Tait† d.
1901		Merle Tuve b.
1901	6 Jan.	Philip Danforth Armour d.
1901	10 Feb.	Max Josef von Pettenkofer d.
1901	16 Feb.	John Rex Whinfield b.
1901	18 Feb.	Egide Walschaerts d.
1901	22 Feb.	George Francis Fitzgerald d.
1901	28 Feb.	Linus Carl Pauling b.
1901	1 Apr.	François Marie Raoult d.
1901	16 Apr.	Henry Augustus Rowland d.
1901	29 Apr.	Hirohito b.
1901	18 May	Vincent du Vigneaud b.
1901	8 Aug.	Ernest Orlando Lawrence b.
1901	12 Aug.	Nils Adolf Erik Nordenskiöld d.
1901	29 Sept.	Enrico Fermi b.
1901	22 Nov.	Alexandre Onoufrievitch Kovalevsky d.
1901	5 Dec.	Werner Karl Heisenberg b.
1901	20 Dec.	Robert Jemison van de Graaff b.
1902		Walter H. Brattain† b.
1902		Hans Buchner† d.
1902		F. Goltz† d.
1902		A. M. Lwoff† b.
1902		Friedrich Krupp† d.
1902		Ernesto Parona† d.
1902		John A. Ratcliffe b.
1902		F. W. Strassmann† b.
1902	14 Jan.	Cato Maximilian Guldberg d.
1902	2 Mar.	Edward Uhler Condon b.
1902	16 May	Tetsuo Nozoe b.
1902	16 June	Barbara McClintock b.
1902	28 June	Maria Goeppert Mayer b.
1902	10 July	Kurt Alder b.
1902	11 July	Samuel Abraham Goudsmit b.
1902	8 Aug.	P. A. M. Dirac b.
1902	10 Aug.	Arne Wilhelm Kaurin Tiselius b.
1902	13 Aug.	Felix Wankel b.
1902	28 Aug.	Sir Reginald Patrick Linstead b.
1902	5 Sept.	Rudolf Ludwig Carl Virchow d.
1902	18 Oct.	Ernst Pascual Jordan b.
1902	17 Nov.	Eugene Paul Wigner b.
1902	22 Nov.	Walter Reed d.
1902	22 Nov.	Sir William Chandler Roberts-Austen d.
1902	5 Dec.	Johannes Adolph Wislicenus d.
1903		C. A. Bjerknes† d.
1903		C. Gegenbaur† d.
1903		A. Rollett† d.
1903		F. O. Schmitt† b.
1903		E. T. S. Walton† b.
1903	28 Jan.	Kathleen Lonsdale b.
1903	1 Feb.	George Gabriel Stokes d.
1903	26 Feb.	Richard John Gatling d.
1903	26 Feb.	Guilio Natta b.
1903	9 Apr.	Gregory Goodwin Pincus b.
1903	28 Apr.	Josiah Willard Gibbs d.
1903	8 June	Evan James Williams b.
1903	6 July	A. H. T. Theorell b.
1903	7 Aug.	L. S. B. Leakey b.
1903	22 Oct.	George Wells Beadle b.
1903	7 Nov.	Konrad Lorenz b.
1903	27 Nov.	Lars Onsager b.
1903	5 Dec.	Cecil Frank Powell b.
1903	8 Dec.	Herbert Spencer d.
1903	28 Dec.	John von Neumann b.
1904		Lowthian Bell† d.
1904		W. Lee Dickinson† d.
1904		Norman Feather† b.

1904		Lu Gwei-Djen† b.
1904		V. V. Markovnikov† d.
1904		Joseph Edward Mayer† b.
1904		Sir John Simon† d.
1904		Wendell M. Stanley† b.
1904		Carl Weigert† d.
1904	1 Mar.	Wilhelm His d.
1904	10 Mar.	Charles J. Pedersen b.
1904	22 Apr.	J. Robert Oppenheimer b.
1904	6 May	Alexander William Williamson d.
1904	8 May	Eadweard James Muybridge d.
1904	15 May	Etienne-Jules Marey d.
1904	24 May	Friedrich Siemens d.
1904	28 July	Pavel Aleksejevic Cherenkov b.
1904	18 Aug.	William A. S. Butement b.
1904	28 Aug.	Eduard Hitzig d.
1904	1 Oct.	Otto Robert Frisch b.
1904	8 Oct.	Clemens Alexander Winkler d.
1904	22 Nov.	L. E. F. Néel b.
1905		Alexander Melville Bell† d.
1905		George Hitchings† b.
1905		Severo Ochoa† b.
1905		Franz Reuleaux† d.
1905		Sir J. S. Burdon Sanderson† d.
1905		I. M. Sechenov† d.
1905		Otto Struve† d.
1905		C. H. Waddington† b.
1905		H. Marshall Ward† d.
1905		C. T. Yerkes† d.
1905	14 Jan.	Ernst Abbe d.
1905	1 Feb.	Emilio Gino Segrè b.
1905	7 Feb.	Ulf Svante von Euler b.
1905	7 June	Karl Kellner d.
1905	4 Aug.	Walther Flemming d.
1905	11 Aug.	Edwin Chargaff b.
1905	3 Sept.	Carl David Anderson b.
1905	30 Sept.	Sir Nevill Mott b.
1905	22 Oct.	Karl G. Jansky b.
1905	23 Oct.	Felix Bloch b.
1905	2 Nov.	Rudolph Albert von Kölliker d.
1905	19 Nov.	Robert Whitehead d.
1906		P. K. L. Drude† d.
1906		K. A. G. Mendelssohn† b.
1906		J. A. Wanklyn† d.
1906		Walter H. Zinn† b.
1906	14 Jan.	Hermann Johann Philipp Sprengel d.
1906	2 Feb.	Samuel Cunliffe Lister d.
1906	8 Feb.	Chester Floyd Carlson b.
1906	31 Mar.	Sin-Itiro Tomonaga b.
1906	19 Apr.	Pierre Curie d.
1906	12 May	William Maurice Ewing b.
1906	19 June	Sir Ernst Boris Chain b.
1906	22 June	Fritz Richard Schaudinn d.
1906	2 July	Hans Albrecht Bethe b.
1906	23 July	Vladimir Prelog b.
1906	4 Sept.	M. L. H. Delbrück b.
1906	5 Sept.	Ludwig Boltzmann d.
1906	18 Oct.	Fredrich Konrad Beilstein d.
1906	2 Dec.	Peter Carl Goldmark b.
1906	25 Dec.	Ernst A. F. Ruska b.
1906	30 Dec.	Sergei Pavlovich Korolev b.
1907		A. M. Clerke† d.
1907		J. Carroll† d.
1907		Ernst von Bergmann† d.
1907		Sir Michael Foster† d.
1907		J. H. D. Jensen b.
1907		N. A. Menschutkin† d.
1907		G. P. S. Occhialini† b.
1907		R. E. Paley† d.
1907		Aleksandr Vasil'evich Topchiev b.
1907		J. W. Wilson† d.
1907	20 Jan.	Dmitry Ivanovich Mendeléeff d.
1907	23 Jan.	Hideki Yukawa b.
1907	8 Feb.	Hendrik Willem Bakhuis

		Roozeboom d.
1907	20 Feb.	Ferdinand Frédéric Henri Moissan d.
1907	16 Mar.	Alexander Solomon Wiener b.
1907	18 Mar.	Pierre Eugène Marcel(1)in Berthelot d.
1907	23 Mar.	Daniele Bovet b.
1907	15 Apr.	Nikolaas Tinbergen b.
1907	1 June	Sir Frank Whittle b.
1907	5 June	Sir Rudolf Peierls b.
1907	14 July	Sir William Henry Perkin d.
1907	18 Aug.	John Kerr d.
1907	18 Sept.	Edwin Mattison McMillan b.
1907	21 Sept.	Sir Edward Bullard b.
1907	2 Oct.	Alexander Robertus Todd (Lord Todd) b.
1907	28 Nov.	Robert Russell Race b.
1907	17 Dec.	William Thomson (Baron Kelvin of Largs) d.
1907	23 Dec.	Pierre Jules Janssen d.
1908		C. E. Chamberland† d.
1908		M. C. Chang† b.
1908		Ilya Frank† b.
1908		George Gore† d.
1908		N. Kurti† b.
1908		J. von Mering† d.
1908		R. Panhard† d.
1908		W. A. Shenstone† d.
1908		Carl Voit† d.
1908	15 Jan.	Edward Teller b.
1908	22 Jan.	Lev Davidovich Landau b.
1908	10 Mar.	Henry Clifton Sorby d.
1908	23 May	John Bardeen b.
1908	24 May	Harry Hammond Hess b.
1908	30 May	Hannes Olof Jösten Alfvén b.
1908	24 Aug.	Antoine Henri Becquerel d.
1908	8 Nov.	William Edward Ayrton d.
1908	4 Dec.	Alfred Day Hershey b.
1908	17 Dec.	Willard Frank Libby b.
1909		Holbrook Gaskell† d.
1909		Robert Hoe† d.
1909		H. F. P. Limpricht† d.
1909		Bindon Blood Stoney† d.
1909		E. L. Tatum† b.
1909	12 Jan.	Hermann Minkowski d.
1909	22 Apr.	Rita Levi-Montalcini b.
1909	7 May	Edwin H. Land b.
1909	21 May	Theodor Wilhelm Engelmann d.
1909	11 July	Simon Newcomb d.
1909	15 July	H. B. G. Casimir b.
1909	30 Oct.	Homi Jehangir Bhabha b.
1909	11 Dec.	Ludwig Mond d.
1910		C. Fahlenberg† d.
1910		J. G. Galle† d.
1910		F. D. Recklinghausen† d.
1910		J. Volhard† d.
1910	17 Jan.	Fredrich Wilhelm Kohlrausch d.
1910	9 Feb.	Jacques Monod b.
1910	13 Feb.	William Shockley b.
1910	1 Mar.	A. J. P. Martin b.
1910	15 Mar.	Hans Heinrich Landolt d.
1910	3 Apr.	Richard Abegg d.
1910	28 Apr.	Edouard Joseph Louis-Marie van Beneden d.
1910	1 May	Alexandre Léon Étard d.
1910	3 May	Howard Taylor Ricketts d.
1910	10 May	Stanislao Cannizzaro d.
1910	11 May	Dorothy Crowfoot Hodgkin b.
1910	12 May	Sir William Huggins d.
1910	27 May	Robert Koch d.
1910	19 June	Paul John Flory b.
1910	4 July	Giovanni Virginio Schiaparelli d.
1910	10 Sept.	Zdenko Hans Skraup d.
1910	19 Oct.	Subrahmanyan Chandrasekhar b.
1910	19 Nov.	Rudolph Fittig d.

1910	13 Dec.	Charles Alfred Coulson b.
1911		J. M. van Bemmelen† d.
1911		Christian Bohr† d.
1911		H. Caro† d.
1911		James Norman Davidson† b.
1911		Norman G. Heatley† b.
1911		J. Hughlings Jackson† d.
1911		N. K. Jerne† b.
1911		Hans von Ohain† b.
1911		William H. Stein† b.
1911		L. J. Troost† d.
1911	17 Jan.	Francis Galton d.
1911	1 Mar.	Jacobus Henricus Van't Hoff d.
1911	8 Apr.	Melvin Calvin b.
1911	13 June	Walter Luis Alvarez b.
1911	5 July	George Johnstone Stoney d.
1911	18 Oct.	Alfred Binet d.
1911	10 Dec.	Sir Joseph Dalton Hooker d.
1911	22 Dec.	Grote Reber b.
1912		P. E. L. de Boisbaudran† d.
1912		Sir George Darwin† d.
1912		Salvador E. Luria† b.
1912	10 Feb.	Joseph Lister (first Baron Lister) d.
1912	21 Feb.	Osborne Reynolds d.
1912	19 Apr.	Glen Theodore Seaborg b.
1912	19 May	Eduard Adolf Strasburger d.
1912	30 May	Wilbur Wright d.
1912	31 May	Chien-Sung Wu b.
1912	7 June	Alan Mathison Turing b.
1912	17 July	Henri Poincaré d.
1912	15 Aug.	Sir Monty Finniston b.
1912	30 Aug.	Edward Mills Purcell b.
1912	13 Sept.	Horace Welcome Babcock b.
1912	19 Nov.	George Emil Palade b.
1912	21 Dec.	Paul Albert Gordan d.
1913		S. W. Kuffler† b.
1913		Bernard Lovell† b.
1913	5 Jan.	Louis Paul Cailletet d.
1913	2 Feb.	Carl Gustaf Patrik de Laval d.
1913	10 June	Sir Edward Abraham b.
1913	20 Aug.	Roger Wolcott Sperry b.
1913	4 Sept.	Stanford Moore b.
1913		29/30 Sept. Rudolf Diesel d.
1913	7 Nov.	Alfred Russel Wallace d.
1914		R. Ahlquist† b.
1914		Å. Åkeson† b.
1914		D. D. Cunningham† d.
1914		F. J. Fenner† b.
1914		A. van Gehuchten d.
1914		J. Gibson† d.
1914		G. L. Y. Ingram† d.
1914		S. M. Jørgensen† d.
1914		A. Lieben† d.
1914		C. T. Liebermann† d.
1914		K. Voelckers† d.
1914	5 Feb.	Sir Alan Hodgkin b.
1914	22 Feb.	Renato Dulbecco b.
1914	12 Mar.	George Westinghouse d.
1914	16 Mar.	Sir John Murray d.
1914	30 Mar.	John Henry Poynting d.
1914	1 May	Herman Frasch d.
1914	9 May	Paul Louis Toussaint Héroult d.
1914	19 May	Max Ferdinand Perutz b.
1914	7 Sept.	James Alfred van Allen b.
1914	7 Sept.	Walter Holbrook Gaskell d.
1914	5 Nov.	August Weismann d.
1914	28 Nov.	Johann Wilhelm Hittorf d.
1914	27 Dec.	Charles Martin Hall d.
1915		E. H. Amagat† d.
1915		V. C. Driffield† d.
1915		F. Hasenöhrl† d.
1915		James Hillier† b.
1915		Robert Hofstadter† b.
1915		Friedrich Loeffler† d.
1915		George Oliver† d.
1915		Sir A. Rücker† d.
1915	23 May	Pierre Emile Martin d.
1915	24 June	Sir Fred Hoyle b.
1915	28 July	Charles Hard Townes b.
1915	10 Aug.	Henry Gwyn Jeffreys Moseley d.
1915	20 Aug.	Carlos J. Finlay d.
1915	20 Aug.	Paul Ehrlich d.
1915	15 Oct.	Theodor Boveri d.
1915	18 Dec.	Sir Henry Enfield Roscoe d.
1916		Christian Anfinsen† b.
1916		W. Esson† d.
1916		John Ferguson† d.
1916		Victor Horsley† d.
1916		Keith Lucas† d.
1916		Aleksandr M. Prokhorov† b.
1916		T. Purdie† d.
1916		Silvanus Thompson† d.
1916	10 Jan.	Sune Bergström b.
1916	12 Feb.	J. W. R. Dedekind d.
1916	19 Feb.	Ernst Mach d.
1916	15 Mar.	Ivan Levinstein d.
1916	30 Apr.	Claude Elwood Shannon b.
1916	6 May	Robert Henry Dicke b.
1916	8 June	Francis H. C. Crick b.
1916	23 July	Sir William Ramsay d.
1916	12 Nov.	Percival Lowell d.
1916	24 Nov.	Sir Hiram Stevens Maxim d.
1916	15 Dec.	Ilya (Elie) Mechnikov d.
1917		John W. Cornforth† b.
1917		Christian De Duve† b.
1917		A. Einhorn† d.
1917		A. F. Huxley† b.
1917		Allan W. Johnson† b.
1917		Alexander Macomb Chance d.
1917	25 Jan.	Ilya Prigogine b.
1917	24 Mar.	John Cowdery Kendrew b.
1917	31 Mar.	Emil Adolf von Behring d.
1917	10 Apr.	Robert Burns Woodward b.
1917	8 May	Count Ferdinand von Zeppelin d.
1917	27 May	Sir Joseph Wilson Swan d.
1917	15 June	Kristian Olaf Bernhard Birkeland d.
1917	20 June	James Mason Crafts d.
1917	28 June	Ernst Pringsheim d.
1917	27 July	Emil Theodor Kocher d.
1917	13 Aug.	Eduard Buchner d.
1917	20 Aug.	Johann Friedrich Adolf von Baeyer d.
1917	8 Oct.	Rodney Robert Porter b.
1917	9 Dec.	Leo James Rainwater b.
1918		K. F. Braun† d.
1918		Gertrude Elion† b.
1918		Georg Gaffky† d.
1918		B. Hopkinson† d.
1918		V. B. Mountcastle† b.
1918	6 Jan.	Georg Ferdinand Ludwig Philip Cantor d.
1918	3 Mar.	Arthur Kornberg b.
1918	20 Apr.	Karl Ferdinand Braun d.
1918	11 May	Richard Phillips Feynman b.
1918	6 June	Edwin G. Krebs b.
1918	6 June	Ruth Ann Sanger b.
1918	31 July	Francis Edgar Stanley d.
1918	13 Aug.	Frederick Sanger b.
1918	8 Sept.	Sir Derek H. R. Barton d.
1918	27 Sept.	Sir Martin Ryle b.
1918	14 Oct.	Kenichi Fukui b.
1919		E. J. Hanson† b.
1919		Sir William Osler† d.
1919		W. K. H. Panofsky† b.
1919		Woldemar Voigt d.
1919	3 Feb.	Edward Charles Pickering d.
1919	4 Apr.	Sir William Crookes d.
1919	8 Apr.	Roland Eötvös d.
1919	9 Apr.	John Presper Eckert b.

1919	22 Apr.	Donald James Cram *b.*
1919	26 June	Michel Tswett *d.*
1919	30 June	Lord Rayleigh (John William Strutt) *d.*
1919	15 July	Emil Fischer *d.*
1919	8 Aug.	Ernst Heinrich Haeckel *d.*
1919	11 Aug.	Andrew Carnegie *d.*
1919	28 Aug.	Sir Godfrey Hounsfield *b.*
1919	1 Nov.	Sir Hermann Bondi *b.*
1919	15 Nov.	Alfred Werner *d.*
1919	28 Dec.	Johannes Robert Rydberg *d.*
1920		O. Butschli† *d.*
1920		Edmond H. Fischer† *b.*
1920		François Jacob† *b.*
1920		J. E. W. Peary† *d.*
1920		John Perry† *d.*
1920	31 Jan.	Wilhelm Pfeffer *d.*
1920	13 Mar.	Charles Lapworth *d.*
1920	18 Apr.	Rudolph Messel *d.*
1920	26 Apr.	Srinivasa Ramanujan *d.*
1920	10 May	John Welsey Hyatt *d.*
1920	22 May	Thomas Gold *b.*
1920	20 June	Ludwig Gattermann *d.*
1920	3 July	William Crawford Gorgas *d.*
1920	25 July	Rosalind Elsie Franklin *b.*
1920	16 Aug.	Sir Joseph Norman Lockyer *d.*
1920	6 Dec.	George Porter (Baron Porter of Luddenham) *b.*
1921		C. L. Reimer† *d.*
1921	23 Jan.	Heinrich Wilhelm Waldeyer-Hartz *d.*
1921	3 Feb.	Ralph Asher Alpher *b.*
1921	17 Feb.	William Odling *d.*
1921	5 May	William Friese-Greene *d.*
1921	21 May	Andrei Sakharov *b.*
1921	25 May	Jack Steinberger *b.*
1921	13 July	Gabriel Lippmann *d.*
1921	14 July	Sir Geoffrey Wilkinson *b.*
1921	17 July	Alick Isaacs *b.*
1921	19 July	Rosalyn Yalow *b.*
1921	17 Oct.	Edward John Bevan *d.*
1921	23 Oct.	John Boyd Dunlop *d.*
1921	12 Dec.	Henrietta Swan Leavitt *d.*
1922		P. A. Barbier† *d.*
1922		F. S. Exner† *d.*
1922		P. A. Guye† *d.*
1922		William S. Halsted† *d.*
1922		R. W. Holley† *b.*
1922		A. B. Kempe† *d.*
1922		Leon Lederman† *b.*
1922		Corrado Parona† *d.*
1922		H. Rubens† *d.*
1922		A. D. Waller† *d.*
1922	9 Jan.	Has Gobind Khorana *b.*
1922	22 Feb.	Reinhard Mannesmann *d.*
1922	9 Apr.	Sir Patrick Manson *d.*
1922	18 May	Charles Louis Alphonse Laveran *d.*
1922	26 May	Ernest Solvay *d.*
1922	19 June	Aage Niels Bohr *b.*
1922	22 July	Jokichi Takamine *d.*
1922	2 Aug.	Alexander Graham Bell *d.*
1922	22 Sept.	Chen Ning Yang *b.*
1922	28 Oct.	Alexander Crum Brown *d.*
1922	14 Dec.	Nikolai Gennadievich Basov *b.*
1923		C. D. Harries† *d.*
1923		P. Jacobson† *d.*
1923		C. Longuet-Higgins† *b.*
1923		Phoebe Marks† *d.*
1923		J. Orth† *d.*
1923	10 Feb.	William Konrad Röntgen *d.*
1923	24 Feb.	Edward Williams Morley *d.*
1923	8 Mar.	Johannes Diderik van der Waals *d.*
1923	27 Mar.	Sir James Dewar *d.*
1923	21 May	Johann (Hans) Wilhelm Goldschmidt *d.*

1923	12 July	Ernst Otto Beckman *d.*
1923	21 July	Rudolph A. Marcus *b.*
1923	9 Sept.	Daniel Carleton Gajdusek *b.*
1923	13 Dec.	Philip Warren Anderson *b.*
1924		F. A. Janssens† *d.*
1924		G. D. Liveing† *d.*
1924		Robert Gail Mills† *b.*
1924		Julius Morgenroth† *d.*
1924		Wilhelm Roux† *d.*
1924		John Clive Ward† *b.*
1924		Torsten Nils Wiesel† *b.*
1924	23 Feb.	Allan Macleod Cormack *b.*
1924	25 Feb.	Hugh Esmor Huxley *b.*
1924	22 Mar.	Siegmund Gabriel *d.*
1924	22 Mar.	Sir William Macewen *d.*
1924	5 Apr.	Victor Hensen *d.*
1924	11 May	Antony Hewish *b.*
1924	14 June	Sir James Black *b.*
1924	1 Aug.	Sir George Thomas Beilby *d.*
1924	1 Aug.	Georges Charpak *b.*
1924	27 Aug.	Sir William Maddock Bayliss *d.*
1924	10 Nov.	Sir Archibald Geikie *d.*
1924	3 Dec.	John Backus *b.*
1925		Sir William Barrett† *d.*
1925		J. Breuer† *d.*
1925		H. R. Carter† *d.*
1925		Rickman Godlee† *d.*
1925		W. F. Hillebrand† *d.*
1925		W. Körner† *d.*
1925		J. N. Langley† *d.*
1925		J. Lederberg† *b.*
1925		Sir James Mackenzie† *d.*
1925	22 Jan.	Christian Felix Klein† *d.*
1925	3 Feb.	Oliver Heaviside *d.*
1925	23 Feb.	Sir William Edward Thorpe *d.*
1925	16 Mar.	August von Wassermann *d.*
1925	25 Mar.	Leo Esaki *b.*
1925	15 Apr.	David Talbot Day *d.*
1925	4 May	Giovanni Battista Grassi *d.*
1925	11 May	Koji Nakanishi *b.*
1925	5 July	Otto Lummer *d.*
1925	5 Nov.	John Newport Langley *d.*
1925	17 Nov.	Johann August Brinell *d.*
1926		A. Caton† *d.*
1926		Ben Mottelson† *b.*
1926		Oberlin Smith† *d.*
1926		A. Van den Broek† *d.*
1926		Franz Ziehl† *d.*
1926	21 Jan.	Camillo Golgi *d.*
1926	29 Jan.	Abdus Salam *b.*
1926	8 Feb.	William Bateson *d.*
1926	21 Feb.	Kamerlingh Heike Onnes *d.*
1926	27 Feb.	David Hunter Hubel *b.*
1926	2 June	Sir William Boog Leishman *d.*
1926	18 June	Alan Rex Sandage *b.*
1926	30 June	Paul Berg *b.*
1926	21 Sept.	Donald Arthur Glaser *b.*
1926	24 Nov.	Tsung Dao Lee *b.*
1926	9 Dec.	Henry W. Kendall *b.*
1926	11 Dec.	Sir William Augustus Tilden *d.*
1927		Manfred Eigen† *b*
1927		Charles Manley† *d.*
1927		H. W. Nirenberg† *b.*
1927		Gerard K. O'Neill† *b.*
1927		F. B. Power† *d.*
1927		John R. Vane† *b.*
1927		H. Wichelhaus† *d.*
1927	13 Jan.	Sydney Brenner *b.*
1927	19 Jan.	Carl Graebe *d.*
1927	4 Mar.	Ira Remsen *d.*
1927	2 May	Ernest Henry Starling *d.*
1927	12 June	Gustav Theodor Fritsch *d.*
1927	5 July	Albrecht Kossel *d.*
1927	11 July	Theodore H. Maiman *b.*

1927	15 Aug.	Bertram Borden Boltwood d.
1927	15 Aug.	William Platt Jencks b.
1927	17 Aug.	Eric Ivar Fredholm d.
1927	28 Sept.	Willem Einthoven d.
1927	2 Oct.	Svante August Arrhenius d.
1927	8 Oct.	César Milstein b.
1928		T. C. Curtius† d.
1928		D. Nathans† b.
1928		F. M. Perkin† d.
1928		E. E. G. Wiedermann† d.
1928		E. C. T. Zincke d.
1928	30 Jan.	Johannes Andreas Grib Fibiger d.
1928	4 Feb.	Hendrik Antoon Lorentz d.
1928	19 Mar.	Sir David Ferrier d.
1928	2 Apr.	Theodore William Richards d.
1928	6 Apr.	James Dewey Watson b.
1928	16 June	Roald Engelbregt Gravning Amundsen d.
1928	12 July	Elias J. Corey b.
1928	30 Aug.	Wilhelm Wien d.
1928	28 Dec.	J. von Neumann b.
1929		W. Arber† b.
1929		Amico Bignami† d.
1929		G. M. Edelman† b.
1929		Ivar Giaever† b.
1929		Peter Ware Higgs† b.
1929		J. L. Reverdin† d.
1929		R. E. Taylor† b.
1929	31 Jan.	Rudolf Ludwig Mossbauer b.
1929	4 Apr.	Karl Benz d.
1929	27 July	Raoul Pierre Pictet d.
1929	4 Aug.	Baron Carl Auer von Welsbach d.
1929	15 Aug.	Edwin Ray Lankester d.
1929	17 Sept.	William Henry Perkin, jun. d.
1929	29 Sept.	Richard Adolf Zsigmondy d.
1929	17 Nov.	Herman Hollerith d.
1929	Dec.	Wilhelm Maybach d.
1930		Florian Cajori† d.
1930		J. I. Friedman† b.
1930	5 Jan.	Ludwig Claisen d.
1930	13 Jan.	Sebastian Ziani de Ferranti d.
1930	19 Feb.	A. A. Campbell Swinton d.
1930	28 Feb.	Leon N. Cooper b.
1930	13 May	Fridtjof Nansen d.
1930	16 June	Elmer Ambrose Sperry d.
1930	6 Aug.	Joseph Achille Le Bel d.
1930	30 Aug.	Allvar Gullstrand d.
1930	17 Sept.	Harold Bailey Dixon d.
1930	10 Oct.	Heinrich Gustav Adolf Engler d.
1930	Nov.	Alfred Lothar Wegener d.
1930	5 Nov.	Christiaan Eijkman d.
1930	13 Dec.	Fritz Pregl d.
1930	25 Dec.	Eugen Goldstein d.
1931		Andrew Balfour† d.
1931		Sir Jesse Boot (Lord Trent)† d.
1931		Martin Flack† d.
1931		Oskar Minkowski† d.
1931		R. Schrieffer† b.
1931		James Lorrain Smith† d.
1931	5 Feb.	Drummond Hoyle Matthews b.
1931	13 Feb.	Sir Charles Algernon Parsons d.
1931	26 Feb.	Otto Wallach d.
1931	22 Mar.	Burton Richter b.
1931	9 May	Albert Abraham Michelson d.
1931	13 June	Shibasaburo Kitasato d.
1931	2 July	Stephen Moulton Babcock d.
1931	6 July	Edward Goodrich Acheson d.
1931	8 Aug.	Roger Penrose b.
1931	23 Aug.	Hamilton Othanel Smith b.
1931	18 Oct.	Thomas Alva Edison d.
1931	20 Nov.	Sir David Bruce d.
1932		Dugald Clerk† d.
1932		E. Bamberger† d.
1932		George Eastman† d.
1932		A. von Ettinghausen† d.
1932		Otto Fischer† d.
1932		G. A. Neuber† d.
1932		G. Peano† d.
1932		Max Rubner† d.
1932		Melvin Schwarz† b.
1932	21 Mar.	Walter Gilbert b.
1932	4 Apr.	Friedrich Wilhelm Oswald d.
1932	18 July	Graham Lusk d.
1932	22 July	R. A. Fessenden d.
1932	23 July	Alberto Santos Dumont d.
1932	15 Sept.	Neil Bartlett b.
1932	16 Sept.	Sir Ronald Ross d.
1932	3 Oct.	Max Wolf d.
1932	24 Oct.	Pierre-Gilles de Gennes b.
1932	5 Dec.	Sheldon Lee Glashow b.
1933		P. Ehrenfest† d.
1933		W. Morley Fletcher† d.
1933		R. E. Paley† d.
1933	22 Feb.	Ernst Johannes Schmidt d.
1933	26 Apr.	Arno Allan Penzias b.
1933	3 May	Steven Weinberg b.
1933	6 June	Heinrich Rohrer b.
1933	14 Aug.	Richard Ernst b.
1933	29 Oct.	L. C. A. Calmette d.
1933	3 Nov.	Pierre Paul Émile Roux d.
1933	8 Dec.	John Joly d.
1934		Yuri Gagarin† b.
1934		Wilhelm His† d.
1934		Bengt J. Samuelsson† b.
1934		A. Schuster† d.
1934		E. W. Washburn† d.
1934		Thomas Watson† d.
1934	29 Jan.	Fritz Haber d.
1934	30 Apr.	William Henry Welch d.
1934	4 July	Marie Curie d.
1934	18 Oct.	Santiago Ramón y Cajal d.
1934	16 Nov.	Carl von Linde d.
1934	10 Dec.	Howard Martin Temin b.
1934	20 Dec.	Theobald Smith d.
1935		Stanley Cohen† b.
1935		K. E. Correns† d.
1935		H. W. Dudley d.
1935		Wilhelm Kolle† d.
1935		Ettore Marchiafava† d.
1935		Lafayette Mendel† d.
1935		Otto Schott† d.
1935		K. Tsiolkovskii† d.
1935		L. Vaillard† d.
1935	14 Mar.	Arthur Rudolf Hantzsch d.
1935	16 Mar.	John James Rickard Macleod d.
1935	29 Mar.	Sir Edward Albert Sharpey-Schafer d.
1935	15 Apr.	Charles Frederick Cross d.
1935	6 May	Sir James Walker d.
1935	21 May	Hugo de Vries d.
1935	1 Aug.	A. D. Little d.
1935	1 Dec.	Bernhard Voldemar Schmidt d.
1935	4 Dec.	Charles Robert Richet d.
1935	13 Dec.	François Auguste Victor Grignard d.
1935	15 Dec.	Percy Carlyle Gilchrist d.
1936		Cyrus Hall McCormick† d.
1936		Karl Pearson† d.
1936	10 Jan.	Sir Walter Bodmer b.
1936	27 Jan.	Samuel Chao Chung Ting b.
1936	27 Feb.	Ivan Petrovich Pavlov d.
1936	28 Feb.	Charles Jules Henri Nicolle d.
1936	14/15 Mar.	John Scott Haldane d.
1936	28 Mar.	Sir Archibald Garrod d.
1936	8 Apr.	Robert Bárány d.
1936	8 June	Kenneth Geddes Wilson b.
1936	11 June	Julius Arthur Nieuwland d.
1936	10 July	Herbert Wayne Boyer b.

1936	15 July	Richard Dixon Oldham *d.*
1936	25 July	Sir Henry Wellcome *d.*
1936	17 Sept.	Henri Louis Le Chatelier *d.*
1936	26 Sept.	Jean-Baptiste Senderens (The Abbé) *d.*
1936	2 Nov.	Thomas Martin Lowry *d.*
1936	18 Dec.	Andrija Mohorovičić *d.*
1937		Julius Bredt† *d.*
1937		Richard Hertwig† *d.*
1937		Roald Hoffmann† *b.*
1937		A. Hutchinson† *d.*
1937		G. H. F. Nuttall† *d.*
1937		A. G. Perkin† *d.*
1937	12 Mar.	Amé Pictet *d.*
1937	29 Apr.	Wallace Hume Carothers *d.*
1937	28 May	Alfred Adler *d.*
1937	13 July	Henry Edward Armstrong *d.*
1937	20 July	Guglielmo Marconi *d.*
1937	19 Oct.	Sir Ernest Rutherford (Lord Rutherford of Nelson) *d.*
1938		J. J. Abel† *d.*
1938		David Baltimore† *b.*
1938		C. B. Bridges *d.*
1938		Edward Charles Edgar† *d.*
1938		Edmund Husserl *d.*
1938		E. Landau† *d.*
1938		Felix Mesnil† *d.*
1938	17 Jan.	William Henry Pickering *d.*
1938	21 Feb.	George Ellery Hale *d.*
1938	13 June	Charles Edouard Guillaume *d.*
1938	5 Nov.	Georges Urbain *d.*
1938	11 Nov.	Hans Christian Joachim Gram *d.*
1939		Jean-Marie Lehn† *b.*
1939		George Redmayne Murray† *d.*
1939	5 Jan.	George Barger *d.*
1939	13 Feb.	Sören Peter Lauritz Sörensen *d.*
1939	25 May	Sir Frank Watson Dyson *d.*
1939	17 June	Frederick John Vine *b.*
1939	18 July	Arthur Edwin Kennelly *d.*
1939	24 Sept.	Sigmund Freud *d.*
1939	7 Oct.	Harvey Cushing *d.*
1939	17 Oct.	Sir William Jackson Pope *d.*
1940		F. Emich† *d.*
1940		P. P. Laidlaw† *d.*
1940		Paul Gottlieb Nipkow† *d.*
1940		G. Sanarelli† *d.*
1940		H. W. F. Siedentopf† *d.*
1940		F. O. Stanley† *d.*
1940		F. Swarts† *d.*
1940		Vito Volterra† *d.*
1940		Pierre Weiss† *d.*
1940	15 Feb.	Rookes Evelyn Bell Crompton *d.*
1940	26 Apr.	Carl Bosch *d.*
1940	17 June	Sir Arthur Harden *d.*
1940	21 June	Samuel Eyde *d.*
1940	30 July	Sir Clive Sinclair *b.*
1940	22 Aug.	Sir Oliver Joseph Lodge *d.*
1940	30 Aug.	Sir Joseph John Thomson *d.*
1940	6 Sept.	Phoebus Aaron Theodor Levene *d.*
1940	30 Sept.	Sir Robert Abbott Hadfield *d.*
1941		William Bullock† *d.*
1941		O. Foerster† *d.*
1941		John Gillies Priestley† *d.*
1941		R. Robinson† *d.*
1941		A. C. Seward† *d.*
1941	21 Feb.	Sir Frederick Grant Banting *d.*
1941	30 Mar.	Herbert Max Finlay Freundlich *d.*
1941	5 Apr.	Arthur Lapworth *d.*
1941	16 Apr.	Hans Adolf Eduard Driesch *d.*
1941	1 June	Hans Berger *d.*
1941	14 Aug.	Paul Sabatier *d.*
1941	9 Sept.	Hans Spemann *d.*
1941	18 Nov.	Hermann Walther Nernst *d.*
1942		A. D. Hall† *d.*

1942		Sir Henry Miers† *d.*
1942		Sir Flinders Petrie† *d.*
1942		K. F. O. Seubert† *d.*
1942		W. J. Young† *d.*
1942	8 Jan.	Stephen William Hawking *b.*
1942	12 Mar.	Sir William Henry Bragg *d.*
1942	17 Apr.	Jean Baptiste Perrin *d.*
1942	12 June	Bert Sakman *b.*
1942	24 June	Karl Albert Ludwig Aschoff *d.*
1942		July Valdemar Poulsen *d.*
1942	3 Aug.	Richard Willstätter *d.*
1943		D. Hilbert† *d.*
1943		H. A. Kelly† *d.*
1943		Wolfgang Ostwald† *d.*
1943		Alexandre Yersin† *d.*
1943	7 Jan.	Nikola Tesla *d.*
1943	26 Jan.	Nikolai Ivanovitch Vavilov *d.*
1943	26 June	Karl Landsteiner *d.*
1943	24 July	Gerard Jacob de Geer *d.*
1943	9 Oct.	Pieter Zeeman *d.*
1943	26 Dec.	Russell Henry Chittenden *d.*
1944		M. Bergmann† *d.*
1944		Ralph Howard Fowler† *d.*
1944		Erwin Neher† *b.*
1944	23 Feb.	Leo Hendrik Baekeland *d.*
1944	22 Mar.	Carl Koller *d.*
1944	30 Mar.	Sir Charles Vernon Boys *d.*
1944	23 Oct.	Charles Glover Barkla *d.*
1944	2 Nov.	Thomas Midgley *d.*
1944	5 Nov.	Alexis Carrel *d.*
1944	22 Nov.	Sir Arthur Stanley Eddington *d.*
1945		E. F. Armstrong† *d.*
1945		Oscar Heinroth† *d.*
1945		H. Kiliani† *d.*
1945		T. Lewis† *d.*
1945		F. Paschen† *d.*
1945		Pio del Rio-Hortega† *d.*
1945	23 Mar.	Sir William Napier Shaw *d.*
1945	31 Mar.	Hans Fischer *d.*
1945	18 Apr.	Sir John Ambrose Fleming *d.*
1945	10 Aug.	Robert Hutchings Goddard *d.*
1945	15 Sept.	Richard Friedrich Johannes Pfeiffer *d.*
1945	24 Sept.	Hans Wilhelm Geiger *d.*
1945	29 Sept.	Evan James Williams *d.*
1945	20 Nov.	Francis William Aston *d.*
1945	4 Dec.	Thomas Hunt Morgan *d.*
1946		W. Dandy† *d.*
1946		P. F. Frankland† *d.*
1946		G. J. F. Kohler† *b.*
1946	8 Mar.	Frederick William Lanchester *d.*
1946	24 Mar.	Gilbert Newton Lewis *d.*
1946	14 June	John Logie Baird *d.*
1946	16 Sept.	Sir James Hopwood Jeans *d.*
1946	19 Dec.	Paul Langevin *d.*
1947		Gerd Binnig† *b.*
1947		G. H. Hardy† *d.*
1947		Johannes Lindhard† *d.*
1947		W. W. Watts† *d.*
1947		Sir Almroth Wright† *d.*
1947	20 Mar.	Victor Moritz Goldschmidt *d.*
1947	21 Mar.	Sir Joseph Barcroft *d.*
1947	7 Apr.	Henry Ford *d.*
1947	16 May	Sir Frederick Gowland Hopkins *d.*
1947	20 May	Philipp Eduard Anton Lenard *d.*
1947	3 Oct.	Max Carl Ernst Ludwig Planck *d.*
1947	17 Dec.	Johannes Nicolaus Brønsted *d.*
1947	30 Dec.	Alfred North Whitehead *d.*
1948		Henri Deslandres *d.*
1948		D'Arcy Thompson† *d.*
1948	30 Jan.	Orville Wright *d.*
1948	11 Apr.	Frederick Orpen Bower *d.*
1948	6 June	Louis Lumière *d.*
1948	14 July	Harry Brearley *d.*

1949		A. Debiernet† d.
1949		Félix d'Hérellet† d.
1949		W. Garstang† d.
1949		G. Komppa† d.
1949		Julius Ruska† d.
1949	31 Mar.	Friedrich Bergius d.
1949	1 May	Frederic Stanley Kipping d.
1949	12 July	Sir Rowland Harry Biffen d.
1949	13 Sept.	Schack August Steenberg Krògh d.
1949	25 Oct.	Joseph Edwin Barnard d.
1950		Constantin Caratheodory d.
1950		John Alfred Ryle† d.
1950	14 Feb.	Karl Guthe Jansky d.
1950	25 Feb.	George Richards Minot d.
1950	19 Mar.	Sir Walter Norman Haworth d.
1950	20 Mar.	Frederick William Twort d.
1950	16 May	Georg Bednorz b.
1950	21 Sept.	Edward Arthur Milne d.
1950	20 Oct.	Samuel Sugden d.
1951		V. F. K. Bjerknes† d.
1951		L. Cuénot† d.
1951		Charles Donovan† d.
1951		Y. Nishina† d.
1951		F. W. Oliver† d.
1951	6 Apr.	Robert Broom d.
1951	26 Apr.	Arnold Sommerfeld d.
1951	6 Oct.	Otto Fritz Meyerhof d.
1952		Hugh Cairns d.
1952		Hendrik Anthony Kramers† d.
1952		Mervyn O'Gorman† d.
1952	4 Mar.	Sir Charles Scott Sherrington d.
1952	15 Mar.	Nevil Vincent Sidgwick d.
1952	12 June	James Colquhoun Irvine d.
1953	28 Sept.	Edwin Powell Hubble d.
1952	29 Nov.	Vladimir Nikolaievich Ipatieff d.
1953	19 Dec.	Robert Andrews Millikan d.
1954		James Herrick† d.
1954	1 Feb.	Edwin Howard Armstrong d.
1954	7 Mar.	Otto Diels d.
1954	10 Apr.	Auguste Lumière d.
1954	7 June	Alan Mathison Turing d.
1954	11 Oct.	Theodore Lyman d.
1954	1 Nov.	Sir Alan Wallace Akers d.
1954	16 Nov.	Albert Francis Blakeslee d.
1954	28 Nov.	Enrico Fermi d.
1955		J. Clay† d.
1955		John Batcheller Sumner† d.
1955		H. Weyl† d.
1955	8 Jan.	Sir Arthur Keith d.
1955	30 Jan.	Sir Edward Mellanby d.
1955	20 Feb.	Oswald Theodore Avery d.
1955	11 Mar.	Sir Alexander Fleming d.
1955	18 Apr.	Albert Einstein d.
1955	11 Aug.	Robert Williams Wood d.
1955	11 Aug.	A. Hagenbach† d.
1955	12 Aug.	James Batcheller Sumner d.
1955	25 Nov.	Sir Arthur George Tansley d.
1955	13 Dec.	Antonio Egas Moniz d.
1956		Walter Kossel† d.
1956	16 Feb.	Meghnad Saha d.
1956	17 Mar.	Irène Joliot-Curie d.
1956	24 Mar.	Sir Edmund Taylor Whittaker d.
1956	11 May	Walter Sydney Adams d.
1956	22 Sept.	Frederick Soddy d.
1956	7 Oct.	Clarence Birdseye d.
1956	31 Oct.	Sir Francis Eugene (Franz Eugen) Simon d.
1956	16 Dec.	Frederick George Donnan d.
1957		Walter Bothe† d.
1957	22 Jan.	Paul Walden d.
1957	7 Feb.	John von Neumann d.
1957	16 Feb.	Sir John Sealy Edward Townsend d.
1957	21 June	Johannes Stark d.
1957	3 July	Frederick Alexander Lindemann

1957		(Viscount Cherwell) d.
1957	5 Aug.	Heinrich Wieland d.
1957	16 Aug.	Irving Langmuir d.
1957	19 Aug.	Carl-Gustav Arvid Rossby d.
1957	26 Oct.	Gerty Cori d.
1957	24 Dec.	Arthur James Ewins d.
1958		Sir John Anderson† d.
1958		Clinton Joseph Davisson† d.
1958		Charles Kettering† d.
1958		J. M. Nuttall† d.
1958		Lord Waverley† d.
1958		Sir Robert Whytlaw-Gray† d.
1958	27 Jan.	Motonori Matsuyama d.
1958	30 Mar.	Sir James Swinburne d.
1958	16 Apr.,	Rosalind Elsie Franklin d.
1958	19 June	Cyril Henry Desch d.
1958	20 June	Kurt Alder d.
1958	14 Aug.	Jean-Frédéric Joliot d.
1958	27 Aug.	Ernest Orlando Lawrence d.
1958	17 Sept.	Friedrich Adolf Paneth d.
1958	15 Dec.	Wolfgang Ernst Pauli d.
1959		Giuseppe Bastianelli† d.
1959		S. S. Chetverikov† d.
1959		E. F. DuBois† d.
1959		Paul Erich Hoffmann† d.
1959		E. J. Holmyard† d.
1959	9 June	Adolf Windaus d.
1959	14 Sept.	Sir Ian Morris Heilbron d.
1959	30 Sept.	Ross Granville Harrison d.
1959	9 Oct.	Sir Henry Thomas Tizard d.
1959	15 Nov.	Charles Thomson Rees Wilson d.
1960		J. F. Fulton† d.
1960		Abram Joffe† d.
1960		D. R. Pye† d.
1960		Charles Singer† d.
1960	24 Apr.	Max Theodor Felix von Laue d.
1960	23 May	Georges Claude d.
1960	25 June	W. H. W. Baade d.
1960	3 Nov.	Sir Harold Spencer Jones d.
1961		T. R. Elliott† d.
1961		A. M. Tyndall† d.
1961	4 Jan.	Erwin Schrödinger d.
1961	6 Apr.	Jules Jean Baptiste Vincent Bordet d.
1961	4 June	William Thomas Astbury d.
1961	6 June	Carl Gustav Jung d.
1961	30 June	Lee de Forest d.
1961	20 Aug.	Percy Williams Bridgman d.
1961	25 Aug.	Morris William Travers d.
1961	24 Nov.	Axel Leonard Wenner-Gren d.
1961	25 Dec.	Otto Loewi d.
1962		Sir Charles Galton Darwin d.
1962		Camille Guérin† d.
1962		E. von Tschermak† d.
1962		T. S. Wheeler† d.
1962	15 Mar.	Arthur Holly Compton d.
1962	20 Mar.	Andrew Elliott Douglass d.
1962	25 Mar.	Auguste Piccard d.
1962	4 June	Charles William Beebe d.
1962	8 June	M. E. L. Freyssinet d.
1962	18 July	Eugene Jules Houdry d.
1962	29 July	Sir Ronald Aylmer Fisher d.
1962	19 Aug.	Riko Majina d.
1962	18 Dec.	Niels Bohr d.
1962	27 Dec.	Aleksandr Vasil'evich Topchiev d.
1963		J. Read† d.
1963		Theodor von Karman d.
1963	27 Feb.	David Keilin d.
1963	11 May	Herbert Spencer Gasser d.
1964		Herbert C. Hoover† d.
1964		Hans von Euler-Cheplin† d.
1964	18 Mar.	Norbert Wiener d.
1964	24 Apr.	Gerhard Domagk d.
1964	21 May	James Franck d.
1964	30 May	Leo Szilard d.

1964	1 Dec.	John Burdon Sanderson Haldane d.
1964	18 Dec.	Victor Francis Hess d.
1965		Philip Showalter Hench† d.
1965		W. Wilson† d.
1965	1 Jan.	Sir George Clarke Simpson d.
1965	21 Apr.	Sir Edward Victor Appleton d.
1965	21 May	Sir Geoffrey de Havilland d.
1965	12 July	Sir Edward John Russell d.
1965	9 Aug.	Thomas Percy Hilditch d.
1965	8 Sept.	Hermann Staudinger d.
1965	20 Sept.	Arthur Holmes d.
1965	9 Oct.	James Riddick Partington d.
1965	5 Dec.	Joseph Erlanger d.
1966		A. N. Richards† d.
1966	14 Jan.	Sergei Pavlovich Korolev d.
1966	22 Jan	Albert Wallace Hull d.
1966	24 Jan.	Homi Jehangir Bhabha d.
1966	10 Mar.	Fritz Zernike d.
1966	29 Apr.	William Henry Eccles d.
1966	20 June	Georges Edouard Lemaître d.
1966	5 July	Georg von Hevesy d.
1966	6 July	John Rex Whinfield d.
1966	11 Aug.	Felix Andries Vening Meinesz d.
1966	22 Sept.	Sir Reginald Patrick Linstead d.
1966	2 Nov.	Petrus (Pieter) Josephus Wilhelmus Debye d.
1966	2 Dec.	Luitzen Egbertus Jan Brouwer d.
1967		R. Kuhn† d.
1967		Reginald C. Punnett† d.
1967	16 Jan.	Robert Jemison van de Graaff d.
1967	26 Jan.	Alick Isaacs d.
1967	18 Feb.	J. Robert Oppenheimer d.
1967	27 Mar.	Jaroslav Heyrovsky d.
1967	5 Apr.	Hermann Joseph Muller d.
1967	22 Aug.	Gregory Goodwin Pincus d.
1967	18 Sept.	Sir John Douglas Cockcroft d.
1967	9 Oct.	Sir Cyril Norman Hinshelwood d.
1968		W. Friedrich† d.
1968		Yuri Gagarin† d.
1968	21 Feb.	Howard Walter Florey (Baron Florey of Adelaide and Marston) d.
1968	1 Apr.	Lev Davidovich Landau d.
1968	23 July	Sir Henry Hallett Dale d.
1968	28 July	Otto Hahn d.
1968	19 Sept.	Chester Floyd Carlson d.
1968	27 Oct.	Lise Meitner d.
1969		Paul Scherrer† d.
1969	9 Aug.	Cecil Frank Powell d.
1969	17 Aug.	Otto Stern d.
1969	25 Aug.	Harry Hammond Hess d.
1970		Bertrand Russell† d.
1970	5 Jan.	Max Born d.
1970	16 Feb.	Francis Peyton Rous† d.
1970	18 Mar.	Boris Petrovitch Uvarov d.
1970	5 Apr.	Alfred Henry Sturtevant d.
1970	1 Aug.	Otto Heinrich Warburg d.
1970	21 Nov.	Sir Chandrasekhara Venkata Raman d.
1971		J. D. Bernal† d.
1971		Wendell M. Stanley† d.
1971		The Svedberg†d.
1971		Igor Tamm† d.
1971		J. Timmermanns† d.
1971	18 June	Paul Karrer d.
1971	1 July	Sir William Lawrence Bragg d.
1971	29 Oct.	Arne Wilhelm Kaurin Tiselius d.
1972		James Norman Davidson† d.
1972		C. R. Harington† d.
1972	20 Feb.	Maria Goeppert Mayer d.
1972	4 May	Edward Calvin Kendall d.
1972	1 Oct.	L. S. B. Leakey d.
1972	26 Oct.	Igor Ivanovich Sikorsky d.
1972	23 Dec.	Andrei Nikolaevich Tupolev d.
1973		E. J. Hanson† d.

1973		W. R. Hesse†d.
1973		J. H. D. Jensen† d.
1973	11 Aug.	Karl Ziegler d.
1973	16 Aug.	Selman Abraham Waksman d.
1974		F. Zwicky† d.
1974	7 Jan.	Charles Alfred Coulson d.
1974	4 Feb.	Satyendra Nath Bose d.
1974	26 Mar.	Edward Uhler Condon d.
1974	4 May	William Maurice Ewing d.
1974	18 May	Harry Ralph Ricardo d.
1974	28 June	Vannevar Bush d.
1974	13 July	Patrick Maynard Stuart Blackett (Baron Blackett of Chelsea) d.
1974	24 July	Sir James Chadwick d.
1975		D. W. Bronk† d.
1975		Kasimir Fajans† d.
1975		E. L. Hirst† d.
1975		J. S. Huxley† d.
1975		E. L. Tatum† d.
1975		C. H. Waddington† d.
1975	3 Feb.	William David Coolidge d.
1975	8 Feb.	Sir Robert Robinson d.
1975	7 July	Jacob Aall Bonnevie Bjerknes d.
1975	10 Sept.	Sir George Paget Thomson d.
1975	30 Oct.	Gustav Ludwig Hertz d.
1975	18 Dec.	Theodosius Grigorievich Dobzhansky d.
1976		Leopold Ruzicka† d.
1976	1 Feb.	Werner Karl Heisenberg d.
1976	2 Feb.	George Hoyt Whipple d.
1976	5 Apr.	Wilder Graves Penfield d.
1976	17 Apr.	Carl Peter Henrik Dam d.
1976	31 May	Jacques Lucien Monod d.
1976	5 Oct.	Lars Onsager d.
1976	6 Nov.	Alexander Solomon Wiener d.
1976	20 Nov.	Trofim Denisovich Lysenko d.
1977		L. F. Fiesert d.
1977		Oskar Benjamin Klein† d.
1977	3 June	Archibald Vivian Hill d.
1977	4 Aug.	Edgar Douglas Adrian (Baron Adrian of Cambridge) d.
1977	7 Dec.	Peter Carl Goldmark d.
1978		Norman Feather† d.
1978		Warren Weaver† d.
1978	7 June	Ronald George Wreyford Norrish d.
1978	26 Sept.	Karl Manne Georg Siegbahn d.
1978	4 Dec.	Samuel Abraham Goudsmit d.
1978	11 Dec.	Vincent du Vigneaud d.
1979	8 Feb.	Dennis Gabor d.
1979	1 May	Giulio Natta d.
1979	8 July	Sin-Itiro Tomonaga d.
1979	8 July	Robert Burns Woodward d.
1979	12 Aug.	Sir Ernst Boris Chain d.
1979	22 Sept.	Otto Robert Frisch d.
1979	30 Oct.	Barnes Neville Wallis d.
1980		S. W. Kuffler† d.
1980		K. A. G. Mendelssohn† d.
1980		K. H. van Vleck† d.
1980	3 Apr.	Sir Edward Bullard d.
1980	31 July	Pascual Jordan d.
1980	8 Sept.	William Frank Libby d.
1981		Odd Hassell† d.
1981	5 Jan.	Harold Clayton Urey d.
1981	10 Mar.	M. L. H. Delbrück d.
1981	8 Sept.	Hideki Yukawa d.
1981	13 Sept.	Gregory Breit d.
1981	22 Nov.	Hans Adolf Krebs d.
1982		Allan W. Johnson† d.
1982		Merle Tuve d.
1982	28 Mar.	William Francis Giauque d.
1982	12 June	Karl Ritter von Frisch d.
1982	29 July	Vladimir Zworykin d.
1982	5 Aug.	Axel Hugo Theorell d.
1982	23 Aug.	Stanford Moore d.

1983	10 Mar.	Ulf Svante von Euler d.
1983	10 Sept.	Felix Bloch d.
1984		Carl Cori† d.
1984		John Rock† d.
1984	8 Apr.	Piotr Leonidovich Kapitza d.
1984	15 Apr.	Robert Russell Race d.
1984	14 Oct.	Sir Martin Ryle d.
1984	20 Oct.	Paul Adrian Maurice Dirac d.
1985	31 Aug.	Sir Frank Macfarlane Burnet d.
1985	6 Sept.	Rodney Robert Porter d.
1986		Fritz Lipmann† d.
1986	31 May	Leo James Rainwater d.
1986	22 Oct.	Albert von Szent-Györgi d.
1986	23 Oct.	Edward Adelbert Doisy d.
1987		Walter H. Brattain† d.
1987		W. P. Murphy† d.
1987		John A. Ratcliffe† d.
1987	19 Mar.	Louis de Broglie d.
1987	17 May	John Howard Northrop d.
1988		Å. Åkeson† d.
1988	11 Jan.	Isidor Isaac Rabi d.
1988	15 Feb.	Richard Phillips Feynman d.
1988	27 May	E. A. F. Ruska d.
1988	1 Sept.	Walter Luis Alvarez d.
1988	9 Oct.	Felix Wankel d.

1988	22 Nov.	Raymond Arthur Dart d.
1988	21 Dec.	Nikolaas Tinbergen d.
1989	7 Jan	Hirohito d.
1989	27 Feb.	Konrad Zacharias Lorenz d.
1989	22 Apr.	Emilio Gino Segrè d.
1989	9 June	George Wells Beadle d.
1989	12 Aug.	William Shockley d.
1989	26 Oct.	Charles John Pedersen d.
1989	14 Dec.	Andrei Dimitrievich Sakharov d.
1990	6 Jan.	Pavel Aleksejevic Cherenkov d.
1990	25 Jan.	William Alan Stewart Butement d.
1991		M. C. Chang† d.
1991		Salvador E. Luria† d.
1991		Lu Gwei-Djen† d.
1991	11 Jan.	Carl David Anderson d.
1991	30 Jan.	John Bardeen d.
1991	2 Feb.	Sir Monty Finniston d.
1991	1 Mar.	Edwin Herbert Land d.
1991	15 Mar.	Robert (Robin) Hill d.
1991	7 Sept.	Edwin Mattison McMillan d.
1992	8 Apr.	Daniele Buvet d.
1992	2 Sept.	Barbara McClintock d.
1992	5 Nov.	Jan Hendrik Oort d.
1993		R. W. Holley† d

APPENDIX

A List of Scientists whose names occur in the book but for whom no full biographies are included, with references to the entry or entries in which each appears and to additional sources.

ABEL, J. J. (1857–1938). See Whipple, G. H.
 Obituary Notices of Fellows of the Royal Society.
 1939
 Dictionary of Scientific Biography
ABERNETHY, John (1764–1831). See Brodie, Sir B. C.
 Dictionary of National Biography
ABU MUSA JABIR IBN HAYYAN (fl. 8th cent.). See
 Geber
 Dictionary of American Biography
ADAMS, W. S. (1876–1956). See Hale, G. E.
 Dictionary of Scientific Biography
 Biographical Memoirs. National Academy of
 Science. 1958
AEPINUS, F. U. T. (1724–1802). See Wilcke, J. C.
 Dictionary of Scientific Biography
AHLQUIST, R. (1914–). See Black, J. W.
 A. G. Debus (Ed.), World Who's Who in Science.
 1968
AIRY, Sir George (1801–92). See Adams, J. C.
 Dictionary of Scientific Biography
 W. Airy, Ed. Autobiography of Sir George Airy. 1896
ÅKASON, Å. (1914–88). See Theorell, A. H. T.
AL-QUSHCHI (AL-KASHI), Muhammad (d. c.1430).
 See Stevinus, S.
 Dictionary of Scientific Biography
ALSTRÖMER, Baron Clas (1736–96). See Dahl, A.
 Poggendorff, Handwörterbuch zur Geschichte der
 Exakten Wissenschaften
AMAGAT, E. H. (1841–1915). See Bridgman, P. W.
 Dictionary of Scientific Biography
AMONTONS, G. (1663–1705). See Fahrenheit, G. D.
 Dictionary of Scientific Biography
ANDERSON, Sir John (1882–1958). See Bohr, N.
 Dictionary of National Biography
ANFINSEN, Christian B. (1916–). See Moore, S.
 Tyler Wasson (Ed.), Nobel Prize Winners. 1987
ANGLADA, Joseph (1775–1833). See Balard, A. J.
 Poggendorff, Handwörterbuch zur Geschichte der
 Exakten Wissenschaften
APIAN (1531–89). See Richard of Wallingford
ARBER, W. (1929–). See Smith, H. C.
 Tyler Wasson (Ed.), Nobel Prize Winners. 1987
ARFWEDSON, J. A. (1792–1841). See Berzelius, J. J.
 Dictionary of Scientific Biography, Supp. I
ARGAND, J. R. (1768–1822). See Hamilton, Sir W. R.;
 Kennelly, A. E.
 Dictionary of Scientific Biography
ARMSTRONG, E. F. (1878–1945). See Armstrong,
 H. E.
 Obituary Notices of Fellows of the Royal Society.
 1948
 Dictionary of Scientific Biography
ARMSTRONG, Sir William (1810–1900). See
 Whitworth, Sir J.
 Dictionary of National Biography
ARNOLD, John (1736–99). See Berthoud, F.
 Dictionary of National Biography
ARTEDI, Petrus (1705–35). See Linnaeus, C.
 Dictionary of Scientific Biography
ASCLEPIADES (c.124– c.40 BC). See Hoffmann, F.
 Dictionary of Scientific Biography
ASHMOLE, Elias (1617–92). See Norton, T.

Dictionary of National Biography
AUBURTIN, S. A. E. (1825–?1893). See Hitzig, E.
 W. Haymaker and F. Schiller (Eds.), Founders of
 Neurology. 1970
AUBREY, John (1626–97). See Wallis, J.
 Dictionary of National Biography
 A. Powell, John Aubrey and His Friends. Rev.
 ed. 1970
AUENBRUGGER, L. (1722–1809). See Morgagni, G. B.
 Dictionary of Scientific Biography

BABCOCK, Harold Delos (1882–). See Babcock,
 H. W.
 A. G. Debus (Ed.), World Who's Who in Science. 1968
BACHET, C. G. (1581–1638). See Fermat, P. de
 Dictionary of Scientific Biography
BACHMAN, John (1790–1874). See Audubon, J. J.
 Dictionary of American Biography
BACON, Richard (1775–1844). See Donkin, B.
 Dictionary of National Biography
BALFOUR, Andrew (1873–1931). See Wellcome, H. S.
 Dictionary of National Biography
BALL, William (1627–90). See Cassini, G. D.
 A. Armitage, Notes and Records of the Royal Society
 of London, 15, 167, 1960
BALTIMORE, D. (1938–). See Temin, H. M.
 Tyler Wasson (Ed.), Nobel Prize Winners. 1987
BAMBERGER, E. (1857–1932). See Hantzsch, A. R.
 Dictionary of Scientific Biography
BANCROFT, Joseph (1836–94). See Lewis, T. R.
 Dictionary of National Biography
BARBARO, Daniel (1528–69). See Belon, P.
 Nouvelle Biographie Universelle. 1852–66
BARBIER, P. A. (1848–1922). See Grignard, F. A. V.
 J. R. Partington, A History of Chemistry. Vol. 4. 1964
BARLOW, Edward (1639–1719). See Tompion, T.
 Dictionary of National Biography
BARRETT, Sir William (1844–1925). See Hadfield, Sir
 R. A.
 Who Was Who
BARRINGTON, Daines (1727–1800). See White, G.
 Dictionary of National Biography
BARTELS, J. M. C. (1769–1836). See Lobachevski, N. I.
BARTHOLIN, Thomas (1616–80). See Bartholin, R.;
 Rudbeck, O.
 Dictionary of Scientific Biography
BASSI, Laura (1711–78). See Spallanzani, L.
BASTIANELLI, Giuseppe (1862–1959). See Grassi,
 G. B.
BATEMAN, Thomas (1778–1821). See Addison, T.
 Dictionary of National Biography
BAUMÉ, A. (1728–1804). See Bergman, T. O.
 Dictionary of Scientific Biography
BEADLE, Clayton (1868–1917). See Bevan, E. J.
BEAUNE, F. de (1601–52). See Descartes, R.
 Nouvelle Biographie Universelle. 1852–66
BEAUNIS, Henri (1830–1921). See Binet, A.
BECCARIA, G. B. (1716–81). See Volta, A.
 Dictionary of Scientific Biography
BECQUEREL, Edmond (1820–91). See Becquerel,
 A. H.; Lippmann, G.
BEECKMAN, Isaac (1588–1637). See Descartes, R.
 Dictionary of Scientific Biography

BELL, Alexander Melville (1819–1905). *See* Bell, A. G.
Dictionary of American Biography
BELL, John (1763–1820). *See* Bell, Sir C.
Dictionary of National Biography
BELL, Lowthian (1816–1904). *See* Thomas, S. G.
Dictionary of National Biography
BELL, Susan J. (BURNELL) (1943–   ). *See* Gold
Who's Who. 1993
BELLINI, Lorenzo (1643–1704). *See* Malpighi, M.
Dictionary of Scientific Biography
BEMMELEN, J. M. van (1830–1911). *See* Roozeboom,
H. W. B.
Poggendorff, *Handwörterbuch zur Geschichte der
Exakten Wissenschaften*
BENIVIENI, Antonio (1443–1502). *See* Morgagni, G. B.
Dictionary of Scientific Biography
BENTHAM, Jeremy (1748–1832). *See* Bentham, G.;
Priestley, J.
Dictionary of National Biography
BENTHAM, Sir Samuel (1757–1831). *See* Brunel, Sir
M. I.
Dictionary of National Biography
BENTLEY, Thomas (1731–80). *See* Wedgwood, J.
Dictionary of National Biography
BERGIER, N. (1567–1623). *See* Trésaguet, P.
Nouvelle Biographie Universelle. 1852–66
BERGMANN, Ernst von (1836–1907). *See* Macewen,
Sir W.
R. H. Major, *A History of Medicine*. 1954
BERGMANN, M. (1886–1944). *See* Du Vigneaud, V.
BERKELEY, George (1685–1753). *See* Fitzgerald, G. F.;
Maclaurin, C.
Dictionary of Scientific Biography
BERNAL, J. D. (1901–71). *See* Hodgkin, D. M. C.;
Perutz, M. F.
*Biographical Memoirs of Fellows of the Royal
Society*. 1980
BERNOULLI, Nicolaus (1695–1726). *See* Bernoulli, D.
Dictionary of Scientific Biography
BESSY, Frénicle de (*c*.1602–75). *See* Fermat, P. de
Dictionary of Scientific Biography
BIDDER, G. P. (1806–78). *See* Stephenson, R.
Dictionary of National Biography
BIGNAMI, Amico (1862–1929). *See* Grassi, G. B.
R.H. Major, *A History of Medicine*. 1954
BILLROTH, Theodor (1829–94). *See* Kocher, E. T.
Dictionary of Scientific Biography
BINNIG, Gerd (1947–   ). *See* Ruska, E. A. F.; Rohrer,
H.
Tyler Wasson (Ed.), *Nobel Prize Winners*. 1987
BIRAIN, M. F. P. G. de (1766–1824). *See* Ampère,
A. M.
BIRKBECK, George (1776–1841). *See* Graham, T.; Ure,
A.
Dictionary of National Biography
BISSELL, G. H. (1821–84). *See* Drake, E. L.
Dictionary of American Biography
BJERKNES, C. A. (1825–1903) *See* Bjerknes, J. A. L.
Dictionary of Scientific Biography
BJERKNES, V. F. K. (1862–1951. *See* Bjerknes, J. A. L.;
Spörer, G. F. W.
Dictionary of Scientific Biography
BOCK, Hieronymus (1498–1554). *See* Fuchs, L.
Dictionary of Scientific Biography
A. Arber, *Herbals* (Pbk). 1986
BOHR, Christian (1855–1911). *See* Haldane, J. S.;
Krogh, S. A. S.
A. G. Debus (Ed.), *World Who's Who in Science*.
1968
BOISBAUDRAN, P. E. L. de (1838–1912). *See* Gadolin,
J.
Dictionary of Scientific Biography
BOLL, Franz (1849–79). *See* Kuhne, W.
BONET, Theophilus (1620–89). *See* Morgagni, G. B.

Bulletin of the History of Medicine, **12**, 623, 1943
BONPLAND, A. J. A. (1773–1858). *See* Humboldt,
Baron F. H. A. von
Nouvelle Biographie Universelle. 1852–66
BOOT (or BOATE), Arnold (1600?–1653?). *See*
Glisson, F.
Dictionary of National Biography
BOOT, Sir Jesse, Lord Trent (1850–1931). *See*
Kipping, F. S.
Dictionary of National Biography
BOSCOVICH, R. J. (1711–87). *See* Faraday, M.
Dictionary of Scientific Biography
BOTHE, Walther (1891–1957). *See* Chadwick, J.;
Geiger, H. W.; Peierls, R. E.
Dictionary of Scientific Biography
Tyler Wasson (Ed.), *Nobel Prize Winners*, 1987
BOUILLAUD, J. B. (1796–1881). *See* Hitzig, E.
Nouvelle Biographie Universelle. 1852–66
BOUQUER, Pierre (1698–1758). *See* Cavendish, H.;
Celsius, A.; La Condamine, C-M. de
Dictionary of Scientific Biography
BOURDELIN, L. C. (1696–1777). *See* Rouelle, G. F.
BOURNE, William (d. 1583). *See* Digges, L. & T.
Dictionary of National Biography
BOUTON, Charles-Marie (1781–1835). *See* Daguerre,
L. J. M.
BOUVART, Alexis (1767–1843). *See* Adams, J. C.; Le
Verrier, U. J. J.
Dictionary of Scientific Biography
BRASSAVOLA, Antonio Musa (1500–55). *See*
Falloppio, G.
Nouvelle Biographie Universelle. 1852–66
BRATTAIN, Walter Houser (1902–87). *See* Bardeen,
J.; Shockley, W.
Tyler Wasson (Ed.), *Nobel Prize Winners*. 1987
BREDT, Julius (1855–1937). *See* Perkin, W. H., jun.
A. G. Debus (Ed.), *World Who's Who in Science*. 1968
BREGUET, L. F. C. (1804–83). *See* Fizeau, A. H. L.
Dictionary of Scientific Biography
BREUER, J. (1842–1925). *See* Freud, S.
Neue Österreichische Biographie. 1923–25
BRIANCHON, C. J. (1783–1864). *See* Pascal, B.
BRIDGES, C. B. (1889–1938). *See* Morgan, T. H.
A. G. Debus (Ed.), *World Who's Who in Science*. 1968
Dictionary of Scientific Biography
BROCKLESBY, R. (1722–97). *See* Young, T.
Journal of the History of Medicine, **17**, 509, 1962
BRONGNIART, A. T. (1801–76). *See* Brongniart, A.
Dictionary of Scientific Biography
BRONK, D. W. (1897–1975). *See* Adrian, E. D.
Dictionary of Scientific Biography, Supp. II
BROWN, John (1735–88). *See* Hoffmann, F.
BRÜCKE, E. W. von (1819–92). *See* Freud, S.
Dictionary of Scientific Biography
BRUNFELS, Otto (1464–1534). *See* Fuchs, L.
Dictionary of Scientific Biography
BUCHNER, Hans (1850–1902). *See* Mechnikov, I.
A. G. Debus (Ed.), *World Who's Who in Science*. 1968
BUCKLAND, W. (1800–74). *See* Agassiz, J. L. R.
BUCKLAND, William (1784–1856). *See* Harcourt,
W. V. V.; Lyell, Sir C.
Dictionary of Scientific Biography
BUCQUET, J. B. M. (1746–89). *See* Fourcroy, A. F. de
Dictionary of Scientific Biography
BULLOCK, William (1813–67). *See* Hoe, R. M.
BULLOCK, William (1868–1941). *See* Twort, F. W.
Dictionary of Scientific Biography
BURDIN, Claude (1790–1873). *See* Fourneyron, B.
A. G. Debus (Ed.), *World Who's Who in Science*. 1968
BÜTSCHLI, O. (1848–1920). *See* Grassi, G. B.
Dictionary of Scientific Biography

CABANIS, P. J. G. (1757–1808). *See* Ampère, A. M.
Dictionary of Scientific Biography

CADET, L. C. (1731–99). *See* Bunsen, R. W.
Dictionary of Scientific Biography
CAHN, R. S. (1899–1981). *See* Prelog, V.
CAHOURS, A. A. T. (1813–91). *See* Étard, A. E.
Dictionary of Scientific Biography
CAIRNS, Hugh (1896–1952). *See* Florey, H. W.
Dictionary of National Biography
CAJORI, Florian (1859–1930). *See* Huygens, C.
R. C. Archibald, *Isis*, **17**, 384, 1932
A. G. Debus (Ed.), *World Who's Who in Science*. 1968
CALCAR, Jan Stefan van (1499–1546). *See* Vesalius,
A.
Nouvelle Biographie Universelle. 1852–66
Dictionary of American Biography
CAMPBELL, John (*c*.1720–90). *See* Hadley, J.
Dictionary of National Biography
CAMUS, C. E. L. (1699–1768). *See* Celsius, A.
Dictionary of Scientific Biography
CANDOLLE, Alphonse de (1806–93). *See* Candolle,
A. P. de
Dictionary of Scientific Biography
CANTON, John (1718–72). *See* Priestley, J.
Dictionary of Scientific Biography
CAPITO, Fabricius (1478–1541). *See* Gesner, C.
Nouvelle Biographie Universelle. 1852–66
CARATHEODORY, Constantin (1873–1950). *See*
Born, M.
Dictionary of Scientific Biography
CARLISLE, A. (1768–1840). *See* Volta, A.
Dictionary of Scientific Biography
CARO, H. (1834–1911). *See* Graebe, C.; Perkin, Sir
W. H.
Dictionary of Scientific Biography
CARROLL, J. (1854–1907). *See* Reed, W.
Dictionary of Scientific Biography
CARTER, H. R. (1852–1925). *See* Reed, W.
Dictionary of American Biography
CASSERIUS (1561–1616). *See* Fabricius, H.
Dictionary of Scientific Biography
CASSINI, J. (1677–1756). *See* Belidor, B. F. de
Dictionary of Scientific Biography
CASTELLI, Benedetto (1577–1644). *See* Borelli, G. A.;
Torricelli, E.
Dictionary of Scientific Biography
CATON, R. (1842–1926). *See* Berger, H.
W. Haymaker and F. Schiller (Eds.), *The Founders of
Neurology*. 1970
CAVANILLES, A. J. (1745–1804). *See* Dahl, A.
Dictionary of Scientific Biography
CHABANEAU, P. F. (1754–1842). *See* Wollaston,
W. H.
D. McDonald, *A History of Platinum*. 1960
CHALLIS, James (1803–82). *See* Adams, J. C.
Dictionary of Scientific Biography
CHAMBERLAND, C. E. (1851–1908). *See* Roux,
P. P. E.
Dictionary of Scientific Biography
CHAMBERLAIN, Owen (1920–). *See* Segrè, E.
Tyler Wasson (Ed.), *Nobel Prize Winners*. 1987
CHANG, M. C. (1908–91). *See* Pincus, G. G.
A. G. Debus (Ed.), *World Who's Who in Science*. 1968
CHESELDEN, William (1688–1752). *See* Hunter, J.;
Monro, A., *primus*; Whytt, R.
Dictionary of National Biography
CHETVERIKÓV, S. S. (1880–1959). *See* Dhobzhansky,
T. G.
CHEVALIER, C. (1804–50). *See* Rühmkorff, H. D.
A. G. Debus (Ed.), *World Who's Who in Science*. 1968
CHLADNI, E. F. F. (1756–1824). *See* Wheatstone, C.
Dictionary of Scientific Biography
CLAIRAUT, A. C. (1713–65). *See* Celsius, A.;
Maclaurin, C.
Dictionary of Scientific Biography
CLANNY, W. R. (1776–1850). *See* Stephenson, G.

Dictionary of National Biography
CLAPEYRON, B. P. E. (1799–1864). *See* Carnot,
N. L. S.
Dictionary of Scientific Biography
CLARK, A. G. (1804–87). *See* Bessel, F. W.
Dictionary of Scientific Biography
CLARKE, Samuel (1675–1729). *See* Leibniz, G. W.
Dictionary of Scientific Biography
CLAUDE, Albert (1899–1983). *See* Palade, G. E.
Tyler Wasson (Ed.), *Nobel Prize Winners*. 1987
CLAVIUS, Christopher (1537–1612). *See* Galilei, G.;
Viète, F.
Dictionary of Scientific Biography
CLAY, J. (1882–1955). *See* Compton, A. H.
Dictionary of Scientific Biography
CLEBSCH, Rudolph (1833–72). *See* Gordan, P. A.
Dictionary of Scientific Biography
CLEGHORN, William (1754–83). *See* Gamble, J. C.
J. R. Partington, *A History of Chemistry*. Vol. 3,
1962
CLÉMENT-DÉSORMES, Nicolas (1779–1841). *See*
Désormes, C. B.
Dictionary of Scientific Biography
CLERK, Dugald (1854–1932). *See* Benz, K.
Dictionary of National Biography
CLERKE, A. M. (1842–1907). *See* Saha, M.
Who Was Who
CLIFT, William (1775–1849). *See* Baillie, M.
Dictionary of Scientific Biography
COHEN, Stanley (1935–). *See* Boyer, H. W.;
Levi-Montalcini, R.
Tyler Wasson (Ed.), *Nobel Prize Winners*. 1987
COLLET-DESCOTILS, H. V. (1773–1815). *See*
Tennant, S.
Dictionary of Scientific Biography
COLLINS, John (1625–83). *See* Gregory, J.
Dictionary of Scientific Biography
COMTE, A. M. F. X. (1798–1857). *See* Williamson,
A. W.
Dictionary of Scientific Biography
CONDORCET, Marquis de (1743–94). *See* Fresnel,
A. J.; Macquer, P. J.
Dictionary of Scientific Biography
COOKE, J. P. (1827–94). *See* Richards, T. W.
Dictionary of Scientific Biography
CORDUS, Valerius (1515–44). *See* Belon, P.
Dictionary of Scientific Biography
CORI, C. F. (1896–1984). *See* Cori, G. T. R.; Krebs,
E. G.
CORNFORTH, John W. (1917–). *See* Prelog, V.
Tyler Wasson (Ed.), *Nobel Prize Winners*. 1987
CORRENS, K. E. (1864–1935). *See* Bateson, W.;
Mendel, J. G.; Vries, H. de
Dictionary of Scientific Biography
CORVISART, J. N. (1775–1821). *See* Laënnec, R. T. H.
Dictionary of Scientific Biography
COTES, Roger (1682–1716). *See* Demoivre, A.;
Wallis, J.
Dictionary of National Biography
Dictionary of Scientific Biography
CRAWFORD, A. (1748/9–1795). *See* Gadolin, J.
Dictionary of Scientific Biography
CRELLE, Leopold (1780–1855). *See* Abel, N. H.
Dictionary of Scientific Biography
CROSFIELD, James (1787–1852). *See* Gamble, J. C.
A. E. Musson, *Enterprise in Soap and Chemicals*.
1965
CROSFIELD, Joseph (1792–1844). *See* Gamble, J. C.
A. E. Musson, *Enterprise in Soap and Chemicals*.
1965
CRUVEILHIER, Jean (1791–1874). *See* Charcot, J-M.
Dictionary of Scientific Biography
CUÉNOT, L. (1866–1951). *See* Morgan, T. H.
Dictionary of Scientific Biography

CULLEN, William (1710–90). *See* Black, J.; Hoffmann, F.; Rush, B.
Dictionary of National Biography
Dictionary of Scientific Biography
CUNNINGHAM, D. D. (1843–1914). *See* Lewis, T. R.
A. G. Debus (Ed.), *World Who's Who in Science.* 1968
CURTIUS, T. C. (1857–1928). *See* Buchner, E.
Dictionary of Scientific Biography

d'ABBANS, Marquis Claude de Jouffroy (1751–1832). *See* Fulton, R.
DALYELL, Sir John Graham (1775–1851). *See* Bell, P.
Dictionary of National Biography
DAM, Carl Peter Henrik (1895–1976). *See* Doisy, E. A.
Dictionary of Scientific Biography, Supp. II
DANDY, W. (1886–1946). *See* Moniz, A. E.
R. H. Major, *A History of Medicine*. 1954
DARBY, Abraham III (1750–91). *See* Darby, A.
Dictionary of National Biography
D'ARCET, J. P. J. (1725–1801). *See* Rouelle, H. M.
Dictionary of Scientific Biography
DARWIN, Sir Charles Galton (1887–1962). *See* Born, M.
Dictionary of National Biography
DARWIN, Sir George (1845–1912). *See* Jeans, Sir J. H.
Dictionary of National Biography
DAUBENTON, L. J. M. (1716–1800). *See* Buffon, Comte G. L. L. de
Dictionary of Scientific Biography
DAVIDSON, J. N. (1911–72). *See* Chargaff, E.
DAVISSON, Clinton Joseph (1881–1958). *See* De Broglie, L.
Dictionary of Scientific Biography
Tyler Wasson (Ed.), *Nobel Prize Winners*. 1987
DAY, Thomas (1748–89). *See* Edgeworth, R. L.
R. G. Schofield, *The Lunar Society of Birmingham.* 1963
DEBIERNE, A. (1874–1949). *See* Curie, M.
A. G. Debus (Ed.), *World Who's Who in Science.* 1968
DEBRAY, Henri Jules (1827–88). *See* Moissan, F. F. H.
Dictionary of Scientific Biography
DE DUVE, Christian (1917–). *See* Palade, G. E.
Tyler Wasson (Ed.), *Nobel Prize Winners*, 1987
DEE, John (1527–1608). *See* Digges, L. & T.
Dictionary of National Biography
DELAUNAY, C. E. (1816–72). *See* Le Verrier, U. J. J.
Dictionary of Scientific Biography
de l'HÔPITAL, G. F. A. (1661–1704). *See* Bernoulli, Jean
Dictionary of Scientific Biography
della TORRE, Marcantonio (1478 ? 1481–1511). *See* Leonardo da Vinci
DEMARQUAY, J. N. (1811–75). *See* Lewis, T. R.
DEMOCRITUS OF ABDERA (d. 361 BC). *See* Epicurus
Dictionary of Scientific Biography
DE MORGAN, A. (1806–71). *See* Hamilton, Sir W. R.
Dictionary of National Biography
DENYS, Jean (1625?–1704). *See* Lower, R.
DESAULT, P. J. (1744–95). *See* Bichat, M. F. X.
B. B. Beeson, *Annals of Medical History*, 5, 342, 1933
DESCROIZILLES, F. A. H. (1751–1825). *See* Berthollet, C. L.
C. Duval, *Journal of Chemical Education*, 28, 508, 1951
DESLANDRES, Henri (1853–1948). *See* Janssen, P. J. C.
Dictionary of Scientific Biography
DESTUTT DE TRACY, A. L. C. (1754–1836). *See* Ampère, A. M.
d'HÉRELLE, Félix (1873–1949). *See* Twort, F. W.
H. J. Parish, *A History of Immunization*. 1965
DEWAR, M. J. S. (1918–). *See* Nozoe, T.
Who's Who. 1993

DICKINSON, W. Lee (1862–1904). *See* Langley, J. N.
DIRICHLET, Peter Gustav Lejeune (1805–59). *See* Dedekind, J. W., Fourier, J. B. J.
Dictionary of Scientific Biography
DIXON, Jeremiah (c.1741–1771). *See* Maskelyne, N.
Dictionary of Scientific Biography
DJERASSI, C. (1923–). *See* Woodward, R.B.
C Djerassi, *Autobiography*. 1992
DODOENS, R. (1517–85). *See* Gerard, J.
A. Arber, *Herbals* (Pbk). 1986
DOISY, Edward (1893–1986). *See* Dam, C. P. H.
Tyler Wasson (Ed.), *Nobel Prize Winners*. 1987
DONATI, G. B. (1826–73). *See* Huggins, Sir W.
Dictionary of Scientific Biography
DONOVAN, Charles (1863–1951). *See* Leishman, W. B.
DRIFFIELD, V. C. (1848–1915). *See* Hurter, F.
D. W. F. Hardie, *A History of the Chemical Industry in Widnes*. 1950
DRUDE, P. K. L. (1863–1906). *See* Lowry, T. M.
Dictionary of Scientific Biography
DUBOIS, É. F. (1882–1959). *See* Lusk, G.
DUCHENNE DE BOULOGNE, G. B. A. (1806–75). *See* Charcot, J-M.
V. Robinson, *Medical Life*, 36, 287, 1929
DUDLEY, Dud (1599–1684). *See* Darby, A.
Dictionary of National Biography
DUDLEY, Harold Ward (1887–1935). *See* Dale, H. H.
DUFOUR, Henri (1787–1875). *See* Seguin, M.
Dictionary of Scientific Biography
DUMÉRIL, A. M. C. (1774–1860). *See* Cuvier, Baron G. L. C. F. D.
Dictionary of Scientific Biography
DUPIN, C. (1784–1873). *See* Monge, G.
Dictionary of Scientific Biography
DUPPA, B. F. (1828–73). *See* Perkin, Sir W. H.
A. G. Debus (Ed.), *World Who's Who in Science*. 1968
DUPUYTREN, G. (1777–1835). *See* Thenard, L. J.
A. G. Debus (Ed.), *World Who's Who in Science.* 1968
DUVERNOY, G. L. (1777–1855). *See* Cuvier, Baron G. L. C. F. D.
A. G. Debus (Ed.), *World Who's Who in Science*. 1968
DWIGHT, Timothy (1752–1817). *See* Silliman, B.
Dictionary of American Biography

EARNSHAW, Thomas (1749–1829). *See* Berthoud, F.
Dictionary of National Biography
EASTMAN, George (1854–1932). *See* Baekeland, L. H.
Dictionary of American Biography
EATON, Amos (1776–1842). *See* Hall, J.
Dictionary of Amrican Biography
EDELMAN, G. M. (1929–). *See* Porter, R. N.
Tyler Wasson (Ed.), *Nobel Prize Winners*. 1987
EDGAR, Edward Charles (1881–1938). *See* Dixon, H. B.
A. G. Debus (Ed.), *World Who's Who in Science*. 1968
EDLUND, E. (1819–88). *See* Arrhenius, S. A.
A. G. Debus (Ed.), *World Who's Who in Science.* 1968
EDWARDS, Sydenham (1769?–1819). *See* Curtis, W.
Dictionary of National Biography
EHRENFEST, Paul (1880–1933). *See* Tinbergen, N.; Breit, G.; Peierls, R. E.; Casimir, H. B. G., Fermi, E.
Dictionary of Scientific Biography
EIGEN, Manfred (1927–). *See* Porter, G.
Tyler Wasson (Ed.), *Nobel Prize Winners*. 1987
EINHORN, A. (1857–1917). *See* Willstätter, R.
EISENSTEIN, F. G. M. (1823–52). *See* Riemann, G. F. B.
Dictionary of Scientific Biography
ELION, Gertrude Belle (1918–). *See* Black, J. W.
Who's Who. 1993
ELKINGTON, Henry (1810–52). *See* Elkington, G. R.
Dictionary of National Biography

ELLIOTT, T. R. (1877–1961). *See* Loewi, O.
Biographical Memoirs of Fellows of the Royal Society. 1961
Dictionary of National Biography
EMICH, F. (1860–1940). *See* Pregl, F.
A. G. Debus (Ed.), *World Who's Who in Science.* 1968
ENCKE, J. F. (1791–1865). *See* Schiaparelli, G. V.
Dictionary of Scientific Biography
ERASMUS (1466–1536). *See* Paracelsus
R. S. Bainton, *Erasmus.* 1970
ESSON, W. (1839–1916). *See* Guldberg, C. M.
Dictionary of Scientific Biography
ETTINGHAUSEN, A. von (1850–1932). *See* Nernst, H. W.
Poggendorff, *Handwörterbuch zur Geschichte der Exakten Wissenschaften*
EUCLID OF MEGARA (5th cent. BC). *See* Euclid
T. C. Heath, *Greek Mathematics.* 1921
Dictionary of Scientific Biography
EWALD, Paul (1888–1985). *See* Born, M.; von Laue, M. T. F.
Dictionary of Scientific Biography, Supp. II
EXNER, F. S. (1849–1922). *See* Freud, S.
A. G. Debus (Ed.), *World Who's Who in Science.* 1968

FAHLBERG, C. (1850–1910). *See* Remsen, I.
A. G. Debus (Ed.), *World Who's Who in Science.* 1968
FAJANS, Kasimir (1887–1975). *See* Soddy, F.
Dictionary of Scientific Biography
FEATHER, Norman (1904–78). *See* Wilson, C. T. R.
Biographical Memoirs of Fellows of the Royal Society. 1981
FENNER, F. J. (1914–   ). *See* Burnet, F. M.
Who's Who. 1993
FERGUSON, John (1837–1916). *See* Desch, C. H.
FERRARI, Luigi (1522–65). *See* Cardano, G.
Dictionary of Scientific Biography
FIELD, C. W. (1819–92). *See* Morse, S. F. B.
Dictionary of American Biography
FIESER, L. F. (1899–1977). See Nakanishi, K.
Dictionary of Scientific Biography, Supp. II
FILHOL, Edward (1814–83). *See* Senderens, J-B.
Poggendorff, *Handwörterbuch zur Geschichte der Exakten Wissenschaften*
FISCHER, Edmond H. (1920–   ). See Krebs, E. G.
Les Prix Nobel en 1992. 1993
FISCHER, Otto (1852–1932). *See* Fischer, E.
A. G. Debus (Ed.), *World Who's Who in Science.* 1968
FLACK, Martin (1882–1931). *See* Keith, Sir A.
Who Was Who
FLETCHER, W. Morley (1873–1933). *See* Hill, A. V.; Hopkins, Sir F. G.
Dictionary of National Biography
FLEXNER, S. (1863–1946), See Rous, F. P.
Obituary Notices of Fellows of the Royal Society. 1948–9
FOERSTER, O. (1873–1941). *See* Penfield, W. G.
A. G. Debus (Ed.), *World Who's Who in Science.* 1968
FORBES, J. D. (1809–68). *See* Dewar, J.
A. G. Debus (Ed.), *World Who's Who in Science.* 1968
FORSTER, J. G. A. (1754–94). *See* Humboldt, Baron F. H. A. von
Dictionary of Scientific Biography
FOSTER, Sir Michael (1836–1907). *See* Balfour, F. M.; Gaskell, W. H.; Langley, J. N.; Sherrington, C. S.
Dictionary of Scientific Biography
FOWLER, Ralph Howard (1889–1944). *See* Dirac, P. A. M.; Milne, E. A.
Biographical Memoirs of Fellows of the Royal Society. 1945
Dictionary of Scientific Biography
FRANK, Ilya (1908–   ). *See* Cherenkov, P. A.

Tyler Wasson (Ed.), *Nobel Prize Winners.* 1987
FRANKLAND, P. F. (1859–1946). *See* Aston, F. W.; Frankland, Sir E.
Dictionary of Scientific Biography
FRÉMY, Edmond (1814–94). *See* Moissan, F. F. H.
Dictionary of Scientific Biography
FRERICHS, F. T. von (1819–85). *See* Ehrlich, P.
R. H. Major, *A History of Medicine.* 1954
FRIEDLÄNDER, C. (1847–87). *See* Gram, H. C. J.
FRIEDMAN, J. I. (1930–   ). *See* Kendall, H. W.
Les Prix Nobel en 1992. 1993
FRIEDRICH, W. (1883–1968). *See* Bragg, W. H.; Bragg, W. L.
P. Forman, *Archive for History of Exact Sciences*, **6**, 38, 1969
FRISIUS, Gemma (1508–55). *See* Mercator, G.
Dictionary of Scientific Biography
FULTON, J. F. (1899–1960). *See* Moniz, A. E.
Dictionary of Scientific Biography
FUST, Johann (*c.* 1400–66). *See* Gutenberg, J.
Allgemeine Deutsche Biographie. 1875–1912

GADD, P. A. (1727–97). *See* Gadolin, J.
Poggendorff, *Handwörterbuch zur Geschichte der Exakten Wissenschaften*
GADOLIN, Jacob (1719–1802). *See* Gadolin, J.
Poggendorff, *Handwörterbuch zur Geschichte der Exakten Wissenschaften*
GAERTNER, J. (1732–91). *See* Cesalpino, A.
A. G. Debus (Ed.), *World Who's Who in Science.* 1968
GAFFKY, Georg (1850–1918). *See* Koch, R.
Dictionary of Scientific Biography
GAGARIN, Yuri (1934–68). *See* Korolev, S. P.
Y. Gagarin, *My Brother Yuri.* 1974
GAHN, J. G. (1745–1818). *See* Scheele, C. W.; Thenard, L. J.
Dictionary of Scientific Biography
GALE, L. D. (1800–83). *See* Morse, S. F. B.
GALL, F. J. (1758–1828). *See* Flourens, J. P. M.
Dictionary of Scientific Biography
GALLE, J. G. (1812–1910). *See* Adams, J. C.
Dictionary of Scientific Biography
GALOIS, Évarist (1811–32). *See* Abel, N. H.; Dedekind, J. W. R.
Dictionary of Scientific Biography
GARBETT, Samuel (1717–1805). *See* Roebuck, J.
GARSTANG, W. (1868–1949). *See* Haeckel, E. H.
Who Was Who
GASKELL, Holbrook (1813–1909). *See* Deacon, H.; Solvay, E.
Dictionary of National Biography (Missing Persons). 1993
GAUDIN, M. A. A. (1804–80). *See* Avogadro, A.
Dictionary of Scientific Biography
GAUTIER, H. (1660–1713). *See* Trésaguet, P.
Nouvelle Biographie Universelle. 1852–66
GEGENBAUR, C. (1826–1903). *See* Grassi, G. B.
Dictionary of Scientific Biography
GEHUCHTEN, A. van (1861–1914). *See* Ramón y Cajal, S.
W. Haymaker and F. Schiller (Eds.), *The Founders of Neurology.* 1970
GEISSLER, H. (1814–79). *See* Rühmkorff, H. D.; Sprengel, H. J. P.
Poggendorff, *Handwörterbuch zur Geschichte der exakten Wissenschaften*
GERLACH, Walther (1889–   ). *See* Stern, O.
A. G. Debus (Ed.), *World Who's Who in Science.* 1968
GERMER, Lester Halbert (1896–   ). *See* De Broglie, L.
A. G. Debus (Ed.), *World Who's Who in Science.* 1968
GHINI, L. (1500–56). *See* Cesalpino, A.
Dictionary of Scientific Biography

GIAEVER, Ivar (1929–). *See* Josephson, B. D.; Esaki, L.
Tyler Wasson (Ed.), *Nobel Prize Winners.* 1987
GIBSON, J. (1855–1914). *See* Brown, A. C.
GILBERT (formerly GIDDY), Davies (1767–1839). *See* Beddoes, T.
Dictionary of National Biography
GILBERT, J. H. (1817–1901). *See* Lawes, J. B.; Liebig, Baron J. von
Dictionary of Scientific Biography
GODFREY, Thomas (1704–49). *See* Hadley, J.
Dictionary of Scientific Biography
GODIN, L. (1704–60). *See* La Condamine, C-M. de
Dictionary of Scientific Biography
GODLEE, Rickman (1849–1925). *See* Macewen, Sir W.
Dictionary of National Biography
GOEPPERT, H. R. (1800–84). *See* Engler, H. G. A.
Dictionary of Scientific Biography
GOETZ, J. C. (1688–1733). *See* Stahl, G. E.
Dictionary of Scientific Biography
GOLTZ, F. (1834–1902). *See* Sherrington, C. S.
Dictionary of Scientific Biography
GOLTZIUS, Hendrik (1558–1617). *See* Drebbel, C.
Nouvelle Biographie Universelle. 1852–66
GOODSIR, J. (1814–67). *See* Virchow, R. L. C.
Dictionary of Scientific Biography
GORE, George (1826–1908). *See* Moissan, F. F. H.
Dictionary of Scientific Biography
GOUGH, John (1757–1825). *See* Dalton, J.
Dictionary of National Biography
GRAEFE, Albrecht von (1828–70). *See* Bowman, Sir W.
R. H. Major, *A History of Medicine.* 1954
GRAHAM, George (1673–1751). *See* Harrison, J.; Tompion, T.
Dictionary of National Biography
GRAMME, Z. T. (1826–1901). *See* Crompton, R. E. B.
Dictionary of Scientific Biography
GRASSMANN, H. G. (1809–77). *See* Whitehead, A. N.
Dictionary of Scientific Biography
GREGORY, D. F. (1813–44). *See* Boole, G.
Dictionary of Scientific Biography
GREGORY, Olinthus (1774–1841). *See* Evans, O.
Dictionary of Scientific Biography
GRIMAUX, L. E. (1835–1900). *See* Laurent, A.
A. G. Debus (Ed.), *World Who's Who in Science.* 1968
GUERIN, Camille (1872–1961). *See* Calmette, L. C. A.
H. J. Parish, *A History of Immunization.* 1965
GUETTARD, J. E. (1715–86). *See* Lavoisier, A. L.
Dictionary of Scientific Biography
GUINTHER, Johann (1505–74). *See* Servetus, M.; Vesalius, A.
Dictionary of Scientific Biography
GULDIN, Paul (1577–1643). *See* Cavalieri, B.; Pappus
Dictionary of Scientific Biography
GUTHRIE, F. (1833–86). *See* Boys, Sir C. V.
Dictionary of National Biography
GUYE, P. A. (1862–1922). *See* Guldberg, C. M.
A. G. Debus (Ed.), *World Who's Who in Science.* 1968
GUYOT, Arnold Henry (1807–84). *See* Hess, H. H.
A. G. Debus (Ed.), *World Who's Who in Science.* 1968
GUYTON DE MORVEAU, L. B. (1737–1816). *See* Désormes, C. B.; Lavoisier, A. L.
Dictionary of Scientific Biography
W. A. Smeaton, *Ambix,* **6**, 18, 1957

HACHETTE, J. N. P. (1769–1834). *See* Désormes, C. B.; Fortin, N.
Dictionary of Scientific Biography
HAGENBACH, A. (1871–1955). *See* Balmer, J. J.
A. G. Debus (Ed.), *World Who's Who in Science.* 1968
HALL, A. D. (1864–1942). *See* Russell, E. J.
Obituary Notices of Fellows of the Royal Society. 1942
HALL, Chester Moor (1703–71). *See* Dollond, J.

Dictionary of National Biography
HALSKE, J. G. (1814–90). *See* Siemens, E. W. von
A. G. Debus (Ed.), *World Who's Who in Science.* 1968
HALSTED, William S. (1852–1922). *See* Cushing, H.; Welch, W. H.
Dictionary of Scientific Biography
HAMBURGER, V. (1900–). *See* Levi-Montalcini, R.
A. G. Debus (Ed.), *World Who's Who in Science.* 1968
HAMPSON, William (c.1854–1926). *See* Claude, G.
HANSON, E. J. (1919–73). *See* Huxley, H. E.
Biographical Memoirs of Fellows of the Royal Society. 1975
HARDY, G. H. (1877–1947). *See* Ramanujan, S.; Wiener, N.
Dictionary of Scientific Biography
HARINGTON, C. R. (1897–1972). *See* Chain, E. B.; Du Vigneaud, V.
Biographical Memoirs of Fellows of the Royal Society. 1972
HARRIES, C. D. (1865–1923). *See* Staudinger, H.
J. R. Partington, *A History of Chemistry.* Vol. 4, 1964
HASENÖHRL, F. (1874–1915). *See* Schrödinger, E.
Dictionary of Scientific Biography
HASSELL, Odd (1897–1981). *See* Barton, D. H. R.
Tyler Wasson (Ed.), *Nobel Prize Winners.* 1987
HAUKSBEE, Francis, the younger (1687–1763). *See* Hauksbee, F.
Dictionary of National Biography
HAÜY, R. J. (1743–1822). *See* Brongniart, A.; Smithson, J.; Vauquelin, L. N.
Dictionary of Scientific Biography
HAWKINS, John (*fl.* 1686–1707). *See* Cocker, E.
E. G. R. Taylor, *Mathematical Practitioners of Tudor and Stuart England.* 1967
HAYWARD, Nathaniel (1808–65). *See* Goodyear, C.
Dictionary of American Biography
HEATLEY, Norman (1911–). *See* Chain, E. B.; Florey, H. W.
HEBRA, F. (1816–80). *See* Semmelweis, I. P.
R. H. Major, *A History of Medicine.* 1954
HEDLEY, William (1779–1843). *See* Stephenson, G.
Dictionary of National Biography
HEGEL, G. W. F. (1770–1831). *See* Nägeli, K. W. von
C. Taylor, *Hegel.* 1975
HEINROTH, Oscar (1871–1945). *See* Lorenz, K. Z.
A. G. Debus (Ed.), *World Who's Who in Science.* 1968
HELIODORUS OF LARISSA (1st cent. AD). *See* Bartholin, R.
A. G. Debus (Ed.), *World Who's Who in Science.* 1968
HENCH, Philip Showalter (1896–1965). *See* Kendall, E. C.
Tyler Wasson (Ed.), *Nobel Prize Winners.* 1987
HENLE, Jacob (1809–84). *See* Müller, J. P.; von Kölliker, R. A.
Dictionary of Scientific Biography
HENRY, Thomas (1734–1816). *See* Henry W.
Dictionary of Scientific Biography
HENSON, W. S. (1805–88). *See* Cayley, Sir G.
HERMITE, C. (1822–1901). *See* Cantor, G. F. L. P.; Fourier, J. B. J.; Poincaré, H.
Dictionary of Scientific Biography
HERRICK, James (1861–1954). *See* Einthoven, W.
A. G. Debus (Ed.), *World Who's Who in Science.* 1968
HERTWIG, Richard (1850–1937). *See* Boveri, T.
Dictionary of Scientific Biography
HESSE, W. R. (1881–1973). *See* Moniz, A. E.
Tyler Wasson (Ed.), *Nobel Prize Winners.* 1987
HEVELIUS (1611–87). *See* Halley, E.
Dictionary of Scientific Biography
HIGGINS, Bryan (c.1741–1818). *See* Higgins, W.
Dictionary of Scientific Biography
HIGGS, Peter Ware (1929–). *See* Salam, A.
Who's Who. 1993

HILBERT, D. (1862–1943). *See* Born, M.; Gordan, P. A.; Wiener, N.
Dictionary of Scientific Biography
HILLEBRAND, W. F. (1853–1925). *See* Ramsay, Sir W.
A. G. Debus (Ed.), *World Who's Who in Science*. 1968
HILLIER, James (1915–). *See* Zworykin, V. K.
A. G. Debus (Ed.), *World Who's Who in Science*. 1968
HINDLEY, Henry (1701–71). *See* Smeaton, J.
M. Daumas, *Scientific Instruments of the 17th and 18th Centuries and their Makers*. 1972
HIRST, E. L. (1898–1975). *See* Haworth, W. N.
Biographical Memoirs of Fellows of the Royal Society. 1976
HIS, Wilhelm (1863–1934). *See* His, W.
HISINGER, W. (1766–1852). *See* Berzelius, J. J.
Dictionary of Scientific Biography
HITCHINGS, George (1905–). *See* Black, J. W.
Les Prix Nobel en 1988. 1989
HJARNE, U. (1641–1724). *See* Cronstedt, A. F.
A. G. Debus (Ed.), *World Who's Who in Science*. 1968
HOAGLAND, Hudson (1899–). *See* Pincus, G. G.
A. G. Debus (Ed.), *World Who's Who in Science*. 1968
HOBBES, Thomas (1588–1679). *See* Wallis, J.
Dictionary of National Biography
HOE, Robert, (1784–1832). *See* Hoe, R. M.
Dictionary of American Biography
HOE, Robert, (1839–1909). *See* Hoe, R. M.
Dictionary of American Biography
HOFFMANN, Paul Erich (1868–1959). *See* Schaudinn, F. R.
A. G. Debus (Ed.), *World Who's Who in Science*. 1968
HOFFMANN, Roald (1937–). *See* Fukui, K.; Woodward, R. B.
Tyler Wasson (Ed.), *Nobel Prize Winners*. 1987
HOFSTADTER, Robert (1915–). *See* Mossbauer, R. L.
Tyler Wasson (Ed.), *Nobel Prize Winners*. 1987
HOLDEN, Isaac (1807–97). *See* Lister, S. C.
Dictionary of National Biography
HOLDER, William (1616–98). *See* Wallis, J.
Dictionary of Scientific Biography
HOLLEY, R. W. (1922–93). *See* Khorana, H. G.
Tyler Wasson (Ed.), *Nobel Prize Winners*. 1987
The Times, 16 February 1993
HOLMYARD, E. J. (1891–1959). *See* Geber
Dictionary of National Biography
HOLYWOOD, John (otherwise Sacrobosco), (d. 1256). *See* Grosseteste, R.
Dictionary of Scientific Biography
HOOKER, Sir William J. (1785–1865). *See* Bentham, G.; Hooker, Sir J. D.
Dictionary of National Biography
HOOVER, Herbert, C. (1874–1964). *See* Agricola
Dictionary of American Biography
HOPE, John (1725–1826). *See* Hope, T. C.
Dictionary of National Biography
HOPKINSON, B. (1874–1918). *See* Ricardo, H. R.
Dictionary of National Biography
HORNER, Leonard (1785–1864). *See* Lyell, Sir C.
Dictionary of National Biography
HORNER, W. G. (1786–1837). *See* Viète, F.
Dictionary of National Biography
HORSLEY, Victor (1857–1916). *See* Macewen, Sir W.; Schiff, M.; Sharpey-Schafer, Sir E. A.
Dictionary of Scientific Biography
HUDDART, Joseph (1741–1816). *See* Cotton, W.
Dictionary of National Biography
HUGGINS, Charles (1901–). *See* Rous, F. P.
Tyler Wasson (Ed.), *Nobel Prize Winners*. 1987
Who's Who. 1993
HUGHLINGS JACKSON, J. (1834–1911). *See* Charcot, J-M.; Ferrier, Sir D.; Hitzig, E.; Sherrington, C. S.

W. Haymaker and F. Schiller (Eds.), *The Founders of Neurology*. 1970
HUME, David (1711–76). *See* Malthus, T. R.
Dictionary of National Biography
J. Y. T. Greig, *David Hume*. 1931
HUNTER, William (1718–83). *See* Baillie, M.; Hunter, J.
Dictionary of Scientific Biography
HUSSERL, Edmund (1859–1938). *See* Born, M.
A. G. Debus (Ed.), *World Who's Who in Science*, 1968
HUTCHINSON, A. (1866–1937). *See* Astbury, W. T.
Obituary Notices of Fellows of the Royal Society. 1939
Dictionary of National Biography
HUTCHINSON, John (1825–65). *See* Brunner, Sir J. T.; Deacon, H.; Mond, L.
D. W. F. Hardie, *A History of the Chemical Industry in Widnes*. 1950
HUXLEY, A. F. (1917–). *See* Hodgkin, A. L.; Huxley, H. E.
Who's Who. 1993
HUXLEY, J. S. (1887–1975). *See* Muller, H. J.
Biographical Memoirs of Fellows of the Royal Society. 1976
K. R. Dronamraju, *If I am to be Remembered: The Life and Works of Julian Huxley, with Selected Correspondence*. 1993

INGRAM, G. L. Y. (1884–1914). *See* Twort, F. W.

JACKSON, C. T. (1805–80). *See* Morton, W. T. G.; Wells, H.
Dictionary of American Biography
JACOB, François (1920–). *See* Gilbert, Walter; Monod, J. L.
Tyler Wasson (Ed.), *Nobel Prize Winners*. 1987
JACOBI, Moritz (1801–74). *See* Jacobi, C. G. J.
Dictionary of Scientific Biography
JACOBSON, P. (1859–1923). *See* Meyer, V.
A. G. Debus (Ed.), *World Who's Who in Science*. 1968
JAMES, Robert (1705–76). *See* Diderot, D.
Dictionary of National Biography
JAMIN, J. C. (1818–86). *See* Lippmann, G.
A. G. Debus (Ed.), *World Who's Who in Science*. 1968
JANSSENS, F. A. (1863–1924). *See* Bateson, W.; Morgan, T. H.
JENSEN, J. H. D. (1907–73). *See* Bohr, A. N.; Goeppert Mayer, M.; Wellcome, H. S.
Tyler Wasson (Ed.), *Nobel Prize Winners*. 1987
JERNE, Nils Kaj (1911–). *See* Milstein, C.
Tyler Wasson (Ed.), *Nobel Prize Winners*. 1987
JESSOP, William (1745–1814). *See* Smeaton, J.
Dictionary of National Biography (Missing Persons). 1993
JOFFÉ, Abram Feodorovich (1880–1960). *See* Kapitza, P.
H. Kant, *Abram Fedorovič Joffe*. 1991
JOHN OF GMÜNDEN (*fl.* 1430). *See* Richard of Wallingford
Dictionary of Scientific Biography
JOHNSON, Allan Woodworth (1917–82). *See* Todd, A. R.
Biographical Memoirs of Fellows of the Royal Society. 1987
JØRGENSEN, S. M. (1837–1914). *See* Brønsted, J. N.; Werner, A.
Dictionary of Scientific Biography
JOWETT, Benjamin (1817–93). *See* Smith, H. J. S.
Dictionary of National Biography
JUNCKER, Johann (1679–1759). *See* Stahl, G. E.
Dictionary of Scientific Biography
JUSSIEU, Adrien de (1797–1853). *See* Jussieu, A. L. de

Dictionary of Scientific Biography
JUSSIEU, Bernard de (c.1699–1777). *See* Duhamel du Monceau, H. L.; Jussieu, A. L. de

KAEMPFER, Engelbert (1651–1715). *See* Thunberg, C. P.
Dictionary of Scientific Biography
KATER, H. (1777–1835). *See* Sabine, Sir E.
Dictionary of Scientific Biography
KAY, John (fl. 1733–64). *See* Arkwright, Sir R.
Dictionary of National Biography
KELLY, H. A. (1858–1943). *See* Welch, W. H.
R. H. Major, *A History of Medicine*. 1954
KEMPE, A. B. (1849–1922). *See* Gordan, P. A.
A. G. Debus (Ed.), *World Who's Who in Science*. 1968
KENDALL, Larcum (1721–95). *See* Harrison, J.
E. G. R. Taylor, *Mathematical Practitioners in Hanoverian England*. 1966
KETTERING, Charles Franklin (1876–1958). *See* Midgley, T.
Dictionary of Scientific Biography
KHALID IBN YAZID, Prince (d. c.704). *See* Robert of Chester
KIDD, John (1775–1851). *See* Harcourt, W. V. V.
Dictionary of Scientific Biography
KILIANI, H. (1855–1945). *See* Windaus, A.
Journal of Chemical Education, **9**, 1909, 1932
KITAIBEL, P. (1757–1817). *See* Klaproth, M. H.
Dictionary of Scientific Biography
KLAUS, K. K. (1796–1864). *See* Butlerov, A. M.
A. G. Debus (Ed.), *World Who's Who in Science*. 1968
KLEIN, Felix (1849–1925). *See* Baade, W. H. W.
Dictionary of Scientific Biography
KLEIN, Oskar Benjamin (1894–1977). *See* Jordan, E. P.
Dictionary of Scientific Biography
KNIPPING, P. (1883–1935). *See* Bragg, W. H.
P. Forman, *Archive for History of Exact Sciences*, **6**, 38, 1969
KNIGHT, T. A. (1759–1838). *See* Dutrochet, R. J. H.
Dictionary of Scientific Biography
KOHLER, G. J. F. (1946–). *See* Milstein, C.
Tyler Wasson (Ed.), *Nobel Prize Winners*. 1987
KOLLE, Wilhelm (1868–1935). *See* Wassermann, A. von
KOLLETSCHKA, J. (1803–47). *See* Semmelweis, I. P.
KOHLRAUSCH, R. H. A. (1809–58). *See* Kohlrausch, F. W.; Weber, W. E.
J. R. Partington, *A History of Chemistry*. Vol. 4. 1964
KOMPPA, G. (1867–1949). *See* Perkin, W. H., jun.
Poggendorff, Handwörterbuch zur Geschichte der Exakten Wissenschaften
KÖRNER, W. (1839–1925). *See* Kekulé, F. A.
A. G. Debus (Ed.), *World Who's Who in Science*. 1968
KOSSEL, Walter, (1888–1956). *See* Lewis, G. N.
Dictionary of Scientific Biography
KRAMERS, Hendrik Anthony (1844–1952. *See* Peierls, R. E.
Dictionary of Scientific Biography
KRONECKER, L. (1823–91). *See* Cantor, G. F. L. P.
Dictionary of Scientific Biography
KRÖNIG, A. K. (1822–79). *See* Clausius, R. J. E.
Dictionary of Scientific Biography
KRUPP, Friedrich (1787–1826). *See* Krupp, A.
G. von Klass, *Krupps: Story of an Industrial Empire*. 1954
KRUPP, Friedrich (1854–1902). *See* Diesel, R.
G. von Klass, *Krupps: Story of an Industrial Empire*. 1954
KUFFLER, S. W. (1913–80). *See* Hubel, D. H.
A. G. Debus (Ed.), *World Who's Who in Science*. 1968
KUHN, R. (1900–67). *See* Tswett, M. S.
Dictionary of Scientific Biography
KUNDT, A. E. E. (1839–94). *See* Röntgen, W. K.
Dictionary of Scientific Biography

KURTI, N. (1908–). *See* Simon, F. E.
Who's Who. 1993
LACEPÈDE, B. G. E. de la ville (1756–1825). *See* Buffon, Comte G. L. L. de
Dictionary of Scientific Biography
LAHIRE, P. de (1640–1718). *See* Belidor, B. F. de; Desargues, G.
Dictionary of Scientific Biography
LAIDLAW, Patrick Playfair (1881–1940). *See* Dale, H. H.
Obituary Notices of Fellows of the Royal Society. 1941
LALANDE, J. J. Le F. de (1732–1807). *See* Arago, D. F. J.; Delambre, J. B. J.; Lacaille, N. L. de
Dictionary of Scientific Biography
LAMONT, J. (1805–79). *See* Sabine, Sir E.
Dictionary of National Biography
LAMY, C. A. (1820–78). *See* Crookes, Sir W.
Poggendorff, Handwörterbuch zur Geschichte der Exakten Wissenschaften
LANDAU, L. D. (1877–1947). *See* Ramanujan, S.
LANGLEY, J. N. (1852–1925). *See* Hill, A. V.; Dale, H. H.
A. G. Debus (Ed.), *World Who's Who in Science.* 1968
LANKESTER, Edwin (1814–74). *See* Lankester, E. R.
Dictionary of National Biography
LAZEAR, J. W. (1866–1900). *See* Read, W.
H. Wain, *History of Preventive Medicine*. 1970
LEDERBERG, J. (1925–). *See* Beadle, G. W.
Tyler Wasson (Ed.), *Nobel Prize Winners*. 1987
LEDERMAN, Leon (1922–). *See* Steinberger, J.
Les Prix Nobel en 1988. 1989
LEGALLOIS, César (1770–1814). *See* Flourens, J. P. M.
Dictionary of Scientific Biography
LEGENDRE, A. M. (1752–1833). *See* Cauchy, A. L.; Gauss, K. F.
Dictionary of Scientific Biography
LEHN, Jean-Marie (1939–). *See* Pedersen, C. J.; Cram, D. J.
Les Prix Nobel en 1987. 1988
LEJEUNE-DIRICHLET, P. G. (1805–59). *See* Riemann, G. F. B.
LÉMERY, Louis (1677–1743). *See* Lémery, N.
Dictionary of Scientific Biography
LEMONNIER, P. C. (1715–99). *See* Celsius, A.
Dictionary of Scientific Biography
LE PÈRE, J. B. (1761–1844). *See* Lesseps, Vicomte F. M. de
Nouvelle Biographie Universelle. 1852–66
LEUCIPPUS (fl. 480 BC). *See* Epicurus
Dictionary of Scientific Biography
LEUCKHART, K. G. F. R. (1822–98). *See* Mechnikov, I.; Weismann, A.
Dictionary of Scientific Biography
LEVASSOR, E. (1844–97). *See* Daimler, G.
LEVI BEN GERSON (1288–1344). *See* Regiomontanus
Dictionary of Scientific Biography
LEWES, G. H. (1817–78). *See* Spencer, H.
Dictionary of National Biography
LEWIS, Thomas (1881–1945). *See* Einthoven, W.
R. H. Major, *A History of Medicine*. 1954
LIEBEN, A. (1836–1914). *See* Skraup, Z. H.
Poggendorff, Handwörterbuch zur Geschichte der Exakten Wissenschaften
LIEBERMANN, C. T. (1842–1914). *See* Graebe, C.; Perkin, Sir W. H.
Dictionary of Scientific Biography
LIMPRICHT, H. F. P. (1827–1909). *See* Fittig, R.
Poggendorff, Handwörterbuch zur Geschichte der Exakten Wissenschaften
LIND, James (1736–1812). *See* Watt, J.
Dictionary of National Biography

LINDHARD, Johannes (1870–1947). *See* Krogh,
S. A. S.
LINNAEUS, the younger (1741–83). *See* Thunberg,
C. P.
E. Nordenskiöld, *History of Biology.* 1928
LIPPMAN, Fritz (1899–1986). *See* Krebs, H.; Jencks,
W. P.
Tyler Wasson (Ed.), *Nobel Prize Winners.* 1987
A. G. Debus (Ed.), *World Who's Who in Science.* 1968
LISTER, Joseph Jackson (1786–1869). *See* Lister, J.
Dictionary of National Biography
LISTON, Robert (1794–1847). *See* Lister, J.; Monro,
A., *tertius*
Dictionary of National Biography
LIVEING, G. D. (1827–1924). *See* Dewar, J.
Dictionary of National Biography
LIVINGSTON, Robert R. (1746–1813). *See* Fulton, R.
Dictionary of American Biography
LLOYD, Humphrey (1800–81). *See* Hamilton, Sir
W. R.
Dictionary of Scientific Biography
LOEFFLER, Friedrich (1852–1915). *See* Koch, R.;
Roux, P. P. E.
Dictionary of Scientific Biography
LONG, Crawford W. (1815–78). *See* Wells, H.
Dictionary of American Biography
LONGOMONTANUS (1562–1647). *See* Gassendi, P.
Dictionary of Scientific Biography
LONGUET-HIGGINS, H. C. (1923–). *See* Fukui, K.
Who's Who. 1993
LOUIS, P. C. A. (1787–1872). *See* Holmes, O. W.
A. G. Debus (Ed.), *World Who's Who in Science.* 1968
LOUYET, Paulin (1818–50). *See* Moissan, F. F. H.
J. R. Partington, *A History of Chemistry.* Vol. 4, 1964
LOVELL, Bernard (1913–). *See* Blackett, P. M. S.
Who's Who. 1993.
LU Gwei-Djen (1904–91). *See* Needham, N. J. T. M.
The Times, 3rd December 1991
LUCAS, K. (1879–1916). *See* Adrian, E. D.
Dictionary of Scientific Biography
LURIA, Salvador Edward (1912–91). *See* Delbrück,
M. L. H.; Dulbecco, R.; Hershey, A.D.; Watson, J.D.
Tyler Wasson (Ed.), *Nobel Prize Winners.* 1987
LWOFF, André Michael (1902–). *See* Monod, J. L.
Tyler Wasson (Ed.), *Nobel Prize Winners.* 1987
LYONS, Israel (1739–75). *See* Banks, Sir J.
Dictionary of National Biography

MACKENZIE, Sir James (1853–1925). *See* Keith, Sir
A.
Dictionary of National Biography
MACLEAN, John (1800–86). *See* Henry, J.
Dictionary of American Biography
MACNEILL, Sir John (?1793–1880). *See* Bazalgette, Sir
J. W.; Rankine, W. J. M.
Dictionary of National Biography
MAESTLIN, Michael (1550–1631). *See* Kepler, J.
MAGLIABECHI, A. (1633–1714). *See* Leeuwenhoek,
A. van
Nouvelle Biographie Universelle. 1852–66
MAGNUS, H. G. (1802–70). *See* Helmholtz, H. L. F.
von; Tyndall, J.
Dictionary of Scientific Biography
MALEBRANCHE, N. (1638–1715). *See* Bernoulli, Jean
Dictionary of Scientific Biography
MANLEY, Charles (1876–1927). *See* Langley, S. P.
Dictionary of American Biography
MARCHIAFAVA, Ettore (1847–1935). *See* Golgi, C.;
Grassi, G. B.; Laveran, C. L. A.
Dictionary of Scientific Biography
MARIGNAN, Marquis de (1497–1555). *See* Ramelli,
A.
Nouvelle Biographie Universelle. 1852–66
MARINUS OF TYRE (*fl.* 150 AD). *See* Ptolemy of
Alexandria

A. G. Debus (Ed.), *World Who's Who in Science.* 1968
MARKOVNIKOV, V. V. (1838–1904). *See* Butlerov,
A. M.
Dictionary of Scientific Biography
MARKS, Phoebe (1854–1923). *See* Ayrton, W. E.
A. G. Debus (Ed.), *World Who's Who in Science.* 1968
MARTIUS, C. F. P. von (1794–1868). *See* Agassiz,
J. L. R.
Dictionary of Scientific Biography
MASON, Charles (*c.* 1730–1789). *See* Maskelyne, N.
Dictionary of National Biography
MASON, Sir Josiah (1795–1881). *See* Elkington, G. R.
Dictionary of National Biography
MASSARI, Bartolomeo (1603–55). *See* Malpighi, M.
MASSON, Francis (1741–1805). *See* Thunberg, C. P.
MAUDSLAY, Joseph (1801–61). *See* Maudslay, H.
Dictionary of National Biography
MAUDSLAY, Thomas Henry (1792–1864). *See*
Maudslay, H.
Dictionary of National Biography
MAYER, Joseph Edward (1904–). *See* Goeppert
Mayer, M.
A. G. Debus (Ed.), *World Who's Who in Science.* 1968
MAYER, Tobias (1723–62). *See* Herschel. Sir W.
Dictionary of Scientific Biography
McCORMICK, Cyrus Hall, jnr. (1859–1936). *See*
McCormick, C. H.
Dictionary of American Biography
McCORMICK, Robert (1780–1846). *See* McCormick,
C. H.
Dictionary of American Biography
MÉCHAIN, P. F. A. (1744–1804). *See* Borda, J. C. (de)
Dictionary of Scientific Biography
MELLONI, M. (1798–1854). *See* Cannizzaro, S.
Dictionary of Scientific Biography
MENAECHMUS (*fl.* 365–350 BC). *See* Descartes, R.
Dictionary of Scientific Biography
MENDEL, Lafayette (1872–1935). *See* Chittenden,
R. H.
Dictionary of Scientific Biography
MENDELSSOHN, K. A. G. (1906–80). *See* Simon, F. E.
*Biographical Memoirs of Fellows of the Royal
Society.* 1983
MENSCHUTKIN, N. A. (1842–1907). *See* Mendeléeff,
D. I.
Dictionary of Scientific Biography
MERCURIUS, Franciscus (1614–99). *See* van
Helmont, J. B.
MERING, J. von (1849–1908). *See* Macleod, J. J. R.
A. G. Debus (Ed.), *World Who's Who in Science.* 1968
MERSENNE, Marin (1588–1648). *See* Borda, J. C. (de);
Brouncker, W.; Desargues, G.; Descartes, R.; Fermat,
P. de; Pascal, B.; Torricelli, E.
Dictionary of Scientific Biography
MESNIL, Felix (1868–1938). *See* Laveran, C. L. A.
Dictionary of Scientific Biography
METIUS, J. (d. 1628). *See* Drebbel, C.
Dictionary of Scientific Biography
MICHELL, John (1724–93). *See* Cavendish, H.
Dictionary of Scientific Biography
MIERS, Sir Henry (1858–1942). *See* Ramsay, Sir W.
Obituary Notices of Fellows of the Royal Society.
1943
Dictionary of National Biography
MILL, John Stuart (1806–73). *See* Bacon, F.
Dictionary of National Biography
MILLER, Hugh (1802–56). *See* Geikie, Sir A.
Dictionary of National Biography
MILLER, W. A. (1817–70). *See* Huggins, Sir W.
Dictionary of National Biography
MILLS, Robert Gail (1924–). *See* Yang, C. N.
A. G. Debus (Ed.), *World Who's Who in Science.* 1968
MINKOWSKI, Oskar (1859–1931). *See* Macleod, J. J. R.
A. G. Debus (Ed.), *World Who's Who in Science.* 1968

MOHL, Hugo von (1805–72). *See* Hofmeister, W. F. B.
Dictionary of Scientific Biography
MOLLWEIDER, K. B. (1774–1825). *See* Delambre,
J. B. J.
A. G. Debus (Ed.), *World Who's Who in Science*. 1968
MOLYNEUX, Samuel (1689–1728). *See* Bradley, J.;
Hadley, J.
Dictionary of National Biography
MONRO, John (1670–1740). *See* Monro. A., *primus*
MORE, Sir Thomas (1478–1535). *See* Kratzer, N.
Dictionary of National Biography
MORGAN, G. C. (1754–98). *See* Cayley, Sir G.
Dictionary of National Biography
MORGAN, John (1797–1847). *See* Addison, T.
MORGENROTH, Julius (1871–1924). *See* Ehrlich, P.
A. G. Debus (Ed.), *World Who's Who in Science*. 1968
MOSELEY, Benjamin (1742–1819). *See* Moseley,
H. G. J.
Dictionary of National Biography
MOSELEY, H. (1801–72). *See* Moseley, H. G. J.
Dictionary of National Biography
MOSELEY, H. N. (1844–91). *See* Moseley, H. G. J.;
Thomson, Sir C. W.
Dictionary of National Biography
MOTTELSON, Ben (1926–). *See* Rainwater, L. J.;
Bohr, A. N.
Tyler Wasson (Ed.), *Nobel Prize Winners*. 1987
MOUNTCASTLE, V. B. (1918–). *See* Hubel, D. H.
A. G. Debus (Ed.), *World Who's Who in Science*. 1968
MUDGE, John (1721–93). *See* Mudge, T.
Dictionary of National Biography
MULLER, John (1699–1784). *See* Belidor, B. F. de
Dictionary of National Biography
MURPHY, W. P. (1892–1987). *See* Minot, G. R.;
Whipple, G. H.
Tyler Wasson (Ed.), *Nobel Prize Winners*. 1987
MURRAY, George Redmayne (1865–1939). *See* Schiff,
M.
R. H. Major, *A History of Medicine*. 1954
MURRAY, James (1788–1871). *See* Lawes, J. B.
Dictionary of National Biography
MUSSCHENBROEK, P. van (1692–1761). *See*
Coulomb, C. A. de; de Geer, C.; Nollet, Abbé J. A.;
Snell, W.
Dictionary of Scientific Biography
MYDORGE, Claude C. (1585–1647). *See* Descartes, R.
Dictionary of Scientific Biography
MYLNE, Robert (1734–1811). *See* Perronet, J-R.;
Smeaton, J.
Dictionary of National Biography

NATHANS, D. (1928–). *See* Smith, H. O.
Tyler Wasson (Ed.), *Nobel Prize Winners*. 1987
NATTERER, K. (1821–1901). *See* Andrews, T.
Poggendorff, *Handwörterbuch zur Geschichte der
Exakten Wissenschaften*
NEEDHAM, John Turberville (1713–81). *See*
Spallanzani, L.
Dictionary of Scientific Biography
NEELSEN, Friedrich (1854–94). *See* Ehrlich, P.
NEHER, Erwin (1944–). *See* Sakmann, B.
Les Prix Nobel en 1991. 1992
NEILSON, J. B. (1792–1865). *See* Macintosh, C.
Dictionary of National Biography
NEMORARIUS, Jordanus (*c*.1220). *See* Tartaglia, N.
Dictionary of Scientific Biography
NEUBER, G. A. (1850–1932). *See* Macewen, Sir W.
A. G. Debus (Ed.), *World Who's Who in Science*. 1968
NEUMANN, Caspar (1683–1737). *See* Marggraf, A. S.
Dictionary of Scientific Biography
NICHOLAS OF CUSA (1401–64). *See* Kepler, J.
Dictionary of Scientific Biography
NICHOLSON, W. (1753–1815). *See* Volta, A.
Dictionary of National Biography

NILSON, L. F. (1840–99). *See* Mendeléeff, D. I.
A. G. Debus (Ed.), *World Who's Who in Science*. 1968
NIPKOW, Paul Gottlieb (1860–1940). *See* Zworykin,
V. K.
A. G. Debus (Ed.), *World Who's Who in Science*. 1968
NIRENBERG, D. (1928–). *See* Khorana, H. G.
Tyler Wasson (Ed.), *Nobel Prize Winners*. 1987
NISHINA, Y. (1890–1951). *See* Tomonaga, S-I.
A. G. Debus (Ed.), *World Who's Who in Science*. 1968
NORTH, Simeon (1802–84). *See* Whitney, E.
Dictionary of American Biography
NUNEZ, Pedro (1492–1577). *See* Vernier, P.
Dictionary of Scientific Biography
NUTTALL, G. H. F. (1862–1937). *See* Keilin, D.;
Mechnikov, I.; Welch, W. H.
Obituary Notices of Fellows of the Royal Society.
1939
Dictionary of National Biography
NUTTALL, J. M. (1890–1958). *See* Geiger, H. W.

OBERTH, Hermann (1894–). *See* Von Braun, W.
F. H. Winter, *Rockets into Space*. 1990 (pbk 1993)
Hans Barth, *Hermann Oberth: Leben, Werk, Wirkung*.
1985.
OCCHIALINI, G. P. S. (1907–). *See* Powell, C. F.
McGraw-Hill Modern Men of Science. 1968.
OCHOA, Severo (1905–). *See* Kornberg, A.
Tyler Wasson (Ed.), *Nobel Prize Winners*. 1987
OECOLAMPADIUS (1482–1531). *See* Paracelsus
Allgemeine Deutsche Biographie
O'GORMAN, Mervyn (1871–1952). *See* Lindemann,
F. A. (Viscount Cherwell)
OHAIN, Hans von (1911–). *See* Whittle, F.
C. Joyce, *New Scientist*, 5 Oct. 1991
OKEN, Lorenz (1779–1851). *See* Nägeli, K. W. von
Dictionary of Scientific Biography
OLBERS, H. W. M. (1758–1840). *See* Bessel, F. W.
Dictionary of Scientific Biography
OLDENBURG, Henry (*c*.1615–77). *See* Grew, N.;
Steno, N.
Dictionary of Scientific Biography
OLDHAM, Thomas (1816–78). *See* Oldham, R. D.
Dictionary of Scientific Biography
OLIPHANT, Mark (1901–). *See* Peierls, R. E.
Who's Who. 1993
OLIVER, F. W. (1864–1915). *See* Tansley, Sir A. G.
A. G. Debus (Ed.), *World Who's Who in Science*.
1968
OLIVER, George (1841–1915). *See* Sharpey-Schafer,
Sir E. A.
Dictionary of Scientific Biography
O'NEILL, Gerard Kitchen (1927–). *See* Richter, B.
OPORINUS, Johannes (1507–68). *See* Vesalius, A.
ORTH, J. (1847–1923). *See* Aschoff, K. A. L.
R. H. Major, *A History of Medicine*. 1954
OSLER, Sir William (1849–1919). *See* Cushing, H.;
Einthoven, W.; Garrod, A. E.; Penfield, W. G.; Welch,
W. H.
Dictionary of National Biography
OSTWALD, Wolfgang (1883–1943). *See* Ostwald,
F. W.
Dictionary of Scientific Biography
OTHO, Lucius Valentine (d. 1597). *See* Rheticus

PAGE, C. G. (1812–68). *See* Rühmkorff, H. D.
A. G. Debus (Ed.), *World Who's Who in Science*. 1968
PALEY, R. E. (1907–33). *See* Wiener, N.
PANHARD, R. (1841–1908). *See* Daimler, G.
A. G. Debus (Ed.), *World Who's Who in Science*. 1968
PANOFSKY, Wolfgang Kurt Hermann (1919–). *See*
Richter, B.
A. G. Debus (Ed.), *World Who's Who in Science*. 1968
PARMENIDES (*c*.515–*c*.450 BC). *See* Empedocles
Dictionary of Scientific Biography

PARONA, Corrado (1848–1922). *See* Grassi, G. B.
PARONA, Ernesto (1849–1902). *See* Grassi, G. B.
PARRY, Sir William (1790–1855). *See* Sabine, Sir E.
Dictionary of National Biography
PASCHEN, F. (1865–1945). *See* Sommerfeld, A.
Dictionary of Scientific Biography
PEACOCK, George (1791–1858). *See* Babbage, C.;
Hamilton, Sir W. R.; Herschel, Sir J. F. W.
Dictionary of Scientific Biography
PEANO, G. (1858–1932). *See* Whitehead, A. N.
Dictionary of Scientific Biography
PEARSON, Karl (1857–1936). *See* Fisher, Sir R. A.
Dictionary of Scientific Biography
PEARY, J. E. W. (1856–1920). *See* Amundsen, R. E. G.
Dictionary of American Biography
PEASE, Edward (1767–1858). *See* Stephenson, G.;
Stephenson, R.
Dictionary of National Biography
PEEL, Robert (1750–1830). *See* Hargreaves, J.
Dictionary of National Biography
PENNANT, Thomas (1726–98). *See* White, G.
Dictionary of Welsh Biography. 1959
PERCY, John (1817–89). *See* Roberts-Austen, Sir W. C.
Dictionary of Scientific Biography
PERKIN, A. G. (1861–1937). *See* Perkin, Sir W. H.;
Perkin, W. H., jun.
R. Robinson, *Endeavour*, **15**, 92, 1956
PERKIN, F. M. (d. 1928). *See* Perkin, Sir W. H.; Perkin,
W. H., jun.
R. Robinson, *Endeavour*, **15**, 92, 1956
PERKIN, Thomas (b. 1757). *See* Perkin, Sir W. H.
PERRY, John (1850–1920). *See* Ayrton, W. E.
PETRIE, Sir Flinders (1853–1942). *See* Desch, C. H.
Obituary Notices of Fellows of the Royal Society.
1945
Dictionary of National Biography
PETRUCCI, Pendolfo (1450–1511). *See* Biringuccio, V.
Nouvelle Biographie Universelle. 1852–66
PETTUS, Sir John (1613–90). *See* Ercker, L.
Dictionary of National Biography
PETTY, Sir William (1623–87). *See* Boyle, R.;
Willis, T.
Dictionary of Scientific Biography
PEURBACH, G. von (1423–61). *See* Gassendi, P.;
Regiomontanus
Dictionary of Scientific Biography
PHILO OF BYZANTIUM (*fl.* 150 BC). *See* Ctesibius of
Alexandria; Hero of Alexandria; Vitruvius
Dictionary of Scientific Biography
PILKINGTON, William (1800–72). *See* Deacon, H.
PINGRE, A. G. (1711–96). *See* Maskelyne, N.
Dictionary of Scientific Biography
PIRIA, R. (1815–65). *See* Cannizzaro, S.
Poggendorff, *Handwörterbuch zur Geschichte der
Exakten Wissenschaften*
PLATO (*c.*427–*c.*347 BC). *See* Aristotle; Eudoxus of
Cnidus; Fernel, J.; Malthus, T. R.; Theophrastus
Dictionary of Scientific Biography
PLOT, Robert (1640–96). *See* Lluyd, E.
Dictionary of National Biography
PONTIN, M. M. (1781–1858). *See* Berzelius, J. J.
Poggendorff, *Handwörterbuch zur Geschichte der
Exakten Wissenschaften*
POTT, Percivall (1714–88). *See* Hunter, J.
Dictionary of National Biography
POUCHET, F. A. (1800–72). *See* Pasteur, L.
Dictionary of Scientific Biography
POUND, James (1669–1724). *See* Bradley, J.
Dictionary of National Biography
POWER, F. B. (1853–1927). *See* Wellcome, H. S.
Dictionary of American Biography
PRIESTLEY, John Gillies (1880–1941). *See* Haldane,
J. S.

PROKHOROV, Aleksander M. (1916–   ). *See* Basov,
N. G.; Townes, C. H.
Tyler Wasson (Ed.), *Nobel Prize Winners.* 1987
PUNNETT, Reginald Crundall (1875–1967). *See*
Sturtevant, A. H.
Dictionary of Scientific Biography
PURDIE, T. (1843–1916). *See* Haworth, W. N.; Irvine,
J. C.
Who Was Who
PYE, D. R. (1886–1960). *See* Tizard, Sir H. T.
*Biographical Memoirs of Fellows of the Royal
Society.* 1961
Dictionary of National Biography

RACE, R. R. (1907–1984). *See* Sanger, R. A.
RADCLIFFE, John (1650–1714). *See* Baillie, M.
RAMSAY, Sir Andrew (1814–91). *See* Geikie, Sir A.
Dictionary of National Biography
RATCLIFFE, John Ashworth (1902–87). *See* Ryle, M.
*Biographical Memoirs of Fellows of the Royal
Society.* 1988
RAU, J. J. (1668–1719). *See* Albinus, B. S.
RAYER, P. F. O. (1793–1867). *See* Davaine, C. J.
A. G. Debus (Ed.), *World Who's Who in Science.* 1968
READ, J. (1884–1963). *See* Page, Sir W. J.
*Biographical Memoirs of Fellows of the Royal
Society.* 1963
Dictionary of National Biography
RECKLINGHAUSEN, F. D. von (1833–1910). *See*
Aschoff, K. A. L.
R. H. Major, *A History of Medicine.* 1954
REDMAN, John (1772–1808). *See* Rush, B.
Dictionary of American Biography
REDOUTÉ, P. J. (1759–1840). *See* Candolle, A. P. de
Dictionary of Scientific Biography
REICHENBACH, Carl (1788–1869). *See* Unverdorben,
O.
Dictionary of Scientific Biography
REICHENBACH, Georg (1771–1826). *See* Gambey,
H. P.
Dictionary of Scientific Biography
REICHERT, K. B. (1811–84). *See* Du Bois Reymond,
E.; Müller, J. P.
Dictionary of Scientific Biography
REICHSTEIN, Tadeus (1897–   ). *See* Kendall, E. C.
Tyler Wasson (Ed.), *Nobel Prize Winners.* 1987
REIMER, C. L. (1856–1921). *See* Tiemann, J. C. W. F.
Poggendorff, *Handwörterbuch zur Geschichte der
Exakten Wissenschaften*
RETZIUS, A. J. (1742–1821). *See* Scheele, C. W.
J. R. Partington, *A History of Chemistry.* Vol. 3, 1962
REULEAUX, Franz (1829–1905). *See* Otto, N. A.
Dictionary of Scientific Biography
REVERDIN, J. L. (1842–1929). *See* Schiff, M.
A. G. Debus (Ed.), *World Who's Who in Science.* 1968
RICARDO, David (1772–1823). *See* Malthus, T. R.
Dictionary of National Biography
RICCATI, J. F. (1676–1754). *See* Bernoulli, D.
Dictionary of Scientific Biography
RICCI, Michelangelo (1619–92). *See* Torricelli, E.
Dictionary of Scientific Biography
RICHARDS, A. N. (1876–1966). *See* Dale, H. H.
Who Was Who
RICHMANN, G. W. (1711–53). *See* Wilcke, J. C.
Dictionary of Scientific Biography
RIGGS, J. M. (1810–85). *See* Wells, H.
Dictionary of American Biography
RIO-ORTEGA, Pio del (1882–1945). *See* Penfield, W.
W. Haymaker and F. Schiller (Eds), *The Founders of
Neurology.* 1970
RIPLEY, George (d. *c.*1490). *See* Norton, T.
A. G. Debus (Ed.), *World Who's Who in Science.* 1968
RIVE, A. A. de la (1801–73). *See* Ampère, A. M.

ROBERVAL, G. P. de (1602–75). *See* Descartes, R.;
Fermat, P. de; Pascal, B.; Torricelli, E.
Dictionary of Scientific Biography
ROBISON, John (1739–1805). *See* Black, J.;
Newcomen, T.; Rennie, J.; Watt, J.
Dictionary of National Biography
Dictionary of Scientific Biography
ROBISON, Sir John (1778–1843). *See* Gilbert, William
Dictionary of National Biography
ROBISON, R. (1883–1941). *See* Harden, Sir A.
Obituary Notices of Fellows of the Royal Society.
1941
ROCHAS, Alphonse Beau de (1815–93). *See* Otto,
N. A.
A. G. Debus (Ed.), *World Who's Who in Science.*
1968
ROCHLEDER, F. (1819–74). *See* Skraup, Z. H.
J. R. Partington, *A History of Chemistry.* Vol. 4, 1964
ROCK, John (1890–1984). *See* Pincus, G. G.
A. G. Debus (Ed.), *World Who's Who in Science.* 1968
RODNEY, Lord (1719–92). *See* Blane, Sir G.
Dictionary of National Biography
ROHRER, Heinrich (1933–   ). *See* Ruska, E. A. F.
Tyler Wasson (Ed.), *Nobel Prize Winners.* 1987
ROLLETT, A. (1834–1903). *See* Engelmann, T. W.
ROSE, G. (1798–1873). *See* Mitscherlich, E.
Dictionary of Scientific Biography
ROSE, H. (1795–1864). *See* Unverdorben, O.
Dictionary of Scientific Biography
ROSS, Sir James (1800–62). *See* Herschel, Sir J. F. W.
Dictionary of Scientific Biography
Dictionary of National Biography
ROSS, Sir John (1777–1856). *See* Sabine, Sir, E.
Dictionary of National Biography
ROSSE, Lord (1800–67). *See* Parsons, Sir C. A.;
Stoney, G. J.
Dictionary of National Biography
ROTHE, G. (1679–1710). *See* Rouelle, G. F.
Poggendorff, *Handwörterbuch zur Geschichte der
Exakten Wissenschaften*
ROTHMAN, Christopher (d. 1599). *See* Brahe, T.
Dictionary of Scientific Biography
ROUS, Peyton (1879–1970). *See* Temin, H. M.
Tyler Wasson (Ed.), *Nobel Prize Winners.* 1987
ROUX, Wilhelm (1850–1924). *See* Driesch, H. A. E.;
Spemann, H.
Dictionary of Scientific Biography
RUBENS, H. (1865–1922). *See* Franck, J.
Dictionary of Scientific Biography
RUBNER, Max (1854–1932). *See* Lusk, G.
Dictionary of Scientific Biography
RÜCKER, Sir A. (1848–1915). *See* Thorpe, Sir T. E.
Who Was Who 1897–1915. (Addendum)
RUDOLFF, C. (*fl.* 16th cent.). *See* Stevinus, S.
Dictionary of Scientific Biography
RUDOLPHI, C. A. (1771–1832). *See* Müller, J. P.
Dictionary of Scientific Biography
RUFFINI, P. (1765–1822). *See* Abel, N. H.
Dictionary of Scientific Biography
RUSKA, Julius (1867–1949). *See* Ruska, E. A. F.
Osiris, **5**, 1, 1938
RUSSELL, Bertrand (1872–1970). *See* Whitehead,
A. N.; Wiener, H.
Dictionary of Scientific Biography
RUYSCH, F. (1638–1731). *See* Morgagni, G. B.
Dictionary of Scientific Biography
RUZICKA, Leopold (1887–1976). *See* Prelog, V.
*Biographical Memoirs of Fellows of the Royal
Society.* 1980
RYLE, John Alfred (1889–1950). *See* Ryle, M.
Dictionary of National Biography

SACROBOSCO (otherwise John Holywood), (d. 1256).
See Grosseteste, R.

Dictionary of Scientific Biography
ST. FOND, Faujas de (1741–1819). *See* Smithson, J.
A. G. Debus (Ed.), *World Who's Who in Science.* 1968
SAINT-GILLES, L. Péan de (1832–63). *See* Berthelot,
P. E. M.; Guldberg, C. M.
SAINT-HILAIRE, Geoffroy (1772–1844). *See* Cuvier,
Baron G. L. C. F. D.
Nouvelle Biographie Universelle. 1852–66
ST. MARTIN, Alexis (1804?–80). *See* Beaumont, W.
R. H. Major, *A History of Medicine.* 1954
SAINT-SIMON, Comte de (1760–1825). *See* Lesseps,
Viscomte F. M. de
Nouvelle Biographie Universelle. 1852–66
SAMUELSSON, Bengt I. (1934–   ). *See* Euler, U. von
Tyler Wasson (Ed.), *Nobel Prize Winners.* 1987
SANARELLI, G. (1865–1940). *See* Reed, W.
A. G. Debus (Ed.), *World Who's Who in Science.* 1968
SANDERSON, Sir J. S. Burdon (1828–1905). *See*
Haldane, J. S.; Sharpey-Schafer, Sir E. A.; Villemin,
J. A.
Dictionary of National Biography
SAVART, F. (1791–1841). *See* Ampère, A. M.
Dictionary of Scientific Biography
SCARPA, A. (1747?–1832). *See* Bassi, A.
Dictionary of Scientific Biography
SCHERRER, Paul (1890–1969). *See* Debye, P. J. W.;
Hull, A. W.
A. G. Debus (Ed.), *World Who's Who in Science.* 1968
SCHICKART, Guillaume (1592–1635). *See* Pascal, B.
Dictionary of Scientific Biography
SCHIMMELBUSCH, Curt (1860–95). *See* Macewen,
Sir W.
SCHLIEMANN, H. (1822–90). *See* Virchow, R. L. C.
Dictionary of Scientific Biography
SCHMITT, F. O. (1903–   ). *See* Huxley, F. E.
A. G. Debus (Ed.), *World Who's Who in Science.* 1968
SCHNEIDER, C. V. (1610–80). *See* Lower, R.
R. H. Major, *A History of Medicine.* 1954
SCHOEFFER, Peter (*c.* 1425–1502). *See* Gutenberg, J.
Allgemeine Deutsche Biographie. 1875–1912
SCHÖNER, Johan (1477–1547). *See* Rheticus
Dictionary of Scientific Biography
SCHÖNLEIN, Lucas (1793–1864). *See* Remak, R.
Dictionary of Scientific Biography
SCHOOTEN, F. van (1615–60). *See* Bernoulli, Jacques
Dictionary of Scientific Biography
SCHOOTEN, P. van (1634–79). *See* Bartholin, R.;
Descartes, R.
SCHORLEMMER, C. W. (1839–92). *See* Frankland, Sir
E.
Dictionary of National Biography
Dictionary of Scientific Biography
SCHOTT, Kaspar (1608–66). *See* Boyle, R.; Guericke,
O. von
Dictionary of Scientific Biography
SCHOTT, Otto (1851–1935). *See* Abbe, E.; Zeiss, C.
Dictionary of Scientific Biography
SCHRIEFFER, R. (1931–   ). *See* Bardeen, J.
Tyler Wasson (Ed.), *Nobel Prize Winners.* 1987
SCHRÖTER, J. H. (1745–1816). *See* Bessel, F. W.
Dictionary of Scientific Biography
SCHULTES, J. A. (1773–1831). *See* Thunberg, C. P.
SCHUSTER, A. (1851–1934). *See* Blackett, P. M. S.;
Geiger, H. W.; Simpson, Sir G. C.
Obituary Notices of Fellows of the Royal Society.
1934
Dictionary of National Biography
SCHWARTZ, Melvin (1932–   ). *See* Steinberger, J.
Les Prix Nobel en 1988. 1989
SCHWINGER, Julian Seymour (1918–   ). *See*
Glashow, S. L.; Feynman, R. P.; Gilbert, Walter;
Tomonaga, S-I.
Tyler Wasson (Ed.), *Nobel Prize Winners.* 1987
SCIPIO DEL FERRO (*c.*1510). *See* Tartaglia, N.

Dictionary of Scientific Biography
SCOTUS, Duns (c.1265–1308). *See* Ockham, William of
Dictionary of National Biography
SECHENOV, I. M. (1829–1905). *See* Pavlov, I. P.
Dictionary of Scientific Biography
SEEBECK, T. J. (1770–1831). *See* Peltier, J. C. A.
Dictionary of Scientific Biography
SEFSTRÖM, N. G. (1787–1845). *See* Berzelius, J. J.
A. G. Debus (Ed.), *World Who's Who in Science*. 1968
SÉGUIN, Armand (c.1765–1835). *See* Lavoisier, A. L.
Dictionary of Scientific Biography
SEUBERT, K. F. O. (1851–1942). *See* Meyer, J. L.
Poggendorff, *Handwörterbuch zur Geschichte der Exakten Wissenschaften*
SEWARD, A. C. (1863–1941). *See* Tansley, Sir A. G.
Dictionary of Scientific Biography
SHARPEY, William (1802–80). *See* Sharpey-Schafer, Sir E. A.
Dictionary of National Biography
Dictionary of Scientific Biography
SHEEHAN, J. C. (1915–92). *See* Du Vigneaud
Chemistry in Britain, **29**, 152, 1993
SHENSTONE, W. A. (1850–1908). *See* Tilden, Sir W. A.
Dictionary of National Biography
SHORT, James (1710–68). *See* Cassegrain, N.
Dictionary of Scientific Biography
SIBTHORP, Humphry (1713–97). *See* Banks, Sir J.
SIBTHORP, John (1758–96). *See* Dioscorides, P.
Dictionary of National Biography
SIEDENTOPF, H. F. W. (1872–1940). *See* Zsigmondy, R. A.
Dictionary of Scientific Biography
SIEGBAHN, M. (1886–1978). *See* Meitner, L.; von Laue, M. T. F.
Dictionary of Scientific Biography, Supp. II
SILLIMAN, Benjamin, jun. (1816–85). *See* Silliman, B.
Dictionary of American Biography
W. D. Miles (Ed.), *American Chemists and Chemical Engineers*. 1976
SIMON, Sir John (1816–1904). *See* Villemin, J. A.
Dictionary of National Biography
SINGER, Charles (1876–1960). *See* Ingenhousz, J.
Dictionary of National Biography
SKODA, J. (1805–81). *See* Semmelweis, I. P.
Dictionary of Scientific Biography
SMALL, William (1734–75). *See* Boulton, M.; Edgeworth, R. L.; Watt, J.; Withering, W.
R. E. Schofield, *The Lunar Society of Birmingham*. 1963
SMITH, Sir Francis (1808–79). *See* Ericsson, J.
Dictionary of National Biography
SMITH, George (1800–68). *See* Bickford, W.
Dictionary of National Biography
SMITH, Sir James Edward (1759–1828). *See* Linnaeus, C.; Thunberg, C. P.
Dictionary of National Biography
SMITH, James Lorrain (1862–1931). *See* Haldane, J. S.
Proceedings of the Royal Society, **109**, iv, 1932
SMITH, Oberlin (1840–1926). *See* Poulsen, A. W.
Revue d'Histoire des Sciences et de leurs Applications, **22**, 78, 1969
SNELL, Rudolph (1546–1613). *See* Snell, W.
SOCRATES (5th cent. BC). *See* Euclid
W. K. C. Guthrie, *A History of Greek Philosophy*. 1969
SOLANDER, Daniel (1736–82). *See* Banks, Sir J.
Dictionary of Scientific Biography
Dictionary of National Biography
SORBIÈRE, S. (1615–70). *See* Gassendi, P.
SOUTH, Sir James (1785–1867). *See* Herschel, Sir J. F. W.

Dictionary of Scientific Biography
Dictionary of National Biography
SPIX, J. B. von (1781–1826). *See* Agassiz, J. L. R.
Dictionary of Scientific Biography
SPURZHEIM, J. C. (1776–1832). *See* Flourens, J. P. M.
Dictionary of Scientific Biography
STANLEY, F. O. (1849–1940). *See* Stanley, F. E.
STANLEY, Wendell Meredith (1904–71). *See* Northrop, J. H.
Tyler Wasson (Ed.), *Nobel Prize Winners*. 1987
STANNIUS, Hermann (1808–83). *See* Siebold, C. T. E. von
Dictionary of Scientific Biography
STARR, J. W. (c.1822–47). *See* Swan, Sir J. W.
STEIN, William H. (1911–). *See* Moore, S.
Tyler Wasson (Ed.), *Nobel Prize Winners*. 1987
STEINER, J. (1796–1863). *See* Riemann, G. F. B.
Dictionary of Scientific Biography
STENHOUSE, J. (1809–80). *See* Kekulé, F. A.; Tilden, Sir W. A.
A. G. Debus (Ed.), *World Who's Who in Science*. 1968
STEWART, Balfour (1828–87). *See* De la Rue, W.; Poynting, J. H.
Dictionary of Scientific Biography
STONEY, Bindon Blood (1828–1909). *See* Stoney, G. J.
Dictionary of National Biography
STRABO, (63 BC– c.AD 21). *See* Hipparchus of Rhodes; Ptolemy of Alexandria
Dictionary of Scientific Biography
STRASSMANN, Friedrich Wilhelm (1902–80). *See* Hahn, O.; Meitner, L. Peierls, R. E.
Dictionary of Scientific Biography, Supp. II
STRECKER, Adolf (1822–71). *See* Waage, P.
J. R. Partington, *A History of Chemistry*. Vol. 4, 1964
STROMEYER, F. (1776–1835). *See* Wöhler, F.
Poggendorff, *Handwörterbuch zur Geschichte der Exakten Wissenschaften*
STRUTT, Jedediah (1726–97). *See* Arkright, Sir R.
Dictionary of National Biography
STRUVE, Otto (1819–1905). *See* Struve, F. G. W.
Dictionary of Scientific Biography
SUMNER, John Batcheller (1887–1955). *See* Northrop, J. H.
Dictionary of Scientific Biography
SVEDBERG, The (1874–1971). *See* Tiselius, A. W. K.
Biographical Memoirs of Fellows of the Royal Society. 1972
SWARTS, F. (1866–1940). *See* Baekeland, L. H.
Dictionary of Scientific Biography
SYLVIUS, Jacobus (1478–1555). *See* Vesalius, A.
R. H. Major, *A History of Medicine*. 1954
SYME, James (1799–1870). *See* Lister, J.
Dictionary of National Biography
SYNGE, Richard Laurence (1897–). *See* Martin, A. J. P.
Tyler Wasson (Ed.), *Nobel Prize Winners*. 1987

TACHENIUS, Otto (d. c.1699). *See* Rouelle, G. F.
Dictionary of Scientific Biography
TAIT, P. G. (1831–1901). *See* Dewar, J.
Dictionary of Scientific Biography
Dictionary of National Biography
TAMM, Igor (1895–1971). *See* Cherenkov, P. A.; Sakharov, A. D.
Tyler Wasson (Ed.), *Nobel Prize Winners*. 1987
TATUM, E. L. (1909–75). *See* Beadle, G. W.
Tyler Wasson (Ed.), *Nobel Prize Winners*. 1987
TAYLOR, R. E. (1929–). *See* Kendall, H. W.
Les Prix Nobel en 1992. 1993
TESSIER, A. H. (1741–1837). *See* Cuvier, Baron G. L. C. F. D.

A. G. Debus (Ed.), *World Who's Who in Science.* 1968
THOMPSON, D'Arcy (1860–1948). *See* Ray, J.
Biographical Memoirs of Fellows of the Royal Society. 1949
THOMPSON, Silvanus (1851–1916). *See* Desch, C. H.
Dictionary of Scientific Biography
THOMSON, James (1786–1849). *See* Thomson, W.
Dictionary of National Biography
THOMSON, Thomas (1773–1852). *See* Anderson, T.
Dictionary of National Biography
TIEDEMANN, F. (1781–1861). *See* Gmelin, L.
Dictionary of Scientific Biography
TIMMERMANNS, J. (1882–1971). *See* Prigogine, I.
Dictionary of Scientific Biography
TISSANDIER, Gaston (1843–99). *See* Bert, P.
TITIUS, Johann Daniell (1729–96). *See* Bode, J. E.
Dictionary of Scientific Biography
TODD, Robert Bentley (1809–60). *See* Bowman, Sir W.
Dictionary of National Biography
TORREY, John (1796–1873). *See* Gray, A.
Dictionary of American Biography
TOURNEFORT, J. P. de (1656–1708). *See* Dioscorides, P.
Dictionary of Scientific Biography
TOWNELEY, Richard (1629–1707). *See* Boyle, R.
Dictionary of Scientific Biography
TRAUBE, Ludwig (1818–76). *See* Traube, M.
A. G. Debus (Ed.), *World Who's Who in Science.* 1968
TROOST, L. J. (1825–1911). *See* Deville, H. É. St-C.
Dictionary of Scientific Biography
TROUSSEAU, A. (1801–67). *See* Broca, P. P.
R. H. Major, *A History of Medicine.* 1954
TSCHERMAK, E. von (1871–1962). *See* Bateson, W.; Mendel, J. G.; Vries, H. de
Dictionary of Scientific Biography
TSIOLKOVSKII, K. (1857–1935). *See* Von Braun, W.
F. H. Winter, *Rockets into Space.* 1990 (pbk 1993)
Arkady Kosmodemyansky, *Konstantin Tsiolkovsky.* 1985.
TURGOT, A. R. (1727–81). *See* Trésaguet, P.
Dictionary of Scientific Biography
TUVE, Merle (1901–82). *See* Breit, G.; Watson-Watt, R. A.
A. G. Debus (Ed.), *World Who's Who in Science.* 1968
TYNDALL, Arthur Mannering (1881–1961). *See* Powell, C. F.
Biographical Memoirs of Fellows of the Royal Society. 1962

UNZER, J. A. (1727–99). *See* Hall, M.
Dictionary of Scientific Biography
UTZSCHNEIDER, J. von (1763–1840). *See* Fraunhofer, J. von; Guinand, P. L.
Poggendorff, *Handwörterbuch zur Geschichte der Exakten Wissenschaften*

VAIL, Alfred (1807–59). *See* Morse, S. F. B.
Dictionary of American Biography
VAILLARD, L. (1850–1935). *See* Roux, P. P. E.
VALENCIENNES, A. (1794–1865). *See* Cuvier, Baron G. L. C. F. D.
Dictionary of Scientific Biography
VALENCY, Charles (1721–1812). *See* Belidor, B. F. de
VALENTIN, G. G. (1810–83). *See* Purkinje, J. E.
Dictionary of Scientific Biography
VALSALVA, A. M. (1666–1723). *See* Morgagni, G. B.
Dictionary of Scientific Biography
VAN DEN BROEK, A. (1870–1926). *See* Moseley, H. G. J.; Soddy, F.
VANE, John R. (1927–). *See* Euler, U. von
Tyler Wasson (Ed.), *Nobel Prize Winners.* 1987

VAN S'GRAVESANDE, W. J. S. (1688–1742). *See* Charles, J. A. C.; Nollet, Abbé J.A.
Dictionary of Scientific Biography
VAN VLECK, J. H. (1899–1980). *See* Mott, N. F.
Tyler Wasson (Ed.), *Nobel Prize Winners.* 1987
VASARI, G. (1511–74). *See* Leonardo da Vinci
H. Osborne (Ed.), *Oxford Companion to Art.* 1970
VERROCCHIO, Andrea del (1435–88). *See* Leonardo da Vinci
H. Osborne (Ed.), *Oxford Companion to Art.* 1970
VICQ D'AZYR F. (1748–94). *See* Fourcroy, A. F. de
Dictionary of Scientific Biography
VIEUSSENS, R. de (1641–1715). *See* Morgagni, G. B.
Dictionary of Scientific Biography
VOELCKERS, K. (1836–1914). *See* Hensen, V.
VOGEL, H. A. (1778–1867). *See* Schrötter, A.
VOIGT, Waldemar (1850–1919). *See* Born, M.
Dictionary of Scientific Biography
VOIT, Carl (1831–1908). *See* Lusk, G.
Dictionary of Scientific Biography
VOLHARD, J. (1834–1910). *See* Remsen, I.; Thiele, F. K. J.
A. G. Debus (Ed.), *World Who's Who in Science.* 1968
VOLTERRA, Vito (1860–1940). *See* Fredholm, E. I.
Dictionary of Scientific Biography
VON EULER-CHEPLIN, Hans (1873–1964). *See* Euler, U. von
A. G. Debus (Ed.), *World Who's Who in Science.* 1968
VON HERTWIG, K. W. T. R. (1850–1937). *See* Frisch, K. R. von
Dictionary of Scientific Biography
VON KARMAN, Theodor (1881–1963). *See* Born, M.
Dictionary of Scientific Biography
VULPIAN, E. F. A. (1826–87). *See* Brown-Séquard, C. E.
A. G. Debus (Ed.), *World Who's Who in Science.* 1968

WACKENRODER, Heinrich Wilhelm Ferdinand (1798–1854). *See* Karrer, P.
Dictionary of Scientific Biography
WADDINGTON, C. H. (1905–75). *See* Needham, N. J. T. M.
Biographical Memoirs of Fellows of the Royal Society. 1977
WALKER, George (c.1734–1807). *See* Cayley, Sir G.
Dictionary of National Biography
WALLER, A. D. (1856–1922). *See* Einthoven, W.
A. G. Debus (Ed.), *World Who's Who in Science.* 1968
WALLICH, N. (1786–1854). *See* Bentham, G.
Dictionary of National Biography
WALTHER, Bernard (1430–1504). *See* Regiomontanus
A. G. Debus (Ed.), *World Who's Who in Science.* 1968
WALTON, Ernest Thomas Silton (1903–). *See* Cockcroft, J. D.; Peierls, R. E.
Who's Who. 1993
WANDELAAR, Jan (1690–1759). *See* Albinus, B. S.
WANKLYN, J. A. (1834–1906). *See* Playfair, L.
Dictionary of National Biography
WARD, H. Marshall (1854–1905). *See* Biffen, Sir R. H.
A. G. Debus (Ed.), *World Who's Who in Science.* 1968
WARD, John Clive (1924–). *See* Salam, A.
Who's Who. 1993
WARINGTON, Robert (1807–67). *See* Graham, T.
Dictionary of National Biography
WARLTIRE, John (1739–1810). *See* Gregor, W.
Dictionary of National Biography (Missing Persons). 1993

SUBJECT INDEX

Geometry: Apollonius, Archimedes, Aristarchus, Bolyai, Cayley, Cauchy, Desargues, Demoivre, Descartes, Euclid, Eudoxus, Fermat, Gauss, Hero, Lobachevski, Monge, Pappus, Pascal, Poncelet, Pythagoras, Regiomontanus, Riemann, Sylvester, Thales

Geophysics: Bullard, Ewings, Hess, H. H., Matsuyama

Germanium: Winkler

Glass, Optical: Abbe, Alter, Dollond, Faraday, Guinand

Gluon: Ting

Gold: Beilby, Castner

Graphite: Acheson

Gravitation: Copernicus, Descartes, Einstein, Eötvös, Galilei, Hooke, Kepler, Laplace, Maclaurin, Maskelyn, Newton, Poynting, Vening Meinesz

Great Exhibition: Playfair

Grignard compounds: Grignard, Kipping

Gyroscope: Sommerfeld, Sperry, E. A.

Haematology: Barcroft, Ehrlich, Krogh, Landsteiner, Lower, Sanger, R. A., Whipple, Wiener, A. S.

Hardness: Brinell, Mohs

H-bomb: Teller

Helicopter: Sikorsky

Heliocentric Universe: Aristarchus, Copernicus, Rheticus

Helium: Crooks, Lockyer, Onnes, Ramsay, Rutherford, Soddy, Travers

Herbalism: Alpini, Celsus, Cesalpino, Culpeper, Dioscorides, Fuchs, L., Galen, Gerard, Turner

Histamine: Dale

History of science and technology: Delambre, Kopp, Lowry, Needham, Ostwald, Partington, Poggendorf, Schiaparelli, Thorpe, Tilden, Wellcome, Whittaker

Holography: Gabor

Hormones: Banting, Kendall, E. C., Macleod

Horology: Anaximander, Aristarchus, Berthoud, Dondi, Harrison, J., Hooke, Huygens, Jones, Mudge, Richard of Wallingford, Thiout, Tompion

Human Genome Organization (HUGO): Bodmer, Dulbecco, Gilbert (Walter)

Hydrogen: Cavendish

Hydrogen blowpipe: Hare, Langmuir

Hygrometer: Daniell, Sanctorius, Saussure

Hydrostatics: Archimedes, D'Alembert, Descartes, Euler, Pascal, Stevinus, Stokes, Torricelli

Iatrochemistry: Glauber, Paracelsus, Sylvius

Ichthyology: Agassiz, Lankester, Schmidt, E. J.

Immunology: Behring, Bordet, Burnet, Calmette, Dale, Jenner, Kitasato, La Condamine, Pasteur, Pfeiffer, Porter, R., Roux, Wassermann, Watson, Wiener, A. S.

Indigo: Baeyer

Information theory: Shannon, Wiener, N.

Infusoria: Dujardin

Instrument making: Abbe, Fortin, Gambey, Hadley, Kratzer, Pixii, Pregl, Ramsden, Smeaton, Thiout, Vernier

Insulin: Banting, Macleod, Sanger

Interferon: Isaacs

Internal combustion engine: Benz, Daimler, Diesel, Lebon, Lenoir, Otto, Ricardo

Iridium: Tennant, S.

Iron: Cort, Darby, Wilkinson

Isomerism: Berzelius, Meyer, Pasteur, Wislicenus, Wöhler

Isomorphism: Mitscherlich

Isotopes: Aston, Beilby, Hahn, Hertz, Hevesy, Lawrence, Soddy, Thomson, J. J., Urey, Zeeman

Jet propulsion: Whittle

Josephson effect: Josephson

J-psi particle: Richter, Ting

Jupiter: Bessel, Cassini, Galilei

Lacteals: Aselli, Pecquet

Laser: Basov, Maiman, Townes

Latent heat: Black, Wilcke

Lead, desilverization: Pattinson

Lead-chamber process: Roebuck

Light, Aberration of: Bradley, Rømer, Struve

Light, Pressure of: Lebedev

Light, Refraction of: Descartes, Hariot, Kepler, Klingenstierna, Snell

Light, Velocity of: Cassini, Fitzgerald, Fizeau, Foucault, Lorentz, Michelson, Morley, Rømer, Weber

Light, Wave theory of: Cauchy, Fizeau, Foucault, Fresnel, Huygens, Young, T.

Lighting, Electric: Coolidge, Edison, Jablochkoff, Langmuir, Sprengel, Swan

Lighting, Gas: Lebon, Murdoch, Welsbach, Winsor

Liquid crystals: De Gennes

Lissajous figures: Lissajous

Locust control: Uvarov

Logarithms: Briggs, Cavalieri, Kepler, Napier

Longitude: Cook, Flamsteed, Galilei, Hadley, Harrison, Maskelyne, Poisson, Ptolemy

LP records: Goldmark

Lunar Society: Beddoes, Boulton, Darwin, E., Edgworth, Keir, Priestly, Watt, Wedgwood, Withering

Lymphatic system: Aselli, Rudbeck, Starling, Florey

Lysozyme: Chain, Fleming, A., Florey

Machine tools: Boulton, Bramah, Mannesmann, Maudslay, Mushet, Nasmyth, Polhem, Ramelli, Roberts, Whitney, Whitworth, Wilkinson, J.

Magic numbers: Goeppert Mayer

Magnetism: Blackett, Coulomb, Eötvös, Faraday, Gilbert (Wm), Kohlrausch, Langevin, Néel, Peregrinus, Sabine, Thales, Tyndall

Magnetohydrodynamics: Alfvén

Magneto-optics: Zeeman

Magnetron: Hull, Tomonaga

Malaria: Golgi, Laveran, Manson, Pfeiffer, Ross

Manganese: Scheele, Weldon

Manhattan Project: Akers, Bush, Feynman, Fuchs, K. E. J., Peierls, Seaborg, Segrè, Teller